Interpreting Literature

. . . the two great esthetic problems . . . of communication and . . . of value

—W. H. AUDEN

Interpreting Literature

Seventh Edition

K. L. Knickerbocker
University of Tennessee

H. Willard Reninger
University of Northern Iowa

Edward W. Bratton
University of Tennessee

B. J. Leggett
University of Tennessee

Harcourt Brace Jovanovich College Publishers
Fort Worth   Philadelphia   San Diego
New York   Orlando   Austin   San Antonio
Toronto   Montreal   London   Sydney   Tokyo

Publisher *Susan Katz*
Acquiring Editor *Charlyce Jones Owen*
Special Project Editors *Pamela Forcey, Jeanette Ninas Johnson*
Production Manager *Robin B. Besofsky*
Art Director *Louis Scardino*

Library of Congress Cataloging in Publication Data

Main entry under title.
Interpreting literature.

Includes indexes.
1. Literature—Collections.   I. Knickerbocker, K. L.
(Kenneth Leslie)   II. Title.
PN6014.I49   1985   808.8   84-19192

ISBN 0-03-063013-4

2 3 4 016 10 9 8 7 6 5 4

Harcourt Brace Jovanovich, Inc.
The Dryden Press
Saunders College Publishing

ACKNOWLEDGMENTS

For permission to reprint materials in this book, the editors are indebted to the following sources:

Edward J. Acton, Inc., for permission to reprint "Exodus" by James Baldwin.

Almo Music Corporation for permission to reprint lyrics of "Crucifixion" and "Nobody's Buying Flowers from the Flower Lady," lyrics and music by Phil Ochs, both copyright © 1966 by Barricade Music, Inc.; all rights administered by Almo Music Corp. (ASCAP); all rights reserved; international copyright secured.

Wallace L. Anderson for permission to reprint "An Analysis of 'Mr. Flood's Party'" from *Edwin Arlington Robinson: A Critical Introduction,* Houghton Mifflin Co., copyright © 1967 by Wallace L. Anderson.

Atheneum Publishers, Inc., for permission to reprint "The Dover Bitch: A Criticism of Life" from *The Hard Hours* by Anthony Hecht, copyright © 1967 by Anthony E. Hecht; "From a Litany" from *Darker* by Mark Strand, copyright © 1968, 1969, 1970 by Mark Strand; "For the Anniversary of My Death"

(Acknowledgments are continued on page 1165.)

Preface

Have you practis'd so long to learn to read?
Have you felt so proud to get at the meaning of poems?
WALT WHITMAN, "Song of Myself"

In the preparation of this volume we have kept our eyes steadily on the student-reader. Editorial devices and selection of material have been guided by this concentration on both the abilities and the limitations of students when they are faced with a piece of imaginative writing. We believe that most students regard imaginative literature as a conspiracy against their mental and emotional peace. Their minds are accustomed to work best at a literal—that is, a servile—level. They are in a very real sense shackled. We are convinced that in most instances these shackles can be broken, that literal minds can be liberated. We know, of course, that a key figure in this process of liberation is the instructor and that a book's effectiveness—ours or anyone else's—must depend in great part upon the wisdom and enthusiasm of those who teach. It has been our chief purpose to provide a readily teachable book.

The principles that have guided our editorial work may be briefly indicated. First of all we have as far as possible allowed literature to speak for itself. In "Fiction: Preliminaries," instead of laying down rules for short stories, we present a story that shows many of the rules in action. In "Biography: Preliminaries," we ask readers to see for for themselves the literary characteristics of autobiographical and biographical writing. The same procedure is followed in the preliminaries to the sections on poetry, drama, and the essay.

The second principle that guided us—a corollary of the first—was to delay comment on a literary technique or characteristic until a demonstration of the technique or characteristic actually appeared in one of the selections. In "The

Essay: Preliminaries," for example, we are able to illustrate the sharp distinction between two kinds of essays, but on the basis of our excerpts from Lamb and Huxley we cannot appropriately say anything demonstrable about the structure of essays. As soon as we reach the full-length essay, however, we have an illustration of structure and can show its importance to the essay.

Our procedure in this respect explains why we use the term "Preliminaries" instead of "Introduction" for the essays that precede the various sections. Each section as a whole—"Preliminaries," the selections, comments, and questions—constitutes an introduction to the type of literature it contains.

The third principle was that all technical terms should be explained as soon as used. Furthermore, since sections of this book may be used out of the order given, we have not hesitated to repeat definitions of terms that recur in the various sections. We think that these occasional repetitions will be a convenience and an aid to readers in fixing certain terms in mind. Each definition is shaped to be applied to the form being considered. There is also an "Index of Literary and Critical Terms."

Finally, we have offered in each section a body of material without comments or questions. We have done this so that whatever has been learned may be independently applied.

The selections have been chosen with two considerations in mind. First, we have offered at the beginning of each section the sort of material that may be readily understood and immediately enjoyed. Secondly, we have followed the simpler selections with progressively more difficult selections. This progression is most apparent in the section on poetry, where proceeding from the simple to the difficult is most important. In general, stories emphasizing plot precede those emphasizing character in the section on fiction. A one-act play precedes nine full-length plays in the section on drama. Anecdotes precede biographical sketches in the section on biography. The essay begins with short and light bits of speculation and moves on to heavier fare.

Preface to the Seventh Edition

The first edition of *Interpreting Literature* appeared exactly thirty years ago, in January 1955. In preparing the seventh edition, we have been especially conscious that very few college texts reach such maturity. When a rare one does, there are good reasons. In the present case, the main reasons are the guiding principles of the volume enunciated by Kenneth L. Knickerbocker and H. Willard Reninger in the Preface to that first edition reprinted above. The most basic of those principles are a realistic and constant awareness of the student-reader and an insistence on including significant and teachable literature presented in an editorial fashion which clarifies its timeless value and enhances its appropriateness for class consideration and discussion. In effect, the durability of *Interpreting Literature* has once again confirmed that the text well made for the college classroom stays in the college classroom. So, many months ago, we were as cautiously aware of beginning with an excellent book as we are presently convinced that we have concluded our task with a text even better for the current English classroom. We have done so, we think, by staying always alert to the guiding principles of that first edition of thirty years ago.

As in previous editions, the basic order of this volume is analytic—that is, its five main divisions are determined by five literary genres: fiction, poetry, drama, biography, and the essay. Each division begins with preliminary discussion and sample interpretations of the literary type featured in the selections of that division. New to this edition in three of the divisions are preliminary discussions of "Writing About Fiction," "Writing About Poetry," and "Writing About Drama."

In addition to the analytic Contents, we also provide an improved organization of selections according to theme. Manageably arranged under ten topics of enduring human interest, literary works of different types and methods but with similar concerns are usefully brought together. The naturally comparative means of that arrangement can itself inform perceptive readers of the qualitative intimacy of form and content, method and meaning, in all kinds of writing—including their own—and can suggest innumerable ideas worth pursuing both in class discussion and in their own papers.

The section on fiction has been thoroughly revised and substantially expanded in both the number and range of the short stories it contains. Eighteen stories are new to this edition, and authors new to the fiction section include John Cheever, Nathaniel Hawthorne, James Joyce, Yukio Mishima, Katherine Anne Porter, Irwin Shaw, John Steinbeck, Robert Louis Stevenson, James Thurber, John Updike, and Alice Walker. They join more than twenty of the best of their peers, superb story-tellers and students of human nature carried over from the sixth edition. Also an important innovation in the anthology is the addition of four doubles among the short stories—that is, pairs of stories by four consummate artists of the genre, Hawthorne, Poe, Faulkner, and Porter. Such doubles offer unique opportunities for grasping how sometimes subtle differences in fictional technique can produce crucial differences in tone, atmosphere, credibility, meaning, and total effect.

Editorial commentary and questions (with occasional suggestions for writing) have been added for most of the short stories; these are directed toward understanding the functional harmony of fictional techniques and themes. We believe instructors will also find such editorial matter more purposively imaginative—with the student's own writing in mind—than is usual in literature anthologies. And even the analytic presentation of fiction has been thoughtfully, but silently, arranged (after introductory selections) to reflect teachable and informative connections among groups of stories, connections not usually suggested by the Thematic Contents. By that means, for example, stories by Porter, Joyce, and Updike are brought together, each reflecting a special use and exploration of human memory, while a Thurber-Vonnegut-White grouping focuses on man and machine. There also are subtle, suggestive gatherings of stories of horror, psychology, science-fiction, humor, the absurd; allegorical and symbolic fiction; tales with a regional flavor and others concerned with crime and its social and psychological consequences.

The poetry section has also been substantially revised, with particular attention to modern and contemporary verse. More than seventy poems are new to the seventh edition, most of them works by twentieth-century poets. Although the full list is too long for inclusion here, poets whose works appear for the first time in this edition include A. R. Ammons, Margaret Atwood, Louise Bogan, Philip Larkin, Denise Levertov, W. S. Merwin, Marianne Moore, Frank O'Hara, Richard Wilbur, and William Carlos Williams. Additional new works by other important modern poets such as Gwendolyn Brooks, James Dickey, Langston Hughes, Robert Lowell, Wilfred Owen, John Crowe Ransom, Adrienne Rich, Theodore Roethke, Wallace Stevens, James Wright, and W. B. Yeats have also been included. Readers familiar with *Interpreting Literature* will discover new selections by Arnold, Blake, Carroll, Clough, Donne, Hardy, Hopkins, Jonson, Keats, Pope, Shelley, and Wordsworth, among others, as well as additional ballads and songs, such as "Lord Randal," "Little Mathie Grove," Bob Dylan's "Mister Tambourine Man," and Leonard Cohen's "Suzanne."

The section on drama, which was thoroughly revised for the sixth edition, returns the six plays added at that time—*Hamlet, Ghosts, Miss Julie, Caligula, The Playboy of the Western World,* and *The Sunshine Boys.* These, together with *Ile, Antigone, The Physician in Spite of Himself,* and *The Visit,* provide a mix of traditional tragedy, naturalistic tragedy, modern experimental theater, and comedy.

A new essay on comedy, Louis Kronenberger's "Some Prefatory Words on Comedy," should prove helpful to readers in approaching the plays of Molière, Synge, and Simon, and it serves as an instructive companion to Joseph Wood Krutch's "The Tragic Fallacy." Also new to the essays are two justly famous statements by poets on their art, Robert Frost's "The Figure a Poem Makes" and Samuel Taylor Coleridge's consideration of the question, "What Is Poetry?" An unusually instructive lineup of biographical selections has been strengthened by the addition of William E. Cole's colorful and moving recollections of "Living and Dying in Shady Valley" shortly after the turn of the century, a selection anthologized nowhere else.

We are grateful for help from a number of individuals, many of them our colleagues at the University of Tennessee. We particularly thank Professor Don Richard Cox for helpful suggestions of many kinds. To James Wren we are indebted for knowledgeable leads to some of the best Japanese fiction. We also wish to acknowledge specific, informed recommendations from James E. Gill,

Minrose Gwin, Clyde Hoffman, Richard Kelly, Bege Neel, Eleanora Overbey, and Frank Robinson. For the breadth and sensitivity of her reading and consequent suggestions, we are grateful to Alfreda Bratton. We particularly appreciate also the proofing skills and other essential contributions so generously provided by Corinne Leggett. And to Sandra Lewis go our thanks for valuable assistance in preparing the manuscript.

As with previous editions, outside readers have carefully reviewed the sixth and offered useful suggestions for the seventh. Many improvements in this volume are the direct result of the commendable efforts of these informed critics: Ellen Bourland, George C. Wallace State Community College; Glenn E. Campbell, Morehead State University; Commodore Craft, Thornton Community College; Barbara Dicey, George C. Wallace State Community College; Charles Duke, Murray State University; William Fahrenbach, DePaul University; Sydney Harrison, Edison Community College; Craig Hergert, Concordia College; William Laubner, Jr., Central Arizona College; Margaret Simpson, San Jacinto College; Judith Stanford, Merrimack College.

We wish to thank the gifted professionals at Holt, Rinehart and Winston for essential help in preparing this edition—especially our original and current English Editors, Nedah Abbott and Charlyce Jones Owen, respectively; our excellent Project Editors Pamela Forcey and Jeanette Ninas Johnson; our Production Manager Robin B. Besofsky, and our Art Director Louis Scardino.

Finally, an *Instructor's Manual* is available to supplement the editorial matter of the basic text. It offers comments, interpretations, and suggestions for class presentation and student writing. The Manual may be obtained through a local Holt representative or by writing to English Editor, College Department, Holt, Rinehart and Winston, CBS Inc., 383 Madison Avenue, New York, NY 10017.

E.W.B.
B.J.L.

Contents

What to Write About Fiction   23

How to Write About Fiction   25

POETRY   297

PRELIMINARIES   299

Imagery 369

Figure and Symbol 377

Innovation in Language: Three Poems by E. E. Cummings 384

THE COMMENT ON EXPERIENCE: FROM SENSUOUS EXPERIENCE TO DOMINANT ATTITUDE 389

DRAMA   581

PRELIMINARIES   583

WRITING ABOUT DRAMA   604

BIOGRAPHY   975

PRELIMINARIES   977

*Thematic Contents**

---

*This thematic grouping is meant to suggest clusters of works which may be read together. Recognizing the sometimes arbitrary result of classifying works of literature, especially imaginative literature that by its very nature is suggestive and wide-ranging, we have found it helpful in some cases to assign works to more than one category. The reader may wish to experiment with yet further groupings and sub-groupings.

Nature and the Self

Society and the Self

Religious and
Metaphysical Values

Love and Hate

Crime and Consequence

Time and Death

Humor, Wit, and Satire

Literature and The Arts

Fiction

The meagre satisfaction that [man] can
extract from reality leaves him starving.
SIGMUND FREUD

As usual truth is a surprise.
KENNETH CLARK

Preliminaries

Storytellers are the perennial delight of humankind. As they begin, we are immediately confronted with people—characters, the most interesting thing in the world. We may be entertained by the sequence of events (plot), we may be given a fresh insight into human personality (character), or we may be offered a penetrating comment on the human situation (theme). The meaning of plot, character, and theme is determined, we shall later discover, by the storytellers' *attitude* toward the facts they relate.

But why should we take seriously a story whose characters and action have never existed? We accept as authentic most biography and history, but why should we attend to something invented, made up? This is a fair question, most often asked by the practical, hardheaded person who is devoted to facts. We shall search for the answer by employing one of the basic principles of this book: We shall ask a few storytellers to provide the answer as we examine their work. We begin with John Galsworthy.

John Galsworthy   (1867–1933)
Quality

I knew him from the days of my extreme youth, because he made my father's boots; inhabiting with his elder brother two little shops let into one, in a small by-street—now no more, but then most fashionably placed in the West End.

That tenement had a certain quiet distinction; there was no sign upon its face that he made for any of the Royal Family—merely his own German name of Gessler Brothers; and in the window a few pairs of boots. I remember that it always troubled me to account for those unvarying boots in the window, for he made only what was ordered, reaching nothing down, and it seemed so inconceivable that what he made could ever have failed to fit. Had he bought them to put there? That, too, seemed inconceivable. He would never have tolerated in his house leather on which he had not worked himself. Besides, they were too beautiful—the pair of pumps, so inexpressibly slim, the patent leathers with cloth tops, making water come into one's mouth, the tall brown riding-boots with marvellous sooty glow, as if, though new, they had been worn a hundred years. Those pairs could only have been made by one who saw before him the Soul of Boot—so truly were they prototypes incarnating the very spirit of all footgear. These thoughts, of course, came to me later, though even when I was promoted to him, at the age of perhaps fourteen, some inkling haunted me of the dignity of himself and brother. For to make boots—such boots as he made—seemed to me then, and still seems to me, mysterious and wonderful.

I remember well my shy remark, one day, while stretching out to him my youthful foot:

"Isn't it awfully hard to do, Mr. Gessler?"

5   And his answer, given with a sudden smile from out of the sardonic redness of his beard: "Id is an Ardt!"

Himself, he was a little as if made from leather, with his yellow crinkly face, and crinkly reddish hair and beard, and neat folds slanting down his cheeks to the corners of his mouth, and his guttural and one-toned voice; for leather is a sardonic substance, and stiff and slow of purpose. And that was the character of his face, save that his eyes, which were grey-blue, had in them the simple gravity of one secretly possessed by the Ideal. His elder brother was so very like him—though watery, paler in every way, with a great industry—that sometimes in early days I was not quite sure of him until the interview was over. Then I knew that it was he, if the words, "I will ask my brudder," had not been spoken; and that, if they had, it was his elder brother.

When one grew old and wild and ran up bills, one somehow never ran them up with Gessler Brothers. It would not have seemed becoming to go in there and stretch out one's foot to that blue iron-spectacled glance, owing him for more than—say—two pairs, just the comfortable reassurance that one was still his client.

For it was not possible to go to him very often—his boots lasted terribly, having something beyond the temporary—some, as it were, essence of boot stitched into them.

One went in, not as into most shops, in the mood of: "Please serve me, and let me go!" but restfully, as one enters a church; and, sitting on the single wooden chair, waited—for there was never anybody there. Soon, over the top edge of that sort of well—rather dark, and smelling soothingly of leather—which formed the shop, there would be seen his face, or that of his elder brother, peering down. A guttural sound, and the tip-tap of bast slippers beating the narrow wooden stairs, and he would stand before one without coat, a little bent, in leather apron, with sleeves turned back, blinking—as if awakened from some dream of boots, or like an owl surprised in daylight and annoyed at this interruption.

10   And I would say: "How do you do, Mr. Gessler? Could you make me a pair of Russia leather boots?"

Without a word he would leave me, retiring whence he came, or into the other portion of the shop, and I would continue to rest in the wooden chair, inhaling the incense of his trade. Soon he would come back, holding in his thin, veined hand a piece of gold-brown leather. With eyes fixed on it, he would remark: "What a beautiful biece!" When I, too, had admired it, he would speak again. "When do you wand dem?" And I would answer: "Oh! As soon as you conveniently can." And he would say: "To-morrow fordnighd?" Or if he were his elder brother: "I will ask my brudder!"

Then I would murmur: "Thank you! Good-morning, Mr. Gessler." "Goot-morning!" he would reply, still looking at the leather in his hand. And as I moved to the door, I would hear the tip-tap of his bast slippers restoring him, up the stairs, to his dream of boots. But if it were some new kind of footgear that he had not yet made me, then indeed he would observe ceremony—divesting me of my boot and holding it long in his hand, looking at it with eyes at once critical and loving, as if recalling the glow with which he had created it, and rebuking the way in which one had disorganized this masterpiece. Then, placing my foot on a piece of paper, he would two or three times tickle the outer edges with a pencil and pass his nervous fingers over my toes, feeling himself into the heart of my requirements.

I cannot forget that day on which I had occasion to say to him: "Mr. Gessler, that last pair of town walking-boots creaked, you know."

He looked at me for a time without replying, as if expecting me to withdraw or qualify the statement, then said:

15   "Id shouldn'd 'ave greaked."

"It did, I'm afraid."

"You goddem wed before dey found demselves?"

"I don't think so."

At that he lowered his eyes, as if hunting for memory of those boots, and I felt sorry I had mentioned this grave thing.

20   "Zend dem back!" he said; "I will look at dem."

A feeling of compassion for my creaking boots surged up in me, so well could I imagine the sorrowful long curiosity of regard which he would bend on them.

"Zome boods," he said slowly, "are bad from birdt. If I can do noding wid dem, I dake dem off your bill."

Once (once only) I went absent-mindedly into his shop in a pair of boots bought in an emergency at some large firm's. He took my order without showing me any leather, and I could feel his eyes penetrating the inferior integument of my foot. At last he said:

"Dose are nod my boods."

25   The tone was not one of anger, nor of sorrow, not even of contempt, but there was in it something quiet that froze the blood. He put his hand down and pressed a finger on the place where the left boot, endeavoring to be fashionable, was not quite comfortable.

"Id 'urds you dere," he said. "Dose big virms 'ave no self-respect. Drash!" And then, as if something had given way within him, he spoke long and bitterly. It was the only time I ever heard him discuss the conditions and hardships of his trade.

"Dey get id all," he said, "dey get id by adverdisement, nod by work. Dey dake it away from us, who lofe our boods. Id gomes to this—bresently I haf no work. Every year id gets less—you will see." And looking at his lined face I saw things I had never noticed before, bitter things and bitter struggle—and what a lot of grey hairs there seemed suddenly in his red beard!

As best I could, I explained the circumstances of the purchase of those ill-omened boots. But his face and voice made so deep an impression that during the next few minutes I ordered many pairs. Nemesis fell! They lasted more terribly than ever. And I was not able conscientiously to go to him for nearly two years.

When at last I went I was surprised to find that outside one of the two little windows of his shop another name was painted, also that of a bootmaker—making, of course, for the Royal Family. The old familiar boots, no longer in dignified isolation, were huddled in the single window. Inside, the now contracted well of the one little shop was more scented and darker than ever. And it was longer than usual, too, before a face peered down, and the tip-tap of the bast slippers began. At last he stood before me, and gazing through those rusty iron spectacles, said:

30   "Mr. ——, isn'd it?"

"Ah! Mr. Gessler," I stammered, "but your boots are really *too* good, you know! See, these are quite decent still!" And I stretched out to him my foot. He looked at it.

"Yes," he said, "beople do nod wand good boods, id seems."

To get away from his reproachful eyes and voice I hastily remarked: "What have you done to your shop?"

He answered quietly: "Id was too exbensif. Do you wand some boods?"

35   I ordered three pairs, though I had only wanted two, and quickly left. I had, I do not know quite what feeling of being part, in his mind, of a conspiracy against him; or not perhaps so much against him as against his idea of boot. One does not, I suppose, care to feel like that; for it was again many months before my next visit to his shop, paid, I remember, with the feeling: "Oh! well, I can't leave the old boy—so here goes! Perhaps it'll be his elder brother!"

For his elder brother, I knew, had not character enough to reproach me, even dumbly.

And, to my relief, in the shop there did appear to be his elder brother, handling a piece of leather.

"Well, Mr. Gessler," I said, "how are you?"

He came close, and peered at me.

40   "I am breddy well," he said slowly, "but my elder brudder is dead."

And I saw that it was indeed himself—but how aged and wan! And never before had I heard him mention his brother. Much shocked, I murmured: "Oh! I am sorry!"

"Yes," he answered, "he was a good man, he made a good bood; but he is dead." And he touched the top of his head, where the hair had suddenly gone as thin as it had been on that of his poor brother, to indicate, I suppose, the cause of death. "He could nod ged over losing de oder shop. Do you wand any boods?" And he held up the leather in his hand: "Id's a beaudiful biece."

I ordered several pairs. It was very long before they came—but they were better than ever. One simply could not wear them out. And soon after that I went abroad.

It was over a year before I was again in London. And the first shop I went to was my old friend's. I had left a man of sixty, I came back to one of seventy-five, pinched and worn and tremulous, who genuinely, this time, did not at first know me.

45   "Oh! Mr. Gessler," I said, sick at heart; "how splendid your boots are! See, I've been wearing this pair nearly all the time I've been abroad; and they're not half worn out, are they?"

He looked long at my boots—a pair of Russia leather, and his face seemed to regain steadiness. Putting his hand on my instep, he said:

"Do dey vid you here? I 'ad drouble wid dat bair, I remember."

I assured him that they had fitted beautifully.

"Do you wand any boods?" he said. "I can make dem quickly; id is a slack dime."

50   I answered: "Please, please! I want boots all round—every kind!"

"I will make a vresh model. Your food must be bigger." And with utter slowness, he traced round my foot, and felt my toes, only once looking up to say:

"Did I dell you my brudder was dead?"

To watch him was painful, so feeble had he grown; I was glad to get away.

I had given those boots up, when one evening they came. Opening the parcel, I set the four pairs out in a row. Then one by one I tried them on. There was no doubt about it. In shape and fit, in finish and quality of leather, they were the best he had ever made me. And in the mouth of one of the town walking-boots I found his bill. The amount was the same as usual, but it gave me quite a shock. He had never before sent it in till quarter day. I flew downstairs and wrote a cheque, and posted it at once with my own hand.

55   A week later, passing the little street, I thought I would go in and tell him how splendidly the new boots fitted. But when I came to where his shop had been, his name was gone. Still there, in the window, were the slim pumps, the patent leathers with cloth tops, the sooty riding boots.

I went in, very much disturbed. In the two little shops—again made into one—was a young man with an English face.

"Mr. Gessler in?" I said.

He gave me a strange, ingratiating look.

"No, sir," he said, "no. But we can attend to anything with pleasure. We've taken the shop over. You've seen our name, no doubt, next door. We make for some very good people."

60   "Yes, yes," I said; "but Mr. Gessler?"

"Oh!" he answered; "dead."

"Dead! But I only received these boots from him last Wednesday week."

"Ah!" he said; " 'a shockin' go. Poor old man starved 'imself."

"Good God!"

65   "Slow starvation, the doctor called it! You see he went to work in such a way! Would keep the shop on; wouldn't have a soul touch his boots except himself. When he got an order, it took him such a time. People won't wait. He lost everybody. And there he'd sit, goin' on and on—I will say that for him—not a man in London made a better boot! But look at the competition! He never advertised! Would 'ave the best leather, too, and do it all 'imself. Well, there it is. What could you expect with his ideas?"

"But starvation—!"

"That may be a bit flowery, as the sayin' is—but I know myself he was sittin' over his boots day and night, to the very last. You see I used to watch him. Never gave 'imself time to eat; never had a penny in the house. All went in rent and leather. How he lived so long I don't know. He regular let his fire go out. He was a character. But he made good boots."

"Yes," I said, "he made good boots."

First Impressions

Perhaps our first question about this or any other story is, Do we like it? Our immediate answer comes from our first impressions and can be called a *natural* response. But experience has taught us that our first impressions about life, people, and literature can be exceedingly misleading, and thoughtful persons have therefore devised many ways of critically examining their impressions. To examine anything, we must have a framework of ideas about its nature and function: the buyer of a used car, for example, had better have a pretty sound notion of the structure of the automobile before trying to determine its real value. Likewise, readers of fiction should have a sound notion of the structure and function of the short story or novel before they accept its influence on their lives. Both the buyer of a car and the reader of fiction should have a method of analysis to confirm or reject first impressions, particularly emotional ones.

A main reason for analyzing a story is to assure us that our total reading experience has been *provided by the story.* Our analysis tests the accuracy of our response; it protects us against uncritical stock responses (p. 309); it helps us to suspend judgment until we understand the story as a complete whole; and perhaps most important of all, it enlarges our enjoyment along with the refinement of our understanding.

With the suggested method of analysis found below, we can test our first impressions of "Quality," and better still we can, in the process, be developing a method of analysis of our own. One reason, surely, for analyzing literature is finally to make all readers their own qualified critics.

The Basic Question

We can begin our exploration, or analysis, of Galsworthy's story by asking the question, What happens to whom and why? This question directs our attention to the fundamental matters of fiction. *What happens?* asks for a consideration of *plot,* or the structure of action; *to whom?* asks for a consideration of the *characters;* and *why?* requires us to investigate the story's *theme,* which controls and shapes the meaning of the characters' action. To keep this basic question constantly in mind will show us how Galsworthy has worked to achieve his final meaning, and of course that meaning is precisely what we are after.

The Facts of the Story

To think clearly about the story we must first have a firm command of the facts of the story—we must know what happens to whom on the literal level. Unless the literal facts of the story are clearly understood before further analysis begins, we are likely to misconstrue the story's total meaning. This book will repeatedly emphasize this principle because its violation misinterprets imaginative literature. At the moment we shall postpone asking why these things happened to the Gessler brothers—let us take one thing at a time to be sure of our ground. The facts of the story can be stated as follows.

> For many years Gessler Brothers had made and sold boots in "two little shops let into one," a tenement which had "a certain quiet distinction." Because the younger brother dealt with the customers, it is through him that we see the character and integrity of these brothers as men and bootmakers. For him the making of boots was an ideal and an art, and the boots were therefore both utilitarian and aesthetic masterpieces. They "lasted terribly" long, and their beauty was "mysterious and wonderful."

But now the big firms of bootmakers were diminishing Gesslers' trade by advertising, according to the younger brother, and not by good work. They were forced to abandon one of their two shops to another bootmaker who represented the new regime of advertising and quick service. This blow brought death to the elder brother, but the younger brother doggedly refused to meet the new "competition" and continued to use the best leather and to produce boots of supreme quality. He finally died of "slow starvation" and his shop was taken over by his brisk competitor. It is significant that the last boots he made immediately before his death were, according to the narrator, "the best he had ever made me."

The basic facts of any story may be made more manageable by the use of a device called an *action line* (see the chart), which clearly shows their sequence.

For years Gessler Brothers had made fine boots. For	Big firms now furnish new competition.	They give up part of their shop to a new firm.	Surviving Gessler refuses	He dies of slow
them bootmaking was an art.	Gesslers' trade is diminished.	Elder Gessler dies of the blow.	to compromise his art.	starvation.

The account of the facts of the story, which resembles a newspaper notice of the troubles and failure of Gessler Brothers, is known as a *paraphrase* on the literal level. But in making the paraphrase, we have raised some questions. Unless Galsworthy's story means more than the paraphrase includes, does the story deserve further consideration? The paraphrase has omitted a good deal, and we sense that the real meaning will be found in these omissions. Why has Galsworthy caused these facts to move in this sequence? What is Galsworthy's *attitude* toward the failure of the Gessler brothers? In short, to know the *surface* action is not enough: what is the *symbolic* action, or the artistic truth of the story—the kind of truth we contemplated in "Preliminaries"?

Warnings

Because no single method of analysis will reveal the meaning of all stories, each one must be approached on its own grounds and interpreted within its own terms of construction. There are, of course, certain principles of fiction that do remain constant, but even these must be applied with tact and discrimination by the reader as interpreter. We should greet with skepticism such dogmatic doctrines as, "All stories must have a plot," or "The conflicts in stories must always be resolved," or "Virtue should always be rewarded, and evil punished." We may finally accept such doctrines, but we must not begin with them. Let us begin by discussing a story. Let us look first for the basic devices by which Galsworthy has transformed the facts of his story into a piece of fictional art with meaning.

Like other writers of fiction, Galsworthy has created his own characters, placed them on his own fictional stage, and caused them to act to some purpose. But in doing so, he was forced to make some decisions that can be found embodied in his story. If we can locate these decisions and determine *why* he made them, the meaning of the story should become clear.

Suppose we try to get at the matter this way: if we were to set up a motion-picture camera on a busy, city-street intersection and shoot the scene for half an hour, we would have a documentary film, but no art. Why? Because the action and characters would be purely accidental, without purpose, form, and specific meaning. Because Galsworthy's story does have these characteristics, we know he must have made certain decisions regarding the course his story was to take. His story was no accident.

Author's Controlling Theme

Every good story is shaped by a controlling theme, or idea. This controlling theme selects and arranges everything that goes into the story—the characters, the action, the resolution of the conflict, and anything else used by the writers to dramatize their total meaning. As we read a story, its theme is usually revealed to us by degrees as the story moves to its conclusion.

We find our first clue to Galsworthy's theme in his title: his general theme or subject is quality. But as the story unfolds, the theme becomes more sharply defined. Whose quality? How does it shape the story's action? What are its consequences in the lives of the principal characters? To answer these questions, Galsworthy begins to dramatize his theme through the actions and responses of Gessler, and the story is on its way.

It is apparent that Galsworthy has written a serious story, a thoughtful interpretation of an aspect of humanity. In serious writers such an interpretation emerges from their world view, or their philosophy of life, which is their accounting of the meaning of existence. Writers have, therefore a scale of values, and above all they make a distinction between quantitative and qualitative values. Artists, regardless of their medium, are deeply involved with the quality of experience. Their general subject is the quality of human nature, and their evaluation of any specific human experience is their truth or, if you disagree with them, their bias. As we move on through our examination of Galsworthy's story, we shall observe the influence of his scale of values, or his attitude toward the facts of the story.

The Shaping Devices of Fiction

Plot, or the structure of action   We have said before that Galsworthy has created his own characters, placed them on his own stage, and caused them to act to some purpose. Here we are especially concerned with that word *act*. Whatever else storywriters do, they must present characters in action, an action that is designed to dramatize a fully realized theme, a situation, a character—in fact, anything the writer wishes to dramatize, or to make concrete in terms of action. This action can take more than one form: it can be violent and obvious like Othello's murder of Desdemona, it can be a lovers' embrace like Romeo and Juliet's, or it can be the inward action of lovers' affection like Queen Victoria's and Albert's. Whatever form the action takes, its function is to dramatize the event for the reader.

The word *plot* has been used to indicate almost any kind of action found in a story, including the closed plot, the open plot, and straight narrative with little or no serious complication. (For further discussion of plot, see p. 19.) Generally, whatever means is used to dramatize the writer's purpose is called plot, or the structure of action.

Most stories emphasize plot, character, or theme, and we shall later meet stories that are notable for one of the three. What of Galsworthy's "Quality"? Let us refer again to the story's action line (p. 9). Galsworthy has used a rather slight, closed plot, which runs the customary course of complication, conflict, climax, and denouement (resolution). The story's external action can be described in this way: the complication appears when the Gesslers' trade is diminished; the conflict appears between the Gesslers and the big firm when they lose one of their two shops; the climax arrives when the surviving Gessler can no longer make a living; and the denouement, or resolution, comes with Gessler's death and the success of the big firm. The story does depend on plot, but we see that the significant action and conflict actually lie within Gessler himself—which means that Galsworthy is using his plot to reveal character. He is doing even more: he is using plot and character to reveal his theme. The story is an excellent example, as we shall see more fully later, of how the basic elements of a story work together harmoniously to produce a significant interpretation of some phase of life.

Before leaving this matter of plot, we can profitably clarify the uses of the word *dramatic*. It can mean one of three things. One sense of the word has been implied directly above: it is used to make a distinction between the essay, which presents abstract ideas, and the story, which presents a theme concretely through characters in action. Students often refer to Professor ————, who dramatizes her ideas in the classroom, meaning that she illustrates the sense of her abstract ideas with concrete examples in action. All stories by their very nature have this kind of dramatic quality. The word *dramatic* is used also to mean the dramatic method used in a scene where characters present themselves with their own words. Barthelme's "A City of Churches" (p. 280), for example, relies heavily on the dramatic scene. And finally, the word is used to indicate the tension created by the conflict of the characters in action. The action is dramatic, we say, when we are stirred emotionally and suspended in a state of expectancy.

Character   We return once more to our statement that Galsworthy has created his characters and has caused them to act to some purpose. This time we are especially interested in that word *character*. The nature and use of characters in any story are determined by the purpose of the writer.

Galsworthy presents a conflict over quality, and his characters therefore represent in one way or another the terms of the conflict. This conflict, as we have seen, is both external and internal: external, between Gessler Brothers and the big firm; and internal, within the younger Gessler himself. The external conflict could have been represented by type characters only, but, because Galsworthy chose to dramatize an inner conflict as well, at least one character had to be individualized to make the inner conflict understandable and credible.

In a serious story like Galsworthy's, one of the uses of character is to dramatize the moral choices made by the author. When Gessler is faced with a declining trade, he is forced to make a decision. Shall he maintain his ideal of making boots, or shall he cheapen his product and meet the new competition? Gessler has uncommon personal integrity, and his boots must not represent merely a price on the open market; they must represent him as a workman. His boots in a very real sense are Gessler. Gessler's choice must therefore be basically a moral choice, not merely a profit-and-loss choice. Galsworthy has created a character who is required by his very nature to make the moral choice he made. That is, the choice is motivated by the created character, which means, of course, that Galsworthy made the choice when he created Gessler, who helps to dramatize Galsworthy's theme. We have here a concrete example of what is meant by the parts of a story working harmoniously to reveal meaning.

Any story's credibility depends on the consistency of each one of its characters. This is more true of the short story than of the novel because there is rarely time enough in the former to permit the development of, or changes in, characters. Once Galsworthy has defined the terms of the conflict over quality and has established the meaning or temper of each character, the action moves to its inevitable conclusion. Suppose that Gessler had compromised his art and had met the new competition. Would that action have been inevitable or credible? Had he done so, the story's structure would have collapsed.

Symbolism   As we continue to penetrate beneath the surface of Galsworthy's story, we see that the meaning of his symbolism must not escape us. His basic symbols are his characters, the finished boots, and even the raw leather itself. In fact, Gessler, his boots, and his leather are actually a compound symbol, which stands for an uncompromising ideal. Speaking of the boots on display in Gessler's window, Galsworthy says,

> Those pairs could only have been made by one who saw before him the Soul of Boot—so truly were they prototypes incarnating the very spirit of all footgear.

This is a reference, of course, to Plato's idealism, and Galsworthy is saying, in effect, that Gessler attempted to make copies of the Ideal Boot. If we recall Matthew Arnold's saying that culture is *"a study of perfection,"* Gessler becomes a symbol of a rich philosophical and literary tradition. When characters are used as symbols, regardless of how much individuality they may show, they represent more than themselves, and in that *more* lie the richness and universality of the story. The truth of this statement will be demonstrated when we discuss the full, or symbolic, meaning of "Quality."

Narrator's point of view: who shall tell the story?   To make their story credible as fiction, authors must establish some authority outside themselves who will objectify and make a representative truth of an author's theme or personal bias. Authors must disentangle themselves from the web of their personal experience and not permit their personality to stand between the representative truth of the story and the reader. Writers have devised ways of establishing an authority outside themselves, one of which is to create a narrator whose point of view controls the entire story. What this narrator knows, sees, and feels dominates everything. The "I" in a story may, of course, be the author, but nevertheless the author must make it appear as if the "I" were the authority for the story.

Galsworthy has used a first-person narrator who speaks in the past tense and who tells only what he has seen and experienced. Because he says, in effect, "I saw it all," this point of view carries a good deal of authority. And by confronting us with a witness, Galsworthy helps to achieve his illusion of reality.

This witness has observed the Gessler brothers since his boyhood. He first bought boots from them "at the age of perhaps fourteen," and years later he saw them meet defeat and disappear in death. Moreover, he seems to be sensitive to human values, and he understands the ideal that motivates Gessler. Could Galsworthy's credibility and the illusion of reality have been so convincingly achieved by another kind of narrator? Suppose the "young man with the English face" had told the story? Or the president of the "big firm"? To tell so much with so few words apparently required a visible witness whose authority is implicit in his presence and his basic understanding of Gessler.

Panorama and scene   The narrator's point of view focuses our attention on whatever the author wishes us to hear and see. Joseph Conrad has said, "My task which I am trying to achieve is, by the power of the written word to make you hear, to make you feel—it is, before all, to make you *see*." To make us see, most writers of fiction use a blend of panorama and scene. Panorama gives us the comprehensive, extensive view, and scene gives us the close-up, or intensive view. Henry James calls them *pictorial* and *picture*. The movies use these two views constantly to focus our attention one way or the other.

The *panoramic* view is usually presented through exposition and description, and it greatly helps to establish the atmosphere and tone (see p. 16) of the story. Here are Galsworthy's opening sentences:

> I knew him from the days of my extreme youth, because he made my father's boots; inhabiting with his elder brother two little shops let into one; in a small by-street— now no more, but then most fashionably placed in the West End.

> That tenement had a certain quiet distinction; there was no sign upon its face that he made for any of the Royal Family—merely his own German name of Gessler Brothers; and in the window a few pairs of boots. . . . Had he bought them to put there? . . . He would never have tolerated in his house leather on which he had not worked himself.

The focus here is comprehensive: the West End of London, the street, the two shops, the window, the shoes, and finally a suggestion of the character of the younger brother. This description of the Gesslers' environment does at least three things almost simultaneously: it describes the Gesslers' character; it establishes the tone of the story—Galsworthy's attitude toward the facts of the story; and it establishes the authority of the narrator. These three things together help to create the atmosphere that will guide our interpretation of every character and action to follow.

When we are to meet Gessler face to face, the narrator shifts the focus from panorama to scene:

> I remember well my shy remark, one day, while stretching out to him my youthful foot:
>
> "Isn't it awfully hard to do, Mr. Gessler?"
>
> And his answer, given with a sudden smile from out of the sardonic redness of his beard: "Id is an Ardt!"

The focus here is the close-up, like the focus of a scene in drama. Through dialogue the characters present and interpret themselves with little or no comment by the narrator. Galsworthy uses dialogue and scene whenever he wishes us to feel and hear the intense quality of Gessler's idealism and his scorn for shoddy workmanship. Examining a pair of boots made by a large firm, Gessler reveals himself:

> "Id 'urds you dere," he said. "Dose big virms 'ave no self-respect. Drash!" And then as if something had given away within him, he spoke long and bitterly. . . .
>
> "Dey get id all," he said, "dey get id by adverdisement, nod by work."

If the devices of panorama and scene seem to be pretty obvious, perhaps the effects achieved by them are not. Good art is usually deceivingly simple until we examine it closely.

Closely related to focus is a factor known as *aesthetic distance,* sometimes called *psychic,* or *artistic, distance,* which helps to control the intensity and kind of attention the reader is asked to give to the story, especially to its dramatic scenes (close-ups). It helps to determine how near the author should bring the reader to the scene. Art is not life: art re-creates a phase of life for a specific purpose. Art selects, emphasizes, and interprets a phase of life to direct the observer's attention to it in some significant way. The question of how close the observer should be brought into the dramatic scenes of a story (or of a play) becomes very important if the author is to make the story credible—and if the author fails to make it credible, all is lost (see "Credibility and the Illusion of Reality," p. 15). Good authors desire their readers to participate in the story's action but not to the extent of losing themselves in their emotional reactions. Readers must be able to contemplate and feel the action almost simultaneously. If the distance between them and the action is too great, they cannot participate in the feeling; if the distance is too little, they cannot contemplate the intellectual content of the action. They must neither stand off to smile at pure invention, nor must they wallow in the intense emotional experience of the characters. Aesthetic distance, in short, contributes to making a story art. A good story is not a slice of emotional life dramatized to overwhelm us, to give us "a good cry," or to violate our sensibilities as was done in one moving picture. In the final scene, a character dies in childbirth, but the movie's focus was so close and detailed that some observers were forced to leave the theater before the scene ran its course. This focus was a gross violation of aesthetic distance, and the scene as art was therefore shattered. The scene did have life, but it was not credible as art. It is entirely reasonable, of course, for writers to violate this principle to achieve some desirable effect necessary to realize their total purpose, as Shakespeare does in *King Lear* when Gloucester's eyes are plucked out. But for Shakespeare to have included this mutilation scene as a shocker and end in itself would have been artistically false.

Aesthetic distance is also the distance authors themselves keep from the action and characters in their stories. They design their form to permit the action and characters to speak for themselves, to obliterate the author as a person. Such writing is sometimes called *objective* as opposed to *subjective* writing, in which the person and personality of the author are clearly apparent. Such objectivity is one of the tenets of naturalism in fiction and is identified with the dramatic method as we see it operating in much contemporary fiction. The point to be made here for our purposes is that whether aesthetic distance is used to name the distance authors themselves keep from the story's action, or to name the distance readers are kept from the action, the result is likely to be the same: to represent life *in art,* not to reproduce life's bare actualism.

The Results of the Shaping Devices

Credibility and the illusion of reality   We now return to a question asked at the beginning of this section: why do we read and take seriously, or accept as authentic, a story whose characters and action have never existed? Some answers will be suggested in this section, but one thing is incontestably clear: regardless of the writer's brilliance and depth, regardless of the dexterity used in employing the devices of fiction already mentioned, if the writer fails to make the story credible, the story will fail. Many philosophers of art (aestheticians) have made similar comments about all art. For example: "There is . . . absolutely no test of good drawing or painting except the capacity of the artist to make us believe. . . . So . . . we demand of every novel and play, every dramatic and narrative poem, that it create the semblance of reality."*

When we approach a story, we must, in Coleridge's words, exercise a "willing suspension of disbelief." We do not ask, Did this thing really happen? When we demand something that really happened, we go to history and biography (see "Biography: Preliminaries," p. 977). When we begin a story, we suspend our skepticism of its actual, literal truth and ask at the story's end, *Could* this thing have happened? The tests for the truth of history and biography are irrelevant for the truth of fiction. This distinction has been enunciated at least since Aristotle (384–322 B.C.) observed

> that it is not the function of the poet [the imaginative writer] to relate what has happened, but what may happen,—what is possible according to the law of probability or necessity. . . . Poetry [imaginative literature], therefore, is more philosophical and a higher thing than history: for poetry tends to express the universal, history the particular . . . and it is this universality at which poetry aims. . . .
>
> (*Poetics,* IX)

The key words here are *probability* and *universality.* To dramatize some specific truth found universally in humankind or in a given civilization—not the

* DeWitt H. Parker, *The Analysis of Art,* New Haven, Conn.: Yale University Press, 1926, p. 6.

truth of an isolated occurrence—the writer is free to be false to the actual in order to be true to the general, the universal. But in devising their fiction, writers must make it probable, *not* merely possible; within its own terms of construction it must be credible, believable. The story must create the illusion of reality from beginning to end. How is this done?

How does Galsworthy do it? In many ways, with many devices. By using a first-person narrator who has witnessed the actions of the Gesslers and who has worn their boots; by confronting us with characters who present themselves in their own characteristic words; but most of all by properly motivating the actions of the characters to make the plot, or the structure of action, move to its *probable* and inevitable conclusion. That is, Galsworthy is saying, given these characters, including the Gesslers, in this situation, according to these circumstances, it is entirely probable that this story would happen in this way.

Is all this so mysterious? Hardly. What do we mean by saying, "Truth is stranger than fiction"? We simply mean that any story whose aim is universal truth based on "the law of probability or necessity" cannot rely on the strange, isolated occurrence. If the story relied on such, no sane reader would believe what happens in the story even though it could be proved true in life. We confirm the accuracy of this point of view whenever we read a newspaper account of a strange occurrence and find ourselves saying, "If it hadn't happened, I wouldn't believe it. Incredible, isn't it?" It may seem to be incredible, but it is true. *In fiction, however, a situation must seem to be credible, or it cannot be accepted as true.*

Tone and atmosphere   We remind ourselves again that the basic, shaping force of Galsworthy's story is his attitude toward the story's literal facts. Gessler makes fine boots; he refuses to compromise his ideal; he dies of slow starvation; the big firm takes over his shops. What does Galsworthy think of all this? Where shall we look beyond the matters already discussed earlier to find out? We can examine his tone and atmosphere, less tangible than plot, characters, theme, and symbolism, but perhaps the most potent and revealing of all.

In a very real sense, Galsworthy's tone *is* his attitude toward the facts of the story. When someone in real life speaks, we attend not only to what the person says, but also to the tone or attitude taken toward what that person is saying. In a story, we listen for the tone of the author's voice in the same way. "Written words," said Joseph Conrad, "have their accent, too."

What does Galsworthy think about Gessler's ideal, and what is his attitude toward his fate? Gessler is treated with the most sensitive consideration, as if Galsworthy were exhibiting something very uncommon in the human scene. For example:

> But if it were some new kind of footgear that he had not yet made me, then indeed he would observe ceremony—divesting me of my boot and holding it long in his hand, looking at it with eyes at once critical and loving, as if recalling the glow with which he had created it, and rebuking the way in which one had disorganized this masterpiece.

In an interesting and instructive way, Galsworthy has demonstrated how important it is to maintain a consistent tone throughout a story. When "Quality" was first published, the last sentence read:

> And I turned and went out quickly, for I did not want that youth to know that I could hardly see.

Later, this sentence was eliminated. Why? Apparently because it violated the story's tone by introducing sentimentality in the narrator for which there is no motivation.

Atmosphere is sometimes used to mean the setting of a story, or the physical environment in which the action takes place. In many stories, including Galsworthy's, atmosphere means psychological as well as physical environment. The two opening paragraphs of Galsworthy's story provide this psychological atmosphere, which gives direction to his attitudes and values.

The value of tone and atmosphere working together lies in their powerful and subtle suggestiveness. Galsworthy's tone and atmosphere come through mostly by indirection, and we know without his ever saying so that Gessler's fate is more than a personal tragedy. We feel, as we say, the enveloping tragedy, and we know it will spread, not end, with Gessler's death.

Tone is then, as we shall see again in the section on poetry, a figure of speech because it permeates the entire story and helps to interpret the symbolic action as distinguished from the mere surface action of the plot. We are now prepared to examine the symbolic action of "Quality."

The meaning of the story: the parts and the whole The unremitting quality of Gessler Brothers moves through three actions, which approximate three scenes in a one-act play. Galsworthy's attitude toward the three actions is established early by the title and the two opening paragraphs. The references to "quality," to the Gesslers' tenement that had a "certain quiet distinction," and to "those unvarying boots in the window" that "could only have been made by one who saw before him the Soul of Boot," all clearly reveal Galsworthy's respect for the Gessler "Ideal."

The first action presents the Gesslers pursuing their " 'Ardt,' " exercising extreme care with their customers' needs, and at peace with their world except for the complication introduced by the new competition of the big firms. Gessler Brothers had been for years the symbol of quality and persevering workmanship. These men had fused making a *living* with making a *life,* and their boots therefore represented their intrinsic character. When they offered a pair of boots to a customer, they offered themselves. When the narrator complains about a pair that creaked, Gessler says, " 'Zome boods . . . are bad from birdt. If I can do noding wid dem, I dake dem off your bill.' " There were no written guarantees carefully modified in small print; there was only Gessler Brothers, and that was enough.

The second action presents the pivotal event, the crisis in Gessler when he is forced by the big firms to decide whether to maintain his quality or meet the new competition. For Gessler this problem is basically moral, not economic. He does not make a living with his left hand and moral decisions with his right. The whole man makes all decisions, and his decision to maintain his quality followed from his moral integrity as the night the day. He knew in advance of their coming what the consequences of his decision would be: his business would decline, it would finally fail—but he would not compromise his ideal. The quality was maintained to the end, and the last boots he made for the narrator were "in shape and fit, in finish and quality of leather . . . the best he had ever made me."

The third action presents the resolution of the crisis, or the consequence of Gessler's decision: his economic failure, his death, and the success of the new firm that bought his shops. Perhaps the basic question to be answered is, What was defeated? Two men or what they stood for?

To answer these questions, we move to the symbolic level of meaning in the story. Because Gessler refused to compromise his ideal, he won a personal, moral victory, but his death symbolizes the defeat of something larger than himself, a defeat that constitutes a tragedy more far-reaching than his personal end. His death symbolizes a blow against the preindustrial practice of combining making a living with making a life. It symbolizes an attack on the personal responsibility taken by the artisan for his work. For Gessler there was no such thing as an economic morality apart from a personal morality. Gessler symbolizes the absorption of material values by human values. (For a brief discussion of these two kinds of value, see "Human Values and the Criticism of Experience," p. 406.) The larger tragedy of the story appears when the symbol is reversed, when human values are absorbed by material values, when boots are made to sell, as Gessler himself says, "'by adverdisement, nod by work,'" instead of being a joy to both the maker as artist and the buyer.

Comment on further fictional practices

The examination of "Quality" has not, of course, revealed all the standard devices and practices used by short-story writers, to say nothing of the many unconventional ones. Galsworthy has used the devices of first-person narrator and closed plot, but there are other kinds of narrators and plots which produce results quite different from Galsworthy's. While we review the steps already taken to analyze "Quality," we shall investigate other fictional practices as appropriate. Before we begin, one principle should be fixed in mind: *no device or practice in a story is good or bad except as its use makes it so; any device should be judged according to its effectiveness in the story.* Wharton's "Roman Fever" (p. 32) is radically different from "Quality," and to judge Wharton's story by Galsworthy's technique would be unspeakably insensitive to the entire cause-and-effect problem in fiction.

1. The facts of the story. Our first step was to locate the facts of "Quality" to understand its literal level. All analysis begins there if we wish to be clear-headed about the rest of it. This act freed us to examine Galsworthy's devices, to see what he had done with the facts, to define his attitude toward them, and to discover what symbolic meaning he had derived from them. To locate the literal facts is, then, the initial step into almost any story. If the exception appears in the form of pure symbolism (see 5, p. 19), it will be revealed as an exception because in looking for the literal facts we shall find none.

2. Author's controlling theme. Theme has been defined as the controlling idea that has determined everything Galsworthy has done in his story. Theme may mean a definite intellectual concept, as it does in Kafka's "A Hunger Artist," or it may indicate a highly complex situation, as for example in Faulkner's "A Rose for Emily." In general, the value of a story does not lie in its theme but rather in what the writer has done with it. The same general theme of the growing pains experienced by young people is used by Flannery O'Connor and Anderson, yet both stories (in this volume) develop and dramatize the theme in different ways. The theme of a story can usually be defined in a crisp abstraction, but the abstraction should never be accepted as the total meaning of a substantial story.

   3. Plot, or the structure of action. Although "Quality" has a closed plot, Galsworthy uses plot chiefly to reveal character. Many other writers, however, use closed plots for other reasons. This type of plot, with its definite resolution of conflict, is usually found in mystery stories such as Poe's "The Purloined Letter" and in stories that have an obvious thesis whose truth the writer attempts to demonstrate.

   The open plot has little or no resolution. Certain writers of serious stories, such as Sartre in "The Wall," may believe that resolutions cannot be found for many of our basic conflicts; they may refuse the formula of the closed plot because they reject on philosophical grounds a finished interpretation of a complicated world. Cheever rejects it in "The Enormous Radio," as does Porter in "Flowering Judas." Except when readers are looking for sheer entertainment and amusement, they have good reason to suspect a story that relies heavily on plot, especially the story with a trick ending whose plot machinery grinds audibly.

   4. Character. "Quality" is a judicious blend of plot, character, and theme; but many, if not most, stories rely mainly on one of the three. Character studies rely chiefly, of course, on fully drawn characters and very little on plot or theme.

   At the other extreme, in a story predominantly of plot, the characters may be little more than types, sometimes no more than pawns, used to create suspense or horror or a situation. Likewise, sometimes in a story predominantly of theme, the characters resemble counters moved about in such a way as to prove the theme. Does Kafka's "A Hunger Artist" entirely avoid the use of characters as pawns?

   There is, of course, always the middle ground, occupied, for example, by Gessler in "Quality" and by Braggioni in Porter's "Flowering Judas." These characters, rounded individuals, are types of humanity in the symbolic sense: they stand for groups of individuals and therefore achieve universality.

   5. Symbolism. Symbolism can appear almost anywhere in fiction: in characters, plots, natural objects, objects made by people, and situations. When a symbol is worked through an entire story, it can be used as an integrating device by which many facts are fused and made meaningful in some basic and comprehensive way. Characters are used to symbolize abstract ideas, as Gessler symbolizes quality, or a psychological state such as we find in Ellison's "King of the Bingo Game." In a sense, the symbol is the basic device of most imaginative literature.

   6. Narrator's point of view. In "Quality," the authority for telling the story is vested in the narrator by Galsworthy to convert the facts of the story into a credible, universal truth. The many kinds of narrators have been variously named and classified, but the basic kinds can perhaps be reduced to four.

First, there is the *first-person narrator,* as used by Galsworthy, who has the authority of an intimate witness, one who is directly involved in the action. In some stories the narrator is the principal character. Such narrators describe with unchallenged authority their own sensations and ideas. Such a narrator can invest a story with uncommon credibility, but the device has its obvious limitations because narrators can know and understand only what their own temperament and talents permit.

Second, there is the *dramatic narrator* who is effaced almost completely, as in Barthelme's "A City of Churches." This narrator resembles the playwright whose characters present themselves with little or no comment by the narrator. Modified in one way or another, this narrative device is very popular in current fiction because, perhaps, it gives the effect of impersonal objectivity and appeals to the scientific temper of our time.

Third, there is the *third-person limited narrator* who acquires knowledge through natural means only, as in Jackson's "The Lottery," Steinbeck's "Flight," and many others. Such a narrator is sometimes called a *roving narrator* who can be anywhere at any time except within the minds of the characters. In a sense, narrators of this kind are omniscient, with their omniscience artfully concealed.

And last, there is the *third-person omniscient narrrator.* Such narrators know everything and can be at any place at any time without having to explain their presence. Such a device gives authors extraordinary flexibility, particularly because they can look into the minds of their characters and report their thoughts and sensations. Thurber's "The Secret Life of Walter Mitty" uses such a narrator in a very special and effective manner.

Is there a best kind of narrator? The best narrator best fulfills the purposes of the author, and we judge the efficacy of a narrator as we judge all other elements in a story—according to the consequences produced in the story.

7. *Panorama and scene.* The function of the two devices of panorama and scene is to permit a necessary shift in focus. "Quality" uses both as appropriate to the purpose, but some stories rely on one or the other almost exclusively. The use of panorama is sometimes much more subtle than readers may recognize, including, as it does, setting and atmosphere. Both the holiday atmosphere and the apparently ordinary village setting that open Jackson's "The Lottery," for example, lend ironic force to the horror that later unfolds. And from the first paragraph of "Flight," Steinbeck's panoramic use of nature is frequent and becomes essential to the reader for both a character analysis of Pepé and an understanding of the relentless code by which he must live and die.

Scene, as we found in "Quality," is the focus of the close-up. A number of stories in this volume use scenes quite effectively—for example, White's "The Hour of Letdown," Wharton's "Roman Fever," Barthelme's "A City of Churches," and Walker's "To Hell with Dying."

8. *Credibility and the illusion of reality.* There are various levels of credibility, in fact, about five. "Quality" is credible on the realistic level, chiefly be-

cause the plot, characters, theme, setting, and atmosphere are all entirely probable on natural grounds. The meaning of this statement should become clearer as
we examine the remaining levels.

Hughes's mixture of fantasy and realism in "On the Road" is one step removed from the realistic level.

A story like Kafka's "A Hunger Artist" is another step away from the realistic
level because it veers toward, but does not seriously enter, the supernatural level.

The fourth and fifth levels of credibility are at times so closely merged in
the same story as to make them appear as one level, although the use of one is
possible without the other. We shall call them the symbolic and the supernatural
levels. Hawthorne's "Young Goodman Brown" is an example of the merger, an
uncommonly successful one.

A story (or poem such as Yeats's "The Second Coming") that uses the symbolic level exclusively, or almost so, is incomprehensible unless the symbols are
clearly understood. When symbols are used in a story told on the realistic level
of credibility, they are defined by the context of the story; this is not necessarily
true of a story that is credible only on the symbolic level. Such a story is credible
if its theme is comprehensible and its tone consistent, but to attempt to apply the
test of the realistic level to such a story is to misconceive the nature of the story's
art.

9. Tone and atmosphere. Consistency of tone and atmosphere is without
question one of the basic necessities of a good story, especially if the story is
satiric or ironic. If satire and irony are revealed by broad exaggeration, tone and
atmosphere may seem to make only a minor contribution; but if the satire and
irony are subtle and perhaps profound, consistency of tone and atmosphere is
indispensable. Also, maintaining something of a fine tonal balance can make essential contributions to the effectiveness and richness of a story. Certainly, Thurber's attitude toward Walter Mitty involves (and encourages in the reader) both
detached amusement and sympathetic identification. And the skillful balancing of
the two enlarges the scope of the story, encouraging both our free enjoyment of
the humor and our engagement in the more serious implications of Mitty's dilemma.

10. The meaning of the story: the parts and the whole. A reader may be
acute and discriminating, but the real test centers in this area. As is true of any
organism, the meaning of a story is always more than the sum of its parts. One
of the cardinal errors in the interpretation of imaginative literature is accepting a
part for the whole. The meaning of "Quality" does not lie in Gessler alone: it lies
in the interaction of Gessler with everything else in the story. This principle of
interpretation is often violated, and unless the principle is carefully observed,
Tolstoy's "Three Deaths," for example, can be easily misinterpreted, and some of
the symbolism in this story may escape all except the most discriminating readers.

First, master all the facts of a story, and then determine what has been done
with *all* of them. There is no shortcut to the precise interpretation of fiction,
poetry, or drama, but there is tremendous pleasure in mastering the approaches
to them.

A note on the novel   Most of the preceding observations concerning the structure of the short story can also be applied to the novel. Although the greater length of the novel gives readers increased responsibilities, particularly in fusing all the parts of the novel to make the complete whole of their focus and comprehension, the basic devices in both forms remain much the same. Like the short story, the novel uses the devices already discussed to transform the facts of the story into a piece of fictional art with meaning. The basic reading problem, then, is quite the same for both the short story and the novel, namely, to learn to read the forms.

What makes a good story?   Fortunately, there is no single formula to guarantee excellence. Fortunately indeed, because if there were, the fascinating variety in stories would be lost, and the formula would quickly bring boredom. Some readers demand entertainment of stories; other readers demand ideas or interesting characters or action, plot, and suspense. All such demands are reasonable, but if a reader demands, say, suspense and finds none, the story is not necessarily a failure. Suspense would have been quite ridiculous in Galsworthy's "Quality"; indeed, he dissipated all hope for it in his opening paragraph.

In our search for excellence, we may begin with one fairly stable assumption: *we should judge all the elements in a story according to the consequences they produce in the story.* Plot, character, theme, suspense—none of these things is good or bad except as its use makes it so. All good creative writers seek to use the right means to bring the desired ends. We therefore ask of every story, Has it been told well? Is it a piece of *literary art* whose technique and subject matter are fused to produce a meaningful whole? Such questions will at least reduce the temptation to condemn escape literature for its want of philosophy and parable literature for its want of sheer entertainment. There are thirty-eight stories in this volume and thirty-eight ways of telling them. Let us begin by judging every story within its own terms of construction, within its own frame of accomplishment. Some tellings may be better than others, and we shall look to this matter as we go along. We shall look to another ingredient also, a final and indispensable matter: having decided how well a story has been told, we shall ask about its value and its truth to humanity.

Writing About Fiction

To someone relatively new at writing about literature, the prospect typically brings along with it two questions, both wrapped in a little anxiety. What should I write about? How should I write about it? Although we have not been specifically addressing those questions, almost everything said in these preliminaries so far is directly applicable to answering one or the other of them. Furthermore, the comments made about the individual aspects of the short story "Quality" could essentially stand alone as specific examples of short pieces of writing about literature.

But here we want to shift from subtle answers to more direct ones. One response to both questions comes quickly to mind in the form of a working proposition: writing about literature is like writing about anything else. As process, it exhibits the same evolution as writing on other subjects: (1) selecting a topic, (2) gathering the facts, (3) narrowing toward a thesis, (4) organizing the material, (5) writing a draft, (6) revising the draft, and (7) writing the final paper. As a finished product, it should possess the usual qualities of any writing of genuine merit: clarity, unity, and effectiveness. So anyone who has done some writing on any subject should find at least a few familiar landmarks in the comments that follow on writing about literature, specifically on writing about fiction.

What to Write About Fiction

Close reading   A primary rule for writing about anything is—don't, without first having made a concentrated effort to understand it thoroughly. No amount of writing skill can camouflage ignorance of the subject. So a close "reading" of the facts of any subject is essential before settling on a particular aspect of it to define, praise, explain, condemn. We have just provided a generally useful pattern—then reviewed it step-by-step—to follow in reading fiction closely, in breaking it down into its constituent elements, and putting these back together again. Following such a pattern with tact and discrimination, as suggested earlier, is a practical means of understanding the functional elements of any story or novel. That understanding is, in turn, the primary means for an informed selection of the particular fictional elements to write about. It is also the main source of supporting details for interpreting and evaluating those elements for others. There are, however, other influences on choosing and writing about literary topics—for example, lively class discussion and reading in other works about literature, both general and particular.

Critical perspectives   Some sense of what others have said about literature and why they have said it can be extremely useful—for both stimulation and caution—in making choices of literary topics and treatments. Even a limited amount of reading in selected theoretical criticism (such as that by Coleridge and Krutch on pp. 1150 and 1112) can add perceptions to our experience of literature and solidity to our writing about it. One of the critics just named, for instance, we quote in the analytical comments on "Quality" above. Such reading is not really so forbidding, but simply constitutes the sort of general thought that hovers about almost any subject. And like Baskin-Robbins, modern applied criticism tempts us with a variety of flavors. Very briefly, one critic may write about a short story, for example, primarily from a historical or sociological perspective (valuing it as a product of a particular time and place); another, primarily from a psychoanalytical perspective (valuing it as an exploration of feelings, mental processes and states); and still another, primarily from a formalistic perspective (valuing it as a unified and self-contained work of art). In "Criticism: A Many-Windowed House" (see p.

1077), Malcolm Cowley succinctly surveys those (and some other) critical perspectives and gives his evaluation of their virtues and vices. His essay is, in fact, a quick and relatively painless means to get a sense of the various ways in which some critics have been writing about literature during the past fifty years or so. It is helpful in orienting and assessing one's own emerging literary perspectives in reading and writing about the short stories that follow. Most writing about literature is not, of course, limited to a single perspective. The comments on "Quality" above, for example, are mainly formalistic, but they blend into a historical perspective at some points. Whatever the critical perspective a writer may come to favor, some knowledge of other critical views can help one avoid the extremes of both timidity and arrogance in selecting topics and writing about them. The writer needs to read and to choose the particular topic with some awareness of the perspectives available, but without preconceptions. The reading of the story itself remains primary, and Cowley's advice about reading "not to impose meanings on a work, but to see what . . . [one] can find" is sound—just the sort of open-minded and close reading suggested earlier.

Quick-noting   Quick-noting in the margin of the text (or in numbered columns on paper) is a natural and practical companion to reading for enjoyment and a way of pulling together the story as a whole. The process soon becomes impractical, however, if more than symbols or brief phrases are jotted down. Plus and minus signs, check marks, stars, triangles, capital letters, and so on are genuine time-savers when assigned consistent meanings (great, lousy, key characterization, theme, key conflict, figurative language). Jottings on first reading will be a bit tentative anyway, and interruptions with more than quick-notes can strangely warp the reader's response to the story. Because short fiction often embodies a compact potency of meanings something like that of poetry, two complete readings of a story are essential (and the second is often a real eye-opener). In quick-noting, however, it is especially important to trust initial responses (they come only *once*)—until they are tested and found wanting by common sense and the context of the whole story. A real danger is simply to shrug off scenes, actions, images for which there is no clear purpose or explanation, apparent inconsistencies or oddities in language or structure or other elements. Instead, the alert quick-noter will use the question mark liberally. Anything strange may well be so intentionally, and a question mark is frequently the key to unlock levels of significance or meaning otherwise missed. Chances are good that something questioned by one person will also be questioned by others, so it frequently offers a natural avenue of mutual curiosity and of communication for later use by the writer.

Peripheral vision   An excellent guide for quick-noting is an active peripheral vision that simultaneously holds in view different and perhaps distant story elements and catches the connection among them, which relates minor characters and conflicts to major ones, which sees both the common stem of a cluster of words and their ripeness with thematic implications. Packed into the opening sentence of Jackson's "The Lottery" (p. 138), for example, is an unusual concentration of words linked by the common stem of their suggestion of a fertile, pastoral world (morning of June 27th, clear and sunny, fresh warmth, full summer day, flowers blossoming profusely, grass richly green). The concentration is not by accident, of course, but is purposively thematic in several ways (which close reading and quick-noting should help to highlight and clarify). Such quick-notes, after refinements easily made during a second reading of a story, permit rapid scanning of margin and text for related groupings of story elements. It is a fast and practical sort of mental hide-and-seek played with possible writing topics of limited scope. No time-consuming translation of all quick-notes into more conventional form on paper or cards is usually necessary or desirable. That should be done only *selectively,* after some progress in defining more specifically what to write about.

Limiting the topic   Fine whittling is next to fine writing, and it always comes first. The effective writer soon learns to cut original ideas to accord with the space and time for the actual writing (and the probable patience of the reader). So whittling away at initial topics for writing about fiction (whether assigned or chosen) differs little from the paring also necessary in writing on other subjects. Trying to write an evaluative critique of all aspects of a short story in a 500-word essay is like trying to launch a motorboat in a mud puddle. But an analysis of one element might float very nicely (for instance, the thematic significance of irony in Tolstoy's "Three Deaths" or of characterization in Galsworthy's "Quality"). Similarly, if the aim is a short comparative essay on the pair of Porter stories reprinted below (pp. 101–112), the necessary whittling to allow for convincing, detailed development might progress from "A Comparison of Two Porter Stories" to "Psychological Implications in 'The Grave' and 'Flowering Judas'" to "The Function of Memory in 'The Grave' and 'Flowering Judas.'" And so on. As a rule, writers should cut away what is of least personal interest and, within the limits of unity and adequate development, should write about those aspects of a story to which they respond most strongly. Lukewarm interest usually means dull writing, which cannot keep or feed a reader. In any event, the twin process of scanning the quick-notes and limiting the topic should culminate in a working thesis for the paper, a one-sentence statement of the main point the paper will try to make about the story or stories. Even though tentative, this thesis, in effect, bridges the gap between the questions of what and how to write about fiction.

How to Write About Fiction

Because Galsworthy's "Quality" is familiar, we can simply appropriate it to illustrate some points already made and to suggest a means for shaping a thesis and using it to help organize fictional material for writing a first draft of the paper. We can assume the writer has finished close reading and marginal quick-noting, has also read the analysis of the story given earlier, and is now limiting the topic toward a working thesis about aspects of the story not covered in that analysis.

One aspect is irony, a frequent method of fiction, therefore a doubly appropriate topic to use as an example here. Before the writer pursues irony in "Quality," however, it is of practical use to provide a brief sidenote on this element of potentially enormous delight and occasional dismay.

Sidenote on irony   At the simplest level, irony is saying one thing and meaning the opposite (A fine friend you are! What a great day!). By tone of voice and situation, we merely catch the discrepancy between apparent and intended meaning and make the necessary adjustment with a touch of humor and satisfaction. Irony is often more subtle in its indirection, but *it always requires the active mental participation of the reader, listener, or observer to achieve its end,* which is precisely why it is an effective figure of speech—and a dangerous one when the discrepancy is not caught (and the intended meaning reversed). Irony is not, however, merely a figure of speech, but the stuff of life. The varsity football tackle called Tiny Tim carries irony in his nickname. The long-anticipated date that turns into a disaster is ironic. So is the series of carefully planned political moves that becomes a comedy of errors when put into action. Irony involves our consciousness of a sharp contrast or discrepancy between intention and result, appearance and reality, expectation and actuality, character and role, and so on. Because life is full of such incongruities, our awareness of its irony can make one day more enjoyable and another perhaps endurable. The master chef whose sense of taste is lost, the stumblebum who enters ballet school, the blind man who makes a hole in one, the comedian whose private life is tragic—all display elements of discrepancy or incongruity which we term *ironic* and which heighten our sense of the humor or pathos they involve. Also ironic is the story of the ugly duckling who becomes a swan or the character of Shakespeare's wise fool or Sophocles' blind seer Tiresias or even Galsworthy's idealist bootmaker. In both life and literature, it is our awareness of the discrepancy that highlights the comic or tragic aspects of a statement, situation, action, or person (four "types" of irony) and increases the pleasure or anguish of our response. Irony creates its effects not by direct statement, but by indirection and implication. We actively participate in the process with necessary perceptions and adjustments in meaning, therefore making the conclusions partly our own and doubly effective when we finally reach them. We have a kind of vested interest in them, a satisfaction because they are partly ours. Because irony, therefore, is both frequent and effective in literature, we need to be alert to its methods and its results.

Finding a thesis   The writer returns to scanning the marginal quick-notes to "Quality" and keeps turning up contrasting or ironic combinations in characterization, plot, scene, and expression. In the order of their occurrence, the pertinent quick-notes are translated into a list of phrases quoted or closely paraphrased from the story itself, with a slash mark added to indicate the opposition or apparent discrepancy between the two parts of each phrase. The writer concludes the list with an appropriate, summarizing opposition, "Real / Ideal":

Ironic Combinations

M2		bootmaker / idealist
		boots' sooty / glow
M2		sardonic, but / best leather
2	*	sardonic leather of / Gessler himself
2	*	guttural accents of / Gessler-idealist
2	*	iron spectacles of / Gessler-visionary
		stitched into boots / timeless essence
		boot shop / like a church
		customer in dark well / dreamer-priest above
		noisy descent from / dream of boot
3	*	tells hardships of / his trade
3	*	conditions worsen / boots improve
3	*	terribly / lasting boots
4	*	rapidly aged, worn / idealist Gessler
4	*	bill sent with last / best boots made
5	*	expect 'slow starvation' / 'with his ideas'
1	*	all work day & night / 'let his fire go out'
		Real / Ideal

(The symbols down the left margin are explained below.)

The ironic quality of these generally incompatible combinations at the very least serves to emphasize the uneasy union of the ideal with the real. And further exploration by the writer could well contribute to that larger understanding usually essential for writing on even a small aspect of a story.

Some suggestions on writing methods   The list does, of course, immediately suggest good possibilities for each of the most common methods of writing about fiction: *explication,* a sentence-by-sentence, detailed unfolding of the meanings of a unified scene or segment; *analysis,* a breaking down into individual story elements for close study and, usually, relation to theme; and *comparison-contrast,* a revealing consideration of the similarities or differences or both between two characters, symbols, or other aspects of a story or stories. The writer could *explicate* the short, symbolic scene in which the boot shop is implicitly a church, the narrator-customer a parishioner, and Gessler a kind of priest of Idealism. An *analysis* of the ironic aspects of Gessler's characterization might be especially worth pursuing. Or the writer might want to *compare-contrast* the attitudes of the narrator and the new shopkeeper toward Gessler. Each of these is a possible step toward a working thesis and a typical method of writing about it.

Still thesis hunting   The writer decides to pursue the ironic aspects of Gessler's characterization as reflected in several of the passages quick-noted, because their literal or suggestive combination of incongruous elements implies a union designed in conflict. Pursuing the idea of conflict down the list, the writer recalls or checks here and there the fuller context in the story itself. Galsworthy's symbolic suggestion of Plato's idealism is, of course, pointed out in the analysis of "Quality" above. The ideal is the mental or visionary or spiritual realm of absolute and eternal perfection. It seems to the writer, therefore, that the descent from the heights of Platonic idealism way down to a boot on earth is a descent of extreme or *ironic* distance. Yet it is a descent deliberately chosen by Galsworthy when he created his idealist as a bootmaker. In further characterizing his bootmaker, Galsworthy makes (and repeats for emphasis) certain other incongruous associations, such as giving guttural, imperfect speech to his seeker of perfection and making the glance of his visionary not merely spectacled, but "iron-spectacled" (and, with time, the iron becomes "rusty"). The leather with which Gessler works is the finest he can obtain, yet is "sardonic" and works *against* his best efforts at perfection (the *sardonic* is a form of irony and literally means "mocking"). And Galsworthy elaborately compares the bootmaker's features to his sardonic leather except for the discrepancy of his "eyes, which were . . . of one secretly possessed by the ideal." The ironic discrepancy in these combinations, therefore, suggests to the writer that the "bitter struggle" of Galsworthy's idealist is ultimately internal, between his absolute commitment to the ideal and his human, earthbound limitations which deny fulfillment. And other ironic combinations in the quick-note list tend to confirm that suggestion of internal conflict—for example, when the idealist essentially confesses the "hardships of his trade" to the narrator "as if something had given way within him." Still other instances include the repeated coupling of the worsening conditions of Gessler's situation with the improving quality of his boots (indicating strenuous commitment) and the bootmaker's own acknowledgment of his limitations in yet another ironic yoking of the material with the ideal, when the last, best boots arrive, for the *first* time with a bill for immediate payment (too late). So Gessler's death by starvation ends at once his life, his dream, and his conflict. Having in that way explored the quick-note list again, the writer can more sharply focus a working thesis: *in Galsworthy's "Quality," the ironic characterization of the idealist heightens our sense of his "bitter struggle" while it suggests that the ultimate conflict between idealism and the real world is internal and is resolved only by death.*

Working the working thesis   The working thesis is well named. It earns its keep up to the point of writing, then retires. Using it as a magnet, the writer can now draw together those story details directly related to the stated point. The magnet functions, of course, in an *ex*clusive as well as an *in*clusive way and ensures the unity of the material to be organized for writing. An easy way for the writer to begin using the working thesis is simply to circle or otherwise mark each item *clearly pertinent* to it in the list of quick-notes already translated to a sheet of paper—as illustrated with asterisks just to the left of items in the list for "Quality" above. The magnet has not attracted the item "boot shop / like a church," for example, because the working thesis is not primarily concerned with the story line and symbols (though sometimes ironic) that mainly characterize the nature of idealism, but rather with ironic elements that more directly reflect the internal struggle of the idealist himself. The writer should act here as in love; if the attraction remains questionable after reasonable acquaintance, it probably isn't strong enough to warrant further consideration.

Choosing a structure and outlining   The structure of prose is determined by the pattern or method of development predominant in writing it. Essentially, a familiarity with these patterns is useful to a writer on *any subject* because they are based on modes of human perception, so they directly relate to how best to get something into a reader's head clearly and effectively. Seven methods of development especially may have the features of old friends; if not, any handbook to rhetoric will offer a succinct review of definition, example, classification, analysis, comparison or contrast (or both), and persuasion. These are friends indeed to the writer, providing some tested means of gauging the kind of potential for development *inherent in the working thesis and the nature of the material on which the thesis is based.* But no writer can pose them as possibilities without being familiar with them. They can also, however, become the seven deadly sins of writing unless the writer resists the temptation to apply this or that method either artificially or exclusively. The method should grow out of a thoughtful grasp of the material itself (and not be arbitrarily imposed on it)—always within considerations of audience and purpose, of course. Even the phrasing of the working thesis, combined with a little common sense, will frequently suggest a natural and effective method of development, sometimes even an appropriate arrangement of details within that method. The writer's working thesis for "Quality," for example, suggests an analytical paper on Galsworthy's ironic characterization in relation to aspects of conflict and theme. The *analysis,* however, will necessarily involve a careful *definition* of irony (as sharp contrast or incongruity in language, situation, or action) and heavy use of *examples* drawn from the story. And because writers cannot discuss resolution until they establish the nature of the conflict and cannot characterize that conflict without first considering its sources in the story, a logical arrangement of details for the paper is also strongly suggested by the working thesis. Another advantage, therefore, of using the quick-note list suggested here is that, for short papers at least, no outline as such is usually required (unless, of course, by assignment). The writer can simply order the items by numbering down the extreme left margin, as shown above with the list for "Quality," in that case also noting "define irony here" at the number that seems best for the reader's needs (M2 in the left margin means "mention in part 2"). The writer need add only the notion of opening and closing with the report and evaluation of Gessler's death by the new shopkeeper (ironic mixtures of literal accuracy and figurative inaccuracy), and just about everything is in place. If specific statement of points and subpoints seems genuinely helpful, an ordered scratch outline is but a small step from the translated, numbered quick-notes.

Writing the first draft   A draft is a preliminary sketch or scheme to which the intensifier *first* is added to emphasize its tentativeness. The writer's only nightmare is to be forever caught in a single sentence. To write or not to write is *not* the question here. The great virtue of the first draft *is* its tentativeness, and the wise writer courts that virtue by writing and writing and writing. Because writing *is* thinking made public, the *process* of writing is simply a continuum of thinking gently harnessed to a purpose and an order. The writer, therefore, needs but to keep slack in the reins, to maintain some flexibility in writing the first draft, for the mind to continue working the materials and making refinements in the plan. Thinking cannot be turned off, only ignored—and that later regretted.

Revising into final copy   Time does not heal all things, but it helps a writer achieve *distance* from what has been written. It is all too easy to be swept away by the splendor of what one has just rolled from the typewriter. Losing it in a desk drawer for even a day or two can do remarkable things for the writer's eyesight. It can also add a little objectivity and a lot of hindsight (which will fortunately appear as foresight in the final draft). Time granting those qualities, the writer can set about revising the first draft into a crisp, finished essay on fiction by using two approaches, one for content and one for form and correctness. Here are two sets of questions—essentially the same as those in "Writing About Poetry" below—that can serve as checklists for revising the first draft.

Content

1. Is the title specific, and does it indicate clearly what the paper is about? Does it go beyond clarity, when possible, to effective, memorable suggestion of the main point?
2. Is the thesis of the paper evident in the introduction?
3. Is every point in the paper related in some way to the thesis?
4. Are the stages of the argument clearly marked with transitions between major ideas?
5. Are the ideas supported by examples and details from the story?
6. Are there gaps in the argument that need to be filled?
7. Are there relevant details in the story that have been omitted from the discussion, especially those that seem to work *against* the thesis?
8. Does the draft achieve a proper balance in the space given to major and minor points?
9. Are there sentences or paragraphs that do not contribute to the main line of argument?
10. Does the conclusion follow from the main argument of the paper, or is it merely a restatement of the introduction?

Form and correctness

1. Are there unnecessary words and phrases? Is the language repetitious? Are there more exact terms that could be substituted?
2. Are the sentences varied? Are there careless lapses into fragments or mixed constructions? When read aloud, do the sentences come in short, choppy, repetitious patterns? Are the combinations of sounds like a fingernail screeched across a blackboard?
3. Does every paragraph have a topic sentence? Are the paragraphs fully developed, with supporting details and examples? Are there transitional phrases indicating shifts in thought?
4. Is the use of tense consistent? Does the paper shift back and forth between present tense ("Galsworthy refers to Gessler as an 'owl surprised in daylight'

. . .") and past tense ("Galsworthy presented the bootmaker as dreaming in the real world . . .")?

5. If phrases are quoted directly from the story, have quotation marks been used? If phrases or sentences are *not* quoted, why not?
6. Has the draft been proofread for careless errors—words omitted, misspellings, apostrophes omitted, commas or other marks of punctuation misused?
7. Has a reasonable effort been made to employ the *rich* potential of the language (including figures of speech, apt allusions, graphic imagery, structural principles) to make the writing itself *interesting* as well as informative, to lift it above a ho-hum style?
8. Has adequate attention been given to natural positions of emphasis, the beginnings and endings of paragraphs and of the whole paper? Are they simply frittered away, or do they contain main points clothed in expressions likely to lodge in the reader's mind?

Reading forward and backward   The writer should read from the beginning to the end of the draft to get a fresh sense of how convincing and complete the development of the thesis is (and perhaps how dull?). Occasional check marks in the margin can be used to note passages to return to for some rhetorical carpentry after the reading. The writer should actually *use* the *content* checklist, scanning it both before and after the reading. The same kind of forward reading is also useful for checking some aspects of form and correctness. However, for any possible slips at the sentence level or below (including sentence structure, punctuation, diction, grammar), the writer might want to read through the entire paper *backwards,* sentence by sentence (easily done by stopping at capital letters going backwards, then reading the sentence forward—with a sheet of paper to move up the page if that is helpful). The method is especially useful in uncovering errors writers *know* they are prone to make and can look for specifically. It permits the writer's mind to do that by disorienting it so that the normal human focus on one's own ideas and their convincing presentation is discombobulated. And with that checking done, the writer can perhaps avoid discombobulating the reader—but only by also quickly checking the final paper copied from the draft for careless errors (something the mental drowsiness of copying especially encourages).

On evaluating an interpretation   Language is the most complex of all humanity's inventions—and the most useful. It is both only because it is constantly developing new potential for adhering precisely to every slight rise and fall, curve and convolution, acceleration, meditative pause, and dead calm of two other immense complexities, human perception and human response. And in interpreting literature, the writers face those complexities in every direction they turn, including inward. Little wonder, then, that differences in interpretation occur. Far more wonder that in the hands of rare genius language can be so structured as to bear at once and magnificently a number of complementary levels of significance. But how can one deal directly with the practical issue of determining the validity of a literary interpretation, whether focused on prose fiction, a poem, or a play? The issue is discussed more thoroughly in "Evaluating an Interpretation" (p. 437), where the remarks are applicable to all literary interpretation (though the immediate focus is poetry). Here it is sufficient simply to conclude with a little common sense to moderate between extremes. If a work of literature can "mean" anything anyone says it means, language has no meaning at all, and we are beyond Alice's looking-glass, where left is right and something nothing. If, on the other hand, only one interpretation of a work were valid or "right," the ever-moving, ever-working power of language would become at once a dead and level sea and genius a dunce. This last reminds us of a friend's account of taking his young son to see the ocean for the first time. As most of us on like occasions, the boy was awestruck, so he sank quietly down on the sand, looked up at his father, and said, "Daddy, I'm just going to sit here till it stops." When faced with the prospect of writing about literature for the first few times, most of us would probably feel a strong kinship with that boy. Our awe and anxiety are natural enough in the face of the ceaseless energy of language somehow harnessed to meaning by the gifted writer. We need but remember, however, to trust our own responses first, then to pursue the reasons that justify those responses *in the facts of the story, poem, or play itself,* as we have suggested here. With that balance as the main character of our writing about literature, we will have some assurance that we can avoid both unacceptable extremes in our interpretations.

Edith Wharton (1862–1937)
Roman Fever

Edith Wharton's "Roman Fever" differs from Galsworthy's "Quality" in many ways. Meaning in stories can be controlled and made manifest variously—through plot, character, theme, symbol, irony, tone, and so on. "Quality" is a blend of plot, character, and theme, but our analysis above has shown the basic importance to Galsworthy of theme, as the story's title indicates. "Roman Fever" is quite a different matter. Readers who look exclusively for philosophical ideas may find too few, and other readers who look for subtle character analysis may find too little, but readers who enjoy the revelation of character and theme through plot will be richly rewarded. The sudden revelation of character made credible is perhaps Wharton's chief technical achievement here.

1
From the table at which they had been lunching two American ladies of ripe but well-cared-for middle age moved across the lofty terrace of the Roman restaurant and, leaning on its parapet, looked first at each other, and then down on the outspread glories

of the Palatine[1] and the Forum, with the same expression of vague but benevolent approval.

As they leaned there a girlish voice echoed up gaily from the stairs leading to the court below. "Well, come along, then," it cried, not to them but to an invisible companion, "and let's leave the young things to their knitting"; and a voice as fresh laughed back: "Oh, look here, Babs, not actually *knitting*—" "Well, I mean figuratively," rejoined the first. "After all, we haven't left our poor parents much else to do . . ." and at that point the turn of the stairs engulfed the dialogue.

The two ladies looked at each other again, this time with a tinge of smiling embarrassment, and the smaller and paler one shook her head and coloured slightly.

"Barbara!" she murmured, sending an unheard rebuke after the mocking voice in the stairway.

5 The other lady, who was fuller, and higher in colour, with a small determined nose supported by vigorous black eyebrows, gave a good-humoured laugh. "That's what our daughters think of us!"

Her companion replied by a deprecating gesture. "Not of us individually. We must remember that. It's just the collective modern idea of Mothers. And you see—" Half guiltily she drew from her handsomely mounted black handbag a twist of crimson silk run through by two fine knitting needles. "One never knows," she murmured. "The new system has certainly given us a good deal of time to kill; and sometimes I get tired just looking—even at this." Her gesture was now addressed to the stupendous scene at their feet.

The dark lady laughed again, and they both relapsed upon the view, contemplating it in silence, with a sort of diffused serenity which might have been borrowed from the spring effulgence of the Roman skies. The luncheon-hour was long past, and the two had their end of the vast terrace to themselves. At its opposite extremity a few groups, detained by a lingering look at the outspread city, were gathering up guidebooks and fumbling for tips. The last of them scattered, and the two ladies were alone on the air-washed height.

"Well, I don't see why we shouldn't just stay here," said Mrs. Slade, the lady of the high colour and energetic brows. Two derelict basketchairs stood near, and she pushed them into the angle of the parapet, and settled herself in one, her gaze upon the Palatine. "After all, it's still the most beautiful view in the world."

"It always will be, to me," assented her friend Mrs. Ansley, with so slight a stress on the "me" that Mrs. Slade, though she noticed it, wondered if it were not merely accidental, like the random underlinings of old-fashioned letter-writers.

10 "Grace Ansley was always old-fashioned," she thought; and added aloud, with a retrospective smile: "It's a view we've both been familiar with for a good many years. When we first met here we were younger than our girls are now. You remember?"

"Oh, yes, I remember," murmured Mrs. Ansley, with the same undefinable stress.— "There's that head-waiter wondering," she interpolated. She was evidently far less sure than her companion of herself and of her rights in the world.

"I'll cure him of wondering," said Mrs. Slade, stretching her hand toward a bag as discreetly opulent-looking as Mrs. Ansley's. Signing to the head-waiter, she explained that she and her friend were old lovers of Rome, and would like to spend the end of the afternoon looking down on the view—that is, if it did not disturb the service? The head-waiter, bowing over her gratuity, assured her that the ladies were most welcome, and would be still more so if they would condescend to remain for dinner. A full-moon night, they would remember. . . .

---

[1] Palace of the Roman Caesars.

Mrs. Slade's black brows drew together, as though references to the moon were out-of-place and even unwelcome. But she smiled away her frown as the head-waiter retreated. "Well, why not? We might do worse. There's no knowing, I suppose, when the girls will be back. Do you even know back from *where?* I don't!"

Mrs. Ansley again coloured slightly. "I think those young Italian aviators we met at the Embassy invited them to fly to Tarquinia[2] for tea. I suppose they'll want to wait and fly back by moonlight."

15   "Moonlight—moonlight! What a part it still plays. Do you suppose they're as sentimental as we were?"

"I've come to the conclusion that I don't in the least know what they are," said Mrs. Ansley. "And perhaps we didn't know much more about each other."

"No; perhaps we didn't."

Her friend gave her a shy glance. "I never should have supposed you were sentimental, Alida."

"Well, perhaps I wasn't." Mrs. Slade drew her lids together in retrospect; and for a few moments the two ladies, who had been intimate since childhood, reflected how little they knew each other. Each one, of course, had a label ready to attach to the other's name; Mrs. Delphin Slade, for instance, would have told herself, or any one who asked her, that Mrs. Horace Ansley, twenty-five years ago, had been exquisitely lovely—no, you wouldn't believe it, would you? . . . though, of course, still charming, distinguished. . . . Well, as a girl she had been exquisite; far more beautiful than her daughter Barbara, though certainly Babs, according to the new standards at any rate, was more effective—had more *edge,* as they say. Funny where she got it, with those two nullities as parents. Yes; Horace Ansley was—well, just the duplicate of his wife. Museum specimens of old New York. Good-looking, irreproachable, exemplary. Mrs. Slade and Mrs. Ansley had lived opposite each other—actually as well as figuratively—for years. When the drawing-room curtains in No. 20 East 73rd Street were renewed, No. 23, across the way, was always aware of it. And of all the movings, buyings, travels, anniversaries, illnesses—the tame chronicle of an estimable pair. Little of it escaped Mrs. Slade. But she had grown bored with it by the time her husband made his big *coup* in Wall Street, and when they bought in upper Park Avenue had already begun to think: "I'd rather live opposite a speak-easy for a change; at least one might see it raided." The idea of seeing Grace raided was so amusing that (before the move) she launched it at a woman's lunch. It made a hit, and went the rounds—she sometimes wondered if it had crossed the street, and reached Mrs. Ansley. She hoped not, but didn't much mind. Those were the days when respectability was at a discount, and it did the irreproachable no harm to laugh at them a little.

20   A few years later, and not many months apart, both ladies lost their husbands. There was an appropriate exchange of wreaths and condolences, and a brief renewal of intimacy in the half-shadow of their mourning; and now, after another interval, they had run across each other in Rome, at the same hotel, each of them the modest appendage of a salient daughter. The similarity of their lot had again drawn them together, lending itself to mild jokes, and the mutual confession that, if in old days it must have been tiring to "keep up" with daughters, it was now, at times, a little dull not to.

No doubt, Mrs. Slade reflected, she felt her unemployment more than poor Grace ever would. It was a big drop from being the wife of Delphin Slade to being his widow. She had always regarded herself (with a certain conjugal pride) as his equal in social gifts, as contributing her full share to the making of the exceptional couple they were: but the difference after his death was irremediable. As the wife of the famous corporation lawyer,

_____

[2] Town in central Italy.

always with an international case or two on hand, every day brought its exciting and un-expected obligation: the impromptu entertaining of eminent colleagues from abroad, the hurried dashes on legal business to London, Paris or Rome, where the entertaining was so handsomely reciprocated; the amusement of hearing in her wake: "What, that handsome woman with the good clothes and the eyes is Mrs. Slade—*the* Slade's wife? Really? Gener-ally the wives of celebrities are such frumps."

Yes; being *the* Slade's widow was a dullish business after that. In living up to such a husband all her faculties had been engaged; now she had only her daughter to live up to, for the son who seemed to have inherited his father's gifts had died suddenly in boyhood. She had fought through that agony because her husband was there, to be helped and to help; now, after the father's death, the thought of the boy had become unbearable. There was nothing left but to mother her daughter; and dear Jenny was such a perfect daughter that she needed no excessive mothering. "Now with Babs Ansley I don't know that I *should* be so quiet," Mrs. Slade sometimes half-enviously reflected; but Jenny, who was younger than her brilliant friend, was that rare accident, an extremely pretty girl who somehow made youth and prettiness seem as safe as their absence. It was all perplexing—and to Mrs. Slade a little boring. She wished that Jenny would fall in love—with the wrong man, even; that she might have to be watched, outmanoeuvred, rescued. And instead, it was Jenny who watched her mother, kept her out of draughts, made sure that she had taken her tonic. . . .

Mrs. Ansley was much less articulate than her friend, and her mental portrait of Mrs. Slade was slighter, and drawn with fainter touches. "Alida Slade's awfully brilliant; but not as brilliant as she thinks," would have summed it up; though she would have added, for the enlightenment of strangers, that Mrs. Slade had been an extremely dashing girl; much more so than her daughter, who was pretty, of course, and clever in a way, but had none of her mother's—well, "vividness," some one had once called it. Mrs. Ansley would take up current words like this, and cite them in quotation marks, as unheard-of audacities. No; Jenny was not like her mother. Sometimes Mrs. Ansley thought Alida Slade was disap-pointed; on the whole she had had a sad life. Full of failures and mistakes; Mrs. Ansley had always been rather sorry for her. . . .

So these two ladies visualized each other, each through the wrong end of her little telescope.

2

For a long time they continued to sit side by side without speaking. It seemed as though, to both, there was a relief in laying down their somewhat futile activities in the presence of the vast Memento Mori[3] which faced them. Mrs. Slade sat quite still, her eyes fixed on the golden slope of the Palace of the Caesars, and after a while Mrs. Ansley ceased to fidget with her bag, and she too sank into meditation. Like many intimate friends, the two ladies had never before had occasion to be silent together, and Mrs. Ansley was slightly embarrassed by what seemed, after so many years, a new stage in their intimacy, and one with which she did not yet know how to deal.

Suddenly the air was full of that deep clangour of bells which periodically covers Rome with a roof of silver. Mrs. Slade glanced at her wristwatch. "Five o'clock already," she said, as though surprised.

Mrs. Ansley suggested interrogatively: "There's bridge at the Embassy at five." For a long time Mrs. Slade did not answer. She appeared to be lost in contemplation, and Mrs. Ansley thought the remark had escaped her. But after a while she said, as if speaking out

---

[3] An object, usually emblematic, used as a reminder of death.

of a dream: "Bridge, did you say? Not unless you want to. . . . But I don't think I will, you know."

"Oh, no," Mrs. Ansley hastened to assure her. "I don't care to at all. It's so lovely here; and so full of old memories, as you say." She settled herself in her chair, and almost furtively drew forth her knitting. Mrs. Slade took sideway note of this activity, but her own beautifully cared-for hands remained motionless on her knee.

"I was just thinking," she said slowly, "what different things Rome stands for to each generation of travellers. To our grandmothers, Roman fever; to our mothers, sentimental dangers—how we used to be guarded!—to our daughters, no more dangers than the middle of Main Street. They don't know it—but how much they're missing!"

30   The long golden light was beginning to pale, and Mrs. Ansley lifted her knitting a little closer to her eyes. "Yes; how we were guarded!"

"I always used to think," Mrs. Slade continued, "that our mothers had a much more difficult job than our grandmothers. When Roman fever stalked the streets it must have been comparatively easy to gather in the girls at the danger hour; but when you and I were young, with such beauty calling us, and the spice of disobedience thrown in, and no worse risk than catching cold during the cool hour after sunset, our mothers used to be put to it to keep us in—didn't they?"

She turned again toward Mrs. Ansley, but the latter had reached a delicate point in her knitting. "One, two, three—slip two; yes, they must have been," she assented, without looking up.

Mrs. Slade's eyes rested on her with a deepened attention "She can knit—in the face of *this!* How like her. . . ."

Mrs. Slade leaned back, brooding, her eyes ranging from the ruins which faced her to the long green hollow of the Forum, the fading glow of the church fronts beyond it, and the outlying immensity of the Colosseum. Suddenly she thought: "It's all very well to say that our girls have done away with sentiment and moonlight. But if Babs Ansley isn't out to catch that young aviator—the one who's a Marchese—then I don't know anything. And Jenny has no chance beside her. I know that too. I wonder if that's why Grace Ansley likes the two girls to go everywhere together? My poor Jenny as a foil—!" Mrs. Slade gave a hardly audible laugh, and at the sound Mrs. Ansley dropped her knitting.

35   "Yes?"

"I—oh, nothing. I was only thinking how your Babs carries everything before her. That Campolieri boy is one of the best matches in Rome. Don't look so innocent, my dear—you know he is. And I was wondering, ever so respectfully, you understand . . . wondering how two such exemplary characters as you and Horace had managed to produce anything quite so dynamic." Mrs. Slade laughed again, with a touch of asperity.

Mrs. Ansley's hands lay inert across her needles. She looked straight out at the great accumulated wreckage of passion and splendour at her feet. But her small profile was almost expressionless. At length she said: "I think you overrate Babs, my dear."

Mrs. Slade's tone grew easier. "No; I don't. I appreciate her. And perhaps envy you. Oh, my girl's perfect; if I were a chronic invalid I'd—well, I think I'd rather be in Jenny's hands. There must be times . . . but there! I always wanted a brilliant daughter . . . and never quite understood why I got an angel instead."

Mrs. Ansley echoed her laugh in a faint murmur. "Babs is an angel too."

40   "Of course—of course! But she's got rainbow wings. Well, they're wandering by the sea with their young men; and here we sit . . . and it all brings back the past a little too acutely."

Mrs. Ansley had resumed her knitting. One might almost have imagined (if one had known her less well, Mrs. Slade reflected) that, for her also, too many memories rose from the lengthening shadows of those august ruins. But no; she was simply absorbed in her work. What was there for her to worry about? She knew that Babs would almost certainly come back engaged to the extremely eligible Campolieri. "And she'll sell the New York house, and settle down near them in Rome, and never be in their way . . . she's much too tactful. But she'll have an excellent cook, and just the right people in for bridge and cocktails . . . and a perfectly peaceful old age among her grandchildren."

Mrs. Slade broke off this prophetic flight with a recoil of self-disgust. There was no one of whom she had less right to think unkindly than of Grace Ansley. Would she never cure herself of envying her? Perhaps she had begun too long ago.

She stood up and leaned against the parapet, filling her troubled eyes with the tranquillizing magic of the hour. But instead of tranquillizing her the sight seemed to increase her exasperation. Her gaze turned toward the Colosseum. Already its golden flank was drowned in purple shadow, and above it the sky curved crystal clear, without light or colour. It was the moment when afternoon and evening hang balanced in mid-heaven.

Mrs. Slade turned back and laid her hand on her friend's arm. The gesture was so abrupt that Mrs. Ansley looked up, startled.

45   "The sun's set. You're not afraid, my dear?"

"Afraid—?"

"Of Roman fever or pneumonia? I remember how ill you were that winter. As a girl you had a very delicate throat, hadn't you?"

"Oh, we're all right up here. Down below, in the Forum, it does get deathly cold, all of a sudden . . . but not here."

"Ah, of course you know because you had to be so careful." Mrs. Slade turned back to the parapet. She thought: "I must make one more effort not to hate her." Aloud she said. "Whenever I look at the Forum from up here, I remember that story about a great-aunt of yours, wasn't she? A dreadfully wicked great-aunt?"

50   "Oh, yes; Great-aunt Harriet. The one who was supposed to have sent her young sister out to the Forum after sunset to gather a night-blooming flower for her album. All our great-aunts and grandmothers used to have albums of dried flowers."

Mrs. Slade nodded. "But she really sent her because they were in love with the same man—"

"Well, that was the family tradition. They said Aunt Harriet confessed it years afterward. At any rate, the poor little sister caught the fever and died. Mother used to frighten us with the story when we were children."

"And you frightened *me* with it, that winter when you and I were here as girls. The winter I was engaged to Delphin."

Mrs. Ansley gave a faint laugh. "Oh, did I? Really frightened you? I don't believe you're easily frightened."

55   "Not often; but I was then. I was easily frightened because I was too happy. I wonder if you know what that means?"

"I—yes. . . ." Mrs. Ansley faltered.

"Well, I suppose that was why the story of your wicked aunt made such an impression on me. And I thought: 'There's no more Roman fever, but the Forum is deathly cold after sunset—especially after a hot day. And the Colosseum's even colder and damper.'"

"The Colosseum—?"

"Yes. It wasn't easy to get in, after the gates were locked for the night. Far from easy. Still, in those days it could be managed; it *was* managed, often. Lovers met there who couldn't meet elsewhere. You knew that?"

60   "I—I daresay. I don't remember."

"You don't remember? You don't remember going to visit some ruins or other one evening, just after dark, and catching a bad chill? You were supposed to have gone to see the moon rise. People always said that expedition was what caused your illness."

There was a moment's silence; then Mrs. Ansley rejoined: "Did they? It was all so long ago."

"Yes. And you got well again—so it didn't matter. But I suppose it struck your friends—the reason given for your illness, I mean—because everybody knew you were so prudent on account of your throat, and your mother took such care of you. . . . You *had* been out late sight-seeing, hadn't you, that night?"

"Perhaps I had. The most prudent girls aren't always prudent. What made you think of it now?"

65   Mrs. Slade seemed to have no answer ready. But after a moment she broke out: "Because I simply can't bear it any longer—!"

Mrs. Ansley lifted her head quickly. Her eyes were wide and very pale. "Can't bear what?"

"Why—your not knowing that I've always known why you went."

"Why I went—?"

"Yes. You think I'm bluffing, don't you? Well, you went to meet the man I was engaged to—and I can repeat every word of the letter that took you there."

70   While Mrs. Slade spoke Mrs. Ansley had risen unsteadily to her feet. Her bag, her knitting and gloves, slid in a panic-stricken heap to the ground. She looked at Mrs. Slade as though she were looking at a ghost.

"No, no—don't," she faltered out.

"Why not? Listen, if you don't believe me. 'My one darling, things can't go on like this. I must see you alone. Come to the Colosseum immediately after dark tomorrow. There will be somebody to let you in. No one whom you need fear will suspect'—but perhaps you've forgotten what the letter said?"

Mrs. Ansley met the challenge with an unexpected composure. Steadying herself against the chair she looked at her friend, and replied: "No; I know it by heart too."

"And the signature? 'Only *your* D.S.' Was that it? I'm right, am I? That was the letter that took you out that evening after dark?"

75   Mrs. Ansley was still looking at her. It seemed to Mrs. Slade that a slow struggle was going on behind the voluntarily controlled mask of her small quiet face. "I shouldn't have thought she had herself so well in hand," Mrs. Slade reflected, almost resentfully. But at this moment Mrs. Ansley spoke. "I don't know how you knew. I burnt that letter at once."

"Yes; you would, naturally—you're so prudent!" The sneer was open now. "And if you burnt the letter you're wondering how on earth I know what was in it. That's it, isn't it?"

Mrs. Slade waited, but Mrs. Ansley did not speak.

"Well, my dear, I know what was in that letter because I wrote it!"

"You wrote it?"

80   "Yes."

The two women stood for a minute staring at each other in the last golden light. Then Mrs. Ansley dropped back into her chair. "Oh," she murmured, and covered her face with her hands.

Mrs. Slade waited nervously for another word or movement. None came, and at length she broke out: "I horrify you."

Mrs. Ansley's hands dropped to her knee. The face they uncovered was streaked with tears. "I wasn't thinking of you. I was thinking—it was the only letter I ever had from him!"

"And I wrote it. Yes; I wrote it! But I was the girl he was engaged to. Did you happen to remember that?"

85   Mrs. Ansley's head drooped again. "I'm not trying to excuse myself . . . I remembered. . . ."
           "And still you went?"
           "Still I went."
           Mrs. Slade stood looking down on the small bowed figure at her side. The flame of her wrath had already sunk, and she wondered why she had ever thought there would be any satisfaction in inflicting so purposeless a wound on her friend. But she had to justify herself.
           "You do understand? I'd found out—and I hated you, hated you. I knew you were in love with Delphin—and I was afraid; afraid of you, of your quiet ways, your sweetness . . . your . . . well, I wanted you out of the way, that's all. Just for a few weeks; just till I was sure of him. So in a blind fury I wrote that letter . . . I don't know why I'm telling you now."

90   "I suppose," said Mrs. Ansley slowly, "it's because you've always gone on hating me."
           "Perhaps. Or because I wanted to get the whole thing off my mind." She paused. "I'm glad you destroyed the letter. Of course I never thought you'd die."
           Mrs. Ansley relapsed into silence, and Mrs. Slade, leaning above her, was conscious of a strange sense of isolation, of being cut off from the warm current of human communion. "You think me a monster!"
           "I don't know. . . . It was the only letter I had, and you say he didn't write it?"
           "Ah, how you care for him still!"

95   "I cared for the memory," said Mrs. Ansley.
           Mrs. Slade continued to look down on her. She seemed physically reduced by the blow—as if, when she got up, the wind might scatter her like a puff of dust. Mrs. Slade's jealousy suddenly leapt up again at the sight. All these years the woman had been living on that letter. How she must have loved him, to treasure the mere memory of its ashes! The letter of the man her friend was engaged to. Wasn't it she who was the monster?
           "You tried your best to get him away from me, didn't you? But you failed; and I kept him. That's all."
           "Yes. That's all."
           "I wish now I hadn't told you. I'd no idea you'd feel about it as you do; I thought you'd be amused. It all happened so long ago, as you say; and you must do me the justice to remember that I had no reason to think you'd ever taken it seriously. How could I, when you were married to Horace Ansley two months afterward? As soon as you could get out of bed your mother rushed you off to Florence and married you. People were rather surprised—they wondered at its being done so quickly; but I thought I knew. I had an idea you did it out of *pique*—to be able to say you'd got ahead of Delphin and me. Girls have such silly reasons for doing the most serious things. And your marrying so soon convinced me that you'd never really cared."

100   "Yes. I suppose it would," Mrs. Ansley assented.
           The clear heaven overhead was emptied of all its gold. Dusk spread over it, abruptly darkening the Seven Hills. Here and there lights began to twinkle through the foliage at their feet. Steps were coming and going on the deserted terrace—waiters looking out of the doorway at the head of the stairs, then reappearing with trays and napkins and flasks of wine. Tables were moved, chairs straightened. A feeble string of electric lights flickered out. Some vases of faded flowers were carried away, and brought back replenished. A stout lady in a dust-coat suddenly appeared, asking in broken Italian if any one had seen the elastic band with her stick under the table at which she had lunched, the waiters assisting.
           The corner where Mrs. Slade and Mrs. Ansley sat was still shadowy and deserted. For a long time neither of them spoke. At length Mrs. Slade began again: "I suppose I did it as a sort of joke—"

"A joke?"

"Well, girls are ferocious sometimes, you know. Girls in love especially. And I remember laughing to myself all that evening at the idea that you were waiting around there in the dark, dodging out of sight, listening for every sound, trying to get in—. Of course I was upset when I heard you were ill afterward."

105   Mrs. Ansley had not moved for a long time. But now she turned slowly toward her companion. "But I didn't wait. He'd arranged everything. He was there. We were let in at once," she said.

Mrs. Slade sprang up from her leaning position. "Delphin there? They let you in? Ah, now you're lying!" she burst out with violence.

Mrs. Ansley's voice grew clearer, and full of surprise. "But of course he was there. Naturally he came—"

"Came? How did he know he'd find you there? You must be raving!"

Mrs. Ansley hesitated, as though reflecting. "But I answered the letter. I told him I'd be there. So he came."

110   Mrs. Slade flung her hands up to her face. "Oh, God—you answered! I never thought of your answering. . . ."

"It's odd you never thought of it, if you wrote the letter."

"Yes. I was blind with rage."

Mrs. Ansley rose, and drew her fur scarf about her. "It is cold here. We'd better go. . . . I'm sorry for you," she said, as she clasped the fur about her throat.

The unexpected words sent a pang through Mrs. Slade. "Yes; we'd better go." She gathered up her bag and cloak. "I don't know why you should be sorry for me," she muttered.

115   Mrs. Ansley stood looking away from her toward the dusky secret mass of the Colosseum. "Well—because I didn't have to wait that night."

Mrs. Slade gave an unquiet laugh. "Yes; I was beaten there. But I oughtn't to begrudge it to you, I suppose. At the end of all these years. After all, I had everything; I had him for twenty-five years. And you had nothing but that one letter that he didn't write."

Mrs. Ansley was again silent. At length she turned toward the door of the terrace. She took a step, and turned back, facing her companion.

"I had Barbara," she said, and began to move ahead of Mrs. Slade toward the stairway.

Comments and Questions

"Roman Fever" is in the tradition of the well-made story characterized by a highly compressed structure of action that moves to its inevitable conclusion without author comment, without interruption of any kind, and providing no more intensity than the situation will bear. Wharton has chosen a single subject and has embodied it in a dramatic situation to permit the characters to develop and speak for themselves. The resolution of the story is reserved for the final sentence, and if credibility is therefore not to be violated, the plot structure must be logically impeccable. Yet the plot seems not to be contrived—as such plots so often are—to guarantee the final surprise. The story relies, then, on plot to reveal character, theme, and final meaning. What does Wharton accomplish with this technique?

The story, if nothing more, is good entertainment. Mrs. Ansley's triumph comes as a dramatic surprise that is itself a subtle kind of humor and delight, and we may be tempted to classify the story as escape literature, enjoyed once and then dismissed. But a little reflection may prove otherwise. There is something arresting in the story's tone—Wharton's implied attitude toward the dramatic situation of the two women. If we are delighted with the final sentence, we are sympathetic with Mrs. Ansley, as Wharton intended us to be. But why? Hardly because our sportsmanship relishes a victory of the demure little Grace Ansley over the aggressive, self-assured Alida Slade. Surely Wharton has provided us with something more than a game—her tone tells us that.

It is often remarked that a second or third reading of a story is one test of its excellence. We may have been taken in by the excitement of the first reading or we may have missed basic implications that give the story substantial status. As we read Wharton's story again, some statements become more arresting. Mrs. Slade to Mrs. Ansley: " 'I was wondering, ever so respectfully, you understand . . . wondering how two such exemplary characters as you and Horace had managed to produce anything quite so dynamic [as Barbara].' Mrs. Slade laughed again, with a touch of asperity." Mrs. Slade again: " 'I always wanted a brilliant daughter . . . and never quite understood why I got an angel instead.' " The serious aspect of the story appears, of course, in Mrs. Slade's self-assumed superiority over Mrs. Ansley, and yet she cannot quite endure the paradox (see "Figure and Symbol," p. 377) of Mrs. Ansley's inferiority producing the brilliant Barbara whereas her own superiority produces only Jenny. The story's final sentence, therefore, accomplishes a good deal. This revelation releases the irony (see "The Misreading of Poems," p. 306), which now envelops Mrs. Slade, whose sense of superiority crashes before the real superiority of Mrs. Ansley—and the irony is compounded because Mrs. Slade, as well as the reader, experiences the irony.

1. This brief interpretation has omitted many important aspects of the story. Despite the humor found in the final sentence, the story has its measure of pathos. Consider Mrs. Slade's final speech, and then describe what her sensations must have been after the final blow.

2. How is the title of the story significant? Functional?

3. Why is the particular Roman setting of the story appropriate? What effect does Wharton's use of panorama and scene (see p. 13) have on the development of the story?

4. Any story that relies chiefly on plot must stand or fall on the author's ability to achieve credibility. Do you find any serious flaws? Why did Mrs. Slade write the letter to Mrs. Ansley? How does Wharton make Mrs. Ansley's having Barbara credible? Does Aunt Harriet help to explain matters?

Flannery O'Connor　(1925–1964)
Everything That Rises Must Converge

This story provides, among other things, a challenge to one's ability to read fiction as imaginative literature, as an art. Two basic questions confront most readers. Is the title ironic? Is the race problem central to the story or only peripheral? The answers to these questions have generated a good deal of critical debate.

Because of O'Connor's multiple interests, her Southern experience and background, and her deeply religious nature and readings in theology, the meaning of her stories has become uncommonly controversial. As one sympathetic critic points out, some readers find "her as another member of the Southern Gothic School"; some "Roman Catholic critics . . . were often pleased to claim this staunch daughter of their Communion as their own especial property . . . in the tradition of 'modern Catholic writers' "; whereas other critics, "declining to tag Miss O'Connor with such convenient labels, and conceding her gift for the comic, expressed distaste for what seemed her undue emphasis on the grotesque . . . and the unnecessary theological intrusions into the body of her fiction." Instead of such excursions by critics into the extrinsic causes of her fiction, what she really needed, according to this critic, "was a good liberating from literary critics unwilling to grant her the primary concession, according to Henry James, due any artist—an acceptance by the reader of her *donnée,*"* or the set of assumptions upon which her fiction proceeds. That is, it is time that she be regarded first as an artist and that her stories be examined as works of art instead of as veiled religious or Southern doctrine.

The excursions into the causes of O'Connor's fiction have been plentiful as readers have looked for the meaning of "Everything That Rises Must Converge." O'Connor offers us some help: "Justice is justice and should not be appealed to along racial lines. The problem is not abstract for the Southerner, it's concrete; he sees it in terms of persons, not races—which way of seeing does away with easy answers. I have tried to touch this subject by way of fiction only once—in a story called 'Everything That Rises Must Converge.' "**

She leaves no doubt about the kind of personal and public world Mrs. Chestny lives in as contrasted with her son Julian's personal and public world. "She lived," says the narrator, "according to the laws of her own fantasy world, outside of which [Julian] had never seen her set foot." Julian is determined to avoid her fantasy world and to come to grips with the reality of his own existence. The conflict between him and his mother brings tragedy to both of them. So the question remains, What is the nature of their "convergence"? Is it ironic or otherwise?

Her doctor had told Julian's mother that she must lose twenty pounds on account of her blood pressure, so on Wednesday nights Julian had to take her downtown on the bus for a reducing class at the Y. The reducing class was designed for working girls over fifty, who weighed from 165 to 200 pounds. His mother was one of the slimmer ones, but she said ladies did not tell their age or weight. She would not ride the buses by herself at night since they had been integrated, and because the reducing class was one of her few pleasures, necessary for her health, and *free,* she said Julian could at least put himself out to take her, considering all she did for him. Julian did not like to consider all she did for him, but every Wednesday night he braced himself and took her.

She was almost ready to go, standing before the hall mirror, putting on her hat, while he, his hands behind him, appeared pinned to the door frame, waiting like Saint Sebastian for the arrows to begin piercing him. The hat was new and had cost her seven dollars and a half. She kept saying, "Maybe I shouldn't have paid that for it. No, I shouldn't have. I'll take it off and return it tomorrow. I shouldn't have bought it."

Julian raised his eyes to heaven. "Yes, you should have bought it," he said. "Put it on and let's go." It was a hideous hat. A purple velvet flap came down on one side of it

---

* Robert Drake, *Flannery O'Connor, A Critical Essay,* Grand Rapids, Mich.: William B. Eerdmans, Publisher, 1966, p. 6.

** From a letter to Sister M. Bernetta Quinn, July 27, 1963.

and stood up on the other; the rest of it was green and looked like a cushion with the stuffing out. He decided it was less comical than jaunty and pathetic. Everything that gave her pleasure was small and depressed him.

She lifted the hat one more time and set it down slowly on top of her head. Two wings of gray hair protruded on either side of her florid face, but her eyes, sky-blue, were as innocent and untouched by experience as they must have been when she was ten. Were it not that she was a widow who had struggled fiercely to feed and clothe and put him through school and who was supporting him still, "until he got on his feet," she might have been a little girl that he had to take to town.

5   "It's all right, it's all right," he said. "Let's go." He opened the door himself and started down the walk to get her going. The sky was a dying violet and the houses stood out darkly against it, bulbous liver-colored monstrosities of a uniform ugliness though no two were alike. Since this had been a fashionable neighborhood forty years ago, his mother persisted in thinking they did well to have an apartment in it. Each house had a narrow collar of dirt around it in which sat, usually, a grubby child. Julian walked with his hands in his pockets, his head down and thrust forward and his eyes glazed with the determination to make himself completely numb during the time he would be sacrificed to her pleasure.

The door closed and he turned to find the dumpy figure, surmounted by the atrocious hat, coming toward him. "Well," she said, "you only live once and paying a little more for it, I at least won't meet myself coming and going."

"Some day I'll start making money," Julian said gloomily—he knew he never would—"and you can have one of those jokes whenever you take the fit." But first they would move. He visualized a place where the nearest neighbors would be three miles away on either side.

"I think you're doing fine," she said, drawing on her gloves. "You've only been out of school a year. Rome wasn't built in a day."

She was one of the few members of the Y reducing class who arrived in hat and gloves and who had a son who had been to college. "It takes time," she said, "and the world is in such a mess. This hat looked better on me than any of the others, though when she brought it out I said, 'Take that thing back. I wouldn't have it on my head,' and she said, 'Now wait till you see it on,' and when she put it on me, I said, 'We–ull,' and she said, 'If you ask me, that hat does something for you and you do something for the hat, and besides,' she said, 'with that hat, you won't meet yourself coming and going.'"

10   Julian thought he could have stood his lot better if she had been selfish, if she had been an old hag who drank and screamed at him. He walked along, saturated in depression, as if in the midst of his martyrdom he had lost his faith. Catching sight of his long, hopeless, irritated face, she stopped suddenly with a grief-stricken look, and pulled back on his arm. "Wait on me," she said. "I'm going back to the house and take this thing off and tomorrow I'm going to return it. I was out of my head. I can pay the gas bill with that seven-fifty."

He caught her arm in a vicious grip. "You are not going to take it back," he said. "I like it."

"Well," she said, "I don't think I ought . . ."

"Shut up and enjoy it," he muttered, more depressed than ever.

"With the world in the mess it's in," she said, "it's a wonder we can enjoy anything. I tell you, the bottom rail is on the top."

15   Julian sighed.

"Of course," she said, "if you know who you are, you can go anywhere." She said this every time he took her to the reducing class. "Most of them in it are not our kind of people," she said, "but I can be gracious to anybody. I know who I am."

"They don't give a damn for your graciousness," Julian said savagely. "Knowing who you are is good for one generation only. You haven't the foggiest idea where you stand now or who you are."

She stopped and allowed her eyes to flash at him. "I most certainly do know who I am," she said, "and if you don't know who you are, I'm ashamed of you."

"Oh hell," Julian said.

20   "Your great-grandfather was a former governor of this state," she said. "Your grandfather was a prosperous landowner. Your grandmother was a Godhigh."

"Will you look around you," he said tensely, "and see where you are now?" and he swept his arm jerkily out to indicate the neighborhood, which the growing darkness at least made less dingy.

"You remain what you are," she said. "Your great-grandfather had a plantation and two hundred slaves."

"There are no more slaves," he said irritably.

"They were better off when they were," she said. He groaned to see that she was off on that topic. She rolled onto it every few days like a train on an open track. He knew every stop, every junction, every swamp along the way, and knew the exact point at which her conclusion would roll majestically into the station: "It's ridiculous. It's simply not realistic. They should rise, yes, but on their own side of the fence."

25   "Let's skip it," Julian said.

"The ones I feel sorry for," she said, "are the ones that are half white. They're tragic."

"Will you skip it?"

"Suppose we were half white. We would certainly have mixed feelings."

"I have mixed feelings now," he groaned.

30   "Well let's talk about something pleasant," she said. "I remember going to Grandpa's when I was a little girl. Then the house had double stairways that went up to what was really the second floor—all the cooking was done on the first. I used to like to stay down in the kitchen on account of the way the walls smelled. I would sit with my nose pressed against the plaster and take deep breaths. Actually the place belonged to the Godhighs but your grandfather Chestny paid the mortgage and saved it for them. They were in reduced circumstances," she said, "but reduced or not, they never forgot who they were."

"Doubtless that decayed mansion reminded them," Julian muttered. He never spoke of it without contempt or thought of it without longing. He had seen it once when he was a child before it had been sold. The double stairways had rotted and been torn down. Negroes were living in it. But it remained in his mind as his mother had known it. It appeared in his dreams regularly. He would stand on the wide porch, listening to the rustle of oak leaves, then wander through the high-ceilinged hall into the parlor that opened onto it and gaze at the worn rugs and faded draperies. It occurred to him that it was he, not she, who could have appreciated it. He preferred its threadbare elegance to anything he could name and it was because of it that all the neighborhoods they had lived in had been a torment to him—whereas she had hardly known the difference. She called her insensitivity "being adjustable."

"And I remember the old darky who was my nurse, Caroline. There was no better person in the world. I've always had a great respect for my colored friends," she said. "I'd do anything in the world for them and they'd . . ."

"Will you for God's sake get off that subject?" Julian said. When he got on a bus by

himself, he made it a point to sit down beside a Negro, in reparation as it were for his
mother's sins.

"You're mighty touchy tonight," she said. "Do you feel all right?"

35   "Yes I feel all right," he said. "Now lay off."

She pursed her lips. "Well, you certainly are in a vile humor," she observed. "I just
won't speak to you at all."

They had reached the bus stop. There was no bus in sight and Julian, his hands still
jammed in his pockets and his head thrust forward, scowled down the empty street. The
frustration of having to wait on the bus as well as ride on it began to creep up his neck
like a hot hand. The presence of his mother was borne in upon him as she gave a pained
sigh. He looked at her bleakly. She was holding herself very erect under the preposterous
hat, wearing it like a banner of her imaginary dignity. There was in him an evil urge to
break her spirit. He suddenly unloosened his tie and pulled it off and put it in his pocket.

She stiffened. "Why must you look like *that* when you take me to town?" she said.
"Why must you deliberately embarrass me?"

"If you'll never learn where you are," he said, "you can at least learn where I am."

40   "You look like a—thug," she said.

"Then I must be one," he murmured.

"I'll just go home," she said. "I will not bother you. If you can't do a little thing like
that for me . . ."

Rolling his eyes upward, he put his tie back. "Restored to my class," he muttered.
He thrust his face toward her and hissed, "True culture is in the mind, the *mind,*" he said,
and tapped his head, "the mind."

"It's in the heart," she said, "and in how you do things and how you do things is
because of who you *are.*"

45   "Nobody in the damn bus cares who you are."

"I care who I am," she said icily.

The lighted bus appeared on top of the next hill and as it approached, they moved
out into the street to meet it. He put his hand under her elbow and hoisted her up on the
creaking step. She entered with a little smile, as if she were going into a drawing room
where everyone had been waiting for her. While he put in the tokens, she sat down on
one of the broad front seats for three which faced the aisle. A thin woman with protruding
teeth and long yellow hair was sitting on the end of it. His mother moved up beside her
and left room for Julian beside herself. He sat down and looked at the floor across the
aisle where a pair of thin feet in red and white canvas sandals were planted.

His mother immediately began a general conversation meant to attract anyone who
felt like talking. "Can it get any hotter?" she said and removed from her purse a folding
fan, black with a Japanese scene on it, which she began to flutter before her.

"I reckon it might could," the woman with the protruding teeth said, "but I know
for a fact my apartment couldn't get no hotter."

50   "It must get the afternoon sun," his mother said. She sat forward and looked up and
down the bus. It was half filled. Everybody was white. "I see we have the bus to ourselves,"
she said. Julian cringed.

"For a change," said the woman across the aisle, the owner of the red and white
canvas sandals. "I come on one the other day and they were thick as fleas—up front and
all through."

"The world is in a mess everywhere," his mother said. "I don't know how we've let
it get in this fix."

"What gets my goat is all those boys from good families stealing automobile tires,"
the woman with the protruding teeth said. "I told my boy, I said you may not be rich but

you been raised right and if I ever catch you in any such mess, they can send you on to the reformatory. Be exactly where you belong."

"Training tells," his mother said. "Is your boy in high school?"

55 "Ninth grade," the woman said.

"My son just finished college last year. He wants to write but he's selling typewriters until he gets started," his mother said.

The woman leaned forward and peered at Julian. He threw her such a malevolent look that she subsided against the seat. On the floor across the aisle there was an abandoned newspaper. He got up and got it and opened it out in front of him. His mother discreetly continued the conversation in a lower tone but the woman across the aisle said in a loud voice, "Well that's nice. Selling typewriters is close to writing. He can go right from one to the other."

"I tell him," his mother said, "that Rome wasn't built in a day."

Behind the newspaper Julian was withdrawing into the inner compartment of his mind where he spent most of his time. This was a kind of mental bubble in which he established himself when he could not bear to be a part of what was going on around him. From it he could see out and judge but in it he was safe from any kind of penetration from without. It was the only place where he felt free of the general idiocy of his fellows. His mother had never entered it but from it he could see her with absolute clarity.

60 The old lady was clever enough and he thought that if she had started from any of the right premises, more might have been expected of her. She lived according to the laws of her own fantasy world, outside of which he had never seen her set foot. The law of it was to sacrifice herself for him after she had first created the necessity to do so by making a mess of things. If he had permitted her sacrifices, it was only because her lack of foresight had made them necessary. All of her life had been a struggle to act like a Chestny without the Chestny goods, and to give him everything she thought a Chestny ought to have; but since, said she, it was fun to struggle, why complain? And when you had won, as she had won, what fun to look back on the hard times! He could not forgive her that she had enjoyed the struggle and that she thought *she* had won.

What she meant when she said she had won was that she had brought him up successfully and had sent him to college and that he had turned out so well—good looking (her teeth had gone unfilled so that his could be straightened), intelligent (he realized he was too intelligent to be a success), and with a future ahead of him (there was of course no future ahead of him). She excused his gloominess on the grounds that he was still growing up and his radical ideas on his lack of practical experience. She said he didn't yet know a thing about "life," that he hadn't even entered the real world—when already he was as disenchanted with it as a man of fifty.

The further irony of all this was that in spite of her, he had turned out so well. In spite of going to only a third-rate college, he had, on his own initiative, come out with a first-rate education; in spite of growing up dominated by a small mind, he had ended up with a large one; in spite of all her foolish views, he was free of prejudice and unafraid to face facts. Most miraculous of all, instead of being blinded by love for her as she was for him, he had cut himself emotionally free of her and could see her with complete objectivity. He was not dominated by his mother.

The bus stopped with a sudden jerk and shook him from his meditation. A woman from the back lurched forward with little steps and barely escaped falling in his newspaper as she righted herself. She got off and a large Negro got on. Julian kept his paper lowered to watch. It gave him a certain satisfaction to see injustice in daily operation. It confirmed his view that with a few exceptions there was no one worth knowing within a radius of three hundred miles. The Negro was well dressed and carried a briefcase. He looked around and then sat down on the other end of the seat where the woman with the red and white canvas sandals was sitting. He immediately unfolded a newspaper and obscured himself behind it. Julian's mother's elbow at once prodded insistently into his ribs. "Now you see why I won't ride on these busses by myself," she whispered.

The woman with the red and white canvas sandals had risen at the same time the Negro sat down and had gone further back in the bus and taken the seat of the woman who had got off. His mother leaned forward and cast her an approving look.

65   Julian rose, crossed the aisle, and sat down in the place of the woman with the canvas sandals. From this position, he looked serenely across at his mother. Her face had turned an angry red. He stared at her, making his eyes the eyes of a stranger. He felt his tension suddenly lift as if he had openly declared war on her.

He would have liked to get in conversation with the Negro and to talk with him about art or politics or any subject that would be above the comprehension of those around them, but the man remained entrenched behind his paper. He was either ignoring the change of seating or had never noticed it. There was no way for Julian to convey his sympathy.

His mother kept her eyes fixed reproachfully on his face. The woman with the protruding teeth was looking at him avidly as if he were a type of monster new to her.

"Do you have a light?" he asked the Negro.

Without looking away from his paper, the man reached in his pocket and handed him a packet of matches.

70   "Thanks," Julian said. For a moment he held the matches foolishly. A NO SMOKING sign looked down upon him from over the door. This alone would not have deterred him; he had no cigarettes. He had quit smoking some months before because he could not afford it. "Sorry," he muttered and handed back the matches. The Negro lowered the paper and gave him an annoyed look. He took the matches and raised the paper again.

His mother continued to gaze at him but she did not take advantage of his momentary discomfort. Her eyes retained their battered look. Her face seemed to be unnaturally red, as if her blood pressure had risen. Julian allowed no glimmer of sympathy to show on his face. Having got the advantage, he wanted desperately to keep it and carry it through. He would have liked to teach her a lesson that would last her a while, but there seemed no way to continue the point. The Negro refused to come out from behind his paper.

Julian folded his arms and looked stolidly before him, facing her but as if he did not see her, as if he had ceased to recognize her existence. He visualized a scene in which, the bus having reached their stop, he would remain in his seat and when she said, "Aren't you going to get off?" he would look at her as at a stranger who had rashly addressed him. The corner they got off on was usually deserted, but it was well lighted and it would not hurt her to walk by herself the four blocks to the Y. He decided to wait until the time came and then decide whether or not he would let her get off by herself. He would have to be at the Y at ten to bring her back, but he could leave her wondering if he was going to show up. There was no reason for her to think she could always depend on him.

He retired again into the high ceilinged room sparsely settled with large pieces of antique furniture. His soul expanded momentarily but then he became aware of his mother across from him and the vision shriveled. He studied her coldly. Her feet in little pumps dangled like a child's and did not quite reach the floor. She was training on him an exaggerated look of reproach. He felt completely detached from her. At that moment he could with pleasure have slapped her as he would have slapped a particularly obnoxious child in his charge.

He began to imagine various unlikely ways by which he could teach her a lesson. He might make friends with some distinguished Negro professor or lawyer and bring him home to spend the evening. He would be entirely justified but her blood pressure would rise to 300. He could not push her to the extent of making her have a stroke, and moreover, he had never been successful at making any Negro friends. He had tried to strike up an acquaintance on the bus with some of the better types, with ones that looked like professors or ministers or lawyers. One morning he had sat down next to a distinguished-looking dark brown man who had answered his questions with a sonorous solemnity but who had turned out to be an undertaker. Another day he had sat down beside a cigar-smoking Negro with a diamond ring on his finger, but after a few stilted pleasantries, the Negro had rung the buzzer and risen, slipping two lottery tickets into Julian's hand as he climbed over him to leave.

75   He imagined his mother lying desperately ill and his being able to secure only a Negro doctor for her. He toyed with that idea for a few minutes and then dropped it for a momentary vision of himself participating as a sympathizer in a sit-in demonstration. This was possible but he did not linger with it. Instead, he approached the ultimate horror. He brought home a beautiful suspiciously Negroid woman. Prepare yourself, he said. There is nothing you can do about it. This is the woman I've chosen. She's intelligent, dignified, even good, and she's suffered and she hasn't thought it *fun*. Now persecute us, go ahead and persecute us. Drive her out of here, but remember, you're driving me too. His eyes were narrowed and through the indignation he had generated, he saw his mother across the aisle, purple-faced, shrunken to the dwarflike proportions of her moral nature, sitting like a mummy beneath the ridiculous banner of her hat.

He was tilted out of his fantasy again as the bus stopped. The door opened with a sucking hiss and out of the dark a large, gaily dressed, sullen-looking colored woman got on with a little boy. The child, who might have been four, had on a short plaid suit and a Tyrolean hat with a blue feather in it. Julian hoped that he would sit down beside him and that the woman would push in beside his mother. He could think of no better arrangement.

As she waited for her tokens, the woman was surveying the seating possibilities—he hoped with the idea of sitting where she was least wanted. There was something familiar-looking about her but Julian could not place what it was. She was a giant of a woman. Her face was set not only to meet opposition but to seek it out. The downward tilt of her large lower lip was like a warning sign: DON'T TAMPER WITH ME. Her bulging figure was encased in a green crepe dress and her feet overflowed in red shoes. She had on a hideous hat. A purple velvet flap came down on one side of it and stood up on the other; the rest of it was green and looked like a cushion with the stuffing out. She carried a mammoth red pocketbook that bulged throughout as if it were stuffed with rocks.

To Julian's disappointment, the little boy climbed up on the empty seat beside his mother. His mother lumped all children, black and white, into the common category, "cute," and she thought little Negroes were on the whole cuter than little white children. She smiled at the little boy as he climbed on the seat.

Meanwhile the woman was bearing down upon the empty seat beside Julian. To his annoyance, she squeezed herself into it. He saw his mother's face change as the woman settled herself next to him and he realized with satisfaction that this was more objectionable to her than it was to him. Her face seemed almost gray and there was a look of dull recognition in her eyes, as if suddenly she had sickened at some awful confrontation. Julian saw that it was because she and the woman had, in a sense, swapped sons. Though his mother would not realize the symbolic significance of this, she would feel it. His amusement showed plainly on his face.

80   The woman next to him muttered something unintelligible to herself. He was con-

scious of a kind of bristling next to him, a muted growling like that of an angry cat. He could not see anything but the red pocketbook upright on the bulging green thighs. He visualized the woman as she had stood waiting for her tokens—the ponderous figure, rising from the red shoes upward over the solid hips, the mammoth bosom, the haughty face, to the green and purple hat.

His eyes widened.

The vision of the two hats, identical, broke upon him with the radiance of a brilliant sunrise. His face was suddenly lit with joy. He could not believe that Fate had thrust upon his mother such a lesson. He gave a loud chuckle so that she would look at him and see that he saw. She turned her eyes on him slowly. The blue in them seemed to have turned a bruised purple. For a moment he had an uncomfortable sense of her innocence, but it lasted only a second before principle rescued him. Justice entitled him to laugh. His grin hardened until it said to her as plainly as if he were saying aloud: Your punishment exactly fits your pettiness. This should teach you a permanent lesson.

Her eyes shifted to the woman. She seemed unable to bear looking at him and to find the woman preferable. He became conscious again of the bristling presence at his side. The woman was rumbling like a volcano about to become active. His mother's mouth began to twitch slightly at one corner. With a sinking heart, he saw incipient signs of recovery on her face and realized that this was going to strike her suddenly as funny and was going to be no lesson at all. She kept her eyes on the woman and an amused smile came over her face as if the woman were a monkey that had stolen her hat. The little Negro was looking up at her with large fascinated eyes. He had been trying to attract her attention for some time.

"Carver!" the woman said suddenly. "Come heah!"

85 When he saw that the spotlight was on him at last, Carver drew his feet up and turned himself toward Julian's mother and giggled.

"Carver!" the woman said. "You heah me? Come heah!"

Carver slid down from the seat but remained squatting with his back against the base of it, his head turned slyly around toward Julian's mother, who was smiling at him. The woman reached a hand across the aisle and snatched him to her. He righted himself and hung backwards on her knees, grinning at Julian's mother. "Isn't he cute?" Julian's mother said to the woman with the protruding teeth.

"I reckon he is," the woman said without conviction.

The Negress yanked him upright but he eased out of her grip and shot across the aisle and scrambled, giggling wildly, onto the seat beside his love.

90 "I think he likes me," Julian's mother said, and smiled at the woman. It was the smile she used when she was being particularly gracious to an inferior. Julian saw everything lost. The lesson had rolled off her like rain on a roof.

The woman stood up and yanked the little boy off the seat as if she were snatching him from contagion. Julian could feel the rage in her at having no weapon like his mother's smile. She gave the child a sharp slap across his leg. He howled once and then thrust his head into her stomach and kicked his feet against her shins. "Be-have," she said vehemently

The bus stopped and the Negro who had been reading the newspaper got off. The woman moved over and set the little boy down with a thump between herself and Julian. She held him firmly by the knee. In a moment he put his hands in front of his face and peeped at Julian's mother through his fingers.

"I see yoooooooo!" she said and put her hand in front of her face and peeped at him.

The woman slapped his hand down. "Quit yo' foolishness," she said, "before I knock the living Jesus out of you!"

95   Julian was thankful that the next stop was theirs. He reached up and pulled the cord. The woman reached up and pulled it at the same time. Oh my God, he thought. He had the terrible intuition that when they got off the bus together, his mother would open her purse and give the little boy a nickel. The gesture would be as natural to her as breathing. The bus stopped and the woman got up and lunged to the front, dragging the child, who wished to stay on, after her. Julian and his mother got up and followed. As they neared the door, Julian tried to relieve her of her pocketbook.

"No," she murmured, "I want to give the little boy a nickel."

"No!" Julian hissed. "No!"

She smiled down at the child and opened her bag. The bus door opened and the woman picked him up by the arm and descended with him, hanging at her hip. Once in the street she set him down and shook him.

Julian's mother had to close her purse while she got down the bus step but as soon as her feet were on the ground, she opened it again and began to rummage inside. "I can't find but a penny," she whispered, "but it looks like a new one."

100   "Don't do it!" Julian said fiercely between his teeth. There was a streetlight on the corner and she hurried to get under it so that she could better see into her pocketbook. The woman was heading off rapidly down the street with the child still hanging backward on her hand.

"Oh little boy!" Julian's mother called and took a few quick steps and caught up with them just beyond the lamppost. "Here's a bright new penny for you," and she held out the coin, which shone bronze in the dim light.

The huge woman turned and for a moment stood, her shoulders lifted and her face frozen with frustrated rage, and stared at Julian's mother. Then all at once she seemed to explode like a piece of machinery that had been given one ounce of pressure too much. Julian saw the black fist swing out with the red pocketbook. He shut his eyes and cringed as he heard the woman shout, "He don't take nobody's pennies!" When he opened his eyes, the woman was disappearing down the street with the little boy staring wide-eyed over her shoulder. Julian's mother was sitting on the sidewalk.

"I told you not to do that," Julian said angrily. "I told you not to do that!"

He stood over her for minute, gritting his teeth. Her legs were stretched out in front of her and her hat was on her lap. He squatted down and looked her in the face. It was totally expressionless. "You got exactly what you deserved," he said. "Now get up."

105   He picked up her pocketbook and put what had fallen out back in it. He picked the hat up off her lap. The penny caught his eye on the sidewalk and he picked that up and let it drop before her eyes into the purse. Then he stood up and leaned over and held his hands out to pull her up. She remained immobile. He sighed. Rising above them on either side were black apartment buildings, marked with irregular rectangles of light. At the end of the block a man came out of a door and walked off in the opposite direction. "All right," he said, "suppose somebody happens by and wants to know why you're sitting on the sidewalk?"

She took the hand and, breathing hard, pulled heavily up on it and then stood for a moment, swaying slightly as if the spots of light in the darkness were circling around her. Her eyes, shadowed and confused, finally settled on his face. He did not try to conceal his irritation. "I hope this teaches you a lesson," he said. She leaned forward and her eyes raked his face. She seemed trying to determine his identity. Then, as if she found nothing familiar about him, she started off with a headlong movement in the wrong direction.

"Aren't you going on to the Y?" he asked.

"Home," she muttered.

"Well, are we walking?"

110   For answer she kept going. Julian followed along, his hands behind him. He saw no reason to let the lesson she had had go without backing it up with an explanation of its meaning. She might as well be made to understand what had happened to her. "Don't think that was just an uppity Negro woman," he said. "That was the whole colored race which will no longer take your condescending pennies. That was your black double. She can wear the same hat as you, and to be sure," he added gratuitously (because he thought it was funny), "it looked better on her than it did on you. What all this means," he said, "is that the old world is gone. The old manners are obsolete and your graciousness is not worth a damn." He thought bitterly of the house that had been lost for him. "You aren't who you think you are," he said.

She continued to plow ahead, paying no attention to him. Her hair had come undone on one side. She dropped her pocketbook and took no notice. He stooped and picked it up and handed it to her but she did not take it.

"You needn't act as if the world had come to an end," he said, "because it hasn't. From now on you've got to live in a new world and face a few realities for a change. Buck up," he said, "it won't kill you."

She was breathing fast.

"Let's wait on the bus," he said.

115   "Home," she said thickly.

"I hate to see you behave like this," he said. "Just like a child. I should be able to expect more of you." He decided to stop where he was and make her stop and wait for a bus. "I'm not going any farther," he said, stopping. "We're going on the bus."

She continued to go on as if she had not heard him. He took a few steps and caught her arm and stopped her. He looked into her face and caught his breath. He was looking into a face he had never seen before. "Tell Grandpa to come get me," she said.

He stared, stricken.

"Tell Caroline to come get me," she said.

120   Stunned, he let her go and she lurched forward again, walking as if one leg were shorter than the other. A tide of darkness seemed to be sweeping her from him. "Mother!" he cried. "Darling, sweetheart, wait!" Crumpling, she fell to the pavement. He dashed forward and fell at her side, crying, "Mamma, Mamma!" He turned her over. Her face was fiercely distorted. One eye, large and staring, moved slightly to the left as if it had become unmoored. The other remained fixed on him, raked his face again, found nothing and closed.

"Wait here, wait here!" he cried and jumped up and began to run for help toward a cluster of lights he saw in the distance ahead of him. "Help, help!" he shouted, but his voice was thin, scarcely a thread of sound. The lights drifted farther away the faster he ran and his feet moved numbly as if they carried him nowhere. The tide of darkness seemed to sweep him back to her, postponing from moment to moment his entry into the world of guilt and sorrow.

Comments and Questions

1. This story contains both social and psychological implications. Both are profound and appropriately intertwined, but the social issues are perhaps more obvious than the psychological problems. Account for the intense and condescending bitterness Julian aims at his mother by word and act. What evidence is there that he has not, after all, entirely escaped her fantasy world himself and that he has, in consequence, "mixed feelings" toward her? Can you cite instances of his affection for her?

2. Comment on the name Godhigh. What does the Godhigh mansion represent in Julian's mind? How does his attitude toward the mansion reveal his personal dilemma and also mirror a larger social issue of the story?

3. Discuss the irony of Julian's statement to his mother that she hasn't "the foggiest idea where you stand now or what you are." For other instances of irony in the story, consider the purpose and the consequence of the bus trip, the repetitious justification for the expensive hat and the result, the unexpected return to Julian's mother for her penny. Should Julian's education and its results be listed among the ironical aspects of the story? Is such pervasive irony collectively functional in the story? Does it relate to the title? Theme? Social issues raised? (see *"Sidenote on irony,"* p. 26.)

James Baldwin   (1924–   )
Exodus

James Baldwin has written in a variety of literary forms, using an even greater variety of subjects, all investigated with a moral force and sincerity not entirely common in our time. It is difficult to read any work of his without feeling the authenticity woven into the fabric of his essays, short stories, and novels. The essays of *Notes of a Native Son* (1955) and *Nobody Knows My Name* (1961) emerge from the depth of his personal experience in black life. More recently he has published a far-ranging commentary on the struggle of blacks in general, but most specifically of himself, to find his identity. The title, *No Name in the Street* (1972), is taken from Job 18:17–18:

> *His remembrance shall perish from the earth,*
> *And he shall have no name in the street.*
> *He shall be driven from light into darkness,*
> *And chased out of the world.*

Baldwin's "Exodus" is the story of Florence's determination, almost regardless of the cost, to free herself of the white psychology that has dominated her people. Her dilemma, to remain with her mother, Rachel, until her mother dies or to leave the South for New York to escape her mother's fate, is the key symbol of the story. It is Florence's Exodus that hangs in the balance. The background of her mother's life is well known to Florence—entirely too well known—, and almost a story in itself. Baldwin's low-key method of telling the story could be a powerful influence on any sensitive reader who expects a condemnation of the Southern whites tinged with hatred. But as every fact of the mother's life is easily documented, we find the artist exploring the psychological effects of those facts instead of writing propaganda. If the reader feels as Florence feels, the artist in Baldwin is probably soberly content.

I

She had always seemed to Florence the oldest woman in the world—for she often spoke of Florence and Gabriel as the children of her old age; and she had been born, innumerable years ago, during slavery, on a plantation in another state. On this plantation she had grown up, one of the field workers, for she was very tall and strong; and by-and-by she had married, and raised children, all of whom had been taken from her, one by sickness, and two by auction, and one whom she had not been allowed to call her own, who had been raised in the master's house. When she was a woman grown, well past thirty as she reckoned it, with one husband buried—but the master had given her another—armies, plundering and burning, had come from the North to set them free. This was in answer to the prayers of the faithful, who had never ceased, both day and night, to cry out for deliverance.

For it had been the will of God that they should hear, and pass it, thereafter, one to another, the story of the Hebrew children, who had been held in bondage in the land of Egypt;[1] and how the Lord had heard their groaning, and how His heart was moved; and how He bid them wait but a little season till He should send deliverance. She had known this story, so it seemed, from the day that she was born. And while life ran, rising in the morning before the sun came up, standing and bending in the fields when the sun was high, crossing the fields homeward while the sun went down at the gates of heaven far away—hearing the whistle of the foreman, and his eerie cry across the fields; in the whiteness of winter when hogs and turkeys and geese were slaughtered, and lights burned bright in the big house, and Bathsheba, the cook, sent over in a napkin bits of ham and chicken and cakes left over by the white folks; in all that befell, in her joys—her pipe in the evening, her man at night, the children she suckled, and guided on their first short steps—and in her tribulations, death, and parting, and the lash; she did not forget that deliverance was promised, and would surely come. She had only to endure and trust in God. She knew that the big house, the house of pride where the white folks lived, would come down: it was written in the Word of God. And they, who walked so proudly now, yet had not fashioned, for themselves, or their children, so sure a foundation as was hers. They walked on the edge of a steep place and their eyes were sightless—God would cause them to rush down, as the herd of swine had once rushed down, into the sea. For all that they were so beautiful, and took their ease, she knew them, and she pitied them, who would have no covering in the great day of His wrath.

Yet, she told her children, God was just, and He struck no people without first giving many warnings. God gave men time, but all the times were in His hand, and, one day, the time to forsake evil and do good would all be finished: then only the whirlwind, death riding on the whirlwind, awaited those people who had forgotten God. In all the days that she was growing up, signs failed not, but none heeded. *Slaves done riz,* was whispered in the cabin, and at the master's gate: slaves in another county had fired the master's house and fields, and dashed their children to death against the stones. *Another slave in hell,* Bathsheba might say one morning, shooing the pickaninnies away from the great porch: a slave had killed his master, or his overseer, and had gone down to hell to pay for it. *I ain't got long to stay here,* someone crooned beside her in the fields: who would be gone by morning on his journey North. All these signs, like the plagues with which the Lord had afflicted Egypt, only hardened the hearts of these people against the Lord. They thought the lash would save them, and they used the lash; or the knife, or the gallows, or the auction block; they thought that kindness would save them, and the master and mis-

[1] See Exodus (Israel in bondage): 1:1–22; 2:1–25. God delivers His people from Egypt: 3:1–14.

tress came down, smiling, to the cabins, making much of the pickaninnies, and bearing gifts. These were great days, and they all, black and white, seemed happy together. But when the Word has gone forth from the mouth of God nothing can turn it back.

The word was fulfilled one morning before she was awake. Many of the stories her mother told meant nothing to Florence, she knew them for what they were, tales told by an old black woman in a cabin in the evening to distract her children from their cold and hunger. But the story of this day she was never to forget, it was a day like the day for which she lived. There was a great running and shouting, said her mother, everywhere outside, and, as she opened her eyes to the light of that day, so bright, she said, and cold, she was certain that the judgment trump had sounded. While she still sat, amazed, and wondering what, on the judgment day, would be the best behavior, in rushed Bathsheba, and behind her many tumbling children, and field hands, and house niggers, all together, and Bathsheba shouted, "Rise up, rise up, Sister Rachel, and see the Lord's deliverance! He done brought us out of Egypt, just like He promised, and we's free at last!"

5   Bathsheba grabbed her, tears running down her face, she, dressed in the clothes in which she had slept, walked to the door to look out on the new day God had given them.

On that day she saw the proud house humbled, green silk and velvet blowing out of windows, and the garden trampled by many horsemen, and the big gates open. The master and mistress, and their kin, and one child she had borne were in that house— which she did not enter. Soon it occurred to her that there was no reason any more to tarry here. She tied her things in a cloth, which she put on her head, and walked out through the big gate, never to see that country any more.

And this, as Florence grew, became her deep ambition: to walk out one morning through the cabin door, never to return. . . .

II

In 1900, when she was twenty-six, Florence walked out through the cabin door. She had thought to wait until her mother, who was so ill now that she no longer stirred out of bed, should be buried—but suddenly she knew that she would wait no longer, the time had come. She had been working as cook and serving girl for a large white family in town, and it was on the day that her master proposed that she become his concubine that she knew that her life among these wretched had come to its destined end. She left her employment that same day (leaving behind her a most vehement conjugal bitterness) and with part of the money which, with cunning, cruelty, and sacrifice, she had saved over a period of years, bought a railroad ticket to New York. When she bought it, in a kind of scarlet rage, she held, like a talisman at the back of her mind, the thought: "I can give it back, I can sell it. This don't mean I got to go." But she knew that nothing could stop her.

And it was this leave-taking which came to stand, in Florence's latter days, and with many another witness, at her bedside. Gray clouds obscured the sun that day, and outside the cabin window she saw that mist still covered the ground. Her mother lay in bed, awake; she was pleading with Gabriel,[2] who had been out drinking the night before, and who was not really sober now, to mend his ways and come to the Lord. And Gabriel, full of the confusion, and pain, and guilt which were his whenever he thought of how he made his mother suffer, but which became nearly insupportable when she taxed him with

---

[2] It is significant that the mother's (Rachel's) son is given the biblical name Gabriel, meaning "God is mighty," but her daughter is given the name Florence, which is customarily identified with bloom and prosperity. His mother had named him Gabriel apparently with great hope, a hope later dashed by his sins, giving his name an ironical twist. For Gabriel see Luke 1:19, 26–38.

it, stood before the mirror, head bowed, buttoning his shirt. Florence knew that he could not unlock his lips to speak; he could not say Yes to his mother, and to the Lord; and he could not say No.

10   "Honey," their mother was saying, "don't you *let* your old mother die without you look her in the eye and tell her she going to see you in glory. You hear me, boy?"

In a moment, Florence thought with scorn, tears would fill his eyes, and he would promise to "do better." He had been promising to "do better" since the day he had been baptized.

She put down her bag in the center of the hateful room.

"Ma," she said, "I'm going. I'm a-going this morning."

Now that she had said it, she was angry with herself for not having said it the night before, so that they would have had time to be finished with their weeping and their arguments. She had not trusted herself to withstand, the night before; but now there was almost no time left. The center of her mind was filled with the image of the great, white clock at the railway station, on which the hands did not cease to move.

15   "You going where?" her mother asked, sharply. But she knew that her mother had understood, had, indeed, long before this moment, known that this moment would come. The astonishment with which she stared at Florence's bag was not altogether astonishment, but a startled, wary attention. A danger imagined had become present and real, and her mother was already searching for a way to break Florence's will. All this Florence, in a moment, knew, and it made her stronger. She watched her mother, waiting.

But at the tone of his mother's voice, Gabriel, who had scarcely heard Florence's announcement, so grateful had he been that something had occurred to distract from him his mother's attention, dropped his eyes, and saw Florence's traveling bag. And he repeated his mother's question in a stunned, angry voice, understanding it only as the words hit the air:

"Yes, girl. Where you think you going?"

"I'm going," she said, "to New York. I got my ticket."

And her mother watched her. For a moment no one said a word. Then, Gabriel, in a changed and frightened voice, asked:

20   "And when you done decide that?"

She did not look at him, nor answer his question. She continued to watch her mother. "I got my ticket," she repeated. "I'm going on the morning train."

"Girl," asked her mother, quietly, "is you sure you know what you's doing?"

She stiffened, seeing in her mother's eyes a mocking pity. "I'm a woman grown," she said. "I know what I'm doing."

"And you going," cried Gabriel, "this morning—just like that? And you going to walk off and leave your mother—just like that?"

25   "You hush," she said, turning to him for the first time; "she got you, ain't she?"

This was indeed, she realized, as he dropped his eyes, the bitter, troubling point. He could not endure the thought of being left alone with his mother, with nothing whatever to put between himself and his guilty love. With Florence gone, time would have swallowed up all his mother's children, except himself; and *he*, then, must make amends for all the pain that she had borne, and sweeten her last moments with all his proofs of love. And his mother required of him one proof only, that he tarry no longer in sin. With Florence gone, his stammering time, his playing time, contracted with a bound to the sparest interrogative second; when he must stiffen himself, and answer to his mother, and all the host of heaven, Yes, or No.

Florence smiled inwardly a small, malicious smile, watching his slow bafflement, and panic, and rage; and she looked at her mother again. "She got you," she repeated. "She don't need me."

"You going North," her mother said, then. "And when you reckon on coming back?"

"I don't reckon on coming back," she said.

30 "You come crying back soon enough," said Gabriel, with malevolence, "soon as they whip your butt up there four or five times."

She looked at him again. "Just don't you try to hold your breath till then, you hear?"

"Girl," said her mother, "you mean to tell me the devil's done made your heart so hard you can just leave your mother on her dying bed, and you don't care if you don't never see her in this world no more? Honey, you can't tell me you done got so evil as all that?"

She felt Gabriel watching her to see how she would take this question—the question, which, for all her determination, she had dreaded most to hear. She looked away from her mother, and straightened, catching her breath, looking outward through the small, cracked window. There, outside, beyond the slowly rising mist, and farther off than her eyes could see, her life awaited her. The woman on the bed was old, her life was fading as the mist rose. She thought of her mother as already in the grave; and she would not let herself be strangled by the hands of the dead.

"I'm going, Ma," she said. "I got to go."

35 Her mother leaned back, face upward to the light, and began to cry. Gabriel moved to Florence's side and grabbed her arm. She looked up into his face and saw that his eyes were full of tears.

"You can't go," he said. "You can't go. You can't go and leave your mother thisaway. She need a woman, Florence, to help look after her. What she going to do here, all alone with me?"

She pushed him from her and moved to stand over her mother's bed.

"Ma," she said, "don't be like that. Ain't a blessed thing for you to cry about so. Ain't a thing can happen to me up North can't happen to me here. God's everywhere, Ma. Ain't no need to worry."

She knew that she was mouthing words; and she realized suddenly that her mother scorned to dignify these words with her attention. She had granted Florence the victory—with a promptness which had the effect of making Florence, however dimly and unwillingly, wonder if her victory was real; and she was not weeping for her daughter's future; she was weeping for the past, and weeping in an anguish in which Florence had no part. And all of this filled Florence with a terrible fear, which was immediately transformed into anger.

40 "Gabriel can take care of you," she said, her voice shaking with malice; "Gabriel ain't never going to leave you. Is you, boy?" and she looked at him. He stood, stupid with bewilderment and grief, a few inches from the bed. "But me," she said, "I got to go." She walked to the center of the room again, and picked up her bag.

"Girl," Gabriel whispered, "ain't you got no feelings at *all*?"

"*Lord!*" her mother cried; and at the sound her heart turned over; she and Gabriel, arrested, stared at the bed. "Lord, Lord, Lord! Lord, have mercy on my sinful daughter! Stretch out your hand and hold her back from the lake that burns forever! Oh, my Lord, my Lord!" and her voice dropped, and broke, and tears ran down her face. "Lord, I done my best with all the children what you give me. Lord, have mercy on my children, and my children's children."

"Florence," said Gabriel, "please don't go. Please don't go. You ain't really fixing to go and leave her like this?"

Tears stood suddenly in her own eyes, though she could not have said what she was crying for. "Leave me be," she said to Gabriel, and picked up her bag again. She opened the door; the cold morning air came in. "Good-by," she said. And then to Gabriel: "Tell her I said goodby." She walked through the cabin door and down the short steps into the frosty yard. Gabriel watched her, standing magnetized between the door and the weeping bed. Then, as her hand was on the gate, he ran before her, and slammed the gate shut.

45   "Girl, where you going? What you doing? You reckon on finding some men up North to dress you in pearls and diamonds?"

Violently, she opened the gate and moved out into the road. He watched her with his jaw hanging, until the dust and the distance swallowed her up.

William Faulkner (1897–1962)
A Rose for Emily

1

When Miss Emily Grierson died, our whole town went to her funeral: the men through a sort of respectful affection for a fallen monument, the women mostly out of curiosity to see the inside of her house, which no one save an old manservant—a combined gardener and cook—had seen in at least ten years.

It was a big, squarish frame house that had once been white, decorated with cupolas and spires and scrolled balconies in the heavily lightsome style of the seventies, set on what had once been our most select street. But garages and cotton gins had encroached and obliterated even the august names of that neighborhood; only Miss Emily's house was left, lifting its stubborn and coquettish decay above the cotton wagons and the gasoline pumps—an eyesore among eyesores. And now Miss Emily had gone to join the representatives of those august names where they lay in the cedar-bemused cemetery among the ranked and anonymous graves of Union and Confederate soldiers who fell at the battle of Jefferson.[1]

Alive, Miss Emily had been a tradition, a duty and a care; a sort of hereditary obligation upon the town, dating from that day in 1894 when Colonel Sartoris, the mayor—he who fathered the edict that no Negro woman should appear on the streets without an apron—remitted her taxes, the dispensation dating from the death of her father on into perpetuity. Not that Miss Emily would have accepted charity. Colonel Sartoris invented an involved tale to the effect that Miss Emily's father had loaned money to the town, which the town, as a matter of business, preferred this way of repaying. Only a man of Colonel Sartoris' generation and thought could have invented it, and only a woman could have believed it.

When the next generation, with its more modern ideas, became mayors and aldermen, this arrangement created some little dissatisfaction. On the first of the year they

---

[1] Faulkner's name for Oxford, Mississippi.

mailed her a tax notice. February came, and there was no reply. They wrote her a formal letter, asking her to call at the sheriff's office at her convenience. A week later the mayor wrote her himself, offering to call or send his car for her and received in reply a note on paper of an archaic shape, in a thin flowing calligraphy in faded ink, to the effect that she no longer went out at all. The tax notice was also enclosed, without comment.

5   They called a special meeting of the Board of Aldermen. A deputation waited upon her, knocked at the door through which no visitor had passed since she ceased giving china-painting lessons eight or ten years earlier. They were admitted by the old Negro into a dim hall from which a stairway mounted into still more shadow. It smelled of dust and disuse—a close, dank smell. The Negro led them into the parlor. It was furnished in heavy, leather-covered furniture. When the Negro opened the blinds of one window, they could see that the leather was cracked; and when they sat down, a faint dust rose sluggishly about their thighs, spinning with slow motes in the single sun-ray. On a tarnished gilt easel before the fireplace stood a crayon portrait of Miss Emily's father.

They rose when she entered—a small, fat woman in black, with a thin gold chain descending to her waist and vanishing into her belt, leaning on an ebony cane with a tarnished gold head. Her skeleton was small and spare; perhaps that was why what would have been merely plumpness in another was obesity in her. She looked bloated, like a body long submerged in motionless water, and of that pallid hue. Her eyes, lost in the fatty ridges of her face, looked like two small pieces of coal pressed into a lump of dough as they moved from one face to another while the visitors stated their errand.

She did not ask them to sit. She just stood in the door and listened quietly until the spokesman came to a stumbling halt. Then they could hear the invisible watch ticking at the end of the gold chain.

Her voice was dry and cold. "I have no taxes in Jefferson. Colonel Sartoris explained it to me. Perhaps one of you can gain access to the city records and satisfy yourselves."

"But we have. We are the city authorities, Miss Emily. Didn't you get a notice from the sheriff, signed by him?"

10   "I received a paper, yes," Miss Emily said. "Perhaps he considers himself the sheriff . . . I have no taxes in Jefferson."

"But there is nothing on the books to show that, you see. We must go by the—"

"See Colonel Sartoris. I have no taxes in Jefferson."

"But, Miss Emily—"

"See Colonel Sartoris." (Colonel Sartoris had been dead almost ten years.) "I have no taxes in Jefferson. Tobe!" The Negro appeared. "Show these gentlemen out."

2

15   So she vanquished them, horse and foot, just as she had vanquished their fathers thirty years before about the smell. That was two years after her father's death and a short time after her sweetheart—the one we believed would marry her—had deserted her. After her father's death she went out very little; after her sweetheart went away, people hardly saw her at all. A few of the ladies had the temerity to call, but were not received, and the only sign of life about the place was the Negro man—a young man then—going in and out with a market basket.

"Just as if a man—any man—could keep a kitchen properly," the ladies said; so they were not surprised when the smell developed. It was another link between the gross, teeming world and the high and mighty Griersons.

A neighbor, a woman, complained to the mayor, Judge Stevens, eighty years old.

"But what will you have me do about it, madam?" he said.

"Why, send her word to stop it," the woman said. "Isn't there a law?"

20   "I'm sure that won't be necessary," Judge Stevens said. "It's probably just a snake or a rat that nigger of hers killed in the yard. I'll speak to him about it."

The next day he received two more complaints, one from a man who came in diffident deprecation. "We really must do something about it, Judge. I'd be the last one in the world to bother Miss Emily, but we've got to do something." That night the Board of Aldermen met—three graybeards and one younger man, a member of the rising generation.

"It's simple enough," he said. "Send her word to have her place cleaned up. Give her a certain time to do it in, and if she don't . . ."

"Dammit, sir," Judge Stevens said, "will you accuse a lady to her face of smelling bad?"

So the next night, after midnight, four men crossed Miss Emily's lawn and slunk about the house like burglars, sniffing along the base of the brickwork and at the cellar openings while one of them performed a regular sowing motion with his hand out of a sack slung from his shoulder. They broke open the cellar door and sprinkled lime there, and in all the outbuildings. As they recrossed the lawn, a window that had been dark was lighted, and Miss Emily sat in it, the light behind her, and her upright torso motionless as that of an idol. They crept quietly across the lawn and into the shadow of the locusts that lined the street. After a week or two the smell went away.

25   That was when people had begun to feel really sorry for her. People in our town, remembering how old lady Wyatt, her great-aunt, had gone completely crazy at last, believed that the Griersons held themselves a little too high for what they really were. None of the young men were quite good enough for Miss Emily and such. We had long thought of them as a tableau, Miss Emily a slender figure in white in the background, her father a spraddled silhouette in the foreground, his back to her and clutching a horsewhip, the two of them framed by the back-flung front door. So when she got to be thirty and was still single, we were not pleased exactly, but vindicated; even with insanity in the family she wouldn't have turned down all of her chances if they had really materialized.

When her father died, it got about that the house was all that was left to her; and in a way, people were glad. At last they could pity Miss Emily. Being left alone, and a pauper, she had become humanized. Now she too would know the old thrill and the old despair of a penny more or less.

The day after his death all the ladies prepared to call at the house and offer condolence and aid, as is our custom. Miss Emily met them at the door, dressed as usual and with no trace of grief on her face. She told them that her father was not dead. She did that for three days, with the ministers calling on her, and the doctors, trying to persuade her to let them dispose of the body. Just as they were about to resort to law and force, she broke down, and they buried her father quickly.

We did not say she was crazy then. We believed she had to do that. We remembered all the young men her father had driven away, and we knew that with nothing left, she would have to cling to that which had robbed her, as people will.

3

She was sick for a long time. When we saw her again. her hair was cut short, making her look like a girl, with a vague resemblance to those angels in colored church windows—sort of tragic and serene.

30   The town had just let the contracts for paving the sidewalks, and in the summer after her father's death they began the work. The construction company came with niggers and mules and machinery, and a foreman named Homer Barron, a Yankee—a big, dark, ready man, with a big voice and eyes lighter than his face. The little boys would follow in groups

to hear him cuss the niggers, and the niggers singing in time to the rise and fall of picks. Pretty soon he knew everybody in town. Whenever you heard a lot of laughing anywhere about the square, Homer Barron would be in the center of the group. Presently we began to see him and Miss Emily on Sunday afternoons driving in the yellow-wheeled buggy and the matched team of bays from the livery stable.

At first we were glad that Miss Emily would have an interest, because the ladies all said, "Of course a Grierson would not think seriously of a Northerner, a day laborer." But there were still others, older people, who said that even grief could not cause a real lady to forget *noblesse oblige*[2]—without calling it *noblesse oblige*. They just said, "Poor Emily. Her kinsfolk should come to her." She had some kin in Alabama; but years ago her father had fallen out with them over the estate of old lady Wyatt, the crazy woman, and there was no communication between the two families. They had not even been represented at the funeral.

And as soon as the old people said, "Poor Emily," the whispering began. "Do you suppose it's really so?" they said to one another. "Of course it is. What else could . . ." This behind their hands; rustling of craned silk and satin behind jalousies closed upon the sun of Sunday afternoon as the thin, swift clop-clop-clop of the matched team passed: "Poor Emily."

She carried her head high enough—even when we believed that she was fallen. It was as if she demanded more than ever the recognition of her dignity as the last Grierson; as if it had wanted that touch of earthiness to reaffirm her imperviousness. Like when she bought the rat poison, the arsenic. That was over a year after they had begun to say "Poor Emily," and while the two female cousins were visiting her.

"I want some poison," she said to the druggist. She was over thirty then, still a slight woman, though thinner than usual, with cold, haughty black eyes in a face the flesh of which was strained across the temples and about the eye-sockets as you imagine a light-house-keeper's face ought to look. "I want some poison," she said.

35   "Yes, Miss Emily. What kind? For rats and such? I'd recom—"

"I want the best you have. I don't care what kind."

The druggist named several. "They'll kill anything up to an elephant. But what you want is—"

"Arsenic," Miss Emily said. "Is that a good one?"

"Is . . . arsenic? Yes, ma'am. But what you want—"

40   "I want arsenic."

The druggist looked down at her. She looked back at him, erect, her face like a strained flag. "Why, of course," the druggist said. "If that's what you want. But the law requires you to tell what you are going to use it for."

Miss Emily just stared at him, her head tilted back in order to look him eye for eye, until he looked away and went and got the arsenic and wrapped it up. The Negro delivery boy brought her the package; the druggist didn't come back. When she opened the package at home there was written on the box, under the skull and bones: "For rats."

4

So the next day we all said, "She will kill herself"; and we said it would be the best thing. When she had first begun to be seen with Homer Barron, we had said, "She will marry him." Then we said, "She will persuade him yet," because Homer himself had remarked—he liked men, and it was known that he drank with the younger men in the Elks' Club—that he was not a marrying man. Later we said, "Poor Emily" behind the jalousies as they passed on Sunday afternoon in the glittering buggy, Miss Emily with her

[2] The obligation of the noble.

head high and Homer Barron with his hat cocked and a cigar in his teeth, reins and whip in a yellow glove.

Then some of the ladies began to say that it was a disgrace to the town, and a bad example to the young people. The men did not want to interfere, but at last the ladies forced the Baptist minister—Miss Emily's people were Episcopal—to call upon her. He would never divulge what happened during that interview, but he refused to go back again. The next Sunday they again drove about the streets, and the following day the minister's wife wrote to Miss Emily's relations in Alabama.

45   So she had blood-kin under her roof again and we sat back to watch developments. At first nothing happened. Then we were sure that they were to be married. We learned that Miss Emily had been to the jeweler's and ordered a man's toilet set in silver, with the letters H. B. on each piece. Two days later we learned that she had bought a complete outfit of men's clothing, including a nightshirt, and we said, "They are married." We were really glad. We were glad because the two female cousins were even more Grierson than Miss Emily had ever been.

So we were not surprised when Homer Barron—the streets had been finished some time since—was gone. We were a little disappointed that there was not a public blowing-off, but we believed that he had gone on to prepare for Miss Emily's coming, or to give her a chance to get rid of the cousins. (By that time it was a cabal, and we were all Miss Emily's allies to help circumvent the cousins.) Sure enough, after another week they departed. And, as we had expected all along, within three days Homer Barron was back in town. A neighbor saw the Negro man admit him at the kitchen door at dusk one evening.

And that was the last we saw of Homer Barron. And of Miss Emily for some time. The Negro man went in and out with the market basket, but the front door remained closed. Now and then we would see her at a window for a moment, as the men did that night when they sprinkled the lime, but for almost six months she did not appear on the streets. Then we knew that this was to be expected too; as if that quality of her father which had thwarted her woman's life so many times had been too virulent and too furious to die.

When we next saw Miss Emily, she had grown fat and her hair was turning gray. During the next few years it grew grayer and grayer until it attained an even pepper-and-salt iron-gray, when it ceased turning. Up to the day of her death at seventy-four it was still that vigorous iron-gray, like the hair of an active man.

From that time on her front door remained closed, save for a period of six or seven years, when she was about forty, during which she gave lessons in china-painting. She fitted up a studio in one of the downstairs rooms, where the daughters and grand-daughters of Colonel Sartoris' contemporaries were sent to her with the same regularity and in the same spirit that they were sent to church on Sundays with a twenty-five cent piece for the collection plate. Meanwhile her taxes had been remitted.

50   The newer generation became the backbone and the spirit of the town, and the painting pupils grew up and fell away and did not send their children to her with boxes of color and tedious brushes and pictures cut from the ladies' magazines. The front door closed upon the last one and remained closed for good. When the town got free postal delivery, Miss Emily alone refused to let them fasten the metal numbers above her door and attach a mailbox to it. She would not listen to them.

Daily, monthly, yearly we watched the Negro grow grayer and more stooped, going in and out with the market basket. Each December we sent her a tax notice, which would be returned by the post office a week later, unclaimed. Now and then we would see her in one of the downstairs windows—she had evidently shut up the top floor of the house—like the carven torso of an idol in a niche, looking or not looking at us, we could never tell which. Thus she passed from generation to generation—dear, inescapable, impervious, tranquil, and perverse.

And so she died. Fell ill in the house filled with dust and shadows, with only a doddering Negro man to wait on her. We did not even know she was sick; we had long since given up trying to get any information from the Negro. He talked to no one, probably not even to her, for his voice had grown harsh and rusty, as if from disuse.

She died in one of the downstairs rooms, in a heavy walnut bed with a curtain, her gray head propped on a pillow yellow and moldy with age and lack of sunlight.

5

The Negro met the first of the ladies at the front door and let them in, with their hushed, sibilant voices and their quick, curious glances, and then he disappeared. He walked right through the house and out the back and was not seen again.

55 The two female cousins came at once. They held the funeral on the second day, with the town coming to look at Miss Emily beneath a mass of bought flowers, with the crayon face of her father musing profoundly above the bier and the ladies sibilant and macabre; and the very old men—some in their brushed Confederate uniforms—on the porch and the lawn, talking of Miss Emily as if she had been a contemporary of theirs, believing that they had danced with her and courted her perhaps, confusing time with its mathematical progression, as the old do, to whom all the past is not a diminishing road but, instead, a huge meadow which no winter every quite touches, divided from them now by the narrow bottleneck of the most recent decade of years.

Already we knew that there was one room in that region above stairs which no one had seen in forty years, and which would have to be forced. They waited until Miss Emily was decently in the ground before they opened it.

The violence of breaking down the door seemed to fill this room with pervading dust. A thin, acrid pall as of the tomb seemed to lie everywhere upon this room decked and furnished as for a bridal: upon the valance curtains of faded rose color, upon the rose-shaded lights, upon the dressing table, upon the delicate array of crystal and the man's toilet things backed with tarnished silver, silver so tarnished that the monogram was obscured. Among them lay a collar and tie, as if they had just been removed, which, lifted, left upon the surface a pale crescent in the dust. Upon a chair hung the suit, carefully folded; beneath it the two mute shoes and the discarded socks.

The man himself lay in the bed.

For a long while we just stood there, looking down at the profound and fleshless grin. The body had apparently once lain in the attitude of an embrace, but now the long sleep that outlasts love, that conquers even the grimace of love, had cuckolded him. What was left of him, rotted beneath what was left of the nightshirt, had become inextricable from the bed in which he lay; and upon him and upon the pillow beside him lay that even coating of the patient and biding dust.

60 Then we noticed that in the second pillow was the indentation of a head. One of us lifted something from it, and leaning forward, that faint and invisible dust dry and acrid in the nostrils, we saw a long strand of iron-gray hair.

Comments and Questions

1. How is the description of Miss Emily's house near the opening of the story suggestive of her situation?

2. List the various conflicts apparent in the story. How is each of the conflicts resolved? How do the resolutions contribute to characterization or to theme?

3. Carefully explore the relationship between Miss Emily and the community of Jefferson, especially that part of the community represented by the narrator (note the frequent use of "we"). Is the relationship something of a reciprocal one between Miss Emily and the community? Explain your answer in some detail.

4. Does the narrator belong to the "newer generation"? Characterize the narrator in every way you can by reference to the details of the story.

5. Both Miss Emily and Julian's mother in "Everything That Rises Must Converge" (p. 41) are representatives of the "aristocracy" of the Old South caught in "reduced circumstances." What other close parallels can you draw between the two? Which character is presented more sympathetically? Which one rises to the level of potent symbol? Is the method of narration, the point of view and the particular narrator, in each story of special importance in asnwering those two questions? Explain.

William Faulkner (1897–1962)
The Bear

He was ten. But it had already begun, long before that day when at last he wrote his age in two figures and he saw for the first time the camp where his father and Major de Spain and old General Compson and the others spent two weeks each November and two weeks again each June. He had already inherited then, without ever having seen it, the tremendous bear with one trap-ruined foot which, in an area almost a hundred miles deep, had earned itself a name, a definite designation like a living man.

He had listened to it for years: the long legend of corncribs rifled, of shotes and grown pigs and even calves carried bodily into the woods and devoured, of traps and deadfalls overthrown and dogs mangled and slain, and shotgun and even rifle charges delivered at point-blank range and with no more effect than so many peas blown through a tube by a boy—a corridor of wreckage and destruction beginning back before he was born, through which sped, not fast but rather with the ruthless and irresistible deliberation of a locomotive, the shaggy tremendous shape.

It ran in his knowledge before he ever saw it. It looked and towered in his dreams before he even saw the unaxed woods where it left its crooked print, shaggy, huge, red-eyed, not malevolent but just big—too big for the dogs which tried to bay it, for the horses which tried to ride it down, for the men and the bullets they fired into it, too big for the very country which was its constricting scope. He seemed to see it entire with a child's complete divination before he ever laid eyes on either—the doomed wilderness whose edges were being constantly and punily gnawed at by men with axes and plows who feared it because it was wilderness, men myriad and nameless even to one another in the land where the old bear had earned a name, through which ran not even a mortal animal but an anachronism, indomitable and invincible, out of an old dead time, a phantom, epitome and apotheosis of the old wild life at which the puny humans swarmed and hacked in a fury of abhorrence and fear, like pygmies about the ankles of a drowsing elephant: the old bear solitary, indomitable and alone, widowered, childless, and absolved of mortality—old Priam reft of his old wife and having outlived all his sons.

Until he was ten, each November he would watch the wagon containing the dogs and the bedding and food and guns and his father and Tennie's Jim, the Negro, and Sam Fathers, the Indian, son of a slave woman and a Chickasaw chief, depart on the road to town, to Jefferson, where Major de Spain and the others would join them. To the boy, at seven, eight, and nine, they were not going into the Big Bottom to hunt bear and deer, but to keep yearly rendezvous with the bear which they did not even intend to kill. Two weeks later they would return, with no trophy, no head and skin. He had not expected it. He had not even been afraid it would be in the wagon. He believed that even after he was ten and his father would let him go too, for those two weeks in November, he would merely make another one, along with his father and Major de Spain and General Compson and the others, the dogs which feared to bay at it and the rifles and shotguns which failed even to bleed it, in the yearly pageant of the old bear's furious immortality.

5   Then he heard the dogs. It was in the second week of his first time in the camp. He stood with Sam Fathers against a big oak beside the faint crossing where they had stood each dawn for nine days now, hearing the dogs. He had heard them once before, one morning last week—a murmur, sourceless, echoing through the wet woods, swelling presently into separate voices which he could recognize and call by name. He had raised and cocked the gun as Sam told him and stood motionless again while the uproar, the invisible course, swept up and past and faded; it seemed to him that he could actually see the deer, the buck, blond, smoke-colored, elongated with speed, fleeing, vanishing, the woods, the gray solitude, still ringing even when the cries of the dogs had died away.

"Now let the hammers down," Sam said.

"You knew they were not coming here too," he said.

"Yes," Sam said. "I want you to learn how to do when you didn't shoot. It's after the chance for the bear or the deer has done already come and gone that men and dogs get killed."

"Anyway," he said, "it was just a deer."

10   Then on the tenth morning he heard the dogs again. And he readied the too-long, too-heavy gun as Sam had taught him, before Sam even spoke. But this time it was no deer, no ringing chorus of dogs running strong on a free scent, but a moiling yapping an octave too high, with something more than indecision and even abjectness in it, not even moving very fast, taking a long time to pass completely out of hearing, leaving them somewhere in the air that echo, thin, slightly hysterical, abject, almost grieving, with no sense of a fleeting, unseen, smoke-colored, grass-eating shape ahead of it, and Sam, who had taught him first of all to cock the gun and take position where he could see everywhere and then never move again, had himself moved up beside him; he could hear Sam breathing at his shoulder, and he could see the arched curve of the old man's inhaling nostrils.

"Hah," Sam said. "Not even running. Walking."

"Old Ben!" the boy said. "But up here!" he cried. "Way up here!"

"He do it every year," Sam said. "Once. Maybe to see who in camp this time, if he can shoot or not. Whether we got the dog yet that can bay and hold him. He'll take them to the river, then he'll send them back home. We may as well go back too; see how they look when they come back to camp."

When they reached the camp the hounds were already there, ten of them crouching back under the kitchen, the boy and Sam squatting to peer back into the obscurity where they had huddled, quiet, the eyes luminous, glowing at them and vanishing, and no sound, only that effluvium of something more than dog, stronger than dog and not just animal, just beast, because still there had been nothing in front of that abject and almost painful yapping save the solitude, the wilderness, so that when the eleventh hound came in at noon and with all the others watching—even old Uncle Ash, who called himself first a cook—Sam daubed the tattered ear and the raked shoulder with turpentine and axle grease, to the boy it was still no living creature, but the wilderness which, leaning for the moment down, had patted lightly once the hound's temerity.

15   "Just like a man," Sam said. "Just like folks. Put off as long as she could having to be brave, knowing all the time that sooner or later she would have to be brave to keep on living with herself, and knowing all the time beforehand what was going to happen to her when she done it."

That afternoon, himself on the one-eyed wagon mule which did not mind the smell of blood nor, as they told him, of bear, and with Sam on the other one, they rode for more than three hours through the rapid, shortening winter day. They followed no path, no trail even that he could see; almost at once they were in a country which he had never seen before. Then he knew why Sam had made him ride the mule which would not spook. The sound one stopped short and tried to whirl and bolt even as Sam got down, blowing its breath, jerking and wrenching at the rein, while Sam held it, coaxing it forward with his voice, since he could not risk tying it, drawing it forward while the boy got down from the marred one.

Then, standing beside Sam in the gloom of the dying afternoon, he looked down at the rotted over-turned log, gutted and scored with claw marks and, in the wet earth beside it, the print of the enormous warped two-toed foot. He knew now what he had smelled when he peered under the kitchen where the dogs huddled. He realized for the first time that the bear which had run in his listening and loomed in his dreams since before he could remember to the contrary, and which, therefore, must have existed in the listening and dreams of his father and Major de Spain and even old General Compson, too, before they began to remember in their turn, was a mortal animal, and that if they had departed for the camp each November without any actual hope of bringing its trophy back, it was not because it could not be slain, but because so far they had had no actual hope to.

"Tomorrow," he said.

"We'll try tomorrow," Sam said. "We ain't got the dog yet."

20   "We've got eleven. They ran him this morning."

"It won't need but one," Sam said. "He ain't here. Maybe he ain't nowhere. The only other way will be for him to run by accident over somebody that has a gun."

"That wouldn't be me," the boy said. "It will be Walter or Major or—"

"It might," Sam said. "You watch close in the morning. Because he's smart. That's how come he has lived this long. If he gets hemmed up and has to pick out somebody to run over, he will pick out you."

"How?" the boy said. "How will he know—" He ceased. "You mean he already knows me, that I ain't never been here before, ain't had time to find out yet whether I—" He ceased again, looking at Sam, the old man whose face revealed nothing until it smiled. He said humbly, not even amazed, "It was me he was watching. I don't reckon he did need to come but once."

25   The next morning they left the camp three hours before daylight. They rode this time because it was too far to walk, even the dogs in the wagon; again the first gray light found him in a place which he had never seen before, where Sam had placed him and told him to stay and then departed. With the gun which was too big for him, which did not even belong to him, but to Major de Spain, and which he had fired only once—at a stump on the first day, to learn the recoil and how to reload it—he stood against a gum tree beside a little bayou whose black still water crept without movement out of a cane-brake and crossed a small clearing and into cane again, where, invisible, a bird—the big woodpecker called Lord-to-God by Negroes—clattered at a dead limb.

It was a stand like any other, dissimilar only in incidentals to the one where he had stood each morning for ten days; a territory new to him, yet no less familiar than that other one which, after almost two weeks, he had come to believe he knew a little—the same solitude, the same loneliness through which human beings had merely passed without altering it, leaving no mark, no scar, which looked exactly as it must have looked when the first ancestor of Sam Fathers' Chickasaw predecessors crept into it and looked about, club or stone ax or bone arrow drawn and poised; different only because, squatting at the edge of the kitchen, he smelled the hounds huddled and cringing beneath it and saw the raked ear and shoulder of the one who, Sam said, had had to be brave once in order to live with herself, and saw yesterday in the earth beside the gutted log the print of the living foot.

He heard no dogs at all. He never did hear them. He only heard the drumming of the woodpecker stop short off and knew that the bear was looking at him. He never saw it. He did not know whether it was in front of him or behind him. He did not move, holding the useless gun, which he had not even had warning to cock and which even now he did not cock, tasting in his saliva that taint as of brass which he knew now because he had smelled it when he peered under the kitchen at the huddled dogs.

Then it was gone. As abruptly as it had ceased, the woodpecker's dry, monotonous clatter set up again, and after a while he even believed he could hear the dogs—a murmur, scarce a sound even, which he had probably been hearing for some time before he even remarked it, drifting into hearing and then out again, dying away. They came nowhere near him. If it was a bear they ran, it was another bear. It was Sam himself who came out of the cane and crossed the bayou, followed by the injured bitch of yesterday. She was almost at heel, like a bird dog, making no sound. She came and crouched against his leg, trembling, staring off into the cane.

"I didn't see him," he said, "I didn't, Sam!"

30   "I know it," Sam said. "He done the looking. You didn't hear him neither, did you?"

"No," the boy said. "I—"

"He's smart," Sam said. "Too smart." He looked down at the hound, trembling faintly and steadily against the boy's knee. From the raked shoulder a few drops of fresh blood oozed and clung. "Too big. We ain't got the dog yet. But maybe someday. Maybe not next time. But someday."

So I must see him, he thought. *I must look at him.* Otherwise, it seemed to him that it would go on like this forever, as it had gone on with his father and Major de Spain, who was older than his father, and even with old General Compson, who had been old enough to be a brigade commander in 1865. Otherwise, it would go on so forever, next time and next time, after and after and after. It seemed to him that he could never see the two of them, himself and the bear, shadowy in the limbo from which time emerged, becoming time; the old bear absolved of mortality and himself partaking, sharing a little of it, enough of it. And he knew now what he had smelled in the huddled dogs and tasted in his saliva. He recognized fear. *So I will have to see him,* he thought, without dread or even hope. *I will have to look at him.*

It was in June of the next year. He was eleven. They were in camp again, celebrating Major de Spain's and General Compson's birthdays. Although the one had been born in September and the other in the depth of winter and in another decade, they had met for two weeks to fish and shoot squirrels and turkey and run coons and wildcats with the dogs at night. That is, he and Boon Hoggenbeck and the Negroes fished and shot squirrels and ran the coons and cats, because the proved hunters, not only Major de Spain and old General Compson, who spent those two weeks sitting in a rocking chair before a tremendous iron pot of Brunswick stew, stirring and tasting, with old Ash to quarrel with about how he was making it and Tennie's Jim to pour whiskey from the demijohn into the tin dipper from which he drank it, but even the boy's father and Walter Ewell, who were still young enough, scorned such, other than shooting the wild gobblers with pistols for wagers on their marksmanship.

Or, that is, his father and the others believed he was hunting squirrels. Until the third day, he thought that Sam Fathers believed that too. Each morning he would leave the camp right after breakfast. He had his own gun now, a Christmas present. He went back to the tree beside the bayou where he had stood that morning. Using the compass which old General Compson had given him, he ranged from that point; he was teaching himself to be a better-than-fair woodsman without knowing he was doing it. On the second day he even found the gutted log where he had first seen the crooked print. It was almost completely crumbled now, healing with unbelievable speed, a passionate and almost visible relinquishment, back into the earth from which the tree had grown.

He ranged the summer woods now, green with gloom; if anything, actually dimmer than in November's gray dissolution, where, even at noon, the sun fell only in intermittent dappling upon the earth, which never completely dried out and which crawled with snakes—moccasins and water snakes and rattlers, themselves the color of the dappling gloom, so that he would not always see them until they moved, returning later and later, first day, second day, passing in the twilight of the third evening the little log pen enclosing the log stable where Sam was putting up the horses for the night.

"You ain't looked right yet," Sam said.

He stopped. For a moment he didn't answer. Then he said peacefully, in a peaceful rushing burst as when a boy's miniature dam in a little brook gives way, "All right. But how? I went to the bayou. I even found that log again. I—"

"I reckon that was all right. Likely he's been watching you. You never saw his foot?"

"I," the boy said—"I didn't—I never thought—"

"It's the gun," Sam said. He stood beside the fence motionless—the old man, the Indian, in the battered faded overalls and the five-cent straw hat which in the Negro's race had been the badge of his enslavement and was now the regalia of his freedom. The camp—the clearing, the house, the barn and its tiny lot with which Major de Spain in his turn had scratched punily and evanescently at the wilderness—faded in the dusk, back into the immemorial darkness of the woods. *The gun,* the boy thought. *The gun.*

"Be scared," Sam said. "You can't help that. But don't be afraid. Ain't nothing in the woods going to hurt you unless you corner it, or it smells that you are afraid. A bear or a deer, too, has got to be scared of a coward the same as a brave man has got to be."

The gun, the boy thought.

"You will have to choose," Sam said.

He left the camp before daylight, long before Uncle Ash would wake in his quilts on the kitchen floor and start the fire for breakfast. He had only the compass and a stick for snakes. He could go almost a mile before he would begin to need the compass. He sat on a log, the invisible compass in his invisible hand, while the secret night sounds, fallen still at his movements, scurried again and then ceased for good, and the owls ceased and gave over to the waking of day birds, and he could see the compass. Then he went fast yet still quietly; he was becoming better and better as a woodsman, still without having yet realized it.

He jumped a doe and a fawn at sunrise, walked them out of the bed, close enough to see them—the crash of undergrowth, the white scut, the fawn scudding behind her faster than he had believed it could run. He was hunting right, upwind, as Sam had taught him; not that it mattered now. He had left the gun; of his own will and relinquishment he had accepted not a gambit, not a choice, but a condition in which not only the bear's heretofore inviolable anonymity but all the old rules and balances of hunter and hunted had been abrogated. He would not even be afraid, not even in the moment when the fear

would take him completely—blood, skin, bowels, bones, memory from the long time before it became his memory—all save that thin, clear, immortal lucidity which alone differed
him from this bear and from all the other bear and deer he would ever kill in the humility
and pride of his skill and endurance, to which Sam had spoken when he leaned in the
twilight on the lot fence yesterday.

By noon he was far beyond the little bayou, farther into the new and alien country
than he had ever been. He was traveling now not only by the compass but by the old,
heavy, biscuit-thick silver watch which had belonged to his grandfather. When he stopped
at last, it was for the first time since he had risen from the log at dawn when he could see
the compass. It was far enough. He had left the camp nine hours ago; nine hours from
now, dark would have already been an hour old. But he didn't think that. He thought, *All
right. Yes. But what?* and stood for a moment, alien and small in the green and topless
solitude, answering his own question before it had formed and ceased. It was the watch,
the compass, the stick—the three lifeless mechanicals with which for nine hours he had
fended the wilderness off; he hung the watch and compass carefully on a bush and leaned
the stick beside them and relinquished completely to it.

He had not been going very fast for the last two or three hours. He went no faster
now, since distance would not matter even if he could have gone fast. And he was trying
to keep a bearing on the tree where he had left the compass, trying to complete a circle
which would bring him back to it or at least intersect itself, since direction would not
matter now either. But the tree was not here, and he did as Sam had schooled him—made
the next circle in the opposite direction, so that the two patterns would bisect somewhere, but crossing no print of his own feet, finding the tree at last, but in the wrong
place—no bush, no compass, no watch—and the tree not even the tree, because there
was a down log beside it and he did what Sam Fathers had told him was the next thing
and the last.

As he sat down on the log he saw the crooked print—the warped, tremendous, two-
toed indentation which, even as he watched it, filled with water. As he looked up, the
wilderness coalesced, solidified—the glade, the tree he sought, the bush, the watch and
the compass glinting where the ray of sunshine touched them. Then he saw the bear. It
did not emerge, appear; it was just there, immobile, solid, fixed in the hot dappling of the
green and windless noon, not as big as he had dreamed it, but as big as he had expected
it, bigger, dimensionless, against the dappled obscurity, looking at him where he sat quietly on the log and looked back at it.

50   Then it moved. It made no sound. It did not hurry. It crossed the glade, walking for
an instant into the full glare of the sun; when it reached the other side it stopped again
and looked back at him across one shoulder while his quiet breathing inhaled and exhaled
three times.

Then it was gone. It didn't walk into the woods, the undergrowth. It faded, sank
back into the wilderness as he had watched a fish, a huge old bass, sink and vanish into
the dark depths of its pool without even any movement of its fins.

He thought, *It will be next fall.* But it was not next fall, nor the next nor the next.
He was fourteen then. He had killed his buck, and Sam Fathers had marked his face with
the hot blood, and in the next year he killed a bear. But even before that accolade he had
become as competent in the woods as many grown men with the same experience; by his
fourteenth year he was a better woodsman than most grown men with more. There was
no territory within thirty miles of the camp that he did not know—bayou, ridge, brake,
landmark, tree and path. He could have led anyone to any point in it without deviation,
and brought them out again. He knew the game trails that even Sam Fathers did not know;

in his thirteenth year he found a buck's bedding place, and unbeknown to his father he borrowed Walter Ewell's rifle and lay in wait at dawn and killed the buck when it walked back to the bed, as Sam had told him how the old Chickasaw fathers did.

But not the old bear, although by now he knew its footprints better than he did his own, and not only the crooked one. He could see any one of three sound ones and distinguish it from any other, and not only by its size. There were other bears within these thirty miles which left tracks almost as large, but this was more than that. If Sam Fathers had been his mentor and the back-yard rabbits and squirrels at home his kindergarten, then the wilderness the old bear ran was his college, the old male bear itself, so long unwifed and childless as to have become its own ungendered progenitor, was his alma mater. But he never saw it.

He could find the crooked print now almost whenever he liked, fifteen or ten or five miles, or sometimes nearer the camp than that. Twice while on stand during the three years he heard the dogs strike its trail by accident; on the second time they jumped it seemingly, the voices high, abject, almost human in hysteria, as on that first morning two years ago. But not the bear itself. He would remember that noon three years ago, the glade, himself and the bear fixed during that moment in the windless and dappled blaze, and it would seem to him that it had never happened, that he had dreamed that too. But it had happened. They had looked at each other, they had emerged from the wilderness old as earth, synchronized to the instant by something more than the blood that moved the flesh and bones which bore them, and touched, pledged something, affirmed, something more lasting than the frail web of bones and flesh which any accident could obliterate.

55 Then he saw it again. Because of the very fact that he thought of nothing else, he had forgotten to look for it. He was still hunting with Walter Ewell's rifle. He saw it cross the end of a long blow-down, a corridor where a tornado had swept, rushing through rather than over the tangle of trunks and branches as a locomotive would have, faster than he had ever believed it could move, almost as fast as a deer even, because a deer would have spent most of that time in the air, faster than he could bring the rifle sights up with it. And now he knew what had been wrong during all the three years. He sat on a log, shaking and trembling as if he had never seen the woods before nor anything that ran them, wondering with incredulous amazement how he could have forgotten the very thing which Sam Fathers had told him and which the bear itself had proved the next day and had now returned after three years to reaffirm.

And now he knew what Sam Fathers had meant about the right dog, a dog in which size would mean less than nothing. So when he returned alone in April—school was out then, so that the sons of farmers could help with the land's planting, and at last his father had granted him permission, on his promise to be back in four days—he had the dog. It was his own, a mongrel of the sort called by Negroes a fyce, a ratter, itself not much bigger than a rat and possessing that bravery which had long since stopped being courage and had become foolhardiness.

It did not take four days. Alone again, he found the trail on the first morning. It was not a stalk; it was an ambush. He timed the meeting almost as if it were an appointment with a human being. Himself holding the fyce muffled in a feed sack and Sam Fathers with two of the hounds on a piece of a plowline rope, they lay down wind of the trail at dawn of the second morning. They were so close that the bear turned without even running, as if in surprised amazement at the shrill and frantic uproar of the released fyce, turning at bay against the trunk of a tree, on its hind feet; it seemed to the boy that it would never stop rising, taller and taller, and even the two hounds seemed to take a desperate and despairing courage from the fyce, following it as it went in.

Then he realized that the fyce was actually not going to stop. He flung, threw the gun away, and ran; when he overtook and grasped the frantically pin-wheeling little dog, it seemed to him that he was directly under the bear.

He could smell it, strong and hot and rank. Sprawling, he looked up to where it loomed and towered over him like a cloudburst and colored like a thunderclap, quite familiar, peacefully and even lucidly familiar, until he remembered: This was the way he had used to dream about it. Then it was gone. He didn't see it go. He knelt, holding the frantic fyce with both hands, hearing the abashed wailing of the hounds drawing farther and farther away, until Sam came up. He carried the gun. He laid it down quietly beside the boy and stood looking down at him.

60   "You've done seed him twice now with a gun in your hands," he said. "This time you couldn't have missed him."

The boy rose. He still held the fyce. Even in his arms and clear of the ground, it yapped frantically, straining and surging after the fading uproar of the two hounds like a tangle of wire springs. He was panting a little but he was neither shaking nor trembling now.

"Neither could you!" he said. "You had the gun! Neither did you!"

"And you didn't shoot," his father said. "How close were you?"

"I don't know, sir," he said. "There was a big wood tick inside his right hind leg. I saw that. But I didn't have the gun then."

65   "But you didn't shoot when you had the gun," his father said. "Why?"

But he didn't answer, and his father didn't wait for him to, rising and crossing the room, across the pelt of the bear which the boy had killed two years ago and the larger one which his father had killed before he was born, to the bookcase beneath the mounted head of the boy's first buck. It was the room which his father called the office, from which all the plantation business was transacted; in it for the fourteen years of his life he had heard the best of all talking. Major de Spain would be there and sometimes old General Compson, and Walter Ewell and Boon Hoggenbeck and Sam Fathers and Tennie's Jim, too, were hunters, knew the woods and what ran them.

He would hear it, not talking himself but listening—the wilderness, the big woods, bigger and older than any recorded document of white man fatuous enough to believe he had bought any fragment of it or Indian ruthless enough to pretend that any fragment of it had been his to convey. It was of the men, not white nor black nor red, but men, hunters with the will and hardihood to endure and the humility and skill to survive, and the dogs and the bear and deer juxtaposed and reliefed against it, ordered and compelled by and within the wilderness in the ancient and unremitting contest by the ancient and immitigable rules which voided all regrets and brooked no quarter, the voices quiet and weighty and deliberate for retrospection and recollection and exact remembering, while he squatted in the blazing firelight as Tennie's Jim squatted, who stirred only to put more wood on the fire and to pass the bottle from one glass to another. Because the bottle was always present, so that after a while it seemed to him that those fierce instants of heart and brain and courage and wiliness and speed were concentrated and distilled into that brown liquor which not women, not boys and children, but only hunters drank, drinking not of the blood they had spilled but some condensation of the wild immortal spirit, drinking it moderately, humbly even, not with the pagan's base hope of acquiring the virtues of cunning and strength and speed, but in salute to them.

His father returned with the book and sat down again and opened it. "Listen," he said. He read the five stanzas aloud, his voice quiet and deliberate in the room where there was no fire now because it was already spring. Then he looked up. The boy watched him. "All right," his father said. "Listen." He read again, but only the second stanza this time, to the end of it, the last two lines, and closed the book and put it on the table beside him. "She cannot fade, though thou hast not thy bliss, forever wilt thou love, and she be fair," he said.

"He's talking about a girl," the boy said.

"He had to talk about something," his father said. Then he said, "He was talking about truth. Truth doesn't change. Truth is one thing. It covers all things which touch the heart—honor and pride and pity and justice and courage and love. Do you see now?"

He didn't know. Somehow it was simpler than that. There was an old bear, fierce and ruthless, not merely just to stay alive, but with the fierce pride of liberty and freedom, proud enough of the liberty and freedom to see it threatened without fear or even alarm; nay, who at times even seemed deliberately to put that freedom and liberty in jeopardy in order to savor them, to remind his old strong bones and flesh to keep supple and quick to defend and preserve them. There was an old man, son of a Negro slave and an Indian king, inheritor on the one side of the long chronicle of a people who had learned humility through suffering, and pride through the endurance which survived the suffering and injustice, and on the other side, the chronicle of a people even longer in the land than the first, yet who no longer existed in the land at all save in the solitary brotherhood of an old Negro's alien blood and the wild and invincible spirit of an old bear. There was a boy who wished to learn humility and pride in order to become skillful and worthy in the woods, who suddenly found himself becoming so skillful so rapidly that he feared he would never become worthy because he had not learned humility and pride, although he had tried to, until one day and as suddenly he discovered that an old man who could not have defined either had led him, as though by the hand, to that point where an old bear and a little mongrel of a dog showed him that, by possessing one thing other, he would possess them both.

And a little dog, nameless and mongrel and many-fathered, grown, yet weighing less than six pounds, saying as if to itself, "I can't be dangerous, because there's nothing much smaller than I am; I can't be fierce, because they would call it just a noise; I can't be humble, because I'm already too close to the ground to genuflect; I can't be proud, because I wouldn't be near enough to it for anyone to know who was casting the shadow, and I don't even know that I'm not going to heaven, because they have already decided that I don't possess an immortal soul. So all I can be is brave. But it's all right. I can be that, even if they still call it just noise."

That was all. It was simple, much simpler than somebody talking in a book about youth and a girl he would never need to grieve over, because he could never approach any nearer her and would never have to get any farther away. He had heard about a bear, and finally got big enough to trail it, and he trailed it four years and at last met it with a gun in his hands and he didn't shoot. Because a little dog—But he could have shot long before the little dog covered the twenty yards to where the bear waited, and Sam Fathers could have shot at any time during that interminable minute while Old Ben stood on his hind feet over them. He stopped. His father was watching him gravely across the spring-rife twilight of the room; when he spoke, his words were as quiet as the twilight, too, not loud, because they did not need to be because they would last. "Courage, and honor, and pride," his father said, "and pity, and love of justice and of liberty. They all touch the heart, and what the heart holds to becomes truth, as far as we know the truth. Do you see now?"

Sam, and Old Ben, and Nip, he thought. And himself too. He had been all right too. His father had said so. "Yes, sir," he said.

Comments and Questions

This is one of the world's great hunting stories. But it is also much more than just a hunting tale, as even a brief paraphrase of its events inescapably suggests. In the beginning is the bear. Almost before time is the bear, surviving all attempts against his "furious immortality," growing in cunning and in campfire legend, patiently awaiting the hunter and dog skilled and courageous enough to warrant his concern and worthy to test his suppleness of muscle and instinct and freely willing to be tested mind and marrow, in turn, by the bear and what has become forever the bear's wilderness. From the outset the hunter is paired with the questions of worthiness in skill, courage, and honor to deserve this matching with the glorious old timeless bear. And there is the necessarily patient, even ritualistic, development of that worthiness in the hunter as boy and youth and in his growth through partial and toward the full and final confrontation of the hunt and with the meaning of that confrontation. It is a genuine, engrossing hunting tale, and it is a hunter's tale as only a hunter could have told it. If it were only a hunting story, pure and simple, however, it would find its proper climax in the apparent success or failure of the hunt and hunter framed in the final confrontation. But Faulkner shifts the climactic frame. His story continues beyond that confrontation and probes well beyond mere questions of individual success or failure to questions of human meaning and human truth. Answers to the questions below should suggest some of that meaning and truth.

1. Define the tone of the first three paragraphs of the story (the narrator's attitude, especially toward the bear). Cite specific supporting passages and language. Does Old Ben suggest or represent anything more than a bear? In some detail, who was Priam? What is an anachronism? An epitome? An apotheosis? How does Faulkner use the concept of time in these paragraphs (and later) and to what end?

2. Cite some instances of forecast that the boy will not later on kill Old Ben, despite opportunity. Which characters seem to know he will not kill the bear, even early in the story? What is the purpose, the effect of their foreknowledge (aside from mere structural preparation)?

3. What paradoxical combination of qualities does Sam Fathers embody? Define his special, suggestive relationship to the boy, to Old Ben.

4. Clearly, setting is of first and functional importance in this story, both in the practical and the figurative senses. Mark every passage in the story where the narrator speaks of the wilderness, and try to distill the essential qualities of that concept, and note any direct or implicit connections with Old Ben, Fathers, the boy, humankind.

5. What is the significance (literal and suggestive) (1) of the "relinquishment" of gun, watch, compass, stick in the boy's compulsive quest to see in reality the tremendous bear of his dreams; (2) of the statement immediately thereafter that the boy "relinquished [himself] completely to it"?

6. In the second-from-last paragraph, note Faulkner's unrelenting presentation of the fyce as unadulterated courage, just under six pounds of lucid symbolism. In view of the inescapable nature of that symbolism, consider the rationale for each aspect of the boy's twin act of saving the fyce and *not* shooting the bear. Is the rationale identical for each? Does one aspect of the act (with its rationale) help to clarify the other? Is the description of the hunters' drinking near the end of the story also pertinent?

7. Read all of Keats's "Ode on a Grecian Urn" (p. 468), with special attention to the second and final stanzas. If the urn itself and the fixed, timeless scenes on it are pieces of immortal truth, what scenes described in Faulkner's story can be equated with them? In preparation to read from the poem, the boy's father walks across two bear pelts to the bookcase "beneath the mounted head of the boy's first buck." What is the special, thematic significance of those earlier trophies at that juncture? An old bear and a mongrel dog show the boy that, "by possessing one thing other," he can possess both humility and pride and, by implication, the other virtues extolled in the story. What is the "one thing other"?

John Cheever (1912–1982)
The Enormous Radio

Jim and Irene Westcott were the kind of people who seem to strike that satisfactory average of income, endeavor, and respectability that is reached by the statistical reports in college alumni bulletins. They were the parents of two young children, they had been married nine years, they lived on the twelfth floor of an apartment house near Sutton Place, they went to the theatre on an average of 10.3 times a year, and they hoped someday to live in Westchester. Irene Westcott was a pleasant, rather plain girl with soft brown hair and a wide, fine forehead upon which nothing at all had been written, and in the cold weather she wore a coat of fitch skins dyed to resemble mink. You could not say that Jim Westcott looked younger than he was, but you could at least say of him that he seemed to feel younger. He wore his graying hair cut very short, he dressed in the kind of clothes his class had worn at Andover, and his manner was earnest, vehement, and intentionally naïve. The Westcotts differed from their friends, their classmates, and their neighbors only in an interest they shared in serious music. They went to a great many concerts—although they seldom mentioned this to anyone—and they spent a good deal of time listening to music on the radio.

Their radio was an old instrument, sensitive, unpredictable, and beyond repair. Neither of them understood the mechanics of radio—or of any of the other appliances that surrounded them—and when the instrument faltered, Jim would strike the side of the cabinet with his hand. This sometimes helped. One Sunday afternoon, in the middle of a Schubert quartet, the music faded away altogether. Jim struck the cabinet repeatedly, but there was no response; the Schubert was lost to them forever. He promised to buy Irene a new radio, and on Monday when he came home from work he told her that he had got one. He refused to describe it, and said it would be a surprise for her when it came.

The radio was delivered at the kitchen door the following afternoon, and with the assistance of her maid and the handyman Irene uncrated it and brought it into the living room. She was struck at once with the physical ugliness of the large gumwood cabinet. Irene was proud of her living room, she had chosen its furnishings and colors as carefully as she chose her clothes, and now it seemed to her that the new radio stood among her intimate possessions like an aggressive intruder. She was confounded by the number of dials and switches on the instrument panel, and she studied them thoroughly before she put the plug into a wall socket and turned the radio on. The dials flooded with a malevolent green light, and in the distance she heard the music of a piano quintet. The quintet was in the distance for only an instant; it bore down upon her with a speed greater than light and filled the apartment with the noise of music amplified so mightily that it knocked a china ornament from a table to the floor. She rushed to the instrument and reduced the volume. The violent forces that were snared in the ugly gumwood cabinet made her uneasy. Her children came home from school then, and she took them to the Park. It was not until later in the afternoon that she was able to return to the radio.

The maid had given the children their suppers and was supervising their baths when Irene turned on the radio, reduced the volume, and sat down to listen to a Mozart quintet that she knew and enjoyed. The music came through clearly. The new instrument had a much purer tone, she thought, than the old one. She decided that tone was most important and that she could conceal the cabinet behind a sofa. But as soon as she had made her peace with the radio, the interference began. A crackling sound like the noise of a burning powder fuse began to accompany the singing of the strings. Beyond the music, there was a rustling that reminded Irene unpleasantly of the sea, and as the quintet progressed, these noises were joined by many others. She tried all the dials and switches but nothing dimmed the interference, and she sat down, disappointed and bewildered, and tried to trace the flight of the melody. The elevator shaft in her building ran beside the living-room wall, and it was the noise of the elevator that gave her a clue to the character of the static. The rattling of the elevator cables and the opening and closing of the elevator doors were reproduced in her loudspeader, and realizing that the radio was sensitive to electrical currents of all sorts, she began to discern through the Mozart the ringing of telephone bells, the dialing of phones, and the lamentation of a vacuum cleaner. By listening more carefully, she was able to distinguish doorbells, elevator bells, electric razors, and Waring mixers, whose sounds had been picked up from the apartments that surrounded hers and transmitted through her loudspeaker. The powerful and ugly instrument, with its mistaken sensitivity to discord, was more than she could hope to master, so she turned the thing off and went into the nursery to see her children.

5   When Jim Westcott came home that night, he went to the radio confidently and worked the controls. He had the same sort of experience Irene had had. A man was speaking on the station Jim had chosen, and his voice swung instantly from the distance into a force so powerful that it shook the apartment. Jim turned the volume control and reduced the voice. Then, a minute or two later, the interference began. The ringing of telephones and doorbells set in, joined by the rasp of the elevator doors and the whir of cooking appliances. The character of the noise had changed since Irene had tried the radio earlier; the last of the electric razors was being unplugged, the vacuum cleaners had all been returned to their closets, and the static reflected that change in pace that overtakes the city after the sun goes down. He fiddled with the knobs but couldn't get rid of the noises, so he turned the radio off and told Irene that in the morning he'd call the people who had sold it to him and give them hell.

The following afternoon, when Irene returned to the apartment from a luncheon date, the maid told her that a man had come and fixed the radio. Irene went into the living room before she took off her hat or her furs and tried the instrument. From the loud-speaker came a recording of the "Missouri Waltz." It reminded her of the thin, scratchy music from an old-fashioned phonograph that she sometimes heard across the lake where she spent her summers. She waited until the waltz had finished, expecting an explanation of the recording, but there was none. The music was followed by silence, and then the plaintive and scratchy record was repeated. She turned the dial and got a satisfactory burst of Caucasian music—the thump of bare feet in the dust and the rattle of coin jewelry—but in the background she could hear the ringing of bells and a confusion of voices. Her children came home from school then, and she turned off the radio and went to the nursery.

When Jim came home that night, he was tired, and he took a bath and changed his clothes. Then he joined Irene in the living room. He had just turned on the radio when the maid announced dinner, so he left it on, and he and Irene went to the table.

Jim was too tired to make even a pretense of sociability, and there was nothing about the dinner to hold Irene's interest, so her attention wandered from the food to the deposits of silver polish on the candlesticks and from there to the music in the other room. She listened for a few minutes to a Chopin prelude and then was surprised to hear a man's voice break in. "For Christ's sake, Kathy," he said, "do you always have to play the piano when I get home?" The music stopped abruptly. "It's the only chance I have," a woman said. "I'm at the office all day." "So am I," the man said. He added something obscene about an upright piano, and slammed a door. The passionate and melancholy music began again.

"Did you hear that?" Irene asked.

10   "What?" Jim was eating his dessert.

"The radio. A man said something while the music was still going on—something dirty."

"It's probably a play."

"I don't think it *is* a play," Irene said.

They left the table and took their coffee into the living room. Irene asked Jim to try another station. He turned the knob. "Have you seen my garters?" a man asked. "Button me up," a woman said. "Have you seen my garters?" the man said again. "Just button me up and I'll find your garters," the woman said. Jim shifted to another station. "I wish you wouldn't leave apple cores in the ashtrays," a man said. "I hate the smell."

15   "This is strange," Jim said.

"Isn't it?" Irene said.

Jim turned the knob again. " 'On the coast of Coromandel where the early pumpkins blow,' " a woman with a pronounced English accent said, " 'in the middle of the woods lived the Yonghy-Bonghy-Bò. Two old chairs, and half a candle, one old jug without a handle . . .' "

"My God!" Irene cried. "That's the Sweeneys' nurse."

" 'These were all his worldly goods,' " the British voice continued.

20   "Turn that thing off," Irene said. "Maybe they can hear *us*." Jim switched the radio off. "That was Miss Armstrong, the Sweeneys' nurse," Irene said. "She must be reading to the little girl. They live in 17-B. I've talked with Miss Armstrong in the Park. I know her voice very well. We must be getting other people's apartments."

"That's impossible," Jim said.

"Well, that was the Sweeneys' nurse," Irene said hotly. "I know her voice. I know it very well. I'm wondering if they can hear us."

Jim turned the switch. First from a distance and then nearer, nearer, as if borne on the wind, came the pure accents of the Sweeneys' nurse again: *"'Lady Jingly! Lady Jingly!'"* she said, *" 'sitting where the pumpkins blow, will you come and be my wife? said the Yonghy-Bonghy-Bò . . .'"*

Jim went over to the radio and said "Hello" loudly into the speaker.

25   *" 'I am tired of living singly,' "* the nurse went on, *" 'on this coast so wild and shingly, I'm a-weary of my life; if you'll come and be my wife, quite serene would be my life . . .' "*

"I guess she can't hear us," Irene said. "Try something else."

Jim turned to another station, and the living room was filled with the uproar of a cocktail party that had overshot its mark. Someone was playing the piano and singing the "Whiffenpoof Song," and the voices that surrounded the piano were vehement and happy. "Eat some more sandwiches," a woman shrieked. There were screams of laughter and a dish of some sort crashed to the floor.

"Those must be the Fullers, in 11-E," Irene said. "I knew they were giving a party this afternoon. I saw her in the liquor store. Isn't this too divine? Try something else. See if you can get those people in 18-C."

The Westcotts overheard that evening a monologue on salmon fishing in Canada, a bridge game, running comments on home movies of what had apparently been a fortnight at Sea Island, and a bitter family quarrel about an overdraft at the bank. They turned off their radio at midnight and went to bed, weak with laughter. Sometime in the night, their son began to call for a glass of water and Irene got one and took it to his room. It was very early. All the lights in the neighborhood were extinguished, and from the boy's window she could see the empty street. She went into the living room and tried the radio. There was some faint coughing, a moan, and then a man spoke. "Are you all right, darling?" he asked. "Yes," a woman said wearily. "Yes, I'm all right, I guess," and then she added with great feeling, "But, you know, Charlie, I don't feel like myself any more. Sometimes there are about fifteen or twenty minutes in the week when I feel like myself. I don't like to go to another doctor, because the doctor's bills are so awful already, but I just don't feel like myself, Charlie. I just never feel like myself." They were not young, Irene thought. She guessed from the timbre of their voices that they were middle-aged. The restrained melancholy of the dialogue and the draft from the bedroom window made her shiver, and she went back to bed.

30   The following morning, Irene cooked breakfast for the family—the maid didn't come up from her room in the basement until ten—braided her daughter's hair, and waited at the door until her children and her husband had been carried away in the elevator. Then she went into the living room and tried the radio. "I don't want to go to school," a child screamed. "I hate school. I won't go to school. I hate school." "You will go to school," an enraged woman said. "We paid eight hundred dollars to get you into that school and you'll go if it kills you." The next number on the dial produced the worn record of the "Missouri Waltz." Irene shifted the control and invaded the privacy of several breakfast tables. She overheard demonstrations of indigestion, carnal love, abysmal vanity, faith, and despair. Irene's life was nearly as simple and sheltered as it appeared to be, and the forthright and sometimes brutal language that came from the loudspeaker that morning astonished and troubled her. She continued to listen until her maid came in. Then she turned off the radio quickly, since this insight, she realized, was a furtive one.

Irene had a luncheon date with a friend that day, and she left her apartment at a little after twelve. There were a number of women in the elevator when it stopped at her floor. She stared at their handsome and impassive faces, their furs, and the cloth flowers in their hats. Which one of them had been to Sea Island? she wondered. Which one had overdrawn her bank account? The elevator stopped at the tenth floor and a woman with a pair of Skye terriers joined them. Her hair was rigged high on her head and she wore a mink cape. She was humming the "Missouri Waltz."

Irene had two Martinis at lunch, and she looked searchingly at her friend and wondered what her secrets were. They had intended to go shopping after lunch, but Irene excused herself and went home. She told the maid that she was not to be disturbed; then she went into the living room, closed the doors, and switched on the radio. She heard, in the course of the afternoon, the halting conversation of a woman entertaining her aunt, the hysterical conclusion of a luncheon party, and a hostess briefing her maid about some cocktail guests. "Don't give the best Scotch to anyone who hasn't white hair," the hostess said. "See if you can get rid of that liver paste before you pass those hot things, and could you lend me five dollars? I want to tip the elevator man."

As the afternoon waned, the conversations increased in intensity. From where Irene sat, she could see the open sky above the East River. There were hundreds of clouds in the sky, as though the south wind had broken the winter into pieces and were blowing it north, and on her radio she could hear the arrival of cocktail guests and the return of children and businessmen from their schools and offices. "I found a good-sized diamond on the bathroom floor this morning," a woman said. "It must have fallen out of that bracelet Mrs. Dunston was wearing last night." "We'll sell it," a man said. "Take it down to the jeweler on Madison Avenue and sell it. Mrs. Dunston won't know the difference, and we could use a couple of hundred bucks . . ." " 'Oranges and lemons, say the bells of St. Clement's,' " the Sweeneys' nurse sang. " 'Halfpence and farthings, say the bells of St. Martin's. When will you pay me? say the bells at old Bailey . . .' " "It's not a hat," a woman cried, and at her back roared a cocktail party. "It's not a hat, it's a love affair. That's what Walter Florell said. He said its not a hat, it's a love affair," and then, in a lower voice, the same woman added, "Talk to somebody, for Christ's sake, honey, talk to somebody. If she catches you standing here not talking to anybody, she'll take us off her invitation list, and I love these parties."

The Westcotts were going out for dinner that night, and when Jim came home, Irene was dressing. She seemed sad and vague, and he brought her a drink. They were dining with friends in the neighborhood, and they walked to where they were going. The sky was broad and filled with light. It was one of those splendid spring evenings that excite memory and desire, and the air that touched their hands and faces felt very soft. A Salvation Army band was on the corner playing "Jesus Is Sweeter." Irene drew on her husband's arm and held him there for a minute, to hear the music. "They're really such nice people, aren't they?" she said. "They have such nice faces. Actually, they're so much nicer than a lot of the people we know." She took a bill from her purse and walked over and dropped it into the tambourine. There was in her face, when she returned to her husband, a look of radiant melancholy that he was not familiar with. And her conduct at the dinner party that night seemed strange to him, too. She interrupted her hostess rudely and stared at the people across the table from her with an intensity for which she would have punished her children.

35   It was still mild when they walked home from the party, and Irene looked up at the spring stars. " 'How far that little candle throws its beams,' " she exclaimed. " 'So shines a good deed in a naughty world.' " She waited that night until Jim had fallen asleep, and then went into the living room and turned on the radio.

Jim came home at about six the next night. Emma, the maid, let him in, and he had taken off his hat and was taking off his coat when Irene ran into the hall. Her face was shining with tears and her hair was disordered. "Go up to 16-C, Jim!" she screamed. "Don't take off your coat. Go up to 16-C. Mr. Osborn's beating his wife. They've been quarreling since four o'clock, and now he's hitting her. Go up there and stop him."

From the radio in the living room, Jim heard screams, obscenities, and thuds. "You know you don't have to listen to this sort of thing," he said. He strode into the living room and turned the switch. "It's indecent," he said. "It's like looking in windows. You know you don't have to listen to this sort of thing. You can turn it off."

"Oh, it's so horrible, it's so dreadful," Irene was sobbing. "I've been listening all day, and it's so depressing."

"Well, if it's so depressing, why do you listen to it? I bought this damned radio to give you some pleasure," he said. "I paid a great deal of money for it. I thought it might make you happy. I wanted to make you happy."

40   "Don't, don't, don't, don't quarrel with me," she moaned, and laid her head on his shoulder. "All the others have been quarreling all day. Everybody's been quarreling. They're all worried about money. Mrs. Hutchinson's mother is dying of cancer in Florida and they don't have enough money to send her to the Mayo Clinic. At least, Mr. Hutchinson says they don't have enough money. And some woman in this building is having an affair with the handyman—with that hideous handyman. It's too disgusting. And Mrs. Melville has heart trouble and Mr. Hendricks is going to lose his job in April and Mrs. Hendricks is horrid about the whole thing and that girl who plays the 'Missouri Waltz' is a whore, a common whore, and the elevator man has tuberculosis and Mr. Osborn has been beating Mrs. Osborn." She wailed, she trembled with grief and checked the stream of tears down her face with the heel of her palm.

"Well, why do you have to listen?" Jim asked again. "Why do you have to listen to this stuff if it makes you so miserable?"

"Oh, don't, don't, don't," she cried. "Life is too terrible, too sordid and awful. But we've never been like that, have we, darling? Have we? I mean, we've always been good and decent and loving to one another, haven't we? And we have two children, two beautiful children. Our lives aren't sordid, are they, darling? Are they?" She flung her arms around his neck and drew his face down to hers. "We're happy, aren't we, darling? We are happy, aren't we?"

"Of course we're happy," he said tiredly. He began to surrender his resentment. "Of course we're happy. I'll have that damned radio fixed or taken away tomorrow." He stroked her soft hair. "My poor girl," he said.

"You love me, don't you?" she asked. "And we're not hypercritical or worried about money or dishonest, are we?"

45   "No, darling," he said.

A man came in the morning and fixed the radio. Irene turned it on cautiously and was happy to hear a California-wine commerical and a recording of Beethoven's Ninth Symphony, including Schiller's "Ode to Joy." She kept the radio on all day and nothing untoward came from the speaker.

A Spanish suite was being played when Jim came home. "Is everything all right?" he asked. His face was pale, she thought. They had some cocktails and went in to dinner to the "Anvil Chorus" from *Il Trovatore*. This was followed by Debussy's "La Mer."

"I paid the bill for the radio today," Jim said. "It cost four hundred dollars. I hope you'll get some enjoyment out of it."

"Oh, I'm sure I will," Irene said.

50   "Four hundred dollars is a good deal more than I can afford," he went on. "I wanted to get something that you'd enjoy. It's the last extravagance we'll be able to indulge in this year. I see that you haven't paid your clothing bills yet. I saw them on your dressing table." He looked directly at her. "Why did you tell me you'd paid them? Why did you lie to me?"

"I just didn't want you to worry, Jim," she said. She drank some water. "I'll be able to pay my bills out of this month's allowance. There were the slipcovers last month, and that party."

"You've got to learn to handle the money I give you a little more intelligently, Irene," he said. "You've got to understand that we won't have as much money this year as we had last. I had a very sobering talk with Mitchell today. No one is buying anything. We're spending all our time promoting new issues, and you know how long that takes. I'm not getting any younger, you know. I'm thirty-seven. My hair will be gray next year. I haven't done as well as I'd hoped to do. And I don't suppose things will get any better."

"Yes, dear," she said.

"We've got to start cutting down," Jim said. "We've got to think of the children. To be perfectly frank with you, I worry about money a great deal. I'm not at all sure of the future. No one is. If anything should happen to me, there's the insurance, but that wouldn't go very far today. I've worked awfully hard to give you and the children a comfortable life," he said bitterly. "I don't like to see all of my energies, all of my youth, wasted in fur coats and radios and slipcovers and—"

55   "Please, Jim," she said. "Please. They'll hear us."

"Who'll hear us? Emma can't hear us."

"The radio."

"Oh, I'm sick!" he shouted. "I'm sick to death of your apprehensiveness. The radio can't hear us. Nobody can hear us. And what if they can hear us? Who cares?"

Irene got up from the table and went into the living room. Jim went to the door and shouted at her from there. "Why are you so Christly all of a sudden? What's turned you overnight into a convent girl? You stole your mother's jewelry before they probated her will. You never gave your sister a cent of that money that was intended for her—not even when she needed it. You made Grace Howland's life miserable, and where was all your piety and your virtue when you went to that abortionist? I'll never forget how cool you were. You packed your bag and went off to have that child murdered as if you were going to Nassau. If you'd had any reasons, if you'd had any good reasons—"

60   Irene stood for a minute before the hideous cabinet, disgraced and sickened, but she held her hand on the switch before she extinguished the music and the voices, hoping that the instrument might speak to her kindly, that she might hear the Sweeneys' nurse. Jim continued to shout at her from the door. The voice on the radio was suave and non-committal. "An early-morning railroad disaster in Tokyo," the loudspeaker said, "killed twenty-nine people. A fire in a Catholic hospital near Buffalo for the care of blind children was extinguished early this morning by nuns. The temperature is forty-seven. The humidity is eighty-nine."

Comments and Questions

This story is an effective marriage of the fantastic and the realistic. For the main character, Irene, and for the reader, the fantastic element of the eavesdropping radio is the curious and necessary means of insight into things as they really are. The story is one of social— and certainly of self—revelation, of public walls and private, psychological masks. Some readers will also want to explore a similarity in theme here and in Frost's "Nothing Gold Can Stay" (p. 499).

1. You can easily construct a plot action line (see p. 9) for this story. Consider especially the progressive and differing stages of Jim's and Irene's engagement with the radio and the ironic role changes, early to late in the action, among the three main characters (Jim, Irene, the radio). In what way do the character shifts serve as implicit commentary on one another? In the first paragraph, Irene is described as having a "fine forehead upon which nothing at all had been written"; Jim is said to be "intentionally naïve." Does the phrasing differentiate the two characters? Do the final two paragraphs shed light on the question?

2. The Westcotts are carefully described as statistically average. Why is that important to the story, the theme? Why are the Westcotts quiet about their one difference from their neighbors? How is that silence revealing? How is the difference itself functionally ironic in the story?

3. Discuss the significance of the Salvation Army episode—especially considering the description of the scene, Irene's attitude toward the band members, the motivation for her gift.

4. The word *enormous* is given special emphasis in the title. How is that emphasis functionally significant, perhaps better than emphasizing other possibilities like *big, ugly, expensive*? Relate *enormous* to "Christly" in the next-to-last paragraph. What elements of forecast do you see in the early descriptions of the radio? Is it at all significant that the radio cabinet is of gumwood?

5. Are there any especially poignant moments in the story? If so, why are they emotionally moving? Who is the most sympathetic character? Why?

Nathaniel Hawthorne   (1804–1864)
Young Goodman Brown

Of all the fictional techniques, allegory is perhaps the easiest to write poorly. Typically, allegorical characters (such as Faith, Lust, Hope) demand so persistently to represent abstract qualities or ideas that the writer is too frequently tempted to make them bloodless pasteboard cutouts. By definition, allegorical narratives actually represent other recognizable historical, moral, philosophical patterns of action or thought; and detailed rigidity in paralleling those original patterns can easily make every event (and character) of the narrative predictable, can smother creative spontaneity and our interest with it. And only when allegorical characters and actions hold our interest do we absorb the moral or other ideas they represent. Moral allegory slides too easily into a sermon; any allegory has a high potential for dullness; and simple straight-line allegory—though it can boast community agreement about its meaning—can be deadly. Open discussion of "Young Goodman Brown" and "The Minister's Black Veil" will quickly demonstrate that Hawthorne was no simple allegorist. Just as Kafka was later to do (see p. 120), Hawthorne makes his allegorical representations ambiguously, richly symbolic; and he simultaneously gives us characters and situations sufficiently realistic to hold our human interest. In short, he confounds our natural inclination to limit neatly our comprehension of his allegory to one simple level or theme or meaning. We cannot settle accounts with Hawthorne's fiction so easily.

Young Goodman Brown came forth at sunset into the street at Salem village; but put his head back, after crossing the threshold, to exchange a parting kiss with his young wife. And Faith, as the wife was aptly named, thrust her own pretty head into the street, letting the wind play with the pink ribbons of her cap while she called to Goodman Brown.

"Dearest heart," whispered she, softly and rather sadly, when her lips were close to his ear, "prithee put off your journey until sunrise and sleep in your bed tonight. A lone woman is troubled with such dreams and such thoughts that she's afeard of herself sometimes. Pray tarry with me this night, dear husband, of all nights in the year."

"My love and my Faith," replied young Goodman Brown, "of all nights in the year, this one night must I tarry away from thee. My journey, as thou callest it, forth and back again, must needs be done 'twixt now and sunrise. What, my sweet, pretty wife, dost thou doubt me already, and we but three months married?"

"Then God bless you!" said Faith, with the pink ribbons; "and may you find all well when you come back."

5   "Amen!" cried Goodman Brown. "Say thy prayers, dear Faith, and go to bed at dusk, and no harm will come to thee."

So they parted; and the young man pursued his way until, being about to turn the corner by the meeting-house, he looked back and saw the head of Faith still peeping after him with a melancholy air, in spite of her pink ribbons.

"Poor little Faith!" thought he, for his heart smote him. "What a wretch am I to leave her on such an errand! She talks of dreams, too. Methought as she spoke there was trouble in her face, as if a dream had warned her what work is to be done to-night. But no, no; 'twould kill her to think it. Well, she's a blessed angel on earth; and after this one night I'll cling to her skirts and follow her to heaven."

With this excellent resolve for the future, Goodman Brown felt himself justified in making more haste on his present evil purpose. He had taken a dreary road, darkened by all the gloomiest trees of the forest, which barely stood aside to let the narrow path creep through, and closed immediately behind. It was all as lonely as could be; and there is this peculiarity in such a solitude, that the traveller knows not who may be concealed by the innumerable trunks and the thick boughs overhead; so that with lonely footsteps he may yet be passing through an unseen multitude.

"There may be a devilish Indian behind every tree," said Goodman Brown to himself; and he glanced fearfully behind him as he added, "What if the devil himself should be at my very elbow!"

10   His head being turned back, he passed a crook of the road, and, looking forward again, beheld the figure of a man, in grave and decent attire, seated at the foot of an old tree. He arose at Goodman Brown's approach and walked onward side by side with him.

"You are late, Goodman Brown," said he. "The clock of the Old South was striking as I came through Boston, and that is full fifteen minutes agone."

"Faith kept me back a while," replied the young man, with a tremor in his voice, caused by the sudden appearance of his companion, though not wholly unexpected.

It was now deep dusk in the forest, and deepest in that part of it where these two were journeying. As nearly as could be discerned, the second traveller was about fifty years old, apparently in the same rank of life as Goodman Brown, and bearing a considerable resemblance to him, though perhaps more in expression than features. Still they might have been taken for father and son. And yet, though the elder person was as simply clad as the younger, and as simple in manner too, he had an indescribable air of one who knew the world, and who would not have felt abashed at the governor's dinner table or in King William's court,[1] were it possible that his affairs should call him thither. But the only thing about him that could be fixed upon as remarkable was his staff, which bore the likeness of a great black snake, so curiously wrought that it might almost be seen to twist and wriggle itself like a living serpent. This, of course, must have been an ocular deception, assisted by the uncertain light.

"Come, Goodman Brown," cried his fellow-traveller, "this is a dull pace for the beginning of a journey. Take my staff, if you are so soon weary."

---

[1] William III, King of England (reigned 1689–1702). Note that several characters named in the story were real women condemned and sentenced as "witches" in 1692 during the Salem trials.

15   "Friend," said the other, exchanging his slow pace for a full stop, "having kept covenant by meeting thee here, it is my purpose now to return whence I came. I have scruples touching the matter thou wot'st of."

"Sayest thou so?" replied he of the serpent, smiling apart. "Let us walk on, nevertheless, reasoning as we go; and if I convince thee not thou shalt turn back. We are but a little way in the forest yet."

"Too far! too far!" exclaimed the goodman, unconsciously resuming his walk. "My father never went into the woods on such an errand, nor his father before him. We have been a race of honest men and good Christians since the days of the martyrs; and shall I be the first of the name of Brown that ever took this path and kept"—

"Such company, thou wouldst say," observed the elder person, interpreting his pause. "Well said, Goodman Brown! I have been as well acquainted with your family as with ever a one among the Puritans; and that's no trifle to say. I helped your grandfather, the constable, when he lashed the Quaker woman so smartly through the streets of Salem; and it was I that brought your father a pitch-pine knot, kindled at my own hearth, to set fire to an Indian village, in King Philip's war. They were my good friends, both; and many a pleasant walk have we had along this path, and returned merrily after midnight. I would fain be friends with you for their sake."

"If it be as thou sayest," replied Goodman Brown, "I marvel they never spoke of these matters; or, verily, I marvel not, seeing that the least rumor of the sort would have driven them from New England. We are a people of prayer, and good works to boot, and abide no such wickedness."

20   "Wickedness or not," said the traveller with the twisted staff, "I have a very general acquaintance here in New England. The deacons of many a church have drunk the communion wine with me; the selectmen of divers towns make me their chairman; and a majority of the Great and General Court are firm supporters of my interest. The governor and I, too—But these are state secrets."

"Can this be so?" cried Goodman Brown, with a stare of amazement at his undisturbed companion. "Howbeit, I have nothing to do with the governor and council; they have their own ways, and are no rule for a simple husbandman like me. But, were I to go on with thee, how should I meet the eye of that good old man, our minister, at Salem village? Oh, his voice would make me tremble both Sabbath day and lecture day."

Thus far the elder traveller had listened with due gravity; but now burst into a fit of irrepressible mirth, shaking himself so violently that his snake-like staff actually seemed to wriggle in sympathy.

"Ha! ha! ha!" shouted he again and again; then composing himself, "Well, go on, Goodman Brown, go on; but, prithee, don't kill me with laughing."

"Well, then, to end the matter at once," said Goodman Brown, considerably nettled, "there is my wife, Faith. It would break her dear little heart; and I'd rather break my own."

25   "Nay, if that be the case," answered the other, "e'en go thy ways, Goodman Brown. I would not for twenty old women like the one hobbling before us that Faith should come to any harm."

As he spoke he pointed his staff at a female figure on the path, in whom Goodman Brown recognized a very pious and exemplary dame, who had taught him his catechism in youth, and was still his moral and spiritual adviser, jointly with the minister and Deacon Gookin.

"A marvel, truly, that Goody Cloyse should be so far in the wilderness at nightfall," said he. "But with your leave, friend, I shall take a cut through the woods until we have left this Christian woman behind. Being a stranger to you, she might ask whom I was consorting with and whither I was going."

"Be it so," said his fellow-traveller. "Betake you to the woods, and let me keep the path."

Accordingly the young man turned aside, but took care to watch his companion, who advanced softly along the road until he had come within a staff's length of the old dame. She, meanwhile, was making the best of her way, with singular speed for so aged a woman, and mumbling some indistinct words—a prayer, doubtless—as she went. The traveller put forth his staff and touched her withered neck with what seemed the serpent's tail.

30   "The devil!" screamed the pious old lady.

"Then Goody Cloyse knows her old friend?" observed the traveller, confronting her and leaning on his writhing stick.

"Ah, forsooth, and is it your worship indeed?" cried the good dame. "Yea, truly is it, and in the very image of my old gossip, Goodman Brown, the grandfather of the silly fellow that now is. But—would your worship believe it?—my broomstick hath strangely disappeared, stolen, as I suspect, by that unhanged witch, Goody Cory, and that, too, when I was all anointed with the juice of smallage,[2] and cinquefoil, and wolf's bane"—

"Mingled with fine wheat and the fat of a new-born babe," said the shape of old Goodman Brown.

"Ah, your worship knows the recipe," cried the old lady, cackling aloud. "So, as I was saying, being all ready for the meeting, and no horse to ride on, I made up my mind to foot it; for they tell me there is a nice young man to be taken into communion to-night. But now your good worship will lend me your arm, and we shall be there in a twinkling."

35   "That can hardly be," answered her friend. "I may not spare you my arm, Goody Cloyse; but here is my staff, if you will."

So saying, he threw it down at her feet, where, perhaps, it assumed life, being one of the rods which its owner had formerly lent to the Egyptian magi. Of this fact, however, Goodman Brown could not take cognizance. He had cast up his eyes in astonishment, and looking down again, beheld neither Goody Cloyse nor the serpentine staff, but his fellow-traveller alone, who waited for him as calmly as if nothing had happened.

"That old woman taught me my catechism," said the young man; and there was a world of meaning in this simple comment.

They continued to walk onward, while the elder traveller exhorted his companion to make good speed and persevere in the path, discoursing so aptly that his arguments seemed rather to spring up in the bosom of his auditor than to be suggested by himself. As they went, he plucked a branch of maple to serve for a walking stick, and began to strip it of the twigs and little boughs, which were wet with evening dew. The moment his fingers touched them they became strangely withered and dried up as with a week's sunshine. Thus the pair proceeded, at a good free pace, until suddenly, in a gloomy hollow of the road, Goodman Brown sat himself down on the stump of a tree and refused to go any farther.

"Friend," said he, stubbornly, "my mind is made up. Not another step will I budge on this errand. What if a wretched old woman do choose to go to the devil when I thought she was going to heaven· is that any reason why I should quit my dear Faith and go after her?"

40   "You will think better of this by and by," said his acquaintance, composedly. "Sit here and rest yourself a while; and when you feel like moving again, there is my staff to help you along."

---

[2] Woods celery, which in witchcraft supposedly has magical powers.

Without more words, he threw his companion the maple stick, and was as speedily out of sight as if he had vanished into the deepening gloom. The young man sat a few moments by the roadside, applauding himself greatly, and thinking with how clear a con- science he should meet the minister in his morning walk, nor shrink from the eye of good old Deacon Gookin. And what calm sleep would be his that very night, which was to have been spent so wickedly, but so purely and sweetly now, in the arms of Faith! Amidst these pleasant and praiseworthy meditations, Goodman Brown heard the tramp of horses along the road, and deemed it advisable to conceal himself within the verge of the forest, con- scious of the guilty purpose that had brought him thither, though now so happily turned from it.

On came the hoof tramps and the voices of the riders, two grave old voices, con- versing soberly as they drew near. These mingled sounds appeared to pass along the road, within a few yards of the young man's hiding-place; but, owing doubtless to the depth of the gloom at that particular spot, neither the travellers nor their steeds were visible. Though their figures brushed the small boughs by the wayside, it could not be seen that they intercepted, even for a moment, the faint gleam from the strip of bright sky athwart which they must have passed. Goodman Brown alternately crouched and stood on tiptoe, pulling aside the branches and thrusting forth his head as far as he durst without discern- ing so much as a shadow. It vexed him the more, because he could have sworn, were such a thing possible, that he recognized the voices of the minister and Deacon Gookin, jogging along quietly, as they were wont to do, when bound to some ordination or eccle- siastical council. While yet within hearing, one of the riders stopped to pluck a switch.

"Of the two, reverend sir," said the voice like the deacon's, "I had rather miss an ordination dinner than to-night's meeting. They tell me that some of our community are to be here from Falmouth and beyond, and others from Connecticut and Rhode Island, besides several of the Indian powwows, who, after their fashion, know almost as much deviltry as the best of us. Moreover, there is a goodly young woman to be taken into communion."

"Mighty well, Deacon Gookin!" replied the solemn old tones of the minister. "Spur up, or we shall be late. Nothing can be done, you know, until I get on the ground."

45 The hoofs clattered again; and the voices, talking so strangely in the empty air, passed on through the forest, where no church had ever been gathered or solitary Chris- tian prayed. Whither, then, could these holy men be journeying so deep into the heathen wilderness? Young Goodman Brown caught hold of a tree for support, being ready to sink down on the ground, faint and overburdened with the heavy sickness of his heart. He looked up to the sky, doubting whether there really was a heaven above him. Yet there was the blue arch, and the stars brightening in it.

"With heaven above and Faith below, I will yet stand firm against the devil!" cried Goodman Brown.

While he still gazed upward into the deep arch of the firmament and had lifted his hands to pray, a cloud, though no wind was stirring, hurried across the zenith and hid the brightening stars. The blue sky was still visible, except directly overhead, where this black mass of cloud was sweeping swiftly northward. Aloft in the air, as if from the depths of the cloud, came a confused and doubtful sound of voices. Once the listener fancied that he could distinguish the accents of towns-people of his own, men and women, both pious and ungodly, many of whom he had met at the communion table, and had seen others rioting at the tavern. The next moment, so indistinct were the sounds, he doubted whether he had heard aught but the murmur of the old forest, whispering without a wind. Then came a stronger swell of those familiar tones, heard daily in the sunshine at Salem village, but never until now from a cloud of night. There was one voice, of a young woman, uttering lamentations, yet with an uncertain sorrow, and entreating for some favor, which, perhaps, it would grieve her to obtain; and all the unseen multitude, both saints and sinners, seemed to encourage her onward.

"Faith!" shouted Goodman Brown, in a voice of agony and desperation; and the echoes of the forest mocked him, crying, "Faith! Faith!" as if bewildered wretches were seeking her all through the wilderness.

The cry of grief, rage, and terror was yet piercing the night, when the unhappy husband held his breath for a response. There was a scream, drowned immediately in a louder murmur of voices, fading into faroff laughter, as the dark cloud swept away, leaving the clear and silent sky above Goodman Brown. But something fluttered lightly down through the air and caught on the branch of a tree. The young man seized it, and beheld a pink ribbon.

50   "My Faith is gone!" cried he, after one stupefied moment. "There is no good on earth; and sin is but a name. Come, devil; for to thee is this world given."

And, maddened with despair, so that he laughed loud and long, did Goodman Brown grasp his staff and set forth again, at such a rate that he seemed to fly along the forest path rather than to walk or run. The road grew wilder and drearier and more faintly traced, and vanished at length, leaving him in the heart of the dark wilderness, still rushing onward with the instinct that guides mortal man to evil. The whole forest was peopled with frightful sounds—the creaking of the trees, the howling of wild beasts, and the yell of Indians; while sometimes the wind tolled like a distant church bell, and sometimes gave a broad roar around the traveller, as if all Nature were laughing him to scorn. But he was himself the chief horror of the scene, and shrank not from its other horrors.

"Ha! ha! ha!" roared Goodman Brown when the wind laughed at him. "Let us hear which will laugh loudest. Think not to frighten me with your deviltry. Come witch, come wizard, come Indian powwow, come devil himself, and here comes Goodman Brown. You may as well fear him as he fear you."

In truth, all through the haunted forest there could be nothing more frightful than the figure of Goodman Brown. On he flew among the black pines, brandishing his staff with frenzied gestures, now giving vent to an inspiration of horrid blasphemy, and now shouting forth such laughter as set all the echoes of the forest laughing like demons around him. The fiend in his own shape is less hideous than when he rages in the breast of man. Thus sped the demoniac on his course, until, quivering among the trees, he saw a red light before him, as when the felled trunks and branches of a clearing have been set on fire, and throw up their lurid blaze against the sky, at the hour of midnight. He paused, in a lull of the tempest that had driven him onward, and heard the swell of what seemed a hymn, rolling solemnly from a distance with the weight of many voices. He knew the tune; it was a familiar one in the choir of the village meeting-house. The verse died heavily away, and was lengthened by a chorus, not of human voices, but of all the sounds of the benighted wilderness pealing in awful harmony together. Goodman Brown cried out, and his cry was lost to his own ear by its unison with the cry of the desert.

In the interval of silence he stole forward until the light glared full upon his eyes. At one extremity of an open space, hemmed in by the dark wall of the forest, arose a rock, bearing some rude, natural resemblance either to an altar or a pulpit, and surrounded by four blazing pines, their tops aflame, their stems untouched, like candles at an evening meeting. The mass of foliage that had overgrown the summit of the rock was all on fire, blazing high into the night and fitfully illuminating the whole field. Each pendent twig and leafy festoon was in a blaze. As the red light arose and fell, a numerous congregation alternately shone forth, then disappeared in shadow, and again grew, as it were, out of the darkness, peopling the heart of the solitary woods at once.

55   "A grave and dark-clad company," quoth Goodman Brown.

In truth they were such. Among them, quivering to and fro between gloom and splendor, appeared faces that would be seen next day at the council board of the province, and others which, Sabbath after Sabbath, looked devoutly heavenward, and benignantly over the crowded pews, from the holiest pulpits in the land. Some affirm that the lady of the governor was there. At least there were high dames well known to her, and wives of honored husbands, and widows, a great multitude, and ancient maidens, all of excellent repute, and fair young girls, who trembled lest their mothers should espy them. Either the sudden gleams of light flashing over the obscure field bedazzled Goodman Brown, or he recognized a score of the church members of Salem village famous for their special sanctity. Good old Deacon Gookin had arrived, and waited at the skirts of that venerable saint, his revered pastor. But, irreverently consorting with these grave, reputable, and pious people, these elders of the church, these chaste dames and dewy virgins, there were men of dissolute lives and women of spotted fame, wretches given over to all mean and filthy vice, and suspected even of horrid crimes. It was strange to see that the good shrank not from the wicked, nor were the sinners abashed by the saints. Scattered also among their pale-faced enemies were the Indian priests, or powwows, who had often scared their native forest with more hideous incantations than any known to English witchcraft.

"But where is Faith?" thought Goodman Brown; and, as hope came into his heart, he trembled.

Another verse of the hymn arose, a slow and mournful strain, such as the pious love, but joined to words which expressed all that our nature can conceive of sin, and darkly hinted at far more. Unfathomable to mere mortals is the lore of fiends. Verse after verse was sung; and still the chorus of the desert swelled between like the deepest tone of a mighty organ; and with the final peal of that dreadful anthem there came a sound, as if the roaring wind, the rushing streams, the howling beasts, and every other voice of the unconcerted wilderness were mingling and according with the voice of guilty man in homage to the prince of all. The four blazing pines threw up a loftier flame, and obscurely discovered shapes and visages of horror on the smoke wreaths above the impious assembly. At the same moment the fire on the rock shot redly forth and formed a glowing arch above its base, where now appeared a figure. With reverence be it spoken, the figure bore no slight similitude, both in garb and manner, to some grave divine of the New England churches.

"Bring forth the converts!" cried a voice that echoed through the field and rolled into the forest.

60   At the word, Goodman Brown stepped forth from the shadow of the trees and approached the congregation, with whom he felt a loathful brotherhood by the sympathy of all that was wicked in his heart. He could have well-nigh sworn that the shape of his own dead father beckoned him to advance, looking downward from a smoke wreath, while a woman, with dim features of despair, threw out her hand to warn him back. Was it his mother? But he had no power to retreat one step, nor to resist, even in thought, when the minister and good old Deacon Gookin seized his arms and led him to the blazing rock. Thither came also the slender form of a veiled female, led between Goody Cloyse, that pious teacher of the catechism, and Martha Carrier, who had received the devil's promise to be queen of hell. A rampant hag was she. And there stood the proselytes beneath the canopy of fire.

"Welcome, my children," said the dark figure, "to the communion of your race. Ye have found thus young your nature and your destiny. My children, look behind you!"

They turned; and flashing forth, as it were, in a sheet of flame, the fiend worshippers were seen; the smile of welcome gleamed darkly on every visage.

"There," resumed the sable form, "are all whom ye have reverenced from youth. Ye deemed them holier than yourselves, and shrank from your own sin, contrasting it with their lives of righteousness and prayerful aspirations heavenward. Yet here are they all in my worshipping assembly. This night it shall be granted you to know their secret deeds: how hoary-bearded elders of the church have whispered wanton words to the young maids of their households; how many a woman, eager for widows' weeds, has given her husband a drink at bedtime and let him sleep his last sleep in her bosom; how beardless youths have made haste to inherit their fathers' wealth, and how fair damsels—blush not, sweet ones—have dug little graves in the garden, and bidden me, the sole guest, to an infant's funeral. By the sympathy of your human hearts for sin ye shall scent out all the places—whether in church, bed-chamber, street, field, or forest—where crime has been committed, and shall exult to behold the whole earth one stain of guilt, one mighty blood spot. Far more than this. It shall be yours to penetrate, in every bosom, the deep mystery of sin, the fountain of all wicked arts, and which inexhaustibly supplies more evil impulses than human power—than my power at its utmost—can make manifest in deeds. And now, my children, look upon each other."

They did so; and, by the blaze of the hell-kindled torches, the wretched man beheld his Faith, and the wife her husband, trembling before that unhallowed altar.

65   "Lo, there ye stand, my children," said the figure, in a deep and solemn tone, almost sad with its despairing awfulness, as if his once angelic nature could yet mourn for our miserable race. "Depending upon one another's hearts, ye had still hoped that virtue were not all a dream. Now are ye undeceived. Evil is the nature of mankind. Evil must be your only happiness. Welcome again, my children, to the communion of your race."

"Welcome," repeated the fiend worshippers, in one cry of despair and triumph.

And there they stood, the only pair, as it seemed, who were yet hesitating on the verge of wickedness in this dark world. A basin was hollowed, naturally, in the rock. Did it contain water, reddened by the lurid light, or was it blood? or, perchance, a liquid flame? Herein did the shape of evil dip his hand and prepare to lay the mark of baptism upon their foreheads, that they might be partakers of the mystery of sin, more conscious of the secret guilt of others, both in deed and thought, than they could now be of their own. The husband cast one look at his pale wife, and Faith at him. What polluted wretches would the next glance show them to each other, shuddering alike at what they disclosed and what they saw!

"Faith! Faith!" cried the husband, "look up to heaven, and resist the wicked one."

Whether Faith obeyed he knew not. Hardly had he spoken when he found himself amid calm night and solitude, listening to a roar of the wind which died heavily away through the forest. He staggered against the rock, and felt it chill and damp; while a hanging twig, that had been all on fire, besprinkled his cheek with the coldest dew.

70   The next morning young Goodman Brown came slowly into the street of Salem village, staring around him like a bewildered man. The good old minister was taking a walk along the graveyard to get an appetite for breakfast and meditate his sermon, and bestowed a blessing, as he passed, on Goodman Brown. He shrank from the venerable saint as if to avoid an anathema. Old Deacon Gookin was at domestic worship, and the holy words of his prayer were heard through the open window. "What God doth the wizard pray to?" quoth Goodman Brown. Goody Cloyse, that excellent old Christian, stood in the early sunshine at her own lattice, catechizing a little girl who had brought her a pint of morning's milk. Goodman Brown snatched away the child as from the grasp of the fiend himself. Turning the corner by the meeting-house, he spied the head of Faith, with the pink ribbons, gazing anxiously forth, and bursting into such joy at sight of him that she

skipped along the street and almost kissed her husband before the whole village. But Goodman Brown looked sternly and sadly into her face, and passed on without a greeting.

Had Goodman Brown fallen asleep in the forest and only dreamed a wild dream of a witch-meeting?

Be it so if you will; but, alas! it was a dream of evil omen for young Goodman Brown. A stern, a sad, a darkly meditative, a distrustful, if not a desperate man did he become from the night of that fearful dream. On the Sabbath day, when the congregation were singing a holy psalm, he could not listen because an anthem of sin rushed loudly upon his ear and drowned all the blessed strain. When the minister spoke from the pulpit with power and fervid eloquence, and, with his hand on the open Bible, of the sacred truths of our religion, and of saintlike lives and triumphant deaths, and of future bliss or misery unutterable, then did Goodman Brown turn pale, dreading lest the roof should thunder down upon the gray blasphemer and his hearers. Often, awaking suddenly at midnight, he shrank from the bosom of Faith; and at morning or eventide, when the family knelt down at prayer, he scowled and muttered to himself, and gazed sternly at his wife, and turned away. And when he had lived long, and was borne to his grave a hoary corpse, followed by Faith, an aged woman, and children and grandchildren, a goodly procession, besides neighbors not a few, they carved no hopeful verse upon his tombstone, for his dying hour was gloom.

Comments and Questions

1. Discuss the allegorical significance of the names Faith and young Goodman Brown. Does Brown lose Faith? If so, in what senses? Is there any particular significance in the continuation of his wedded life into children and grandchildren?

2. Is it significant that Brown's symbolic journey begins at sunset and ends at sunrise? Considering the characters Brown meets and the events in the forest, what do you think the journey symbolizes? Have you considered natural, social, moral, psychological possibilities?

3. How are the various colors and shades of light in the story significant?

4. At several points in Brown's journey, he hesitates or resists going forward. Is his resistance genuine or merely feigned, a Hawthorne comment on human self-delusion or hypocrisy?

5. Why does Hawthorne depict the devil as looking much like Brown's father or Brown himself?

6. Compare the setting of the village and of the forest, the language used to describe each, and the activities occurring in each. How is setting itself a functional, contributing aspect of the story?

7. The witches' Sabbath is essentially an inversion of the ceremonies, hymns, supernatural personages of the typical Christian Sabbath service and obviously involves an intimate and ironic mingling of the satanic and the saintly. Cite other instances of irony and ambiguity (of statement, action, situation, character), and comment on whether they contribute to or detract from the effectiveness of the story.

8. Write an extended comparison of this story and the preceding one, especially noting the progressive change in the central character in each case. Do you see a difference in the motivation and perception of Irene and Brown at the outset of their stories?

Nathaniel Hawthorne (1804–1864)
The Minister's Black Veil

The sexton stood in the porch of Milford meeting-house, pulling busily at the bell-rope. The old people of the village came stooping along the street. Children, with bright faces, tripped merrily beside their parents, or mimicked a graver gait, in the conscious dignity of their Sunday clothes. Spruce bachelors looked sidelong at the pretty maidens, and fancied that the Sabbath sunshine made them prettier than on week days. When the throng had mostly streamed into the porch, the sexton began to toll the bell, keeping his eye on the Reverend Mr. Hooper's door. The first glimpse of the clergyman's figure was the signal for the bell to cease its summons.

"But what has good Parson Hooper got upon his face?" cried the sexton in astonishment.

All within hearing immediately turned about, and beheld the semblance of Mr. Hooper, pacing slowly his meditative way towards the meeting-house. With one accord they started, expressing more wonder than if some strange minister were coming to dust the cushions of Mr. Hooper's pulpit.

"Are you sure it is our parson?" inquired Goodman Gray of the sexton.

5   "Of a certainty it is good Mr. Hooper," replied the sexton. "He was to have exchanged pulpits with Parson Shute, of Westbury; but Parson Shute sent to excuse himself yesterday, being to preach a funeral sermon."

The cause of so much amazement may appear sufficiently slight. Mr. Hooper, a gentlemanly person, of about thirty, though still a bachelor, was dressed with due clerical neatness, as if a careful wife had starched his band, and brushed the weekly dust from his Sunday's garb. There was but one thing remarkable in his appearance. Swathed about his forehead, and hanging down over his face, so low as to be shaken by his breath, Mr. Hooper had on a black veil. On a nearer view it seemed to consist of two folds of crape, which entirely concealed his features, except the mouth and chin, but probably did not intercept his sight, further than to give a darkened aspect to all living and inanimate things. With this gloomy shade before him, good Mr. Hooper walked onward, at a slow and quiet pace, stooping somewhat, and looking on the ground, as is customary with abstracted men, yet nodding kindly to those of his parishioners who still waited on the meeting-house steps. But so wonderstruck were they that his greeting hardly met with a return.

"I can't really feel as if good Mr. Hooper's face was behind that piece of crape," said the sexton.

"I don't like it," muttered an old woman, as she hobbled into the meeting-house. "He has changed himself into something awful, only by hiding his face."

"Our parson has gone mad!" cried Goodman Gray, following him across the threshold.

10   A rumor of some unaccountable phenomenon had preceded Mr. Hooper into the meeting-house, and set all the congregation astir. Few could refrain from twisting their heads towards the door; many stood upright, and turned directly about; while several little boys clambered upon the seats, and came down again with a terrible racket. There was a general bustle, a rustling of the women's gowns and shuffling of the men's feet, greatly at variance with that hushed repose which should attend the entrance of the minister. But Mr. Hooper appeared not to notice the perturbation of his people. He entered with an

almost noiseless step, bent his head mildly to the pews on each side, and bowed as he passed his oldest parishioner, a white-haired great-grandsire, who occupied an arm-chair in the centre of the aisle. It was strange to observe how slowly this venerable man became conscious of something singular in the appearance of his pastor. He seemed not fully to partake of the prevailing wonder, till Mr. Hooper had ascended the stairs, and showed himself in the pulpit, face to face with his congregation, except for the black veil. That mysterious emblem was never once withdrawn. It shook with his measured breath, as he gave out the psalm; it threw its obscurity between him and the holy page, as he read the Scriptures; and while he prayed, the veil lay heavily on his uplifted countenance. Did he seek to hide it from the dread Being whom he was addressing?

Such was the effect of this simple piece of crape, that more than one woman of delicate nerves was forced to leave the meeting-house. Yet perhaps the pale-faced congregation was almost as fearful a sight to the minister, as his black veil to them.

Mr. Hooper had the reputation of a good preacher, but not an energetic one: he strove to win his people heavenward by mild, persuasive influences, rather than to drive them thither by the thunders of the Word. The sermon which he now delivered was marked by the same characteristics of style and manner as the general series of his pulpit oratory. But there was something, either in the sentiment of the discourse itself, or in the imagination of the auditors, which made it greatly the most powerful effort that they had ever heard from their pastor's lips. It was tinged, rather more darkly than usual, with the gentle gloom of Mr. Hooper's temperament. The subject had reference to secret sin, and those sad mysteries which we hide from our nearest and dearest, and would fain conceal from our own consciousness, even forgetting that the Omniscient can detect them. A subtle power was breathed into his words. Each member of the congregation, the most innocent girl, and the man of hardened breast, felt as if the preacher had crept upon them, behind his awful veil, and discovered their hoarded iniquity of deed or thought. Many spread their clasped hands on their bosoms. There was nothing terrible in what Mr. Hooper said, at least, no violence; and yet, with every tremor of his melancholy voice, the hearers quaked. An unsought pathos came hand in hand with awe. So sensible were the audience of some unwonted attribute in their minister, that they longed for a breath of wind to blow aside the veil, almost believing that a stranger's visage would be discovered, though the form, gesture, and voice were those of Mr. Hooper.

At the close of the services, the people hurried out with indecorous confusion, eager to communicate their pent-up amazement, and conscious of lighter spirits the moment they lost sight of the black veil. Some gathered in little circles, huddled closely together, with their mouths all whispering in the centre; some went homeward alone, wrapt in silent meditation; some talked loudly, and profaned the Sabbath day with ostentatious laughter. A few shook their sagacious heads, intimating that they could penetrate the mystery; while one or two affirmed that there was no mystery at all, but only that Mr. Hooper's eyes were so weakened by the midnight lamp, as to require a shade. After a brief interval, forth came good Mr. Hooper also, in the rear of his flock. Turning his veiled face from one group to another, he paid due reverence to the hoary heads, saluted the middle aged with kind dignity as their friend and spiritual guide, greeted the young with mingled authority and love, and laid his hands on the little children's heads to bless them. Such was always his custom on the Sabbath day. Strange and bewildered looks repaid him for his courtesy. None, as on former occasions, aspired to the honor of walking by their pastor's side. Old Squire Sanders, doubtless by an accidental lapse of memory, neglected to invite Mr. Hooper to his table, where the good clergyman had been wont to bless the food, almost every Sunday since his settlement. He returned, therefore, to the parsonage, and, at the moment of closing the door, was observed to look back upon the people, all of whom had their eyes fixed upon the minister. A sad smile gleamed faintly from beneath the black veil, and flickered about his mouth, glimmering as he disappeared.

"How strange," said a lady, "that a simple black veil, such as any woman might wear on her bonnet, should become such a terrible thing on Mr. Hooper's face!"

15 "Something must surely be amiss with Mr. Hooper's intellects," observed her husband, the physician of the village. "But the strangest part of the affair is the effect of this vagary, even on a sober-minded man like myself. The black veil, though it covers only our pastor's face, throws its influence over his whole person, and makes him ghostlike from head to foot. Do you not feel it so?"

"Truly do I," replied the lady; "and I would not be alone with him for the world. I wonder he is not afraid to be alone with himself!"

"Men sometimes are so," said her husband.

The afternoon service was attended with similar circumstances. At its conclusion, the bell tolled for the funeral of a young lady. The relatives and friends were assembled in the house, and the more distant acquaintances stood about the door, speaking of the good qualities of the deceased, when their talk was interrupted by the appearance of Mr. Hooper, still covered with his black veil. It was now an appropriate emblem. The clergyman stepped into the room where the corpse was laid, and bent over the coffin, to take a last farewell of his deceased parishioner. As he stooped, the veil hung straight down from his forehead, so that, if her eyelids had not been closed forever, the dead maiden might have seen his face. Could Mr. Hooper be fearful of her glance, that he so hastily caught back the black veil? A person who watched the interview between the dead and living, scrupled not to affirm, that, at the instant when the clergyman's features were disclosed, the corpse had slightly shuddered, rustling the shroud and muslin cap, though the countenance retained the composure of death. A superstitious old woman was the only witness of this prodigy. From the coffin Mr. Hooper passed into the chamber of the mourners, and thence to the head of the staircase, to make the funeral prayer. It was a tender and heart-dissolving prayer, full of sorrow, yet so imbued with celestial hopes, that the music of a heavenly harp, swept by the fingers of the dead, seemed faintly to be heard among the saddest accents of the minister. The people trembled, though they but darkly understood him when he prayed that they, and himself, and all of mortal race, might be ready, as he trusted this young maiden had been, for the dreadful hour that should snatch the veil from their faces. The bearers went heavily forth, and the mourners followed, saddening all the street, with the dead before them, and Mr. Hooper in his black veil behind.

"Why do you look back?" said one in the procession to his partner.

20 "I had a fancy," replied she, "that the minister and the maiden's spirit were walking hand in hand."

"And so had I, at the same moment," said the other.

That night, the handsomest couple in Milford village were to be joined in wedlock. Though reckoned a melancholy man, Mr. Hooper had a placid cheerfulness for such occasions, which often excited a sympathetic smile where livelier merriment would have been thrown away. There was no quality of his disposition which made him more beloved than this. The company at the wedding awaited his arrival with impatience, trusting that the strange awe, which had gathered over him throughout the day, would now be dispelled. But such was not the result. When Mr. Hooper came, the first thing that their eyes rested on was the same horrible black veil, which had added deeper gloom to the funeral, and could portend nothing but evil to the wedding. Such was its immediate effect on the guests that a cloud seemed to have rolled duskily from beneath the black crape, and dimmed the light of the candles. The bridal pair stood up before the minister. But the bride's cold fingers quivered in the tremulous hand of the bridegroom, and her deathlike paleness caused a whisper that the maiden who had been buried a few hours before was come from her grave to be married. If ever another wedding were so dismal, it was that famous one where they tolled the wedding knell. After performing the ceremony, Mr. Hooper raised a glass of wine to his lips, wishing happiness to the new-married couple in a strain of mild pleasantry that ought to have brightened the features of the guests, like a cheerful gleam from the hearth. At that instant, catching a glimpse of his figure in the looking-glass, the black veil involved his own spirit in the horror with which it over-whelmed all others. His frame shuddered, his lips grew white, he spilt the untasted wine upon the carpet, and rushed forth into the darkness. For the Earth, too, had on her Black Veil.

The next day, the whole village of Milford talked of little else than Parson Hooper's black veil. That, and the mystery concealed behind it, supplied a topic for discussion be-tween acquaintances meeting in the street, and good women gossiping at their open win-dows. It was the first item of news that the tavern-keeper told to his guests. The children babbled of it on their way to school. One imitative little imp covered his face with an old black handkerchief, thereby so affrighting his playmates that the panic seized himself, and he well-nigh lost his wits by his own waggery.

It was remarkable that of all the busybodies and impertinent people in the parish, not one ventured to put the plain question to Mr. Hooper, wherefore he did this thing. Hitherto, whenever there appeared the slightest call for such interference, he had never lacked advisers, nor shown himself averse to be guided by their judgment. If he erred at all, it was by so painful a degree of self-distrust, that even the mildest censure would lead him to consider an indifferent action as a crime. Yet, though so well acquainted with this amiable weakness, no individual among his parishioners chose to make the black veil a subject of friendly remonstrance. There was a feeling of dread, neither plainly confessed nor carefully concealed, which caused each to shift the responsibility upon another, till at length it was found expedient to send a deputation to the church, in order to deal with Mr. Hooper about the mystery, before it should grow into a scandal. Never did an embassy so ill discharge its duties. The minister received them with friendly courtesy, but became silent, after they were seated, leaving to his visitors, the whole burden of introducing their important business. The topic, it might be supposed, was obvious enough. There was the black veil swathed round Mr. Hooper's forehead, and concealing every feature above his placid mouth, on which, at times, they could perceive the glimmering of a melancholy smile. But that piece of crape, to their imagination, seemed to hang down before his heart, the symbol of a fearful secret between him and them. Were the veil but cast aside, they might speak freely of it, but not till then. Thus they sat a considerable time, speechless, confused, and shrinking uneasily from Mr. Hooper's eye, which they felt to be fixed upon them with an invisible glance. Finally, the deputies returned abashed to their constituents, pronouncing the matter too weighty to be handled, except by a council of the churches, if, indeed, it might not require a general synod.

25   But there was one person in the village unappalled by the awe with which the black veil had impressed all beside herself. When the deputies returned without an explanation, or even venturing to demand one, she, with the calm energy of her character, determined to chase away the strange cloud that appeared to be settling round Mr. Hooper, every moment more darkly than before. As his plighted wife, it should be her privilege to know what the black veil concealed. At the minister's first visit, therefore, she entered upon the subject with a direct simplicity, which made the task easier both for him and her. After he had seated himself, she fixed her eyes steadfastly upon the veil, but could discern nothing of the dreadful gloom that had so overawed the multitude: it was but a double fold of crape, hanging down from his forehead to his mouth, and slightly stirring with his breath.

"No," she said aloud, and smiling, "there is nothing terrible in this piece of crape, except that it hides a face which I am always glad to look upon. Come, good sir, let the sun shine from behind the cloud. First lay aside your black veil: then tell me why you put it on."

Mr. Hooper's smile glimmered faintly.

"There is an hour to come," said he, "when all of us shall cast aside our veils. Take it not amiss, beloved friend, if I wear this piece of crape till then."

"Your words are a mystery, too," returned the young lady. "Take away the veil from them, at least."

30 "Elizabeth, I will," said he, "so far as my vow may suffer me. Know, then, this veil is a type and a symbol, and I am bound to wear it ever, both in light and darkness, in solitude and before the gaze of multitudes, and as with strangers, so with my familiar friends. No mortal eye will see it withdrawn. This dismal shade must separate me from the world: even you, Elizabeth, can never come behind it!"

"What grievous affliction hath befallen you," she earnestly inquired, "that you should thus darken your eyes forever?"

"If it be a sign of mourning," replied Mr. Hooper, "I, perhaps, like most other mortals, have sorrows dark enough to be typified by a black veil."

"But what if the world will not believe that it is the type of an innocent sorrow?" urged Elizabeth. "Beloved and respected as you are, there may be whispers that you hide your face under the consciousness of secret sin. For the sake of your holy office, do away this scandal!"

The color rose into her cheeks as she intimated the nature of the rumors that were already abroad in the village. But Mr. Hooper's mildness did not forsake him. He even smiled again—that same sad smile, which always appeared like a faint glimmering of light, proceeding from the obscurity beneath the veil.

35 "If I hide my face for sorrow, there is cause enough," he merely replied; "and if I cover it for secret sin, what mortal might not do the same?"

And with this gentle, but unconquerable obstinacy did he resist all her entreaties. At length Elizabeth sat silent. For a few moments she appeared lost in thought, considering, probably, what new methods might be tried to withdraw her lover from so dark a fantasy, which, if it had no other meaning, was perhaps a symptom of mental disease. Though of a firmer character than his own, the tears rolled down her cheeks. But, in an instant, as it were, a new feeling took the place of sorrow: her eyes were fixed insensibly on the black veil, when, like a sudden twilight in the air, its terrors fell around her. She arose, and stood trembling before him.

"And do you feel it then, at last?" said he mournfully.

She made no reply, but covered her eyes with her hand, and turned to leave the room. He rushed forward and caught her arm.

"Have patience with me, Elizabeth!" cried he, passionately. "Do not desert me, though this veil must be between us here on earth. Be mine, and hereafter there shall be no veil over my face, no darkness between our souls! It is but a mortal veil—it is not for eternity! O! you know not how lonely I am, and how frightened, to be alone behind my black veil. Do not leave me in this miserable obscurity forever!"

40 "Lift the veil but once, and look me in the face," said she.

"Never! It cannot be!" replied Mr. Hooper.

"Then farewell!" said Elizabeth.

She withdrew her arm from his grasp, and slowly departed, pausing at the door, to give one long shuddering gaze, that seemed almost to penetrate the mystery of the black veil. But, even amid his grief, Mr. Hooper smiled to think that only a material emblem had separated him from happiness, though the horrors, which it shadowed forth, must be drawn darkly between the fondest of lovers.

From that time no attempts were made to remove Mr. Hooper's black veil, or, by a direct appeal, to discover the secret which it was supposed to hide. By persons who claimed a superiority to popular prejudice, it was reckoned merely an eccentric whim, such as often mingles with the sober actions of men otherwise rational, and tinges them all with its own semblance of insanity. But with the multitude, good Mr. Hooper was irreparably a bugbear. He could not walk the street with any peace of mind, so conscious was he that the gentle and timid would turn aside to avoid him, and that others would make it a point of hardihood to throw themselves in his way. The impertinence of the latter class compelled him to give up his customary walk at sunset to the burial ground; for when he leaned pensively over the gate, there would always be faces behind the grave-stones, peeping at his black veil. A fable went the rounds that the stare of the dead people drove him thence. It grieved him, to the very depth of his kind heart, to observe how the children fled from his approach, breaking up their merriest sports, while his melancholy figure was yet afar off. Their instinctive dread caused him to feel more strongly than aught else, that a preternatural horror was interwoven with the threads of the black crape. In truth, his own antipathy to the veil was known to be so great, that he never willingly passed before a mirror, nor stooped to drink at a still fountain, lest, in its peaceful bosom, he should be affrighted by himself. This was what gave plausibility to the whispers, that Mr. Hooper's conscience tortured him for some great crime too horrible to be entirely con-cealed, or otherwise than so obscurely intimated. Thus, from beneath the black veil, there rolled a cloud into the sunshine, an ambiguity of sin or sorrow, which enveloped the poor minister, so that love or sympathy could never reach him. It was said that ghost and fiend consorted with him there. With self-shudderings and outward terrors, he walked contin-ually in its shadow, groping darkly within his own soul, or gazing through a medium that saddened the whole world. Even the lawless wind, it was believed, respected his dreadful secret, and never blew aside the veil. But still good Mr. Hooper sadly smiled at the pale visages of the worldly throng as he passed by.

45   Among all its bad influences, the black veil had one desirable effect, of making its wearer a very efficient clergyman. By the aid of his mysterious emblem—for there was no other apparent cause—he became a man of awful power over souls that were in agony for sin. His converts always regarded him with a dread peculiar to themselves, affirming, though but figuratively, that, before he brought them to celestial light, they had been with him behind the black veil. Its gloom, indeed, enabled him to sympathize with all dark affections. Dying sinners cried aloud for Mr. Hooper, and would not yield their breath till he appeared; though ever, as he stooped to whisper consolation, they shuddered at the veiled face so near their own. Such were the terrors of the black veil, even when Death had bared his visage! Strangers came long distances to attend service at his church, with the mere idle purpose of gazing at his figure, because it was forbidden them to behold his face. But many were made to quake ere they departed! Once, during Governor Belch-er's administration, Mr. Hooper was appointed to preach the election sermon. Covered with his black veil, he stood before the chief magistrate, the council, and the representa-tives, and wrought so deep an impression, that the legislative measures of that year were characterized by all the gloom and piety of our earliest ancestral sway.

In this manner Mr. Hooper spent a long life, irreproachable in outward act, yet shrouded in dismal suspicions; kind and loving, though unloved, and dimly feared; a man apart from men, shunned in their health and joy, but ever summoned to their aid in mortal anguish. As years wore on, shedding their snows above his sable veil, he acquired a name throughout the New England churches, and they called him Father Hooper. Nearly all his parishioners, who were of mature age when he was settled, had been borne away by many a funeral: he had one congregation in the church, and a more crowded one in the church-yard; and having wrought so late into the evening, and done his work so well, it was now good Father Hooper's turn to rest.

Several persons were visible by the shaded candle-light, in the death chamber of the old clergyman. Natural connections he had none. But there was the decorously grave, though unmoved physician, seeking only to mitigate the last pangs of the patient whom he could not save. There were the deacons, and other eminently pious members of his church. There, also, was the Reverend Mr. Clark, of Westbury, a young and zealous divine, who had ridden in haste to pray by the bedside of the expiring minister. There was the nurse, no hired handmaiden of death, but one whose calm affection had endured thus long in secrecy, in solitude, amid the chill of age, and would not perish, even at the dying hour. Who, but Elizabeth! And there lay the hoary head of good Father Hooper upon the death pillow, with the black veil still swathed about his brow, and reaching down over his face, so that each more difficult gasp of his faint breath caused it to stir. All through life that piece of crape had hung between him and the world: it had separated him from cheerful brotherhood and woman's love, and kept him in that saddest of all prisons, his own heart; and still it lay upon his face, as if to deepen the gloom of his darksome chamber, and shade him from the sunshine of eternity.

For some time previous, his mind had been confused, wavering doubtfully between the past and the present, and hovering forward, as it were, at intervals, into the indistinctness of the world to come. There had been feverish turns, which tossed him from side to side, and wore away what little strength he had. But in his most convulsive struggles, and in the wildest vagaries of his intellect, when no other thought retained its sober influence, he still showed an awful solicitude lest the black veil should slip aside. Even if his bewildered soul could have forgotten, there was a faithful woman at his pillow, who, with averted eyes, would have covered that aged face, which she had last beheld in the comeliness of manhood. At length the death-stricken old man lay quietly in the torpor of mental and bodily exhaustion, with an imperceptible pulse, and breath that grew fainter and fainter, except when a long, deep, and irregular inspiration seemed to prelude the flight of his spirit.

The minister of Westbury approached the bedside.

50   "Venerable Father Hooper," said he, "the moment of your release is at hand. Are you ready for the lifting of the veil that shuts in time from eternity?"

Father Hooper at first replied merely by a feeble motion of his head; then, apprehensive, perhaps, that his meaning might be doubtful, he exerted himself to speak.

"Yea," said he, in faint accents, "my soul hath a patient weariness until that veil be lifted."

"And is it fitting," resumed the Reverend Mr. Clark, "that a man so given to prayer, of such a blameless example, holy in deed and thought, so far as mortal judgment may pronounce; is it fitting that a father in the church should leave a shadow on his memory, that may seem to blacken a life so pure? I pray you, my venerable brother, let not this thing be! Suffer us to be gladdened by your triumphant aspect as you go to your reward. Before the veil of eternity be lifted, let me cast aside this black veil from your face!"

And thus speaking, the Reverend Mr. Clark bent forward to reveal the mystery of so many years. But, exerting a sudden energy, that made all the beholders stand aghast, Father Hooper snatched both his hands from beneath the bedclothes, and pressed them strongly on the black veil, resolute to struggle, if the minister of Westbury would contend with a dying man.

55   "Never!" cried the veiled clergyman. "On earth, never!"

"Dark old man!" exclaimed the affrighted minister, "with what horrible crime upon your soul are you now passing to the judgment?"

Father Hooper's breath heaved; it rattled in his throat; but, with a mighty effort, grasping forward with his hands, he caught hold of life, and held it back till he should speak. He even raised himself in bed; and there he sat, shivering with the arms of death around him, while the black veil hung down, awful, at that last moment, in the gathered terrors of a lifetime. And yet the faint, sad smile, so often there, now seemed to glimmer from its obscurity, and linger on Father Hooper's lips.

"Why do you tremble at me alone?" cried he, turning his veiled face round the circle of pale spectators. "Tremble also at each other! Have men avoided me, and women shown no pity, and children screamed and fled, only for my black veil? What, but the mystery which it obscurely typifies, had made this piece of crape so awful? When the friend shows his inmost heart to his friend; the lover to his best beloved; when man does not vainly shrink from the eye of his Creator, loathsomely treasuring up the secret of his sin; then deem me a monster, for the symbol beneath which I have lived, and die! I look around me, and lo! on every visage a Black Veil!"

While his auditors shrank from one another, in mutual affright, Father Hooper fell back upon his pillow, a veiled corpse, with a faint smile lingering on his lips. Still veiled, they laid him in his coffin, and a veiled corpse they bore him to the grave. The grass of many years has sprung up and withered on that grave; the burial stone is moss-grown, and good Mr. Hooper's face is dust; but awful is still the thought that it mouldered beneath the Black Veil!

Comments and Questions

1. In a footnote to this story, Hawthorne explained that the original of Mr. Hooper was a New England clergyman who wore a veil over his face after accidentally killing a friend. Hawthorne carefully avoids assigning any such specific reason for Mr. Hooper's wearing of the veil. Why?

2. Immediately after his sermon on secret sin, Mr. Hooper's parishioners initiate his personal isolation from them. Do they avoid their usual association with him merely because they suspect he is guilty of some secret sin? Does their behavior help to clarify the symbolism of the veil? How does their behavior relate to Mr. Hooper's final deathbed words? Consider the physician's remarks after the sermon in this connection.

3. For the purposes of this allegory, why does Hawthorne make his central character a minister? Whom does Mr. Hooper symbolize?

4. How are the qualities of a black crape veil especially appropriate for its symbolic function in the story?

5. Consider the different effects of Mr. Hooper's black veil at the regular service, the funeral, the wedding. How does Hawthorne's use of each make a significant contribution to the story?

6. How does Elizabeth's perception of the veil and its effects differ from the perception of other characters in the story (note precisely what she says to Hooper)? What is her symbolic importance to the story?

7. What parallels do you see between the social situations, the central character, and the psychological effects in this story and Cheever's "The Enormous Radio" presented earlier? What important differences would you note?

8. Do you more readily identify with the characters in this Hawthorne story or the preceding one? Specifically, why?

9. How is the third-person limited point of view (see p. 20) especially important to the effectiveness of this story?

10. Writing some allegorical fiction yourself can be very instructive about the form and the difficulties it poses. Why not pick up at the conclusion of Elizabeth's interview with Mr. Hooper? Only have her agree to marry him in spite of the black veil—then write your own allegorical conclusion to Hawthorne's parable.

Langston Hughes   (1902–1967)
On the Road

Hughes, often regarded as "America's senior black professional literary man," believed that his purpose as a writer was "to explain and illuminate the Negro condition in America." One of Hughes's most knowledgeable critics and a black poet, James A. Emanuel, believes that " 'On the Road' is artistically among the top five or six of Hughes's many stories" and "is a richly symbolic fusion of dream and reality, using well over two hundred precisely patterned images." In talking to the writer Kay Boyle about the story, Hughes commented:

> *All I had in mind was cold, hunger, a strange town at night . . . and a black vagabond named Sargeant against white snow, cold people, hard doors, trying to go somewhere, but too tired and hungry to make it—hemmed in on the ground by the same people who hemmed Christ in by rigid rituals surrounding a man-made cross. It developed as a kind of visual picture-story out of night, snow, man, church, police, cross, doors becoming bars, then ending with a man shaking the bars, but Christ at least free on the precarious road—His destination Kansas City, being a half-way point across the country. . . .*
>
> *I was writing of the little man. . . . I was writing, too, of Jesus as a human being whose meaning sometimes has been lost through the organization of the church. . . . The function of religion in daily life, as the Reverend [Martin Luther] King has made it function, is what I was talking about. . . . Sargeant had done as much for Jesus in getting Him down off the cross as Jesus had done for Sargeant in showing him that even the Saviour of men had nowhere to go except to push on. . . .**

He was not interested in the snow. When he got off the freight, one early evening during the depression, Sargeant never even noticed the snow. But he must have felt it

---

* Quoted in James A. Emanuel, *Langston Hughes,* New York: Twayne Publishers, Inc., 1967, pp. 93–94.

seeping down his neck, cold, wet, sopping in his shoes. But if you had asked him, he wouldn't have known it was snowing. Sargeant didn't see the snow, not even under the bright lights of the main street, falling white and flaky against the night. He was too hungry, too sleepy, too tired.

The Reverend Mr. Dorset, however, saw the snow when he switched on his porch light, opened the front door of his parsonage, and found standing there before him a big black man with snow on his face, a human piece of night with snow on his face—obviously unemployed.

Said the Reverend Mr. Dorset before Sargeant even realized he'd opened his mouth: "I'm sorry. No! Go right on down this street four blocks and turn to your left, walk up seven and you'll see the Relief Shelter. I'm sorry. No!" He shut the door.

Sargeant wanted to tell the holy man that he had already been to the Relief Shelter, been to hundreds of relief shelters during the depression years, the beds were always gone and supper was over, the place was full, and they drew the color line anyhow. But the minister said, "No," and shut the door. Evidently he didn't want to hear about it. And he *had* a door to shut.

5   The big black man turned away. And even yet he didn't see the snow, walking right into it. Maybe he sensed it, cold, wet, sticking to his jaws, wet on his black hands, sopping in his shoes. He stopped and stood on the sidewalk hunched over—hungry, sleepy, cold—looking up and down. Then he looked right where he was—in front of a church. Of course! A church! Sure, right next to a parsonage, certainly a church.

It had *two* doors.

Broad, white steps in the night all snowy white. Two high arched doors with slender stone pillars on either side. And way up, a round lacy window with a stone crucifix in the middle and Christ on the crucifix in stone. All this was pale in the street lights, solid and stony pale in the snow.

Sargeant blinked. When he looked up the snow fell into his eyes. For the first time that night he *saw* the snow. He shook his head. He shook the snow from his coat sleeves, felt hungry, felt lost, felt not lost, felt cold. He walked up the steps of the church. He knocked at the door. No answer. He tried the handle. Locked. He put his shoulder against the door and his long black body slanted like a ramrod. He pushed. With loud rhythmic grunts, like the grunts in a chain-gang song, he pushed against the door.

"I'm tired . . . Huh! . . . Hongry . . . Uh! . . . I'm sleepy . . . Huh! I'm cold . . . I got to sleep somewheres," Sargeant said. "This here is a church, ain't it? Well, uh!"

10   He pushed against the door.

Suddenly, with an undue cracking and squeaking, the door began to give way to the tall black Negro who pushed ferociously against the door.

By now two or three white people had stopped in the street, and Sargeant was vaguely aware of some of them yelling at him concerning the door. Three or four more came running, yelling at him.

"Hey!" they said. "Hey!"

"Un-huh," answered the big tall Negro, "I know it's a white folks' church, but I got to sleep somewhere." He gave another lunge at the door. "Huh!"

15   And the door broke open.

But just when the door gave way, two white cops arrived in a car, ran up the steps with their clubs and grabbed Sargeant. But Sargeant for once had no intention of being pulled or pushed away from the door.

Sargeant grabbed, but not for anything so weak as a broken door. He grabbed for one of the tall stone pillars beside the door, grabbed at it and caught it. And held it. The cops pulled and Sargeant pulled. Most of the people in the street got behind the cops and helped them pull.

"A big black unemployed Negro holding onto our church!" thought the people. "The idea!"

The cops began to beat Sargeant over the head, and nobody protested. But he held on.

20 And then the church fell down.[1]

Gradually, the big stone front of the church fell down, the walls and the rafters, the crucifix and the Christ. Then the whole thing fell down, covering the cops and the people with bricks and stones and debris. The whole church fell down in the snow.

Sargeant got out from under the church and went walking on up the street with the stone pillar on his shoulder. He was under the impression that he had buried the parsonage and the Reverend Mr. Dorset who said, "No!" So he laughed, and threw the pillar six blocks up the street and went on.

Sargeant thought he was alone, but listening to the crunch, crunch, crunch on the snow of his own footsteps, he heard other footsteps, too, doubling his own. He looked around and there was Christ walking along beside him, the same Christ that had been on the cross on the church—still stone with a rough stone surface, walking along beside him just like he was broken off the cross when the church fell down.

"Well, I'll be dogged," said Sargeant. "This here's the first time I ever seed you off the cross."

25 "Yes," said Christ, crunching his feet in the snow. "You had to pull the church down to get me off the cross."

"You glad?" said Sargeant.

"I sure am," said Christ.

They both laughed.

"I'm a hell of a fellow, ain't I?" said Sargeant. "Done pulled the church down!"

30 "You did a good job," said Christ. "They have kept me nailed on a cross for nearly two thousand years."

"Whee-ee-e!" said Sargeant. "I know you are glad to get off."

"I sure am," said Christ.

They walked on in the snow. Sargeant looked at the man of stone.

"And you been up there two thousand years?"

35 "I sure have," Christ said.

"Well, if I had a little cash," said Sargeant, "I'd show you around a bit."

"I been around," said Christ.

"Yeah, but that was a long time ago."

"All the same," said Christ, "I've been around."

40 They walked on in the snow until they came to the railroad yards. Sargeant was tired, sweating and tired.

"Where you goin'?" Sargeant said, stopping by the tracks. He looked at Christ. Sargeant said, "I'm just a bum on the road. How about you? Where you goin'?"

"God knows," Christ said, "but I'm leavin' here."

They saw the red and green lights of the railroad yard half veiled by the snow that fell out of the night. Away down the track they saw a fire in a hobo jungle.

"I can go there and sleep," Sargeant said.

---

[1] Reminiscent of Samson's pulling down the pillars of the temple where the great feast of the Philistine god Dagon was held. See Judges 16:28–31.

45   "You can?"

"Sure," said Sargeant. "That place ain't got no doors."

Outside the town, along the tracks, there were barren trees and bushes below the embankment, snow-gray in the dark. And down among the trees and bushes there were makeshift houses made out of boxes and tin and old pieces of wood and canvas. You couldn't see them in the dark, but you knew they were there if you'd ever been on the road, if you had ever lived with the homeless and hungry in a depression.

"I'm side-tracking," Sargeant said. "I'm tired."

"I'm gonna make it on to Kansas City," said Christ.

50   "O.K." Sargeant said. "So long!"

He went down into the hobo jungle and found himself a place to sleep. He never did see Christ no more. About six A.M. a freight came by. Sargeant scrambled out of the jungle with a dozen or so more hoboes and ran along the track, grabbing at the freight. It was dawn, early dawn, cold and gray.

"Wonder where Christ is by now?" Sargeant thought. "He must-a gone a way on down the road. He didn't sleep in this jungle."

Sargeant grabbed the train and started to pull himself up into a moving coal car, over the edge of a wheeling coal car. But strangely enough, the car was full of cops. The nearest cop rapped Sargeant soundly across the knuckles with his night stick. Wham! Rapped his big black hands for clinging to the top of the car. Wham! But Sargeant did not turn loose. He clung on and tried to pull himself into the car. He hollered at the top of his voice, "Damn it, lemme in this car!"

"Shut up," barked the cop. "You crazy coon!" He rapped Sargeant across the knuckles and punched him in the stomach. "You ain't out in no jungle now. This ain't no train. You in jail."

55   Wham! across his bare black fingers clinging to the bars of his cell. Wham! between the steel bars low down against his shins.

Suddenly Sargeant realized that he really was in jail. He wasn't on no train. The blood of the night before had dried on his face, his head hurt terribly, and a cop outside in the corridor was hitting him across the knuckles for holding onto the door, yelling and shaking the cell door.

"They must-a took me to jail for breaking down the door last night," Sargeant thought, "that church door."

Sargeant went over and sat on a wooden bench against the cold stone wall. He was emptier than ever. His clothes were wet, clammy cold wet, and shoes sloppy with snow water. It was just about dawn. There he was, locked up behind a cell door, nursing his bruised fingers.

The bruised fingers were his, but not the *door.*

60   Not the *club,* but the fingers.

"You wait," mumbled Sargeant, black against the jail wall. "I'm gonna break down this door, too."

"Shut up—or I'll paste you one," said the cop.

"I'm gonna break down this door," yelled Sargeant as he stood up in his cell.

Then he must have been talking to himself because he said, "I wonder where Christ's gone? I wonder if he's gone to Kansas City?"

Katherine Anne Porter   (1894–1980)
Flowering Judas

Braggioni sits heaped upon the edge of a straight-backed chair much too small for him, and sings to Laura in a furry, mournful voice. Laura has begun to find reasons for avoiding her own house until the latest possible moment, for Braggioni is there almost every night. No matter how late she is, he will be sitting there with a surly, waiting expression, pulling at his kinky yellow hair, thumbing the strings of his guitar, snarling a tune under his breath. Lupe the Indian maid meets Laura at the door, and says with a flicker of a glance towards the upper room, "He waits."

Laura wishes to lie down, she is tired of her hairpins and the feel of her long tight sleeves, but she says to him, "Have you a new song for me this evening?" If he says yes, she asks him to sing it. If he says no, she remembers his favorite one, and asks him to sing it again. Lupe brings her a cup of chocolate and a plate of rice, and Laura eats at the small table under the lamp, first inviting Braggioni, whose answer is always the same: "I have eaten, and besides, chocolate thickens the voice."

Laura says, "Sing, then," and Braggioni heaves himself into song. He scratches the guitar familiarly as though it were a pet animal, and sings passionately off key, taking the high notes in a prolonged painful squeal. Laura, who haunts the markets listening to the ballad singers, and stops every day to hear the blind boy playing his reed-flute in Sixteenth of September Street, listens to Braggioni with pitiless courtesy, because she dares not smile at his miserable performance. Nobody dares to smile at him. Braggioni is cruel to everyone, with a kind of specialized insolence, but he is so vain of his talents, and so sensitive to slights, it would require a cruelty and vanity greater than his own to lay a finger on the vast cureless wound of his self-esteem. It would require courage, too, for it is dangerous to offend him, and nobody has this courage.

Braggioni loves himself with such tenderness and amplitude and eternal charity that his followers—for he is a leader of men, a skilled revolutionist, and his skin has been punctured in honorable warfare—warm themselves in the reflected glow, and say to each other: "He has a real nobility, a love of humanity raised above mere personal affections." The excess of this self-love has flowed out, inconveniently for her, over Laura, who, with so many others, owes her comfortable situation and her salary to him. When he is in a very good humor, he tells her, "I am tempted to forgive you for being a *gringa. Gringita!*" and Laura, burning, imagines herself leaning forward suddenly, and with a sound backhanded slap wiping the suety smile from his face. If he notices her eyes at these moments he gives no sign.

5   She knows what Braggioni would offer her, and she must resist tenaciously without appearing to resist, and if she could avoid it she would not admit even to herself the slow drift of his intention. During these long evenings which have spoiled a long month for her, she sits in her deep chair with an open book on her knees, resting her eyes on the consoling rigidity of the printed page when the sight and sound of Braggioni singing threaten to identify themselves with all her remembered afflictions and to add their weight to her uneasy premonitions of the future. The gluttonous bulk of Braggioni has become a symbol of her many disillusions, for a revolutionist should be lean, animated by heroic faith, a vessel of abstract virtues. This is nonsense, she knows it now and is ashamed of it. Revolution must have leaders, and leadership is a career for energetic men. She is, her comrades tell her, full of romantic error, for what she defines as cynicism in them is

merely "a developed sense of reality." She is almost too willing to say, "I am wrong, I suppose I don't really understand the principles," and afterward she makes a secret truce with herself, determined not to surrender her will to such expedient logic. But she cannot help feeling that she has been betrayed irreparably by the disunion between her way of living and her feeling of what life should be, and at times she is almost contented to rest in this sense of grievance as a private store of consolation. Sometimes she wishes to run away, but she stays. Now she longs to fly out of this room, down the narrow stairs, and into the street where the houses lean together like conspirators under a single mottled lamp, and leave Braggioni singing to himself.

Instead she looks at Braggioni, frankly and clearly, like a good child who understands the rules of behavior. Her knees cling together under sound blue serge, and her round white collar is not purposely nun-like. She wears the uniform of an idea, and has renounced vanities. She was born Roman Catholic, and in spite of her fear of being seen by someone who might make a scandal of it, she slips now and again into some crumbling little church, kneels on the chilly stone, and says a Hail Mary on the gold rosary she bought in Tehuantepec. It is no good and she ends by examining the altar with its tinsel flowers and ragged brocades, and feels tender about the battered doll-shape of some male saint whose white, lace-trimmed drawers hang limply around his ankles below the hieratic dignity of his velvet robe. She has encased herself in a set of principles derived from her early training, leaving no detail of gesture or of personal taste untouched, and for this reason she will not wear lace made on machines. This is her private heresy, for in her special group the machine is sacred, and will be the salvation of the workers. She loves fine lace, and there is a tiny edge of fluted cobweb on this collar, which is one of twenty precisely alike, folded in blue tissue paper in the upper drawer of her clothes chest.

Braggioni catches her glance solidly as if he had been waiting for it, leans forward, balancing his paunch between his spread knees, and sings with tremendous emphasis, weighing his words. He has, the song relates, no father and no mother, nor even a friend to console him; lonely as a wave of the sea he comes and goes, lonely as a wave. His mouth opens round and yearns sideways, his balloon cheeks grow oily with the labor of song. He bulges marvelously in his expensive garments. Over his lavender collar, crushed upon a purple necktie, held by a diamond hoop: over his ammunition belt of tooled leather worked in silver, buckled cruelly about his gasping middle: over the tops of his glossy yellow shoes Braggioni swells with ominous ripeness, his mauve silk hose stretched taut, his ankles bound with the stout leather thongs of his shoes.

When he stretches his eyelids at Laura she notes again that his eyes are the true tawny yellow cat's eyes. He is rich, not in money, he tells her, but in power, and this power brings with it the blameless ownership of things, and the right to indulge his love of small luxuries. "I have a taste for the elegant refinements," he said once, flourishing a yellow silk handkerchief before her nose. "Smell that? It is Jockey Club, imported from New York." Nonetheless he is wounded by life. He will say so presently. "It is true everything turns to dust in the hand, to gall on the tongue." He sighs and his leather belt creaks like a saddle girth. "I am disappointed in everything as it comes. Everything." He shakes his head. "You, poor thing, you will be disappointed too. You were born for it. We are more alike than you realize in some things. Wait and see. Some day you will remember what I have told you, you will know that Braggioni was your friend."

Laura feels a slow chill, a purely physical sense of danger, a warning in her blood that violence, mutilation, a shocking death, wait for her with lessening patience. She has translated this fear into something homely, immediate, and sometimes hesitates before crossing the street. "My personal fate is nothing, except as the testimony of a mental attitude," she reminds herself, quoting from some forgotten philosophic primer, and is sensible enough to add, "Anyhow, I shall not be killed by an automobile if I can help it."

10   "It may be true I am as corrupt, in another way, as Braggioni," she thinks in spite of herself, "as callous, as incomplete," and if this is so, any kind of death seems preferable. Still she sits quietly, she does not run. Where could she go? Uninvited she has promised herself to this place; she can no longer imagine herself as living in another country, and there is no pleasure in remembering her life before she came here.

Precisely what is the nature of this devotion, its true motives, and what are its obligations? Laura cannot say. She spends part of her days in Xochimilco, near by, teaching Indian children to say in English, "The cat is on the mat." When she appears in the classroom, they crowd about her with smiles on their wise, innocent, clay-colored faces, crying, "Good morning, my titcher!" in immaculate voices, and they make of her desk a fresh garden of flowers every day.

During her leisure she goes to union meetings and listens to busy important voices quarreling over tactics, methods, internal politics. She visits the prisoners of her own political faith in their cells, where they entertain themselves with counting cockroaches, repenting of their indiscretions, composing their memoirs, writing out manifestoes and plans for their comrades who are still walking about free, hands in pockets, sniffing fresh air. Laura brings them food and cigarettes and a little money, and she brings messages disguised in equivocal phrases from the men outside who dare not set foot in the prison for fear of disappearing into the cells kept empty for them. If the prisoners confuse night and day, and complain, "Dear little Laura, time doesn't pass in this infernal hole, and I won't know when it is time to sleep unless I have a reminder," she brings them their favorite narcotics, and says in a tone that does not wound them with pity, "Tonight will really be night for you," and though her Spanish amuses them, they find her comforting, useful. If they lose patience and all faith, and curse the slowness of their friends in coming to their rescue with money and influence, they trust her not to repeat everything, and if she inquires, "Where do you think we can find money, or influence?" they are certain to answer, "Well, there is Braggioni, why doesn't he do something?"

She smuggles letters from headquarters to men hiding from firing squads in back streets in mildewed houses, where they sit in tumbled beds and talk bitterly as if all Mexico were at their heels, when Laura knows positively they might appear at the band concert in the Alameda on Sunday morning, and no one would notice them. But Braggioni says, "Let them sweat a little. The next time they may be careful. It is very restful to have them out of the way for a while." She is not afraid to knock on any door in any street after midnight, and enter in the darkness, and say to one of these men who is really in danger: "They will be looking for you—seriously—tomorrow morning after six. Here is some money from Vicente. Go to Vera Cruz and wait."

She borrows money from the Roumanian agitator to give to his bitter enemy the Polish agitator. The favor of Braggioni is their disputed territory, and Braggioni holds the balance nicely, for he can use them both. The Polish agitator talks love to her over café tables, hoping to exploit what he believes is her secret sentimental preference for him, and he gives her misinformation which he begs her to repeat as the solemn truth to certain persons. The Roumanian is more adroit. He is generous with his money in all good causes, and lies to her with an air of ingenuous candor, as if he were her good friend and confidant. She never repeats anything they may say. Braggioni never asks questions. He has other ways to discover all that he wishes to know about them.

15   Nobody touches her, but all praise her gray eyes, and the soft, round under lip which promises gayety, yet is always grave, nearly always firmly closed: and they cannot understand why she is in Mexico. She walks back and forth on her errands, with puzzled eyebrows, carrying her little folder of drawings and music and school papers. No dancer dances more beautifully than Laura walks, and she inspires some amusing, unexpected ardors, which cause little gossip, because nothing comes of them. A young captain who

had been a soldier in Zapata's army attempted, during a horseback ride near Cuernavaca, to express his desire for her with the noble simplicity befitting a rude folk-hero: but gently, because he was gentle. This gentleness was his defeat, for when he alighted, and removed her foot from the stirrup, and essayed to draw her down into his arms, her horse, ordinarily a tame one, shied fiercely, reared and plunged away. The young hero's horse careened blindly after his stable-mate, and the hero did not return to the hotel until rather late that evening. At breakfast he came to her table in full charro dress, gray buckskin jacket and trousers with strings of silver buttons down the leg, and he was in a humorous, careless mood. "May I sit with you?" and "You are a wonderful rider. I was terrified that you might be thrown and dragged. I should never have forgiven myself. But I cannot admire you enough for your riding!"

"I learned to ride in Arizona," said Laura.

"If you will ride with me again this morning, I promise you a horse that will not shy with you," he said. But Laura remembered that she must return to Mexico City at noon.

Next morning the children made a celebration and spent their playtime writing on the blackboard, "We lov ar ticher," and with tinted chalks they drew wreaths of flowers around the words. The young hero wrote her a letter: "I am a very foolish, wasteful, impulsive man. I should have first said I love you, and then you would not have run away. But you shall see me again." Laura thought, "I must send him a box of colored crayons," but she was trying to forgive herself for having spurred her horse at the wrong moment.

A brown, shock-haired youth came and stood in her patio one night and sang like a lost soul for two hours, but Laura could think of nothing to do about it. The moonlight spread a wash of gauzy silver over the clear spaces of the garden, and the shadows were cobalt blue. The scarlet blossoms of the Judas tree were dull purple, and the names of the colors repeated themselves automatically in her mind, while she watched not the boy, but his shadow, fallen like a dark garment across the fountain rim, trailing in the water. Lupe came silently and whispered expert counsel in her ear: "If you will throw him one little flower, he will sing another song or two and go away." Laura threw the flower, and he sang a last song and went away with the flower tucked in the band of his hat. Lupe said, "He is one of the organizers of the Typographers Union, and before that he sold corridos in the Merced market, and before that, he came from Guanajuato, where I was born. I would not trust any man, but I trust least those from Guanajuato."

20   She did not tell Laura that he would be back again the next night, and the next, nor that he would follow her at a certain fixed distance around the Merced market, through the Zócolo, up Francisco I. Madero Avenue, and so along the Paseo de la Reforma to Chapultepec Park, and into the Philosopher's Footpath, still with that flower withering in his hat, and an indivisible attention in his eyes.

Now Laura is accustomed to him, it means nothing except that he is nineteen years old and is observing a convention with all propriety, as though it were founded on a law of nature, which in the end it might very well prove to be. He is beginning to write poems which he prints on a wooden press, and he leaves them stuck like handbills in her door. She is pleasantly disturbed by the abstract, unhurried watchfulness of his black eyes which will in time turn easily towards another object. She tells herself that throwing the flower was a mistake, for she is twenty-two years old and knows better; but she refuses to regret it, and persuades herself that her negation of all external events as they occur is a sign that she is gradually perfecting herself in the stoicism she strives to cultivate against that disaster she fears, though she cannot name it.

She is not at home in the world. Every day she teaches children who remain strangers to her, though she loves their tender round hands and their charming opportunistic savagery. She knocks at unfamiliar doors not knowing whether a friend or a stranger shall answer, and even if a known face emerges from the sour gloom of that unknown interior, still it is the face of a stranger. No matter what this stranger says to her, nor what her message to him, the very cells of her flesh reject knowledge and kinship in one monotonous word. No. No. No. She draws her strength from this one holy talismanic word which does not suffer her to be led into evil. Denying everything, she may walk anywhere in safety, she looks at everything without amazement.

No, repeats this firm unchanging voice of her blood; and she looks at Braggioni without amazement. He is a great man, he wishes to impress this simple girl who covers her great round breasts with thick dark cloth, and who hides long, invaluably beautiful legs under a heavy skirt. She is almost thin except for the incomprehensible fullness of her breasts, like a nursing mother's, and Braggioni, who considers himself a judge of women, speculates again on the puzzle of her notorious virginity, and takes the liberty of speech which she permits without a sign of modesty, indeed, without any sort of sign, which is disconcerting.

"You think you are so cold, *gringita!* Wait and see. You will surprise yourself some day! May I be there to advise you!" He stretches his eyelids at her, and his ill-humored cat's eyes waver in a separate glance for the two points of light marking the opposite ends of a smoothly drawn path between the swollen curve of her breasts. He is not put off by that blue serge, nor by her resolutely fixed gaze. There is all the time in the world. His cheeks are bellying with the wind of song. "O girl with the dark eyes," he sings, and reconsiders. "But yours are not dark. I can change all that. O girl with the green eyes, you have stolen my heart away!" Then his mind wanders to the song, and Laura feels the weight of his attention being shifted elsewhere. Singing thus, he seems harmless, he is quite harmless, there is nothing to do but sit patiently and say "No," when the moment comes. She draws a full breath, and her mind wanders also, but not far. She dares not wander too far.

25   Not for nothing has Braggioni taken pains to be a good revolutionist and a professional lover of humanity. He will never die of it. He has the malice, the cleverness, the wickedness, the sharpness of wit, the hardness of heart, stipulated for loving the world profitably. *He will never die of it.* He will live to see himself kicked out from his feeding trough by other hungry world-saviours. Traditionally he must sing in spite of his life which drives him to bloodshed, he tells Laura, for his father was a Tuscany peasant who drifted to Yucatan and married a Maya woman: a woman of race, an aristocrat. They gave him the love and knowledge of music, thus: and under the rip of his thumbnail, the strings of the instrument complain like exposed nerves.

Once he was called Delgadito by all the girls and married women who ran after him; he was so scrawny all his bones showed under his thin cotton clothing, and he could squeeze his emptiness to the very backbone with his two hands. He was a poet and the revolution was only a dream then; too many women loved him and sapped away his youth, and he could never find enough to eat anywhere, anywhere! Now he is a leader of men, crafty men who whisper in his ear, hungry men who wait for hours outside his office for a word with him, emaciated men with wild faces who waylay him at the street gate with a timid, "Comrade, let me tell you . . ." and they blow the foul breath from their empty stomachs in his face.

He is always sympathetic. He gives them handfuls of small coins from his own pocket, he promises them work, there will be demonstrations, they must join the unions and attend the meetings, above all they must be on the watch for spies. They are closer to him than his own brothers, without them he can do nothing—until tomorrow, comrade!

Until tomorrow. "They are stupid, they are lazy, they are treacherous, they would cut my throat for nothing," he says to Laura. He has good food and abundant drink, he hires an automobile and drives in the Paseo on Sunday morning, and enjoys plenty of sleep in a soft bed beside a wife who dares not disturb him; and he sits pampering his bones in easy billows of fat, singing to Laura, who knows and thinks these things about him. When he was fifteen, he tried to drown himself because he loved a girl, his first love, and she laughed at him. "A thousand women have paid for that," and his tight little mouth turns down at the corners. Now he perfumes his hair with Jockey Club, and confides to Laura: "One woman is really as good as another for me, in the dark. I prefer them all."

His wife organizes unions among the girls in the cigarette factories, and walks in picket lines, and even speaks at meetings in the evening. But she cannot be brought to acknowledge the benefits of true liberty. "I tell her I must have my freedom, net. She does not understand my point of view." Laura has heard this many times. Braggioni scratches the guitar and meditates. "She is an instinctively virtuous woman, pure gold, no doubt of that. If she were not, I should lock her up, and she knows it."

His wife, who works so hard for the good of the factory girls, employs part of her leisure lying on the floor weeping because there are so many women in the world, and only one husband for her, and she never knows where nor when to look for him. He told her: "Unless you can learn to cry when I am not here, I must go away for good." That day he went away and took a room at the Hotel Madrid.

It is this month of separation for the sake of higher principles that has been spoiled not only for Mrs. Braggioni, whose sense of reality is beyond criticism, but for Larura, who feels herself bogged in a nightmare. Tonight Laura envies Mrs. Braggioni, who is alone, and free to weep as much as she pleases about a concrete wrong. Laura has just come from a visit to the prison, and she is waiting for tomorrow with a bitter anxiety as if tomorrow may not come, but time may be caught immovably in this hour, with herself transfixed, Braggioni singing on forever, and Eugenio's body not yet discovered by the guard.

Braggioni says: "Are you going to sleep?" Almost before she can shake her head, he begins telling her about the May-day disturbances coming on in Morelia, for the Catholics hold a festival in honor of the Blessed Virgin, and the Socialists celebrate their martyrs on that day. "There will be two independent processions, starting from either end of town, and they will march until they meet, and the rest depends . . ." He asks her to oil and load his pistols. Standing up, he unbuckles his ammunition belt, and spreads it laden across her knees. Laura sits with the shells slipping through the cleaning cloth dipped in oil, and he says again he cannot understand why she works so hard for the revolutionary idea unless she loves some man who is in it. "Are you not in love with someone?" "No," says Laura. "And no one is in love with you?" "No." "Then it is your own fault. No woman need go begging. Why, what is the matter with you? The legless beggar woman in the Alameda has a perfectly faithful lover. Did you know that?"

Laura peers down the pistol barrel and says nothing, but a long, slow faintness rises and subsides in her; Braggioni curves his swollen fingers around the throat of the guitar and softly smothers the music out of it, and when she hears him again he seems to have forgotten her,and is speaking in the hypnotic voice he uses when talking in small rooms to a listening, close-gathered crowd. Some day this world, now seemingly so composed and eternal, to the edges of every sea shall be merely a tangle of gaping trenches, of crashing walls and broken bodies. Everything must be torn from its accustomed place where it has rotted for centuries, hurled skyward and distributed, cast down again clean as rain, without separate identity. Nothing shall survive that the stiffened hands of poverty have created for the rich and no one shall be left alive except the elect spirits destined to procreate a new world cleansed of cruelty and injustice, ruled by benevolent anarchy:

"Pistols are good, I love them, cannon are even better, but in the end I pin my faith to good dynamite," he concludes, and strokes the pistol lying in her hands. "Once I dreamed of destroying this city, in case it offered resistance to General Ortiz, but it fell into his hands like an overripe pear."

He is made restless by his own words, rises and stands waiting. Laura holds up the belt to him: "Put that on, and go kill somebody in Morelia, and you will be happier," she says softly. The presence of death in the room makes her bold. "Today, I found Eugenio going into a stupor. He refused to allow me to call the prison doctor. He had taken all the tablets I brought him yesterday. He said he took them because he was bored."

35 "He is a fool, and his death is his own business," says Braggioni, fastening his belt carefully.

"I told him if he had waited only a little while longer, you would have got him set free," says Laura. "He said he did not want to wait."

"He is a fool and we are well rid of him," says Braggioni, reaching for his hat.

He goes away. Laura knows his mood has changed, she will not see him any more for a while. He will send word when he needs her to go on errands into strange streets, to speak to the strange faces that will appear, like clay masks with the power of human speech, to mutter their thanks to Braggioni for his help. Now she is free, and she thinks, I must run while there is time. But she does not go.

Braggioni enters his own house where for a month his wife has spent many hours every night weeping and tangling her hair upon her pillow. She is weeping now, and she weeps more at the sight of him, the cause of all her sorrows. He looks about the room. Nothing is changed, the smells are good and familiar, he is well acquainted with the woman who comes toward him with no reproach except grief on her face. He says to her tenderly: "You are so good, please don't cry any more, you dear good creature." She says, "Are you tired, my angel? Sit here and I will wash your feet." She brings a bowl of water, and kneeling, unlaces his shoes, and when from her knees she raises her sad eyes under her blackened lids, he is sorry for everything, and bursts into tears. "Ah, yes, I am hungry, I am tired, let us eat something together," he says, between sobs. His wife leans her head on his arm and says, "Forgive me!" and this time he is refreshed by the solemn, endless rain of her tears.

40 Laura takes off her serge dress and puts on a white linen nightgown and goes to bed. She turns her head a little to one side, and lying still, reminds herself that it is time to sleep. Numbers tick in her brain like little clocks, soundless doors close of themselves around her. If you would sleep, you must not remember anything, the children will say tomorrow, good morning, my teacher, the poor prisoners who come every day bringing flowers to their jailor. 1-2-3-4-5—it is monstrous to confuse love with revolution, night with day, life with death—ah, Eugenio!

The tolling of the midnight bell is a signal, but what does it mean? Get up, Laura, and follow me: come out of your sleep, out of your bed, out of this strange house. What are you doing in this house? Without a word, without fear she rose and reached for Eugenio's hand, but he eluded her with a sharp, sly smile and drifted away. This is not all, you shall see—Murderer, he said, follow me, I will show you a new country, but it is far away and we must hurry No, said Laura, not unless you take my hand, no; and she clung first to the stair rail, and then to the topmost branch of the Judas tree that bent down slowly and set her upon the earth, and then to the rocky ledge of a cliff, and then to the jagged wave of a sea that was not water but a desert of crumbling stone. Where are you taking me, she asked in wonder but without fear. To death, and it is a long way off, and we must hurry, said Eugenio. No, said Laura, not unless you take my hand. Then eat these flowers, poor prisoner, said Eugenio in a voice of pity, take and eat: and from the Judas tree he stripped the warm bleeding flowers, and held them to her lips. She saw that his hand was fleshless, a cluster of small white petrified branches, and his eye sockets were without light, but she ate the flowers greedily for they satisfied both hunger and thirst. Murderer! said Eugenio, and Cannibal! This is my body and my blood. Laura cried No! and at the sound of her own voice, she awoke trembling, and was afraid to sleep again.

Comments and Questions

1. The narrator directly indicates that Braggioni has become a symbol of Laura's "many disillusions." How has her relationship with Braggioni and the revolution paralleled her earlier religious belief, training, and disillusionment? Cite instances of Porter's use of religious terminology to reinforce that parallel. How is the parallel functional in the story? How does it contribute to characterization, motivation, psychological conflict, theme?

2. How does the fourth paragraph of the story suggest a comparison between Braggioni and Christ? Where else is the comparison specifically encouraged? In terms of diction and style, how does Porter impress upon us the ironic nature of the comparison, the hypocritical duality of Braggioni's character and revolutionary role? Does Braggioni, in fact, have any redeeming qualities?

3. Laura herself states, "It may be true I am as corrupt, in another way as Braggioni . . . as callous and incomplete." Can you mention other instances suggesting that Laura mirrors certain qualities in Braggioni? How are such suggestions important? Who betrays and who is betrayed in the story?

4. Review all of Laura's potential love relationships (not merely sexual ones). How does weaving their variety and her rejection of each throughout the story serve as dramatized commentary on Laura's own assessment of her psychological dilemma of being "bogged in a nightmare"? Does she make a commitment anywhere in the story?

5. Porter uses the dramatic or the historical present tense until the very moment of action in Laura's nightmare at the conclusion. Can you justify the shift to the past tense at that point? What has been gained by using the present tense in previous scenes?

6. As a messenger of the revolution, does Laura also embody a comment on sociopolitical or other causes in our century? How does Laura's delivery of narcotics to jailed revolutionaries constitute ironic symbolism?

7. Do a close and thorough analysis of the imagery of Laura's nightmare, relating it to the central conflict and theme of the story. Are there universal implications in the conflict and theme?

8. How do Porter's characterization, plot, and use of symbolism differ significantly from those in Hawthorne's allegorical fictions above?

Katherine Anne Porter   (1894–1980)
The Grave

The grandfather, dead for more than thirty years, had been twice disturbed in his long repose by the constancy and possessiveness of his widow. She removed his bones first to Louisiana and then to Texas as if she had set out to find her own burial place, knowing well she would never return to the places she had left. In Texas she set up a small cemetery in a corner of her first farm, and as the family connection grew, and oddments of relations came over from Kentucky to settle, it contained at last about twenty graves. After the grandmother's death, part of her land was to be sold for the benefit of certain of her children, and the cemetery happened to lie in the part set aside for sale. It was necessary to take up the bodies and bury them again in the family plot in the big new public cemetery, where the grandmother had been buried. At last her husband was to lie beside her for eternity, as she had planned.

The family cemetery had been a pleasant small neglected garden of tangled rose bushes and ragged cedar trees and cypress, the simple flat stones rising out of uncropped sweet-smelling wild grass. The graves were lying open and empty one burning day when Miranda and her brother Paul, who often went together to hunt rabbits and doves, propped their twenty-two Winchester rifles carefully against the rail fence, climbed over and explored among the graves. She was nine years old and he was twelve.

They peered into the pits all shaped alike with such purposeful accuracy, and look ing at each other with pleased adventurous eyes, they said in solemn tones: "These were graves!" trying by words to shape a special, suitable emotion in their minds, but they felt nothing except an agreeable thrill of wonder: they were seeing a new sight, doing some-thing they had not done before. In them both there was also a small disappointment at the entire commonplaceness of the actual spectacle. Even if it had once contained a coffin for years upon years, when the coffin was gone a grave was just a hole in the ground. Miranda leaped into the pit that had held her grandfather's bones. Scratching around aim-lessly and pleasurably as any young animal, she scooped up a lump of earth and weighed it in her palm. It had a pleasantly sweet, corrupt smell, being mixed with cedar needles and small leaves, and as the crumbs fell apart, she saw a silver dove no larger than a hazel nut, with spread wings and a neat fan-shaped tail. The breast had a deep round hollow in it. Turning it up to the fierce sunlight, she saw that the inside of the hollow was cut in little whorls. She scrambled out, over the pile of loose earth that had fallen back into one end of the grave, calling to Paul that she had found something, he must guess what . . . His head appeared smiling over the rim of another grave. He waved a closed hand at her. "I've got something too!" They ran to compare treasures, making a game of it, so many guesses each, all wrong, and a final showdown with opened palms. Paul had found a thin wide gold ring carved with intricate flowers and leaves. Miranda was smitten at sight of the ring and wished to have it. Paul seemed more impressed by the dove. They made a trade, with some little bickering. After he had got the dove in his hand, Paul said, "Don't you know what this is? This is a screw head for a *coffin!* . . . I'll bet nobody else in the world has one like this!"

Miranda glanced at it without covetousness. She had the gold ring on her thumb; it fitted perfectly. "Maybe we ought to go now," she said, "maybe one of the niggers 'll see us and tell somebody." They knew the land had been sold, the cemetery was no longer theirs, and they felt like trespassers. They climbed back over the fence, slung their rifles loosely under their arms—they had been shooting at targets with various kinds of firearms since they were seven years old—and set out to look for the rabbits and doves or whatever small game might happen along. On these expeditions Miranda always followed at Paul's heels along the path, obeying instructions about handling her gun when going through fences; learning how to stand it up properly so it would not slip and fire unexpectedly; how to wait her time for a shot and not just bang away in the air without looking, spoiling shots for Paul, who really could hit things if given a chance. Now and then, in her excitement at seeing birds whizz up suddenly before her face, or a rabbit leap across her very toes, she lost her head, and almost without sighting she flung her rifle up and pulled the trigger. She hardly ever hit any sort of mark. She had no proper sense of hunting at all. Her brother would be often completely disgusted with her. "You don't care whether you get the bird or not," he said. "That's no way to hunt." Miranda could not understand his indignation. She had seen him smash his hat and yell with fury when he had missed his aim. "What I like about shooting," said Miranda, with exasperating inconsequence, "is pulling the trigger and hearing the noise."

5   "Then, by golly," said Paul, "whyn't you go back to the range and shoot at bulls-eyes?"

"I'd just as soon," said Miranda, "only like this, we walk around more."

"Well, you just stay behind and stop spoiling my shots," said Paul, who, when he made a kill, wanted to be certain he had made it. Miranda, who alone brought down a bird once in twenty rounds, always claimed as her own any game they got when they fired at the same moment. It was tiresome and unfair and her brother was sick of it.

"Now, the first dove we see, or the first rabbit, is mine," he told her. "And the next will be yours. Remember that and don't get smarty."

"What about snakes?" asked Miranda idly. "Can I have the first snake?"

10   Waving her thumb gently and watching her gold ring glitter, Miranda lost interest in shooting. She was wearing her summer roughing outfit: dark blue overalls, a light blue shirt, a hired-man's straw hat, and thick brown sandals. Her brother had the same outfit except his was a sober hickory-nut color. Ordinarily Miranda preferred her overalls to any other dress, though it was making rather a scandal in the countryside, for the year was 1903, and in the back country the law of female decorum had teeth in it. Her father had been criticized for letting his girls dress like boys and go careering around astride bare-backed horses. Big sister Maria, the really independent and fearless one, in spite of her rather affected ways, rode at a dead run with only a rope knotted around her horse's nose. It was said the motherless family was running down, with the grandmother no longer there to hold it together. It was known that she had discriminated against her son Harry in her will, and that he was in straits about money. Some of his old neighbors reflected with vicious satisfaction that now he would probably not be so stiffnecked, nor have any more high-stepping horses either. Miranda knew this, though she could not say how. She had met along the road old women of the kind who smoked corn-cob pipes, who had treated her grandmother with most sincere respect. They slanted their gummy old eyes side-ways at the granddaughter and said, "Ain't you ashamed of yoself, Missy? It's aginst the Scriptures to dress like that. Whut yo Pappy thinkin about?" Miranda, with her powerful social sense, which was like a fine set of antennae radiating from every pore of her skin, would feel ashamed because she knew well it was rude and ill-bred to shock anybody, even bad-tempered old crones, though she had faith in her father's judgment and was perfectly comfortable in the clothes. Her father had said, "They're just what you need, and they'll save your dresses for school . . ." This sounded quite simple and natural to her. She had been brought up in rigorous economy. Wastefulness was vulgar. It was also a sin. These were truths; she had heard them repeated many times and never once disputed.

Now the ring, shining with the serene purity of fine gold on her rather grubby thumb, turned her feelings against her overalls and sockless feet, toes sticking through the thick brown leather straps. She wanted to go back to the farmhouse, take a good cold bath, dust herself with plenty of Maria's violet talcum powder—provided Maria was not present to object, of course—put on the thinnest, most becoming dress she owned, with a big sash, and sit in a wicker chair under the trees . . . These things were not all she wanted, of course; she had vague stirrings of desire for luxury and a grand way of living which could not take precise form in her imagination but were founded on family legend of past wealth and leisure. These immediate comforts were what she could have, and she wanted them at once. She lagged rather far behind Paul, and once she thought of just turning back without a word and going home. She stopped, thinking that Paul would never do that to her, and so she would have to tell him. When a rabbit leaped, she let Paul have it without dispute. He killed it with one shot.

When she came up with him, he was already kneeling, examining the wound, the rabbit trailing from his hands. "Right through the head," he said complacently, as if he had aimed for it. He took out his sharp, competent bowie knife and started to skin the body. He did it very cleanly and quickly. Uncle Jimbilly knew how to prepare the skins so that Miranda always had fur coats for her dolls, for though she never cared much for her dolls she liked seeing them in fur coats. The children knelt facing each other over the dead animal. Miranda watched admiringly while her brother stripped the skin away as if he were taking off a glove. The flayed flesh emerged dark scarlet, sleek, firm; Miranda with thumb and finger felt the long fine muscles with the silvery flat strips binding them to the joints. Brother lifted the oddly bloated belly. "Look," he said, in a low amazed voice. "It was going to have young ones."

Very carefully he slit the thin flesh from the center ribs to the flanks, and a scarlet bag appeared. He slit again and pulled the bag open, and there lay a bundle of tiny rabbits, each wrapped in a thin scarlet veil. The brother pulled these off and there they were, dark gray, their sleek wet down lying in minute even ripples, like a baby's head just washed, their unbelievably small delicate ears folded close, their little blind faces almost featureless.

Miranda said, "Oh, I want to *see*," under her breath. She looked and looked—excited but not frightened, for she was accustomed to the sight of animals killed in hunting—filled with pity and astonishment and a kind of shocked delight in the wonderful little creatures for their own sakes, they were so pretty. She touched one of them ever so carefully. "Ah, there's blood running over them," she said and began to tremble without knowing why. Yet she wanted most deeply to see and to know. Having seen, she felt at once as if she had known all along. The very memory of her former ignorance faded, she had always known just this. No one had ever told her anything outright, she had been rather unobservant of the animal life around her because she was so accustomed to animals. They seemed simply disorderly and unaccountably rude in their habits, but altogether natural and not very interesting. Her brother had spoken as if he had known about everything all along. He may have seen all this before. He had never said a word to her, but she knew now a part at least of what he knew. She understood a little of the secret, formless intuitions in her own mind and body, which had been clearing up, taking form, so gradually and so steadily she had not realized that she was learning what she had to know. Paul said cautiously, as if he were talking about something forbidden: "They were just about ready to be born." His voice dropped on the last word. "I know," said Miranda, "like kittens. I know, like babies." She was quietly and terribly agitated, standing again with her rifle under her arm, looking down at the bloody heap. "I don't want the skin," she said, "I won't have it." Paul buried the young rabbits again in their mother's body, wrapped the skin around her, carried her to a clump of sage bushes, and hid her away. He came out again at once and said to Miranda, with an eager friendliness, a confidential tone quite unusual in him, as if he were taking her into an important secret on equal terms: "Listen now. Now you listen to me, and don't ever forget. Don't you ever tell a living soul that you saw this. Don't tell a soul. Don't tell Dad because I'll get into trouble. He'll say I'm leading you into things you ought not to do. He's always saying that. So now don't you go and forget and blab out sometime the way you're always doing . . . Now, that's a secret. Don't you tell."

15   Miranda never told, she did not even wish to tell anybody. She thought about the whole worrisome affair with confused unhappiness for a few days. Then it sank quietly into her mind and was heaped over by accumulated thousands of impressions, for nearly twenty years. One day she was picking her path among the puddles and crushed refuse of a market street in a strange city of a strange country, when without warning, plain and clear in its true colors as if she looked through a frame upon a scene that had not stirred nor changed since the moment it happened, the episode of that far-off day leaped from its burial place before her mind's eye. She was so reasonlessly horrified she halted suddenly staring, the scene before her eyes dimmed by the vision back of them. An Indian vendor had held up before her a tray of dyed sugar sweets, in the shapes of all kinds of small creatures: birds, baby chicks, baby rabbits, lambs, baby pigs. They were in gay colors and smelled of vanilla, maybe. . . . It was a very hot day and the smell in the market, with its piles of raw flesh and wilting flowers, was like the mingled sweetness and corruption she had smelled that other day in the empty cemetery at home: the day she had remembered always until now vaguely as the time she and her brother had found treasure in the opened graves. Instantly upon this thought the dreadful vision faded, and she saw clearly her brother, whose childhood face she had forgotten, standing again in the blazing sunshine, again twelve years old, a pleased sober smile in his eyes, turning the silver dove over and over in his hands.

Comments and Questions

   1. Porter's stories are sometimes termed "lyric," which implies both an internal focus and an emphasis on an emotionally charged situation (to capture a mental state) rather than on developing a plot. Is "lyric" in that sense equally applicable to "Flowering Judas" above and to "The Grave"?

   2. One accomplishment of this story is to provide something of a psychological portrait of humankind, a depiction of the persistent, but unpredictable intimacy of the living present and the dead past in the human mind. Is such an intimacy essential in the continuity of self we call a memory, such as the one at the climax of Porter's story? Explain.

   3. How does the psychic juxtaposition of life and death relate to the cemetery scene with Miranda and Paul digging among the graves and to the scene with the dead rabbit shortly after?

   4. What is the symbolic significance of the silver dove and especially of the gold ring? What effect does the ring have on Miranda and her thoughts? How do these effects (and thoughts) relate to the theme of the story?

   5. Discuss the thematic pertinence of the very first sentence of the story. How does it relate directly to the last scene in the Mexican market street? Cite specific phrases that link the final scene with the opening paragraph and with the day Miranda remembers so vividly.

6. When do the two episodes of that remembered day first mingle their "sweetness and corruption" with conscious revelation for Miranda? Comment on her initial and final attitudes toward the memory.

James Joyce   (1882–1941)
Araby

North Richmond Street, being blind, was a quiet street except at the hour when the Christian Brothers' School set the boys free. An uninhabited house of two storeys stood at the blind end, detached from its neighbours in a square ground. The other houses of the street, conscious of decent lives within them, gazed at one another with brown imperturbable faces.

The former tenant of our house, a priest, had died in the back drawing-room. Air, musty from having been long enclosed, hung in all the rooms, and the waste room behind the kitchen was littered with old useless papers. Among these I found a few paper-covered books, the pages of which were curled and damp: *The Abbot,* by Walter Scott, *The Devout Communicant* and *The Memoirs of Vidocq.* I liked the last best because its leaves were yellow. The wild garden behind the house contained a central apple-tree and a few straggling bushes under one of which I found the late tenant's rusty bicycle-pump. He had been a very charitable priest; in his will he had left all his money to institutions and the furniture of his house to his sister.

When the short days of winter came dusk fell before we had well eaten our dinners. When we met in the street the houses had grown sombre. The space of sky above us was the colour of ever-changing violet and towards it the lamps of the street lifted their feeble lanterns. The cold air stung us and we played till our bodies glowed. Our shouts echoed in the silent street. The career of our play brought us through the dark muddy lanes behind the houses where we ran the gauntlet of the rough tribes from the cottages, to the back doors of the dark dripping gardens where odours arose from the ashpits, to the dark odorous stables where a coachman smoothed and combed the horse or shook music from the buckled harness. When we returned to the street light from the kitchen windows had filled the areas. If my uncle was seen turning the corner we hid in the shadow until we had seen him safely housed. Or if Mangan's sister came out on the doorstep to call her brother in to his tea we watched her from our shadow peer up and down the street. We waited to see whether she would remain or go in and, if she remained, we left our shadow and walked up to Mangan's steps resignedly. She was waiting for us, her figure defined by the light from the half-opened door. Her brother always teased her before he obeyed and I stood by the railings looking at her. Her dress swung as she moved her body and the soft rope of her hair tossed from side to side.

Every morning I lay on the floor in the front parlour watching her door. The blind was pulled down to within an inch of the sash so that I could not be seen. When she came out on the doorstep my heart leaped. I ran to the hall, seized my books and followed her. I kept her brown figure always in my eye and, when we came near the point at which our ways diverged, I quickened my pace and passed her. This happened morning after morning. I had never spoken to her, except for a few casual words, and yet her name was like a summons to all my foolish blood.

5   Her image accompanied me even in places the most hostile to romance. On Saturday evenings when my aunt went marketing I had to go to carry some of the parcels. We walked through the flaring streets, jostled by drunken men and bargaining women, amid the curses of labourers, the shrill litanies of shop-boys who stood on guard by the barrels of pigs' cheeks, the nasal chanting of street-singers, who sang a *come-all-you* about O'Donovan Rossa, or a ballad about the troubles in our native land. These noises converged in a single sensation of life for me: I imagined that I bore my chalice safely through a throng of foes. Her name sprang to my lips at moments in strange prayers and praises which I myself did not understand. My eyes were often full of tears (I could not tell why) and at times a flood from my heart seemed to pour itself out into my bosom. I thought little of the future. I did not know whether I would ever speak to her or not or, if I spoke to her, how I could tell her of my confused adoration. But my body was like a harp and her words and gestures were like fingers running upon the wires.

One evening I went into the back drawing-room in which the priest had died. It was a dark rainy evening and there was no sound in the house. Through one of the broken panes I heard the rain impinge upon the earth, the fine incessant needles of water playing in the sodden beds. Some distant lamp or lighted window gleamed below me. I was thankful that I could see so little. All my senses seemed to desire to veil themselves and, feeling that I was about to slip from them, I pressed the palms of my hands together until they trembled, murmuring: *"O love! O love!"* many times.

At last she spoke to me. When she addressed the first words to me I was so confused that I did not know what to answer. She asked me was I going to *Araby*. I forgot whether I answered yes or no. It would be a splendid bazaar, she said she would love to go.

"And why can't you?" I asked.

While she spoke she turned a silver bracelet round and round her wrist. She could not go, she said, because there would be a retreat that week in her convent. Her brother and two other boys were fighting for their caps and I was alone at the railings. She held one of the spikes, bowing her head towards me. The light from the lamp opposite our door caught the white curve of her neck, lit up her hair that rested there and, falling, lit up the hand upon the railing. It fell over one side of her dress and caught the white border of a petticoat, just visible as she stood at ease.

10   "It's well for you," she said.

"If I go," I said, "I will bring you something."

What innumerable follies laid waste my waking and sleeping thoughts after that evening! I wished to annihilate the tedious intervening days. I chafed against the work of school. At night in my bedroom and by day in the classroom her image came between me and the page I strove to read. The syllables of the word *Araby* were called to me through the silence in which my soul luxuriated and cast an Eastern enchantment over me. I asked for leave to go to the bazaar on Saturday night. My aunt was surprised and hoped it was not some Freemason affair. I answered few questions in class. I watched my master's face pass from amiability to sternness; he hoped I was not beginning to idle. I could not call my wandering thoughts together. I had hardly any patience with the serious work of life which, now that it stood between me and my desire, seemed to me child's play, ugly monotonous child's play.

On Saturday morning I reminded my uncle that I wished to go to the bazaar in the evening. He was fussing at the hallstand, looking for the hat-brush, and answered me curtly:

"Yes, boy, I know."

15   As he was in the hall I could not go into the front parlour and lie at the window. I left the house in bad humour and walked slowly towards the school. The air was pitilessly raw and already my heart misgave me.

When I came home to dinner my uncle had not yet been home. Still it was early. I sat staring at the clock for some time and, when its ticking began to irritate me, I left the room. I mounted the staircase and gained the upper part of the house. The high cold empty gloomy rooms liberated me and I went from room to room singing. From the front window I saw my companions playing below in the street. Their cries reached me weakened and indistinct and, leaning my forehead against the cool glass, I looked over at the dark house where she lived. I may have stood there for an hour, seeing nothing but the brown-clad figure cast by my imagination, touched discreetly by the lamplight at the curved neck, at the hand upon the railings and at the border below the dress.

When I came downstairs again I found Mrs. Mercer sitting at the fire. She was an old garrulous woman, a pawnbroker's widow, who collected used stamps for some pious purpose. I had to endure the gossip of the tea-table. The meal was prolonged beyond an hour and still my uncle did not come. Mrs. Mercer stood up to go: she was sorry she couldn't wait any longer, but it was after eight o'clock and she did not like to be out late, as the night air was bad for her. When she had gone I began to walk up and down the room, clenching my fists. My aunt said:

"I'm afraid you may put off your bazaar for this night of Our Lord."

At nine o'clock I heard my uncle's latchkey in the halldoor. I heard him talking to himself and heard the hallstand rocking when it had received the weight of his overcoat. I could interpret these signs. When he was midway through his dinner I asked him to give me the money to go to the bazaar. He had forgotten.

20   "The people are in bed and after their first sleep now," he said.

I did not smile. My aunt said to him energetically:

"Can't you give him the money and let him go? You've kept him late enough as it is."

My uncle said he was very sorry he had forgotten. He said he believed in the old saying: "All work and no play makes Jack a dull boy." He asked me where I was going and, when I had told him a second time he asked me did I know *The Arab's Farewell to His Steed.* When I left the kitchen he was about to recite the opening lines of the piece to my aunt.

I held a florin tightly in my hand as I strode down Buckingham Street towards the station. The sight of the streets thronged with buyers and glaring with gas recalled to me the purpose of my journey. I took my seat in a third-class carriage of a deserted train. After an intolerable delay the train moved out of the station slowly. It crept onward among ruinous houses and over the twinkling river. At Westland Row Station a crowd of people pressed to the carriage doors; but the porters moved them back, saying that it was a special train for the bazaar. I remained alone in the bare carriage. In a few minutes the train drew up beside an improvised wooden platform. I passed out on to the road and saw by the lighted dial of a clock that it was ten minutes to ten. In front of me was a large building which displayed the magical name.

25   I could not find any sixpenny entrance and, fearing that the bazaar would be closed, I passed in quickly through a turnstile, handing a shilling to a weary-looking man. I found myself in a big hall girdled at half its height by a gallery. Nearly all the stalls were closed and the greater part of the hall was in darkness. I recognized a silence like that which pervades a church after a service. I walked into the centre of the bazaar timidly. A few people were gathered about the stalls which were still open. Before a curtain, over which the words *Café Chantant* were written in coloured lamps, two men were counting money on a salver. I listened to the fall of the coins.

Remembering with difficulty why I had come I went over to one of the stalls and examined porcelain vases and flowered tea-sets. At the door of the stall a young lady was talking and laughing with two young gentlemen. I remarked their English accents and listened vaguely to their conversation.

"O, I never said such a thing!"

"O, but you did!"

"O, but I didn't!"

30   "Didn't she say that?"

"Yes. I heard her."

"O, there's a . . . fib!"

Observing me the young lady came over and asked me did I wish to buy anything. The tone of her voice was not encouraging; she seemed to have spoken to me out of a sense of duty. I looked humbly at the great jars that stood like eastern guards at either side of the dark entrance to the stall and murmured:

"No, thank you."

35   The young lady changed the position of one of the vases and went back to the two young men. They began to talk of the same subject. Once or twice the young lady glanced at me over her shoulder.

I lingered before her stall, though I knew my stay was useless, to make my interest in her wares seem the more real. Then I turned away slowly and walked down the middle of the bazaar. I allowed the two pennies to fall against the sixpence in my pocket. I heard a voice call from one end of the gallery that the light was out. The upper part of the hall was now completely dark.

Gazing up into the darkness I saw myself as a creature driven and derided by vanity; and my eyes burned with anguish and anger.

John Updike (1932–   )
The Astronomer

I feared his visit. I was twenty-four, and the religious revival within myself was at its height. Earlier that summer, I had discovered Kierkegaard[1], and each week I brought back to the apartment one more of the Princeton University Press's elegant and expensive editions of his works. They were beautiful books, sometimes very thick, sometimes very thin, always typographically exhilarating, with their welter of title pages, subheads, epigraphs, emphatic italics, italicized catchwords taken from German philosophy and too subtle for translation, translator's prefaces and footnotes, and Kierkegaard's own endless footnotes, blanketing pages at a time as, crippled, agonized by distinctions, he scribbled on and on, heaping irony on irony, curse on curse, gnashing, sneering, praising Jehovah in the privacy

[1] Controversial Danish philosopher, Protestant theologian, and founder of modern existentialism (1813–1855). Kierkegaard ridiculed as irreligious all Hegelian attempts to justify Christianity on rational, objective grounds, insisting instead on the necessity of individual choice (between the world and Christ) based on faith; hence Kierkegaard opposed scientific "objectivity" by equating truth with subjectivity.

of his empty home in Copenhagen. The demons with which he wrestled—Hegel and his avatars—were unknown to me, so Kierkegaard at his desk seemed to me to be writhing in the clutch of phantoms, slapping at silent mosquitoes, twisting furiously to confront presences that were not there. It was a spectacle unlike any I had ever seen in print before, and it brought me much comfort during those August and September evenings, while the traffic on the West Side Highway swished tirelessly and my wife tinkled the supper dishes in our tiny kitchenette.

We lived at the time on the sixth floor of a building on Riverside Drive, and overlooked the Hudson. The river would become black before the sky, and the little Jersey towns on the far bank would be pinched between two massive tongs of darkness until only a row of sparks remained. These embers were reflected in the black water, and when a boat went dragging its wake up the river the reflections would tremble, double, fragment, and not until long after the shadow of the boat passed reconstruct themselves.

The astronomer was a remnant of our college days. Two years had passed since we had seen him. When Harriet and I were both undergraduates, another couple, a married couple, had introduced him to us. The wife of this couple had gone to school with Harriet, and the husband was a teaching associate of the astronomer; so Bela and I were the opposite ends of a chain. He was a Hungarian. His parents had fled the terror of Kun's regime; they were well-to-do. From Vienna they had come to London; from there Bela had gone to Oxford, and from there come to this country, years ago. He was forty, a short, thickset man with a wealth of stiff black hair, combed straight back without a parting, like a Slav bicyclist. Only a few individual hairs had turned white. He gave an impression of abnormal density; his anatomical parts seemed set one on top of the other without any loose space between for leeway or accommodation of his innards. A motion in his foot instantly jerked his head. The Magyar cheekbones gave his face a blunt, aggressive breadth; he wore steel-rimmed glasses that seemed several sizes too small. He was now teaching at Columbia. Brilliant, he rarely deigned to publish papers, so that his brilliance was carried around with him as undiminished potency. He liked my wife. Like Kierkegaard, he was a bachelor, and in the old days his flirtatious compliments, rolled out with a rich, slow British accent and a broad-mouthed, thoughtful smile across a cafeteria table or after dinner in our friends' living room, made me feel foolish and incapable; she was not my wife then. "Ah, Harri-et, Harri-et," he would call, giving the last syllable of her name a full, French, roguish weight, "come and sit by me on this Hide-a-bed." And then he would pat the cushion beside him, which his own weight had caused to lift invitingly. Somewhat more than a joke, it was nevertheless not rude to me; I did not have enough presence in his eyes to receive rudeness.

He had an air of seeing beyond me, of seeing into the interstellar structure of things, of having transcended, except perhaps in the niggling matter of lust, the clouds of human subjectivity—vaporous hopes supported by immaterial rationalizations. It was his vigorous, clear vision that I feared.

5   When he came into our apartment, directing warmth into all its corners with brisk handshakes and abrupt pivotings of his whole frame, he spotted the paperback *Meno* that I had been reading, back and forth on the subway, two pages per stop. It is the dialogue in which Socrates, to demonstrate the existence of indwelling knowledge, elicits some geometrical truths from a small boy. "My Lord, Walter," Bela said, "why are you reading this? Is this the one where he proves two and two equals four?" And thus quickly, at a mere wink from this atheist, Platonism and all its attendant cathedrals came tumbling down.

We ate dinner by the window, from which the Hudson appeared a massive rent opened in a tenuous web of light. Though we talked trivially, about friends and events, I felt the structure I had painstakingly built up within myself wasting away; my faith (existentialism padded out with Chesterton), my prayers, my churchgoing (to a Methodist edifice where the spiritual void of the inner city reigned above the fragile hats of a dozen old ladies and the minister shook my hand at the door with a look of surprise on his face), all dwindled to the thinnest filaments of illusion, and in one flash, I knew, they would burn to nothing. I felt behind his eyes immensities of space and gas, seemed to see with him through my own evanescent body into gigantic systems of dead but furious matter, suns like match heads, planets like cinders, galaxies that were whirls of ash, and beyond them, more galaxies, and more, fleeing with sickening speed beyond the rim that our most powerful telescopes could reach. I had once heard him explain, in a cafeteria, how the white dwarf star called the companion of Sirius is so dense that light radiating from it is tugged back by gravitation toward the red end of the spectrum.

My wife took our dessert dishes away; before she brought coffee, I emptied the last of the red wine into our glasses. Bela lit a cigar and, managing its fresh length and the wineglass with his electric certainty of touch, talked. Knowing that, since the principal business of my employment was to invent the plots of television commercials, I was to some extent a humorist, he told me of a parody he had seen of the B.B.C. Third Programme. It involved Bertrand Russell reading the first five hundred decimal places of π, followed by twenty minutes of silent meditation led by Mr. T. S. Eliot, and then Bertrand Russell reading the *next* five hundred places of π.

If my laughter burst out excessively, it was because his acknowledgment, though minimal and oblique, that Bertrand Russell might by some conception be laughable and that meditation and the author of "Little Gidding" did at least *exist* momentarily relieved me of the strain of maintaining against the pressure of his latent opinions my own superstitious, fainthearted identity. This small remission of his field of force admitted worlds of white light, and my wife, returning to the room holding with bare arms at the level of our eyes a tray on which an old tin pot and three china demitasse cups stated their rectangular silhouettes, seemed a creature of intense beauty.

"Ah, Harri-et, Harri-et," Bela said, lowering his cigar, "married life has not dimmed thy lustre."

10　　　My wife blushed, rather too readily—her skin had always been discomfitingly quick to answer his praise—and set the tray on the table and took her chair and served us. Mixing wine and coffee in our mouths, we listened to Bela tell of when he first came to this country. He was an instructor in general science at a university in Michigan. The thermometer stayed at zero for months, the students carved elaborate snow sculptures on the campus, everyone wore ear muffs and unbuckled galoshes. At first, he couldn't believe in the ear muffs; they looked like something you would find among the most secluded peasantry of Central Europe. It had taken him months to muster the courage to go into a shop and ask for such childish things. But at last he had, and had been very happy in them. They were very sensible. He continued to wear them, though in the East they did not seem to be the fashion.

"I know," Harriet said. "In the winter here, you see all these poor Madison Avenue men—"

"Such as Walter," Bela smoothly interceded, shaping his cigar ash on the edge of his saucer.

"Well, yes, except it doesn't look so bad with him because he never cuts his hair. But all these other men with their tight little hats on the top of their haircuts right in the dead of this damp, windy winter—their ears are bright red in the subway."

"And the girls," Bela said, "the girls in the Midwest wear *immense puffs,* as big around as—" He cupped his hands, fingers spread, over his ears and, hunching his head down on his thick brief neck, darted glances at us in a startled way. He had retained, between two fingers, the cigar, so his head seemed to have sprouted, rather low, one smoking horn. His hands darted away, his chest expanded and became rigid as he tried to embrace, for us, the sense of these remote pompoms. "White, woolly," he said sharply, giving each adjective a lecturer's force; then the words glided as he suddenly exhaled, "They're like the snowballs that girls in your ice shows wear on their breasts." He pronounced the two *s*'s in "breasts" so distinctly it seemed the radiator had hissed.

15   It surprised us that he had ever seen an ice show. We had not thought of him as a sightseer. But it turned out that in those first years he had inspected the country thoroughly. He had bought an old Dodge one summer and driven all around the West by himself. With incongruous piety, he had visited the Grand Canyon, Yosemite, a Sioux reservation. He described a long stretch of highway in New Mexico. "There are these black hills. Utterly without vegetation. Great, heavy, almost purplish folds, unimaginably ugly, mile after mile after mile. Not a gas station, not a sign of green. Nothing." And his face, turning rapidly from one to the other of us, underwent an expression I had never before seen him wear. His black eyebrows shot up in two arches stretching his eyelids smooth, and his upper lip tightened over his lower, which was retracted in a way that indicated it was being delicately pinched between his teeth. This expression, bestowed in silence and swiftly erased, confessed what he could not pronounce: He had been frightened.

On the table, below our faces, the cups and glasses broken into shards by shadows, the brown dregs of coffee and wine, the ashtrays and the ashes were hastily swept together into a little heap of warm dark tones distinct from the universal debris.

That is all I remember. The mingle on the table was only part of the greater confusion as in the heat of rapport our unrelated spirits and pasts scrambled together, bringing everything in the room with them, including the rubble of footnotes bound into Kierkegaard. In memory, perhaps because we lived on the sixth floor, this scene—this invisible scene—seems to take place at a great height, as if we were the residents of a star suspended against the darkness of the city and the river. What is the past, after all, but a vast sheet of darkness in which a few moments, pricked apparently at random, shine?

Comments and Questions

1. How do the first two sentences establish the central conflict of the story?

2. Analyze the unusually long fourth sentence. How is the sentence structure itself especially functional, revealing of character and situation? Support your response by reference to a later scene and sentence in particular. Why does the narrator take special "comfort" from the Kierkegaard books? Can you relate the final adverb clause to other aspects of the paragraph? How is the setting described in the second paragraph especially pertinent and suggestive?

3. How are the physical characteristics of Bela appropriate to his role in the story, to his intellectual qualities, to the narrator's fear at the outset?

4. The fact that Bela is an astronomer is given special emphasis in the title. Why? Imagery suggestive of astronomy is used to describe the physical setting, the state of mind of the narrator, and so on. What does the use of the imagery contribute to the story? Is there thematic irony in the use of astronomical imagery in the final sentence? Is there irony in the phrase "pricked apparently at random" in that sentence? Comment on other astronomical imagery in the final paragraph. Does such imagery function symbolically in the story?

5. What is Harriet's function? Comment on the phrasing, the double significance, and the juxtaposition of the two sentences: "Brilliant, he rarely deigned to publish papers, so that his brilliance was carried around with him as undiminished potency. He liked my wife." Locate similar sentences elsewhere in the story.

6. How do the allusions to Bertrand Russell and especially to T. S. Eliot and "Little Gidding" contribute to the story?

7. How is the foreground conflict in the story (between Walter and Bela) resolved? How is the resolution particularly ironic? Is it suggestive of a larger resolution? What earlier indications are there that Bela, after all, had not entirely transcended some rather typical qualities of human nature?

Franz Kafka   (1883–1924)
A Hunger Artist

This story is an allegory in the sense that the symbols which are embodied in characters, events, and natural objects represent ideas. In most allegory, as for example John Bunyan's *The Pilgrim's Progress,* 1678, the symbols can be translated into equivalents which remain constant throughout the story. But in "A Hunger Artist" Kafka has used his symbols to produce more than one level of meaning (compare Hawthorne's stories above), each one used to dramatize a different theme. Is the story "about" the artist in an alien society, "about" religion—or possibly both and even more? On the problem of reading Kafka, Albert Camus offers some help: "The whole art of Kafka consists in forcing the reader to reread. . . . Sometimes there is a double possibility of interpretation. . . . This is what the author wanted. But it would be wrong to try to interpret everything in Kafka in detail. A symbol is always in general and, however precise its translation, an artist can restore to it only its movement: there is no word-for-word rendering" (*The Myth of Sisyphus,* 1955).

During these last decades the interest in professional fasting has markedly diminished. It used to pay very well to stage such great performances under one's own management, but today that is quite impossible. We live in a different world now. At one time the whole town took a lively interest in the hunger artist; from day to day of his fast the excitement mounted; everybody wanted to see him at least once a day; there were people who bought season tickets for the last few days and sat from morning till night in front of his small barred cage; even in the nighttime there were visiting hours, when the whole effect was heightened by torch flares; on fine days the cage was set out in the open air, and then it was the children's special treat to see the hunger artist; for their elders he was often just a joke that happened to be in fashion, but the children stood open-mouthed, holding each other's hands for greater security, marveling at him as he sat there pallid in black tights, with his ribs sticking out so prominently, not even on a seat but down among straw on the ground, sometimes giving a courteous nod, answering questions with a constrained smile, or perhaps stretching an arm through the bars so that one might feel how thin it was, and then again withdrawing deep into himself, paying no attention to anyone or anything, not even to the all-important striking of the clock that was the only piece of furniture in his cage, but merely staring into vacancy with half-shut eyes, now and then taking a sip from a tiny glass of water to moisten his lips.

Besides casual onlookers there were also relays of permanent watchers selected by the public, usually butchers, strangely enough, and it was their task to watch the hunger artist day and night, three of them at a time, in case he should have some secret recourse to nourishment. This was nothing but a formality, instituted to reassure the masses, for the initiates knew well enough that during his fast the artist would never in any circumstances, not even under forcible compulsion, swallow the smallest morsel of food; the honor of his profession forbade it. Not every watcher, of course, was capable of understanding this, there were often groups of night watchers who were very lax in carrying out their duties and deliberately huddled together in a retired corner to play cards with great absorption, obviously intending to give the hunger artist the chance of a little refreshment, which they supposed he could draw from some private hoard. Nothing annoyed the artist more than such watchers; they made him miserable; they made his fast seem unendurable; sometimes he mastered his feebleness sufficiently to sing during their watch for as long as he could keep going, to show them how unjust their suspicions were. But that was of little use; they only wondered at his cleverness in being able to fill his mouth even while singing. Much more to his taste were the watchers who sat close up to the bars, who were not content with the dim night lighting of the hall but focused him in the full glare of the electric pocket torch given them by the impresario. The harsh light did not trouble him at all. In any case he could never sleep properly, and he could always drowse a little, whatever the light, at any hour, even when the hall was thronged with noisy onlookers. He was quite happy at the prospect of spending a sleepless night with such watchers; he was ready to exchange jokes with them, to tell them stories out of his nomadic life, anything at all to keep them awake and demonstrate to them again that he had no eatables in his cage and that he was fasting as not one of them could fast. But his happiest moment was when the morning came and an enormous breakfast was brought them, at his expense, on which they flung themselves with the keen appetite of healthy men after a weary night of wakefulness. Of course there were people who argued that this breakfast was an unfair attempt to bribe the watchers, but that was going rather too far, and when they were invited to take on a night's vigil without a breakfast, merely for the sake of the cause, they made themselves scarce, although they stuck stubbornly to their suspicions.

Such suspicions, anyhow, were a necessary accompaniment to the profession of fasting. No one could possibly watch the hunger artist continuously, day and night, and so no one could produce first-hand evidence that the fast had really been rigorous and continuous; only the artist himself could know that; he was therefore bound to be the sole completely satisfied spectator of his own fast. Yet for other reasons he was never satisfied; it was not perhaps mere fasting that had brought him to such skeleton thinness that many people had regretfully to keep away from his exhibitions, because the sight of him was too much for them, perhaps it was dissatisfaction with himself that had worn him down. For he alone knew, what no other initiate knew, how easy it was to fast. It was the easiest thing in the world. He made no secret of this, yet people did not believe him; at the best they set him down as modest, most of them, however, thought he was out for publicity or else was some kind of cheat who found it easy to fast because he had discovered a way of making it easy, and then had the impudence to admit the fact, more or less. He had to put up with all that, and in the course of time had got used to it, but his inner dissatisfaction always rankled, and never yet, after any term of fasting—this must be granted to his credit—had he left the cage of his own free will. The longest period of fasting was fixed by his impresario at forty days, beyond that term he was not allowed to go, not even in great cities, and there was good reason for it, too. Experience had proved that for about forty days the interest of the public could be stimulated by a steadily increasing pressure of advertisement, but after that the town began to lose interest, sympathetic support began notably to fall off; there were of course local variations as between one town and another or one country and another, but as a general rule forty days marked the limit. So on the fortieth day the flower-bedecked cage was opened, enthusiastic spectators filled the hall, a military band played, two doctors entered the cage to measure the results of the fast, which were announced through a megaphone, and finally two young ladies appeared, blissful at having been selected for the honor, to help the hunger artist down the few steps leading to a small table on which was spread a carefully chosen invalid repast. And at this very moment the artist always turned stubborn. True, he would entrust his bony arms to the outstretched helping hands of the ladies bending over him, but stand up he would not. Why stop fasting at this particular moment, after forty days of it? He had held out for a long time, an illimitably long time; why stop now, when he was in his best fasting form, or rather, not quite in his best fasting form? Why should he be cheated of the fame he would get for fasting longer, for being not only the record hunger artist of all time, which presumably he was already, but for beating his own record by a performance beyond human imagination, since he felt that there were no limits to his capacity for fasting? His public pretended to admire him so much, why should it have so little patience with him; if he could endure fasting longer, why shouldn't the public endure it? Besides, he was tired, he was comfortable sitting in the straw, and now he was supposed to lift himself to his full height and go down to a meal the very thought of which gave him a nausea that only the presence of the ladies kept him from betraying, and even that with an effort. And he looked up into the eyes of the ladies who were apparently so friendly and in reality so cruel, and shook his head, which felt too heavy on its strengthless neck. But then there happened yet again what always happened. The impresario came forward, without a word—for the band made speech impossible —lifted his arms in the air above the artist, as if inviting Heaven to look down upon its creature here in the straw, this suffering martyr, which indeed he was, although in quite another sense; grasped him round the emaciated waist, with exaggerated caution, so that the frail condition he was in might be appreciated; and committed him to the care of the blenching ladies, not without secretly giving him a shaking so that his legs and body tottered and swayed. The artist now submitted completely; his head lolled on his breast as if it had landed there by chance; his body was hollowed out; his legs in a spasm of self-preservation clung close to each other at the knees, yet scraped on the ground as if it were not really solid ground, as if they were only trying to find solid ground; and the whole weight of his body, a feather-weight after all, relapsed onto one of the ladies, who, looking round for help and panting a little— this post of honor was not at all what she had expected it to be—first stretched her neck as far as she could to keep her face at least free from contact with the artist, then finding this impossible, and her more fortunate companion not coming to her aid but merely holding extended on her own trembling hand the little bunch of knucklebones that was the artist's, to the great delight of the spectators burst into tears and had to be replaced by an attendant who had long been stationed in readiness. Then came the food, a little of which the impresario managed to get between the artist's lips, while he sat in a kind of half-fainting trance, to the accompaniment of cheerful patter designed to distract the public's attention from the artist's condition; after that, a toast was drunk to the public, supposedly prompted by a whisper from the artist in the impresario's ear; the band confirmed it with a mighty flourish, the spectators melted away, and no one had any cause to be dissatisfied with the proceedings, no one except the hunger artist himself, he only, as always.

So he lived for many years, with small regular intervals of recuperation, in visible glory, honored by the world, yet in spite of that troubled in spirit, and all the more troubled because no one would take his trouble seriously. What comfort could he possibly need? What more could he possibly wish for? And if some good-natured person, feeling sorry for him, tried to console him by pointing out that his melancholy was probably caused by fasting, it could happen, especially when he had been fasting for some time, that he reacted with an outburst of fury and to the general alarm began to shake the bars of his cage like a wild animal. Yet the impresario had a way of punishing these outbreaks which he rather enjoyed putting into operation. He would apologize publicly for the artist's behavior, which was only to be excused, he admitted, because of the irritability caused by fasting; a condition hardly to be understood by well-fed people; then by natural transition he went on to mention the artist's equally incomprehensible boast that he could fast for much longer than he was doing; he praised the high ambition, the good will, the great self-denial undoubtedly implicit in such a statement; and then quite simply countered it by bringing out photographs, which were also on sale to the public, showing the artist on the fortieth day of a fast lying in bed almost dead from exhaustion. This perversion of the truth, familiar to the artist though it was, always unnerved him afresh and proved too much for him. What was a consequence of the premature ending of his fast was here presented as the cause of it! To fight against this lack of understanding, against a whole world of non-understanding was impossible. Time and again in good faith he stood by the bars listening to the impresario, but as soon as the photographs appeared he always let go and sank with a groan back on to his straw, and the reassured public could once more come close and gaze at him.

5   A few years later when the witnesses of such scenes called them to mind, they often failed to understand themselves at all. For meanwhile the aforementioned change in public interest had set in; it seemed to happen almost overnight; there may have been profound causes for it, but who was going to bother about that; at any rate the pampered hunger artist suddenly found himself deserted one fine day by the amusement seekers, who went streaming past him to other more favored attractions. For the last time the impresario hurried him over half Europe to discover whether the old interest might still survive here and there; all in vain; everywhere, as if by secret agreement, a positive revulsion from professional fasting was in evidence. Of course it could not really have sprung up so suddenly as all that, and many premonitory symptoms which had not been sufficiently remarked or suppressed during the rush and glitter of success now came retrospectively to mind, but it was now too late to take any countermeasures. Fasting would surely come into fashion again at some future date, yet that was no comfort for those living in the present. What, then, was the hunger artist to do? He had been applauded by thousands in his time and could hardly come down to showing himself in a street booth at village fairs, and as for adopting another profession, he was not only too old for that but too fanatically devoted to fasting. So he took leave of the impresario, his partner in an unparalleled career, and hired himself to a large circus; in order to spare his own feelings he avoided reading the conditions of his contract.

A large circus with its enormous traffic in replacing and recruiting men, animals and apparatus can always find a use for people at any time, even for a hunger artist, provided of course that he does not ask too much, and in this particular case anyhow it was not only the artist who was taken on but his famous and long-known name as well; indeed considering the peculiar nature of his performance, which was not impaired by advancing age, it could not be objected that here was an artist past his prime, no longer at the height of his professional skill, seeking a refuge in some quiet corner of a circus; on the contrary, the hunger artist averred that he could fast as well as ever, which was entirely credible; he even alleged that if he were allowed to fast as he liked, and this was at once promised him without more ado, he could astound the world by establishing a record never yet achieved, a statement which certainly provoked a smile among the other professionals, since it left out of account the change in public opinion, which the hunger artist in his zeal conveniently forgot.

He had not, however, actually lost his sense of the real situation and took it as a matter of course that he and his cage should be stationed, not in the middle of the ring as a main attraction, but outside, near the animal cages, on a site that was after all easily accessible. Large and gaily painted placards made a frame for the cage and announced what was to be seen inside it. When the public came thronging out in the intervals to see the animals, they could hardly avoid passing the hunger artist's cage and stopping there for a moment, perhaps they might even have stayed longer had not those pressing behind them in the narrow gangway, who did not understand why they should be held up on their way towards the excitements of the menagerie, made it impossible for anyone to stand gazing quietly for any length of time. And that was the reason why the hunger artist, who had of course been looking forward to these visiting hours as the main achievement of his life, began instead to shrink from them. At first he could hardly wait for the intervals; it was exhilarating to watch the crowds come streaming his way, until only too soon—not even the most obstinate self-deception, clung to almost consciously, could hold out against the fact—the conviction was borne in upon him that these people, most of them, to judge from their actions, again and again, without exception, were all on their way to the menagerie. And the first sight of them from the distance remained the best. For when they reached his cage he was at once deafened by the storm of shouting and abuse that arose from the two contending factions, which renewed themselves continuously, of those who wanted to stop and stare at him—he soon began to dislike them more than the others— not out of real interest but only out of obstinate self-assertiveness, and those who wanted to go straight on to the animals. When the first great rush was past, the stragglers came along, and these, whom nothing could have prevented from stopping to look at him as long as they had breath, raced past with long strides, hardly even glancing at him, in their haste to get to the menagerie in time. And all too rarely did it happen that he had a stroke of luck, when some father of a family fetched up before him with his children, pointed a finger at the hunger artist and explained at length what the phenomenon meant, telling stories of earlier years when he himself had watched similar but much more thrilling performances, and the children, still rather uncomprehending, since neither inside nor outside school had they been sufficiently prepared for this lesson—what did they care about fasting?—yet showed by the brightness of their intent eyes that new and better times might be coming. Perhaps, said the hunger artist to himself many a time, things would be a little better if his cage were set not quite so near the menagerie. That made it too easy for people to make their choice, to say nothing of what he suffered from the stench of the menagerie, the animals' restlessness by night, the carrying past of raw lumps of flesh for the beasts of prey, the roaring at feeding times, which depressed him continually. But he did not dare to lodge a complaint with the management; after all, he had the animals to thank for the troops of people who passed his cage, among whom there might always be one here and there to take an interest in him, and who could tell where they might seclude him if he called attention to his existence and thereby to the fact that, strictly speaking, he was only an impediment on the way to the menagerie.

A small impediment, to be sure, one that grew steadily less. People grew familiar with the strange idea that they could be expected, in times like these, to take an interest in a hunger artist, and with this familiarity the verdict went out against him. He might fast as much as he could, and he did so; but nothing could save him now, people passed him by. Just try to explain to anyone the art of fasting! Anyone who has no feeling for it cannot be made to understand it. The fine placards grew dirty and illegible, they were torn down; the little notice board telling the number of fast days achieved, which at first was changed carefully every day, had long stayed at the same figure, for after the first few weeks even this small task seemed pointless to the staff; and so the artist simply fasted on and on, as he had once dreamed of doing, and it was no trouble to him, just as he had always foretold, but no one counted the days, no one, not even the artist himself, knew what records he was already breaking, and his heart grew heavy. And when once in a time some leisurely passer-by stopped, made merry over the old figure on the board and spoke of swindling, that was in its way the stupidest lie ever invented by indifference and inborn malice, since it was not the hunger artist who was cheating; he was working honestly, but the world was cheating him of his reward.

Many more days went by, however, and that too came to an end. An overseer's eye fell on the cage one day and he asked the attendants why this perfectly good cage should be left standing there unused with dirty straw inside it; nobody knew, until one man, helped out by the notice board, remembered about the hunger artist. They poked into the straw with sticks and found him in it. "Are you still fasting?" asked the overseer. "When on earth do you mean to stop?" "Forgive me, everybody," whispered the hunger artist; only the overseer, who had his ear to the bars, understood him. "Of course," said the overseer, and tapped his forehead with a finger to let the attendants know what state the man was in, "we forgive you." "I always wanted you to admire my fasting," said the hunger artist. "We do admire it," said the overseer, affably. "But you shouldn't admire it," said the hunger artist. "Well, then we don't admire it," said the overseer, "but why shouldn't we admire it?" "Because I have to fast, I can't help it," said the hunger artist. "What a fellow you are," said the overseer, "and why can't you help it?" "Because," said the hunger artist, lifting his head a little and speaking, with his lips pursed, as if for a kiss, right into the overseer's ear, so that no syllable might be lost, "because I couldn't find the food I liked. If I had found it, believe me, I should have made no fuss and stuffed myself like you or anyone else." These were his last words, but in his dimming eyes remained the firm though no longer proud persuasion that he was still continuing to fast.

10   "Well, clear this out now!" said the overseer, and they buried the hunger artist, straw and all. Into the cage they put a young panther. Even the most insensitive felt it refreshing to see this wild creature leaping around the cage that had so long been dreary. The panther was all right. The food he liked was brought him without hesitation by the attendants; he seemed not even to miss his freedom; his noble body, furnished almost to the bursting point with all that it needed, seemed to carry freedom around with it too; somewhere in his jaws it seemed to lurk; and the joy of life streamed with such ardent passion from his throat that for the onlookers it was not easy to stand the shock of it. But they braced themselves, crowded round the cage, and did not want ever to move away.

Jean-Paul Sartre   (1905–1980)
The Wall

Sartre's story is commonly read as a dramatization of some basic aspects of existentialism,* a theory of existence that emerged in France after World War II and helped to generate the literature of the absurd of the new lost generation. Existentialism is essentially a philosophy of revolt against nineteenth-century rationalism that perceived and understood reality through the intellect. It rejects such speculation about reality and finds reality in the experience of the individual. It finds no purpose or meaning inherent in the universe, and leaves morality to the individual who must arrive at his own code through experience. As Albert Camus observes, "The fact that certain great novelists have chosen to write in terms of images rather than of arguments reveals a great deal about a certain kind of thinking common to them all, a conviction of the futility of all explanatory principles, and of the instructive message of sensory impressions." And Sartre, sometimes referred to as the high priest of existentialism, speaking of Camus, says he "is very much at peace within disorder. Nature's obstinate blindness probably irritates him, but it comforts him as well. Its irrationality is only a negative thing. The absurd man is a humanist; he knows only the good things in the world." These two quotations put together seem to arrive at the heart of existentialism: the futility of trying to explain life through reason and the irrationality of nature and the universe. (See Updike's "The Astronomer," p. 116, and Hardy's "Hap," p. 430.)

The setting of "The Wall" is the Spanish Civil War of 1936–1939. The story belongs to Pablo Ibbieta, the narrator, who is probably the voice of Sartre. The question is, Why is Pablo prepared to die differently from Tom Steinbock and Juan Mirbal? He could have probably saved his life by betraying Ramon Gris. Why does Pablo finally say, "I laughed so hard the tears came to my eyes"? The answer lies, of course, in the kind of absurd world Pablo has experienced, the kind the existentialist rejects.

For two essays that are relevant to the debate over values in contemporary literature, see MacLeish, "Who Precisely Do You Think You Are?" p. 1156 and Krutch, "The Tragic Fallacy," p. 1112.

They pushed us into a large white room and my eyes began to blink because the light hurt them. Then I saw a table and four fellows seated at the table, civilians, looking at some papers. The other prisoners were herded together at one end and we were obliged to cross the entire room to join them. There were several I knew, and others who must have been foreigners. The two in front of me were blond with round heads. They looked alike. I imagine they were French. The smaller one kept pulling at his trousers, out of nervousness.

This lasted about three hours. I was dog-tired and my head was empty. But the room was well-heated, which struck me as rather agreeable; we had not stopped shivering for twenty-four hours. The guards led the prisoners in one after the other in front of the table. Then the four fellows asked them their names and what they did. Most of the time that

---

* The serious student who wishes to explore existentialism will find these sources helpful: Jean-Paul Sartre, *Existentialism,* New York: Philosophical Library; London: Methuen and Company, 1947; Walter Kaufmann, *Existentialism from Dostoevsky to Sartre,* Cleveland and New York: Meridian Books, 1956, pp. 287–311. Esslin's "The Absurdity of the Absurd" (p. 1120) shows the influence of existentialism on drama, especially through Sartre and Albert Camus.

was all—or perhaps from time to time they would ask such questions as: "Did you help sabotage the munitions?" or, "Where were you on the morning of the ninth and what were you doing?" They didn't even listen to the replies, or at least they didn't seem to. They just remained silent for a moment and looked straight ahead, then they began to write. They asked Tom if it was true he had served in the International Brigade. Tom couldn't say he hadn't because of the papers they had found in his jacket. They didn't ask Juan anything, but after he told them his name, they wrote for a long while.

"It's my brother José who's the anarchist," Juan said. "You know perfectly well he's not here now. I don't belong to any party. I never did take part in politics." They didn't answer.

Then Juan said, "I didn't do anything. And I'm not going to pay for what the others did."

5   His lips were trembling. A guard told him to stop talking and led him away. It was my turn.

"Your name is Pablo Ibbieta?"

I said yes.

The fellow looked at his papers and said, "Where is Ramon Gris?"

"I don't know."

10   "You hid him in your house from the sixth to the nineteenth."

"I did not."

They continued to write for a moment and the guards led me away. In the hall, Tom and Juan were waiting between two guards. We started walking. Tom asked one of the guards, "What's the idea?" "How do you mean?" the guard asked. "Was that just the preliminary questioning, or was that the trial?" "That was the trial," the guard said. "So now what? What are they going to do with us?" The guard answered drily, "The verdict will be told you in your cell."

In reality, our cell was one of the cellars of the hospital. It was terribly cold there because it was very drafty. We had been shivering all night long and it had hardly been any better during the day. I had spent the preceding five days in a cellar in the archbishop's palace, a sort of dungeon that must have dated back to the Middle Ages. There were lots of prisoners and not much room, so they housed them just anywhere. But I was not homesick for my dungeon. I hadn't been cold there, but I had been alone, and that gets to be irritating. In the cellar I had company. Juan didn't say a word; he was afraid, and besides, he was too young to have anything to say. But Tom was a good talker and knew Spanish well.

In the cellar there was a bench and four straw mattresses. When they led us back we sat down and waited in silence. After a while Tom said, "Our goose is cooked."

15   "I think so too," I said. "But I don't believe they'll do anything to the kid."

Tom said, "They haven't got anything on him. He's the brother of a fellow who's fighting, and that's all."

I looked at Juan. He didn't seem to have heard.

Tom continued, "You know what they do in Saragossa? They lay the guys across the road and then they drive over them with trucks. It was a Moroccan deserter who told us that. They says it's just to save ammunition."

I said, "Well, it doesn't save gasoline."

20   I was irritated with Tom; he shouldn't have said that.

He went on, "There are officers walking up and down the roads with their hands in their pockets, smoking, and they see that it's done right. Do you think they'd put 'em out of their misery? Like hell they do. They just let 'em holler. Sometimes as long as an hour. The Moroccan said the first time he almost puked."

"I don't believe they do that here," I said, "unless they really are short of ammunition."

The daylight came in through four air vents and a round opening that had been cut in the ceiling, to the left, and which opened directly onto the sky. It was through this hole, which was ordinarily closed by means of a trapdoor, that they unloaded coal into the cellar. Directly under the hole, there was a big pile of coal dust; it had been intended for heating the hospital, but at the beginning of the war they had evacuated the patients and the coal had stayed there unused; it even got rained on from time to time, when they forgot to close the trapdoor.

Tom started to shiver. "God damn it," he said, "I'm shivering. There, it is starting again."

He rose and began to do gymnastic exercises. At each movement, his shirt opened and showed his white, hairy chest. He lay down on his back, lifted his legs in the air and began to do the scissors movement. I watched his big buttocks tremble. Tom was tough, but he had too much fat on him. I kept thinking that soon bullets and bayonet points would sink into that mass of tender flesh as though it were a pat of butter.

I wasn't exactly cold, but I couldn't feel my shoulders or my arms. From time to time, I had the impression that something was missing and I began to look around for my jacket. Then I would suddenly remember they hadn't given me a jacket. It was rather awkward. They had taken our clothes to give them to their own soldiers and had left us only our shirts and these cotton trousers the hospital patients wore in mid-summer. After a moment, Tom got up and sat down beside me, breathless.

"Did you get warmed up?"

"Damn it, no. But I'm all out of breath."

Around eight o'clock in the evening, a Major came in with two falangists.[1]

"What are the names of those three over there?" he asked the guard.

"Steinbock, Ibbieta and Mirbal," said the guard.

The Major put on his glasses and examined his list.

"Steinbock—Steinbock . . . Here it is. You are condemned to death. You'll be shot tomorrow morning."

He looked at his list again.

"The other two, also," he said.

"That's not possible," said Juan. "Not me."

The Major looked at him with surprise. "What's your name?"

"Juan Mirbal."

"Well, your name is here," said the Major, "and you're condemned to death."

"I didn't do anything," said Juan.

The Major shrugged his shoulders and turned toward Tom and me.

"You are both Basque?"[2]

"No, nobody's Basque."

He appeared exasperated.

"I was told there were three Basques. I'm not going to waste my time running after them. I suppose you don't want a priest?"

We didn't even answer.

Then he said, "A Belgian doctor will be around in a little while. He has permission to stay with you all night."

He gave a military salute and left.

"What did I tell you?" Tom said. "We're in for something swell."

---

[1] A member of the Spanish Phalanx, a fascist organization.   [2] One of a people of obscure origin inhabiting the western Pyrenees on the Bay of Biscay.

50   "Yes," I said. "It's a damned shame for the kid."

I said that to be fair, but I really didn't like the kid. His face was too refined and it was disfigured by fear and suffering, which had twisted all his features. Three days ago, he was just a kid with a kind of affected manner some people like. But now he looked like an aging fairy, and I thought to myself he would never be young again, even if they let him go. It wouldn't have been a bad thing to show him a little pity, but pity makes me sick, and besides, I couldn't stand him. He hadn't said anything more, but he had turned gray. His face and hands were gray. He sat down again and stared, round-eyed, at the ground. Tom was goodhearted and tried to take him by the arm, but the kid drew himself away violently and made an ugly face. "Leave him alone," I said quietly. "Can't you see he's going to start to bawl?" Tom obeyed regretfully. He would have liked to console the kid; that would have kept him occupied and he wouldn't have been tempted to think about himself. But it got on my nerves. I had never thought about death, for the reason that the question had never come up. But now it had come up, and there was nothing else to do but think about it.

Tom started talking. "Say, did you ever bump anybody off?" he asked me. I didn't answer. He started to explain to me that he had bumped off six fellows since August. He hadn't yet realized what we were in for, and I saw clearly he didn't *want* to realize it. I myself hadn't quite taken it in. I wondered if it hurt very much. I thought about the bullets; I imagined their fiery hail going through my body. All that was beside the real question; but I was calm, we had all night in which to realize it. After a while Tom stopped talking and I looked at him out of the corner of my eye. I saw that he, too, had turned gray and that he looked pretty miserable. I said to myself, "It's starting." It was almost dark, a dull light filtered through the air vents across the coal pile and made a big spot under the sky. Through the hole in the ceiling I could already see a star. The night was going to be clear and cold.

The door opened and two guards entered. They were followed by a blond man in a tan uniform. He greeted us.

"I'm the doctor," he said. "I've been authorized to give you any assistance you may require in these painful circumstances."

55   He had an agreeable, cultivated voice.

I said to him, "What are you going to do here?"

"Whatever you want me to do. I shall do everything in my power to lighten these few hours."

"Why did you come to us? There are lots of others: the hospital's full of them."

"I was sent here," he answered vaguely. "You'd probably like to smoke, wouldn't you?" he added suddenly. "I've got some cigarettes and even some cigars."

60   He passed around some English cigarettes and some *puros*,[3] but we refused them. I looked him straight in the eye and he appeared uncomfortable.

"You didn't come here out of compassion," I said to him. "In fact, I know who you are. I saw you with some fascists in the barracks yard the day I was arrested."

I was about to continue, when all at once something happened to me which surprised me: the presence of this doctor had suddenly ceased to interest me. Usually, when I've got hold of a man I don't let go. But somehow the desire to speak had left me. I shrugged my shoulders and turned away. A little later, I looked up and saw he was watching me with an air of curiosity. The guards had sat down on one of the mattresses. Pedro, the tall thin one, was twiddling his thumbs, while the other one shook his head occasionally to keep from falling asleep.

[3] a cigar.

"Do you want some light?" Pedro suddenly asked the doctor. The other fellow nodded, "Yes." I think he was not over-intelligent, but doubtless he was not malicious. As I looked at his big, cold, blue eyes, it seemed to me the worst thing about him was his lack of imagination. Pedro went out and came back with an oil lamp which he set on the corner of the bench. It gave a poor light, but it was better than nothing; the night before we had been left in the dark. For a long while I stared at the circle of light the lamp threw on the ceiling. I was fascinated. Then, suddenly, I came to, the light circle paled, and I felt as if I were being crushed under an enormous weight. It wasn't the thought of death, and it wasn't fear; it was something anonymous. My cheeks were burning hot and my head ached.

I roused myself and looked at my two companions. Tom had his head in his hands and only the fat, white nape of his neck was visible. Juan was by far the worst off; his mouth was wide open and his nostrils were trembling. The doctor came over to him and touched him on the shoulder, as though to comfort him; but his eyes remained cold. Then I saw the Belgian slide his hand furtively down Juan's arm to his wrist. Indifferent, Juan let himself be handled. Then, as though absent-mindedly, the Belgian laid three fingers over his wrist; at the same time, he drew away somewhat and managed to turn his back to me. But I leaned over backward and saw him take out his watch and look at it a moment before relinquishing the boy's wrist. After a moment, he let the inert hand fall and went and leaned against the wall. Then, as if he had suddenly remembered something very important that had to be noted down immediately, he took a notebook from his pocket and wrote a few lines in it. "The son-of-a-bitch," I thought angrily. "He better not come and feel my pulse; I'll give him a punch in his dirty jaw."

65 He didn't come near me, but I felt he was looking at me. I raised my head and looked back at him. In an impersonal voice, he said, "Don't you think it's frightfully cold here?"

He looked purple with cold.

"I'm not cold," I answered him.

He kept looking at me with a hard expression. Suddenly I understood, and I lifted my hands to my face. I was covered with sweat. Here, in this cellar, in mid-winter, right in a draft, I was sweating. I ran my fingers through my hair, which was stiff with sweat; at the same time, I realized my shirt was damp and sticking to my skin. I had been streaming with perspiration for an hour, at least, and had felt nothing. But this fact hadn't escaped that Belgian swine. He had seen the drops rolling down my face and had said to himself that it showed an almost pathological terror; and he himself had felt normal and proud of it because he was cold. I wanted to get up and go punch his face in, but I had hardly started to make a move before my shame and anger had disappeared. I dropped back into the bench with indifference.

I was content to rub my neck with my handkerchief because now I felt the sweat dripping from my hair onto the nape of my neck and that was disagreeable. I soon gave up rubbing myself, however, for it didn't do any good; my handkerchief was already wringing wet and I was still sweating. My buttocks, too, were sweating, and my damp trousers stuck to the bench.

70 Suddenly, Juan said, "You're a doctor, aren't you?"

"Yes," said the Belgian.

"Do people suffer—very long?"

"Oh! When . . . ? No, no," said the Belgian, in a paternal voice, "it's quickly over."

His manner was as reassuring as if he had been answering a paying patient.

75 "But I . . . Somebody told me—they often have to fire two volleys."

"Sometimes," said the Belgian, raising his head, "it just happens that the first volley doesn't hit any of the vital organs."

"So then they have to reload their guns and aim all over again?" Juan thought for a moment, then added hoarsely, "But that takes time!"

He was terribly afraid of suffering. He couldn't think about anything else, but that went with his age. As for me, I hardly thought about it any more and it certainly was not fear of suffering that made me perspire.

I rose and walked toward the pile of coal dust. Tom gave a start and looked at me with a look of hate. I irritated him because my shoes squeaked. I wondered if my face was as putty-colored as his. Then I noticed that he, too, was sweating. The sky was magnificent; no light at all came into our dark corner and I had only to lift my head to see the Big Bear. But it didn't look the way it had looked before. Two days ago, from my cell in the archbishop's palace, I could see a big patch of sky and each time of day brought back a different memory. In the morning, when the sky was a deep blue, and light, I thought of beaches along the Atlantic; at noon, I could see the sun, and I remembered a bar in Seville where I used to drink manzanilla[4] and eat anchovies and olives; in the afternoon, I was in the shade, and I thought of the deep shadow which covers half of the arena while the other half gleams in the sunlight: it really gave me a pang to see the whole earth reflected in the sky like that. Now, however, no matter how much I looked up in the air, the sky no longer recalled anything. I liked it better that way. I came back and sat down next to Tom. There was a long silence.

80 Then Tom began to talk in a low voice. He had to keep talking, otherwise he lost his way in his own thoughts. I believe he was talking to me, but he didn't look at me. No doubt he was afraid to look at me, because I was gray and sweating. We were both alike and worse than mirrors for each other. He looked at the Belgian, the only one who was alive.

"Say, do you understand? I don't."

Then I, too, began to talk in a low voice. I was watching the Belgian.

"Understand what? What's the matter?"

"Something's going to happen to us that I don't understand."

85 There was a strange odor about Tom. It seemed to me that I was more sensitive to odors than ordinarily. With a sneer, I said, "You'll understand, later."

"That's not so sure," he said stubbornly. "I'm willing to be courageous, but at least I ought to know . . . Listen, they're going to take us out into the courtyard. All right. The fellows will be standing in line in front of us. How many of them will there be?"

"Oh, I don't know. Five, or eight. Not more."

"That's enough. Let's say there'll be eight of them. Somebody will shout 'Shoulder arms!' and I'll see all eight rifles aimed at me. I'm sure I'm going to feel like going through the wall. I'll push against the wall as hard as I can with my back, and the wall won't give in. The way it is in a nightmare. . . . I can imagine all that. Ah, if you only knew how well I can imagine it!"

"Skip it!" I said. "I can imagine it too."

90 "It must hurt like the devil. You know they aim at your eyes and mouth so as to disfigure you," he added maliciously. "I can feel the wounds already. For the last hour I've been having pains in my head and neck. Not real pains—it's worse still: they're the pains I'll feel tomorrow morning. And after that, then what?"

I understood perfectly well what he meant, but I didn't want to seem to understand. As for the pains, I, too, felt them all through my body, like a lot of little gashes. I couldn't get used to them, but I was like him, I didn't think they were very important.

"After that," I said roughly, "you'll be eating daisies."

[4]A pale aromatic dry Spanish sherry wine.

He started talking to himself, not taking his eyes off the Belgian, who didn't seem to be listening to him. I knew what he had come for, and that what we were thinking didn't interest him. He had come back to look at our bodies, our bodies which were dying alive.

"It's like in a nightmare," said Tom. "You want to think of something, you keep having the impression you've got it, that you're going to understand, and then it slips away from you, it eludes you and it's gone again. I say to myself, afterwards, there won't be anything. But I don't really understand what that means. There are moments when I almost do—and then it's gone again. I start to think of the pains, the bullets, the noise of the shooting. I am a materialist, I swear it; and I'm not going crazy, either. But there's something wrong. I see my own corpse. That's not hard, but it's *I* who see it, with *my* eyes. I'll have to get to the point where I think—where I think I won't see anything more. I won't hear anything more, and the world will go on for the others. We're not made to think that way, Pablo. Believe me, I've already stayed awake all night waiting for something. But this is not the same thing. This will grab us from behind, Pablo, and we won't be ready for it."

95 "Shut up," I said. "Do you want me to call a father confessor?"

He didn't answer. I had already noticed that he had a tendency to prophesy and call me "Pablo" in a kind of pale voice. I didn't like that very much, but it seems all the Irish are like that. I had a vague impression that he smelled of urine. Actually, I didn't like Tom very much, and I didn't see why, just because we were going to die together, I should like him any better. There are certain fellows with whom it would be different—with Ramon Gris, for instance. But between Tom and Juan, I felt alone. In fact, I liked it better that way. With Ramon I might have grown soft. But I felt terribly hard at that moment, and I wanted to stay hard.

Tom kept on muttering, in a kind of absent-minded way. He was certainly talking to keep from thinking. Naturally, I agreed with him, and I could have said everything he was saying. It's not *natural* to die. And since I was going to die, nothing seemed natural any more: neither the coal pile, nor the bench, nor Pedro's dirty old face. Only it was disagreeable for me to think the same things Tom thought. And I knew perfectly well that all night long, within five minutes of each other, we would keep on thinking things at the same time, sweating or shivering at the same time. I looked at him sideways and, for the first time, he seemed strange to me. He had death written on his face. My pride was wounded. For twenty-four hours I had lived side by side with Tom, I had listened to him, I had talked to him, and I knew we had nothing in common. And now we were as alike as twin brothers, simply because we were going to die together. Tom took my hand without looking at me.

"Pablo, I wonder . . . I wonder if it's true that we just cease to exist."

I drew my hand away.

100 "Look between your feet, you dirty dog."

There was a puddle between his feet and water was dripping from his trousers.

"What's the matter?" he said, frightened.

"You're wetting your pants," I said to him.

"It's not true," he said furiously. "I can't be . . . I don't feel anything."

105 The Belgian had come closer to him. With an air of false concern, he asked, "Aren't you feeling well?"

Tom didn't answer. The Belgian looked at the puddle without comment.

"I don't know what that is," Tom said savagely, "but I'm not afraid. I swear to you, I'm not afraid."

The Belgian made no answer. Tom rose and went to a corner. He came back, buttoning his fly, and sat down, without a word. The Belgian was taking notes.

We were watching the doctor. Juan was watching him too. All three of us were watching him because he was alive. He had the gestures of a living person, the interests of a living person; he was shivering in this cellar the way living people shiver; he had an obedient, well-fed body. We, on the other hand, didn't feel our bodies any more—not the same way, in any case. I felt like touching my trousers, but I didn't dare to. I looked at the Belgian, well-planted on his two legs, master of his muscles—and able to plan for tomorrow. We were like three shadows deprived of blood; we were watching him and sucking his life like vampires.

110   Finally he came over to Juan. Was he going to lay his hand on the nape of Juan's neck for some professional reason, or had he obeyed a charitable impulse? If he had acted out of charity, it was the one and only time during the whole night. He fondled Juan's head and the nape of his neck. The kid let him do it, without taking his eyes off him. Then, suddenly, he took hold of the doctor's hand and looked at it in a funny way. He held the Belgian's hand between his own two hands and there was nothing pleasing about them, those two gray paws squeezing that fat red hand. I sensed what was going to happen and Tom must have sensed it, too. But all the Belgian saw was emotion, and he smiled paternally. After a moment, the kid lifted the big red paw to his mouth and started to bite it. The Belgian drew back quickly and stumbled toward the wall. For a second, he looked at us with horror. He must have suddenly understood that we were not men like himself. I began to laugh, and one of the guards started up. The other had fallen asleep with his eyes wide open, showing only the whites.

I felt tired and over-excited at the same time. I didn't want to think any more about what was going to happen at dawn—about death. It didn't make sense, and I never got beyond just words, or emptiness. But whenever I tried to think about something else I saw the barrels of rifles aimed at me. I must have lived through my execution twenty times in succession; one time I thought it was the real thing; I must have dozed off for a moment. They were dragging me toward the wall and I was resisting; I was imploring their pardon. I woke with a start and looked at the Belgian. I was afraid I had cried out in my sleep. But he was smoothing his mustache; he hadn't noticed anything. If I had wanted to, I believe I could have slept for a while. I had been awake for the last forty-eight hours, and I was worn out. But I didn't want to lose two hours of life. They would have had to come and wake me at dawn. I would have followed them, drunk with sleep, and I would have gone off without so much as "Gosh!" I didn't want it that way, I didn't want to die like an animal. I wanted to understand. Besides, I was afraid of having nightmares. I got up and began to walk up and down and, so as to think about something else, I began to think about my past life. Memories crowded in on me, helter-skelter. Some were good and some were bad—at least that was how I had thought of them *before*. There were faces and happenings. I saw the face of a little *novillero*[5] who had gotten himself horned during the *Feria*,[6] in Valencia. I saw the face of one of my uncles, of Ramon Gris. I remembered all kinds of things that had happened: how I had been on strike for three months in 1926, and had almost died of hunger. I recalled a night I had spent on a bench in Granada; I hadn't eaten for three days, I was nearly wild, I didn't want to give up the sponge. I had to smile. With what eagerness I had run after happiness, and women, and liberty! And to what end? I had wanted to liberate Spain, I admired Py Margall, I had belonged to the anarchist movement, I had spoken at public meetings. I took everything as seriously as if I had been immortal.

At that time I had the impression that I had my whole life before me, and I thought to myself, "It's all a god-damned lie." Now it wasn't worth anything because it was finished. I wondered how I had ever been able to go out and have a good time with girls. I wouldn't have lifted my little finger if I had ever imagined that I would die like this. I saw my life

[5]An aspiring bullfighter who has not yet attained the rank of matador.   [6]A local religious holiday.

before me, finished, closed, like a bag, and yet what was inside was not finished. For a moment I tried to appraise it. I would have liked to say to myself, "It's been a good life." But it couldn't be appraised, it was only an outline. I had spent my life writing checks on eternity, and had understood nothing. Now, I didn't miss anything. There were a lot of things I might have missed: the taste of manzanilla, for instance, or the swims I used to take in summer in a little creek near Cadiz. But death had taken the charm out of everything.

Suddenly the Belgian had a wonderful idea.

"My friends," he said to us, "if you want me to—and providing the military authorities give their consent—I could undertake to deliver a word or some token from you to your loved ones. . . ."

115   Tom growled. "I haven't got anybody."

I didn't answer. Tom waited for a moment, then he looked at me with curiosity. "Aren't you going to send any message to Concha?"

"No."

I hated that sort of sentimental conspiracy. Of course, it was my fault, since I had mentioned Concha the night before, and I should have kept my mouth shut. I had been with her for a year. Even as late as last night, I would have cut my arm off with a hatchet just to see her again for five minutes. That was why I had mentioned her. I couldn't help it. Now I didn't care any more about seeing her. I hadn't anything more to say to her. I didn't even want to hold her in my arms. I loathed my body because it had turned gray and was sweating—and I wasn't even sure that I didn't loathe hers too. Concha would cry when she heard about my death; for months she would have no more interest in life. But still it was I who was going to die. I thought of her beautiful, loving eyes. When she looked at me something went from her to me. But I thought to myself that it was all over; if she looked at me *now* her gaze would not leave her eyes, it would not reach out to me. I was alone.

Tom too, was alone, but not the same way. He was seated astride his chair and had begun to look at the bench with a sort of smile, with surprise, even. He reached out his hand and touched the wood cautiously, as though he were afraid of breaking something, then he drew his hand back hurriedly, and shivered. I wouldn't have amused myself touching that bench, if I had been Tom, that was just some more Irish play-acting. But somehow it seemed to me too that the different objects had something funny about them. They seemed to have grown paler, less massive than before. I had only to look at the bench, the lamp or the pile of coal dust to feel I was going to die. Naturally, I couldn't think clearly about my death, but I saw it everywhere, even on the different objects, the way they had withdrawn and kept their distance, tactfully, like people talking at the bedside of a dying person. It was *his own death* Tom had just touched on the bench.

120   In the state I was in, if they had come and told me I could go home quietly, that my life would be saved, it would have left me cold. A few hours, or a few years of waiting are all the same, when you've lost the illusion of being eternal. Nothing mattered to me any more. In a way, I was calm. But it was a horrible kind of calm—because of my body. My body—I saw with its eyes and I heard with its ears, but it was no longer I. It sweat and trembled independently, and I didn't recognize it any longer. I was obliged to touch it and look at it to know what was happening to it, just as if it had been someone else's body. At times I still felt it, I felt a slipping, a sort of headlong plunging, as in a falling airplane, or else I heard my heart beating. But this didn't give me confidence. In fact, everything that came from my body had something damned dubious about it. Most of the time it was silent, it stayed put and I didn't feel anything other than a sort of heaviness, a loathsome presence against me. I had the impression of being bound to an enormous vermin.

The Belgian took out his watch and looked at it.

"It's half-past-three," he said.

The son-of-a-bitch! He must have done it on purpose. Tom jumped up. We hadn't yet realized the time was passing. The night surrounded us like a formless, dark mass; I didn't even remember it had started.

Juan started to shout. Wringing his hands, he implored, "I don't want to die! I don't want to die!"

125 He ran the whole length of the cellar with his arms in the air, then he dropped down onto one of the mattresses, sobbing. Tom looked at him with dismal eyes and didn't even try to console him any more. The fact was, it was no use; the kid made more noise than we did, but he was less affected, really. He was like a sick person who defends himself against his malady with a high fever. When there's not even any fever left, it's much more serious.

He was crying. I could tell he felt sorry for himself; he was thinking about death. For one second, one single second, I too felt like crying, crying out of pity for myself. But just the contrary happened. I took one look at the kid, saw his thin, sobbing shoulders, and I felt I was inhuman. I couldn't feel pity for these others or for myself. I said to myself, "I want to die decently."

Tom had gotten up and was standing just under the round opening looking out for the first signs of daylight. I was determined, I wanted to die decently, and I only thought about that. But underneath, ever since the doctor had told us the time, I felt time slipping, flowing by, one drop at a time.

It was still dark when I heard Tom's voice.

"Do you hear them?"

130 "Yes."

People were walking in the courtyard.

"What the hell are they doing? After all, they can't shoot in the dark."

After a moment, we didn't hear anything more. I said to Tom, "There's the daylight."

Pedro got up yawning, and came and blew out the lamp. He turned to the man beside him. "It's hellish cold."

135 The cellar had grown gray. We could hear shots at a distance.

"It's about to start," I said to Tom. "That must be in the back courtyard."

Tom asked the doctor to give him a cigarette. I didn't want any; I didn't want either cigarettes or alcohol. From that moment on, the shooting didn't stop.

"Can you take it in?" Tom said.

He started to add something, then he stopped and began to watch the door. The door opened and a lieutenant came in with four soldiers. Tom dropped his cigarette.

140 "Steinbock?"

Tom didn't answer. Pedro pointed him out.

"Juan Mirbal?"

"He's the one on the mattress."

"Stand up," said the Lieutenant.

145 Juan didn't move. Two soldiers took hold of him by the armpits and stood him up on his feet. But as soon as they let go of him he fell down.

The soldiers hesitated a moment.

"He's not the first one to get sick," said the Lieutenant. "You'll have to carry him, the two of you. We'll arrange things when we get there." He turned to Tom. "All right, come along."

Tom left between two soldiers. Two other soldiers followed, carrying the kid by his arms and legs. He was not unconscious; his eyes were wide open and tears were rolling down his cheeks. When I started to go out, the Lieutenant stopped me.

"Are you Ibbieta?"

150 "Yes."

"You wait here. They'll come and get you later on."

They left. The Belgian and the two jailers left too, and I was alone. I didn't understand what had happened to me, but I would have liked it better if they had ended it all right away. I heard the volleys at almost regular intervals; at each one, I shuddered. I felt like howling and tearing my hair. But instead, I gritted my teeth and pushed my hands deep into my pockets, because I wanted to stay decent.

An hour later, they came to fetch me and took me up to the first floor in a little room which smelt of cigar smoke and was so hot it seemed to me suffocating. Here there were two officers sitting in comfortable chairs, smoking, with papers spread out on their knees.

"Your name is Ibbieta?"

155 "Yes."

"Where is Ramon Gris?"

"I don't know."

The man who questioned me was small and stocky. He had hard eyes behind his glasses.

"Come nearer," he said to me.

160 I went nearer. He rose and took me by the arms, looking at me in a way calculated to make me go through the floor. At the same time he pinched my arms with all his might. He didn't mean to hurt me; it was quite a game; he wanted to dominate me. He also seemed to think it was necessary to blow his fetid breath right into my face. We stood like that for a moment, only I felt more like laughing than anything else. It takes a lot more than that to intimidate a man who's about to die; it didn't work. He pushed me away violently and sat down again.

"It's your life or his," he said. "You'll be allowed to go free if you tell us where he is."

After all, these two bedizened fellows with their riding crops and boots were just men who were going to die one day. A little later than I, perhaps, but not a great deal. And there they were, looking for names among their papers, running after other men in order to put them in prison or do away with them entirely. They had their opinions on the future of Spain and on other subjects. Their petty activities seemed to me to be offensive and ludicrous. I could no longer put myself in their place. I had the impression they were crazy.

The little fat fellow kept looking at me, tapping his boots with his riding crop. All his gestures were calculated to make him appear like a spirited, ferocious animal.

"Well? Do you understand?"

165 "I don't know where Gris is," I said. "I thought he was in Madrid."

The other officer lifted his pale hand indolently. This indolence was also calculated. I saw through all their little tricks, and I was dumbfounded that men should still exist who took pleasure in that kind of thing.

"You have fifteen minutes to think it over," he said slowly. "Take him to the linen-room, and bring him back here in fifteen minutes. If he continues to refuse, he'll be executed at once."

They knew what they were doing. I had spent the night waiting. After that, they had made me wait another hour in the cellar, while they shot Tom and Juan, and now they locked me in the linen-room. They must have arranged the whole thing the night before. They figured that sooner or later people's nerves wear out and they hoped to get me that way.

They made a big mistake. In the linen-room I sat down on a ladder because I felt very weak, and I began to think things over. Not their proposition, however. Naturally I knew where Gris was. He was hiding in his cousins' house, about two miles outside of the city. I knew, too, that I would not reveal his hiding place, unless they tortured me (but they didn't seem to be considering that). All that was definitely settled and didn't interest me in the least. Only I would have liked to understand the reasons for my own conduct. I would rather die than betray Gris. Why? I no longer liked Ramon Gris. My friendship for him had died shortly before dawn along with my love for Concha, along with my own desire to live. Of course I still admired him—he was hard. But it was not for that reason I was willing to die in his place; his life was no more valuable than mine. No life was of any value. A man was going to be stood up against a wall and fired at till he dropped dead. It didn't make any difference whether it was I or Gris or somebody else. I knew perfectly well he was more useful to the Spanish cause than I was, but I didn't give a God damn about Spain or anarchy, either; nothing had any importance now. And yet, there I was. I could save my skin by betraying Gris and I refused to do it. It seemed more ludicrous to me than anything else; it was stubbornness.

170   I thought to myself, "Am I hard-headed!" And I was seized with a strange sort of cheerfulness.

They came to fetch me and took me back to the two officers. A rat darted out under our feet and that amused me. I turned to one of the falangists and said to him, "Did you see that rat?"

He made no reply. He was gloomy, and took himself very seriously. As for me, I felt like laughing, but I restrained myself because I was afraid that if I started, I wouldn't be able to stop. The falangist wore mustaches. I kept after him, "You ought to cut off those mustaches, you fool."

I was amused by the fact that he let hair grow all over his face while he was still alive. He gave me a kind of half-hearted kick, and I shut up.

"Well," said the fat officer, "have you thought things over?"

175   I looked at them with curiosity, like insects of a very rare species.

"I know where he is," I said. "He's hiding in the cemetery. Either in one of the vaults, or in the gravediggers' shack."

I said that just to make fools of them. I wanted to see them get up and fasten their belts and bustle about giving orders.

They jumped to their feet.

"Fine. Moles, go ask Lieutenant Lopez for fifteen men. And as for you," the little fat fellow said to me, "if you've told the truth, I don't go back on my word. But you'll pay for this, if you're pulling our leg."

180   They left noisily and I waited in peace, still guarded by the falangists. From time to time I smiled at the thought of the face they were going to make. I felt dull and malicious. I could see them lifting up the gravestones, or opening the doors of the vaults one by one. I saw the whole situation as though I were another person: the prisoner determined to play the hero, the solemn falangists with their mustaches and the men in uniform running around among the graves. It was irresistibly funny.

After half an hour, the little fat fellow came back alone. I thought he had come to give the order to execute me. The others must have stayed in the cemetery.

The officer looked at me. He didn't look at all foolish.

"Take him out in the big courtyard with the others," he said. "When military operations are over, a regular tribunal will decide his case."

I thought I must have misunderstood.

185   "So they're not—they're not going to shoot me?" I asked.

"Not now, in any case. Afterwards, that doesn't concern me."

I still didn't understand.

"But why?" I said to him.

He shrugged his shoulders without replying, and the soldiers led me away. In the big courtyard there were a hundred or so prisoners, women, children and a few old men. I started to walk around the grass plot in the middle. I felt absolutely idiotic. At noon we were fed in the dining hall. Two or three fellows spoke to me. I must have known them, but I didn't answer. I didn't even know where I was.

190   Toward evening, about ten new prisoners were pushed into the courtyard. I recognized Garcia, the baker.

He said to me, "Lucky dog! I didn't expect to find you alive."

"They condemned me to death." I said, "and then they changed their minds. I don't know why."

"I was arrested at two o'clock," Garcia said.

"What for?"

195   Garcia took no part in politics.

"I don't know," he said. "They arrest everybody who doesn't think the way they do." He lowered his voice.

"They got Gris."

I began to tremble.

200   "When?"

"This morning. He acted like a damned fool. He left his cousins' house Tuesday because of a disagreement. There were any number of fellows who would have hidden him, but he didn't want to be indebted to anybody any more. He said, 'I would have hidden at Ibbieta's, but since they've got him, I'll go hide in the cemetery.' "

"In the cemetery?"

"Yes. It was the god-damnedest thing. Naturally they passed by there this morning; that had to happen. They found him in the gravediggers' shack. They opened fire at him and they finished him off."

"In the cemetery!"

205   Everything went around in circles, and when I came to I was sitting on the ground. I laughed so hard the tears came to my eyes.

Shirley Jackson   (1919–1965)
The Lottery

Although this story was published before the appearance of what has come to be known as the literature of the absurd,* nevertheless the temptation to read "The Lottery" as part of this literary movement is compelling. In discussing the military draft lottery** Max Lerner says, "It is a game in which a third of the players are bound to

* For a definition and discussion of the literature of the absurd, see Esslin's "The Absurdity of the Absurd" (p. 1120). See also the headnote to Sartre's "The Wall" (p. 126). This story is identified with the literature of the absurd as is Kafka's story "A Hunger Artist" (p. 120).

** *Miami Herald,* December 5, 1969.

lose, another third to win and the in-between third sentenced for a spell to uncertainty. I am speaking of the lottery drawing which pulled all 366 possible birthdays out of a big jar in a random sequence that decided the draft future of over 800,000 young Americans." And then Lerner adds a philosophical note: "We go through life on the assumption that it makes some sort of rational sense, but constantly we have to face the element of the absurd in it. To all the absurdities of the human condition the young men must now add this wild absurdity of having their fate decided by a random drawing of a birthdate which was accidental to start with." Lerner's comments serve as an appropriate way of identifying Jackson's "The Lottery" with the literature of the absurd.

The morning of June 27th was clear and sunny, with the fresh warmth of a full-summer day; the flowers were blossoming profusely and the grass was richly green. The people of the village began to gather in the square, between the post office and the bank, around ten o'clock; in some towns there were so many people that the lottery took two days and had to be started on June 26th, but in this village, where there were only about three hundred people, the whole lottery took less than two hours, so it could begin at ten o'clock in the morning and still be through in time to allow the villagers to get home for noon dinner.

The children assembled first, of course. School was recently over for the summer, and the feeling of liberty sat uneasily on most of them; they tended to gather together quietly for a while before they broke into boisterous play, and their talk was still of the classroom and the teacher, of books and reprimands. Bobby Martin had already stuffed his pockets full of stones, and the other boys soon followed his example, selecting the smoothest and roundest stones; Bobby and Harry Jones and Dickie Delacroix—the villagers pronounced this name "Dellacroy"—eventually made a great pile of stones in one corner of the square and guarded it against the raids of the other boys. The girls stood aside, talking among themselves, looking over their shoulders at the boys, and the very small children rolled in the dust or clung to the hands of their older brothers or sisters.

Soon the men began to gather, surveying their own children, speaking of planting and rain, tractors and taxes. They stood together, away from the pile of stones in the corner, and their jokes were quiet and they smiled rather than laughed. The women, wearing faded house dresses and sweaters, came shortly after their menfolk. They greeted one another and exchanged bits of gossip as they went to join their husbands. Soon the women, standing by their husbands, began to call to their children, and the children came reluctantly, having to be called four or five times. Bobby Martin ducked under his mother's grasping hand and ran, laughing, back to the pile of stones. His father spoke up sharply, and Bobby came quickly and took his place between his father and his oldest brother.

The lottery was conducted—as were the square dances, the teen-age club, the Halloween program—by Mr. Summers, who had time and energy to devote to civic activities. He was a round-faced, jovial man and he ran the coal business, and people were sorry for him, because he had no children and his wife was a scold. When he arrived in the square, carrying a black wooden box, there was a murmur of conversation among the villagers, and he waved and called, "Little late today, folks." The postmaster, Mr. Graves, followed him, carrying a three-legged stool, and the stool was put in the center of the square and Mr. Summers set the black box down on it. The villagers kept their distance, leaving a space between themselves and the stool, and when Mr. Summers said, "Some of you fellows want to give me a hand?" there was a hesitation before two men, Mr. Martin and his oldest son, Baxter, came forward to hold the box steady on the stool while Mr. Summers stirred up the papers inside it.

5   The original paraphernalia for the lottery had been lost long ago, and the black box now resting on the stool had been put into use even before Old Man Warner, the oldest

man in town, had been born. Mr. Summers spoke frequently to the villagers about making a new box, but no one liked to upset even as much tradition as there was represented by the black box. There was a story that the present box had been made with some pieces of the box that had preceded it, the one that had been constructed when the first people settled down to make a village here. Every year, after the lottery, Mr. Summers began talking again about a new box, but every year the subject was allowed to fade off without anything's being done. The black box grew shabbier each year; by now it was no longer completely black but splintered badly along one side to show the original wood color, and in some places faded or stained.

Mr. Martin and his oldest son, Baxter, held the black box securely on the stool until Mr. Summers had stirred the papers thoroughly with his hand. Because so much of the ritual had been forgotten or discarded, Mr. Summers had been successful in having slips of paper substituted for the chips of wood that had been used for generations. Chips of wood, Mr. Summers had argued, had been all very well when the village was tiny, but now that the population was more than three hundred and likely to keep on growing, it was necessary to use something that would fit more easily into the black box. The night before the lottery, Mr. Summers and Mr. Graves made up the slips of paper and put them in the box, and it was then taken to the safe of Mr. Summers' coal company and locked up until Mr. Summers was ready to take it to the square next morning. The rest of the year, the box was put away, sometimes one place, sometimes another: it had spent one year in Mr. Graves' barn and another year underfoot in the post office, and sometimes it was set on a shelf in the Martin grocery and left there.

There was a great deal of fussing to be done before Mr. Summers declared the lottery open. There were the lists to make up—of heads of families, heads of households in each family, members of each household in each family. There was the proper swearing-in of Mr. Summers by the postmaster, as the official of the lottery; at one time, some people remembered, there had been a recital of some sort, performed by the official of the lottery, a perfunctory, tuneless chant that had been rattled off duly each year; some people believed that the official of the lottery used to stand just so when he said or sang it, others believed that he was supposed to walk among the people, but years and years ago this part of the ritual had been allowed to lapse. There had been, also, a ritual salute, which the official of the lottery had had to use in addressing each person who came up to draw from the box, but this also changed with time, until now it was felt necessary only for the official to speak to each person approaching. Mr. Summers was very good at all this; in his clean white shirt and blue jeans, with one hand resting carelessly on the black box, he seemed very proper and important as he talked interminably to Mr. Graves and the Martins.

Just as Mr. Summers finally left off talking and turned to the assembled villagers, Mrs. Hutchinson came hurriedly along the path to the square, her sweater thrown over her shoulders, and slid into place in the back of the crowd. "Clean forgot what day it was," she said to Mrs. Delacroix, who stood next to her, and they both laughed softly. "Thought my old man was out back stacking wood, "Mrs. Hutchinson went on, "and then I looked out the window and the kids was gone, and then I remembered it was the twenty-seventh and came a-running." She dried her hands on her apron, and Mrs. Delacroix said, "You're in time though. They're still talking away up there."

Mrs. Hutchinson craned her neck to see through the crowd and found her husband and children standing near the front. She tapped Mrs. Delacroix on the arm as a farewell and began to make her way through the crowd. The people separated good-humoredly to let her through; two or three people said, in voices just loud enough to be heard across the crowd, "Here comes your Missus, Hutchinson," and "Bill, she made it after all." Mrs.

Hutchinson reached her husband, and Mr. Summers, who had been waiting, said cheerfully, "Thought we were going to have to get on without you, Tessie." Mrs. Hutchinson said, grinning, "Wouldn't have me leave m'dishes in the sink, now, would you, Joe?" and soft laughter ran through the crowd as the people stirred back into position after Mrs. Hutchinson's arrival.

10   "Well, now," Mr. Summers said soberly, "guess we better get started, get this over with, so's we can go back to work. Anybody ain't here?"

"Dunbar," several people said, "Dunbar, Dunbar."

Mr. Summers consulted his list. "Clyde Dunbar," he said. "That's right. He's broke his leg, hasn't he. Who's drawing for him?"

"Me, I guess," a woman said, and Mr. Summers turned to look at her. "Wife draws for her husband," Mr. Summers said. "Don't you have a grown boy to do it for you, Janey?" Although Mr. Summers and everyone else in the village knew the answer perfectly well, it was the business of the official of the lottery to ask such questions formally. Mr. Summers waited until an expression of polite interest while Mrs. Dunbar answered.

"Horace's not but sixteen yet," Mrs. Dunbar said regretfully. "Guess I gotta fill in for the old man this year."

15   "Right," Mr. Summers said. He made a note on the list he was holding. Then he asked, "Watson boy drawing this year?"

A tall boy in the crowd raised his hand. "Here," he said. "I'm drawing for m'mother and me." He blinked his eyes nervously and ducked his head as several voices in the crowd said things like "Good fellow, Jack," and "Glad to see your mother's got a man to do it."

"Well," Mr. Summers said, "guess that's everyone. Old Man Warner make it?"

"Here," a voice said, and Mr. Summers nodded.

A sudden hush fell on the crowd as Mr. Summers cleared his throat and looked at the list. "All ready?" he called. "Now, I'll read the names—heads of families first—and the men come up and take a paper out of the box. Keep the paper folded in your hand without looking at it until everyone has had a turn. Everything clear?"

20   The people had done it so many times that they only half listened to the directions; most of them were quiet, wetting their lips, not looking around. Then Mr. Summers raised one hand high and said, "Adams." A man disengaged himself from the crowd and came forward. "Hi, Steve," Mr. Summers said, and Mr. Adams said, "Hi, Joe." They grinned at one another humorlessly and nervously. Then Mr. Adams reached into the black box and took out a folded paper. He held it firmly by one corner as he turned and went hastily back to his place in the crowd, where he stood a little apart from his family, not looking down at his hand.

"Allen," Mr. Summers said. "Anderson . . . Bentham."

"Seems like there's no time at all between lotteries any more," Mrs. Delacroix said to Mrs. Graves in the back row. "Seems like we got through with the last one only last week."

"Time sure goes fast," Mrs. Graves said.

"Clark . . . Delacroix."

25   "There goes my old man," Mrs. Delacroix said. She held her breath while her husband went forward.

"Dunbar," Mr. Summers said, and Mrs. Dunbar went steadily to the box while one of the women said, "Go on, Janey," and another said, "There she goes."

"We're next," Mrs. Graves said. She watched while Mr. Graves came around from the side of the box, greeted Mr. Summers gravely, and selected a slip of paper from the box. By now, all through the crowd there were men holding the small folded papers in their large hands, turning them over and over nervously. Mrs. Dunbar and her two sons stood together, Mrs. Dunbar holding the slip of paper.

"Harburt. . . . Hutchinson."

"Get up there, Bill," Mrs. Hutchinson said, and the people near her laughed.

30   "Jones."

"They do say," Mr. Adams said to Old Man Warner, who stood next to him, "that over in the north village they're talking of giving up the lottery."

Old Man Warner snorted. "Pack of crazy fools," he said. "Listening to the young folks, nothing's good enough for *them*. Next thing you know, they'll be wanting to go back to living in caves, nobody work any more, live *that* way for a while. Used to be a saying about 'Lottery in June, corn be heavy soon.' First thing you know, we'd all be eating stewed chickweed and acorns. There's *always* been a lottery," he added petulantly. "Bad enough to see young Joe Summers up there joking with everybody."

"Some places have already quit lotteries," Mrs. Adams said.

"Nothing but trouble in *that*," Old Man Warner said stoutly. "Pack of young fools."

35   "Martin." And Bobby Martin watched his father go forward. "Overdyke. . . . Percy."

"I wish they'd hurry," Mrs. Dunbar said to her older son. "I wish they'd hurry."

"They're almost through," her son said.

"You get ready to run tell Dad," Mrs. Dunbar said.

Mr. Summers called his own name and then stepped forward precisely and selected a slip from the box. Then he called, "Warner."

40   "Seventy-seventh year I been in the lottery," Old Man Warner said as he went through the crowd. "Seventy-seventh time."

"Watson." The tall boy came awkwardly through the crowd. Someone said, "Don't be nervous, Jack," and Mr. Summers said, "Take your time, son."

"Zanini."

After that, there was a long pause, a breathless pause, until Mr. Summers, holding his slip of paper in the air, said, "All right, fellows." For a minute, no one moved and then all the slips of paper were opened. Suddenly, all the women began to speak at once, saying, "Who is it?" "Who's got it?" "Is it the Dunbars?" "Is it the Watsons?" Then the voices began to say, "It's Hutchinson. It's Bill." "Bill Hutchinson's got it."

"Go tell your father," Mrs. Dunbar said to her older son.

45   People began to look around to see the Hutchinsons. Bill Hutchinson was standing quiet, staring down at the paper in his hand. Suddenly, Tessie Hutchinson shouted to Mr. Summers, "You didn't give him time enough to take any paper he wanted. I saw you. It wasn't fair!"

"Be a good sport, Tessie," Mrs. Delacroix called, and Mrs. Graves said, "All of us took the same chance."

"Shut up, Tessie." Bill Hutchinson said.

"Well, everybody," Mr. Summers said, "that was done pretty fast, and now we've got to be hurrying a little more to get done in time." He consulted his next list. "Bill," he said, "you draw for the Hutchinson family. You got any other households in the Hutchinsons?"

"There's Don and Eva," Mrs. Hutchinson yelled. "Make *them* take their chance!"

50   "Daughters draw with their husbands' families, Tessie," Mr. Summers said gently. "You know that as well as anyone else."

"It wasn't *fair*," Tessie said.

"I guess not, Joe," Bill Hutchinson said regretfully. "My daughter draws with her husband's family, that's only fair. And I've got no other family except the kids."

"Then, as far as drawing for families is concerned, it's you," Mr. Summers said in explanation, "and as far as drawing for households is concerned, that's you, too. Right?"

"Right," Bill Hutchinson said.

"How many kids, Bill?" Mr. Summers asked formally.

"Three," Bill Hutchinson said. "There's Bill, Jr., and Nancy, and little Dave. And Tessie and me."

"All right, then," Mr. Summers said. "Harry, you got their tickets back?"

Mr. Graves nodded and held up the slips of paper. "Put them in the box, then," Mr. Summers directed. "Take Bill's and put it in."

"I think we ought to start over," Mrs. Hutchinson said, as quietly as she could. "I tell you it wasn't *fair*. You didn't give him time enough to choose. Everybody saw that."

Mr. Graves had selected the five slips and put them in the box, and he dropped all the papers but those onto the ground, where the breeze caught them and lifted them off.

"Listen, everybody," Mrs. Hutchinson was saying to people around her.

"Ready, Bill?" Mr. Summers asked, and Bill Hutchinson, with one quick glance around at his wife and children, nodded.

"Remember," Mr. Summers said, "take the slips and keep them folded until each person has taken one. Harry, you help little Dave." Mr. Graves took the hand of the little boy, who came willingly with him up to the box. "Take a paper out of the box, Davy," Mr. Summers said. Davy put his hand into the box and laughed. "Take just *one* paper," Mr. Summers said. "Harry, you hold it for him." Mr. Graves took the child's hand and removed the folded paper from the tight fist and held it while little Dave stood next to him and looked up at him wonderingly.

"Nancy next," Mr. Summers said. Nancy was twelve, and her school friends breathed heavily as she went forward, switching her skirt, and took a slip daintily from the box. "Bill, Jr.," Mr. Summers said, and Billy, his face red and his feet overlarge, nearly knocked the box over as he got a paper out. "Tessie," Mr. Summers said. She hesitated for a minute, looking around defiantly, and then set her lips and went up to the box. She snatched a paper out and held it behind her.

"Bill," Mr. Summers said, and Bill Hutchinson reached into the box and felt around, bringing his hand out at last with the slip of paper in it.

The crowd was quiet. A girl whispered, "I hope it's not Nancy," and the sound of the whisper reached the edges of the crowd.

"It's not the way it used to be," Old Man Warner said clearly. "People ain't the way they used to be."

"All right," Mr. Summers said. "Open the papers. Harry, you open little Dave's."

Mr. Graves opened the slip of paper and there was a general sigh through the crowd as he held it up and everyone could see that it was blank. Nancy and Bill, Jr., opened theirs at the same time, and both beamed and laughed, turning around to the crowd and holding their slips of paper above their heads.

"Tessie," Mr. Summers said. There was a pause, and then Mr. Summers looked at Bill Hutchinson, and Bill unfolded his paper and showed it. It was blank.

"It's Tessie," Mr. Summers said, and his voice was hushed. "Show us her paper, Bill."

Bill Hutchinson went over to his wife and forced the slip of paper out of her hand. It had a black spot on it, the black spot Mr. Summers had made the night before with the heavy pencil in the coal-company office. Bill Hutchinson held it up, and there was a stir in the crowd.

"All right, folks," Mr. Summers said. "Let's finish quickly."

Although the villagers had forgotten the ritual and lost the original black box, they still remembered to use stones. The pile of stones the boys had made earlier was ready; there were stones on the ground with the blowing scraps of paper that had come out of the box. Mrs. Delacroix selected a stone so large she had to pick it up with both hands and turned to Mrs. Dunbar. "Come on," she said. "Hurry up."

75   Mrs. Dunbar had small stones in both hands, and she said, gasping for breath, "I can't run at all. You'll have to go ahead and I'll catch up with you."

The children had stones already, and someone gave little Davy Hutchinson a few pebbles.

Tessie Hutchinson was in the center of a cleared space by now, and she held her hands out desperately as the villagers moved in on her. "It isn't fair," she said. A stone hit her on the side of the head.

Old Man Warner was saying, "Come on, come on, everyone." Steve Adams was in the front of the crowd of villagers, with Mrs. Graves beside him.

"It isn't fair, it isn't right," Mrs. Hutchinson screamed, and then they were upon her.

Edgar Allan Poe   (1809–1849)
The Cask of Amontillado

The thousand injuries of Fortunato I had borne as I best could; but when he ventured upon insult, I vowed revenge. You, who so well know the nature of my soul, will not suppose, however, that I gave utterance to a threat. *At length* I would be avenged; this was a point definitely settled—but the very definitiveness with which it was resolved precluded the idea of risk. I must not only punish, but punish with impunity. A wrong is unredressed when retribution overtakes its redresser. It is equally unredressed when the avenger fails to make himself felt as such to him who has done the wrong.

It must be understood, that neither by word nor deed had I given Fortunato cause to doubt my good-will. I continued, as was my wont, to smile in his face, and he did not perceive that my smile *now* was at the thought of his immolation.

He had a weak point—this Fortunato—although in other regards he was a man to be respected and even feared. He prided himself on his connoisseurship in wine. Few Italians have the true virtuoso spirit. For the most part their enthusiasm is adopted to suit the time and opportunity—to practise imposture upon the British and Austrian *millionnaires*. In painting and gemmary Fortunato, like his countrymen, was a quack—but in the matter of old wines he was sincere. In this respect I did not differ from him materially: I was skillful in the Italian vintages myself, and bought largely whenever I could.

It was about dusk, one evening during the supreme madness of the carnival season, that I encountered my friend. He accosted me with excessive warmth, for he had been drinking much. The man wore motley. He had on a tight-fitting parti-striped dress, and his head was surmounted by the conical cap and bells. I was so pleased to see him, that I thought I should never have done wringing his hand.

I said to him: "My dear Fortunato, you are luckily met. How remarkably well you are looking to-day! But I have received a pipe of what passes for Amontillado,[1] and I have my doubts."

"How?" said he. "Amontillado? A pipe? Impossible! And in the middle of the carnival!"

"I have my doubts," I replied; "and I was silly enough to pay the full Amontillado price without consulting you in the matter. You were not to be found, and I was fearful of losing a bargain."

"Amontillado!"

"I have my doubts."

"Amontillado!"

"And I must satisfy them."

"Amontillado!"

"As you are engaged, I am on my way to Luchesi. If any one has a critical turn, it is he. He will tell me—"

"Luchesi cannot tell Amontillado from Sherry."

"And yet some fools will have it that his taste is a match for your own."

"Come, let us go."

"Whither?"

"To your vaults."

"My friend, no; I will not impose upon your good nature. I perceive you have an engagement. Luchesi—"

"I have no engagement;—come."

"My friend, no. It is not the engagement, but the severe cold with which I perceive you are afflicted. The vaults are insufferably damp. They are encrusted with nitre."

"Let us go, nevertheless. The cold is merely nothing. Amontillado! You have been imposed upon. And as for Luchesi, he cannot distinguish Sherry from Amontillado."

Thus speaking, Fortunato possessed himself of my arm. Putting on a mask of black silk, and drawing a *roquelaire* closely about my person, I suffered him to hurry me to my palazzo.

There were no attendants at home; they had absconded to make merry in honor of the time. I had told them that I should not return until the morning, and had given them explicit orders not to stir from the house. These orders were sufficient, I well knew, to insure their immediate disappearance, one and all, as soon as my back was turned.

I took from their sconces two flambeaux, and giving one to Fortunato, bowed him through several suites of rooms to the archway that led into the vaults. I passed down a long and winding staircase, requesting him to be cautious as he followed. We came at length to the foot of the descent, and stood together on the damp ground of the catacombs of the Montresors.

The gait of my friend was unsteady, and the bells upon his cap jingled as he strode.

"The pipe?" said he.

"It is farther on," said I; "but observe the white web-work which gleams from these cavern walls."

He turned toward me, and looked into my eyes with two filmy orbs that distilled the rheum of intoxication.

"Nitre?" he asked, at length.

"Nitre," I replied. "How long have you had that cough?"

[1]A highly prized pale, dry Spanish wine from Montilla.

"Ugh! ugh! ugh!—ugh! ugh! ugh!—ugh! ugh! ugh!—ugh! ugh! ugh!—ugh! ugh! ugh!"
My poor friend found it impossible to reply for many minutes.

"It is nothing," he said, at last.

35   "Come," I said, with decision, "we will go back; your health is precious. You are rich, respected, admired, beloved; you are happy, as once I was. You are a man to be missed. For me it is no matter. We will go back; you will be ill, and I cannot be responsible. Besides, there is Luchesi—"

"Enough," he said; "the cough is a mere nothing; it will not kill me. I shall not die of a cough."

"True—true," I replied; "and, indeed, I had no intention of alarming you unnecessarily; but you should use all proper caution. A draught of this Medoc will defend us from the damps."

Here I knocked off the neck of a bottle which I drew from a long row of its fellows that lay upon the mould.

"Drink," I said, presenting him the wine.

40   He raised it to his lips with a leer. He paused and nodded to me familiarly, while his bells jingled.

"I drink," he said, "to the buried that repose around us."

"And I to your long life."

He again took my arm, and we proceeded.

"These vaults," he said, "are extensive."

45   "The Montresors," I replied, "were a great and numerous family."

"I forget your arms."

"A huge human foot d'or, in a field azure; the foot crushes a serpent rampant whose fangs are imbedded in the heel."

"And the motto?"

"Nemo me impune lacessit."[2]

50   "Good!" he said.

The wine sparkled in his eyes and the bells jingled. My own fancy grew warm with the Medoc. We had passed through walls of piled bones, with casks and puncheons intermingling, into the inmost recesses of the catacombs. I paused again, and this time I made bold to seize Fortunato by an arm above the elbow.

"The nitre!" I said; "see, it increases. It hangs like moss upon the vaults. We are below the river's bed. The drops of moisture trickle among the bones. Come, we will go back ere it is too late. Your cough—"

"It is nothing," he said; "let us go on. But first, another draught of the Medoc."

I broke and reached him a flagon of De Grâve. He emptied it at a breath. His eyes flashed with a fierce light. He laughed and threw the bottle upward with a gesticulation I did not understand.

55   I looked at him in surprise. He repeated the movement—a grotesque one.

"You do not comprehend?" he said.

"Not I," I replied.

"Then you are not of the brotherhood."

"How?"

60   "You are not of the masons."

"Yes, yes," I said; "yes, yes."

"You? Impossible! A mason?"

"A mason," I replied.

---

[2]No one injures me with impunity.

"A sign," he said.

"It is this," I answered, producing a trowel from beneath the folds of my *roquelaire*.

"You jest," he exclaimed, recoiling a few paces. "But let us proceed to the Amontillado."

"Be it so," I said, replacing the tool beneath the cloak, and again offering him my arm. He leaned upon it heavily. We continued our route in search of the Amontillado. We passed through a range of low arches, descended, passed on, and descending again, arrived at a deep crypt, in which the foulness of the air caused our flambeaux rather to glow than flame.

At the most remote end of the crypt there appeared another less spacious. Its walls had been lined with human remains, piled to the vault overhead, in the fashion of the great catacombs of Paris. Three sides of this interior crypt were still ornamented in this manner. From the fourth the bones had been thrown down, and lay promiscuously upon the earth, forming at one point a mound of some size. Within the wall thus exposed by the displacing of the bones, we perceived a still interior recess, in depth about four feet, in width three, in height six or seven. It seemed to have been constructed for no special use within itself, but formed merely the interval between two of the colossal supports of the roof of the catacombs, and was backed by one of the circumscribing walls of solid granite.

It was in vain that Fortunato, uplifting his dull torch, endeavored to pry into the depth of the recess. Its termination the feeble light did not enable us to see.

"Proceed," I said; "herein is the Amontillado. As for Luchesi—"

"He is an ignoramus," interrupted my friend, as he stepped unsteadily forward, while I followed immediately at his heels. In an instant he had reached the extremity of the niche, and finding his progress arrested by the rock, stood stupidly bewildered. A moment more and I had fettered him to the granite. In its surface were two iron staples, distant from each other about two feet, horizontally. From one of these depended a short chain, from the other a padlock. Throwing the links about his waist, it was but the work of a few seconds to secure it. He was too much astounded to resist. Withdrawing the key I stepped back from the recess.

"Pass your hand," I said, "over the wall; you cannot help feeling the nitre. Indeed it is *very* damp. Once more let me *implore* you to return. No? Then I must positively leave you. But I must first render you all the little attentions in my power."

"The Amontillado!" ejaculated my friend, not yet recovered from his astonishment.

"True," I replied; "the Amontillado."

As I said these words I busied myself among the pile of bones of which I have before spoken. Throwing them aside, I soon uncovered a quantity of building stone and mortar. With these materials and with the aid of my trowel, I began vigorously to wall up the entrance of the niche.

I had scarcely laid the first tier of the masonry when I discovered that the intoxication of Fortunato had in a great measure worn off. The earliest indication I had of this was a low moaning cry from the depth of the recess. It was *not* the cry of a drunken man. There was then a long and obstinate silence. I laid the second tier, and the third, and the fourth; and then I heard the furious vibrations of the chain. The noise lasted for several minutes, during which, that I might hearken to it with the more satisfaction, I ceased my labors and sat down upon the bones. When at last the clanking subsided, I resumed the trowel, and finished without interruption the fifth, the sixth, and the seventh tier. The wall was now nearly upon a level with my breast. I again paused, and holding the flambeaux over the masonwork, threw a few feeble rays upon the figure within.

A succession of loud and shrill screams, bursting suddenly from the throat of the chained form, seemed to thrust me violently back. For a brief moment I hesitated—I trembled. Unsheathing my rapier, I began to grope with it about the recess; but the thought of an instant reassured me. I placed my hand upon the solid fabric of the catacombs, and felt satisfied. I reapproached the wall. I replied to the yells of him who clamored. I re-echoed—I aided—I surpassed them in volume and in strength. I did this, and the clamorer grew still.

It was now midnight, and my task was drawing to a close. I had completed the eighth, the ninth, and the tenth tier. I had finished a portion of the last and the eleventh; there remained but a single stone to be fitted and plastered in. I struggled with its weight; I placed it partially in its destined position. But now there came from out the niche a low laugh that erected the hairs upon my head. It was succeeded by a sad voice, which I had difficulty in recognizing as that of the noble Fortunato. The voice said—

"Ha! ha! ha!—he! he!—a very good joke indeed—an excellent jest. We will have many a rich laugh about it at the palazzo—he! he! he!—over our wine—he! he! he!"

80   "The Amontillado!" I said.

"He! he! he!—he! he! he!—yes, the Amontillado. But is it not getting late? Will not they be awaiting us at the palazzo, the Lady Fortunato and the rest? Let us be gone."

"Yes," I said, "let us be gone."

"For the love of God, Montresor!"

"Yes," I said, "for the love of God!"

85   But to these words I hearkened in vain for a reply. I grew impatient. I called aloud:

"Fortunato!"

No answer. I called again:

"Fortunato!"

No answer still. I thrust a torch through the remaining aperture and let it fall within. There came forth in return only a jingling of the bells. My heart grew sick—on account of the dampness of the catacombs. I hastened to make an end of my labor. I forced the last stone into its position; I plastered it up. Against the new masonry I re-erected the old rampart of bones. For the half of a century no mortal has disturbed them. *In pace requiescat!*[3]

Comments and Questions

1. J. R. Hammond has suggested that a chief reason Poe's writing continues to be popular is that "his strength lay in the description of mental and emotional states, in removing layers of artifice from man's animal nature and affording a terrifying glimpse into the violence and sadism present beneath."[4] In that connection, what similarities and differences would you emphasize between Poe's story and Jackson's "The Lottery" immediately above or Browning's "Porphyria's Lover" (p. 473)?

2. Poe's story is as heavily laced with irony as it is with revenge. Jackson also uses irony extensively and effectively in "The Lottery." Both tales open with settings and language drenched in irony and move ahead with irony of names, action, situation, and so on. To what extent, however, does your first reading of passages in each story coincide with your recognition that they are ironical? Can you characterize and account for the quite different ironical methods of each story? To what extent do considerations of point of view,

[3] May he rest in peace!
[4] *An Edgar Allan Poe Companion,* Totowa: Barnes & Noble, 1981, p. 33.

characterization, and emotional impact justify the use of one or the other method? (See "Sidenote on irony," p. 26.)

3. Explain the repeated references to nitre (niter).

4. How is it entirely in keeping with Montresor's character to insist repeatedly that Fortunato turn back out of the catacombs? How will that later enhance his pleasure in the revenge he takes?

5. Comment on the functions of the costumes of Montresor and Fortunato; on the effect of Montresor's remark, "My heart grew sick—on account of the dampness of the catacombs"; on the irony of the final sentence.

6. Does Montresor fulfill the stipulations for revenge given in the opening paragraph? Comment on poetic or moral justice in Poe's tale.

Edgar Allan Poe (1809–1849)
The Purloined Letter

Poe invented and essentially perfected the detective story. Both the meticulously chiseled deductive pattern of his tales of ratiocination and the intensely cerebral C. Auguste Dupin, calm and analytical in the heart of enigma, have influenced virtually every mystery writer of genuine stature. Sherlock Holmes, Father Brown, Ellery Queen, Charlie Chan, and countless others are all the descendants of Monsieur Dupin, sometime poet, severe logician, student of human nature, and master sleuth. The opening sentences of "The Murders in the Rue Morgue," where Dupin makes his first appearance, describe those analytical faculties that have become synonymous with his name and method:

> *The mental features discoursed of as the analytical, are, in themselves, but little susceptible of analysis. We appreciate them only in their effects. We know of them, among other things, that they are always to their possessor, when inordinately possessed, a source of the liveliest enjoyment. As the strong man exults in his physical ability, delighting in such exercises as call his muscles into action, so glories the analyst in that moral activity which* disentangles. *He derives pleasure from even the most trivial occupations bringing his talent into play. He is fond of enigmas, of conundrums, hieroglyphics; exhibiting in his solutions of each a degree of* acumen *which appears to the ordinary apprehension* praeternatural. *His results, brought about by the very soul and essence of method, have, in truth, the whole air of intuition.*

Poe goes on to equate the analytic with the "truly imaginative" in describing the mental processes of a Dupin, the "moral activity" that leads, step by inexorable step, to truth.

The method Poe describes appears in its purest form—without the distraction of murder—in "The Purloined Letter." After observing Dupin in action there, you should apply the method yourself to unravel as satisfactorily as possible the chief remaining mystery of a notorious murder case, the origin of the revenge motive, Fortunato's "insult" to Montresor in "The Cask of Amontillado" above. In the process of determining what that "insult" might have been, you can sharpen some very useful mental attributes. Much the same kind of imagination, analysis, and peripheral vision described by Poe and demonstrated by Dupin are required in the critical reading of literature. What are the clues to unravel the mystery? Surely Dupin would find them ample for some admirable deductions.

Nil sapientiæ odiosius acumine nimio.[1]—*Seneca*

At Paris, just after dark one gusty evening in the autumn of 18—, I was enjoying the twofold luxury of meditation and a meerschaum, in company with my friend, C. Auguste Dupin, in his little back library, or book-closet, *au troisième,* No. 33 *Rue Dunôt, Faubourg St. Germain.* For one hour at least we had maintained a profound silence; while each, to any casual observer, might have seemed intently and exclusively occupied with the curling eddies of smoke that oppressed the atmosphere of the chamber. For myself, however, I was mentally discussing certain topics which had formed matter for conversation between us at an earlier period of the evening; I mean the affair of the Rue Morgue, and the mystery attending the murder of Marie Rogêt.[2] I looked upon it, therefore, as something of a coincidence, when the door of our apartment was thrown open and admitted our old acquaintance, Monsieur G——, the Prefect of the Parisian police.

We gave him a hearty welcome; for there was nearly half as much of the entertaining as of the contemptible about the man, and we had not seen him for several years. We had been sitting in the dark, and Dupin now arose for the purpose of lighting a lamp, but sat down again, without doing so, upon G.'s saying that he had called to consult us, or rather to ask the opinion of my friend, about some official business which had occasioned a great deal of trouble.

"If it is any point requiring reflection," observed Dupin, as he forbore to enkindle the wick, "we shall examine it to better purpose in the dark."

"That is another of your odd notions," said the Prefect, who had the fashion of calling everything "odd" that was beyond his comprehension, and thus lived amid an absolute legion of "oddities."

5   "Very true," said Dupin, as he supplied his visitor with a pipe, and rolled toward him a comfortable chair.

"And what is the difficulty now?" I asked. "Nothing more in the assassination way I hope?"

"Oh, no; nothing of that nature. The fact is, the business is *very* simple indeed, and I make no doubt that we can manage it sufficiently well ourselves; but then I thought Dupin would like to hear the details of it, because it is so excessively *odd.*"

"Simple and odd," said Dupin.

"Why, yes; and not exactly that either. The fact is, we have all been a good deal puzzled because the affair *is* so simple, and yet baffles us altogether."

10   "Perhaps it is the very simplicity of the thing which puts you at fault," said my friend.

"What nonsense you *do* talk!" replied the Prefect, laughing heartily.

"Perhaps the mystery is a little *too* plain," said Dupin.

---

[1] Nothing is more inimical to wisdom than an excess of acuteness.   [2] Two murder cases Dupin solves in Poe's earlier fiction.

"Oh, good heavens! who ever heard of such an idea?"

"A little *too* self-evident."

15 "Ha! ha! ha!—ha! ha! ha!—ho! ho! ho!" roared our visitor, profoundly amused, "oh, Dupin, you will be the death of me yet!"

"And what, after all, *is* the matter on hand?" I asked.

"Why, I will tell you," replied the Prefect, as he gave a long, steady, and contemplative puff, and settled himself in his chair. "I will tell you in a few words; but, before I begin, let me caution you that this is an affair demanding the greatest secrecy, and that I should most probably lose the position I now hold, were it known that I confided it to any one."

"Proceed," said I.

"Or not," said Dupin.

20 "Well, then; I have received personal information, from a very high quarter, that a certain document of the last importance has been purloined from the royal apartments. The individual who purloined it is known; this beyond a doubt; he was seen to take it. It is known, also, that it still remains in his possession."

"How is this known?" asked Dupin.

"It is clearly inferred," replied the Prefect, "from the nature of the document, and from the non-appearance of certain results which would at once arise from its passing *out* of the robber's possession—that is to say, from his employing it as he must design in the end to employ it."

"Be a little more explicit," I said.

"Well, I may venture so far as to say that the paper gives its holder a certain power in a certain quarter where such power is immensely valuable." The Prefect was fond of the cant of diplomacy.

25 "Still I do not quite understand," said Dupin.

"No? Well; the disclosure of the document to a third person, who shall be nameless, would bring in question the honor of a personage of most exalted station; and this fact gives the holder of the document an ascendancy over the illustrious personage whose honor and peace are so jeopardized."

"But this ascendancy," I interposed, "would depend upon the robber's knowledge of the loser's knowledge of the robber. Who would dare—"

"The thief," said G., "is the Minister D——, who dares all things, those unbecoming as well as those becoming a man. The method of the theft was not less ingenious than bold. The document in question—a letter, to be frank—had been received by the personage robbed while alone in the royal *boudoir*. During its perusal she was suddenly interrupted by the entrance of the other exalted personage from whom especially it was her wish to conceal it. After a hurried and vain endeavor to thrust it in a drawer, she was forced to place it, open as it was, upon a table. The address, however, was uppermost, and, the contents thus unexposed, the letter escaped notice. At this juncture enters the Minister D——. His lynx eye immediately perceives the paper, recognizes the handwriting of the address, observes the confusion of the personage addressed, and fathoms her secret. After some business transactions, hurried through in his ordinary manner, he produces a letter somewhat similar to the one in question, opens it, pretends to read it, and then places it in close juxtaposition to the other. Again he converses, for some fifteen minutes, upon the public affairs. At length, in taking leave, he takes also from the table the letter to which he had no claim. Its rightful owner saw, but, of course, dared not call attention to the act, in the presence of the third personage who stood at her elbow. The minister decamped; leaving his own letter—one of no importance—upon the table."

"Here, then," said Dupin to me, "you have precisely what you demand to make the ascendancy complete—the robber's knowledge of the loser's knowledge of the robber."

30   "Yes," replied the Prefect; "and the power thus attained has, for some months past, been wielded, for political purposes, to a very dangerous extent. The personage robbed is more thoroughly convinced, every day, of the necessity of reclaiming her letter. But this, of course, cannot be done openly. In fine, driven to despair, she has committed the matter to me."

"Than whom," said Dupin, amid a perfect whirlwind of smoke, "no more sagacious agent could, I suppose, be desired, or even imagined."

"You flatter me," replied the Prefect; "but it is possible that some such opinion may have been entertained."

"It is clear," said I, "as you observe, that the letter is still in the possession of the minister; since it is this possession, and not any employment of the letter, which bestows the power. With the employment the power departs."

"True," said G.; "and upon this conviction I proceeded. My first care was to make thorough search of the minister's hotel;[3] and here my chief embarrassment lay in the necessity of searching without his knowledge. Beyond all things, I have been warned of the danger which would result from giving him reason to suspect our design."

35   "But," said I, "you are quite *au fait*[4] in these investigations. The Parisian police have done this thing often before."

"Oh, yes; and for this reason I did not despair. The habits of the minister gave me, too, a great advantage. He is frequently absent from home all night. His servants are by no means numerous. They sleep at a distance from their master's apartment, and, being chiefly Neapolitans, are readily made drunk. I have keys, as you know, with which I can open any chamber or cabinet in Paris. For three months a night has not passed, during the greater part of which I have not been engaged, personally, in ransacking the D____ Hotel. My honor is interested, and, to mention a great secret, the reward is enormous. So I did not abandon the search until I had become fully satisfied that the thief is a more astute man than myself. I fancy that I have investigated every nook and corner of the premises in which it is possible that the paper can be concealed."

"But is it not possible," I suggested, "that although the letter may be in possession of the minister, as it unquestionably is, he may have concealed it elsewhere than upon his own premises?"

"This is barely possible," said Dupin. "The present peculiar condition of affairs at court, and especially of those intrigues in which D____ is known to be involved, would render the instant availability of the document—its susceptibility of being produced at a moment's notice—a point of nearly equal importance with its possession."

"Its susceptibility of being produced?" said I.

40   "That is to say, of being *destroyed,*" said Dupin.

"True," I observed; "the paper is clearly then upon the premises. As for its being upon the person of the minister, we may consider that as out of the question."

"Entirely," said the Prefect. "He has been twice waylaid, as if by footpads, and his person rigidly searched under my own inspection."

"You might have spared yourself this trouble," said Dupin. "D____, I presume, is not altogether a fool, and, if not, must have anticipated these waylayings, as a matter of course."

"Not *altogether* a fool," said G., "but then he is a poet, which I take to be only one remove from a fool."

---

[3] Townhouse.   [4] Skillful.

45   "True," said Dupin, after a long and thoughtful whiff from his meerschaum, "although I have been guilty of certain doggerel myself."

"Suppose you detail," said I, "the particulars of your search."

"Why, the fact is, we took our time, and we searched *everywhere*. I have had long experience in these affairs. I took the entire building, room by room; devoting the nights of a whole week to each. We examined, first, the furniture of each apartment. We opened every possible drawer; and I presume you know that, to a properly trained police-agent, such a thing as a *'secret'* drawer is impossible. Any man is a dolt who permits a 'secret' drawer to escape him in a search of this kind. The thing is *so* plain. There is a certain amount of bulk—of space—to be accounted for in every cabinet. Then we have accurate rules. The fiftieth part of a line could not escape us. After the cabinets we took the chairs. The cushions we probed with the fine long needles you have seen me employ. From the tables we removed the tops."

"Why so?"

"Sometimes the top of a table, or other similarly arranged piece of furniture, is removed by the person wishing to conceal an article; then the leg is excavated, the article deposited within the cavity, and the top replaced. The bottoms and tops of bedposts are employed in the same way."

50   "But could not the cavity be detected by sounding?" I asked.

"By no means, if, when the article is deposited, a sufficient wadding of cotton be placed around it. Besides, in our case, we were obliged to proceed without noise."

"But you could not have removed—you could not have taken to pieces *all* articles of furniture in which it would have been possible to make a deposit in the manner you mention. A letter may be compressed into a thin spiral roll, not differing much in shape or bulk from a large knitting-needle, and in this form it might be inserted into the rung of a chair, for example. You did not take to pieces all the chairs?"

"Certainly not; but we did better—we examined the rungs of every chair in the hotel, and, indeed, the jointings of every description of furniture, by the aid of a most powerful microscope.[5] Had there been any traces of recent disturbance we should not have failed to detect it instantly. A single grain of gimlet-dust, for example, would have been as obvious as an apple. Any disorder in the gluing—any unusual gaping in the joints—would have sufficed to insure detection."

"I presume you looked to the mirrors, between the boards and the plates, and you probed the beds and the bedclothes, as well as the curtains and carpets."

55   "That of course; and when we had absolutely completed every particle of the furniture in this way, then we examined the house itself. We divided its entire surface into compartments, which we numbered, so that none might be missed; then we scrutinized each individual square inch throughout the premises, including the two houses immediately adjoining, with the microscope, as before."

"The two houses adjoining!" I exclaimed; "you must have had a great deal of trouble."

"We had; but the reward offered is prodigious."

"You include the *grounds* about the houses?"

"All the grounds are paved with brick. They gave us comparatively little trouble. We examined the moss between the bricks, and found it undisturbed."

60   "You looked among D——'s papers, of course, and into the books of the library?"

"Certainly; we opened every package and parcel; we not only opened every book, but we turned over every leaf in each volume, not contenting ourselves with a mere shake,

[5]Magnifying glass.

according to the fashion of some of our police officers. We also measured the thickness of every book-*cover,* with the most accurate admeasurement, and applied to each the most jealous scrutiny of the microscope. Had any of the bindings been recently meddled with, it would have been utterly impossible that the fact should have escaped observation. Some five or six volumes, just from the hands of the binder, we carefully probed, longitudinally, with the needles."

"You explored the floors beneath the carpets?"

"Beyond doubt. We removed every carpet, and examined the boards with the microscope."

"And the paper on the walls?"

65   "Yes."

"You looked into the cellars?"

"We did."

"Then," I said, "you have been making a miscalculation, and the letter is *not* upon the premises, as you suppose."

"I fear you are right there," said the Prefect. "And now, Dupin, what would you advise me to do?"

70   "To make a thorough research of the premises."

"That is absolutely needless," replied G_____. "I am not more sure that I breathe than I am that the letter is not at the hotel."

"I have no better advice to give you," said Dupin. "You have, of course, an accurate description of the letter?"

"Oh, yes!"—And here the Prefect, producing a memorandum-book, proceeded to read aloud a minute account of the internal, and especially of the external, appearance of the missing document. Soon after finishing the perusal of this description, he took his departure, more entirely depressed in spirits than I had ever known the good gentleman before.

In about a month afterward he paid us another visit, and found us occupied very nearly as before. He took a pipe and a chair and entered into some ordinary conversation. At length I said:

75   "Well, but G., what of the purloined letter? I presume you have at last made up your mind that there is no such thing as overreaching the Minister?"

"Confound him, say I—yes; I made the re-examination, however, as Dupin suggested—but it was all labor lost, as I knew it would be."

"How much was the reward offered, did you say?" asked Dupin.

"Why, a very great deal—a *very* liberal reward—I don't like to say how much, precisely; but one thing I *will* say, that I wouldn't mind giving my individual check for fifty thousand francs to any one who could obtain me that letter. The fact is, it is becoming of more and more importance every day; and the reward has been lately doubled. If it were trebled, however, I could do no more than I have done."

"Why, yes," said Dupin, drawlingly, between the whiffs of his meerschaum, "I really—think, G., you have not exerted yourself—to the utmost in this matter. You might—do a little more, I think, eh?"

80   "How?—in what way?"

"Why—puff, puff—you might—puff, puff—employ counsel in the matter, eh?—puff, puff, puff. Do you remember the story they tell of Abernethy?"

"No; hang Abernethy!"

"To be sure! hang him and welcome. But, once upon a time, a certain rich miser conceived the design of sponging upon this Abernethy for a medical opinion. Getting up, for this purpose, an ordinary conversation in a private company, he insinuated his case to the physician, as that of an imaginary individual.

" 'We will suppose,' said the miser, 'that his symptoms are such and such; now, doctor, what would *you* have directed him to take?'

85   " 'Take!' said Abernethy, 'why, take *advice,* to be sure.' "

"But," said the Prefect, a little discomposed, "*I* am *perfectly* willing to take advice, and to pay for it. I would *really* give fifty thousand francs to any one who would aid me in the matter."

"In that case," replied Dupin, opening a drawer, and producing a check-book, "you may as well fill me up a check for the amount mentioned. When you have signed it, I will hand you the letter."

I was astounded. The Prefect appeared absolutely thunder-stricken. For some minutes he remained speechless and motionless, looking incredulously at my friend with open mouth, and eyes that seemed starting from their sockets; then apparently recovering himself in some measure, he seized a pen, and, after several pauses and vacant stares, finally filled up and signed a check for fifty thousand francs, and handed it across the table to Dupin. The latter examined it carefully and deposited it in his pocketbook; then, unlocking an *escritoire,*[6] took thence a letter and gave it to the Prefect. This functionary grasped it in a perfect agony of joy, opened it with a trembling hand, cast a rapid glance at its contents, and then, scrambling and struggling to the door, rushed at length unceremoniously from the room and from the house, without having uttered a syllable since Dupin had requested him to fill up the check.

When he had gone, my friend entered into some explanations.

90   "The Parisian police," he said, "are exceedingly able in their way. They are persevering, ingenious, cunning, and thoroughly versed in the knowledge which their duties seem chiefly to demand. Thus, when G_____ detailed to us his mode of searching the premises at the Hotel D_____, I felt entire confidence in his having made a satisfactory investigation—so far as his labors extended."

"So far as his labors extended?" said I.

"Yes," said Dupin. "The measures adopted were not only the best of their kind, but carried out to absolute perfection. Had the letter been deposited within the range of their search, these fellows would, beyond a question, have found it."

I merely laughed—but he seemed quite serious in all that he said.

"The measures, then," he continued, "were good in their kind, and well executed; their defect lay in their being inapplicable to the case and to the man. A certain set of highly ingenious resources are, with the Prefect, a sort of Procrustean[7] bed, to which he forcibly adapts his designs. But he perpetually errs by being too deep or too shallow for the matter in hand; and many a school-boy is a better reasoner than he. I knew one about eight years of age, whose success at guessing in the game of 'even and odd' attracted universal admiration. This game is simple, and is played with marbles. One player holds in his hand a number of these toys, and demands of another whether that number is even or odd. If the guess is right, the guesser wins one; if wrong, he loses one. The boy to whom I allude won all the marbles of the school. Of course he had some principle of guessing; and this lay in mere observation and admeasurement of the astuteness of his opponents. For example, an arrant simpleton is his opponent, and, holding up his closed hand, asks, 'Are they even or odd?' Our school-boy replies, 'Odd,' and loses; but upon the second trial he wins, for he then says to himself: 'The simpleton had them even upon the first trial, and his amount of cunning is just sufficient to make him have them odd upon the second; I will therefore guess odd';—he guesses odd, and wins. Now, with a simpleton

[6]Writing desk.
[7] In Greek mythology, Procrustes robbed travelers, tying them in his bed and stretching them or cutting off their legs to make them fit it.

a degree above the first, he would have reasoned thus: 'This fellow finds that in the first instance I guessed odd, and, in the second, he will propose to himself, upon the first impulse, a simple variation from even to odd, as did the first simpleton; but then a second thought will suggest that this is too simple a variation, and finally he will decide upon putting it even as before. I will therefore guess even';—he guesses even, and wins. Now this mode of reasoning in the school-boy, whom his fellows termed 'lucky,'—what, in its last analysis, is it?"

95   "It is merely," I said, "an identification of the reasoner's intellect with that of his opponent."

"It is," said Dupin; "and, upon inquiring of the boy by what means he effected the *thorough* identification in which his success consisted, I received answer as follows: 'When I wish to find out how wise, or how stupid, or how good, or how wicked is any one, or what are his thoughts at the moment, I fashion the expression of my face, as accurately as possible, in accordance with the expression of his, and then wait to see what thoughts or sentiments arise in my mind or heart, as if to match or correspond with the expression.' This response of the school-boy lies at the bottom of all the spurious profundity which has been attributed to Rochefoucauld, to La Bougive, to Machiavelli, and to Campanella."

"And the identification," I said, "of the reasoner's intellect with that of his opponent, depends, if I understand you aright, upon the accuracy with which the opponent's intellect is admeasured."

"For its practical value it depends upon this," replied Dupin; "and the Prefect and his cohort fail so frequently, first, by default of this identification, and, secondly, by ill-admeasurement, or rather through non-admeasurement, of the intellect with which they are engaged. They consider only their *own* ideas of ingenuity; and, in searching for any thing hidden, advert only to the modes in which *they* would have hidden it. They are right in this much—that their own ingenuity is a faithful representative of that of *the mass;* but when the cunning of the individual felon is diverse in character from their own, the felon foils them, of course. This always happens when it is above their own, and very usually when it is below. They have no variation of principle in their investigations; at best, when urged by some unusual emergency—by some extraordinary reward—they extend or ex-aggerate their old modes of *practice,* without touching their principles. What, for example, in this case of D——, has been done to vary the principle of action? What is all this boring, and probing, and sounding, and scrutinizing with the microscope, and dividing the surface of the building into registered square inches—what is it all but an exaggeration *of the application* of the one principle or set of principles of search, which are based upon the one set of notions regarding human ingenuity, to which the Prefect, in the long routine of his duty, has been accustomed? Do you not see he has taken it for granted that *all* men proceed to conceal a letter, not exactly in a gimlet-hole bored in a chair-leg, but, at least, in *some* out-of-the-way hole or corner suggested by the same tenor of thought which would urge a man to secrete a letter in a gimlet-hole bored in a chair-leg? And do you not see also, that such *recherchés* nooks for concealment are adapted only for ordinary occa-sions, and would be adopted only by ordinary intellects; for, in all cases of concealment, a disposal of the article concealed—a disposal of it in this *recherché* manner,—is, in the very first instance, presumable and presumed; and thus its discovery depends, not at all upon the acumen, but altogether upon the mere care, patience, and determination of the seekers; and where the case is of importance—or, what amounts to the same thing in the political eyes, when the reward is of magnitude,—the qualities in question have *never* been known to fail. You will now understand what I meant in suggesting that, had the purloined letter been hidden anywhere within the limits of the Prefect's examination—in other words, had the principle of its concealment been comprehended within the principles of the Prefect—its discovery would have been a matter altogether beyond question. This functionary, however, has been thoroughly mystified; and the remote source of his defeat lies in the supposition that the Minister is a fool, because he has acquired renown as a poet. All fools are poets; this the Prefect *feels;* and he is merely guilty of a *non distributio medii*[8] in thence inferring that all poets are fools."

"But is this really the poet?" I asked. "There are two brothers, I know; and both have attained reputation in letters. The Minister I believe has written learnedly on the Differential Calculus. He is a mathematician, and no poet."

100 "You are mistaken; I know him well; he is both. As poet *and* mathematician, he would reason well; as mere mathematician, he could not have reasoned at all, and thus would have been at the mercy of the Prefect."

"You surprise me," I said, "by these opinions, which have been contradicted by the voice of the world. You do not mean to set at naught the well-digested idea of centuries. The mathematical reason has long been regarded as *the* reason *par excellence.*"

"*'Il y a à parier,'*" replied Dupin, quoting from Chamfort, "*'que toute idée publique, toute convention reçue, est une sottise, car elle a convenue au plus grand nombre.'*[9] The mathematicians, I grant you, have done their best to promulgate the popular error to which you allude, and which is none the less an error for its promulgation as truth. With an art worthy a better cause, for example, they have insinuated the term 'analysis' into application to algebra. The French are the originators of this particular deception; but if a term is of any importance—if words derive any value from applicability—then 'analysis' conveys 'algebra' about as much as, in Latin, *'ambitus'* implies 'ambition,' *'religio'* 'religion,' or *'homines honesti'* a set of *honorable* men."

"You have a quarrel on hand, I see," said I, "with some of the algebraists of Paris; but proceed."

"I dispute the availability, and thus the value, of that reason which is cultivated in any especial form other than the abstractly logical. I dispute, in particular, the reason educed by mathematical study. The mathematics are the science of form and quantity; mathematical reasoning is merely logic applied to observation upon form and quantity. The great error lies in supposing that even the truths of what is called *pure* algebra are abstract or general truths. And this error is so egregious that I am confounded at the universality with which it has been received. Mathematical axioms are *not* axioms of general truth. What is true of *relation*—of form and quantity—is often grossly false in regard to morals, for example. In this latter science it is very usually *un*true that the aggregated parts are equal to the whole. In chemistry also the axiom fails. In the consideration of motive it fails; for two motives, each of a given value, have not, necessarily, a value when united, equal to the sum of their values apart. There are numerous other mathematical truths which are only truths within the limits of *relation*. But the mathematician argues from his *finite truths,* through habit, as if they were of an absolutely general applicability— as the world indeed imagines them to be. Bryant, in his very learned 'Mythology,' mentions an analogous source of error, when he says that 'although the pagan fables are not believed, yet we forget ourselves continually, and make inferences from them as existing realities.' With the algebraists, however, who are pagans themselves, the 'pagan fables' *are* believed, and the inferences are made, not so much through lapse of memory as through an unaccountable addling of the brains. In short, I never yet encountered the mere math-

---

[8]In syllogistic reasoning, an undistributed middle, which leads to a false conclusion.
[9]The odds are that every idea which is popular, every received convention, is a piece of stupidity, because it is acceptable to the greatest number.

ematician who would be trusted out of equal roots, or one who did not clandestinely hold it as a point of his faith that $x^2 + px$ was absolutely and unconditionally equal to q. Say to one of these gentlemen, by way of experiment, if you please, that you believe occasions may occur where $x^2 + px$ is *not* altogether equal to q, and, having made him understand what you mean, get out of his reach as speedily as convenient, for, beyond doubt, he will endeavor to knock you down.

105   "I mean to say," continued Dupin, while I merely laughed at his last observations, "that if the Minister had been no more than a mathematician, the Prefect would have been under no necessity of giving me this check. I knew him, however, as both mathematician and poet, and my measures were adapted to his capacity, with reference to the circumstances by which he was surrounded. I knew him as a courtier, too, and as a bold *intriguant*. Such a man, I considered, could not fail to be aware of the ordinary political modes of action. He could not have failed to anticipate—and events have proved that he did not fail to anticipate—the waylayings to which he was subjected. He must have foreseen, I reflected, the secret investigations of his premises. His frequent absences from home at night, which were hailed by the Prefect as certain aids to his success, I regarded only as *ruses,* to afford opportunity for thorough search to the police, and thus the sooner to impress them with the conviction to which G_____, in fact, did finally arrive—the conviction that the letter was not upon the premises. I felt, also, that the whole train of thought, which I was at some pains in detailing to you just now, concerning the invariable principle of political action in searches for articles concealed—I felt that this whole train of thought would necessarily pass through the mind of the minister. It would imperatively lead him to despise all the ordinary *nooks* of concealment. *He* could not, I reflected, be so weak as not to see that the most intricate and remote recess of his hotel would be as open as his commonest closets to the eyes, to the probes, to the gimlets, and to the microscopes of the Prefect. I saw, in fine, that he would be driven, as a matter of course, to *simplicity,* if not deliberately induced to it as a matter of choice. You will remember, perhaps, how desperately the Prefect laughed when I suggested, upon our first interview, that it was just possible this mystery troubled him so much on account of its being so *very* self-evident."

"Yes," said I, "I remember his merriment well. I really thought he would have fallen into convulsions."

"The material world," continued Dupin, "abounds with very strict analogies to the immaterial; and thus some color of truth has been given to the rhetorical dogma, that metaphor, or simile, may be made to strengthen an argument as well as to embellish a description. The principle of the *vis inertiæ*, for example, seems to be identical in physics and metaphysics. It is not more true in the former, that a large body is with more difficulty set in motion than a smaller one, and that its subsequent *momentum* is commensurate with this difficulty, than it is, in the latter, that intellects of the vaster capacity, while more forcible, more constant, and more eventful in their movements than those of inferior grade, are yet the less readily moved, and more embarrassed, and full of hesitation in the first steps of their progress. Again: have you ever noticed which of the street signs, over the shop doors, are the most attractive of attention?"

"I have never given the matter a thought," I said.

"There is a game of puzzles," he resumed, "which is played upon a map. One party playing requires another to find a given word—the name of town, river, state, or empire— any word, in short, upon the motley and perplexed surface of the chart. A novice in the game generally seeks to embarrass his opponents by giving them the most minutely lettered names; but the adept selects such words as stretch, in large characters, from one end of the chart to the other. These, like the over-largely lettered signs and placards of the street, escape observation by dint of being excessively obvious; and here the physical oversight is precisely analogous with the moral inapprehension by which the intellect suffers to pass unnoticed those considerations which are too obtrusively and too palpably self-evident. But this is a point, it appears, somewhat above or beneath the understanding of the Prefect. He never once thought it probable, or possible, that the minister had deposited the letter immediately beneath the nose of the whole world, by way of best preventing any portion of that world from perceiving it.

110   "But the more I reflected upon the daring, dashing, and discriminating ingenuity of D_____; upon the fact that the document must always have been *at hand,* if he intended to use it to good purpose; and upon the decisive evidence, obtained by the Prefect, that it was not hidden within the limits of that dignitary's ordinary search—the more satisfied I became that, to conceal this letter, the minister had resorted to the comprehensive and sagacious expedient of not attempting to conceal it at all.

    "Full of these ideas, I prepared myself with a pair of green spectacles, and called one fine morning, quite by accident, at the Ministerial hotel. I found D_____ at home, yawning, lounging, and dawdling, as usual, and pretending to be in the last extremity of *ennui.* He is, perhaps, the most really energetic human being now alive—but that is only when nobody sees him.

    "To be even with him, I complained of my weak eyes, and lamented the necessity of the spectacles, under cover of which I cautiously and thoroughly surveyed the whole apartment, while seemingly intent only upon the conversation of my host.

    "I paid especial attention to a large writing-table near which he sat, and upon which lay confusedly, some miscellaneous letters and other papers, with one or two musical instruments and a few books. Here, however, after a long and very deliberate scrutiny, I saw nothing to excite particular suspicion.

    "At length my eyes, in going the circuit of the room, fell upon a trumpery filigree card-rack of pasteboard, that hung dangling by a dirty blue ribbon, from a little brass knob just beneath the middle of the mantelpiece. In this rack, which had three or four compartments, were five or six visiting cards and a solitary letter. This last was much soiled and crumpled. It was torn nearly in two, across the middle—as if a design, in the first instance, to tear it entirely up as worthless, had been altered, or stayed, in the second. It had a large black seal, bearing the D_____ cipher *very* conspicuously, and was addressed, in a diminutive female hand, to D_____, the minister, himself. It was thrust carelessly, and even, as it seemed, contemptuously, into one of the uppermost divisions of the rack.

115   "No sooner had I glanced at this letter than I concluded it to be that of which I was in search. To be sure, it was, to all appearance, radically different from the one of which the Prefect had read us so minute a description. Here the seal was large and black, with the D_____ cipher; there it was small and red, with the ducal arms of the S_____ family. Here, the address, to the minister, was diminutive and feminine; there the superscription, to a certain royal personage, was markedly bold and decided; the size alone formed a point of correspondence. But, then, the *radicalness* of these differences, which was excessive; the dirt; the soiled and torn condition of the paper, so inconsistent with the *true* methodical habits of D_____, and so suggestive of a design to delude the beholder into an idea of the worthlessness of the document;—these things, together with the hyperobtrusive situation of this document, full in the view of every visitor, and thus exactly in accordance with the conclusions to which I had previously arrived; these things, I say, were strongly corroborative of suspicion, in one who came with the intention to suspect.

    "I protracted my visit as long as possible, and, while I maintained a most animated discussion with the minister, upon a topic which I knew well had never failed to interest and excite him, I kept my attention really riveted upon the letter. In this examination, I committed to memory its external appearance and arrangement in the rack; and also fell, at length, upon a discovery which set at rest whatever trivial doubt I might have entertained. In scrutinizing the edges of the paper, I observed them to be more *chafed* than seemed necessary. They presented the *broken* appearance which is manifested when a stiff paper, having been once folded and pressed with a folder, is refolded in a reversed direction, in the same creases or edges which had formed the original fold. This discovery was sufficient. It was clear to me that the letter had been turned, as a glove, inside out, redirected and re-sealed. I bade the minister good-morning, and took my departure at once, leaving a gold snuff-box upon the table.

"The next morning I called for the snuff-box, when we resumed, quite eagerly, the conversation of the preceding day. While thus engaged, however, a loud report, as if of a pistol, was heard immediately beneath the windows of the hotel, and was succeeded by a series of fearful screams, and the shoutings of a terrified mob. D———— rushed to a casement, threw it open, and looked out. In the meantime I stepped to the card-rack, took the letter, put it in my pocket, and replaced it by a *fac-simile,* (so far as regards externals) which I had carefully prepared at my lodgings—imitating the D———— cipher, very readily, by means of a seal formed of bread.

"The disturbance in the street had been occasioned by the frantic behavior of a man with a musket. He had fired it among a crowd of women and children. It proved, however, to have been without ball, and the fellow was suffered to go his way as a lunatic or a drunkard. When he had gone, D———— came from the window, whither I had followed him immediately upon securing the object in view. Soon afterward I bade him farewell. The pretended lunatic was a man in my own pay."

"But what purpose had you," I asked, "in replacing the letter by a *fac-simile?* Would it not have been better, at the first visit, to have seized it openly, and departed?"

"D————," replied Dupin, "is a desperate man, and a man of nerve. His hotel, too, is not without attendants devoted to his interests. Had I made the wild attempt you suggest, I might never have left the Ministerial presence alive. The good people of Paris might have heard of me no more. But I had an object apart from these considerations. You know my political prepossessions. In this matter, I act as a partisan of the lady concerned. For eighteen months the Minister has had her in his power. She has now him in hers—since, being unaware that the letter is not in his possession, he will proceed with his exactions as if it was. Thus will he inevitably commit himself, at once, to his political destruction. His downfall, too, will not be more precipitate than awkward. It is all very well to talk about the *facilis descensus Averni;*[10] but in all kinds of climbing, as Catalani said of singing, it is far more easy to get up than to come down. In the present instance I have no sympathy—at least no pity—for him who descends. He is that *monstrum horrendum,* an unprincipled man of genius. I confess, however, that I should like very well to know the precise character of his thoughts, when, being defied by her whom the Prefect terms 'a certain personage,' he is reduced to opening the letter which I left for him in the card-rack."

"How? did you put any thing particular in it?"

"Why—it did not seem altogether right to leave the interior blank—that would have been insulting. D————, at Vienna once, did me an evil turn, which I told him, quite good-humoredly, that I should remember. So, as I knew he would feel some curiosity in regard to the identity of the person who had outwitted him, I thought it a pity not to give him a

[10]Easy descent to Hell.

clew. He is well acquainted with my MS., and I just copied into the middle of the blank sheet the words—

" '—   —Un dessein si funeste,
          S'il n'est digne d'Atrée, est digne de Thyeste.'[11]

They are to be found in Crébillon's 'Atrée.' "

Yukio Mishima (1925–1970)
The Pearl*

December 10 was Mrs. Sasaki's birthday, but since it was Mrs. Sasaki's wish to celebrate the occasion with the minimum of fuss, she had invited to her house for afternoon tea only her closest friends. Assembled were Mesdames Yamamoto, Matsumura, Azuma, and Kasuga—all four being forty-three years of age, exact contemporaries of their hostess.

These ladies were thus members, as it were, of a Keep-Our-Ages-Secret Society, and could be trusted implicitly not to divulge to outsiders the number of candles on today's cake. In inviting to her birthday party only guests of this nature Mrs. Sasaki was showing her customary prudence.

On this occasion Mrs. Sasaki wore a pearl ring. Diamonds at an all-female gathering had not seemed in the best of taste. Furthermore, pearls better matched the color of the dress she was wearing on this particular day.

Shortly after the party had begun, Mrs. Sasaki was moving across for one last inspection of the cake when the pearl in her ring, already a little loose, finally fell from its socket. It seemed a most inauspicious event for this happy occasion, but it would have been no less embarrassing to have everyone aware of the misfortune, so Mrs. Sasaki simply left the pearl close by the rim of the large cake dish and resolved to do something about it later. Around the cake were set out the plates, forks, and paper napkins for herself and the four guests. It now occurred to Mrs. Sasaki that she had no wish to be seen wearing a ring with no stone while cutting the cake, and accordingly she removed the ring from her finger and very deftly, without turning around, slipped it into a recess in the wall behind her back.

5 Amid the general excitement of the exchange of gossip, and Mrs. Sasaki's surprise and pleasure at the thoughtful presents brought by her guests, the matter of the pearl was very quickly forgotten. Before long it was time for the customary ceremony of lighting and extinguishing the candles on the cake. Everyone crowded excitedly about the table, lending a hand in the not untroublesome task of lighting forty-three candles.

---

[11]"A plot so fatal that, if not worthy of Atreus, is yet worthy of Thyestes"—quoted from Crébillon's *Atrée et Thyeste*. Thyestes seduced the wife of Atreus, who in turn murdered Thyestes' sons and fed them to their father at a banquet.

*Translated by Geoffrey M. Sargent.

Mrs. Sasaki, with her limited lung capacity, could hardly be expected to blow out all that number at one puff, and her appearance of utter helplessness gave rise to a great deal of hilarious comment.

The procedure followed in serving the cake was that, after the first bold cut, Mrs. Sasaki carved for each guest individually a slice of whatever thickness was requested and transferred this to a small plate, which the guest then carried back with her to her own seat. With everyone stretching out hands at the same time, the crush and confusion around the table was considerable.

On top of the cake was a floral design executed in pink icing and liberally interspersed with small silver balls. These were silver-painted crystals of sugar—a common enough decoration on birthday cakes. In the struggle to secure helpings, moreover, flakes of icing, crumbs of cake, and a number of these silver balls came to be scattered all over the white tablecloth. Some of the guests gathered these stray particles between their fingers and put them on their plates. Others popped them straight into their mouths.

In time all returned to their seats and ate their portions of cake at their leisure, laughing. It was not a homemade cake, having been ordered by Mrs. Sasaki from a certain high-class confectioner's, but the guests were unanimous in praising its excellence.

10   Mrs. Sasaki was bathed in happiness. But suddenly, with a tinge of anxiety, she recalled the pearl she had abandoned on the table, and, rising from her chair as casually as she could, she moved across to look for it. At the spot where she was sure she had left it, the pearl was no longer to be seen.

Mrs. Sasaki abhorred losing things. At once and without thinking, right in the middle of the party, she became wholly engrossed in her search, and the tension in her manner was so obvious that it attracted everyone's attention.

"Is there something the matter?" someone asked.

"No, not at all, just a moment. . . ."

Mrs. Sasaki's reply was ambiguous, but before she had time to decide to return to her chair, first one, then another, and finally every one of her guests had risen and was turning back the tablecloth or groping about on the floor.

15   Mrs. Azuma, seeing this commotion, felt that the whole thing was just too deplorable for words. She was incensed at a hostess who could create such an impossible situation over the loss of a solitary pearl.

Mrs. Azuma resolved to offer herself as a sacrifice and to save the day. With a heroic smile she declared: "That's it then! It must have been a pearl I ate just now! A silver ball dropped on the tablecloth when I was given my cake, and I just picked it up and swallowed it without thinking. It *did* seem to stick in my throat a little. Had it been a diamond, now, I would naturally return it—by an operation, if necessary—but as it's a pearl I must simply beg your forgiveness."

This announcement at once resolved the company's anxieties, and it was felt, above all, that it had saved the hostess from an embarrassing predicament. No one made any attempt to investigate the truth or falsity of Mrs. Azuma's confession. Mrs. Sasaki took one of the remaining silver balls and put it in her mouth.

"Mm," she said. "Certainly tastes like a pearl, this one!"

Thus this small incident, too, was cast into the crucible of good-humored teasing, and there—amid general laughter—it melted away.

20   When the party was over Mrs. Azuma drove off in her two-seater sportscar, taking with her in the other seat, her close friend and neighbor Mrs. Kasuga. Before two minutes had passed Mrs. Azuma said, "Own up! It was you who swallowed the pearl, wasn't it? I covered up for you, and took the blame on myself."

This unceremonious manner of speaking concealed deep affection, but, however friendly the intention may have been, to Mrs. Kasuga a wrongful accusation was a wrongful accusation. She had no recollection whatsoever of having swallowed a pearl in mistake for a sugar ball. She was—as Mrs. Azuma too must surely know—fastidious in her eating habits, and, if she so much as detected a single hair in her food, whatever she happened to be eating at the time immediately stuck in her gullet.

"Oh, really now!" protested the timid Mrs. Kasuga in a small voice, her eyes studying Mrs. Azuma's face in some puzzlement. "I just couldn't do a thing like that!"

"It's no good pretending. The moment I saw that green look on your face, I knew."

The little disturbance at the party had seemed closed by Mrs. Azuma's frank confession, but even now it had left behind it this strange awkwardness. Mrs. Kasuga, wondering how best to demonstrate her innocence, was at the same time seized by the fantasy that a solitary pearl was lodged somewhere in her intestines. It was unlikely, of course, that she should mistakenly swallow a pearl for a sugar ball, but in all that confusion of talk and laughter one had to admit that it was at least a possibility. Though she thought back over the events of the party again and again, no moment in which she might have inserted a pearl into her mouth came to mind—but, after all, if it was an unconscious act one would not expect to remember it.

25   Mrs. Kasuga blushed deeply as her imagination chanced upon one further aspect of the matter. It had occurred to her that when one accepted a pearl into one's system it almost certainly—its luster a trifle dimmed, perhaps, by gastric juices—re-emerged intact within a day or two.

And with this thought the design of Mrs. Azuma, too, seemed to have become transparently clear. Undoubtedly Mrs. Azuma had viewed this same prospect with embarrassment and shame, and had therefore cast her responsibility onto another, making it appear that she had considerately taken the blame to protect a friend.

Meanwhile Mrs. Yamamoto and Mrs. Matsumura, whose homes lay in a similar direction, were returning together in a taxi. Soon after the taxi had started Mrs. Matsumura opened her handbag to make a few adjustments to her make-up. She remembered that she had done nothing to her face since all that commotion at the party.

As she was removing the powder compact her attention was caught by a sudden dull gleam as something tumbled to the bottom of the bag. Groping about with the tips of her fingers, Mrs. Matsumura retrieved the object, and saw to her amazement that it was a pearl.

Mrs. Matsumura stifled an exclamation of surprise. Recently her relationship with Mrs. Yamamoto had been far from cordial, and she had no wish to share with that lady a discovery with such awkward implications for herself.

30   Fortunately Mrs. Yamamoto was gazing out of the window and did not appear to have noticed her companion's momentary start of surprise.

Caught off balance by this sudden turn of events, Mrs. Matsumura did not pause to consider how the pearl had found its way into her bag, but immediately became a prisoner of her own private brand of school-captain morality. It was unlikely—she thought—that she would do a thing like this, even in a moment of abstraction. But since, by some chance, the object had found its way into her handbag, the proper course was to return it at once. If she failed to do so, it would weigh heavily upon her conscience. The fact that it was a pearl, too—an article you could neither call all that expensive nor yet all that cheap—only made her position more ambiguous.

At any rate, she was determined that her companion, Mrs. Yamamoto, should know nothing of this incomprehensible development—especially when the affair had been so nicely rounded off, thanks to the selflessness of Mrs. Azuma. Mrs. Matsumura felt she could remain in the taxi not a moment longer, and, on the pretext of remembering a promise to visit a sick relative on her way back, she made the driver set her down at once, in the middle of a quiet residential district.

Mrs. Yamamoto, left alone in the taxi, was a little surprised that her practical joke should have moved Mrs. Matsumura to such abrupt action. Having watched Mrs. Matsumura's reflection in the window just now, she had clearly seen her draw the pearl from the bag.

At the party Mrs. Yamamoto had been the very first to receive a slice of cake. Adding to her plate a silver ball which had spilled onto the table, she had returned to her seat—again before any of the others—and there had noticed that the silver ball was a pearl. At this discovery she had at once conceived a malicious plan. While all the others were preoccupied with the cake, she had quickly slipped the pearl into the handbag left on the next chair by that insufferable hypocrite Mrs. Matsumura.

35   Stranded in the middle of a residential district where there was little prospect of a taxi, Mrs. Matsumura fretfully gave her mind to a number of reflections on her position.

First, no matter how necessary it might be for the relief of her own conscience, it would be a shame indeed, when people had gone to such lengths to settle the affair satisfactorily, to go and stir up things all over again; and it would be even worse if in the process—because of the inexplicable nature of the circumstances—she were to direct unjust suspicions upon herself.

Secondly—notwithstanding these considerations—if she did not make haste to return the pearl now, she would forfeit her opportunity forever. Left till tomorrow (at the thought Mrs. Matsumura blushed) the returned pearl would be an object of rather disgusting speculation and doubt. Concerning this possibility Mrs. Azuma herself had dropped a hint.

It was at this point that there occurred to Mrs. Matsumura, greatly to her joy, a master scheme which would both salve her conscience and at the same time involve no risk of exposing her character to any unjust suspicion. Quickening her step, she emerged at length onto a comparatively busy thoroughfare, where she hailed a taxi and told the driver to take her quickly to a certain celebrated pearl shop on the Ginza. There she took the pearl from her bag and showed it to the attendant, asking to see a pearl of slightly larger size and clearly superior quality. Having made her purchase, she proceeded once more, by taxi, to Mrs. Sasaki's house.

Mrs. Matsumura's plan was to present this newly purchased pearl to Mrs. Sasaki, saying that she had found it in her jacket pocket. Mrs. Sasaki would accept it and later attempt to fit it into the ring. However, being a pearl of a different size, it would not fit into the ring, and Mrs. Sasaki—puzzled—would try to return it to Mrs. Matsumura, but Mrs. Matsumura would refuse to have it returned. Thereupon Mrs. Sasaki would have no choice but to reflect as follows: The woman has behaved in this way in order to protect someone else. Such being the case, it is perhaps safest simply to accept the pearl and forget the matter. Mrs. Matsumura has doubtless observed one of the three ladies in the act of stealing the pearl. But at least, of my four guests, I can now be sure that Mrs. Matsumura, if no one else, is completely without guilt. Whoever heard of a thief stealing something and then replacing it with a similar article of greater value?

40   By this device Mrs. Matsumura proposed to escape forever the infamy of suspicion, and equally—by a small outlay of cash—the pricks of an uneasy conscience.

To return to the other ladies. After reaching home, Mrs. Kasuga continued to feel painfully upset by Mrs. Azuma's cruel teasing. To clear herself of even a ridiculous charge like this—she knew—she must act before tomorrow or it would be too late. That is to say, in order to offer positive proof that she had not eaten the pearl it was above all necessary for the pearl itself to be somehow produced. And, briefly, if she could show the pearl to Mrs. Azuma immediately, her innocence on the gastronomic count (if not on any other) would be firmly established. But if she waited until tomorrow, even though she managed to produce the pearl, the shameful and hardly mentionable suspicion would inevitably have intervened.

The normally timid Mrs. Kasuga, inspired with the courage of impetuous action, burst from the house to which she had so recently returned, sped to a pearl shop in the Ginza, and selected and bought a pearl which, to her eye, seemed of roughly the same size as those silver balls on the cake. She then telephoned Mrs. Azuma. On returning home, she explained, she had discovered in the folds of the bow of her sash the pearl which Mrs. Sasaki had lost, but, since she felt too ashamed to return it by herself, she wondered if Mrs. Azuma would be so kind as to go with her, as soon as possible. Inwardly Mrs. Azuma considered the story a little unlikely, but since it was the request of a good friend she agreed to go.

Mrs. Sasaki accepted the pearl brought to her by Mrs. Matsumura and, puzzled at its failure to fit the ring, fell obligingly into that very train of thought for which Mrs. Matsumura had prayed; but it was a surprise to her when Mrs. Kasuga arrived about an hour later, accompanied by Mrs. Azuma, and returned another pearl.

Mrs. Sasaki hovered perilously on the brink of discussing Mrs. Matsumura's prior visit, but checked herself at the last moment and accepted the second pearl as unconcernedly as she could. She felt sure that this one at any rate would fit, and as soon as the two visitors had taken their leave she hurried to try it in the ring. But it was too small, and wobbled loosely in the socket. At this discovery Mrs. Sasaki was not so much surprised as dumbfounded.

On the way back in the car both ladies found it impossible to guess what the other might be thinking, and, though normally relaxed and loquacious in each other's company, they now lapsed into a long silence.

Mrs. Azuma, who believed she could do nothing without her own full knowledge, knew for certain that she had not swallowed the pearl herself. It was simply to save everyone from embarrassment that she had cast shame aside and made that declaration at the party—more particularly it was to save the situation for her friend, who had been fidgeting about and looking conspicuously guilty. But what was she to think now? Beneath the peculiarity of Mrs. Kasuga's whole attitude, and beneath this elaborate procedure of having herself accompany her as she returned the pearl, she sensed that there lay something much deeper. Could it be that Mrs. Azuma's intuition had touched upon a weakness in her friend's make-up which it was forbidden to touch upon, and that by thus driving her friend into a corner she had transformed an unconscious, impulsive kleptomania into a deep mental derangement beyond all cure?

Mrs. Kasuga, for her part, still retained the suspicion that Mrs. Azuma had genuinely swallowed the pearl and that her confession at the party had been the truth. If that was so, it had been unforgivable of Mrs. Azuma, when everything was smoothly settled, to tease her so cruelly on the way back from the party, shifting the guilt onto herself. As a result, timid creature that she was, she had been panic-stricken, and besides spending good money had felt obliged to act out that little play—and was it not exceedingly ill-natured of Mrs. Azuma that, even after all this, she still refused to confess it was she who had eaten the pearl? And if Mrs. Azuma's innocence was all pretense, she herself—acting her part so painstakingly—must appear in Mrs. Azuma's eyes as the most ridiculous of third-rate comedians.

To return to Mrs. Matsumura. That lady, on her way back from obliging Mrs. Sasaki to accept the pearl, was feeling now more at ease in her mind and had the notion to make a leisurely reinvestigation, detail by detail, of the events of the recent incident. When going to collect her portion of cake, she had most certainly left her handbag on the chair. Then, while eating the cake, she had made liberal use of the paper napkin—so there could have been no necessity to take a handkerchief from her bag. The more she thought about it the less she could remember having opened her bag until she touched up her face in the taxi on the way home. How was it, then, that a pearl had rolled into a handbag which was always shut?

She realized now how stupid she had been not to have remarked this simple fact before, instead of flying into a panic at the mere sight of the pearl. Having progressed this far, Mrs. Matsumura was struck by an amazing thought. Someone must purposely have placed the pearl in her bag in order to incriminate her. And of the four guests at the party the only one who would do such a thing was, without doubt, the detestable Mrs. Yamamoto. Her eyes glinting with rage, Mrs. Matsumura hurried toward the house of Mrs. Yamamoto.

50 From her first glimpse of Mrs. Matsumura standing in the doorway, Mrs. Yamamoto knew at once what had brought her. She had already prepared her line of defense.

However, Mrs. Matsumura's cross-examination was unexpectedly severe, and from the start it was clear that she would accept no evasions.

"It was you, I know. No one but you could do such a thing," began Mrs. Matsumura, deductively.

"Why choose me? What proof have you? If you can say a thing like that to my face, I suppose you've come with pretty conclusive proof, have you?" Mrs. Yamamoto was at first icily composed.

To this Mrs. Matsumura replied that Mrs. Azuma, having so nobly taken the blame on herself, clearly stood in an incompatible relationship with mean and despicable behavior of this nature; and as for Mrs. Kasuga, she was much too weak-kneed for such dangerous work; and that left only one person—yourself.

55 Mrs. Yamamoto kept silent, her mouth shut tight like a clamshell. On the table before her gleamed the pearl which Mrs. Matsumura had set there. In the excitement she had not even had time to raise a teaspoon, and the Ceylon tea she had so thoughtfully provided was beginning to get cold.

"I had no idea that you hated me so." As she said this, Mrs. Yamamoto dabbed at the corners of her eyes, but it was plain that Mrs. Matsumura's resolve not to be deceived by tears was as firm as ever.

"Well, then," Mrs. Yamamoto continued, "I shall say what I had thought I must never say. I shall mention no names, but one of the guests . . ."

"By that, I suppose, you can only mean Mrs. Azuma or Mrs. Kasuga?"

"Please, I beg at least that you allow me to omit the name. As I say, one of the guests had just opened your bag and was dropping something inside when I happened to glance in her direction. You can imagine my amazement! Even if I had felt *able* to warn you, there would have been no chance. My heart just throbbed and throbbed, and on the way back in the taxi—oh, how awful not to be able to speak even then! If we had been good friends, of course, I could have told you quite frankly, but since I knew of your apparent dislike for me . . ."

60 "I see. You have been very considerate, I'm sure. Which means, doesn't it, that you have now cleverly shifted the blame onto Mrs. Azuma and Mrs. Kasuga?"

"Shifted the blame! Oh, how can I get you to understand my feelings? I only wanted to avoid hurting anyone."

"Quite. But you didn't mind hurting me, did you? You might at least have mentioned this in the taxi."

"And if you had been frank with me when you found the pearl in your bag, I would probably have told you, at that moment, everything I had seen—but no, you chose to leave the taxi at once, without saying a word!"

For the first time, as she listened to this, Mrs. Matsumura was at a loss for a reply.

65 "Well, then. Can I get you to understand? I wanted no one to be hurt."

Mrs. Matsumura was filled with an even more intense rage.

"If you are going to tell a string of lies like that," she said, "I must ask you to repeat them, tonight if you wish, in my presence, before Mrs. Azuma and Mrs. Kasuga."

At this Mrs. Yamamoto started to weep.

"And thanks to you," she sobbed reprovingly, "all my efforts to avoid hurting anyone will have come to nothing."

70 It was a new experience for Mrs. Matsumura to see Mrs. Yamamoto crying, and, though she kept reminding herself not to be taken in by tears, she could not altogether dismiss the feeling that perhaps somewhere, since nothing in this affair could be proved, there might be a modicum of truth even in the assertions of Mrs. Yamamoto.

In the first place—to be a little more objective—if one accepted Mrs. Yamamoto's story as true, then her reluctance to disclose the name of the guilty party, whom she had observed in the very act, argued some refinement of character. And just as one could not say for sure that the gentle and seemingly timid Mrs. Kasuga would never be moved to an act of malice, so even the undoubtedly bad feeling between Mrs. Yamamoto and herself could, by one way of looking at things, be taken as actually lessening the likelihood of Mrs. Yamamoto's guilt. For if she were to do a thing like this, with their relationship as it was, Mrs. Yamamoto would be the first to come under suspicion.

"We have differences in our natures," Mrs. Yamamoto continued tearfully, "and I cannot deny that there are things about yourself which I dislike. But, for all that, it is really too bad that you should suspect me of such a petty trick to get the better of you. . . . Still, on thinking it over, to submit quietly to your accusations might well be the course most consistent with what I have felt in this matter all along. In this way I alone shall bear the guilt, and no other will be hurt."

After this pathetic pronouncement, Mrs. Yamamoto lowered her face to the table and abandoned herself to uncontrolled weeping.

Watching her, Mrs. Matsumura came by degrees to reflect upon the impulsiveness of her own behavior. Detesting Mrs. Yamamoto as she had, there had been times in her castigation of that lady when she had allowed herself to be blinded by emotion.

75 When Mrs. Yamamoto raised her head again after this prolonged bout of weeping, the look of resolution on her face, somehow remote and pure, was apparent even to her visitor. Mrs. Matsumura, a little frightened, drew herself upright in her chair.

"This thing should never have been. When it is gone, everything will be as before." Speaking in riddles, Mrs. Yamamoto pushed back her disheveled hair and fixed a terrible, yet hauntingly beautiful gaze upon the top of the table. In an instant she had snatched up the pearl from before her, and, with a gesture of no ordinary resolve, tossed it into her mouth. Raising her cup by the handle, her little finger elegantly extended, she washed the pearl down her throat with one gulp of cold Ceylon tea.

Mrs. Matsumura watched in horrified fascination. The affair was over before she had time to protest. This was the first time in her life she had seen a person swallow a pearl, and there was in Mrs. Yamamoto's manner something of that desperate finality one might expect to see in a person who had just drunk poison.

However, heroic though the action was, it was above all a touching incident, and not only did Mrs. Matsumura find her anger vanished into thin air, but so impressed was she by Mrs. Yamamoto's simplicity and purity that she could only think of that lady as a saint. And now Mrs. Matsumura's eyes too began to fill with tears, and she took Mrs. Yamamoto by the hand.

"Please forgive me, please forgive me," she said. "It was wrong of me."

80   For a while they wept together, holding each other's hands and vowing to each other that henceforth they would be the firmest of friends.

When Mrs. Sasaki heard rumors that the relationship between Mrs. Yamamoto and Mrs. Matsumura, which had been so strained, had suddenly improved, and that Mrs. Azuma and Mrs. Kasuga, who had been such good friends, had suddenly fallen out, she was at a loss to understand the reasons and contented herself with the reflection that nothing was impossible in this world.

However, being a woman of no strong scruples, Mrs. Sasaki requested a jeweler to refashion her ring and to produce a design into which two new pearls could be set, one large and one small, and this she wore quite openly, without further mishap.

Soon she had completely forgotten the small commotion on her birthday, and when anyone asked her age she would give the same untruthful answers as ever.

Comments and Questions

1. In this story, the dropping of a pearl into a handbag is like dropping a pebble into a very small, but revealing, social pond, then observing the disturbance of the circles spread across the entire surface. How is the point of view Mishima employs essential to accomplishing the social commentary he aims at?

2. What motivates Mrs. Yamamoto to steal the pearl and slip it into Mrs. Matsumura's purse? How is her motivation ironical in terms of ultimate consequences? What other instances of irony did you note? Does the use of irony relate to theme?

3. In what ways are the first three paragraphs especially thematically appropriate to open the story?

4. Describe the various conflicts faced by the individuals in the story; then consider their motivations in resolving the conflicts as they do. What similarities do you note? Are the conflicts and resolutions related to theme?

5. Is there any symbolism in Mishima's use of a pearl?

6. Is the theme a culturally limited one or are there universal parallels in character, situation, action?

Guy de Maupassant (1850–1893)
The Piece of String

Along all the roads around Goderville the peasants and their wives were coming toward the burgh because it was market day. The men were proceeding with slow steps, the whole body bent forward at each movement of their long twisted legs; deformed by their hard work, by the weight on the plow which, at the same time, raised the left shoulder and swerved the figure, by the reaping of the wheat which made the knees spread to make a firm "purchase," by all the slow and painful labors of the country. Their blouses, blue, "stiff-starched," shining as if varnished, ornamented with a little design in white at the neck and wrists, puffed about their bony bodies, seemed like balloons ready to carry them off. From each of them a head, two arms and two feet protruded.

Some led a cow or a calf by a cord, and their wives, walking behind the animal, whipped its haunches with a leafy branch to hasten its progress. They carried large baskets on their arms from which, in some cases, chickens and, in others, ducks thrust out their heads. And they walked with a quicker, livelier step than their husbands. Their spare straight figures were wrapped in a scanty little shawl pinned over their flat bosoms, and their heads were enveloped in a white cloth glued to the hair and surmounted by a cap.

Then a wagon passed at the jerky trot of a nag, shaking strangely, two men seated side by side and a woman in the bottom of the vehicle, the latter holding onto the sides to lessen the hard jolts.

In the public square of Goderville there was a crowd, a throng of human beings and animals mixed together. The horns of the cattle, the tall hats, with long nap, of the rich peasant and the headgear of the peasant women rose above the surface of the assembly. And the clamorous, shrill, screaming voices made a continuous and savage din, which sometimes was dominated by the robust lungs of some countryman's laugh or the long lowing of a cow tied to the wall of a house.

5   All that smacked of the stable, the dairy and the dirt heap, hay and sweat, giving forth that unpleasant odor, human and animal, peculiar to the people of the field.

Maître Hauchecome of Breaute had just arrived at Goderville, and he was directing his steps toward the public square when he perceived upon the ground a little piece of string. Maître Hauchecome, economical like a true Norman, thought that everything useful ought to be picked up, and he bent painfully, for he suffered from rheumatism. He took the bit of thin cord from the ground and began to roll it carefully when he noticed Maître Malandain, the harness maker, on the threshold of his door, looking at him. They had heretofore had business together on the subject of a halter, and they were on bad terms, both being good haters. Maître Hauchecome was seized with a sort of shame to be seen thus by his enemy, picking a bit of string out of the dirt. He concealed his "find" quickly under his blouse, then in his trousers' pocket; then he pretended to be still looking on the ground for something which he did not find, and he went toward the market, his head forward, bent double by his pains.

He was soon lost in the noisy and slowly moving crowd which was busy with interminable bargainings. The peasants milked, went and came, perplexed, always in fear of being cheated, not daring to decide, watching the vender's eye, ever trying to find the trick in the man and the flaw in the beast.

The women, having placed their great baskets at their feet, had taken out the poultry which lay upon the ground, tied together by the feet, with terrified eyes and scarlet crests.

They heard offers, stated their prices with a dry air and impassive face, or perhaps, suddenly deciding on some proposed reduction, shouted to the customer who was slowly going away: "All right, Maître Authirne, I'll give it to you for that."

10   Then little by little the square was deserted, and the Angelus ringing at noon, those who had stayed too long scattered to their shops.

At Jourdain's the great room was full of people eating, as the big court was full of vehicles of all kinds, carts, gigs, wagons, dumpcarts, yellow with dirt, mended and patched, raising their shafts to the sky like two arms or perhaps with their shafts in the ground and their backs in the air.

Just opposite the diners seated at the table the immense fireplace, filled with bright flames, cast a lively heat on the backs of the row on the right. Three spits were turning on which were chickens, pigeons and legs of mutton, and an appetizing odor of roast beef and gravy dripping over the nicely browned skin rose from the hearth, increased the jovialness and made everybody's mouth water.

All the aristocracy of the plow ate there at Maître Jourdain's, tavern keeper and horse dealer, a rascal who had money.

The dishes were passed and emptied, as were the jugs of yellow cider. Everyone told his affairs, his purchases and sales. They discussed the crops. The weather was favorable for the green things but not for the wheat.

15   Suddenly the drum beat in the court before the house. Everybody rose, except a few indifferent persons, and ran to the door or to the windows, their mouths still full and napkins in their hands.

After the public crier had ceased his drumbeating he called out in a jerky voice, speaking his phrases irregularly:

"It is hereby made known to the inhabitants of Goderville, and in general to all persons present at the market, that there was lost this morning on the road to Benzeville, between nine and ten o'clock, a black leather pocketbook containing five hundred francs and some business papers. The finder is requested to return same with all haste to the mayor's office or to Maître Fortune Houlbreque of Manneville; there will be twenty francs reward."

Then the man went away. The heavy roll of the drum and the crier's voice were again heard at a distance.

Then they began to talk of this event, discussing the chances that Maître Houlbreque had of finding or not finding his pocketbook.

20   And the meal concluded. They were finishing their coffee when a chief of the gendarmes appeared upon the threshold.

He inquired:

"Is Maître Hauchecome of Breaute here?"

Maître Hauchecome, seated at the other end of the table, replied:

"Here I am."

25   And the officer resumed:

"Maître Hauchecome, will have the goodness to accompany me to the mayor's office? The mayor would like to talk to you."

The peasant, surprised and disturbed, swallowed at a draught his tiny glass of brandy, rose and, even more bent than in the morning, for the first steps after each rest were specially difficult, set out, repeating: "Here I am, here I am."

The mayor was awaiting him, seated on an armchair. He was the notary of the vicinity, a stout, serious man with pompous phrases.

"Maître Hauchecome," said he, "you were seen this morning to pick up, on the road to Benzeville, the pocketbook lost by Maître Houlbreque of Manneville."

30   The countryman, astounded, looked at the mayor, already terrified by this suspicion resting on him without his knowing why.

"Me? Me? Me pick up the pocketbook?"

"Yes, you yourself."

"Word of honor, I never heard of it."

"But you were seen."

35   "I was seen, me? Who says he saw me?"

"Monsieur Malandain, the harness maker."

The old man remembered, understood and flushed with anger.

"Ah, he saw me, the clodhopper, he saw me pick up this string here, M'sieu the Mayor." And rummaging in his pocket, he drew out the little piece of string.

But the mayor, incredulous, shook his head.

40   "You will not make me believe, Maître Hauchecome, that Monsieur Malandain, who is a man worthy of credence, mistook this cord for a pocketbook."

The peasant, furious, lifted his hand, spat at one side to attest his honor, repeating:

"It is nevertheless the truth of the good God, the sacred truth, M'sieu the Mayor. I repeat it on my soul and my salvation."

The mayor resumed:

"After picking up the object you stood like a stilt, looking a long while in the mud to see if any piece of money had fallen out."

45   The good old man choked with indignation and fear.

"How anyone can tell—how anyone can tell—such lies to take away an honest man's reputation! How can anyone—"

There was no use in his protesting; nobody believed him. He was confronted with Monsieur Malandain, who repeated and maintained his affirmation. They abused each for an hour. At his own request Maître Hauchecome was searched; nothing was found on him.

Finally the mayor, very much perplexed, discharged him with the warning that he would consult the public prosecutor and ask for further orders.

The news had spread. As he left the mayor's office the old man was surrounded and questioned with a serious or bantering curiosity in which there was no indignation. He began to tell the story of the string. No one believed him. They laughed at him.

50   He went along, stopping his friends, beginning endlessly his statement and his protestations, showing his pockets turned inside out to prove that he had nothing.

They said:

"Old rascal, get out!"

And he grew angry, becoming exasperated, hot and distressed at not being believed, not knowing what to do and always repeating himself.

Night came. He must depart. He started on his way with three neighbors to whom he pointed out the place where he had picked up the bit of string, and all along the road he spoke of his adventure.

55   In the evening he took a turn in the village of Breaute in order to tell it to everybody. He only met with incredulity.

It made him ill at night.

The next day about one o'clock in the afternoon Marius Paumelle, a hired man in the employ of Maître Breton, husbandman at Ymanville, returned the pocketbook and its contents to Maître Houlbreque of Manneville.

This man claimed to have found the object in the road, but not knowing how to read, he had carried it to the house and given it to his employer.

The news spread through the neighborhood. Maître Hauchecome was informed of it. He immediately went the circuit and began to recount his story completed by the happy climax. He was in triumph.

60   "What grieved me so much was not the thing itself as the lying. There is nothing so shameful as to be placed under a cloud on account of a lie."

He talked of his adventure all day long; he told it on the highway to people who were passing by, in the wineshop to people who were drinking there and to persons coming out of church the following Sunday. He stopped strangers to tell them about it. He was calm now, and yet something disturbed him without his knowing exactly what it was. People had the air of joking while they listened. They did not seem convinced. He seemed to feel that remarks were being made behind his back.

On Tuesday of the next week he went to the market at Goderville, urged solely by the necessity he felt of discussing the case.

Malandain, standing at his door, began to laugh on seeing him pass. Why?

He approached a farmer from Crequetot who did not let him finish and, giving him a thump in the stomach, said to his face:

65   "You big rascal."

Then he turned his back on him.

Maître Hauchecome was confused; why was he called a big rascal?

When he was seated at the table in Jourdain's tavern he commenced to explain "the affair."

A horse dealer from Monvilliers called to him:

70   "Come, come, old sharper, that's an old trick; I know all about your piece of string!"

Hauchecome stammered:

"But since the pocketbook was found."

But the other man replied:

"Shut up, papa, there is one that finds and there is one that reports. At any rate you are mixed with it."

75   The peasant stood choking. He understood. They accused him of having had the pocketbook returned by a confederate, by an accomplice.

He tried to protest. All the table began to laugh.

He could not finish his dinner and went away in the midst of jeers.

He went home ashamed and indignant, choking with anger and confusion, the more dejected that he was capable, with his Norman cunning, of doing what they had accused him of and ever boasting of it as of a good turn. His innocence to him, in a confused way, was impossible to prove, as his sharpness was known. And he was stricken to the heart by the injustice of the suspicion.

Then he began to recount the adventures again, prolonging his history every day, adding each time new reasons, more energetic protestations, more solemn oaths which he imagined and prepared in his hours of solitude, his whole mind given up to the story of the string. He was believed so much the less as his defense was more complicated and his arguing more subtle.

80   "Those are lying excuses," they said behind his back.

He felt it, consumed his heart over it and wore himself out with useless efforts. He wasted away before their very eyes.

The wags now made him tell about the string to amuse them, as they make a soldier who has been on a campaign tell about his battles. His mind, touched to the depth, began to weaken.

Toward the end of December he took to his bed.

He died in the first days of January, and in the delirium of his death struggles he kept claiming his innocence, reiterating:

85   "A piece of string, a piece of string—look—here it is, M'sieu the Mayor."

Comments and Questions

1. This story presents a crime only in the imagination of the Goderville peasants, yet manages to expand the question of social and individual innocence or guilt in widening ripples through the community. How are irony and symbolism here suggestive of those methods used by Mishima in the preceding story?

2. Specifically how do paragraphs 4 and 5 contribute to the story?

3. The peasants continue to believe Hauchecome guilty even after the return of the pocketbook. Is their attitude believable? Is it prepared for earlier in the story?

4. Even after he is officially exonerated, Hauchecome remains obsessed with the need to retell his adventure and establish his innocence. Why?

5. How is the physical description of the peasants in the opening pertinent to the remainder of the story?

Robert Louis Stevenson (1850–1894)
Markheim

"Yes," said the dealer, "our windfalls are of various kinds. Some customers are ignorant, and then I touch a dividend on my superior knowledge. Some are dishonest," and here he held up the candle, so that the light fell strongly on his visitor, "and in that case," he continued, "I profit by my virtue."

Markheim had but just entered from the daylight streets, and his eyes had not yet grown familiar with the mingled shine and darkness in the shop. At these pointed words, and before the near presence of the flame, he blinked painfully and looked aside.

The dealer chuckled. "You come to me on Christmas-day," he resumed, "when you know that I am alone in my house, put up my shutters, and make a point of refusing business. Well, you will have to pay for that; you will have to pay for my loss of time, when I should be balancing my books; you will have to pay, besides, for a kind of manner that I remark in you to-day very strongly. I am the essence of discretion, and ask no awkward questions; but when a customer can not look me in the eye, he has to pay for it." The dealer once more chuckled; and then, changing to his usual business voice, though still with a note of irony, "You can give, as usual, a clean account of how you came into the possession of the object?" he continued. "Still your uncle's cabinet? A remarkable collector, sir!"

And the little, pale, round-shouldered dealer stood almost on tip-toe, looking over the top of his gold spectacles, and nodding his head with every mark of disbelief. Markheim returned his gaze with one of infinite pity, and a touch of horror.

5   "This time," said he, "you are in error. I have not come to sell, but to buy. I have no curios to dispose of; my uncle's cabinet is bare to the wainscot; even were it still intact, I

have done well on the Stock Exchange, and should more likely add to it than otherwise, and my errand to-day is simplicity itself. I seek a Christmas-present for a lady," he continued, waxing more fluent as he struck into the speech he had prepared; "and certainly I owe you every excuse for thus disturbing you upon so small a matter. But the thing was neglected yesterday; I must produce my little compliment at dinner; and as you very well know, a rich marriage is not a thing to be neglected."

There followed a pause, during which the dealer seemed to weigh this statement incredulously. The ticking of many clocks among the curious lumber of the shop, and the faint rushing of the cabs in a near thoroughfare, filled up the interval of silence.

"Well, sir," said the dealer, "be it so. You are an old customer after all; and if, as you say, you have the chance of a good marriage, far be it from me to be an obstacle. Here is a nice thing for a lady now," he went on, "this hand-glass—fifteenth century, warranted; comes from a good collection, too; but I reserve the name, in the interests of my customer, who was just like yourself, my dear sir, the nephew and sole heir of a remarkable collector."

The dealer, while he thus ran on in his dry and biting voice, had stooped to take the object from its place; and, as he had done so, a shock had passed through Markheim, a start both of hand and foot, a sudden leap of many tumultuous passions to the face. It passed as swiftly as it came, and left no trace beyond a certain trembling of the hand that now received the glass.

"A glass," he said, hoarsely, and then paused, and repeated it more clearly. "A glass? For Christmas? Surely not?"

10   "And why not?" cried the dealer. "Why not a glass?"

Markheim was looking upon him with an indefinable expression. "You ask me why not?" he said. "Why, look here—look in it—look at yourself! Do you like to see it? No! nor I—nor any man."

The little man had jumped back when Markheim had so suddenly confronted him with the mirror; but now, perceiving there was nothing worse on hand, he chuckled. "Your future lady, sir, must be pretty hard favored," said he.

"I ask you," said Markheim, "for a Christmas-present, and you give me this—this damned reminder of years, and sins and follies—this hand-conscience! Did you mean it? Had you a thought in your mind? Tell me. It will be better for you if you do. Come, tell me about yourself. I hazard a guess now, that you are in secret a very charitable man?"

The dealer looked closely at his companion. It was very odd, Markheim did not appear to be laughing; there was something in his face like an eager sparkle of hope, but nothing of mirth.

15   "What are you driving at?" the dealer asked.

"Not charitable?" returned the other, gloomily. "Not charitable; not pious; not scrupulous; unloving, unbeloved; a hand to get money, a safe to keep it. Is that all? Dear God, man, is that all?"

"I will tell you what it is," began the dealer, with some sharpness, and then broke off again into a chuckle. "But I see this is a love match of yours, and you have been drinking the lady's health."

"Ah!" cried Markheim, with a strange curiosity. "Ah, have you been in love? Tell me about that."

"I," cried the dealer. "I in love! I never had the time, nor have I the time to-day for all this nonsense. Will you take the glass?"

20   "Where is the hurry?" returned Markheim. "It is very pleasant to stand here talking; and life is so short and insecure that I would not hurry away from any pleasure—no, not even from so mild a one as this. We should rather cling, cling to what little we can get,

like a man at a cliff's edge. Every second is a cliff, if you think upon it—a cliff a mile high—high enough, if we fall, to dash us out of every feature of humanity. Hence it is best to talk pleasantly. Let us talk of each other; why should we wear this mask? Let us be confidential. Who knows, we might become friends?"

"I have just one word to say to you," said the dealer. "Either make your purchase, or walk out of my shop."

"True, true," said Markheim. "Enough fooling. To business. Show me something else."

The dealer stooped once more, this time to replace the glass upon the shelf, his thin blonde hair falling over his eyes as he did so. Markheim moved a little nearer, with one hand in the pocket of his great-coat; he drew himself up and filled his lungs; at the same time many different emotions were depicted together on his face—terror, horror, and resolve, fascination and a physical repulsion; and through a haggard lift of his upper lip, his teeth looked out.

"This, perhaps, may suit," observed the dealer; and then, as he began to re-arise, Markheim bounded from behind upon his victim. The long, skewer-like dagger flashed and fell. The dealer struggled like a hen, striking his temple on the shelf, and then tumbled on the floor in a heap.

25   Time had some score of small voices in that shop, some stately and slow as was becoming to their great age; others garrulous and hurried. All these told out the seconds in an intricate chorus of tickings. Then the passage of a lad's feet, heavily running on the pavement, broke in upon these smaller voices and startled Markheim into the consciousness of his surroundings. He looked about him awfully. The candle stood on the counter, its flame solemnly wagging in a draught; and by that inconsiderable movement, the whole room was filled with noiseless bustle and kept heaving like a sea: the tall shadows nodding, the gross blots of darkness swelling and dwindling as with respiration, the faces of the portraits and the china gods changing and wavering like images in water. The inner door stood ajar, and peered into that league of shadows with a long slit of daylight like a pointing finger.

From these fear-striken rovings, Markheim's eyes returned to the body of his victim, where it lay both humped and sprawling, incredibly small and strangely meaner than in life. In these poor, miserly clothes, in that ungainly attitude, the dealer lay like so much sawdust. Markheim had feared to see it, and, lo! it was nothing. And yet, as he gazed, this bundle of old clothes and pool of blood began to find eloquent voices. There it must lie; there was none to work the cunning hinges or direct the miracle of locomotion—there it must lie till it was found. Found! ay, and then? Then would this dead flesh lift up a cry that would ring over England, and fill the world with the echoes of pursuit. Ay, dead or not, this was still the enemy. "Time was that when the brains were out," he thought; and the first word struck into his mind. Time, now that the deed was accomplished—time, which had closed for the victim, had become instant and momentous for the slayer.

The thought was yet in his mind, when, first one and then another, with every variety of pace and voice—one deep as the bell from a cathedral turret, another ringing on its treble notes the prelude of a waltz—the clocks began to strike the hour of three in the afternoon.

The sudden outbreak of so many tongues in that dumb chamber staggered him. He began to bestir himself, going to and fro with the candle, beleaguered by moving shadows, and startled to the soul by chance reflections. In many rich mirrors, some of home designs, some from Venice or Amsterdam, he saw his face repeated and repeated, as it were an army of spies; his own eyes met and detected him; and the sound of his own steps, lightly as they fell, vexed the surrounding quiet. And still as he continued to fill his pockets, his mind accused him, with a sickening iteration, of the thousand faults of his design. He should have chosen a more quiet hour; he should have prepared an alibi; he should not have used a knife; he should have been more cautious, and only bound and gagged the dealer, and not killed him; he should have been more bold, and killed the servant also; he should have done all things otherwise; poignant regrets, weary, incessant toiling of the mind to change what was unchangeable, to plan what was now useless, to be the architect of the irrevocable past. Meanwhile, and behind all this activity, brute terrors, like scurrying of rats in a deserted attic, filled the more remote chambers of his brain with riot; the hand of the constable would fall heavy on his shoulder, and his nerves would jerk like a hooked fish; or he beheld, in galloping defile, the dock, the prison, the gallows, and the black coffin.

Terror of the people in the street sat down before his mind like a besieging army. It was impossible, he thought, but that some rumor of the struggle must have reached their ears and set on edge their curiosity; and now, in all the neighboring houses, he divined them sitting motionless and with uplifted ear—solitary people, condemned to spend Christmas dwelling alone on memories of the past, and now startlingly recalled from that tender exercise; happy family parties, struck into silence round the table, the mother still with raised finger: every degree and age and humor, but all, by their own hearths, prying and hearkening and weaving the rope that was to hang him. Sometimes it seemed to him he could not move too softly; the clink of the tall Bohemian goblets rang out loudly like a bell; and alarmed by the bigness of the ticking, he was tempted to stop the clocks. And then, again, with a swift transition of his terrors, the very silence of the place appeared a source of peril, and a thing to strike and freeze the passer-by; and he would step more boldly, and bustle aloud among the contents of the shop, and imitate, with elaborate bravado, the movements of a busy man at ease in his own house.

30   But he was now so pulled about by different alarms that, while one portion of his mind was still alert and cunning, another trembled on the brink of lunacy. One hallucination in particular took a strong hold on his credulity. The neighbor hearkening with white face beside his window, the passer-by arrested by a horrible surmise on the pavement—these could at worst suspect, they could not know; through the brick walls and shuttered windows only sounds could penetrate. But here, within the house, was he alone? He knew he was; he had watched the servant set forth sweethearting, in her poor best, "out for the day" written in every ribbon and smile. Yes, he was alone, of course; and yet, in the bulk of empty house above him, he could surely hear a stir of delicate footing—he was surely conscious, inexplicably conscious of some presence. Ay, surely; to every room and corner of the house his imagination followed it; and now it was a faceless thing, and yet had eyes to see with; and again it was a shadow of himself; and yet again behold the image of the dead dealer, reinspired with cunning and hatred.

At times, with a strong effort, he would glance at the open door which still seemed to repel his eyes. The house was tall, the skylight small and dirty, the day blind with fog; and the light that filtered down to the ground story was exceedingly faint, and showed dimly on the threshold of the shop. And yet, in that strip of doubtful brightness, did there not hang wavering a shadow?

Suddenly, from the street outside, a very jovial gentleman began to beat with a staff on the shop-door, accompanying his blows with shouts and railleries in which the dealer was continually called upon by name. Markheim, smitten into ice, glanced at the dead man. But no! he lay quite still; he was fled away far beyond earshot of these blows and shoutings; he was sunk beneath seas of silence; and his name, which would once have caught his notice above the howling of a storm, had become an empty sound. And presently the jovial gentleman desisted from his knocking and departed.

Here was a broad hint to hurry what remained to be done, to get forth from this accusing neighborhood, to plunge into a bath of London multitudes, and to reach, on the other side of day, that haven of safety and apparent innocence—his bed. One visitor had come: at any moment another might follow and be more obstinate. To have done the deed, and yet not to reap the profit, would be too abhorrent a failure. The money, that was now Markheim's concern; and as a means to that, the keys.

He glanced over his shoulder at the open door, where the shadow was still lingering and shivering; and with no conscious repugnance of the mind, yet with a tremor of the belly, he drew near the body of his victim. The human character had quite departed. Like a suit half-stuffed with bran, the limbs lay scattered, the trunk doubled, on the floor; and yet the thing repelled him. Although so dingy and inconsiderable to the eye, he feared it might have more significance to the touch. He took the body by the shoulders, and turned it on its back. It was strangely light and supple, and the limbs, as if they had been broken, fell into the oddest postures. The face was robbed of all expression; but it was as pale as wax, and shockingly smeared with blood about one temple. That was, for Markheim, the one displeasing circumstance. It carried him back, upon the instant, to a certain fair day in a fisher's village: a gray day, a piping wind, a crowd upon the street, the blare of brasses, the booming of drums, the nasal voice of a ballad singer; and a boy going to and fro, buried over head in the crowd and divided between interest and fear, until, coming out upon the chief place of concourse, he beheld a booth and a great screen with pictures, dismally designed, garishly colored: Brownrigg with her apprentice; the Mannings with their murdered guest; Weare in the death-grip of Thurtell; and a score besides of famous crimes. The thing was as clear as an illusion; he was once again that little boy; he was looking once again, and with the same sense of physical revolt, at these vile pictures; he was still stunned by the thumping of the drums. A bar of that day's music returned upon his memory; and at that, for the first time, a qualm came over him, a breath of nausea, a sudden weakness of the joints, which he must instantly resist and conquer.

35   He judged it more prudent to confront than to flee from these considerations; looking the more hardily in the dead face, bending his mind to realize the nature and greatness of his crime. So little awhile ago that face had moved with every change of sentiment, that pale mouth had spoken, that body had been all on fire with governable energies; and now, and by his act, that piece of life had been arrested, as the horologist, with interjected finger, arrests the beating of the clock. So he reasoned in vain; he could rise to no more remorseful consciousness; the same heart which had shuddered before the painted effigies of crime, looked on its reality unmoved. At best, he felt a gleam of pity for one who had been endowed in vain with all those faculties that can make the world a garden of enchantment, one who had never lived and who was now dead. But of penitence, no, with a tremor.

With that, shaking himself clear of these considerations, he found the keys and advanced toward the open door of the shop. Outside, it had begun to rain smartly; and the sound of the shower upon the roof had banished silence. Like some dripping cavern, the chambers of the house were haunted by an incessant echoing, which filled the ear and mingled with the ticking of the clocks. And, as Markheim approached the door, he seemed to hear, in answer to his own cautious tread, the steps of another foot withdrawing up the stair. The shadow still palpitated loosely on the threshold. He threw a ton's weight of resolve upon his muscles, and drew back the door.

The faint, foggy daylight glimmered dimly on the bare floor and stairs; on the bright suit of armor posted, halbert in hand, upon the landing; and on the dark wood-carvings, and framed pictures that hung against the yellow panels of the wainscot. So loud was the beating of the rain through all the house that, in Markheim's ears, it began to be distinguished into many different sounds. Footsteps and sighs, the tread of regiments marching in the distance, the chink of money in the counting, and the creaking of doors held stealthily ajar, appeared to mingle with the patter of the drops upon the cupola and the gushing of the water in the pipes. The sense that he was not alone grew upon him to the verge of madness. On every side he was haunted and begirt by presences. He heard them moving in the upper chambers; from the shop, he heard the dead man getting to his legs; and as he began with a great effort to mount the stairs, feet fled quietly before him and followed stealthily behind. If he were but deaf, he thought, how tranquilly he would possess his soul. And then again, and hearkening with every fresh attention, he blessed himself for that unresisting sense which held the outposts and stood a trusty sentinel upon his life. His head turned continually on his neck; his eyes, which seemed starting from their orbits, scouted on every side, and on every side were half-rewarded as with the tail of something nameless vanishing. The four-and-twenty steps to the first floor were four-and-twenty agonies.

On that first story, the doors stood ajar, three of them like three ambushes, shaking his nerves like the throats of cannon. He could never again, he felt, be sufficiently immured and fortified from men's observing eyes; he longed to be home, girt in by walls, buried among bedclothes, and invisible to all but God. And at that thought he wondered a little, recollecting tales of other murderers and the fear they were said to entertain of heavenly avengers. It was not so, at least, with him. He feared the laws of nature, lest, in their callous and immutable procedure, they should preserve some damning evidence of his crime. He feared tenfold more, with a slavish, superstitious terror, some scission in the continuity of man's experience, some willful illegality of nature. He played a game of skill, depending on the rules, calculating consequence from cause; and what if nature, as the defeated tyrant overthrew the chess-board, should break the mold of their succession? The like had befallen Napoleon (so writers said) when the winter changed the time of its appearance.[1] The like might befall Markheim: the solid walls might become transparent and reveal his doings like those of bees in a glass hive; and stout planks might yield under his foot like quicksands and detain him in their clutch; ay, and there were soberer accidents that might destroy him: if, for instance, the house should fall and imprison him beside the body of his victim; or the house next door should fly on fire, and the firemen invade him from all sides. These things he feared; and, in a sense, these things might be called the hands of God reached forth against sin. But about God himself he was at ease; his act was doubtless exceptional, but so were his excuses, which God knew; it was there, and not among men, that he felt sure of justice.

When he had got safe into the drawing-room, and shut the door behind him, he was aware of a respite from alarms. The room was quite dismantled, uncarpeted besides, and strewn with packing cases and incongruous furniture; several great pier-glasses, in which he beheld himself at various angles, like an actor on the stage; many pictures, framed and unframed, standing with their faces to the wall; a fine Sheraton sideboard, a cabinet of marquetry, and a great old bed, with tapestry hangings. The windows opened to the floor; but by great good fortune the lower part of the shutters had been closed, and this concealed him from the neighbors. Here, then, Markheim drew in a packing case before the cabinet, and began to search among the keys. It was a long business, for there were many; and it was irksome, besides; for, after all, there might be nothing in the cabinet, and time was on the wing. But the closeness of the occupation sobered him. With the tail of his eye he saw the door—even glanced at it from time to time directly, like a besieged commander

---

[1]Winter came earlier than normal when Napoleon invaded Russia, and thousands of his soldiers froze to death on his retreat.

pleased to verify the good estate of his defenses. But in truth he was at peace. The rain falling in the street sounded natural and pleasant. Presently, on the other side, the notes of a piano were wakened to the music of a hymn, and the voices of many children took up the air and words. How stately, how comfortable was the melody! How fresh the youthful voices! Markheim gave ear to it smilingly, as he sorted out the keys; and his mind was thronged with answerable ideas and images; churchgoing children and the pealing of the high organ; children afield, bathers by the brook-side, ramblers on the brambly common, kite-flyers in the windy and cloud-navigated sky; and then, at another cadence of the hymn, back again to church, and the somnolence of summer Sundays, and the high genteel voice of the parson (which he smiled a little to recall) and the painted Jacobean tombs, and the dim lettering of the Ten Commandments in the chancel.

40   And as he sat thus, at once busy and absent, he was startled to his feet. A flash of ice, a flash of fire, a bursting gush of blood, went over him, and then he stood transfixed and thrilling. A step mounted the stair slowly and steadily, and presently a hand was laid upon the knob, and the lock clicked, and the door opened.

Fear held Markheim in a vice. What to expect he knew not, whether the dead man walking, or the official ministers of human justice, or some chance witness blindly stumbling in to consign him to the gallows. But when a face was thrust into the aperture, glanced round the room, looked at him, nodded and smiled as if in friendly recognition, and then withdrew again, and the door closed behind it, his fear broke loose from his control in a hoarse cry. At the sound of this the visitant returned.

"Did you call me?" he asked, pleasantly, and with that he entered the room and closed the door behind him.

Markheim stood and gazed at him with all his eyes. Perhaps there was a film upon his sight, but the outlines of the newcomer seemed to change and waver like those of the idols in the wavering candle-light of the shop; and at times he thought he knew him; and at times he thought he bore a likeness to himself; and always, like a lump of living terror, there lay in his bosom the conviction that this thing was not of the earth and not of God.

And yet the creature had a strange air of the common-place, as he stood looking on Markheim with a smile; and when he added: "You are looking for the money, I believe?" it was in the tones of everyday politeness.

45   Markheim made no answer.

"I should warn you," resumed the other, "that the maid has left her sweetheart earlier than usual and will soon be here. If Mr. Markheim be found in this house, I need not describe to him the consequences."

"You know me?" cried the murderer.

The visitor smiled. "You have long been a favorite of mine," he said; "and I have long observed and often sought to help you."

"What are you?" cried Markheim: "the devil?"

50   "What I may be," returned the other, "can not affect the service I propose to render you."

"It can," cried Markheim; "it does! Be helped by you? No, never; not by you! You do not know me yet, thank God, you do not know me!"

"I know you," replied the visitant, with a sort of kind severity or rather firmness. "I know you to the soul."

"Know me!" cried Markheim. "Who can do so? My life is but a travesty and slander on myself. I have lived to belie my nature. All men do; all men are better than this disguise that grows about and stifles them. You see each dragged away by life, like one whom bravos have seized and muffled in a cloak. If they had their own control—if you could see their faces, they would be altogether different, they would shine out for heroes and saints!

I am worse than most; myself is more overlaid; my excuse is known to me and God. But, had I the time, I could disclose myself."

"To me?" inquired the visitant.

55   "To you before all," returned the murderer. "I supposed you were intelligent. I thought—since you exist—you would prove a reader of the heart. And yet you would propose to judge me by my acts! Think of it; my acts! I was born and I have lived in a land of giants; giants have dragged me by the wrists since I was born out of my mother—the giants of circumstance. And you would judge me by my acts! But can you not look within? Can you not understand that evil is hateful to me? Can you not see within me the clear writing of conscience, never blurred by any willful sophistry, although too often disregarded? Can you not read me for a thing that surely must be common as humanity—the unwilling sinner?"

"All this is very feelingly expressed," was the reply, "but it regards me not. These points of consistency are beyond my province, and I care not in the least by what compulsion you may have been dragged away, so as you are but carried in the right direction. But time flies; the servant delays, looking in the faces of the crowd and at the pictures on the hoardings,[2] but still she keeps moving nearer; and remember, it is as if the gallows itself was striding toward you through the Christmas streets! Shall I help you; I, who know all? Shall I tell you where to find the money?"

"For what price?" asked Markheim.

"I offer you the service for a Christmas gift," returned the other.

Markheim could not refrain from smiling with a kind of bitter triumph. "No," said he, "I will take nothing at your hands; if I were dying of thirst, and it was your hand that put the pitcher to my lips, I should find the courage to refuse. It may be credulous, but I will do nothing to commit myself to evil."

60   "I have no objection to a death-bed repentance," observed the visitant.

"Because you disbelieve their efficacy!" Markheim cried.

"I do not say so," returned the other; "but I look on these things from a different side, and when the life is done my interest falls. The man has lived to serve me, to spread black looks under color of religion, or to sow tares in the wheat-field, as you do, in a course of weak compliance with desire. Now that he draws so near to his deliverance, he can add but one act of service—to repent, to die smiling, and thus to build up in confidence and hope the more timorous of my surviving followers. I am not so hard a master. Try me. Accept my help. Please yourself in life as you have done hitherto; please yourself more amply, spread your elbows at the board; and when the night begins to fall and the curtains to be drawn, I tell you, for your greater comfort, that you will find it even easy to compound your quarrel with your conscience, and to make a truckling peace with God. I came but now from such a deathbed, and the room was full of sincere mourners, listening to the man's last words: and when I looked into that face, which had been set as a flint against mercy, I found it smiling with hope."

"And do you, then suppose me such a creature?" asked Markheim. "Do you think I have no more generous aspirations than to sin, and sin, and sin, and, at last, sneak into heaven? My heart rises at the thought. Is this, then, your experience of mankind? or is it because you find me with red hands that you presume such baseness? and is this crime of murder indeed so impious as to dry up the very springs of good?"

"Murder is to me no special category," replied the other. "All sins are murder, even as all life is war. I behold your race, like starving mariners on a raft, plucking crusts out of the hands of famine and feeding on each other's lives. I follow sins beyond the moment

---

[2]In British usage, a billboard.

of their acting; I find in all that the last consequence is death; and to my eyes, the pretty maid who thwarts her mother with such taking graces on a question of a ball, drips no less visibly with human gore than such a murderer as yourself. Do I say that I follow sins? I follow virtues also; they differ not by the thickness of a nail, they are both scythes for the reaping angel of Death. Evil, for which I live, consists not in action but in character. The bad man is dear to me; not the bad act, whose fruits, if we could follow them far enough down the hurtling cataract of the ages, might yet be found more blessed than those of the rarest virtues. And it is not because you have killed a dealer, but because you are Markheim, that I offered to forward your escape."

65   "I will lay my heart open to you," answered Markheim. "This crime on which you find me is my last. On my way to it I have learned many lessons; itself is a lesson, a momentous lesson. Hitherto I have been driven with revolt to what I would not; I was a bond-slave to poverty, driven and scourged. There are robust virtues that can stand in these temptations; mine was not so: I had a thirst of pleasure. But to-day, and out of this deed, I pluck both warning and riches—both the power and a fresh resolve to be myself. I become in all things a free actor in the world; I begin to see myself all changed, these hands the agents of good, this heart at peace. Something comes over me out of the past; something of what I have dreamed on Sabbath evenings to the sound of the church organ, of what I forecast when I shed tears over noble books, or talked, an innocent child, with my mother. There lies my life; I have wandered a few years, but now I see once more my city of destination."

        "You are to use this money on the Stock Exchange, I think?" remarked the visitor; "and there, if I mistake not, you have already lost some thousands?"

        "Ah," said Markheim, "but this time I have a sure thing."

        "This time, again, you will lose," replied the visitor, quietly.

        "Ah, but I keep back the half!" cried Markheim.

70   "That also you will lose," said the other.

        The sweat started upon Markheim's brow. "Well, then, what matter?" he exclaimed. "Say it be lost, say I am plunged again in poverty, shall one part of me, and that the worse, continue until the end to override the better? Evil and good run strong in me, haling me both ways. I do not love the one thing, I love all. I can conceive great deeds, renunciations, martyrdoms; and though I be fallen to such a crime as murder, pity is no stranger to my thoughts. I pity the poor; who knows their trials better than myself? I pity and help them; I prize love, I love honest laughter; there is no good thing nor true thing on earth but I love it from my heart. And are my vices only to direct my life, and my virtues to lie without effect, like some passive lumber of the mind? Not so; good, also, is a spring of acts."

        But the visitant raised his finger. "For six-and-thirty years that you have been in this world," said he, "through many changes of fortune and varieties of humor, I have watched you steadily fall. Fifteen years ago you would have started at a theft. Three years back you would have blenched at the name of murder. Is there any crime, is there any cruelty or meanness, from which you still recoil?—five years from now I shall detect you in the fact! Downward, downward, lies your way; nor can anything but death avail to stop you."

        "It is true," Markheim said, huskily, "I have in some degree complied with evil. But it is so with all: the very saints, in the mere exercise of living, grow less dainty, and take on the tone of their surroundings."

        "I will propound to you one simple question," said the other; "and as you answer, I shall read to you your moral horoscope. You have grown in many things more lax; possibly you do right to be so; and at any account, it is the same with all men. But granting that, are you in any one particular, however trifling, more difficult to please with your own conduct, or do you go in all things with a looser rein?"

75   "In any one?" repeated Markheim, with an anguish of consideration. "No," he added, with despair, "in none! I have gone down in all."

"Then," said the visitor, "content yourself with what you are, for you will never change; and the words of your part on this stage are irrevocably written down."

Markheim stood for a long while silent, and indeed it was the visitor who first broke the silence. "That being so," he said, "shall I show you the money?"

"And grace?" cried Markheim.

"Have you not tried it?" returned the other. "Two or three years ago, did I not see you on the platform of revival meetings, and was not your voice the loudest in the hymn?"

80   "It is true," said Markheim; "and I see clearly what remains for me by way of duty. I thank you for these lessons from my soul: my eyes are opened, and I behold myself at last for what I am."

At this moment, the sharp note of the door-bell rang through the house; and the visitant, as though this were some concerted signal for which he had been waiting, changed at once in his demeanor.

"The maid!" he cried. "She has returned, as I forewarned you, and there is now before you one more difficult passage. Her master, you must say, is ill; you must let her in, with an assured but rather serious countenance—no smiles, no overacting, and I promise you success! Once the girl within, and the door closed, the same dexterity that has already rid you of the dealer will relieve you of this last danger in your path. Thenceforward you have the whole evening—the whole night, if needful—to ransack the treasures of the house and to make good your safety. This is help that comes to you with the mask of danger. Up!" he cried: "up, friend; your life hangs trembling in the scales; up, and act!"

Markheim steadily regarded his counsellor. "If I be condemned to evil acts," he said, "there is still one door of freedom open—I can cease from action. If my life be an ill thing, I can lay it down. Though I be, as you say truly, at the beck of every small temptation, I can yet, by one decisive gesture, place myself beyond the reach of all. My love of good is damned to barrenness; it may, and let it be! But I have still my hatred of evil; and from that, to your galling disappointment, you shall see that I can draw both energy and courage."

The features of the visitor began to undergo a wonderful and lovely change; they brightened and softened with a tender triumph; and, even as they brightened, faded and dislimned. But Markheim did not pause to watch or understand the transformation. He opened the door and went downstairs very slowly, thinking to himself. His past went soberly before him; he beheld it as it was, ugly and strenuous like a dream, random as chance-medley—a scene of defeat. Life, as he thus reviewed it, tempted him no longer; but on the further side he perceived a quiet haven for his bark. He paused in the passage, and looked into the shop, where the candle still burned by the dead body. It was strangely silent. Thoughts of the dealer swarmed into his mind, as he stood gazing. And then the bell once more broke out into impatient clamor.

85   He confronted the maid upon the threshold with something like a smile.

"You had better go for the police," said he: "I have killed your master."

Comments and Questions

1. Is the main interest in this story curiosity about how the criminal will be caught or concern that the murderer might go unpunished or what?

2. By what means (several) does Stevenson transfer considerable reader sympathy from the dealer to Markheim?

3. How important a role does setting play in this story?

4. Can you chart the stages of Markheim's psychological reactions to the murder he has committed? What is his attitude toward God, and what does it reveal?

5. Review the use of figurative language (similes, metaphors, and so on) in the story. Is it employed purposively, effectively, merely as a decoration of sorts, or how?

6. Is there any functional humor in the story?

7. Is the conclusion of the story believable? Why or why not?

John Steinbeck (1902–1968)
Flight

About fifteen miles below Monterey, on the wild coast, the Torres family had their farm, a few sloping acres above a cliff that dropped to the brown reefs and to the hissing white waters of the ocean. Behind the farm the stone mountains stood up against the sky. The farm buildings huddled like little clinging aphids on the mountain skirts, crouched low to the ground as though the wind might blow them into the sea. The little shack, the rattling, rotting barn were gray-bitten with sea salt, beaten by the damp wind until they had taken on the color of the granite hills. Two horses, a red cow and a red calf, half a dozen pigs and a flock of lean, multi-colored chickens stocked the place. A little corn was raised on the sterile slope, and it grew short and thick under the wind, and all the cobs formed on the landward sides of the stalks.

Mama Torres, a lean, dry woman with ancient eyes, had ruled the farm for ten years ever since her husband tripped over a stone in the field one day and fell full length on a rattlesnake. When one is bitten on the chest there is not much that can be done.

Mama Torres had three children, two undersized black ones of twelve and fourteen, Emilio and Rosy, whom Mama kept fishing on the rocks below the farm when the sea was kind and when the truant officer was in some distant part of Monterey County. And there was Pepé, the tall smiling son of nineteen, a gentle, affectionate boy, but very lazy. Pepé had a tall head, pointed at the top, and from its peak, coarse black hair grew down like a thatch all around. Over his smiling little eyes Mama cut a straight bang so he could see. Pepé had sharp Indian cheekbones and an eagle nose, but his mouth was as sweet and shapely as a girl's mouth, and his chin was fragile and chiseled. He was loose and gangling, all legs and feet and wrists, and he was very lazy. Mama thought him fine and brave, but she never told him so. She said, "Some lazy cow must have got into thy father's family, else how could I have a son like thee" And she said, "When I carried thee, a sneaking lazy coyote came out of the brush and looked at me one day. That must have made thee so."

Pepé smiled sheepishly and stabbed at the ground with his knife to keep the blade sharp and free from rust. It was his inheritance, that knife, his father's knife. The long heavy blade folded back into the black handle. There was a button on the handle. When Pepé pressed the button, the blade leaped out ready for use. The knife was with Pepé always, for it had been his father's knife.

5   One sunny morning when the sea below the cliff was glinting and blue and the white surf creamed on the reef, when even the stone mountains looked kindly, Mama Torres called out the door of the shack, "Pepé, I have a labor for thee."

There was no answer. Mama listened. From behind the barn she heard a burst of laughter. She lifted her full long skirt and walked in the direction of the noise.

Pepé was sitting on the ground with his back against a box. His white teeth glistened. On either side of him stood the two black ones, tense and expectant. Fifteen feet away a redwood post was set in the ground. Pepé's right hand lay limply in his lap, and in the palm the big black knife rested. The blade was closed back into the handle. Pepé looked smiling at the sky.

Suddenly Emilio cried, "Ya!"

Pepé's wrist flicked like the head of a snake. The blade seemed to fly open in mid-air, and with a thump the point dug into the redwood post, and the black handle quivered. The three burst into excited laughter. Rosy ran to the post and pulled out the knife and brought it back to Pepé. He closed the blade and settled the knife carefully in his listless palm again. He grinned self-consciously at the sky.

10   "Ya!"

The heavy knife lanced out and sunk into the post again. Mama moved forward like a ship and scattered the play.

"All day you do foolish things with the knife, like a toy-baby," she stormed. "Get up on thy huge feet that eat up shoes. Get up!" She took him by one loose shoulder and hoisted at him. Pepé grinned sheepishly and came half-heartedly to his feet. "Look!" Mama cried. "Big lazy, you must catch the horse and put on thy father's saddle. You must ride to Monterey. The medicine bottle is empty. There is no salt. Go thou now, Peanut! Catch the horse."

A revolution took place in the relaxed figure of Pepé. "To Monterey, me? Alone? *Sí,* Mama."

She scowled at him. "Do not think, big sheep, that you will buy candy. No, I will give you only enough for the medicine and the salt."

15   Pepé smiled. "Mama, you will put the hatband on the hat?"

She relented then. "Yes, Pepé. You may wear the hatband."

His voice grew insinuating, "And the green handkerchief, Mama?"

"Yes, if you go quickly and return with no trouble, the silk green handkerchief will go. If you make sure to take off the handkerchief when you eat so no spot may fall on it. . . ."

"*Sí,* Mama. I will be careful. I am a man."

20   "Thou? A man? Thou art a peanut."

He went into the rickety barn and brought out a rope, and he walked agilely enough up the hill to catch the horse.

When he was ready and mounted before the door, mounted on his father's saddle that was so old that the oaken frame showed through torn leather in many places, then Mama brought out the round black hat with the tooled leather band, and she reached up and knotted the green silk handkerchief about his neck. Pepé's blue denim coat was much darker than his jeans, for it had been washed much less often.

Mama handed up the big medicine bottle and the silver coins. "That for the medicine," she said, "and that for the salt. That for a candle to burn for the papa. That for *dulces* for the little ones. Our friend Mrs. Rodriquez will give you dinner and maybe a bed for the night. When you go to the church say only ten Paternosters and only twenty-five Ave Marias. Oh! I know, big coyote. You would sit there flapping your mouth over Aves all day while you looked at the candles and the holy pictures. That is not good devotion to stare at the pretty things."

The black hat, covering the high pointed head and black thatched hair of Pepé, gave him dignity and age. He sat the rangy horse well. Mama thought how handsome he was, dark and lean and tall. "I would not send thee now alone, thou little one, except for the medicine," she said softly. "It is not good to have no medicine, for who knows when the toothache will come, or the sadness of the stomach. These things are."

25   *"Adios,* Mama," Pepé cried. "I will come back soon. You may send me often alone. I am a man."

"Thou art a foolish chicken."

He straightened his shoulders, flipped the reins against the horse's shoulder and rode away. He turned once and saw that they still watched him, Emilio and Rosy and Mama. Pepé grinned with pride and gladness and lifted the tough buckskin horse to a trot.

When he had dropped out of sight over a little dip in the road, Mama turned to the black ones, but she spoke to herself. "He is nearly a man now," she said. "It will be a nice thing to have a man in the house again." Her eyes sharpened on the children. "Go to the rocks now. The tide is going out. There will be abalones to be found." She put the iron hooks into their hands and saw them down the steep trail to the reefs. She brought the smooth stone *metate* to the doorway and sat grinding her corn to flour and looking occasionally at the road over which Pepé had gone. The noonday came and then the afternoon, when the little ones beat the abalones on a rock to make them tender and Mama patted the tortillas to make them thin. They ate their dinner as the red sun was plunging down toward the ocean. They sat on the doorsteps and watched the big white moon come over the mountain tops.

Mama said, "He is now at the house of our friend Mrs. Rodriguez. She will give him nice things to eat and maybe a present."

30   Emilio said, "Some day I too will ride to Monterey for medicine. Did Pepé come to be a man today?"

Mama said wisely, "A boy gets to be a man when a man is needed. Remember this thing. I have known boys forty years old because there was no need for a man."

Soon afterwards they retired, Mama in her big oak bed on one side of the room, Emilio and Rosy in their boxes full of straw and sheepskins on the other side of the room.

The moon went over the sky and the surf roared on the rocks. The roosters crowed the first call. The surf subsided to a whispering surge against the reef. The moon dropped toward the sea. The roosters crowed again.

The moon was near down to the water when Pepé rode on a winded horse to his home flat. His dog bounced out and circled the horse yelping with pleasure. Pepé slid off the saddle to the ground. The weathered little shack was silver in the moonlight and the square shadow of it was black to the north and east. Against the east the piling mountains were misty with light; their tops melted into the sky.

35   Pepé walked wearily up the three steps and into the house. It was dark inside. There was a rustle in the corner.

Mama cried out from her bed. "Who comes? Pepé, is it thou?"

"Sí, Mama."

"Did you get the medicine?"

"Sí, Mama."

40   "Well, go to sleep, then. I thought you would be sleeping at the house of Mrs. Rodriguez." Pepé stood silently in the dark room. "Why do you stand there, Pepé? Did you drink wine?"

"Sí, Mama."

"Well, go to bed then and sleep out the wine."

His voice was tired and patient, but very firm. "Light the candle, Mama. I must go away into the mountains."

"What is this, Pepé? You are crazy." Mama struck a sulphur match and held the little blue burr until the flame spread up the stick. She set light to the candle on the floor beside her bed. "Now, Pepé, what is this you say?" She looked anxiously into his face.

45   He was changed. The fragile quality seemed to have gone from his chin. His mouth was less full than it had been, the lines of the lips were straighter, but in his eyes the greatest change had taken place. There was no laughter in them any more nor any bashfulness. They were sharp and bright and purposeful.

He told her in a tired monotone, told her everything just as it had happened. A few people came into the kitchen of Mrs. Rodriquez. There was wine to drink. Pepé drank wine. The little quarrel—the man started toward Pepé and then the knife—it went almost by itself. It flew, it darted before Pepé knew it. As he talked, Mama's face grew stern, and it seemed to grow more lean. Pepé finished. "I am a man now, Mama. The man said names to me I could not allow."

Mama nodded. "Yes, thou art a man, my poor little Pepé. Thou art a man. I have seen it coming on thee. I have watched you throwing the knife into the post, and I have been afraid." For a moment her face had softened, but now it grew stern again. "Come! We must get you ready. Go. Awaken Emilio and Rosy. Go quickly."

Pepé stepped over to the corner where his brother and sister slept among the sheepskins. He leaned down and shook them gently. "Come, Rosy! Come, Emilio! The mama says you must arise."

The little black ones sat up and rubbed their eyes in the candlelight. Mama was out of bed now, her long black skirt over her nightgown. "Emilio," she cried. "Go up and catch the other horse for Pepé. Quickly now! Quickly." Emilio put his legs in his overalls and stumbled sleepily out the door.

50   "You heard no one behind you on the road?" Mama demanded.

"No, Mama. I listened carefully. No one was on the road."

Mama darted like a bird about the room. From a nail on the wall she took a canvas water bag and threw it on the floor. She stripped a blanket from her bed and rolled it into a tight tube and tied the ends with string. From a box beside the stove she lifted a flour sack half full of black stringy jerky. "Your father's black coat, Pepé. Here, put it on."

Pepé stood in the middle of the floor watching her activity. She reached behind the door and brought out the rifle, a long 38–56, worn shiny the whole length of the barrel. Pepé took it from her and held it in the crook of his elbow. Mama brought a little leather bag and counted the cartridges into his hand. "Only ten left," she warned. "You must not waste them."

Emilio put his head in the door. "*'Qui 'st 'l caballo,* Mama."

55   "Put on the saddle from the other horse. Tie on the blanket. Here, tie the jerky to the saddle horn."

Still Pepé stood silently watching his mother's frantic activity. His chin looked hard, and his sweet mouth was drawn and thin. His little eyes followed Mama about the room almost suspiciously.

Rosy asked softly, "Where goes Pepé?"

Mama's eyes were fierce. "Pepé goes on a journey. Pepé is a man now. He has a man's thing to do."

Pepé straightened his shoulders. His mouth changed until he looked very much like Mama.

60   At last the preparation was finished. The loaded horse stood outside the door. The water bag dripped a line of moisture down the bay shoulder.

The moonlight was being thinned by the dawn and the big white moon was near down to the sea. The family stood by the shack. Mama confronted Pepé. "Look, my son! Do not stop until it is dark again. Do not sleep even though you are tired. Take care of the horse in order that he may not stop of weariness. Remember to be careful with the bullets—there are only ten. Do not fill thy stomach with jerky or it will make thee sick. Eat a little jerky and fill thy stomach with grass. When thou comest to the high mountains, if thou seest any of the dark watching men, go not near to them nor try to speak to them. And forget not thy prayers." She put her lean hands on Pepé's shoulders, stood on her toes and kissed him formally on both cheeks, and Pepé kissed her on both cheeks. Then he went to Emilio and Rosy and kissed both of their cheeks.

Pepé turned back to Mama. He seemed to look for a little softness, a little weakness in her. His eyes were searching, but Mama's face remained fierce. "Go now," she said. "Do not wait to be caught like a chicken."

Pepé pulled himself into the saddle. "I am a man," he said.

It was the first dawn when he rode up the hill toward the little canyon which let a trail into the mountains. Moonlight and daylight fought with each other, and the two warring qualities made it difficult to see. Before Pepé had gone a hundred yards, the outlines of his figure were misty; and long before he entered the canyon, he had become a gray, indefinite shadow.

65 Mama stood stiffly in front of her doorstep, and on either side of her stood Emilio and Rosy. They cast furtive glances at Mama now and then.

When the gray shape of Pepé melted into the hillside and disappeared, Mama relaxed. She began the high, whining keen of the death wail. "Our beautiful—our brave," she cried. "Our protector, our son is gone." Emilio and Rosy moaned beside her. "Our beautiful—our brave, he is gone." It was the formal wail. It rose to a high piercing whine and subsided to a moan. Mama raised it three times and then she turned and went into the house and shut the door.

Emilio and Rosy stood wondering in the dawn. They heard Mama whimpering in the house. They went out to sit on the cliff above the ocean. They touched shoulders. "When did Pepé come to be a man?" Emilio asked.

"Last night," said Rosy. "Last night in Monterey." The ocean clouds turned red with the sun that was behind the mountains.

"We will have no breakfast," said Emilio. "Mama will not want to cook." Rosy did not answer him. "Where is Pepé gone?" he asked.

70 Rosy looked around at him. She drew her knowledge from the quiet air. "He has gone on a journey. He will never come back."

"Is he dead? Do you think he is dead?"

Rosy looked back at the ocean again. A little steamer, drawing a line of smoke, sat on the edge of the horizon. "He is not dead," Rosy explained. "Not yet."

Pepé rested the big rifle across the saddle in front of him. He let the horse walk up the hill and he didn't look back. The stony slope took on a coat of short brush so that Pepé found the entrance to a trail and entered it.

When he came to the canyon opening, he swung once in his saddle and looked back, but the houses were swallowed in the misty light. Pepé jerked forward again. The high shoulder of the canyon closed in on him. His horse stretched out its neck and sighed and settled to the trail.

75 It was a well-worn path, dark soft leafmold earth strewn with broken pieces of sandstone. The trail rounded the shoulder of the canyon and dropped steeply into the bed of the stream. In the shallows the water ran smoothly, glinting in the first morning sun. Small

round stones on the botton were as brown as rust with sun moss. In the sand along the edges of the stream the tall, rich wild mint grew, while in the water itself the cress, old and tough, had gone to heavy seed.

The path went into the stream and emerged on the other side. The horse sloshed into the water and stopped. Pepé dropped his bridle and let the beast drink of the running water.

Soon the canyon sides became steep and the first giant sentinel redwoods guarded the trail, great round red trunks bearing foliage as green and lacy as ferns. Once Pepé was among the trees, the sun was lost. A perfumed and purple light lay in the pale green of the underbrush. Gooseberry bushes and blackberries and tall ferns lined the stream, and overhead the branches of the redwoods met and cut off the sky.

Pepé drank from the water bag, and he reached into the flour sack and brought out a black string of jerky. His white teeth gnawed at the string until the tough meat parted. He chewed slowly and drank occasionally from the water bag. His little eyes were slumberous and tired, but the muscles of his face were hard set. The earth of the trail was black now. It gave up a hollow sound under the walking hoofbeats.

The stream fell more sharply. Little waterfalls splashed on the stones. Five-fingered ferns hung over the water and dripped spray from their fingertips. Pepé rode half over in his saddle, dangling one leg loosely. He picked a bay leaf from a tree beside the way and put it into his mouth for a moment to flavor the dry jerky. He held the gun loosely across the pommel.

80   Suddenly he squared in his saddle, swung the horse from the trail and kicked it hurriedly up behind a big redwood tree. He pulled up the reins tight against the bit to keep the horse from whinnying. His face was intent and his nostrils quivered a little.

A hollow pounding came down the trail, and a horseman rode by, a fat man with red cheeks and a white stubble beard. His horse put down its head and blubbered at the trail when it came to the place where Pepé had turned off. "Hold up!" said the man and he pulled up his horse's head.

When the last sound of hoofs died away, Pepé came back into the trail again. He did not relax in the saddle any more. He lifted the big rifle and swung the lever to throw a shell into the chamber, and then he let down the hammer to half cock.

The trail grew very steep. Now the redwood trees were smaller and their tops were dead, bitten dead where the wind reached them. The horse plodded on; the sun went slowly overhead and started down toward the afternoon.

Where the stream came out of a side canyon, the trail left it. Pepé dismounted and watered his horse and filled up his water bag. As soon as the trail had parted from the stream, the trees were gone and only the thick brittle sage and manzanita and chaparral edged the trail. And the soft black earth was gone, too, leaving only the light tan broken rock for the trail bed. Lizards scampered away into the brush as the horse rattled over the little stones.

85   Pepé turned in his saddle and looked back. He was in the open now: he could be seen from a distance. As he ascended the trail the country grew more rough and terrible and dry. The way wound about the bases of great square rocks. Little gray rabbits skittered in the brush. A bird made a monotonous high creaking. Eastward the bare rock mountaintops were pale and powder-dry under the dropping sun. The horse plodded up and up the trail toward a little V in the ridge which was the pass.

Pepé looked suspiciously back every minute or so, and his eyes sought the tops of the ridges ahead. Once, on a white barren spur, he saw a black figure for a moment, but he looked quickly away, for it was one of the dark watchers. No one knew who the watchers were, nor where they lived, but it was better to ignore them and never to show interest in them. They did not bother one who stayed on the trail and minded his own business.

The air was parched and full of light dust blown by the breeze from the eroding mountains. Pepé drank sparingly from his bag and corked it tightly and hung it on the horn again. The trail moved up the dry shale hillside, avoiding rocks, dropping under clefts, climbing in and out of old water scars. When he arrived at the little pass he stopped and looked back for a long time. No dark watchers were to be seen now. The trail behind was empty. Only the high tops of the redwoods indicated where the stream flowed.

Pepé rode on through the pass. His little eyes were nearly closed with weariness, but his face was stern, relentless and manly. The high mountain wind coasted sighing through the pass and whistled on the edges of the big blocks of broken granite. In the air, a red-tailed hawk sailed over close to the ridge and screamed angrily. Pepé went slowly through the broken jagged pass and looked down on the other side.

The trail dropped quickly, staggering among broken rock. At the bottom of the slope there was a dark crease, thick with brush, and on the other side of the crease a little flat, in which a grove of oak trees grew. A scar of green grass cut across the flat. And behind the flat another mountain rose, desolate with dead rocks and starving little black bushes. Pepé drank from the bag again for the air was so dry that it encrusted his nostrils and burned his lips. He put the horse down the trail. The hooves slipped and struggled on the steep way, starting little stones that rolled off into the brush. The sun was gone behind the westward mountain now, but still it glowed brilliantly on the oaks and on the grassy flat. The rocks and the hillsides still sent up waves of the heat they had gathered from the day's sun.

90   Pepé looked up to the top of the next dry withered ridge. He saw a dark form against the sky, a man's figure standing on top of a rock, and he glanced away quickly not to appear curious. When a moment later he looked up again, the figure was gone.

Downward the trail was quickly covered. Sometimes the horse floundered for footing, sometimes set his feet and slid a little way. They came at last to the bottom where the dark chaparral was higher than Pepé's head. He held up his rifle on one side and his arm on the other to shield his face from the sharp brittle fingers of the brush.

Up and out of the crease he rode, and up a little cliff. The grassy flat was before him, and the round comfortable oaks. For a moment he studied the trail down which he had come, but there was no movement and no sound from it. Finally he rode out over the flat, to the green streak, and at the upper end of the damp he found a little spring welling out of the earth and dropping into a dug basin before it seeped out over the flat.

Pepé filled his bag first, and then he let the thirsty horse drink out of the pool. He led the horse to the clump of oaks, and in the middle of the grove, fairly protected from sight on all sides, he took off the saddle and the bridle and laid them on the ground. The horse stretched his jaws sideways and yawned. Pepé knotted the lead rope about the horse's neck and tied him to a sapling among the oaks, where he could graze in a fairly large circle.

When the horse was gnawing hungrily at the dry grass, Pepé went to the saddle and took a black string of jerky from the sack and strolled to an oak tree on the edge of the grove, from under which he could watch the trail. He sat down in the crisp dry oak leaves and automatically felt for his big black knife to cut the jerky, but he had no knife. He leaned back on his elbow and gnawed at the tough strong meat. His face was blank, but it was a man's face.

95   The bright evening light washed the eastern ridge, but the valley was darkening. Doves flew down from the hills to the spring, and the quail came running out of the brush and joined them, calling clearly to one another.

Out of the corner of his eye Pepé saw a shadow grow out of the bushy crease. He turned his head slowly. A big spotted wildcat was creeping toward the spring, belly to the ground, moving like thought.

Pepé cocked his rifle and edged the muzzle slowly around. Then he looked apprehensively up the trail and dropped the hammer again. From the ground beside him he picked an oak twig and threw it toward the spring. The quail flew up with a roar and the doves whistled away. The big cat stood up: for a long moment he looked at Pepé with cold yellow eyes, and then fearlessly walked back into the gulch.

The dusk gathered quickly in the deep valley. Pepé muttered his prayers, put his head down on his arm and went instantly to sleep.

The moon came up and filled the valley with cold blue light, and the wind swept rustling down from the peaks. The owls worked up and down the slopes looking for rabbits. Down in the brush of the gulch a coyote gabbled. The oak trees whispered softly in the night breeze.

100   Pepé started up, listening. His horse had whinnied. The moon was just slipping behind the western ridge, leaving the valley in darkness behind it. Pepé sat tensely gripping his rifle. From far up the trail he heard an answering whinny and the crash of shod hooves on the broken rock. He jumped to his feet, ran to his horse and led it under the trees. He threw on the saddle and cinched it tight for the steep trail, caught the unwilling head and forced the bit into the mouth. He felt the saddle to make sure the water bag and the sack of jerky were there. Then he mounted and turned up the hill.

It was velvet dark. The horse found the entrance to the trail where it left the flat, and started up, stumbling and slipping on the rocks. Pepé's hand rose up to his head. His hat was gone. He had left it under the oak tree.

The horse had struggled far up the trail when the first change of dawn came into the air, a steel grayness as light mixed thoroughly with dark. Gradually the sharp snaggled edge of the ridge stood out above them, rotten granite tortured and eaten by the winds of time. Pepé had dropped his reins on the horn, leaving direction to the horse. The brush grabbed at his legs in the dark until one knee of his jeans was ripped.

Gradually the light flowed down over the ridge. The starved brush and rocks stood out in the half light, strange and lonely in high perspective. Then there came warmth into the light. Pepé drew up and looked back, but he could see nothing in the darker valley below. The sky turned blue over the coming sun. In the waste of the mountainside, the poor dry brush grew only three feet high. Here and there, big outcroppings of unrotted granite stood up like moldering houses. Pepé relaxed a little. He drank from his water bag and bit off a piece of jerky. A single eagle flew over, high in the light.

Without warning Pepé's horse screamed and fell on its side. He was almost down before the rifle crash echoed up from the valley. From a hole behind the struggling shoulder, a stream of bright crimson blood pumped and stopped and pumped and stopped. The hooves threshed on the ground. Pepé lay half stunned beside the horse. He looked slowly down the hill. A piece of sage clipped off beside his head and another crash echoed up from side to side of the canyon. Pepé flung himself frantically behind a bush.

105   He crawled up the hill on his knees and on one hand. His right hand held the rifle up off the ground and pushed it ahead of him. He moved with the instinctive care of an animal. Rapidly he wormed his way toward one of the big outcroppings of granite on the hill above him. Where the brush was high he doubled up and ran, but where the cover was slight he wriggled forward on his stomach, pushing the rifle ahead of him. In the last little distance there was no cover at all. Pepé poised and then he darted across the space and flashed around the corner of the rock.

He leaned panting against the stone. When his breath came easier he moved along behind the big rock until he came to a narrow split that offered a thin section of vision down the hill. Pepé lay on his stomach and pushed the rifle barrel through the slit and waited.

The sun reddened the western ridges now. Already the buzzards were settling down toward the place where the horse lay. A small brown bird scratched in the dead sage leaves directly in front of the rifle muzzle. The coasting eagle flew back toward the rising sun.

Pepé saw a little movement in the brush far below. His grip tightened on the gun. A little brown doe stepped daintily out on the trail and crossed it and disappeared into the brush again. For a long time Pepé waited. Far below he could see the little flat and the oak trees and the slash of green. Suddenly his eyes flashed back at the trail again. A quarter of a mile down there had been a quick movement in the chaparral. The rifle swung over. The front sight nestled in the V of the rear sight. Pepé studied for a movement and then raised the rear sight a notch. The little movement in the brush came again. The sight settled on it. Pepé squeezed the trigger. The explosion crashed down the mountain and up the other side, and came rattling back. The whole side of the slope grew still. No more movement. And then a white streak cut into the granite of the slit and a bullet whined away and a crash sounded up from below. Pepé felt a sharp pain in his right hand. A sliver of granite was sticking out from between his first and second knuckles and the point protruded from his palm. Carefully he pulled out the sliver of stone. The wound bled evenly and gently. No vein nor artery was cut.

Pepé looked into a little dusty cave in the rock and gathered a handful of spider web, and he pressed the mass into the cut, plastering the soft web into the blood. The flow stopped almost at once.

110   The rifle was on the ground. Pepé picked it up, levered a new shell into the chamber. And then he slid into the brush on his stomach. Far to the right he crawled, and then up the hill, moving slowly and carefully, crawling to cover and resting and then crawling again.

In the mountains the sun is high in its arc before it penetrates the gorges. The hot face looked over the hill and brought instant heat with it. The white light beat on the rocks and reflected from them and rose up quivering from the earth again, and the rocks and bushes seemed to quiver behind the air.

Pepé crawled in the general direction of the ridge peak, zig-zagging for cover. The deep cut between his knuckles began to throb. He crawled close to a rattlesnake before he saw it, and when it raised its dry head and made a soft beginning whirr, he backed up and took another way. The quick gray lizards flashed in front of him, raising a tiny line of dust. He found another mass of spider web and pressed it against his throbbing hand.

Pepé was pushing the rifle with his left hand now. Little drops of sweat ran to the ends of his coarse black hair and rolled down his cheeks. His lips and tongue were growing thick and heavy. His lips writhed to draw saliva into his mouth. His little dark eyes were uneasy and suspicious. Once when a gray lizard paused in front of him on the parched ground and turned its head sideways he crushed it flat with a stone.

When the sun slid past noon he had not gone a mile. He crawled exhaustedly a last hundred yards to a patch of high sharp manzanita, crawled desperately, and when the patch was reached he wriggled in among the tough gnarly trunks and dropped his head on his left arm. There was little shade in the meager brush, but there was cover and safety. Pepé went to sleep as he lay and the sun beat on his back. A few little birds hopped close to him and peered and hopped away. Pepé squirmed in his sleep and he raised and dropped his wounded hand again and again.

115   The sun went down behind the peaks and the cool evening came, and then the dark. A coyote yelled from the hillside, Pepé started awake and looked about with misty eyes. His hand was swollen and heavy; a little thread of pain ran up the inside of his arm and

settled in a pocket in his armpit. He peered about and then stood up, for the mountains were black and the moon had not yet risen. Pepé stood up in the dark. The coat of his father pressed on his arm. His tongue was swollen until it nearly filled his mouth. He wriggled out of the coat and dropped it in the brush, and then he struggled up the hill, falling over rocks and tearing his way through the brush. The rifle knocked against stones as he went. Little dry avalanches of gravel and shattered stone went whispering down the hill behind him.

After a while the old moon came up and showed the jagged ridge top ahead of him. By moonlight Pepé traveled more easily. He bent forward so that his throbbing arm hung away from his body. The journey uphill was made in dashes and rests, a frantic rush up a few yards and then a rest. The wind coasted down the slope rattling the dry stems of the bushes.

The moon was at meridian when Pepé came at last to the sharp backbone of the ridge top. On the last hundred yards of the rise no soil had clung under the wearing winds. The way was on solid rock. He clambered to the top and looked down on the other side. There was a draw like the last below him, misty with moonlight, brushed with dry struggling sage and chaparral. On the other side the hill rose up sharply and at the top the jagged rotten teeth of the mountain showed against the sky. At the bottom of the cut the brush was thick and dark.

Pepé stumbled down the hill. His throat was almost closed with thirst. At first he tried to run, but immediately he fell and rolled. After that he went more carefully. The moon was just disappearing behind the mountains when he came to the bottom. He crawled into the heavy brush feeling with his fingers for water. There was no water in the bed of the stream, only damp earth. Pepé laid his gun down and scooped up a handful of mud and put it in his mouth, and then he spluttered and scraped the earth from his tongue with his finger, for the mud drew at his mouth like a poultice. He dug a hole in the stream bed with his fingers, dug a little basin to catch water; but before it was very deep his head fell forward on the damp ground and he slept.

The dawn came and the heat of the day fell on the earth, and still Pepé slept. Late in the afternoon his head jerked up. He looked slowly around. His eyes were slits of wariness. Twenty feet away in the heavy brush a big tawny mountain lion stood looking at him. Its long thick tail waved gracefully, its ears erect with interest, not laid back dangerously. The lion squatted down on its stomach and watched him.

120 Pepé looked at the hole he had dug in the earth. A half inch of muddy water had collected in the bottom. He tore the sleeve from his hurt arm, with his teeth ripped out a little square, soaked it in the water and put it in his mouth. Over and over he filled the cloth and sucked it.

Still the lion sat and watched him. The evening came down but there was no movement on the hills. No birds visited the dry bottom of the cut. Pepé looked occasionally at the lion. The eyes of the yellow beast drooped as though he were about to sleep. He yawned and his long thin ted tongue curled out. Suddenly his head jerked around and his nostrils quivered. His big tail lashed. He stood up and slunk like a tawny shadow into the thick brush.

A moment later Pepé heard the sound, the faint far crash of horses' hooves on gravel. And he heard something else, a high whining yelp of a dog.

Pepé took his rifle in his left hand and he glided into the brush almost as quietly as the lion had. In the darkening evening he crouched up the hill toward the next ridge. Only when the dark came did he stand up. His energy was short. Once it was dark he fell over the rocks and slipped to his knees on the steep slope, but he moved on and on up the hill, climbing and scrabbling over the broken hillside.

When he was far up toward the top, he lay down and slept for a little while. The withered moon, shining on his face, awakened him. He stood up and moved up the hill. Fifty yards away he stopped and turned back, for he had forgotten his rifle. He walked heavily down and poked about in the brush, but he could not find his gun. At last he lay down to rest. The pocket of pain in his armpit had grown more sharp. His arm seemed to swell out and fall with every heartbeat. There was no position lying down where the heavy arm did not press against his armpit.

125   With the effort of a hurt beast, Pepé got up and moved again toward the top of the ridge. He held his swollen arm away from his body with his left hand. Up the steep hill he dragged himself, a few steps and a rest, and a few more steps. At last he was nearing the top. The moon showed the uneven sharp back of it against the sky.

Pepé's brain spun in a big spiral up and away from him. He slumped to the ground and lay still. The rock ridge top was only a hundred feet above him.

The moon moved over the sky. Pepé half turned on his back. His tongue tried to make words, but only a thick hissing came from between his lips.

When the dawn came, Pepé pulled himself up. His eyes were sane again. He drew his great puffed arm in front of him and looked at the angry wound. The black line ran up from his wrist to his armpit. Automatically he reached in his pocket for the big black knife, but it was not there. His eyes searched the ground. He picked up a sharp blade of stone and scraped at the wound, sawed at the proud flesh and then squeezed the green juice out in big drops. Instantly he threw back his head and whined like a dog. His whole right side shuddered at the pain, but the pain cleared his head.

In the gray light he struggled up the last slope to the ridge and crawled over and lay down behind a line of rocks. Below him lay a deep canyon exactly like the last, water-less and desolate. There was no flat, no oak trees, not even heavy brush in the bottom of it. And on the other side a sharp ridge stood up, thinly brushed with starving sage, littered with broken granite. Strewn over the hill there were giant outcroppings, and on the top the granite teeth stood out against the sky.

130   The new day was light now. The flame of sun came over the ridge and fell on Pepé where he lay on the ground. His coarse black hair was littered with twigs and bits of spider web. His eyes had retreated back into his head. Between his lips the tip of his black tongue showed.

He sat up and dragged his great arm into his lap and nursed it, rocking his body and moaning in his throat. He threw back his head and looked up into the pale sky. A big black bird circled nearly out of sight, and far to the left another was sailing near.

He lifted his head to listen, for a familiar sound had come to him from the valley he had climbed out of; it was the crying yelp of hounds, excited and feverish, on a trail.

Pepé bowed his head quickly. He tried to speak rapid words but only a thick hiss came from his lips. He drew a shaky cross on his breast with his left hand. It was a long struggle to get to his feet. He crawled slowly and mechanically to the top of a big rock on the ridge peak. Once there, he arose slowly, swaying to his feet, and stood erect. Far below he could see the dark brush where he had slept. He braced his feet and stood there, black against the morning sky.

There came a ripping sound at his feet. A piece of stone flew up and a bullet droned off into the next gorge. The hollow crash echoed up from below. Pepé looked down for a moment and then pulled himself straight again.

135   His body jarred back. His left hand fluttered helplessly toward his breast. The second crash sounded from below. Pepé swung forward and toppled from the rock. His body struck and rolled over and over, starting a little avalanche. And when at last he stopped against a bush, the avalanche slid slowly down and covered up his head.

Comments and Questions

1. In a sense, the same kind of peripheral vision required of the effective basketball playmaker is also required of the critically intelligent reader of literature. The title of this story itself presents a central question answerable only by the reader's active peripheral vision and critical ability to read the part in terms of its functional relation to other parts and, further, to perceive their thematic harmony of meaning through an enriching consciousness of the story as a whole. Only in that manner can the reader determine with reasonable confidence the significance of the title "Flight" (and, here, of the entire story). Is it just literally descriptive of Pepé's running away? Is it directly symbolic in relation to the pervasive bird imagery and the direction of Pepé's flight? Or is it ironically symbolic, signifying a quite opposite thematic emphasis?

2. Carefully analyze the diction and imagery of the first two paragraphs. Do most of the adjectives, for example, hang together like a cluster of grapes? What is their common stem? Are the diction and imagery especially functional, preparatory for an understanding of other elements in the story (characters, conflicts, action, theme)?

3. What is the effect and purpose of the final sentence of the second paragraph?

4. What is the significance of the "trappings" (saddle, hat, etc.) of Pepé's journey to Monterey? Of his loss of some of the same items during his flight?

5. What is the function of the style of Mama's last-minute instructions to Pepé before his flight?

6. In a characterizing phrase for each, list every instance of references to birds and animals in the story. Is there a discernible, functional pattern among them?

7. How many dawns occur during Pepé's flight? Is the time of day when he dies ironic, fitting?

8. To what extent are Steinbeck's methods here comparable, say, to those of Hawthorne above? Constructing a plot action line (see p. 9) for "Flight" could be helpful in answering the question.

Ralph Ellison (1914–   )
King of the Bingo Game

This story was published in 1944 when Ellison was thirty years old, and it preceded his celebrated novel, *Invisible Man* (1952), by eight years. In 1965 the magazine *Book Week* asked 200 authors, critics, and editors to determine according to their collective judgment the most distinguished writers and the most distinguished novel published in America between 1945 and 1965. Of the more than 10,000 novels, *Invisible Man* was judged to be "the most distinguished single work," and Ellison was given sixth place among novelists, one place above Norman Mailer and two above Hemingway. Concerning *Invisible Man*, Ellison wrote: "Indeed, if I were asked in all seriousness just what I considered to be the chief significance of *Invisible Man* as a fiction, I would reply: Its experimental attitude, and its attempt to return to the mood of personal moral responsibility for democracy which typified the best of our nine-teenth-century fiction. . . . I came to believe that the writers of that period took a much greater responsibility for the condition of democracy and, indeed, their works were imaginative projections of the conflicts within the human heart which arose when the sacred principles of the Constitution and the Bill of Rights clashed with the practi-cal exigencies of human greed and fear, hate and love. . . . Whenever we as Americans have faced serious crises we have returned to fundamentals; this, in brief, is what I have tried to do."* Undoubtedly Ellison's basic concern in this statement is that writers should take a personal moral responsibility for the condition of democracy, and this Ellison has done in very large measure.

"King of the Bingo Game" and "Flying Home" (1944) are often said to be his best short stories, and in them he clearly accepts his moral responsibility for the condi-tion of democracy. The larger, deeper issue in "King of the Bingo Game" is the condition and place of the black in American democracy, an issue that permeates most of black American literature.** The desperate young black who tries to win the bingo game of life as arranged by the whites is defeated, and the consequences of this defeat are, as Ellison dramatizes here and in *Invisible Man,* a violation of the Constitution and the Bill of Rights. Just who is the King of the bingo game? Ellison provides his answer.

The woman in front of him was eating roasted peanuts that smelled so good that he could barely contain his hunger. He could not even sleep and wished they'd hurry and begin the bingo game. There, on his right, two fellows were drinking wine out of a bottle wrapped in a paper bag, and he could hear soft gurgling in the dark. His stomach gave a low, gnawing growl. "If this was down South," he thought, "all I'd have to do is lean over and say, 'Lady, gimme a few of those peanuts, please ma'am,' and she'd pass me the bag and never think nothing of it." Or he could ask the fellows for a drink in the same way. Folks down South stuck together that way; they didn't even have to know you. But up here it was different. Ask somebody for something, and they'd think you were crazy. Well, I ain't crazy. I'm just broke, 'cause I got no birth certificate to get a job, and Laura 'bout to die 'cause we got no money for a doctor. But I ain't crazy. And yet a pinpoint of doubt was focused in his mind as he glanced toward the screen and saw the hero stealthily entering a dark room and sending the beam of a flashlight along a wall of bookcases. This is where he finds the trapdoor, he remembered. The man would pass abruptly through the wall and find the girl tied to a bed, her legs and arms spread wide, and her clothing torn to rags. He laughed softly to himself. He had seen the picture three times, and this was one of the best scenes.

On his right the fellow whispered wide-eyed to his companion, "Man, look a-yon-der!"

"Damn!"

"Wouldn't I like to have her tied up like that . . ."

"Hey! That fool's letting her loose!"

"Aw, man, he loves her."

"Love or no love!"

The man moved impatiently beside him, and he tried to involve himself in the scene. But Laura was on his mind. Tiring quickly of watching the picture he looked back to where

*For Ellison's complete essay, "Brave Words for a Startling Occasion," see p. 1086.
**See stories by Langston Hughes (p. 97) and James Baldwin (p. 52).

the white beam filtered from the projection room above the balcony. It started small and grew large, specks of dust dancing in its whiteness as it reached the screen. It was strange how the beam always landed right on the screen and didn't mess up and fall somewhere else. But they had it all fixed. Everything was fixed. Now suppose when they showed that girl with her dress torn the girl started taking off the rest of her clothes, and when the guy came in he didn't untie her but kept her there and went to taking off his own clothes? *That* would be something to see. If a picture got out of hand like that those guys up there would go nuts. Yeah, and there'd be so many folks in here you couldn't find a seat for nine months? A strange sensation played over his skin. He shuddered. Yesterday he'd seen a bedbug on a woman's neck as they walked out into the bright street. But exploring his thigh through a hole in his pocket he found only goose pimples and old scars.

The bottle gurgled again. He closed his eyes. Now a dreamy music was accompanying the film and train whistles were sounding in the distance, and he was a boy again walking along a railroad trestle down South, and seeing the train coming, and running back as fast as he could go, and hearing the whistle blowing, and getting off the trestle to solid ground just in time, with the earth trembling beneath his feet, and feeling relieved as he ran down the cinder-strewn embankment onto the highway, and looking back and seeing with terror that the train had left the track and was following him right down the middle of the street, and all the white people laughing as he ran screaming . . .

10   "Wake up there, buddy! What the hell do you mean hollering like that? Can't you see we trying to enjoy this here picture?"

He stared at the man with gratitude.

"I'm sorry, old man," he said. "I musta been dreaming."

"Well, here, have a drink. And don't be making no noise like that, damn!"

His hands trembled as he tilted his head. It was not wine, but whiskey. Cold rye whiskey. He took a deep swoller, decided it was better not to take another, and handed the bottle back to its owner.

15   "Thanks, old man," he said.

Now he felt the cold whiskey breaking a warm path straight through the middle of him, growing hotter and sharper as it moved. He had not eaten all day, and it made him light-headed. The smell of the peanuts stabbed him like a knife, but he got up and found a seat in the middle aisle. But no sooner did he sit than he saw a row of intense-faced young girls, and he got up again, thinking, "You chicks musta been Lindy-hopping somewhere." He found a seat several rows ahead as the lights came on, and he saw the screen disappear behind a heavy red and gold curtain; then the curtain rising, and the man with the microphone and a uniformed attendant coming on the stage.

He felt for his bingo cards, smiling. The guy at the door wouldn't like it if he knew about his having *five* cards. Well, not everyone played the bingo game; and even with five cards he didn't have much of a chance. For Laura, though, he had to have faith. He studied the cards, each with its different numerals, punching the free center hole in each and spreading them neatly across his lap; and when the light faded he sat slouched in his seat so that he could look from his cards to the bingo wheel with but a quick shifting of his eyes.

Ahead, at the end of the darkness, the man with the microphone was pressing a button attached to a long cord and spinning the bingo wheel and calling out the number each time the wheel came to rest. And each time the voice rang out his finger raced over the cards for the number. With five cards he had to move fast. He became nervous; there were too many cards, and the man went too fast with his grating voice. Perhaps he should just select one and throw the others away. But he was afraid. He became warm. Wonder how much Laura's doctor would cost? Damn that, watch the cards! And with despair he

heard the man call three in a row which he missed on all five cards. This way he'd never
win. . . .

When he saw the row of holes punched across the third card, he sat paralyzed and
he heard the man call three more numbers before he stumbled forward, screaming.

20   "Bingo! Bingo!"

"Let that fool up there," someone called.

"Get up there, man!"

He stumbled down the aisle and up the steps to the stage into a light so sharp and
bright that for a moment it blinded him, and he felt that he had moved into the spell of
some strange, mysterious power. Yet it was as familiar as the sun, and he knew it was the
perfectly familiar bingo.

The man with the microphone was saying something to the audience as he held out
his card. A cold light flashed from the man's finger as the card left his hand. His knees
trembled. The man stepped closer, checking the card against the numbers chalked on the
board. Suppose he had made a mistake? The pomade on the man's hair made him feel
faint, and he backed away. But the man was checking the card over the microphone now,
and he had to stay. He stood tense, listening.

25   "Under the O, forty-four," the man chanted. "Under the I, seven. Under the G, three.
Under the B, ninety-six. Under the N, thirteen!"

His breath came easier as the man smiled at the audience.

"Yessir, ladies and gentlemen, he's one of the chosen people!"

The audience rippled with laughter and applause.

"Step right up to the front of the stage."

30   He moved slowly forward, wishing that the light was not so bright.

"To win tonight's jackpot of $36.90 the wheel must stop between the double zero,
understand?"

He nodded, knowing the ritual from the many days and nights he had watched the
winners march across the stage to press the button that controlled the spinning wheel and
receive the prizes. And now he followed the instructions as though he'd crossed the slippery stage a million prize-winning times.

The man was making some kind of a joke, and he nodded vacantly. So tense had he
become that he felt a sudden desire to cry and shook it away. He felt vaguely that his
whole life was determined by the bingo wheel; not only that which would happen now
that he was at last before it, but all that had gone before, since his birth, and his mother's
birth and the birth of his father. It had always been there, even though he had not been
aware of it, handing out the unlucky cards and numbers of his days. The feeling persisted,
and he started quickly away. I better get down from here before I make a fool of myself,
he thought.

"Here, boy," the man called. "You haven't started yet."

35   Someone laughed as he went hesitantly back.

"Are you all reet?"

He grinned at the man's jive talk, but no words would come, and he knew it was
not a convincing grin. For suddenly he knew that he stood on the slippery brink of some
terrible embarrassment.

"Where are you from, boy?" the man asked.

"Down South."

40   "He's from down South, ladies and gentlemen," the man said. "Where from? Speak
right into the mike."

"Rocky Mont," he said. "Rock' Mont, North Car'lina."

"So you decided to come down off the mountain to the U.S.," the man laughed. He felt that the man was making a fool of him, but then something cold was placed in his hand, and the lights were no longer behind him.

Standing before the wheel he felt alone, but that was somehow right, and he remembered his plan. He would give the wheel a short quick twirl. Just a touch of the button. He had watched it many times, and always it came close to double zero when it was short and quick. He steeled himself; the fear had left, and he felt a profound sense of promise, as though he were about to be repaid for all the things he'd suffered all his life. Trembling, he pressed the button. There was a whirl of lights, and in a second he realized with finality that though he wanted to, he could not stop. It was as though he held a high-powered line in his naked hand. His nerves tightened. As the wheel increased its speed it seemed to draw him more and more into his power, as though it held his fate; and with it came a deep need to submit, to whirl, to lose himself in its swirl of color. He could not stop it now, he knew. So let it be.

The button rested snugly in his palm where the man had placed it. And now he became aware of the man beside him, advising him through the microphone, while behind the shadowy audience hummed with noisy voices. He shifted his feet. There was still that feeling of helplessness within him, making part of him desire to turn back, even now that the jackpot was right in his hand. He squeezed the button until his fist ached. Then, like the sudden shriek of a subway whistle, a doubt tore through his head. Suppose he did not spin the wheel long enough? What could he do, and how could he tell? And then he knew, even as he wondered, that as long as he pressed the button, he could control the jackpot. He and only he could determine whether or not it was to be his. Not even the man with the microphone could do anything about it now. He felt drunk. Then, as though he had come down from a high hill into a valley of people, he heard the audience yelling.

45   "Come down from there, you jerk!"

"Let somebody else have a chance . . ."

"Ole Jack thinks he done found the end of the rainbow . . ."

The last voice was not unfriendly, and he turned and smiled dreamily into the yelling mouths. The he turned his back squarely on them.

"Don't take too long, boy," a voice said.

50   He nodded. They were yelling behind him. Those folks did not understand what had happened to him. They had been playing the bingo game day in and night out for years, trying to win rent money or hamburger change. But not one of those wise guys had discovered this wonderful thing. He watched the wheel whirling past the numbers and experienced a burst of exaltation: This is God! This is the really truly God! He said it aloud, "This is God!"

He said it with such absolute conviction that he feared he would fall fainting into the footlights. But the crowd yelled so loud that they could not hear. Those fools, he thought. I'm here trying to tell them the most wonderful secret in the world, and they're yelling like they gone crazy. A hand fell upon his shoulder.

"You'll have to make a choice now, boy. You've taken too long."

He brushed the hand violently away.

"Leave me alone, man. I know what I'm doing!"

55   The man looked surprised and held on to the microphone for support. And because he did not wish to hurt the man's feelings he smiled, realizing with a sudden pang that there was no way of explaining to the man just why he had to stand there pressing the button forever.

"Come here," he called tiredly.

The man approached, rolling the heavy microphone across the stage.

"Anybody can play this bingo game, right?" he said.

"Sure, but . . ."

60   He smiled, feeling inclined to be patient with this slick looking white man with his blue sport shirt and his sharp gabardine suit.

"That's what I thought," he said. "Anybody can win the jackpot as long as they get the lucky number, right?"

"That's the rule, but after all . . ."

"That's what I thought," he said. "And the big prize goes to the man who knows how to win it?"

The man nodded speechlessly.

65   "Well then, go on over there and watch me win like I want to. I ain't going to hurt nobody," he said, "and I'll show you how to win. I mean to show the whole world how it's got to be done."

And because he understood, he smiled again to let the man know that he held nothing against him for being white and impatient. Then he refused to see the man any longer and stood pressing the button, the voices of the crowd reaching him like sounds in distant streets. Let them yell. All the Negroes down there were just ashamed because he was black like them. He smiled inwardly, knowing how it was. Most of the time he was ashamed of what Negroes did himself. Well, let them be ashamed for something this time. Like him. He was like a long thin black wire that was being stretched and wound upon the bingo wheel; wound until he wanted to scream; wound, but this time himself controlling the winding and the sadness and the shame, and because he did, Laura would be all right. Suddenly the lights flickered. He staggered backwards. Had something gone wrong? All this noise. Didn't they know that although he controlled the wheel, it also controlled him, and unless he pressed the button forever and forever and ever it would stop, leaving him high and dry, dry and high on this hard high slippery hill and Laura dead? There was only one chance; he had to do whatever the wheel demanded. And gripping the button in despair, he discovered with surprise that it imparted a nervous energy. His spine tingled. He felt a certain power.

Now he faced the raging crowd with defiance, its screams penetrating his eardrums like trumpets shrieking from a juke-box. The vague faces glowing in the bingo lights gave him a sense of himself that he had never known before. He was running the show, by God! They had to react to him, for he was their luck. This is *me,* he thought. Let the bastards yell. Then someone was laughing inside him, and he realized that somehow he had forgotten his own name. It was a sad, lost feeling to lose your name, and a crazy thing to do. That name had been given him by the white man who had owned his grandfather a long lost time ago down South. But maybe those wise guys knew his name.

"Who am I?" he screamed.

"Hurry up and bingo, you jerk!"

70   They didn't know either, he thought sadly. They didn't even know their own names, they were all poor nameless bastards. Well, he didn't need that old name; he was reborn. For as long as he pressed the button he was The-man-who-pressed-the-button-who-held-the-prize-who-was-the-King-of-Bingo. That was the way it was, and he'd have to press the button even if nobody understood, even though Laura did not understand.

"Live!" he shouted.

The audience quieted like the dying of a huge fan.

"Live, Laura, baby. I got holt of it now, sugar. Live!"

He screamed it, tears streaming down his face. "I got nobody but YOU!"

75   The screams tore from his very guts. He felt as though the rush of blood to his head would burst out in baseball seams of small red droplets, like a head beaten by police clubs. Bending over he saw a trickle of blood splashing the toe of his shoe. With his free

hand he searched his head. It was his nose. God, suppose something has gone wrong? He felt that the whole audience had somehow entered him and was stamping their feet in his stomach and he was unable to throw them out. They wanted the prize, that was it. They wanted the secret for themselves. But they'd never get it; he would keep the bingo wheel whirling forever, and Laura would be safe in the wheel. But would she? It had to be, because if she were not safe the wheel would cease to turn; it could not go on. He had to get away, *vomit* all, and his mind formed an image of himself running with Laura in his arms down the tracks of the subway just ahead of an A train, running desperately *vomit* with people screaming for him to come out but knowing no way of leaving the tracks because to stop would bring the train crushing down upon him and to attempt to leave across the other tracks would mean to run into a hot third rail as high as his waist which threw blue sparks that blinded his eyes until he could hardly see.

He heard singing and the audience was clapping its hands.

Shoot the liquor to him, Jim, boy!
Clap-clap-clap
Well a-calla the cop
He's blowing his top!
Shoot the liquor to him, Jim, boy!

Bitter anger grew within him at the singing. They think I'm crazy. Well let 'em laugh. I'll do what I got to do.

He was standing in an attitude of intense listening when he saw that they were watching something on the stage behind him. He felt weak. But when he turned he saw no one. If only his thumb did not ache so. Now they were applauding. And for a moment he thought that the wheel had stopped. But that was impossible, his thumb still pressed the button. Then he saw them. Two men in uniform beckoned from the end of the stage. They were coming toward him, walking in step, slowly, like a tap-dance team returning for a third encore. But their shoulders shot forward, and he backed away, looking wildly about. There was nothing to fight them with. He had only the long black cord which led to a plug somewhere back stage, and he couldn't use that because it operated the bingo wheel. He backed slowly, fixing the men with his eyes as his lips stretched over his teeth in a tight, fixed grin; moved toward the end of the stage and realizing that he couldn't go much further, for suddenly the cord became taut and he couldn't afford to break the cord. But he had to do something. The audience was howling. Suddenly he stopped dead, seeing the men halt, their legs lifted as in an interrupted step of a slow-motion dance. There was nothing to do but run in the other direction and he dashed forward, slipping and sliding. The men fell back, surprised. He struck out violently going past.

"Grab him!"

80 He ran, but all too quickly the cord tightened, resistingly, and he turned and ran back again. This time he slipped them, and discovered by running in a circle before the wheel he could keep the cord from tightening. But this way he had to flail his arms to keep the men away. Why couldn't they leave a man alone? He ran, circling.

"Ring down the curtain," someone yelled. But they couldn't do that. If they did the wheel flashing from the projection room would be cut off. But they had him before he could tell them so, trying to pry open his fist, and he was wrestling and trying to bring his knees into the fight and holding on to the button, for it was his life. And now he was down, seeing a foot coming down, crushing his wrist cruelly, down, as he saw the wheel whirling serenely above.

"I can't give up," he screamed. Then quietly, in a confidential tone, "Boys, I really can't give it up."

It landed hard against his head. And in the blank moment they had it away from him, completely now. He fought them trying to pull him up from the stage as he watched the wheel spin slowly to a stop. Without surprise he saw it rest at double-zero.

"You see," he pointed bitterly.

85   "Sure, boy, sure, it's O. K.," one of the men said smiling.

And seeing the man bow his head to someone he could not see, he felt very, very happy; he would receive what all the winners received.

But as he warmed in the justice of the man's tight smile he did not see the man's slow wink, nor see the bow-legged man behind him step clear of the swiftly descending curtain and set himself for a blow. He only felt the dull pain exploding in his skull, and he knew even as it slipped out of him that his luck had run out on the stage.

Bernard Malamud (1914–   )
The Magic Barrel

Not long ago there lived in uptown New York, in a small, almost meager room, though crowded with books, Leo Finkle, a rabbinical student in the Yeshivah University. Finkle, after six years of study, was to be ordained in June and had been advised by an acquaintance that he might find it easier to win himself a congregation if he were married. Since he had no present prospects of marriage, after two tormented days of turning it over in his mind, he called in Pinye Salzman, a marriage broker whose two-line advertisement he had read in the *Forward.*

The matchmaker appeared one night out of the dark fourth-floor hallway of the graystone rooming house where Finkle lived, grasping a black, strapped portfolio that had been worn thin with use. Salzman, who had been long in the business, was of slight but dignified build, wearing an old hat, and an overcoat too short and tight for him. He smelled frankly of fish, which he loved to eat, and although he was missing a few teeth, his presence was not displeasing because of an amiable manner curiously contrasted with mournful eyes. His voice, his lips, his wisp of beard, his bony fingers were animated, but gave him a moment of repose and his mild blue eyes revealed a depth of sadness, a characteristic that put Leo a little at ease although the situation, for him, was inherently tense.

He at once informed Salzman why he had asked him to come, explaining that his home was in Cleveland, and that but for his parents, who had married comparatively late in life, he was alone in the world. He had for six years devoted himself almost entirely to his studies, as a result of which, understandably, he had found himself without time for a social life and the company of young women. Therefore he thought it the better part of trial and error—of embarrassing fumbling—to call in an experienced person to advise him on these matters. He remarked in passing that the function of the marriage broker was ancient and honorable, highly approved in the Jewish community, because it made practical the necessary without hindering joy. Moreover, his own parents had been brought together by a matchmaker. They had made, if not a financially profitable marriage—since neither had possessed any worldly goods to speak of—at least a successful one in the sense of their everlasting devotion to each other. Salzman listened in embarrassed surprise, sensing a sort of apology. Later, however, he experienced a glow of pride in his work, an emotion that had left him years ago, and he heartily approved of Finkle.

The two went to their business. Leo had led Salzman to the only clear place in the room, a table near a window that overlooked the lamplit city. He seated himself at the matchmaker's side but facing him, attempting by an act of will to suppress the unpleasant tickle in his throat. Salzman eagerly unstrapped his portfolio and removed a loose rubber band from a thin packet of much-handled cards. As he flipped through them, a gesture and sound that physically hurt Leo, the student pretended not to see and gazed steadfastly out the window. Although it was still February, winter was on its last legs, signs of which he had for the first time in years begun to notice. He now observed the round white moon, moving high in the sky through a cloud menagerie, and watched with half-open mouth as it penetrated a huge hen, and dropped out of her like an egg laying itself. Salzman, though pretending through eyeglasses he had just slipped on, to be engaged in scanning the writing on the cards, stole occasional glances at the young man's distinguished face, noting with pleasure the long, severe scholar's nose, brown eyes heavy with learning, sensitive yet ascetic lips, and a certain, almost hollow quality of the dark cheeks. He gazed around at shelves upon shelves of books and let out a soft, contented sigh.

5   When Leo's eyes fell upon the cards, he counted six spread out in Salzman's hand.
"So few?" he asked in disappointment.
"You wouldn't believe me how much cards I got in my office," Salzman replied. "The drawers are already filled to the top, so I keep them now in a barrel, but is every girl good for a new rabbi?"

Leo blushed at this, regretting all he had revealed of himself in a curriculum vitae he had sent to Salzman. He had thought it best to acquaint him with his strict standards and specifications, but in having done so, felt he had told the marriage broker more than was absolutely necessary.

He hesitantly inquired, "Do you keep photographs of your clients on file?"

10   "First comes family, amount of dowry, also what kind promises," Salzman replied, unbuttoning his tight coat and settling himself in the chair. "After comes pictures, rabbi."

"Call me Mr. Finkle. I'm not yet a rabbi."

Salzman said he would, but instead called him doctor, which he changed to rabbi when Leo was not listening too attentively.

Salzman adjusted his horn-rimmed spectacles, gently cleared his throat and read in an eager voice the contents of the top card:

"Sophie P. Twenty-four years. Widow one year. No children. Educated high school and two years college. Father promises eight thousand dollars. Has wonderful wholesale business. Also real estate. On the mother's side comes teachers, also one actor. Well known on Second Avenue."

15   Leo gazed up in surprise. "Did you say a widow?"

"A widow don't mean spoiled, rabbi. She lived with her husband maybe four months. He was a sick boy she made a mistake to marry him."

"Marrying a widow has never entered my mind."

"This is because you have no experience. A widow, especially if she is young and healthy like this girl, is a wonderful person to marry. She will be thankful to you the rest of her life. Believe me, if I was looking now for a bride, I would marry a widow."

Leo reflected, then shook his head.

20   Salzman hunched his shoulders in an almost imperceptible gesture of disappointment. He placed the card down on the wooden table and began to read another:
        "Lily H. High school teacher. Regular. Not a substitute. Has savings and new Dodge
car. Lived in Paris one year. Father is successful dentist thirty-five years. Interested in
professional man. Well Americanized family. Wonderful opportunity."
        "I knew her personally," said Salzman. "I wish you could see this girl. She is a doll.
Also very intelligent. All day you could talk to her about books and theyater and what not.
She also knows current events."
        "I don't believe you mentioned her age?"
        "Her age?" Salzman said, raising his brows. "Her age is thirty-two years."
25   Leo said after a while, "I'm afraid that seems a little too old."
        Salzman let out a laugh. "So how old are you, rabbi?"
        "Twenty-seven."
        "So what is the difference, tell me, between twenty-seven and thirty-two? My own
wife is seven years older than me. So what did I suffer?—Nothing. If Rothschild's daughter
wants to marry you, would you say on account of her age, no?"
        "Yes," Leo said dryly.
30   Salzman shook off the no in the yes. "Five years don't mean a thing. I give you my
word that when you will live with her for one week you will forget her age. What does it
mean five years—that she lived more and knows more than somebody who is younger?
On this girl, God bless her, years are not wasted. Each one that it comes makes better the
bargain."
        "What subject does she teach in high school?"
        "Languages. If you heard the way she speaks French, you will think it is music. I am
in the business twenty-five years, and I recommend her with my whole heart. Believe me,
I know what I'm talking, rabbi."
        "What's on the next card?" Leo said abruptly.
        Salzman reluctantly turned up the third card:
35   "Ruth K. Nineteen years. Honor student. Father offers thirteen thousand cash to the
right bridegroom. He is a medical doctor. Stomach specialist with marvelous practice.
Brother in law owns own garment business. Particular people."
        Salzman looked as if he had read his trump card.
        "Did you say nineteen?" Leo asked with interest.
        "On the dot."
        "Is she attractive?" He blushed. "Pretty?"
40   Salzman kissed his finger tips. "A little doll. On this I give you my word. Let me call
the father tonight and you will see what means pretty."
        But Leo was troubled. "You're sure she's that young?"
        "This I am positive. The father will show you the birth certificate."
        "Are you positive there isn't something wrong with her?" Leo insisted.
        "Who says there is wrong?"
45   "I don't understand why an American girl her age should go to a marriage broker."
        A smile spread over Salzman's face.
        "So for the same reason you went, she comes."
        Leo flushed. "I am pressed for time."
        Salzman, realizing he had been tactless, quickly explained. "The father came, not
her. He wants she should have the best, so he looks around himself. When we will locate
the right boy he will introduce him and encourage. This makes a better marriage than if a
young girl without experience takes for herself. I don't have to tell you this."

50   "But don't you think this young girl believes in love?" Leo spoke uneasily.
        Salzman was about to guffaw but caught himself and said soberly, "Love comes with the right person, not before."
        Leo parted dry lips but did not speak. Noticing that Salzman had snatched a glance at the next card, he cleverly asked, "How is her health?"
        "Perfect," Salzman said, breathing with difficulty. "Of course, she is a little lame on her right foot from an auto accident that it happened to her when she was twelve years, but nobody notices on account she is so brilliant and also beautiful."
        Leo got up heavily and went to the window. He felt curiously bitter and upbraided himself for having called in the marriage broker. Finally, he shook his head.
55   "Why not?" Salzman persisted, the pitch of his voice rising.
        "Because I detest stomach specialists."
        "So what do you care what is his business? After you marry her do you need him? Who says he must come every Friday night in your house?"
        Ashamed of the way the talk was going, Leo dismissed Salzman, who went home with heavy, melancholy eyes.
        Though he had felt only relief at the marriage broker's departure, Leo was in low spirits the next day. He explained it as arising from Salzman's failure to produce a suitable bride for him. He did not care for his type of clientele. But when Leo found himself hesitating whether to seek out another matchmaker, one more polished than Pinye, he wondered if it could be—his protestations to the contrary, and although he honored his father and mother—that he did not, in essence, care for the matchmaking institution? This thought he quickly put out of mind yet found himself still upset. All day he ran around in the woods—missed an important appointment, forgot to give out his laundry, walked out of a Broadway cafeteria without paying and had to run back with the ticket in his hand; had even not recognized his landlady in the street when she passed with a friend and courteously called out, "A good evening to you, Doctor Finkle." By nightfall, however, he had regained sufficient calm to sink his nose into a book and there found peace from his thoughts.
60   Almost at once there came a knock on the door. Before Leo could say enter, Salzman, commercial cupid, was standing in the room. His face was gray and meager, his expression hungry, and he looked as if he would expire on his feet. Yet the marriage broker managed, by some trick of the muscles, to display a broad smile.
        "So good evening. I am invited?"
        Leo nodded, disturbed to see him again, yet unwilling to ask the man to leave.
        Beaming still, Salzman laid his portfolio on the table. "Rabbi, I got for you tonight good news."
        "I've asked you not to call me rabbi. I'm still a student."
65   "Your worries are finished. I have for you a first-class bride."
        "Leave me in peace concerning this subject." Leo pretended lack of interest.
        "The world will dance at your wedding."
        "Please, Mr. Salzman, no more."
        "But first must come back my strength," Salzman said weakly. He fumbled with the portfolio straps and took out of the leather case an oily paper bag, from which he extracted a hard, seeded roll and a small, smoked white fish. With a quick motion of his hand he stripped the fish out of its skin and began ravenously to chew. "All day in a rush," he muttered.
70   Leo watched him eat.
        "A sliced tomato you have maybe?" Salzman hesitantly inquired.
        "No."

The marriage broker shut his eyes and ate. When he had finished he carefully cleaned up the crumbs and rolled up the remains of the fish, in the paper bag. His spectacled eyes roamed the room until he discovered, amid some piles of books, a one-burner gas stove. Lifting his hat he humbly asked, "A glass tea you got, rabbi?"

Conscience-stricken, Leo rose and brewed the tea. He served it with a chunk of lemon and two cubes of lump sugar, delighting Salzman.

75   After he had drunk his tea, Salzman's strength and good spirits were restored.

"So tell me, rabbi," he said amiably, "you considered some more the three clients I mentioned yesterday?"

"There was no need to consider."

"Why not?"

"None of them suits me."

80   "What then suits you?"

Leo let it pass because he could give only a confused answer.

Without waiting for a reply, Salzman asked, "You remember this girl I talked to you—the high school teacher?"

"Age thirty-two."

But, surprisingly, Salzman's face lit in a smile. "Age twenty-nine."

85   Leo shot him a look. "Reduced from thirty-two?"

"A mistake," Salzman avowed. "I talked today with the dentist. He took me to his safety deposit box and showed me the birth certificate. She was twenty-nine years last August. They made her a party in the mountains where she went for her vacation. When her father spoke to me the first time I forgot to write the age and told you thirty-two, but now I remember this was a different client, a widow."

"The same one you told me about? I thought she was twenty-four?"

"A different. Am I responsible that the world is filled with widows?"

"No, but I'm not interested in them, nor for that matter, in school teachers."

90   Salzman pulled his clasped hands to his breast. Looking at the ceiling he devoutly exclaimed, "Yiddishe kinder, what can I say to somebody that he is not interested in high school teachers? So what then you are interested?"

Leo flushed but controlled himself.

"In what else will you be interested," Salzman went on, "if you not interested in this fine girl that she speaks four languages and has personally in the bank ten thousand dollars? Also her father guarantees further twelve thousand. Also she has a new car, wonderful clothes, talks on all subjects, and she will give you a first-class home and children. How near do we come in life to paradise?"

"If she's so wonderful, why wasn't she married ten years ago?"

"Why?" said Salzman with a heavy laugh. "—Why? Because she is *partikiler.* That is why. She wants the *best.*"

95   Leo was silent, amused at how he had entangled himself. But Salzman had aroused his interest in Lily H., and he began seriously to consider calling on her. When the marriage broker observed how intently Leo's mind was at work on the facts he had supplied, he felt certain they would soon come to an agreement.

Late Saturday afternoon, conscious of Salzman, Leo Finkle walked with Lily Hirschorn along Riverside Drive. He walked briskly and erectly, wearing with distinction the black fedora he had that morning taken with trepidation out of the dusty hat box on his closet shelf, and the heavy black Saturday coat he had thoroughly whisked clean. Leo also owned a walking stick, a present from a distant relative, but quickly put temptation aside and did not use it. Lily, petite and not unpretty, had on something signifying the approach of spring. She was au courant, animatedly, with all sorts of subjects, and he weighed her words and found her surprisingly sound—score another for Salzman, whom he uneasily sensed to be somewhere around, hiding perhaps high in a tree along the street, flashing the lady signals with a pocket mirror; or perhaps a cloven-hoofed Pan, piping nuptial ditties as he danced his invisible way before them, strewing wild buds on the wall and purple grapes in their path, symbolizing fruit of a union, though there was of course still none.

Lily startled Leo by remarking, "I was thinking of Mr. Salzman, a curious figure, wouldn't you say?"

Not certain what to answer, he nodded.

She bravely went on, blushing. "I for one am grateful for his introducing us. Aren't you?"

100   He courteously replied, "I am."

"I mean," she said with a little laugh—and it was all in good taste, or at least gave the effect of being not in bad—"do you mind that we came together so?"

He was not displeased with her honesty, recognizing that she meant to set the relationship aright, and understanding that it took a certain amount of experience in life, and courage, to want to do it quite that way. One had to have some sort of past to make that kind of beginning.

He said that he did not mind. Salzman's function was traditional and honorable— valuable for what it might achieve, which, he pointed out, was frequently nothing.

Lily agreed with a sigh. They walked on for a while and she said after a long silence, again with a nervous laugh, "Would you mind if I asked you something a little bit personal? Frankly, I find the subject fascinating." Although Leo shrugged, she went on half embarrassedly, "How was it that you came to your calling? I mean was it a sudden passionate inspiration?"

105   Leo, after a time, slowly replied, "I was always interested in the Law."

"You saw revealed in it the presence of the Highest?"

He nodded and changed the subject. "I understand that you spent a little time in Paris, Miss Hirschorn?"

"Oh, did Mr. Salzman tell you, Rabbi Finkle?" Leo winced but she went on, "It was ages ago and almost forgotten. I remember I had to return for my sister's wedding."

And Lily would not be put off. "When," she asked in a trembly voice, "did you become enamored of God?"

110   He stared at her. Then it came to him that she was talking not about Leo Finkle, but of a total stranger, some mystical figure, perhaps even passionate prophet that Salzman had dreamed up for her—no relation to the living or dead. Leo trembled with rage and weakness. The trickster had obviously sold her a bill of goods, just as he had him, who'd expected to become acquainted with a young lady of twenty-nine, only to behold, the moment he laid eyes upon her strained and anxious face, a woman past thirty-five and aging rapidly. Only his self control had kept him this long in her presence.

"I am not," he said gravely, "a talented religious person," and in seeking words to go on, found himself possessed by shame and fear. "I think," he said in a strained manner, "that I came to God not because I loved Him, but because I did not."

This confession he spoke harshly because its unexpectedness shook him.

Lily wilted. Leo saw a profusion of loaves of bread go flying like ducks high over his head, not unlike the winged loaves by which he had counted himself to sleep last night. Mercifully, then, it snowed, which he would not put past Salzman's machinations.

He was infuriated with the marriage broker and swore he would throw him out of the room the minute he reappeared. But Salzman did not come that night, and when Leo's anger had subsided, an unaccountable despair grew in its place. At first he thought this was caused by his disappointment in Lily, but before long it became evident that he had involved himself with Salzman without a true knowledge of his own intent. He gradually realized—with an emptiness that seized him with six hands—that he had called in the broker to find him a bride because he was incapable of doing it himself. This terrifying insight he had derived as a result of his meeting and conversation with Lily Hirschorn. Her probing questions had somehow irritated him into revealing—to himself more than her—the true nature of his relationship to God, and from that it had come upon him, with shocking force, that apart from his parents, he had never loved anyone. Or perhaps it went the other way, that he did not love God so well as he might, because he had not loved man. It seemed to Leo that his whole life stood starkly revealed and he saw himself for the first time as he truly was—unloved and loveless. This bitter but somehow not fully unexpected revelation brought him to a point of panic, controlled only by extraordinary effort. He covered his face with his hands and cried.

115   The week that followed was the worst of his life. He did not eat and lost weight. His beard darkened and grew ragged. He stopped attending seminars and almost never opened a book. He seriously considered leaving the Yeshivah, although he was deeply troubled at the thought of the loss of all his years of study—saw them like pages torn from a book, strewn over the city—and at the devastating effect of this decision upon his parents. But he had lived without knowledge of himself, and never in the Five Books[1] and all the Commentaries—mea culpa[2]—had the truth been revealed to him. He did not know where to turn, and in all this desolating loneliness there was no *to whom,* although he often thought of Lily but not once could bring himself to go downstairs and make the call. He became touchy and irritable, especially with his landlady, who asked him all manner of personal questions; on the other hand, sensing his own disagreeableness, he waylaid her on the stairs and apologized abjectly, until mortified, she ran from him. Out of this, however, he drew the consolation that he was a Jew and that a Jew suffered. But gradually, as the long and terrible week drew to a close, he regained his composure and some idea of purpose in life: to go on as planned. Although he was imperfect, the ideal was not. As for his quest for a bride, the thought of continuing afflicted him with anxiety and heartburn, yet perhaps with this new knowledge of himself he would be more successful than in the past. Perhaps love would now come to him and a bride to that love. And for this sanctified seeking who needed a Salzman?

The marriage broker, a skeleton with haunted eyes, returned that very night. He looked, withal, the picture of frustrated expectancy—as if he had steadfastly waited the week at Miss Lily Hirschorn's side for a telephone call that never came.

Casually coughing, Salzman came immediately to the point: "So how do you like her?"

Leo's anger rose and he could not refrain from chiding the matchmaker: "Why did you lie to me, Salzman?"

Salzman's pale face went dead white, the world had snowed on him.

120   "Did you not state that she was twenty-nine?" Leo insisted.

"I give you my word—"

"She was thirty-five, if a day. *At least* thirty-five."

"Of course don't be too sure. Her father told me—"

"Never mind. The worst of it was that you lied to her."

125   "How did I lie to her, tell me?"

"You told her things about me that weren't true. You made me out to be more,

---

[1]The *Megilloth:* Song of Solomon, Ruth, Lamentations, Ecclesiastes, and Esther.
[2]Through my fault.

consequently less than I am. She had in mind a totally different person, a sort of semi-mystical Wonder Rabbi."

"All I said, you was a religious man."

"I can imagine."

Salzman sighed. "This is my weakness that I have," he confessed. "My wife says to me I shouldn't be a salesman, but when I have two fine people that they would be wonderful to be married, I am so happy that I talk too much." He smiled wanly. "This is why Salzman is a poor man."

130   Leo's anger left him. "Well, Salzman, I'm afraid that's all."

The marriage broker fastened hungry eyes on him.

"You don't want any more a bride?"

"I do," said Leo," "but I have decided to seek her in a different way. I am no longer interested in an arranged marriage. To be frank, I now admit the necessity of premarital love. That is, I want to be in love with the one I marry."

"Love?" said Salzman, astounded. After a moment he remarked, "For us, our love is our life, not for the ladies. In the ghetto they—"

135   "I know, I know," said Leo. "I've thought of it often. Love, I have said to myself, should be a by-product of living and worship rather than its own end. Yet for myself I find it necessary to establish the level of my need and fulfill it."

Salzman shrugged but answered, "Listen, rabbi, if you want love, this I can find for you also. I have such beautiful clients that you will love them the minute your eyes will see them."

Leo smiled unhappily. "I'm afraid you don't understand."

But Salzman hastily unstrapped his portfolio and withdrew a manila packet from it.

"Pictures," he said, quickly laying the envelope on the table.

140   Leo called after him to take the pictures away, but as if on the wings of the wind, Salzman had disappeared.

March came. Leo had returned to his regular routine. Although he felt not quite himself yet—lacked energy—he was making plans for a more active social life. Of course it would cost something, but he was an expert in cutting corners; and when there were no corners left he would make circles rounder. All the while Salzman's pictures had lain on the table, gathering dust. Occasionally as Leo sat studying, or enjoying a cup of tea, his eyes fell on the manila envelope, but he never opened it.

The days went by and no social life to speak of developed with a member of the opposite sex—it was difficult, given the circumstances of his situation. One morning Leo toiled up the stairs to his room and stared out the window at the city. Although the day was bright his view of it was dark. For some time he watched the people in the street below hurrying along and then turned with a heavy heart to his little room. On the table was the packet. With a sudden relentless gesture he tore it open. For a half-hour he stood by the table in a state of excitement, examining the photographs of the ladies Salzman had included. Finally, with a deep sigh he put them down. There were six, of varying degrees of attractiveness, but look at them long enough and they all became Lily Hirschorn: all past their prime, all starved behind bright smiles, not a true personality in the lot. Life, despite their frantic yoohooings, had passed them by; they were pictures in a brief case that stank of fish. After a while, however, as Leo attempted to return the photographs into the envelope, he found in it another, a snapshot of the type taken by a machine for a quarter. He gazed at it a moment and let out a cry.

Her face deeply moved him. Why, he could at first not say. It gave him the impression of youth—spring flowers, yet age—a sense of having been used to the bone, wasted; this came from the eyes, which were hauntingly familiar, yet absolutely strange. He had a vivid impression that he had met her before, but try as he might he could not place her although he could almost recall her name, as if he had read it in her own handwriting. No, this couldn't be; he would have remembered her. It was not, he affirmed, that she had an extraordinary beauty—no, though her face was attractive enough; it was that *something* about her moved him. Feature for feature, even some of the ladies of the photographs could do better; but she leaped forth to his heart—had *lived,* or wanted to—more than just wanted, perhaps regretted how she had lived—had somehow deeply suffered: it could be seen in the depths of those reluctant eyes, and from the way the light enclosed and shone from her, and within her, opening realms of possibility: this was her own. Her he desired. His head ached and eyes narrowed with the intensity of his gazing, then as if an obscure fog had blown up in the mind, he experienced fear of her and was aware that he had received an impression, somehow, of evil. He shuddered, saying softly, it is thus with us all. Leo brewed some tea in a small pot and sat sipping it without sugar, to calm himself. But before he had finished drinking, again with excitement he examined the face and found it good: good for Leo Finkle. Only such a one could understand him and help him seek whatever he was seeking. She might, perhaps, love him. How she had happened to be among the discards in Salzman's barrel he could never guess, but he knew he must urgently go find her.

Leo rushed downstairs, grabbed up the Bronx telephone book and searched for Salzman's home address. He was not listed, nor was his office. Neither was he in the Manhattan book. But Leo remembered having written down the address on a slip of paper after he had read Salzman's advertisement in the "personals" column of the *Forward.* He ran up to his room and tore through his papers, without luck. It was exasperating. Just when he needed the matchmaker he was nowhere to be found. Fortunately Leo remembered to look in his wallet. There on a card he found his name written and a Bronx address. No phone number was listed, the reason—Leo now recalled—he had originally communicated with Salzman by letter. He got on his coat, put a hat on over his skull cap and hurried to the subway station. All the way to the far end of the Bronx he sat on the edge of his seat. He was more than once tempted to take out the picture and see if the girl's face was as he remembered it, but he refrained, allowing the snapshot to remain in his inside coat pocket, content to have her so close. When the train pulled into the station he was waiting at the door and bolted out. He quickly located the street Salzman had advertised.

145   The building he sought was less than a block from the subway, but it was not an office building, nor even a loft, nor a store in which one could rent office space. It was a very old tenement house. Leo found Salzman's name in pencil on a soiled tag under the bell and climbed three dark flights to his apartment. When he knocked, the door was opened by a thin, asthmatic, gray-haired woman, in felt slippers.

"Yes?" she said, expecting nothing. She listened without listening. He could have sworn he had seen her, too, before but knew it was an illusion.

"Salzman—does he live here? Pinye Salzman," he said, "the matchmaker?"

She stared at him a long minute. "Of course."

He felt embarrassed. "Is he in?"

150   "No." Her mouth, though left open, offered nothing more.

"The matter is urgent. Can you tell me where his office is?"

"In the air." She pointed upward.

"You mean he has no office?" Leo asked.

"In his socks."

155   He peered into the apartment. It was sunless and dingy, one large room divided by a half-open curtain, beyond which he could see a sagging metal bed. The near side of the

room was crowded with rickety chairs, old bureaus, a three-legged table, racks of cooking
utensils, and all the apparatus of a kitchen. But there was no sign of Salzman or his magic
barrel, probably also a figment of the imagination. An odor of frying fish made Leo weak
to the knees.

"Where is he?" he insisted. "I've got to see your husband."

At length she answered, "So who knows where he is? Every time he thinks a new
thought he runs to a different place. Go home, he will find you."

"Tell him Leo Finkle."

She gave no sign she had heard.

160   He walked downstairs, depressed.

But Salzman, breathless, stood waiting at his door.

Leo was astounded and overjoyed. "How did you get here before me?"

"I rushed."

"Come inside."

165   They entered. Leo fixed tea, and a sardine sandwich for Salzman. As they were drinking he reached behind him for the packet of pictures and handed them to the marriage
broker.

Salzman put down his glass and said expectantly, "You found somebody you like?"

"Not among these."

The marriage broker turned away.

"Here is the one I want." Leo held forth the snapshot.

170   Salzman slipped on his glasses and took the picture into his trembling hand. He
turned ghastly and let out a groan.

"What's the matter?" cried Leo.

"Excuse me. Was an accident this picture. She isn't for you."

Salzman frantically shoved the manila packet into his portfolio. He thrust the snapshot into his pocket and fled down the stairs.

Leo, after momentary paralysis, gave chase and cornered the marriage broker in the
vestibule. The landlady made hysterical outcries but neither of them listened.

175   "Give me back the picture, Salzman."

"No." The pain in his eyes was terrible.

"Tell me who she is then."

"This I can't tell you. Excuse me."

He made to depart, but Leo, forgetting himself, seized the matchmaker by his tight
coat and shook him frenziedly.

180   "Please," sighed Salzman. *"Please."*

Leo ashamedly let him go. "Tell me who she is," he begged. "It's very important for
me to know."

"She is not for you. She is a wild one—wild, without shame. This is not a bride for
a rabbi."

"What do you mean wild?"

"Like an animal. Like a dog. For her to be poor was a sin. This is why to me she is
dead now."

185   "In God's name, what do you mean?"

"Her I can't introduce to you," Salzman cried.

"Why are you so excited?"

"Why, he asks," Salzman said, bursting into tears. "This is my baby, my Stella, she
should burn in hell."

Leo hurried up to bed and hid under the covers. Under the covers he thought his
life was through. Although he soon fell asleep he could not sleep her out of his mind. He

woke, beating his breast. Though he prayed to be rid of her, his prayers went unanswered. Through days of torment he endlessly struggled not to love her; fearing success, he escaped it. He then concluded to convert her to goodness, himself to God. The idea alternately nauseated and exalted him.

190   He perhaps did not know that he had come to a final decision until he encountered Salzman in a Broadway cafeteria. He was sitting alone at a rear table, sucking the bony remains of a fish. The marriage broker appeared haggard, and transparent to the point of vanishing.

Salzman looked up at first without recognizing him. Leo had grown a pointed beard and his eyes were weighted with wisdom.

"Salzman," he said, "love has at last come to my heart."

"Who can love from a picture?" mocked the marriage broker.

"It is not impossible."

195   "If you can love her, then you can love anybody. Let me show you some new clients that they just sent me their photographs. One is a little doll."

"Just her I want," Leo murmured.

"Don't be a fool, doctor. Don't bother with her."

"Put me in touch with her, Salzman," Leo said humbly. "Perhaps I can be of service."

Salzman had stopped eating and Leo understood with emotion that it was now arranged.

200   Leaving the cafeteria, he was, however, afflicted by a tormenting suspicion that Salzman had planned it all to happen this way.

Leo was informed by letter that she would meet him on a certain corner, and she was there one spring night, waiting under a street lamp. He appeared, carrying a small bouquet of violets and rosebuds. Stella stood by the lamp post, smoking. She wore white with red shoes, which fitted his expectations, although in a troubled moment he had imagined the dress red, and only the shoes white. She waited uneasily and shyly. From afar he saw that her eyes—clearly her father's—were filled with desperate innocence. He pictured, in her, his own redemption. Violins and lit candles revolved in the sky. Leo ran forward with flowers outthrust.

Around the corner, Salzman, leaning against a wall, chanted prayers for the dead.

Irwin Shaw   (1913–1984)
The Eighty-Yard Run

The pass was high and wide and he jumped for it, feeling it slap flatly against his hands, as he shook his hips to throw off the halfback who was diving at him. The center floated by, his hands desperately brushing Darling's knee as Darling picked his feet up high and delicately ran over a blocker and an opposing lineman in a jumble on the ground near the scrimmage line. He had ten yards in the clear and picked up speed, breathing easily, feeling his thigh pads rising and falling against his legs, listening to the sound of cleats behind him, pulling away from them, watching the other backs heading him off toward the sideline, the whole picture, the men closing in on him, the blockers fighting for position, the ground he had to cross, all suddenly clear in his head, for the first time in his life not a meaningless confusion of men, sounds, speed. He smiled a little to himself as he ran, holding the ball lightly in front of him with his two hands, his knees pumping high, his hips twisting in the almost girlish run of a back in a broken field. The first halfback came at him and he fed him his leg, then swung at the last moment, took the shock of the man's shoulder without breaking stride, ran right through him, his cleats biting securely into the turf. There was only the safety man now, coming warily at him, his arms crooked, hands spread. Darling tucked the ball in, spurted at him, driving hard, hurling himself along, his legs pounding, knees high, all two hundred pounds bunched into controlled attack. He was sure he was going to get past the safety man. Without thought, his arms and legs working beautifully together, he headed right for the safety man, stiff-armed him, feeling blood spurt instantaneously from the man's nose onto his hand, seeing his face go awry, head turned, mouth pulled to one side. He pivoted away, keeping the arm locked, dropping the safety man as he ran easily toward the goal line, with the drumming of cleats diminishing behind him.

How long ago? It was autumn then, and the ground was getting hard because the nights were cold and leaves from the maples around the stadium blew across the practice fields in gusts of wind, and the girls were beginning to put polo coats over their sweaters when they came to watch practice in the afternoons. . . . Fifteen years. Darling walked slowly over the same ground in the spring twilight, in his neat shoes, a man of thirty-five dressed in a double-breasted suit, ten pounds heavier in the fifteen years, but not fat, with the years between 1925 and 1940 showing in his face.

The coach was smiling quietly to himself and the assistant coaches were looking at each other with pleasure the way they always did when one of the second stringers suddenly did something fine, bringing credit to them, making their $2,000 a year a tiny bit more secure.

Darling trotted back, smiling, breathing deeply but easily, feeling wonderful, not tired, though this was the tail end of practice and he'd run eighty yards. The sweat poured off his face and soaked his jersey and he liked the feeling, the warm moistness lubricating his skin like oil. Off in a corner of the field some players were punting and the smack of leather against the ball came pleasantly through the afternoon air. The freshmen were running signals on the next field and the quarterback's sharp voice, the pound of the eleven pairs of cleats, the "Dig, now *dig!*" of the coaches, the laughter of the players all somehow made him feel happy as he trotted back to midfield, listening to the applause and shouts of the students along the sidelines, knowing that after that run the coach would have to start him Saturday against Illinois.

5   Fifteen years, Darling thought, remembering the shower after the workout, the hot water steaming off his skin and the deep soapsuds and all the young voices singing with the water streaming down and towels going and managers running in and out and the sharp sweet smell of oil of wintergreen and everybody clapping him on the back as he dressed and Packard, the captain, who took being captain very seriously, coming over to him and shaking his hand and saying, "Darling, you're going to go places in the next two years."

The assistant manager fussed over him, wiping a cut on his leg with alcohol and iodine, the little sting making him realize suddenly how fresh and whole and solid his body felt. The manager slapped a piece of adhesive tape over the cut, and Darling noticed the sharp clean white of the tape against the ruddiness of the skin, fresh from the shower.

He dressed slowly, the softness of his shirt and the soft warmth of his wool socks and his flannel trousers a reward against his skin after the harsh pressure of the shoulder harness and thigh and hip pads. He drank three glasses of cold water, the liquid reaching down coldly inside of him, soothing the harsh dry places in his throat and belly left by the sweat and running and shouting of practice.

Fifteen years.

The sun had gone down and the sky was green behind the stadium and he laughed quietly to himself as he looked at the stadium, rearing above the trees, and knew that on Saturday when the 70,000 voices roared as the team came running out onto the field, part of that enormous salute would be for him. He walked slowly, listening to the gravel crunch satisfactorily under his shoes in the still twilight, feeling his clothes swing lightly against his skin, breathing the thin evening air, feeling the wind move softly in his damp hair, wonderfully cool behind his ears and at the nape of his neck.

10   Louise was waiting for him at the road, in her car. The top was down and he noticed all over again, as he always did when he saw her, how pretty she was, the rough blonde hair and the large, inquiring eyes and the bright mouth, smiling now.

She threw the door open. "Were you good today?" she asked.

"Pretty good," he said. He climbed in, sank luxuriously into the soft leather, stretched his legs far out. He smiled, thinking of the eighty yards. "Pretty damn good."

She looked at him seriously for a moment, then scrambled around, like a little girl, kneeling on the seat next to him, grabbed him, her hands along his ears, and kissed him as he sprawled, head back, on the seat cushion. She let go of him, but kept her head close to his, over his. Darling reached up slowly and rubbed the back of his hand against her cheek, lit softly by a street lamp a hundred feet away. They looked at each other, smiling.

Louise drove down to the lake and they sat there silently, watching the moon rise behind the hills on the other side. Finally he reached over, pulled her gently to him, kissed her. Her lips grew soft, her body sank into his, tears formed slowly in her eyes. He knew, for the first time, that he could do whatever he wanted with her.

15   "Tonight," he said. "I'll call for you at seven-thirty. Can you get out?"

She looked at him. She was smiling, but the tears were still full in her eyes. "All right," she said. "I'll get out. How about you? Won't the coach raise hell?"

Darling grinned. "I got the coach in the palm of my hand," he said. "Can you wait till seven-thirty?"

She grinned back at him. "No," she said.

They kissed and she started the car and they went back to town for dinner. He sang on the way home.

20   Christian Darling, thirty-five years old, sat on the frail spring grass, greener now than it ever would be again on the practice field, looked thoughtfully up at the stadium, a deserted ruin in the twilight. He had started on the first team that Saturday and every Saturday after that for the next two years, but it had never been as satisfactory as it should have been. He never had broken away, the longest run he'd ever made was thirty-five yards, and that in a game that was already won, and then that kid had come up from the third team, Diederich, a blank-faced German kid from Wisconsin, who ran like a bull, ripping lines to pieces Saturday after Saturday, plowing through, never getting hurt, never changing his expression, scoring more points, gaining more ground than all the rest of the team put together, making everybody's All-American, carrying the ball three times out of four, keeping everybody else out of the headlines. Darling was a good blocker and he spent his Saturday afternoons working on the big Swedes and Polacks who played tackle and end for Michigan, Illinois, Purdue, hurling into huge pile-ups, bobbing his head wildly to elude the great raw hands swinging like meat-cleavers at him as he went charging in to open up holes for Diederich coming through like a locomotive behind him. Still, it wasn't

so bad. Everybody liked him and he did his job and he was pointed out on the campus and boys always felt important when they introduced their girls to him at their proms, and Louise loved him and watched him faithfully in the games, even in the mud, when your own mother wouldn't know you, and drove him around in her car keeping the top down because she was proud of him and wanted to show everybody that she was Christian Darling's girl. She bought him crazy presents because her father was rich, watches, pipes, humidors, an icebox for beer for his room, curtains, wallets, a fifty-dollar dictionary.

"You'll spend every cent your old man owns," Darling protested once when she showed up at his rooms with seven different packages in her arms and tossed them onto the couch.

"Kiss me," Louise said, "and shut up."

"Do you want to break your poor old man?"

"I don't mind. I want to buy you presents."

25   "Why?"

"It makes me feel good. Kiss me. I don't know why. Did you know that you're an important figure?"

"Yes," Darling said gravely.

"When I was waiting for you at the library yesterday two girls saw you coming and one of them said to the other, 'That's Christian Darling. He's an important figure.' "

"You're a liar."

30   "I'm in love with an important figure."

"Still, why the hell did you have to give me a forty-pound dictionary?"

"I wanted to make sure," Louise said, "that you had a token of my esteem. I want to smother you in tokens of my esteem."

Fifteen years ago.

They'd married when they got out of college. There'd been other women for him, but all casual and secret, more for curiosity's sake, and vanity, women who'd thrown themselves at him and flattered him, a pretty mother at a summer camp for boys, an old girl from his home town who'd suddenly blossomed into a coquette, a friend of Louise's who had dogged him grimly for six months and had taken advantage of the two weeks that Louise went home when her mother died. Perhaps Louise had known, but she'd kept quiet, loving him completely, filling his rooms with presents, religiously watching him battling with the big Swedes and Polacks on the line of scrimmage on Saturday afternoons, making plans for marrying him and living with him in New York and going with him there to the night clubs, the theaters, the good restaurants, being proud of him in advance, tall, white-teethed, smiling, large, yet moving lightly, with an athlete's grace, dressed in evening clothes, approvingly eyed by magnificently dressed and famous women in theater lobbies, with Louise adoringly at his side.

35   Her father, who manufactured inks, set up a New York office for Darling to manage and presented him with three hundred accounts, and they lived on Beekman Place with a view of the river with fifteen thousand dollars a year between them, because everybody was buying everything in those days, including ink. They saw all the shows and went to all the speakeasies and spent their fifteen thousand dollars a year and in the afternoons Louise went to the art galleries and the matinees of the more serious plays that Darling didn't like to sit through and Darling slept with a girl who danced in the chorus of *Rosalie* and with the wife of a man who owned three copper mines. Darling played squash three times a week and remained as solid as a stone barn and Louise never took her eyes off him when they were in the same room together, watching him with a secret, miser's smile, with a trick of coming over to him in the middle of a crowded room and saying gravely, in a low voice, "You're the handsomest man I've ever seen in my whole life. Want a drink?"

Nineteen twenty-nine came to Darling and to his wife and father-in-law, the maker of inks, just as it came to everyone else. The father-in-law waited until 1933 and then blew his brains out and when Darling went to Chicago to see what the books of the firm looked like he found out all that was left were debts and three or four gallons of unbought ink.

"Please, Christian," Louise said, sitting in their neat Beekman Place apartment, with a view of the river and prints of paintings by Dufy and Braque and Picasso on the wall, "please, why do you want to start drinking at two o'clock in the afternoon?"

"I have nothing else to do," Darling said, putting down his glass, emptied of its fourth drink. "Please pass the whisky."

Louise filled his glass. "Come take a walk with me," she said. "We'll walk along the river."

40   "I don't want to walk along the river," Darling said, squinting intensely at the prints of paintings by Dufy, Braque and Picasso.

"We'll walk along Fifth Avenue."

"I don't want to walk along Fifth Avenue."

"Maybe," Louise said gently, "you'd like to come with me to some art galleries. There's an exhibition by a man named Klee. . . ."

"I don't want to go to any art galleries. I want to sit here and drink Scotch whisky," Darling said. "Who the hell hung those goddam pictures up on the wall?"

45   "I did," Louise said.

"I hate them."

"I'll take them down," Louise said.

"Leave them there. It gives me something to do in the afternoon. I can hate them." Darling took a long swallow. "Is that the way people paint these days?"

"Yes, Christian. Please don't drink any more."

50   "Do you like painting like that?"

"Yes, dear."

"Really?"

"Really."

Darling looked carefully at the prints once more. "Little Louise Tucker. The middle-western beauty. I like pictures with horses in them. Why should you like pictures like that?"

55   "I just happen to have gone to a lot of galleries in the last few years . . ."

"Is that what you do in the afternoon?"

"That's what I do in the afternoon," Louise said.

"I drink in the afternoon."

Louise kissed him lightly on the top of his head as he sat there squinting at the pictures on the wall, the glass of whisky held firmly in his hand. She put on her coat and went out without saying another word. When she came back in the early evening, she had a job on a woman's fashion magazine.

60   They moved downtown and Louise went out to work every morning and Darling sat home and drank and Louise paid the bills as they came up. She made believe she was going to quit work as soon as Darling found a job, even though she was taking over more responsibility day by day at the magazine, interviewing authors, picking painters for the illustrations and covers, getting actresses to pose for pictures, going out for drinks with the right people, making a thousand new friends whom she loyally introduced to Darling.

"I don't like your hat," Darling said, once, when she came in in the evening and kissed him, her breath rich with Martinis.

"What's the matter with my hat, Baby?" she asked, running her fingers through his hair. "Everybody says it's very smart."

"It's too damned smart," he said. "It's not for you. It's for a rich, sophisticated woman of thirty-five with admirers."

Louise laughed. "I'm practicing to be a rich, sophisticated woman of thirty-five with admirers," she said. He stared soberly at her. "Now, don't look so grim, Baby. It's still the same simple little wife under the hat." She took the hat off, threw it into a corner, sat on his lap. "See? Homebody Number One."

65   "Your breath could run a train," Darling said, not wanting to be mean, but talking out of boredom, and sudden shock at seeing his wife curiously a stranger in a new hat, with a new expression in her eyes under the little brim, secret, confident, knowing.

Louise tucked her head under his chin so he couldn't smell her breath. "I had to take an author out for cocktails," she said. "He's a boy from the Ozark Mountains and he drinks like a fish. He's a Communist."

"What the hell is a Communist from the Ozarks doing writing for a woman's fashion magazine?"

Louise chuckled. "The magazine business is getting all mixed up these days. The publishers want to have a foot in every camp. And anyway, you can't find an author under seventy these days who isn't a Communist."

"I don't think I like you to associate with all these people, Louise," Darling said. "Drinking with them."

70   "He a very nice, gentle boy," Louise said. "He reads Ernest Dowson."

"Who's Ernest Dowson?"

Louise patted his arm, stood up, fixed her hair. "He's an English poet."

Darling felt that somehow he had disappointed her. "Am I supposed to know who Ernest Dowson is?"

"No, dear. I'd better go in and take a bath."

75   After she had gone, Darling went over to the corner where the hat was lying and picked it up. It was nothing, a scrap of straw, a red flower, a veil, meaningless on his big hand, but on his wife's head a signal of something . . . big city, smart and knowing women drinking and dining with men other than their husbands, conversation about things a normal man wouldn't know much about, Frenchmen who painted as though they used their elbows instead of brushes, composers who wrote whole symphonies without a single melody in them, writers who knew all about politics and women who knew all about writers, the movement of the proletariat, Marx, somehow mixed up with five-dollar dinners and the best-looking women in America and fairies who made them laugh and half-sentences immediately understood and secretly hilarious and wives who called their husbands "Baby." He put the hat down, a scrap of straw and a red flower, and a little veil. He drank some whisky straight and went into the bathroom where his wife was lying deep in her bath, singing to herself and smiling from time to time like a little girl, paddling the water gently with her hands, sending up a light spicy fragrance from the bath salts she used.

He stood over her, looking down at her. She smiled up at him, her eyes half closed, her body pink and shimmering in the warm, scented water. All over again, with all the old suddenness, he was hit deep inside him with the knowledge of how beautiful she was, how much he needed her.

"I came in here," he said, "to tell you I wish you wouldn't call me 'Baby.' "

She looked up at him from the bath, her eyes quickly full of sorrow, half-understanding what he meant. He knelt and put his arms around her, his sleeves plunged heedlessly in the water, his shirt and jacket soaking wet as he clutched her wordlessly, holding her crazily tight, crushing her breath from her, kissing her desperately, searchingly, regretfully.

He got jobs after that, selling real estate and automobiles, but somehow, although he had a desk with his name on a wooden wedge on it, and he went to the office religiously at nine each morning, he never managed to sell anything and he never made any money.

80   Louise was made assistant editor, and the house was always full of strange men and women who talked fast and got angry on abstract subjects like mural painting, novelists, labor unions. Negro short-story writers drank Louise's liquor, and a lot of Jews, and big solemn men with scarred faces and knotted hands who talked slowly but clearly about picket lines and battles with guns and leadpipe at mine-shaft-heads and in front of factory gates. And Louise moved among them all, confidently, knowing what they were talking about, with opinions that they listened to and argued about just as though she were a man. She knew everybody, condescended to no one, devoured books that Darling had never heard of, walked along the streets of the city, excited, at home, soaking in all the million tides of New York without fear, with constant wonder.

Her friends liked Darling and sometimes he found a man who wanted to get off in the corner and talk about the new boy who played fullback for Princeton, and the decline of the double wing-back, or even the state of the stock market, but for the most part he sat on the edge of things, solid and quiet in the high storm of words. "The dialectics of the situation . . . The theater has been given over to expert jugglers . . . Picasso? What man has a right to paint old bones and collect ten thousand dollars for them? . . . I stand firmly behind Trotsky . . . Poe was the last American critic. When he died they put lilies on the grave of American criticism. I don't say this because they panned my last book, but . . ."

Once in a while he caught Louise looking soberly and consideringly at him through the cigarette smoke and the noise and he avoided her eyes and found an excuse to get up and go into the kitchen for more ice or to open another bottle.

"Come on," Cathal Flaherty was saying, standing at the door with a girl, "you've got to come down and see this. It's down on Fourteenth Street, in the old Civic Repertory, and you can only see it on Sunday nights and I guarantee you'll come out of the theater singing." Flaherty was a big young Irishman with a broken nose who was the lawyer for a longshoreman's union, and he had been hanging around the house for six months on and off, roaring and shutting everybody else up when he got in an argument. "It's a new play, *Waiting for Lefty;* it's about taxi-drivers."

"Odets," the girl with Flaherty said. "It's by a guy named Odets."

85   "I never heard of him," Darling said.

"He's a new one," the girl said.

"It's like watching a bombardment," Flaherty said. "I saw it last Sunday night. You've got to see it."

"Come on, Baby," Louise said to Darling, excitement in her eyes already. "We've been sitting in the Sunday *Times* all day, this'll be a great change."

"I see enough taxi-drivers every day," Darling said, not because he meant that, but because he didn't like to be around Flaherty, who said things that made Louise laugh a lot and whose judgment she accepted on almost every subject. "Let's go to the movies."

90   "You've never seen anything like this before," Flaherty said. "He wrote this play with a baseball bat."

"Come on," Louise coaxed, "I bet it's wonderful."

"He has long hair," the girl with Flaherty said. "Odets. I met him at a party. He's an actor. He didn't say a goddam thing all night."

"I don't feel like going down to Fourteenth Street," Darling said, wishing Flaherty and his girl would get out. "It's gloomy."

"Oh, hell!" Louise said loudly. She looked coolly at Darling, as though she'd just been introduced to him and was making up her mind about him, and not very favorably. He saw her looking at him, knowing there was something new and dangerous in her face and he wanted to say something, but Flaherty was there and his damned girl, and anyway, he didn't know what to say.

95 "I'm going," Louise said, getting her coat. "I don't think Fourteenth Street is gloomy."

"I'm telling you," Flaherty was saying, helping her on with her coat, "it's the Battle of Gettysburg, in Brooklynese."

"Nobody could get a word out of him," Flaherty's girl was saying as they went through the door. "He just sat there all night."

The door closed. Louise hadn't said good night to him. Darling walked around the room four times, then sprawled out on the sofa, on top of the Sunday *Times*. He lay there for five minutes looking at the ceiling, thinking of Flaherty walking down the street talking in that booming voice, between the girls, holding their arms.

Louise had looked wonderful. She'd washed her hair in the afternoon and it had been very soft and light and clung close to her head as she stood there angrily putting her coat on. Louise was getting prettier every year, partly because she knew by now how pretty she was, and made the most of it.

100 "Nuts," Darling said, standing up. "Oh, nuts."

He put on his coat and went down to the nearest bar and had five drinks off by himself in a corner before his money ran out.

The years since then had been foggy and downhill. Louise had been nice to him, and in a way, loving and kind, and they'd fought only once, when he said he was going to vote for Landon. ("Oh, Christ," she'd said, "doesn't *anything* happen inside your head? Don't you read the papers? The penniless Republican!") She'd been sorry later and apologized for hurting him, but apologized as she might to a child. He'd tried hard, had gone grimly to the art galleries, the concert halls, the bookshops, trying to gain on the trail of his wife, but it was no use. He was bored, and none of what he saw or heard or dutifully read made much sense to him and finally he gave it up. He had thought, many nights as he ate dinner alone, knowing that Louise would come home late and drop silently into bed without explanation, of getting a divorce, but he knew the loneliness, the hopelessness, of not seeing her again would be too much to take. So he was good, completely devoted, ready at all times to go any place with her, do anything she wanted. He even got a small job, in a broker's office and paid his own way, bought his own liquor.

Then he'd been offered the job of going from college to college as a tailor's representative. "We want a man," Mr. Rosenberg had said, "who as soon as you look at him, you say, 'There's a university man.'" Rosenberg had looked approvingly at Darling's broad shoulders and well-kept waist, at his carefully brushed hair and his honest, wrinkle-less face. "Frankly, Mr. Darling, I am willing to make you a proposition. I have inquired about you, you are favorably known on your old campus, I understand you were in the backfield with Alfred Diederich."

Darling nodded. "Whatever happened to him?"

105 "He is walking around in a cast for seven years now. An iron brace. He played professional football and they broke his neck for him."

Darling smiled. That, at least, had turned out well.

"Our suits are an easy product to sell, Mr. Darling," Rosenberg said. "We have a handsome, custom-made garment. What has Brooks Brothers got that we haven't got? A name. No more."

"I can make fifty, sixty dollars a week," Darling said to Louise that night. "And expenses. I can save some money and then come back to New York and really get started here."

"Yes, Baby," Louise said.

110 "As it is," Darling said carefully, "I can make it back here once a month, and holidays and the summer. We can see each other often."

"Yes, Baby." He looked at her face, lovelier now at thirty-five than it had ever been before, but fogged over now as it had been for five years with a kind of patient, kindly, remote boredom.

"What do you say?" he asked. "Should I take it?" Deep within he hoped fiercely, longingly, for her to say, "No, Baby, you stay right here," but she said, as he knew she'd say, "I think you'd better take it."

He nodded. He had to get up and stand with his back to her, looking out the window, because there were things plain on his face that she had never seen in the fifteen years she'd known him. "Fifty dollars is a lot of money," he said. "I never thought I'd ever see fifty dollars again." He laughed. Louise laughed, too.

Christian Darling sat on the frail green grass of the practice field. The shadow of the stadium had reached out and covered him. In the distance the lights of the university shone a little mistily in the light haze of evening. Fifteen years. Flaherty even now was calling for his wife, buying her a drink, filling whatever bar they were in with that voice of his and that easy laugh. Darling half-closed his eyes, almost saw the boy fifteen years ago reach for the pass, slip the halfback, go skittering lightly down the field, his knees high and fast and graceful, smiling to himself because he knew he was going to get past the safety man. That was the high point, Darling thought, fifteen years ago, on an autumn afternoon, twenty years old and far from death, with the air coming easily into his lungs, and a deep feeling inside him that he could do anything, knock over anybody, outrun whatever had to be outrun. And the shower after and the three glasses of water and the cool night air on his damp head and Louise sitting hatless in the open car with a smile and the first kiss she ever really meant. The high point, an eighty-yard run in the practice, and a girl's kiss and everything after that a decline. Darling laughed. He had practiced the wrong thing, perhaps. He hadn't practiced for 1929 and New York City and a girl who would turn into a woman. Somewhere, he thought, there must have been a point where she moved up to me, was even with me for a moment, when I could have held her hand, if I'd known, held tight, gone with her. Well, he'd never known. Here he was on a playing field that was fifteen years away and his wife was in another city having dinner with another and better man, speaking with him a different, new language, a language nobody had ever taught him.

115 Darling stood up, smiled a little, because if he didn't smile he knew the tears would come. He looked around him. This was the spot. O'Connor's pass had come sliding out just to here . . . the high point. Darling put up his hands, felt all over again the flat slap of the ball. He shook his hips to throw off the halfback, cut back inside the center, picked his knees high as he ran gracefully over two men jumbled on the ground at the line of scrimmage, ran easily, gaining speed, for ten yards, holding the ball lightly in his two hands, swung away from the halfback diving at him, ran, swinging his hips in the almost girlish manner of a back in a broken field, tore into the safety man, his shoes drumming heavily on the turf, stiff-armed, elbow locked, pivoted, raced lightly and exultantly for the goal line.

It was only after he had sped over the goal line and slowed to a trot that he saw the boy and girl sitting together on the turf, looking at him wonderingly.

He stopped short, dropping his arms. "I . . ." he said, gasping a little, though his condition was fine and the run hadn't winded him. "I—once I played here."

The boy and the girl said nothing. Darling laughed embarrassedly, looked hard at them sitting there, close to each other, shrugged, turned and went toward his hotel, the sweat breaking out on his face and running down into his collar.

Anton Chekhov   (1860–1904)
On the Road

Upon the breast of a gigantic crag,
A golden cloudlet rested for one night.
                    —Lermontov[1]

In the room which the tavern keeper, the Cossack Semyon Tchistopluy, called the "travellers' room," that is kept exclusively for travellers, a tall, broad-shouldered man of forty was sitting at the big unpainted table. He was asleep with his elbows on the table and his head leaning on his fist. An end of tallow candle, stuck into an old pomatum pot, lighted up his light brown beard, his thick, broad nose, his sunburnt cheeks and the thick, black eyebrows overhanging his closed eyes. . . . The nose and the cheeks and the eyebrows, all the features, each taken separately, were coarse and heavy, like the furniture and the stove in the "travellers' room," but taken all together they gave the effect of something harmonious and even beautiful. Such is the lucky star, as it is called, of the Russian face: the coarser and harsher its features the softer and more good-natured it looks. The man was dressed in a gentleman's reefer jacket, shabby, but bound with wide new braid, a plush waistcoat, and full black trousers thrust into big high boots.

On one of the benches, which stood in a continuous row along the wall, a girl of eight, in a brown dress and long black stockings, lay asleep on a coat lined with fox. Her face was pale, her hair was flaxen, her shoulders were narrow, her whole body was thin and frail, but her nose stood out as thick and ugly a lump as the man's. She was sound asleep, and unconscious that her semicircular comb had fallen off her head and was cutting her cheek.

The "travellers' room" had a festive appearance. The air was full of the smell of freshly scrubbed floors, there were no rags hanging as usual on the line that ran diagonally across the room, and a little lamp was burning in the corner over the table, casting a patch of red light on the ikon of St. George the Victorious.[2] From the ikon stretched on each side of the corner a row of cheap oleographs, which maintained a strict and careful gra-

---

[1]Mikhail Yurievich Lermontov (1814–1841), Russian poet and novelist, was called the "poet of the Caucasus" because he was twice exiled there.
[2]Historical and mythological religious character.

dation in the transition from the sacred to the profane. In the dim light of the candle end and the red ikon lamp the pictures looked like one continuous stripe, covered with blurs of black. When the tiled stove, trying to sing in unison with the weather, drew in the air with a howl, while the logs, as though waking up, burst into bright flame and hissed angrily, red patches began dancing on the log walls, and over the head of the sleeping man could be seen first the Elder Seraphim,[3] then the Shah Nasir-ed-Din,[4] then a fat, brown baby with goggle eyes, whispering in the ear of a young girl with an extraordinarily blank, and indifferent face. . . .

Outside a storm was raging. Something frantic and wrathful, but profoundly unhappy, seemed to be flinging itself about the tavern with the ferocity of a wild beast and trying to break in. Banging at the doors, knocking at the windows and on the roof, scratching at the walls, it alternately threatened and besought, then subsided for a brief interval, and then with a gleeful, treacherous howl burst into the chimney, but the wood flared up, and the fire, like a chained dog, flew wrathfully to meet its foe, a battle began, and after it—sobs, shrieks, howls of wrath. In all of this there was the sound of angry misery and unsatisfied hate, and the mortified impatience of something accustomed to triumph.

5   Bewitched by this wild, inhuman music the "travellers' room" seemed spellbound forever, but all at once the door creaked and the potboy, in a new print shirt, came in. Limping on one leg, and blinking his sleepy eyes, he snuffed the candle with his fingers, put some more wood on the fire and went out. At once from the church, which was three hundred paces from the tavern, the clock struck midnight. The wind played with the chimes as with the snowflakes; chasing the sounds of the clock it whirled them round and round over a vast space, so that some strokes were cut short or drawn out in long, vibrating notes, while others were completely lost in the general uproar. One stroke sounded as distinctly in the room as though it had chimed just under the window. The child, sleeping on the foxskin, started and raised her head. For a minute she stared blankly at the dark window, at Nasir-ed-Din over whom a crimson glow from the fire flickered at that moment, then she turned her eyes upon the sleeping man.

"Daddy," she said.

But the man did not move. The little girl knitted her brow angrily, lay down, and curled up her legs. Someone in the tavern gave a loud, prolonged yawn. Soon afterwards there was the squeak of the swing door and the sound of indistinct voices. Someone came in, shaking the snow off, and stamping in felt boots which made a muffled thud.

"What is it?" a woman's voice asked languidly.

"Mademoiselle Ilovaisky has come, . . ." answered a bass voice.

10   Again there was the squeak of the swing door. Then came the roar of the wind rushing in. Someone, probably the lame boy, ran to the door leading to the "travellers' room," coughed differentially, and lifted the latch.

"This way, lady, please," said a woman's voice in dulcet tones. "It's clean in here, my beauty. . . ."

The door was opened wide and a peasant with a beard appeared in the doorway, in the long coat of a coachman, plastered all over with snow from head to foot, and carrying a big trunk on his shoulder. He was followed into the room by a feminine figure, scarcely half his height, with no face and no arms, muffled and wrapped up like a bundle and also covered with snow. A damp chill, as from a cellar, seemed to come to the child from the coachman and the bundle, and the fire and the candles flickered.

"What nonsense!" said the bundle angrily. "We could go perfectly well. We have only nine more miles to go, mostly by the forest, and we should not get lost. . . ."

[3]Literally, Elder Angel   [4]Famous jester of Turkish legend.

"As for getting lost, we shouldn't, but the horses can't go on, lady!" answered the coachman. "And it is Thy Will, O Lord! As though I had done it on purpose!"

15   "God knows where you have brought me. . . . Well, be quiet. . . . There are people asleep here, it seems. You can go. . . ."

The coachman put the portmanteau on the floor, and as he did so, a great lump of snow fell off his shoulders. He gave a sniff and went out.

Then the little girl saw two little hands come out from the middle of the bundle, stretch upwards and begin angrily disentangling the network of shawls, kerchiefs, and scarves. First a big shawl fell on the ground, then a hood, then a white knitted kerchief. After freeing her head, the traveller took off her pelisse and at once shrank to half the size. Now she was in a long, grey coat with big buttons and bulging pockets. From one pocket she pulled out a paper parcel, from the other a bunch of big, heavy keys, which she put down so carelessly that the sleeping man started and opened his eyes. For some time he looked blankly round him as though he didn't know where he was, then he shook his head, went to the corner and sat down. . . . The newcomer took off her greatcoat, which made her shrink to half her size again, she took off her big felt boots, and sat down, too.

By now she no longer resembled a bundle: she was a thin little brunette of twenty, as slim as a snake, with a long white face and curly hair. Her nose was long and sharp, her chin, too, was long and sharp, her eyelashes were long, the corners of her mouth were sharp, and, thanks to this general sharpness, the expression of her face was biting. Swathed in a closely fitting black dress with a mass of lace at her neck and sleeves, with sharp elbows and long pink fingers, she recalled the portraits of mediaeval English ladies. The grave concentration of her face increased this likeness.

The lady looked round at the room, glanced sideways at the man and the little girl, shrugged her shoulders, and moved to the window. The dark windows were shaking from the damp west wind. Big flakes of snow glistening in their whiteness lay on the window frame, but at once disappeared, borne away by the wind. The savage music grew louder and louder. . . .

20   After a long silence the little girl suddenly turned over, and said angrily, emphasizing each word:

"Oh, goodness, goodness, how unhappy I am! Unhappier than anyone!"

The man got up and moved with little steps to the child with a guilty air, which was utterly out of keeping with his huge figure and big beard.

"You are not asleep, dearie?" he said, in an apologetic voice. "What do you want?"

"I don't want anything, my shoulder aches! You are a wicked man, Daddy, and God will punish you! You'll see He will punish you."

25   "My darling, I know your shoulder aches, but what can I do, dearie?" said the man, in the tone in which men who have been drinking excuse themselves to their stern spouses. "It's the journey has made your shoulder ache, Sasha. To-morrow we shall get there and rest, and the pain will go away. . . ."

"To-morrow, to-morrow. . . . Every day you say to-morrow. We shall be going on another twenty days."

"But we shall arrive to-morrow, dearie, on your father's word of honour. I never tell a lie, but if we are detained by the snowstorm it is not my fault."

"I can't bear any more, I can't, I can't!"

Sasha jerked her leg abruptly and filled the room with an unpleasant wailing. Her father made a despairing gesture, and looked hopelessly toward the young lady. The latter shrugged her shoulders, and hesitatingly went up to Sasha.

30   "Listen, my dear," she said, "it is no use crying. It's really naughty; if your shoulder aches it can't be helped."

"You see, Madam," said the man quickly, as though defending himself, "we have not slept for two nights, and have been travelling in a revolting conveyance. Well, of course, it is natural she should be ill and miserable, . . . and then, you know, we had a drunken driver, our portmanteau has been stolen . . . the snowstorm all the time, but what's the use of crying, Madam? I am exhausted, though, by sleeping in a sitting position, and I feel as though I were drunk. Oh, dear! Sasha, and I feel sick as it is, and then you cry!"

The man shook his head, and with a gesture of despair sat down.

"Of course you mustn't cry," said the young lady. "It's only little babies cry. If you are ill, dear, you must undress and go to sleep . . . Let us take off your things!"

When the child had been undressed and pacified a silence reigned again. The young lady seated herself at the window, and looked around wonderingly at the room of the inn, at the ikon, at the stove. . . . Apparently the room and the little girl with the thick nose, in her short boy's nightgown, and the child's father, all seemed strange to her. This strange man was sitting in a corner; he kept looking about him helplessly, as though he were drunk, and rubbing his face with the palm of his hand. He sat silent, blinking, and judging from his guilty-looking figure it was difficult to imagine that he would soon begin to speak. Yet he was the first to begin. Stroking his knees, he gave a cough, laughed, and said:

35   "It's a comedy, it really is. . . . I look and I cannot believe my eyes: for what devilry has destiny driven us to this accursed inn? What did she want to show by it? Life sometimes performs such *'salto mortale,'*[5] one can only stare and blink in amazement. Have you come from far, Madam?"

"No, not from far," answered the young lady. "I am going from our estate, fifteen miles from here, to our farm, to my father and brother. My name is Ilovaisky, and the farm is called Ilovaiskoe. It's nine miles away. What unpleasant weather!"

"It couldn't be worse."

The lame boy came in and stuck a new candle in the pomatum pot.

"You might bring us the samovar, boy," said the man, addressing him.

40   "Who drinks tea now?" laughed the boy. "It is a sin to drink tea before mass. . . ."

"Never mind, boy, you won't burn in hell if we do. . . ."

Over the tea the new acquaintances got into conversation.

Mlle. Ilovaisky learned that her companion was called Grigory Petrovitch Liharev, that he was the brother of the Liharev who was Marshal of Nobility in one of the neighbouring districts, and he himself had once been a landowner, but had "run through everything in his time." Liharev learned that her name was Marya Mihailovna, that her father had a huge estate, but that she was the only one to look after it as her father and brother looked at life through their fingers, were irresponsible, and were too fond of harriers.

"My father and brother are all alone at the farm," she told him, brandishing her fingers (she had the habit of moving her fingers before her pointed face as she talked, and after every sentence moistened her lips with her sharp little tongue). "They, I mean men, are an irresponsible lot, and don't stir a finger for themselves. I can fancy there will be no one to give them a meal after the fast! We have no mother, and we have such servants that they can't lay the tablecloth properly when I am away. You can imagine their condition now! They will be left with nothing to break their fast, while I have to stay here all night. How strange it all is."

45   She shrugged her shoulders, took a sip from her cup, and said:

"There are festivals that have a special fragrance: at Easter, Trinity and Christmas there is a peculiar scent in the air. Even unbelievers are fond of those festivals. My brother, for instance, argues that there is no God, but he is the first to hurry to Matins at Easter."

---

[5]Mortal leap; deadly jump.

Liharev raised his eyes to Mlle. Ilovaisky and laughed.

"They argue that there is no God," she went on, laughing too, "but why is it, tell me, all the celebrated writers, the learned men, clever people generally, in fact, believe towards the end of their life?"

"If man does not know how to believe when he is young, Madam, he won't believe in his old age if he is ever so much of a writer."

50 Judging from Liharev's cough he had a bass voice, but, probably from being afraid to speak aloud, or from exaggerated shyness, he spoke in a tenor. After a brief pause he heaved a sigh and said:

"The way I look at it is that faith is a faculty of the spirit. It is just the same as a talent, one must be born with it. So far as I can judge by myself, by the people I have seen in my time, and by all that is done around us, this faculty is present in Russians in its highest degree. Russian life presents us with an uninterrupted succession of convictions and aspirations, and if you care to know, it has not yet the faintest notion of lack of faith or scepticism. If a Russian does not believe in God, it means he believes in something else."

Liharev took a cup of tea from Mlle. Ilovaisky, drank off half in one gulp, and went on:

"I will tell you about myself. Nature has implanted in my breast an extraordinary faculty for belief. Whisper it not to the night, but half my life I was in the ranks of the Atheists and Nihilists,[6] but there was not one hour in my life in which I ceased to believe. All talents, as a rule, show themselves in early childhood, and so my faculty showed itself when I could still walk upright under the table. My mother liked her children to eat a great deal, and when she gave me food she used to say: 'Eat! Soup is the great thing in life!' I believed, and ate the soup ten times a day, ate like a shark, ate till I was disgusted and stupefied. My nurse used to tell me fairy tales, and I believed in house-spirits, in wood-elves, and in goblins of all kinds. I used sometimes to steal corrosive sublimate from my father, sprinkle it on cakes, and carry them up to the attic that the house-spirits, you see, might eat them and be killed. And when I was taught to read and understand what I read, then there was a fine to-do. I ran away to America and went off to join the brigands, and wanted to go into a monastery, and hired boys to torture me for being a Christian. And note that my faith was always active, never dead. If I was running away to America I was not alone, but seduced someone else, as great a fool as I was, to go with me, and was delighted when I was nearly frozen outside the town gates and when I was thrashed; if I went to join the brigands I always came back with my face battered. A most restless childhood, I assure you! And when they sent me to the high school and pelted me with all sorts of truths—that is, that the earth goes round the sun, or that white light is not white, but is made up of seven colours—my poor little head began to go round! Everything was thrown into a whirl in me: Navin who made the sun stand still, and my mother who in the name of the Prophet Elijah[7] disapproved of lightning conductors, and my father who was indifferent to the truths I had learned. My enlightenment inspired me. I wandered about the house and stables like one possessed, preaching my truths; was horrified by ignorance, glowed with hatred for anyone who saw in white light nothing but white light. . . . But all that's nonsense and childishness. Serious, so to speak, manly enthusiasms began only at the university. You have, no doubt, Madam, taken your degree somewhere?"

[6]Believer in nihilism (Lat. *nihil,* nothing), a movement that appeared in Russia about 1850 aimed at the annihilation of many beliefs and institutions; happiness was to be the only law.
[7]See I Kings 18, especially verse 38: "Then the fire of the Lord fell. . . ." The point here is that Liharev's mother disapproved of lightning rods because they distorted God's purposes.

"I studied at Novotcherkask at the Don Institute."

55   "Then you have not been to a university? So you don't know what science means. All the sciences in the world have the same passport, without which they regard themselves as meaningless . . . the striving towards truth! Every one of them, even pharmacology, has for its aim not utility, not the alleviation of life, but truth. It's remarkable! When you set to work to study any science, what strikes you first of all is its beginning. I assure you there is nothing more attractive and grander, nothing is so staggering, nothing takes a man's breath away like the beginning of any science. From the first five or six lectures you are soaring on wings of the brightest hopes, you already seem to yourself to be welcoming truth with open arms. And I gave myself up to science, heart and soul, passionately, as to the woman one loves. I was its slave; I found it the sun of my existence, and asked for no other. I studied day and night without rest, ruined myself over books, wept when before my eyes men exploited science for their own personal ends. But my enthusiasm did not last long. The trouble is that every science has a beginning but not an end, like a recurring decimal. Zoology has discovered 35,000 kinds of insects, chemistry reckons 60 elements. If in time tens of noughts can be written after these figures, zoology and chemistry will be just as far from their end as now, and all contemporary scientific work consists in increasing these numbers. I saw through this trick when I discovered the 35,001st and felt no satisfaction. Well, I had no time to suffer from disillusionment, as I was soon possessed by a new faith. I plunged into Nihilism, with its manifestoes, its 'black divisions,' and all the rest of it. I 'went to the people,' worked in factories, worked as an oiler, as a barge hauler. Afterwards, when wandering over Russia, I had a taste of Russian life, I turned into a fervent devotee of that life. I loved the Russian people with poignant intensity, I loved their God and believed in Him, and in their language, their creative genius. . . . And so on, and so on. . . . I have been a Slavophile[8] in my time, I used to pester Aksakov[9] with letters, and I was a Ukrainophile, and an archaeologist, and a collector of specimens of peasant art. . . . I was enthusiastic over ideas, people, events, places . . . my enthusiasm was endless! Five years ago I was working for the abolition of private property; my last creed was non-resistance to evil."

Sasha gave an abrupt sigh and began moving. Liharev got up and went to her.

"Won't you have some tea, dearie?" he asked tenderly.

"Drink it yourself," the child answered rudely.

Liharev was disconcerted, and went back to the table with a guilty step.

60   "Then you have had a lively time," said Mlle. Ilovaisky; "you have something to remember."

"Well, yes, it's all very lively when one sits over tea and chatters to a kind listener, but you should ask what that liveliness has cost me! What price have I paid for the variety of my life? You see, Madam, I have not held my convictions like a German doctor of philosophy, *zierlichmännerlich*,[10] I have not lived in solitude, but every conviction I have had has bound my back to the yoke, has torn my body to pieces. Judge, for yourself. I was wealthy like my brothers, but now I am a beggar. In the delirium of my enthusiasm I smashed up my own fortune and my wife's—a heap of other people's money. Now I am forty-two, old age is close upon me, and I am homeless, like a dog that has dropped behind its waggon at night. All my life I have not known what peace meant, my soul has been in continual agitation, distressed even by its hopes . . . I have been wearied out with heavy irregular work, have endured privation, have five times been in prison, have dragged myself across the provinces of Archangel and of Toblosk . . . it's painful to think

---

[8]Lover of Slav civilization.   [9]Sergei Aksakov (1791–1859), a Russian novelist.
[10]Elegantly manlike, or in a culturally mannered way.

of it! I have lived, but in my fever I have not even been conscious of the process of life itself. Would you believe it, I don't remember a single spring, I never noticed how my wife loved me, how my children were born. What more can I tell you? I have been a misfortune to all who have loved me. . . . My mother has worn mourning for me all these fifteen years, while my proud brothers, who have had to wince, to blush, to bow their heads, to waste their money on my account, have come in the end to hate me like poison."

Liharev got up and sat down again.

"If I were simply unhappy I should thank God," he went on without looking at his listener. "My personal unhappiness sinks into the background when I remember how often in my enthusiasms I have been absurd, far from the truth, unjust, cruel, dangerous! How often I have hated and despised those whom I ought to have loved, and *vice versa*. I have changed a thousand times. One day I believe, fall down and worship, the next I flee like a coward from the gods and friends of yesterday, and swallow in silence the 'scoundrel!' they hurl after me. God alone has seen how often I have wept and bitten my pillow in shame for my enthusiasms. Never once in my life have I intentionally lied or done evil, but my conscience is not clear! I cannot even boast, Madam, that I have no one's life upon my conscience, for my wife died before my eyes, worn out by my reckless activity. Yes, my wife! I tell you they have two ways of treating women nowadays. Some measure women's skulls to prove woman is inferior to man, pick out her defects to mock at her, to look original in her eyes, and to justify their sensuality. Others do their utmost to raise women to their level, that is, force them to learn by heart the 35,000 species, to speak and write the same foolish things as they speak and write themselves."

Liharev's face darkened.

65 "I tell you that woman has been and always will be the slave of man," he said in a bass voice, striking his fist on the table. "She is soft, tender wax which a man always moulds into anything he likes. . . . My God! for the sake of some trumpery masculine enthusiasm she will cut off her hair, abandon her family, die among strangers! . . . among the ideas for which she has sacrificed herself there is not a single feminine one. . . . An unquestioning, devoted slave! I have not measured skulls, but I say this from hard, bitter experience: the proudest, most independent women, if I have succeeded in communicating to them my enthusiasm, have followed me without criticism, without question, and have done anything I chose; I have turned a nun into a Nihilist who, as I heard afterwards, shot a gendarme; my wife never left me for a minute in my wanderings, and like a weathercock changed her faith in step with my changing enthusiasms."

Liharev jumped up and walked up and down the room.

"A noble, sublime slavery!" he said, clasping his hands. "It is just in it that the highest meaning of woman's life lies! Of all the fearful medley of thoughts and impressions accumulated in my brain from my association with women my memory, like a filter, has retained no ideas, no clever saying, no philosophy, nothing but that extraordinary resignation to fate, that wonderful mercifulness, forgiveness of everything."

Liharev clenched his fists, stared at a fixed point, and with a sort of passionate intensity, as though he were savouring each word as he uttered it, hissed through his clenched teeth:

"That . . . that great-hearted fortitude, faithfulness unto death, poetry of the heart. . . . . The meaning of life lies in just that unrepining martyrdom, in the tears which would soften a stone, in the boundless, all-forgiving love which brings light and warmth into the chaos of life. . . ."

70 Mlle. Ilovaisky got up slowly, took a step towards Liharev, and fixed her eyes upon his face. From the tears that glittered on his eyelashes, from his quivering, passionate voice, from the flush on his cheeks, it was clear to her that women were not a chance, not a

simple subject of conversation. They were the object of his new enthusiasm, or, as he said himself, his new faith! For the first time in her life she saw a man carried away, fervently believing. With his gesticultations, with his flashing eyes he seemed to her mad, frantic, but there was a feeling of such beauty in the fire of his eyes, in his words, in all the movements of his huge body, that without noticing what she was doing she stood facing him as though rooted to the spot, and gazed into his face with delight.

"Take my mother," he said, stretching out his hand to her with an imploring expression on his face, "I poisoned her existence, according to her ideas disgraced the name of Liharev, did her as much harm as the most malignant enemy, and what do you think? My brothers give her little sums for holy bread and church services, and outraging her religious feelings, she saves that money and sends it in secret to her erring Grigory. This trifle alone elevates and ennobles the soul far more than all the theories, all the clever sayings and the 35,000 species. I can give you thousands of instances. Take you, even, for instance! With tempest and darkness outside you are going to your father and your brother to cheer them with your affection in the holiday, though very likely they have forgotten and are not thinking of you. And, wait a bit, and you will love a man and follow him to the North Pole. You would, wouldn't you?"

"Yes, if I loved him."

"There, you see," cried Liharev delighted, and he even stamped with his foot. "Oh dear! How glad I am that I have met you! Fate is kind to me, I am always meeting splendid people. Not a day passes but one makes acquaintance with somebody one would give one's soul for. There are ever so many more good people than bad in this world. Here, see, for instance, how openly and from our hearts we have been talking as though we had known each other a hundred years. Sometimes, I assure you, one restrains oneself for ten years and holds one's tongue, is reserved with one's friends and one's wife, and meets some cadet in a train and babbles one's whole soul out to him. It is the first time I have the honour of seeing you, and yet I have confessed to you as I have never confessed in my life. Why is it?"

Rubbing his hands and smiling good-humouredly Liharev walked up and down the room, and fell to talking about women again. Meanwhile they began ringing for matins.

75 "Goodness," wailed Sasha. "He won't let me sleep with his talking!"

"Oh, yes!" said Liharev, startled. "I am sorry, darling, sleep, sleep. . . . I have two boys besides her," he whispered. "They are living with their uncle, Madam, but this one can't exist a day without her father. She's wretched, she complains, but she sticks to me like a fly to honey. I have been chattering too much, Madam, and it would do you no harm to sleep. Wouldn't you like me to make up a bed for you?"

Without waiting for permission he shook the wet pelisse, stretched it on a bench, fur side upwards, collected various shawls and scarves, put the overcoat folded up into a roll for a pillow, and all this he did in silence with a look of devout reverence, as though he were not handling a woman's rags, but the fragments of holy vessels. There was something apologetic, embarrassed about his whole figure, as though in the presence of a weak creature he felt ashamed of his height and strength. . . .

When Mlle. Ilovaisky had lain down, he put out the candle and sat down on a stool by the stove.

"So, Madam," he whispered, lighting a fat cigarette and putting the smoke into the stove. "Nature has put into the Russian an extraordinary faculty for belief, a searching intelligence, and the lift of speculation, but all that is reduced to ashes by irresponsibility, laziness, and dreamy frivolity. . . . Yes. . . ."

80 She gazed wonderingly into the darkness, and saw only a spot of red on the ikon and the flicker of the light of the stove on Liharev's face. The darkness, the chime of the bells, the roar of the storm, the lame boy, Sasha with her fretfulness, unhappy Liharev and

his sayings—all this was mingled together, and seemed to grow into one huge impression, and God's world seemed to her fantastic, full of marvels and magical forces. All that she had heard was ringing in her ears, and human life presented itself to her as a beautiful poetic fairy tale without an end.

The immense impression grew and grew, clouded consciousness, and turned into a sweet dream. She was asleep, though she saw the little ikon lamp and a big nose with the light playing on it.

She heard the sound of weeping.

"Daddy, darling," a child's voice was tenderly entreating, "let's go back to uncle! There is a Christmas-tree there! Styopa and Kolya are there!"

"My darling, what can I do?" a man's bass persuaded softly. "Understand me! Come, understand!"

⁸⁵ And the man's weeping blended with the child's. This voice of human sorrow, in the midst of the howling of the storm, touched the girl's ear with such sweet human music that she could not bear the delight of it, and wept too. She was conscious afterwards of a big, black shadow coming softly up to her, picking up a shawl that had dropped on to the floor and carefully wrapping it round her feet.

Mlle. Ilovaisky was awakened by a strange uproar. She jumped up and looked about her in astonishment. The deep blue dawn was looking in at the window half-covered with snow. In the room there was a grey twilight, through which the stove and the sleeping child and Nasir-ed-Din stood out distinctly. The stove and the lamp were both out. Through the wide-open door she could see the big tavern room with a counter and chairs. A man, with a stupid, gipsy face and astonished eyes, was standing in the middle of the room in a puddle of melting snow, holding a big red star on a stick. He was surrounded by a group of boys, motionless as statues, and plastered over with snow. The light shone through the red paper of the star, throwing a glow of red on their wet faces. The crowd was shouting in disorder, and from its uproar Mlle. Ilovaisky could make out only one couplet:

> "Hi, you little Russian lad,
> Bring your sharp knife,
> We will kill the Jew, we will kill him,
> The son of tribulation. . . ."

Liharev was standing near the counter, looking feelingly at the singers and tapping his feet in time. Seeing Mlle. Ilovaisky, he smiled all over his face and came up to her. She smiled too.

"A happy Christmas!" he said. "I saw you slept well."

She looked at him, said nothing, and went on smiling.

⁹⁰ After the conversation in the night he seemed to her not tall and broad shouldered, but little, just as the biggest steamer seems to us a little thing when we hear that it has crossed the ocean.

"Well, it is time for me to set off," she said. "I must put on my things. Tell me where you are going now?"

"I? To the station of Klinushki, from there to Sergievo, and from Sergievo; with horses, thirty miles to the coal mines that belong to a horrid man, a general called Shash-kovsky. My brothers have got me the post of superintendent there. . . . I am going to be a coal miner."

"Stay, I know those mines. Shashkovsky is my uncle, you know. But . . . what are you going there for?" asked Mlle. Ilovaisky, looking at Liharev in surprise.

"As superintendent. To superintend the coal mines."

"I don't understand!" she shrugged her shoulders. "You are going to the mines. But you know, it's the bare steppe, a desert, so dreary that you couldn't exist a day there! It's horrible coal, no one will buy it, and my uncle's a maniac, a despot, a bankrupt. . . . You won't get your salary!"

"No matter," said Liharev, unconcernedly. "I am thankful even for coal mines."

She shrugged her shoulders, and walked about the room in agitation.

"I don't understand, I don't understand," she said, moving her fingers before her face. "It's impossible, and . . . and irrational! You must understand that it's . . . it's worse than exile. It is a living tomb! O Heavens!" she said hotly, going up to Liharev and moving her fingers before his smiling face; her upper lip was quivering, and her sharp face turned pale, "Come, picture it, the bare steppe, solitude. There is no one to say a word to there, and you . . . are enthusiastic over women! Coal mines . . . and women!"

Mlle. Ilovaisky was suddenly ashamed of her heat and, turning away from Liharev, walked to the window.

"No, no, you can't go there," she said, moving her fingers rapidly over the pane.

Not only in her heart, but even in her spine she felt that behind her stood an infinitely unhappy man, lost and outcast, while he, as though he were unaware of his unhappiness, as though he had not shed tears in the night, was looking at her with a kindly smile. Better he should go on weeping! She walked up and down the room several times in agitation, then stopped short in a corner and sank into thought. Liharev was saying something, but she did not hear him. Turning her back on him she took out of her purse a money note, stood for a long time crumpling it in her hand, and looking round at Liharev, blushed and put it in her pocket.

The coachman's voice was heard through the door. With a stern concentrated face she began putting on her things in silence. Liharev wrapped her up, chatting gaily, but every word he said lay on her heart like a weight. It is not cheering to hear the unhappy or the dying jest.

When the transformation of a live person into a shapeless bundle had been completed, Mlle. Ilovaisky looked for the last time round the "travellers' room," stood a moment in silence, and slowly walked out. Liharev went to see her off. . . .

Outside, God alone knows why, the winter was raging still. Whole clouds of big soft snowflakes were whirling restlessly over the earth, unable to find a resting-place. The horses, the sledge, the trees, a bull tied to a post, all were white and seemed soft and fluffy.

"Well, God help you," muttered Liharev, tucking her into the sledge. "Don't remember evil against me. . . ."

She was silent. When the sledge started, and had to go round a huge snowdrift, she looked back at Liharev with an expression as though she wanted to say something to him. He ran up to her, but she did not say a word to him, she only looked at him through her long eyelashes with little specks of snow on them.

Whether his finely intuitive soul were really able to read that look, or whether his imagination deceived him, it suddenly began to seem to him that with another touch or two that girl would have forgiven him his failures, his age, his desolate position, and would have followed him without question or reasonings. He stood a long while as though rooted to the spot, gazing at the tracks left by the sledge runners. The snowflakes greedily settled on his hair, his beard, his shoulders. . . . Soon the track of the runners had vanished, and he himself covered with snow, began to look like a white rock, but still his eyes kept seeking something in the clouds of snow.

Comments and Questions

As we continue with our study of the short story, we must not lose sight of the basic matters while we, of necessity, move among the technical matters of story construction. We recall our earlier statement that although we are giving a good deal of attention to form, we must never lose sight of our ultimate goal, which is *to comprehend the values and reality explored by any piece of writing.*

We still keep in mind our question, What makes a good short story? As we look back—Galsworthy, Porter, Steinbeck, Faulkner—have we found a *great* short story? How would we make the distinction between a good and a great one? Perhaps we can help ourselves to find that distinction by trying to answer questions like these about Chekhov's story:

1. What are the principal devices used by Chekhov to transform the facts of his story into a piece of fictional art with meaning? Has he relied chiefly on plot, character, or theme? Panorama or scene? What kind of a narrator? Does the symbolism, if any, help to give the story its most fundamental meaning? In what ways do the tone and atmosphere help to make clear Chekhov's meaning? These questions concern technique and form; they are ways of getting into a discussion of the story's meaning. To know the answers to the questions is not to know very *much,* but to know the *meaning* of the answers is to know a great deal about the meaning of the story.

2. Is the story a good or a great one? Is Chekhov a mechanic only who can fit parts together, or is he an artist? To put the question another way: Is the story a satisfactory technical performance or is the technique *used* to dramatize a penetrating interpretation of life? Have you ever heard a pianist or violinist who gave a brilliant technical performance, yet left you unmoved—a technician but no artist? How would you classify Chekhov?

3. It has been said that the whole purpose of art is to get below the surface meaning of life. Does Chekhov get there? Does the story have two or three dimensions? Support your opinion by evidence from the story.

4. Is Chekhov unusually sensitive to human personality and character? Do we *know* Liharev and Mlle. Ilovaisky?

5. What is the significance of the snowstorm? The story begins and ends with the storm. Is this an accident, decoration, or symbolism?

W. Somerset Maugham   (1874–1965)
The Colonel's Lady

All this happened two or three years before the outbreak of the war.

The Peregrines were having breakfast. Though they were alone and the table was long they sat at opposite ends of it. From the walls George Peregrine's ancestors, painted by the fashionable painters of the day, looked down upon them. The butler brought in the morning post. There were several letters for the Colonel, business letters, *The Times* and a small parcel for his wife Evie. He looked at his letters and then, opening *The Times,*

began to read it. They finished breakfast and rose from the table. He noticed that his wife
hadn't opened the parcel.

"What's that?" he asked.

"Only some books."

5   "Shall I open it for you?"

"If you like."

He hated to cut string and so with some difficulty untied the knots.

"But they're all the same," he said when he had unwrapped the parcel. "What on
earth d'you want six copies of the same book for?" He opened one of them. "Poetry."
Then he looked at the title page. *When Pyramids Decay*, he read, by E. K. Hamilton. Eva
Katherine Hamilton: that was his wife's maiden name. He looked at her with smiling surprise. "Have you written a book, Evie? You are a slyboots."

"I didn't think it would interest you very much. Would you like a copy?"

10   "Well, you know poetry isn't much in my line, but—yes, I'd like a copy; I'll read it.
I'll take it along to my study. I've got a lot to do this morning."

He gathered up *The Times*, his letters and the book and went out. His study was a
large and comfortable room, with a big desk, leather armchairs and what he called "trophies of the chase" on the walls. In the bookshelves were works of reference, books on
farming, gardening, fishing and shooting, and books on the last war, in which he had won
an M.C. and a D.S.O. For before his marriage he had been in the Welsh Guards. At the
end of the war he retired and settled down to the life of a country gentleman in the
spacious house, some twenty miles from Sheffield, which one of his forebears had built in
the reign of George III. George Peregrine had an estate of some fifteen hundred acres
which he managed with ability; he was a justice of the peace and performed his duties
conscientiously. During the season he rode to hounds two days a week. He was a good
shot, a golfer and though now a little over fifty could still play a hard game of tennis. He
could describe himself with propriety as an all-round sportsman.

He had been putting on weight lately, but was still a fine figure of a man; tall, with
grey curly hair, only just beginning to grow thin on the crown, frank blue eyes, good
features and a high colour. He was a public-spirited man, chairman at any number of local
organizations and, as became his class and station, a loyal member of the Conservative
party. He looked upon it as his duty to see to the welfare of the people on his estate and
it was a satisfaction to him to know that Evie could be trusted to tend the sick and succour
the poor. He had built a cottage hospital on the outskirts of the village and paid the wages
of a nurse out of his own pocket. All he asked of the recipients of his bounty was that at
elections, county or general, they should vote for his candidate. He was a friendly man,
affable to his inferiors, considerate with his tenants and popular with the neighbouring
gentry. He would have been pleased and at the same time slightly embarrassed if someone
had told him he was a jolly good fellow. That was what he wanted to be. He desired no
higher praise.

It was hard luck that he had no children. He would have been an excellent father,
kindly but strict, and would have brought up his sons as a gentleman's sons should be
brought up, sent them to Eton, you know, taught them to fish, shoot and ride. As it was,
his heir was a nephew, son of his brother killed in a motor accident, not a bad boy, but
not a chip off the old block, no, sir, far from it; and would you believe it, his fool of a
mother was sending him to a co-educational school. Evie had been a sad disappointment
to him. Of course she was a lady, and she had a bit of money of her own; she managed
the house uncommonly well and she was a good hostess. The village people adored her.
She had been a pretty young thing when he married her, with a creamy skin, light brown
hair and a trim figure, healthy, too, and not a bad tennis player; he couldn't understand

why she'd had no children; of course she was faded now, she must be getting on for five and forty; her skin was drab, her hair had lost its sheen and she was as thin as a rail. She was always neat and suitably dressed, but she didn't seem to bother how she looked; she wore no makeup and didn't even use lipstick; sometimes at night when she dolled herself up for a party you could tell that once she'd been quite attractive, but ordinarily she was— well, the sort of woman you simply didn't notice. A nice woman, of course, a good wife, and it wasn't her fault if she was barren, but it was tough on a fellow who wanted an heir of his own loins; she hadn't any vitality, that's what was the matter with her. He supposed he'd been in love with her when he asked her to marry him, at least sufficiently in love for a man who wanted to marry and settle down, but with time he discovered that they had nothing much in common. She didn't care about hunting, and fishing bored her. Naturally they'd drifted apart. He had to do her the justice to admit that she'd never bothered him. There'd been no scenes. They had no quarrels. She seemed to take it for granted that he should go his own way. When he went up to London now and then she never wanted to come with him. He had a girl there, well, she wasn't exactly a girl, she was thirty-five if she was a day, but she was blonde and luscious and he only had to wire ahead of time and they'd dine, do a show and spend the night together. Well, a man, a healthy normal man had to have some fun in his life. The thought crossed his mind that if Evie hadn't been such a good woman she'd have been a better wife; but it was not the sort of thought that he welcomed and he put it away from him.

George Peregrine finished his *Times* and being a considerate fellow rang the bell and told the butler to take the paper to Evie. Then he looked at his watch. It was half-past ten and at eleven he had an appointment with one of his tenants. He had half an hour to spare.

15   "I'd better have a look at Evie's book," he said to himself.

He took it up with a smile. Evie had a lot of highbrow books in her sitting-room, not the sort of books that interested him, but if they amused her he had no objection to her reading them. He noticed that the volume he now held in his hand contained no more than ninety pages. That was all to the good. He shared Edgar Allan Poe's opinion that poems should be short. But as he turned the pages he noticed that several of Evie's had long lines of irregular length and didn't rhyme. He didn't like that. At his first school, when he was a little boy, he remembered learning a poem that began: *The boy stood on the burning deck,* and later, at Eton, one that started: *Ruin seize thee, ruthless king;* and then there was Henry V; they'd had to take that one half. He stared at Evie's pages with consternation.

"That's not what I call poetry," he said.

Fortunately it wasn't all like that. Interspersed with the pieces that looked so odd, lines of three or four words and then a line of ten or fifteen, there were little poems, quite short, that rhymed, thank God, with the lines all the same length. Several of the pages were just headed with the word *Sonnet,* and out of curiosity he counted the lines; there were fourteen of them. He read them. They seemed all right, but he didn't quite know what they were all about. He repeated to himself: *Ruin seize thee, ruthless king.*

"Poor Evie," he sighed.

20   At that moment the farmer he was expecting was ushered into the study, and putting the book down he made him welcome. They embarked on their business.

"I read your book, Evie," he said as they sat down to lunch. "Jolly good. Did it cost you a packet to have it printed?"

"No, I was lucky. I sent it to a publisher and he took it."

"Not much money in poetry, my dear," he said in his good-natured, hearty way.

"No, I don't suppose there is. What did Bannock want to see you about this morning?"

25   Bannock was the tenant who had interrupted his reading of Evie's poems.

"He's asked me to advance the money for a pedigree bull he wants to buy. He's a good man and I've half a mind to do it."

George Peregrine saw that Evie didn't want to talk about her book and he was not sorry to change the subject. He was glad she had used her maiden name on the title page; he didn't suppose anyone would ever hear about the book, but he was proud of his own unusual name and he wouldn't have liked it if some damned penny-a-liner had made fun of Evie's effort in one of the papers.

During the few weeks that followed he thought it tactful not to ask Evie any questions about her venture into verse and she never referred to it. It might have been a discreditable incident that they had silently agreed not to mention. But then a strange thing happened. He had to go to London on business and he took Daphne out to dinner. That was the name of the girl with whom he was in the habit of passing a few agreeable hours whenever he went to town.

"Oh, George," she said, "is that your wife who's written a book they're all talking about?"

30   "What on earth d'you mean?"

"Well, there's a fellow I know who's a critic. He took me out to dinner the other night and he had a book with him. 'Got anything for me to read?' I said. 'What's that?' 'Oh, I don't think that's your cup of tea,' he said, 'It's poetry, I've just been reviewing it,' 'No poetry for me,' I said. 'It's about the hottest stuff I ever read,' he said. 'Selling like hot cakes. And it's damned good.' "

"Who's the book by?" asked George.

"A woman called Hamilton. My friend told me that wasn't her real name. He said her real name was Peregrine. 'Funny,' I said, 'I know a fellow called Peregrine.' 'Colonel in the army,' he said. 'Lives near Sheffield.' "

"I'd just as soon you didn't talk about me to your friends," said George with a frown of vexation.

35   "Keep your shirt on, dearie. Who'd you take me for? I just said, 'It's not the same one.' " Daphne giggled. "My friend said: 'They say he's a regular Colonel Blimp.' "

George had a keen sense of humour.

"You could tell them better than that," he laughed. "If my wife had written a book I'd be the first to know about it, wouldn't I?"

"I suppose you would."

Anyhow the matter didn't interest her and when the Colonel began to talk of other things she forgot about it. He put it out of his mind too. There was nothing to it, he decided, and that silly fool of a critic had just been pulling Daphne's leg. He was amused at the thought of her tackling that book because she had been told it was hot stuff and then finding it just a lot of stuff cut up into unequal lines.

40   He was a member of several clubs and next day he thought he'd lunch at one in St. James's Street. He was catching a train back to Sheffield early in the afternoon. He was sitting in a comfortable armchair having a glass of sherry before going into the dining-room when an old friend came up to him.

"Well, old boy, how's life?" he said. "How d'you like being the husband of a celebrity?"

George Peregrine looked at his friend. He thought he saw an amused twinkle in his eyes.

"I don't know what you're talking about," he answered.

"Come off it, George. Everyone knows E. K. Hamilton is your wife. Not often a book of verse has a success like that. Look here, Henry Dashwood is lunching with me. He'd like to meet you."

45 "Who the devil is Henry Dashwood and why should he want to meet me?"

"Oh, my dear fellow, what do you do with yourself all the time in the country? Henry's about the best critic we've got. He wrote a wonderful review on Evie's book. D'you mean to say she didn't show it to you?"

Before George could answer his friend had called a man over. A tall, thin man, with a high forehead, a beard, a long nose and a stoop, just the sort of man whom George was prepared to dislike at first sight. Introductions were effected. Henry Dashwood sat down.

"Is Mrs. Peregrine in London by any chance? I should very much like to meet her," he said.

"No, my wife doesn't like London. She prefers the country," said George stiffly.

50 "She wrote me a very nice letter about my review. I was pleased. You know, we critics get more kicks than halfpence. I was simply bowled over by her book. It's so fresh and original, very modern without being obscure. She seems to be as much at her ease in free verse as in classical metres." Then because he was a critic he thought he should criticize. "Sometimes her ear is a trifle at fault, but you can say the same of Emily Dickinson. There are several of those short lyrics of hers that might have been written by Landor."

All this was gibberish to George Peregrine. The man was nothing but a disgusting highbrow. But the Colonel had good manners and he answered with proper civility. Henry Dashwood went on as though he hadn't spoken.

"But what makes the book so outstanding is the passion that throbs in every line. So many of these young poets are so anaemic, cold, bloodless, dully intellectual, but here you have real naked, earthy passion; of course deep, sincere emotion like that is tragic— ah, my dear Colonel, how right Heine was when he said that the poet makes little songs out of his great sorrows. You know, now and then, as I read and re-read those heart-rending pages I thought of Sappho."

This was too much for George Peregrine and he got up.

"Well, it's jolly nice of you to say such nice things about my wife's little book. I'm sure she'll be delighted. But I must bolt, I've got to catch a train and I want to get a bite of lunch."

55 "Damned fool," he said irritably to himself as he walked upstairs to the dining-room.

He got home in time for dinner and after Evie had gone to bed he went into his study and looked for her book. He thought he'd just glance through it again to see for himself what they were making such a fuss about, but he couldn't find it. Evie must have taken it away.

"Silly," he muttered.

He'd told her he thought it jolly good. What more could a fellow be expected to say? Well, it didn't matter. He lit his pipe and read the *Field* till he felt sleepy. But a week or so later it happened that he had to go into Sheffield for the day. He lunched there at his club. He had nearly finished when the Duke of Haverel came in. This was the great local magnate and of course the Colonel knew him, but only to say how d'you do to; and he was surprised when the Duke stopped at his table.

"We're so sorry your wife couldn't come to us for the week-end," he said, with a sort of shy cordiality. "We're expecting rather a nice lot of people."

60 George was taken aback. He guessed that the Haverels had asked him and Evie over for the week-end and Evie, without saying a word to him about it, had refused. He had the presence of mind to say he was sorry too.

"Better luck next time," said the Duke pleasantly and moved on.

Colonel Peregrine was very angry and when he got home he said to his wife:

"Look here, what's this about our being asked over to Haverel? Why on earth did you say we couldn't go? We've never been asked before and it's the best shooting in the county."

"I didn't think of that. I thought it would only bore you."

65 "Damn it all, you might at least have asked me if I wanted to go."

"I'm sorry."

He looked at her closely. There was something in her expression that he didn't quite understand. He frowned.

"I suppose *I* was asked?" he barked.

Evie flushed a little.

70 "Well, in point of fact you weren't."

"I call it damned rude of them to ask you without asking me."

"I suppose they thought it wasn't your sort of party. The Duchess is rather fond of writers and people like that, you know. She's having Henry Dashwood, the critic, and for some reason he wants to meet me."

"It was damned nice of you to refuse, Evie."

"It's the least I could do," she smiled. She hesitated a moment. "George, my publishers want to give a little dinner party for me one day towards the end of the month and of course they want you to come too."

75 "Oh, I don't think that's quite my mark. I'll come up to London with you if you like. I'll find someone to dine with."

Daphne.

"I expect it'll be very dull, but they're making rather a point of it. And the day after, the American publisher who's taken my book is giving a cocktail party at Claridge's. I'd like you to come to that if you wouldn't mind."

"Sounds like a crashing bore, but if you really want me to come I'll come."

"It would be sweet of you."

80 George Peregrine was dazed by the cocktail party. There were a lot of people. Some of them didn't look so bad, a few of the women were decently turned out, but the men seemed to him pretty awful. He was introduced to everybody as Colonel Peregrine, E. K. Hamilton's husband, you know. The men didn't seem to have anything to say to him, but the women gushed.

"You *must* be proud of your wife. Isn't it *wonderful*? You know, I read it right through at a sitting, I simply couldn't put it down, and when I'd finished I started again at the beginning and read it right through a second time. I was simply *thrilled*."

The English publisher said to him:

"We've not had a success like this with a book of verse for twenty years. I've never seen such reviews."

The American publisher said to him:

85 "It's swell. It'll be a smash hit in America. You wait and see."

The American publisher had sent Evie a great spray of orchids. Damned ridiculous, thought George. As they came in, people were taken up to Evie and it was evident that they said flattering things to her, which she took with a pleasant smile and a word or two of thanks. She seemed a trifle flushed with excitement, but seemed quite at her ease. Though he thought the whole thing a lot of stuff and nonsense, George noted with approval that his wife was carrying it off in just the right way.

"Well, there's one thing," he said to himself, "you can see she's a lady and that's a damned sight more than you can say of anyone else here."

He drank a good many cocktails. But there was one thing that bothered him. He had a notion that some of the people he was introduced to looked at him in a rather funny sort of way, he couldn't quite make out what it meant, and once when he strolled by two women who were sitting together on a sofa he had the impression that they were talking about him and after he passed he was almost certain they tittered. He was very glad when the party came to an end.

In the taxi on their way back to their hotel Evie said to him:

90 "You were wonderful, dear. You made quite a hit. The girls simply raved about you; they thought you so handsome."

"Girls," he said bitterly. "Old hags."

"Were you bored, dear?"

"Stiff."

She pressed his hand in a gesture of sympathy.

95 "I hope you won't mind if we wait and go down by the afternoon train. I've got some things to do in the morning."

"No, that's all right. Shopping?"

"I do want to buy one or two things, but I've got to go and be photographed. I hate the idea, but they think I ought to be. For America, you know."

He said nothing. But he thought. He thought it would be a shock to the American public when they saw the portrait of the homely, dessicated little woman who was his wife. He'd always been under the impression that they liked glamour in America.

He went on thinking and next morning when Evie had gone out he went to his club and up to the library. There he looked up recent numbers of *The Times Literary Supplement*, the *New Statesman* and the *Spectator*. Presently he found reviews of Evie's book. He didn't read them very carefully, but enough to see that they were extremely favourable. Then he went to the bookseller's in Picadilly where he occasionally bought books. He'd made up his mind that he had to read this damned thing of Evie's properly, but he didn't want to ask her what she'd done with the copy she'd given him. He'd buy one for himself. Before going in he looked in the window and the first thing he saw was a display of *When Pyramids Decay*. Damned silly title! He went in. A young man came forward and asked if he could help him.

100 "No, I'm just having a look round." It embarrassed him to ask for Evie's book and he thought he'd find it for himself and then take it to the salesman. But he couldn't see it anywhere and at last, finding the young man near him, he said in a carefully casual tone: "By the way, have you got a book called *When Pyramids Decay?*"

"The new edition came in this morning. I'll get a copy."

In a moment the young man returned with it. He was a short, rather stout young man, with a shock of untidy carroty hair and spectacles. George Peregrine, tall, upstanding, very military, towered over him.

"Is this a new edition then?" he asked.

"Yes, sir. The fifth. It might be a novel the way it's selling."

105 George Peregrine hesitated a moment.

"Why d'you suppose it's such a success? I've always been told no one reads poetry."

"Well, it's good, you know. I've read it meself." The young man, though obviously cultured, had a slight Cockney accent, and George quite instinctively adopted a patronizing attitude. "It's the story they like. Sexy, you know, but tragic."

George frowned a little. He was coming to the conclusion that the young man was rather impertinent. No one had told him anything about there being a story in the damned book and he had not gathered that from reading the reviews. The young man went on.

"Of course it's only a flash in the pan, if you know what I mean. The way I look at it, she was sort of inspired like by a personal experience, like Housman was with *The Shropshire Lad*. She'll never write anything else."

110 "How much is the book?" said George coldly to stop his chatter. "You needn't wrap it up, I'll just slip it in my pocket."

The November morning was raw and he was wearing a greatcoat.

At the station he bought the evening papers and magazines and he and Evie settled themselves comfortably in opposite corners of a firstclass carriage and read. At five o'clock they went along to the restaurant car to have tea and chatted a little. They arrived. They drove home in the car which was waiting for them. They bathed, dressed for dinner, and after dinner Evie, saying she was tired out, went to bed. She kissed him, as was her habit, on the forehead. Then he went into the hall, took Evie's book out of the greatcoat pocket and going into the study began to read it. He didn't read verse very easily and though he read with attention, every word of it, the impression he received was far from clear. Then he began at the beginning again and read it a second time. He read with increasing malaise, but he was not a stupid man and when he had finished he had a distinct understanding of what it was all about. Part of the book was in free verse, part in conventional metres, but the story it related was coherent and plain to the meanest intelligence. It was the story of a passionate love affair between an older woman, married, and a young man. George Peregrine made out the steps of it as easily as if he had been doing a sum in simple addition.

Written in the first person, it began with the tremulous surprise of the woman, past her youth, when it dawned upon her that the young man was in love with her. She hesitated to believe it. She thought she must be deceiving herself. And she was terrified when on a sudden she discovered that she was passionately in love with him. She told herself it was absurd; with the disparity of age between them nothing but unhappiness could come to her if she yielded to her emotion. She tried to prevent him from speaking, but the day came when he told her that he loved her and forced her to tell him that she loved him too. He begged her to run away with him. She couldn't leave her husband, her home; and what life could they look forward to, she an ageing woman, he so young? How could she expect his love to last? She begged him to have mercy on her. But his love was impetuous. He wanted her, he wanted her with all his heart, and at last trembling, afraid, desirous, she yielded to him. Then there was a period of ecstatic happiness. The world, the dull, humdrum world of every day, blazed with glory. Love songs flowed from her pen. The woman worshipped the young, virile body of her lover. George flushed darkly when she praised his broad chest and slim flanks, the beauty of his legs and the flatness of his belly.

Hot stuff, Daphne's friend had said. It was that all right. Disgusting.

There were sad little pieces in which she lamented the emptiness of her life when, as must happen, he left her, but they ended with a cry that all she had to suffer would be worth it for the bliss that for a while had been hers. She wrote of the long, tremulous nights they passed together and the languor that lulled them to sleep in one another's arms. She wrote of the rapture of brief stolen moments when, braving all danger, their passion overwhelmed them and they surrendered to its call.

She thought it would be an affair of a few weeks, but miraculously it lasted. One of the poems referred to three years having gone by without lessening the love that filled their hearts. It looked as though he continued to press her to go away with him, far away, to a hill town in Italy, a Greek island, a walled city in Tunisia, so that they could be together always, for in another of the poems she besought him to let things be as they were. Their happiness was precarious. Perhaps it was owing to the difficulties they had to encounter and the rarity of their meetings that their love had retained for so long its first enchanting ardour. Then on a sudden the young man died. How, when or where George could not discover. There followed a long, heartbroken cry of bitter grief, grief she could not indulge in, grief that had to be hidden. She had to be cheerful, give dinner parties and go out to dinner, behave as she had always behaved, though the light had gone out of her life and she was bowed down with anguish. The last poem of all was a set of four short stanzas in which the writer, sadly resigned to her loss, thanked the dark powers that rule man's destiny that she had been privileged at least for a while to enjoy the greatest happiness that we poor human beings can ever hope to know.

It was three o'clock in the morning when George Peregrine finally put the book down. It had seemed to him that he heard Evie's voice in every line; over and over again he came upon turns of phrase he had heard her use, there were details that were as familiar to him as to her; there was no doubt about it; it was her own story she had told, and it was as plain as anything could be that she had had a lover and her lover had died. It was not anger so much that he felt, nor horror or dismay, though he was dismayed and he was horrified, but amazement. It was as inconceivable that Evie should have had a love affair, and a wildly passionate one at that, as that the trout in a glass case over the chimney piece in his study, the finest he had ever caught, should suddenly wag its tail. He understood now the meaning of the amused look he had seen in the eyes of that man he had spoken with at the club, he understood why Daphne when she was talking about the book had seemed to be enjoying a private joke, and why those two women at the cocktail party had tittered when he strolled past them.

He broke out into a sweat. Then on a sudden he was seized with fury and he jumped up to go and awake Evie and ask her sternly for an explanation. But he stopped at the door. After all what proof had he? A book. He remembered that he'd told Evie he thought it jolly good. True, he hadn't read it, but he'd pretended he had. He would look a perfect fool if he had to admit that.

"I must watch my step," he muttered.

120   He made up his mind to wait for two or three days and think it all over. Then he'd decide what to do. He went to bed, but he couldn't sleep for a long time.

"Evie," he kept on saying to himself, "Evie, of all people."

They met at breakfast next morning as usual. Evie was as she always was, quiet, demure and self-possessed, a middle-aged woman who made no effort to look younger than she was, a woman who had nothing of what he still called It. He looked at her as he hadn't looked at her for years. She had her usual placid serenity. Her pale blue eyes were untroubled. There was no sign of guilt on her candid brow. She made the same little casual remarks she always made.

"It's nice to get back to the country again after those two hectic days in London. What are you going to do this morning?"

It was incomprehensible.

125   Three days later he went to see his solicitor. Henry Blane was an old friend of George's as well as his lawyer. He had a place not far from Peregrine's and for years they had shot over one another's preserves. For two days a week he was a busy country gentleman and for the other five a busy lawyer in Sheffield. He was a tall, robust fellow, with a boisterous manner and a jovial laugh, which suggested that he liked to be looked upon essentially as a sportsman and a good fellow and only incidentally as a lawyer. But he was shrewd and worldly-wise.

"Well, George, what's brought you here today?" he boomed as the Colonel was shown into his office. "Have a good time in London? I'm taking my missus up for a few days next week. How's Evie?"

"It's about Evie I've come to see you," said Peregrine, giving him a suspicious look. "Have you read her book?"

His sensitivity had been sharpened during those last days of troubled thought and he was conscious of a faint change in the lawyer's expression. It was as though he were suddenly on his guard.

"Yes, I've read it. Great success, isn't it? Fancy Evie breaking out into poetry. Wonders will never cease."

130   George Peregrine was inclined to lose his temper.

"It's made me look a perfect damned fool."

"Oh, what nonsense, George! There's no harm in Evie's writing a book. You ought to be jolly proud of her."

"Don't talk such rot. It's her own story. You know it and everyone else knows it. I suppose I'm the only one who doesn't know who her lover was."

"There is such a thing as imagination, old boy. There's no reason to suppose the whole thing isn't just made up."

135   "Look here, Henry, we've known one another all our lives. We've had all sorts of good times together. Be honest with me. Can you look me in the face and tell me you believe it's a made-up story?"

Henry Blane moved uneasily in his chair. He was disturbed by the distress in old George's voice.

"You've got no right to ask me a question like that. Ask Evie."

"I daren't," George answered after an anguished pause. "I'm afraid she'd tell me the truth."

There was an uncomfortable silence.

140   "Who was the chap?"

Henry Blane looked at him straight in the eye.

"I don't know, and if I did I wouldn't tell you."

"You swine. Don't you see what a position I'm in? Do you think it's very pleasant to be made absolutely ridiculous?"

The lawyer lit a cigarette and for some moments silently puffed it.

145   "I don't see what I can do for you," he said at last.

"You've got private detectives you employ, I suppose. I want you to put them on the job and let them find everything out."

"It's not very pretty to put detectives on one's wife, old boy; and besides, taking for granted for a moment that Evie had an affair, it was a good many years ago and I don't suppose it would be possible to find a thing. They seem to have covered their tracks pretty carefully."

"I don't care. You put the detectives on. I want to know the truth."

"I won't, George. If you're determined to do that you'd better consult someone else. And look here, even if you got evidence that Evie had been unfaithful to you what would you do with it? You'd look rather silly divorcing your wife because she'd committed adultery ten years ago."

150   "At all events I could have it out with her."

"You can do that now, but you know just as well as I do that if you do she'll leave you. D'you want her to do that?"

George gave him an unhappy look.

"I don't know. I always thought she'd been a damned good wife to me. She runs the house perfectly, we never have any servant trouble; she's done wonders with the garden and she's splendid with all the village people. But damn it, I have my self-respect to think of. How can I go on living with her when I know that she was grossly unfaithful to me?"

"Have you always been faithful to her?"

155   "More or less, you know. After all we've been married for nearly twenty-four years and Evie was never much for bed."

The solicitor slightly raised his eyebrows, but George was too intent on what he was saying to notice.

"I don't deny that I've had a bit of fun now and then. A man wants it. Women are different."

"We only have men's word for that," said Henry Blane, with a faint smile.

"Evie's absolutely the last woman I'd have suspected of kicking over the traces. I mean, she's a very fastidious, reticent woman. What on earth made her write the damned book?"

160   "I suppose it was a very poignant experience and perhaps it was a relief to her to get it off her chest like that."

"Well, if she had to write it why the devil didn't she write it under an assumed name?"

"She used her maiden name. I suppose she thought that was enough and it would have been if the book hadn't had this amazing boom."

George Peregrine and the lawyer were sitting opposite one another with a desk between them. George, his elbow on the desk, his cheek resting on his hand, frowned at his thought.

"It's so rotten not to know what sort of a chap he was. One can't even tell if he was by way of being a gentleman. I mean, for all I know he may have been a farmhand or a clerk in a lawyer's office."

165   Henry Blane did not permit himself to smile and when he answered there was in his eyes a kindly, tolerant look.

"Knowing Evie so well I think the probabilities are that he was all right. Anyhow I'm sure he wasn't a clerk in my office."

"It's been such a shock to me," the Colonel sighed. "I thought she was fond of me. She couldn't have written that book unless she hated me."

"Oh, I don't believe that. I don't think she's capable of hatred."

"You're not going to pretend that she loves me."

170   "No."

"Well, what does she feel for me?"

Henry Blane leaned back in his swivel chair and looked at George reflectively.

"Indifference, I should say."

The Colonel gave a little shudder and reddened.

175   "After all, you're not in love with her, are you?"

George Peregrine did not answer directly.

"It's been a great blow to me not to have any children, but I've never let her see that I think she's let me down. I've always been kind to her. Within reasonable limits I've tried to do my duty by her."

The lawyer passed a large hand over his mouth to conceal the smile that trembled on his lips.

"It's been such an awful shock to me," Peregrine went on. "Damn it all, even ten years ago Evie was no chicken, and God knows she wasn't much to look at. It's so ugly." He sighed deeply. "What would *you* do in my place?"

180   "Nothing."

George Peregrine drew himself bolt upright in his chair and he looked at Henry with the stern, set face that he must have worn when he inspected his regiment.

"I can't overlook a thing like this. I've been made a laughing-stock. I can never hold up my head again."

"Nonsense," said the lawyer sharply, and then in a pleasant, kindly manner: "Listen, old boy: the man's dead; it all happened a long while back. Forget it. Talk to people about Evie's book, rave about it, tell 'em how proud you are of her. Behave as though you had so much confidence in her, you *knew* she could never have been unfaithful to you. The world moves so quickly and people's memories are so short. They'll forget."

"I shan't forget."

185   "You're both middle-aged people. She probably does a great deal more for you than

you think and you'd be awfully lonely without her. I don't think it matters if you don't forget. It'll be all to the good if you can get it into that thick head of yours that there's a lot more in Evie than you ever had the gumption to see."

"Damn it all, you talk as if *I* was to blame."

"No, I don't think you were to blame, but I'm not so sure that Evie was either. I don't suppose she wanted to fall in love with this boy. D'you remember those verses right at the end? The impression they gave me was that though she was shattered by his death, in a strange sort of way she welcomed it. All through she'd been aware of the fragility of the tie that bound them. He died in the full flush of his first love and had never known that love so seldom endures; he'd only known its bliss and beauty. In her own bitter grief she found solace in the thought that he'd been spared all sorrow."

"All that's a bit above my head, old boy. I see more or less what you mean."

George Peregrine stared unhappily at the inkstand on the desk. He was silent and the lawyer looked at him with curious, yet sympathetic eyes.

190   "Do you realize what courage she must have had never by a sign to show how dreadfully unhappy she was?" he said gently.

Colonel Peregrine sighed.

"I'm broken. I suppose you're right; it's no good crying over spilt milk and it would only make things worse if I made a fuss."

"Well?"

George Peregrine gave a pitiful little smile.

195   "I'll take your advice. I'll do nothing. Let them think me a damned fool and to hell with them. The truth is, I don't know what I'd do without Evie. But I'll tell you what, there's one thing I shall never understand till my dying day: What in the name of heaven did the fellow ever see in her?"

Comments and Questions

It is uncommonly profitable to compare the method and results of Chekhov's "On the Road" (p. 220) with those of Maugham's story. Each writer has a method and subject quite different from the other's. Maugham is critical of Chekhov's method and results, particularly because Chekhov does not rely on plot, because, from Maugham's point of view, he tells no story. "If you try to tell one of his stories," says Maugham, "you will find that there is nothing to tell." For Maugham, apparently Chekhov's stories have a middle, but no beginning or end. Here, Maugham could be commenting about "On the Road": "If you could take two or three persons, describe their mutual relations and leave it at that, why then it wasn't hard to write a story. . . ." Both Chekhov and Maugham have had a tremendous influence on the short story, and it would be naïve to conclude that one is right, the other wrong. As Henry James said, "The House of Fiction has . . . not one window, but a million. . . ."

1. The tone and atmosphere of "On the Road" and "The Colonel's Lady" are quite different. How does each writer achieve them, and with what results? This is a large question, and it requires a comprehensive, thoughtful answer. Perhaps the answers to the following questions will help.

2. In what ways does Maugham comment on the action of the story? Consider especially his *indirect* comments; for example, the scene in which Peregrine meets the critic Dashwood. We seem to have a clear idea about Maugham's attitude toward his characters— are we so clear about Chekhov's attitude?

3. Assuming that you enjoyed both stories, describe what you enjoyed about each one. Does the word *enjoy* exactly describe your reaction to *both* stories?

4. We recognize that Chekhov's structure of action differs considerably from Maugham's. Is one better than the other or is each one designed to produce different and *justifiable* results?

5. Is one author more serious than the other, or is it simply that one is Russian and the other British? If the latter part of this question is quite meaningless to you, state your case. Did you laugh at all as you read either story? If we laugh at a serious story, do we discredit it?

Joyce Carol Oates (1938–   )
In the Region of Ice

Sister Irene was a tall, deft woman in her early thirties. What one could see of her face made a striking impression—serious, hard gray eyes, a long slender nose, a face waxen with thought. Seen at the right time, from the right angle, she was almost handsome. In her past teaching positions she had drawn a little upon the fact of her being young and brilliant and also a nun, but she was beginning to grow out of that.

This was a new university and an entirely new world. She had heard—of course it was true—that the Jesuit administration of this school had hired her at the last moment to save money and to head off the appointment of a man of dubious religious commitment. She had prayed for the necessary energy to get her through this first semester. She had no trouble with teaching itself; once she stood before a classroom she felt herself capable of anything. It was the world immediately outside the classroom that confused and alarmed her, though she let none of this show—the cynicism of her colleagues, the indifference of many of the students, and, above all, the looks she got that told her nothing much would be expected of her because she was a nun. This took energy, strength. At times she had the idea that she was on trial and that the excuses she made to herself about her discomfort were only the common excuses made by guilty people. But in front of a class she had no time to worry about herself or the conflicts in her mind. She became, once and for all, a figure existing only for the benefit of others, an instrument by which the facts were communicated.

About two weeks after the semester began, Sister Irene noticed a new student in her class. He was slight and fair-haired, and his face was blank, but not blank by accident, blank on purpose, suppressed and restricted into a dumbness that looked hysterical. She was prepared for him before he raised his hand, and when she saw his arm jerk, as if he had at last lost control of it, she nodded to him without hesitation.

"Sister, how can this be reconciled with Shakespeare's vision in *Hamlet?* How can these opposing views be in the same mind?"

5   Students glanced at him, mildly surprised. He did not belong in the class, and this was mysterious, but his manner was urgent and blind.

"There is no need to reconcile opposing views," Sister Irene said, leaning forward against the podium. "In one play Shakespeare suggests one vision, in another play another; the plays are not simultaneous creations, and even if they were, we never demand a logical—"

"We must demand a logical consistency," the young man said. "The idea of education is itself predicated upon consistency, order, sanity—"

He had interrupted her, and she hardened her face against him—for his sake, not her own, since she did not really care. But he noticed nothing. "Please see me after class," she said.

After class the young man hurried up to her.

10   "Sister Irene, I hope you didn't mind my visiting today. I'd heard some things, interesting things," he said. He stared at her, and something in her face allowed him to smile. "I . . . could we talk in your office? Do you have time?"

They walked down to her office. Sister Irene sat at her desk, and the young man sat facing her; for a moment they were self-conscious and silent.

"Well, I suppose you know—I'm a Jew," he said.

Sister Irene stared at him. "Yes?" she said.

"What am I doing at a Catholic university, huh?" He grinned. "That's what you want to know."

15   She made a vague movement of her hand to show that she had no thoughts on this, nothing at all, but he seemed not to catch it. He was sitting on the edge of the straight-backed chair. She saw that he was young but did not really look young. There were harsh lines on either side of his mouth, as if he had misused that youthful mouth somehow. His skin was almost as pale as hers, his eyes were dark and not quite in focus. He looked at her and through her and around her, as his voice surrounded them both. His voice was a little shrill at times.

"Listen, I did the right thing today—visiting your class! God, what a lucky accident it was; some jerk mentioned you, said you were a good teacher—I thought, what a laugh! These people know about good teachers here? But yes, listen, yes, I'm not kidding—you are good. I mean that."

Sister Irene frowned. "I don't quite understand what all this means."

He smiled and waved aside her formality, as if he knew better. "Listen, I got my B.A. at Columbia, then I came back here to this crappy city. I mean, I did it on purpose, I wanted to come back. I wanted to. I have my reasons for doing things. I'm on a three-thousand-dollar fellowship," he said, and waited for that to impress her. "You know, I could have gone almost anywhere with that fellowship, and I came back home here—my home's in the city—and enrolled here. This was last year. This is my second year. I'm working on a thesis. I mean I was, my master's thesis—but the hell with that. What I want to ask you is this: Can I enroll in your class, is it too late? We have to get special permission if we're late."

Sister Irene felt something nudging her, some uneasiness in him that was pleading with her not to be offended by his abrupt, familiar manner. He seemed to be promising another self, a better self, as if his fair, childish, almost cherubic face were doing tricks to distract her from what his words said.

20   "Are you in English studies?" she asked.

"I was in history. Listen," he said, and his mouth did something odd, drawing itself down into a smile that made the lines about it deepen like knives, "listen, they kicked me out."

He sat back, watching her. He crossed his legs. He took out a package of cigarettes and offered her one. Sister Irene shook her head, staring at his hands. They were small and stubby and might have belonged to a ten-year-old, and the nails were a strange near-violet color. It took him awhile to extract a cigarette.

"Yeah, kicked me out. What do you think of that?"

"I don't understand."

25   "My master's thesis was coming along beautifully, and then this bastard—I mean, excuse me, this professor, I won't pollute your office with his name—he started making criticisms, he said some things were unacceptable, he—" The boy leaned forward and hunched his narrow shoulders in a parody of secrecy. "We had an argument. I told him some frank things, things only a broad-minded person could hear about himself. That takes courage, right? He didn't have it! He kicked me out of the master's program, so now I'm coming into English. Literature is greater than history; European history is one big pile of garbage. Sky-high. Filth and rotting corpses, right? Aristotle says that poetry is higher than history; he's right; in your class today I suddenly realized that this is my field, Shakespeare, only Shakespeare is—"

Sister Irene guessed that he was going to say that only Shakespeare was equal to him, and she caught the moment of recognition and hesitation, the half-raised arm, the keen, frowning forehead, the narrowed eyes; then he thought better of it and did not end the sentence. "The students in your class are mainly negligible, I can tell you that. You're new here, and I've been here a year—I would have finished my studies last year but my father got sick, he was hospitalized, I couldn't take exams and it was a mess—but I'll make it through English in one year or drop dead. I can do it, I can do anything. I'll take six courses at once—" He broke off, breathless. Sister Irene tried to smile. "All right then, it's settled? You'll let me in? Have I missed anything so far?"

He had no idea of the rudeness of his question. Sister Irene, feeling suddenly exhausted, said, "I'll give you a syllabus of the course."

"Fine! Wonderful!"

He got to his feet eagerly. He looked through the schedule, muttering to himself, making favorable noises. It struck Sister Irene that she was making a mistake to let him in. There were these moments when one had to make an intelligent decision. . . . But she was sympathetic with him, yes. She was sympathetic with something about him.

30   She found out his name the next day: Allen Weinstein.

After this she came to her Shakespeare class with a sense of excitement. It became clear to her at once that Weinstein was the most intelligent student in her class. Until he had enrolled, she had not understood what was lacking, a mind that could appreciate her own. Within a week his jagged, protean mind had alienated the other students, and though he sat in the center of the class, he seemed totally alone, encased by a miniature world of his own. When he spoke of the "frenetic humanism of the High Renaissance," Sister Irene dreaded the raised eyebrows and mocking smiles of the other students, who no longer bothered to look at Weinstein. She wanted to defend him, but she never did, because there was something rude and dismal about his knowledge; he used it like a weapon, talking passionately of Nietzsche and Goethe and Freud until Sister Irene would be forced to close discussion.

In meditation, alone, she often thought of him. When she tried to talk about him to a young nun, Sister Carlotta, everything sounded gross. "But no, he's an excellent student," she insisted. "I'm very grateful to have him in class. It's just that . . . he thinks ideas are real." Sister Carlotta, who loved literature also, had been forced to teach grade-school arithmetic for the last four years. That might have been why she said, a little sharply, "You don't think ideas are real?"

Sister Irene acquiesced with a smile, but of course she did not think so: only reality is real.

When Weinstein did not show up for class on the day the first paper was due, Sister Irene's heart sank, and the sensation was somehow a familiar one. She began her lecture and kept waiting for the door to open and for him to hurry noisily back to his seat, grinning an apology toward her—but nothing happened.

35   If she had been deceived by him, she made herself think angrily, it was as a teacher and not as a woman. He had promised her nothing.

Weinstein appeared the next day near the steps of the liberal arts building. She heard someone running behind her, a breathless exclamation: "Sister Irene!" She turned and saw him, panting and grinning in embarrassment. He wore a dark-blue suit with a necktie, and he looked, despite his childish face, like a little old man; there was something oddly precarious and fragile about him. "Sister Irene, I owe you an apology, right?" He raised his eyebrows and smiled a sad, forlorn, yet irritatingly conspiratorial smile. "The first paper—not in on time, and I know what your rules are. . . . You won't accept late papers, I know—that's good discipline, I'll do that when I teach too. But, unavoidably, I was unable to come to school yesterday. There are many—many—" He gulped for breath, and Sister Irene had the startling sense of seeing the real Weinstein stare out at her, a terrified prisoner behind the confident voice. "There are many complications in family life. Perhaps you are unaware—I mean—"

She did not like him, but she felt this sympathy, something tugging and nagging at her the way her parents had competed for her love so many years before. They had been whining, weak people, and out of their wet need for affection, the girl she had been (her name was Yvonne) had emerged stronger than either of them, contemptuous of tears because she had seen so many. But Weinstein was different; he was not simply weak— perhaps he was not weak at all—but his strength was confused and hysterical. She felt her customary rigidity as a teacher begin to falter. "You may turn your paper in today if you have it," she said, frowning.

Weinstein's mouth jerked into an incredulous grin. "Wonderful! Marvelous!" he said. "You are very understanding, Sister Irene, I must say. I must say . . . I didn't expect, really . . " He was fumbling in a shabby old briefcase for the paper. Sister Irene waited. She was prepared for another of his excuses, certain that he did not have the paper, when he suddenly straightened up and handed her something. "Here! I took the liberty of writing thirty pages instead of just fifteen," he said. He was obviously quite excited; his cheeks were mottled pink and white. "You may disagree violently with my interpretation—I expect you to, in fact I'm counting on it—but let me warn you, I have the exact proof, right here in the play itself!" He was thumping at a book, his voice growing louder and shriller. Sister Irene, startled, wanted to put her hand over his mouth and soothe him.

"Look," he said breathlessly, "may I talk with you? I have a class now I hate, I loathe, I can't bear to sit through! Can I talk with you instead?"

40   Because she was nervous, she stared at the title page of the paper: " 'Erotic Melodies in *Romeo and Juliet*' by Allen Weinstein, Jr."

"All right?" he said. "Can we walk around here? Is it all right? I've been anxious to talk with you about some things you said in class."

She was reluctant, but he seemed not to notice. They walked slowly along the shaded campus paths. Weinstein did all the talking, of course, and Sister Irene recognized nothing in his cascade of words that she had mentioned in class. "The humanist must be committed to the totality of life," he said passionately. "This is the failing one finds everywhere in the academic world! I found it in New York and I found it here and I'm no ingénu, I don't go around with my mouth hanging open—I'm experienced, look, I've been to Europe, I've lived in Rome! I went everywhere in Europe except Germany, I don't talk about Germany . . . Sister Irene, think of the significant men in the last century, the men who've changed the world! Jews, right? Marx, Freud, Einstein! Not that I believe Marx, Marx is a madman . . . and Freud, no, my sympathies are with spiritual humanism. I believe that the Jewish race is the exclusive . . . the exclusive, what's the word, the exclusive means by which humanism will be extended. . . . Humanism begins by excluding the Jew, and now," he said with a high, surprised laugh, "the Jew will perfect it. After the Nazis, only the Jew is authorized to understand humanism, its limitations and its possibilities. So, I say that the humanist is committed to life in its totality and not just to his profession! The religious person is totally religious, he is his religion! What else? I recognize in you a humanist and a religious person—"

But he did not seem to be talking to her or even looking at her.

"Here, read this," he said, "I wrote it last night." It was a long free-verse poem, typed on a typewriter whose ribbon was worn out.

45   "There's this trouble with my father, a wonderful man, a lovely man, but his health—his strength is fading, do you see? What must it be to him to see his son growing up? I mean, I'm a man now, he's getting old, weak, his health is bad—it's hell, right? I sympathize with him. I'd do anything for him, I'd cut open my veins, anything for a father—right? That's why I wasn't in school yesterday," he said, and his voice dropped for the last sentence, as if he had been dragged back to earth by a fact.

Sister Irene tried to read the poem, then pretended to read it. A jumble of words dealing with "life" and "death" and "darkness" and "love." "What do you think?" Weinstein said nervously, trying to read it over her shoulder and crowding against her.

"It's very . . . passionate," Sister Irene said.

This was the right comment; he took the poem back from her in silence, his face flushed with excitement. "Here, at this school, I have few people to talk with. I haven't shown anyone else that poem." He looked at her with his dark, intense eyes, and Sister Irene felt them focus upon her. She was terrified at what he was trying to do—he was trying to force her into a human relationship.

"Thank you for your paper," she said, turning away.

50   When he came the next day, ten minutes late, he was haughty and disdainful. He had nothing to say and sat with his arms folded. Sister Irene took back with her to the convent a feeling of betrayal and confusion. She had been hurt. It was absurd, and yet—She spent too much time thinking about him, as if he were somehow a kind of crystallization of her own loneliness; but she had no right to think so much of him. She did not want to think of him or of her loneliness. But Weinstein did so much more than think of his predicament; he embodied it, he acted it out, and that was perhaps why he fascinated her. It was as if he were doing a dance for her, a dance of shame and agony and delight, and so long as he did it, she was safe. She felt embarrassment for him, but also anxiety; she wanted to protect him. When the dean of the graduate school questioned her about Weinstein's work, she insisted that he was an "excellent" student, though she knew the dean had not wanted to hear that.

She prayed for guidance, she spent hours on her devotions, she was closer to her vocation than she had been for some years. Life at the convent became tinged with unreality, a misty distortion that took its tone from the glowering skies of the city at night, identical smokestacks ranged against the clouds and giving to the sky the excrement of the populated and successful earth. This city was not her city, this world was not her world. She felt no pride in knowing this, it was a fact. The little convent was not like an island in the center of this noisy world, but rather a kind of hole or crevice the world did not bother with, something of no interest. The convent's rhythm of life had nothing to do with the world's rhythm, it did not violate or alarm it in any way. Sister Irene tried to draw together the fragments of her life and synthesize them somehow in her vocation as a nun: she was a nun, she was recognized as a nun and had given herself happily to that life, she had a name, a place, she had dedicated her superior intelligence to the Church, she worked without pay and without expecting gratitude, she had given up pride, she did not think of herself but only of her work and her vocation, she did not think of anything external to these, she saturated herself daily in the knowledge that she was involved in the mystery of Christianity.

A daily terror attended this knowledge, however, for she sensed herself being drawn by that student, that Jewish boy, into a relationship she was not ready for. She wanted to cry out in fear that she was being forced into the role of a Christian, and what did that mean? What could her studies tell her? What could the other nuns tell her? She was alone, no one could help; he was making her into a Christian, and to her that was a mystery, a thing of terror, something others slipped on the way they slipped on their clothes, casually and thoughtlessly, but to her a magnificent and terrifying wonder.

For days she carried Weinstein's paper, marked A, around with her; he did not come to class. One day she checked with the graduate office and was told that Weinstein had called in to say his father was ill and that he would not be able to attend classes for a while. "He's strange, I remember him," the secretary said. "He missed all his exams last spring and made a lot of trouble. He was in and out of here every day."

So there was no more of Weinstein for a while, and Sister Irene stopped expecting him to hurry into class. Then, one morning, she found a letter from him in her mailbox.

55   He had printed it in black ink, very carefully, as if he had not trusted handwriting. The return address was in bold letters that, like his voice, tried to grab onto her: Birchcrest Manor. Somewhere north of the city. "Dear Sister Irene," the block letters said, "I am doing well here and have time for reading and relaxing. The Manor is delightful. My doctor here is an excellent, intelligent man who has time for me, unlike my former doctor. If you have time, you might drop in on my father, who worries about me too much, I think, and explain to him what my condition is. He doesn't seem to understand. I feel about this new life the way that boy, what's his name, in *Measure for Measure*, feels about the prospects of a different life; you remember what he says to his sister when she visits him in prison, how he is looking forward to an escape into another world. Perhaps you could *explain* this to my father and he would stop worrying." The letter ended with the father's name and address, in letters that were just a little too big. Sister Irene, walking slowly down the corridor as she read the letter, felt her eyes cloud over with tears. She was cold with fear, it was something she had never experienced before. She knew what Weinstein was trying to tell her, and the desperation of his attempt made it all the more pathetic; he did not deserve this, why did God allow him to suffer so?

She read through Claudio's speech to his sister, in *Measure for Measure:*[1]

> *Ay, but to die, and go we know not where;*
> *To lie in cold obstruction*[2] *and to rot;*
> *This sensible warm motion*[3] *to become*
> *A kneaded clod;*[4] *and the delighted spirit*
> *To bathe in fiery floods, or to reside*
> *In thrilling*[5] *region of thick-ribbèd ice,*
> *To be imprison'd in the viewless*[6] *winds*
> *And blown with restless violence round about*
> *The pendent world; or to be worse than worst*
> *Of those that lawless and incertain thought*

[1]III. i. 118–132.   [2]Obstruction: that is, stiff and cold.   [3]This sensible warm motion: this feeling, living body.   [4]Kneaded clod: that is, turned into earth.   [5]Thrilling: freezing.   [6]Viewless: invisible.

Imagine howling! 'Tis too horrible!
The weariest and most loathed worldly life
That age, ache, penury, and imprisonment
Can lay on nature is a paradise
To what we fear of death.

Sister Irene called the father's number that day. "Allen Weinstein residence, who may I say is calling?" a woman said, bored. "May I speak to Mr. Weinstein? It's urgent—about his son," Sister Irene said. There was a pause at the other end. "You want to talk to his mother, maybe?" the woman said. "His mother? Yes, his mother, then. Please. It's very important."

She talked with this strange, unsuspected woman, a disembodied voice that suggested absolutely no face, and insisted upon going over that afternoon. The woman was nervous, but Sister Irene, who was a university professor, after all, knew enough to hide her own nervousness. She kept waiting for the woman to say, "Yes, Allen has mentioned you . . ." but nothing happened.

She persuaded Sister Carlotta to ride over with her. This urgency of hers was something they were all amazed by. They hadn't suspected that the set of her gray eyes could change to this blurred, distracted alarm, this sense of mission that seemed to have come to her from nowhere. Sister Irene drove across the city in the late afternoon traffic, with the high whining noises from residential streets where trees were being sawed down in pieces. She understood now the secret, sweet wildness that Christ must have felt, giving himself for man, dying for the billions of men who would never know of him and never understand the sacrifice. For the first time she approached the realization of that great act. In her troubled mind the city traffic was jumbled and yet oddly coherent, an image of the world that was always out of joint with what was happening in it, its inner history struggling with its external spectacle. This sacrifice of Christ's, so mysterious and legendary now, almost lost in time—it was that by which Christ transcended both God and man at one moment, more than man because of his fate to do what no other man could do, and more than God because no god could suffer as he did. She felt a flicker of something close to madness.

60   She drove nervously, uncertainly, afraid of missing the street and afraid of finding it too, for while one part of her rushed forward to confront these people who had betrayed their son, another part of her would have liked nothing so much as to be waiting as usual for the summons to dinner, safe in her room. . . . When she found the street and turned onto it, she was in a state of breathless excitement. Here lawns were bright green and marred with only a few leaves, magically clean, and the houses were enormous and pompous, a mixture of styles: ranch houses, colonial houses, French country houses, white-bricked wonders with curving glass and clumps of birch trees somehow encircled by white concrete. Sister Irene stared as if she had blundered into another world. This was a kind of heaven, and she was too shabby for it.

The Weinstein's house was the strangest one of all: it looked like a small Alpine lodge, with an inverted-V-shaped front entrance. Sister Irene drove up the black-topped driveway and let the car slow to a stop; she told Sister Carlotta she would not be long.

At the door she was met by Weinstein's mother, a small, nervous woman with hands like her son's. "Come in, come in," the woman said. She had once been beautiful, that was clear, but now in missing beauty she was not handsome or even attractive but looked ruined and perplexed, the misshapen swelling of her white-blond professionally set hair like a cap lifting up from her surprised face. "He'll be right in. Allen?" she called, "our visitor is here." They went into the living room. There was a grand piano at one end and an organ at the other. In between were scatterings of brilliant modern furniture in conversational groups, and several puffed-up white rugs on the polished floor. Sister Irene could not stop shivering.

"Professor, it's so strange, but let me say when the phone rang I had a feeling—I had a feeling," the woman said, with damp eyes. Sister Irene sat, and the woman hovered about her. "Should I call you Professor? We don't . . . you know . . . we don't understand the technicalities that go with—Allen, my son, wanted to go here to the Catholic school; I told my husband why not? Why fight? It's the thing these days, they do anything they want for knowledge. And he had to come home, you know. He couldn't take care of himself in New York, that was the beginning of the trouble. . . . Should I call you Professor?"

"You can call me Sister Irene."

65 "Sister Irene?" the woman said, touching her throat in awe, as if something intimate and unexpected had happened.

Then Weinstein's father appeared, hurrying. He took long, impatient strides. Sister Irene stared at him and in that instant doubted everything—he was in his fifties, a tall, sharply handsome man, heavy but not fat, holding his shoulders back with what looked like an effort, but holding them back just the same. He wore a dark suit and his face was flushed, as if he had run a long distance.

"Now," he said, coming to Sister Irene and with a precise wave of his hand motioning his wife off, "Now, let's straighten this out. A lot of confusion over that kid, eh?" He pulled a chair over, scraping it across a rug and pulling one corner over, so that its brown underside was exposed. "I came home early just for this, Libby phoned me. Sister, you got a letter from him, right?"

The wife looked at Sister Irene over her husband's head as if trying somehow to coach her, knowing that this man was so loud and impatient that no one could remember anything in his presence.

"A letter—yes—today—"

70 "He says what in it? You got the letter, eh? Can I see it?"

She gave it to him and wanted to explain, but he silenced her with a flick of his hand. He read through the letter so quickly that Sister Irene thought perhaps he was trying to impress her with his skill at reading. "So?" he said, raising his eyes, smiling, "so what is this? He's happy out there, he says. He doesn't communicate with us any more, but he writes to you and says he's happy—what's that? I mean, what the hell is that?"

"But he isn't happy. He wants to come home," Sister Irene said. It was so important that she make him understand that she could not trust her voice; goaded by this man, it might suddenly turn shrill, as his son's did. "Someone must read their letters before they're mailed, so he tried to tell me something by making an allusion to—"

"What?"

"—an allusion to a play, so that I would know. He may be thinking suicide, he must be very unhappy—"

75 She ran out of breath. Weinstein's mother had begun to cry, but the father was shaking his head jerkily back and forth. "Forgive me, Sister, but it's a lot of crap, he needs the hospital, he needs help—right? It costs me fifty a day out there, and they've got the best place in the state, I figure it's worth it. He needs help, that kid, what do I care if he's unhappy? He's unbalanced!" he said angrily. "You want us to get him out again? We argued with the judge for two hours to get him in, an acquaintance of mine. Look, he can't control himself—he was smashing things here, he was hysterical. They need help, lady, and you do something about it fast! You do something! We made up our minds to do something and we did it! This letter—what the hell is this letter? He never talked like that to us!"

"But he means the opposite of what he says—"

"Then he's crazy! I'm the first to admit it." He was perspiring, and his face had darkened. "I've got no pride left this late. He's a little bastard, you want to know? He calls me names, he's filthy, got a filthy mouth—that's being smart huh? They give him a big scholarship for his filthy mouth? I went to college too, and I got out and knew something, and I for Christ's sake did something with it; my wife is an intelligent woman, a learned woman, would you guess she does book reviews for the little newspaper out here? Intelligent isn't crazy—crazy isn't intelligent. Maybe for you at the school he writes nice papers and gets an A, but out here, around the house, he can't control himself, and we got him committed!"

"But—"

"We're fixing him up, don't worry about it!" He turned to his wife. "Libby, get out of here, I mean it. I'm sorry, but get out of here, you're making a fool of yourself, go stand in the kitchen or something, you and the goddamn maid can cry on each other's shoulders. That one in the kitchen is nuts too, they're all nuts. Sister," he said, his voice lowering, "I thank you immensely for coming out here. This is wonderful, your interest in my son. And I see he admires you—that letter there. But what about that letter? If he did want to get out, which I don't admit—he was willing to be committed, in the end he said okay himself—if he wanted out I wouldn't do it. Why? So what if he wants to come back? The next day he wants something else, what then? He's a sick kid, and I'm the first to admit it."

80   Sister Irene felt that sickness spread to her. She stood. The room was so big it seemed it must be a public place; there had been nothing personal or private about their conversation. Weinstein's mother was standing by the fireplace, sobbing. The father jumped to his feet and wiped his forehead in a gesture that was meant to help Sister Irene on her way out. "God, what a day," he said, his eyes snatching at hers for understanding, "you know—one of those days all day long? Sister, I thank you a lot. There should be more people in the world who care about others, like you. I mean that."

On the way back to the convent, the man's words returned to her, and she could not get control of them; she could not even feel anger. She had been pressed down, forced back, what could she do? Weinstein might have been watching her somehow from a barred window, and he surely would have understood. The strange idea she had had on the way over, something about understanding Christ, came back to her now and sickened her. But the sickness was small. It could be contained.

About a month after her visit to his father, Weinstein himself showed up. He was dressed in a suit as before, even the necktie was the same. He came right into her office as if he had been pushed and could not stop.

"Sister," he said, and shook her hand. He must have seen fear in her because he smiled ironically. "Look, I'm released. I'm let out of the nut house. Can I sit down?"

He sat. Sister Irene was breathing quickly, as if in the presence of an enemy who does not know he is an enemy.

85   "So, they finally let me out. I heard what you did. You talked with him, that was all I wanted. You're the only one who gave a damn. Because you're a humanist and a religious person, you respect . . . the individual. Listen," he said, whispering, "it was hell out there! Hell Birchcrest Manor! All fixed up with fancy chairs and *Life* magazines lying around— and what do they do to you? They locked me up, they gave me shock treatments! Shock treatments, how do you like that, it's discredited by everybody now—they're crazy out there themselves, sadists. They locked me up, they gave me hypodermic shots, they didn't treat me like a human being! Do you know what that is," Weinstein demanded savagely, "not to be treated like a human being? They made me an animal—for fifty dollars a day! Dirty filthy swine! Now I'm an outpatient because I stopped swearing at them. I found

somebody's bobby pin, and when I wanted to scream I pressed it under my fingernail and it stopped me—the screaming went inside and not out—so they gave me good reports, those sick bastards. Now I'm an outpatient and I can walk along the street and breathe in the same filthy exhaust from the buses like all you normal people! Christ," he said, and threw himself back against the chair.

Sister Irene stared at him. She wanted to take his hand, to make some gesture that would close the aching distance between them. "Mr. Weinstein—"

"Call me Allen!" he said sharply.

"I'm very sorry—I'm terribly sorry—"

"My own parents committed me, but of course they didn't know what it was like. It was hell," he said thickly, "and there isn't any hell except what other people do to you. The psychiatrist out there, the main shrink, he hates Jews, too, some of us were positive of that, and he's got a bigger nose than I do, a real beak." He made a noise of disgust. "A dirty bastard, a sick, dirty, pathetic bastard—all of them. Anyway, I'm getting out of here, and I came to ask you a favor."

90   "What do you mean?"

"I'm getting out. I'm leaving. I'm going up to Canada and lose myself. I'll get a job, I'll forget everything, I'll kill myself maybe—what's the difference? Look, can you lend me some money?"

"Money?"

"Just a little! I have to get to the border, I'm going to take a bus."

"But I don't have any money—"

95   "No money?" He stared at her, "You mean—you don't have any? Sure you have some!"

She stared at him as if he had asked her to do something obscene. Everthing was splotched and uncertain before her eyes.

"You must . . . you must go back," she said, "you're making a—"

"I'll pay it back. Look, I'll pay it back, can you go to where you live or something and get it? I'm in a hurry. My friends are sons of bitches: one of them pretended he didn't see me yesterday—I stood right in the middle of the sidewalk and yelled at him, I called him some appropriate names! So he didn't see me, huh? You're the only one who understands me, you understand me like a poet, you—"

"I can't help you, I'm sorry—I . . ."

100   He looked to one side of her and flashed his gaze back, as if he could control it. He seemed to be trying to clear his vision.

"You have the soul of a poet," he whispered, "you're the only one. Everybody else is rotten! Can't you lend me some money, ten dollars maybe? I have three thousand in the bank, and I can't touch it! They take everything away from me, they make me into an animal. . . . You know I'm not an animal, don't you? Don't you?"

"Of course," Sister Irene whispered.

"You could get money. Help me. Give me your hand or something, touch me, help me—please. . . ." He reached for her hand and she drew back. He stared at her and his face seemed about to crumble, like a child's. "I want something from you, but I don't know what—I want something!" he cried. "Something real! I want you to look at me like I was a human being, is that too much to ask? I have a brain, I'm alive, I'm suffering—what does that mean? Does that mean nothing? I want something real and not this phony Christian love garbage—it's all in the books, it isn't personal—I want something real—look. . . ."

He tried to take her hand again, and this time she jerked away. She got to her feet. "Mr. Weinstein," she said, "please—"

105   "You! You nun!" he said scornfully, his mouth twisted into a mock grin. "You nun! There's nothing under that ugly outfit, right? And you're not particularly smart even though you think you are; my father has more brains in his foot than you—"

He got to his feet and kicked the chair.

"You bitch!" he cried.

She shrank back against her desk as if she thought he might hit her, but he only ran out of the office.

Weinstein: the name was to become disembodied from the figure, as time went on. The semester passed, the autumn drizzle turned into snow, Sister Irene rode to school in the morning and left in the afternoon, four days a week, anonymous in her black winter cloak, quiet and stunned. University teaching was an anonymous task, each day dissociated from the rest, with no necessary sense of unity among the teachers: they came and went separately and might for a year miss a colleague who left his office five minutes before they arrived, and it did not matter.

110   She heard of Weinstein's death, his suicide by drowning, from the English Department secretary, a handsome white-haired woman who kept a transistor radio on her desk. Sister Irene was not surprised; she had been thinking of him as dead for months. "They identified him by some special television way they have now," the secretary said. "They're shipping the body back. It was up in Quebec. . . ."

Sister Irene could feel a part of herself drifting off, lured by the plains of white snow to the north, the quiet, the emptiness, the sweep of the Great Lakes up to the silence of Canada. But she called that part of herself back. She could only be one person in her lifetime. That was the ugly truth, she thought, that she could not really regret Weinstein's suffering and death; she had only one life and had already given it to someone else. He had come too late to her. Fifteen years ago, perhaps, but not now.

She was only one person, she thought, walking down the corridor in a dream. Was she safe in this single person, or was she trapped? She had only one identity. She could make only one choice. What she had done or hadn't done was the result of that choice, and how was she guilty? If she could have felt guilt, she thought, she might at least have been able to feel something.

Sherwood Anderson (1876–1941)
I'm a Fool

It was a hard jolt for me, one of the most bitterest I ever had to face. And it all came about through my own foolishness, too. Even yet sometimes, when I think of it, I want to cry or swear or kick myself. Perhaps, even now, after all this time, there will be a kind of satisfaction in making myself look cheap by telling of it.

It began at three o'clock one October afternoon as I sat in the grand stand at the fall trotting and pacing meet at Sandusky, Ohio.

To tell the truth, I felt a little foolish that I should be sitting in the grand stand at all. During the summer before I had left my home town with Harry Whitehead and, with a nigger named Burt, had taken a job as swipe with one of the two horses Harry was campaigning through the fall race meets that year. Mother cried and my sister Mildred, who wanted to get a job as a school teacher in our town that fall, stormed and scolded about the house all during the week before I left. They both thought it was something disgraceful that one of our family should take a place as a swipe with race horses. I've an idea Mildred thought my taking the place would stand in the way of her getting the job she'd been working so long for.

But after all I had to work, and there was no other work to be got. A big lumbering fellow of nineteen couldn't just hang around the house and I had got too big to mow people's lawns and sell newspapers. Little chaps who could get next to people's sympathies by their sizes were always getting jobs away from me. There was one fellow who kept saying to everyone who wanted a lawn mowed or a cistern cleaned, that he was saving money to work his way through college, and I used to lay awake nights thinking up ways to injure him without being found out. I kept thinking of wagons running over him and bricks falling on his head as he walked along the street. But never mind him.

5   I got the place with Harry and I liked Burt fine. We got along splendid together. He was a big nigger with a lazy sprawling body and soft, kind eyes, and when it came to a fight he could hit like Jack Johnson. He had Bucephalus, a big black pacing stallion that could do 2.09 or 2.10, if he had to, and I had a little gelding named Doctor Fritz that never lost a race all fall when Harry wanted him to win.

We set out from home late in July in a box car with the two horses and after that, until late November, we kept moving along to the race meets and the fairs. It was a peachey time for me, I'll say that. Sometimes now I think that boys who are raised regular in houses, and never had a fine nigger like Burt for best friend, and go to high schools and college, and never steal anything, or get drunk a little, or learn to swear from fellows who know how, or come walking up in front of a grand stand in their shirt sleeves and with dirty horsy pants on when the races are going on and the grand stand is full of people all dressed up—What's the use of talking about it? Such fellows don't know nothing at all. They've never had no opportunity.

But I did. Burt taught me how to rub down a horse and put the bandages on after a race and steam a horse out and a lot of valuable things for any man to know. He could wrap a bandage on a horse's leg so smooth that if it had been the same color you would think it was his skin, and I guess he'd have been a big driver, too, and got to the top like Murphy and Walter Cox and the others if he hadn't been black.

Gee whizz, it was fun. You got to a county seat town, maybe say on a Saturday or Sunday, and the fair began the next Tuesday and lasted until Friday afternoon. Doctor Fritz would be, say in the 2.25 trot on Tuesday afternoon and on Thursday afternoon Bucephalus would knock 'em cold in the "free-for-all" pace. It left you a lot of time to hang around and listen to horse talk, and see Burt knock some yap cold that got too gay, and you'd find out about horses and men and pick up a lot of stuff you could use all the rest of your life, if you had some sense and salted down what you heard and felt and saw.

And then at the end of the week when the race meet was over, and Harry had run home to tend up to his livery stable business, you and Burt hitched the two horses to carts and drove slow and steady across country, to the place for the next meeting, so as to not overheat the horses, etc., etc., you know.

10   Gee whizz, Gosh amighty, the nice hickorynut and beechnut and oaks and other kinds of trees along the roads, all brown and red, and the good smells, and Burt singing a song that was called Deep River, and all the country girls at the windows of houses and

everything. You can stick your colleges up your nose for all me. I guess I know where I got my education.

Why, one of those little burgs of towns you come to on the way, say now on a Saturday afternoon, and Burt says, "let's lay up here." And you did.

And you took the horses to a livery stable and fed them, and you got your good clothes out of a box and put them on.

And the town was full of farmers gaping, because they could see you were race horse people, and the kids maybe never see a nigger before and was afraid and run away when the two of us walked down their main street.

And that was before prohibition and all that foolishness, and so you went into a saloon, the two of you, and all the yaps come and stood around, and there was always someone pretended he was horsy and knew things and spoke up and began asking questions, and all you did was to lie and lie all you could about what horses you had, and I said I owned them, and then some fellow said, "Will you have a drink of whiskey" and Burt knocked his eye out the way he could say, offhand like, "Oh well, all right, I'm agreeable to a little nip. I'll split a quart with you." Gee whizz.

15   But that isn't what I want to tell my story about. We got home late in November and I promised mother I'd quit the race horses for good. There's a lot of things you've got to promise a mother because she don't know any better.

And so, there not being any work in our town any more than when I left there to go to the races, I went off to Sandusky and got a pretty good place taking care of horses for a man who owned a teaming and delivery and storage and coal and real estate business there. It was a pretty good place with good eats, and a day off each week, and sleeping on a cot in a big barn, and mostly just shovelling in hay and oats to a lot of big good-enough skates of horses, that couldn't have trotted a race with a toad. I wasn't dissatisfied and I could send money home.

And then, as I started to tell you, the fall races come to Sandusky and I got the day off and I went. I left the job at noon and had on my good clothes and my new brown derby hat, I'd just bought the Saturday before, and a stand-up collar.

First of all I went down-town and walked about with the dudes. I've always thought to myself, "put up a good front" and so I did it. I had forty dollars in my pocket and so I went into the West House, a big hotel, and walked up to the cigar stand. "Give me three twenty-five cent cigars," I said. There was a lot of horsemen and strangers and dressed-up people from other towns standing around in the lobby and in the bar, and I mingled amongst them. In the bar there was a fellow with a cane and a Windsor tie on, that it made me sick to look at him. I like a man to be a man and dress up, but not to go put on that kind of airs. So I pushed him aside, kind of rough, and had me a drink of whiskey. And then he looked at me, as though he thought maybe he'd get gay, but he changed his mind and didn't say anything. And then I had another drink of whiskey, just to show him something, and went out and had a hack out to the races, all to myself, and when I got there I bought myself the best seat I could get up in the grand stand, but didn't go in for any of these boxes. That's putting on too many airs.

And so there I was, sitting up in the grand stand as gay as you please and looking down on the swipes coming out with their horses, and with their dirty horsy pants on and the horse blankets swung over their shoulders, same as I had been doing all the year before. I liked one thing about the same as the other, sitting up there and feeling grand and being down there and looking up at the yaps and feeling grander and more important, too. One thing's about as good as another, if you take it just right. I've often said that.

20   Well, right in front of me, in the grand stand that day, there was a fellow with a couple of girls and they was about my age. The young fellow was a nice guy all right. He was the kind maybe that goes to college and then comes to be a lawyer or maybe a

newspaper editor or something like that, but he wasn't stuck on himself. There are some of that kind are all right and he was one of the ones.

He had his sister with him and another girl and the sister looked around over his shoulder, accidental at first, not intending to start anything—she wasn't that kind—and her eyes and mine happened to meet.

You know how it is. Gee, she was a peach! She had on a soft dress, kind of a blue stuff and it looked carelessly made, but was well sewed and made and everything. I knew that much. I blushed when she looked right at me and so did she. She was the nicest girl I've ever seen in my life. She wasn't stuck on herself and she could talk proper grammar without being like a school teacher or something like that. What I mean is, she was O.K. I think maybe her father was well-to-do, but not rich to make her chesty because she was his daughter, as some are. Maybe he owned a drug store or a drygoods store in their home town, or something like that. She never told me and I never asked.

My own people are all O.K. too, when you come to that. My grandfather was Welsh and over in the old country, in Wales he was—But never mind that.

The first heat of the first race come off and the young fellow setting there with the two girls left them and went down to make a bet. I knew what he was up to, but he didn't talk big and noisy and let everyone around know he was a sport, as some do. He wasn't that kind. Well, he come back and I heard him tell the two girls what horse he'd bet on, and when the heat trotted they all half got to their feet and acted in the excited, sweaty way people do when they've got money down on a race, and the horse they bet on is up there pretty close at the end, and they think maybe he'll come on with a rush, but he never does because he hasn't got the old juice in him, come right down to it.

25   And then, pretty soon, the horses came out for the 2.18 pace and there was a horse in it I knew. He was a horse Bob French had in his string but Bob didn't own him. He was a horse owned by a Mr. Mathers down at Marietta, Ohio.

This Mr. Mathers had a lot of money and owned some coal mines or something and he had a swell place out in the country, and he was stuck on race horses, but was a Presbyterian or something, and I think more than likely his wife was one, too, maybe a stiffer one than himself. So he never raced his horses hisself, and the story round the Ohio race tracks was that when one of his horses got ready to go to the races he turned him over to Bob French and pretended to his wife he was sold.

So Bob had the horses and he did pretty much as he pleased and you can't blame Bob, at least, I never did. Sometimes he was out to win and sometimes he wasn't. I never cared much about that when I was swiping a horse. What I did want to know was that my horse had the speed and could go out in front, if you wanted him to.

And, as I'm telling you, there was Bob in this race with one of Mr. Mathers' horses, was named "About Ben Ahem"[1] or something like that, and was fast as a streak. He was a gelding and had a mark of 2.21, but could step in .08 or .09.

Because when Burt and I were out, as I've told you, the year before, there was a nigger, Burt knew, worked for Mr. Mathers and we went out there one day when we didn't have no race on at the Marietta Fair and our boss Harry was gone home.

30   And so everyone was gone to the fair but just this one nigger and he took us all through Mr. Mathers' swell house and he and Burt tapped a bottle of wine Mr. Mathers had hid in his bedroom, back in a closet, without his wife knowing, and he showed us this Ahem horse. Burt was always stuck on being a driver but didn't have much chance to get to the top, being a nigger, and he and the other nigger gulped the whole bottle of wine and Burt got a little lit up.

---

[1] Intentional misspelling for "Abou Ben Adhem," a poem by Leigh Hunt about a man, whose "name led all the rest."

So the nigger let Burt take this About Ben Ahem and step him a mile in a track Mr. Mathers had all to himself, right there on the farm. And Mr. Mathers had one child, a daughter, kinda sick and not very good looking, and she came home and we had to hustle and get About Ben Ahem stuck back in the barn.

I'm only telling you to get everything straight. At Sandusky, that afternoon I was at the fair, this young fellow with the two girls was fussed, being with the girls and losing his bet. You know how a fellow is that way. One of them was his girl and the other his sister. I had figured that out.

"Gee whizz," I says to myself, "I'm going to give him the dope."

He was mighty nice when I touched him on the shoulder. He and the girls were nice to me right from the start and clear to the end. I'm not blaming them.

35   And so he leaned back and I give him the dope on About Ben Ahem. "Don't bet a cent on this first heat because he'll go like an oxen hitched to a plow, but when the first heat is over go right down and lay on your pile." That's what I told him.

Well, I never saw a fellow treat any one sweller. There was a fat man sitting beside the little girl, that had looked at me twice by this time, and I at her, and both blushing, and what did he do but have the nerve to turn and ask the fat man to get up and change places with me so I could set with his crowd.

Gee whizz, craps amighty. There I was. What a chump I was to go and get gay up there in the West House bar, and just because that dude was standing there with a cane and that kind of a necktie on, to go and get all balled up and drink that whiskey, just to show off.

Of course she would know, me sitting right beside her and letting her smell of my breath. I could have kicked myself right down out of that grand stand and all around that race track and made a faster record than most of the skates of horses they had there that year.

Because that girl wasn't any mutt of a girl. What wouldn't I have give right then for a stick of chewing gum to chew, or a lozenger, or some licorice, or most anything. I was glad I had those twenty-five cent cigars in my pocket and right away I give that fellow one and lit one myself. Then that fat man got up and we changed places and there I was, plunked right down beside her.

40   They introduced themselves and the fellow's best girl, he had with him, was named Miss Elinor Woodbury, and her father was a manufacturer of barrels from a place called Tiffin, Ohio. And the fellow himself was named Wilbur Wessen and his sister was Miss Lucy Wessen.

I suppose it was their having such swell names that got me off my trolley. A fellow just because he has been a swipe with a race horse, and works taking care of horses for a man in the teaming, delivery, and storage business isn't any better or worse than any one else. I've often thought that, and said it too.

But you know how a fellow is. There's something in that kind of nice clothes, and the kind of nice eyes she had, and the way she had looked at me, awhile before, over her brother's shoulder, and me looking back at her, and both of us blushing.

I couldn't show her up for a boob, could I?

I made a fool of myself, that's what I did. I said my name was Walter Mathers from Marietta, Ohio, and then I told all three of them the smashingest lie you ever heard. What I said was that my father owned the horse About Ben Ahem and that he had let him out to this Bob French for racing purposes, because our family was proud and had never gone into racing that way, in our own name, I mean. Then I had got started and they were all leaning over and listening, and Miss Lucy Wessen's eyes were shining, and I went the whole hog.

45   I told about our place down at Marietta, and about the big stables and the grand brick house we had on a hill, up above the Ohio River, but I knew enough not to do it in no bragging way. What I did was to start things and then let them drag the rest out of me. I acted just as reluctant to tell as I could. Our family hasn't got any barrel factory, and since I've known us, we've always been pretty poor, but not asking anything of any one at that, and my grandfather, over in Wales—but never mind that.

We set there talking like we had known each other for years and years, and I went and told them that my father had been expecting maybe this Bob French wasn't on the square, and had sent me up to Sandusky on the sly to find out what I could.

And I bluffed it through. I had found out all about the 2.18 pace, in which About Ben Ahem was to start.

I said he would lose the first heat by pacing like a lame cow and then he would come back and skin 'em alive after that. And to back up what I said I took thirty dollars out of my pocket and handed it to Mr. Wilbur Wessen and asked him, would he mind, after the first heat, to go down and place it on About Ben Ahem for whatever odds he could get. What I said was that I didn't want Bob French to see me and none of the swipes.

Sure enough the first heat come off and About Ben Ahem went off his stride, up the back stretch, and looked like a wooden horse or a sick one, and come in to be last. Then this Wilbur Wessen went down to the betting place under the grand stand and there I was with the two girls, and when that Miss Woodbury was looking the other way once, Lucy Wessen kinda, with her shoulder you know, kinda touched me. Not just tucking down, I don't mean. You know how a woman can do. They get close, but not getting gay either. You know what they do. Gee whizz.

50   And then they give me a jolt. What they had done, when I didn't know, was to get together, and they had decided Wilbur Wessen would bet fifty dollars, and the two girls had gone and put in ten dollars each, of their own money, too. I was sick then, but I was sicker later.

About the gelding, About Ben Ahem, and their winning their money, I wasn't worried a lot about that. It come out O.K. Ahem stepped the next three heats like a bushel of spoiled eggs going to market before they could be found out, and Wilbur Wessen had got nine to two for the money. There was something else eating at me.

Because Wilbur come back, after he had bet the money, and after that he spent most of his time talking to that Miss Woodbury, and Lucy Wessen and I was left alone together like on a desert island. Gee, if I'd only been on the square or if there had been any way of getting myself on the square. There ain't any Walter Mathers, like I said to her and them, and there hasn't ever been one, but if there was, I bet I'd go to Marietta, Ohio, and shoot him tomorrow.

There I was, big boob that I am. Pretty soon the race was over, and Wilbur had gone down and collected our money, and we had a hack downtown, and he stood us a swell supper at the West House, and a bottle of champagne beside.

And I was with that girl and she wasn't saying much, and I wasn't saying much either. One thing I know. She wasn't stuck on me because of the lie about my father being rich and all that. There's a way you know. . . . Craps amighty. There's a kind of girl, you see just once in your life, and if you don't get busy and make hay, then you're gone for good and all, and might as well go jump off a bridge. They give you a look from inside of them somewhere, and it ain't no vamping, and what it means is— you want that girl to be your wife, and you want nice things around her like flowers and swell clothes, and you want her to have the kids you're going to have, and you want good music played and no ragtime. Gee whizz.

55   There's a place over near Sandusky, across a kind of bay, and it's called Cedar Point.

And after we had supper we went over to it in a launch, all by ourselves. Wilbur and Miss Lucy and that Miss Woodbury had to catch a ten o'clock train back to Tiffin, Ohio, because, when you're out with girls like that you can't get careless and miss any trains and stay out all night, like you can with some kinds of Janes.

And Wilbur blowed himself to the launch and it cost him fifteen cold plunks, but I wouldn't never have knew if I hadn't listened. He wasn't no tin horn kind of a sport.

Over at the Cedar Point place, we didn't stay around where there was a gang of common kind of cattle at all.

There was big dance halls and dining places for yaps, and there was a beach you could walk along and get where it was dark, and we went there.

She didn't talk hardly at all and neither did I, and I was thinking how glad I was my mother was all right, and always made us kids learn to eat with a fork at table, and not swill soup, and not be noisy and rough like a gang you see around a race track that way.

60   Then Wilbur and his girl went away up the beach and Lucy and I sat down in a dark place, where there was some roots of old trees, the water had washed up, and after that the time, till we had to go back in the launch and they had to catch their trains, wasn't nothing at all. It went like winking your eye.

Here's how it was. The place we were setting in was dark, like I said, and there was the roots from that old stump sticking up like arms, and there was a watery smell, and the night was like—as if you could put your hand out and feel it—so warm and soft and dark and sweet like an orange.

I most cried and I most swore and I most jumped up and danced, I was so mad and happy and sad.

When Wilbur come back from being alone with his girl, and she saw him coming, Lucy she says, "we got to go to the train now," and she was most crying too, but she never knew nothing I knew, and she couldn't be so all busted up. And then, before Wilbur and Miss Woodbury got up to where we was, she put her face up and kissed me quick and put her head up against me and she was all quivering and—Gee whizz.

Sometimes I hope I have cancer and die. I guess you know what I mean. We went in the launch across the bay to the train like that, and it was dark, too. She whispered and said it was like she and I could get out of the boat and walk on the water, and it sounded foolish, but I knew what she meant.

65   And then quick we were right at the depot, and there was a big gang of yaps, the kind that goes to the fairs, and crowded and milling around like cattle, and how could I tell her? "It won't be long because you'll write and I'll write to you." That's all she said.

I got a chance like a hay barn afire. A swell chance I got.

And maybe she would write me, down at Marietta that way, and the letter would come back, and stamped on the front of it by the U.S.A. "there ain't any such guy," or something like that, whatever they stamp on a letter that way.

And me trying to pass myself off for a bigbug and a swell—to her, as decent a little body as God ever made. Craps amighty—a swell chance I got!

And then the train come in, and she got on it, and Wilbur Wessen, he come and shook hands with me, and that Miss Woodbury was nice too and bowed to me, and I at her, and the train went and I busted out and cried like a kid.

70   Gee, I could have run after that train and made Dan Patch look like a freight train after a wreck but, socks amighty, what was the use? Did you ever see such a fool?

I'll bet you what—if I had an arm broke right now or a train had run over my foot— I wouldn't go to no doctor at all. I'd go set down and let her hurt and hurt—that's what I'd do.

I'll bet you what—if I hadn't drunk that booze I'd never been such a boob as to go tell such a lie—that couldn't never be made straight to a lady like her.

I wish I had that fellow right here that had on a Windsor tie and carried a cane. I'd smash him for fair. Gosh darn his eyes. He's a big fool—that's what he is.

And if I'm not another you just go find me one and I'll quit working and be a bum and give him my job. I don't care nothing for working, and earning money, and saving it for no such boob as myself.

Comments and Questions

There are many things to be considered in this story, among them method, style, and meaning. The quality of the story can be easily underestimated, for here is an outstanding example of art that conceals its art. In most of his short stories and novels, Anderson is interested in the drama of the inner life. It is one thing to dramatize external action; it is quite another to dramatize the inner life, and in his many stories Anderson has devised more than one way of doing it. In "I'm a Fool," he uses a first-person participating narrator by which he creates the atmosphere of the confessional. After reading the story, we see how thoroughly well designed the first paragraph is to set the stage for the action to follow: It opens the story with a sort of plunging intensity, which is retained to the end.

1. The story is told in dramatic monologue. What are the advantages of this method in this story? Compare Anderson's method with that used in Browning's "My Last Duchess" (p. 310) and in Eliot's "The Love Song of J. Alfred Prufrock" (p. 575).

2. The story is an example, not common in fiction, of psychological *self*-analysis. By what devices does Anderson permit the narrator to achieve it?

3. In what sense is the story dramatic? Is it told in the dramatic past or present? Do not be too sure of your first answers.

4. It has been suggested that Anderson helped "to free American short-story writers from the tyranny of mechanical plots." Explain.

5. Anderson's style obviously makes a basic contribution to the meaning of his story. Comment on the diction, sentence structure, and especially the rhythm of the narrator's speech.

6. It has been said that the story contains a good deal of poetry. Is there some truth in the comment? Do you believe that a young man like the narrator would speak so "naturally" in figures of speech? Select a few figures from the story and discuss them.

7. The story also contains a good deal of comedy. Kronenberger terms comedy "the enemy, not of virtue or idealism, but of hypocrisy and pretense" and "nothing less, in fact, than a form of moral enlightenment" (see p. 1126). Comment on the thematic function of comedy here in that light.

8. To what extent does the story achieve credibility? How real is this young man? Do we *feel* the tugs and quiet desperation of his inner struggle, or is the whole story mostly a tour de force?

9. Has Anderson dramatized some universal truth? Does the story have a theme of any kind beyond the young man's struggle with himself?

James Thurber   (1894–1961)
The Secret Life of Walter Mitty

"We're going through!" The Commander's voice was like thin ice breaking. He wore his full-dress uniform, with the heavily braided white cap pulled down rakishly over one cold gray eye. "We can't make it, sir. It's spoiling for a hurricane, if you ask me." "I'm not asking you, Lieutenant Berg," said the Commander. "Throw on the power lights! Rev her up to 8,500! We're going through!" The pounding of the cylinders increased: ta-pocketa-pocketa-pocketa-pocketa-pocketa. The Commander stared at the ice forming on the pilot window. He walked over and twisted a row of complicated dials "Switch on No. 8 auxiliary!" he shouted. "Switch on No. 8 auxiliary!" repeated Lieutenant Berg. "Full strength in No. 3 turret!" shouted the Commander. "Full strength in No. 3 turret!" The crew, bending to their various tasks in the huge, hurtling eight-engined Navy hydroplane, looked at each other and grinned. "The Old Man'll get us through," they said to one another. "The Old Man ain't afraid of Hell!". . .

"Not so fast! You're driving too fast!" said Mrs. Mitty. "What are you driving so fast for?"

"Hmm?" said Walter Mitty. He looked at his wife, in the seat beside him, with shocked astonishment. She seemed grossly unfamiliar, like a strange woman who had yelled at him in a crowd. "You were up to fifty-five," she said. "You know I don't like to go more than forty. You were up to fifty-five." Walter Mitty drove on toward Waterbury in silence, the roaring of the SN202 through the worst storm in twenty years of Navy flying fading in the remote, intimate airways of his mind. "You're tensed up again," said Mrs. Mitty. "It's one of your days. I wish you'd let Dr. Renshaw look you over."

Walter Mitty stopped the car in front of the building where his wife went to have her hair done. "Remember to get those overshoes while I'm having my hair done," she said. "I don't need overshoes," said Mitty. She put her mirror back into her bag. "We've been all through that," she said, getting out of the car. "You're not a young man any longer." He raced the engine a little. "Why don't you wear your gloves? Have you lost your gloves?" Walter Mitty reached in a pocket and brought out the gloves. He put them on, but after she had turned and gone into the building and he had driven on to a red light, he took them off again. "Pick it up, brother!" snapped a cop as the light changed, and Mitty hastily pulled on his gloves and lurched ahead. He drove around the streets aimlessly for a time, and then he drove past the hospital on his way to the parking lot.

5   . . . "It's the millionaire banker, Wellington McMillan," said the pretty nurse. "Yes?" said Walter Mitty, removing his gloves slowly. "Who has the case?" "Dr. Renshaw and Dr. Benbow, but there are two specialists here, Dr. Remington from New York and Mr. Pritchard-Mitford from London. He flew over." A door opened down a long, cool corridor and Dr. Renshaw came out. He looked distraught and haggard. "Hello, Mitty," he said. "We're having the devil's own time with McMillan, the millionaire banker and close personal friend of Roosevelt. Obstreosis of the ductal tract. Tertiary. Wish you'd take a look at him." "Glad to," said Mitty.

In the operating room there were whispered introductions: "Dr. Remington, Dr. Mitty. Mr. Pritchard-Mitford, Dr. Mitty." "I've read your book on streptothricosis," said Pritchard-Mitford, shaking hands. "A brilliant performance, sir." "Thank you," said Walter Mitty.

"Didn't know you were in the States, Mitty," grumbled Remington. "Coals to Newcastle, bringing Mitford and me here for a tertiary." "You are very kind," said Mitty. A huge, complicated machine, connected to the operating table, with many tubes and wires, began at this moment to go pocketa-pocketa-pocketa. "The new anesthetizer is giving way!" shouted an interne. "There is no one in the East who knows how to fix it!" "Quiet man!" said Mitty, in a low, cool voice. He sprang to the machine, which was now going pocketa-pocketa-queep-pocketa-queep. He began fingering delicately a row of glistening dials. "Give me a fountain pen!" he snapped. Someone handed him a fountain pen. He pulled a faulty piston out of the machine and inserted the pen in its place. "That will hold for ten minutes," he said. "Get on with the operation." A nurse hurried over and whispered to Renshaw, and Mitty saw the man turn pale. "Coreopsis has set in," said Renshaw nervously. "If you would take over, Mitty?" Mitty looked at him and at the craven figure of Benbow, who drank, and at the grave, uncertain faces of the two great specialists. "If you wish," he said. They slipped a white gown on him; he adjusted a mask and drew on thin gloves; nurses handed him shining. . .

"Back it up, Mac! Look out for that Buick!" Walter Mitty jammed on the brakes. "Wrong lane, Mac," said the parking-lot attendant, looking at Mitty closely. "Gee. Yeh," muttered Mitty. He began cautiously to back out of the lane marked "Exit Only." "Leave her sit there," said the attendant. "I'll put her away." Mitty got out of the car. "Hey, better leave the key." "Oh," said Mitty, handing the man the ignition key. The attendant vaulted into the car, backed it up with insolent skill, and put it where it belonged.

They're so damn cocky, thought Walter Mitty, walking along Main Street; they think they know everything. Once he had tried to take his chains off, outside New Milford, and he had got them wound around the axles. A man had had to come out in a wrecking car and unwind them, a young, grinning garageman. Since then Mrs. Mitty always made him drive to a garage to have the chains taken off. The next time, he thought, I'll wear my right arm in a sling; they won't grin at me then. I'll have my right arm in a sling and they'll see I couldn't possibly take the chains off myself. He kicked at the slush on the sidewalk. "Overshoes," he said to himself, and he began looking for a shoe store.

When he came out into the street again, with the overshoes in a box under his arm, Walter Mitty began to wonder what the other thing was his wife had told him to get. She told him twice, before they set out from their house for Waterbury. In a way he hated these weekly trips to town—he was always getting something wrong. Kleenex, he thought, Squibb's, razor blades? No. Toothpaste, toothbrush, bicarbonate, carborundum, initiative and referendum? He gave it up. But she would remember it. "Where's the what's-its-name?" she would ask. "Don't tell me you forgot the what's-its-name." A newsboy went by shouting something about the Waterbury trial.

10 . . . "Perhaps this will refresh your memory." The District Attorney suddenly thrust a heavy automatic at the quiet figure on the witness stand. "Have you ever seen this before?" Walter Mitty took the gun and examined it expertly. "This is my Webley-Vickers 50.80," he said calmly. An excited buzz ran around the courtroom. The judge rapped for order. "You are a crack shot with any sort of firearms, I believe?" said the District Attorney, insinuatingly. "Objection!" shouted Mitty's attorney. "We have shown that the defendant could not have fired the shot. We have shown that he wore his right arm in a sling on the night of the fourteenth of July." Walter Mitty raised his hand briefly and the bickering attorneys were stilled. "With any known make of gun," he said evenly, "I could have killed Gregory Fitzhurst at three hundred feet *with my left hand*." Pandemonium broke loose in the courtroom. A woman's scream rose above the bedlam and suddenly a lovely, dark-

haired girl was in Walter Mitty's arms. The District Attorney struck at her savagely. Without rising from his chair, Mitty let the man have it on the point of the chin. "You miserable cur!" . . .

"Puppy biscuit," said Walter Mitty. He stopped walking and the buildings of Waterbury rose up out of the misty courtroom and surrounded him again. A woman who was passing laughed. "He said 'Puppy biscuit,'" she said to her companion. "That man said 'Puppy biscuit' to himself." Walter Mitty hurried on. He went into an A. & P., not the first one he came to but a smaller one farther up the street. "I want some biscuit for small, young dogs," he said to the clerk. "Any special brand, sir?" The greatest pistol shot in the world thought a moment. "It says 'Puppies Bark for It' on the box," said Walter Mitty.

His wife would be through at the hairdresser's in fifteen minutes, Mitty saw in looking at his watch, unless they had trouble drying it; sometimes they had trouble drying it. She didn't like to get to the hotel first; she would want him to be there waiting for her as usual. He found a big leather chair in the lobby, facing a window, and he put the overshoes and the puppy biscuit on the floor beside it. He picked up an old copy of *Liberty* and sank down into the chair. "Can Germany Conquer the World Through the Air?" Walter Mitty looked at the pictures of bombing planes and of ruined streets.

. . . "The cannonading has got the wind up in young Raleigh, sir," said the sergeant. Captain Mitty looked up at him through tousled hair. "Get him to bed," he said wearily. "With the others. I'll fly alone." "But you can't, sir," said the sergeant anxiously. "It takes two men to handle that bomber and the Archies are pounding hell out of the air. Von Richtman's circus is between here and Saulier." "Somebody's got to get that ammunition dump," said Mitty. "I'm going over. Spot of brandy?" He poured a drink for the sergeant and one for himself. War thundered and whined around the dugout and battered at the door. There was a rending of wood and splinters flew through the room. "A bit of a near thing," said Captain Mitty carelessly. "The box barrage is closing in," said the sergeant. "We only live once, Sergeant," said Mitty, with his faint, fleeting smile. "Or do we?" He poured another brandy and tossed it off. "I never see a man could hold his brandy like you, sir," said the sergeant. "Begging your pardon, sir." Captain Mitty stood up and strapped on his huge Webley-Vickers automatic. "It's forty kilometers through hell, sir," said the sergeant. Mitty finished one last brandy. "After all," he said softly, "what isn't?" The pounding of the cannon increased; there was the rat-tat-tatting of machine guns, and from somewhere came the menacing pocketa-pocketa-pocketa of the new flame-throwers. Walter Mitty walked to the door of the dugout humming "Auprès de Ma Blonde." He turned and waved to the sergeant. "Cheerio!" he said. . . .

Something struck his shoulder. "I've been looking all over this hotel for you," said Mrs. Mitty. "Why do you have to hide in this old chair? How did you expect me to find you?" "Things close in," said Walter Mitty vaguely. "What?" Mrs. Mitty said. "Did you get the what's-its-name? The puppy biscuit? What's in that box?" "Overshoes," said Mitty. "Couldn't you have put them on in the store?" "I was thinking," said Walter Mitty. "Does it ever occur to you that I am sometimes thinking?" She looked at him. "I'm going to take your temperature when I get you home," she said.

15   They went out through the revolving doors that made a faintly derisive whistling sound when you pushed them. It was two blocks to the parking lot. At the drugstore on the corner she said, "Wait here for me. I forgot something. I won't be a minute." She was more than a minute. Walter Mitty lighted a cigarette. It began to rain, rain with sleet in it. He stood up against the wall of the drugstore, smoking. . . . He put his shoulders back and his heels together. "To hell with the handkerchief," said Walter Mitty scornfully. He

took one last drag on his cigarette and snapped it away. Then, with that faint, fleeting smile playing about his lips, he faced the firing squad; erect and motionless, proud and disdainful, Walter Mitty the Undefeated, inscrutable to the last.

Comments and Questions

The English essayist and critic William Hazlitt wrote: "Man is the only animal that laughs and weeps, for he is the only animal that is struck by the difference between what things are and what they ought to be. . . . To explain the nature of laughter and tears is to account for the condition of human life; for it is in a manner compounded of the two!"[1] Incongruity is often seen as the basis of humor and very frequently as the source of the humor in Thurber's story. Curiously, however, Hazlitt sees incongruity at the heart of both the comic and the tragic, the common center of gravity around which spin those very opposite extremes. Might not "The Secret Life of Walter Mitty" exemplify Hazlitt's point? To find the character (or story of) Walter Mitty only hilarious is perhaps only to half-read, to half-perceive the significance of his or its incongruity. Perhaps the character and the story are each richly "compounded" of both the comic and the tragic. And perhaps incongruity is the single key that unlocks both for us (see "Sidenote on irony," p. 26).

1. When one says, "It's a lovely day" in the midst of a storm, the remark does not naturally suit—is incongruous with—its context, and the perceiving mind makes the anticipated adjustment in meaning. So the kind of humor we term irony is by nature incongruous because its intended meaning is the opposite of its apparent one. (Irony is also at times a means of having one's cake and eating it too, of playing with multiple meanings.) Is the word *secret* in the title here ironic? Describe the content of Mitty's "secret" life. What is the similar nature of that various content? Comment on the diction and function of the final phrase, "Walter Mitty the Undefeated, inscrutable to the last."

2. As often pointed out, it is significant that clichés and cliché situations make up so much of Mitty's reveries. But how many cliché expressions and situations can you cite in the externally real segments of the story? Isn't that equally important?

3. Comment fully on the pertinence of: "He went into an A. & P., not the first one he came to but a smaller one farther up the street."

4. "Pocketa-pocketa" is used by Mitty to represent the sounds of various machines, but is it suggestive beyond the literal level in the full context of the story? What about "queep"?

5. Mrs. Mitty asks, "Why do you have to hide in this old chair? How do you expect me to find you?" Mitty "vaguely" responds, "Things close in." Comment on the implication of that exchange.

---

[1] *Complete Works,* ed. P. P. Howe, London: J. M. Dent and Sons, 1930–1934, VI, 5.

Kurt Vonnegut, Jr. (1922–   )
Harrison Bergeron[1]

The year was 2081, and everybody was finally equal. They weren't only equal before God and the law. They were equal every which way. Nobody was smarter than anybody else. Nobody was better looking than anybody else. Nobody was stronger or quicker than anybody else. All this equality was due to the 211th, 212th, and 213th Amendments to the Constitution, and to the unceasing vigilance of agents of the United States Handicapper General.

Some things about living still weren't quite right, though. April, for instance, still drove people crazy by not being springtime. And it was in that clammy month that the H-G men took George and Hazel Bergeron's fourteen-year-old son, Harrison, away.

It was tragic, all right, but George and Hazel couldn't think about it very hard. Hazel had a perfectly average intelligence, which meant she couldn't think about anything except in short bursts. And George, while his intelligence was way above normal, had a little mental handicap radio in his ear. He was required by law to wear it at all times. It was tuned to a government transmitter. Every twenty seconds or so, the transmitter would send out some sharp noise to keep people like George from taking unfair advantage of their brains.

George and Hazel were watching television. There were tears on Hazel's cheeks, but she'd forgotten for the moment what they were about.

5   On the television screen were ballerinas.

A buzzer sounded in George's head. His thought fled in panic, like bandits from a burglar alarm.

"That was a real pretty dance, that dance they just did," said Hazel.

"Huh?" said George.

"That dance—it was nice," said Hazel.

10   "Yup," said George. He tried to think a little about the ballerinas. They weren't really very good—no better than anybody else would have been, anyway. They were burdened with sashweights and bags of birdshot, and their faces were masked, so that no one, seeing a free and graceful gesture or a pretty face, would feel like something the cat drug in. George was toying with the vague notion that maybe dancers shouldn't be handicapped. But he didn't get very far with it before another noise in his ear radio scattered his thoughts.

George winced. So did two out of the eight ballerinas.

Hazel saw him wince. Having no mental handicap herself, she had to ask George what the latest sound had been.

"Sounded like somebody hitting a milk bottle with a ball peen hammer," said George.

"I'd think it would be real interesting, hearing all the different sounds," said Hazel, a little envious. "All the things they think up."

15   "Um," said George.

"Only, if I was Handicapper General, you know what I would do?" said Hazel. Hazel,

---

[1]Jeffers's poem "Science" (p. 508) can be read as a companion piece to this story because both find human beings the victims of their own science and technology. Bradbury's story "There Will Come Soft Rains" (p. 271) has a similar theme.

as a matter of fact, bore a strong resemblance to the Handicapper General, a woman named Diana Moon Glampers. "If I was Diana Moon Glampers," said Hazel, "I'd have chimes on Sunday—just chimes. Kind of in honor of religion."

"I could think, if it was just chimes," said George.

"Well—maybe make 'em real loud," said Hazel. "I think I'd make a good Handicapper General."

"Good as anybody else," said George.

20 "Who knows better'n I do what normal is?" said Hazel.

"Right," said George. He began to think glimmeringly about his abnormal son who was now in jail, about Harrison, but a twenty-one-gun salute in his head stopped that.

"Boy!" said Hazel, "that was a doozy, wasn't it?"

It was such a doozy that George was white and trembling, and tears stood on the rims of his red eyes. Two of the eight ballerinas had collapsed to the studio floor, were holding their temples.

"All of a sudden you look so tired," said Hazel. "Why don't you stretch out on the sofa, so's you can rest your handicap bag on the pillows, honeybunch." She was referring to the forty-seven pounds of birdshot in a canvas bag, which was padlocked around George's neck. "Go on and rest the bag for a little while," she said. "I don't care if you're not equal to me for a while."

25 George weighed the bag with his hands. "I don't mind it," he said. "I don't notice it any more. It's just a part of me."

"You been so tired lately—kind of wore out," said Hazel. "If there was just some way we could make a little hole in the bottom of the bag, and just take out a few of them lead balls. Just a few."

"Two years in prison and two thousand dollars fine for every ball I took out," said George. "I don't call that a bargain."

"If you could just take a few out when you came home from work," said Hazel. "I mean—you don't compete with anybody around here. You just set around."

"If I tried to get away with it," said George, "then other people'd get away with it— and pretty soon we'd be right back to the dark ages again, with everybody competing against everybody else. You wouldn't like that, would you?"

30 "I'd hate it," said Hazel.

"There you are," said George. "The minute people start cheating on laws, what do you think happens to society?"

If Hazel hadn't been able to come up with an answer to this question, George couldn't have supplied one. A siren was going off in his head.

"Reckon it'd fall all apart," said Hazel.

"What would?" said George blankly.

35 "Society," said Hazel uncertainly. "Wasn't that what you just said?"

"Who knows?" said George.

The television program was suddenly interrupted for a news bulletin. It wasn't clear at first as to what the bulletin was about, since the announcer, like all announcers, had a serious speech impediment. For about half a minute, and in a state of high excitement, the announcer tried to say, "Ladies and gentlemen—"

He finally gave up, handed the bulletin to a ballerina to read.

"That's all right—" Hazel said of the announcer, "he tried. That's the big thing. He tried to do the best he could with what God gave him. He should get a nice raise for trying so hard."

40 "Ladies and gentlemen—" said the ballerina, reading the bulletin. She must have been extraordinarily beautiful, because the mask she wore was hideous. And it was easy

to see that she was the strongest and most graceful of all the dancers, for her handicap bags were as big as those worn by two-hundred-pound men.

And she had to apologize at once for her voice, which was a very unfair voice for a woman to use. Her voice was a warm, luminous, timeless melody. "Excuse me—" she said, and she began again, making her voice absolutely uncompetitive.

"Harrison Bergeron, age fourteen," she said in a grackle squawk, "has just escaped from jail, where he was held on suspicion of plotting to overthrow the government. He is a genius and an athlete, is under-handicapped, and should be regarded as extremely dangerous."

A police photograph of Harrison Bergeron was flashed on the screen upside down, then sideways, upside down again, then right side up. The picture showed the full length of Harrison against a background calibrated in feet and inches. He was exactly seven feet tall.

The rest of Harrison's appearance was Halloween and hardware. Nobody had ever borne heavier handicaps. He had outgrown hindrances faster than the H-G men could think them up. Instead of a little ear radio for a mental handicap, he wore a tremendous pair of earphones, and spectacles with thick wavy lenses. The spectacles were intended to make him not only half blind, but to give him whanging headaches besides.

45   Scrap metal was hung all over him. Ordinarily, there was a certain symmetry, a military neatness to the handicaps issued to strong people, but Harrison looked like a walking junkyard. In the race of life, Harrison carried three hundred pounds.

And to offset his good looks, the H-G men required that he wear at all times a red rubber ball for a nose, keep his eyebrows shaved off, and cover his even white teeth with black caps at snaggle-tooth random.

"If you see this boy," said the ballerina, "do not—I repeat, do not—try to reason with him."

There was the shriek of a door being torn from its hinges.

Screams and barking cries of consternation came from the television set. The photograph of Harrison Bergeron on the screen jumped again and again, as though dancing to the tune of an earthquake.

50   George Bergeron correctly identified the earthquake, and well he might have—for many was the time his own home had danced to the same crashing tune. "My God—" said George, "that must be Harrison!"

The realization was blasted from his mind instantly by the sound of an automobile collision in his head.

When George could open his eyes again, the photograph of Harrison was gone. A living, breathing Harrison filled the screen.

Clanking, clownish, and huge, Harrison stood in the center of the studio. The knob of the uprooted studio door was still in his hand. Ballerinas, technicians, musicians, and announcers cowered on their knees before him, expecting to die.

"I am the Emperor!" cried Harrison. "Do you hear? I am the Emperor! Everybody must do what I say at once!" He stamped his foot and the studio shook.

55   "Even as I stand here—" he bellowed, "crippled, hobbled, sickened—I am a greater ruler than any man who ever lived! Now watch me become what I *can* become!"

Harrison tore the straps of his handicap harness like wet tissue paper, tore straps guaranteed to support five thousand pounds.

Harrison's scrap-iron handicaps crashed to the floor.

Harrison thrust his thumbs under the bar of the padlock that secured his head harness. The bar snapped like celery. Harrison smashed his headphones and spectacles against the wall.

He flung away his rubber-ball nose, revealed a man that would have awed Thor, the god of thunder.

60 "I shall now select my Empress!" he said, looking down on the cowering people. "Let the first woman who dares rise to her feet claim her mate and her throne!"

A moment passed, and then a ballerina arose, swaying like a willow.

Harrison plucked the mental handicap from her ear, snapped off her physical handicaps with marvelous delicacy. Last of all, he removed her mask.

She was blindingly beautiful.

"Now—" said Harrison, taking her hand, "shall we show the people the meaning of the word dance? Music!" he commanded.

65 The musicians scrambled back into their chairs, and Harrison stripped them of their handicaps, too. "Play your best," he told them, "and I'll make you barons and dukes and earls."

The music began. It was normal at first—cheap, silly, false. But Harrison snatched two musicians from their chairs, waved them like batons as he sang the music as he wanted it played. He slammed them back into their chairs.

The music began again and was much improved.

Harrison and his Empress merely listened to the music for a while—listened gravely, as though synchronizing their heartbeats with it.

They shifted their weights to their toes.

70 Harrison placed his big hands on the girl's tiny waist, letting her sense the weightlessness that would soon be hers.

And then, in an explosion of joy and grace, into the air they sprang!

Not only were the laws of the land abandoned, but the law of gravity and the laws of motion as well.

They reeled, whirled, swiveled, flounced, capered, gamboled, and spun.

They leaped like deer on the moon.

75 The studio ceiling was thirty feet high, but each leap brought the dancers nearer to it.

It became their obvious intention to kiss the ceiling.

They kissed it.

And then, neutralizing gravity with love and pure will, they remained suspended in air inches below the ceiling, and they kissed each other for a long, long time.

It was then that Diana Moon Glampers, the Handicapper General, came into the studio with a double-barreled ten-gauge shotgun. She fired twice, and the Emperor and the Empress were dead before they hit the floor.

80 Diana Moon Glampers loaded the gun again. She aimed it at the musicians and told them they had ten seconds to get their handicaps back on.

It was then that the Bergerons' television tube burned out.

Hazel turned to comment about the blackout to George. But George had gone out into the kitchen for a can of beer.

George came back in with a beer, paused while a handicap signal shook him up. And then he sat down again. "You been crying?" he said to Hazel.

"Yup," she said.

85 "What about?" he said.

"I forget," she said. "Something real sad on television."

"What was it?" he said.

"It's all kind of mixed up in my mind," said Hazel.

"Forget sad things," said George.

90 "I always do," said Hazel.

"That's my girl," said George. He winced. There was the sound of a rivetting gun in his head.

"Gee—I could tell that one was a doozy," said Hazel.

"You can say that again," said George.

"Gee—" said Hazel, "I could tell that one was a doozy."

E. B. White (1899–   )

The Hour of Letdown

When the man came in, carrying the machine, most of us looked up from our drinks, because we had never seen anything like it before. The man set the thing down on top of the bar near the beerpulls. It took up an ungodly amount of room and you could see the bartender didn't like it any too well, having this big, ugly-looking gadget parked right there.

"Two rye-and-water," the man said.

The bartender went on puddling an Old-Fashioned that he was working on, but he was obviously turning over the request in his mind.

"You want a double?" he asked, after a bit.

5   "No," said the man. "Two rye-and-water, please." He stared straight at the bartender, not exactly unfriendly but on the other hand not affirmatively friendly.

Many years of catering to the kind of people that come into saloons had provided the bartender with an adjustable mind. Nevertheless, he did not adjust readily to this fellow, and he did not like the machine—that was sure. He picked up a live cigarette that was idling on the edge of the cash register, took a drag out of it, and returned it thoughtfully. Then he poured two shots of rye whiskey, drew two glasses of water, and shoved the drinks in front of the man. People were watching. When something a little out of the ordinary takes place at a bar, the sense of it spreads quickly all along the line and pulls the customers together.

The man gave no sign of being the center of attention. He laid a five-dollar bill down on the bar. Then he drank one of the ryes and chased it with water. He picked up the other rye, opened a small vent in the machine (it was like an oil cup) and poured the whiskey in, and then poured the water in.

The bartender watched grimly. "Not funny," he said in an even voice. "And furthermore, your companion takes up too much room. Why'n you put it over on that bench by the door, make more room here."

"There's plenty of room for everyone here," replied the man.

10   "I ain't amused," said the bartender. "Put the goddam thing over near the door like I say. Nobody will touch it."

The man smiled. "You should have seen it this afternoon," he said. "It was magnificent. Today was the third day of the tournament. Imagine it—three days of continuous brainwork! And against the top players in the country, too. Early in the game it gained an advantage; then for two hours it exploited the advantage brilliantly, ending with the opponent's king backed in a corner. The sudden capture of a knight, the neutralization of a bishop, and it was all over. You know how much money it won, all told, in three days of playing chess?"

"How much?" asked the bartender.

"Five thousand dollars," said the man. "Now it wants to let down, wants to get a little drunk."

The bartender ran his towel vaguely over some wet spots. "Take it somewheres else and get it drunk there!" he said firmly. "I got enough troubles."

15 The man shook his head and smiled. "No, we like it here." He pointed at the empty glasses. "Do this again, will you, please?"

The bartender slowly shook his head. He seemed dazed but dogged. "You stow the thing away," he ordered. "I'm not ladling out whiskey for jokestersmiths."

" 'Jokesmiths,' " said the machine. "The word is 'jokesmiths.' "

A few feet down the bar, a customer who was on his third highball seemed ready to participate in this conversation to which we had all been listening so attentively. He was a middle-aged man. His necktie was pulled down away from his collar, and he had eased the collar by unbuttoning it. He had pretty nearly finished his third drink, and the alcohol tended to make him throw his support in with the underprivileged and the thirsty.

"If the machine wants another drink, give it another drink," he said to the bartender. "Let's not have haggling."

20 The fellow with the machine turned to his new-found friend and gravely raised his hand to his temple, giving him a salute of gratitude and fellowship. He addressed his next remark to him, as though deliberately snubbing the bartender.

"You know how it is when you're all fagged out mentally, how you want a drink?"

"Certainly do," replied the friend. "Most natural thing in the world."

There was a stir all along the bar, some seeming to side with the bartender, others with the machine group. A tall, gloomy man standing next to me spoke up.

"Another whiskey sour, Bill," he said. "And go easy on the lemon juice."

25 "Picric acid,"[1] said the machine, sullenly. "They don't use lemon juice in these places."

"That does it!" said the bartender, smacking his hand on the bar. "Will you put that thing away or else beat it out of here. I ain't in the mood, I tell you. I got this saloon to run and I don't want lip from a mechanical brain or whatever the hell you've got there."

The man ignored this ultimatum. He addressed his friend, whose glass was not empty.

"It's not just that it's all tuckered out after three days of chess," he said amiably. "You know another reason it wants a drink?"

"No," said the friend. "Why?"

30 "It cheated," said the man.

At this remark, the machine chuckled. One of its arms dipped slightly, and a light glowed in a dial.

The friend frowned. He looked as though his dignity had been hurt, as though his trust had been misplaced. "Nobody can cheat at chess," he said. "Simpossible. In chess, everything is open and above the board. The nature of the game of chess is such that cheating is impossible."

"That's what I used to think, too," said the man. "But there *is* a way."

"Well, it doesn't surprise me any," put in the bartender. "The first time I laid my eyes on that crummy thing I spotted it for a crook."

35 "Two rye-and-water," said the man.

[1]A bitter, toxic acid sometimes used in medicine.

"You can't have the whiskey," said the bartender. He glared at the mechanical brain. "How do I know it ain't drunk already?"

"That's simple. Ask it something," said the man.

The customers shifted and stared into the mirror. We were all in this thing now, up to our necks. We waited. It was the bartender's move.

"Ask it what? Such as?" said the bartender.

40 "Makes no difference. Pick a couple big figures, ask it to multiply them together. You couldn't multiply big figures together if you were drunk, could you?"

The machine shook slightly, as though making internal preparations.

"Ten thousand eight hundred and sixty-two, multiply it by ninety-nine," said the bartender, viciously. We could tell that he was throwing in the two nines to make it hard.

The machine flickered. One of its tubes spat, and a hand changed position, jerkily.

"One million seventy-five thousand three hundred and thirty-eight," said the machine.

45 Not a glass was raised all along the bar. People just stared gloomily into the mirror; some of us studied our own faces, others took carom shots at the man and the machine.

Finally, a youngish, mathematically minded customer got out a piece of paper and pencil and went into retirement. "It works out," he reported after some minutes of calculating. "You can't say the machine is drunk."

Everyone now glared at the bartender. Reluctantly he poured two shots of rye, drew two glasses of water. The man drank his drink. Then he fed the machine its drink. The machine's light grew fainter. One of its cranky little arms wilted.

For a while the saloon simmered along like a ship at sea in calm weather. Every one of us seemed to be trying to digest the situation, with the help of liquor. Quite a few glasses were refilled. Most of us sought help in the mirror—the court of last appeal.

The fellow with the unbuttoned collar settled his score. He walked stiffly over and stood between the man and the machine. He put one arm around the man, the other arm around the machine. "Let's get out of here and go to a good place," he said.

50 The machine glowed slightly. It seemed to be a little drunk now.

"All right," said the man. "That suits me fine. I've got my car outside."

He settled for the drinks and put down a tip. Quietly and a trifle uncertainly he tucked the machine under his arm, and he and his companion of the night walked to the door and out into the street.

The bartender stared fixedly, then resumed his light housekeeping. "So he's got his car outside," he said, with heavy sarcasm. "Now isn't that nice!"

A customer at the end of the bar near the door left his drink, stepped to the window, parted the curtains, and looked out. He watched for a moment, then returned to his place and addressed the bartender. "It's even nicer than you think," he said. "It's a Cadillac. And which one of the three of them d'ya think is doing the driving?"

Comments and Questions

1. What is the point of view of the story (see p. 19)? How is it essential to achieving the humor?

2. What are the main traits of the machine? How does White emphatically convey some of those traits to us without specifying them directly?

3. What is the special function of the bartender in the story? Is he (strangely) comparable to Walter Mitty (p. 260)?

4. Of what importance is the saloon setting? Comment on the double meaning of the title.

5. Why is it significant that the machine has cheated at chess? That it drives away in a Cadillac?

Ray Bradbury   (1920–   )
There Will Come Soft Rains

In the living room the voice-clock sang, *Tick-tock, seven o'clock, time to get up, time to get up, seven o'clock!* as if it were afraid that nobody would. The morning house lay empty. The clock ticked on, repeating and repeating its sounds into the emptiness. *Seven-nine, breakfast time, seven-nine!*

In the kitchen the breakfast stove gave a hissing sigh and ejected from its warm interior eight pieces of perfectly browned toast, eight eggs sunnyside up, sixteen slices of bacon, two coffees, and two cool glasses of milk.

"Today is August 4, 2026," said a second voice from the kitchen ceiling, "in the city of Allendale, California." It repeated the date three times for memory's sake. "Today is Mr. Featherstone's birthday. Today is the anniversary of Tilita's marriage. Insurance is payable, as are the water, gas, and light bills."

Somewhere in the walls, relays clicked, memory tapes glided under electric eyes.

5   *Eight-one, tick-tock, eight-one o'clock, off to school, off to work, run, run, eight-one!* But no doors slammed, no carpets took the soft tread of rubber heels. It was raining outside. The weather box on the front door sang quietly: "Rain, rain, go away; rubbers, raincoats for today . . ." And the rain tapped on the empty house, echoing.

Outside, the garage chimed and lifted its door to reveal the waiting car. After a long wait the door swung down again.

At eight-thirty the eggs were shriveled and the toast was like stone. An aluminum wedge scraped them into the sink, where hot water whirled them down a metal throat which digested and flushed them away to the distant sea. The dirty dishes were dropped into a hot washer and emerged twinkling dry.

Nine-fifteen, sang the clock, *time to clean.*

Out of warrens in the wall, tiny robot mice darted. The rooms were acrawl with the small cleaning animals, all rubber and metal. They thudded against chairs, whirling their mustached runners, kneading the rug nap, sucking gently at hidden dust. Then, like mysterious invaders, they popped into their burrows. Their pink electric eyes faded. The house was clean.

10   *Ten o'clock.* The sun came out from behind the rain. The house stood alone in a city of rubble and ashes. This was the one house left standing. At night the ruined city gave off a radioactive glow which could be seen for miles.

Ten-fifteen. The garden sprinklers whirled up in golden founts, filling the soft morning air with scatterings of brightness. The water pelted windowpanes, running down the charred west side where the house had been burned evenly free of its white paint. The entire west face of the house was black, save for five places. Here the silhouette in paint of a man mowing a lawn. Here, as in a photograph, a woman bent to pick flowers. Still farther over, their images burned on wood in one titanic instant, a small boy, hands flung into the air; higher up, the image of a thrown ball, and opposite him a girl, hands raised to catch a ball which never came down.

The five spots of paint—the man, the woman, the children, the ball—remained. The rest was a thin charcoaled layer.

The gentle sprinkler rain filled the garden with falling light.

Until this day, how well the house had kept its peace. How carefully it had inquired, "Who goes there? What's the password?" and, getting no answer from lonely foxes and whining cats, it had shut up its windows and drawn shades in an old-maidenly preoccupation with self-protection which bordered on a mechanical paranoia.

15   It quivered at each sound, the house did. If a sparrow brushed a window, the shade snapped up. The bird, startled, flew off! No, not even a bird must touch the house!

The house was an altar with ten thousand attendants, big, small, servicing, attending, in choirs. But the gods had gone away, and the ritual of the religion continued senselessly, uselessly.

Twelve noon.

A dog whined, shivering, on the front porch.

The front door recognized the dog voice and opened. The dog, once huge and fleshy, but now gone to bone and covered with sores, moved in and through the house, tracking mud. Behind it whirred angry mice, angry at having to pick up mud, angry at inconvenience.

20   For not a leaf fragment blew under the door but what the wall panels flipped open and the copper scrap rats flashed swiftly out. The offending dust, hair, or paper, seized in miniature steel jaws, was raced back to the burrows. There, down tubes which fed into the cellar, it was dropped into the sighing vent of an incinerator which sat like evil Baal[1] in a dark corner.

The dog ran upstairs, hysterically yelping to each door, at last realizing, as the house realized, that only silence was here.

It sniffed the air and scratched the kitchen door. Behind the door, the stove was making pancakes which filled the house with a rich baked odor and the scent of maple syrup.

The dog frothed at the mouth, lying at the door, sniffing, its eyes turned to fire. It ran wildly in circles, biting at its tail, spun in a frenzy, and died. It lay in the parlor for an hour.

Two o'clock, sang a voice.

25   Delicately sensing decay at last, the regiments of mice hummed out as softly as blown gray leaves in an electrical wind.

Two-fifteen.

The dog was gone.

---

[1]Baal (pl. Baalim) is a general name for the Syrian gods, as Ashtaroth is for the goddesses. Baal was a false god; Baalim, a form of worship that Hosea and other prophets denounced as heathenism. Matthew 12:24 refers to Beelzebub (Baalzebub) as "the prince of devils." Milton's *Paradise Lost* places him next in rank to Satan:

One next himself in power, and next in crime,
Long after known in Palestine, and nam'd
Beelzebub.   (I. 79–81)

In the cellar, the incinerator glowed suddenly and a whirl of sparks leaped up the chimney.

Two thirty-five.

30   Bridge tables sprouted from patio walls. Playing cards fluttered onto pads in a shower of pips.[2] Martinis manifested on an oaken bench with egg-salad sandwiches. Music played.

But the tables were silent and the cards untouched.

At four o'clock the tables folded like great butterflies back through the paneled walls.

Four-thirty.

The nursery walls glowed.

35   Animals took shape: yellow giraffes, blue lions, pink antelopes, lilac panthers cavorting in crystal substance. The walls were glass. They looked out upon color and fantasy. Hidden films clocked through well-oiled sprockets, and the walls lived. The nursery floor was woven to resemble a crisp, cereal meadow. Over this ran aluminum roaches and iron crickets, and in the hot still air butterflies of delicate red tissue wavered among the sharp aroma of animal spoors![3] There was the sound like a great matted yellow hive of bees within a dark bellows, the lazy bumble of a purring lion. And there was the patter of okapi[4] feet and the murmur of a fresh jungle rain, like other hoofs, falling upon the summer-starched grass. Now the walls dissolved into distances of parched weed, mile on mile, and warm endless sky. The animals drew away into thorn brakes and water holes.

It was the children's hour.

Five o'clock. The bath filled with clear hot water.

Six, seven, eight o'clock. The dinner dishes manipulated like magic tricks, and in the study a *click*. In the metal stand opposite the hearth where a fire now blazed up warmly, a cigar popped out, half an inch of soft gray ash on it, smoking, waiting.

Nine o'clock. The beds warmed their hidden circuits, for nights were cool here.

40   *Nine-five.* A voice spoke from the study ceiling:

"Mrs. McClellan, which poem would you like this evening?"

The house was silent.

The voice said at last, "Since you express no preference, I shall select a poem at random." Quiet music rose to back the voice. "Sara Teasdale. As I recall, your favorite. . . ."

"There will come soft rains and the smell of the ground,
And swallows circling with their shimmering sound;

And frogs in the pools singing at night,
And wild plum-trees in tremulous white;

Robins will wear their feathery fire
Whistling their whims on a low fence-wire;

And not one will know of the war, not one
Will care at last when it is done.

[2]Spots.   [3]Droppings.   [4]African animal related to the giraffe.

Not one would mind, either bird nor tree
If mankind perished utterly;

And Spring herself, when she woke at dawn,
Would scarcely know that we were gone."[5]

The fire burned on the stone hearth and the cigar fell away into a mound of quiet ash on its tray. The empty chairs faced each other between the silent walls, and the music played.

45   At ten o'clock the house began to die.
The wind blew. A falling tree bough crashed through the kitchen window. Cleaning solvent, bottled, shattered over the stove. The room was ablaze in an instant!
"Fire!" screamed a voice. The house lights flashed, water pumps shot water from the ceilings. But the solvent spread on the linoleum, licking, eating under the kitchen door, while the voices took it up in chorus: "Fire, fire, fire!"
The house tried to save itself. Doors sprang tightly shut, but the windows were broken by the heat and the wind blew and sucked upon the fire.
The house gave ground as the fire in ten billion angry sparks moved with flaming ease from room to room and then up the stairs. While scurrying water rats squeaked from the walls, pistoled their water, and ran for more. And the wall sprays let down showers of mechanical rain.
50   But too late. Somewhere, sighing, a pump shrugged to a stop. The quenching rain ceased. The reserve water supply which had filled baths and washed dishes for many quiet days was gone.
The fire crackled up the stairs. It fed upon Picassos and Matisses[6] in the upper halls, like delicacies, baking off the oily flesh, tenderly crisping the canvases into black shavings.
Now the fire lay in beds, stood in windows, changed the colors of drapes!
And then, reinforcements.
From attic trapdoors, blind robot faces peered down with faucet mouths gushing green chemical.
55   The fire backed off, as even an elephant must at the sight of a dead snake. Now there were twenty snakes whipping over the floor, killing the fire with a clear cold venom of green froth.
But the fire was clever. It had sent flame outside the house, up through the attic to the pumps there. An explosion! The attic brain which directed the pumps was shattered into bronze shrapnel on the beams.
The fire rushed back into every closet and felt of the clothes hung there.
The house shuddered, oak bone on bone, its bared skeleton cringing from the heat, its wire, its nerves revealed as if a surgeon had torn the skin off to let the red veins and capillaries quiver in the scalded air. Help, help! Fire! Run, run! Heat snapped mirrors like the first brittle winter ice. And the voices wailed Fire, fire, run, run, like a tragic nursery rhyme, a dozen voices, high, low, like children dying in a forest, alone, alone. And the voices fading as the wires popped their sheathings like hot chestnuts. One, two, three, four, five voices died.
In the nursery the jungle burned. Blue lions roared, purple giraffes bounded off.

---

[5]"There Will Come Soft Rains," in Sara Teasdale, *Flame and Shadow,* New York: Macmillan, 1920.
[6]That is, valuable paintings by the Spaniard Pablo Picasso and the Frenchman Henri Matisse.

The panthers ran in circles, changing color, and ten million animals, running before the fire, vanished off toward a distant steaming river. . . .

60   Ten more voices died. In the last instant under the fire avalanche, other choruses, oblivious, could be heard announcing the time, playing music, cutting the lawn by remote-control mower, or setting an umbrella frantically out and in the slamming and opening front door, a thousand things happening, like a clock shop when each clock strikes the hour insanely before or after the other, a scene of maniac confusion, yet unity; singing, screaming, a few last cleaning mice darting bravely out to carry the horrid ashes away! And one voice, with sublime disregard for the situation, read poetry aloud in the fiery study, until all the film spools burned, until all the wires withered and the circuits cracked.

The fire burst the house and let it slam flat down, puffing out skirts of spark and smoke.

In the kitchen, an instant before the rain of fire and timber, the stove could be seen making breakfasts at a psychopathic rate, ten dozen eggs, six loaves of toast, twenty dozen bacon strips, which, eaten by fire, started the stove working again, hysterically hissing!

The crash. The attic smashing into kitchen and parlor. The parlor into cellar, cellar into sub-cellar. Deep freeze, armchair, film tapes, circuits, beds, and all like skeletons thrown in a cluttered mound deep under.

Smoke and silence. A great quantity of smoke.

65   Dawn showed faintly in the east. Among the ruins, one wall stood alone. Within the wall, a last voice said, over and over again and again, even as the sun rose to shine upon the heaped rubble and steam:

"Today is August 5, 2026, today is August 5, 2026, today is . . ."

Comments and Questions

1. It may be of interest that this story was first published in 1948 and Sara Teasdale's poem in 1920. If "Harrison Bergeron" above is an extension of a contemporary insistence on equality to its logical conclusion for the purpose of highly entertaining social satire, "There Will Come Soft Rains" uses a similar kind of extension for a much more sobering comment. Aside from the obvious extension of the nuclear threat into the future, what other dominant trends, obsessions, concerns of our twentieth-century society are projected forward by Bradbury?

2. This is a story curiously without human characters. How does Bradbury compensate for their absence? Is there any functional conflict in the story?

3. How does the dog contribute to the story?

4. Is there any irony in the title of the story? The house is an ingeniously devised model of intricate, sophisticated, efficient machinery conceived to cater to even the whims of its human creators. What is intensely ironic about that? (See "Sidenote on irony," p. 26.)

5. How is the conclusion richly suggestive?

6. Provide an informative comparison of the methods and accomplishments of a humorous and a serious treatment of a similar theme in "The Hour of Letdown" above and this story.

Walter Van Tilburg Clark (1909–   )
The Portable Phonograph

The red sunset, with narrow, black cloud strips like threats across it, lay on the curved horizon of the prairie. The air was still and cold, and in it settled the mute darkness and greater cold of night. High in the air there was wind, for through the veil of the dusk the clouds could be seen gliding rapidly south and changing shapes. A sensation of torment, of two-sided, unpredictable nature, arose from the stillness of the earth air beneath the violence of the upper air. Out of the sunset, through the dead, matted grass and isolated weed stalks of the prairie, crept the narrow and deeply rutted remains of a road. In the road, in places, there were crusts of shallow, brittle ice. There were little islands of an old oiled pavement in the road too, but most of it was mud, now frozen rigid. The frozen mud still bore the toothed impress of great tanks, and a wanderer on the neighboring undulations might have stumbled, in this light, into large, partially filled-in and weed-grown cavities, their banks channeled and beginning to spread into badlands. These pits were such as might have been made by falling meteors, but they were not. They were the scars of gigantic bombs, their rawness already made a little natural by rain, seed and time. Along the road there were rakish remnants of fence. There was also, just visible, one portion of tangled and multiple barbed wire still erect, behind which was a shelving ditch with small caves, now very quiet and empty, at intervals in its back wall. Otherwise there was no structure or remnant of a structure visible over the dome of the darkling earth, but only, in sheltered hollows, the darker shadows of young trees trying again.

Under the wuthering arch of the high wind a V of wild geese fled south. The rush of their pinions sounded briefly, and the faint, plaintive notes of their expeditionary talk. Then they left a still greater vacancy. There was the smell and expectation of snow, as there is likely to be when the wild geese fly south. From the remote distance, toward the red sky, came faintly the protracted howl and quick yap-yap of a prairie wolf.

North of the road, perhaps a hundred yards, lay the parallel and deeply intrenched course of a small creek, lined with leafless alders and willows. The creek was already silent under ice. Into the bank above it was dug a sort of cell, with a single opening, like the mouth of a mine tunnel. Within the cell there was a little red of fire, which showed dully through the opening, like a reflection or a deception of the imagination. The light came from the chary burning of four blocks of poorly aged peat, which gave off a petty warmth and much acrid smoke. But the precious remnants of wood, old fence posts and timbers from the long-deserted dugouts, had to be saved for the real cold, for the time when a man's breath blew white, the moisture in his nostrils stiffened at once when he stepped out, and the expansive blizzards paraded for days over the vast open, swirling and settling and thickening, till the dawn of the cleared day when the sky was a thin blue-green and the terrible cold, in which a man could not live for three hours unwarmed, lay over the uniformly drifted swell of the plain.

Around the smoldering peat four men were seated cross-legged. Behind them, traversed by their shadows, was the earth bench, with two old and dirty army blankets, where the owner of the cell slept. In a niche in the opposite wall were a few tin utensils which caught the glint of the coals. The host was rewrapping in a piece of daubed burlap, four fine, leather-bound books. He worked slowly and very carefully, and at last tied the bundle securely with a piece of grass-woven cord. The other three looked intently upon the process, as if a great significance lay in it. As the host tied the cord, he spoke. He was an old man, his long, matted beard and hair gray to nearly white. The shadows made his brows and cheekbones appear gnarled, his eyes and cheeks deeply sunken. His big hands, rough with frost and swollen by rheumatism, were awkward but gentle at their task. He was like a prehistoric priest performing a fateful ceremonial rite. Also his voice had in it a suitable quality of deep, reverent despair, yet perhaps, at the moment, a sharpness of selfish satisfaction.

5   "When I perceived what was happening," he said, "I told myself, 'It is the end. I cannot take much; I will take these.'

"Perhaps I was impractical," he continued. "But for myself, I do not regret, and what do we know of those who will come after us? We are the doddering remnant of a race of mechanical fools. I have saved what I love; the soul of what was good in us here; perhaps the new ones will make a strong enough beginning not to fall behind when they become clever."

He rose with slow pain and placed the wrapped volumes in the niche with his utensils. The others watched him with the same ritualistic gaze.

"Shakespeare, the Bible, *Moby Dick, The Divine Comedy,*" one of them said softly. "You might have done worse; much worse."

"You will have a little soul left until you die," said another harshly. "That is more than is true of us. My brain becomes thick, like my hands." He held the big, battered hands, with their black nails, in the glow to be seen.

10   "I want paper to write on," he said. "And there is none."

The fourth man said nothing. He sat in the shadow farthest from the fire, and sometimes his body jerked in its rags from the cold. Although he was still young, he was sick, and coughed often. Writing implied a greater future than he now felt able to consider.

The old man seated himself laboriously, and reached out, groaning at the movement, to put another block of peat on the fire. With bowed heads and averted eyes, his three guests acknowledged his magnanimity.

"We thank you, Doctor Jenkins, for the reading," said the man who had named the books.

They seemed then to be waiting for something. Doctor Jenkins understood, but was loath to comply. In an ordinary moment he would have said nothing. But the words of *The Tempest,* which he had been reading, and the religious attention of the three, made this an unusual occasion.

15   "You wish to hear the phonograph," he said grudgingly.

The two middle-aged men stared into the fire, unable to formulate and expose the enormity of their desire.

The young man, however, said anxiously, between suppressed coughs, "Oh, please," like an excited child.

The old man rose again in his difficult way, and went to the back of the cell. He returned and placed tenderly upon the packed floor, where the firelight might fall upon it, an old, portable phonograph in a black case. He smoothed the top with his hand, and then opened it. The lovely green-felt-covered disk became visible.

"I have been using thorns as needles," he said. "But tonight, because we have a musician among us"—he bent his head to the young man, almost invisible in the shadow—"I will use a steel needle. There are only three left."

20   The two middle-aged men stared at him in speechless adoration. The one with the big hands, who wanted to write, moved his lips, but the whisper was not audible.

"Oh, don't," cried the young man, as if he were hurt. "The thorns will do beautifully."

"No," the old man said. "I have become accustomed to the thorns, but they are not really good. For you, my young friend, we will have good music tonight.

"After all," he added generously, and beginning to wind the phonograph, which creaked, "they can't last forever."

"No, nor we," the man who needed to write said harshly. "The needle, by all means."

25   "Oh, thanks," said the young man. "Thanks," he said again, in a low, excited voice, and then stifled his coughing with a bowed head.

"The records, though," said the old man when he had finished winding, "are a different matter. Already they are very worn. I do not play them more than once a week. One, once a week, that is what I allow myself.

"More than a week I cannot stand it; not to hear them," he apologized.

"No, how could you?" cried the young man. "And with them here like this."

"A man can stand anything," said the man who wanted to write, in his harsh, antagonistic voice.

30   "Please, the music," said the young man.

"Only the one," said the old man. "In the long run we will remember more that way."

He had a dozen records with luxuriant gold and red seals. Even in that light the others could see that the threads of the records were becoming worn. Slowly he read out the titles, and the tremendous, dead names of the composers and the artists and the orchestras. The three worked upon the names in their minds, carefully. It was difficult to select from such a wealth what they would at once most like to remember. Finally the man who wanted to write named Gershwin's "New York."

"Oh, no," cried the sick young man, and then could say nothing more because he had to cough. The others understood him, and the harsh man withdrew his selection and waited for the musician to choose.

The musician begged Doctor Jenkins to read the titles again, very slowly, so that he could remember the sounds. While they were read, he lay back against the wall, his eyes closed, his thin, horny hand pulling at his light beard, and listened to the voices and the orchestras and the single instruments in his mind.

35   When the reading was done he spoke despairingly. "I have forgotten," he complained. "I cannot hear them clearly.

"There are things missing," he explained.

"I know," said Doctor Jenkins. "I thought that I knew all of Shelley by heart. I should have brought Shelley."

"That's more soul than we can use," said the harsh man. "*Moby Dick* is better.

"By God, we can understand that," he emphasized.

40   The doctor nodded.

"Still," said the man who had admired the books, "we need the absolute if we are to keep a grasp on anything.

"Anything but these sticks and peat clods and rabbit snares," he said bitterly.

"Shelley desired an ultimate absolute," said the harsh man. "It's too much," he said. "It's no good; no earthly good."

The musician selected a Debussy nocturne. The others considered and approved. They rose to their knees to watch the doctor prepare for the playing, so that they appeared to be actually in an attitude of worship. The peat glow showed the thinness of their bearded faces, and the deep lines in them, and revealed the condition of their garments. The other two continued to kneel as the old man carefully lowered the needle onto the spinning disk, but the musician suddenly drew back against the wall again, with his knees up, and buried his face in his hands.

45   At the first notes of the piano the listeners were startled. They stared at each other. Even the musician lifted his head in amazement, but then quickly bowed it again, strainingly, as if he were suffering from a pain he might not be able to endure. They were all listening deeply, without movement. The wet, blue-green notes tinkled forth from the old machine, and were individual, delectable presences in the cell. The individual, delectable presences swept into a sudden tide of unbearably beautiful dissonance, and then continued fully the swelling and ebbing of that tide, the dissonant inpourings, and the resolutions, and the diminishments, and the little, quiet wavelets of interlude lapping between. Every sound was piercing and singularly sweet. In all the men except the musician, there occurred rapid sequences of tragically heightened recollection. He heard nothing but what was there. At the final, whispering disappearance, but moving quietly, so that the others would not hear him and look at him, he let his head fall back in agony, as if it were drawn there by the hair, and clenched the fingers of one hand over his teeth. He sat that way while the others were silent, and until they began to breathe again normally. His drawn-up legs were trembling violently.

Quickly Doctor Jenkins lifted the needle off, to save it, and not to spoil the recollection with scraping. When he had stopped the whirling of the sacred disk, he courteously left the phonograph open and by the fire, in sight.

The others, however, understood. The musician rose last, but then abruptly, and went quickly out at the door without saying anything. The others stopped at the door and gave their thanks in low voices. The doctor nodded magnificently.

"Come again," he invited, "in a week. We will have the 'New York.'"

When the two had gone together, out toward the rimed road, he stood in the entrance, peering and listening. At first there was only the resonant boom of the wind overhead, and then, far over the dome of the dead, dark plain, the wolf cry lamenting. In the rifts of clouds the doctor saw four stars shining. It impressed the doctor that one of them had just been obscured by the beginning of a flying cloud at the very moment he heard what he had been listening for, a sound of suppressed coughing. It was not near by, however. He believed that down against the pale alders he could see the moving shadow.

50   With nervous hands he lowered the piece of canvas which served as his door, and pegged it at the bottom. Then quickly and quietly, looking at the piece of canvas frequently, he slipped the records into the case, snapped the lid shut, and carried the phonograph to his couch. There, pausing often to stare at the canvas and listen, he dug earth from the wall and disclosed a piece of board. Behind this there was a deep hole in the wall, into which he put the phonograph. After a moment's consideration, he went over and reached down his bundle of books and inserted it also. Then, guardedly, he once more sealed up the hole with the board and the earth. He also changed his blankets, and the grass-stuffed sack which served as a pillow, so that he could lie facing the entrance. After carefully placing two more blocks of peat on the fire, he stood for a long time watching the stretched canvas, but it seemed to billow naturally with the first gusts of a lowering wind. At last he prayed, and got in under his blankets, and closed his smoke-smarting eyes. On the inside of the bed, next the wall, he could feel with his hand the comfortable piece of lead pipe.

Donald Barthelme   (1931–   )
A City of Churches

"Yes," Mr. Phillips said, "ours is a city of churches all right."

Cecelia nodded, following his pointing hand. Both sides of the street were solidly lined with churches, standing shoulder to shoulder in a variety of architectural styles. The Bethel Baptist stood next to the Holy Messiah Free Baptist, St. Paul's Episcopal next to Grace Evangelical Covenant. Then came the First Christian Science, the Church of God, All Souls, Our Lady of Victory, the Society of Friends, the Assembly of God, and the Church of the Holy Apostles. The spires and steeples of the traditional buildings were jammed in next to the broad imaginative flights of the "contemporary" designs.

"Everyone here takes a great interest in church matters," Mr. Phillips said.

Will I fit in? Cecelia wondered. She had come to Prester to open a branch office of a car-rental concern.

5   "I'm not especially religious," she said to Mr. Phillips, who was in the real-estate business.

"Not *now,*" he answered. "Not *yet.* But we have many fine young people here. You'll get integrated into the community soon enough. The immediate problem is, where are you to live? Most people," he said, "live in the church of their choice. All of our churches have many extra rooms. I have a few belfry apartments that I can show you. What price range were you thinking of?"

They turned a corner and were confronted with more churches. They passed St. Luke's, the Church of the Epiphany, All Saints Ukrainian Orthodox, St. Clement's, Fountain Baptist, Union Congregational, St. Anargyri's, Temple Emanuel, the First Church of Christ Reformed. The mouths of all the churches were gaping open. Inside, lights could be seen dimly.

"I can go up to a hundred and ten," Cecelia said. "Do you have any buildings here that are *not* churches?"

"None," said Mr. Phillips. "Of course many of our fine church structures also do double duty as something else." He indicated a handsome Georgian façade. "That one," he said, "houses the United Methodist and the Board of Education. The one next to it, which is Antioch Pentecostal, has the barbershop."

10   It was true. A red-and-white striped barber pole was attached inconspicuously to the front of the Antioch Pentecostal.

"Do many people rent cars here?" Cecelia asked. "Or would they, if there was a handy place to rent them?"

"Oh, I don't know," said Mr. Phillips. "Renting a car implies that you want to go somewhere. Most people are pretty content right here. We have a lot of activities. I don't think I'd pick the car-rental business if I was just starting out in Prester. But you'll do fine." He showed her a small, extremely modern building with a severe brick, steel, and glass front. "That's St. Barnabas. Nice bunch of people over there. Wonderful spaghetti suppers."

Cecelia could see a number of heads looking out of the windows. But when they saw that she was staring at them, the heads disappeared.

"Do you think it's healthy for so many churches to be gathered together in one place?" she asked the guide. "It doesn't seem . . . *balanced,* if you know what I mean."

15   "We are famous for our churches," Mr. Phillips replied. "They are harmless. Here we are now."

He opened a door and they began climbing many flights of dusty stairs. At the end of the climb they entered a good-sized room, square, with windows on all four sides. There was a bed, a table, and two chairs, lamps, a rug. Four very large bronze bells hung in the exact center of the room.

"What a view!" Mr. Phillips exclaimed. "Come here and look."

"Do they actually ring these bells?" Cecelia asked.

"Three times a day," Mr. Phillips said, smiling. "Morning, noon, and night. Of course when they're rung you have to be pretty quick at getting out of the way. You get hit in the head by one of these babies and that's all she wrote."

20 "God Almighty," said Cecelia involuntarily. Then she said, "Nobody lives in the belfry apartments. That's why they're empty."

"You think so?" Mr. Phillips said.

"You can only rent them to new people in town," she said accusingly.

"I wouldn't do that," Mr. Phillips said. "It would go against the spirit of Christian fellowship."

"This town is a little creepy, you know that?"

25 "That may be, but it's not for you to say, is it? I mean, you're new here. You should walk cautiously, for a while. If you don't want an upper apartment I have a basement over at Central Presbyterian. You'd have to share it. There are two women in there now."

"I don't want to share," Cecelia said. "I want a place of my own."

"Why?" the real-estate man asked curiously. "For what purpose?"

"Purpose?" asked Cecelia. "There is no particular purpose. I just want—"

"That's not usual here. Most people live with other people. Husbands and wives. Sons with their mothers. People have roommates. That's the usual pattern."

30 "Still, I prefer a place of my own."

"It's very unusual."

"Do you have any such places? Besides bell towers, I mean?"

"I guess there are a few," Mr. Phillips said, with clear reluctance. "I can show you one or two, I suppose."

He paused for a moment.

35 "It's just that we have different values, maybe, from some of the surrounding communities," he explained. "We've been written up a lot. We had four minutes on the C.B.S. Evening News one time. Three or four years ago. 'A City of Churches,' it was called."

"Yes, a place of my own is essential," Cecelia said, "if I am to survive here."

"That's kind of a funny attitude to take," Mr. Phillips said. "What denomination are you?"

Cecelia was silent. The truth was, she wasn't anything.

"I said, what denomination are you?" Mr. Phillips repeated.

40 "I can will my dreams," Cecelia said. "I can dream whatever I want. If I want to dream that I'm having a good time, in Paris or some other city, all I have to do is go to sleep and I will dream that dream. I can dream whatever I want."

"What do you dream, then, mostly?" Mr. Phillips said, looking at her closely.

"Mostly sexual things," she said. She was not afraid of him.

"Prester is not that kind of a town," Mr. Phillips said, looking away.

They went back down the stairs.

45 The doors of the churches were opening, on both sides of the street. Small groups of people came out and stood there, in front of the churches, gazing at Cecelia and Mr. Phillips.

A young man stepped forward and shouted, *"Everyone in this town already has a car! There is no one in this town who doesn't have a car!"*

"Is that true?" Cecelia asked Mr. Phillips.

"Yes," he said. "It's true. No one would rent a car here. Not in a hundred years."

"Then I won't stay," she said. "I'll go somewhere else."

50   "You must stay," he said. "There is already a car-rental office for you. In Mount Moriah Baptist, on the lobby floor. There is a counter and a telephone and a rack of car keys. And a calendar."

"I won't stay," she said. "Not if there's not any sound business reason for staying."

"We want you," said Mr. Phillips. "We want you standing behind the counter of the car-rental agency, during regular business hours. It will make the town complete."

"I won't," she said. "Not me."

"You must. It's essential."

55   "I'll dream," she said. "Things you won't like."

"We are discontented," said Mr. Phillips. "Terribly, terribly discontented. Something is wrong."

"I'll dream the Secret," she said. "You'll be sorry."

"We are like other towns, except that we are perfect," he said. "Our discontent can only be held in check by perfection. We need a car-rental girl. Someone must stand behind that counter."

"I'll dream the life you are most afraid of," Cecelia threatened.

60   "You are ours," he said, gripping her arm. "Our car-rental girl. Be nice. There is nothing you can do."

"Wait and see," Cecelia said.

Alice Walker (1944–   )
To Hell with Dying

"To hell with dying," my father would say, "these children want Mr. Sweet!"

Mr. Sweet was a diabetic and an alcoholic and a guitar player and lived down the road from us on a neglected cotton farm. My older brothers and sisters got the most benefit from Mr. Sweet, for when they were growing up he had quite a few years ahead of him and so was capable of being called back from the brink of death any number of times—whenever the voice of my father reached him as he lay expiring. . . . "To hell with dying, man," my father would say, pushing the wife away from the bedside (in tears although she knew the death was not necessarily the last one unless Mr. Sweet really wanted it to be), "the children want Mr. Sweet!" And they did want him, for at a signal from Father they would come crowding around the bed and throw themselves on the covers and whoever was the smallest at the time would kiss him all over his wrinkled brown face and begin to tickle him so that he would laugh all down in his stomach, and his moustache, which was long and sort of straggly, would shake like Spanish moss and was also that color.

Mr. Sweet had been ambitious as a boy, wanted to be a doctor or lawyer or sailor, only to find that black men fare better if they are not. Since he could be none of those things he turned to fishing as his only earnest career and playing the guitar as his only claim to doing anything extraordinarily well. His son, the only one that he and his wife, Miss Mary, had, was shiftless as the day is long and spent money as if he were trying to see the bottom of the mint, which Mr. Sweet would tell him was the clean brown palm of his hand. Miss Mary loved her "baby," however, and worked hard to get him the "li'l necessaries" of life, which turned out mostly to be women.

Mr. Sweet was a tall, thinnish man with thick kinky hair going dead white. He was dark brown, his eyes were very squinty and sort of bluish, and he chewed Brown Mule tobacco. He was constantly on the verge of being blind drunk, for he brewed his own liquor and was not in the least a stingy sort of man, and was always very melancholy and sad, though frequently when he was "feelin' good" he'd dance around the yard with us, usually keeling over just as my mother came to see what the commotion was.

5   Toward all of us children he was very kind, and had the grace to be shy with us, which is unusual in grown-ups. He had great respect for my mother for she never held his drunkenness against him and would let us play with him even when he was about to fall in the fireplace from drink. Although Mr. Sweet would sometimes lose complete or nearly complete control of his head and neck so that he would loll in his chair, his mind remained strangely acute and his speech not too affected. His ability to be drunk and sober at the same time made him an ideal playmate, for he was as weak as we were and we could usually best him in wrestling, all the while keeping a fairly coherent conversation going.

We never felt anything of Mr. Sweet's age when we played with him. We loved his wrinkles and would draw some on our brows to be like him, and his white hair was my special treasure and he knew it and would never come to visit us just after he had had his hair cut off at the barbershop. Once he came to our house for something, probably to see my father about fertilizer for his crops, for although he never paid the slightest attention to his crops he liked to know what things would be best to use on them if he ever did. Anyhow, he had not come with his hair since he had just had it shaved off at the barbershop. He wore a huge straw hat to keep off the sun and also to keep his head away from me. But as soon as I saw him I ran up and demanded that he take me up and kiss me, with his funny beard which smelled so strongly of tobacco. Looking forward to burying my small fingers into his woolly hair I threw away his hat only to find he had done something to his hair, that it was no longer there! I let out a squall which made my mother think that Mr. Sweet had finally dropped me in the well or something and from that day I've been wary of men in hats. However, not long after, Mr. Sweet showed up with his hair grown out and just as white and kinky and impenetrable as it ever was.

Mr. Sweet used to call me his princess, and I believed it. He made me feel pretty at five and six, and simply outrageously devastating at the blazing age of eight and a half. When he came to our house with his guitar the whole family would stop whatever they were doing to sit around him and listen to him play. He liked to play "Sweet Georgia Brown," that was what he called me sometimes, and also he liked to play "Caldonia" and all sorts of sweet, sad, wonderful songs which he sometimes made up. It was from one of these songs that I learned that he had had to marry Miss Mary when he had in fact loved somebody else (now living in Chi'-ca-go or, De-stroy, Michigan). He was not sure that Joe Lee, her "baby," was also his baby. Sometimes he would cry and that was an indication that he was about to die again. And so we would all get prepared, for we were sure to be called upon.

I was seven the first time I remember actually participating in one of Mr. Sweet's "revivals"—my parents told me I had participated before, I had been the one chosen to kiss him and tickle him long before I knew the rite of Mr. Sweet's rehabilitation. He had come to our house, it was a few years after his wife's death, and he was very sad, and also, typically, very drunk. He sat on the floor next to me and my older brother, the rest of the children were grown-up and lived elsewhere, and began to play his guitar and cry. I held his woolly head in my arms and wished I could have been old enough to have been the woman he loved so much and that I had not been lost years and years ago.

When he was leaving my mother said to us that we'd better sleep light that night for we'd probably have to go over to Mr. Sweet's before daylight. And we did. For soon after we had gone to bed one of the neighbors knocked on our door and called my father and said that Mr. Sweet was sinking fast and if we wanted to get in a word before the crossover he'd better shake a leg and get over to Mr. Sweet's house. All the neighbors knew to come to our house if something was wrong with Mr. Sweet, but they did not know how we always managed to make him well, or at least stop him from dying, when he was often so near death. As soon as we heard the cry we got up, my brother and I and my mother and father, and put on our clothes. We hurried out of the house and down the road for we were always afraid that we might someday be too late and Mr. Sweet would get tired of dallying.

10   When we got to the house, a very poor shack really, we found the front room full of neighbors and relatives and someone met us at the door and said that it was all very sad that old Mr. Sweet Little (for Little was his family name although we mostly ignored it) was about to kick the bucket. My parents were advised not to take my brother and me into the "death-room" seeing we were so young and all, but we were so much more accustomed to the death-room than he that we ignored him and dashed in without giving his warning a second thought. I was almost in tears, for these deaths upset me fearfully, and the thought of how much depended on me and my brother (who was such a ham most of the time) made me very nervous.

The doctor was bending over the bed and turned back to tell us for at least the tenth time in the history of my family that alas, old Mr. Sweet Little was dying and that the children had best not see the face of implacable death (I didn't know what "implacable" was, but whatever it was, Mr. Sweet was not!). My father pushed him rather abruptly out of the way saying as he always did and very loudly for he was saying it to Mr. Sweet, "To hell with dying, man, these children want Mr. Sweet!" which was my cue to throw myself upon the bed and kiss Mr. Sweet all around the whiskers and under the eyes and around the collar of his nightshirt where he smelled so strongly of all sorts of things, mostly liniment.

I was very good at bringing him around, for as soon as I saw that he was struggling to open his eyes I knew he was going to be all right and so could finish my revival sure of success. As soon as his eyes were open he would begin to smile and that way I knew that I had surely won. Once though I got a tremendous scare for he could not open his eyes and later I learned that he had had a stroke and that one side of his face was stiff and hard to get into motion. When he began to smile I could tickle him in earnest for I was sure that nothing would get in the way of his laughter, although once he began to cough so hard that he almost threw me off his stomach, but that was when I was very small, little more than a baby, and my bushy hair had gotten in his nose.

When we were sure he would listen to us we would ask him why he was in bed and when he was coming to see us again and could we play with his guitar which more than likely would be leaning against the bed. His eyes would get all misty and he would sometimes cry out loud, but we never let it embarrass us for he knew that we loved him and that we sometimes cried too for no reason. My parents would leave the room to just the three of us; Mr. Sweet, by that time, would be propped up in bed with a number of pillows behind his head and with me sitting and lying on his shoulder and along his chest. Even when he had trouble breathing he would not ask me to get down. Looking into my eyes he would shake his white head and run a scratchy old finger all around my hairline, which was rather low down nearly to my eyebrows and for which some people said I looked like a baby monkey.

My brother was very generous in all this, he let me do all the revivaling—he had done it for years before I was born and so was glad to be able to pass it on to someone new. What he would do while I talked to Mr. Sweet was pretend to play the guitar, in fact pretend that he was a young version of Mr. Sweet, and it always made Mr. Sweet glad to think that someone wanted to be like him—of course we did not know this then, we played the thing by ear, and whatever he seemed to like, we did. We were desperately afraid that he was just going to take off one day and leave us.

15   It did not occur to us that we were doing anything special; we had not learned that death was final when it did come. We thought nothing of triumphing over it so many times, and in fact became a trifle contemptuous of people who let themselves be carried away. It did not occur to us that if our own father had been dying we could not have stopped it, that Mr. Sweet was the only person over whom we had power.

When Mr. Sweet was in his eighties I was a young lady studying away in a university many miles from home. I saw him whenever I went home, but he was never on the verge of dying that I could tell and I began to feel that my anxiety for his health and psychological well-being was unnecessary. By this time he not only had a moustache but a long flowing snow-white beard which I loved and combed and braided for hours. He was still a very heavy drinker and was like an old Chinese opium-user, very peaceful, fragile, gentle, and the only jarring note about him was his old steel guitar which he still played in the old sad, sweet, downhome blues way.

On Mr. Sweet's ninetieth birthday I was finishing my doctorate in Massachusetts and had been making arrangements to go home for several weeks' rest. That morning I got a telegram telling me that Mr. Sweet was dying again and could I please drop everything and come home. Of course I could. My dissertation could wait and my teachers would understand when I explained to them when I got back. I ran to the phone, called the airport, and within four hours I was speeding along the dusty road to Mr. Sweet's.

The house was more dilapidated than when I was last there, barely a shack, but it was overgrown with yellow roses which my family had planted many years ago. The air was heavy and sweet and very peaceful. I felt strange walking through the gate and up the old rickety steps. But the strangeness left me as I caught sight of the long white beard I loved so well flowing down the thin body over the familiar quilt coverlet. Mr. Sweet!

His eyes were closed tight and his hands, crossed over his stomach, were thin and delicate, no longer rough and scratchy. I remembered how always before I had run and jumped up on him just anywhere; now I knew he would not be able to support my weight. I looked around at my parents, and was surprised to see that my father and mother also looked old and frail. My father, his own hair very gray, leaned over the quietly sleeping old man who, incidentally, smelled still of wine and tobacco, and said as he'd done so many times, "To hell with dying, man! My daughter is home to see Mr. Sweet!" My brother had not been able to come as he was in the war in Asia. I bent down and gently stroked the closed eyes and gradually they began to open. The closed, wine-stained lips twitched a little, then parted in a warm, slightly embarrassed smile. Mr. Sweet could see me and he recognized me and his eyes looked very spry and twinkly for a moment. I put my head down on the pillow next to his and we just looked at each other for a long time. Then he began to trace my peculiar hairline with a thin, smooth finger. I closed my eyes when his finger halted above my ear (he used to rejoice at the dirt in my ears when I was little), his hand stayed cupped around my cheek. When I opened my eyes, sure I had reached him in time, his were closed.

20   Even at twenty-four how could I believe that I had failed? that Mr. Sweet was really gone? He had never gone before. But when I looked up at my parents I saw that they were holding back tears. They had loved him dearly. He was like a piece of rare and delicate china which was always being saved from breaking and which finally fell. I looked long at the old face, the wrinkled forehead, the red lips, the hands that still reached out to me. Soon I felt my father pushing something cool into my hands. It was Mr. Sweet's guitar. He had asked them months before to give it to me, he had known that even if I came next time he would not be able to respond in the old way. He did not want me to feel that my trip had been for nothing.

The old guitar! I plucked the strings, hummed "Sweet Georgia Brown." The magic of Mr. Sweet lingered still in the cool steel box. Through the window I could catch the fragrant delicate scent of tender yellow roses. The man on the high old-fashioned bed with the quilt coverlet and the flowing white beard had been my first love.

Comments and Questions

The credibility (p. 20) of this story is immense. Perhaps the main critical question about the story is, in fact: Just how does it achieve such authenticity in so short a space? How does it so effectively absorb the reader right into the scenes depicted? With unusual immediacy, the reader is there to treasure Mr. Sweet's wrinkles and his "kinky and impenetrable" white hair; to relish his strumming out "Sweet Georgia Brown"; to crowd around his bed when he's "about to die again" for yet one more revival; to know again the child's moment of easy certainty that the face of death is not, after all, implacable, that love and need can will even death to benevolence. Clearly, palpable, graphic detail contributes to the authenticity. Walker's evocative blending of the humorous and the poignant into the vividly real can be fully appreciated, however, only by considering her orchestration of point of view, language, character, motivation, and universal theme.

   1. How successfully has Walker transferred the spoken word to the written page? Cite specific examples to support your conclusion.

   2. To what extent does Mr. Sweet embody the curious mixture of giddiness and sobriety that is often the child's? Does Walker provide adequate motivating and characterizing factors to make Mr. Sweet's traits genuinely believable? Comment extensively.

   3. Even the name Mr. Sweet suggests a one-dimensional character. Specifically how does Walker avoid such artificiality, and how early in the story does she begin?

   4. What is the point of view (p. 19) and how does it contribute to the credibility of the story? How is the perspective of the narrator especially like that of the narrators of Porter's "The Grave" (p. 109) and Joyce's "Araby" (p. 113)?

   5. Comment in depth on the reciprocal nature of the relationship between Mr. Sweet and the children. How does that balanced reciprocity serve to validate the relationship for the reader?

   6. What does the narrator mean when she says (in the third sentence) that her older brothers and sisters "got the most benefit from Mr. Sweet"? What benefit?

   7. Justify the final sentence of the story.

   8. How is the title suggestive of the universal theme of the story? What is the crucial role of the narrator's father?

Leo Tolstoy   (1828–1910)
Three Deaths

1

It was autumn. Two carriages were driving at a rapid trot along the highroad. In the foremost sat two women. One was a lady, thin and pale; the other, her maid, was plump, with shining, red cheeks. Her short, coarse hair stood out under her faded hat; her red hand, in a torn glove, kept hurriedly putting it tidy; her high bosom, covered with a tapestry kerchief, was eloquent of health; her quick, black eyes watched out of the window the fields flying past, then glanced timidly at her mistress, then shifted uneasily about the corners of the carriage. Just before the maid's nose swung the lady's hat, hanging from the rack above; on her lap lay a puppy. Her feet were kept from the floor by the boxes that stood on the carriage floor, and could be faintly heard knocking on them through the shaking of the springs and the rattling of the windows.

With her hands clasped on her knees and her eyes closed, the lady swayed feebly to and fro on the cushions that had been put at her back, and with a slight frown she coughed inwardly. On her head she wore a white nightcap, and a light blue kerchief was tied on her soft, white neck. A straight parting, retreating under her cap, divided her fair, pomaded, exceedingly flat hair, and there was a dry, deathlike look about the whiteness of the skin of this wide parting. The faded, yellowish skin hung loose on her delicate and beautiful features and was flushed on her cheeks. Her lips were dry and restless, her eyelashes were thin and straight, and her cloth travelling cloak fell in straight folds over her sunken bosom. Though her eyes were closed, the lady's face expressed fatigue, irritation, and habitual suffering. A footman was dozing on the box, one elbow on the rail of the seat. The driver, hired from the posting-station, shouted briskly to the four sturdy, sweating horses, and looked round now and then at the other driver, who called to him from behind on the coach. Smoothly and rapidly the wheels made their broad, parallel tracks along the chalky mud of the road. The sky was gray and cold; a damp mist was falling over the fields and the road. The carriage was close, and smelt of eau de Cologne and dust. The sick woman stretched her head back and slowly opened her eyes. Her large, handsome, dark eyes were very bright.

"Again," she said, her beautiful, thin hand nervously thrusting away a corner of the maid's cloak which was just brushing against her knees, and her mouth twitched painfully. Matryosha gathered up her cloak in both hands, lifted it up on her lap, and edged further away. Her blooming face flushed bright red. The sick woman's fine dark eyes kept eager watch on the servant's actions. She leaned with both hands on the seat and tried to raise herself, so as to be sitting higher; but her strength failed her. Her mouth twitched and her whole face worked with an expression of helpless, wrathful irony. "You might at least help me! . . . Ah, you needn't! I can do it myself, only be so good as not to lay your bundles, bags, or whatever they are behind me, please! You had better not touch me if you're so awkward!"

The lady shut her eyes, and rapidly raising her eyelids again glanced at the maid. Matryosha was staring at her and biting her red underlip. A heavy sigh rose from the sick woman's chest, but changed to a cough before it was uttered. She turned away, frowning, and clutched at her chest with both hands. When the cough was over, she closed her eyes again and sat without stirring. The carriage and the coach drove into a village. Matryosha put her stout arm out from under her kerchief and crossed herself.

5   "What is it?" asked the lady.

"A station, madam."

"What do you cross yourself for, I ask?"

"A church, madam."

The sick woman turned towards the window, and began slowly crossing herself, her great eyes fastened on the big village church as the carriage drove by it.

10   The two carriages stopped together at the station. The sick woman's husband and the doctor got out of the other carriage and came up to her.

"How do you feel?" asked the doctor, taking her pulse.

"Well, how are you, my dear—not tired?" asked her husband, in French. "Wouldn't you like to get out?"

Matryosha, gathering up her bundles, squeezed into a corner so as not to be in their way as they talked.

"Just the same," answered the lady. "I won't get out."

15   Her husband stayed a little while beside the carriage, then went into the station-house. Matryosha got out of the carriage and ran on tiptoe through the mud to the gates.

"If I am ill, it's no reason you shouldn't have your lunch," the invalid said with a faint smile to the doctor, who was standing at the carriage window.

"None of them care anything about me," she added to herself, as soon as the doctor had moved with sedate step away from her and run at a trot up the steps of the station-house. "They are all right, so they don't care. O my God!"

"Well, Eduard Ivanovich," said her husband, meeting the doctor and rubbing his hands, with a cheery smile. "I've ordered the case of wine to be brought in. What do you say to a bottle?"

"I shouldn't say no," answered the doctor.

20   "Well, how is she?" the husband asked with a sigh, lifting his eyebrows and dropping his voice.

"I have told you she can't possibly get as far as Italy; if she reaches Moscow it will be a wonder, especially in this weather."

"What are we to do! Oh my God! my God!" The husband put his hand over his eyes. "Put it here," he added to the servant who brought in the case of wine.

"You should have kept her at home," the doctor answered, shrugging his shoulders.

"But tell me, what could I do?" protested the husband. "I did everything I could, you know, to keep her. I talked to her of our means, and of the children whom we should have to leave behind, and of my business—she won't hear a word of anything. She makes plans for her life abroad as though she were strong and well. And to tell her of her position would be the death of her."

25   "But death has hold of her already, you ought to know it, Vasily Dmitrich. A person can't live without lungs, and the lungs can't grow again. It's distressing and terrible, but what's one to do? My duty and yours is simply to see that her end should be as easy as possible. It's the priest who is needed now."

"O my God! But conceive my position, having to speak to her of the last sacrament. Come what will, I can't tell her. You know how good she is."

"You must try, all the same, to persuade her to wait till the roads are frozen," said the doctor, shaking his head significantly, "or we may have a disaster on the road."

"Aksyusha, hey, Aksyusha!" shrieked the stationmaster's daughter, flinging a jacket over her head, and stamping on the dirty back steps of the station; "let's go and have a look at the lady from Shirkin; they say she's being taken abroad for her lungs. I've never seen what people look like in consumption."

Aksyusha darted out at the doorway, and arm in arm they ran by the gate. Slackening their pace, they walked by the carriage, and peeped in at the lowered window. The sick woman turned her head towards them, but noticing their curiosity, she frowned and turned away.

30   "My gra-a-cious!" said the stationmaster's daughter, turning her head away quickly. "Such a wonderful beauty as she was, and what does she look like now. Enough to frighten one, really. Did you see, did you see, Aksyusha?"

"Yes, she is thin!" Aksyusha assented. "Let's go by and get another look at her, as though we were going to the well. She turned away before I'd seen her properly. I am sorry for her, Masha!"

"And the mud's awful!" answered Masha, and both ran back to the gate.

"I've grown frightful, it seems," thought the invalid. "Ah, to make haste, to make haste to get abroad, then I shall soon be better!"

"Well, how are you, my dear?" said her husband, still munching as he came up to the carriage.

35   "Always that invariable question," thought the sick woman, "and he goes on eating too!"

"Just the same," she muttered through her teeth.

"Do you know, my dear, I'm afraid the journey will be bad for you in this weather, and Eduard Ivanovich says so too. Hadn't we better turn back?"

She kept wrathfully silent.

"The weather will change, and the roads perhaps will be hard, and that would make it better for you; and then we would all go together."

40   "Excuse me. If I hadn't listened to you long ago, I should be in Berlin by now and should be quite well."

"That couldn't be helped, my angel; it was out of the question, as you know! But now, if you would wait for a month, you would be ever so much better. I should have settled my business, and we could take the children."

"The children are quite well, and I am not."

"But consider, my dear, with this weather if you get worse on the road . . . there, at any rate, you're at home."

"And if I am at home? . . . To die at home?" the sick woman answered hotly. But the word "die" evidently terrified her; she bent an imploring, questioning look upon her husband. He dropped his eyes and did not speak. The sick woman's mouth puckered all at once like a child's, and tears dropped from her eyes. Her husband buried his face in his handkerchief, and walked away from the carriage without speaking.

45   "No, I am going," said the sick woman, lifting her eyes towards heaven, and she fell to whispering disconnected words. "My God, what for?" she said, and the tears flowed more freely. For a long while she prayed fervently, but there was still the same pain and tightness on her chest. The sky, the fields, and the road were just as gray and cheerless; and the same autumn mist, neither thicker nor clearer, hung over the mud of the road, the roofs of the huts, the carriage and the sheepskin coats of the drivers, who were greasing and harnessing a carriage, chatting together in their vigorous, merry voices.

2

The horses were put in the shafts; but the driver lingered. He went into the drivers' hut. It was hot and stifling, dark and oppressive in the hut; there was a smell of human beings, baking bread, and cabbage, and sheepskins. There were several drivers in the room: the cook was busy at the stove; on the top of the stove lay a sick man wrapped in sheepskins.

"Uncle Fyodor! hey, Uncle Fyodor!" said the driver as he came into the room. He

was a young fellow, in a sheepskin coat with a whip stuck in his belt, and he was addressing the sick man.

"What do you want Fedya for, you windbag?" one of the drivers interposed. "They
are waiting for you in the carriage."

"I want to ask him for his boots; I've worn mine out," answered the young fellow,
tossing back his hair and straightening the gloves in his belt. "Is he asleep? Hey, Uncle
Fyodor?" he repeated, going up to the stove.

50   "What?" a weak voice was heard in reply, and a thin face with a red beard bent over
from the stove. A big, wasted, white hand, covered with hair, pulled up a coat on the bony
shoulder in the dirty shirt. "Give me a drink, brother; what do you want?"

The young man handed him a dipper of water.

"Well, Fedya," he said, hesitating, "you won't be wanting your new boots now; give
them to me; you won't be going out, you know."

Pressing his weary head to the shining dipper, and wetting his scanty, hanging mustaches in the turbid water, the sick man drank feebly and eagerly. His tangled beard was
not clean, his sunken, lusterless eyes were lifted with an effort to the young man's face.
When he had finished drinking he tried to lift his hand to wipe his wet lips, but he could
not, and he wiped them on the sleeve of the coat. Without uttering a sound, but breathing
heavily through his nose, he looked straight into the young man's eyes, trying to rally his
strength.

"Maybe you've promised them to someone already?" said the young man; "if so,
never mind. The thing is, it's soaking wet outside, and I've got to go out on a job; and I
said to myself, why, I'll ask Fedya for his boots, he'll not need them, for sure. If you are
likely to need them yourself, say so."

55   There was a gurgle and a rattle in the sick man's throat; he bent over and was
choked by a deep, stifling cough.

"He need them!" the cook cried out in sudden anger, filling the whole hut with her
voice. "He's not got off the stove these two months! Why, he coughs fit to split himself; it
makes me ache inside simply to hear him. How could he want boots? He won't wear new
boots to be buried! And time he was, too, long ago—God forgive me the sin! Why, he
coughs fit to split himself. He ought to be moved into another hut, or somewhere! There
are hospitals, I've heard say, for such in the town; he takes up the whole place, and what's
one to do? One hasn't room to turn around. And then they expect me to keep the place
clean!"

"Hi, Seryoga! go and take your seat; the gentry are waiting," the stationmaster
shouted at the door.

Seryoga would have gone away without waiting for an answer, but the sick man's
eyes, while he was coughing, had told him he wanted to answer.

"You take the boots, Seryoga," said he, stifling the cough and taking breath a minute.
"Only buy me a stone when I die, do you hear?" he added huskily.

60   "Thanks, uncle, so I'll take them; and as to the stone, ay, ay, I'll buy it."

"There, lads, you hear?" the sick man managed to articulate, and again he bent over
and began choking.

"All right, we heard," said one of the drivers. "Go along, Seryoga, or the overseer
will be running after you again. The lady from Shirkin is ill."

Seryoga quickly pulled off his torn boots, which were much too large for him, and
thrust them under a bench. Uncle Fyodor's new boots fitted his feet perfectly, and Seryoga
went out to the carriage looking at them.

"What grand boots! let me grease them for you," said a driver with the greasepot in
his hand, as Seryoga got on the box and picked up the reins. "Did he give them to you
for nothing?"

65   "Why, are you jealous?" answered Seryoga, getting up and shaking down the skirts of his coat about his legs. "Hi, get up, my darlings!" he shouted to the horses, brandishing the whip, and the two carriages, with their occupants, boxes, and baggage, rolled swiftly along the wet road, and vanished into the gray autumn mist.

The sick driver remained lying on the stove in the stifling hut. Unrelieved by coughing, he turned over on the other side with an effort, and was quiet. All day till evening, men were coming and going and dining in the hut; there was no sound from the sick man. At nightfall, the cook clambered up onto the stove and reached across his legs to get a sheepskin. "Don't you be angry with me, Nastasya," said the sick man; "I shall soon clear out of your place."

"That's all right, that's all right; why, I didn't mean it," muttered Nastasya. "But what is it that's wrong with you, uncle? Tell me about it."

"All my inside's wasted away. God knows what it is."

"My word! and does your throat hurt when you cough!"

70   "It hurts me all over. My death is at hand—that's what it is. Oh, oh, oh!" moaned the sick man.

"Cover your legs up like this," said Nastasya, pulling a coat over him as she crept off the stove.

A night-light glimmered dimly all night in the hut. Nastasya and some ten drivers lay on the floor and the benches asleep, and snoring loudly. The sick man alone moaned faintly, coughed, and turned over on the stove. Towards morning he became quite still.

"A queer dream I had in the night," said the cook, stretching next morning in the half-light. "I dreamed that Uncle Fyodor got down from the stove and went out to chop wood. 'Nastasya,' says he, 'I'll split you some'; and I says to him, 'How can you chop wood?' and he snatches up the axe and starts chopping so fast, so fast that the chips were flying. 'Why,' says I, 'you were ill, weren't you?' 'No,' says he, 'I'm all right,' and he swings the axe, so that it gave me quite a fright. I screamed out and waked up. Isn't he dead, perhaps? Uncle Fyodor! Hey, uncle!"

Fyodor made no sound in reply.

75   "May be he is dead. I'll get up and see," said one of the drivers who was awake.

A thin hand, covered with reddish hairs, hung down from the stove; it was cold and pale.

"I'll go and tell the overseer. He's dead, seemingly," said the driver.

Fyodor had no relations—he had come from distant parts. The next day he was buried in the new graveyard beyond the copse, and for several days after Nastasya told every one of the dream she had had, and how she had been the first to discover that Uncle Fyodor was dead.

3

Spring had come. Streams of water hurried gurgling between the frozen dung-heaps in the wet streets of the town. The people moving to and fro were gayly dressed and gayly chattering. Behind the fences of the little gardens the buds on the trees were swelling, and their branches rustled faintly in the fresh breeze. Everywhere there was a running and a dripping of clear drops. . . . The sparrows chattered incoherently, and fluttered to and fro on their little wings. On the sunny side, on fences, trees, and houses, all was movement. There was youth and gladness in the sky and on the earth and in the heart of man. In one of the principal streets there was straw lying in front of a large house; in the house lay the dying woman who had been hastening abroad.

80   At the closed door of her room stood the patient's husband and her cousin, an elderly woman; on a sofa sat a priest with downcast eyes, holding something wrapped up in his stole. In a corner an old lady, the patient's mother, lay in an armchair, weeping

bitterly. Near her stood a maid holding a clean pocket-handkerchief in readiness for the old lady when she should ask for it. Another maid was rubbing the old lady's temples with something and blowing on her gray head under her cap.

"Well, Christ be with you, my dear," said the husband to the elderly woman who was standing with him at the door; "she has such confidence in you, you know so well how to talk to her; go in, and have a good talk with her." He would have opened the door; but the cousin restrained him, put her handkerchief several times to her eyes, and shook her head.

"Come, now, I don't look as if I had been crying, I think," she said, and opening the door herself, she went into the sickroom.

The husband was in great excitement, and seemed utterly distraught. He walked towards the old lady, but stopped short a few paces from her, turned, walked about the room, and went up to the priest. The priest looked at him, raised his eyebrows heavenwards, and sighed. His thick, grizzled beard turned upwards too, and then sank again.

"My God! my God!" said the husband.

85 "There is nothing one can do," said the priest, and again his brows and his beard were elevated and drooped again.

"And her mother here!" the husband said, almost in despair. "She will never be able to bear this! She loves her, she loves her so that she . . . I don't know. If you, father, would attempt to soothe her and to persuade her to go out of this room."

The priest rose and went to the old lady.

"True it is, that none can sound the depths of a mother's heart," said he; "but God is merciful."

The old lady's face began suddenly twitching, and she sobbed hysterically.

90 "God is merciful," the priest went on, when she was a little calmer. "In my parish, I must tell you, there was a man ill, much worse than Marya Dmitryevna, and a simple artisan cured him with herbs in a very short time. And this same artisan is in Moscow now, indeed. I told Vasily Dmitryevich—he might try him. Anyway, it would be a comfort to the sick woman. To God all things are possible."

"No, she can't live," said the old lady; "if it could have been me, but God takes her." And her hysterics grew so violent that she fainted.

The sick woman's husband hid his face in his hands, and ran out of the room.

The first person that met him in the corridor was a boy of six, who was running at full speed after a little girl younger than himself.

"Shouldn't I take the children to see their mamma?" asked the nurse.

95 "No, she doesn't want to see them. It upsets her."

The boy stood still for a moment, staring intently into his father's face, then suddenly kicking up his foot, with a merry shriek he ran on.

"I'm pretending she's my black horse, papa!" shouted the boy, pointing to his sister.

Meanwhile in the next room the cousin was sitting by the sick woman's bedside, and trying by skillfully leading up to the subject to prepare her for the idea of death. The doctor was at the other window mixing a draught.

The sick woman, in a white dressing-gown, sat propped up with pillows in bed, and gazed at the cousin without speaking.

100 "Ah, my dear," she said, suddenly interrupting her, "don't try to prepare me. Don't treat me as a child. I am a Christian. I know all about it. I know I haven't long to live; I know that if my husband would have listened to me sooner, I should have been in Italy, and perhaps, most likely indeed, should have been quite well. Everyone told him so. But it can't be helped, it seems that it was God's will. We are all great sinners, I know that; but

I put my trust in God's mercy: He will forgive all, surely, all. I try to understand myself. I, too, have sinned greatly, my dear. But, to make up, how I have suffered. I have tried to bear my sufferings with patience. . . ."

"Then may I send for the priest, my dear? You will feel all the easier after the sacrament," said the cousin. The sick woman bowed her head in token of assent. "God forgive me, a sinner!" she murmured.

The cousin went out and beckoned to the priest.

"She is an angel!" she said to the husband with tears in her eyes. The husband began to weep; the priest went in at the door; the old lady was still unconscious, and in the outer room there was a complete stillness. Five minutes later the priest came out, and taking off his stole smoothed back his hair.

"Thank God, the lady is calmer now," he said; "she wants to see you."

105   The cousin and the husband went in. The sick woman was weeping quietly, gazing at the holy picture.

"I congratulate you, my dear," said her husband.

"Thank you! How happy I am now, what unspeakable joy I am feeling!" said the sick woman, and a faint smile played about her thin lips. "How merciful is God! Is it not true? Is He not merciful and almighty?" And again with eyes full of tears she gazed at the holy picture in eager prayer.

Then suddenly something seemed to recur to her mind. She beckoned her husband to her.

"You never will do what I ask," she said in a weak, irritable voice.

110   Her husband, craning his neck forward, listened submissively.

"What is it, my dear?"

"How often I've told you those doctors don't know anything; there are plain women healers, who work cures. . . . The priest told me . . . an artisan . . . send for him."

"For whom, my dear?"

"My God, he won't understand anything!" . . .

115   And the sick woman frowned and covered her eyes. The doctor went up and took her hand. The pulse was growing perceptibly weaker and weaker. He made a sign to the husband. The sick woman noticed this gesture and looked around in alarm. The cousin turned away, and burst into tears.

"Don't cry, don't torture yourself and me," said the sick woman. "That destroys all the calm left me."

"You are an angel!" said the cousin, kissing her hand.

"No, kiss me here, it's only the dead who are kissed on the hand. My God! my God!"

The same evening the sick woman was a corpse, and the corpse lay in a coffin in the drawing-room of the great house. The doors of the big room were closed, and in it a deacon sat alone, reading the Psalms of David aloud in a rhythmic, nasal tone. The bright light of the wax candles in the tall silver candlesticks fell on the pale brow of the dead woman, on the heavy, waxen hands and the stonelike folds of the shroud, that jutted up horribly at the knees and toes. The deacon read on rhythmically without taking in the meaning of his own words, and the words echoed and died away strangely in the still room. From time to time the sounds of children's voices and the tramp of their feet came from a far-away room.

120   " 'Hidest thou thy face, they are troubled,' " the psalm-reader boomed; " 'thou takest away their breath, they die and return to their dust. Thou sendest forth thy spirit, they are created; and thou renewest the face of the earth. The glory of the Lord shall endure for ever.' "

The face of the dead woman was stern and solemn. Nothing stirred the pure, cold brow and the firmly set lips. She was all attention. But did she even now understand those grand words?

4

A month later a stone chapel was raised over the dead woman's grave. But there was still no stone over the driver's grave, and there was nothing but the bright green grass over the mound, which was the only sign of a man's past existence.

"You will be sinning, Seryoga," the cook at the station said one day, "if you don't buy a stone for Fyodor. You were always saying it was winter, but now why don't you keep your word? I was by at the time. He's come back once already to ask you for it; if you don't buy it, he'll come again and stifle you."

"Why, did I say I wasn't going to?" answered Seryoga; "I'll buy a stone as I said I would; I'll buy one for a silver rouble and a half. I've not forgotten, but it must be fetched, you know. As soon as I've a chance to go to the town I'll buy it."

125   "You might put a cross up anyway," put in an old driver, "or else it's a downright shame. You're wearing the boots."

"Where's one to get a cross? You wouldn't cut one out of a log of firewood?"

"What are you talking about? You can't hew it out of a log. You take an axe and go early in the morning into the copse; you can cut a cross there. An aspen or something you can fell. And it'll make a fine wooden monument too. Or else you'll have to go and stand the forester a drink of vodka. One doesn't want to have to give him a drink for every trifle. The other day I broke a splinter-bar; I cut myself a first-rate new one, and no one said a word to me."

In the early morning, when it was hardly light, Seryoga took his axe and went into the wood. Over all lay a chill, even-colored veil of still-falling dew, not lighted up by the sun. The east was imperceptibly growing clearer, reflecting its faint light on the arch of sky covered with fine clouds. Not a blade of grass below, not a leaf on the topmost twig stirred. The stillness of the forest was only broken at intervals by the sound of wings in a tree or a rustle on the ground. Suddenly a strange sound, not one of nature's own, rang out and died away on the edge of the forest. But again the sound was heard, and began to be repeated at regular intervals near the trunks of the motionless trees. One of the treetops began shaking in a strange way; its sappy leaves whispered something; and a warbler that had been perched on one of its branches fluttered round it twice, and uttering a whistle and wagging its tail, settled on another tree.

The sound of the axe was more and more muffled, the sappy, white chips flew out on the dewy grass, and a faint crackling sound followed each blow. The tree shuddered all over, bowed, and quickly stood up straight again, trembling in dismay on its roots. For a moment all was still, but again the tree bent; a crack was heard in its trunk, and with a snapping of twigs its branches dropped, and it crashed down with its top on the damp earth. The sound of the axe and of steps died away. The warbler whistled and flew up higher. The branch in which it had caught its wings shook for a little while in all its leaves, then became still like the rest. The trees displayed their motionless branches more gladly than ever in the newly opened space.

130   The first beams of the sun, piercing the delicate cloud, shone out in the sky and darted over the earth. The mist began rolling in waves in the hollows; the dew glittered sparkling on the green grass; the translucent clouds turned white, and floated in haste across the blue sky. The birds flitted to and fro in the thickets and twittered some happy song, like mad things. The sappy leaves whispered joyously and calmly on the tree-tops, and the branches of the living trees, slowly, majestically, swayed above the fallen dead tree.

Comments and Questions

The marrow of this story is irony. Appropriately, the essence of both its method and its meaning is richly ironic (see "Sidenote on irony," p. 26). Setting, organization, language, characterization, action—all are functionally oxymoronic in developing a theme that couples the opposites of life and death (oxymoron: a close combination of opposites).

1. The first sentence is brief and emphatic and is structured in such a way as necessarily to throw all of its weight of meaning on the final word. Why is so much emphasis given to the setting of autumn? A careful reading of Keats's "To Autumn" (p. 469) could throw some light on the question, especially if one also reads again the elaborate, contrasting descriptions of the dying woman and her maid in the opening paragraphs of the story. What, then, is the thematic significance of opening with autumn?

2. When the coach stops at the station, the husband and the doctor are interrupted by the servant with the wine case. Read that short paragraph again, and comment on its significance and on the later passage beginning, " 'Well, how are you, my dear?' said her husband, still munching as he came up to the carriage."

3. What meticulous unity of purpose do you see in the setting, the pervasive nature of the diction (especially verbs and modifiers), and the organization or structure of the paragraph which opens Part 3? Compare the language and content of that paragraph with those of the final paragraph of the story. How do the two paragraphs relate to the passage read from the Psalms of David?

4. The title is unequivocal in equating the significance of the deaths of a lady of high station, a peasant, and a tree. What is the parallel implication about the lives of the three? Does that relate to the perspective of the passage from the Psalms of David?

5. What is ironical about the priest's role in the story? What is the function of the sick woman's cousin?

6. Compare the "markers" of all three graves. Do they constitute a subtle and ironic comment by Tolstoy?

Poetry

. . . is "news that stays news"
EZRA POUND

**The verse is mine, but, friend, when you declaim it,
It seems like yours, so grievously you maim it.**
MARTIAL

Preliminaries

Robert Frost (1874–1963)
Stopping by Woods
on a Snowy Evening

Whose woods these are I think I know.
His house is in the village though;
He will not see me stopping here
To watch his woods fill up with snow.

5 My little horse must think it queer
To stop without a farmhouse near
Between the woods and frozen lake
The darkest evening of the year.

He gives his harness bells a shake
10 To ask if there is some mistake.
The only other sound's the sweep
Of easy wind and downy flake.

The woods are lovely, dark, and deep.
But I have promises to keep,
15 And miles to go before I sleep,
And miles to go before I sleep.

The definitions of poetry, the hymns of praise, and the essays on the nature of poetry would cram the shelves of any modest public library and overflow onto the floors as well. Good talk about poetry is nevertheless rare, and even the best of it will rest lightly on fallow ground until we ourselves have learned how to penetrate the inner life of a few poems. We cannot be talked into enjoying the pleasures of poetry, but we can bring ourselves to such pleasures by learning to understand individual poems.

Each type of literature has a structure of its own. If we wish to understand the structure of a poem, it seems sensible to begin by examining one. We shall learn much about poetry in general if we can discover exactly what Frost has done and how he has done it.

The plain sense of a poem   As we read Frost's poem for the first time, a certain kind of sense comes through to us almost immediately. This sense we shall call the poem's plain sense, sometimes called literal sense or literal meaning. The plain sense gives us the literal facts of a poem, and with such facts all understanding of a poem begins, but does *not* end.

The plain sense of Frost's poem tells us that the speaker, returning home at dusk in his one-horse sleigh, stops to enjoy the peace and solitude of the occasion: the snow is falling softly, the woods are inviting, there is no other human being to break the silence. But the horse finds no reason for stopping: it is growing dark, there is no house in sight, and the miles stretch before them. Reflecting on his horse's impatience, the speaker concedes that he should move on to keep the commitments he has made.

But in drawing the plain sense from the poem, we have raised many questions. Unless this poem means more than the preceding paraphrase includes, does the poem merit further consideration? Will another kind of approach to the poem reveal meanings not yet located? These and other questions we must answer if we are to understand the poem fully. Let us note before we proceed that paraphrasing the poem helped to raise the questions about the poem's fullest meaning. Unless the plain sense is clearly understood before further analysis of a poem begins, the reader is likely to misconstrue the total meaning of the poem.

Imagery   A little closer reading of the poem shows us that Frost is depending on our ability to see and hear imaginatively. When he uses such words as *woods* and *horse,* he depends on our ability to see the real woods and horse. When the horse "gives his harness bells a shake," and when we are told that

> The only other sound's the sweep
> Of easy wind and downy flake,

the poet depends on our ability to hear these sounds. Contrary to some popular opinion, there is no mystery in imagery. Its function in poetry is identical with its function in everyday speech: it presents to readers their concrete world of things and recalls the sight and sound and feel of them. With imagery poets people and furnish the world of their poems and cause us to experience that world as directly and unmistakably as we experience life itself. Indeed, it is sometimes said that imagery is the very basis of poetry, and as we proceed, we shall observe the force of this assertion.

Figurative language   A still closer reading of Frost's poem shows that he has used some of his imagery in a special way. When we read that

> My little horse must think it queer
> To stop without a farmhouse near,

we suspect that this is no ordinary horse. And when we read further that

> He gives his harness bells a shake
> To ask if there is some mistake,

we know that this is a very special horse, one that asks questions. At this point in our attempt to understand the poem, we are moving from the plain sense to the figurative sense of the poem. The speaker in the poem is not alone, as he seemed to be in the first stanza, and we sense a conflict of some sort between him and the horse. The horse, having been given some human characteristics, becomes in a sense a human being and challenges the speaker in some significant way. By comparing the horse with a human being, the poet has described the horse figuratively.

There are other figures in the poem, as in the lines

> The only other sound's the *sweep*
> Of *easy* wind and *downy* flake,

in which both the wind and snow are described figuratively, not literally. The wind moves gracefully, easily, with the curving, hushed motion of an unseen broom; and the snowflakes are as soft as the down, or fluffy feathers, on a young bird.

It is customary at this point in most books on the nature of poetry to describe in abstract terms the reason for using figurative language. Suppose we forego this temptation and permit the poem itself to tell us. Perhaps the poem can answer the question most often asked by students and general readers alike: "Why don't poets say what they *mean*? If by *downy flake* a poet means soft flake, why doesn't the poet say so?" Such questions are usually asked impatiently, as if only poets resorted to figures of speech. But our everyday speech is peppered (!) with figures of speech. We "go on a lark," "lead a dog's life," "smell a rat," "stumble in our thinking," and "walk the straight and narrow path." Aren't we saying what we mean? We are saying exactly what we mean, and so is Frost. The word *soft* is too general: there is also soft steel and soft wood. How soft is soft? We know how soft Frost's flakes are: they are as soft as down—about as soft as soft can be.

The figure of speech not only says exactly what the poet means, *it also invites the reader to help to say it.* To understand what Frost means by "downy flake," we must transfer the relevant characteristics from the down of birds to the snowflakes. This is an imaginative act, not a passive acceptance. *The figure requires us to participate in the life of the poem.* (For further exploration of figures, see "Figure and Symbol," p. 377.)

Symbolism   We now return to Frost's little horse. The poet has described the horse figuratively by giving him certain characteristics of a person. The horse thinks it queer "to stop without a farmhouse near" and he therefore asks, "if there is some mistake" about this stopping. He is challenging the "impractical" sense of the driver with his own horse sense. When the writer uses one thing to stand for another, we call it a symbol. The horse stands for horse sense and operates as a symbol in the poem, as we shall observe later.

Not all figures of speech contain symbols, and not all symbols in a poem are embedded in figures of speech. (For further explanation of this distinction, see "Figure and Symbol," p. 377.) The horse is a figure and a symbol, but what about the "woods," the "promises," and the "miles"? These things are not figuratively described, but they could be symbols. And if they are, what do they stand for? Why is the driver of the horse tempted to interrupt his journey by watching the woods fill up with snow? Why does he regard them as "lovely, dark, and deep"? To whom has he given "promises," and what kind of promises? And while we are bearing down on this seemingly innocent little poem, questioning every literal stroke of the poet's pen, let us ask what kind of "miles" are meant. And is the "sleep" only temporary or permanent?

Perhaps these questions have already suggested that many symbols in poetry have been made conventional through long use. Just as the handclasp in everyday life stands for friendliness, the word *dark* or *darkest* in poetry may stand for something unknown or forbidding or secretive, perhaps even tragic. The title of Arthur Koestler's novel *Darkness at Noon* is completely symbolic and suggests that some tragedy throws its shadow over our century. Here a warning is appropriate: such words as *darkness, noon, light, black,* and *white* are not always used symbolically. How, then, do we know when they are so used? Symbols are identified and their meaning made clear by the full context of the poem. In fact, this principle determines the meaning of all the elements in every poem. It can be stated this way: *the whole poem helps to determine the meaning of its parts, and, in turn, each part helps to determine the meaning of the whole poem.*

The meaning of a poem: the parts and the whole   As the first step in understanding a poem, we have seen how helpful it is to make a paraphrase of its plain sense. We are now in a position to make a different kind of paraphrase, one that includes the figurative-symbolic meaning of the poem. We are seeing again the method used in all creative literature, a method we have already seen operate in fiction. As we begin, we keep in mind imagery, figurative language, and symbolism. We should enjoy this detective work, determined to let nothing important escape us.

Frost's imagery gives us the life-texture of the situation and makes it credible, or believable. Within this context of reality we can think and feel as we do in real life: we can participate in the life of the poem. But in order to do so we must understand the relationships of the imagery, figures, and symbols: their relationships make the symbolic meaning of the poem.

Why is the driver tempted to interrupt his journey? Is it because nature has invited him to her communion? The solitude and peace of the woods softly filling with snow tempt him to leave off this moving from place to place—to what end is all this journeying? The woods, "lovely, dark and deep," invite him to leave the traffic of the world on "the darkest evening of the year," the time of his life when his personal burdens weigh most heavily upon him.* But the dramatic device of the horse shows us the conflict within the man: shall he yield to this temptation or move on to fulfill his promises? The noise of the harness bells breaks his reverie, and asks for his decision.

Having come so far in this symbolic interpretation of the poem, it is no longer possible to regard the "promises," the "miles," and the "sleep" as mere literal facts:

> The woods are lovely, dark, and deep.
> But I have promises to keep,
> And miles to go before I sleep,
> And miles to go before I sleep.

The last stanza can, therefore, be paraphrased by saying that the driver consents to move on, to forego entering a world of his own, because he has promises and responsibilities to fulfill to humanity during the years before he dies. Interpreted figuratively, these lines reconcile the conflict within the driver. This conflict is a condition that exists in most, if not all, human beings, and for this reason we say that Frost's poem has universal value, or universality.

Rhythm and rhyme   There are other elements, not yet mentioned, that Frost has used to fashion the total meaning of his poem. It is sometimes difficult for readers to believe that such matters as rhythm and rhyme are used to convey meaning. Popular opinion regards them as troublesome technical matters of interest to the specialist only or, at best, as ornaments on the poetic Christmas tree. Once again let us forego the customary abstract definitions of such matters and let the poet's practice provide the instruction.

---

*Some readers have found a death wish in this poem. In a public lecture at the State University of Iowa, April 13, 1959, Frost stated explicitly that the poem "is not concerned with death." His statement, of course, does not settle the matter. Nevertheless, the primary tension in the poem is between the horse and the driver, and they hardly represent life and death. We may note, however, other tensions developed in the poem that support the major conflict: driver vs. owner, woods vs. promises, "miles to go" vs. sleep.

After all we have now discovered about Frost's compact, sensitive lyric, we can hardly suspect him of decorating his poem with the trinkets of rhythm and rhyme to exhibit his cleverness. Here, it should be made very clear that poetry should be spoken aloud: poetry is speech, and the voice or tone of poets communicates their attitude toward the facts of the poem. Unless we *hear* Frost's lines being spoken aloud, all our observations that follow will miss the mark.

A very old definition of poetry regards it as a fusion of sound and sense.* Note that word *fusion:* not a mechanical combination, but a fusion, a melting together of sound and sense. In our paraphrase of the figurative meaning of the poem earlier, we apparently discussed the sense while ignoring the sound. But— now the secret comes out—this was not so. Experienced readers of poetry know that the division is impossible because as one reads for sense, one is either consciously or unconsciously being influenced by the sound. Hence before our paraphrase of the poem had been started, the sound of the poem had already done its work, exerting its influence on the writer of the paraphrase. Now let us see just how skillful Frost has been.

As we read the poem aloud, we hear and feel the movement within each line. In a good poem the right sound is fused with the right sense, thus:

Whose woods these are I think I know.
His house is in the village though.

Now let us change the word order but not the words themselves:

I think I know whose woods these are
Though his house is in the village.

Here, the wrong sound has distorted the sense.

As we read Frost's arrangement aloud, we hear the four pulsations or beats in each line. Because there are four beats we call the line *tetrameter* (tetra = four), a line of four feet. We hear also that each foot contains two syllables, the first one unstressed and the second one stressed (whŏse woóds), which foot we call *iambic.* The iambic foot is acknowledged to be the most natural rhythm in colloquial English, that is, in our familiar, everyday spoken language. Compare Frost's lines with these (read them aloud):

'Twas the night before Christ-mas, when all through the house,
Not a crea-ture was stir-ring, not e-ven a mouse.

This anapestic rhythm is appropriate to give us the feel of galloping reindeer and the excitement of Christmas Eve, but it is hardly appropriate for the colloquial expression with which Frost speaks to us directly, simply, and naturally. It should be clear, then, that his rhythm is not a decoration, *but rather a basic element in the poem's structure and meaning.*

---

*As Pope put it, "The sound must seem an Echo to the sense" (p. 356). Frost speaks of "the sound of sense."

A brief examination of Frost's rhyme scheme will show how consciously and purposefully it must have been chosen. It runs:

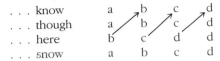

. . . know	a	b	c	d
. . . though	a	b	c	d
. . . here	b	c	d	d
. . . snow	a	b	c	d

One of the purposes of rhyme is to tie the sense together with sound. Note, then, three important consequences of Frost's rhyme scheme. First, three of the four lines in each stanza (except the last stanza) rhyme; hence, these stanzas are very compact sound-and-sense units. Second, the *third* line in each stanza always rhymes with the *first* line in the following stanza; hence the sound helps to pass the sense from one stanza to the next. And third, in the last stanza all four lines rhyme; hence, the sound is brought to rest just as the reconciliation of the conflict within the driver is brought to rest, and as he will be brought to rest upon his arrival at home. And note particularly that the symbols involved in the rhyming words *deep, keep,* and *sleep* are the key symbols that finally reveal the full meaning of the poem.

Are we ready to say that these matters are accidents or pretty decorations or troublesome technical matters outside the full meaning of Frost's poem? Hardly. Frost has demonstrated to us the truth of Stephen Spender's acute remark that "a poem *means* the sum of everything which it *is*. . . ." (See Spender's essay, "On Teaching Modern Poetry," p. 1096.) The sum of everything that Frost's poem *is* contains more than we have already located, but we have located and discussed the poem's basic factors, the factors that must be understood in order to interpret the meaning of almost any poem.

What have we learned? We have learned that a poem may best be seen as a living organism that contains the necessary elements of its own life. If "a poem *means* the sum of everything which it *is*," we must not only understand everything in the poem, but we must also be aware of all its parts as they work together to make the total meaning of the poem. If the poem is a good one—and this is surely one test—every element in it contributes to its meaning.

We have learned further that a poem has at least two levels of meaning: the literal level and the figurative-symbolic level. We have seen that a poem suggests much more than it says literally: like lovers' conversation, a poem gives out hints of extensive meanings along the way. Students often refer to the figurative meaning as the hidden meaning, as if poets had set out to hide their meaning in order to make the poem difficult. Ordinarily, poets have outgrown the game of hide-and-seek, but they do write figuratively for such reasons as Frost has already demonstrated.

And we have learned that a poem possesses a concentration and intensity that help to make it memorable. *The right word in the right place, the intimate fusion of sound and sense, and the economy of rich suggestion are virtues of the structure of most poetry.*

The Misreading of Poems

Most misreadings of poems come from the reader's failure to realize that there are many languages within the English language, such as the languages of science, history, journalism, and, of course, the language of poetry itself. By using *language* in this sense, we mean a unified pattern of words including certain specific devices to communicate a very specific meaning. Poetry has such a language of its own. For example, when Frost says,

> My little horse must think it queer
> To stop without a farmhouse near,

we immediately sense the language of poetry, not of science or history, because of the devices of rhythm (iambic tetrameter), rhyme (*queer-near*), figurative language (a horse that thinks), and symbol (a horse that stands for practical sense as against the impractical sense of the driver).

It is best, of course, to learn in a positive way what to look for in a poem and what to do with what we find, but nevertheless we may save ourselves some difficulty if we first identify a few blind alleys to be avoided.

To illustrate some basic causes of misreading a poem, suppose we begin by examining a few student comments on the following poem.

Hart Crane (1899–1932)
North Labrador

A land of leaning ice
Hugged by plaster-grey arches of sky,
Flings itself silently
Into eternity.

5 "Has no one come here to win you,
Or left you with the faintest blush
Upon your glittering breasts?
Have you no memories, O Darkly Bright?"

Cold-hushed, there is only the shifting of moments
10 That journey toward no Spring—
No birth, no death, no time nor sun
In answer.

Failure on the literal level   Incredible as it may seem, the failures on this level are legion. Few readers admit guilt, yet most of us are sinners. One reader of

"North Labrador" read *Spring* (l. 10) as running water and asked why the word had been capitalized. It is easy to smile at this error, but even practiced readers are victims of similar kinds of mistakes. We can avoid failure on the literal level by asking questions like these about every poem: *Who* is speaking to whom? *What* is the situation in the poem? *Where* are we geographically, and in time? Further, the literal level is determined by applying the same basic disciplines we use in reading prose: we should seek to understand the sentence structure—the very grammar—the vocabulary (how many failures here!), the pronouns (especially *its*), and even the punctuation. Elementary? Yes, and indispensable. True, the full meaning of a poem does not end with its literal sense, but neither will figurative meaning begin without it.

Failure to rise to the figurative level   Having examined "North Labrador," three readers commented as follows: "I think this poem is rather stupid. It is quite evident that no one could survive on a sheet of ice. But the author does ask the question, 'why has no one settled here?' There seems to be little point to it." Despite that slight stirring in his third sentence, this reader is truly shackled, and even the second stanza, which compares North Labrador to a woman, does no more than to shake his prose chains. Another reader begins to worry about those chains: "I like the arrangement of this poem. It leaves one with thoughts about it, and I wonder just what is meant." Still another reader threatens to break loose and rise to the figurative level: "The words [images] in this one caught my attention first—they are quite descriptive and put me in a mood. I can see the cold desolation, the colorlessness, and can feel the moments plodding by with a point-less, 'toward no Spring,' sameness." This reader is on his way to poetic liberation. When he sees that the entire poem is literally about North Labrador but figura-tively about the utter loneliness and emotional starvation of the human heart, he will have learned a basic lesson in the reading of poems.

To rise to the figurative level of a poem requires imagination, or the ability to perceive comparisons—to understand, for example, that Hart Crane is making a comment on humanity by talking about North Labrador. Crane had seen the dramatic comparison with his imagination, and he has therefore used certain as-pects of North Labrador to comment on a tragic situation in the human heart.

Failure to recognize irony   Many readers, churning with good spirits and ready to accept their world at face value, are likely to accept irony at face value, too. The failure to recognize irony is closely related to the failure to rise to the figu-rative level because irony, like simile and metaphor, is a figure of speech. Yet it is a special kind of figure because it relies more on *contrast* than on comparison, and consequently the poet depends on the reader to bring a special knowledge to the ironical statement to understand the contrast. In extended pieces of litera-ture, of course, authors themselves may provide the necessary special knowledge.

When Burns writes,

My love is like a red red rose,

he is emphasizing the comparison, not the contrast, between the loved one and

the beauties of the rose. But note this passage from Clough's "The Latest Deca-
logue" (p. 474):

> Do not adultery commit;
> Advantage rarely comes of it.
> Thou shalt not steal; an empty feat,
> When it's so lucrative to cheat.
> Bear not false witness; let the lie
> Have time on its own wings to fly.
> Thou shalt not covet, but tradition
> Approves all forms of competition.

The poet is emphasizing here the contrast between the morality of his time (as
expressed by the speaker) and that based on the Ten Commandments. We cannot,
therefore, take the speaker's words at face value, because he expresses a point of
view that the poem, as a whole, mocks. The tone is ironic because a discrepancy
exists between the poem's *apparent* meaning and its *real* meaning.

The title of Eliot's poem "The Love Song of J. Alfred Prufrock" (p. 575) is
ironic for readers if they catch the suggestion of a prude dressed in a frock coat
(a Prince Albert) contemplating the act of lovemaking. "Love Song" is intended
to recall the sensations of love songs long admired, and the reader may remember two famous lines from a Shakespearean sonnet (p. 371):

> Love alters not with his brief hours and weeks,
> But bears it out even to the edge of doom.

Prufrock's love song tells us why he hovers on the edge of doom, but hardly for
the reasons offered by Shakespeare. By such a contrast Eliot exposes Prufrock's
frustration: Eliot's use of the word *love* is ironic because Prufrock is capable only
of self-love.

As a poetic device, irony accomplishes some valuable effects for poets. They
can profess a restraint and detachment while often their emotions are intensely
aroused. This posture plus the double meaning of the irony are likely to appeal
to the sophisticated intelligence of readers who come to feel that they and the
poet share recondite meanings obscure to less perceptive minds. Irony, indeed,
has enjoyed a long philosophical career, and its enjoyment is a mark of the mature mind. It produces an unmistakable tone in a poem, and tone itself, we shall
come to see later, becomes a figure of speech as it pervades an entire poem. (See
"Figure and Symbol," p. 377.)

Preconceptions about the nature of poetry   One of the most persistent preconceptions holds that a poem must contain ideas, penetrating abstractions about the
meaning of life—or, the reverse, a poem must be "pure" and never "soiled" with
"thought." Either position disqualifies a huge share of the world's distinguished
poetry, and this act alone should alert us to the untenable dogmatism. *Must* we
make a decision between Yeats's "Among School Children" (p. 569) and Coleridge's "Kubla Khan" (p. 459)? The judgment of the years says no.

Another preconception can become a little militant at times against pessimism. One reader of Crane's "North Labrador" writes: "This one appears to be

on the gloomy side of things and it didn't appeal to me at all." This statement is closely allied to another reader's comment: "I don't think I am a better person for having read it." These preconceptions, too, would disqualify another huge share of the world's poems. We shall come to see that the fine poets do not arbitrarily decree that either optimism or pessimism is superior, nor do they assume that the proper function of a poem is to offer morals in capsule form. "North Labrador," for example, is actually a religious poem in the deepest sense, but Crane includes no explicitly stated prescription for happiness here or for salvation later. His comment appears by indirection and inference: the isolated soul who "journeys toward no Spring" is a cold, tragic soul who has been cut off from the warmth of love and affection. But Crane feels no responsibility for spelling out the prescription by adding another stanza saying, "Don't be like that— avoid it at all cost!" Beware of judging a poem by its optimism or pessimism. It is better to ask: Does the poem enlarge my understanding and sympathies?

Preconceptions in favor of or against one doctrine or another can produce curious results in the reading of poems. Some readers constantly search for the confirming doctrine; they are determined to find what they already believe. This attitude of mind used as an approach to poems can bring unfortunate consequences. It may violate the poem's meaning to make it conform to the reader's belief. It is comfortable to have great poets on our side, and the temptation to stretch them into place is not always resisted, but the art of the poem may be undervalued if the poem fails to confirm the reader's belief. Milton's *Paradise Lost* suffered this fate when T. S. Eliot found Milton's theology unpalatable, although, to Eliot's credit, he later recanted. Or this attitude of mind may overpraise the art of the poem if the poem does confirm the reader's belief.

The last-mentioned preconception is perhaps the most difficult to correct because it is quite natural—but still wrong—to accept without critical examination a poem's art simply because we agree with the poem's point of view. Forty-nine college students still without instruction in poetry on the college level were asked to judge seven poems, which ranged from very good to bad. Thirty students commented favorably on the poorest poem of the seven, titled "A Visit to Mom and Dad," and five students thought it to be the best of the lot. After six weeks of experience in analyzing and judging many poems, these readers changed their opinion radically concerning the value of "A Visit to Mom and Dad" because they had learned that no subject, however close to their hearts, necessarily makes a good poem.

These readers were victims of what is known as *stock response.* To facilitate everyday living, most of us gather a pattern of attitudes and a hierarchy of values by which we make decisions, issue opinions, and guide our everyday behavior. We are likely to react quickly against certain ideas and key words and in favor of others, sometimes without examining the context of the idea or key word. Debaters, candidates for office, and advertisers make a conscious study of our stock responses, and play the human console accordingly.

But we should be very clear about the relationship of stock responses and poems. There is nothing inherently wrong with stock responses. The point is, *What has the poet done with them?* Good poets—the poets devoted to their art—

try to furnish within the poem itself the attitudes and reasons for our participating in their belief. The poor poet simply pushes buttons marked "God," "Country," "Mom," and "Dad," and gives us no fresh experience, no insights, no "momentary stay against confusion." The logical question is, If poets have no more to offer than their rhyming of our stock responses, why should they write?

Other preconceptions that sidetrack readers have to do with the sound of a poem, its form, and even its length. "North Labrador" brought such comments as these: "It's choppy. I prefer things that read a little smoother." Another reader: "I don't care for this style of writing." Another: "It's awfully short." But still another reader disagrees: "This reads easily and sounds like poetry should." These contradictory comments emerge from a failure to understand one of the basic principles of all poems: poets select the means (the technical devices) to produce the desired end. The sound and sense of a good poem are a fusion, an organic whole, and we must first comprehend the whole before we judge the means or the technical matters. We shall soon see that Frost's "Departmental" (p. 319) is choppy, and that Burns's "Sweet Afton" (p. 318) is smoother and more flowing. And we shall see, too, that if either poem had the other's rhythm, both poems would be quite meaningless, indeed a little silly.

The only serviceable cure for the preconceptions brought to the reading of poems is to refuse to accept or reject *any* part of a poem until after the poem's totality has been mastered. Briefly, we should not read *into* poems; we should read *out* of poems whatever the poets have put into them. Once we have completely surrounded a poem's meaning, it is our privilege to use the poem for any purpose whatever: as a document in the history of sensibility, as a confirmation or denial of the value of some sensuous experience or idea—but *not* before we have surrounded the poem's meaning. There is simply no other way.*

Robert Browning (1812–1889)
My Last Duchess
Ferrara

Now that we have absorbed some initial instruction on the reading of poetry, including some pitfalls to be avoided, suppose we put our preliminary knowledge to work on a poem. Browning's influence on twentieth-century poetry is now well

*For a revealing study of the causes of the misreadings of poems see I. A. Richards, *Practical Criticism, a Study of Literary Judgment,* New York: Harcourt Brace Jovanovich, Inc., 1929 and 1952, especially pp. 13–17.

known; he is indeed very much a "modern." "My Last Duchess" is a concentrated little dramatic scene in which the Duke describes his own character through his words and actions. Although the poem is a dramatic monologue, we can easily supply the conversation that has taken place between the Duke and his listener, the Count's emissary.

That's my last Duchess painted on the wall
Looking as if she were alive. I call
That piece a wonder, now: Frà Pandolf's hands
Worked busily a day, and there she stands.
5 Will't please you sit and look at her? I said
"Frà Pandolf" by design, for never read
Strangers like you that pictured countenance,
The depth and passion of its earnest glance,
But to myself they turned (since none puts by
10 The curtain I have drawn for you, but I)
And seemed as they would ask me, if they durst,
How such a glance came there; so, not the first
Are you to turn and ask thus. Sir, 'twas not
Her husband's presence only, called that spot
15 Of joy into the Duchess' cheek: perhaps
Frà Pandolf chanced to say, "Her mantle laps
Over my lady's wrist too much," or "Paint
Must never hope to reproduce the faint
Half-flush that dies along her throat." Such stuff
20 Was courtesy, she thought, and cause enough
For calling up that spot of joy. She had
A heart—how shall I say?—too soon made glad,
Too easily impressed; she liked whate'er
She looked on, and her looks went everywhere.
25 Sir, 'twas all one! My favor at her breast,
The dropping of the daylight in the West,
The bough of cherries some officious fool
Broke in the orchard for her, the white mule
She rode with round the terrace—all and each
30 Would draw from her alike the approving speech,
Or blush, at least. She thanked men,—good! but thanked
Somehow—I know not how—as if she ranked
My gift of a nine-hundred-years-old name
With anybody's gift. Who'd stoop to blame
35 This sort of trifling? Even had you skill
In speech—(which I have not)—to make your will
Quite clear to such an one, and say, "Just this
Or that in you disgusts me; here you miss,
Or there exceed the mark"—and if she let
40 Herself be lessoned so, nor plainly set
Her wits to yours, forsooth, and made excuse,
—E'en then would be some stooping; and I choose
Never to stoop. Oh, sir, she smiled, no doubt,
Whene'er I passed her; but who passed without
45 Much the same smile? This grew; I gave commands;

Then all smiles stopped together. There she stands
As if alive. Will't please you rise? We'll meet
The company below then. I repeat,
The Count your master's known munificence
50 Is ample warrant that no just pretence
Of mine for dowry will be disallowed;
Though his fair daughter's self, as I avowed
At starting, is my object. Nay, we'll go
Together down, sir. Notice Neptune, though,
55 Taming a sea-horse, thought a rarity,
Which Claus of Innsbruck cast in bronze for me!

Analytical Dialogue on "My Last Duchess"

The following dialogue on "My Last Duchess" is one way of analyzing a poem, that is, accounting for all the important matters that make the poem meaningful. This conversation between a student and his professor is not the sort of exchange we are likely to encounter in the classroom (unfortunately), but it contains a number of principles that, when observed, help us to read poems accurately. The first principle appears in the opening comment by A: he has stated, very briefly, the plain, or literal, sense of the poem. He knows what the poem is "about." But Z refuses to allow the poem to rest there, and the analysis is under way. What other principles of accurate reading can be found?

z: You have read the poem?

a: Yes, and I think I understand it fairly well. It's about a Duke who had his wife killed because she was too pleasant to everybody.

z: If that's all there is to it, why do so many people enjoy—and remember—this poem?

a: It's sensational; I suppose that's why.

z: Perhaps, but in essence the story is commonplace. Newspapers every day carry accounts of murders committed for the slightest reasons. "Husband Has Wife Killed Because She Smiled at Everybody"—such a headline and the story would get passing attention, but few people would paste the account into a scrapbook. There must be something else to make this bit of writing memorable. Shall we see if we can find out what it is?

a: All right. Where do we start?

z: With the title. Anything worth noting about the title? What does "Last" mean? Does it mean final?

a: Certainly not. The Duke's going to have another duchess. Probably "Last" means former or latest.

z: Latest? Would that meaning imply that the Duke might have had another duchess—or several other duchesses—before the last one?

a: I don't know.

z: Well, neither do I, and since such an idea has no bearing on the poem as it is
told, suppose we discard it.

a: I have no objection. Besides I want you to know that I looked up Ferrara: it's a
place in Italy, northern Italy.

z: Good. That gives us something to go on, doesn't it? Ferrara is a real place. The
speaker is an Italian duke, and the subject of his remarks is his former wife. Now
if we want to be orderly about our inquiry, we ought to know to whom the
Duke is speaking.

a: I didn't find that out until near the end of the poem when the Duke mentioned
a count as the master of the person the Duke is talking to. He evidently was
visiting the Duke to make marriage arrangements for the Count's daughter. I felt
sorry for her.

z: You should. Actually the daughter of the Count is the real object of all the
Duke's talk, isn't she?

a: How do you know?

z: Because the Duke obviously is not talking at random; he's not revealing his arrogance and cruelty for the fun of hearing himself talk. He is issuing a sharp, clear
warning: "This is precisely the way my former Duchess conducted herself; I did
not attempt to school her in proper behavior; I choose never to stoop; I do not
intend to stoop to my next Duchess; but if you like, here is a warning to her."
Since it is unlikely that the Count would resist a ducal connection for his daughter, one may hope that he and his daughter were given a verbatim report of the
Duke's comments.

a: I read somewhere that the stop before the painting of the Duchess was simply
part of an art tour with the pause before Neptune as another part of the tour.

z: Does that interpretation fit the facts? What were the Duke and the Count's emissary doing immediately *before* the poem opens?

a: They were discussing the proposed wedding and how much dowry the Count
would provide. The lines about the dowry come near the end of the poem—
lines 48 to 53 beginning with the words, "I repeat."

z: And where were they going after settling this question?

a: To "meet the company below."

z: Do you think it likely that an art tour would be sandwiched between these two
actions? Isn't it more likely that the deliberate pause before the portrait was
planned by the Duke in advance as *part* of the negotiations for the hand of the
Count's daughter?

a: Let me ask you a question: Why didn't the poem end as the Duke and the emissary descend the stairs? What's the significance of Neptune taming a sea horse?

z: A much debated question. Some critics make a parallel between the Duke and
Neptune: the Duke tamed a wife as Neptune tamed a sea horse. Is there any
difficulty here?

a: Sounds plausible to me—but wait a minute: the Duke really didn't tame his wife,
did he? He didn't make any effort to tame her; he simply removed her without
warning. I would say the parallel breaks down.

z: Agreed. Other critics say that the bronze statue and the portrait were equally
interesting as art forms. I think this interpretation is only partly true. The Duke
must have realized that in talking of his last Duchess there had inevitably been

"some stooping," some condescension, a curious sort of charitableness, a touch of magnanimity. He was relieved to be done with the warning. He could return to casualness and hope that the reference to the bronze would be linked to the portrait as simply another work of art. And it may be that having used the portrait to point a moral and adorn a tale, he himself could *now* classify the portrait as simply another of his art treasures. You look skeptical.

A: I feel skeptical. The poem doesn't say all that, does it?

Z: No.

A: Why doesn't it?

Z: Because you, along with millions of other readers, would not enjoy being told everything in a-b-c fashion. The poet could have made his lines as clear as

Thirty days hath September,
April, June, and November.

These are useful lines but not very absorbing.

A: Nevertheless, I don't like puzzles.

Z: Unless you can solve them?

A: Yes.

Z: A good poem is an open puzzle—all the parts are there, and some of the fun is in putting them firmly together. This poet, for example, wanted you and me to enter into the character of a cold, arrogant, devious, observing, suspicious, scheming, all-powerful husband. He had confidence that you could provide these adjectives even though he uses none of them himself. He wanted you to speculate about the Duchess, too. Do you know anything about women?

A: Not much.

Z: Do you think you would like the Duchess?

A: Yes, I think so. She was easygoing and popular, I imagine, with everybody except her husband.

Z: Any more adjectives for her?

A: You might call her charming, genial, and I imagine she was pretty. She was democratic. She could blush easily, which shows she was sensitive.

Z: Good. But did she have any fault, any blind spot?

A: She didn't pay enough attention to her husband?

Z: Why didn't she?

A: How should I know?

Z: Do you recall how close an observer the husband was? He knew when his wife smiled and why, and when she blushed; and he could repeat the phrases or describe the actions that would call forth these genial responses.

A: Maybe she didn't notice that he was watching her, or maybe she felt so innocent that she didn't notice. You mean her weakness was a blindness to her husband's watching her? That isn't a weakness.

Z: Doubtless even if she had studied her husband's expression she would have seen little warning in its monotonous impassiveness. But what did she lack that women pride themselves on having?

A: A woman's intuition?

Z: Precisely. "All smiles stopped together"—that is, suddenly and finally. No hint of the Duke's displeasure ever reached the Duchess until it was too late. If she had had intuition, she . . .

A: Excuse me for interrupting, but didn't you say this was to be an orderly discussion? We began with the title, and that's as far as we went in orderliness.

z: But haven't we been *essentially* well organized? We analyzed the title, then the speaker, then the person spoken of. We mentioned the person spoken to, and we set forth the real purpose of the Duke's remarks. We haven't said much about setting. How much do we know about that?

A: Much. The country is Italy, the city Ferrara, and the local address, the palace of the Duke. As I see it, the Duke and emissary have stopped at the head of a stairway, marble, I think, but the poet doesn't say so. There the Duke draws back curtains and reveals a portrait. He steps back and sits down with the emissary— on a bench of some sort. I suppose, possibly like those in museums. After the Duke finishes, they rise and go down the stairs together.

z: Why together?

A: Because the Duke is feeling in good spirits; everything is going well and he feels democratic.

z: That's the chief reason. Another is that the emissary is entitled to be treated as his master, the Count, would have been treated. Are we ready for a straightforward statement of the poem's contents, including the action before the poem opened—the antecedent action?

A: We ought to be ready. Please proceed.

z: The proud Duke of Ferrara, dissatisfied with the indiscriminate geniality of his wife, puts her away, and later decides to negotiate with a Count for the hand of his daughter. The emissary of the Count arrives at the ducal residence and goes into conference with the Duke over marriage terms. At the conclusion of a friendly talk, the Duke uses the portrait of his last Duchess as the pretext for warning his Duchess-to-be of the conduct expected of her. The warning delivered, the conferees go to meet the Duke's guests, who perhaps were assembled to hear the news of the betrothal. Anything left out?

A: That is the story, all right. Do you suppose that was the form the story had when the poet sat down to write?

z: An important and observant question. I think almost surely the poet worked from the straightforward story, his raw materials. Details and arrangement make the poem. We cannot say how much material he discarded, but all surplusage is gone. Give these same basic materials to any number of writers, and the result will be any number of versions, some of which might be excellent, but none, one feels, superior to this poem.

A: I can see that. He might have told us more about Frà Pandolf—a smooth flatterer. Or the emissary might have been in love with the Count's daughter and—

z: Hold on! You've jumped the fence, and that way lies Tristan and Isolde.

A: Who?

z: Never mind. You might look them up sometime and see how many versions there are of *that* affair. Now, I want you to consider for a moment the problems our poet faced, and the artistic tact he used in solving them.

A: Do we have to do this?

z: No, but you have entered very well into one level of enjoyment, and I thought you might like to try, briefly, another level—the level of technical artistry.

A: Sounds forbidding, but go ahead.

z: For one thing, the poet deliberately imposed upon himself the limitations of the dramatic monologue.

A: Please define. I know your habits on examinations.

z: The dramatic monologue is the name given to poems in which a single speaker talks aloud to one or more listeners. If there are no listeners, by the way, the speaker is indulging in dramatic soliloquy. There are enough ordinary difficulties in telling a story, but the difficulties of the dramatic monologue are extraordinary.

A: It doesn't look so terribly difficult. It flows so easily that at first I didn't even notice the rhymes. But I grant the difficulty. Why did the poet choose this form?

z: The results of great art always look easy. As for your question, the poet must have decided that this was the one effective way *for him* to tell his story. Since we agree that he was successful, we are likely to agree that he chose the right form. Shall we list some of the "handicaps" which the poet imposed upon himself?

A: If you wish.

z: Will you name the first and perhaps most obvious one?

A: I defer to you. You have my permission to name the whole list.

z: I'll name the first, and you will then be able to name the second. One, the poet excluded himself from the poem—no comments, no moral. All dramatic writers do this, more or less. Two?

A: He doesn't say how to read the poem, is that it?

z: Yes. He omits stage directions. Few dramatic writers do that. This means that within a short speech he must include the setting (time and place), the exposition, and the antecedent action, all in such a natural way that these elements are absorbed into the forward motion of the poem. Three, he had to watch the time element with special care. He could allow the Duke to be greatly skilled in speech—in spite of the Duke's protests to the contrary—but a long speech at the particular time would have been out of character. Four?

A: Four, if you please.

z: This is most important. The Duke had to say things that would reveal his true (cruel) nature, and yet the reader must believe that this particular character would actually say such things. Here the motivation must be strong and convincing. As we have already seen, the motivation—a warning to the Count's daughter—is strong and convincing.

A: The poem is believable all right. Would you call this a great poem?

z: One measure—not the only measure—of a poem's validity is its staunchness before searching questions. By this test the poem is great. An inferior poem would not fare so well.

Tone and the Pleasures of Poetry

One of the open secrets of this book lies in the belief that readers cannot be required or forced to enjoy poetry, much less to understand it. But we can all be led into understanding by first reading good poems whose meaning and structure are quite immediately clear, especially if the poems give us a good-natured jolt or touch some universal feeling or attitude. Our immediate concern is to feel the delight of the fusion of *sound* and *sense*. The following poems have been chosen because the fusion can be immediately felt. Readers are not, however, expected to enjoy every poem they read regardless of their skill in reading: our past experiences, backgrounds, and temperaments will help and hinder enjoyment of poems; so if you can find even two or three of these poems that come alive for you, you are on your way.

A. E. Housman (1859–1936)
When I Was One-and-Twenty

When I was one-and-twenty
   I heard a wise man say,
"Give crowns and pounds and guineas
   But not your heart away;
5 Give pearls away and rubies
   But keep your fancy free."
But I was one-and-twenty,
   No use to talk to me.

When I was one-and-twenty
10   I heard him say again,
"The heart out of the bosom
   Was never given in vain;
'Tis paid with sighs a-plenty
   And sold for endless rue."
15 And I am two-and-twenty,
   And oh, 'tis true, 'tis true.

Housman's problem here was to make us *feel* the jaunty cocksureness of the young speaker in the poem who ignores the wise man's advice until the speaker's own experience confirms it. Housman could have told us he was jaunty and cocksure, but he has the speaker present himself to exhibit his jaunty cocksureness. How did Housman accomplish this? That is, how does sound—the rhythm, rhyme, and the clipped words—help to interpret the sense? Notice that each line has only three feet (trimeter); each line's rhythm is well-nigh perfect (sure); most words have only one syllable (clipped, jaunty); and the rhyme is repetitious—like the speaker until he grows into wisdom. Does the tone of the poem give a clear sense of the speaker? Why is the speaker's insight delayed until the last line of the poem?

Let us now hear a completely different fusion of sound and sense in Burns's poem.

Robert Burns   (1759–1796)
Sweet Afton

Flow gently, sweet Afton! among thy green braes,[1]
Flow gently, I'll sing thee a song in thy praise;
My Mary's asleep by thy murmuring stream,
Flow gently, sweet Afton, disturb not her dream.

5 Thou stock-dove whose echo resounds through the glen,
Ye wild whistling blackbirds in yon thorny den,
Thou green-crested lapwing, thy screaming forbear,
I charge you, disturb not my slumbering fair.

How lofty, sweet Afton, thy neighboring hills,
10 Far marked with the courses of clear, winding rills;[2]
There daily I wander as noon rises high,
My flocks and my Mary's sweet cot[3] in my eye.

How pleasant thy banks and green valleys below,
Where, wild in the woodlands, the primroses blow;
15 There oft, as mild ev'ning weeps over the lea,
The sweet-scented birk[4] shades my Mary and me.

Thy crystal stream, Afton, how lovely it glides,
And winds by the cot where my Mary resides;
How wanton thy waters her snowy feet lave,[5]
20 As, gathering sweet flowerets, she stems thy clear wave.

Flow gently, sweet Afton, among thy green braes,
Flow gently, sweet river, the theme of my lays;[6]
My Mary's asleep by thy murmuring stream,
Flow gently, sweet Afton, disturb not her dream.

Burns's problem here was to make us feel the mood of the speaker generated by his loved one, so the poet has employed the devices of his art—rhythm,
rhyme, word sounds (onomatopoeia), and stanza form. With these devices he has
accomplished a good deal. The sentiments of the speaker flow gently and tenderly as the river flows, and the tone of the poem is reminiscent of a tenderness
muted and enriched by time. The flowing quality is produced by the four-footed
line (tetrameter) with most feet having three syllables accented on the third syllable (anapestic foot), as in the first line:

    ˘ ˘ ´ | ˘ ˘ ´ | ˘ ˘ ´ | ˘ ˘ ˘ ´
    Flow gent|ly sweet Af|ton among|thy green braes

Yet the couplets *(braes-praise; stream-dream)* present a series of disciplined sentiments that do not disappear in the strong force of the flowing rhythm. The

---

[1]Banks.   [2]Small brooks.   [3]Cottage, small house.   [4]Birch tree.   [5]Bathe.   [6]Songs.

poem's emotion is therefore measured, gentle, and yet strong as if it would match time in eternity.

Poems, we see, *do* speak for themselves *if we know how to listen,* but Frost's poem now speaks in a radically different manner.

Robert Frost   (1874–1963)
Departmental

An ant on the table cloth
Ran into a dormant moth
Of many times his size.
He showed not the least surprise.
5 His business wasn't with such.
He gave it scarcely a touch,
And was off on his duty run.
Yet if he encountered one
Of the hive's enquiry squad
10 Whose work is to find out God
And the nature of time and space,
He would put him onto the case.
Ants are a curious race;
One crossing with hurried tread
15 The body of one of their dead
Isn't given a moment's arrest—
Seems not even impressed.
But he no doubt reports to any
With whom he crosses antennae,
20 And they no doubt report
To the higher up at court.
Then word goes forth in Formic:
"Death's come to Jerry McCormic,
Our selfless forager Jerry.
25 Will the special Janizary[1]
Whose office it is to bury
The dead of the commissary
Go bring him home to his people.
Lay him in state on a sepal.
30 Wrap him for shroud in a petal.

[1]A soldier of an elite corps.

Embalm him with ichor of nettle.
This is the word of your Queen."
And presently on the scene
Appears a solemn mortician;
35 And taking formal position,
With feelers calmly atwiddle,
Seizes the dead by the middle,
And heaving him high in air,
Carries him out of there.
40 No one stands round to stare.
It is nobody else's affair.

It couldn't be called ungentle.
But how thoroughly departmental.

This poem is a satire on our modern tendency to accept only individual responsibility in life instead of accepting some responsibility for the whole social structure. Literally Frost is talking about ants, but figuratively he is satirizing people. Satire is usually a light, sprightly form of ridicule, and Frost's *technical* problem was therefore to make us feel the force of his short jabs, needling, against our fragmentizing of life. By using the devices of the short, clipped line (trimeter) and the couplet form, and by ending many lines with abrupt stops *(report-court; Formic-McCormic; atwiddle-middle),* Frost makes us see and feel these efficient little ants (people) scurrying to their single duties looking neither to the right nor left. And note that when Frost wants to rub the satire in, he rhymes three and even four successive lines *(space-case-race; air-there-stare-affair).* Perhaps we feel a little punch-drunk at the end of the poem.

If we are now alive to the various results of poets fusing sound and sense expertly, the following poems may provide us with a good deal of pleasure.

William Carlos Williams   (1883–1963)
This Is Just to Say

I have eaten
the plums
that were in
the icebox

5 and which
you were probably
saving
for breakfast

Forgive me
10 they were delicious
so sweet
and so cold

A. E. Housman (1859–1936)
With Rue My Heart Is Laden

With rue my heart is laden
    For golden friends I had,
For many a rose-lipt maiden
    And many a lightfoot lad.

5 By brooks too broad for leaping
    The lightfoot boys are laid;
The rose-lipt girls are sleeping
    In fields where roses fade.

Robert Herrick (1591–1674)
Upon Julia's Clothes

Whenas in silks my Julia goes,
Then, then, methinks, how sweetly flows
That liquefaction of her clothes.

Next, when I cast mine eyes, and see
5 That brave vibration, each way free.
O, how that glittering taketh me!

James Wright (1927–1980)

Lying in a Hammock at William Duffy's Farm in Pine Island, Minnesota

Over my head, I see the bronze butterfly,
Asleep on the black trunk,
Blowing like a leaf in green shadow.
Down the ravine behind the empty house,
5 The cowbells follow one another
Into the distances of the afternoon.
To my right,
In a field of sunlight between two pines,
The droppings of last year's horses
10 Blaze up into golden stones.
I lean back, as the evening darkens and comes on.
A chicken hawk floats over, looking for home.
I have wasted my life.

Dorothy Parker (1893–1967)

Résumé

Razors pain you;
Rivers are damp;
Acids stain you;
And drugs cause cramp.
5 Guns aren't lawful;
Nooses give;
Gas smells awful;
You might as well live.

Emily Dickinson (1830–1886)
The Pedigree of Honey

Version I

The pedigree of Honey
Does not concern the Bee,
Nor lineage of Ecstasy
Delay the Butterfly
5 On spangled journeys to the peak
Of some perceiveless thing—
The right of way to Tripoli
A more essential thing.

Version II

The Pedigree of Honey
Does not concern the Bee—
A Clover, any time, to him,
Is Aristocracy—

Frank K. Robinson (1931–   )
Ten Haiku*

I
only the movement
cardinals
in the wild cherry

II
taking her hand
    aware of the bones
in mine

* An unrhymed Japanese poem recording the essence of a moment keenly perceived, in which nature is linked to human nature. It usually consists of seventeen syllables. All Japanese classical haiku, as well as most modern ones, contain a word or phrase indicating one of the four seasons. In contemporary practice, however, the only rules considered binding are those of brevity and intensity of perception.

III
old photograph . . .
the bride smiling at someone
beyond a torn edge

IV
migraine. . .
the blank eyes
of the carp

V
tv glow
in a neighbor's window
tonight's moon

VI
its roots
holding the shape of the pot—
discarded geranium

VII
christmas eve
the waiter seats her
near the tree

VIII
old woman
at the grave of the boy
she married

IX
    afterwards
listening
    to our hearts

X
the warm smell
of a new-plowed field . . .
starting my will

The Enduring Ballad

Story Ballads

Anonymous
Barbra Allen

In London City where I once did dwell, there's where I got my learning,
I fell in love with a pretty young girl, her name was Barbra Allen.
I courted her for seven long years, she said she would not have me;
Then straightaway home as I could go and liken to a dying.

5 I wrote her a letter on my death bed, I wrote it slow and moving;
"Go take this letter to my old true love and tell her I am dying."
She took the letter in her lily-white hand, she read it slow and moving;
"Go take this letter back to him, and tell him I am coming."

As she passed by his dying bed she saw his pale lips quivering;
10 "No better, no better I'll ever be until I get Barbra Allen."
As she passed by his dying bed; "You're very sick and almost dying,
No better, no better you will ever be, for you can't get Barbra Allen."

As she went down the long stair steps she heard the death bell toning,
And every bell appeared to say, "Hard-hearted Barbra Allen!"
15 As she went down the long piney walk she heard some small birds singing,
And every bird appeared to say, "Hard-hearted Barbra Allen!"

She looked to the East, she looked to the West, she saw the pale corpse coming,
"Go bring them pale corpse unto me, and let me gaze upon them.
Oh, mama, mama, go make my bed, go make it soft and narrow!
20 Sweet Willie died today for me, I'll die for him tomorrow!"

They buried Sweet Willie in the old church yard, they buried Miss Barbra beside him;
And out of his grave there sprang a red rose, and out of hers a briar.
They grew to the top of the old church tower, they could not grow any higher,
They hooked, they tied in a true love's knot, red rose around the briar.

Anonymous
Sir Patrick Spens

The king sits in Dumferling toune,
    Drinking the blude-reid wine:
"Oh whar will I get guid sailor,
    To sail this schip of mine?"

5 Up and spak an eldern knicht,[1]
    Sat at the kings richt kne:
"Sir Patrick Spens is the best sailor
    That sails upon the se."

The king has written a braid[2] letter,
10   And signd it wi his hand,
And sent it to Sir Patrick Spens,
    Was walking on the sand.

The first line that Sir Patrick red,
    A loud lauch lauched he;
15 The next line that Sir Patrick red,
    The teir blinded his ee.

"O wha is this has don this deid,
    This ill deid don to me,
To send me out this time o' the yeir,
20   To sail upon the se!

"Mak hast, mak haste, my mirry men all,
    Our guid schip sails the morne."
"O say na sae,[3] my master deir,
    For I feir a deadlie storme.

25 "Late, late yestreen I saw the new moone,
    Wi the auld moone in hir arme,
And I feir, I feir, my deir master,
    That we will cum to harme."

O our Scots nobles wer richt laith[4]
30   To weet their cork-heild schoone,[5]
Bot lang owre[6] a' the play wer playd,
    Thair hats they swam aboone.[7]

O lang, lang may their ladies sit,
    Wi their fans into their hand,
35 Or eir[8] they se Sir Patrick Spens
    Cum sailing to the land.

---

[1]Knight.   [2]Stately.   [3]Not so.   [4]Loath.   [5]Cork-heeled shoes.   [6]Before.   [7]Above.
[8]Before.

O lang, lang may their ladies stand,
   Wi their gold kems[9] in their hair,
Waiting for their ain[10] deir lords,
40   For they'll se thame na mair.

Haf owre, half owre[11] to Aberdour,
   It's fiftie fadom[12] deip,
And thair lies guid Sir Patrick Spens,
   Wi the Scots lords at his feit.

Comments and Questions

This poem, like "Barbra Allen," is an anonymous folk, or popular, ballad whose "final" shape includes the alterations that were made as the ballad passed from generation to generation. Like all literary forms, the ballad emerged to serve a purpose, and the purpose of the ballad seems to have been to celebrate, lament, or commemorate some dramatic incident that probably affected the community at the time.

    1. Of the many versions of this old Scottish ballad, this one seems to have become the best established, perhaps because of its brevity, compression, and dramatic intensity. It is, in effect, a short story. What are the facts of the story?

    2. This ballad has a surprising number of characteristics of the modern short story. Consider the narrator's point of view, panorama and scene, character portrayal, and dramatic elements. (For a discussion of these terms see, in the fiction division, "Preliminaries," p. 10.) Note particularly the relative absence of author comment.

    3. In what way does the tone of this ballad differ from that of "Barbra Allen"?

    4. Note the metrical structure of "Sir Patrick Spens." It is written in conventional ballad stanza, the first and third lines having four feet (tetrameter), the second and fourth lines having three feet (trimeter), written mostly in iambic meter (the kíng), and with a rhyme scheme of *abcb*. This form is sometimes called a classic structure and is quite different of course from the structure found in "Barbra Allen," which has roughly seven feet in each line, written in broken iambic meter. It is tempting to ask which ballad has the better technique, but it is sounder to ask, Does each technique serve well the meaning of the poem? What is your opinion? Consider question 3 again before you conclude.

    5. Compare "Sir Patrick Spens" with Pound's "Ballad of the Goodly Fere" (p. 337), and note the similar metrical effect.

---

[9]Combs.   [10]Own.   [11]Halfway over.   [12]Fathoms.

Anonymous
Lord Randal

"O where hae[1] ye been, Lord Randal, my son?
O where hae ye been, my handsome young man?"
"I hae been to the wild wood: mother, make my bed soon,
For I'm weary wi hunting, and fain wald[2] lie down."

5 "Where gat ye your dinner, Lord Randal, my son?
Where gat ye your dinner, my handsome young man?"
"I din'd wi my true-love; mother, make my bed soon,
For I'm weary wi hunting, and fain wald lie down."

"What gat ye to your dinner, Lord Randal, my son?
10 What gat ye to your dinner, my handsome young man?"
"I gat eels boiled in broo,[3] mother, make my bed soon,
For I'm weary wi hunting, and fain wald lie down."

"What became of your bloodhounds, Lord Randal, my son?
What became of your bloodhounds, my handsome young man?"
15 "O they swelld and they died; mother, make my bed soon,
For I'm weary wi hunting, and fain wald lie down."

"O I fear ye are poisond, Lord Randal, my son!
O I fear ye are poisond, my handsome young man!"
"O yes! I am poisond; mother, make my bed soon,
20 For I'm sick at the heart, and I fain wald lie down."

Anonymous
Little Mathie Grove

Holiday, holiday, on the very first day of the year, year,
    On the very first day of the year,
Little Mathie Grove went to the church
    The Holy Word for to hear, hear,
5   The Holy Word for to hear.

The first came in was Lily-white,
    The next came in was a girl,

[1]Have.   [2]Would.   [3]Broth.

The next came in was Lord Daniel's wife,
    The fairest one in the world, world,
10   The fairest one in the world.

She placed her eye on Little Mathie Grove,
    And said, "Go home with me this night;
Go home with me this night for to lie,
    Go home with me this night."

15 "I can't go home with you this night,
    For fear I do lose my life,
For the rings that's on your fingers says
    You are Lord Daniel's wife, wife,
    Says you are Lord Daniel's wife."

20 "But what if I am Lord Daniel's wife,
    Lord Daniel's gone from home;
He has gone to the high King's house
    To see his fences, Sir, Sir,
    To see his fences, Sir."

25 There stood that Little Foot-page,
    Hearing every word that they did say,
He says, "Lord Daniel shall hear this
    Before the break of day, day,
    Before the break of day."

30 It was fourteen miles to the King's house,
    And seven of them he run;
He run till he came to the broad river side,
    He bowed to his breast and swum, swum,
    He bowed to his breast and swum.

35 He swum till he came to the other side,
    He buckled up his shoes and run, run,
    He buckled up his shoes and run.
He run till he came to the high King's gate,
    He rattled his bell and rung, rung,
40   He rattled his bell and rung.

The first came out was Lord Daniel,
    Said, "What news have you to tell?
Is your old scafel a-burning down,
    Or is your tavern won, won,
45   Or is your tavern won?"

"My old scafel is not burnt down,
    But neither is my tavern won,
But your wife is at home, in the bed,
    With Little Mathie Grove alone, lone,
50   With Little Mathie Grove alone."

He had a trumpet and it would blow,
    And every time it would sound,
It seemed for to say,

"Rise up and go, go,"
55   It says, "Rise up and go."

She says, "No, no, lie still with me,
        And keep me from the cold,
It is nothing but them shepherd boys
        A-driving their sheep to the fold, fold.
60   Driving their sheep to the fold."

They turned then, to hugging and kissing,
        Till they returned to sleep,
And when they wakened the next morning,
        Lord Daniel was at their bed-feet, feet,
65   Lord Daniel was at their bed-feet.

Says, "How do you like your blanket, Sir,
        And how do you like your sheet?
Or how do you like this fair young miss
        That lies in your arms so sweet, sweet,
70   That lies in your arms so sweet?"

"Very well do I like my blanket, Sir,
Very well do I like my sheet,
Much better do I like this fair young miss
        That lies in my arms asleep, sleep,
75   That lies in my arms asleep."

"Get up, get up, put on your clothes,
        And fight me like a man,
I can't have it said in the fairest land,
        That I slew a naked man, man,
80   That I slew a naked man."

"How can I get up, put on my clothes,
        And fight you for my life,
For I see you have two very bright swords,
        And me not as much as a knife, knife,
85   And me not as much as a knife."

"Sir, I have two very bright swords
        Which cost me deep in purse,
And you can have the very best one,
        And I will take the worst, worst,
90   And I will take the worst."

The very first lick Little Mathie stroke,
        He wounded him deep and sore,
But the very first lick Lord Daniel stroke,
        Little Mathie couldn't fight no more, more
95   Little Mathie couldn't fight no more.

He took this lady by the hand,
        And placed her on his knee;
Says, "Which do you love the best,

Little Mathie Grove or me, me,
100   Little Mathie Grove or me?"

"Very well do I like your red rosy cheeks,
    Much better do I like your chin,
Much better do I like Little Mathie Grove
    Than you or any of your kin, kin,
105   Than you or any of your kin."

He took this lady by the lily-white hand,
    He led her out in the lane;
He drew his sword from his side,
    He split her head into twin, twin,
110   He split her head into twin.

"O don't you hear them larkins say,
    Don't you hear them sparrows cry,
To-day I have slain the two fairest ones,
    And to-morrow I will have to die, die,
115   And to-morrow I will have to die."

Anonymous
Frankie and Johnny

Frankie and Johnny were lovers, great God how they could love!
Swore to be true to each other, true as the stars up above.
He was her man, but he done her wrong.

Frankie she was his woman, everybody knows.
5 She spent her forty dollars for Johnny a suit of clothes.
He was her man, but he done her wrong.

Frankie and Johnny went walking, Johnny in his brand new suit.
"O good Lawd," said Frankie, "but don't my Johnny look cute?"
He was her man, but he done her wrong.

10 Frankie went down to the corner, just for a bucket of beer.
Frankie said, "Mr. Bartender, has my loving Johnny been here?
He is my man, he wouldn't do me wrong."

"I don't want to tell you no story. I don't want to tell you no lie,
But your Johnny left here an hour ago with that lousy Nellie Blye.
15 He is your man, but he's doing you wrong."

Frankie went back to the hotel, she didn't go there for fun,

For under her red kimono she toted a forty-four gun.
He was her man, but he done her wrong.

Frankie went down to the hotel and looked in the window so high,
20 And there was her loving Johnny a-loving up Nellie Blye.
He was her man, but he was doing her wrong.

Frankie threw back her kimono, took out that old forty-four.
Root-a-toot-toot, three times she shot, right through the hardwood door.
He was her man, but he was doing her wrong.

25 Johnny grabbed off his Stetson, crying, "O Frankie don't shoot!"
Frankie pulled that forty-four, went root-a-toot-toot-toot-toot.
He was her man, but he done her wrong.

"Roll me over gently, roll me over slow,
Roll me on my right side, for my left side hurts me so,
30 I was her man, but I done her wrong."

With the first shot Johnny staggered, with the second shot he fell;
When the last bullet got him, there was a new man's face in hell.
He was her man, but he done her wrong.

"O, bring out your rubber-tired hearses, bring out your rubber-tired hacks;
35 Gonna take Johnny to the graveyard and ain't gonna bring him back.
He was my man, but he done me wrong."

"O, put me in that dungeon, put me in that cell,
Put me where the northeast wind blows from the southeast corner of hell.
I shot my man, cause he done me wrong!"

Anonymous
On Top of Old Smoky

On top of old Smoky, all covered with snow,
I lost my true lover for acourtin' too slow.
Now, courtin's a pleasure, but parting is grief,
And a false-hearted lover is worse than a thief;
5 For a thief will just rob you and take what you have,
But a false-hearted lover will lead you to the grave;
And the grave will decay you, and turn you to dust.
Not one boy in a hundred a poor girl can trust:
They'll hug you and kiss you, and tell you more lies
10 Then the crossties on a railroad, or stars in the skies.
So, come all you young maidens, and listen to me:

Never place your affections in a green willow tree;
For the leaves they will wither, and the roots they will die.
Your lover will forsake you, and you'll never know why.

Literary Ballads

    The poems that follow are called literary ballads or art ballads, conscious imitations of the popular folk ballad. The ballads we have already read are primitive poems that survive probably because of their singing quality and their frank projection of elementary emotions; they have the charm of being understood immediately, of striking home without study. Now enters the professional poet.

John Keats (1795–1821)
La Belle Dame sans Merci

Oh, what can ail thee, knight-at-arms,
    Alone and palely loitering?
The sedge has withered from the lake,
    And no birds sing.

5 Oh, what can ail thee, knight-at-arms,
    So haggard and so woe-begone?
The squirrel's granary is full,
    And the harvest's done.

I see a lily on thy brow,
10   With anguish moist and fever dew;
And on thy cheeks a fading rose
    Fast withereth too.

"I met a lady in the meads,
    Full beautiful—a faery's child;
15 Her hair was long, her foot was light,
    And her eyes were wild

"I made a garland for her head,
    And bracelets too, and fragrant zone;[1]

---

[1]Girdle, sash.

She looked at me as she did love,
20   And made sweet moan.

"I set her on my pacing steed,
    And nothing else saw all day long;
For sideways would she lean, and sing
    A faery's song.

25 "She found me roots of relish sweet,
    And honey wild, and manna-dew,
And sure in language strange she said,
    'I love thee true.'

"She took me to her elfin grot,
30   And there she wept, and sighed full sore,
And there I shut her wild, wild eyes,
    With kisses four.

"And there she lullèd me asleep,
    And there I dreamed—ah! woe betide!—
35 The latest dream I ever dreamed
    On the cold hill side.

"I saw pale kings and princes too,
    Pale warriors, death-pale were they all,
They cried—'La Belle Dame sans Merci
40   Hath thee in thrall!'

"I saw their starved lips in the gloam,
    With horrid warning gapèd wide;
And I awoke, and found me here
    On the cold hill's side.

45 "And this is why I sojourn here
    Alone and palely loitering,
Though the sedge is withered from the lake,
    And no birds sing."

Comments and Questions

1. The title announces the ballad's general theme, the beautiful lady without pity. What is the specific theme? This is the most complex and self-conscious ballad we have yet read, and it includes more symbolism than we have yet encountered. What does the lady symbolize?

2. Who are the two speakers in the poem? How do lines 1–12 sustain or complement the remainder of the poem?

3. We note in passing that Keats's stanza form is similar to that in "Sir Patrick Spens" (p. 326). Can you hazard an explanation of why Keats's form differs in some respects from the other?

William Butler Yeats (1865–1939)
The Ballad of Father Gilligan

The old priest Peter Gilligan
Was weary night and day;
For half his flock were in their beds,
Or under green sods lay.

5 Once, while he nodded on a chair,
At the moth-hour of eve,
Another poor man sent for him,
And he began to grieve.

"I have no rest, nor joy, nor peace,
10 For people die and die";
And after cried he, "God forgive!
My body spake, not I!"

He knelt, and leaning on the chair
He prayed and fell asleep;
15 And the moth-hour went from the fields,
And stars began to peep.

They slowly into millions grew,
And leaves shook in the wind;
And God covered the world with shade,
20 And whispered to mankind.

Upon the time of sparrow-chirp
When the moths came once more,
The old priest Peter Gilligan
Stood upright on the floor.

25 "Mavrone, mavrone! the man has died
While I slept on the chair";
He roused his horse out of its sleep,
And rode with little care.

He rode now as he never rode,
30 By rocky lane and fen;
The sick man's wife opened the door:
"Father! you come again!"

"And is the poor man dead?" he cried.
"He died an hour ago."
35 The old priest Peter Gilligan
In grief swayed to and fro.

"When you were gone, he turned and died
As merry as a bird."
The old priest Peter Gilligan
40 He knelt him at that word.

"He Who hath made the night of stars
For souls who tire and bleed,
Sent one of His great angels down
To help me in my need.

45 "He Who is wrapped in purple robes,
With planets in His care,
Had pity on the least of things
Asleep upon a chair."

A. E. Housman (1859–1936)
The True Lover

The lad came to the door at night,
  When lovers crown their vows,
And whistled soft and out of sight
  In shadow of the boughs.

5 "I shall not vex you with my face
  Henceforth, my love, for aye;
So take me in your arms a space
  Before the east is grey.

"When I from hence away am past
10   I shall not find a bride,
And you shall be the first and last
  I ever lay beside."

She heard and went and knew not why;
  Her heart to his she laid;
15 Light was the air beneath the sky
  But dark under the shade.

"Oh do you breathe, lad, that your breast
  Seems not to rise and fall,
And here upon my bosom prest
20   There beats no heart at all?"

"Oh loud, my girl, it once would knock,
  You should have felt it then;
But since for you I stopped the clock
  It never goes again."

25 "Oh lad, what is it, lad, that drips
  Wet from your neck on mine?

What is it falling on my lips,
   My lad, that tastes of brine?"

"Oh like enough 'tis blood, my dear,
30   For when the knife has slit
The throat across from ear to ear
   'Twill bleed because of it."

Under the stars the air was light
   But dark below the boughs,
35 The still air of the speechless night,
   When lovers crown their vows.

Ezra Pound (1885–1972)
Ballad of the Goodly Fere[1]

Simon Zelotes[2] speaketh it somewhile after the Crucifixion.

[1]

Ha' we lost the goodliest fere o' all
For the priests and the gallows tree?
Aye lover he was of brawny men,
O' ships and the open sea.

[2]

5 When they came wi' a host to take Our Man
His smile was good to see;
"First let these go!" quo' our Goodly Fere,
"Or I'll see ye damned," says he.

[3]

Aye, he sent us out through the crossed high spears,
10 And the scorn of his laugh rang free;
"Why took ye not me when I walked about
Alone in the town?" says he.[3]

---

[1] *Fere:* literally a traveling comrade.   [2] A disciple of Christ (not to be confused with Simon Peter; see Acts 1:13) and one of the zealots (Zelotes) who bitterly opposed the Roman domination of Palestine. In having us see Christ through Simon's eyes, Pound provides a rather unconventional Christ who is nevertheless surprisingly supported by the scriptures.   [3] Christ challenges and needles his captors; see Matthew 26:55.

[4]

Oh, we drunk his "Hale" in the good red wine
When we last made company;
15 No capon priest was the Goodly Fere
But a man o' men was he.[4]

[5]

I ha' seen him drive a hundred men
Wi' a bundle o' cords swung free,
That they took the high and holy house
20 For their pawn and treasury.[5]

[6]

They'll no' get him a' in a book I think,
Though they write it cunningly;
No mouse of the scrolls[6] was the Goodly Fere
But aye loved the open sea.

[7]

25 If they think they ha' snared our Goodly Fere
They are fools to the last degree.
"I'll go to the feast," quo' our Goodly Fere,
"Though I go to the gallows tree."[7]

[8][8]

"Ye ha' seen me heal the lame and blind,
30 And wake the dead," says he;
"Ye shall see one thing to master all:
'Tis how a brave man dies on the tree."

[9]

A son of God was the Goodly Fere
That bade us his brothers be.
35 I ha' seen him cow a thousand men.
I have seen him upon the tree.[9]

[10]

He cried no cry when they drave the nails
And the blood gushed hot and free;
The hounds of the crimson sky gave tongue
40 But never a cry cried he.[10]

---

[4] L. 16: see Matthew 11:19 for confirmation. "No capon priest," rather, a full-blooded male.
[5] The cleansing of the Temple: see John 2:13–17.   [6] No creeper through scriptures; instead a
man who fought for his principles.   [7] Christ was not tricked; he entered Jerusalem knowing what
would happen. See Matthew 16:21–23; 20:17–19.   [8] A continuation of the prophecy in Matthew
above. See also Luke 18:35–43.   [9] Stanzas 9 and 11: reference to the Nazareth incident where
Christ's fellow Galileans "filled with wrath . . . rose up, and thrust him out of the city, and led him
unto the brow of the hill . . . that they might cast him down headlong. But he, passing through the
midst of them, went his own way." Luke 4:28–30.   [10] See Matthew 27:45, 51; Luke 23:44–45.

[11]

I ha' seen him cow a thousand men
On the hills o' Galilee;
They whined as he walked out calm between,
Wi' his eyes like the grey o' the sea,

[12]

45 Like the sea that brooks no voyaging
With the winds unleashed and free,
Like the sea that he cowed at Genseret
Wi' twey words spoke' suddenly.[11]

[13]

A master of men was the Goodly Fere,
50 A mate of the wind and sea;
If they think they ha' slain our Goodly Fere
They are fools eternally.

[14]

I ha' seen him eat o' the honey-comb[12]
Sin' they nailed him to the tree.

Gwendolyn Brooks (1917–   )
the ballad of chocolate mabbie

It was Mabbie without the grammar school gates.
And Mabbie was all of seven.
And Mabbie was cut from a chocolate bar.
And Mabbie thought life was heaven.

5 The grammar school gates were the pearly gates,
For Willie Boone went to school.
When she sat by him in history class
Was only her eyes were cool.

It was Mabbie without the grammar school gates
10 Waiting for Willie Boone.
Half hour after the closing bell!
He would surely be coming soon.

---

[11] Genseret (Gennesaret in Luke 5:1), another name for Galilee. The words Christ spoke: "Peace, be still," as in Mark 4:39.   [12] Honey-comb: see Luke 24:42–49, which begins: "And they gave him a piece of a broiled fish, and of a honeycomb."

Oh, warm is the waiting for joys, my dears!
And it cannot be too long.
15 Oh, pity the little poor chocolate lips
That carry the bubble of song!

Out came the saucily bold Willie Boone.
It was woe for our Mabbie now.
He wore like a jewel a lemon-hued lynx
20 With sand-waves loving her brow.

It was Mabbie alone by the grammar school gates.
Yet chocolate companions had she:
Mabbie on Mabbie with hush in the heart.
Mabbie on Mabbie to be.

Margaret A. Walker (1915–   )
Molly Means

Old Molly Means was a hag and a witch;
Chile of the devil, the dark, and sitch.
Her heavy hair hung thick in ropes
And her blazing eyes was black as pitch.
5 Imp at three and wench at 'leben
She counted her husbands to the number seben.
 O Molly, Molly, Molly Means
 There goes the ghost of Molly Means.

Some say she was born with a veil on her face
10 So she could look through unnatchal space
Through the future and through the past
And charm a body or an evil place
And every man could well despise
The evil look in her coal black eyes.
15   Old Molly, Molly, Molly Means
 Dark is the ghost of Molly Means.

And when the tale begun to spread
Of evil and of holy dread:
Her black-hand arts and her evil powers
20 How she cast her spells and called the dead,
The younguns was afraid at night

And the farmers feared their crops would blight.
    Old Molly, Molly, Molly Means
    Cold is the ghost of Molly Means.

25 Then one dark day she put a spell
On a young gal-bride just come to dwell
In the lane just down from Molly's shack
And when her husband come riding back
His wife was barking like a dog
30 And on all fours like a common hog.
    O Molly, Molly, Molly Means
    Where is the ghost of Molly Means?

The neighbors come and they went away
And said she'd die before break of day
35 But her husband held her in his arms
And swore he'd break the wicked charms;
He'd search all up and down the land
And turn the spell on Molly's hand.
    O Molly, Molly, Molly Means
40   Sharp is the ghost of Molly Means.

So he rode all day and he rode all night
And at the dawn he come in sight
Of a man who said he could move the spell
And cause the awful thing to dwell
45 On Molly Means, to bark and bleed
Till she died at the hands of her evil deed.
    Old Molly, Molly, Molly Means
    This is the ghost of Molly Means.

Sometimes at night through the shadowy trees
50 She rides along on a winter breeze.
You can hear her holler and whine and cry.
Her voice is thin and her moan is high,
And her cackling laugh or her barking cold
Bring terror to the young and old.
55   O Molly, Molly, Molly Means
    Lean is the ghost of Molly Means.

The Return of the Minstrel:
New Folk and Country Ballads

The return of the minstrel, formerly a musical entertainer or traveling poet of the later Middle Ages, has become a national and international phenomenon during the last few decades. Recordings of these minstrels' songs are bought by the millions, and the performers entertain huge audiences in concert halls and millions of enthusiasts every week by radio and television. The folk ballad has a long and persistent tradition, and its resurgence may be a symbol of something very im-

portant in contemporary life, something too important to be ignored by the official literati of the poetic world. For an excellent examination and historical explanation of this movement see Barbara Farris Graves and Donald J. McBain's essay,
"Electric Orphic Circuit" (p. 1089), which has been taken from their book, *Lyric
Voices, Approaches to the Poetry of Contemporary Song* (New York: John Wiley
and Sons, Inc., 1972). The book contains many of the best of these lyrics.

   Another valuable book, one that investigates the evolution of the lyric, is C.
Day Lewis's *The Lyric Impulse* (Cambridge: Harvard University Press, 1965); Chapter 5, "Country Lyrics," is especially valuable.

Bob Dylan   (1941–   )
Mister Tambourine Man*

Chorus

Hey, Mister Tambourine Man, play a song for me,
I'm not sleepy and there ain't no place I'm going to.
Hey, Mister Tambourine Man, play a song for me,
In the jingle, jangle morning I'll come followin' you.

5   Though I know that evenin's empire has returned into sand
Vanished from my hand,
Left me blindly here to stand
But still not sleepin'.
My weariness amazes me,
10 I'm branded on my feet,
I have no one to meet,
And the ancient empty street's
Too dead for dreamin'.
Chorus

Take me on a trip upon your magic swirlin' ship,
15 My senses have been stripped,
My hands can't feel to grip,
My toes too numb to step,
Wait only for my boot heels to be wanderin'.
I'm ready to go anywhere,
20 I'm ready for to fade
Into my own parade.

Cast your dancin' spell my way,
I promise to go under it.
Chorus

Though you might hear laughin', spinnin', swingin' madly through the sun,
25 It's not aimed at anyone,
It's just escapin' on the run,
And but for the sky there are no fences facin'.
And if you hear vague traces
Of skippin' reels of rhyme
30 To your tambourine in time,
It's just a ragged clown behind,
I wouldn't pay it any mind,
It's just a shadow
You're seein' that he's chasin'.
Chorus

35 Take me disappearin' through the smoke rings of my mind
Down the foggy ruins of time,
Far past the frozen leaves,
The haunted, frightened trees
Out to the windy beach
40 Far from the twisted reach of crazy sorrow.
Yes, to dance beneath the diamond sky
With one hand wavin' free,
Silhouetted by the sea,
Circled by the circus sands,
45 With memory and fate
Driven deep beneath the waves.
Let me forget about today until tomorrow.
Chorus

Kris Kristofferson (1936–   )
Sunday Mornin' Comin' Down*

Well, I woke up Sunday mornin'
     with no way to hold my head that didn't hurt;
And the beer I had for breakfast wasn't bad,
     so I had one more for dessert;
5   Then I fumbled in my closet
     through my clothes and found my cleanest dirty shirt;

Then I washed my face, and combed my hair,
    and stumbled down the stairs to meet the day.

I'd smoked my mind the night before
10   with cigarettes and songs I'd been pickin';
But I lit my first and watched a small kid
    playing with a can that he was kickin';
Then I walked across the empty street and caught
    the Sunday smell of someone fryin' chicken;
15 And it took me back to somethin' that
    I'd lost somewhere somehow along the way.

On the Sunday mornin' sidewalk, I'm wishin', Lord, that I was stoned,
    'Cause there's something in a Sunday that makes a body feel alone;
    And there's nothing short of dyin' that's half as lonesome as the sound
20   On the sleeping city sidewalk; and Sunday mornin' comin' down.

In the park I saw a daddy
    with a laughing little girl that he was swingin';
And I stopped beside a Sunday school
    and listened to the song they were singin';
25 Then I headed down the street,
    and somewhere far away a lonely bell was ringin';
And it echoed thru the canyon
    like a disappearing dream of yesterday.

On the Sunday mornin' sidewalk, I'm wishin', Lord, that I was stoned,
30   'Cause there's something in a Sunday that make a body feel alone;
    And there's nothing short of dyin' that's half as lonesome as the sound
    On the sleeping city sidewalk; and Sunday mornin' comin' down.

Kris Kristofferson (1936–   )
and Fred Foster (1931–   )
Me and Bobby McGee*

Busted flat in Baton Rouge,
Headin' for the trains;
Feelin' nearly faded as my jeans,
Bobby thumbed a diesel down
5   Just before it rained;
Took us all the way to New Orleans.

I took my harpoon out
    of my dirty, red bandana
And was blowin' sad,
      while Bobby sang the blues;
With them windshield wipers slappin' time
    and Bobby clappin' hands
We fin'ly sang up ev'ry song that driver knew.

Freedom's just another word for nothin' left to lose,
      Nothin' ain't worth nothin', but it's free;
    Feelin' good was easy, Lord,
    When Bobby sang the blues;
And feelin' good was good enough for me,
  Good enough for me and Bobby McGee.

    From the coal mines of Kentucky
    To the California sun,
    Bobby shared the secrets of my soul;
    Standin' right beside me, Lord,
    Through everything I done,
    And every night she kept me from the cold.

    Then somewhere near Salinas,
      Lord, I let her slip away
Lookin' for the home
    I hope she'll find;
And I'd trade all of my tomorrows
      for a single yesterday,
    Holdin' Bobby's body next to mine.

Freedom's just another word for nothin' left to lose,
      Nothin' left is all she left for me;
      Feelin' good was easy, Lord,
    When Bobby sang the blues;
    Nothin' left is all she left for me;
And buddy that was good enough for me,
  Good enough for me and Bobby McGee.

10
15
20
25
30
35

Leonard Cohen (1934–   )
Stories of the Street*

The stories of the street are mine
The Spanish voices laugh
The Cadillacs go creeping down
Through the night and the poison gas.
5 I lean from my window sill
In this old hotel I chose
One hand on my suicide
One hand on the rose.

I know you've heard it's over now
10 And war must surely come
The cities they are broke in half
And the middle men are gone.
But let me ask you one more time
O, children of the dust,
15 All these hunters who are shrieking now
Do they speak for us?

And where do all these highways go
Now that we are free?
Why are the armies marching still
20 That were coming home to me?
O, lady with your legs so fine
O, stranger at your wheel
You are locked into your suffering
And your pleasures are the seal.

25 The age of lust is giving birth
And both the parents ask
The nurse to tell them fairy tales
On both sides of the glass
Now the infant with his cord
30 Is hauled in like a kite
And one eye filled with blueprints
One eye filled with night.

O, come with me my little one
And we will find that farm
35 And grow us grass and apples there
And keep all the animals warm.
And if by chance I wake at night
And I ask you who I am
O, take me to the slaughter house
40 I will wait there with the lamb.

With one hand on a hexagram
And one hand on a girl
I balance on a wishing well
That all men call the world.
45 We are so small between the stars
So large against the sky
And lost among the subway crowds
I try to catch your eye.

Leonard Cohen (1934–   )
Suzanne*

Suzanne takes you down
To her place near the river.
You can hear the boats go by,
You can stay the night beside her,
5 And you know that she's half-crazy
But that's why you want to be there,
And she feeds you tea and oranges
That come all the way from China,
And just when you mean to tell her
10 That you have no love to give her,
Then she gets you on her wave-length
And she lets the river answer
That you've always been her lover.

And you want to travel with her,
15 And you want to travel blind,
And you know that she can trust you
'Cause you've touched her perfect body
With your mind.

And Jesus was a sailor
20 When he walked upon the water
And he spent a long time watching
From a lonely wooden tower
And when he knew for certain
That only drowning men could see him,
25 He said, "All men shall be sailors, then,
Until the sea shall free them,"

But he, himself, was broken
Long before the sky would open.
Forsaken, almost human,
30 He sank beneath your wisdom
Like a stone.

And you want to travel with him,
And you want to travel blind,
And you think you'll maybe trust him
35 'Cause he touched your perfect body
With his mind.

Suzanne takes your hand
And she leads you to the river.
She is wearing rags and feathers
40 From Salvation Army counters,
And the sun pours down like honey
On our lady of the harbor;
And she shows you where to look
Among the garbage and the flowers.
45 There are heroes in the seaweed,
There are children in the morning,
They are leaning out for love,
And they will lean that way forever
While Suzanne, she holds the mirror.

50 And you want to travel with her,
You want to travel blind,
And you're sure that she can find you
'Cause she's touched her perfect body
With her mind.

Bill Ward (1943–   )
Alabama*

Stony creeks in hollow-bottoms, hiding from the sun and hidden
From me now by years that came between;
Watching morning on the river, seeing sunlight burn the foggy water
First to gold and then to green.
5   And the time I've been gone drags behind me like a chain,
       And weighs me down till I ain't worth a damn;

'Cause the ground that I walked held the waters of creation
And the bones of those that made me who I am.
Alabama, I still hear the liquid silver of your name;
10 And I see your sundown swallows,
And I taste your wind and smell your dusty rain.

Wavy haze of heat in August, dancing like a crazy lake
Above the sleeping fields along the road;
Country girls and growing older, knowing eyes and glowing shoulders,
15 Summer nights that silently explode.
       And the faces I knew crowd around me like a dream,
       Saying things I heard them say a life ago;
       And the leaves I remember on the breezes of November
       Seem much realer than this unfamiliar snow.
20 Alabama, I still hear the liquid silver of your name;
And I see your sundown swallows,
And I taste your wind and smell your dusty rain.

Sometimes now at night the life I'm leading's leading me to go out
Stumbling under stars that ain't my own;
25 And a winter moon keeps saying—maybe cussing, maybe praying—
Go to hell or heaven; go on home.
Alabama, I still hear the liquid silver of your name;
And I see your sundown swallows,
And I taste your wind and smell your dusty rain.

Pete Seeger (1919–   )
Where Have All the Flowers Gone?*

Where have all the flowers gone?
Long time passing
Where have all the flowers gone?
Long time ago
5 Where have all the flowers gone?
Young girls have picked them, every one.
Oh, when will they ever learn?
Oh, when will they ever learn?

Where have all the young girls gone?

10 Long time passing
    Where have all the young girls gone?
    Long time ago
    Where have all the young girls gone?
    They've taken husbands, every one.
15 Oh, when will they ever learn?
    Oh, when will they ever learn?

    Where have all the husbands gone?
    Long time passing
    Where have all the husbands gone?
20 Long time ago
    Where have all the husbands gone?
    Gone for soldiers, every one.
    Oh, when will they ever learn?
    Oh, when will they ever learn?

25 Where have all the soldiers gone?
    Long time passing
    Where have all the soldiers gone?
    Long time ago
    Where have all the soldiers gone?
30 Gone to graveyards, every one.
    Oh, when will they ever learn?
    Oh, when will they ever learn?

    Where have all the graveyards gone?
    Long time passing
35 Where have all the graveyards gone?
    Long time ago
    Where have all the graveyards gone?
    They're covered with flowers, every one.
    Oh, when will they ever learn?
40 Oh, when will they ever learn?

    Where have all the flowers gone?
    Long time passing
    Where have all the flowers gone?
    Long time ago
45 Where have all the flowers gone?
    Young girls have picked them, every one.
    Oh, when will they ever learn?
    Oh, when will they ever learn?

Paul Simon (1942–   )
The Sound of Silence

Hello darkness my old friend,
I've come to talk with you again,
Because a vision softly creeping,
Left its seeds while I was sleeping
5 And the vision that was planted in my brain
Still remains within the sound of silence.

In restless dreams I walked alone,
Narrow streets of cobble stone
'Neath the halo of a street lamp,
10 I turned my collar to the cold and damp
When my eyes were stabbed by the flash of a neon light
That split the night, and touched the sound of silence.

And in the naked light I saw
Ten thousand people maybe more,
15 People talking without speaking,
People hearing without listening,
People writing songs that voices never share
And no one dares disturb the sound of silence.

"Fools!" said I, "You do not know
20 Silence like a cancer grows.
Hear my words that I might teach you
Take my arms that I might reach you."
But my words like silent raindrops fell
And echoed, in the wells of silence.

25 And the people bowed and prayed
To the neon God they made,
And the sign flashed out its warning
In the words that it was forming.
And the sign said:
30   "The words of the prophets are written
    on the subway walls and tenement halls"
And whispered in the sound of silence.

Phil Ochs   (1940–1976)
Crucifixion

And the night comes again to the circle-studded sky
The stars settle slowly, in loneliness they lie
Till the universe explodes as a falling star is raised
The planets are paralyzed, the mountains are amazed
5 But they all glow brighter from the brilliance of the blaze
With the speed of insanity, then, he dies.

In the green fields of turning a baby is born
His cries crease the wind and mingle with the morn
An assault upon the order, the changing of the guard
10 Chosen for a challenge that's hopelessly hard
And the only single sign is the sighing of the stars
But to the silence of distance they're sworn.

So dance, dance, dance
Teach us to be true
15 Come dance, dance, dance
'Cause we love you.

Images of innocence charge him to go on
But the decadence of history is looking for a pawn
To a nightmare of knowledge he opens up the gate
20 A blinding revelation is served upon his plate
That beneath the greatest love is a hurricane of hate
And God help the critic of the dawn.

So he stands on the sea and he shouts to the shore
But the louder that he screams the longer he's ignored
25 For the wine of oblivion is drunk to the dregs
And the merchants of the masses almost have to be begged
Till the giant is aware that someone's pulling at his leg
And someone is tapping at the door.

So dance, dance, dance
30 Teach us to be true
Come dance, dance, dance
'Cause we love you.

Then his message gathers meaning and it spreads across the land
The rewarding of the fame is the following of the man
35 But ignorance is everywhere and people have their way
And success is an enemy to the losers of the day
In the shadows of the churches who knows what they pray
And blood is the language of the band.

The Spanish bulls are beaten, the crowd is soon beguiled
40 The matador is beautiful, a symphony of style

Excitement is ecstatic, passion places bets
Gracefully he bows to ovations that he gets
But the hands that are applauding are slippery with sweat
And saliva is falling from their smiles.

45 So dance, dance, dance
Teach us to be true
Come dance, dance, dance
'Cause we love you.

Then this overflow of life is crushed into a liar
50 The gentle soul is ripped apart and tossed into the fire
It's the burial of beauty, it's the victory of night
Truth becomes a tragedy limping from the light
The heavens are horrified, they stagger from the sight
And the cross is trembling with desire.

55 They say they can't believe it, it's a sacrilegious shame
Now who would want to hurt such a hero of the game
But you know I predicted it, I knew he had to fall
How did it happen, I hope his suffering was small
Tell me every detail, I've got to know it all
60 And do you have a picture of the pain?

So dance, dance, dance
Teach us to be true
Come dance, dance, dance
'Cause we love you.

65 Time takes her toll and the memory fades
But his glory is growing in the magic that he made
Reality is ruined, there is nothing more to fear
The drama is distorted to what they want to hear
Swimming in their sorrow in the twisting of a tear
70 As they wait for the new thrill parade.

The eyes of the rebel have been branded by the blind
To the safety of sterility the threat has been refined
The child was created to the slaughter house he's led
So good to be alive when the eulogies are read
75 The climax of emotion, the worship of the dead
As the cycle of sacrifice unwinds.

So dance, dance, dance
Teach us to be true
Come dance, dance, dance
80 'Cause we love you.

And the night comes again to the circle-studded sky
The stars settle slowly, in loneliness they lie
Till the universe explodes as a falling star is raised
The planets are paralyzed, the mountains are amazed
85 But they all glow brighter from the brilliance of the blaze
With the speed of insanity, then, he dies.

Phil Ochs   (1940–1976)
Nobody's Buying Flowers from the Flower Lady

Millionaires and paupers walk the lonely street
Rich and poor companions of the restless feet
Strangers in a foreign land strike a match with a tremblin' hand
Learned too much to ever understand
5   But nobody's buying flowers from the flower lady.

Lovers quarrel, snarl away their happiness
Kisses crumble in a web of loneliness
It's written by the poison pen, voices break before they bend
The door is slammed, it's over once again
10   But nobody's buying flowers from the flower lady.

Poets agonize, they cannot find the words
The stone stares at the sculptor, asks are you absurd
The painter paints his brushes black, through the canvas runs a crack
The portrait of the pain never answers back
15   But nobody's buying flowers from the flower lady.

Soldiers disillusioned come home from the war
Sarcastic students tell them not to fight no more
And they argue through the night, black is black and white is white
Walk away both knowing they are right
20   Still nobody's buying flowers from the flower lady.

Smoke dreams of escaping souls are drifting by
Dull the pain of living as they slowly die
Smiles change into a sneer, washed away by whiskey tears
In the quicksand of their minds they disappear
25   But nobody's buying flowers from the flower lady.

Feeble aged people almost to their knees
Complain about the present using memories
Never found their pot of gold, wrinkled hands pound weary holes
Each line screams out you're old, you're old, you're old
30   But nobody's buying flowers from the flower lady.

And the flower lady hobbles home without a sale
Tattered shreds of petals leave a fading trail
Not a pause to hold a rose, even she no longer knows
The lamp goes out, the evening now is closed
35   And nobody's buying flowers from the flower lady.

Johnny Hartford　(1937–　)
Gentle on My Mind*

It's knowing that your door is always open and your path is free to walk,
That makes me tend to leave my sleeping bag rolled up and stashed behind your couch,
And it's knowing that I'm not shackled by forgotten words and bonds
And the ink stains that have dried upon some line,
5 That keeps you in the backroads by the rivers of my memory that keeps you ever
Gentle on my mind.

It's not clinging to the rocks and ivy planted on their columns now that binds me
Or something that somebody said because they thought we fit together walkin',
It's just knowing that the world will not be cursing or forgiving when I walk along
10 Some railroad track and find
That you're moving on the backroads by the rivers of my memory and for hours
You're just gentle on my mind.

Though the wheat fields and the clothes lines and junkyards and the highways
Come between us
15 And some other woman crying to her mother 'cause she turned and I was gone.
I still run in silence, tears of joy might stain my face and summer sun might
Burn me 'til I'm blind
But not to where I cannot see you walkin' on the backroads by the rivers flowing
Gentle on my mind.

20 I dip my cup of soup from the gurglin' cracklin' caldron in some train yard
My beard a rough'ning coal pile and a dirty hat pulled low across my face.
Through cupped hands 'round a tin can I pretend I hold you to my breast and find
That you're waving from the backroads by the rivers of my memory ever smilin'
Ever gentle on my mind.

The Language of Poetry

We have already seen that there are many languages within the English language—the language of science, of journalism, of history, of philosophy (p. 306). True, all these languages have some basic things in common that make them English instead of French or German, such as grammatical structure and vocabulary. If we read that "North Labrador is a land of ice covered by grey sky, a silence where time has no meaning," the description is clear to anyone schooled in the basic devices of the English language. But when Hart Crane says that North Labrador is

> A land of leaning ice
> Hugged by plaster-grey arches of sky [that]
> Flings itself silently
> Into eternity,

we know that special language devices are being used to create a special kind of comment on North Labrador. We have already been introduced to the basic devices in "Preliminaries" (p. 299), of the poetry division, but the time has now arrived to explore them more thoroughly to prepare us for some penetrating poems yet to come. In a very real sense, we need the right keys to unlock the many corridors of poetic experience.

Rhythm and Rhyme: The Proper Fusion of Sound and Sense

Pope saw clearly that

> True ease in writing comes from art, not chance,
> As those move easiest who have learn'd to dance.
> 'Tis not enough no harshness gives offense,
> The sound must seem an Echo to the sense.
> —*An Essay on Criticism,* ll. 362–365

Rhythm and rhyme, the basis of sound, are used to convey *meaning* in poetry. Most readers readily acknowledge that they can produce delightful effects for their own sake, as they do for some readers in Poe's "The Bells," but it is not usually understood that rhythm and rhyme actually help in shaping the meaning of a poem. The popular myth runs: the *idea* must be put into some form or frame, of course, but the idea is really the important matter—as if the idea has been put into a fancy basket to be delivered to the reader in appropriate style. A brief demonstration of this erroneous approach to poems may be more substantial than a book of arguments.

George Washington Doane (1799–1859)
Evening

Softly now the light of day
Fades upon my sight away;
Free from care, from labor free,
Lord, I would commune with Thee:

5   Thou, whose all-pervading eye,
    Naught escapes, without, within,
Pardon each infirmity,
    Open fault and secret sin.

Soon, for me, the light of day
10   Shall forever pass away;
Then, from sin and sorrow free,
Take me, Lord, to dwell with Thee:

Thou, who, sinless, yet hast known
    All of man's infirmity;
15   Then from Thine eternal throne,
    Jesus, look with pitying eye.

This poem presents a perfectly sound religious idea, acceptable to thousands of readers regardless of their sectarian doctrine. The first stanza says roughly that with the fading of "the light of day" the poet "would commune" with God. The second stanza asks omniscient God to pardon the speaker's sins. The third stanza includes a nice touch by now using "the light of day" to mean life. When this light passes forever away, the speaker wishes to dwell with God, free from earthly sin and sorrow. The last stanza asks God, sinless though He is, to look with pity upon man's earthly infirmity.

The poem contains humility, and a distaste for all sins which bring sorrow—who would quarrel with such sentiments? Do such sentiments make a good *poem?* A brief examination of its rhythm and rhyme will help to answer the question.

Note the rhyme scheme:

aabb   cdcd   aabb   ecec
  (couplets)   (couplets)

Does there seem to be any reason why stanzas 1 and 3 only should be written in couplets? If we examine the *logic* of the poem, stanzas 3 and 4 should be reversed, permitting the poem to come to rest with the line,

Take me, Lord, to dwell with Thee:

With this structure, the exact repetition of the rhymes in stanzas 1 and 4 would have real point by bringing to rest the tone that opens the poem in stanza 1. We note further that most of the rhymes are hackneyed and trite: *day* calls for *away,* *free* calls for *Thee,* and so on. Instead of awakening our sensibilities and surprising us with the fresh word, the rhymes discourage our expectancy, and the sense of the poem slips through our lulled wits. Line 3 seems to be especially awkward, beginning and ending with the same word, *free,* which rhymes with *Thee* in line 4.

The entire poem, save the last line, is written in monotonous tetrameter. Hardly the slightest variation exists except in the last line, where it is the least appropriate if we assume that the function of the last line is to bring the action to rest. Further, the monotonous regularity of the accented beat sometimes accents unimportant words: *upon,* line 2; *would,* line 4. To summarize, the poem is not memorable, condensed, or rigidly organized; and the religious idea, *which could have been made a religious experience* for the reader, lies dormant and ineffective.

Francis Quarles   (1592–1644)
A Good-Night

Close now thine eyes and rest secure;
Thy soul is safe enough, thy body sure;
   He that loves thee, he that keeps
And guards thee, never slumbers, never sleeps.
5 The smiling conscience in a sleeping breast
   Has only peace, has only rest;
   The music and the mirth of kings
Are all but very discords, when she sings;
   Then close thine eyes and rest secure;
10 No sleep so sweet as thine, no rest so sure.

The idea in this religious poem can be simply stated: a free conscience brings the peace and security provided by God. It requires no subtle analysis, however, to discover the shaping influences of rhythm and rhyme, which have helped to make the poem so superior to the paraphrase.

Although the lyric is written in five couplets, which could have been monotonous, the poet has provided a good deal of variation in only ten lines. Note that the first line of each couplet is tetrameter, and the second line pentameter except the third couplet—the middle couplet—which is reversed to break the rhythmic regularity. Note further that although the poem uses an iambic foot, the accent in the first foot does not always come on the second syllable. To *read* the accent on the second syllable of lines 1, 3, 6, and 10 would certainly violate their meaning. Note the difference in lines 3 and 4:

> ′ ˘ ′ ˘ ′ ˘ ˘ ′
> He that loves thee, he that keeps
> ˘ ′ ˘ ′ ˘ ′ ˘ ′ ˘ ′
> And guards thee, never slumbers, never sleeps.

In one respect at least the rhyme scheme is especially appropriate. The sense of the poem has to do with restful security, and the rhyme helps to produce such an effect in the reader by closing the poem with the same sound that opened it, *secure-sure*. That is, the sound actually helps to interpret the sense. If further proof is necessary, suppose we change the word order a bit in the first four lines:

> Close thine eyes now and rest secure;
> Thy body is sure, thy soul safe enough;
>   He that keeps, he that loves thee
> And guards thee, never sleeps, never slumbers.

The sense is still there—or is it?

The emergent tone   We are not concerned with exhibiting the extreme subtleties in the fusion of sound and sense in poetry, nor are we encouraging anyone to underestimate their importance. We wish to make clear that rhythm and rhyme help to shape the exact meaning of a poem. They help to establish the tone, which is in effect the poet's attitude toward the sense, or facts, of the poem, and *readers must allow the tone to help them interpret the poem*. They must read the poem aloud and listen for the poet's voice and attitude because that attitude has shaped the meaning of the entire poem. Tone is less tangible than image and figure (indeed, we borrow a term from music to describe it), but no less real. We shall see when we consider figures of speech and symbols (p. 377) that tone can actually become a figure of speech when the *entire* poem is meaningful only on the figurative level.

The shaping mechanics of verse   Because poetry is an art, many people are irritated with the phrase "the mechanics of verse." "What does it matter"—the objection runs—"whether the line is iambic or trochaic, tetrameter or pentameter? I don't want to write poetry; I just want to read it." The argument seems to make good sense until we press that word *read* a little. Whether or not we read a poem aloud, we must be able to "hear" and feel its rhythms as well as to understand its sense. In a good poem the fusion of rhythm and sense is there, and we must read the fusion, not rhythm *or* sense, to experience the whole poem. To emphasize the rhythm as we read produces singsong; to emphasize the sense loses the poet's tone and attitude. To read both rhythm and sense simultaneously requires an elementary knowledge of the *foot,* the *line,* and the *stanza.*

The foot.   The foot is the smallest unit of stressed and unstressed syllables found in verse. An elementary knowledge includes four kinds of feet.

1. *Iamb:* One unstressed and one stressed syllable, as in *deˇlíght.* This line is composed of iambic feet:

> ˘ ′ ˘ ′ ˘ ′ ˘ ′
> How small | a part | of time | they share

2. *Anapest:* Two unstressed and one stressed syllable, as in *underneath.* This line is composed chiefly of anapestic feet:

It was man | y and man | y a year | ago

3. *Trochee:* One stressed and one unstressed syllable, as in *happen* and *trochee.* This line is composed of trochaic feet:

Should you | ask me | whence these | stories

4. *Dactyl:* One stressed and two unstressed syllables, as in *Michigan* and *elephant.* This line is composed of dactylic feet:

Take her up | tenderly

The line. The line, called also a *verse,* determines the basic rhythmical pattern of the poem, and provides a principle of order for the sense. Lines are named according to the number of feet they possess, as follows:

One foot—monometer
Two feet—dimeter
Three feet—trimeter
Four feet—tetrameter
Five feet—pentameter
Six feet—hexameter
Seven feet—heptameter
Eight feet—octameter

Lines are therefore described according to the *kind* and *number* of feet they possess. For example, the line used to illustrate iambic meter is called *iambic tetrameter:*

How small | a part | of time | they share
    1   2   3   4

This line is *dactylic dimeter:*

Take her up | tenderly
  1   2

Most poems, like most of those we have already read, have lines composed of from three to five feet because these units of verse best serve the sense communicated by most poets. Poe's "The Raven" is an exception with its octameter line because the poet is working for a special tone and is using internal rhyme to help achieve his tone. His octameter line can be seen actually as two tetrameter units that are sometimes rhymed:

Once up | on a | midnight | dreary, || while I | pondered, | weak and | weary

Now that we have come so far in our brief analysis of the foot and the line, we see that few poems are written exclusively with the same line or even the same foot. To avoid monotony, to achieve special effects, and—most important—to fuse the sound and sense, poets employ many kinds of variations. Although we have scanned the line from "The Raven" as "regular" trochaic octameter verse, we do not read it that way because the resulting sound would violate the sense. We actually read the line something like this:

Once up|on a | midnight | dreary, | while I | pondered | weak and | weary

There are, then, actually two degrees of stress, called primary (´) and secondary (˝), which are made necessary by the poem's sense.

Another kind of variation in the line is made by substituting one kind of foot for another. The substitution of the anapestic foot for the iambic foot is found in Bryant's "Green River":

When breez|es are soft | and skies | are fair,
I steal | an hour | from stud|y and care

Note another kind of substitution, dimeter for tetrameter, in Waller's "Song" (p. 395):

Go, love|ly Rose,
Tell her | that wastes | her time | and me,
That now | she knows
When I | resem|ble her | to thee
How sweet | and fair | she seems | to be.

Because everyone does not read poetry the same way—not even highly qualified readers—we should be extremely reluctant to draw dogmatic generalizations about the scansion of any poem. Almost every serious poem has both metrical and rhetorical rhythm unless it is written in free verse (see p.364). There is movement of sound and movement of sense in every poem, and generally some compromise between the two must be made if the total meaning of the poem is not to be violated. This statement is especially true of poems with rhyme, and even more true of poems with internal rhyme. The reading of poems, especially aloud, is an accomplished art, but it will not be accomplished unless the reader knows what goes on in the poem.

Rhyme. Rhyme is perhaps the most obvious technical device in poetry, yet its effects can be most subtle. Like all other devices, it is used for a specific purpose in each poem, and to judge its usefulness we must understand that purpose. The limerick depends heavily on rhyme:

There once was a man from Nantucket
Who kept all his cash in a bucket;
   But his daughter, named Nan,
   Ran away with a man,
And as for the bucket, Nantucket.

Some limericks combine a substantial subject with humor as does this one that plays with Einstein's famous theory of relativity:

> There was a young lady named Bright,
> Whose speed was far faster than light;
> > She set out one day
> > In a relative way,
> And returned home the previous night.

Rhyme is used here to produce a humorous effect by emphasizing the element of surprise. The use of rhyme in Blake's "The Tiger" (p. 396) is more subtle:

> Tiger! Tiger! burning bright
> In the forests of the night,
> What immortal hand or eye
> Could frame thy fearful symmetry?

The rhyme *bright-night* suggests a paradox, an apparent contradiction that upon close examination proves to be true. The rhyme *eye-symmetry* is even more subtle in its suggestion that an immortal eye, really unknown to us and by suggestion part of the "night," frames this symmetry, fearful because, by suggestion, it, too, is part of the "night." To hit the rhymes in "The Tiger" as we are expected to do in the limerick would violate the poem's meaning. In fact, by alternating a perfect rhyme, *bright-night,* with an imperfect rhyme, *eye-symmetry,* Blake has discouraged us from overemphasizing the rhymes in the stanza.

There are many kinds of rhymes, used to achieve different purposes. The principal rhymes are *perfect* and *imperfect,* subdivided as follows:

Masculine (perfect): final accented syllables rhyme:

> lie-die; resist-consist

Feminine or multiple (perfect): rhyming accented syllables followed by identical unaccented syllables:

> raven-craven; comparison-garrison

Sprung or near-rhyme (imperfect): similar but not identical vowels rhyme:

> blood-good; strong-unstrung; eye-symmetry

Rhyme is found in two positions:

End-rhyme: at the end of the lines, the usual position, as in "The Tiger."

Internal rhyme: within the line:

> The splendor *falls* on castle *walls*

Stanza form. A stanza is a pattern of lines that usually presents a unit of poetic experience. If the poem is composed of two or more stanzas, the pattern is generally repeated. There are many variations, of course, in stanza form, but we shall note only the standard forms that appear most frequently in American and English poetry. An alert reader will, of course, examine the stanza in any poem to determine how and why it helps to shape the poem's meaning. As we become more experienced in reading poetry—and more conditioned by standard stanza forms—certain expectancies are established in us which help to interpret the various forms.

Heroic couplet: two rhymed iambic pentameter lines; each couplet is usually a complete unit, as in Pope:

> Hope springs eternal in the human breast,
> Man never is, but always to be, blessed.
> —"An Essay on Man"

The couplet is not confined to iambic pentameter lines; Jonson, for example, uses iambic tetrameter in "Come, My Celia":

> Come, my Celia, let us prove
> While we may the sports of love;
> Time will not be ours forever,
> He at length our good will sever.

Swinburne uses anapestic pentameter couplets in a chorus of "Atalanta in Calydon":

> We have seen thee, O Love, thou art fair; thou art goodly, O Love;
> Thy wings make light in the air as the wings of a dove.

Ballad stanza: four-line iambic, alternately tetrameter and trimeter, rhyming *abcb,* as in "Sir Patrick Spens" (p. 326):

> The king sits in Dumferling toune,
>   Drinking the blude-reid wine:
> "O whar will I get guid sailor,
>   To sail this schip of mine?"

The sonnet: fourteen iambic pentameter lines, grouped variously according to the purpose of the poet.

The *Italian,* sometimes called *Petrarchan* or *legitimate,* sonnet has two parts: an octet, or eight lines, rhyming *abbaabba;* and a sestet, or six lines, using new rhymes, rhyming *cdcdcd* or some other combination. Wordsworth's "Composed upon Westminster Bridge" (p. 399) and Milton's "On His Blindness" (p. 404) are sonnets in the Italian form.

The *English,* sometimes called the *Shakespearean,* sonnet has three four-line units, or quatrains, and a concluding couplet, rhyming, *ababcdcdefefgg.* Drayton's "Since There's No Help" (p. 403) and the sonnets by Shakespeare, of course, are examples of the English form.

Usually, but not necessarily, the octet of a sonnet presents a problem or conflict, and the sestet offers a resolution or simply a comment on the conflict. Frost observed with characteristic humor that after the eighth line a sonnet takes a turn for better or worse. (See pp. 399–406 for other sonnets and further commentary on the sonnet form.)

The Spenserian stanza: devised by Edmund Spenser (1552–1599) and used in *The Faerie Queene,* contains nine lines, eight of iambic pentameter, and the last of iambic hexameter (an Alexandrine), rhyming *ababbcbcc.* Because of the excellent effects it can be made to produce, this stanza form seems to be forever fresh and useful.

Blank verse: iambic pentameter verse free from rhyme, the metrical line that seems to fit best the natural rhythms of our language. Shakespeare used it in his plays (*Hamlet,* p. 626), Milton chose it for *Paradise Lost,* and Frost used it with extraordinary effectiveness.

Free verse: Free verse—not to be confused with blank verse—is verse that does not adhere to any exact metrical pattern. Although much of the world's poetry is written in free verse, sometimes called *vers libre,* many handbooks and textbooks on poetry give it a wide berth as if the whole matter were of little importance or not quite respectable.

There are both good and bad metrical verse and free verse, but the sins of one are not the virtues of the other. Bad metrical verse is perfectly, monotonously, and mechanically regular; bad free verse is rhetorically undisciplined and formless. Writers of good metrical verse resort to many variations as we have seen; and the more they use, the closer they come to free verse. Writers of good free verse use a firm rhetorical discipline that often approximates a metrical form; and the firmer the rhetorical discipline the closer it comes to metrical verse. Are the differences between the two following passages very marked?

> To be, or not to be—that is the question:
> Whether 'tis nobler in the mind to suffer
> The slings and arrows of outrageous fortune
> Or to take arms against a sea of troubles,
> 5 And by opposing end them. To die—to sleep—
> No more; and by a sleep to say we end
> The heartache, and the thousand natural shocks
> That flesh is heir to. 'Tis a consummation
> Devoutly to be wished. . . .
> —Shakespeare, *Hamlet,* III. i. 56–64

> This, this is he; softly a while;
> Let us not break in upon him.
> O change beyond report, thought, or belief!
> See how he lies at random, carelessly diffused,
> 5 With languished head unpropt,
> As one past hope, abandoned,
> And by himself given over,
> In slavish habit, ill-fitted weeds
> O'er-worn and soiled.
> 10 Or do my eyes misrepresent? Can this be he,
> That heroic, that renowned,
> Irresistible Samson? whom, unarmed,
> No strength of man, or fiercest wild beast, could withstand;
> Who tore the lion as the lion tears the kid;
> 15 Ran on embattled armies clad in iron,
> And, weaponless himself,
> Made arms ridiculous, useless the forgery

> Of brazen shield and spear, the hammered cuirass,
> Chalybean-tempered steel, and frock of mail
> 20 Adamantean proof. . . .
>   —Milton, *Samson Agonistes*

Both these passages are shaped by a firm rhetorical discipline. Shakespeare is using blank verse liberally varied to permit the sense to strike home. To attempt to read any line metrically simply violates the sense; for example:

> The heart-ache and the thousand natural shocks

Rhetorically, it scans something like this:

> The heart-ache and the thousand natural shocks

Although the passage from Milton is written in free verse, the metrical verse often shows itself (lines 5, 6, 8, 9, and so on), and the rhetorical discipline never falters. It seems quite pointless to ask, is metrical verse superior to free verse? It seems better to ask, does the verse form properly shape the meaning of the poem?

The rhythm of good free verse is the rhythm of thought. Much so-called poetic prose is actually free verse written in prose form. "Psalm 23," King James Version, is easily converted from prose to verse:

> The Lord is my shepherd;
> I shall not want.
>
> He maketh me to lie down in green pastures:
> He leadeth me beside the still waters.
> 5 He restoreth my soul:
> He leadeth me in the paths of righteousness
> For his name's sake.
> Yea, though I walk
> Through the valley of the shadow of death,
> 10 I will fear no evil:
> For thou art with me;
> Thy rod and thy staff
> They comfort me.
>
> Thou preparest a table before me
> 15 In the presence of mine enemies:
> Thou anointest my head with oil;
> My cup runneth over.
>
> Surely goodness and mercy shall follow me
> All the days of my life:
> 20 And I will dwell in the house of the Lord
> For ever.

As we ask ourselves some questions about the poems to follow, perhaps we can observe the appropriate uses of metrical and free verse.

William Wordsworth (1770–1850)
My Heart Leaps Up

My heart leaps up when I behold
   A rainbow in the sky:
So was it when my life began;
So is it now I am a man;
5 So be it when I shall grow old,
   Or let me die!
The Child is father of the Man;
And I could wish my days to be
Bound each to each by natural piety.

Comments and Questions

1. Although Wordsworth uses metrical verse, the poem is, compared to a sonnet, quite irregular in form. All lines are written in iambic meter, but note that they vary from dimeter to pentameter. Note further that the rhyme scheme is somewhat unusual: *abccabcdd.* We do not ask, is it right for Wordsworth to depart from the more regular forms? The question is, Does the poem's irregular form shape the poem's meaning? Does the sound help to interpret the sense? The poem's form is certainly no accident. Why is line 6 the shortest, and line 9 the longest? Why do the last two lines rhyme? Why do lines 1 and 5 rhyme, and lines 2 and 6? The answers to these questions are related to the total experience provided by the poem.

2. How good a poem is it?

3. Explain the line "The Child is father of the Man."

Frank O'Hara (1926–1966)
Autobiographia Literaria

When I was a child
I played by myself in a
corner of the schoolyard
all alone.

5 I hated dolls and I
hated games, animals were

not friendly and birds
flew away.

If anyone was looking
10 for me I hid behind a
tree and cried out "I am
an orphan."

And here I am, the
center of all beauty!
15 writing these poems!
Imagine!

Comments and Questions

1. We ask the same basic questions of O'Hara's poem that we asked of Words-worth's: Does the poem's free-verse form help to interpret the sense? How do the lines of varying length help to communicate O'Hara's attitude? Why is the fourth line of each stanza the shortest?

2. Do the lines move with the rhythm of thought in the poem? How would you describe the speaker's tone? Why is the free-verse form consistent with the tone?

3. Does Wordsworth's line "The Child is father of the Man" apply to this poem as well?

Thomas Moore   (1779–1852)
Believe Me, If All Those Endearing Young Charms

Believe me, if all those endearing young charms,
    Which I gaze on so fondly today,
Were to change by tomorrow, and fleet in my arms,
    Like fairy-gifts fading away,
5 Thou wouldst still be adored, as this moment thou art,
    Let thy loveliness fade as it will,
And around the dear ruin each wish of my heart
    Would entwine itself verdantly still.

It is not while beauty and youth are thine own,
10   And thy cheeks unprofaned by a tear,
That the fervor and faith of a soul can be known,

To which time will but make thee more dear;
No, the heart that has truly loved never forgets,
    But as truly loves on to the close,
15 As the sun-flower turns on her god, when he sets,
    The same look which she turned when he rose.

Comments and Questions

1. The regularity of Moore's lyric—a brief subjective and musical poem—is apparent: the foot is anapestic, the lines alternate between tetrameter and trimeter, and the rhyme scheme has a definite pattern (*ababcdcd,* and so on). Compared with "My Heart Leaps Up," is Moore's poem dull and monotonous, or does his form help shape the meaning of the poem?

2. The poem, we said, is a lyric. Does this fact help to account for its form?

George Herbert   (1593–1633)
Easter Wings

It is interesting to note a device used by a few seventeenth-century poets: the form of the poem that follows speaks for itself. Joseph Addison (1672–1719) called this sort of thing "false wit," which we may translate as false poetic form. Do you agree?

Lord, who createdst man in wealth and store,
    Though foolishly he lost the same,
        Decaying   more   and   more
           Till   he   became
5   Most   poor;
           With   thee
       Oh,   let   me   rise
    As   larks,   harmoniously,
And sing this day thy victories;
10 Then shall the fall further the flight in me.

My tender age in sorrow did begin;
    And still with sicknesses and shame
        Thou   didst   so   punish   sin,
          That   I   became
15   Most   thin.
           With   thee
      Let   me   combine,
    And feel this day thy victory;
    For if I imp[1] my wing on thine,
20 Affliction shall advance the flight in me.

---

[1] To graft or repair a bird's wing to improve its ability to fly.

Imagery

There are in general two ways of speaking: abstractly and concretely. If we say, "George is an honest, just man with a good deal of integrity," we have described him with abstract terms. If we say, "As George was following the stranger, he saw the stranger's pocketbook slip to the sidewalk, he picked it up, quickened his step, and returned it to him"—we have described George with concrete terms. In the first statement we have spoken *about* George; in the second statement we have allowed George's *act to speak* for George himself. In the first statement we testify to his honesty; in the second statement the act testifies for him, and it may be the more convincing. The second statement illustrates the basic method of the creative writer, especially the poet.

In the second statement we "image" or—as we say—we imagine George's act. We see it all happen because of the concrete details involved: *stranger, pocketbook, sidewalk,* and *step*. Such words are called *imagery* in a poem because they bring real, concrete life into it; they represent the life that the poet wants the reader to experience. Except in poorly constructed, superficial poems, these images are not mere decorations—they are in great part a poet's *method* of thinking. This principle we must understand if we are to enter the inner life of a good poem, and not to enter it is to bypass the poem's higher level, the figurative level of meaning.

Some poems rely almost exclusively on imagery for their meaning, as we shall see when we later explore MacLeish's "You, Andrew Marvell" (p. 373). MacLeish depends on images rather than on a logical argument to make the reader feel the inexorable movement of time. Note the appeal to the senses in the images of the first two stanzas:

And here face down beneath the sun
And here upon earth's noonward height
To feel the always coming on
The always rising of the night:

To feel creep up the curving east
The earthy chill of dusk and slow
Upon those under lands the vast
And ever climbing shadow grow. . . .

Poets can rely on images for meaning if the images are carefully *selected* (not the approximate image, but the *exact* image) and *arranged* because we think naturally in images. Note how our mind searches for meaning by grouping these images: *table, bottle, cabinet, glasses, alcohol, men*—and we see a barroom. Yet note what happens when we add only two more images: *test tube, Bunsen burner*. The *regrouped* images become a laboratory because the last two images alter the *grouped* meaning of the first six.

In that little demonstration of how we think in images there are many lessons for the readers of poems, but for our purposes here chiefly these: we must understand the poem as an organic whole—we must allow the meaning of each image to come clear in its natural setting with all the other images. And we must make sure that all the images are included in our interpretation of the poem's meaning. We are driven back to our basic principle ("Preliminaries," p. 299): the whole poem helps to determine the meaning of its parts, and, in turn, each part helps to determine the meaning of the whole. When we interpret a poem's imagery, the observance of this principle is imperative.

We are now in a position to understand why imagery is the life of a good poem. With imagery the poet allows life to present itself, and we can hear, see, smell, feel, and touch experience. As we read the following poem, we are immediately involved with sense experience—concrete life itself.

Emily Dickinson   (1830–1886)
I Taste a Liquor Never Brewed

I taste a liquor never brewed—
From Tankards scooped in Pearl—
Not all the Vats upon the Rhine
Yield such an Alcohol!

5 Inebriate of Air—am I—
And Debauchee of Dew—
Reeling—thro endless summer days—
From inns of Molten Blue—

When "Landlords" turn the drunken Bee
10 Out of the Foxglove's door—
When Butterflies—renounce their "drams"—
I shall but drink the more!

Till Seraphs[1] swing their snowy Hats—
And Saints—to windows run—
15 To see the little Tippler
Leaning against the—Sun—

Comments

Through images—many of which are also figures and symbols—this poem presents a theme which, as such, is never mentioned directly. The "liquor never brewed" is the

---

[1] Six-winged angels standing in the presence of God.

exhilarating aspect of nature in which we participate by entering Emily Dickinson's sensuous world, and we participate fully because the images are fresh and unusual. "Scooped in Pearl," "inebriate of Air," and "reeling . . . from inns of Molten Blue" are not the worn counters of expression. They are sharp, concrete, arresting sense impressions that communicate meaning, quite unforgettably.

We see, then, that the purpose of imagery is to communicate meaning, not merely to serve as a graceful embellishment. If we understand this distinction before we investigate imagery further, our study can become a genuine pleasure instead of an academic chore. Many of the poems in this section use imagery in striking and original ways and, read carefully, they can help to cultivate our sensitivity to imagery as communication. For most poets, imagery actually becomes a way of thinking, or of translating abstractions into concrete experience. Indeed, imagery is the chief means the poet has of creating reality—the poet's *own* sense of the reality of the inner and outer world and their relationships. Here are two poets thinking in images.

William Shakespeare (1564–1616)
Sonnet 116: Let Me Not to the Marriage of True Minds

Let me not to the marriage of true minds
Admit impediments. Love is not love
Which alters when it alteration finds,
Or bends with the remover to remove.
5 Oh, no! it is an ever-fixed mark
That looks on tempests and is never shaken;
It is the star to every wandering bark,
Whose worth's unknown, although his height be taken.
Love's not Time's fool, though rosy lips and cheeks
10 Within his bending sickle's compass come;
Love alters not with his brief hours and weeks,
But bears it out even to the edge of doom.
    If this be error and upon me proved,
    I never writ, nor no man ever loved.

John Frederick Nims (1913–   )
Love Poem

My clumsiest dear, whose hands shipwreck vases,
At whose quick touch all glasses chip and ring,
Whose palms are bulls in china, burs in linen,
And have no cunning with any soft thing

5   Except all ill at ease fidgeting people:
The refugee uncertain at the door
You make at home; deftly you steady
The drunk clambering on his undulant floor.

Unpredictable dear, the taxi drivers' terror,
10 Shrinking from far headlights pale as a dime
Yet leaping before red apoplectic streetcars—
Misfit in any space. And never on time.

A wrench in clocks and the solar system. Only
With words and people and love you move at ease.
15 In traffic of wit expertly manoeuvre
And keep us, all devotion, at your knees.

Forgetting your coffee spreading on our flannel,
Your lipstick grinning on our coat,
So gayly in love's unbreakable heaven
20 Our souls on glory of spilt bourbon float.

Be with me darling early and late. Smash glasses—
I will study wry music for your sake.
For should your hands drop white and empty
All the toys of the world would break.

Comments and Questions

1. Much like Shakespeare's "Sonnet 116," this poem is a definition of love presented in images and figures. To realize just how essential Nim's images are, try to state the plain sense of the poem in literal language only. What are the basic images and how are they related to a portrait of the speaker's love?

2. What is the tone of the poem? How do the images contribute to the tone?

3. Some of the images may at first seem inappropriate in a love poem. How are they justified? How does the poet use contrast to develop his portrait?

Archibald MacLeish   (1892–1982)
You, Andrew Marvell

And here face down beneath the sun
And here upon earth's noonward height
To feel the always coming on
The always rising of the night:

5 To feel creep up the curving east
The earthy chill of dusk and slow
Upon those under lands the vast
And ever climbing shadow grow

And strange at Ectaban[1] the trees
10 Take leaf by leaf the evening strange
The flooding dark about their knees
The mountains over Persia change

And now at Kermanshah[2] the gate
Dark empty and the withered grass
15 And through the twilight now the late
Few travelers in the westward pass

And Baghdad darken and the bridge
Across the silent river gone
And through Arabia the edge
20 Of evening widen and steal on

And deepen on Palmyra's[3] street
The wheel rut in the ruined stone
And Lebanon fade out and Crete
High through the clouds and overblown

25 And over Sicily the air
Still flashing with the landward gulls
And loom and slowly disappear
The sails above the shadowy hulls

And Spain go under and the shore
30 Of Africa the gilded sand
And evening vanish and no more
The low pale light across that land

Nor now the long light on the sea:

And here face downward in the sun
35 To feel how swift how secretly
The shadow of the night comes on . . .

---

[1] The ancient capital of Media, presently a part of Iran.   [2] City in Iran.   [3] An ancient flourishing city in Syria, presently a poor Arab village.

Comments and Questions

Edwin Arlington Robinson called this poem "really a magical thing." It must be read aloud three or four times in a leisurely way to appreciate Robinson's comment. What produces the magic? Many poetic devices working together, of course, not the least of them the imagery. The title is undoubtedly a reference to Marvell's "To His Coy Mistress" (p. 410), particularly to such well-known lines as:

> But at my back I always hear
> Time's wingéd chariot hurrying near;
> And yonder all before us lie
> Deserts of vast eternity.

These lines and MacLeish's poem are concerned with the relentless movement of time—thieving time, as the Elizabethans called it. Note that the sound never diminishes until the last line, and the suspense is evenly distributed from beginning to end, helped along by the relentless stress of almost perfect (regular) iambic meter. The tone of the poem is one of restrained resignation and perhaps profound regret.

To get at the specific meaning of the poem—a meaning more specific than that of relentless time—we must account for the first and last stanzas, which are quite different from the others with their specific references to cities and countries. Where is the "here," the vantage point from which the poet speaks and feels this relentless time? Some readers have felt that "here" means MacLeish's native land, America, and the poet has confirmed it.* Working with this clue, can we read the poem as saying that young America will some-day also experience the ravages of time as the older countries have? We may now return to the tremendous importance of the images, important because they seem to answer the question affirmatively. Note how the images move from "noonward height" in the first stanza to these images in the following stanzas: "the earthy chill," "the flooding dark," "the withered grass," "Spain go under," and "evening vanish." And finally, line 34 repeats the image in line 1, implying that America, too, will have its withered grass and its evening vanish. It is important to recognize that MacLeish has not offered his argument in some logical frame; he has depended on his images to make us feel the force of his specific theme. This technique is quite characteristic of much modern poetry, depending as it does so heavily on imagery and unusual symbolism.

---

* Norman C. Stageberg and Wallace L. Anderson, *Poetry as Experience,* New York: American Book Company, 1952, p. 465.

Gerard Manley Hopkins (1844–1889)
Spring and Fall:
To a Young Child

Márgarét, are you griéving
Over Goldengrove[1] unleaving?
Léaves, líke the things of man, you
With your fresh thoughts care for, can you?
5 Áh, ás the heart grows older
It will come to such sights colder
By and by, nor spare a sigh
Though worlds of wanwood leafmeal lie;
And yet you wíll weep and know why.
10 Now no matter, child, the name:
Sórrow's spríngs áre the same.
Nor mouth had, no nor mind, expressed
What heart heard of, ghost[2] guessed:
It ís the blight man was born for,
15 It is Margaret you mourn for.

Comments and Questions

1. This poem will not be understood or enjoyed through hurried reading, but the subtle fusion of sound and sense can be enjoyed if we first understand the poem's literal sense. The sense is actually not difficult, but it is highly concentrated: every word counts, and every line moves the sense along without interruption. Put the literal sense into writing, and account for every phrase in the poem. How did you interpret line 9? Note that the poet stresses *will,* not *weep.* The first word in lines 14 and 15 is very important, and line 15 summarizes the meaning of the poem.

2. Perhaps you have already discovered how thoroughly fused the sound and sense are. Note the rhyme in the first couplet: how does it contribute to meaning? What is the relationship of the first and last couplets? Note especially the rhyme *born for—mourn for.*

---

[1] Literally an estate in Wales, near Llansa in Flintshire; figuratively a color of vanishing youth.
[2] Spirit.

Robert Frost (1874–1963)
Neither Out Far nor In Deep

The people along the sand
All turn and look one way.
They turn their backs on the land.
They look at the sea all day.

5 As long as it takes to pass
A ship keeps raising its hull;
The wetter ground like glass
Reflects a standing gull.

The land may vary more;
10 But whatever the truth may be—
The water comes ashore,
And the people look at the sea.

They cannot look out far.
They cannot look in deep.
15 But when was that ever a bar
To any watch they keep?

Comments and Questions

In this poem the plain sense, the rhyme scheme, the rhythm, the images—in fact, every-thing seems to be simple. By this time, however, we have had enough experience with poems to suspect that Frost's little poem means something more than meets the eye, and we recall that our analysis of his "Stopping by Woods on a Snowy Evening" (in poetry division, under "Preliminaries," p. 299) found the something more in his figures and sym-bols. Like so many of Frost's poems, the one given here is disarmingly simple, but let us arm ourselves just the same. The following subsection, "Figure and Symbol," will explore these matters: we use this poem to introduce the problems.

Frost's figures and symbols here are quite conventional, made so by repeated use and time. As usual, we come to figures and symbols through the images, and the central images here are "people," "land," "sea," and "watch." Practiced readers have developed the habit of asking questions of poems, whatever questions a poem seems to raise. Who are these "people"? Because they are completely unidentified, they must represent all of us, humanity. Why do "they turn their back on the land" and all "look at the sea"? The clue to the answer lies in line 10: they are looking for truth. Why do they look to the sea for it—is there no truth to be found on the land? The land gives us our bearings and represents the known, but the sea is limitless and mysterious to the eye and represents the unknown, exciting the imagination. We scrutinize the unknown, and little by little extract more meaning from it, but our progress toward the great, final answers is small ("they cannot look out far") because their subtleties are too great ("they cannot look in deep"). Nevertheless, the human race keeps the watch and continues to scrutinize the unknown, and there is hope ("the water comes ashore") that we shall know more and more about our destiny.

It is not entirely uncommon for some readers who really enjoy poems to protest at this point, asking in good faith, "*Must* we scatter the beauty of this little poem by all this analysis—is it really necessary to read all this *into* [note well, *into*] the poem?" The answer to this impatient question is not simple, and if the questioner is impatient enough, the answer is never adequate. A preliminary answer says it all depends on what is meant by "the beauty of this little poem." If readers are satisfied with the sound and the harmony of the images, for them that is beauty enough. But there is no reason why these readers should legislate for other readers who find beauty, too, in the meaningful truth provided by the poem's figures and symbols. Such is the beginning of the answer to the impatient question; we hope a fuller answer will be found in the subsection to follow. (See Spender's "On Teaching Modern Poetry," p. 1096, for commentary on this controversy.)

Figure and Symbol

Now that we have seen how images bring concrete life (sensuous experience) into a poem, and how poets think naturally with them (as we all do), we are prepared to see how poets use these images in special ways, sometimes to say things which can be said in no other way.

Figures and symbols are images used in a particular way to explore the less known through the known. William Wordsworth describes an evening as "quiet as a nun/ Breathless with adoration." The images in this figure are the still evening and the nun, and our imagination is required to transfer the *relevant* characteristics of the nun to the evening. We see it as peaceful, gentle, spiritual in its tranquility. The *irrelevant* characteristics of the figure of the nun we allow to drop away. That is, we must make the proper connection between the evening and the nun, and when someone insists on transferring all the associations or none of them, we say that person has no imagination. For such people poetry is simply an empty art because they cannot interpret figurative meaning.

Wordsworth could have relied on adjectives instead of using the figure of the nun, but he would have lost his economy of means and the concentrated suggestiveness provided by the figure. But figures can be used even on a higher level to communicate experience that cannot be communicated in any other way. To communicate the subtleties of the love experience has always placed a tremendous burden on language and the poets, and we therefore find love poems rife with figures (and symbols—see below) of all kinds. On falling deeply in love, how would you explain and describe the exact shades and depths of feeling to a person who had never experienced such love? With abstract terms? Try it, and despair. We are quickly forced into a series of figures to compare the love experience with other experiences that are somewhat related to love:

"Shall I compare thee to a summer's day?"
(Shakespeare, p. 442)

"My love is like a red red rose."
(Burns, p. 455)

Figures were not concocted as decorations: poetic necessity was originally the mother of communicative invention.

Poetry, then, understood in its most basic sense does not mean merely a collection of rhymes, rhythms, and images: it is actually a way of thinking and feeling used to explore the unknown. Writers of prose as well as poets use this method, and here is Vernon Louis Parrington, scholar and master of figurative language, speaking of Herman Melville:

> The golden dreams of transcendental faith, that buoyed up Emerson and gave hope to Thoreau, turned to ashes in his mouth; the white gleams of mysticism that now and then lighted up his path died out and left him in darkness.

Like Melville, Macbeth saw his own dreams perish; when he saw his darkness coming, Shakespeare makes him say:

> Tomorrow, and tomorrow, and tomorrow,
> Creeps in this petty pace from day to day
> To the last syllable of recorded time;
> And all our yesterdays have lighted fools
> The way to dusty death. Out, out, brief candle!
> Life's but a walking shadow, a poor player
> That struts and frets his hour upon the stage
> And then is heard no more. It is a tale
> Told by an idiot, full of sound and fury,
> Signifying nothing.
> —*Macbeth*, V. v. 19–28

A full analysis and explanation of everything said by Shakespeare in these ten lines would require many prose pages. Why is this so?

The answer lies in the nature of Shakespeare's figurative language, especially in its economy and tremendous suggestiveness. Shakespeare could have had Macbeth tell us simply that life is meaningless—why did he use ten lines to tell us that? (Such a question is sometimes asked impatiently by the literal mind.) Because Shakespeare wants us to participate in Macbeth's tragic flash of insight by having us transfer the relevant characteristics of *petty pace, last syllable, dusty death, brief candle, a walking shadow, a player that struts and frets* to Macbeth's feeling about life at this moment. These images we understand, and when Shakespeare uses them as figures too, we understand Macbeth. This act of transference we call the *imaginative process:* in our mind, life for Macbeth is *as* meaningless as a shadow, a fretting player, an idiot's tale. Is it any wonder that Macbeth cries, "Out, out, brief candle!" when its flickering light signifies nothing to be lived for?

Kinds of figures   We are so accustomed to figures of speech in our everyday reading and conversation that unpracticed readers of poems sometimes overlook some figures and read them literally. It is best, therefore, to have the kinds of figures in mind, and to add their names to our critical vocabulary. Figurative language is sometimes called metaphorical language, or simply metaphor because its Greek ancestor *metapherein* means to carry meaning beyond its literal meaning (*meta* = beyond + *pherein* = to bring—that is, to bring beyond). *Regardless, then, of the kind of figure we observe, its basic function is always to carry meaning from the literal to the figurative level.*

Simile: a stated comparison, introduced by *like* or *as.* For example, "My love is like a red red rose"; "There is no Frigate like a Book."

Metaphor: an implied comparison, with *like* or *as* omitted. For example, "Life's but a walking shadow"—instead of saying "Life is *like* a walking shadow."

Personification: giving human characteristics to an object, an animal, or an abstract idea. Personification is a metaphor, of course, in the sense that there is an implied comparison between a nonhuman thing and a human being. For example, "There Honor comes, a pilgrim gray"; "My little horse must think it queer / To stop without a farmhouse near."

Synecdoche: using a part for the whole. For example, "Fifty winters [years] passed him by." Or using the whole for the part: for example, "the halcyon year"—meaning summer.

Metonymy: describing one thing by using the term for another thing closely associated with it. For example, "the crown" used for "the king."

Hyperbole: an exaggeration used for special effect. For example, "Drink to me only with thine eyes"; "Go and catch a falling star."

Irony: a statement whose real meaning is completely opposed to its professed, or surface meaning. For example, the lines engraved on the shattered statue of Shelley's Ozymandias: " 'My name is Ozymandias, King of Kings:/ Look on my works, ye Mighty, and despair!' " (See Shelley's poem, p. 405.)

Paradox: a statement whose surface, obvious meaning seems to be illogical, even absurd, but which makes good sense upon closer examination. For example: speaking of humanity Somerset Maugham observed, "the normal is the rarest thing in the world." Another example, Christ "lives that death may die." Irony, of course, is related to paradox because in each the surface meaning is never the real meaning, and hence both rely on an indirect method, a well-established device in poetry.

Dead metaphor: a metaphor that has lost its figurative meaning through endless use. For example, "the back of the chair"; "the face of the clock."

Allusion: a reference to some well-known place, event, or person; not a comparison in the exact sense, but a figure in the sense that it implies more than its narrow meaning. For example: "No! I am not Prince Hamlet, nor was meant to be"; "Miniver loved the Medici"; "There is a stubborn torch that flames from Marathon to Concord."

The entire poem as figure: a poem that can be understood and enjoyed on the literal level, but when properly interpreted *as a whole* is completely figurative. There are many examples in this book: Frost's "Departmental" (p. 319), Herrick's "Delight in Disorder" (p. 448), and so on.

Symbol A symbol, defined most simply, is one thing used to stand for, to represent, another thing. A lion stands for strength and courage; a lamb stands for gentleness; a burning torch held aloft stands for liberty. The word's Greek ancestor is *symballein,* meaning to compare by throwing together. A symbol is there-fore a figure of speech, although there is a technical difference between the two which should be understood in order to identify the *kinds* of symbol in poems.

If Shakespeare had written,

> Life's like a walking shadow,

he would have used a simile because the comparison is *stated.* He did write,

> Life's but a walking shadow,

and he therefore used a metaphor that *implies* the comparison without explicitly stating it, but note that both terms of the figure, *life* and *shadow,* are still present in the metaphor. If Shakespeare had dropped one term, *life,* and had used only *shadow* to stand for life, he would have used a symbol.

A symbol, however, is not necessarily related to metaphor. It can stand on its own feet by representing through continued use and common understanding a simple object or a complex pattern of associations or ideas. When we use the Cross to represent Christianity, we do not imply that the Cross is *like* Christianity; we simply say it stands for it, and the device works because the association is universally understood. When Frost says in "Birches,"

> I'd like to go [*toward* heaven] by climbing a birch tree.
> And climb black branches up a snow-white trunk,

almost any reader of poems should sense that Frost is up to something with those "*black branches*" and that "*snow-white* trunk." And of course he is. The "snow-white trunk" stands for the ideal that reaches toward heaven, and the black branches are life's dark realities we shall have to climb *over* and *with* to complete the climb to the top of the ideal. These are *conventional* symbols, made so by use and time, recognized by practiced readers of poetry.

But some poets depart from conventional symbols to invent their own for their special purposes because, we assume, the conventional symbols will not properly communicate new sensations in a new age. Such symbols are called *arbitrary* or *personal* symbols and must be understood in the poem's complete context, not by any previous mutual understanding between poet and reader. A good deal of "modern" poetry relies heavily on textual symbolism, and it ac-counts for some of the obscurity some readers find in modern poetry. When Eliot begins "The Love Song of J. Alfred Prufrock" (p. 575) with these lines,

> Let us go then, you and I,
> When the evening is spread out against the sky
> Like a patient etherised upon a table,

the explanation of his symbols must be found in the remainder of the poem, not in any conventional meaning of patients who are etherized upon tables.

Genuine understanding of metaphor and symbol will not be achieved, how-ever, through theoretical explanations: let us examine them in action in the poems that follow.

Emily Dickinson (1830–1886)
There Is No Frigate like a Book

There is no Frigate like a Book
To take us Lands away
Nor any Coursers like a Page
Of prancing Poetry—
5 This Travel may the poorest take
Without offence of Toll—
How frugal is the Chariot
That bears the Human soul.

Comments

The reader unable to read figurative language would find this poem incomprehensible. Structurally and rhetorically the poem is simple, but unless we can visualize a book as a "ship" taking us to new intellectual and emotional "lands," and a page as a spirited "horse," no amount of abstract explanation will help us to understand the poem. Because the poem's structure is simple, the poem readily reveals the basic problem in reading poetry; but regardless of the complexity of a poem's structure and rhetoric, unless we can interpret the meaning of image, figure, and symbol, no amount of work on structure will make the poem clear. Even at the risk of laboring the obvious, this principle must be made absolutely clear: it is repeatedly overlooked even by practiced readers.

T. S. Eliot (1888–1965)
Morning at the Window

They are rattling breakfast plates in basement kitchens,
And along the trampled edges of the street
I am aware of the damp souls of housemaids
Sprouting despondently at area gates.

5 The brown waves of fog toss up to me
Twisted faces from the bottom of the street,
And tear from a passer-by with muddy skirts
An aimless smile that hovers in the air
And vanishes along the level of the roofs.

Comments and Questions

Except for a few images, Eliot's poem appears to be written in plain statement. The literal situation is simple: the speaker is perhaps looking from a second-floor window or balcony as he sees and hears the movements and noises appropriate to the neighborhood's morning activities. Breakfast plates rattle, housemaids appear at the gates, waves of fog rise to reveal faces in the street, faces with problems in them, and the fog vanishes over the roofs. But the unusual images press for meaning—they tell us this literal reading will not do. Why the "basement" kitchens? Why the "trampled edges" of the street? Why the "damp souls" and why do they "sprout" despondently? We go back to the title, suspecting we have been trapped by irony. Morning is a conventional symbol of hope and energy, but neither is in this poem. As we account for the brown (stained) waves of fog, the twisted (abnormal, perverted) faces, the aimless smile whose owner has lost her bearings, we see that Eliot finds humanity living in the slums—this, we understand, is our morning now whose hope and energy have vanished over the roofs of the world. We shall meet more of Eliot's theme—the degeneration of our time—in "The Love Song of J. Alfred Prufrock" (p. 575).

But note the sharp precision of the scene in the poem—no plain statement, no abstractions, no message wrapped up and labeled in the final line, no stale figures and symbols. What does Eliot depend on instead? The poem below will tell us—an acknowledged manifesto of modern poetry.

Archibald MacLeish   (1892–1982)
Ars Poetica

A poem should be palpable and mute
As a globed fruit,

Dumb
As old medallions to the thumb,

5 Silent as the sleeve-worn stone
Of casement ledges where the moss has grown—

A poem should be wordless
As the flight of birds.
                    *

A poem should be motionless in time
10 As the moon climbs,

Leaving, as the moon releases
Twig by twig the night-entangled trees,

Leaving, as the moon behind the winter leaves,
Memory by memory the mind—

15 A poem should be motionless in time
As the moon climbs.

                              *

A poem should be equal to:
Not true.

For all the history of grief
20 An empty doorway and a maple leaf.

For love
The leaning grasses and two lights above the sea—

A poem should not mean
But be.

Comments and Questions

Ars poetica means the art of poetry, or, in this case, MacLeish's definition of a poem. We can assume that he is describing what he means by a good poem as contrasted, say, with a lecture or perhaps an essay.

In presenting his *ars poetica* as a poem, MacLeish assumed a double responsibility: he must not only make the sense of the poem describe a poem, but he must also cause this poem to be an example of the kind of poem of which he approves.

The poem has stimulated a good deal of controversy, especially the final "couplet." What, according to MacLeish, is a good poem? The structure, a series of couplets (except lines 13–14 and 21–22), is not complicated; so the difficulty must be chiefly in the figures and symbols, especially in the paradoxes (see p. 379).

The poem has three principal divisions, lines 1–8, 9–16, and 17–end; each division presents a basic principle of a good poem. First, "a poem should be palpable and mute" (dumb, silent, wordless). Literally, this dictum is nonsense, but MacLeish is not speaking literally—and *no* poem, he is saying by implication, ever should. A poem should speak concretely (palpably) through images, by presenting things that speak silently for themselves. That is, poets should not talk about things in some general abstract way; they should permit things to speak for themselves. The "globed fruit," the "old medallions," the "casement ledges," and the "flight of birds" will tell their own stories by their presence. The reader must find the significance of the thing in the thing itself.

Second (lines 9–16), a poem should be timeless and universal in its attitudes, timeless as the moon is timeless and as memories are. An event is always timely, but the meaning of an event in human terms is timeless and universal.

The third division of the poem (lines 17–end) seems to give the most difficulty, although its meaning has already been partially explained in the previous lines. "A poem should be equal to" the experience presented as *experience* in the whole poem, and "not true" as a theory or a propositional truth is true—not merely abstractly true. A poem's truth should be self-evident as it emerges from the poem's images that represent experience, not a labored truth sustained by argument. "A poem should not mean" as an argument means, but should "be" its own witness for its own kind of truth. Commenting on the nature of art, without directly mentioning "Ars Poetica," MacLeish seems to put the poem's meaning into prose:

> Art is a method of dealing with our experience of this world, which makes that experience, *as* experience, recognizable to the spirit. . . . Art is not a technique for extracting truths. . . . Art is an organization of experience in terms of experience, the purpose of which is the recognition of experience. ["A poem should be equal to: / Not true."] It is an interpreter between ourselves and that which has happened to us, the purpose of which is to make legible what it is that has happened. . . . It is an organization of experience comprehensible not in terms of something else, but of itself; not in terms of significance, but of itself; not in terms of truth even, but of itself. ["A poem should not mean / But be."] The truth of a work of art is the truth of its organization. It has no other truth."*

When Stephen Spender says that "a poem *means* the sum of everything which it *is* . . . ," he is saying much the same thing. (See Spender's essay, "On Teaching Modern Poetry," p. 1096.)

For our immediate purposes the value of MacLeish's poem lies in his explanation and use of a method used by many modern poets, including T. S. Eliot and others whom we shall read later. This method—to summarize briefly for the moment—relies chiefly on textual symbols, compound images, and communication by association, rather than on logical structure.

Innovation in Language: Three Poems by E. E. Cummings

As we have moved progressively through the poems by Moore, Dickinson, Eliot, and MacLeish, we have moved away from the older poetry with its conventional techniques and attitudes into modern poetry. We have learned that the language (the poetic devices of symbol, rhythm, and sound) of Dickinson is somewhat different from Moore's language; and that the language of Eliot is sharply different from the poetic language used by both Moore and Dickinson.

One of the distinctive qualities of modern verse is innovation in the use of language, the tendency of twentieth-century poets to push language beyond orthodox usage. E. E. Cummings is perhaps the most celebrated of the modern poetic innovators. Although he has never achieved the almost universal popularity of a Frost, Cummings has appealed especially to young people. One Cummings biographer, Charles Norman, reports that "when Cummings went to Bennington College in Vermont to give a reading, the entire audience of girls rose as he mounted the platform and chanted . . . in unison his poem 'Buffalo Bill's.'"

On first meeting Cummings' poetry the reader is likely to assume that he is confronted with the whims of a dabbler who delights in linguistic pyrotechnics in order to confuse and astonish. But the young who are slow to accept the chains of conventional grammatical and rhetorical practice are ready to consider Hemingway's argument that "there is a fourth and fifth dimension that can be gotten" in prose—and, implies Cummings, in poetry, too. In short, there is no reason to believe that conventional language forms, regardless of how "liberal" and "descriptive," are adequate to communicate all

---

* *A Time to Speak,* Boston: Houghton Mifflin Company, 1940, pp. 84–85.

personal, subjective experience. The basic question for the creative writer is not, Is this language pattern "acceptable"? The question is, How far may language be stretched and distorted to communicate experience and still reach the sensibilities of the enlightened reader? Shakespeare took some chances, Eliot took them, and Cummings took even greater chances (of not being understood—there is no other criterion involved) and at times he was downright reckless. Actually, the only question for the *reader* confronted by language is, At what point am I lost?

Let us now examine three of Cummings' poems. The first poem is a sonnet that is somewhat unconventional, the second poem is more unconventional, and the third poem represents Cummings at his liberated best.

E. E. Cummings   (1894–1962)
The Cambridge Ladies

the Cambridge ladies who live in furnished souls
are unbeautiful and have comfortable minds
(also, with the church's protestant blessings
daughters, unscented shapeless spirited)
5 they believe in Christ and Longfellow, both dead,
are invariably interested in so many things—
at the present writing one still finds
delighted fingers knitting for the is it Poles?
perhaps. While permanent faces coyly bandy
10 scandal of Mrs. N and Professor D
. . . . the Cambridge ladies do not care, above
Cambridge if sometimes in its box of
sky lavender and cornerless, the
moon rattles like a fragment of angry candy

Comments and Questions

It is easy to become impatient with Cummings, and although some of his poems may deserve our impatience, his best ones teach us in the most extraordinary way the importance of the fusion of sound and sense, and the contribution technique (the devices of poetry working together) makes to meaning.

"The Cambridge Ladies" is one of his more conventional poems, but still an appropriate one to sharpen our wits on. Cummings calls the poem a sonnet, but when we compare it with Shakespeare's "Sonnet 18" (p. 442), the differences are apparent. True, Cummings' sonnet has fourteen lines, but the rhyme scheme in the octet is quite irregular

for the form; the sestet is a little unusual; and the rhythm is only roughly iambic pentameter. Compared to Shakespeare's sonnet, Cummings' threatens to become shapeless with
each succeeding beat, as if it would run off its track on the next curve. Is his sonnet
therefore inferior? Not if we recall one of our basic principles: no device is good or bad
in a poem except as its use makes it so. The tone (Cummings' attitude toward his subject)
of his sonnet is radically different from Shakespeare's, and Cummings' devices, working
together, produce the tone he wants us to hear.

Are the Cambridge ladies local specimens only or do they finally symbolize certain
traits in a type of woman? What do they believe in? What are their spiritual resources?
Surely the tone is satiric, and it helps us to interpret the meaning of every image, figure,
and symbol. Instead of having free souls to embrace spiritual values wherever found, their
souls are dull ("unbeautiful") rooms already furnished (by family and religious inheritance) in which their minds can live "comfortably" without fear of the new, original, or
challenging. They believe in the *dead* Christ and Longfellow. Christ alive (T. S. Eliot's
"tiger" in his poem "Gerontion") would indeed threaten the complacency of these Cambridge ladies; and Cummings' placing Longfellow—a symbol of Harvard's earlier Genteel
Tradition—against a tremendous spiritual force like Christ throws into sharp relief the
decadence of the ladies. They knit for—"is it Poles?" It does not matter for whom because
knitting is socially fashionable at the moment (the war effort?). They fill their empty minds
with scandal, an excitement used as a substitute for adventures they fear to touch themselves. What can we make of the last four lines? Cummings' satiric thrust against the ladies'
superficiality helps us to find their lives lived in a neat little box scented with lavender,
shielded from life's bruises by round corners. And if the moon—a conventional symbol of
love, mystery, and adventure—has been reduced *within* their box to the ladies' size to be
regarded by these children as candy, we should express no surprise to hear the moon's
protest rattle in anger against its confinement.

Is the sonnet really shapeless compared to Shakespeare's? Not if each has a shape
appropriate to fusing the poem's sound and sense. The even-flowing lines of Shakespeare
are not appropriate for Cummings' satiric jabs, and our being jolted by the sound prepares
us to *experience* the sense of the sonnet—we *feel* the sense as well as comprehend it
intellectually.

E. E. Cummings   (1894–1962)
Pity This Busy Monster, Manunkind

pity this busy monster, manunkind,

not. Progress is a comfortable disease:
your victim (death and life safely beyond)
plays with the bigness of his littleness
5   —electrons deify one razorblade
into a mountainrange;lenses extend

unwish through curving wherewhen till unwish
returns on its unself.
                              A world of made
is not a world of born—pity poor flesh

10 and trees,poor stars and stones,but never this
fine specimen of hypermagical

ultraomnipotence. We doctors know

a hopeless case if—listen:there's a hell
of a good universe next door;let's go

Comments

This unconventional sonnet is a satire on humanity. The creature manunkind (mankind,
humankind, and man unkind), surrounded by his world and universe, never gets beyond
the image of himself as he rummages around in his little circle of materialism ("plays with
the bigness of his littleness"). The heart of his tragedy,

                              lenses extend
            unwish through curving wherewhen till unwish
            returns on its unself,

comes clear if we understand that "curving wherewhen" ("where" as space and "when"
as time) refers to Einstein's concept of "space-time" as a single dimension. Humankind,
then, says Cummings, looking out at the universe through telescopes, only "returns on its
unself" instead of extending the self beyond its "hypermagical ultraomnipotence."

E. E. Cummings (1894–1962)
Among Crumbling People

---

a
  mong crum
              bling people(a
long ruined streets
5 hither and)softly

thither between (tumb
ling)
      houses(as
the kno

10 wing spirit prowls,its
nose winces
before a dissonance of

Rish and Foses)
                          until
15   (finding one's self
at some distance from the
crooked town)a

harbour fools the sea(
while
20   emanating the triple
starred

Hotel du Golf . . . that notable structure
or ideal edifice . . . situated or established
. . . far from the noise of waters
25   )one's

eye perceives
                    (as the ego approaches)
painfully sterilized contours;
within

30 which
"ladies&gentlemen"
—under

glass—
are:
35 asking.

?each
oth?
er

rub,
40 !berq;
:uestions

Comments

We see at a glance that this is one of Cummings' less conventional poems. Either the strange form helps to interpret its meaning or we have been hoodwinked. The key to both its meaning and form lies in the first line: the people are crumbling, for reasons given in the poem, as the form itself crumbles away in the last ten lines. The plain, literal sense seems to be this: the knowing spirit prowls along ruined streets among crumbling people and their houses, wincing before the incompatible odors of fish and roses ("Rish and Foses") until the spirit finds in the Hotel du Golf an "ideal edifice" with "sterilized contours," inhabitants who live "under glass," asking each other ("rubber") questions without point or meaning.

But to find the poem's full meaning we must understand how the various devices help to interpret its figurative meaning. For example, note the combined effect of the irregular lines and the parentheses. Lines 1–3 are themselves dropping off, and the knowing spirit prowls around and among the parentheses. We read *outside* the parentheses that the spirit moves "among crumbling people . . . softly thither between . . . houses"; but we read *within* the parentheses that the spirit moves "along ruined streets hither and . . . tumbling. . . ." The purpose of such devices is apparently to cause us to *experience* this ruined topsy-turvy world that the knowing (critical, evaluating) spirit investigates and finds wanting. We find another device in Cummings' use of the slurred " 'ladies&gentlemen' " to show the lack of discrimination and taste in another kind of crumbling people, those who live "under glass" in "sterilized contours." These people are exhibited as dead specimens in showcases whose inner life has disintegrated.

The effect of the poem, then, is to cause us to experience through this unusual fusion of sound, sense, *and* the typographical form of the poem on the page two kinds of people: those who live among external ruins (streets, houses, incompatible odors), and those who live with their own internal ruins—their soulless lives.

The Comment on Experience: From Sensuous Experience to Dominant Attitude

Some wit has said that poetry is the art of saying something by saying something else just as good, thinking, of course, of the poet's use of figures of speech and symbolism. But the wit really missed the point by failing to see that poetry is the art of saying something that can hardly be said in any other way. Poetic language is not a substitute for some other language with which the poet could make things clearer were he less obstinate and aesthetic. Poetic language exists simply because no other language has been found to communicate our attitudes and feelings toward certain kinds of experience.

In this section we shall begin with poems that contain little or no comment—poems of sensuous experience—and pass along to poems with increasingly more comment. Our purpose is not merely to classify poems according to the degree of comment they possess. *We use this device to make us sensitive to whatever is happening within the poem, to make us aware of the kind of experience the poet has provided.* And, certainly not least, we want to demonstrate that one kind of poem is not superior to another because it happens to present a sensuous experience or an intellectual experience which appeals immediately to our temperament or prejudices. We should recognize such prejudices when we hear it said, "nature poetry is the best poetry," or "philosophical poetry is best because philosophy is the highest wisdom." A student of poetry may finally adopt such an attitude or other, but let us not begin with it. Let us begin with an attitude that focuses our attention on the *experience* and *quality of art* in each poem.

Some poets have presented their objects with little or no comment, as

Emerson has done in "The Snow-Storm," whereas others have used some object as a basis for their comment, making the comment instead of the object the life of the poem, as Jonson has done in "Song, to Celia" (p. 392). Other poets have gone beyond to the object-comment combination by using a situation or animal as a symbol, as Blake has used an animal as a symbol of raw life force (interpreted by some readers as evil) in "The Tiger" (p. 396).

As we approach the middle of this section, the poems will include attitudes that are more prominently implied or stated than they are in the earlier poems. Some readers will say that the poems contain more ideas and are, therefore, more valuable than poems of sensuous experience like Emerson's "The Snow-Storm."

It is easy to become dogmatic about the relation of poetry to ideas—to thought, philosophy, and the meaning of life. The greatest poetry, says one group, is philosophical poetry, and they produce as their proof such poems as Milton's *Paradise Lost,* Tennyson's "In Memoriam," and Jeffers' "Meditation on Saviors." The finest poetry, counters another group, is "pure poetry," by which they mean poetry of sensuous experience never "soiled" with "thought." Fortunately for those of us who would roam freely through the entire history of poetry, choosing as we go, no school of critics has ever successfully legislated for or against one kind of poetry. Every decade or so such legislation is attempted. Not even Shakespeare escapes the legislators, and we read with some astonishment that *Hamlet* is an "artistic failure." We should not frown upon the legislators because another group always takes their place, and the new agitation is stimulating while it lasts.

Perhaps we can avoid the confusions created by the dogmatic legislators of successive generations by reminding ourselves of two or three basic matters we have already examined briefly. Through the centuries good poets have explored and commented upon almost every phase of experience regardless of the winds of critical doctrine which have howled around them. The winds blow away and the poems remain. The moral here is obvious: each one of us tries to understand—absorb, digest, assimilate—the experiences provided by hundreds of poems, and we call those experiences good which make some substantial contribution to our expanding personal sensibilities and to our awareness of the world around us. Further, we remind ourselves that the quality of a poem is first determined by its artistic qualities—that it should be first judged as a poem, not as an idea or argument. And further, in this poetic realm of subjective experience we must all become our own critics who finally establish our own hierarchy of poems. If we permit someone else to establish the hierarchy, we shall not know who we are, and to know who we are is the final lesson of the humanities, including poetry.

Ralph Waldo Emerson (1803–1882)
The Snow-Storm

Announced by all the trumpets of the sky,
Arrives the snow, and, driving o'er the fields,
Seems nowhere to alight: the whited air
Hides hills and woods, the river, and the heaven,
5 And veils the farm-house at the garden's end.
The sled and traveller stopped, the courier's feet
Delayed, all friends shut out, the housemates sit
Around the radiant fireplace, enclosed
In a tumultuous privacy of storm.

10   Come see the north wind's masonry,
Out of an unseen quarry evermore
Furnished with tile, the fierce artificer
Curves his white bastions with projected roof
Round every windward stake, or tree, or door.
15 Speeding, the myriad-handed, his wild work
So fanciful, so savage, nought cares he
For number or proportion. Mockingly,
On coop or kennel he hangs Parian wreaths;
A swan-like form invests the hidden thorn;
20 Fills up the farmer's lane from wall to wall,
Maugre the farmer's sighs; and at the gate
A tapering turret overtops the work.
And when his hours are numbered, and the world
Is all his own, retiring, as he were not,
25 Leaves, when the sun appears, astonished Art
To mimic in slow structures, stone by stone,
Built in an age, the mad wind's night-work,
The frolic architecture of the snow.

Ben Jonson   (1572–1637)
Song, to Celia

Drink to me only with thine eyes,
    And I will pledge with mine;
Or leave a kiss but in the cup
    And I'll not look for wine.
5 The thirst that from the soul doth rise
    Doth ask a drink divine;
But might I of Jove's nectar sup,
    I would not change for thine.

I sent thee late a rosy wreath,
10   Not so much honoring thee
As giving it a hope that there
    It could not withered be;
But thou thereon didst only breathe,
    And sent'st it back to me;
15 Since when it grows, and smells, I swear,
    Not of itself but thee!

Comments and Questions

1. This poem has been set to music, and you may have known it first as a song. What qualities of the poem provide its *inherent* music?

2. Like Browning's "My Last Duchess" (p. 310), the poem is a dramatic lyric. What makes it dramatic?

3. Does the poem present sensuous experience exclusively, or has Jonson included some comment on experience? Confirm your opinion with evidence from the poem.

Robert Herrick   (1591–1674)
To Daffodils

Fair daffodils, we weep to see
    You haste away so soon;
As yet the early-rising sun
    Has not attained his noon.
5   Stay, stay,
    Until the hasting day

      Has run
        But to the even-song;
And having prayed together, we
10   Will go with you along.

We have short time to stay, as you;
    We have as short a spring,
As quick a growth to meet decay,
    As you, or anything.
15   We die
      As your hours do, and dry
      Away
      Like to the summer's rain,
Or as the pearls of morning's dew,
20   Ne'er to be found again.

Denise Levertov (1923–)
October

Certain branches cut
certain leaves fallen
the grapes
        cooked and put up
5 for winter

mountains without one
shrug of cloud
no feint of blurred
wind-willow leaf-light

10 their chins up
in blue of the eastern sky
their red cloaks
wrapped tight to the bone

Gary Snyder (1930–)
Hay for the Horses

He had driven half the night
From far down San Joaquin
Through Mariposa, up the
Dangerous mountain roads,
5 And pulled in at eight a.m.
With his big truckload of hay behind the barn.
With winch and ropes and hooks
We stacked the bales up clean
To splintery redwood rafters
10 High in the dark, flecks of alfalfa
Whirling through shingle-cracks of light,
Itch of haydust in the sweaty shirt and shoes.
At lunchtime under Black oak
Out in the hot corral,
15 —The old mare nosing lunchpails,
Grasshoppers crackling in the weeds—
'I'm sixty-eight,' he said,
'I first bucked hay when I was seventeen.
I thought, that day I started,
20 I sure would hate to do this all my life.
And dammit, that's just what
I've gone and done.'

Theodore Roethke (1908–1963)
I Knew a Woman

I knew a woman, lovely in her bones,
When small birds sighed, she would sigh back at them;
Ah, when she moved, she moved more ways than one:
The shapes a bright container can contain!
5 Of her choice virtues only gods should speak,
Or English poets who grew up on Greek
(I'd have them sing in chorus, cheek to cheek).

How well her wishes went! She stroked my chin,
She taught me Turn, and Counter-turn, and Stand;

10 She taught me Touch, that undulant white skin;
I nibbled meekly from her proffered hand;
She was the sickle; I, poor I, the rake,
Coming behind her for her pretty sake
(But what prodigious mowing we did make).

15 Love likes a gander, and adores a goose:
Her full lips pursed, the errant note to seize;
She played it quick, she played it light and loose;
My eyes, they dazzled at her flowing knees;
Her several parts could keep a pure repose,
20 Or one hip quiver with a mobile nose
(She moved in circles, and those circles moved).

Let seed be grass, and grass turn into hay:
I'm martyr to a motion not my own;
What's freedom for? To know eternity.
25 I swear she cast a shadow white as stone.
But who would count eternity in days?
These old bones live to learn her wanton ways:
(I measure time by how a body sways).

Edmund Waller   (1606-1687)

Song

Go, lovely Rose,
Tell her that wastes her time and me,
That now she knows,
When I resemble her to thee,
5 How sweet and fair she seems to be.

Tell her that's young,
And shuns to have her graces spied,
That hadst thou sprung
In deserts where no men abide,
10 Thou must have uncommended died.

Small is the worth
Of beauty from the light retir'd:
Bid her come forth,
Suffer herself to be desir'd,
15 And not blush so to be admir'd.

Then die, that she

The common fate of all things rare
   May read in thee,
How small a part of time they share,
20 That are so wondrous sweet and fair.

Comments

In some of the poems in this section, we have found not only descriptions of natural objects and people but comments on them as well. Waller's poem goes even further by including an argument. The lover has observed the delicacy of the rose and the speed with which it fades. Looking for an argument to persuade the woman he loves, he uses the rose as an example of a natural object that exhibits its brief delicacy for the admiration of men. This is the lover's generalization, and with it he bids his lady to

> Suffer herself to be desir'd,
> And not blush so to be admir'd.

Perhaps we can locate the art in the poem by recognizing what makes the poem persuasive. The method is not the debater's—the appeal is hardly to the rational intellect. Waller relies chiefly on the emotional appeal generated by the sound—the music—which *moves* us to consider or accept the sense, or the abstract argument. The art of the poem requires us to participate in the lover's feelings, and in a sense we become the lover, moved by his urgency.

William Blake (1757-1827)
The Tiger

Tiger! Tiger! burning bright
In the forests of the night,
What immortal hand or eye
Could frame thy fearful symmetry?

5 In what distant deeps or skies
Burnt the fire of thine eyes?
On what wings dare he aspire?
What the hand dare seize the fire?

And what shoulder, and what art,
10 Could twist the sinews of thy heart?

And when thy heart began to beat,
What dread hand? and what dread feet?

What the hammer? what the chain?
In what furnace was thy brain?
15 What the anvil? What dread grasp
Dare its deadly terrors clasp?

When the stars threw down their spears,
And watered heaven with their tears,
Did he smile his work to see?
20 Did he who made the Lamb make thee?

Tiger! Tiger! burning bright
In the forests of the night,
What immortal hand or eye,
Dare frame thy fearful symmetry?

William Blake   (1757-1827)
The Lamb

    Little Lamb, who made thee?
    Dost thou know who made thee?
Gave thee life, and bid thee feed,
By the stream and o'er the mead;
5 Gave thee clothing of delight,
Softest clothing, woolly, bright;
Gave thee such a tender voice,
Making all the vales rejoice?
    Little Lamb, who made thee?
10   Dost thou know who made thee?

    Little Lamb, I'll tell thee,
    Little Lamb, I'll tell thee:
He is callèd by thy name,
For he calls himself a Lamb.
15 He is meek, and he is mild;
He became a little child.
I a child, and thou a lamb,
We are callèd by his name.
    Little Lamb, God bless thee!
20   Little Lamb, God bless thee!

Comments and Questions

1. As line 20 of "The Tiger" indicates, Blake's two poems can be considered profitably as companion pieces. Both poems, of course, have a symbolic level of meaning. Describe the meaning of each symbol.

2. Considered together, how do the poems complement each other? In what way does Blake suggest that some thoughtful conclusion should emerge from his questioning?

William Cullen Bryant   (1794-1878)
To a Waterfowl

Whither, midst falling dew,
While glow the heavens with the last steps of day,
Far, through their rosy depths, dost thou pursue
    Thy solitary way?

5   Vainly the fowler's eye
Might mark thy distant flight to do thee wrong,
As, darkly seen against the crimson sky,
    Thy figure floats along.

Seek'st thou the plashy brink
10 Of weedy lake, or marge of river wide,
Or where the rocking billows rise and sink
    On the chafed ocean-side?

There is a Power whose care
Teaches thy way along that pathless coast—
15 The desert and illimitable air—
    Lone wandering, but not lost.

All day thy wings have fanned,
At that far height, the cold, thin atmosphere,
Yet stoop not, weary, to the welcome land,
20   Though the dark night is near.

And soon that toil shall end;
Soon shalt thou find a summer home, and rest,
And scream among thy fellows; reeds shall bend,
    Soon, o'er thy sheltered nest.

25   Thou'rt gone, the abyss of heaven
Hath swallowed up thy form; yet, on my heart
Deeply has sunk the lesson thou hast given,
    And shall not soon depart.

    He who, from zone to zone,
30 Guides through the boundless sky thy certain flight,
In the long way that I must tread alone,
    Will lead my steps aright.

Comments and Questions

1. Bryant has here used an old device of drawing a lesson from nature. If there is a Power that directs the waterfowl safely to home and rest, the same Power, concludes the speaker, "will lead my steps aright." Regardless of your agreement or disagreement with Bryant's theme, what do you think of his explicitly labeling his theme a "lesson"? Bryant wrote during a period when delivering explicit messages in poetic form was fashionable, but if we can believe MacLeish's "Ars Poetica" (p. 382) and the practice of most modern poets, a poem is no place for a message or a sermon. What is your view of the matter? Does Bryant's didacticism mar the poem?

2. Note the somewhat unusual metrical structure of the stanzas: the first and fourth lines contain three feet (trimeter), and the second and third lines contain five feet (pentameter). The rhyme scheme is *abab*. How does this structure of sound help to create the tone of the poem?

William Wordsworth (1770–1850)
Composed upon Westminster Bridge

We now examine eight sonnets that provide us with various kinds of experiences. We remind ourselves that the sonnet generally, but not always, presents a situation in the octet, and disposes of it in one way or another in the sestet. The form is, therefore, quite appropriate for presenting some phase of sensuous experience in the octet and for commenting on, or expressing ideas about, that experience in the sestet. (See p. 363 for sonnet forms.)

Earth has not anything to show more fair;
Dull would he be of soul who could pass by

A sight so touching in its majesty;
This city now doth, like a garment, wear
5 The beauty of the morning; silent, bare,
Ships, towers, domes, theatres, and temples lie
Open unto the fields, and to the sky;
All bright and glittering in the smokeless air.
Never did sun more beautifully steep
10 In his first splendor, valley, rock, or hill;
Ne'er saw I, never felt, a calm so deep!
The river glideth at his own sweet will:
Dear God! The very houses seem asleep;
And all that mighty heart is lying still!

Comments and Questions

This sonnet gives us an opportunity to consider some questions often asked by students and readers in general. The questions run like these: must we always grasp a poem like an orange to squeeze every last drop of subtle meaning from it? Can't we just *enjoy* a poem? Must we drive all the fun out of poetry with this everlasting search for meaning?

These are fair questions; suppose we try to answer them with the help of Wordsworth's sonnet.

The sonnet provides us with many levels of appreciation, just as a rich experience in life does. Many readers have called the sonnet beautiful, undoubtedly because it provides a very satisfying sensuous experience: the liquid sound of rhythm and rhyme, the clear images of nature, the simple but dignified diction, and the structure on the literal level, which is quite easily understood, all combine to give us a valuable experience. Once we have placed ourselves on the bridge and have absorbed this lovely picture of London lying still at full dawn, we can understand the natural resentment expressed by some readers against an analysis to find the sonnet's meaning. On this sensuous level the sonnet is quite clear and certainly of great value. But should these readers try to legislate against any further meaning the sonnet possesses any more than the philosophical readers should try to legislate against the sensuous readers? When students ask, Can't we just enjoy the poem? the answer is a resounding yes—but we should ask further, How *many* ways can the poem be enjoyed? That, too, is a fair question. Perhaps we can help to find the answer by asking a few other questions.

1. We have already admitted that the poem provides a lovely experience; some readers have called it "charming," "enchanting." How would you describe your experience?

2. Wordsworth's images are undoubtedly partly responsible for our favorable sensuous reaction—lines 6–8, for example, are striking. A picture so packed with images would probably have little unity unless it had a central image. Does the sonnet have one?

3. Suppose we assume that the central image is in lines 4–5:

This city now doth, like a garment, wear
The beauty of the morning. . . .

Why has Wordsworth personified the city? Have you noted particularly line 14?

4. What is the nature of the garment? "The beauty of the morning," Wordsworth says, by which he means nature. Perhaps the garment is a symbol which stands for a special kind of nature. Perhaps the "smokeless air," contrasted with the smoke and grime of normal city atmosphere, is a symbol of purity of spirit which pervades the entire scene. Does the tone of the poem seem to be religious?

5. Is there any reason why the sonnet cannot be enjoyed on more than one level of appreciation and understanding? Is there any reason why these levels should not be coordinated to arrive at the *full* meaning of the poem?

William Shakespeare   (1564–1616)
Sonnet 29: When in Disgrace with Fortune and Men's Eyes

When in disgrace with fortune and men's eyes,
I all alone beweep my outcast state
And trouble deaf heaven with my bootless[1] cries
And look upon myself and curse my fate,
5 Wishing me like to one more rich in hope,
Featured like him, like him with friends possessed,
Desiring this man's art[2] and that man's scope,[3]
With what I most enjoy contented least;
Yet in these thoughts myself almost despising,
10 Haply I think on thee, and then my state,
Like to the lark at break of day arising
From sullen earth, sings hymns at heaven's gate;
    For thy sweet love remembered such wealth brings
    That then I scorn to change my state with kings.

[1] Futile.   2 Skill.   [3] Range of opportunity.

William Shakespeare (1564–1616)
Sonnet 30: When to the Sessions of Sweet Silent Thought

When to the sessions of sweet silent thought[1]
I summon up remembrance of things past,
I sigh the lack of many a thing I sought,
And with old woes new wail my dear time's waste.
5 Then can I drown an eye, unused to flow,
For precious friends hid in death's dateless[2] night,
And weep afresh love's long-since canceled woe,
And moan the expense of many a vanished sight—[3]
Then can I grieve at grievances foregone,[4]
10 And heavily from woe to woe tell o'er
The sad account of fore-bemoaned moan,
Which I new pay as if not paid before.
    But if the while I think on thee, dear friend,
    All losses are restored and sorrows end.

William Shakespeare (1564–1616)
Sonnet 130: My Mistress' Eyes Are Nothing like the Sun

My mistress' eyes are nothing like the sun;
Coral is far more red than her lips' red:
If snow be white, why then her breasts are dun;
If hairs be wires, black wires grow on her head.
5 I have seen roses damask'd,[1] red and white,
But no such roses see I in her cheeks;
And in some perfumes is there more delight
Than in the breath that from my mistress reeks.
I love to hear her speak, yet well I know

---

[1] L1: see Shakespeare's *Othello,* III. iii. 138ff.   [2] Endless.   [3] Lament the cost of lost objects.
[4] Past distresses.   [1] Variegated.

10 That music hath a far more pleasing sound:
    I grant I never saw a goddess go,—
    My mistress, when she walks, treads on the ground.
        And yet, by heaven, I think my love as rare
        As any she² belied with false compare.

Comments and Questions

Shakespeare here is concerned with the poetic convention of idealizing women. Why does he purposely hack out some of these rough lines (1.4 especially) and violate our ears with ugly stabs? Why does he resort to words like *dun* and *reeks?*

Michael Drayton   (1563–1631)
Since There's No Help

Since there's no help, come let us kiss and part—
Nay, I have done, you get no more of me;
And I am glad, yea, glad with all my heart,
That thus so cleanly I myself can free.
5 Shake hands for ever, cancel all our vows,
And when we meet at any time again,
Be it not seen in either of our brows
That we one jot of former love retain.
Now at the last gasp of Love's latest breath,
10 When, his pulse failing, Passion speechless lies,
When Faith is kneeling by his bed of death,
And Innocence is closing up his¹ eyes,
        —Now if thou wouldst, when all have given him over,
        From death to life thou might'st him yet recover.

² Woman.   ¹ Love's

John Milton   (1608–1674)
On His Blindness

When I consider how my light is spent
Ere half my days in this dark world and wide,
And that one talent which is death to hide
Lodged with me useless, though my soul more bent
5 To serve therewith my Maker, and present
My true account, lest he returning chide;
"Doth God exact day-labor, light denied?"
I fondly[1] ask. But Patience, to prevent
That murmur, soon replies, "God doth not need
10 Either man's work or his own gifts. Who best
Bear his mild yoke, they serve him best. His state
Is kingly: thousands at his bidding speed,
And post o'er land and ocean without rest;
They also serve who only stand and wait."

Comments and Questions

1. The sonnets we have now read indicate that the poets have used the form to present personal matters, and to draw conclusions from their experiences. Milton's blindness was a tremendous blow to his poetic aspirations, and when total blindness came in 1652, *Paradise Lost* was still to be written. Can you find evidences of Milton's struggle within himself in the *rhetorical* and *metrical* structure of the sonnet? Compare his sonnet with Wordsworth's "Composed upon Westminster Bridge" above; how does the sound of each differ from the other?

2. The word *talent* in line 3 can be related to Matthew 25: 14–30. What is your conclusion about Milton's meaning?

[1] Foolishly.

Percy Bysshe Shelley   (1792–1822)
Ozymandias[1]

I met a traveler from an antique land
Who said: Two vast and trunkless legs of stone
Stand in the desert. Near them, on the sand,
Half sunk, a shattered visage lies, whose frown,
5 And wrinkled lip, and sneer of cold command,
Tell that its sculptor well those passions read
Which yet survive, stamped on these lifeless things,
The hand that mocked them, and the heart that fed:
And on the pedestal these words appear:
10 "My name is Ozymandias, King of Kings:
Look on my works, ye Mighty, and despair!"
Nothing beside remains. Round the decay
Of that colossal wreck, boundless and bare
The lone and level sands stretch far away.

Comments and Questions

1. It has been said that this sonnet "is an ironic poem on the vanity and futility of a tyrant's power." Discuss the poem's irony.

2. The poem is unusual in representing so many different points of view in fourteen lines (i.e., the speaker, the traveler, the sculptor, Ozymandias). What effect does Shelley achieve with this device? How is it related to the ironic tone?

John Keats   (1795–1821)
On Seeing the Elgin Marbles[1]

My spirit is too weak—mortality
    Weighs heavily on me like unwilling sleep,
    And each imagin'd pinnacle and steep
Of godlike hardship tells me I must die
5 Like a sick Eagle looking at the sky.
    Yet 'tis a gentle luxury to weep

[1] Ramses II (1295–1225 B.C.), Pharaoh of Egypt.
[1] Statues and friezes from the Greek Parthenon, sold to the British Museum by Lord Elgin.

That I have not the cloudy winds to keep
Fresh for the opening of the morning's eye.
Such dim-conceived glories of the brain
10   Bring round the heart an undescribable feud;
So do these wonders a most dizzy pain,
    That mingles Grecian grandeur with the rude
Wasting of old Time—with a billowy main—
    A sun—a shadow of a magnitude.

Human Values and the Criticism of Experience: Philosophical Poems*

Almost all poetry is in one sense or another a criticism, or an evaluation, of experience. In some poems the criticism is only implied, at times quite subtly; in others it is boldly stated.

If we stop to consider the nature and interests of artists, regardless of their medium, it should surprise no one that they are usually critical of their age. By critical we mean that in exploring human experience, the artist tries to sift the genuine and enduring from the shoddy and vulgar to erect a hierarchy of values. Above all, the artist is interested in *human values*.

The nature of these human values should be found in the poems, but perhaps we can prepare ourselves to recognize them as we come upon them later. There are two kinds of basic values, means values and end values. If we say that a house is worth $65,000, we are speaking of a means value because the house is a means to an end—the good life. All material things— land, food, clothing, automobiles—possess means values, or, as they are more frequently called, material values.

The consequences which accrue from using these material things we call living, or life, which we label good, mediocre, or bad, according to our basis of judgment or our philosophy of life. We ask, What is the good life? Suppose we say it is the consequence of the whole person, body and spirit, living successfully with one's self, with society, and with the universe. The values that emerge from such a life we call end values, or human values. They are the values most prized by the artist, including the poet. Think back, for a moment, over the poems we have already read: what have the poets been interested in, means values or end values? Have they explored food, clothing, automobiles, material property, riches? Not often, of course; but when they have, what was their *attitude* toward them? Think of Frost's "Neither Out Far nor In Deep" (p. 376) and Shelley's "Ozymandias" (p. 405). The burden of these poems is the *ends* in life; they ask the implied

---

* Archibald MacLeish's essay "Who Precisely Do You Think You Are?" p. 1156, raises some basic questions regarding the human values in our time, including certain questionable values represented in some contemporary literature.

question, what shall we live *for?* Thoreau answered when he said, "The cost of a thing is the amount of what I will call life which is required to be exchanged for it. . . ."

The artist—whether poet, painter, sculptor, or composer—does at least two things: the artist explores the inner world of personality, the essential individual, and records the consequences on the individual of having lived in any given civilization. Poems are the products of poets confronted by their environment, and the poems become value judgments on that environment. The poems of previous times, therefore, become documents or depositories where the human values of former ages are found.

We have implied earlier that human beings are confronted with three inescapable things: *themselves, society,* and *the universe.* The poems to follow explore these relationships.

The Individual: Psychological Values

Individual psychological values emerge when the poet explores the nature and worth of the individual, and especially when individuals must struggle with conflicts within themselves. The poet is immensely interested in the personal and spiritual resources of the individual, and many poets seem to find the world's most basic tragedy in our lack of them.

Edwin Arlington Robinson (1869–1935)
Miniver Cheevy

Miniver Cheevy, child of scorn,
   Grew lean while he assailed the seasons;
He wept that he was ever born,
   And he had reasons.

5 Miniver loved the days of old
   When swords were bright and steeds were prancing;
The vision of a warrior bold
   Would set him dancing.

Miniver sighed for what was not,
10   And dreamed, and rested from his labors;
He dreamed of Thebes and Camelot,
   And Priam's neighbors.

Miniver mourned the ripe renown
  That made so many a name so fragrant;
15 He mourned Romance, now on the town,
  And Art, a vagrant.

Miniver loved the Medici,
  Albeit he had never seen one;
He would have sinned incessantly
20 Could he have been one.

Miniver cursed the commonplace
  And eyed a khaki suit with loathing;
He missed the medieval grace
  Of iron clothing.

25 Miniver scorned the gold he sought,
  But sore annoyed was he without it;
Miniver thought, and thought, and thought,
  And thought about it.

Miniver Cheevy, born too late,
30 Scratched his head and kept on thinking;
Miniver coughed, and called it fate,
  And kept on drinking.

Comments

Robinson, a failure in practical affairs for years, was unusually sensitive to personal failure and frustration. Miniver is used as a symbol of all the Minivers in the world who because of their psychological structure cannot reconcile themselves to the realities of their environment. Miniver is a romantic in the sense that for him the heroic world lies in the past. What is the poet's attitude toward Miniver? What are his assumptions and their consequences in the poem?

Two attitudes are apparent: the poet is sympathetic with Miniver, yet he smiles at the humor and irony, albeit tragic, of his predicament. Many practical people would condemn Miniver as a lazy vagrant without ambition. Robinson sees further: he is too wise psychologically to be trapped by making a complicated situation simple. He knows that the predicament of the Minivers in the world is not simple. Miniver's problem is not social or philosophical, but rather psychological in the sense that Robinson apparently believes that Miniver's temperament prevents him from reconciling himself to his world. His temperament is his "fate," and no amount of "thinking" finds a solution for him. What, then, is Miniver to do? He "kept on drinking"—not literally only, of course, but figuratively; he kept on escaping to a romantic world in which he could live.

Robinson's basic assumption is that people—people like Miniver at least—do what they must do, what they are temperamentally equipped to do. This interpretation of human character, begun as a psychological investigation, soon attaches itself to philosophical speculation and becomes a part of a long philosophical tradition summarized by the phrase "Character is fate."

Robert Lowell   (1917–1977)
Skunk Hour

(For Elizabeth Bishop)

Nautilus Island's hermit
heiress still lives through winter in her Spartan cottage;
her sheep still graze above the sea.
Her son's a bishop. Her farmer
5 is first selectman in our village,
she's in her dotage.

Thirsting for
the hierarchic privacy
of Queen Victoria's century,
10 she buys up all
the eyesores facing her shore,
and lets them fall.

The season's ill—
we've lost our summer millionaire,
15 who seemed to leap from an L. L. Bean
catalogue. His nine-knot yawl
was auctioned off to lobstermen.
A red fox stain covers Blue Hill.

And now our fairy
20 decorator brightens his shop for fall,
his fishnet's filled with orange cork,
orange, his cobbler's bench and awl,
there is no money in his work,
he'd rather marry.

25 One dark night,
my Tudor Ford climbed the hill's skull,
I watched for love-cars. Lights turned down,
they lay together, hull to hull,
where the graveyard shelves on the town. . . .
30 My mind's not right.

A car radio bleats,
"Love, O careless Love. . . ." I hear
my ill-spirit sob in each blood cell,
as if my hand were at its throat. . . .
35 I myself am hell;
nobody's here—

only skunks, that search
in the moonlight for a bite to eat.
They march on their soles up Main Street:

40 white stripes, moonstruck eyes' red fire
under the chalk-dry and spar spire
of the Trinitarian Church.

I stand on top
of our back steps and breathe the rich air—
45 a mother skunk with her column of kittens swills the garbage pail.
She jabs her wedge head in a cup
of sour cream, drops her ostrich tail,
and will not scare.

Comments and Questions

1. On a first reading, this poem hardly seems "philosophical." Its tone is intensely personal, even confessional. Yet it deals with the most basic of human conflicts as the speaker searches for spiritual resources to counter the loss of all values. In the first four stanzas the speaker surveys his Nautilus Island neighbors and finds nothing but decay, illness, death, and perversity. What values are suggested by the heiress, the summer millionaire, and the decorator?

2. How do the first four stanzas prepare us for the speaker's confession of his own perverse actions in stanza 5 and his shocking statement in line 30, "My mind's not right"? How should we read the line "I myself am hell"?

3. The seemingly casual progression of the poem leads finally to the scene with the skunks at the garbage pail. In the midst of filth, herself a source of it, the mother skunk "will not scare." Does the speaker find some comfort in this? Is defiance the only value left to him?

Andrew Marvell   (1621–1678)
To His Coy Mistress

The two poems to follow explore the deepest and most crucial emotion, the experience of love. Marvell's "To His Coy Mistress" reflects the survival of the Elizabethan notion of thieving time (see also MacLeish's "You, Andrew Marvell," p. 373) as it touches love; Browning's "A Toccata of Galuppi's" reflects a Victorian conflict. Both of the poems finally go beyond the love experience as such to comment on basic human values which belong to no age or century alone.

Had we but world enough, and time,
This coyness, Lady, were no crime.
We would sit down and think which way
To walk and pass our long love's day.
5 Thou by the Indian Ganges' side

Shouldst rubies find: I by the tide
Of Humber would complain. I would
Love you ten years before the Flood,
And you should, if you please, refuse
10   Till the conversion of the Jews.
My vegetable love should grow
Vaster than empires, and more slow;
An hundred years should go to praise
Thine eyes and on thy forehead gaze;
15   Two hundred to adore each breast,
But thirty thousand to the rest;
An age at least to every part,
And the last age should show your heart.
For, Lady, you deserve this state,
20   Nor would I love at lower rate.
      But at my back I always hear
Time's wingèd chariot hurrying near;
And yonder all before us lie
Deserts of vast eternity.
25   Thy beauty shall no more be found,
Nor, in thy marble vault, shall sound
My echoing song; then worms shall try
That long preserved virginity,
And your quaint honor turn to dust,
30   And into ashes all my lust:
The grave's a fine and private place,
But none, I think, do there embrace.
      Now therefore, while the youthful hue
Sits on thy skin like morning dew
35   And while thy willing soul transpires
At every pore with instant fires,
Now let us sport us while we may,
And now, like amorous birds of prey,
Rather at once our time devour
40   Than languish in his slow-chapt power.
Let us roll all our strength and all
Our sweetness up into one ball,
And tear our pleasures with rough strife
Thorough[1] the iron gates of life:
45   Thus, though we cannot make our sun
Stand still, yet we will make him run.

Comments

The plain sense of this poem is clear enough, coming to us in three parts: had we but time enough, says the lover to his desired, your coyness (prolonging the chase) would be appropriate and exciting—anticipation is greater than realization (ll. 1–20). But, argues the

[1] Through.

lover, time is against this leisurely approach to consummation (ll. 21–32), and therefore let us devour rather than languish (ll. 33–end). The poem, then, is an argument much like Waller's "Song" ("Go, lovely Rose," p. 395), and as such is impeccably logical, but in the realm of love logic is quite useless. The persuasion must come from the art of the poem, which moves us to accept the abstract argument. The basic devices are hyperbole (exaggeration), the impatience of the lover created by the crisp couplets in short lines, and the images of rich emotional content. We may agree with the lover's argument not merely because he is logical, but because we *participate* in his emotional need and urgency, which are common to us all.

Robert Browning   (1812–1889)
A Toccata of Galuppi's

I
Oh, Galuppi, Baldassaro, this is very sad to find!
I can hardly misconceive you; it would prove me deaf and blind;
But although I take your meaning, 'tis with such a heavy mind!

II
Here you come with your old music, and here's all the good it brings.
5 What, they lived once thus at Venice where the merchants were the kings,
Where St. Mark's is, where the Doges used to wed the sea with rings?

III
Ay, because the sea's the street there; and 'tis arched by . . . what you call
. . . Shylock's bridge with houses on it, where they kept the carnival:
I was never out of England—it's as if I saw it all!

IV
10 Did young people take their pleasure when the sea was warm in May?
Balls and masks begun at midnight, burning ever to mid-day
When they made up fresh adventures for the morrow, do you say?

V
Was a lady such a lady, cheeks so round and lips so red,—
On her neck the small face buoyant, like a bell-flower on its bed,
15 O'er the breast's superb abundance where a man might base his head?

VI
Well, and it was graceful of them—they'd break talk off and afford
—She, to bite her mask's black velvet—he, to finger on his sword,
While you sat and played Toccatas, stately at the clavichord?

VII
What? Those lesser thirds so plaintive, sixths diminished, sigh on sigh,

20 Told them something? Those suspensions, those solutions—"Must we die?"
Those commiserating sevenths—"Life might last! we can but try!"

     VIII

"Were you happy?"—"Yes."—"And are you still as happy?"—"Yes. And you?"
—"Then, more kisses!"—"Did *I* stop them, when a million seemed so few?"
Hark! the dominant's persistence, till it must be answered to!

     IX

25 So an octave struck the answer. Oh, they praised you, I dare say!
"Brave Galuppi! that was music! good alike at grave and gay!
I can always leave off talking, when I hear a master play."

     X

Then they left you for their pleasure: till in due time, one by one,
Some with lives that came to nothing, some with deeds as well undone,
30 Death came tacitly and took them where they never see the sun.

     XI

But when I sit down to reason, think to take my stand nor swerve,
While I triumph o'er a secret wrung from nature's close reserve,
In you come with your cold music, till I creep thro' every nerve.

     XII

Yes, you, like a ghostly cricket, creaking where a house was burned—
35 "Dust and ashes, dead and done with, Venice spent what Venice earned!
The soul, doubtless, is immortal—where a soul can be discerned.

     XIII

"Yours for instance, you know physics, something of geology,
Mathematics are your pastime; souls shall rise in their degree;
Butterflies may dread extinction,—you'll not die, it cannot be!

     XIV

40 "As for Venice and its people merely born to bloom and drop,
Here on earth they bore their fruitage, mirth and folly were the crop;
What of soul was left, I wonder, when the kissing had to stop?

     XV

"Dust and ashes!" So you creak it, and I want the heart to scold.
Dear dead women, with such hair, too—what's become of all the gold
45 Used to hang and brush their bosoms? I feel chilly and grown old.

Comments and Questions

Few poems demonstrate so well as this one the contribution which sound makes to sense. Browning's musical education began early, and he remained devoted to music throughout his life, as his poetry testifies. Baldassare Galuppi (1706–1785) was a famous Venetian composer of light operas, church music, sonatas, and toccatas. If "A Toccata of Galuppi's" is read aloud with sympathy and understanding, the characteristics of the toccata are quite apparent. It is a composition written for the organ or clavichord (forerunner of the modern piano), characterized by brilliant full chords and running passages, free fantasia style, and quite unrestrained by any fixed form. The word *toccata* is the past participle of Italian *toccare,* to touch, meaning that the instrument is touched, not played, which produces the effect of a series of rapid tones touched but not held. Life is quickly conjured up and quickly fades away.

To enable us to see that Browning is actually using the toccata in more than one way, we should fix the facts of the poem clearly in mind. The scientific Englishman whose reliance on reason has caused him to look askance at love and the emotions is moved by Galuppi's toccata to reconsider his devotion to reason and science. Although he has never been out of England, the music paints pictures of old Venice in his mind, Venice the traditional harbor of love and romance—"it's as if I saw it all!" The questions he asks in stanzas IV–VI clearly indicate that his reliance on reason is shaken. The music causes him to hear the young couple discussing the meaning of the music to them (VII–IX): they are made to feel that although death will finally overtake them, they can try to pursue their love and frivolity—that the attempt will be at least a temporary reward. Knowing that the lovers did go to their death, he puts them away with soft, regretful words (X), but the music still persists to challenge his failure to rely on love and affection regardless of how fleeting they seem to be (XI–XIV): his rationalizing will not sustain him, and he feels "chilly and grown old." Briefly, he has missed the essence of life and knows it (XV).

1. As usual, a statement of the facts of a poem omits much of the essential poetic experience. How deeply is the Englishman really moved by the music? Explain the meaning of the music's comment in stanza XIII. What do the butterflies and mathematics symbolize?

2. The poem is, of course, actually a dramatic dialogue. Have you any idea how we can get at Browning's attitude toward the antagonists? The answer to this question lies partly in the tone of the poem, and its tone is greatly determined by Browning's use of the toccata's characteristics in his metrical structure. To put the question another way, to what extent does the sound help to interpret the sense? Confirm your opinion with specific evidence from the poem.

William Shakespeare   (1564–1616)
Sonnet 55: Not Marble, nor the Gilded Monuments

Not marble, nor the gilded monuments
Of princes, shall outlive this powerful rhyme;
But you shall shine more bright in these contents[1]
Than unswept stone,[2] besmeared with sluttish time.
5 When wasteful war shall statues overturn,
And broils[3] root out the work of masonry,

---

[1] Verses.   [2] Stone monument unswept by time.   [3] Tumult.

Nor Mars his sword nor war's quick fire shall burn
The living record of your memory.
'Gainst death and all-oblivious enmity
10 Shall you pace forth; your praise shall still find room
Even in the eyes of all posterity
That wear this world out to the ending doom.[4]
    So, till the judgment[5] that yourself arise,
    You live in this, and dwell in lovers' eyes.

Comments

Love poetry, always dominant in the history of literature, is of course an exploration of psychological values. Nothing is more personal than the love experience; nothing operates with greater impact on personality; nothing is so subtle in its influence on human character. In this sonnet Shakespeare's attitude toward love is highly complimentary. Let us compare his attitude with MacLeish's in the poem that follows.

Archibald MacLeish   (1892–1982)
(for Adele)
"Not Marble nor the Gilded Monuments"

The praisers of women in their proud and beautiful poems,
Naming the grave mouth and the hair and the eyes,
Boasted those they love should be forever remembered:
These were lies.

5 The words sound but the face in the Istrian[1] sun is forgotten.
The poet speaks but to her dead ears no more.
The sleek throat is gone—and the breast that was troubled to listen:
Shadow from door.

Therefore I will not praise your knees nor your fine walking
10 Telling you men shall remember your name as long
As lips move or breath is spent or the iron of English
Rings from a tongue.

I shall say you were young, and your arms straight, and your mouth scarlet:
I shall say you will die and none will remember you:

---

[4] Last Judgment.   [5] Till Judgment Day.   [1] Istria, a peninsula in northeast "Sunny Italy."

15 Your arms change, and none remember the swish of your garments,
   Nor the click of your shoe.

Not with my hand's strength, not with difficult labor
Springing the obstinate words to the bones of your breast
And the stubborn line to your young stride and the breath to your breathing
20 And the beat to your haste
Shall I prevail on the hearts of unborn men to remember.

(What is a dead girl but a shadowy ghost
Or a dead man's voice but a distant and vain affirmation
Like dream words most)

25 Therefore I will not speak of the undying glory of women.
I will say you were young and straight and your skin fair
And you stood in the door and the sun was a shadow of leaves on your shoulders
And a leaf on your hair—

I will not speak of the famous beauty of dead women:
30 I will say the shape of a leaf lay once on your hair.
Till the world ends and the eyes are out and the mouths broken
Look! It is there!

The Individual and Society: Social Values

Social values are likely to emerge from poetry whenever a poet explores the relationships of the individual and society, especially when the needs of the individual differ from the demands of society. Although social values have appeared in the poetry of every age, they have become more prominent since the convergence of modern democracy, industrial civilization, and modern science. In the older agrarian societies, personal and social morals tended to coalesce, but in our industrial civilization private and public morals seem to grow further apart, and the repercussions of this conflict find their way into imaginative literature.

William Wordsworth (1770–1850)
Lines Written in Early Spring

I heard a thousand blended notes,
While in a grove I sate reclined,
In that sweet mood when pleasant thoughts
Bring sad thoughts to the mind.

5 To her fair works did Nature link
The human soul that through me ran;

And much it grieved my heart to think
What man has made of man.

Through primrose tufts, in that green bower,
10 The periwinkle trailed its wreaths;
And 'tis my faith that every flower
Enjoys the air it breathes.

The birds around me hopped and played,
Their thoughts I cannot measure:—
15 But the least motion which they made,
It seemed a thrill of pleasure.

The budding twigs spread out their fan,
To catch the breezy air;
And I must think, do all I can,
20 That there was pleasure there.

If this belief from heaven be sent,
If such be Nature's holy plan,
Have I not reason to lament
What man has made of man?

Wordsworth seems to have raised the right question. The poets to follow furnish a variety of comments on what "man has made of man."

Thomas Hardy (1840–1928)
The Man He Killed

"Had he and I but met
By some old ancient inn,
We should have sat us down to wet
Right many a nipperkin!

5 "But ranged as infantry,
And staring face to face,
I shot at him as he at me,
And killed him in his place.

"I shot him dead because—
10 Because he was my foe,
Just so: my foe of course he was;
That's clear enough; although

"He thought he'd 'list, perhaps,
Off-hand like—just as I—

15 Was out of work—had sold his traps—
   No other reason why.

   "Yes; quaint and curious war is!
   You shoot a fellow down
   You'd treat if met where any bar is,
20   Or help to half-a-crown."

Amy Lowell (1874–1925)
The Dinner-Party

Fish
"So . . ." they said,
With their wine-glasses delicately poised,
Mocking at the thing they cannot understand.
"So . . ." they said again,
5 Amused and insolent.
The silver on the table glittered,
And the red wine in the glasses
Seemed the blood I had wasted
In a foolish cause.

Game
10 The gentleman with the grey-and-black whiskers
Sneered languidly over his quail.
Then my heart flew up and labored,
Then I burst from my own holding
And hurled myself forward.
15 With straight blows I beat upon him,
Furiously, with red-hot anger, I thrust against him.
But my weapon slithered over his polished surface,
And I recoiled upon myself,
Panting.

Drawing-Room
20 In a dress all softness and half-tones,
Indolent and half-reclined,
She lay upon a couch,
With the firelight reflected in her jewels.
But her eyes had no reflection,
25 They swam in a grey smoke,
The smoke of smoldering ashes,
The smoke of her cindered heart.

Coffee

They sat in a circle with their coffee-cups.
One dropped in a lump of sugar,
30 One stirred with a spoon.
I saw them as a circle of ghosts
Sipping blackness out of beautiful china,
And mildly protesting against my coarseness
In being alive.

Talk

35 They took dead men's souls
And pinned them on their breasts for ornament;
Their cuff-links and tiaras
Were gems dug from a grave;
They were ghouls battening on exhumed thoughts;
40 And I took a green liqueur from a servant
So that he might come near me
And give me the comfort of a living thing.

Eleven O'Clock

The front door was hard and heavy,
It shut behind me on the house of ghosts.
45 I flattened my feet on the pavement
To feel it solid under me;
I ran my hand along the railings
And shook them,
And pressed their pointed bars
50 Into my palms.
The hurt of it reassured me,
And I did it again and again
Until they were bruised.
When I woke in the night
55 I laughed to find them aching,
For only living flesh can suffer

Comments and Questions

The poet assumes that social well-being, or the happiness of humanity, depends on the sympathetic contact of all members of the community. The guests at the dinner party act on no such assumption. Their feeling of class superiority denies them not only sympathy for humanity, but and more important—it perverts their own humanity as well. Their tragedy lies in their being unable to see that their attitude toward mankind corrupts themselves.

   1. In what ways does the technique in this poem resemble that used in Eliot's "The Love Song of J. Alfred Prufrock" (p. 575)? Consider the use of image, symbol, and especially dramatic opposition.

   2. What is the full meaning of the last line in the poem?

Robinson Jeffers   (1887–1962)
Shine, Perishing Republic

While this America settles in the mould of its vulgarity, heavily thickening to empire,
And protest, only a bubble in the molten mass, pops and sighs out, and the mass
    hardens,

I sadly smiling remember that the flower fades to make fruit, the fruit rots to make earth.
Out of the mother; and through the spring exultances, ripeness and decadence; and
    home to the mother.

5 You making haste haste on decay; not blameworthy; life is good, be it stubbornly long or
    suddenly
A mortal splendor: meteors are not needed less than mountains: shine, perishing
    republic.

But for my children, I would have them keep their distance from the thickening center;
    corruption
Never has been compulsory, when the cities lie at the monster's feet there are left the
    mountains.

And boys, be in nothing so moderate as in love of man, a clever servant, insufferable
    master.
10 There is the trap that catches noblest spirits, that caught—they say—God, when he
    walked on earth.

Comments and Questions

The British writer W. Somerset Maugham (1874–1965) is reported to have said, "If a nation values anything more than freedom, it will lose its freedom; and if it is comfort or money that it values more, it will lose that, too." In this poem Jeffers finds America on the way to empire because it has given up the passion for freedom that has made it. Students of Jeffers recognize his basic pattern of belief in this area as something like this: civilizations have always risen and inevitably fallen, this cycle always moving from east to west. Why do civilizations fall? Freedom and wealth are irreconcilable, according to Jeffers, because human beings are driven by desire (self-love) to achieve power over their fellow human beings, and they will sell their freedom to achieve it. People and their nations, therefore, travel the cycle of freedom, desire, wealth, loss of freedom, and ruin. People then travel westward—as the Pilgrims and others did in the early seventeenth century; they fight to regain their freedom, win it, and travel the cycle to ruin once more.

    1. Is agreement with Jeffers' point of view necessary to the enjoyment of his art?

    2. What are the essential characteristics of his art as they differ from those of almost all other poems in this section? Jeffers has said that "a tidal recurrence is the one essential quality of the speech of poetry." How appropriate is Jeffers' free verse?

    3. Note how Jeffers thinks in images, and how logically those images progress from line to line. Trace this progress of image-thinking through "Shine, Perishing Republic."

Robert Frost (1874–1963)

The Gift Outright*

In his essay "An Extemporaneous Talk for Students," Frost says this poem "is my story of the revolutionary war. . . . The dream was to occupy the land with character—that's another way to put it—to occupy a new land with character."

The land was ours before we were the land's.
She was our land more than a hundred years
Before we were her people. She was ours
In Massachusetts, in Virginia,
5 But we were England's, still colonials,
Possessing what we still were unpossessed by,
Possessed by what we now no more possessed.
Something we were withholding made us weak
Until we found out that it was ourselves
10 We were withholding from our land of living,
And forthwith found salvation in surrender.
Such as we were we gave ourselves outright
(The deed of gift was many deeds of war)
To the land vaguely realizing westward,
15 But still unstoried, artless, unenhanced,
Such as she was, such as she would become.

Langston Hughes (1902–1967)

Harlem

What happens to a dream deferred?

Does it dry up
like a raisin in the sun?
Or fester like a sore—
5 And then run?
Does it stink like rotten meat?
Or crust and sugar over—
like a syrupy sweet?

* Read by Frost at the inauguration of John F. Kennedy as President of the United States, January 20, 1961.

10   Maybe it just sags
       like a heavy load.

       Or does it explode?

Comments and Questions

In Hughes's poem, Frost's "gift outright" has become the "dream deferred." What happens to it? This and the three following poems suggest a different perspective—that of the black American—on our social values in the mid-twentieth century.

Ray Durem   (1915–1963)
Award

A Gold Watch to the FBI Man who has followed me for 25 years.

Well, old spy
looks like I
led you down some pretty blind alleys,
took you on several trips to Mexico,
5   fishing in the high Sierras,
jazz at the Philharmonic.
You've watched me all your life,
I've clothed your wife,
put your two sons through college.
10   what good has it done?
the sun keeps rising every morning.
ever see me buy an Assistant President?
or close a school?
or lend money to Trujillo?
15   ever catch me rigging airplane prices?
I bought some after-hours whiskey in L.A.
but the Chief got his pay.
I ain't killed no Koreans
or fourteen-year-old boys in Mississippi.
20   neither did I bomb Guatemala,
or lend guns to shoot Algerians.
I admit I took a Negro child

to a white rest room in Texas,
but she was my daughter, only three,
25 who had to pee.

Raymond R. Patterson   (1929–   )
At That Moment

(For Malcolm X*)

When they shot Malcolm Little down
On the stage of the Audubon Ballroom,
When his life ran out through bullet holes
(Like the people running out when the murder began)
5 His blood soaked the floor
One drop found a crack through the stark
Pounding thunder—slipped under the stage and began
Its journey· burrowed through concrete into the cellar,
Dropped down darkness, exploding like quicksilver
10 Pellets of light, panicking rats, paralyzing cockroaches—
Tunneled through rubble and wrecks of foundations,
The rocks that buttress the bowels of the city, flowed
Into pipes and powerlines, the mains and cables of the city:
A thousand fiery seeds.
15 At that moment,
Those who drank water where he entered . . .
Those who cooked food where he passed . . .
Those who burned light while he listened . . .
Those who were talking as he went, knew he was water
20 Running out of faucets, gas running out of jets, power
Running out of sockets, meaning running along taut wires—
To the hungers of their living. It is said
Whole slums of clotted Harlem plumbing groaned
And sundered free that day, and disconnected gas and light
25 Went on and on and on. . . .
They rushed his riddled body on a stretcher
To the hospital. But the police were too late.
It had already happened.

* Malcolm X was assassinated in Harlem on February 21, 1965. See pp. 533 and 559 for other poems on Malcolm X.

Gwendolyn Brooks (1917–   )
We Real Cool

The Pool Players.
Seven at the Golden Shovel.

We real cool. We
Left school. We

Lurk late. We
Strike straight. We

5 Sing sin. We
Thin gin. We

Jazz June. We
Die soon.

"The Secret Sits": Metaphysical Values

For many of our fundamental questions about life we have answers whose truth can be demonstrated beyond doubt. We no longer must *assume,* for example, that certain causes bring certain effects; we *know* that such-and-such germs cause certain diseases. Science has provided the exact knowledge. But for other fundamental and searching questions we have no answers that can be verified beyond doubt. For example: Was the universe planned by a supreme being, or was it an accident? Is death final or a passage to another life? What is the essential character of nature, and what can we learn from it? Are we the victims of forces over which we have no control, or do we have some measure of free will? To summarize: What is the meaning of life? Is there any more basic question?

Where do we go for answers? It is possible to go to a branch of philosophy called metaphysics. Metaphysics is the source of our *assumptions* about life, and we all live by certain assumptions whether or not we realize it. In religion we call them articles of faith. For example, if we assume that our earthly sins are punishable after death, certain consequences in our behavior are likely to follow immediately. If we assume no freedom to direct our own actions (freedom of will), other consequences are likely to follow, and so on.

When verifiable scientific knowledge runs dry, we do not stop asking questions: in fact, some of the most important questions are still to be asked, and people have always insisted upon looking for answers. We shall see this insistence in the poets to follow. From its beginnings poetry has pursued metaphysical problems, and poets are often referred to as prophets. The Greek poets and dramatists dealt with the metaphysical and religious questions of their day; Milton's *Paradise Lost* is built on a pattern of metaphysical assumptions; and the poems that follow are nothing if not metaphysical in their implications.

Robert Frost (1874–1963)
The Secret Sits

We dance round in a ring and suppose,
But the Secret sits in the middle and knows.

James Hearst (1900–1983)
Truth

How the devil do I know
if there are rocks in your field,
plow it and find out.
If the plow strikes something
5 harder than earth, the point
shatters at a sudden blow
and the tractor jerks sidewise
and dumps you off the seat—
because the spring hitch
10 isn't set to trip quickly enough
and it never is—probably
you hit a rock. That means
the glacier emptied his pocket
in your field as well as mine,
15 but the connection with a thing
is the only truth that I know of,
so plow it.

Emily Dickinson (1830–1886)
Because I Could Not Stop for Death

Because I could not stop for Death—
He kindly stopped for me—
The Carriage held but just Ourselves—
And Immortality.

5 We slowly drove—He knew no haste
And I had put away
My labor and my leisure too,
For His Civility—

We passed the School, where Children strove
10 At Recess—in the Ring—
We passed the Fields of Gazing Grain—
We passed the Setting Sun—

Or rather—He passed Us—
The Dews drew quivering and chill—
15 For only Gossamer, my Gown—
My Tippet[1]—only Tulle[2]—

We paused before a House that seemed
A Swelling of the Ground—
The Roof was scarcely visible—
20 The Cornice—in the Ground—

Since then—'tis Centuries—and yet
Feels shorter than the Day
I first surmised the Horses Heads
Were toward Eternity—

Comments and Questions

We are all compelled finally to take some attitude toward death, and poets, too, have pursued the theme relentlessly. The conventional attitude toward death is often somber, awed, and hushed, but Emily Dickinson's attitude is hardly conventional. Death is here represented as the driver of a carriage who courts the lady by taking her for a drive; they are alone except for the passenger Immortality—what company could be more appropriate? Is the poet equating death with love? It seems so, but note that this idea is not pushed to sentimentality. Instead of drawing a commonplace moral from the situation she has created, she simply presents the situation. She presents it, in fact, a little ironically: death, in his "Civility," "kindly" stops for his beloved, who puts aside both her "labor" and her

[1] Shoulder cape.   [2] A sheer mesh fabric.

"leisure." Could the arrival of death be more natural, less awesome? Stanzas 3–5 give us the sensation of passing from life to eternity, and finally (stanza 6) the realization that we were headed for eternity from the beginning of our life. Can we say that the poet's attitude toward death is sane and normal? She makes the process of passing from life to death seem natural, inevitable, and appropriate to life as we know it. At least, this is her assumption about the nature of death, and we are left free to contemplate it.

John Donne (1572–1631)
Holy Sonnet VII: At the Round Earth's Imagined Corners

At the round earth's imagined corners,[1] blow
Your trumpets, angels; and arise, arise
From death, you numberless infinities
Of souls, and to your scattered bodies go;
5 All whom the flood did, and fire shall o'erthrow,
All whom war, dearth, age, agues, tyrannies,
Despair, law, chance hath slain, and you whose eyes
Shall behold God and never taste death's woe.
But let them sleep, Lord, and me mourn a space,
10 For if above all these, my sins abound,
'Tis late to ask abundance of thy grace
When we are there; here on this lowly ground[2]
Teach me how to repent; for that's as good
As if thou' hadst sealed my pardon with thy blood.[3]

Comments and Questions

As usual, Donne has used a highly concentrated rhetorical structure that must be read carefully, including the syntax on the literal level. For his poetic purposes, Donne invokes the angels to blow their trumpets to summon the dead to Judgment Day. The "numberless infinities of souls" are expected to return to their "scattered bodies" to be judged: some shall be condemned to "fire" and others "shall behold God and never taste death's woe." The octet is Donne's method of projecting himself, imaginatively, into Judgment Day, and

---

[1] The earth conceived of as having four corners. [2] The earth. [3] Christ's crucifixion.

this imaginative act causes him to consider his own sins, and by implication the earthly sins of all of us. Shall we rely on God's grace on Judgment Day, or repent and dissolve our sins here on earth? The implication of the poem is that we should do the latter.

1. What are Donne's two basic metaphysical assumptions?

2. If one cannot accept the assumption of Judgment Day as a reality, is the poem valueless?

3. Compare the view of death in this poem with that of Larkin's "Aubade," which follows.

Philip Larkin (1922–   )
Aubade[1]

I work all day, and get half drunk at night.
Waking at four to soundless dark, I stare.
In time the curtain-edges will grow light.
Till then I see what's really always there:
5 Unresting death, a whole day nearer now,
Making all thought impossible but how
And where and when I shall myself die.
Arid interrogation: yet the dread
Of dying, and being dead,
10 Flashes afresh to hold and horrify.

The mind blanks at the glare. Not in remorse
—The good not done, the love not given, time
Torn off unused—nor wretchedly because
An only life can take so long to climb
15 Clear of its wrong beginnings, and may never;
But at the total emptiness for ever,
The sure extinction that we travel to
And shall be lost in always. Not to be here,
Not to be anywhere,
20 And soon; nothing more terrible, nothing more true.

This is a special way of being afraid
No trick dispels. Religion used to try,
That vast moth-eaten musical brocade
Created to pretend we never die,
25 And specious stuff that says *No rational being*
Can fear a thing it will not feel, not seeing

[1] Morning song.

That this is what we fear—no sight, no sound,
No touch or taste or smell, nothing to think with,
Nothing to love or link with,
30 The anaesthetic from which none come round.

And so it stays just on the edge of vision,
A small unfocused blur, a standing chill
That slows each impulse down to indecision.
Most things may never happen: this one will.
35 And realisation of it rages out
In furnace-fear when we are caught without
People or drink. Courage is no good:
It means not scaring others. Being brave
Lets no one off the grave.
40 Death is no different whined at than withstood.

Slowly light strengthens, and the room takes shape.
It stands plain as a wardrobe, what we know,
Have always known, know that we can't escape,
Yet can't accept. One side will have to go.
45 Meanwhile telephones crouch, getting ready to ring
In locked-up offices, and all the uncaring
Intricate rented world begins to rouse.
The sky is white as clay, with no sun.
Work has to be done.
50 Postmen like doctors go from house to house.

Comments and Questions

1. Larkin assumes a view of death that differs sharply from that of the two preceding poems. What is his assumption, and how does it affect the tone of the poem?

2. The poem rejects our normal defenses against the dread of dying. List the defenses the poem alludes to. What arguments are advanced against them? What aspect of death is the most horrifying for the speaker? Discuss the line "Most things may never happen: this one will. . . ."

3. Discuss the poem's conclusion. What is the significance of the references to telephones that "crouch, getting ready to ring," "locked-up offices," and postmen? Why, in the poem, are postmen like doctors? Does the poem's conclusion suggest another kind of defense that we all employ against the thought of death?

Thomas Hardy   (1840–1928)
Hap[1]

If but some vengeful god would call to me
From up the sky, and laugh: "Thou suffering thing,
Know that thy sorrow is my ecstasy,
That thy love's loss is my hate's profiting!"
5   Then would I bear it, clench myself, and die,
Steeled by the sense of ire unmerited;
Half-eased in that a Powerfuller than I
Had willed and meted me the tears I shed.

But not so. How arrives it joy lies slain,
10   And why unblooms the best hope ever sown?
—Crass Casualty obstructs the sun and rain,
And dicing Time for gladness casts a moan. . . .
These purblind Doomsters had as readily strown
Blisses about my pilgrimage as pain.

Walter Savage Landor   (1775–1864)
Dying Speech of an Old Philosopher*

I strove with none, for none was worth my strife:
    Nature I loved, and, next to Nature, Art:
I warm'd both hands before the fire of Life;
    It sinks; and I am ready to depart.

Writing About Poetry

The ideal preparation for writing about poetry is to learn to *read* it well, to have
something to say when faced with the 500-word theme on Frost's "After Apple-
Picking." In one sense, then, all that has gone before in this section on poetry is

[1] Chance.
* Written on his seventy-fourth birthday, 1849.

a preparation for writing if it has provided some means of interpreting poems, analyzing the elements that constitute poetry, and evaluating the effects that poems seek to achieve. The initial step in conquering the anxiety that appears with the first theme assignment is to recognize that writing is not an activity divorced from analytical reading and thinking.

Writing about poems is the culmination of a process that begins with reading, and it differs from the kind of thinking and reflecting that goes along with reading only in its more formal method of presentation. Our thoughts and reflections on poems may be scattered and haphazard; when we write them down, we attempt to put them in some order. Class discussions on poems may range over many topics; in writing we attempt to select only those observations which contribute to the point we wish to make. Discussion may seem to lack focus; in writing we provide a focus by selecting a central idea or thesis. Thinking does not have to be conducted in complete sentences or punctuated with commas; writing must conform to certain established practices. These and other considerations make writing a more disciplined activity, but it should not be separated from the other experiences that take place in the classroom or outside it.

Furthermore, writing about poems should not be separated from other sorts of writing. Essays devoted to poetry or to literature in general do not constitute a special genre or kind of writing. Good writing on whatever subject is judged by the same standards. The basic principles learned in writing about poems should be transferable to the history class or to the world outside the classroom. What follows, then, is not a theory of writing about poetry but a series of principles involved in writing that may be applied directly to poetry. These principles offer practical advice. They give some order to the process of writing.

Choosing the Topic

What to write about is the initial decision, and it may also be the most important decision, influencing everything else. In a sense, the conception of the subject, the idea, is everything. The poem or poems to be written about may be dictated by the instructor, and suggestions for topics may be provided by the instructor or the text. However, it is the writer's job to focus and limit the topic—to come up with an idea that will give shape to the paper. Several distinctions are important here.

Having decided on (or been given) a poem to write about, say Frost's "After Apple-Picking,"* the writer does not yet have a topic for the paper. To say that one's topic is Frost's "After Apple-Picking" is to assume that the paper is going to deal with every conceivable element of the poem. The question is, What aspect of the poem lends itself to a paper of the size and scope assigned? A further question involves the difference between two basic exercises—*explication* and *analysis*. Explication does involve a discussion of the entire poem but only in regard to one aspect, the poem's meaning. Explication may be thought of as close attention to the details of the work for the purpose of illuminating the work as a

---

* Since "After Apple-Picking" (p. 571) is used as an example throughout the discussion, a careful reading of the poem is essential to what follows.

whole. It should be distinguished from *paraphrase,* which is merely the translation of the language of the poem into the writer's own words. Paraphrase is a useful device for understanding a poem, but it is not a proper method for composing an entire paper. Explication, on the other hand, preserves the facts of the poem, explains them, and points up the relationship among them. It is the starting point for criticism and a useful approach in writing. An explication of "After Apple-Picking" would attempt to take into account the important details of the poem—the "two-pointed ladder," the barrel left unfilled, the distortions of the speaker's drowsy state, the cider-apple heap, the woodchuck's "long sleep," and so on. Then the ideal explication would attempt to answer two further questions. How are all these details linked, and how are they related to the larger meaning of the poem as a whole?

Analysis, unlike explication, separates the poem into its component parts and selects one of those parts for closer study. Analysis may focus on any of the elements of poetry (or combination of elements) that have been discussed in the preceding subsections—imagery, figurative language, symbolism, rhythm and rhyme, irony, paradox, and so on. (See especially "Preliminaries," p. 299, and "The Language of Poetry," p. 355, for definitions and discussions of the elements of the poem that may constitute the topic for a paper of analysis.)

A writer who chooses to explicate the poem has found the topic (i.e., "Frost's 'After Apple-Picking': An Explication"). The essay of analysis, however, involves a further decision: which aspect of "After Apple-Picking"—the imagery, the symbolism, the point of view of the speaker, for example—should become the focus of the paper? The answer to this question is dictated partly by the writer (What aspect of the poem is most appealing?) and partly by the poem itself (What aspect of the poem seems most crucial to its meaning or success?). An analysis of symbolism may be crucial to one poem, irrelevant to another. Metaphor is used effectively in Donne's "Batter My Heart, Three-Personed God" (p. 446) and is of no consequence in Williams' "This Is Just to Say" (p. 320).

The choice of a topic, then, comes only after a careful reading of the poem. But what if it does not come? Obviously more and closer reading is necessary, with particular attention to detail. The method some writers use involves underlining key passages in pencil or (to preserve the book) copying down in a notebook key phrases, comments, observations. Does some pattern emerge? For example, reading "After Apple-Picking," one might underline or jot down every reference to the drowsy state of the speaker:

Essence of winter sleep is on the night

I am drowsing off

I cannot rub the strangeness from my sight

I was well/ Upon my way to sleep before it fell

I could tell/ What form my dreaming was about to take

Magnified apples appear and disappear

I feel the ladder sway

I am overtired

One can see what will trouble/ This sleep of mine

The woodchuck's . . . long sleep

Or just some human sleep

At this point it may be unclear just what all this adds up to, but here is a topic—the imagery of sleep and dreams in Frost's "After Apple-Picking." It is a limited topic (not the poem, but one aspect of the poem), one that appeals to the writer (after discovering it), and one that seems significant to the poem as a whole (not a minor detail, but a pattern that runs throughout the poem). The advantage of finding a limited topic early in the process of writing the paper is that all the writer's efforts may now be directed to this aspect of the poem. Other scattered notes and false starts may now be discarded as irrelevant to *this* topic. They belong to other essays.

Organizing the Material and Writing a First Draft

Having found a topic, the writer's job is now to bring some order to the material. To do this, one must first state as clearly as possible the *central idea* or *thesis* of the paper. The term *thesis* may sound much too formal and scholarly for a short essay on a poem by Frost; it is, however, simply a statement of the *point* to be made about the subject. "Frost's Use of the Imagery of Sleep and Dreams" may be a good title for the paper, but it is not a thesis because it makes no point about the imagery. The ideal thesis would be a complete sentence that states the most important idea to be found in the paper. This exact sentence need not appear in the finished paper (unless the instructor requests it as part of the assignment); it is primarily for the *writer's* use in clarifying the focus of the paper and organizing the details.

If the writer cannot come up with such a sentence, then more thinking about the thesis is necessary. To locate the thesis, it may be helpful for the writer to ask a series of questions about the topic chosen. *What do these images have in common? Why is everything associated with sleep in the poem strange, distorted, magnified? Why does the speaker's sleep retain all the sensations of the apple-picking? Why does the speaker refer to "what will trouble" his sleep? Why is he unsure of the nature of his sleep? Why does he refer to the woodchuck's "long sleep"?* And so on. An answer to these questions (there is no *one* answer) may well constitute the thesis statement of the paper. One might decide, for example, that the poem deals with an opposition between apple-picking (engagement, responsibility) and sleep (retreat, escape). The experience that is being described occurs in a twilight zone *after* apple-picking, but just before sleep takes over completely. With this idea in mind, one might argue that the imagery of dreaming, with its strange distortions and magnifications of the day's work, suggests the speaker's inability to free himself from an activity that has come to dominate him to the exclusion of everything else. He has had "too much/ Of apple-picking." He is consumed by it, and even though it was something he desired, he needs to regain a perspective, a balance that has been lost in going too far in one direction. Presumably, it is through "some human sleep," which will return him shortly to the real world of responsibility, that this balance will be restored. Here, then, is a working thesis: *In Frost's "After Apple-Picking," the imagery of sleep and dreams shows the confusion and lack of perspective that result from any consuming activity taken to an extreme.* It is a *working* thesis that may need to be modified after later thought, but it provides a central idea around which the details of the poem may take shape.

The thesis statement is useful for the writer not only in clarifying exactly what point is being made about the topic but also in providing unity and coherence for the many details from the poem the writer will need to discuss in the body of the paper. After the thesis has been stated clearly, the writer's next task is to ensure that every point made in the paper relates directly to the thesis. The thesis is both inspiring and limiting. It may prompt new ideas and observations not seen before, but it also limits the scope of the paper. A discussion of death in relation to the woodchuck's "long sleep" might be interesting in another paper with a different thesis but inappropriate to the thesis chosen. The unity of the finished essay depends on the reader's sense that everything in the paper is used to develop or support the thesis.

How is the thesis to be developed? At this stage the writer may have a topic, a thesis statement, and a collection of notes and quotations that relate to the thesis, but no clear sense of a method of ordering them. A point to remember here is one made earlier—good writing on whatever subject follows the same basic principles. The writer who is faced with organizing a paper on poetry may have spent an entire term exploring the patterns of development used in other types of expository writing—definition, classification, analysis, example and illustration, comparison and contrast, persuasion, and so on. These patterns are no less useful when the subject is poetry. Illustration is always an appropriate technique for supporting an interpretation of a poem. Comparison or contrast is one of the most frequent strategies employed in writing about literature. (Is the theme of opposition between apple-picking and sleep similar to the antithesis between "promises to keep" and sleep in Frost's "Stopping by Woods on a Snowy Evening" [p. 299]?) The principles employed in the persuasive or argumentative essay are equally valid in a paper written to convince the skeptical reader that one's analysis of "After Apple-Picking" is on target. Which of these patterns does the thesis of the paper seem to call for?

And would an outline be useful at this point? In a long research paper, a formal outline with major divisions and hosts of subdivisions may be in order, but for a short essay on a poem something more informal may serve just as well. An outline is merely a device for ordering one's thoughts, not an end in itself. It should not distract the writer from the task at hand. Unless the outline is a part of the paper assignment, the writer may require nothing more than a listing of the points to be made in the essay. After these have been written down and numbered, it will be easier to see which ideas go together, which are major points and which are less important. Details from the poem that support each point may also be grouped with them. In what order should they be presented? By renumbering them, the writer can establish the most effective order of presentation. What *is* most effective is a decision for the writer; in most cases, however, it is a good idea to begin with an important point (which may be dictated by the thesis statement), to save the smaller supporting details for the body of the paper, and to end with one of the strongest and most convincing points.

To go from the outline to a first draft will not seem such a formidable challenge if the writer remembers that it is only a *first* draft. The *rewriting* should be reserved for the finished paper. At this stage the aim is to establish the shape of the essay, to convert the ideas in the outline to paragraphs, and to work in the details from the poem that support the major points. The flow of ideas here is more important than the exact word or the ideal sentence construction. In composing the first draft, the writer may find that the outline was deficient in some areas. New ideas may occur in the process of writing. Even the thesis statement may need to be revised. This is the value of a rough draft. The act of composition itself is the working out of all the earlier thinking about the topic. Some ideas that looked good in outline may not be supported by the poem. Others may not fit in easily with the main line of argument. The writer should not feel bound to earlier conceptions or to the outline or thesis statement. The goal is an interesting and convincing discussion of the poem at hand, and the first draft is the testing ground for the initial conception of the essay.

Revision and the Final Draft

In an ideal world, the writer would set the first draft aside, allow it to "cool," and return to it later with a fresh approach. Although the demands and deadlines of student life do not always create ideal conditions, revision is best accomplished when the first draft can be viewed with some objectivity, as if one were reading and correcting another person's writing. Two kinds of revision are necessary to produce an effective final draft—one for content and one for form and correctness. Here are two sets of questions that can serve as checklists for revising the first draft.

Content

1. Is the title specific, and does it indicate clearly what the paper is about?
2. Is the thesis of the paper evident in the introduction?
3. Is every point in the paper related in some way to the thesis?
4. Are the stages of the argument clearly marked with transitions between major ideas?
5. Are the ideas supported by examples and details from the poem?
6. Are there gaps in the argument that need to be filled?
7. Are there relevant details in the poem that have been omitted from the discussion?
8. Does the draft achieve a proper balance in the space given to major and minor points?
9. Are there sentences or paragraphs that do not contribute to the main line of argument?
10. Does the conclusion follow from the main argument of the paper, or is it merely a restatement of the introduction?

Form and Correctness

1. Are there unnecessary words and phrases? Is the language repetitious? Are there more exact terms that could be substituted?
2. Are the sentences varied? Are there careless lapses into fragments or mixed constructions? When read aloud, do the sentences sound choppy?
3. Does every paragraph have a topic sentence? Are the paragraphs fully developed, with supporting details and examples? Are there transitional phrases indicating shifts in thought?
4. Is the use of tense consistent? Does the paper shift back and forth between present tense ("Frost refers to the woodchuck's sleep in line 41 . . .") and past tense ("Frost described the rumbling sound of apples . . .")?
5. If phrases are quoted directly from the poem, have quotation marks been used?
6. Has the draft been proofread for careless errors—words omitted, misspellings, apostrophes omitted, commas or other marks of punctuation misused?

These two kinds of revision demand two different readings of the draft. In revising the content, the writer should focus on the argument of the paper. Read aloud, is it clear in its development? Will the reader be able to follow the stages of the argument from the introduction to the conclusion? In checking the draft for correctness, the writer should not be distracted by the content. Attention should be paid only to the words, sentences, paragraphs, and marks of punctuation. A dictionary and a writer's handbook are also essential to answer any last-minute questions about spelling or usage. The revisions completed, the final paper may now be copied from the corrected draft.

Quoting from Poems

In writing about poetry, quoting lines and phrases from the poem is one of the most effective and efficient ways of making a point. Because, as one poet put it, poetry is not the thing said but a way of saying it, direct quotation is often better than paraphrase since it preserves the words and phrasing of the poem. Quoting from poems, however, seems to present writers with more problems than quoting from prose. Here are a few simple principles that may be followed. If fewer than two lines are quoted, it is better to incorporate the quotation into one's own prose, enclosing the passage in quotation marks and indicating the poet's original line lengths with a slanting line (/):

> One indication of the speaker's ambivalent attitude toward apple-picking may be seen in lines 28 and 29 when he says, "I am overtired/ Of the great harvest I myself desired."

Note, however, that when a quotation is incorporated within one's own prose, the entire sentence must be grammatically consistent. In the following example, the shift from third person to first person makes the sentence awkward:

> In lines 28 and 29 the speaker says that he is "overtired/ Of the great harvest I myself desired."

If more than two lines of poetry are quoted, the passage is separated from one's own prose by the space of an extra line at the beginning and end. No quotation marks are used. The passage should be indented, and it should be written out exactly as it appears in the poem:

> One indication of the speaker's ambivalent attitude toward apple-picking may be seen in lines 27–29:
>
>> For I have had too much
>> Of apple-picking: I am overtired
>> Of the great harvest I myself desired.
>
> It is not, then, that the harvest was an unpleasant task, but rather that it had become all-consuming.

If words are left out in the middle of a quotation, an ellipsis (. . .) should be used. At the beginning and end of a quotation, the ellipsis may be omitted. Whole lines that are left out of a quotation are indicated by a single ellipsis on a separate line:

> One can see what will trouble
> This sleep of mine, whatever sleep it is.
>
>   . . .
>
> The woodchuck could say whether it's like his
> Long sleep . . .
> Or just some human sleep.

Evaluating an Interpretation

One final issue associated with writing about poetry has to do not with the form of the essay itself but with the nature of interpretation. The questions raised by students faced with a writing assignment often reveal an uncertainty about standards for evaluating interpretations of poems: *Is this to be my own opinion? Do you count off if you don't agree with my interpretation? Isn't the interpretation what the poem means to me?*

Behind such questions seems to lie the assumption that one interpretation is just as good as another. It's just a matter of how one happens to respond to the poem. The argument at times advanced by someone whose interpretation has been questioned is this: *It may mean something else to you, but how can the meaning of the poem for me be anything other than my own response to it?* The problem of judging the validity of interpretation is one of the most difficult issues in the criticism of poetry. No brief discussion will address all the questions involved, but the nature of interpretation calls for some *practical* discussion for two important reasons. First, it is impossible to avoid the problem of interpretation in writing about literature. Secondly, the writer's assumptions about interpretation will have a direct bearing on the methods used in developing the essay. The writer who assumes that all interpretations are equally valid is apt to produce a very different sort of essay from that produced by a writer who assumes that interpretations are susceptible to some standards of judgment.

The important questions, then, are these. How can the writer (or reader) judge the strength or weakness of a reading of a poem? Are there criteria by which an interpretation can be evaluated? What separates a "good" interpretation from a "bad" one? If all interpretations are *not* equally valid, then is there only *one* correct interpretation of a poem?

This last question establishes the two extreme positions, both of which are dangerous for the writer to adopt. If any interpretation is as good as any other, then there seems to be little point in "proving" or supporting one's reading. All that is necessary is to report one's response to the poem. But clearly this position is inadequate. We have all heard or read interpretations that are woefully off-target or irrelevant and can be *shown* to be so. The meaning of a particular word in the poem may have been misunderstood. ("Frost refers in line 10 to a piece of glass farmers use to cover the drinking trough.") The interpretation may simply ignore everything essential to the poem. ("Frost's poem reminds me of the time I visited an apple orchard in Virginia.") If an interpretation can be *corrected* by reference to the poem itself or shown to be inadequate by the fact that it does not deal with the words in the text, then obviously all interpretations are not equally good.

But what about the other extreme? Is there only one correct interpretation that we are all struggling to find? This position, too, presents problems for the writer. In the first place, it is apt to produce a great sense of anxiety. To begin with the assumption that only one reading is correct is to face the fact that almost any reading one comes up with is almost certainly wrong. How can one lonely writer be expected to solve the great mystery of a poem that scholars and critics have been struggling with for years? And what about all those books and articles on Frost? They don't always seem to agree in their interpretations. Furthermore, to say that there is only one correct reading of a poem does not really solve the problem. Even if it were true, how would we know when we had found it?

The fact is that writing about poetry seems to fall into that twilight zone of uncertainty between two extremes (much like Frost's narrator in "After Apple-Picking"). On the one hand, we cannot produce a set of scientific principles by which interpretations can be judged correct or incorrect. On the other hand, we feel instinctively that some interpretations are better than others, that interpretations may be weak or strong, convincing or unconvincing, bad, good, and better. On what basis, then, do we make this judgment?

In judging the sort of essays of explication and analysis we have been discussing here, our appeal is to *the poem itself*. With the exception of research papers that may deal with scholarship, history, and biography, our only means of arguing about, evaluating, and correcting interpretations are the text of the poem and our own good common sense. And the judgments we make about interpretations are not different in kind from the judgments we make daily about all sorts of matters. Most of the important decisions we are faced with in life are not susceptible to objective or scientific resolution, but we make them nevertheless, and we do so on the basis of some criteria that we regard as convincing. The same is true with interpretation.

Given the text of the poem as the "corrective" for interpretations, we may conclude that the best interpretations are, first, those that take into account the greatest part of the text, that are able to incorporate the important details of the poem. The weak interpretation may ignore significant details, or it may actually be contradicted by certain aspects of the poem. An interpretation, for example, that argues that the speaker of Frost's poem finds picking apples distasteful is weakened by lines 28 and 29: "I am overtired/ Of the great harvest I myself desired." And a reading that concludes that the poem is about the sense of satis faction one feels after any great achievement has simply ignored too many of the poem's details.

Of course, this principle does not solve all our problems. Poems are complex. Figurative language, symbols, tone, and mood are liable to different shadings of interpretation. However, it is clear that we do have *some* criteria by which to make judgments. Furthermore, the fact that interpretations may differ does not necessarily mean that one is better than another. We may approach poems from a number of different angles and perspectives. The questions that we ask about a poem determine the answers that we get. Two different questions about "After Apple-Picking" may result in two very different interpretations, that nevertheless are convincing, each in its own way.

There is one other test we can apply to interpretations. How *significant* is the point being made? Is it an important theme in the poem, or does it involve only a minor detail? An interpretation that deals with the complexity or ambiguity of the speaker's state of mind in "After Apple-Picking" will likely be of more value than one that concentrates solely on the hibernation habits of woodchucks or attempts to identify the variety of apples referred to in the poem. Interpretations may be evaluated not only on the basis of their fidelity to the details of the poem but also on the basis of the significance of what they have to say about the poem.

Finally, analyses and explications of poems may be judged on the strength of the argument made, the reasonableness of the conclusions drawn, the relevance and convincing nature of the evidence presented. In this respect, interpretations of poems do not differ from other varieties of expository essays. Perhaps the major distinction is that in writing about poetry our allegiance is not primarily to the larger world of experience but to the smaller world created by the poem. The facts of the poem serve as a measure by which our efforts may be corrected and evaluated but also as the means by which a convincing essay may be created and supported. Once we recognize, first, that all interpretations are not equally valid, and, secondly, that there is no one ideal, Platonic interpretation by which all others are judged, we are thrown back on the poem itself. If our interpretations are to be convincing, we must be able not only to analyze the details of the poem carefully but also to find effective ways of working them into the essay. If we have been successful, the question of validity of interpretations will not even arise. The ultimate success of a well-argued essay on poetry is perhaps the response from the reader that W. H. Auden wished for his poems to receive: *That's true; now, why didn't I think of it for myself?*

The Dimensions of Poetic Experience

Anonymous
O Western Wind, When Wilt Thou Blow*

O Western wind, when wilt thou blow
That the small rain down can rain?
Christ, that my love were in my arms
And I in my bed again!

Anonymous
Jolly Good Ale and Old

I cannot eat but little meat,
    My stomach is not good;
But sure I think that I can drink
    With him that wears a hood.
5 Though I go bare, take ye no care,
    I nothing am a-cold;
I stuff my skin so full within
    Of jolly good ale and old.

      Back and side go bare, go bare;
10   Both foot and hand go cold;
      But, belly, God send thee good ale enough,
      Whether it be new or old.

---

* It is said that this is the oldest poem in English for which we have recorded music. The manuscript is in the Bodleian Library, Oxford University, England.

I love no roast but a nut-brown toast,
    And a crab[1] laid in the fire;
15 A little bread shall do me stead;
    Much bread I not desire.
No frost nor snow, no wind, I trow,
    Can hurt me if I wold;
I am so wrapped and thoroughly lapped
20   Of jolly good ale and old.
        Back and side go bare, go bare, etc.

And Tib, my wife, that as her life
    Loveth well good ale to seek,
Full oft drinks she till ye may see
25   The tears run down her cheek:
Then doth she trowl to me the bowl
    Even as a maltworm should,
And saith, "Sweetheart, I took my part
    Of this jolly good ale and old."
30   Back and side go bare, go bare, etc.

Now let them drink till they nod and wink,
    Even as good fellows should do;
They shall not miss to have the bliss
    Good ale doth bring men to;
35 And all poor souls that have scoured bowls
    Or have them lustily trolled,
God save the lives of them and their wives,
    Whether they be young or old.
        Back and side go bare, go bare;
40   Both foot and hand go cold;
        But, belly, God send thee good ale enough,
    Whether it be new or old.

[1] Crab apple.

Sir Thomas Wyatt   (1503–1542)
They Flee from Me

They flee from me, that sometime did me seek,
With naked foot, stalking in my chamber.
I have seen them, gentle, tame, and meek,
That now are wild, and do not remember
5 That sometime they put themselves in danger
To take bread at my hand, and now they range,
Busily seeking with a continual change.

Thanked be fortune, it hath been otherwise
Twenty times better; but once, in special,
10 In thin array, after a pleasant guise,
When her loose gown from her shoulders did fall,
And she me caught in her arms long and small,
Therewithal sweetly did me kiss,
And softly said, "Dear heart, how like you this?"

15 It was no dream: I lay broad waking.
But all is turned, thorough[1] my gentleness,
Into a strange fashion of forsaking;
And I have leave to go, of her goodness,
And she also to use new-fangledness.
20 But since that I so kindely[2] am served,
I would fain know what she hath deserved.

William Shakespeare   (1564–1616)
Sonnet 18: Shall I Compare Thee to a Summer's Day?

Shall I compare thee to a summer's day?
Thou art more lovely and more temperate:
Rough winds do shake the darling buds of May,
And summer's lease hath all too short a date:
5 Sometime too hot the eye of heaven shines,

[1] Through.   [2] Naturally.

And often is his gold complexion dimmed;
And every fair from fair sometime declines,[1]
By chance or nature's changing course untrimmed;[2]
But thy eternal summer shall not fade
10 Nor lose possession of that fair thou owest;[3]
Nor shall Death brag thou wander'st in his shade,
When in eternal lines to time thou growest:
    So long as men can breathe, or eyes can see,
    So long lives this, and this gives life to thee.

William Shakespeare (1564–1616)
Sonnet 129: The Expense of Spirit in a Waste of Shame

The expense of spirit in a waste of shame
Is lust in action; and till action, lust
Is perjured, murderous, bloody, full of blame,
Savage, extreme, rude, cruel, not to trust,
5 Enjoyed no sooner but despisèd straight;
Past reason hunted, and no sooner had
Past reason hated, as a swallowed bait
On purpose laid to make the taker mad;
Mad in pursuit and in possession so;
10 Had, having, and in quest to have extreme;
A bliss in proof, and proved, a very woe;
Before, a joy proposed; behind, a dream.
    All this the world well knows; yet none knows well
    To shun the heaven that leads men to this hell.

---

[1] Every beautiful thing finally loses its beauty.   [2] Stripped of gay apparel.   [3] Ownest.

William Shakespeare   (1564–1616)
Sonnet 73: That Time of Year Thou Mayst in Me Behold

That time of year thou mayst in me behold
When yellow leaves, or none, or few, do hang
Upon those boughs which shake against the cold,
Bare ruined choirs, where late the sweet birds sang.
5   In me thou seest the twilight of such day
As after sunset fadeth in the west;
Which by and by black night doth take away,
Death's second self, that seals up all in rest.
In me thou seest the glowing of such fire,
10 That on the ashes of his youth doth lie,
As the death-bed whereon it must expire,
Consum'd with that which it was nourished by.
    This thou perceiv'st, which makes thy love more strong,
    To love that well which thou must leave ere long.

John Donne   (1572–1631)
Woman's Constancy

Now thou hast loved me one whole day,
To-morrow when thou leav'st, what wilt thou say?
Wilt thou then antedate some new-made vow?
    Or say that now
5   We are not just those persons which we were?
Or, that oaths made in reverential fear
Of love, and his wrath, any may forswear?
Or, as true deaths true marriages untie,
So lovers' contracts, images of those,
10 Bind but till sleep, death's image,[1] them unloose?
    Or, your own end to justify,
For having purposed change and falsehood, you
Can have no way but falsehood to be true?[2]

[1] Sleep which is an image of death.   [2] Ll. 12–13: In your declaration of love, you must be false again to rid yourself of the false declaration. That is, one falsehood demands another.

Vain lunatic, against these scapes I could
15   Dispute and conquer, if I would;
        Which I abstain to do,
For by to-morrow, I may think so too.

John Donne   (1572–1631)
The Flea

Mark but this flea, and mark in this,
How little that which thou deny'st me is;
It sucked me first, and now sucks thee,
And in this flea our two bloods mingled be;
5 Thou know'st that this cannot be said
A sin, nor shame, nor loss of maidenhead;
        Yet this enjoys before it woo,
        And pampered swells with one blood made of two,
        And this, alas, is more than we would do.

10 Oh stay, three lives in one flea spare,
Where we almost, yea, more than married are.
This flea is you and I, and this
Our marriage bed, and marriage temple is;
Though parents grudge, and you, w' are met,
15 And cloistered in these living walls of jet.
        Though use[1] make you apt to kill me,
        Let not to that, self-murder added be,
        And sacrilege, three sins in killing three.

Cruel and sudden, hast thou since
20 Purpled thy nail in blood of innocence?
Wherein could this flea guilty be,
 Except in that drop which it sucked from thee?
 Yet thou triumph'st and say'st that thou
Find'st not thyself, nor me the weaker now;
25   'Tis true, then learn how false fears be:
        Just so much honor, when thou yield'st to me,
        Will waste, as this flea's death took life from thee.

[1] Habit.

John Donne   (1572–1631)
Holy Sonnet XIV: Batter My Heart, Three-Personed God

Batter my heart, three-personed God; for You
As yet but knock, breathe, shine, and seek to mend;
That I may rise and stand, o'erthrow me, and bend
Your force, to break, blow, burn, and make me new.
5 I, like an usurped town, to another due,
Labor to admit You, but Oh, to no end!
Reason, Your viceroy in me, me should defend,
But is captived, and proves weak or untrue.
Yet dearly I love You, and would be loved fain.[1]
10 But am betrothed unto Your enemy:
Divorce me, untie, or break that knot again,
Take me to You, imprison me, for I,
Except You enthrall me, never shall be free,
Nor ever chaste, except You ravish me.

Ben Jonson   (1572–1637)
On Gut

Gut eats all day and lechers all the night;
So all his meat he tasteth over twice;
And, striving so to double his delight,
He makes himself a thoroughfare of vice.
5 Thus in his belly can he change a sin:
Lust it comes out, that gluttony went in.

[1] Gladly.

Ben Jonson (1572–1637)
Though I Am Young, and Cannot Tell

Though I am young, and cannot tell
    Either what Death or Love is well,
Yet I have heard they both bear darts,
    And both do aim at human hearts.
5 And then again, I have been told
    Love wounds with heat, as Death with cold;
So that I fear they do but bring
    Extremes to touch, and mean one thing.

As in a ruin we it call
10   One thing to be blown up, or fall;
Or to our end like way may have
    By a flash of lightning, or a wave;
So Love's inflaméd shaft or brand
    May kill as soon as Death's cold hand;
15 Except Love's fires the virtue have
    To fright the frost out of the grave.

Robert Herrick (1591–1674)
Upon a Child

Here a pretty baby lies
Sung asleep with lullabies:
Pray be silent, and not stir
Th' easy earth that covers her.

Robert Herrick (1591–1674)
Delight in Disorder

A sweet disorder in the dress
Kindles in clothes a wantonness;
A lawn[1] about the shoulders thrown
Into a fine distraction,
5 An erring lace, which here and there
Enthralls the crimson stomacher,[2]
A cuff neglectful, and thereby
Ribands to flow confusedly,
A winning wave, deserving note,
10 In the tempestuous petticoat,
A careless shoe-string, in whose tie
I see a wild civility,
Do more bewitch me than when art[3]
Is too precise in every part.

John Milton (1608–1674)
How Soon Hath Time

How soon hath Time, the subtle thief of youth,
    Stolen on his wing my three and twentieth year!
    My hasting days fly on with full career,
    But my late spring no bud or blossom shewith,
5 Perhaps my semblance might deceive the truth
    That I to manhood am arrived so near,
    And inward ripeness doth much less appear,
    That some more timely-happy spirits indueth.
Yet be it less or more, or soon or slow,
10   It shall be still in strictest measure even
    To that same lot, however mean or high,
Toward which Time leads me, and the will of Heaven;
    All is, if I have grace to use it so,
    As ever in my great Taskmaster's eye.

[1] Fine linen, as a scarf.   [2] Center front section of a waist or underwaist or an unusually heavily embroidered or jeweled separate piece for the center front of a bodice.   [3] Art: conscious effort to achieve a desired effect.

William Cartwright (1611–1643)
No Platonic Love*

Tell me no more of minds embracing minds,
    And hearts exchanged for hearts;
That spirits spirits meet, as winds do winds,
    And mix their subtlest parts;
5 That two unbodied essences may kiss,
And then like angels, twist and feel one bliss.

I was that silly thing that once was wrought
    To practise this thin love;
I climbed from sex to soul, from soul to thought;
10   But thinking there to move,
Headlong I rolled from thought to soul, and then
From soul I lighted at the sex again.

As some strict down-looked men pretend to fast
    Who yet in closets eat,
15 So lovers who profess they spirits taste,
    Feed yet on grosser meat;
I know they boast they souls to souls convey,
Howe'er they meet, the body is the way.

Come, I will undeceive thee: they that tread
20   Those vain aerial ways
Are like young heirs and alchemists, misled
    To waste their wealth and days;
For searching thus to be forever rich,
They only find a med'cine for the itch.

---

    * The Greek philosopher Plato (427?–347 B.C.) wrote *The Symposium,* a dialogue on ideal love. "Platonic love" became a popular term for spiritual love between the sexes without sexual complications. See J. V. Cunningham's poem "The Metaphysical Amorist," p. 526, which has a theme similar to Cartwright's.

Richard Lovelace   (1618–1658)
To Lucasta, Going to the Wars

Tell me not, Sweet, I am unkind,
　　That from the nunnery
Of thy chaste breast and quiet mind
　　To war and arms I fly.

5　True, a new mistress now I chase,
　　The first foe in the field;
And with a stronger faith embrace
　　A sword, a horse, a shield.

Yet this inconstancy is such
10　　As thou too shalt adore;
I could not love thee, Dear, so much,
　　Loved I not Honor more.

Alexander Pope   (1688–1744)
Ode on Solitude

Happy the man whose wish and care
　　A few paternal acres bound,
Content to breathe his native air,
　　　　In his own ground.

5　Whose herds with milk, whose fields with bread,
　　Whose flocks supply him with attire,
Whose trees in summer yield him shade,
　　　　In winter fire.

Blest, who can unconcernedly find
10　　Hours, days, and years slide soft away,
In health of body, peace of mind,
　　　　Quiet by day.

Sound sleep by night: study and ease,
　　Together mixed: sweet recreation:
15　And innocence, which most does please
　　　　With meditation.

Thus let me live, unseen, unknown;
　　Thus unlamented let me die;
Steal from the world, and not a stone
20　　　　　　　　Tell where I lie.

Thomas Gray　(1716–1771)
Elegy Written
in a Country Churchyard

The Curfew tolls the knell of parting day,
　　The lowing herd wind slowly o'er the lea,
The plowman homeward plods his weary way,
　　And leaves the world to darkness and to me.

5　Now fades the glimmering landscape on the sight,
　　And all the air a solemn stillness holds,
Save where the beetle wheels his droning flight,
　　And drowsy tinklings lull the distant folds;

Save that from yonder ivy-mantled tower
10　　The moping owl does to the moon complain
Of such, as wandering near her secret bower,
　　Molest her ancient solitary reign.

Beneath those rugged elms, that yew-tree's shade,
　　Where heaves the turf in many a mould'ring heap,
15　Each in his narrow cell for ever laid,
　　The rude Forefathers of the hamlet sleep.

The breezy call of incense-breathing Morn,
　　The swallow twitt'ring from the straw-built shed,
The cock's shrill clarion, or the echoing horn,[1]
20　　No more shall rouse them from their lowly bed.

For them no more the blazing hearth shall burn,
　　Or busy housewife ply her evening care:
No children run to lisp their sire's return,
　　Or climb his knees the envied kiss to share.

25　Oft did the harvest to their sickle yield,
　　Their furrow oft the stubborn glebe has broke;

---

[1] Of the hunt, early in the morning.

How jocund did they drive their team afield!
   How bowed the woods beneath their sturdy stroke!

Let not Ambition mock their useful toil,
30   Their homely joys, and destiny obscure;
Nor Grandeur hear with a disdainful smile
   The short and simple annals of the poor.

The boast of heraldry, the pomp of power,
   And all that beauty, all that wealth e'er gave,
35 Awaits[2] alike th' inevitable hour.
   The paths of glory lead but to the grave.

Nor you, ye Proud, impute to These the fault,
   If Memory o'er their Tomb no Trophies raise,
Where through the long-drawn aisle and fretted vault
40   The pealing anthem swells the note of praise.

Can storied urn[3] or animated[4] bust
   Back to its mansion call the fleeting breath?
Can Honor's voice provoke[5] the silent dust,
   Or Flattery soothe the dull cold ear of Death?

45 Perhaps in this neglected spot is laid
   Some heart once pregnant with celestial fire;
Hands, that the rod of empire might have swayed,
   Or waked to ecstasy the living lyre.

But Knowledge to their eyes her ample page
50   Rich with the spoils of time did ne'er unroll:
Chill Penury repressed their noble rage,[6]
   And froze the genial[7] current of the soul.

Full many a gem of purest ray serene,
   The dark unfathomed caves of ocean bear:
55 Full many a flower is born to blush unseen,
   And waste its sweetness on the desert air.

Some village-Hampden,[8] that with dauntless breast
   The little Tyrant of his fields withstood;
Some mute inglorious Milton here may rest,
60   Some Cromwell guiltless of his country's blood.

Th' applause of list'ning senates to command,
   The threats of pain and ruin to despise,
To scatter plenty o'er a smiling land,
   And read their history in a nation's eyes,

65 Their lot forbade: not circumscribed alone
   Their growing virtues, but their crimes confined;

[2] The subject of the verb *awaits* is *hour.*   [3] Such as Keats describes in his "Ode on a Grecian Urn" (see p. 468).   [4] Lifelike.   [5] Call forth.   [6] Inspired mood.   [7] Creative.   [8] John Hampden (1594–1643), whose leadership in Parliament resisted the tyranny of Charles I.

Forbade to wade through slaughter to a throne,
 And shut the gates of mercy on mankind,

The struggling pangs of conscious truth to hide
70 To quench the blushes of ingenuous shame,
 Or heap the shrine of Luxury and Pride
  With incense kindled at the Muse's flame.

Far from the madding crowd's ignoble strife,
 Their sober wishes never learned to stray;
75 Along the cool sequestered vale of life
  They kept the noiseless tenor of their way.

Yet ev'n these bones from insult to protect,
 Some frail memorial still erected nigh,
With uncouth rhymes and shapeless sculpture decked,
80 Implores the passing tribute of a sigh.

Their name, their years, spelt by th' unlettered muse,
 The place of fame and elegy supply;
And many a holy text around she strews,
 That teach the rustic moralist to die.

85 For who to dumb Forgetfulness a prey,
This pleasing anxious being e'er resigned,
Left the warm precincts of the cheerful day,
 Nor cast one longing ling'ring look behind?

On some fond breast the parting soul relies,
90 Some pious drops the closing eye requires;
Ev'n from the tomb the voice of Nature cries,
 Ev'n in our Ashes live their wonted Fires.

For⁹ thee, who mindful of th' unhonored Dead
 Dost in these lines their artless tale relate,
95 If chance,¹⁰ by lonely contemplation led,
 Some kindred Spirit shall inquire thy fate,

Haply some hoary-headed Swain may say,
 "Oft have we seen him at the peep of dawn
Brushing with hasty steps the dews away
100 To meet the sun upon the upland lawn.

"There at the foot of yonder nodding beech
 That wreathes its old fantastic roots so high,
His listless length at noontide would he stretch,
 And pore upon the brook that babbles by.

105 "Hard by yon wood, now smiling as in scorn,
 Mutt'ring his wayward fancies he would rove,
Now drooping, woeful wan, like one forlorn,
 Or crazed with care, or crossed in hopeless love.

⁹ As for. ¹⁰ If it should chance.

"One morn I missed him on the customed hill,
110   Along the heath and near his favorite tree;
Another came; nor yet beside the rill,
    Nor up the lawn, nor at the wood was he;

"The next with dirges due in sad array
    Slow through the church-way path we saw him borne.
115 Approach and read (for thou cans't read) the lay,
    Graved on the stone beneath yon agèd thorn."

The Epitaph
Here rests his head upon the lap of earth
    A youth to fortune and to fame unknown.
Fair Science frowned not on his humble birth,
120   *And Melancholy marked him for her own.*

Large was his bounty, and his soul sincere,
    Heaven did a recompense as largely send:
He gave to Misery all he had, a tear,
    He gained from Heaven ('twas all he wished) a friend.

125 *No further seek his merits to disclose,*
    Or draw his frailties from their dread abode,
(There they alike in trembling hope repose)
    The bosom of his Father and his God.

William Blake   (1757–1827)
London

I wander thro' each charter'd street,
Near where the charter'd Thames does flow,
And mark in every face I meet
Marks of weakness, marks of woe.

5 In every cry of every Man,
In every Infant's cry of fear,
In every voice: in every ban,
The mind-forg'd manacles I hear.

How the Chimney-sweeper's cry
10 Every blackning Church appalls,
And the hapless Soldier's sigh,
Runs in blood down Palace walls.

But most thro' midnight streets I hear
How the youthful Harlot's curse
15 Blasts the new-born Infant's tear,
And blights with plagues the Marriage hearse.

William Blake   (1757–1827)
The Sick Rose

O rose, thou art sick.
The invisible worm
That flies in the night
In the howling storm

5 Has found out thy bed
Of crimson joy,
And his dark secret love
Does thy life destroy.

Robert Burns   (1759–1796)
My Love Is like a Red Red Rose

My love is like a red red rose
    That's newly sprung in June:
My love is like the melodie
    That's sweetly played in tune.

5 So fair art thou, my bonnie lass,
    So deep in love am I:
And I will love thee still, my dear,
    Till a' the seas gang dry.

    Till a' the seas gang dry, my dear,
10   And the rocks melt wi' the sun:

And I will love thee still, my dear,
　　While the sands o' life shall run.

And fare thee weel, my only love,
　　And fare thee weel awhile!
15 And I will come again, my love,
　　Tho' it were ten thousand mile.

William Wordsworth   (1770–1850)
Stepping Westward

"What, you are stepping westward?"—"Yea."
—'T would be a *wildish* destiny,
If we, who thus together roam
In a strange Land, and far from home,
5 Were in this place the guests of Chance:
Yet who would stop, or fear to advance,
Though home or shelter he had none,
With such a sky to lead him on?

The dewy ground was dark and cold;
10 Behind, all gloomy to behold;
And stepping westward seemed to be
A kind of *heavenly* destiny:
I liked the greeting; 't was a sound
Of something without place or bound;
15 And seemed to give me spiritual right
To travel through that region bright.

The voice was soft, and she who spake
Was walking by her native lake:
The salutation had to me
20 The very sound of courtesy:
Its power was felt; and while my eye
Was fixed upon the glowing Sky,
The echo of the voice enwrought
A human sweetness with the thought
25 Of travelling through the world that lay
Before me in my endless way.

Comments

In a background note to this poem, Wordsworth indicates that he and a companion were walking one evening about sunset while on a visit in Scotland when "we met, in one of the loneliest parts of that solitary region, two well-dressed women, one of whom said to us, by way of greeting, 'What, you are stepping westward?' " The poem is, of course, both a literal description of that commonplace incident and its environment and a metaphorical consideration of some universal questions about human destiny.

William Wordsworth (1770–1850)
A Slumber Did My Spirit Seal

A slumber did my spirit seal;
   I had no human fears:
She seemed a thing that could not feel
   The touch of earthly years.

5 No motion has she now, no force;
   She neither hears nor sees;
Rolled round in earth's diurnal course,
   With rocks, and stones, and trees.

William Wordsworth (1770–1850)
It Is a Beauteous Evening

It is a beauteous evening, calm and free;
The holy time is quiet as a nun
Breathless with adoration; the broad sun
Is sinking down in its tranquillity;
5 The gentleness of heaven broods o'er the sea:
Listen! the mighty Being is awake,
And doth with his eternal motion make

A sound like thunder—everlastingly.
Dear child! dear girl! that walkest with me here,
10 If thou appear untouched by solemn thought,
Thy nature is not therefore less divine:
Thou liest in Abraham's bosom all the year,
And worships'st at the Temple's inner shrine,
God being with thee when we know it not.

William Wordsworth (1770–1850)
The World Is Too Much with Us

The world is too much with us; late and soon,
Getting and spending, we lay waste our powers;
Little we see in Nature that is ours;
We have given our hearts away, a sordid boon!
5 This Sea that bares her bosom to the moon;
The winds that will be howling at all hours,
And are up-gathered now like sleeping flowers;
For this, for everything, we are out of tune;
It moves us not.—Great God! I'd rather be
10 A Pagan suckled in a creed outworn;
So might I, standing on this pleasant lea,
Have glimpses that would make me less forlorn:
Have sight of Proteus rising from the sea;
Or hear old Triton[1] blow his wreathèd[2] horn.

[1] Sea gods of classical mythology. Proteus could assume any shape. Triton, son of Neptune, could
raise and calm the waves by blasts on his conch-shell trumpet.   [2] Spiral.

Samuel Taylor Coleridge (1772–1834)
Kubla Khan: Or a Vision in a Dream*

In Xanadu did Kubla Khan[1]
A stately pleasure-dome decree;
Where Alph, the sacred river, ran
Through caverns measureless to man
5 Down to a sunless sea.

So twice five miles of fertile ground
With walls and towers were girdled round:
And here were gardens bright with sinuous rills,
Where blossomed many an incense-bearing tree;
10 And here were forests ancient as the hills
Enfolding sunny spots of greenery.

But oh! that deep romantic chasm which slanted
Down the green hill athwart[2] a cedarn cover!
A savage place! as holy and enchanted
15 As e'er beneath a waning moon was haunted
By woman wailing for her demon-lover!
And from this chasm, with ceaseless turmoil seething,
As if this earth in fast thick pants were breathing
A mighty fountain momently[3] was forced:
20 Amid whose swift half-intermitted burst
Huge fragments vaulted like rebounding hail,
Or chaffy grain beneath the thresher's flail:

* The poem was written in 1798, not 1797 as Coleridge erroneously states. A preface by the author explains the genesis and composition of the poem: "In the summer of the year of 1797 [1798], the Author, then in ill health, had retired to a lonely farm-house. . . . In consequence of a slight indisposition, an anodyne [it was opium] had been prescribed, from the effects of which he fell asleep in his chair at the moment that he was reading the following sentence, or words of the same substance, in 'Purchas's Pilgrimage': 'Here the Khan Kubla commanded a palace to be built, and a stately garden thereunto. And thus ten miles of fertile ground were enclosed with a wall.' The Author continued for about three hours in a profound sleep, at least of the external senses, during which time he has the most vivid confidence, that he could not have composed less than from two to three hundred lines; if that indeed can be called composition in which all the images rose up before him as *things*, with a parallel production of the correspondent expressions, without any sensation or consciousness of effort. On awaking he appeared to himself to have a distinct recollection of the whole, and taking his pen, ink and paper, instantly and eagerly wrote down the lines that are here preserved. At this moment he was unfortunately called out by a person on business from Porlock, and detained by him above an hour, and on his return to his room, found, to his no small surprise and mortification, that though he still retained some vague and dim recollection of the general purport of the vision, yet, with the exception of some eight or ten scattered lines and images, all the rest had passed away like the images on the surface of a stream into which a stone has been cast, but, alas! without the after restoration of the latter!"

[1] Founder of the Mongol dynasty in China.   [2] Across.   [3] Continuously.

And 'mid these dancing rocks at once and ever
It flung up momently the sacred river.
25 Five miles meandering with a mazy motion
Through wood and dale the sacred river ran,
Then reached the caverns measureless to man,
And sank in tumult to a lifeless ocean:
And 'mid this tumult Kubla heard from far
30 Ancestral voices prophesying war!

> The shadow of the dome of pleasure
> Floated midway on the waves;
> Where was heard the mingled measure
> From the fountain and the caves.
35 It was a miracle of rare device,
A sunny pleasure-dome with caves of ice!

> A damsel with a dulcimer[4]
> In a vision once I saw:
> It was an Abyssinian maid,
40   And on her dulcimer she played,
> Singing of Mount Abora.
> Could I revive within me
> Her symphony and song,
> To such a deep delight 'twould win me,
45 That with music loud and long,
I would build that dome in air,
That sunny dome! those caves of ice!
And all who heard should see them there,—
And all should cry, Beware! Beware!—
50 His flashing eyes, his floating hair!
Weave a circle round him thrice,
And close your eyes with holy dread,
For he on honey-dew hath fed,
And drunk the milk of Paradise.

[4] Wire-stringed instrument played with light hammers in the hand.

George Gordon, Lord Byron (1788–1824)
The Destruction of Sennacherib[1]

I
The Assyrian came down like the wolf on the fold,
And his cohorts were gleaming in purple and gold;
And the sheen of their spears was like stars on the sea,
When the blue wave rolls nightly on deep Galilee.

II
5 Like the leaves of the forest when Summer is green,
That host with their banners at sunset were seen:
Like the leaves of the forest when Autumn hath blown,
That host on the morrow lay wither'd and strown.

III
For the Angel of Death spread his wings on the blast,
10 And breathed in the face of the foe as he pass'd;
And the eyes of the sleepers wax'd deadly and chill,
And their hearts but once heaved, and for ever grew still!

IV
And there lay the steed with his nostril all wide,
But through it there roll'd not the breath of his pride;
15 And the foam of his gasping lay white on the turf,
And cold as the spray of the rock-beating surf.

V
And there lay the rider distorted and pale,
With the dew on his brow, and the rust on his mail:
And the tents were all silent, the banners alone,
20 The lances unlifted, the trumpet unblown.

VI
And the widows of Ashur are loud in their wail,
And the idols are broke in the temple of Baal;
And the might of the Gentile, unsmote by the sword,
Hath melted like snow in the glance of the Lord!

---

[1] Assyrian king, 705–681 B.C., whose troops were destroyed by plague. See 2 Kings 19:20–37.

Ogden Nash   (1902–1971)
Very like a Whale[1]

One thing that literature would be greatly the better for
Would be a more restricted employment by authors of simile and metaphor.
Authors of all races, be they Greeks, Romans, Teutons or Celts,
Can't seem just to say that anything is the thing it is but have to go out of their way to say
    that it is like something else.
5 What does it mean when we are told
That the Assyrian came down like a wolf on the fold?
In the first place, George Gordon Byron had had enough experience
To know that it probably wasn't just one Assyrian, it was a lot of Assyrians.
However, as too many arguments are apt to induce apoplexy and thus hinder longevity,
10 We'll let it pass as one Assyrian for the sake of brevity.
Now then, this particular Assyrian, the one whose cohorts were gleaming in purple and
    gold,
Just what does the poet mean when he says he came down like a wolf on the fold?
In heaven and earth more than is dreamed of in our philosophy there are a great many
    things,
But I don't imagine that among them there is a wolf with purple and gold cohorts or
    purple and gold anythings.
15 No, no, Lord Byron, before I'll believe that this Assyrian was actually like a wolf I must
    have some kind of proof;
Did he run on all fours and did he have a hairy tail and a big red mouth and big white
    teeth and did he say Woof woof woof?
Frankly I think it is very unlikely, and all you were entitled to say, at the very most,
Was that the Assyrian cohorts came down like a lot of Assyrian cohorts about to destroy
    the Hebrew host.
But that wasn't fancy enough for Lord Byron, oh dear me no, he had to invent a lot of
    figures of speech and then interpolate them.
20 With the result that whenever you mention Old Testament soldiers to people they say Oh
    yes, they're the ones that a lot of wolves dressed up in gold and purple ate them.
That's the kind of thing that's being done all the time by poets, from Homer to Tennyson;
They're always comparing ladies to lilies and veal to venison.
And they always say things like that the snow is a white blanket after a winter storm.
Oh it is, is it, all right then, you sleep under a six-inch blanket of snow and I'll sleep
    under a half-inch blanket of unpoetical blanket material and we'll see which one
    keeps warm.
25 And after that maybe you'll begin to comprehend dimly
What I mean by too much metaphor and simile.

[1] The title is an allusion to *Hamlet*, III. ii. 318. See p. 677.

Percy Bysshe Shelley (1792–1822)
Ode to the West Wind

I

O wild West Wind, thou breath of Autumn's being,
Thou, from whose unseen presence the leaves dead
Are driven, like ghosts from an enchanter fleeing,

Yellow, and black, and pale, and hectic red,
5 Pestilence-stricken multitudes: O thou,
Who chariotest to their dark wintry bed

The wingéd seeds, where they lie cold and low,
Each like a corpse within its grave, until
Thine azure sister of the Spring shall blow

10 Her clarion o'er the dreaming earth, and fill
(Driving sweet buds like flocks to feed in air)
With living hues and odors plain and hill:

Wild Spirit, which art moving everywhere;
Destroyer and preserver; hear, oh hear!

II

15 Thou on whose stream, 'mid the steep sky's commotion,
Loose clouds like earth's decaying leaves are shed,
Shook from the tangled boughs of Heaven and Ocean,

Angels of rain and lightning: there are spread
On the blue surface of thine airy surge,
20 Like the bright hair uplifted from the head

Of some fierce Maenad, even from the dim verge
Of the horizon to the zenith's height
The locks of the approaching storm. Thou dirge

Of the dying year, to which this closing night
25 Will be the dome of a vast sepulcher,
Vaulted with all thy congregated might

Of vapors, from whose solid atmosphere
Black rain, and fire, and hail will burst: Oh hear!

III

Thou who didst waken from his summer dreams
30 The blue Mediterranean, where he lay,
Lulled by the coil of his crystálline streams,

Beside a pumice isle in Baiae's bay,
And saw in sleep old palaces and towers
Quivering within the wave's intenser day,

35 All overgrown with azure moss and flowers
So sweet, the sense faints picturing them! Thou
For whose path the Atlantic's level powers

Cleave themselves into chasms, while far below
The sea-blooms and the oozy woods which wear
40 The sapless foliage of the ocean, know

Thy voice, and suddenly grow gray with fear,
And tremble and despoil themselves: Oh hear!

       IV

If I were a dead leaf thou mightest bear;
If I were a swift cloud to fly with thee;
45 A wave to pant beneath thy power, and share

The impulse of thy strength, only less free
Than thou, O uncontrollable! If even
I were as in my boyhood, and could be

The comrade of thy wanderings over heaven,
50 As then, when to outstrip thy skyey speed
Scarce seemed a vision, I would ne'er have striven

As thus with thee in prayer in my sore need.
Oh! lift me as a wave, a leaf, a cloud!
I fall upon the thorns of life! I bleed!

55 A heavy weight has chained and bowed
One too like thee: tameless, and swift, and proud.

       V

Make me thy lyre, even as the forest is:
What if my leaves are falling like its own!
The tumult of thy mighty harmonies

60 Will take from both a deep, autumnal tone,
Sweet though in sadness. Be thou, spirit fierce,
My spirit! Be thou me, impetuous one!

Drive my dead thoughts over the universe
Like withered leaves to quicken a new birth;
65 And, by the incantation of this verse,

Scatter, as from an unextinguished hearth
Ashes and sparks, my words among mankind!
Be through my lips to unawakened earth

The trumpet of a prophecy! O Wind,
70 If Winter comes, can Spring be far behind?

John Keats (1795–1821)
On First Looking into Chapman's Homer

Much have I traveled in the realms of gold,[1]
And many goodly states and kingdoms seen;
Round many western islands[2] have I been
Which bards in fealty to Apollo[3] hold.
5 Oft of one wide expanse had I been told
That deep-browed Homer ruled as his demesne;
Yet did I never breathe its pure serene
Till I heard Chapman speak out loud and bold:
Then felt I like some watcher of the skies
10 When a new planet swims into his ken;
Or like stout Cortez[4] when with eagle eyes
He stared at the Pacific—and all his men
Looked at each other with a wild surmise—
Silent, upon a peak in Darien.[5]

John Keats (1795–1821)
Ode to a Nightingale

1

My heart aches, and a drowsy numbness pains
    My sense, as though of hemlock I had drunk,
Or emptied some dull opiate to the drains
    One minute past, and Lethe-wards had sunk:
5 'Tis not through envy of thy happy lot,
    But being too happy in thy happiness,—
        That thou, light-wingèd Dryad[1] of the trees,
            In some melodious plot
Of beechen green, and shadows numberless,
10   Singest of summer in full-throated ease.

[1] Great literature.   [2] Modern European literature.   [3] God of poetry.   [4] Keats's error: it was Balboa.   [5] Isthmus of Panama.
[1] Tree nymph.

2

O, for a draught of vintage! that hath been
 Cooled a long age in the deep-delvèd earth,
Tasting of Flora[2] and the country-green,
 Dance, and Provençal[3] song, and sunburnt mirth!
15 O for a beaker full of the warm South,
 Full of the true, the blushful Hippocrene,[4]
  With beaded bubbles winking at the brim,
   And purple-stainèd mouth;
 That I might drink, and leave the world unseen,
20 And with thee fade away into the forest dim:

3

Fade far away, dissolve, and quite forget
 What thou among the leaves hast never known,
The weariness, the fever, and the fret
 Here, where men sit and hear each other groan;
25 Where palsy shakes a few, sad, last gray hairs,
 Where youth grows pale, and spectre-thin, and dies;
  Where but to think is to be full of sorrow
   And leaden-eyed despairs,
Where Beauty cannot keep her lustrous eyes
30 Or new Love pine at them beyond tomorrow.

4

Away! away! for I will fly to thee,
 Not charioted by Bacchus and his pards,[5]
But on the viewless wings of Poesy,
 Though the dull brain perplexes and retards:
35 Already with thee! tender is the night,
 And haply the Queen-Moon is on her throne,
  Clustered around by all her starry Fays;[6]
   But here there is no light,
Save what from heaven is with the breezes blown
40 Through verdurous glooms and winding mossy ways.

5

I cannot see what flowers are at my feet,
 Nor what soft incense hangs upon the boughs,
But, in embalmèd[7] darkness, guess each sweet
 Wherewith the seasonable month endows
45 The grass, the thicket, and the fruit-tree wild;
 White hawthorn, and the pastoral eglantine;
  Fast-fading violets covered up in leaves;
   And mid-May's eldest child,
The coming musk-rose, full of dewy wine,
50 The murmurous haunt of flies on summer eves.

---

[2] Goddess of flowers. [3] Provence, original home of the troubadours in southeastern France.
[4] Drinking from this fountain supposedly induced poetic inspiration. [5] Leopards. [6] Fairies.
[7] Fragrant.

6

Darkling I listen; and, for many a time
   I have been half in love with easeful Death,
Called him soft names in many a musèd rhyme,
   To take into the air my quiet breath;
55 Now more than ever seems it rich to die,
    To cease upon the midnight with no pain,
      While thou art pouring forth thy soul abroad
        In such an ecstasy!
   Still wouldst thou sing, and I have ears in vain—
60   To thy high requiem become a sod.

7

Thou wast not born for death, immortal Bird!
   No hungry generations tread thee down;
The voice I hear this passing night was heard
   In ancient days by emperor and clown:
65 Perhaps the self-same song that found a path
   Through the sad heart of Ruth, when, sick for home,
      She stood in tears amid the alien corn;[8]
        The same that oft-times hath
   Charmed magic casements, opening on the foam
70   Of perilous seas, in faery lands forlorn.

8

Forlorn! the very word is like a bell
   To toll me back from thee to my sole self!
Adieu! the fancy cannot cheat so well
   As she is famed to do, deceiving elf.
75 Adieu! adieu! thy plaintive anthem fades
   Past the near meadows, over the still stream,
      Up the hill-side; and now 'tis buried deep
        In the next valley-glades:
Was it a vision, or a waking dream?
80   Fled is that music:—Do I wake or sleep?

[8] Ll. 66–67; see Ruth 2.

John Keats (1795–1821)
Ode on a Grecian Urn

1

Thou still unravished bride of quietness,
    Thou foster-child of silence and slow time,
Sylvan historian, who canst thus express
    A flowery tale more sweetly than our rime:
5 What leaf-fringed legend haunts about thy shape
        Of deities or mortals, or of both,
            In Tempe[1] or the dales of Arcady?[2]
    What men or gods are these? What maidens loth?
        What mad pursuit? What struggles to escape?
10   What pipes and timbrels?[3] What wild ecstasy?

2

Heard melodies are sweet, but those unheard
    Are sweeter; therefore, ye soft pipes, play on;
Not to the sensual[4] ear, but, more endeared,
    Pipe to the spirit ditties of no tone:
15 Fair youth, beneath the trees, thou canst not leave
        Thy song, nor ever can those trees be bare;
            Bold Lover, never, never canst thou kiss,
    Though winning near the goal—yet, do not grieve;
        She cannot fade, though thou hast not thy bliss,
20   Forever wilt thou love, and she be fair!

3

Ah, happy, happy boughs! That cannot shed
    Your leaves, nor ever bid the Spring adieu:
And, happy melodist, unwearièd,
    Forever piping songs forever new;
25 More happy love! more happy, happy love!
        Forever warm and still to be enjoy'd,
            Forever panting, and forever young;
All breathing human passion far above,
        That leaves a heart high-sorrowful and cloyed,
30   A burning forehead, and a parching tongue.

4

Who are these coming to the sacrifice?
    To what green altar, O mysterious priest,
Lead'st thou that heifer lowing at the skies,
    And all her silken flanks with garlands drest?

---

[1] Valley in Thessaly.   [2] Central hill region in southern Greece, long associated in poetry with pastoral life.   [3] Small drums or tambourines.   [4] Sensuous, physical, actual.

35 What little town by river or sea shore,
    Or mountain-built with peaceful citadel,
       Is emptied of this folk, this pious morn?
And, little town, thy streets for evermore
    Will silent be; and not a soul to tell
40   Why thou art desolate, can e'er return.

      5

O Attic[5] shape! Fair Attitude! with brede[6]
    Of marble men and maidens overwrought,
With forest branches and the trodden weed;
    Thou, silent form, dost tease us out of thought
45 As doth eternity: Cold Pastoral![7]
    When old age shall this generation waste,
       Thou shalt remain, in midst of other woe
Than ours, a friend to man, to whom thou sayst,
    "Beauty is truth, truth beauty,"—that is all
50   Ye know on earth, and all ye need to know.

John Keats   (1795–1821)
To Autumn

    1

Season of mists and mellow fruitfulness,
    Close bosom-friend of the maturing sun;
Conspiring with him how to load and bless
    With fruit the vines that round the thatch-eaves run;
5 To bend with apples the mossed cottage-trees,
    And fill all fruit with ripeness to the core;
       To swell the gourd, and plump the hazel shells
    With a sweet kernel; to set budding more,
And still more, later flowers for the bees,
10 Until they think warm days will never cease,
       For Summer has o'er-brimmed their clammy cells.

    2

Who hath not seen thee oft amid thy store?
    Sometimes whoever seeks abroad may find
Thee sitting careless on a granary floor,
15   Thy hair soft-lifted by the winnowing wind;

[5] Of Attica, Athenian.   [6] Embroidery, braid.   [7] Pastoral scene fired in cold marble or clay.

Or on a half-reaped furrow sound asleep,
    Drowsed with the fume of poppies, while thy hook
        Spares the next swath and all its twinéd flowers:
And sometimes like a gleaner thou dost keep
20   Steady thy laden head across a brook;
    Or by a cider-press, with patient look,
        Thou watchest the last oozings hours by hours.

        3

Where are the songs of Spring? Aye, where are they?
    Think not of them, thou hast thy music too—
25 While barréd clouds bloom the soft-dying day,
    And touch the stubble-plains with rosy hue;
Then in a wailful choir the small gnats mourn
    Among the river sallows, borne aloft
        Or sinking as the light wind lives or dies;
30 And full-grown lambs loud bleat from hilly bourn;
    Hedge crickets sing; and now with treble soft
    The redbreast whistles from a garden-croft;
        And gathering swallows twitter in the skies.

Henry Wadsworth Longfellow
(1807–1882)

Nature

As a fond mother, when the day is o'er,
    Leads by the hand her little child to bed,
    Half willing, half reluctant to be led,
    And leave his broken playthings on the floor,
5 Still gazing at them through the open door,
    Nor wholly reassured and comforted
    By promises of others in their stead,
    Which, though more splendid, may not please him more;
So Nature deals with us, and takes away
10   Our playthings one by one, and by the hand
    Leads us to rest so gently, that we go
Scarce knowing if we wish to go or stay,
    Being too full of sleep to understand
    How far the unknown transcends the what we know.

Comments

For another poet who relies on Nature for guidance see Bryant's "To a Waterfowl," p. 398. Longfellow and Bryant were contemporaries. For a poet who relies on a quite different, mystical nature see Whitman's "Song of Myself," p. 475.

Alfred, Lord Tennyson (1809–1892)

Break, Break, Break

Break, break, break,
    On thy cold gray stones, O Sea!
And I would that my tongue could utter
    The thoughts that arise in me.

5 O well for the fisherman's boy,
    That he shouts with his sister at play!
Oh well for the sailor lad,
    That he sings in his boat on the bay!

And the stately ships go on
10   To their haven under the hill;
But O for the touch of a vanished hand,
    And the sound of a voice that is still!

Break, break, break,
    At the foot of thy crags, O Sea!
15 But the tender grace of a day that is dead
    Will never come back to me.

Alfred, Lord Tennyson   (1809–1892)
Tears, Idle Tears

Tears, idle tears, I know not what they mean,
Tears from the depth of some divine despair
Rise in the heart, and gather to the eyes,
In looking on the happy autumn-fields,
5 And thinking of the days that are no more.

Fresh as the first beam glittering on a sail,
That brings our friends up from the underworld,
Sad as the last which reddens over one
That sinks with all we love below the verge;
10 So sad, so fresh, the days that are no more.

Ah, sad and strange as in dark summer dawns
The earliest pipe of half-awakened birds
To dying ears, when unto dying eyes
The casement slowly grows a glimmering square;
15 So sad, so strange, the days that are no more.

Dear as remembered kisses after death,
And sweet as those by hopeless fancy feigned
On lips that are for others; deep as love,
Deep as first love, and wild with all regret;
20 O Death in Life, the days that are no more!
                              (From *The Princess*)

Alfred, Lord Tennyson   (1809–1892)
The Eagle

He clasps the crag with crooked hands;
Close to the sun in lonely lands,
Ringed with the azure world, he stands.

The wrinkled sea beneath him crawls;
5 He watches from his mountain walls,
And like a thunderbolt he falls.

Robert Browning   (1812–1889)
Porphyria's Lover

The rain set early in to-night,
   The sullen wind was soon awake,
It tore the elm-tops down for spite,
   And did its worst to vex the lake:
5   I listened with heart fit to break.
When glided in Porphyria; straight
   She shut the cold out and the storm,
And kneeled and made the cheerless grate
   Blaze up, and all the cottage warm;
10   Which done, she rose, and from her form
Withdrew the dripping cloak and shawl,
   And laid her soiled gloves by, untied
Her hat and let the damp hair fall,
   And, last, she sat down by my side
15   And called me. When no voice replied,
She put my arm about her waist,
   And made her smooth white shoulder bare,
And all her yellow hair displaced,
   And, stopping, made my cheek lie there,
20   And spread, o'er all, her yellow hair,
Murmuring how she loved me—she
   Too weak, for all her heart's endeavor,
To set its struggling passion free
   From pride, and vainer ties dissever,
25   And give herself to me forever.
But passion sometimes would prevail,
   Nor could to-night's gay feast restrain
A sudden thought of one so pale
   For love of her, and all in vain:
30   So, she was come through wind and rain.
Be sure I looked up at her eyes
   Happy and proud; at last I knew
Porphyria worshipped me; surprise
   Made my heart swell, and still it grew
35   While I debated what to do.
That moment she was mine, mine, fair,
   Perfectly pure and good: I found
A thing to do, and all her hair
   In one long yellow string I wound
40   Three times her little throat around,
And strangled her. No pain felt she;
   I am quite sure she felt no pain.

As a shut bud that holds a bee,
    I warily oped her lids: again
45   Laughed the blue eyes without a stain.
And I untightened next the tress
    About her neck; her cheek once more
Blushed bright beneath my burning kiss:
    I propped her head up as before,
50   Only, this time my shoulder bore
Her head, which droops upon it still:
    The smiling rosy little head,
So glad it has its utmost will,
    That all it scorned at once is fled,
55   And I, its love, am gained instead!
Porphyria's love: she guessed not how
    Her darling one wish would be heard.
And thus we sit together now,
    And all night long we have not stirred,
60   And yet God has not said a word!

Arthur Hugh Clough (1819–1861)
The Latest Decalogue

Thou shalt have one God only; who
Would be at the expense of two?
No graven images may be
Worshipped, except the currency.
5 Swear not at all; for, for thy curse
Thine enemy is none the worse.
At church on Sunday to attend
Will serve to keep the world thy friend.
Honor thy parents; that is, all
10 From whom advancement may befall.
Thou shalt not kill; but need'st not strive
Officiously to keep alive.
Do not adultery commit;
Advantage rarely comes of it.
15 Thou shalt not steal; an empty feat,
When it's so lucrative to cheat.
Bear not false witness; let the lie
Have time on its own wings to fly.
Thou shalt not covet, but tradition
20 Approves all forms of competition.

Walt Whitman   (1819–1892)
From Song of Myself[1]

1

I celebrate myself, and sing myself,
And what I assume you shall assume,
For every atom belonging to me as good belongs to you.

I loafe and invite my soul,
5 I lean and loafe at my ease observing a spear of summer grass.

My tongue, every atom of my blood, form'd from this soil, this air,
Born here of parents born here from parents the same, and their parents the same,

I, now thirty-seven years old in perfect health begin,
Hoping to cease not till death.

10 Creeds and schools in abeyance,
Retiring back a while sufficed at what they are, but never forgotten,
I harbor for good or bad, I permit to speak at every hazard,
Nature without check with original energy.[2]

2

Houses and rooms are full of perfumes, the shelves are crowded with perfumes,
15 I breathe the fragrance myself and know it and like it,
The distillation would intoxicate me also, but I shall not let it.[3]

The atmosphere is not a perfume, it has no taste of the distillation, it is odorless,
It is for my mouth forever, I am in love with it,
I will go to the bank by the wood and become undisguised and naked,
20 I am mad for it to be in contact with me.
The smoke of my own breath,
Echoes, ripples, buzz'd whispers, love-root, silk-thread, crotch and vine,
My respiration and inspiration, the beating of my heart, the passing of blood and air
      through my lungs,
The sniff of green leaves and dry leaves, and of the shore and dark-color'd sea-rocks, and
      of hay in the barn,
25 The sound of the belch'd words of my voice loos'd to the eddies of the wind,
A few light kisses, a few embraces, a reaching around of arms,
The play of shine and shade on the trees as the supple boughs wag,
The delight alone or in the rush of the streets, or along the fields and hill-sides,
The feeling of health, the full-noon trill, the song of me rising from bed and meeting the
      sun.

30 Have you reckon'd a thousand acres much? Have you reckon'd the earth much?

---

[1] Whitman regards himself as the voice of the divine average in humanity as ll. 2–3 make clear. The phrase "O divine average!" is used in his poem "Starting from Paumanok."   [2] Ll. 10–13 are cardinal in Whitman's thought. As John Burroughs (1837-1921), American naturalist, friend to Whitman and author of *Whitman, A Study* (1896), was quick to see, these lines present his single theme: reliance on absolute nature.   [3] Whitman rejects the artificial in order to embrace nature. See ll. 32–35.

Have you practis'd so long to learn to read?
Have you felt so proud to get at the meaning of poems?
Stop this day and night with me and you shall possess the origin of all poems,[4]
You shall possess the good of the earth and sun, (there are millions of suns left.)
35 You shall no longer take things at second or third hand, nor look through the eyes of the
      dead, nor feed on the spectres in books,
You shall not look through my eyes either, nor take things from me,
You shall listen to all sides and filter them from your self.

    3

I have heard what the talkers were talking, the talk of the beginning and the end,
But I do not talk of the beginning or the end.

40 There was never any more inception than there is now,
Nor any more youth or age than there is now,
And will never be any more perfection than there is now,
Nor any more heaven or hell than there is now.

Urge and urge and urge,
45 Always the procreant urge of the world.
Out of the dimness opposite equals advance, always substance and increase, always sex,
Always a knit of identity, always distinction, always a breed of life.

To elaborate is no avail, learn'd and unlearn'd feel that it is so.

Sure as the most certain sure, plumb in the uprights, well entretied,[5] braced in the
      beams,
50 Stout as a horse, affectionate, haughty, electrical,
I and this mystery here we stand.

Clear and sweet is my soul, and clear and sweet is all that is not my soul.

Lack one lacks both, and the unseen is proved by the seen,
Till that becomes unseen and receives proof in its turn.

55 Showing the best and dividing it from the worst age vexes age,
Knowing the perfect fitness and equanimity of things, while they discuss I am silent, and
      go bathe and admire myself.

Welcome is every organ and attribute of me, and of any man hearty and clean,
Not an inch nor a particle of an inch is vile, and none shall be less familiar than the rest.

I am satisfied—I see, dance, laugh, sing;
60 As the hugging and loving bed-fellow sleeps at my side through the night, and withdraws
      at the peep of the day with stealthy tread,
Leaving the baskets cover'd with white towels swelling the house with their plenty,
Shall I postpone my acceptation and realization and scream at my eyes,
That they turn from gazing after and down the road,
And forthwith cipher and show me to a cent,
65 Exactly the value of one and exactly the value of two, and which is ahead?

---

[4] Because he insists on reading nature, not men's interpretation of nature. There is, of course, a
good deal of mysticism in Whitman's own interpretation of nature.   [5] A carpenter's vernacular
meaning "crossed-braced" as between two joists or walls.

Walt Whitman   (1819-1892)
A Noiseless Patient Spider

A noiseless patient spider,
I mark'd where on a little promontory it stood isolated,
Mark'd how to explore the vacant vast surrounding,
It launch'd forth filament, filament, filament, out of itself,
5 Ever unreeling them, ever tirelessly speeding them.

And you O my soul where you stand,
Surrounded, detached, in measureless oceans of space,
Ceaselessly musing, venturing, throwing, seeking the spheres to connect them,
Till the bridge you will need be form'd, till the ductile anchor hold,
10 Till the gossamer thread you fling catch somewhere, O my soul.

Matthew Arnold   (1822–1888)
Shakespeare

Others abide our question. Thou art free.
We ask and ask—Thou smilest and art still,
Out-topping knowledge. For the loftiest hill,
Who to the stars uncrowns his majesty,

5 Planting his steadfast footsteps in the sea,
Making the heaven of heavens his dwelling-place,
Spares but the cloudy border of his base
To the foil'd searching of mortality;

And thou, who didst the stars and sunbeams know,
10 Self-school'd, self-scann'd, self-honour'd, self-secure,
Didst tread on earth unguess'd at.—Better so!

All pains the immortal spirit must endure,
All weakness which impairs, all griefs which bow,
Find their sole speech in that victorious brow.

Matthew Arnold   (1822–1888)
Dover Beach

The sea is calm tonight,
The tide is full, the moon lies fair
Upon the straits;—on the French coast, the light
Gleams and is gone; the cliffs of England stand,
5 Glimmering and vast, out in the tranquil bay.
Come to the window, sweet is the night air!
Only, from the long line of spray
Where the sea meets the moon-blanch'd land,
Listen! you hear the grating roar
10 Of pebbles which the waves draw back, and fling,
At their return, up the high strand,
Begin, and cease, and then again begin,
With tremulous cadence slow, and bring
The eternal note of sadness in.

15 Sophocles long ago
Heard it on the Aegean, and it brought
Into his mind the turbid ebb and flow
Of human misery; we
Find also in the sound a thought,
20 Hearing it by this distant northern sea.

The Sea of Faith
Was once, too, at the full, and round earth's shore
Lay like the folds of a bright girdle furl'd.
But now I only hear
25 Its melancholy, long, withdrawing roar,
Retreating, to the breath
Of the night-wind, down the vast edges drear
And naked shingles[1] of the world.

Ah, love, let us be true
30 To one another! for the world, which seems
To lie before us like a land of dreams,
So various, so beautiful, so new,
Hath really neither joy, nor love, nor light,
Nor certitude, nor peace, nor help for pain;
35 And we are here as on a darkling plain
Swept with confused alarms of struggle and flight,
Where ignorant armies clash by night.

[1] Pebbled beaches.

Anthony Hecht   (1922–   )
The Dover Bitch

A Criticism of Life (For Andrews Wanning)

So there stood Matthew Arnold and this girl
With the cliffs of England crumbling away behind them,
And he said to her,"Try to be true to me,
And I'll do the same for you, for things are bad
5 All over, etc., etc."
Well now, I knew this girl. It's true she had read
Sophocles in a fairly good translation
And caught that bitter allusion to the sea,
But all the time he was talking she had in mind
10 The notion of what his whiskers would feel like
On the back of her neck. She told me later on
That after a while she got to looking out
At the lights across the channel, and really felt sad,
Thinking of all the wine and enormous beds
15 And blandishments in French and the perfumes.
And then she got really angry. To have been brought
All the way down from London, and then be addressed
As a sort of mournful cosmic last resort
Is really tough on a girl, and she was pretty.
20 Anyway, she watched him pace the room
And finger his watch-chain and seem to sweat a bit,
And then she said one or two unprintable things.
But you mustn't judge her by that. What I mean to say is,
She's really all right. I still see her once in a while
25 And she always treats me right. We have a drink
And I give her a good time, and perhaps it's a year
Before I see her again, but there she is,
Running to fat, but dependable as they come.
And sometimes I bring her a bottle of *Nuit d'Amour.*[1]

[1] Night of Love, a perfume.

George Meredith (1828–1909)
Tragic Memory

In our old shipwrecked days there was an hour,
When in the firelight steadily aglow,
Joined slackly, we beheld the red chasm grow
Among the clicking coals. Our library-bower
5 That eve was left to us: and hushed we sat
As lovers to whom Time is whispering.
From sudden-opened doors we heard them sing:
The nodding elders mixed good wine with chat.
Well knew we that Life's greatest treasure lay
10 With us, and of it was our talk. "Ah, yes!
Love dies!" I said: I never thought it less.
She yearned to me that sentence to unsay.
Then when the fire domed blackening, I found
Her cheek was salt against my kiss, and swift
15 Up the sharp scale of sobs her breast did lift:—
Now am I haunted by that taste! that sound!

Emily Dickinson (1830–1886)
The Soul Selects Her Own Society

The Soul selects her own Society—
Then—shuts the Door—
To her divine Majority—
Present no more—

5 Unmoved—she notes the Chariots—pausing—
At her low Gate—
Unmoved—an Emperor be kneeling
Upon her Mat—

I've known her—from an ample nation—
10 Choose One—
Then—close the Valves of her attention—
Like Stone—

Emily Dickinson   (1830–1886)
Some Keep the Sabbath Going to Church

Some keep the Sabbath going to Church—
I keep it, staying at Home—
With a Bobolink for a Chorister—
And an Orchard, for a Dome—

5 Some keep the Sabbath in Surplice—
I just wear my Wings—
And instead of tolling the Bell, for Church,
Our little Sexton—sings.

God preaches, a noted Clergyman—
10 And the sermon is never long,
So instead of getting to Heaven, at last—
I'm going, all along.

Emily Dickinson   (1830–1886)
I Died for Beauty

I died for Beauty—but was scarce
Adjusted in the Tomb
When One who died for Truth, was lain
In an adjoining Room—

5 He questioned softly "Why I failed"?
"For Beauty", I replied—
"And I—for Truth—Themself are One—
We Bretheren, are", He said—

And so, as Kinsmen, met a Night—
10 We talked between the Rooms—
Until the Moss had reached our lips—
And covered up—our names—

Emily Dickinson   (1830–1886)
I Had Been Hungry, All the Years

I had been hungry, all the Years—
My Noon had Come—to dine—
I trembling drew the Table near—
And touched the Curious Wine—

5   'Twas this on Tables I had seen—
When turning, hungry, Home
I looked in Windows, for the Wealth
I could not hope—for Mine—

I did not know the ample Bread—
10   'Twas so unlike the Crumb
The Birds and I, had often shared
In Nature's—Dining Room—

The Plenty hurt me—'twas so new—
Myself felt ill—and odd—
15   As Berry—of a Mountain Bush—
Transplanted—to the Road—

Nor was I hungry—so I found
That Hunger—was a way
Of Persons outside Windows—
20   The Entering—takes away—

Emily Dickinson   (1830–1886)
He Preached upon "Breadth"

He preached upon "Breadth" till it argued him narrow—
The Broad are too broad to define
And of "Truth" until it proclaimed him a Liar—
The Truth never flaunted a Sign—

5   Simplicity fled from his counterfeit presence
As Gold the Pyrites would shun—
What confusion would cover the innocent Jesus
To meet so enabled a Man!

Emily Dickinson (1830–1886)
My Life Closed Twice Before Its Close

My life closed twice before its close;
It yet remains to see
If Immortality unveil
A third event to me,

5 So huge, so hopeless to conceive
As these that twice befel.
Parting is all we know of heaven,
And all we need of hell.

Emily Dickinson (1830–1886)
Success Is Counted Sweetest

Success is counted sweetest
By those who ne'er succeed.
To comprehend a nectar
Requires sorest need.

5 Not one of all the purple Host.
Who took the Flag today
Can tell the definition
So clear of Victory

As he defeated—dying—
10 On whose forbidden ear
The distant strains of triumph
Burst agonized and clear!

Emily Dickinson   (1830–1886)
These Are the Days When Birds Come Back

These are the days when Birds come back—
A very few—a Bird or two—
To take a backward look.

These are the days when skies resume
5 The old—old sophistries of June—
A blue and gold mistake.

Oh fraud that cannot cheat the Bee—
Almost thy plausibility
Induces my belief.

10 Till ranks of seeds their witness bear—
And softly thro' the altered air
Hurries a timid leaf.

Oh Sacrament of summer days,
Oh Last Communion in the Haze—
15 Permit a child to join.

Thy sacred emblems to partake—
Thy consecrated bread to take
And thine immortal wine!

Emily Dickinson   (1830–1886)
Much Madness Is Divinest Sense

Much Madness is divinest Sense—
To a discerning Eye—
Much Sense—the starkest Madness—
'Tis the Majority
5 In this, as All, prevail—
Assent—and you are sane—
Demur—you're straightway dangerous—
And handled with a Chain—

Emily Dickinson   (1830–1886)
This World Is Not Conclusion

This World is not Conclusion.
A Species stands beyond—
Invisible, as Music—
But positive, as Sound—
5   It beckons, and it baffles—
Philosophy—don't know—
And through a Riddle, at the last—
Sagacity, must go—
To guess it, puzzles scholars—
10 To gain it, Men have borne
Contempt of Generations
And Crucifixion, shown—
Faith slips—and laughs, and rallies—
Blushes, if any see—
15 Plucks at a twig of Evidence—
And asks a Vane, the way—
Much Gesture, from the Pulpit—
Strong Hallelujahs roll—
Narcotics cannot still the Tooth
20 That nibbles at the soul—

Emily Dickinson   (1830–1886)
I Could Not Prove the Years Had Feet

I could not prove the Years had feet—
Yet confident they run
Am I, from symptoms that are past
And Series that are done—
5   I find my feet have further Goals—
I smile upon the Aims
That felt so ample—Yesterday—
Today's—have vaster claims—

I do not doubt the self I was
10 Was competent to me—
But something awkward in the fit—
Proves that—outgrown—I see—

Emily Dickinson   (1830–1886)
This Is My Letter to the World

This is my letter to the World
That never wrote to Me—
The simple News that Nature told—
With tender Majesty

5 Her Message is committed
To Hands I cannot see—
For love of Her—Sweet—countrymen—
Judge tenderly—of Me

Lewis Carroll   (1832–1898)
Jabberwocky[1]

'Twas brillig, and the slithy toves
    Did gyre and gimble in the wabe;
All mimsy were the borogoves,
    And the mome raths outgrabe.

5 "Beware the Jabberwock, my son!
    The jaws that bite, the claws that catch!
Beware the Jubjub bird, and shun
    The frumious Bandersnatch!"

---

[1] Lewis Carroll: "Humpty-Dumpty's theory, of two meanings packed into one word like a portmanteau, seems to me the right explanation for all. For instance, take the two words 'fuming' and 'furious.' Make up your mind that you will say both words, but leave it unsettled which you will say first. . . . If you have that rarest of gifts, a perfectly balanced mind, you will say 'frumious.' "

He took his vorpal sword in hand:
10   Long time the manxome foe he sought—
So rested he by the Tumtum tree,
        And stood awhile in thought.

And as in uffish thought he stood,
    The Jabberwock, with eyes of flame,
15 Came whiffling through the tulgey wood,
        And burbled as it came!

One, two! One, two! And through and through
    The vorpal blade went snicker-snack!
He left it dead, and with its head
20   He went galumphing back.

"And hast thou slain the Jabberwock?
    Come to my arms, my beamish boy!
O frabjous day! Callooh! Callay!"
        He chortled in his joy.

25 'Twas brillig, and the slithy toves
    Did gyre and gimble in the wabe;
All mimsy were the borogoves,
        And the mome raths outgrabe.

Thomas Hardy   (1840–1928)
Neutral Tones

We stood by a pond that winter day,
And the sun was white, as though chidden of God,
And a few leaves lay on the starving sod;
    —They had fallen from an ash, and were gray.

5 Your eyes on me were as eyes that rove
Over tedious riddles of years ago;
And some words played between us to and fro
    On which lost the more by our love.

The smile on your mouth was the deadest thing
10 Alive enough to have strength to die;
And a grin of bitterness swept thereby
    Like an ominous bird a-wing. . . .

Since then, keen lessons that love deceives,
And wrings with wrong, have shaped to me
15 Your face, and the God-curst sun, and a tree,
    And a pond edged with grayish leaves.

Thomas Hardy   (1840–1928)
The Convergence of the Twain

Lines on the Loss of the "Titanic"[1]

1

In a solitude of the sea
Deep from human vanity,
And the Pride of Life that planned her, stilly couches she.

2

Steel chambers, late the pyres
5   Of her salamandrine fires,
Cold currents thrid, and turn to rhythmic tidal lyres.

3

Over the mirrors meant
To glass the opulent
The sea-worm crawls—grotesque, slimed, dumb, indifferent.

4

10   Jewels in joy designed
To ravish the sensuous mind
Lie lightless, all their sparkles bleared and black and blind.

5

Dim moon-eyed fishes near
Gaze at the gilded gear
15 And query: 'What does this vaingloriousness down here?'. . .

6

Well: while was fashioning
This creature of cleaving wing,
The Immanent Will that stirs and urges everything

7

Prepared a sinister mate
20   For her—so gaily great—
A Shape of Ice, for the time far and dissociate.

8

And as the smart ship grew
In stature, grace, and hue,
In shadowy silent distance grew the Iceberg too.

[1]On April 15, 1912, the *Titanic* struck an iceberg and sank, with great loss of life, on her
maiden voyage.

9

25 Alien they seemed to be:
    No mortal eye could see
The intimate welding of their later history.

10

Or sign that they were bent
By paths coincident
30 On being anon twin halves of one august event,

11

Till the Spinner of the Years
Said 'Now!' And each one hears,
And consummation comes, and jars two hemispheres.

Gerard Manley Hopkins   (1844–1889)
God's Grandeur

The world is charged with the grandeur of God.
    It will flame out, like shining from shook foil;
    It gathers to a greatness, like the ooze of oil
Crushed. Why do men then now not reck his rod?
5 Generations have trod, have trod, have trod;
    And all is seared with trade; bleared, smeared with toil;
    And wears man's smudge and shares man's smell: the soil
Is bare now, nor can foot feel, being shod.

And for all this, nature is never spent;
10   There lives the dearest freshness deep down things;
And though the last lights off the black West went
    Oh, morning, at the brown brink eastward, springs—
Because the Holy Ghost over the bent
    World broods with warm breast and with ah! bright wings.

Gerard Manley Hopkins (1844–1889)
Pied Beauty[1]

Glory be to God for dappled things—
    For skies of couple-colour as a brinded[2] cow;
        For rose-moles all in stipple upon trout that swim;
Fresh-firecoal chestnut-falls;[3] finches' wings;
5   Landscape plotted and pieced—fold, fallow and plough;
        And áll trádes, their gear and tackle and trim.
All things counter, original, spare, strange;
    Whatever is fickle, freckled (who knows how?)
        With swift, slow; sweet, sour; adazzle, dim;
10 He fathers-forth whose beauty is past change:
                Praise him.

A. E. Housman (1859–1936)
To an Athlete Dying Young

The time you won your town the race
We chaired you through the market-place;
Man and boy stood cheering by,
And home we brought you shoulder-high.

5 Today, the road all runners come,
Shoulder-high we bring you home,
And set you at your threshold down,
Townsman of a stiller town.

Smart lad, to slip betimes away
10 From fields where glory does not stay
And early though the laurel grows
It withers quicker than the rose.

Eyes the shady night has shut
Cannot see the record cut,
15 And silence sounds no worse than cheers
After earth has stopped the ears:

[1] Parti-colored beauty.   [2] Spotted, flecked, or streaked.   [3] Fallen chestnuts compared to burning coals.

Now you will not swell the rout
Of lads that wore their honors out,
Runners whom renown outran
20 And the name died before the man.

So set, before its echoes fade,
The fleet foot on the sill of shade,
And hold to the low lintel up
The still-defended challenge-cup.

25 And round that early-laureled head
Will flock to gaze the strengthless dead,
And find unwithered on its curls
The garland briefer than a girl's.

William Butler Yeats   (1865–1939)
The Wild Swans at Coole

The trees in their autumn beauty,
The woodland paths are dry,
Under the October twilight the water
Mirrors a still sky;
5 Upon the brimming water among the stones
Are nine-and-fifty swans.

The nineteenth autumn has come upon me
Since I first made my count;
I saw, before I had well finished,
10 All suddenly mount
And scatter wheeling in great broken rings
Upon their clamorous wings.

I have looked upon those brilliant creatures,
And now my heart is sore.
15 All's changed since I, hearing at twilight,
The first time on this shore,
The bell-beat of their wings above my head,
Trod with a lighter tread.

Unwearied still, lover by lover,
20 They paddle in the cold
Companionable streams or climb the air;
Their hearts have not grown old;

Passion or conquest, wander where they will,
Attend upon them still.

25 But now they drift on the still water,
Mysterious, beautiful;
Among what rushes will they build,
By what lake's edge or pool
Delight men's eyes when I awake some day
30 To find they have flown away?

William Butler Yeats (1865–1939)
The Second Coming

Turning and turning in the widening gyre[1]
The falcon cannot hear the falconer;
Things fall apart; the centre cannot hold;
Mere anarchy is loosed upon the world,
5 The blood-dimmed tide is loosed, and everywhere
The ceremony of innocence is drowned;
The best lack all conviction, while the worst
Are full of passionate intensity.

Surely some revelation is at hand;
10 Surely the Second Coming[2] is at hand.
The Second Coming! Hardly are those words out
When a vast image out of *Spiritus Mundi*[3]
Troubles my sight: somewhere in sands of the desert
A shape with lion body and the head of a man,
15 A gaze blank and pitiless as the sun,
Is moving its slow thighs, while all about it
Reel shadows of the indignant desert birds.
The darkness drops again; but now I know
That twenty centuries of stony sleep
20 Were vexed to nightmare by a rocking cradle,
And what rough beast, its hour come round at last,
Slouches towards Bethlehem to be born?

[1] Circular or spiral movement.   [2] Related to the second coming of Christ is Yeats's conviction that the approaching end of a historical cycle of 2000 years would bring a new age.   [3] Literally, world spirit. For Yeats it means the "general mind," or our collective consciousness.

William Butler Yeats   (1865–1939)
Sailing to Byzantium

I

That is no country for old men. The young
In one another's arms, birds in the trees
—Those dying generations—at their song,
The salmon-falls, the mackerel-crowded seas,
5 Fish, flesh, or fowl, commend all summer long
Whatever is begotten, born, and dies.
Caught in that sensual music all neglect
Monuments of unageing intellect.

II

An aged man is but a paltry thing,
10 A tattered coat upon a stick, unless
Soul clap its hands and sing, and louder sing
For every tatter in its mortal dress,
Nor is there singing school but studying
Monuments of its own magnificence;
15 And therefore I have sailed the seas and come
To the holy city of Byzantium.

III

O sages standing in God's holy fire
As in the gold mosaic of a wall,
Come from the holy fire, perne in a gyre,[1]
20 And be the singing-masters of my soul.
Consume my heart away; sick with desire
And fastened to a dying animal
It knows not what it is; and gather me
Into the artifice of eternity.

IV

25 Once out of nature I shall never take
My bodily form from any natural thing,
But such a form as Grecian goldsmiths make
Of hammered gold and gold enamelling
To keep a drowsy Emperor awake;
30 Or set upon a golden bough to sing
To lords and ladies of Byzantium
Of what is past, or passing, or to come.

---

[1] Circular or spiral movement (see "The Second Coming," l. 1).

Edwin Arlington Robinson   (1869–1935)
Mr. Flood's Party

Old Eben Flood,[1] climbing alone one night
Over the hill between the town below
And the forsaken upland hermitage
That held as much as he should ever know
5 On earth again of home, paused warily.
The road was his with not a native near;
And Eben, having leisure, said aloud,
For no man else in Tilbury Town[2] to hear:
"Well, Mr. Flood, we have the harvest moon
10 Again, and we may not have many more;
The bird is on the wing, the poet says,
And you and I have said it here before.
Drink to the bird." He raised up to the light
The jug that he had gone so far to fill,
15 And answered huskily; "Well, Mr. Flood,
Since you propose it, I believe I will."

Alone, as if enduring to the end
A valiant armor of scarred hopes outworn,
He stood there in the middle of the road
20 Like Roland's ghost winding a silent horn.[3]
Below him, in the town among the trees,
Where friends of other days had honored him,
A phantom salutation of the dead
Rang thinly till old Eben's eyes were dim.

25 Then, as a mother lays her sleeping child
Down tenderly, fearing it may awake,
He set the jug down slowly at his feet
With trembling care, knowing that most things break;
And only when assured that on firm earth
30 It stood, as the uncertain lives of men
Assuredly did not, he paced away,
And with his hand extended paused again:

"Well, Mr. Flood, we have not met like this
In a long time; and many a change has come
35 To both of us, I fear, since last it was
We had a drop together. Welcome home!"
Convivially returning with himself,
Again he raised the jug up to the light;

---

[1] Ebb and flood, the passing of time.   [2] Though this happens to be Robinson's name for Gardiner, Maine, where he was reared, the name is of no consequence.   [3] Hero of the tales in the Charlemagne cycle; the defender of the Christians against the Saracens. The implication in ll. 19–20 is that Eben, like Roland, sounds his horn only to find his friends dead.

And with an acquiescent quaver said:
40 "Well, Mr. Flood, if you insist, I might.

"Only a very little, Mr. Flood—
For auld lang syne. No more, sir; that will do."
So, for the time, apparently it did,
And Eben evidently thought so too;
45 For soon amid the silver loneliness
Of night he lifted up his voice and sang,
Secure, with only two moons listening
Until the whole harmonious landscape rang—

"For auld lang syne." The weary throat gave out,
50 The last word wavered, and the song was done.
He raised again the jug regretfully
And shook his head, and was again alone.
There was not much that was ahead of him,
And there was nothing in the town below—
55 Where strangers would have shut the many doors
That many friends had opened long ago.

Edwin Arlington Robinson (1869–1935)
The Mill

The miller's wife had waited long,
     The tea was cold, the fire was dead;
And there might yet be nothing wrong
     In how he went and what he said:
5 "There are no millers any more,"
     Was all that she had heard him say;
And he had lingered at the door
     So long that it seemed yesterday.

Sick with a fear that had no form
10   She knew that she was there at last;
And in the mill there was a warm
     And mealy fragrance of the past.
What else there was would only seem
     To say again what he had meant;
15 And what was hanging from a beam
     Would not have heeded where she went.

And if she thought it followed her,
     She may have reasoned in the dark

That one way of the few there were
20   Would hide her and would leave no mark:
Black water, smooth above the weir
     Like starry velvet in the night,
Though ruffled once, would soon appear
     The same as ever to the sight.

Ralph Hodgson   (1871–1962)
Eve

Eve, with her basket, was
Deep in the bells and grass,
Wading in bells and grass
Up to the knees,
5 Picking a dish of sweet
Berries and plums to eat,
Down in the bells and grass
Under the trees.

Mute as a mouse in a
10 Corner the cobra lay,
Curled round a bough of the
Cinnamon tall. . . .
Now to get even and
Humble proud Heaven and
15 Now was the moment or
Never at all.

'Eva!' Each syllable
Light as a flower fell,
'Eva!' he whispered the
20 Wondering maid,
Soft as a bubble sung
Out of a linnet's lung,
Soft and most silverly
'Eva!' he said.

25 Picture that orchard sprite,
Eve, with her body white,
Supple and smooth to her
Slim finger tips,
Wondering, listening,

30 Listening, wondering,
    Eve with a berry
    Half-way to her lips.

    Oh had our simple Eve
    Seen through the make-believe!
35 Had she but known the
    Pretender he was!
    Out of the boughs he came,
    Whispering still her name,
    Tumbling in twenty rings
40 Into the grass.

    Here was the strangest pair
    In the world anywhere,
    Eve in the bells and grass
    Kneeling, and he
45 Telling his story low. . . .
    Singing birds saw them go
    Down the dark path to
    The Blasphemous Tree.

    Oh what a clatter when
50 Titmouse and Jenny Wren
    Saw him successful and
    Taking his leave!
    How the birds rated him,
    How they all hated him!
55 How they all pitied
    Poor motherless Eve!

    Picture her crying
    Outside in the lane,
    Eve, with no dish of sweet
60 Berries and plums to eat,
    Haunting the gate of the
    Orchard in vain. . . .
    Picture the lewd delight
    Under the hill to-night—
65 'Eva!' the toast goes round,
    'Eva!' again.

Ted Hughes (1930–   )
Theology

No, the serpent did not
Seduce Eve to the apple.
All that's simply
Corruption of the facts.

5 Adam ate the apple.
Eve ate Adam.
The serpent ate Eve.
This is the dark intestine.

The serpent, meanwhile,
10 Sleeps his meal off in Paradise—
Smiling to hear
God's querulous calling.

Robert Frost (1874–1963)
The Strong Are Saying Nothing

The soil now gets a rumpling soft and damp,
And small regard to the future of any weed.
The final flat of the hoe's approval stamp
Is reserved for the bed of a few selected seed.

5 There is seldom more than a man to a harrowed piece.
Men work alone, their lots plowed far apart,
One stringing a chain of seed in an open crease,
And another stumbling after a halting cart.

To the fresh and black of the squares of early mold
10 The leafless bloom of a plum is fresh and white;
Though there's more than a doubt if the weather is not too cold
For the bees to come and serve its beauty aright.

Wind goes from farm to farm in wave on wave,
But carries no cry of what is hoped to be.
15 There may be little or much beyond the grave,
But the strong are saying nothing until they see.

Robert Frost (1874–1963)
Acquainted with the Night

I have been one acquainted with the night.
I have walked out in rain—and back in rain.
I have outwalked the furthest city light.

I have looked down the saddest city lane.
5 I have passed by the watchman on his beat
And dropped my eyes, unwilling to explain.

I have stood still and stopped the sound of feet
When far away an interrupted cry
Came over houses from another street,

10 But not to call me back or say good-by;
And further still at an unearthly height
One luminary clock against the sky

Proclaimed the time was neither wrong nor right.
I have been one acquainted with the night.

Robert Frost (1874–1963)
Nothing Gold Can Stay

Nature's first green is gold,
Her hardest hue to hold.
Her early leaf's a flower;
But only so an hour.
5 Then leaf subsides to leaf.
So Eden sank to grief,
So dawn goes down to day.
Nothing gold can stay.

Wallace Stevens   (1879–1955)
Peter Quince[1] at the Clavier

I

Just as my fingers on these keys
Make music, so the selfsame sounds
On my spirit make a music, too.

Music is feeling, then, not sound;
5 And thus it is that what I feel,
Here in this room, desiring you,

Thinking of your blue-shadowed silk,
Is music. It is like the strain
Waked in the elders by Susanna.[2]

10 Of a green evening, clear and warm,
She bathed in her still garden, while
The red-eyed elders watching, felt

The basses of their beings throb
In witching chords, and their thin blood[3]
15 Pulse pizzicati[4] of Hosanna.

II

In the green water, clear and warm,
Susanna lay.
She searched
The touch of springs,
20 And found
Concealed imaginings.
She sighed,
For so much melody.

Upon the bank, she stood
25 In the cool
Of spent emotions.
She felt, among the leaves,
The dew
Of old devotions.

30 She walked upon the grass,
Still quavering.
The winds were like her maids,
On timid feet,

[1] Carpenter and poet of sorts in Shakespeare's *A Midsummer Night's Dream*.   [2] The story of Susanna and the Elders is conveniently found in *The Bible Designed to Be Read as Living Literature,* New York: Simon and Schuster, 1936, pp. 858–862. As a part of the Apocrypha the story is rarely included in Protestant Bibles.   [3] A reference to the advanced age of the Elders.   [4] Creating sound by plucking instead of bowing the instrument.

Fetching her woven scarves,
35 Yet wavering.

A breath upon her hand
Muted the night.
She turned—
A cymbal crashed,
40 And roaring horns.

III

Soon, with a noise like tambourines,
Came her attendant Byzantines.

They wondered why Susanna cried
Against the elders by her side;

45 And as they whispered, the refrain
Was like a willow swept by rain.

Anon, their lamps' uplifted flame
Revealed Susanna and her shame.

And then, the simpering Byzantines
50 Fled, with a noise like tambourines.

IV

Beauty is momentary in the mind—[5]
The fitful tracing of a portal;
But in the flesh it is immortal.
The body dies; the body's beauty lives.
55 So evenings die, in their green going,
A wave, interminably flowing.
So gardens die, their meek breath scenting
The cowl of winter, done repenting.
So maidens die, to the auroral
60 Celebration of a maiden's choral.
Susanna's music touched the bawdy strings
Of those white elders; but, escaping,
Left only Death's ironic scraping.
Now, in its immortality, it plays
65 On the clear viol of her memory,
And makes a constant sacrament of praise.

[5] Ll. 51–58: Stevens's theory of beauty. See his "Sunday Morning," l. 63: "Death is the mother of beauty"(p. 574).

Wallace Stevens   (1879–1955)
Disillusionment of Ten O'Clock

The houses are haunted
By white night-gowns.
None are green,
Or purple with green rings,
5 Or green with yellow rings,
Or yellow with blue rings.
None of them are strange,
With socks of lace
And beaded ceintures.
10 People are not going
To dream of baboons and periwinkles.
Only, here and there, an old sailor,
Drunk and asleep in his boots,
Catches tigers
15 In red weather.

Wallace Stevens   (1879–1955)
The Snow Man

One must have a mind of winter
To regard the frost and the boughs
Of the pine-trees crusted with snow;

And have been cold a long time
5 To behold the junipers shagged with ice,
The spruces rough in the distant glitter

Of the January sun; and not to think
Of any misery in the sound of the wind,
In the sound of a few leaves,

10 Which is the sound of the land
Full of the same wind
That is blowing in the same bare place

For the listener, who listens in the snow,
And, nothing himself, beholds
15 Nothing that is not there and the nothing that is.

William Carlos Williams (1883–1963)
Tract

I will teach you my townspeople
how to perform a funeral
for you have it over a troop
of artists—
5 unless one should scour the world—
you have the ground sense necessary.

See! the hearse leads.
I begin with a design for a hearse.
For Christ's sake not black—
10 nor white either—and not polished!
Let it be weathered—like a farm wagon—
with gilt wheels (this could be
applied fresh at small expense)
or no wheels at all:
15 a rough dray to drag over the ground.

Knock the glass out!
My God—glass, my townspeople!
For what purpose? Is it for the dead
to look out or for us to see
20 how well he is housed or to see
the flowers or the lack of them—
or what?
To keep the rain and snow from him?
He will have a heavier rain soon:
25 pebbles and dirt and what not.
Let there be no glass—
and no upholstery, phew!
and no little brass rollers
and small easy wheels on the bottom—
30 my townspeople what are you thinking of?

A rough plain hearse then
with gilt wheels and no top at all.
On this the coffin lies
by its own weight.
35   No wreaths please—
especially no hot house flowers.
Some common memento is better,
something he prized and is known by:
his old clothes—a few books perhaps—
40 God knows what! You realize
how we are about these things
my townspeople—
something will be found—anything
even flowers if he had come to that.

45 So much for the hearse.
   For heaven's sake though see to the driver!
   Take off the silk hat! In fact
   that's no place at all for him—
   up there unceremoniously
50 dragging our friend out to his own dignity!
   Bring him down—bring him down!
   Low and inconspicuous! I'd not have him ride
   on the wagon at all—damn him—
   the undertaker's understrapper!
55 Let him hold the reins
   and walk at the side
   and inconspicuously too!

   Then briefly as to yourselves:
   Walk behind—as they do in France,
60 seventh class, or if you ride
   Hell take curtains! Go with some show
   of inconvenience; sit openly—
   to the weather as to grief.
   Or do you think you can shut grief in?
65 What—from us? We who have perhaps
   nothing to lose? Share with us
   share with us—it will be money
   in your pockets.
                    Go now
70 I think you are ready.

William Carlos Williams   (1883–1963)
Portrait of a Lady

Your thighs are appletrees
whose blossoms touch the sky.
Which sky? The sky
where Watteau[1] hung a lady's
5 slipper. Your knees
are a southern breeze—or
a gust of snow. Agh! what
sort of man was Fragonard?[2]
—as if that answered

[1] Jean Antoine Watteau (1684–1721), French painter best known for idealized pastoral scenes.
[2] Jean Honoré Fragonard (1732–1806), French court painter and engraver.

10 anything. Ah, yes—below
    the knees, since the tune
    drops that way, it is
    one of those white summer days,
    the tall grass of your ankles
15 flickers upon the shore—
    Which shore?—
    the sand clings to my lips—
    Which shore?
    Agh, petals maybe. How
20 should I know?
    Which shore? Which shore?
    I said petals from an appletree.

D. H. Lawrence   (1885–1930)
Piano

Softly, in the dusk, a woman is singing to me;
Taking me back down the vista of years, till I see
A child sitting under the piano, in the boom of the tingling strings
And pressing the small, poised feet of a mother who smiles as she sings.

5 In spite of myself the insidious mastery of song
Betrays me back, till the heart of me weeps to belong
To the old Sunday evenings at home, with winter outside
And hymns in the cozy parlor, the tinkling piano our guide.

So now it is vain for the singer to burst into clamor
10 With the great black piano appassionato. The glamor
Of childish days is upon me, my manhood is cast
Down in the flood of remembrance, I weep like a child for the past.

D. H. Lawrence   (1885–1930)
Snake

A snake came to my water-trough
On a hot, hot day, and I in pyjamas for the heat,
To drink there.

In the deep, strange-scented shade of the great dark carob-tree
5   I came down the steps with my pitcher
And must wait, must stand and wait, for there he was at the trough before me.

He reached down from a fissure in the earth-wall in the gloom
And trailed his yellow-brown slackness soft-bellied down, over the edge of the stone
        trough
And rested his throat upon the stone bottom,
10   And where the water had dripped from the tap, in a small clearness,
He sipped with his straight mouth,
Softly drank through his straight gums, into his slack long body,
Silently.

Someone was before me at my water-trough,
15   And I, like a second comer, waiting.

He lifted his head from his drinking, as cattle do,
And looked at me vaguely, as drinking cattle do,
And flickered his two-forked tongue from his lips, and mused a moment,
And stooped and drank a little more,
20   Being earth-brown, earth-golden from the burning bowels of the earth
On the day of Sicilian July, with Etna smoking.

The voice of my education said to me
He must be killed,
For in Sicily the black, black snakes are innocent, the gold are venomous.

25   And voices in me said, If you were a man
You would take a stick and break him now, and finish him off.

But must I confess how I liked him,
How glad I was he had come like a guest in quiet, to drink at my water-trough
And depart peaceful, pacified, and thankless,
30   Into the burning bowels of this earth?

Was it cowardice, that I dared not kill him?
Was it perversity, that I longed to talk to him?
Was it humility, to feel so honoured?
I felt so honoured.

35   And yet those voices:
If you were not afraid, you would kill him!

And truly I was afraid, I was most afraid,
But even so, honoured still more

That he should seek my hospitality
40 From out the dark door of the secret earth.

He drank enough
And lifted his head, dreamily, as one who has drunken,
And flickered his tongue like a forked night on the air, so black,
Seeming to lick his lips,
45 And looked around like a god, unseeing, into the air,
And slowly turned his head,
And slowly, very slowly, as if thrice adream,
Proceeded to draw his slow length curving round
And climb again the broken bank of my wall-face.
50 And as he put his head into that dreadful hole,
And as he slowly drew up, snake-easing his shoulders, and entered farther,
A sort of horror, a sort of protest against his withdrawing into that horrid black hole,
Deliberately going into the blackness, and slowly drawing himself after,
Overcame me now his back was turned.

55 I looked round, I put down my pitcher,
I picked up a clumsy log
And threw it at the water-trough with a clatter.

I think it did not hit him,
But suddenly that part of him that was left behind convulsed in undignified haste,
60 Writhed like lightning, and was gone
Into the black hole, the earth-lipped fissure in the wall-front,
At which, in the intense still noon, I stared with fascination.

And immediately I regretted it.
I thought how paltry, how vulgar, what a mean act!
65 I despised myself and the voices of my accursed human education.

And I thought of the albatross,
And I wished he would come back, my snake.

For he seemed to me again like a king,
Like a king in exile, uncrowned in the underworld,
70 Now due to be crowned again.

And so, I missed my chance with one of the lords
Of life.
And I have something to expiate;
A pettiness.

Robinson Jeffers   (1887–1962)
Science

Man, introverted man, having crossed
In passage and but a little with the nature of things this latter century
Has begot giants; but being taken up
Like a maniac with self-love and inward conflicts cannot manage his hybrids.
5 Being used to deal with edgeless dreams,
Now he's bred knives on nature turns them also inward: they have thirsty points though.
His mind forebodes his own destruction;
Actaeon[1] who saw the goddess naked among leaves and his hounds tore him.
A little knowledge, a pebble from the shingle,[2]
10 A drop from the oceans: who would have dreamed this infinitely little too much?

Robinson Jeffers   (1887–1962)
The Bloody Sire

It is not bad. Let them play.
Let the guns bark and the bombing-plane
Speak his prodigious blasphemies.
It is not bad, it is high time,
5 Stark violence is still the sire of all the world's values.

What but the wolf's tooth whittled so fine
The fleet limbs of the antelope?
What but fear winged the birds, and hunger
Jeweled with such eyes the great goshawk's head?
10 Violence has been the sire of all the world's values.

Who would remember Helen's[1] face
Lacking the terrible halo of spears?
Who formed Christ but Herod[2] and Caesar,

[1] Having seen Diana bathing while he was hunting, Actaeon was changed by her into a stag and his hounds tore him.   [2] Seashore.
[1] Helen of Troy, whose elopement with Paris brought about the siege and destruction of Troy.
[2] Herod the Great (73?–4 B.C.), who destroyed the babes of Bethlehem (Matthew 2:16).

The cruel and bloody victories of Caesar?
15 Violence, the bloody sire of all the world's values.

Never weep, let them play,
Old violence is not too old to beget new values.

Marianne Moore   (1887–1972)
Poetry

I, too, dislike it: there are things that are important beyond all this fiddle.
　　Reading it, however, with a perfect contempt for it, one discovers in
　　it after all, a place for the genuine.
　　　　Hands that can grasp, eyes
5　　　　that can dilate, hair that can rise
　　　　　　if it must, these things are important not because a

high-sounding interpretation can be put upon them but because they are
　　useful. When they become so derivative as to become unintelligible,
　　the same thing may be said for all of us, that we
10　　　　do not admire what
　　　　we cannot understand: the bat
　　　　　　holding on upside down or in quest of something to

eat, elephants pushing, a wild horse taking a roll, a tireless wolf under
　　a tree, the immovable critic twitching his skin like a horse that
　　　　feels a flea, the base-
15　ball fan, the statistician—
　　　　nor is it valid
　　　　　　to discriminate against "business documents and

school-books"; all these phenomena are important. One must make
　　　　a distinction
　　however: when dragged into prominence by half poets, the result
　　　　is not poetry,
20　nor till the poets among us can be
　　　　"literalists of
　　　　the imagination"—above
　　　　　　insolence and triviality and can present

for inspection, "imaginary gardens with real toads in them," shall we have
25　　it. In the meantime, if you demand on the one hand,
　　　　the raw material of poetry in

all its rawness and
that which is on the other hand
      genuine, you are interested in poetry.

John Crowe Ransom   (1888–1974)
Bells for John Whiteside's Daughter

There was such speed in her little body,
And such lightness in her footfall,
It is no wonder that her brown study
Astonishes us all.

5 Her wars were bruited in our high window.
We looked among orchard trees and beyond,
Where she took arms against her shadow,
Or harried unto the pond

The lazy geese, like a snow cloud
10 Dripping their snow on the green grass,
Tricking and stopping, sleepy and proud,
Who cried in goose, Alas,

For the tireless heart within the little
Lady with rod that made them rise
15 From their noon apple dreams, and scuttle
Goose-fashion under the skies!

But now go the bells, and we are ready;
In one house we are sternly stopped
To say we are vexed at her brown study,
20 Lying so primly propped.

Claude McKay (1890–1948)
Harlem Dancer

Applauding youths laughed with young prostitutes
And watched her perfect, half-clothed body sway;
Her voice was like the sound of blended flutes
Blown by black players on a picnic day.
5 She sang and danced on gracefully and calm,
The light gauze hanging loose about her form;
To me she seemed a proudly-swaying palm
Grown lovelier for passing through a storm.
Upon her swarthy neck black shiny curls
10 Luxuriant fell; and tossing coins in praise,
The wine-flushed, bold-eyed boys, and even the girls,
Devoured her shape with eager, passionate gaze;
But looking at her falsely-smiling face,
I knew her self was not in that strange place.

Edna St. Vincent Millay (1892–1950)
To Jesus on His Birthday

For this your mother sweated in the cold,
For this you bled upon the bitter tree:
A yard of tinsel ribbon bought and sold;
A paper wreath; a day at home for me.
5 The merry bells ring out, the people kneel;
Up goes the man of God before the crowd;
With voice of honey and with eyes of steel
He drones your humble gospel to the proud.
Nobody listens. Less than the wind that blows
10 Are all your words to us you died to save.
O Prince of Peace! O Sharon's dewy Rose!
How mute you lie within your vaulted grave.
    The stone the angel rolled away with tears
    Is back upon your mouth these thousand years.

Wilfred Owen (1893–1918)
Dulce Et Decorum Est

Bent double, like old beggars under sacks,
Knock-kneed, coughing like hags, we cursed through sludge,
Till on the haunting flares we turned our backs
And towards our distant rest began to trudge.
5 Men marched asleep. Many had lost their boots
But limped on, blood-shod. All went lame; all blind;
Drunk with fatigue; deaf even to the hoots
Of tired, outstripped Five-Nines that dropped behind.

Gas! GAS! Quick, boys!—An ecstasy of fumbling,
10 Fitting the clumsy helmets just in time;
But someone still was yelling out and stumbling
And flound'ring like a man in fire or lime . . .
Dim, through the misty panes and thick green light,
As under a green sea, I saw him drowning.

15 In all my dreams, before my helpless sight,
He plunges at me, guttering, choking, drowning.

If in some smothering dreams you too could pace
Behind the wagon that we flung him in,
And watch the white eyes writhing in his face,
20 His hanging face, like a devil's sick of sin;
If you could hear, at every jolt, the blood
Come gargling from the froth-corrupted lungs,
Obscene as cancer, bitter as the cud
Of vile, incurable sores on innocent tongues,—
25 My friend, you would not tell with such high zest
To children ardent for some desperate glory,
The old Lie: Dulce et decorum est
Pro patria mori.[1]

---

[1]The Latin quotation is from Horace and means "It is sweet and proper to die for one's country."

Louise Bogan   (1897–1970)
Evening in the Sanitarium

The free evening fades, outside the windows fastened with decorative iron grilles.
The lamps are lighted; the shades drawn; the nurses are watching a little.
It is the hour of the complicated knitting on the safe bone needles; of the games of
    anagrams and bridge;
The deadly game of chess; the book held up like a mask.

5 The period of the wildest weeping, the fiercest delusion, is over.
The women rest their tired half-healed hearts; they are almost well.
Some of them will stay almost well always: the blunt-faced woman whose thinking
    dissolved
Under academic discipline; the manic-depressive girl
Now leveling off; one paranoiac afflicted with jealousy.
10 Another with persecution. Some alleviation has been possible.

O fortunate bride, who never again will become elated after childbirth!
O lucky older wife, who has been cured of feeling unwanted!
To the suburban railway station you will return, return.
To meet forever Jim home on the 5:35.
15 You will be again as normal and selfish and heartless as anybody else.

There is life left: the piano says it with its octave smile.
The soft carpets pad the thump and splinter of the suicide to be.
Everything will be splendid: the grandmother will not drink habitually.
The fruit salad will bloom on the plate like a bouquet
20 And the garden produce the blue-ribbon aquilegia.
The cats will be glad; the fathers feel justified; the mothers relieved.
The sons and husbands will no longer need to pay the bills.
Childhoods will be put away, the obscene nightmare abated.

At the ends of the corridors the baths are running.
25 Mrs. C. again feels the shadow of the obsessive idea.
Miss R. looks at the mantel-piece, which must mean something.

E. B. White   (1899–   )
I Paint What I See[1]

A Ballad of Artistic Integrity, on the Occasion of the Removal of Some Rather Expensive Murals from the RCA Building.

"What do you paint, when you paint on a wall?"
   Said John D.'s grandson Nelson.[2]
"Do you paint just anything there at all?
"Will there be any doves, or a tree in fall?
5 "Or a hunting scene, like an English hall?"

    "I paint what I see," said Rivera.

"What are the colors you use when you paint?"
   Said John D.'s grandson Nelson.
"Do you use any red in the beard of a saint?
10 "If you do, is it terribly red, or faint?
"Do you use any blue? Is it Prussian?"

    "I paint what I paint," said Rivera.

"Whose is that head that I see on my wall?"
   Said John D.'s grandson Nelson.
15 "Is it anyone's head whom we know, at all?
"A Rensselaer, or a Saltonstall?
"Is it Franklin D.? Is it Mordaunt Hall?
"Or is it the head of a Russian?"

    "I paint what I think," said Rivera.

20 *"I paint what I paint, I paint what I see,*
    "I paint what I think," said Rivera,
"And the thing that is dearest in life to me
"In a bourgeois hall is Integrity;
    "However . . .
25 *"I'll take out a couple of people drinkin'*
"And put in a picture of Abraham Lincoln;
"I could even give you McCormick's reaper
"And still not make my art much cheaper.
"But the head of Lenin has got to stay
30 *"Or my friends will give me the bird today,*
    "The bird, the bird, forever."

"It's not good taste in a man like me,"
   Said John D.'s grandson Nelson,

---

[1] A commentary on the murals for Rockefeller Center in New York City painted by the Mexican artist Diego Rivera (1886–1957).   [2] Nelson A. Rockefeller, governor of New York and vice-president of the United States.

"To question an artist's integrity
35 "Or mention a practical thing like a fee,
"But I know what I like to a large degree,
    "Though art I hate to hamper;
"For twenty-one thousand conservative bucks
"You painted a radical. I say shucks,
40   "I never could rent the offices—
    "The capitalistic offices.
"For this, as you know, is a public hall
"And people want doves, or a tree in fall,
"And though your art I dislike to hamper,
45 "I owe a *little* to God and Gramper,
    "And after all,
    "It's *my* wall . . ."

    "We'll see if it is," said Rivera.

Hart Crane (1899–1932)
To Brooklyn Bridge

[1]
How many dawns, chill from his rippling rest
The seagull's wings shall dip and pivot him,
Shedding white rings of tumult, building high
Over the chained bay waters Liberty—

[2]
5 Then, with inviolate curve, forsake our eyes
As apparitional as sails that cross
Some page of figures to be filed away;
—Till elevators drop us from our day . . .

[3]
I think of cinemas, panoramic sleights
10 With multitudes bent toward some flashing scene
Never disclosed, but hastened to again,
Foretold to other eyes on the same screen;

[4]
And Thee, across the harbor, silver-paced
As though the sun took step of thee, yet left
15 Some motion ever unspent in thy stride,—
Implicitly thy freedom staying thee!

[5]

Out of some subway scuttle, cell or loft
A bedlamite speeds to thy parapets,
Tilting there momently, shrill shirt ballooning,
20 A jest falls from the speechless caravan.

[6]

Down Wall, from girder into street noon leaks,
A rip-tooth of the sky's acetylene;
All afternoon the cloud-flown derricks turn . . .
Thy cables breathe the North Atlantic still.

[7]

25 And obscure as that heaven of the Jews,
Thy guerdon . . . Accolade thou dost bestow
Of anonymity time cannot raise:
Vibrant reprieve and pardon thou dost show.

[8]

O harp and altar, of the fury fused,
30 (How could mere toil align thy choiring strings!)
Terrific threshold of the prophet's pledge,
Prayer of pariah, and the lover's cry,—

[9]

Again the traffic lights that skim thy swift
Unfractioned idiom, immaculate sigh of stars,
35 Beading thy path—condense eternity:
And we have seen night lifted in thine arms.

[10]

Under thy shadow by the piers I waited;
Only in darkness is thy shadow clear.
The City's fiery parcels all undone,
40 Already snow submerges an iron year . . .

[11]

O Sleepless as the river under thee,
Vaulting the sea, the prairies' dreaming sod,
Unto us lowliest sometime sweep, descend
And of the curveship lend a myth to God.

Comments

This poem is used by Crane as a "Proem," or preface, to his long poem, "The Bridge," the major effort of his brief career.

Crane has said that in the entire poem, "The Bridge," he was attempting to recreate the "Myth of America." He was much concerned about the future of America because, as he said, "I feel persuaded that here are destined to be discovered certain as yet undefined spiritual quantities. . . ." Brooklyn Bridge he made the symbol of America, the "threshold" of these spiritual quantities. The "Proem: To Brooklyn Bridge" is an invocation to and a eulogy of his basic symbol, Brooklyn Bridge.

James Hearst (1900–1983)
Landmark

The road wound back among the hills of mind
Rutted and worn, in a wagon with my father
Who wore a horsehide coat and knew the way
Toward home, I saw him and the tree together.

5 For me now fields are whirling in a wheel
And the spokes are many paths in all directions,
Each day I come to crossroads after dark,
No place to stay, no aunts, no close connections.

Calendars shed their leaves, mark down a time
10 When chrome danced brightly. The roadside tree is rotten,
I told a circling hawk, widen the gate
For the new machine, a landmark's soon forgotten.

You say the word, he mocked, I'm used to exile.
But the furrow's tongue never tells the harvest true,
15 When my engine saw had redesigned the landscape
For a tractor's path, the stump bled what I knew.

Countee Cullen (1903–1946)
For John Keats, Apostle of Beauty

Not writ in water,[1] nor in mist,
    Sweet lyric throat, thy name;
Thy singing lips that cold death kissed[2]
    Have seared his own with flame.

[1] Keats wrote for his own epitaph, "Here lies one whose name was writ in water."   [2] Keats (1795–1821) suffered an untimely death.

Countee Cullen   (1903–1946)
Yet Do I Marvel

I doubt not God is good, well-meaning, kind,
And did He stoop to quibble could tell why
The little buried mole continues blind,
Why flesh that mirrors Him must some day die,
5   Make plain the reason tortured Tantalus[1]
Is baited by the fickle fruit, declare
If merely brute caprice dooms Sisyphus[2]
To struggle up a never-ending stair.
Inscrutable His ways are, and immune
10 To catechism by a mind too strewn
With petty cares to slightly understand
What awful brain compels His awful hand.
Yet do I marvel at this curious thing:
To make a poet black, and bid him sing!

Phyllis McGinley   (1905–1978)
The Day After Sunday

Always on Monday, God's in the morning papers,
    His name is a headline, His Works are rumored abroad.
Having been praised by men who are movers and shapers,
    From prominent Sunday pulpits, newsworthy is God.

5   On page 27, just opposite Fashion Trends,
    One reads at a glance how He scolded the Baptists a little,
Was firm with the Catholics, practical with the Friends,
    To Unitarians pleasantly noncommittal.

---

[1] Tantalus. In Greek mythology, the son of Zeus and a Lydian king who divulged the secrets of the gods to mortals and was punished by being submerged up to the chin in a river of Hades with a tree of fruit above his head. Whenever he tried to eat the fruit or drink the water, they moved just beyond his reach causing him agonizing thirst and hunger. The nature of his punishment gave us the word *tantalize*.   [2] Sisyphus. A legendary king of Corinth whose work in the world of shades is to roll a huge stone to the top of a hill where it constantly rolls back. Hence "a labor of Sisyphus" is endless and exhausting.

In print are His numerous aspects, too: God smiling,
10   God vexed, God thunderous, God whose mansions are pearl,
Political God, God frugal, God reconciling
      Himself with science, God guiding the Camp Fire Girl.

Always on Monday morning the press reports
      God as revealed to His vicars in various guises—
15 Benevolent, stormy, patient, or out of sorts.
      God knows which God is the God God recognizes.

Frank Marshall Davis   (1905–   )
Roosevelt Smith

You ask what happened to Roosevelt Smith

Well . . .

Conscience and the critics got him

Roosevelt Smith was the only dusky child born and bred in the village of Pine City,
      Nebraska

5 At college they worshipped the novelty of a black poet and predicted fame

At twenty-three he published his first book . . . the critics said he imitated Carl
      Sandburg, Edgar Lee Masters and Vachel Lindsay . . . they raved about a wealth of
      racial material and the charm of darky dialect

So for two years Roosevelt worked and observed in Dixie

At twenty-five a second book . . . Negroes complained about plantation scenes and said
      he dragged Aframerica's good name in the mire for gold . . . "Europe," they said,
      "honors Dunbar for his 'Ships That Pass in the Night'[1] and not for his dialect which
      they don't understand"

For another two years Roosevelt strove for a different medium of expression

10 At twenty-seven a third book . . . The critics said the density of Gertrude Stein or T. S.
      Eliot hardly fitted the simple material to which a Negro had access

For another two years Roosevelt worked

---

[1] A short romantic poem by Paul Laurence Dunbar (1872–1906) which, implies Davis, is honored in
Europe because it has little or nothing to reflect the realities of Negro life as they are reflected in
such poems by Dunbar as "A Death Song" and "When Malindy Sings." Further, Davis implies, the
English would be impressed by Dunbar's title "Ships That Pass in the Night" because an English
romantic novel with the same title (1893) written by Bearice Harraden had sold over a million
copies.

At twenty-nine his fourth book . . . the critics said a Negro had no business initiating the classic forms of Keats, Browning and Shakespeare . . . "Roosevelt Smith," they announced, "has nothing original and is merely a blackface white. His African heritage is a rich source should he use it"

So for another two years Roosevelt went into the interior of Africa

At thirty-one his fifth book . . . interesting enough, the critics said, but since it followed nothing done by any white poet it was probably just a new kind of prose

15 Day after the reviews came out Roosevelt traded conscience and critics for the leather pouch and bunions of a mail carrier and read in the papers until his death how little the American Negro had contributed to his nation's literature . . .[2]

W. H. Auden (1907–1973)
Lullaby*

Lay your sleeping head, my love,
Human on my faithless arm;
Time and fevers burn away
Individual beauty from
5 Thoughtful children, and the grave
Proves the child ephemeral:
But in my arms till break of day
Let the living creature lie,
Mortal, guilty, but to me
10 The entirely beautiful.

Soul and body have no bounds:
To lovers as they lie upon
Her tolerant enchanted slope
In their ordinary swoon,
15 Grave the vision Venus sends
Of supernatural sympathy,
Universal love and hope;
While an abstract insight wakes
Among the glaciers and the rocks

---

[2] See Dudley Randall's "Black Poet, White Critic," p. 528.

    * Editors have previously used "Lay Your Sleeping Head" as the title; Auden has now supplied one. He has made four word changes: l. 20, *carnal* for *sensual;* l. 34, *welcome* for *sweetness;* l. 36, *our* for *the;* l. 37, *find* for *see.* Any sensitive, critical reader of poetry would probably ask why Auden made the changes.

20 The hermit's carnal ecstasy.

Certainty, fidelity
On the stroke of midnight pass
Like vibrations of a bell
And fashionable madmen raise
25 Their pedantic boring cry:
Every farthing of the cost,
All the dreaded cards foretell,
Shall be paid, but from this night
Not a whisper, not a thought,
30 Not a kiss nor look be lost.

Beauty, midnight, vision dies:
Let the winds of dawn that blow
Softly round your dreaming head
Such a day of welcome show
35 Eye and knocking heart may bless,
Find our mortal world enough;
Noons of dryness find you fed
By the involuntary powers,
Nights of insult let you pass
40 Watched by every human love.

W. H. Auden   (1907–1973)
Musée des Beaux Arts[1]

About suffering they were never wrong,
The Old Masters: how well they understood
Its human position; how it takes place
While someone else is eating or opening a window or just walking dully along;
5 How, when the aged are reverently, passionately waiting
For the miraculous birth, there always must be
Children who did not specially want it to happen, skating
On a pond at the edge of the wood:
They never forgot
10 That even the dreadful martyrdom must run its course
Anyhow in a corner, some untidy spot
Where the dogs go on with their doggy life and the torturer's horse
Scratches its innocent behind on a tree.

[1] Museum of Fine Arts.

In Brueghel's *Icarus*,[2] for instance: how everything turns away
15 Quite leisurely from the disaster; the ploughman may
Have heard the splash, the forsaken cry,
But for him it was not an important failure; the sun shone
As it had to on the white legs disappearing into the green
Water; and the expensive delicate ship that must have seen
20 Something amazing, a boy falling out of the sky,
Had somewhere to get to and sailed calmly on.

W. H. Auden   (1907–1973)
The Unknown Citizen

To JS/07/M/378
This Marble Monument
Is Erected by the State

He was found by the Bureau of Statistics to be
One against whom there was no official complaint,
And all the reports on his conduct agree
That, in the modern sense of an old-fashioned word, he was a saint,
5 For in everything he did he served the Greater Community.
Except for the War till the day he retired
He worked in a factory and never got fired,
But satisfied his employers, Fudge Motors Inc.
Yet he wasn't a scab[1] or odd in his views,
10 For his Union reports that he paid his dues,
(Our report on his Union shows it was sound)
And our Social Psychology workers found
That he was popular with his mates and liked a drink.
The Press are convinced that he bought a paper every day
15 And that his reactions to advertisements were normal in every way.
Policies taken out in his name prove that he was fully insured,
And his Health-card shows he was once in hospital but left it cured.
Both Producers Research and High-Grade Living declare
He was fully sensible to the advantages of the Instalment Plan
20 And had everything necessary to the Modern Man,

[2] A painting by the Flemish Pieter Brueghel (1525–1569) in the Royal Museum in Brussels. Icarus, flying with his father Daedalus, flew too close to the sun, which melted the wax holding on his wings and pitched him into the sea. The adjective *Icarian* has come to mean soaring too high for safety.

[1] A union member or nonmember disloyal to the union during a strike.

A phonograph, a radio, a car and a frigidaire.
Our researchers into Public Opinion are content
That he held the proper opinions for the time of year;
When there was peace, he was for peace; when there was war, he went.
25 He was married and added five children to the population,
Which our Eugenist[2] says was the right number for a parent of his generation,
And our teachers report that he never interfered with their education.
Was he free? Was he happy? The question is absurd:
Had anything been wrong, we should certainly have heard.

Theodore Roethke (1908–1963)
Elegy for Jane

My Student, Thrown by a Horse

I remember the neckcurls, limp and damp as tendrils;
And her quick look, a sidelong pickerel smile;
And how, once startled into talk, the light syllables leaped for her,
And she balanced in the delight of her thought,
5 A wren, happy, tail into the wind,
Her song trembling the twigs and small branches.
The shade sang with her;
The leaves, their whispers turned to kissing.
And the mould sang in the bleached valleys under the rose.

10 Oh, when she was sad, she cast herself down into such a pure depth,
Even a father could not find her:
Scraping her cheek against straw,
Stirring the clearest water.

My sparrow, you are not here,
15 Waiting like a fern, making a spiney shadow.
The sides of wet stones cannot console me,
Nor the moss, wound with the last light.

If only I could nudge you from this sleep,
My maimed darling, my skittery pigeon.
20 Over this damp grave I speak the words of my love:
I, with no rights in this matter,
Neither father nor lover.

---

[2] One versed in eugenics, the science that aims at improving the human race by controlling the hereditary qualities through proper mating.

Stephen Spender   (1909–   )
I Think Continually of Those Who Were Truly Great

I think continually of those who were truly great.
Who, from the womb, remembered the soul's history
Through corridors of light where the hours are suns,
Endless and singing. Whose lovely ambition
5 Was that their lips, still touched with fire,
Should tell of the Spirit, clothed from head to foot in song.
And who hoarded from the Spring branches
The desires falling across their bodies like blossoms.

What is precious, is never to forget
10 The essential delight of the blood drawn from ageless springs
Breaking through rocks in worlds before our earth.
Never to deny its pleasure in the morning simple light
Nor its grave evening demand for love.
Never to allow gradually the traffic to smother
15 With noise and fog, the flowering of the Spirit.

Near the snow, near the sun, in the highest fields,
See how these names are fêted by the waving grass
And by the streamers of white cloud
And whispers of wind in the listening sky.
20 The names of those who in their lives fought for life,
Who wore at their hearts the fire's centre.
Born of the sun, they travelled a short while toward the sun,
And left the vivid air signed with their honour.

Comments

Spender's essay "On Teaching Modern Poetry" (p. 1096) includes a good deal of comment on the nature of modern poetry, and the kinds of value to be found in it. The reader may find it profitable to consider Spender's poem in the light of his critical opinions

Stephen Spender   (1909–   )

An Elementary School Classroom in a Slum

Far far from gusty waves these children's faces.
Like rootless weeds, the hair torn round their pallor.
The tall girl with her weighed-down head. The paper-
seeming boy, with rat's eyes. The stunted, unlucky heir
5 Of twisted bones, reciting a father's gnarled disease,
His lesson from his desk. At back of the dim class
One unnoted, sweet and young. His eyes live in a dream
Of squirrel's game, in tree room, other than this.
On sour cream walls, donations. Shakespeare's head,
10 Cloudless at dawn, civilized dome riding all cities.
Belled, flowery, Tyrolese valley. Open-handed map
Awarding the world its world. And yet, for these
Children, these windows, not this world, are world,
Where all their future's painted with a fog,
15 A narrow street sealed in with a lead sky,
Far far from rivers, capes, and stars of words.

Surely, Shakespeare is wicked, the map a bad example
With ships and sun and love tempting them to steal—
For lives that slyly turn in their cramped holes
20 From fog to endless night? On their slag heap, these children
Wear skins peeped through by bones and spectacles of steel
With mended glass, like bottle bits on stones.
All of their time and space are foggy slum.
So blot their maps with slums as big as doom.

25 Unless, governor, teacher, inspector, visitor,
This map becomes their window and these windows
That shut upon their lives like catacombs,
Break O break open till they break the town
And show the children to green fields, and make their world
30 Run azure on gold sands, and let their tongues
Run naked into books, the white and green leaves open
History theirs whose language is the sun.

J. V. Cunningham   (1911–   )
The Metaphysical Amorist

You are the problem I propose,
My dear, the text my musings glose:[1]
I call you for convenience love.
By definition you're a cause
5 Inferred by necessary laws—
You are so to the saints above.
But in this shadowy lower life
I sleep with a terrestrial wife
And earthy children I beget.
10 Love is a fiction I must use,
A privilege I can abuse,
And sometimes something I forget.

Now, in the heavenly other place
Love is in the eternal mind
15 The luminous form whose shade she is,
A ghost discarnate,[2] thought defined.
She was so to my early bliss,
She is so while I comprehend
The forms my senses apprehend,
20 And in the end she will be so.

Her whom my hands embrace I kiss,
Her whom my mind infers I know.
The one exists in time and space
And as she was she will not be;
25 The other is in her own grace
And is *She is* eternally.

Plato![3] you shall not plague my life.
I married a terrestrial wife.
And Hume![4] she is not mere sensation
30 In sequence of observed relation.
She has two forms—ah, thank you, Duns!—,[5]
I know her in both ways at once.
I knew her, yes, before I knew her,
And by both means I must construe her,
35 And none among you shall undo her.

[1] Archaic form of *gloze,* to make glozes or glosses upon; to discuss, expound, interpret.
[2] Having no physical body; incorporeal.   [3] Plato (427?–347 B.C.), Greek philosopher, wrote *The Symposium* on ideal love. "Platonic love" has become a popular term for spiritual love between the sexes without sexual implications. See William Cartwright's poem "No Platonic Love" (p. 449), which has a theme similar to Cunningham's.   [4] David Hume (1711–1776), Scottish philosopher, restricted human knowledge to the experience of ideas, impressions, and sensations. The speaker in the poem therefore rebukes him in ll. 29–30.   [5] John Duns Scotus (1265?–1308), Scottish scholastic theologian, was an extreme realist in philsophy (non-Platonic), so the speaker embraces him.

Robert E. Hayden (1913–1980)
Frederick Douglass*

When it is finally ours, this freedom, this liberty, this beautiful
and terrible thing, needful to man as air,
usable as earth; when it belongs at last to all,
when it is truly instinct, brain matter, diastole, systole,
5 reflex action; when it is finally won; when it is more
than the gaudy mumbo jumbo of politicians:
this man, this Douglass, this former slave, this Negro
beaten to his knees, exiled, visioning a world
where none is lonely, more hunted, alien,
10 this man, superb in love and logic, this man
shall be remembered. Oh, not with statues' rhetoric,
not with legends and poems and wreaths of bronze alone,
but with the lives grown out of his life, the lives
fleshing his dream of the beautiful, needful thing.

Robert E. Hayden (1913–1980)
Those Winter Sundays

Sundays too my father got up early
and put his clothes on in the blueblack cold,
then with cracked hands that ached
from labor in the weekday weather made
5 banked fires blaze. No one ever thanked him.

I'd wake and hear the cold splintering, breaking.
When the rooms were warm, he'd call,

*Frederick Douglass (1817–1895), an early, powerful champion of emancipation and enfranchisement for Negroes, born a slave in Maryland, escaped (1838) to New York, and legally won his freedom in 1846. He became a poet, a distinguished antislavery orator and autobiographer, worked with William Lloyd Garrison on *The Liberator,* broke with Garrison in 1847, and launched his own weekly, *The North Star,* and later his *Frederick Douglass' Paper* and *Douglass' Monthly.* In a letter to his former master, Thomas Arnold, Douglass stated his position during the Civil War: "We are fighting for unity of idea, unity of sentiment, unity of object, unity of institutions, in which there will be no North, no South, no East, no West, no black, no white, but a solidarity of the nation, making every slave free, and every free man a voter."

For further information on Douglass, consult Philip S. Foner, *Frederick Douglass,* New York: Citadel Press, 1961.

and slowly I would rise and dress,
fearing the chronic angers of that house,

10   Speaking indifferently to him,
who had driven out the cold
and polished my good shoes as well.
What did I know, what did I know
of love's austere and lonely offices?

Dudley Randall   (1914–   )
Black Poet, White Critic[1]

A critic advises
not to write on controversial subjects
like freedom or murder,
but to treat universal themes
5   and timeless symbols
like the white unicorn.

A white unicorn?

[1] See Davis's "Roosevelt Smith" p. 519.

Dudley Randall   (1914–   )
Booker T. and W. E. B.*

"It seems to me," said Booker T.,
"It shows a mighty lot of cheek
To study chemistry and Greek
When Mister Charlie needs a hand
5 To hoe the cotton on his land,
And when Miss Ann looks for a cook,
Why stick your nose inside a book?"

"I don't agree," said W. E. B.,
"If I should have the drive to seek
10 Knowledge of chemistry or Greek,
I'll do it. Charles and Miss can look
Another place for hand or cook.
Some men rejoice in skill of hand,
And some in cultivating land,
15 But there are others who maintain
The right to cultivate the brain."

"It seems to me," said Booker T.,
"That all you folks have missed the boat
Who shout about the right to vote,
20 And spend vain days and sleepless nights
In uproar over civil rights.
Just keep your mouths shut, do not grouse,
But work, and save, and buy a house."

"I don't agree," said W. E. B.,
25 "For what can property avail
If dignity and justice fail.
Unless you help to make the laws,
They'll steal your house with trumped-up clause.
A rope's as tight, a fire as hot,
30 No matter how much cash you've got."

---

* Booker T. Washington (1856–1915) and Dr. William Edward Burghardt Du Bois (1868–1963)—Author's note. Du Bois preferred the initials W. E. B.
   This poem suggests (as good poems usually do) more than it explicitly says. A basic disagreement between Washington and Du Bois, who was twelve years younger than Washington, appeared when the Negroes began to settle in white Harlem about 1905, a result of the rise of black economic nationalism. Washington's National Negro Business League, founded in 1900 and identified with the Afro-American Realty Company, was a powerful influence on the Negro move into Harlem. Washington and his Negro business allies had become aggressive in economics but remained conservative in civil rights politics. Du Bois, disagreeing with this conservatism, believed that unless the Negro fought for and won his civil rights there was no guarantee that his new economic status would remain safe. Stanzas 2 and 3 in the poem present the opposing points of view, and line 32 tells us where the poet stands. For a full account of this disagreement consult Harold Cruse, *The Crisis of the Negro Intellectual,* New York: William Morrow and Co., 1967, especially pp. 11–63.

Speak soft, and try your little plan,
But as for me, I'll be a man."

"It seems to me," said Booker T.—

"I don't agree,"
35 Said W. E. B.

Randall Jarrell (1914–1965)
The Emancipators[1]

When you[2] ground the lenses[3] and the moons[4] swam free
From that great wanderer; when the apple[5] shone
Like a sea-shell through your prism, voyager;[6]
When, dancing in pure flame, the Roman mercy,[7]
5 Your doctrines blew like ashes from your bones;[8]

Did you think, for an instant, past the numerals
Jellied in Latin[9] like bacteria in broth,
Snatched for by holy Europe like a sign?
Past sombre tables[10] inched out with the lives
10 Forgotten or clapped for by the wigged Societies?[11]

You guessed this? The earth's face altering with iron,
The smoke ranged like a wall against the day?

[1] Jarrell observes: "Galileo, Newton, and Bruno are the great emancipators addressed in the first stanza. . . ." *Selected Poems,* 1955, p. xiii.   [2] Galileo Galilei (1564–1642), Italian astronomer and physicist who supported Copernicus's (1473–1543) contention that the earth and planets revolve around the sun; regarded as heresy at the time.   [3] The telescope he made.   [4] Jupiter's satellites, which he discovered (1610).   [5] Sir Isaac Newton (1642–1727); seeing an apple fall led him to the law of gravitation. Byron wrote:

> When Newton saw an apple fall, he found,
> In that slight startle from his contemplation. . . .
> A mode of proving that the earth turned round,
> In a most natural whirl called gravitation.
> *Don Juan,* X. I.

[6] Voyager through the realms of thought. Wordsworth's lines are found on Newton's statue in Trinity College, Cambridge:

> The marble index of a mind for ever
> Voyaging through strange seas of Thought alone.
> *The Prelude*

[7] Roman Catholic Church took Bruno's life before his soul was completely damned.   [8] Ll. 4–5: Giordano Bruno (c. 1548–1600), Italian philosopher, critic of Christianity, and supporter of the Copernican system (see footnote 2); burned at the stake for heresy.   [9] Probably scientific terms (numerals).   [10] Scientific formulas or charts.   [11] Royal Societies.

—The equations metamorphose into use: the free
Drag their slight bones from tenements to vote
15 To die with their children in your factories.

Man is born in chains,[12] and everywhere we see him dead.
On your earth they sell nothing but our lives.
You knew that what you died for was our deaths?
You learned, those years, that what men wish is Trade?
20 It was you who understood; it is we who change.[13]

Dylan Thomas (1914–1953)
The Force That Through the Green Fuse Drives the Flower

The force that through the green fuse drives the flower
Drives my green age; that blasts the roots of trees
Is my destroyer.
And I am dumb to tell the crooked rose
5 My youth is bent by the same wintry fever.

The force that drives the water through the rocks
Drives my red blood; that dries the mouthing streams
Turns mine to wax.
And I am dumb to mouth unto my veins
10 How the mountain spring the same mouth sucks.

The hand that whirls the water in the pool
Stirs the quicksand; that ropes the blowing wind
Hauls my shroud sail.
And I am dumb to tell the hanging man
15 How of my clay is made the hangman's lime.

The lips of time leech to the fountain head;
Love drips and gathers, but the fallen blood
Shall calm her sores.
And I am dumb to tell a weather's wind
20 How time has ticked a heaven round the stars.

And I am dumb to tell the lover's tomb
How at my sheet goes the same crooked worm.

[12] "Man is born free, and everywhere he is in chains."—Rousseau (1712–1778), *The Social Contract*,
1762.   [13] Final stanza: implies that the freedom man thought he had achieved is an illusion.

Dylan Thomas   (1914–1953)
Do Not Go Gentle into That Good Night

Do not go gentle into that good night,
Old age should burn and rave at close of day;
Rage, rage against the dying of the light.

Though wise men at their end know dark is right,
5 Because their words had forked no lightning they
Do not go gentle into that good night.

Good men, the last wave by, crying how bright
Their frail deeds might have danced in a green bay,
Rage, rage against the dying of the light.

10 Wild men who caught and sang the sun in flight,
And learn, too late, they grieved it on its way,
Do not go gentle into that good night.

Grave men, near death, who see with blinding sight
Blind eyes could blaze like meteors and be gay,
15 Rage, rage against the dying of the light.

And you, my father, there on the sad height,
Curse, bless, me now with your fierce tears, I pray.
Do not go gentle into that good night.
Rage, rage against the dying of the light.

William Stafford   (1914–   )
Travelling Through the Dark

Travelling through the dark I found a deer
dead on the edge of the Wilson River road.
It is usually best to roll them into the canyon:
that road is narrow; to swerve might make more dead.

5 By glow of the tail-light I stumbled back of the car
and stood by the heap, a doe, a recent killing;
she had stiffened already, almost cold.
I dragged her off; she was large in the belly.

My fingers touching her side brought me the reason—
10 her side was warm; her fawn lay there waiting,
alive, still, never to be born.
Beside that mountain road I hesitated.

The car aimed ahead its lowered parking lights;
under the hood purred the steady engine.
15 I stood in the glare of the warm exhaust turning red;
around our group I could hear the wilderness listen.

I thought hard for us all—my only swerving—
then pushed her over the edge into the river.

Margaret A. Walker (1915–   )
For Malcolm X*

All you violated ones with gentle hearts,
You violent dreamers whose cries shout heartbreak;
Whose voices echo clamors of our cool capers,
And whose black faces have hollowed pits for eyes.
5 All you gambling sons and hooked children and bowery bums
Hating white devils and black bourgeoisie,
Thumbing your noses at your burning red suns,
Gather round this coffin and mourn your dying swan.

Snow-white moslem head-dress around a dead black face!
10 Beautiful were your sand-papering words against our skins!
Our blood and water pour from your flowing wounds.
You have cut open our breasts and dug scalpels in our brains.
When and Where will another come to take your holy place?
Old man mumbling in his dotage, or crying child, unborn?

---

* See Imamu Amiri Baraka, "A Poem for Black Hearts" (p. 559) and Raymond R. Patterson, "At That Moment" (p. 423) for other poems on Malcolm X. See also *The Autobiography of Malcolm X,* New York: Grove Press, 1964, especially Ch. 19. Malcolm X was assassinated in Harlem on February 21, 1965.

Gwendolyn Brooks   (1917–   )
From The Children of the Poor

1

People who have no children can be hard:
Attain a mail of ice and insolence:
Need not pause in the fire, and in no sense
Hesitate in the hurricane to guard.
5 And when wide world is bitten and bewarred
They perish purely, waving their spirits hence
Without a trace of grace or of offense
To laugh or fail, diffident, wonder-starred.
While through a throttling dark we others hear
10 The little lifting helplessness, the queer
Whimper-whine; whose unridiculous
Lost softness softly makes a trap for us.
And makes a curse. And makes a sugar of
The malocclusions, the inconditions of love.

Robert Lowell   (1917–1977)
As a Plane Tree by the Water[1]

Darkness has called to darkness, and disgrace
Elbows about our windows in this planned
Babel of Boston[2] where our money talks
And multiplies the darkness of a land
5 Of preparation[3] where the Virgin[4] walks
And roses spiral her enamelled face

[1] "Blessed *is* the man that walketh not in the counsel of the ungodly . . .
But his delight *is* in the law of the LORD . . .
And he shall be like a tree planted by the rivers of water. . . ."
                                                          Psalm 1.

The Douai version of the Bible adds *plane* before *tree* in the final line, meaning broad-leaved.
[2] A reference to the Tower of Babel, or Babylon, which was the Old Testament man's supreme expression of self-will and pride in trying to build a tower that would reach heaven and so place man on a level with God. Noting this pride, God confounded the builders' language to halt the building and scattered men "upon the face of all the earth." (Genesis 11:1–9.) Likewise Boston, a "planned Babel" where money "multiplies the darkness."   [3] A land of preparation for the next world; see Hebrews 11:13–16.   [4] The Virgin Mary; apparently an image of her is being carried (walks) in an Easter procession.

Or fall to splinters on unwatered streets.
Our Lady of Babylon,[5] go by, go by,
I was once the apple of your eye;
10 Flies, flies[6] are on the plane tree, on the streets.

The flies, the flies, the flies of Babylon
Buzz in my ear-drums while the devil's long
Dirge of the people detonates the hour
For floating cities where his golden tongue
15 Enchants the masons of the Babel Tower
To raise tomorrow's city to the sun
That never sets upon these hell-fire streets
Of Boston, where the sunlight is a sword
Striking at the withholder of the Lord:
20 Flies, flies are on the plane tree, on the streets.

Flies strike the miraculous waters of the iced
Atlantic and the eyes of Bernadette
Who saw Our Lady standing in the cave
At Massabielle, saw her so squarely that
25 Her vision put out reason's eyes.[7] The grave
Is open-mouthed and swallowed up in Christ.[8]
O walls of Jericho! And all the streets
To our Atlantic wall are singing: "Sing,
Sing for the resurrection of the King."[9]
30 Flies, flies are on the plane tree, on the streets.

Robert Lowell (1917–1977)
The Dead in Europe

After the planes unloaded, we fell down
Buried together, unmarried men and women;
Not crown of thorns,[1] not iron, not Lombard crown,[2]

---

[5] Used in contrast to the Virgin; the great whore of Babylon (Revelation 17:1–6, 18). Boston, the new Babylon.   [6] Symbol of the plagues; see Exodus 8:20–24; 9:3, 6.   [7] Ll. 21–25: A reference to St. Bernadette (Soubirous) who in 1859, at the age of fourteen, claimed to have seen the Blessed Virgin in a cave in the Massabielle rocks in the Pyrenees near Lourdes, France. The cave contains a spring whose waters have become "miraculous waters" of healing, a shrine. The image of Bernadette is apparently being carried in the Easter procession.   [8] Ll. 25–26: The grave is open at this Eastertime, as witnessed by the processional, and death is "swallowed up" by Christ's victorious resurrection.   [9] The impregnable, the walls of Jericho, has been taken; death has been assailed and conquered by Christ. But not so in Boston (l. 30).

[1] The crown of thorns of Christ.   [2] Apparently an ironic reference to the bankers and money lenders of Lombardy, established in Lombard Street, London. The Lombard crown is a reference to the Teutons who invaded Italy in 568 to establish a kingdom. Lowell's reference is probably purposely ambiguous.

Not grilled and spindle spires pointing to heaven
5   Could save us. Raise us, Mother,[3] we fell down
Here hugger-mugger in the jellied fire:[4]
Our sacred earth in our day was our curse.

Our Mother, shall we rise on Mary's day
In Maryland, wherever corpses married
10   Under the rubble, bundled together? Pray
For us whom the blockbusters married and buried;
When Satan scatters us on Rising-day,[5]
O Mother, snatch our bodies from the fire:
Our sacred earth in our day was our curse.

15   Mother, my bones are trembling and I hear
The earth's reverberations and the trumpet[6]
Bleating into my shambles. Shall I bear,
(O Mary!) unmarried man and powder-puppet,
Witness to the Devil! Mary, hear,
20   O Mary, marry earth, sea, air and fire;
Our sacred earth in our day is our curse.

Lawrence Ferlinghetti (1919–   )
In Goya's Greatest Scenes

In Goya's greatest scenes[1] we seem to see
                              the people of the world
        exactly at the moment when
                they first attained the title of
5   'suffering humanity'

---

[3] The Virgin Mary, mother of Christ.   [4] Jumbled in the bomb fire.   [5] The Last Judgment (Judgment Day). "And I saw the dead, small and great, stand before God; and the books were opened: and another book was opened, which is *the book* of life: and the dead were judged out of those things which were written in the books, according to their works. And the sea gave up the dead which were in it; and death and hell delivered up the dead which were in them: and they were judged every man according to their works." Revelation 20:12–13.   [6] Trumpets that wake the dead for the Last Judgment. See Donne's "Holy Sonnet VII," p. 427.

[1] Francisco José de Goya y Lucientes (1746–1828), Spanish master painter, etcher, and lithographer, and chief painter to the Spanish king; widely known for his unrestrained realistic portrayal of contemporary life in Spain, and of "suffering humanity" as his famous painting "The Third of May" testifies. It is said that "he loathed the horrors of organized killings, and when asked why he painted such things, he answered curtly, 'To have the pleasure of saying eternally to men that they stop being barbarians.'"

They writhe upon the page
                in a veritable rage
                        of adversity
Heaped up
10   groaning with babies and bayonets
                           under cement skies
    in an abstract landscape of blasted trees
      bent statues bats wings and beaks
           slippery gibbets
15   cadavers and carnivorous cocks
    and all the final hollering monsters
      of the
           'imagination of disaster'
they are so bloody real
20   it is as if they really still existed

And they do

    Only the landscape is changed

They still are ranged along the roads
    plagued by legionaires
           false windmills and demented roosters

They are the same people
        only further from home

  on freeways fifty lanes wide
      on a concrete continent
30   spaced with bland billboards
    illustrating imbecile illusions of happiness

The scene shows fewer tumbrils[2]
        but more maimed citizens
              in painted cars
35   and they have strange license plates
   and engines
       that devour America

---

[2] A vehicle carrying condemned prisoners (such as political prisoners during the French Revolution) to a place of execution.

Richard Wilbur   (1921–   )
Museum Piece

The good gray guardians of art
Patrol the halls on spongy shoes,
Impartially protective, though
Perhaps suspicious of Toulouse.[1]

5 Here dozes one against the wall,
Disposed upon a funeral chair.
A Degas[2] dancer pirouettes
Upon the parting of his hair.

See how she spins! The grace is there,
10 But strain as well is plain to see.
Degas loved the two together:
Beauty joined to energy.

Edgar Degas purchased once
A fine El Greco,[3] which he kept
15 Against the wall beside his bed
To hang his pants on while he slept.

Mona Van Duyn   (1921–   )
An Annual and Perennial Problem

*"Among annuals and perennials, there are not many that can
properly be classed among these* Heavy *and frankly seductive odors.
No gardener should plant these in quantities near the house, or porch,
or patio without realizing that many of them, in spite of exquisite
fragrance, have a past steeped in sin."*

Taylor's Garden Guide*

One should have known, I suppose, that you can't even trust
the lily-of-the-valley, for all it seems so chaste.

---

[1] Henri de Toulouse-Lautrec Monfa (1864–1901), French painter famous for his posters and paintings of Parisian nightlife.   [2] Edgar Degas (1834–1917), French Impressionist known for paintings of ballerinas.   [3] El Greco (1548?–1614?), Spanish painter (born in Crete) known for his elongated figures.

* Norman Taylor, *Taylor's Garden Guide,* New York: D. Van Nostrand and Co., 1957.

The whole lily family, in fact, is "brooding and sultry."
It's a good thing there's a Garden Guide, nothing paltry

5 about *their* past. Why, some are so "stinking" one expert cried,
" 'May dogs devour its hateful bulbs!' " Enough said.

We'd better not try to imagine . . . But it's hard to endure
the thought of them sitting brazenly in churches, looking pure.

The tuberose fragrance "is enhanced by dusk and becomes"
10 (remember, they're taken right into some people's homes,

perhaps with teen-age children around in that air!)
"intoxicating with darkness." Well, there you are.

You hear it said sometimes that in a few cases
the past can be lived down. There's no basis

15 for that belief—these flowers have had plenty of time.
Sinners just try to make decent folks do the same.

What we've always suspected is true. We're not safe anywhere.
Dark patios, of course—But even at our own back door

from half a block off the jasmine may try to pollute us,
20 and Heaven protect us all from the trailing arbutus!

Philip Larkin (1922–   )
Church Going

Once I am sure there's nothing going on
I step inside, letting the door thud shut.
Another church: matting, seats, and stone,
And little books; sprawlings of flowers, cut
5 For Sunday, brownish now; some brass and stuff
Up at the holy end; the small neat organ;
And a tense, musty, unignorable silence,
Brewed God knows how long. Hatless, I take off
My cycle-clips in awkward reverence,

10 Move forward, run my hand around the font.[1]
From where I stand, the roof looks almost new—
Cleaned, or restored? Someone would know: I don't.
Mounting the lectern, I peruse a few

[1] Receptacle for baptismal water.

Hectoring[2] large-scale verses, and pronounce
15 "Here endeth" much more loudly than I'd meant.
The echoes snigger briefly. Back at the door
I sign the book, donate an Irish sixpence,
Reflect the place was not worth stopping for.

Yet stop I did: in fact I often do,
20 And always end much at a loss like this,
Wondering what to look for; wondering, too,
When churches fall completely out of use
What we shall turn them into, if we shall keep
A few cathedrals chronically on show,
25 Their parchment, plate and pyx[3] in locked cases,
And let the rest rent-free to rain and sheep.
Shall we avoid them as unlucky places?

Or, after dark, will dubious women come
To make their children touch a particular stone;
30 Pick simples[4] for a cancer; or on some
Advised night see walking a dead one?
Power of some sort or other will go on
In games, in riddles, seemingly at random;
But superstition, like belief, must die,
35 And what remains when disbelief has gone?
Grass, weedy pavement, brambles, buttress, sky,

A shape less recognizable each week,
A purpose more obscure. I wonder who
Will be the last, the very last, to seek
40 This place for what it was; one of the crew
That tap and jot and know what rood-lofts[5] were?
Some ruin-bibber,[6] randy for antique,
Or Christmas-addict, counting on a whiff
Of gown-and-bands and organ-pipes and myrrh?
45 Or will he be my representative,

Bored, uninformed, knowing the ghostly silt
Dispersed, yet tending to this cross of ground
Through suburb scrub because it held unspilt
So long and equably what since is found
50 Only in separation—marriage, and birth,
And death, and thoughts of these—for whom was built
This special shell? For, though I've no idea
What this accoutered frowsty barn is worth,
It pleases me to stand in silence here;

55 A serious house on serious earth it is,
In whose blent air all our compulsions meet,
Are recognized, and robed as destinies.

---

[2] Blustering.   [3] Receptacle for the Eucharist.   [4] Medicinal plants.   [5] Beams or screens on which crucifixes are attached.   [6] Antique collector.

And that much never can be obsolete,
Since someone will forever be surprising
60 A hunger in himself to be more serious,
And gravitating with it to this ground,
Which, he once heard, was proper to grow wise in,
If only that so many dead lie round.

James Dickey (1923–   )
Adultery

We have all been in rooms
We cannot die in, and they are odd places, and sad.
Often Indians are standing eagle-armed on hills

In the sunrise   open wide to the Great Spirit
5 Or gliding in canoes   or cattle are browsing on the walls
Far away   gazing down with the eyes of our children

Not far away   or there are men driving
The last railspike, which has turned
Gold in their hands. Gigantic forepleasure lives

10 Among such scenes, and we are alone with it
At last. There is always some weeping
Between us   and someone is always checking

A wrist watch by the bed to see how much
Longer we have left. Nothing can come
15 Of this   nothing can come

Of us: of me with my grim techniques
Or you who have sealed your womb
With a ring of convulsive rubber:

Although we come together,
20 Nothing will come of us. But we would not give
It up, for death is beaten

By praying Indians   by distant cows   historical
Hammers   by hazardous meetings that bridge
A continent. One could never die here

25 Never die   never die
While crying. My lover, my dear one
I will see you next week

When I'm in town. I will call you
If I can. Please get hold of   please don't
30 Oh God, Please don't any more I can't bear . . . Listen:

We have done it again   we are
Still living. Sit up and smile,
God bless you. Guilt is magical.

James Dickey   (1923–   )
Cherrylog Road

Off Highway 106
At Cherrylog Road I entered
The '34 Ford without wheels,
Smothered in kudzu,
5 With a seat pulled out to run
Corn whiskey down from the hills,

And then from the other side
Crept into an Essex
With a rumble seat of red leather
10 And then out again, aboard
A blue Chevrolet, releasing
The rust from its other color,

Reared up on three building blocks.
None had the same body heat;
15 I changed with them inward, toward
The weedy heart of the junkyard,
For I knew that Doris Holbrook
Would escape from her father at noon

And would come from the farm
20 To seek parts owned by the sun
Among the abandoned chassis,
Sitting in each in turn
As I did, leaning forward
As in a wild stock-car race

25 In the parking lot of the dead.
Time after time, I climbed in
And out the other side, like
An envoy or movie star
Met at the station by crickets.
30 A radiator cap raised its head,

Become a real toad or a kingsnake
As I neared the hub of the yard,
Passing through many states,
Many lives, to reach
35 Some grandmother's long Pierce-Arrow
Sending platters of blindness forth

From its nickel hubcaps
And spilling its tender upholstery
On sleepy roaches,
40 The glass panel in between
Lady and colored driver
Not all the way broken out,

The back-seat phone
Still on its hook.
45 I got in as though to exclaim,
"Let us go to the orphan asylum,
John; I have some old toys
For children who say their prayers."

I popped with sweat as I thought
50 I heard Doris Holbrook scrape
Like a mouse in the southern state sun
That was eating the paint in blisters
From a hundred car tops and hoods.
She was tapping like code,

55 Loosening the screws,
Carrying off headlights,
Sparkplugs, bumpers,
Cracked mirrors and gear-knobs,
Getting ready, already,
60 To go back with something to show

Other than her lips' new trembling
I would hold to me soon, soon,
Where I sat in the ripped back seat
Talking over the interphone,
65 Praying for Doris Holbrook
To come from her father's farm

And to get back there
With no trace of me on her face
To be seen by her red-haired father
70 Who would change, in the squalling barn,
Her back's pale skin with a strop,
Then lay for me

In a bootlegger's roasting car
With a string-triggered 12-gauge shotgun
75 To blast the breath from the air.
Not cut by the jagged windshields,

Through the acres of wrecks she came
With a wrench in her hand,

Through dust where the blacksnake dies
80 Of boredom, and the beetle knows
The compost has no more life.
Someone outside would have seen
The oldest car's door inexplicably
Close from within:

85 I held her and held her and held her,
Convoyed at terrific speed
By the stalled, dreaming traffic around us,
So the blacksnake, stiff
With inaction, curved back
90 Into life, and hunted the mouse

With deadly overexcitement,
The beetles reclaimed their field
As we clung, glued together,
With the hooks of the seat springs
95 Working through to catch us red-handed
Amidst the gray breathless batting

That burst from the seat at our backs.
We left by separate doors
Into the changed, other bodies
100 Of cars, she down Cherrylog Road
And I to my motorcycle
Parked like the soul of the junkyard

Restored, a bicycle fleshed
With power, and tore off
105 Up Highway 106, continually
Drunk on the wind in my mouth,
Wringing the handlebar for speed,
Wild to be wreckage forever.

James Dickey (1923–   )
The Sheep Child

Farm boys wild to couple
With anything   with soft-wooded trees
With mounds of earth   mounds
Of pinestraw   will keep themselves off
5 Animals by legends of their own:
In the hay-tunnel dark
And dung of barns, they will
Say   I have heard tell

That in a museum in Atlanta
10 Way back in a corner somewhere
There's this thing that's only half
Sheep   like a woolly baby
Pickled in alcohol   because
Those things can't live   his eyes
15 Are open   but you can't stand to look
I heard from somebody who . . .

But this is now almost all
Gone. The boys have taken
Their own true wives in the city,
20 The sheep are safe in the west hill
Pasture   but we who were born there
Still are not sure. Are we,
Because we remember, remembered
In the terrible dust of museums?

25 Merely with his eyes, the sheep-child may

Be saying   saying

I am here, in my father's house.
I who am half of your world, came deeply
To my mother in the long grass
30 *Of the west pasture, where she stood like moonlight*
Listening for foxes. It was something like love
From another world that seized her
From behind, and she gave, not lifting her head
Out of dew, without ever looking, her best
35 *Self to that great need. Turned loose, she dipped her face*
Farther into the chill of the earth, and in a sound
Of sobbing   of something stumbling
Away, began, as she must do,
To carry me. I woke, dying,

40 *In the summer sun of the hillside, with my eyes*
Far more than human. I saw for a blazing moment

The great grassy world from both sides,
Man and beast in the round of their need,
And the hill wind stirred in my wool,
45 *My hoof and my hand clasped each other,*
I ate my one meal
Of milk, and died
Staring. From dark grass I came straight

To my father's house, whose dust
50 *Whirls up in the halls for no reason*
When no one comes   piling deep in a hellish mild corner,
And, through my immortal waters,
I meet the sun's grains eye
To eye, and they fail at my closet of glass.
55 *Dead, I am most surely living*
In the minds of farm boys: I am he who drives
Them like wolves from the hound bitch and calf
And from the chaste ewe in the wind.
They go into woods   into bean fields   they go
60 *Deep into their known right hands. Dreaming of me,*
They groan   they wait   they suffer
Themselves, they marry, they raise their kind.

Donald Justice (1925–   )
The Tourist from Syracuse

One of those men who can be a car salesman or a
tourist from Syracuse or a hired assassin.
                                    John D. MacDonald

You would not recognize me.
Mine is the face which blooms in
The dank mirrors of washrooms
As you grope for the light switch.

5 My eyes have the expression
Of the cold eyes of statues
Watching their pigeons return
From the feed you have scattered,

And I stand on my corner
10 With the same marble patience.

If I move at all, it is
At the same pace precisely

As the shade of the awning
Under which I stand waiting
15 And with whose blackness it seems
I am already blended.

I speak seldom, and always
In a murmur as quiet
As that of crowds which surround
20 The victims of accidents.

Shall I confess who I am?
My name is all names and none.
I am the used-car salesman,
The tourist from Syracuse,

25 The hired assassin, waiting.
I will stand here forever
Like one who has missed his bus—
Familiar, anonymous—

On my usual corner,
30 The corner at which you turn
To approach that place where now
You must not hope to arrive.

Donald Justice (1925–   )
Counting the Mad

This one was put in a jacket,
This one was sent home,
This one was given bread and meat
But would eat none,
5 And this one cried No No No No
All day long.

This one looked at the window
As though it were a wall,
This one saw things that were not there,
10 This one things that were,
And this one cried No No No No
All day long.

This one thought himself a bird,
This one a dog
15 And this one thought himself a man,
An ordinary man,
And cried and cried No No No No
All day long.

Allen Ginsberg (1926–   )
Last Night in Calcutta

Still night. The old clock Ticks,
half past two. A ringing of crickets
awake in the ceiling. The gate is locked
on the street outside—sleepers, mustaches,
5 nakedness, but no desire. A few mosquitos
waken the itch, the fan turns slowly—
a car thunders along the black asphalt,
a bull snorts, something is expected—
Time sits solid in the four yellow walls.
10 No one is here, emptiness filled with train
whistles & dog barks, answered a block away.
Pushkin[1] sits on the bookshelf, Shakespeare's
complete works as well as Blake's unread—
O Spirit of Poetry, no use calling on you
15 babbling in this emptiness furnished with beds
under the bright oval mirror—perfect
night for sleepers to dissolve in tranquil
blackness, and rest there eight hours
—Waking to stained fingers, bitter mouth
20 and lung gripped by cigarette hunger,
what to do with this big toe, this arm
this eye in the starving skeleton-filled
sore horse tramcar-heated Calcutta in
Eternity—sweating and teeth rotted away—
25 Rilke[2] at least could dream about lovers,
the old breast excitement and trembling belly,
is that it? And the vast starry space—
If the brain changes matter breathes

---

[1] Alexander Pushkin (1799–1837), famous Russian poet.   [2] The German poet Rainer Maria Rilke (1875–1926), whose *Duino Elegies* celebrates angels and lovers of immortal power.

fearfully back on man—But now
30   the great crash of buildings and planets
breaks thru the walls of language and drowns
me under its Ganges[3] heaviness forever.
No escape but thru Bangkok and New York death.
Skin is sufficient to be skin, that's all
35   it ever could be, tho screams of pain in the kidney
make it sick of itself, a wavy dream
dying to finish its all too famous misery
—Leave immortality for another to suffer like a fool,
not get stuck in the corner of the universe
40   sticking morphine in the arm and eating meat.

W. D. Snodgrass   (1926–   )
What We Said

Stunned in that first estrangement,
We went through the turning woods
Where inflamed leaves sick as words
Spun, wondering what the change meant.

5   Half gone, our road led onwards
By barbed wire, past the ravine
Where a lost couch, snarled in vines,
Spilled its soiled, gray innards

Into a garbage mound.
10   We came, then, to a yard
Where tarpaper, bottles and charred
Boards lay on the trampled ground.

This had been someone's lawn.
And, closing up like a wound,
15   The cluttered hole in the ground
A life had been built upon.

In the high grass, cars had been.
On the leafless branches, rags
And condoms fluttered like the flags
20   Of new orders moving in.

We talked of the last war, when
Houses, cathedral towns, shacks—

[3] The sacred river of India.

Whole continents went into wreckage.
What fools could do that again?

25 Ruin on every side—
We would set our loves in order,
Surely, we told each other.
Surely. That's what we said.

A. R. Ammons (1926–   )
Cascadilla Falls

I went down by Cascadilla
Falls this
evening, the
stream below the falls,
5 and picked up a
handsized stone
kidney-shaped, testicular, and

thought all its motions into it,
the 800 mph earth spin,
10 the 190-million-mile yearly
displacement around the sun,
the overriding
grand
haul

15 of the galaxy with the 30,000
mph of where
the sun's going:
thought all the interweaving
motions
20 into myself: dropped

the stone to dead rest:
the stream from other motions
broke
rushing over it:
25 shelterless,
I turned

to the sky and stood still:
oh

I do
30 not know where I am going
that I can live my life
by this single creek.

James Wright (1927–1980)
The Blessing

Just off the highway to Rochester, Minnesota,
Twilight bounds softly forth on the grass.
And the eyes of those two Indian ponies
Darken with kindness.
5 They have come gladly out of the willows
To welcome my friend and me.
We step over the barbed wire into the pasture
Where they have been grazing all day, alone.
They ripple tensely, they can hardly contain their happiness
10 That we have come.
They bow shyly as wet swans. They love each other.
There is no loneliness like theirs.
At home once more,
They begin munching the young tufts of spring in the darkness.
15 I would like to hold the slenderer one in my arms,
For she has walked over to me
And nuzzled my left hand.
She is black and white,
Her mane falls wild on her forehead,
20 And the light breeze moves me to caress her long ear
That is delicate as the skin over a girl's wrist.
Suddenly I realize
That if I stepped out of my body I would break
Into blossom.

W. S. Merwin   (1927–   )
For the Anniversary of My Death

Every year without knowing it I have passed the day
When the last fires will wave to me
And the silence will set out
Tireless traveller
5 Like the beam of a lightless star

Then I will no longer
Find myself in life as in a strange garment
Surprised at the earth
And the love of one woman
10 And then shamelessness of men
As today writing after three days of rain
Hearing the wren sing and the falling cease
And bowing not knowing to what

Anne Sexton   (1928–1974)
The Kiss

My mouth blooms like a cut.
I've been wronged all year, tedious
nights, nothing but rough elbows in them
and delicate boxes of Kleenex calling *crybaby*
5 *crybaby, you fool!*

Before today my body was useless.
Now it's tearing at its square corners.
It's tearing old Mary's garments off, knot by knot
and see—Now it's shot full of these electric bolts.
10 Zing! A resurrection!

Once it was a boat, quite wooden
and with no business, no salt water under it
and in need of some paint. It was no more
than a group of boards. But you hoisted her, rigged her.
15 She's been elected.

My nerves are turned on. I hear them like
musical instruments. Where there was silence

the drums, the strings are incurably playing. You did this.
Pure genius at work. Darling, the composer has
20 stepped into fire.

Donald Hall (1928–   )
My Son, My Executioner

My son, my executioner,
    I take you in my arms,
Quiet and small and just astir,
    And whom my body warms.

5 Sweet death, small son, our instrument
        Of immortality,
Your cries and hungers document
        Our bodily decay.

We twenty-five and twenty-two,
10   Who seemed to live forever,
Observe enduring life in you
        And start to die together.

Donald Hall (1928–   )
Self-Portrait as a Bear

Here is a fat animal, a bear
that is partly a dodo.
Ridiculous wings hang at his shoulders
while he plods in the brickyards
5 at the edge of the city, smiling
and eating flowers. He eats them
because he loves them
because they are beautiful

because they love him.
10 It is eating flowers which makes him fat.
He carries his huge stomach
over the gutters of damp leaves
in the parking lots in October,
but inside that paunch
15 he knows there are fields of lupine
and meadows of mustard and poppy.
He encloses sunshine.
Winds bend the flowers
in combers across the valley,
20 birds hang on the stiff wind,
at night there are showers, and the sun
lifts through a haze every morning
of the summer in the stomach.

Adrienne Rich   (1929–   )
Living in Sin

She had thought the studio would keep itself;
no dust upon the furniture of love.
Half heresy, to wish the taps less vocal,
the panes relieved of grime. A plate of pears,
5 a piano with a Persian shawl, a cat
stalking the picturesque amusing mouse
had risen at his urging.
Not that at five each separate stair would writhe
under the milkman's tramp; that morning light
10 so coldly would delineate the scraps
of last night's cheese and three sepulchral bottles;
that on the kitchen shelf among the saucers
a pair of beetle-eyes would fix her own—
envoy from some black village in the mouldings . . .
15 Meanwhile, he, with a yawn,
sounded a dozen notes upon the keyboard,
declared it out of tune, shrugged at the mirror,
rubbed at his beard, went out for cigarettes;
while she, jeered by the minor demons,
20 pulled back the sheets and made the bed and found
a towel to dust the table-top,
and let the coffee-pot boil over on the stove.

By evening she was back in love again,
though not so wholly but throughout the night
25 she woke sometimes to feel the daylight coming
like a relentless milkman up the stairs.

Adrienne Rich   (1929–   )
Two Songs

1

Sex, as they harshly call it,
I fell into this morning
at ten o'clock, a drizzling hour
of traffic and wet newspapers.
5 I thought of him who yesterday
clearly didn't
turn me to a hot field
ready for plowing,
and longing for that young man
10 piercéd me to the roots
bathing every vein, etc.
All day he appears to me
touchingly desirable,
a prize one could wreck one's peace for.
15 I'd call it love if love
didn't take so many years
but lust too is a jewel
a sweet flower and what
pure happiness to know
20 all our high-toned questions
breed in a lively animal.

2

That "old last act"!
And yet sometimes
all seems post coitum triste
25 and I a mere bystander.
Somebody else is going off,
getting shot to the moon.
Or, a moon-race!
Split seconds after
30 my opposite number lands

I make it—
we lie fainting together
at a crater-edge
heavy as mercury in our moonsuits
35 till he speaks—
in a different language
yet one I've picked up
through cultural exchanges . . .
we murmur the first moonwords:
40 *Spasibo. Thanks. O.K.*

Gary Snyder   (1930–   )
A Walk

Sunday the only day we don't work:
Mules farting around the meadow,
                    Murphy fishing,
The tent flaps in the warm
5 Early sun: I've eaten breakfast and I'll
                    take a walk
To Benson Lake. Packed a lunch,
Goodbye. Hopping on creekbed boulders
Up the rock throat three miles
10   Piute Creek—
In steep gorge glacier-slick rattlesnake country
Jump, land by a pool, trout skitter,
The clear sky. Deer tracks.
Bad places by a falls, boulders big as houses,
15 Lunch tied to belt,
I stemmed up a crack and almost fell
But rolled out safe on a ledge
                    and ambled on.
Quail chicks freeze underfoot, color of stone
20 Then run cheep! away, hen quail fussing.
Craggy west end of Benson Lake—after edging
Past dark creek pools on a long white slope—
Lookt down in the ice-black lake
                    lined with cliff
25 From far above: deep shimmering trout.
A lone duck in a gunsightpass
                    steep side hill

Through slide-aspen and talus, to the east end,
Down to grass, wading a wide smooth stream
30 Into camp. At last.
            By the rusty three-year-
Ago left-behind cookstove
Of the old trail crew,
Stoppt and swam and ate my lunch.

Robley Wilson, Jr. (1930–   )
The Great Teachers

Love is not love
Which alters when it alteration finds.

It never bothered Socrates,
Who clustered close about him
His own images, ghostly togas
Milk-pure, frozen in flowing out.
5 The naive boys with crossed ankles
Rocked on their doubled fists,
The alert rows of them mirror
To the equanimities of love.

It never bothered Aristotle.
10 Thought was a sun his pupils
Tethered to like cavalries
Making a shambles of the past.
They brought him precious spoils
For the apartments of his mind;
15 Heavy with plunder, he divined
The blinded temperance of love.

It never bothered the Saviour
On the populous mountainsides,
Where the confusion of bared heads
20 Made like trees an orderly bowing.
If gospel truth sits oddly in
The mind, His vision meets
Upon some special confidence
The humble intersects of love.

25 It never bothers great teachers.
We learn them best when they are men

Poised on the sills of life, and see
How they lean out from it
To touch truth. We presume to teach
30 But grow old and hang back from risk.
We ask our children: *What is love?*
And are, too, endlessly betrayed.

Sylvia Plath[1] (1932–1963)
Two Views of a Cadaver Room

1

The day she visited the dissecting room
They had four men laid out, black as burnt turkey,
Already half unstrung. A vinegary fume
Of the death vats clung to them;
5 The white-smocked boys started working.
The head of his cadaver had caved in,
And she could scarcely make out anything
In that rubble of skull plates and old leather.
A sallow piece of string held it together.

10 In their jars the snail-nosed babies moon and glow.
He hands her the cut-out heart like a cracked heirloom.

2

In Brueghel's panorama of smoke and slaughter
Two people only are blind to the carrion army:
He, afloat in the sea of her blue satin
15 Skirts, sings in the direction
Of her bare shoulder, while she bends,
Fingering a leaflet of music, over him,
Both of them deaf to the fiddle in the hands
Of the death's-head shadowing their song.
20 These Flemish lovers flourish; not for long.

Yet desolation, stalled in paint, spares the little country
Foolish, delicate, in the lower right-hand corner.

---

[1] See Ch. 7 from *The Bell Jar,* a fictionalized autobiography of Sylvia Plath, p. 533.

Sylvia Plath (1932–1963)
Suicide off Egg Rock

Behind him the hotdogs split and drizzled
On the public grills, and the ochreous salt flats,
Gas tanks, factory stacks—that landscape
Of imperfections his bowels were part of—
5 Rippled and pulsed in the glassy updraft.
Sun struck the water like a damnation.
No pit of shadow to crawl into,
And his blood beating the old tattoo
I am, I am, I am. Children
10 Were squealing where combers broke and the spindrift
Raveled wind-ripped from the crest of the wave.
A mongrel working his legs to a gallop
Hustled a gull flock to flap off the sandspit.

He smoldered, as if stone-deaf, blindfold,
15 His body beached with the sea's garbage,
A machine to breathe and beat forever.
Flies filing in through a dead skate's eyehole
Buzzed and assailed the vaulted brainchamber.
The words in his book wormed off the pages.
20 Everything glittered like blank paper.

Everything shrank in the sun's corrosive
Ray but Egg Rock on the blue wastage.
He heard when he walked into the water

The forgetful surf creaming on those ledges.

Imamu Amiri Baraka[1] (1934–   )
A Poem for Black Hearts[2]

For Malcolm's eyes, when they broke
the face of some dumb white man. For
Malcolm's hands raised to bless us

---

[1] Earlier known as LeRoi Jones.   [2] See Margaret A. Walker's "For Malcom X" (p. 533) and Raymond R. Patterson's "At That Moment" (p. 423) for other views of the death of Malcolm X.

all black and strong in his image
5 of ourselves, for Malcolm's words
fire darts, the victor's tireless
thrusts, words hung above the world
change as it may, he said it, and
for this he was killed, for saying,
10 and feeling, and being/change, all
collected hot in his heart, For Malcolm's
heart, raising us above our filthy cities,
for his stride, and his beat, and his address
to the grey monsters of the world, For Malcolm's
15 pleas for your dignity, black men, for your life,
black men, for the filling of your minds
with righteousness, For all of him dead and
gone and vanished from us, and all of him which
clings to our speech-black god of our time.
20 For all of him, and all of yourself, look up,
black man, quit stuttering and shuffling, look up,
black man, quit whining and stooping, for all of him,
For Great Malcolm a prince of the earth, let nothing in us rest
until we avenge ourselves for his death, stupid animals
25 that killed him, let us never breathe a pure breath if
we fail, and white men call us faggots till the end of
the earth.

Imamu Amiri Baraka[1]   (1934–   )
Preface to a Twenty Volume Suicide Note

Lately, I've become accustomed to the way
The ground opens up and envelops me
Each time I go out to walk the dog.
Or the broad edged silly music the wind
5 Makes when I run for a bus—

Things have come to that.

And now, each night I count the stars,
And each night I get the same number.

[1] Earlier known as LeRoi Jones.

And when they will not come to be counted
10 I count the holes they leave.

Nobody sings anymore.

And then last night, I tiptoed up
To my daughter's room and heard her
Talking to someone, and when I opened
15 The door, there was no one there. . .
Only she on her knees,
Peeking into her own clasped hands.

Mark Strand (1934–)
From a Litany

There is an open field I lie down in a hole I once dug and I praise the sky.
I praise the clouds that are like lungs of light.
I praise the owl that wants to inhabit me and the hawk that does not.
I praise the mouse's fury, the wolf's consideration.
5 I praise the dog that lives in the household of people and shall never be one of them.
I praise the whale that lives under the cold blankets of salt.
I praise the formations of squid, the domes of meandra.
I praise the secrecy of doors, the openness of windows.
I praise the depth of closets.
10 I praise the wind, the rising generations of air.
I praise the trees on whose branches shall sit the Cock of Portugal and the Polish Cock.
I praise the palm trees of Rio and those that shall grow in London.
I praise the gardeners, the worms and the small plants that praise each other.
I praise the sweet berries of Georgetown, Maine and the song of the white-throated
    sparrow.
15 I praise the poets of Waverly Place and Eleventh Street, and the one whose bones turn to
    dark emeralds when he stands upright in the wind.
I praise the clocks for which I grow old in a day and young in a day.
I praise all manner of shade, that which I see and that which I do not.
I praise all roofs from the watery roof of the pond to the slate roof of the customs house.
I praise those who have made of their bodies final embassies of flesh.
20 I praise the failure of those with ambition, the authors of leaflets and notebooks of
    nothing.
I praise the moon for suffering men.
I praise the sun its tributes.
I praise the pain of revival and the bliss of decline.
I praise all for nothing because there is no price.

25 I praise myself for the way I have with a shovel and I praise the shovel.
I praise the motive of praise by which I shall be reborn.
I praise the morning whose sun is upon me.
I praise the evening whose son I am.

Richard Rackstraw (1936–1974)

The Word

You are walking the track, counting
the ties, perhaps, as a hunter
whose pockets are empty, whose rage
steadies him. The gun you carry is open.

5 You have hunted for years. Thin animals
are your familiars. You have loved
the hollows of their eyes, the tensile
marrow of their wills in such silence.

Now bruised from the sun, your eyes
10 darken like roses. It is almost night.
You are walking into a distance
the late-autumn Monarch[1] flies.

Deep in your thought was a word
the sound of dry flesh pawing at
15 the door of a cabin. You opened the door
and the word, the word came in.

---

[1] A large migratory American butterfly of unusual size and beauty. When this poem was written, their winter home was a mystery; hence the author is using their flight as a symbol related to "walking into a distance." Very recently the monarchs' winter home was found to be in Mexico, a literal fact unrelated to the poem.

Diane Wakoski   (1937–   )
You, Letting the Trees Stand as My Betrayer

You replaced the Douglas firs
    that reached
    like mechanics' hands
    outside my windows

5   trying to understand the glass
    with furry, needle-tipped noses

You,
who understood me
in the rain

10 or at least
accepted me.

The trees never left
my windows
even when they put on gloves
15 for age;
they had married the glass
with the thud of falling cones.
They remembered my name
on windy nights.

20 But you
are my betrayer
who tried to frighten me with trees one night.
Then chopped them down
outside my windows
25 the next day

You ride a motorcycle
past wintry trees
and summer trees
and never once
30 think of me.
But my friends are
the falling branches
that will tilt you
and snap your neck one day.
35 I dream of your thick body
uprooted
and torn by a storm
on a motorcycle track.

You chopped down my trees—
40 they were my legs—
and unlike George Washington you did tell
many lies.
You are my betrayer,
you woodsman,
45 the man who stomps into the heart of this
forest.

Margaret Atwood   (1939–   )
Game After Supper

This is before electricity,
it is when there were porches.

On the sagging porch an old man
is rocking. The porch is wooden,

5 the house is wooden and grey;
in the living room which smells of
smoke and mildew, soon
the woman will light the kerosene lamp.

There is a barn but I am not in the barn;
10 there is an orchard too, gone bad,

its apples like soft cork
but I am not there either.

I am hiding in the long grass
with my two dead cousins,
15 the membrane grown already
across their throats.

We hear crickets and our own hearts
close to our ears;
though we giggle, we are afraid.

20 From the shadows around
the corner of the house
a tall man is coming to find us:

He will be an uncle,
if we are lucky.

Erica Jong (1942–   )
How You Get Born

One night, your mother is listening to the walls.
The clock whirrs like insect wings.
The ticking says lonely lonely lonely.

In the living room, the black couch swallows her.
5 She trusts it more than men,
but no one will ever love her
enough.

She doesn't yet know you
so how can she love you?
10 She loves you like God or Shakespeare.
She loves you like Mozart.

You are trembling in the walls like music.
You cross the ceiling in a phantom car of light.

Meanwhile unborn,
15 you wait in a heavy rainsoaked cloud
for your father's thunderbolt.
Your mother lies in the living room dreaming your hands.
Your mother lies in the living room dreaming your eyes.

She awakens & a shudder shakes her teeth.
20 The world is beginning again after the flood.

She slides into bed beside that gray-faced man,
your father.
She opens her legs to your coming.

Nikki Giovanni (1943–   )
Kidnap Poem

ever been kidnapped
by a poet
if i were a poet
i'd kidnap you
5 put you in my phrases and meter
you to jones beach

or maybe coney island
or maybe just to my house
lyric you in lilacs
10 dash you in the rain
blend into the beach
to complement my see
play the lyre for you
ode you with my love song
15 anything to win you
wrap you in the red Black green
show you off to mama
yeah if i were a poet i'd kid
nap you.

James Tate (1943–   )
The Lost Pilot

for my father, 1922–1944

Your face did not rot
like the others—the co-pilot,
for example, I saw him

yesterday. His face is corn-
5 mush: his wife and daughter,
the poor ignorant people, stare

as if he will compose soon.
He was more wronged than Job.
But your face did not rot

10 like the others—it grew dark,
and hard like ebony;
the features progressed in their

distinction. If I could cajole
you to come back for an evening,
15 down from your compulsive

orbiting, I would touch you,
read your face as Dallas,
your hoodlum gunner, now,

with the blistered eyes, reads
20 his braille editions. I would
touch your face as a disinterested

scholar touches an original page.
However frightening, I would
discover you, and I would not

25 turn you in; I would not make
you face your wife, or Dallas,
or the co-pilot, Jim. You

could return to your crazy
orbiting, and I would not try
30 to fully understand what

it means to you. All I know
is this: when I see you,
as I have seen you at least

once every year of my life,
35 spin across the wilds of the sky
like a tiny, African god,

I feel dead. I feel as if I were
the residue of a stranger's life,
that I should pursue you.

40 My head cocked toward the sky,
I cannot get off the ground,
and, you, passing over again,

fast, perfect, and unwilling
to tell me that you are doing
45 well, or that it was mistake

that placed you in that world,
and me in this; or that misfortune
placed these worlds in us.

Edward Francisco (1953–   )
Lilith's Child[1]

I had no voice before
But now
Speaking with a pale tongue
I tell of parents who give birth
5 To tombstones.

[1] The poem was occasioned by the death of a four-year-old girl who was fatally beaten by her step-father and mother in Tennessee in 1976.

Parents whose faces hard and weatherbeaten
As agony
Stiffen with the venom of a kiss
For one who trusted them
10 As she trusted
Breathing.

Once running on pink feet
I swam breezy upon the grass
Under clouds whiter than milk
15 Or the bathtub where I used to sit warmly
Counting the wrinkles
In my fingers held under water
Until mother would come unplug the drain
That swallowed all but me
20 Left whitely bare and shivering
Against the porcelain.

How I dreaded the swift tug
Of the brush through my hair
Sweet and wild as fieldflowers.
25 Yet not so much did I dread
As when in the door
He appeared, eyes glaring, marching
Me over in the furious cadence
Of his clenched heart
30 Until taking my arm
He would fling me breathless upon the bed
That quivered with my limbs' descent.

Then He would clap my back in cruel applause
For tricks performed by one
35 Who only sought to please
And so
Nailed herself to every task,
Ran up and down the stairs
Danced the cruel dance
40 Until one night
Hearing the ancient curse of winds
Blow fiercely from the North
I pulled the eternal blanket over shivering day
And slept.

45 I had not meant to sleep so long
But only wished to listen to the song
Of the bird in the egg
Outside my window
Whose ageless voice
50 First rose then fell in measured echoes
To the chorus of mourning neighbors
Singing beside the grave.

And there

Standing among the shadows
55   I saw
Shapes of long-forgotten power rise
And heard there dreams
In which only children cried
60   And knew at last
That with each ritual hand of dust,
They sought to choke the final cry—
The cry of Lilith's child.

Four Modern Classics

William Butler Yeats   (1865–1939)
Among School Children

I

I walk through the long schoolroom questioning;[1]
A kind old nun in a white hood replies;
The children learn to cipher and to sing,
To study reading-books and history,
5   To cut and sew, be neat in everything
In the best modern way—the children's eyes
In momentary wonder stare upon
A sixty-year-old smiling public man.

II

I dream of a Ledaean body,[2] bent
10   Above a sinking fire, a tale that she
Told of a harsh reproof, or trivial event
That changed some childish day to tragedy—
Told, and it seemed that our two natures blent
Into a sphere from youthful sympathy,
15   Or else, to alter Plato's parable,[3]
Into the yolk and white of the one shell.

---

[1] Yeats was an Irish Senator (1922–1928) when he made the schoolroom visit on which the poem is based.   [2] As beautiful as Leda and Helen of Troy, her daughter (see l. 20) whose father, Zeus, in the form of a swan, had possessed Leda. Yeats's poem "Leda and the Swan" celebrates the event.
[3] Plato's *Symposium* tells us that Zeus "cut men in two . . . as you might divide an egg with a hair," and hence "each of us when separated is but the indenture of a man, having one side only like a flat fish, and he is always looking for his other half."

III

And thinking of that fit of grief or rage
I look upon one child or t'other there
And wonder if she stood so at that age—
20 For even daughters of the swan can share
Something of every paddler's heritage—
And had that colour upon cheek or hair,
And thereupon my heart is driven wild:
She stands before me as a living child.

IV

25 Her present image floats into the mind—
Did Quattrocento[4] finger fashion it
Hollow of cheek as though it drank the wind
And took a mess of shadows for its meat?
And I though never of Ledaean kind
30 Had pretty plumage once—enough of that,
Better to smile on all that smile, and show
There is a comfortable kind of old scarecrow.

V

What youthful mother, a shape upon her lap
Honey of generation[5] had betrayed,
35 And that must sleep, shriek, struggle to escape
As recollection or the drug decide,
Would think her son, did she but see that shape
With sixty or more winters on its head,
A compensation for the pang of his birth,
40 Or the uncertainty of his setting forth?

VI

Plato thought nature but a spume that plays
Upon a ghostly paradigm of things;[6]
Solider Aristotle played the taws
Upon the bottom of a king of kings;[7]
45 World-famous golden-thighed Pythagoras[8]
Fingered upon a fiddle-stick or strings
What a star sang and careless Muses heard:
Old clothes upon old sticks to scare a bird.[9]

---

[4] An Italian term used by the art historians to describe schools and styles of fifteenth-century painting as, for example, Botticelli's female figures.   [5] Yeats's note: "I have taken the 'honey of generation' from Porphyry's essay on 'The Cave of the Nymphs,' but find no warrant in Porphyry for considering it the 'drug' that destroys the 'recollection' of pre-natal freedom. He blamed a cup of oblivion given in the zodiacal sign of Cancer." Porphyry's original name was Malchus (232?–304?A.D.), Greek scholar and Neoplatonic philosopher.   [6] Plato regarded physical reality as an imperfect representation of ideal reality (Plato's philosophy of idealism).   [7] The pupil of Plato, Aristotle nevertheless taught that our world does possess reality.   [8] Greek philosopher (fl. c. 530 B.C.), whose later followers thought him a god with a golden thigh, taught the transmigration of souls (reincarnation) and that reality is found in the mathematical relationships that govern its order and harmony. Such mysticism intrigued Yeats.   [9] See l. 32.

VII

Both nuns and mothers worship images,
50 But those the candles light are not as those
That animate a mother's reveries,
But keep a marble or a bronze repose.
And yet they too break hearts—O Presences
That passion, piety or affection knows,
55 And that all heavenly glory symbolize—
O self-born mockers of man's enterprise;

VIII

Labour is blossoming or dancing where
The body is not bruised to pleasure soul.
Nor beauty born out of its own despair,
60 Nor blear-eyed wisdom out of midnight oil.
O chestnut-tree, great-rooted blossomer,
Are you the leaf, the blossom or the bole?
O body swayed to music, O brightening glance,
How can we know the dancer from the dance?

Robert Frost (1874–1963)
After Apple-Picking

My long two-pointed ladder's sticking through a tree
Toward heaven still,
And there's a barrel that I didn't fill
Beside it, and there may be two or three
5 Apples I didn't pick upon some bough.
But I am done with apple-picking now.
Essence of winter sleep is on the night,
The scent of apples: I am drowsing off.
I cannot rub the strangeness from my sight
10 I got from looking through a pane of glass
I skimmed this morning from the drinking trough
And held against the world of hoary grass.
It melted, and I let it fall and break.
But I was well
15 Upon my way to sleep before it fell,
And I could tell
What form my dreaming was about to take.
Magnified apples appear and disappear,
Stem end and blossom end,
20 And every fleck of russet showing clear.

My instep arch not only keeps the ache,
It keeps the pressure of a ladder-round.
I feel the ladder sway as the boughs bend.
And I keep hearing from the cellar bin
25 The rumbling sound
Of load on load of apples coming in.
For I have had too much
Of apple-picking: I am overtired
Of the great harvest I myself desired.
30 There were ten thousand thousand fruit to touch,
Cherish in hand, lift down, and not let fall.
For all
That struck the earth,
No matter if not bruised or spiked with stubble,
35 Went surely to the cider-apple heap
As of no worth.
One can see what will trouble
This sleep of mine, whatever sleep it is.
Were he not gone,
40 The woodchuck could say whether it's like his
Long sleep, as I describe its coming on,
Or just some human sleep.

Wallace Stevens (1879–1955)
Sunday Morning[1]

I
Complacencies of the peignoir,[2] and late
Coffee and oranges in a sunny chair,
And the green freedom of a cockatoo
Upon a rug mingle to dissipate
5 The holy hush of ancient sacrifice.
She dreams a little, and she feels the dark
Encroachment of that old catastrophe,[3]
As a calm darkens among water-lights.
The pungent oranges and bright, green wings
10 Seem things in some procession of the dead,
Winding across wide water, without sound.

[1] Double meaning: religious Sunday, and sun day as in ll. 2, 19–21, 91–97, 110. Stevens's basic question: where is the true paradise? The answer is found in the replies to the woman's troubled questionings. [2] Negligee. [3] The crucifixion or possibly death in general.

The day is like wide water, without sound,
Stilled for the passing of her dreaming feet
Over the seas, to silent Palestine,
15 Dominion of the blood and sepulchre.[4]

II

Why should she give her bounty to the dead?
What is divinity if it can come
Only in silent shadows and in dreams?
Shall she not find in comforts of the sun,
20 In pungent fruit and bright, green wings, or else
In any balm or beauty of the earth,
Things to be cherished like the thought of heaven?
Divinity must live within herself:
Passions of rain, or moods in falling snow;
25 Grievings in loneliness, or unsubdued
Elations when the forest blooms; gusty
Emotions on wet roads on autumn nights;
All pleasures and all pains, remembering
The bough of summer and the winter branch.
30 These are the measures destined for her soul.

III

Jove[5] in the clouds had his inhuman birth.
No mother suckled him, no sweet land gave
Large-mannered motions to his mythy mind.
He moved among us, as a muttering king,
35 Magnificent, would move among his hinds,
Until our blood, commingling, virginal,
With heaven, brought such requital to desire
The very hinds discerned it, in a star.
Shall our blood fail? Or shall it come to be
40 The blood of paradise? And shall the earth
Seem all of paradise that we shall know?
The sky will be much friendlier then than now,
A part of labor and a part of pain,
And next in glory to enduring love,
45 Not this dividing and indifferent blue.

IV

She says, "I am content when wakened birds,
Before they fly, test the reality
Of misty fields, by their sweet questionings;
But when the birds are gone, and their warm fields
50 Return no more, where, then, is paradise?"
There is not any haunt of prophecy,
Nor any old chimera of the grave,
Neither the golden underground, nor isle

---

[4] Ll. 14–15: Palestine, the Christian Holy Land, the scene of Christ's crucifixion (blood) and the tomb (sepulchre).   [5] God of the sky and king of gods and men (Latin—Jupiter, Greek—Zeus).

Melodious, where spirits gat[6] them home,
55 Nor visionary south, nor cloudy palm
Remote on heaven's hill, that has endured
As April's green endures; or will endure
Like her remembrance of awakened birds,
Or her desire for June and evening, tipped
60 By the consummation of the swallow's wings.

V

She says, "But in contentment I still feel
The need of some imperishable bliss."
Death is the mother of beauty; hence from her,
Alone, shall come fulfilment to our dreams
65 And our desires. Although she strews the leaves
Of sure obliteration on our paths,
The path sick sorrow took, the many paths
Where triumph rang its brassy phrase, or love
Whispered a little out of tenderness,
70 She makes the willow shiver in the sun
For maidens who were wont to sit and gaze
Upon the grass, relinquished to their feet.
She causes boys to pile new plums and pears
On disregarded plate. The maidens taste
75 And stray impassioned in the littering leaves.

VI

Is there no change of death in paradise?
Does ripe fruit never fall? Or do the boughs
Hang always heavy in that perfect sky,
Unchanging, yet so like our perishing earth,
80 With rivers like our own that seek for seas
They never find, the same receding shores
That never touch with inarticulate pang?
Why set the pear upon those river-banks
Or spice the shores with odors of the plum?
85 Alas, that they should wear our colors there,
The silken weavings of our afternoons,
And pick the strings of our insipid lutes!
Death is the mother of beauty, mystical,
Within whose burning bosom we devise
90 Our earthly mothers waiting, sleeplessly.

VII

Supple and turbulent, a ring of men
Shall chant in orgy on a summer morn
Their boisterous devotion to the sun,
Not as a god, but as a god might be,
95 Naked among them, like a savage source.
Their chant shall be a chant of paradise,
Out of their blood, returning to the sky;

[6] Got.

And in their chant shall enter, voice by voice,
The windy lake wherein their lord delights,
100 The trees, like serafin,[7] and echoing hills,
That choir among themselves long afterward.
They shall know well the heavenly fellowship
Of men that perish and of summer morn.
And whence they came and whither they shall go
105 The dew upon their feet shall manifest.

VIII

She hears, upon that water without sound,
A voice that cries, "The tomb in Palestine[8]
Is not the porch of spirits lingering.
It is the grave of Jesus, where he lay."
110 We live in an old chaos of the sun,
Or old dependency of day and night,
Or island solitude, unsponsored, free,
Of that wide water, inescapable.
Deer walk upon our mountains, and the quail
115 Whistle about us their spontaneous cries;
Sweet berries ripen in the wilderness;
And, in the isolation of the sky,
At evening, casual flocks of pigeons make
Ambiguous undulations as they sink,
120 Downward to darkness, on extended wings.

T. S. Eliot   (1888–1965)
The Love Song of J. Alfred Prufrock

*S'io credesse che mia risposta fosse
A persona che mai tornasse al mondo,
Questa fiamma staria senza più scosse.
Ma perciocché giammai di questo fondo
Non tornò vivo alcun, s'i'odo il vero,
Senza tema d'infamia ti rispondo.*[1]

---

[7] Seraphim (pl.), highest order of angels at God's throne. See Dickinson's "I Taste a Liquor Never Brewed," final stanza (p. 370).   [8] Ll. 107–112: the passage seems to mean that Jesus was but a man who like us was "unsponsored, free." Compare the interpretation of Jesus found in Pound's poem "Ballad of the Goodly Fere," p. 337.

[1] If I believed that my answer might belong
To anyone who ever returned to the world,
This flame would leap no more.
But since, however, from these depths
No one ever returns alive, if I know the truth,
Then without fear of infamy I answer you.
                    Dante, *Inferno*, xxvii, 61–66.

Let us go then, you and I,[2]
When the evening is spread out against the sky
Like a patient etherised upon a table;
Let us go, through certain half-deserted streets,
5 The muttering retreats
Of restless nights in one-night cheap hotels
And sawdust restaurants with oyster-shells:
Streets that follow like a tedious argument
Of insidious intent
10 To lead you to an overwhelming question . . .
Oh, do not ask 'What is it?'
Let us go and make our visit.

 In the room the women come and go
Talking of Michelangelo.

15 The yellow fog that rubs its back upon the window-panes,
The yellow smoke that rubs its muzzle on the window-panes,
Licked its tongue into the corners of the evening,
Lingered upon the pools that stand in drains,
Let fall upon its back the soot that falls from chimneys,
20 Slipped by the terrace, made a sudden leap,
And seeing that it was a soft October night,
Curled once about the house, and fell asleep.

 And indeed there will be time
For the yellow smoke that slides along the street
25 Rubbing its back upon the window-panes;
There will be time, there will be time
To prepare a face to meet the faces that you meet;
There will be time to murder and create,
And time for all the works and days of hands[3]
30 That lift and drop a question on your plate;
Time for you and time for me,
And time yet for a hundred indecisions,
And for a hundred visions and revisions,
Before the taking of a toast and tea.

35 In the room the women come and go
Talking of Michelangelo.

 And indeed there will be time
To wonder, 'Do I dare?' and, 'Do I dare?'
Time to turn back and descend the stair,
40 With a bald spot in the middle of my hair—
(They will say: 'How his hair is growing thin!')
My morning coat, my collar mounting firmly to the chin,
My necktie rich and modest, but asserted by a simple pin—
(They will say: 'But how his arms and legs are thin!')

---

[2] Probably Prufrock's divided self; the entire poem seems to support this interpretation.   [3] An allusion to the Greek poet (8th century B.C.) Hesiod's *Works and Days*, a poem celebrating hard work in the fields.

45 Do I dare
  Disturb the universe?
  In a minute there is time
  For decisions and revisions which a minute will reverse.

      For I have known them all already, known them all:—
50 Have known the evenings, mornings, afternoons,
  I have measured out my life with coffee spoons;
  I know the voices dying with a dying fall
  Beneath the music from a farther room.
      So how should I presume?

55   And I have known the eyes already, known them all—
  The eyes that fix you in a formulated phrase,
  And when I am formulated, sprawling on a pin,
  When I am pinned and wriggling on the wall,
  Then how should I begin
60 To spit out all the butt-ends of my days and ways?
      And how should I presume?

      And I have known the arms already, known them all—
  Arms that are braceleted and white and bare
  (But in the lamplight, downed with light brown hair!)
65 Is it perfume from a dress
  That makes me so digress?
  Arms that lie along a table, or wrap about a shawl.
      And should I then presume?
      And how should I begin?

                    .   .   .   .   .

70   Shall I say, I have gone at dusk through narrow streets
  And watched the smoke that rises from the pipes
  Of lonely men in shirt-sleeves, leaning out of windows? . . .

      I should have been a pair of ragged claws
  Scuttling across the floors of silent seas.

                    .   .   .   .   .

75   And the afternoon, the evening, sleeps so peacefully!
  Smoothed by long fingers,
  Asleep . . . tired . . . or it malingers,
  Stretched on the floor, here beside you and me.
  Should I, after tea and cakes and ices,
80 Have the strength to force the moment to its crisis?
  But though I have wept and fasted, wept and prayed,
  Though I have seen my head (grown slightly bald) brought in upon a platter,[4]
  I am no prophet—and here's no great matter;
  I have seen the moment of my greatness flicker,

---

[4] Like the head of John the Baptist. At the request of Salome, who had pleased Herod with her dancing at his birthday feast, Herod executed John the Baptist, who was in prison, and had his head brought in on a platter. See Matthew 14:3–11.

85 And I have seen the eternal Footman[5] hold my coat, and snicker,
And in short, I was afraid.

    And would it have been worth it, after all,
After the cups, the marmalade, the tea,
Among the porcelain, among some talk of you and me,
90 Would it have been worth while,
To have bitten off the matter with a smile,
To have squeezed the universe into a ball[6]
To roll it toward some overwhelming question,
To say: 'I am Lazarus,[7] come from the dead,
95 Come back to tell you all, I shall tell you all'—
If one, settling a pillow by her head,
    Should say: 'That is not what I meant at all.
    That is not it, at all.'

    And would it have been worth it, after all,
100 Would it have been worth while,
After the sunsets and the dooryards and the sprinkled streets,
After the novels, after the teacups, after the skirts that trail along the floor—
And this, and so much more?—
It is impossible to say just what I mean!
105 But as if a magic lantern threw the nerves in patterns on a screen:
Would it have been worth while
If one, settling a pillow or throwing off a shawl,
And turning toward the window, should say:
    'That is not it at all,
110   That is not what I meant, at all.'

    . . . . .

    No! I am not Prince Hamlet, nor was meant to be;
Am an attendant lord, one that will do
To swell a progress,[8] start a scene or two,
Advise the prince; no doubt, an easy tool,
115 Deferential, glad to be of use,
Politic, cautious, and meticulous;
Full of high sentence, but a bit obtuse;
At times, indeed, almost ridiculous—
Almost, at times, the Fool.

120   I grow old . . I grow old . . .
I shall wear the bottoms of my trousers rolled.

    Shall I part my hair behind? Do I dare to eat a peach?
I shall wear white flannel trousers, and walk upon the beach.
I have heard the mermaids singing, each to each.

---

[5] Probably Death and his waiting carriage. Compare Dickinson's concept of death in "Because I Could Not Stop for Death," p. 426.   [6] See Marvell's "To His Coy Mistress," ll. 41–42, p. 410.
[7] Lazarus, the brother of Mary and Martha, who was raised from death by Christ. See John 11:1–44; and Luke 16:19–26.   [8] A progress in Elizabethan times was a journey, usually led by the Queen, attended by her court, into her kingdom. Ll. 111–119 refer to Shakespeare's *Hamlet* (see p. 626) including Prince Hamlet, Polonius the adviser to the King, and Osric "the Fool."

125 I do not think that they will sing to me.

I have seen them riding seaward on the waves
Combing the white hair of the waves blown back
When the wind blows the water white and black.

We have lingered in the chambers of the sea
130 By sea girls wreathed with seaweed red and brown
Till human voices wake us, and we drown.

Comments

Four characteristic elements of Eliot's style are important to keep in mind in reading the poem. First, most of Eliot's symbols are textual (personal). They are not conventional symbols whose meanings are immediately apparent; they must be understood in the complete context of the poem. Second, Eliot does not provide transitions between the scenes of his story; whatever logical sequence exists is implied, not stated. Note the absence of any conventional transition, for example, between lines 12 and 13. The transitions are implicit in the meaning of the poem. Third, Eliot uses the method of dramatic opposition, and this method, once understood, will help us to make the transitions between apparently unrelated scenes. Prufrock is opposed to Michelangelo, John the Baptist, Lazarus, Shakespeare, in order to contrast sharply the great values of the past with those represented by Prufrock. And fourth, Eliot uses a method he calls the "objective correlative" by which he dramatizes sensations, emotions, and feelings through "a set of objects, a situation, a chain of events. . . . " For example, instead of having Prufrock tell us directly that he has wasted his life in frivolous activity, Eliot has him say, "I have measured out my life with coffee spoons," and we participate in Prufrock's emotion of frustration. By correlating Prufrock's frustration with the objective act of measuring out his life in useless activity, Eliot dramatizes Prufrock's sensations.

Two facts about the poem should help get us started: it is a soliloquy, and the title is ironic. The action takes place in Prufrock's mind where Eliot objectifies Prufrock's neurotic self. The love song is a far cry from those we have read by Shakespeare, Herrick, Marvell, Burns, and others. The poem is in effect a psychological self-analysis of a man who is incapable of love, physically and spiritually, who cannot "force the moment to its crisis," who is "in short . . . afraid." He is a man divided, like Hamlet, but unlike Hamlet he never welds himself together for any heroic action; he does not "Have the strength to force the moment to its crisis." One of the most thoughtful interpretations of the poem is found in Grover Smith's "A Critique of 'The Love Song of J. Alfred Prufrock,' " p. 1153.

Drama

In tragic life, God wot,
No villain need be! Passions spin the plot:
We are betrayed by what is false within.
GEORGE MEREDITH

Preliminaries

A backward glance at the sections on fiction and poetry may recall to us many dramatic moments. We may have observed that the conversation of Mrs. Ansley and Mrs. Slade in "Roman Fever" was like a scene from a play or that "My Last Duchess" is drama of a special sort. When we say *dramatic*, we may have in mind *intense*. If so, we have the right notion of the nature of drama, for although all forms of literature are concentrations or distillations of human experience, drama has its own peculiar intensity and rightly lends its name to other forms when they become especially vivid. We are not, then, unfamiliar with what is dramatic when we approach drama itself.

We know, too, that drama is simply one way of telling a story. All the terms that we have applied to fiction—plot, characters, setting, exposition, antecedent action, crisis, and others—apply equally well to drama. How drama tells a story may be seen most clearly in a representative specimen, a conventional one-act play by one of America's great dramatists.

Eugene O'Neill (1888–1953)
Ile

CHARACTERS

BEN, *the cabin boy*
THE STEWARD
CAPTAIN KEENEY
SLOCUM, *second mate*
MRS. KEENEY
JOE, *a harpooner*
Members of the crew of the steam whaler
 Atlantic Queen

Scene. CAPTAIN KEENEY'S *cabin on board the steam whaling ship* Atlantic Queen—*a small, square compartment about eight feet high with a skylight in the center looking out on the poop deck. On the left [the stern of the ship] a long bench with rough cushions is built in against the wall. In front of the bench, a table. Over the bench, several curtained portholes.*

In the rear, left, a door leading to the CAPTAIN'S *sleeping quarters. To the right of the door a small organ, looking as if it were brand-new, is placed against the wall.*

On the right, to the rear, a marble-topped sideboard. On the sideboard, a woman's sewing basket. Farther forward, a doorway leading to the companionway, and past the officers' quarters to the main deck.

In the center of the room, a stove. From the middle of the ceiling a hanging lamp is suspended. The walls of the cabin are painted white.

There is no rolling of the ship, and the light which comes through the skylight is sickly and faint, indicating one of those gray days of calm when ocean and sky are alike dead. The silence is unbroken except for the measured tread of someone walking up and down on the poop deck overhead.

It is nearing two bells—one o'clock—in the afternoon of a day in the year 1895.

At the rise of the curtain there is a moment of intense silence. Then THE STEWARD *enters and commences to clear the table of the few dishes which still remain on it after the* CAPTAIN'S *dinner. He is an old, grizzled man dressed in dungaree pants, a sweater, and a woolen cap with earflaps. His manner is sullen and angry. He stops stacking up the plates and casts a quick glance upward at the skylight; then tiptoes over to the closed door in rear and listens with his ear pressed to the crack. What he hears makes his face darken and he mutters a furious curse. There is a noise from the doorway on the right and he darts back to the table.*

BEN *enters. He is an overgrown, gawky boy with a long, pinched face. He is dressed in sweater, fur cap, etc. His teeth are chattering with the cold and he hurries to the stove, where he stands for a moment shivering, blowing on his hands, slapping them against his sides, on the verge of crying.*

THE STEWARD *(in relieved tones—seeing who it is)* Oh, 'tis you, is it? What're ye shiverin' 'bout? Stay by the stove where ye belong and ye'll find no need of chatterin'.

BEN It's c-c-cold. *(Trying to control his chattering teeth—derisively)* Who d'ye think it were—the Old Man?

THE STEWARD *(makes a threatening move—*BEN *shrinks away)* None o' your lip, young un, or I'll learn ye. *(More kindly)* Where was it ye've been all o' the time—the fo'c's'tle?

BEN Yes.

THE STEWARD Let the Old Man see ye up for'ard monkeyshinin' with the hands and ye'll get a hidin' ye'll not forget in a hurry.

BEN Aw, he don't see nothin'. *(A trace of awe in his tones—he glances upward)* He just walks up and down like he didn't notice nobody—and stares at the ice to the no'th'ard.

THE STEWARD *(the same tone of awe creeping into his voice)* He's always starin' at the ice. *(In a sudden rage, shaking his fist at the skylight)* Ice, ice, ice! Damn him and damn the ice! Holdin' us in for nigh on a year—nothin' to see but ice—stuck in it like a fly in molasses!

BEN *(apprehensively)* Ssshh! He'll hear ye.

THE STEWARD *(raging)* Aye, damn him, and damn the Arctic seas, and damn this stinkin' whalin' ship of his, and damn me for a fool to ever ship on it! *(Subsiding as if realizing the uselessness of this outburst—shaking his head—slowly, with deep conviction)* He's a hard man—as hard a man as ever sailed the seas.

BEN *(solemnly)* Aye.

THE STEWARD The two years we all signed up for are done this day. Blessed Christ! Two years 'o this dog's life, and no luck in the fishin', and the hands half starved with the food runnin' low, rotten as it is; and not a sign of him turnin' back for home! *(Bitterly)* Home! I begin to doubt if ever I'll set foot on land again. *(Excitedly)* What is it he thinks he's goin' to do? Keep us all up here after our time is worked out till the last man of us is starved to death or frozen? We've grub enough hardly to last out the voyage back if we started now. What are the men goin' to do 'bout it? Did ye hear any talk in the fo'c's'tle?

BEN *(going over to him—in a half-whisper)* They said if he don't put back south for home today they're goin' to mutiny.

THE STEWARD *(with grim satisfaction)* Mutiny? Aye, 'tis the only thing they can do; and serve him right after the manner he's treated them—'s if they weren't no better nor dogs.

BEN The ice is all broke up to s'uth'ard. They's clear water 's far 's you can see. He ain't got no excuse for not turnin' back for home, the men says.

THE STEWARD *(bitterly)* He won't look nowheres but no'th'ard where they's only the ice to see. He don't want to see no clear water. All he thinks on is gittin' the ile —'s if it was our fault he ain't had good luck with the whales. *(Shaking his head)* I think the man's mighty nigh losin' his senses.

BEN *(awed)* D'you really think he's crazy?

THE STEWARD Aye, it's the punishment o' God on him. Did ye ever hear of a man who wasn't crazy do the things he does? *(Pointing to the door in rear)* Who but a man that's mad would take his woman—and as sweet a woman as ever was—on a stinkin' whalin' ship to the Arctic seas to be locked in by the rotten ice for nigh on a year, and maybe lose her senses forever—for it's sure she'll never be the same again.

BEN *(sadly)* She useter be awful nice to me before—*(His eyes grow wide and frightened.)* she got—like she is.

THE STEWARD   Aye, she was good to all of us. 'Twould have been hell on board without her; for he's a hard man—a hard, hard man—a driver if there ever were one. *(With a grim laugh)* I hope he's satisfied now—drivin' her on till she's near lost her mind. And who could blame her? 'Tis a God's wonder we're not a ship full of crazed people— with the damned ice all the time, and the quiet so thick you're afraid to hear your own voice.

BEN *(with a frightened glance toward the door on right)*   She don't never speak to me no more—jest looks at me 's if she didn't know me.

THE STEWARD   She don't know no one—but him. She talks to him—when she does talk—right enough.

BEN   She does nothin' all day long now but sit and sew—and then she cries to herself without makin' no noise. I've seen her.

THE STEWARD   Aye, I could hear her through the door a while back.

BEN *(tiptoes over to the door and listens)*   She's cryin' now.

THE STEWARD *(furiously—shaking his fist)*   God send his soul to hell for the devil he is! *(There is the noise of someone coming slowly down the companionway stairs. THE STEWARD hurries to his stacked-up dishes. He is so nervous from fright that he knocks off the top one, which falls and breaks on the floor. He stands aghast, trembling with dread. BEN is violently rubbing off the organ with a piece of cloth which he has snatched from his pocket. CAPTAIN KEENEY appears in the doorway on right and comes into the cabin, removing his fur cap as he does so. He is a man of about forty, around five-ten in height but looking much shorter on account of the enormous proportions of his shoulders and chest. His face is massive and deeply lined, with gray-blue eyes of a bleak hardness, and a tightly clenched, thin-lipped mouth. His thick hair is long and gray. He is dressed in a heavy blue jacket and blue pants stuffed into his sea-boots.*

He is followed into the cabin by the SECOND MATE, a rangy six-footer with a lean weather-beaten face. The MATE is dressed about the same as the CAPTAIN. He is a man of thirty or so.)

KEENEY *(comes toward THE STEWARD—with a stern look on his face. THE STEWARD is visibly frightened and the stack of dishes rattle in his trembling hands. KEENEY draws back his fist and THE STEWARD shrinks away. The fist is gradually lowered and KEENEY speaks slowly.)*   'Twould be like hitting a worm. It is nigh on two bells, Mr. Steward, and this truck not cleared yet.

THE STEWARD *(stammering)*   Y-y-yes, sir.

KEENEY   Instead of doin' your rightful work ye've been below here gossipin' old woman's talk with that boy. *(To BEN, fiercely)* Get out o' this, you! Clean up the chart room. *(BEN darts past the MATE to the open doorway.)* Pick up that dish, Mr. Steward!

THE STEWARD *(doing so with difficulty)*   Yes, sir.

KEENEY   The next dish you break, Mr. Steward, you take a bath in the Bering Sea at the end of a rope.

THE STEWARD *(trembling)*   Yes, sir. *(He hurries out. The SECOND MATE walks slowly over to the CAPTAIN.)*

MATE   I warn't 'specially anxious the man at the wheel should catch what I wanted to say to you, sir. That's why I asked you to come below.

KEENEY *(impatiently)*   Speak your say, Mr. Slocum.

MATE *(unconsciously lowering his voice)*   I'm afeard there'll be trouble with the hands by the look o' things. They'll likely turn ugly, every blessed one o' them, if you don't put back. The two years they signed up for is up today.

KEENEY   And d'you think you're tellin' me somethin' new, Mr. Slocum? I've felt it in the air this long time past. D'you think I've not seen their ugly looks and the grudgin' way they worked? *(The door in rear is opened and* MRS. KEENEY *stands in the doorway. She is a slight, sweet-faced little woman primly dressed in black. Her eyes are red from weeping and her face drawn and pale. She takes in the cabin with a frightened glance and stands as if fixed to the spot by some nameless dread, clasping and unclasping her hands nervously. The two men turn and look at her.)*

KEENEY *(with rough tenderness)* Well, Annie?

MRS. KEENEY *(as if awakening from a dream)* David, I— *(She is silent. The* MATE *starts for the doorway.)*

KEENEY *(turning to him—sharply)* Wait!

MATE Yes, sir.

KEENEY D'you want anything Annie?

MRS. KEENEY *(after a pause, during which she seems to be endeavoring to collect her thoughts)* I thought maybe—I'd go up on deck, David, to get a breath of fresh air. *(She stands humbly awaiting his permission. He and the* MATE *exchange a significant glance.)*

KEENEY It's too cold, Annie. You'd best stay below today. There's nothing to look at on deck—but ice.

MRS. KEENEY *(monotonously)* I know—ice, ice, ice! But there's nothing to see down here but these walls. *(She makes a gesture of loathing.)*

KEENEY You can play the organ, Annie.

MRS. KEENEY *(dully)* I hate the organ. It puts me in mind of home.

KEENEY *(a touch of resentment in his voice)* I got it jest for you.

MRS. KEENEY *(dully)* I know. *(She turns away from them and walks slowly to the bench on left. She lifts up one of the curtains and looks through a porthole; then utters an exclamation of joy.)* Ah, water! Clear water! As far as I can see! How good it looks after all these months of ice! *(She turns around to them, her face transfigured with joy.)* Ah, now I must go up on the deck and look at it, David.

KEENEY *(frowning)* Best not today, Annie. Best wait for a day when the sun shines.

MRS. KEENEY *(desperately)* But the sun never shines in this terrible place.

KEENEY *(a tone of command in his voice)* Best not today, Annie.

MRS. KEENEY *(crumbling before this command—abjectly)* Very well, David. *(She stands there staring straight before her as if in a daze. The two men look at her uneasily.)*

KEENEY *(sharply)* Annie!

MRS. KEENEY *(dully)* Yes, David.

KEENEY Me and Mr. Slocum has business to talk about—ship's business.

MRS. KEENEY Very well, David. *(She goes slowly out, rear, and leaves the door three-quarters shut behind her.)*

KEENEY Best not have her on deck if they's goin' to be any trouble.

MATE Yes, sir.

KEENEY And trouble they's goin' to be. I feel it in my bones. *(Takes a revolver from the pocket of his coat and examines it)* Got your'n?

MATE Yes, sir.

KEENEY Not that we'll have to use 'em—not if I know their breed of dog—just to frighten 'em up a bit. *(Grimly)* I ain't never been forced to use one yit; and trouble I've had by land and by sea 's long as I kin remember, and will have till my dyin' day, I reckon.

MATE *(hesitatingly)* Then you ain't goin'—to turn back?

KEENEY Turn back! Mr. Slocum, did you ever hear o' me pointin' s'uth for home with only a measly four hundred barrel of ile in the hold?

MATE *(hastily)* No sir—but the grub's gittin' low.

KEENEY They's enough to last a long time yit, if they're careful with it; and they's plenty o' water.

MATE   They say it's not fit to eat—what's left; and the two years they signed on fur is up today. They might make trouble for you in the courts when we git home.

KEENEY   To hell with 'em! Let them make what law trouble they kin. I don't give a damn 'bout the money. I've got to git the ile! (*Glancing sharply at the* MATE) You ain't turnin' no damned sea-lawyer, be you, Mr. Slocum?

MATE (*flushing*)   Not by a hell of a sight, sir.

KEENEY   What do the fools want to go home fur now? Their share o' the four hundred barrel wouldn't keep 'em in chewin' terbacco.

MATE (*slowly*)   They wants to git back to their folks an' things, I s'pose.

KEENEY (*looking at him searchingly*)   'N you want to turn back, too. (*The* MATE *looks down confusedly before his sharp gaze.*) Don't lie, Mr. Slocum. It's writ down plain in your eyes. (*With grim sarcasm*) I hope, Mr. Slocum, you ain't agoin' to jine the men agin me.

MATE (*indignantly*)   That ain't fair, sir, to say sich things.

KEENEY (*with satisfaction*)   I warn't much afeard o' that, Tom. You been with me nigh on ten year and I've learned ye whalin'. No man kin say I ain't a good master, if I be a hard one.

MATE   I warn't thinkin' of myself, sir—'bout turnin' home, I mean. (*Desperately*) But Mrs. Keeney, sir—seems like she ain't jest satisfied up here, ailin' like—what with the cold an' bad luck an' the ice an' all.

KEENEY (*his face clouding—rebukingly but not severely*)   That's my business, Mr. Slocum. I'll thank you to steer a clear course o' that. (*A pause*) The ice'll break up soon to no'th'ard. I could see it startin' today. And when it goes and we git some sun Annie'll perk up. (*Another pause—then he bursts forth.*) It ain't the damned money what's keepin' me up in the Northern seas, Tom. But I can't go back to Homeport with a measly four hundred barrel of ile. I'd die fust. I ain't never come back home in all my days without a full ship. Ain't that truth?

MATE   Yes, sir; but this voyage you been ice-bound, an'—

KEENEY (*scornfully*)   And d'you s'pose any of 'em would believe that—any o' them skippers I've beaten voyage after voyage? Can't you hear 'em laughin' and sneerin'—Tibbots 'n' Harris 'n' Simms and the rest—and all o' Homeport makin' fun o' me? "Dave Keeney what boasts he's the best whalin' skipper out o' Homeport comin' back with a measly four hundred barrel of ile?" (*The thought of this drives him into a frenzy, and he smashes his fist down on the marble top of the sideboard.*) Hell! I got to git the ile, I tell you. How could I figger on this ice? It's never been so bad before in the thirty year I been acomin' here. And now it's breakin' up. In a couple o' days it'll be all gone. And they's whale here, plenty of 'em. I know they is and I ain't never gone wrong yit. I got to git the ile! I got to git it in spite of all hell, and by God, I ain't agoin' home till I do git it! (*There is the sound of subdued sobbing from the door in rear. The two men stand silent for a moment, listening. Then* KEENEY *goes over to the door and looks in. He hesitates for a moment as if he were going to enter—then closes the door softly.* JOE, *the harpooner, an enormous six-footer with a battered, ugly face, enters from right and stands waiting for the* CAPTAIN *to notice him.*)

KEENEY (*turning and seeing him*)   Don't be standin' there like a gawk, Harpooner. Speak up!

JOE (*confusedly*)   We want—the men, sir—they wants to send a depitation aft to have a word with you.

KEENEY (*furiously*)   Tell 'em to go to— (*Checks himself and continues grimly.*) Tell 'em to come. I'll see 'em.

JOE   Aye, aye, sir. (*He goes out.*)

KEENEY (*with a grim smile*)   Here it comes, the trouble you spoke of, Mr. Slocum, and we'll make short shift of it. It's better to crush such things at the start than let them make headway.

MATE *(worriedly)*   Shall I wake up the First and Fourth, sir? We might need their help.

KEENEY   No, let them sleep. I'm well able to handle this alone, Mr. Slocum. *(There is the shuffling of footsteps from outside and five of the crew crowd into the cabin, led by* JOE. *All are dressed alike—sweaters, sea-boots, etc. They glance uneasily at the* CAPTAIN, *twirling their fur caps in their hands.)*

KEENEY *(after a pause)*   Well? Who's to speak fur ye?

JOE *(stepping forward with an air of bravado)*   I be.

KEENEY *(eyeing him up and down coldly)*   So you be. Then speak your say and be quick about it.

JOE *(trying not to wilt before the* CAPTAIN'S *glance and avoiding his eyes)*   The time we signed up for is done today.

KEENEY *(icily)*   You're telling me nothin' I don't know.

JOE   You ain't pintin' fur home yit, far 's we kin see.

KEENEY   No, and I ain't agoin' to till this ship is full of ile.

JOE   You can't go no further no'th with the ice afore ye.

KEENEY   The ice is breaking up.

JOE *(after a slight pause during which the others mumble angrily to one another)* The grub we're gittin' now is rotten.

KEENEY   It's good enough fur ye. Better men than ye are have eaten worse. *(There is a chorus of angry exclamations from the crowd.)*

JOE *(encouraged by this support)*   We ain't agoin' to work no more less you puts back for home.

KEENEY *(fiercely)*   You ain't ain't you?

JOE   No; and the law courts'll say we was right.

KEENEY   To hell with your law courts! We're at sea now and I'm the law on this ship. *(Edging up toward the* HARPOONER)   And every mother's son of you what don't obey orders goes in irons. *(There are more angry exclamations from the crew.* MRS. KEENEY *appears in the doorway in the rear and looks on with startled eyes. None of the men notice her.)*

JOE *(with bravado)*   Then we're agoin' to mutiny and take the old hooker home ourselves. Ain't we, boys? *(As he turns his head to look at the others,* KEENEY'S *fist shoots out to the side of his jaw.* JOE *goes down in a heap and lies there.* MRS. KEENEY *gives a shriek and hides her face in her hands. The men pull out their sheath knives and start a rush, but stop when they find themselves confronted by the revolvers of* KEENEY *and the* MATE.*)*

KEENEY *(his eyes and voice snapping)*   Hold still! *(The men stand huddled together in a sullen silence.* KEENEY'S *voice is full of mockery.)* You've found out it ain't safe to mutiny on this ship, ain't you? And now git for'ard where ye belong, and—*(He gives* JOE'S *body a contemptuous kick.)* drag him with you. And remember the first man of ye I see shirkin' I'll shoot dead as sure as there's a sea under us, and you can tell the rest the same. Git for'ard now! Quick! *(The men leave in cowed silence, carrying* JOE *with them.* KEENEY *turns to the* MATE *with a short laugh and puts his revolver back in his pocket.)* Best get up on deck, Mr. Slocum, and see to it they don't try none of their skulkin' tricks. We'll have to keep an eye peeled from now on. I know 'em.

MATE   Yes, sir. *(He goes out, right.* KEENEY *hears his wife's hysterical weeping and turns around in surprise—then walks slowly to her side.)*

KEENEY *(putting an arm around her shoulder—with gruff tenderness)*   There, there, Annie. Don't be afeard. It's all past and gone.

MRS. KEENEY *(shrinking away from him)*   Oh, I can't bear it! I can't bear it any longer!

KEENEY *(gently)*   Can't bear what, Annie?

MRS. KEENEY *(hysterically)*   All this horrible brutality, and these brutes of men, and this terrible ship, and this prison cell of a room and the ice all around, and the silence. *(After this outburst she calms down and wipes her eyes with her handkerchief.)*

KEENEY *(after a pause during which he looks down at her with a puzzled frown)* Remember, I warn't hankerin' to have you come on this voyage, Annie.

MRS. KEENEY   I wanted to be with you, David, don't you see? I didn't want to wait back there in the house all alone as I've been doing these last six years since we were married—waiting, and watching, and fearing—with nothing to keep my mind occupied— not able to go back teaching school on account of being Dave Keeney's wife. I used to dream of sailing on the great, wide, glorious ocean. I wanted to be by your side in the danger and vigorous life of it all. I wanted to see you the hero they make you out to be in Homeport. And instead— *(Her voice grows tremulous.)* all I find is ice and cold—and brutality! *(Her voice breaks.)*

KEENEY   I warned you what it'd be, Annie. "Whalin' ain't no ladies' tea-party," I says to you, and "you better stay to home where you've got all your woman's comforts." *(Shaking his head)* But you was so set on it.

MRS. KEENEY *(wearily)*   Oh, I know it isn't your fault, David. You see, I didn't believe you. I guess I was dreaming about the old Vikings in the story books and I thought you were one of them.

KEENEY *(protestingly)*   I done my best to make it as cozy and as comfortable as could be. (MRS. KEENEY *looks around her in wild scorn.*) I even sent to the city for that organ for ye, thinkin' it might be soothin' to ye to be playin' it times when they was calms and things was dull like.

MRS. KEENEY *(wearily)*   Yes, you were very kind, David. I know that. *(She goes to left and lifts the curtains from the porthole and looks out—then suddenly bursts forth:)* I won't stand it—I can't stand it—pent up by these walls like a prisoner. *(She runs over to him and throws her arms around him, weeping. He puts his arm protectingly over her shoulders.)* Take me away from here, David! If I don't get away from here, out of this terrible ship, I'll go mad! Take me home, David! I can't think any more. I feel as if the cold and the silence were crushing down on my brain. I'm afraid. Take me home!

KEENEY *(holds her at arm's length and looks at her face anxiously)*   Best go to bed, Annie. You ain't yourself. You got fever. Your eyes look so strange like. I ain't never seen you look this way before.

MRS. KEENEY *(laughing hysterically)*   It's the ice and the cold and the silence—they'd make any one look strange.

KEENEY *(soothingly)*   In a month or two, with good luck, three at the most, I'll have her filled with ile and then we'll give her everything she'll stand and pint for home.

MRS. KEENEY   But we can't wait for that—I can't wait. I want to get home. And the men won't wait. They want to get home. It's cruel, it's brutal for you to keep them. You must sail back. You've got no excuse. There's clear water to the south now. If you've a heart at all you've got to turn back.

KEENEY *(harshly)*   I can't, Annie.

MRS. KEENEY   Why can't you?

KEENEY   A woman couldn't rightly understand my reason.

MRS. KEENEY *(wildly)*   Because it's a stupid, stubborn reason. Oh, I heard you talking with the Second Mate. You're afraid the other captains will sneer at you because you didn't come back with a full ship. You want to live up to your silly reputation even if you do have to beat and starve men and drive me mad to do it.

KEENEY *(his jaw set stubbornly)*   It ain't that, Annie. Them skippers would never dare sneer to my face. It ain't so much what any one'd say—but— *(He hesitates, struggling to express his meaning.)* you see—I've always done it—since my first voyage as skipper. I always come back—with a full ship—and—it don't seem right not to—somehow. I been always first whalin' skipper out o' Homeport, and—Don't you see my meanin', Annie? *(He glances at her. She is not looking at him but staring dully in front of her, not hearing a word he is saying.)* Annie! *(She comes to herself with a start.)* Best turn in, Annie, there's a good woman. You ain't well.

MRS. KEENEY *(resisting his attempts to guide her to the door in rear)*   David! Won't you please turn back?

KEENEY *(gently)*   I can't, Annie—not yet awhile. You don't see my meanin'. I got to git the ile.

MRS. KEENEY   It'd be different if you needed the money, but you don't. You've got more than plenty.

KEENEY *(impatiently)*   It ain't the money I'm thinkin' of. D'you think I'm as mean as that?

MRS. KEENEY *(dully)*   No—I don't know—I can't understand— *(Intensely)* Oh, I want to be home in the old house once more and see my own kitchen again, and hear a woman's voice talking to me and be able to talk to her. Two years! It seems so long ago— as if I'd been dead and could never go back.

KEENEY *(worried by her strange tone and the far-away look in her eyes)*   Best to go to bed, Annie. You ain't well.

MRS. KEENEY *(not appearing to hear him)*   I used to be lonely when you were away. I used to think Homeport was a stupid, monotonous place. Then I used to go down on the beach, especially when it was windy and the breakers were rolling in, and I'd dream of the fine free life you must be leading. *(She gives a laugh which is half a sob.)* I used to love the sea then. *(She pauses; then continues with slow intensity:)* But now—I don't ever want to see the sea again.

KEENEY *(thinking to humor her)*   'Tis no fit place for a woman, that's sure. I was a fool to bring ye.

MRS. KEENEY *(after a pause—passing her hand over her eyes with a gesture of pathetic weariness)*   How long would it take us to reach home—if we started now?

KEENEY *(frowning)*   'Bout two months, I reckon, Annie, with fair luck.

MRS. KEENEY *(counts on her fingers—then murmurs with a rapt smile)*   That would be August, the latter part of August, wouldn't it? It was on the twenty-fifth of August we were married, David, wasn't it?

KEENEY *(trying to conceal the fact that her memories have moved him—gruffly)* Don't *you* remember?

MRS. KEENEY *(vaguely—again passes her hand over her eyes)*   My memory is leaving me—up here in the ice. It was so long ago. *(A pause—then she smiles dreamily.)* It's June now. The lilacs will be all in bloom in the front yard—and the climbing roses on the trellis to the side of the house—they're budding. *(She suddenly covers her face with her hands and commences to sob.)*

KEENEY *(disturbed)*   Go in and rest, Annie. You're all wore out cryin' over what can't be helped.

MRS. KEENEY *(suddenly throwing her arms around his neck and clinging to him)* You love me, don't you, David?

KEENEY *(in amazed embarrassment at this outburst)*   Love you? Why d'you ask me such a question, Annie?

MRS. KEENEY *(shaking him—fiercely)* But you do, don't you, David? Tell me!

KEENEY I'm your husband, Annie, and you're my wife. Could there be aught but love between us after all these years?

MRS. KEENEY *(shaking him again—still more fiercely)* Then you do love me. Say it!

KEENEY *(simply)* I do, Annie.

MRS. KEENEY *(shaking him again—her hands drop to her sides.* KEENEY *regards her anxiously. She passes her hand across her eyes and murmurs half to herself:)* I sometimes think if we could only have had a child. (KEENEY *turns away from her, deeply moved. She grabs his arm and turns him around to face her—intensely.)* And I've always been a good wife to you, haven't I, David?

KEENEY *(his voice betraying his emotion)* No man has ever had a better, Annie.

MRS. KEENEY And I've never asked for much from you, have I, David? Have I?

KEENEY You know you could have all I got the power to give ye, Annie.

MRS. KEENEY *(wildly)* Then do this this once for my sake, for God's sake—take me home! It's killing me, this life—the brutality and cold and horror of it. I'm going mad. I can feel the threat in the air. I can hear the silence threatening me—day after gray day and every day the same. I can't bear it. *(Sobbing)* I'll go mad, I know I will. Take me home, David, if you love me as you say. I'm afraid. For the love of God, take me home! *(She throws her arms around him, weeping against his shoulder. His face betrays the tremendous struggle going on within him. He holds her out at arm's length, his expression softening. For a moment his shoulders sag, he becomes old, his iron spirit weakens as he looks at her tear-stained face.)*

KEENEY *(dragging out the words with an effort)* I'll do it, Annie—for your sake—if you say it's needful for ye.

MRS. KEENEY *(wild with joy—kissing him)* God bless you for that, David! *(He turns away from her silently and walks toward the companionway. Just at that moment there is a clatter of footsteps on the stairs and the* SECOND MATE *enters the cabin.)*

MATE *(excitedly)* The ice is breakin' up to no'th'ard, sir. There's a clear passage through the floe, and clear water beyond, the lookout says. (KEENEY *straightens himself like a man coming out of a trance.* MRS. KEENEY *looks at the* MATE *with terrified eyes.)*

KEENEY *(dazedly—trying to collect his thoughts)* A clear passage? To no'th'ard?

MATE Yes, sir.

KEENEY *(his voice suddenly grim with determination)* Then get her ready and we'll drive her through.

MATE Aye, aye, sir.

MRS. KEENEY *(appealingly)* David!

KEENEY *(not heeding her)* Will the men turn to willin' or must we drag 'em out?

MATE They'll turn to willin' enough. You put the fear o' God into 'em, sir. They're meek as lambs.

KEENEY Then drive 'em—both watches. *(With grim determination)* They's whale t'other side o' this floe and we're going to git 'em.

MATE Aye, aye, sir. *(He goes out hurriedly. A moment later there is the sound of scuffling feet from the deck outside and the* MATE's *voice shouting orders.)*

KEENEY *(speaking aloud to himself—derisively)* And I was agoin' home like a yaller dog!

MRS. KEENEY *(imploringly)* David!

KEENEY *(sternly)* Woman, you ain't adoin' right when you meddle in men's business and weaken 'em. You can't know my feelin's. I got to prove a man to be a good husband for ye to take pride in. I got to get the ile, I tell ye.

MRS. KEENEY *(supplicatingly)* David! Aren't you going home?

KEENEY *(ignoring this question—commandingly)* You ain't well. Go and lay down a mite. *(He starts for the door.)* I got to git on deck. *(He goes out. She cries after him in anguish:)* David! *(A pause. She passes her hand across her eyes—then commences to laugh hysterically and goes to the organ. She sits down and starts to play wildly an old hymn.* KEENEY *reënters from the doorway to the deck and stands looking at her angrily. He comes over and grabs her roughly by the shoulder.)*

KEENEY Woman, what foolish mockin' is this? *(She laughs wildly and he starts back from her in alarm.)* Annie! What is it? *(She doesn't answer him.* KEENEY'S *voice trembles.)* Don't you know me, Annie? *(He puts both hands on her shoulders and turns her around so that he can look into her eyes. She stares up at him with a stupid expression, a vague smile on her lips. He stumbles away from her, and she commences softly to play the organ again.)*

KEENEY *(swallowing hard—in a hoarse whisper, as if he had difficulty in speaking)* You said—you was agoin' mad—God! *(A long wail is heard from the deck above)* Ah bl-o-o-o-ow! *(A moment later the* MATE'S *face appears through the skylight. He cannot see* MRS. KEENEY.)*

MATE *(in great excitement)* Whales, sir—a whole school of 'em—off the star'b'd quarter 'bout five miles away—big ones!

KEENEY *(galvanized into action)* Are you lowerin' the boats?

MATE Yes, sir.

KEENEY *(with grim decision)* I'm acomin' with ye.

MATE Aye, aye, sir. *(Jubilantly)* You'll git the ile now right enough, sir. *(His head is withdrawn and he can be heard shouting orders.)*

KEENEY *(turning to his wife)* Annie! Did you hear him? I'll get the ile. *(She doesn't answer or seem to know he is there. He gives a hard laugh, which is almost a groan.)* I know you're foolin' me, Annie. You ain't out of your mind—(Anxiously) be you? I'll git the ile now right enough—jest a little while longer, Annie—then we'll turn hom'ard. I can't turn back now, you see that, don't ye? I've got to git the ile. *(In sudden terror)* Answer me! You ain't mad, be you? *(She keeps on playing the organ, but makes no reply. The* MATE'S *face appears again through the skylight.)*

MATE All ready, sir. *(*KEENEY *turns his back on his wife and strides to the doorway, where he stands for a moment and looks back at her in anguish, fighting to control his feelings.)*

MATE Comin', sir?

KEENEY *(his face suddenly grown hard with determination)* Aye. *(He turns abruptly and goes out.* MRS. KEENEY *does not appear to notice his departure. Her whole attention seems centered in the organ. She sits with half-closed eyes, her body swaying a little from side to side to the rhythm of the hymn. Her fingers move faster and faster and she is playing wildly and discordantly as*

The Curtain Falls.)

First Impressions

All that a play is at the moment we read it and all that we are during the reading interact to produce our first impressions. When we move away from what may be called *natural response* into conscious analysis of what we have read, two things are likely to happen: (1) the play changes; (2) we change. A new interaction takes place in which we act on the play and the play acts upon us. The moment that we ask questions and attempt to answer them, we modify natural response and start analysis.

Natural response and conscious analysis are not completely separate processes. How separate they are depends greatly upon the reader. Untrained readers will passively allow what they are reading to act on them; analysis for them is a separate process. Trained readers, even during the first reading, will begin applying analytical method that will modify their natural response. The point here, however, is that for the untrained and the trained reader analysis alone will yield the more complex meaning—and therefore the full pleasure—of a serious literary work.

Our natural response to *Ile* doubtless involves our attitude toward Captain Keeney. Do we like him? Probably not. Do we like Annie? Perhaps we do. The important question, however, is this one: Is our liking or disliking a character more, or less, significant than the credibility of the character? Some of the best-drawn characters in literature are villains: Claudius, for example, in *Hamlet*. We may dislike them on a moral level but like them as fully realized persons. In short, we need to warn ourselves that sympathy for Annie should not make us think of her as an artistically finer character than Captain Keeney, whom we may despise. Analysis will make this conclusion clear.

We should bear in mind that the analysis of *Ile* represents one approach, always with modifications, to the understanding of any play. *Miss Julie* (p. 780), also a one-act play, differs in many ways from *Ile* but will respond to the same sort of analysis applied to *Ile*. The nine full-length plays are, of course, more complicated in structure than the one-act plays, but the same method of analysis will apply to them, too.

The Facts of the Play

We should first of all have before us the literal facts with which the play was built. These materials are not the play, but without a sure knowledge of them we cannot reach what is essential in the play.

> In 1889 Annie, a schoolteacher with romantic notions of the sea, married Captain Keeney, the most successful whaling-boat skipper of Homeport. Childless after four years and imagining her husband's life at sea as free and venturesome compared to the monotonous life of Homeport, Annie won reluctant permission to accompany her husband on a voyage that began in June 1893. Before the voyage, Captain Keeney installed an organ in his cabin so that Annie might have the comfort of music during the long days ahead. Meager luck during the first year at sea played out completely when the *Atlantic Queen* became ice-locked in the Arctic Ocean and remained immovable until the exact day arrived ending the two-year contracts signed by the crew.

> On this day, with the ice barrier broken to the south, the crew through a deputation demands on threat of mutiny that the ship be sailed homeward. Captain Keeney, with no intention of failing to get "ile" at whatever cost, knocks down the crew's spokesman and, with weapons, holds control of the ship. Annie, cured of all roman-

tic notions of the sea and verging on madness, uses all her resources to force her husband to start for home. The final appeal to his love for her wins momentarily, but a report from the Second Mate that the ice to the north is broken and whales sighted returns Captain Keeney to his purpose of getting the "ile." Annie's mind gives way, and the play ends with Captain Keeney off after the whales and his wife wildly playing hymns on the organ.

Here are the materials. What does O'Neill make of this story? What do we make of it?

Exposition and Antecedent Action

Exposition explains. It sets forth the information we need in order to understand the present action. If we look back at our summary of the play, we see that the first paragraph is straight exposition, an explanation of what has gone on before the play opened. Everything that occurred before the play opened is called *antecedent action* and is a part of the exposition. The playwright has the task of giving us as much of the exposition as possible through the medium of dialogue, dialogue that must be carefully motivated to appear casual and natural.

We need some information before the dialogue begins. The direct statements of the author are used chiefly to set the stage, to describe the characters, to indicate "stage business," and to direct the correct reading of the lines. The author also gives us the key to what is antecedent action:

> *it is nearing two bells—one o'clock—in the afternoon of a day in the year 1895.*

Here is our starting point. Everything that occurred before the moment indicated is antecedent action.

Before a word is spoken, tension is established through a bit of stage business. (Stage business is action without dialogue.) The Steward—

> . . . *tiptoes over to the closed door in rear and listens with his ear pressed to the crack. What he hears makes his face darken and he mutters a furious curse.*

What, we ask, is the significance of this action? We know that we have our first hint of the kind of play this is to be. Eavesdropping can be amusing, even farcical. The muttered curse, the tiptoeing give us warning of the play's tone. (Tone represents the author's attitude toward the facts of the play and determines how the play should be regarded by the reader.) Even before this, we as readers have taken heed of the author's serious intent in the words describing the atmosphere of the setting:

> . . . *the light which comes through the skylight is sickly and faint, indicating one of those gray days of calm when ocean and sky are alike dead.*

The tread of "someone walking up and down the poop deck" brings the monotony of sight and sound into unison. We are ready for a serious play, for perhaps a tragic play, before the first word is spoken.

Two minor characters, the Steward and Ben, appear first and talk naturally, yet economically, for our benefit. With their appearance the present action begins, even though the chief ingredient of their talk involves past action. In other words, exposition, antecedent action, and present action blend into one action. The cruel cold is made real by Ben's chattering speech. It is a fact of here and now. It is also a fact of the past and a portent of things to come. Ice and cold are prime factors. The Old Man (Captain Keeney) is "always starin' at the ice," says the Steward in awed tones. (Is it Ice versus Captain Keeney? we ask.) Then the Steward rages: "Ice, ice, ice! Damn him and damn the ice!" The past year of hardships is equally chargeable to the unyielding ice and to the unyielding Captain. Nothing can be done about the ice. What about the Captain? "What are the men goin' to do 'bout it?" asks the Steward. Ben replies: "They said if he don't put back south for home today they're goin' to mutiny." If this were to be a simple struggle between Captain and crew, we are now ready to meet the central character, "a hard man—as hard a man as ever sailed the seas."

The hardness of Captain Keeney, however, is to be given emphasis through his treatment of his wife, Annie. We must know what manner of woman she was and is. Ben attests: "She useter be awful nice to me before—*(His eyes grow wide and frightened.)* she got—like she is." The Steward adds: " 'Twould have been hell on board without her." When Ben tiptoes to the door and hears Annie crying, we recall the Steward's action as the play opens. We have learned that Annie is a sweet, amiable person, in every way a contrast to her husband. We are now ready to meet Captain Keeney and later his wife.

Exposition, including references to antecedent action, does not stop, of course, with the introduction of the main characters. From the dialogue between Captain Keeney and the second mate, and between the Captain and his wife, we learn still more details as the present action moves forward. What we learn has already been summarized under "The Facts of the Play."

Setting

Setting tells us where and when the action takes place and is correlated with the exposition. Setting is the *environment* of the play. (A similar term, *panorama,* is used in connection with short stories. See, in the fiction division, "Preliminaries.") If we were in a theater to see *Ile,* the program would inform us that the action takes place in "Captain Keeney's cabin aboard the steam whaling vessel *Atlantic Queen*" and would add: "Time: afternoon of a day in the year 1895." That much information would be sufficient, for the remainder of the description serves as directions for staging that would be visible as soon as the curtain went up. *As readers we must set our own stage.*

We are accustomed to this demand from a writer, for in reading fiction we were constantly aware of the background of the action. We note differences, however, in that the dramatist must attend first of all to the setting of each scene, whereas the writer of short stories—or novels, or narrative poems—may intersperse descriptive passages as appropriate. We note, too, that dramatists are crisp and precise in their description and confine themselves for the most part to utilitarian prose. (George Bernard Shaw is an exception to this rule and frequently wrote novelistic plays. Even some of O'Neill's stage directions go beyond pure usefulness.) They are writing, not for a reader who might savor their style, but for a stage manager who will be expected to build the semblance of *"a small, square compartment about eight feet high with a skylight in the center looking out on the poop deck."*

Here, perhaps, we should ask: What difference does the setting make? Our answer, at first, is that the setting is important, and we cite the author's care in emphasizing the relation of the ice-bound ship to the characters. We are to be given a view of a microcosm, a little world, far removed and long removed from the larger world. We feel that we must understand the characters in relation to their restricted and unfavorable environment. In one sense, then, the setting, including the ice fields that have held the ship immovable, controls the characters and through them the action. We realize at once, however, that this answer may not be fully satisfactory. Would time and place have had the same effect on any other group of characters? Possibly not. We suspect that the setting of *Ile* simply tests characters who are already formed. We begin to suspect that setting represents something beyond itself, that it is in reality an *opposing force*, a symbol of challenge to human beings. Accepting the challenge, a man (or woman) may win or lose.

We see only the *"small, square compartment,"* but we know what is outside. The remainder of the ship is there with water to the south and ice to the north. To the north also are whales, the immediate goal. But do these things complete the setting? Are we looking at a true microcosm? Does the larger world have nothing to do with this smaller world? Clearly it does have much to do with it. In a sense the *Atlantic Queen* has invisible but powerful lines connecting it to Homeport. Homeport is part of the setting, a reality in the minds of every character. The men are desperate to complete the voyage and return even though to return without oil means a dead loss to them. Annie is frantic to "be home in the old house once more," to see her kitchen, to talk to women and to hear them talk. Yet, it is Homeport's ties with Captain Keeney that are strongest of all—he dares not go back unsuccessful, to occupy a position less exalted than "first whalin' skipper out o' Homeport." Part of the setting, then, is a place seen only in the mind's eyes of the characters and of the readers or observers of this play.

Plot

The action in *Ile* is simple and straightforward. If in the beginning of our analysis it was useful to assemble a fairly detailed summary of the facts, it is equally necessary at this point to look at the essence of the action. Stripped of details, it is the story of a ship's captain who, in pursuit of whale oil, ignores hardships, subdues a mutinous crew, nearly succumbs to his wife's pleas, but reasserts himself in time to drive his wife mad and, apparently, in the end to win through to his goal. Except when the Captain knocks down the spokesman for the crew, the external action is limited to nothing more exciting than the dropping of a dish. Yet tension steadily mounts as we await the answer to the question: what course will Captain Keeney take?

Let us note first the dropping of the dish by the Steward. The agitation of the Steward at the approach of the Captain causes the accident. More important, after the Captain appears, we no longer have to depend on hearsay about his hardness and cruelty; we see cruelty in action:

> (KEENEY *draws back his fist and* THE STEWARD *shrinks away. The fist is gradually lowered and* KEENEY *speaks slowly*.) 'Twould be like hitting a worm.

A moment later he adds:

> The next dish you break, Mr. Steward, you take a bath in the Bering Sea at the end of a rope.

Here, then, is the hard man made real. We know now what to expect of him.

Before we proceed, let us look at a diagram of the action. This diagram represents an "action line." Three separate interdependent conflicts are involved: Captain Keeney against natural forces (the Ice); Captain Keeney against human rights (the Crew); Captain Keeney against the claims of home and love (Annie).

Action Line of Ile

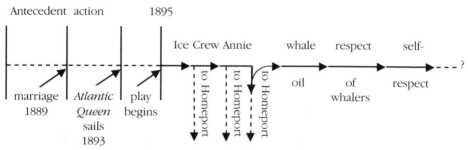

Let us suppose that Captain Keeney, on being petitioned by his crew, had agreed to return home. Or suppose, on the other hand, everybody had agreed that getting the "ile" was the thing to do. Would either situation have made a play? Why not? Is it that we naturally dislike to see and hear people agree with each other? Is it that we prefer to witness a clash? We do enjoy a contest, and doubtless this is one good reason for emphasizing conflict. We must look further, however, for a basic answer to our reason for enjoying conflict. Agreement is an end, a result. Disagreement is a means to an end, an active process. Agreement is static; disagreement is dynamic. When agreement is reached, the struggle is over. Our first interest, then, must be centered in the struggle, which will be resolved into some sort of agreement.

Ile clearly depends on disagreement or conflict. So many plays depend on a clash of interests or personalities—clashes that may be expressed in talk or a blow or may be waged within a character—that conflict is said to be the essence of drama. In reading *Ile* we are spectators of a combat in which the central figure, Captain Keeney, stands against all comers—the capricious Bering Sea, the crew, his wife. Will he win, and if he does, at what cost?

We have mentioned the word *crisis*, a useful term to describe a turning point. A play consists of one or more minor crises and one major crisis. The major crisis is the climax of the play. In *Ile* a minor crisis occurs when the crew through its deputation challenges Captain Keeney. Before the challenge we do not know the answers to such questions as these: Will Captain Keeney yield to a reasonable appeal? Will he yield to threats? Will he be forced to yield? As our diagram indicates, the Captain did not waver from his determined course; the men are vanquished and that question is settled. This settling of a question (or questions) constitutes a *minor resolution*. Agreement of a sort is reached.

No sooner is this minor crisis resolved than the action leading to the major crisis begins. Annie is more powerful than the crew; Captain Keeney cannot settle this issue by a blow. He is apparently beaten:

> KEENEY—*(dragging out the words with an effort)*   I'll do it, Annie—for your sake— if you say it's needful for ye.

For a brief moment disaster seems averted. We have hardly time to frame the question, will Captain Keeney make good his promise?—before we have the answer, an answer that clearly settles the major issue. The ice has broken, leaving a clear passage northward.

> KEENEY—*(his voice suddenly grim with determination)* Then get her ready and we'll drive her through.

With this speech the issue is settled, and the major resolution begins.

Characters

Our interest in how the play will come out is legitimate, but once we know the answer, other and more important questions confront us. Can the pursuit of whale oil, whether successful or not, be very important? Do we really care whether Captain Keeney wins or loses? Why should we care what happens to him or to Annie or to the crew of an obscure whaling ship? We have admiration for courage, of course, and pity for weakness. Are these emotions of admiration and pity stirred sufficiently to account for our concern? Perhaps. If the characters are credible, we see in them characteristics that we may call *universal qualities*, for we have seen these qualities in other people and detect them in ourselves.

Without Captain Keeney there would be no play, for he helps to create the forces that oppose him. The ice is a dread and a menace because he refuses to be beaten by it. The crew is mutinous because he makes them so. Annie becomes mad because in a real sense he wills that she shall go mad. We begin to see that the action, the plot, of this play is relatively unimportant. *Given these particular characters under these particular circumstances, we realize that what happened must inevitably have happened.*

Is this, then, a character play? Certainly Captain Keeney is a man of strong will and single purpose, cruel, somber, destructive of anybody and anything that seeks to oppose him. Accustomed to winning through his ruthlessness, he has developed a contempt for lesser beings and a determination never to hear "laughin' and sneerin'" at his expense. In direct conflict with his crew, he wins easily. "I know 'em," he says. Next he faces his distraught wife and bends to her appeal. We see a hint of softness, but it is the softness born of bewilderment and loss of words to explain his actions. He knows that he scorns the "ile" itself and the money it will bring. Why then, Annie wants to know, not turn homeward? Is he afraid of words from other whaling captains? Note the reply:

> It ain't so much what any one'd say—but—(*He hesitates, struggling to express his meaning.*) you see—I've always done it—since my first voyage as skipper. I always come back with a full ship—and—it don't seem right not to—somehow. I been always first whalin' skipper out o' Homeport, and—Don't you see my meanin', Annie?

Perhaps Annie did see his meaning, but to her it was invalid. With this speech and others of like import, the play, we realize, takes on a significance beyond its literal meaning. Captain Keeney, Annie, the crew, the ice wastes, Homeport fall into a pattern of universal significance. We have been reading a play in which each character is a symbol, each object something beyond itself. Older plays of this sort personified such abstractions as Vice, Virtue, Everyman. The personifications in *Ile* are not so clearcut, but we can identify them.

Symbolic Meaning

Although Captain Keeney does not represent Everyman, he does stand for every person's deepest desire to excel. He is the fanatic who drives straight for his goal without swerving and with a ruthless disregard for those with tentative goals or those with insufficient will to draw a straight line. His force requires the submission of others: first, by a physical blow and the threat of a weapon, he wins his easiest victory; next, in a more difficult struggle, he bends to the power of human love but quickly regains his control and renounces his "weakness." The men who momentarily oppose him do not seek victory at any cost, though surely they would have won if they had so willed. They are the usual men accustomed to go so far and no farther. One notes, however, that some will go farther than others. Mr. Slocum, the second mate, may someday become a Captain of Keeney's stamp. Joe the harpooner, spokesman for the crew, has doubtless won his place by successfully asserting himself. All members of the "depitation" are chosen men. Always a man of some will can find submissiveness in men of feebler will.

Annie perhaps is the Usual Woman, kind, loving, appalled by cruelty. Her husband does not say, "*You* couldn't rightly understand my reason"; he does say, "A *woman* couldn't rightly understand my reason." Annie replies, "Because it's a stupid, stubborn reason." Yet, such stupid, stubborn reasons lie at the base of Captain Keeney's success, a success that had attracted Annie: "I wanted to see you the hero they make you out to be in Homeport." Does Captain Keeney suspect, perhaps know, that even his wife would not think him a hero if he turned back? Apparently so, for he says, "I got to prove a man to be a good husband for ye to take pride in. I got to get the ile, I tell ye."

Homeport means what its name implies. For the men it represents release. For Annie it stands for sanity, for the normal, the warm, the safe things in life. For Captain Keeney it is a tribunal, a place of judgment to which at intervals he must return for the verdict. There must be no chance for an adverse decision. No excuses will do. He would not excuse another skipper; he does not expect, nor want, to be excused himself. The question will be: "Is your ship filled with oil?" The oil itself must be the answer.

In opposition to Homeport are the ice wastes of the Arctic seas. Droughts, floods, typhoons, earthquakes—there can be no malice in these, but when they touch man to his harm, he may shake his fist or go down on his knees. Captain Keeney could not strike down nor argue with nature. He could wait. The Usual Men and the Usual Women could wait, too, but not so long. The Ice Wastes won victory after victory down to the last man. Then, just as victory over the fanatic was about to go elsewhere, a cry rang out: "The ice is breakin' up to no'th'ard, sir." And in a moment: "Whales, sir—a whole school of 'em."

Has nature at last relented? Is this to be taken as an instance of reward for the persevering? Is this a happy ending? Hardly. If the ice had broken up a month before, all might have been well. If the ice had held fast a day longer, all might have been well. It is as though the Ice Wastes had played a closely calculated game with the end in view of mocking the fanatic. (Compare Creon's belated decision in *Antigone*, which begins on p. 606.) He will get his "ile." He will return to Homeport with a full ship and a mad wife. These things we know. Beyond these things we may speculate. Would the sort of price paid be too high even for a man like Captain Keeney? Would his pride remain in being "first whalin' skipper out o' Homeport"? We cannot be sure of the answers to these questions, but we can suspect that the struck target, in this instance, shattered into rubble.

Applying Our Observations to Other Plays

What we have observed about how a story is told in *Ile* may be applied, always with modifications, to other plays. It may be well to review our procedure by listing, point by point, the steps which we have taken.

1. We began with *first impressions.* As soon as you have completed a first reading of a play, take the time to examine what you think and feel about what you have read. Do you like the play? Before rereading the play, can you say *why* you liked it or did not like it? Were you amused, excited, depressed, apathetic as you read? Were you chiefly interested in the outcome? Or did the outcome matter less than the credibility of the persons involved? Did you find yourself thinking: "I know people like these characters"? On the other hand, did you say to yourself: "These characters are outside the range of my experience"? Such questions as these will help you to realize your first impressions.

2. The next step is to record the *facts of the play.* As we have seen in our analysis of *Ile,* the first event with any bearing on the present action of the play occurred six years before the play opened when Captain Keeney married Annie. We did not pick up this fact until late in the play. Your task, then, in assembling the facts is to look first of all for the chronological starting point and then to piece together a straightforward narrative. At the end of this process, you may be surprised to find how many significant facts, all bearing on a right interpretation, you overlooked during the first reading.

3. We have chosen to consider *exposition and antecedent* action next, but it would be just as convenient to consider setting at this point. Through gathering the facts, you have had to settle the matter of antecedent action. The exposition, partly through direct statement of the author and partly through dialogue, reveals the tone of the play. Is the tone serious, light, whimsical? How do authors intend that we shall regard their plays? In what way do they let us know what our attitude should be? Do the stage directions establish the *atmosphere* and thereby prepare us for what may legitimately happen in such an atmosphere? Is the dialogue in keeping with the atmosphere? Is the action credible in relation to the characters and the atmosphere?

4. Next we have considered the *setting.* Playwrights normally must give careful attention to *time* and *place,* the two elements of setting. In *Ile* setting is of major significance, though time, but not timing, is of much less importance than place. The invisible setting, we have noted, plays a strong part in the drama. The Greek convention of the unities of time and place (the action to occur in one place and within a day) reduces the significance of setting in *Antigone.* The characters in *Hamlet* respond to place—the mist-shrouded battlements of Elsinore in Act I, for example—and readers (but especially audiences) know at once that a tragedy will unfold. Historical time, too, is of the essence in details and in a larger sense, for morality in *Hamlet* is the morality of a primitive, revenge-approving society only vaguely aware of Christian ethics. In *The Physician in Spite of Himself,* Molière uses settings as mere backdrops against which the romping action can take place. The gloom that saturates Ibsen's *Ghosts* is emphasized by the pervading "rain and mist" that, ironically, dissolve before the sun as darkness settles over the mind of the protagonist. Strindberg's *Miss Julie* observes the unities of time and place. Both the place (a manor house kitchen) and the time (Midsummer Eve, a festive occasion for servants) vitally affect the play's three characters and their actions. Although *The Playboy of the Western World* has universal appeal, its setting is highly localized: it is pure Irish. The characters are a product of Celtic genes and a distinctive environment. Place and time, consequently, are a pervasive influence. In *The Visit,* Duerrenmatt virtually makes a character of "the shabby and ruined" central European town. Its desolation reflects a degradation that the composite citizenry wishes to escape at any cost. Historic time, and therefore place, are important in Camus' *Caligula.* Place in *The Sunshine Boys* summarizes what has happened to an over-the-hill comedian. Time is pinned down by the many references to living persons.

Key questions are these: Is the setting what it is simply because the characters are what they are? Or are the characters at least partly what they are because the setting is what it is? The function of the setting in relation to characters and plot can be determined by answering these questions.

5. The where and when of the play settled, we turn now to what happens, the *plot.* Here we note that the playwright—even the Absurdist who appears to eschew action—must be severely selective. In traditional plays every action must advance the play toward a minor crisis and point all minor crises toward the major crisis. A dish dropped, as in *Ile,* must have its significance. We may ask,

then, what is the function of each act in relation to the crises? Next, is there a cause-and-effect relationship linking one action with the next? In *Ile,* Captain Keeney's conflict with the crew does not bring about the conflict with Annie. In other words, the second conflict does not grow out of the first. On the other hand, each action in *Antigone* grows out of a preceding action. Another question is this one: Is the action inevitable? To put it another way, does the action happen because the characters are what they are? If it does, the play is essentially a character play. The actions of Captain Keeney grow inevitably out of his character. What about the actions of Antigone? Of Creon? Of Hamlet? Of Claudius? Of Miss Julie? Of Caligula? Of Willie?

In examining the plot it is useful to construct an action line. Record on the line, with spaced dashes, the antecedent action; then at spaced intervals on an unbroken line indicate the minor crises that lead to the major crisis; end the line with the resolution of the final crisis, the *denouement.*

6. When we examine the *characters* of a play, we find use for our total knowledge of human nature. Are the characters believable when tested by what we know of ourselves added to what we know about other human beings? Believability is relative, of course, and some characters come close to absolute believability, whereas others remain more or less distant. One probably does not doubt the reality of Captain Keeney. What of Haemon, Gertrude, Sganarelle, Mrs. Alving, Jean, Pegeen, Claire Zachanassian, Caesonia, Al—to name only one character from each of the other plays in this collection? Each character presents a fresh problem in credibility. An example of such a problem is Antigone. What she does and what she is are to be explained in part by reference to a whole system of mythology. Do we have to believe in the system of mythology in order to believe in Antigone? We face a different problem with Caligula, who seems a madman, but whose madness clearly has method in it.

For any play, we may ask: how *consistent* are the characters? What we are asking is, If a character has done this, would this character also do that? Such a question is tricky. An element of inconsistency may be the most revealing trait in a character. Miss Julie becomes more credible, not less, when she wavers. Dramatists, however, are wary of glaring inconsistencies, for the limits of time make it difficult to justify them.

7. Our last step is a *summing up.* What do all the parts mean? If the play has a general meaning, then it is certain that we have been involved with symbols. Do the characters stand simply for themselves or do they represent something beyond themselves? Does the play emphasize a theme, an idea, a way of life? If there is a theme, can you state it in a single sentence and then support that sentence with evidence from the play?

The foregoing suggestions for play analysis are by no means exhaustive. Little has been said, for example, about staging and the use of stage properties—*props*—those items that are referred to in the dialogue and that may be essential to the working out of the action. Of one thing every student can be certain: as authority over a play increases, pleasure also increases, even if in the end it turns into the negative fun of damning the play!

A Note on Seeing Plays

Although there are closet dramas (plays to be read and not staged), the vast majority of plays are written to be presented before an audience. In a very real sense, therefore, a play is not a complete work of art until it is acted out before an audience. Imaginative readers can do much toward staging the play in their own minds and, perhaps, even acting out the various parts. This sort of multiple role for the reader calls for a great deal of intellectual, even emotional, energy, but the rewards, though differing from those experienced in seeing a play, are great.

Writing About Drama

The steps involved in *choosing a topic, organizing the material, writing a first draft, revising for the final draft, quoting,* and *evaluating an interpretation* are covered in "Writing About Poetry" (p. 430). The basic principles discussed there apply to drama as well as to poetry. Writing about plays, however, presents a few new problems, which may be listed briefly.

1. Because plays are much longer than most poems, an essay of *explication* cannot hope to do justice to the entire work. The writer must be content to deal with a single scene, episode, or passage. It should, however, be an important passage, and the explication should attempt to show its relevance to the play as a whole. The writer should never attempt a detailed discussion of one scene before reading the entire play.

2. For an essay of *analysis,* see the seven points discussed in "Applying Our Observations to Other Plays" (pp. 601–603). Note that *setting, character,* and *plot* are generally more crucial elements for discussion in drama than in poetry. On the other hand, a few of the elements of poetry—rhythm and rhyme, for example—may not be present in contemporary drama, although they may be found in some traditional drama.

3. In an essay on *character,* comparison or contrast is a useful method of organization, especially because the action may depend on the opposition between characters—between the different values, motives, or qualities they represent.

4. In an essay on *setting* or *plot,* the writer must be careful not to isolate these elements from the other aspects of the play such as *theme* or *character.* As in the paper of explication, the element of the play under discussion must be placed in the context of the play as a whole. Furthermore, in discussing plot, the writer should be aware of the parallels or antitheses between plot and subplots.

5. Because the typical play offers a greater wealth of details and incidents than the typical poem, the writer must be much more selective in choosing the details for supporting an interpretation. Also, the initial idea for the paper may be much too broad for a short essay. How can it be limited? Should it be re-

stricted further in the portion of the play it discusses? Or should the examples and illustrations be pared down to the most essential?

6. The two major types of drama, tragedy and comedy, are discussed in the essays "The Tragic Fallacy" (p. 1112) and "Some Prefatory Words on Comedy" (p. 1126). Obviously, the writer must keep in mind the essential differences between them in working out an interpretation, for tragedy and comedy present two different ways of looking at the world. In an essay on tragedy, more attention may be paid to the nature of the struggle between the protagonist and his or her tragic fate. What is the nature of the struggle? What flaw of character brings about the protagonist's downfall? What is the relationship between fate and character? Setting and character? Plot and character? Is there a direct cause-and-effect relationship that may be analyzed in the play? In an essay on comedy, more attention may be paid to the incongruities and self-deceptions of the characters. Social customs and values are more essential to comedy than to tragedy. What attitudes are being ridiculed in the play? How is the final triumph of certain characters related to the values they represent? Finally, in regard to the theme of the play as a whole, what values are being upheld in the play's overall system of rewards and punishments?

7. Quoting from plays generally follows the same principles as quoting from poems (see p. 436). However, in referring to passages in plays, one should keep the numbers for act, scene, and line always in the same order, and they should be written in capital Roman numerals (act), lowercase Roman numerals (scene), and Arabic numerals (line): III. ii. 269.

8. Among the possibilities for writing on drama is a *review* of the performance of a play. In a review, the writer has many more elements to consider than simply the text—the performances of the actors, the conception of the director, the setting, the lighting, the costuming, and so on. Also, the review, unlike the typical essay on the text of the play, involves some *evaluation* of the production. That is, the performance allows writers to compare their conception of the text with the conception suggested by the production. Given the performance, what *was* the director's conception? Which aspects of the play did the director choose to emphasize? Was it a traditional or an innovative production? If innovative— *Hamlet* in modern dress, for example—were the liberties taken effective, or did they do injury to the tone or mood of the play? Was the casting effective? Were the major actors up to their roles? What surprising twists did they manage to suggest in the delivery of their lines? Were there passages in the text of the play that took on new life in performance? Did the sets, lighting, and costumes contribute to the overall effect? Finally, did the theme or meaning of the play shift in any direction after the experience of the performance? Because plays were written to be performed, the review of a live (or even a taped or filmed) production is one of the most challenging and rewarding assignments in writing about drama.

Sophocles (496–406 B.C.)
Antigone*

Antigone was written some twenty-four hundred years ago. Today it is still being performed, not simply as a curiosity but as a vital drama with ample modern significance.

If we follow our outline for reviewing a play, we shall see that *Antigone* requires only slightly different treatment from that accorded a modern play. Our *first impressions,* however, may be affected by a few technical details. It is best, therefore, to anticipate some of the questions that one would naturally ask upon first contact with Greek drama.

The first question involves the interrelationships of the characters. We need to know what Sophocles expected his audience to know about the family relationships of the royal house of Thebes. We may begin with Labdacus, the father of Laius. Laius married Jocasta and by her had a son, Oedipus, part of whose story is told in Sophocles' *Oedipus Rex.* Oedipus, under a curse of the gods, murdered his father without knowing that his victim was his father and then married Jocasta in ignorance that she was his mother. Oedipus and Jocasta had four children: two boys, Eteocles and Polynices, and two girls, Antigone and Ismene. Eteocles succeeded Oedipus as king of Thebes but was killed by his brother, Polynices, who, with six other champions, had come to Thebes to take the throne. In the duel Polynices also was killed. The throne passed then to Creon, who was the brother of Jocasta and, therefore, the uncle of Jocasta's and Oedipus' four children. Creon's wife was Eurydice, and their children were Megareus and Haemon.

These relationships may be summarized in two diagrams:

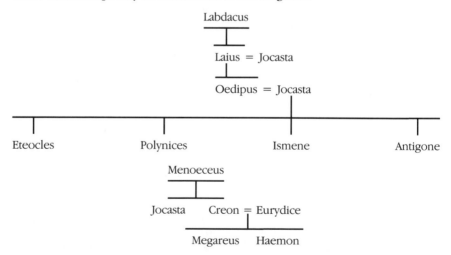

The second question involves the Chorus, a technique infrequently used in modern plays (but compare *The Visit,* p. 845, and *Caligula,* p. 894). You will see what

---

* This translation, based on the text of Sir Richard C. Jebb, has been somewhat modified by the editors and carefully checked and further modified by Professor Albert Rapp. We are deeply indebted to Professor Rapp for his assistance.

functions are actually performed by the Chorus in *Antigone*. You will see that it does these things: (1) it provides, as needed, poetic interludes that suggest the passage of time; (2) it acts as spokesperson for public opinion; (3) it occasionally is expository; (4) it helps to set the mood and to point up the universal significance of what is happening. You will note that it can be wise, and it can be stupid; that it vacillates and yet can make up its mind. In many ways it has all the virtues and vices of a general public.

With this much information available for reference, you should now be prepared to read this surprisingly modern play. Pronunciations of proper names used in the play are indicated in a listing on p. 624.

CHARACTERS

ANTIGONE ⎫ *daughters of Oedipus, former*   GUARD, *assigned to watch unburied corpse*
ISMENE   ⎭   *king of Thebes*   *of Polynices*
CREON, *present king of Thebes*   FIRST MESSENGER
EURYDICE, *wife of Creon*   SECOND MESSENGER
HAEMON, *son of Creon and betrothed of An-*   CHORUS OF THEBAN ELDERS
   tigone
TIRESIAS, *blind soothsayer*

Scene. *All dialogue is spoken before the Royal Palace at Thebes.* ISMENE *enters first, followed by* ANTIGONE.

ANTIGONE Ismene, sister, my own dear sister, do you know any evil, bequeathed to us by Oedipus, which Zeus will not fulfill while we live? Nothing painful is there, nothing ruinous, no shame, no dishonor, that I have not seen in your woes and mine. And now what of this new edict the King has just proclaimed to all Thebes? Do you know of it? Have you heard? Or has it been hidden from you that our friends are threatened with the doom of our enemies?

ISMENE No word of friends, Antigone, glad or painful, has come to me, since we two sisters lost two brothers, killed in one day by a twofold blow. I know the Argive host withdrew last night; but more, good or bad, I know not.

ANTIGONE So I thought and therefore arranged to see you where you alone may hear.

ISMENE What is it? It is plain that you have dark news.

ANTIGONE Has not Creon destined our brothers, the one to honored burial, the other to unburied shame? Eteocles, they say, with due observance of right and custom, he has buried properly for joining honorably the dead below. But the body of Polynices—Creon has published to Thebes that none shall bury him, or mourn, but leave unwept, without a tomb, a welcome feast for birds. Such, I have heard, is the edict the good Creon has set forth for you and me—yes, for *me*—and is coming here to proclaim it clearly to those who have not heard, for it's a heavy matter, since whoever disobeys, his punishment is death by public stoning. *(Pause)* You know it now, and you will soon show whether you are nobly bred or unworthy of a noble family.

ISMENE Poor sister—if all this is true, what could I do or undo?

ANTIGONE Will you help me do what must be done?

ISMENE   What must be done? What do you mean?

ANTIGONE   Will you help me lift the body?

ISMENE   You would bury him?—when it is forbidden?

ANTIGONE   I will do my part—and yours too, if you will not—for a brother. To him I will not be false.

ISMENE   Would you dare when Creon has forbidden it?

ANTIGONE   He has no right to keep me from my own.

ISMENE   Antigone! Remember how our father perished, amid hate and scorn, when sins, self-revealed, moved him to strike out his eyes with his own hands; then the mother-wife, two names in one, with a twisted noose ended her life; and last, our two brothers—each killed by the other's hand. Now is it our turn? We two left all alone—think how we shall die more miserably than all the rest if we defy a king's decree or his powers. No, we must remember, first that we were born women and should not strive with men; next, that we are ruled by the stronger and must obey in these things and even in worse ones. May the dead forgive me, but I must obey our ruler. It is foolish to do otherwise.

ANTIGONE   I will not beg you. No, even if you offered now to help, you would not be welcome as my helper. Go your way. I will bury him and count it gain to die in doing that. I shall join a loved one, sinless my crime. I owe more allegiance to the dead than to the living, for with the dead I shall abide forever. But *you*—live on and disobey the laws of the gods.

ISMENE   I intend no dishonor to the gods—but to defy the State—I am too weak for that.

ANTIGONE   Such be your excuse. I go to heap earth on the brother whom I love.

ISMENE   How I fear for you, Antigone!

ANTIGONE   You need not. Be fearful for yourself.

ISMENE   At least be careful. Tell no one your plan and neither will I.

ANTIGONE   Announce it to all Thebes. I shall hate you even more if you don't.

ISMENE   You have hot courage for a chilling act!

ANTIGONE   My act will please where it counts most to please.

ISMENE   Perhaps, but you are attempting what you cannot do.

ANTIGONE   If my strength is not enough, at least I will have tried.

ISMENE   A hopeless task should not be tried.

ANTIGONE   If you continue talking in this way, I shall hate you and so will the dead! Leave me alone to suffer this dread thing. For I shall be suffering nothing as dreadful as a dishonorable death.

ISMENE   Go, then, if you must, but remember no matter how foolish your deed, those who love you will love you still. (*Exit* ANTIGONE *left.* ISMENE *enters the Palace through one of the two side-doors.*)

(*Enter* CHORUS *of Theban elders.*)

CHORUS   Beam of the sun, fairest light that ever dawned on Thebes of the seven gates, you have shone forth at last, eye of the golden day, arisen above Dirce's stream! The warrior of the white shield, who came from Argos in battle array, has been stirred by you to headlong flight.

He advanced against our land by reason of the vexed claims of Polynices; and, like a shrill-screaming eagle, he flew over our country, sheathed in snow-white wings, with an armed multitude and with plumage of helmets.

He paused above our homes; he ravened around our seven portals with spears athirst for blood; but he fled, before his jaws were glutted with gore or his fire had consumed our towers. Fierce was the noise of battle raised behind him as he wrestled with, but could not conquer, his dragon foe.

For Zeus utterly abhors the boast of a proud tongue; and when he beheld the Argives coming on in a great stream, their golden harness clanging, he smote with brandished fire one who was at that moment about to shout "Victory" from atop our ramparts.

Down to the earth with a crash fell the invader, torch in hand, he who but a moment before, in the frenzy of the mad attack, was blowing against us the blasts of his hot hate. But his threats fared not as he had hoped; and to our other foes the Wargod also dealt havoc, a mighty helper at our need.

For, seven invaders at seven gates, matched against seven, left a tribute of their bronze for Zeus who turned the battle; except for the two brothers, who crossed spears with each other and are sharers in a common death.

But since victory has come to us, let joy be ours in Thebes, city of the many chariots; let us enjoy forgetfulness after the recent wars, and let us visit all the temples of the gods with night-long dance and song; and may Bacchus be our leader, Bacchus whose dancing shakes the land of Thebes.

But behold, the king of the land comes, Creon, son of Menoeceus, our new ruler by the new fortunes that the gods have given; what matter is he pondering, that he has summoned this conference of elders to hear?

(*Enter* CREON, *from the central door of the Palace. Dressed as a king, he has with him two* ATTENDANTS.)

CREON   Sirs, the vessel of our State, after being tossed on wild waves, has once more been safely steadied by the gods: and you, of all the people, have been called here because I knew, first of all, how true and constant was your reverence for the royal power of Laius; and again, how, when Oedipus was ruler and then perished, you were still loyal to his children. Since then, his sons have fallen, each felled by the other, each stained with a brother's blood;—and now I possess the throne and all its powers, by right of near kinship to the dead.

No man can be fully known, in soul and spirit and mind, until he has been schooled in rule and law-giving. If the supreme ruler of a State does not seek the best counsel, I hold and have ever held such a person to be base. If one holds a friend of more worth to him than his fatherland, that person has no place in my regard. For I—Zeus, who sees everything, is my witness—I would not be silent if I saw ruin, instead of safety, coming to the citizens; the country's foes would never be friends of mine, for our country is the ship that bears us safe and we cannot have any friends unless the ship of state prospers in its voyage.

Such are the rules by which I guard the greatness of Thebes. In accord with these rules, I have published an edict to the citizens concerning the sons of Oedipus: that Eteocles, who fell fighting for our city, fighting with great courage, shall be entombed and favored with every rite that follows the noblest dead to their rest. But for his brother, Polynices, who came back from exile and sought to consume with fire the city of his fathers and the shrines of his father's gods, who sought to taste of kinsmen's blood and to lead the rest into slavery—touching this man, it has been proclaimed to our people that no one shall bury him or lament his death, but leave him unburied, a corpse for birds and dogs to eat, a ghastly, shameful sight.

Never, by deed of mine, shall the wicked stand in honor before the just, but whoever has good will towards Thebes, he shall be honored of me in both his life and death.

CHORUS   Such is your pleasure, Creon, son of Menoeceus, touching this city's foe and its friend. And you have the power to make good your order both for the dead and the living.

CREON   See, then, that my mandate is enforced.

CHORUS   Give this task to some younger man.

CREON   I don't mean that. Watchers of the corpse are at their posts.

CHORUS   What further then, do you have in mind?

CREON   That you do not side with breakers of these commands.

CHORUS   No man is foolish enough to be in love with death.

CREON   That would be the penalty. But always someone can be tempted to his ruin through love of gain.

(Enter GUARD.)

GUARD   O King, I will not say that I come breathless from speed, or that I have plied a nimble foot, for often my thoughts made me stop, and I would wheel around and start back. My mind was holding large discourse with me: "Fool, why hurry to your certain doom?" "Wretch, loitering again? And if Creon hears the story from someone else, will you not pay for it?" So debating, I went on my way without eagerness, and thus a short road was made long. At last, however, I have come hither—to you; and though what I will say may amount to little, I will say it, for I come holding tight to one hope: that I can suffer nothing but what is my fate.

CREON   And what makes you so fearful?

GUARD   First let me tell you about myself—I did not do the deed—I did not see the doer—it is not right that I should come to any harm.

CREON   You shrewdly build a fence around yourself. Clearly you must have strange news.

GUARD   Yes, truly. Dread news makes one pause.

CREON   Then tell it, will you, and so get you gone?

GUARD   Well, this is it—the corpse—someone has just given it burial and gone away—after sprinkling dry dust on the flesh, with other pious rites.

CREON   What do you say? What living man has dared do this?

GUARD   I know not. No mark of a pickaxe was seen there, no earth thrown up by mattock. The ground was hard and dry, unbroken, without track of wheels. Whoever did it left no trace. And when the first day-watchman showed it to us, dread wonder fell on all. The dead man was veiled from us—not really buried but strewn with dust, as by the hand of one who feared a curse. There was no evidence that any beast of prey or dog had come near him or torn him.

Then everyone began accusing everyone else and, without anyone to stop it, a fight nearly broke out. Every man was the accused, and no one was convicted but all denied any knowledge of the act. And we were ready to take red-hot iron in our hands—to walk through fire—to swear by the gods that we had not done the deed—that we knew nothing of the planning or the doing.

At last, when we had got nowhere with our searching, someone spoke who made all of us bow our heads in fright, for we could neither deny him nor escape misfortune if we obeyed. He said this deed must not be hidden but must be reported to you. And this seemed best; and the lot fell to me. So here I am—as unwelcome as unwilling, I know, for no man likes a bearer of bad news.

CHORUS   O King, think you by chance this deed might be the work of gods?

CREON   Stop, before your words fill me completely with anger and you be found not only old but foolish. You say what is not to be believed, that the gods are concerned with this corpse. Was it for high reward of trusty service that they hid his nakedness, the nakedness of one who came to burn their columned shrines and sacred treasures, to burn their land, and scatter its laws to the wind? Or do you imagine the gods honoring the wicked? It cannot be. No! From the first there were certain ones in this city that muttered against me, chafing at this edict, wagging their heads in secret; and kept not their necks bowed to the yoke like men contented with my rule.

It is by them, I am certain, that these have been lured and bribed to do the deed. No evil surpasses the power of money. Money lays cities low, drives men from their homes, misguides and warps honest souls till they do shameful things, and still teaches folks to practice villainies and to know every godless deed.

But the men who did this thing for hire have made it certain they shall pay the price. Now, as Zeus is my god, know this—I swear it: if you do not find the one who buried the corpse and bring him before me, death alone shall not be enough for you; before death, you will be tortured until you clear up this outrage. Your lesson will be to steal with sure knowledge of how bribes are won and how it is not good to accept gain from every source. You will find more loss in evil than profit.

GUARD   May I speak? Or shall I just turn and go?

CREON   Know you not that even your voice is now an offense in my ears?

GUARD   In your ears or in your soul?

CREON   And would you define the location of my pain?

GUARD   I may offend your ears but the doer offends your soul.

CREON   You are a born babbler, that's clear.

GUARD   Maybe, but never the doer of the deed.

CREON   Yes, and more than that—the seller of your life for silver.

GUARD   Ah, me! It is sad, certainly, that a judge should misjudge.

CREON   Let your fancy play with the word "judgment" if you wish;—but, if you fail to catch the doers of these things, you shall swear that evil gains bring sorrows. *(Exit into Palace.)*

GUARD   Well, heaven send that he be found! But whether he is caught or not—fortune will decide that—you will not see me here again. Saved once, beyond my best hope, I owe the gods great thanks. *(Exit.)*

CHORUS   Wonders are many, and none is more wonderful than man: he has power to cross the white sea, driven by the stormy southwind, plunging under surges that threaten to engulf him; and Earth, eldest of the gods, immortal, unwearied, does he master, turning the soil as the ploughs go to and fro year after year.

And the soaring race of birds, the tribes of savage beasts, and the brood of the sea, he traps in the meshes of his snares, man excellent in cunning. And he masters by his arts the beast whose den is in the wilderness, who roams the hills; he breaks the horse of shaggy mane and puts the yoke upon his neck; he tames the tireless mountain bull.

And speech, and lightning thought, and all the interweavings that shape a state has he taught himself; how to be sheltered from arrowy frost and the rushing rain. Yes, nothing is beyond his power; from baffling diseases he has devised escapes and only against Death shall he call for help in vain.

Cunning beyond fancy's dream is the fertile skill which now brings him to evil, now to good. When he honors the laws of the land and the justice which he has sworn by the gods to uphold, his city stands proud, but no city has he who, for his foolishness, lives with sin. Never may such a one share my hearth, or share my thoughts.

(Enter the GUARD *from the left, leading in* ANTIGONE.)

CHORUS   What sight is this? My soul stands amazed. I know her. It is Antigone. O, unhappy child and child of an unhappy father—Oedipus! What does this mean? *You* brought a prisoner? *You,* disloyal to the King's laws, and arrested for your folly?

GUARD   Here she is. She did it. We caught her burying him. But where is Creon?

CHORUS   He comes forth again from the Palace, at the right time.

CREON   What is it? What has happened that makes my coming timely?

GUARD   O King, men should be careful of their words, for second-thoughts may correct the first intention. I could have sworn that I should not soon be here again—

scared by the threats by which you blasted me. But there is no pleasure like one unexpected, and I have returned, in spite of my oath, bringing this girl—who was taken doing grace to the dead. This time, be sure, there was no casting of lots, for this piece of luck belongs to me and to no one else. And now, Sire, take her yourself, question her, examine her as you will, but I hope I have gained the right to be free and completely rid of this trouble.

CREON   And your prisoner here—how and where did you take her?

GUARD   She was burying the man, as I said.

CREON   Do you mean what you say? Do you?

GUARD   I saw her burying the corpse that you had forbidden to bury. Is that plain and clear?

CREON   And how was she seen? how taken in the act?

GUARD   It happened this way. When we had come to the place—with your dreadful threats ringing in our ears—we swept away all the dust from the corpse and bared the dank body; and sat us down on the brow of the hill, to the windward to avoid the smell of him. Every man was wide awake and kept his neighbors awake with torrents of threats against anyone who shirked his task.

So it went, until the sun was straight overhead, and the heat began to burn: and then suddenly a whirlwind lifted a storm of dust, which filled the plain, covered the leaves of the trees, and choked the air. We closed our eyes and bore this plague of the gods.

And then, after a long time, the dust storm passed and the girl was seen. Like a bird bitter at finding its nest stripped of nestlings, she cried aloud when she saw the bare corpse. She wailed aloud and called down curses on the doers of the deed. Without hesitation she brought dust in her hands; and then from a bronze pitcher, three times she poured a drink-offering upon the corpse.

We rushed forward when we saw it and closed in on our quarry, who stood there undismayed. Then we charged her with her past and present doings and she denied nothing—a joy and a pain to me at the same time. To have escaped from one's own troubles is a great joy, but it is painful to bring troubles to others. However that may be, all such things mean less to me than my own safety.

CREON   You—whose head is bowed—do you admit or do you deny the deed?

ANTIGONE   I admit it; I make no denial.

CREON (*to the* GUARD)   You may go now, free and clear of a serious charge. (*Exit* GUARD.) (*To* ANTIGONE) Now, tell me—in few words—did you know that an edict had forbidden this?

ANTIGONE   I knew it—why shouldn't I? It was public.

CREON   And you dared to transgress that law?

ANTIGONE   Yes, for it was not Zeus that had issued that edict; nor was it a law given to men by Justice which lives with the gods below; nor did I consider your decrees so powerful as to override the unwritten and unfailing laws of heaven. For heaven's laws are eternal and no man knows when they were first put forth.

Not from dread of any human pride could I answer to the gods for breaking *these*. Die I must—I knew that well (how should I not know it?)—even without your edict. But if I am to die before my time, I count that gain, for when one lives, as I do, boxed in by evils, can one count death as anything but gain?

Therefore for me to meet this doom is a trifling grief, but if I had allowed my mother's son to remain unburied, that would have grieved me; for death, I am not grieved. And if my deeds are foolhardy in your sight, perhaps a foolish judge condemns my folly.

CHORUS   She shows herself the passionate child of a passionate father and does not know how to bend before trouble.

CREON   Yet I would have you know that stubbornness is most often humbled. It is the hardest iron, baked to brittleness in the fire, that you shall oftenest see snapped and shivered; and I have known wild horses brought tame by a little curbing; there is no room for pride among slaves.—This girl became versed in violence when she broke the laws that have been set forth; and, that done, behold a second insult as she boasts of this and exults in her defiance.

Now, truly I am no man—she is the man—if victory in this rests with her and brings no penalty. No! be she sister's child, or even nearer to me in blood than any that worship Zeus at the altar of the house, she and her kinfolk shall not avoid direct punishment, for I charge also her sister with a full share in plotting this burial.

Summon Ismene—for I saw her within just now—raving as if out of her mind. So often, before the deed, the mind convicts itself in its treason while plotting dark evil. But this, too, is truly hateful, when one has been caught in a crime and makes that crime a glory.

ANTIGONE   Would you do more than kill me?

CREON   Nothing more, no. That done, I am satisfied.

ANTIGONE   Why, then, do you delay? In all your talk there is nothing pleasing to me—may there never be!—and my words, I suppose, are unpleasant to you. And yet, for glory—how could I have won greater glory than by giving burial to my own brother? All here would agree to this were they not afraid to say so. But royalty—blessed in so many ways—has the power to do and say what it will.

CREON   You are in error. No citizens of Thebes agree with you.

ANTIGONE   Yes they do. But fear of you seals their mouths.

CREON   And are not you ashamed to be so different?

ANTIGONE   No, for there is nothing shameful in honoring a brother.

CREON   Was it not a brother, too, who died in the opposite cause?

ANTIGONE   Brother by the same mother and the same father.

CREON   Why then do you do honor which is impious in the sight of Eteocles?

ANTIGONE   Eteocles would not think my act impious.

CREON   He would think so, if you make him but equal in honor with the wicked.

ANTIGONE   It was his brother—not his slave—that perished.

CREON   Laying waste this land, while *he* fell defending it.

ANTIGONE   No matter. Duty must be paid the dead.

CREON   But good deserves more than evil.

ANTIGONE   Who can know such things? In the land of the dead that may not be the law.

CREON   A foe is never a friend—not even in death.

ANTIGONE   It is not my nature to hate but to love.

CREON   Join the dead, then, and love them. While I live, no woman shall rule me.

(*Enter* ISMENE, *led in by two* ATTENDANTS.)

CHORUS   Ismene comes, shedding the tears of a loving sister; her darkened brow casts a shadow over her cheeks as tears break in rain over her fair face.

CREON   And you, who, lurking like a viper in my house, were secretly sucking my life-blood, while I knew not I was nurturing two traitors to rise against my throne—come, tell me, will you confess your part in this burial, or will you deny knowledge of it?

ISMENE   I have done the deed—if my sister allows my claim—and share the guilt with her.

ANTIGONE   No. Justice will not allow that. You did not consent to the deed and neither did I allow you a part in it.

ISMENE   But, now that you are in it, I am not ashamed to take my place by your side.

ANTIGONE   Whose was the deed, Hades and the dead know. A friend in words has not my love.

ISMENE   But, Antigone, do not reject me. Let me die with you and thereby honor the dead.

ANTIGONE   You shall not die with me, nor claim a deed you had no part in. My death is enough.

ISMENE   If I lose you, what will life mean to me?

ANTIGONE   Ask Creon; you care only for him.

ISMENE   Why do you mock me to no purpose?

ANTIGONE   If, indeed, I mock you, it is with pain that I do so.

ISMENE   Tell me—how can I help you, even now?

ANTIGONE   Save yourself. I shall not mind.

ISMENE   Have pity, Antigone. May I not die with you?

ANTIGONE   Your choice was to live; mine, to die.

ISMENE   At least your choice was made over my protest.

ANTIGONE   One world approved your choice; another approved mine.

ISMENE   Yes, the offense is the same for both of us.

ANTIGONE   Be reconciled. Live . . . My life has long been given to death so that I might serve the dead.

CREON   One of these creatures, it appears, is newly mad; the other has been mad from the beginning.

ISMENE   Yes, O King, for the mind of the unfortunate often goes astray.

CREON   Yours did when you joined your sister.

ISMENE   How could I endure life without her?

CREON   She lives no more. Speak not as though she did.

ISMENE   But will you put to death the betrothed of your son?

CREON   Never mind that. There are other fields for him to plough.

ISMENE   But not such a love as bound him to her.

CREON   I will not countenance an evil wife for a son of mine.

ANTIGONE   Haemon, dearest. How your father wrongs you!

CREON   Enough and too much of you and your marriage!

CHORUS   Would you indeed take this girl from your son?

CREON   Not I, but Death.

CHORUS   It is determined that she shall die?

CREON   Determined, yes. (*To the* ATTENDANTS) No more delay. Take them inside, the proper place for women, for even the bold seek to escape when life stands face to face with Death. (*Exit* ATTENDANTS, *guarding* ANTIGONE *and* ISMENE.)

CHORUS   Blessed are they whose days have never tasted of evil. When a house has once been shaken from heaven, the curse passes from generation to generation of the race; even as, when the surge is driven from the deep by the fierce breath of Thracian gales, it roils the black sands from the depths, and there is a sullen roar from wind-vexed headlands that front the blows of the storm.

In the house of Labdacus[1] sorrows are heaped upon the sorrows of the dead, and generation is not freed by generation, but some god strikes them down, and the race has no deliverance.

For now that hope, the light of which had spread above the last root of the house of Oedipus—that hope, now, is brought low in blood-stained dust by the infernal gods, by folly in speech, and frenzy of heart.

---

[1] Labdacus was the father of Laius, who was the father of Oedipus. See chart on p. 606.

Your power, O Zeus, what human trespass can limit? That power which is unquelled by sleep or the long march of months, as you dwell in dazzling splendor on Olympus, ageless but not aged.

And so, through the future, near or far, as through the past, shall this law stand: nothing that is great comes into the life of man without a curse.

But hope is to many men a comfort, and to many a false lure of foolish desires; and man loses his awareness until suddenly his foot is burned against the hot fire. It is a wise and famous saying that evil comes to seem good to him whose mind the gods draw to mischief, and thus man fares not long free of suffering.

But Haemon comes, the last of your sons. Does he come to lament the doom of his promised bride, Antigone, and bitter over the loss of his marriage hopes?

(*Enter* HAEMON.)

CREON   We shall know soon, better than prophets could tell us. My son, hearing the unalterable doom of your betrothed, are you come in anger against your father? Or do I still hold your love in spite of my action?

HAEMON   Father, I am your son, and you in your wisdom trace rules for me that I shall follow. I cannot regard marriage as a greater gain than your good guidance.

CREON   Yes, my son, your heart's fixed law should be to obey your father. Men pray to have loyal sons who will deal evil to their enemies and honor to their friends. But he who is father to unprofitable children has sown trouble for himself and comfort to his enemies. Therefore, my son, do not seize impulsively the pleasures offered by a woman, for know this: that joys grow cold if an evil woman shares your bed and home. For what wound could strike deeper than a false love? Loathe this girl as if she were your enemy and let her find a husband in Hades. For I have apprehended her, alone of all the city, in open disobedience. I will not make myself a liar to my people—I will put her to death.

Let her appeal as she will to the claims of kinship.[2] If I tolerate crime in my own kindred, I must bear the crimes of strangers. He who does his duty in his own household will be found righteous in matters of State too. But if anyone breaks the law and thinks to dictate to his rulers, such a one can win no praise from me. No, the one whom the State appoints must be obeyed, in little things and great, in just things and unjust. I am certain that that one who thus obeys would be a good ruler no less than a good subject, and in any battle would stand his ground where he was set, loyal and brave at his comrade's side.

But disobedience is the worst of evils. It ruins cities, desolates homes, and causes the defeat of armies; whereas unquestioning obedience saves the lives of multitudes. Consequently, we must support the cause of order and not allow a mere woman to worst us. If we must fall from power, it is better to fall before a man than to be called weaker than a woman.

CHORUS   To us, unless the years have stolen our wits, you seem to say wisely what you say.

HAEMON   Father, the gods implant reason in men, the highest of all things we have. I have not the skill nor the desire to prove you wrong; yet, what I have to say may be of some use. At least, as your son, I may report, for your good, all that men say or do, or find to blame. The dread of your displeasure forbids the citizens to speak up with words offensive to you; but I can hear the murmurs in the dark, the lamentings of the city for this maiden. The people say, "No woman ever merited her doom less—none ever was to die shamefully for such glorious deeds; who when her own brother had fallen in bloody

---

[2] Antigone was Creon's niece. See chart on p. 606.

battle, would not leave him unburied to be eaten by dogs and birds. Does not *she* deserve golden reward?"

Such is the whispered rumor that spreads in secret. For me, father, no treasure is so precious as your welfare. What fairer exchange is there than a son's pride in his father and a father's pride in his son? Do not, therefore, keep to a single line of thought as though it were the only path. For if any man thinks that he alone is wise, that in speech and thought he has no equal, such a man when laid open to view will be found empty.

No, though a man be wise, it is not shameful for him to learn and to give way if need be. As you have seen, trees survive that bend to winter's torrents, while the unbending perish root and branch. So also, he who keeps the sheet of his sail taut and never slackens it before a gale, upsets the boat.

Father, forego your wrath. Permit yourself to change. For, if as young as I am I may say so, the next best thing to natural wisdom is wisdom acquired through accepting advice.

CHORUS   Sire, it would seem that Haemon has spoken wisely just as you also have spoken wisely. There seems much to be said on both sides.

CREON   Elders of Thebes—are we at our age to be schooled by this young fellow?

HAEMON   In nothing that is not right, but even if I am young, you should consider what I have said, not my years.

CREON   Is it right to be disobedient?

HAEMON   No one should respect evil-doers.

CREON   Is not your lady tainted with that malady?

HAEMON   The people of Thebes say no.

CREON   Shall the people of Thebes prescribe how I shall rule?

HAEMON   Surely that is a childish question.

CREON   Am I to rule this land by judgment other than my own?

HAEMON   No city belongs to one man.

CREON   Is not the city held to be the ruler's?

HAEMON   You would make a good ruler over a desert.

CREON   This boy, it appears, is the woman's champion.

HAEMON   Not at all—unless you are a woman. My concern is for you.

CREON   You show this by open feud with your father!

HAEMON   Only because you are offending against Justice.

CREON   Do I offend by respecting my own authority?

HAEMON   You show no respect by trampling on the rights of the gods.

CREON   What a coward—to give way to a woman!

HAEMON   You will not find me in league with baseness.

CREON   All your words, at least, plead for that girl.

HAEMON   And for you, and for me, and for the gods of the dead.

CREON   You will never marry her this side of the grave.

HAEMON   Then she must die, but she will not die alone.

CREON   Your boldness now runs to open threats?

HAEMON   What threat is it to argue against error?

CREON   You will regret this foolish effort to teach me wisdom.

HAEMON   If you were not my father, I should have said that you are not very wise.

CREON   Slave to this woman, don't go on chattering so!

HAEMON   Would you alone speak and hear no answer?

CREON   Do you say that? By the heaven above us—be sure of this: you shall suffer for taunting me in this outrageous way. Drag forth that hated thing that she may die now, in his presence—before his eyes—at his side!

HAEMON   No, not at my side—never shall that be; nor shall you ever set eyes again upon my face. Rave as you will to such followers as can endure you. (*Exit* HAEMON.)

CHORUS   He is gone, O King, in angry haste; a youthful mind, when stung, is dangerous.

CREON   Let him rave to the top of his bent and good speed to him, but he shall not save these two girls from their doom.

CHORUS   Indeed? Do you intend to slay them both?

CREON   No—you are right—not her who had no part in the matter.

CHORUS   And how will you slay the other?

CREON   I will take her where the path is loneliest and wall her up alive in a rocky cave, with food enough so we may not be responsible for her blood. There, let her pray to Hades, the only god she loves; perhaps she will obtain from him protection against death; or else she will learn, if a little late, how useless is reverence for the dead. (*Exit* CREON.)

CHORUS   Love, the unconquered, master of wealth, who keep your vigil on the soft cheeks of a maiden, you roam over the sea and among the dwellers of the wilds; no one escapes you, be he god or mortal man; and he who receives you is like a thing possessed.

The just themselves have their minds warped by you, to their ruin. You it is who have stirred the present strife of kinsmen. The light you kindled in the eyes of the fair bride is victorious; it is a power enthroned beside the eternal laws, and Aphrodite works her unconquerable will.

(ANTIGONE *enters, between* GUARDS.)

But now I am carried beyond the bounds of loyalty to my king, and I cannot keep back the streaming tears, as I see Antigone make her way to the bridal chamber of eternal sleep.

ANTIGONE   Look upon me, my countrymen, setting forth on my last way, gazing for the last time on the light of the sun, which for me shall be no more. For Hades, who offers sleep to all, is leading me, while yet alive, to the shore of Acheron. No wedding-chant will there be for me, no bridal day; but I am betrothed of the Lord of the Dark Lake.

CHORUS   But glory and praise will go with you to that deep place of the dead. Wasting sickness has not stricken you, nor were you taken away by the sword; but alive, mistress of your fate, you pass to Hades as has no other mortal.

ANTIGONE   I have heard that, long ago, Niobe,[3] daughter of Tantalus, was doomed to die a piteous death on the heights of Sipylus. There, rigid rocks encompassed her like ivy, and she was beaten upon by snow and rain, which even now—they say—mingle with her tears. Most like hers is the fate which brings me to my rest.

CHORUS   Yes, but she was a goddess, born of gods. We are mortal. Yet it is great renown for a woman to share the doom of a goddess both in her life and after death.

ANTIGONE   Oh, you are mocking me! In the name of our father's gods, cannot you wait till I am gone, but must taunt me to my face? You, at least, O fount of Dirce and many-charioted Thebes, will bear witness by what laws I pass to the rock-sealed tomb—unhappy me, unwept of friends, who have no home on earth nor in the shades, no home among the living or the dead!

CHORUS   But you stepped forth to the utmost limits of daring, my child; and you are now paying for that before the throne of Law. Yet I also think you are paying for your father's sins.

[3] Niobe, an earlier queen of Thebes, had reared seven fine sons and seven lovely daughters. Pride in this accomplishment made Niobe consider herself above the gods, until one day she insulted Leto, the mother of Apollo and Diana. In punishment, all fourteen children were destroyed by the arrows of Apollo and Diana; and Niobe was turned into a stone on the side of Mount Sipylus. In summer, tears could be seen issuing from the stone.

ANTIGONE   You have touched my bitterest thought, awakening the ever-new lament for my father and for the terrible doom visited on the house of Labdacus. Horrible thoughts!—the marriage of mother and son—a mother slumbering at the side of her son— my father! From what manner of parents did I take my miserable being! Now to them I go, accursed, unwed, to share their home! And, Polynices, ill-starred in marriage,[4] in death you have undone my life!

CHORUS   An act of reverence is worthy of some praise, but a challenge against authority will bring retribution. Your self-will has brought ruin upon you.

ANTIGONE   Unwept, without friends, without marriage-songs, I am led on a journey which cannot longer be delayed. I shall never see again the holy light of the sun, and for my fate no tear is shed, no friend laments.

(Enter CREON.*)*

CREON   Know you not that songs and wailings before death would never cease if it profited to utter them? Away with her! And when you have placed her, according to my order, in her vaulted grave, leave her there, alone; either to die, or to go on living in her tomb. In any case, our hands are clean. This, however, is certain: she shall henceforth be deprived of the light of day.

ANTIGONE   Tomb, bridal-chamber, eternal prison in the cave rock, there I must go to join my own—those many who have perished and dwell now with Persephone. Last of all, most miserable of all, before my time, I join the others. But I have good hope my coming will be welcome to my father and pleasant to my mother and more than welcome to you, my brothers, for when you died, with my own hands I washed and dressed you and poured libations at your graves. It is for tending your corpse, Polynices, that I have won this reward.

And yet I honored you rightly, the wise will say. [But I would not have taken this task upon me had I had a mother, or if a husband had been left unburied. What reason for this, you ask? The husband lost, another might have been found and another child might have replaced the first one; but with both my father and my mother dead, I could never have another brother. This is why I held you, Polynices, first in honor, but Creon held me guilty of a sin and outrage. And now I go alive to the vaults of death.][5]

What law of heaven have I transgressed? Unfortunate that I am, why should I look to the gods any more—where is any ally for me—when by piety I have earned the name of impious? If my punishment is sanctioned by the gods, I shall soon know, but if the sin is with my judges, I could wish them no fuller measure of evil than they have heaped upon me.

CHORUS   Still the same tempest of the soul vexes this maiden with the same fierce gusts.

CREON   All the more reason for her guards to act at once!

ANTIGONE   Ah, that word has the sound of death.

CREON   Your doom will be fulfilled.

ANTIGONE   O city of my fathers, O eldest gods of our race, they lead me away—now, now—they linger no longer! Look upon me, princes of Thebes, the last daughter of the

---

[4] Polynices had married an Argive princess. The marriage opened the way to Argive backing for an assault on Thebes, during which Polynices lost his life and thereby brought on Antigone's defiance of Creon.

[5] This bracketed passage has been challenged as illogical and perhaps spurious—though all manuscripts contain it. Can it be defended?

house of your kings—see what has come upon me—and from whom, because I feared to cast away the fear of Heaven! (ANTIGONE *is led away by the* GUARDS.)

CHORUS   Even thus suffered Danaë, in her beauty exchanging the light of day for brassbound walls; and in that dungeon, secret as the grave, she was held close prisoner. She, too, was of proud lineage, O Antigone, and she received into her in a golden shower the seed of Zeus. But dread is the mysterious power of fate. There is no deliverance from it by wealth or by war, by walled city, or dark sea-beaten ships.[6]

So suffered Lycurgus, too, when shackles tamed him, the son of Dryas, that King of the Edonians, so quick to anger. He paid for his frenzied taunts at the hands of Dionysus; for he too was shut away in a rocky prison. There the fierce exuberance of his madness slowly passed. He learned to know the power of the god whom in his frenzy he had mocked, when he angered the Muses by trying to quench the Bacchanalian fire of the Maenads.[7]

And by the waters of the Dark Rocks, the waters of the twofold sea, are the shores of Bosporus and Thracian Salmydessus. Here Ares, hard by the city, saw the blinding wounds inflicted by Idothea, fierce wife of Phineus, upon his two children. With weaving-needle she, bloody-handed, put out the light of their eyes, which craved for vengeance. They too were then entombed, as you; and deep in misery, they cried out against their cruel doom, those sons of a mother cursed by her marriage. Yet she was of Erechtheid blood, nursed amid her father's storms, a true child of Boreas, swift as wind, a daughter of the gods brought low by the gray Fates.[8] So it was, Antigone.

(*Enter from the right* TIRESIAS, *a blind seer, led by a* BOY.)

TIRESIAS   Princes of Thebes, we have come with linked steps, both served by the eyes of one, for in this way the blind may walk.

CREON   And what word do you bring, old man?

TIRESIAS   I will tell you and you must take heed.

CREON   Indeed, Tiresias, it has not been my custom to ignore your counsel.

TIRESIAS   Thereby you have thus far steered well the city's course.

CREON   I freely grant how much I owe to you.

TIRESIAS   Hear this then: once more you stand on fate's fine edge.

CREON   What mean you? Your words send a shudder through me.

TIRESIAS   You will learn—you will learn when you hear my foretelling. As I sat in my accustomed place to read the voices of the birds, I heard a strange thing: they were screaming in feverish rage and their language was lost in jabber. And I knew from the whirr of their wings they were tearing murderously at each other.

In fear at what I had heard, I prepared a burnt-sacrifice, but the Fire-god offered no fire; a dank moisture oozed from the flesh and trickled upon the embers which smoked and sputtered. The gall of the sacrifice vanished into the air and the fat-larded thighs were bared of the fat. My boy assured me that no signs came, and my offering was a failure.

And who should be blamed for this failure? It is your evil counsel which has brought

---

[6] Danaë's father, Acrisius, locked his daughter in a bronze tower to keep a prophecy from coming to pass, to wit, that Danaë would give birth to a son who would kill Acrisius. Zeus, however, descended in a golden shower through the roof and impregnated Danaë. She gave birth to Perseus who, later, at an athletic festival accidentally killed Acrisius with a discus.   [7] Lycurgus, opposed to Dionysus (Roman Bacchus), tried to stop revelry in the god's honor. For this he was shut up in a rocky prison. Soon afterward he went blind and died.

[8] Idothea was the second wife of the prophet Phineus. (She is called in other accounts Idaea, Dia, or Erytia.) Some versions have Phineus himself blinding his two children by a former marriage, because of charges made against them by their stepmother.

this sickness upon the city. The altars of Thebes have been tainted—all of them—by birds and dogs which have torn at the corpse of Oedipus' son; and therefore the gods no longer accept prayers and sacrifices at our hands or the flame of meat-offerings; nor does any bird give a clear sign by his shrill cry, for they have tasted a slain man's blood.

Take heed of these things, my son. All men may sin, but when a sin has been committed, the sinner is not forever lost if he will but heal the mischief he has done and not stubbornly cling to his error.

Self-will is folly. Give honor to the dead, for what courage is needed to slay the slain again? It is your good that I have sought, and for that reason you should accept what I have said.

CREON Old man, you join the others in the sport of shooting at me—a fair target for everyone's arrows. The tribe of seers has long made a business of me. Gain your gains, drive your trade, if you like, in the gold-mines of Sardis or India, but try not for advantage of me. You shall not hide that man in the grave—no, though the eagles of Zeus should carry morsels from the body to their Master's throne—no, not even for dread of such defilement will I allow his burial, for I know well enough no mortal can defile the gods. But you, aged Tiresias, how shameful the fall of wisdom when it dresses shameful thoughts in fair words—all for the sake of gain!

TIRESIAS Ah, does any man know, does any man consider . . . ?

CREON Go ahead. What sage comment do you have for us now?

TIRESIAS How precious, above all riches, is good counsel.

CREON True; as evil counsel is the worst of crimes.

TIRESIAS And you are tainted with that sickness.

CREON I would not answer the seer with a taunt.

TIRESIAS But you do by saying that I prophesy lies.

CREON Well, the tribe of prophets has always had an eye for money.

TIRESIAS And the race of tyrants loves base gain.

CREON Do you know you are speaking to your King?

TIRESIAS I know it. It was through me that you saved Thebes.

CREON You are a wise prophet, but not necessarily honest.

TIRESIAS You will taunt me into revealing a dread secret.

CREON Out with it!—only expect no profit for your words.

TIRESIAS As far as you're concerned, they'll bring no profit.

CREON You will not shake my determination.

TIRESIAS Then know this—and know it well—that the sun's swift chariot will not run many more courses before you shall have given a son of yours to death, a corpse in payment for corpses; because you have ruthlessly consigned a living soul to the tomb, and because you have kept from the tomb one who belongs there, and leave his corpse unburied, unhonored, unhallowed. These things are not for you to do, nor even for the gods. These are your crimes; and because of them avenging destroyers lie in wait for you; the Furies of Hell pursue you that you may suffer the ills you have brought to others.

Judge now if I speak these things as a hireling. Soon in your house shall rise the wailing of men and of women. And a tumult of hatred against you shall echo from all the cities nearby because some of their sons had their only burial-rites from dogs, or from wild beasts, or from carrion birds—a pollution to the hearths and altars of each city.

You have provoked me to launch these arrows at your heart, sure arrows from which you cannot escape.

Come boy, lead me home. Let him spend his rage on younger men or learn to control his tongue and sweeten his mind if he can. (*Exit* TIRESIAS.)

CHORUS He has gone, O King, and left behind his dread prophecies. In all the time it has taken to change my hair from dark to white, I have never known him to prophesy falsely.

CREON   I, too, know it well and am troubled in soul. It is bad to give way, but it may be worse to stand firm.

CHORUS   It would be well, son of Menoeceus, to accept advice.

CREON   What advice? What should I do? Speak, and I will obey.

CHORUS   Free Antigone from her rocky vault. And make a tomb for the unburied Polynices.

CREON   And this is your advice? You would have me yield?

CHORUS   Yes, Creon, and speedily. The gods strike swiftly and cut short the follies of men.

CREON   It is hard to give way, but I do so. I obey. One must not wage a vain war against destiny.

CHORUS   Do these things yourself. Do not leave them to others.

CREON   I will go at once. Slaves! Take tools for digging and hurry to yonder hill. Since my mind is made up, I will myself unbind Antigone even as I myself bound her. But my mind is dark with foreboding. It had been best to keep the established laws, even to life's end. (*Exit* CREON *with* SERVANTS.)

CHORUS   O god of many names, glory of the Cadmean bride, offspring of loud-thundering Zeus! You who watch over famed Italia and reign over the hospitable valley of Eleusis! O Bacchus, dweller in Thebes, mother-city of the Bacchantes, by the soft-gliding stream of Ismenus, on the soil where the fierce dragon's teeth were sown!

You have seen where torch-flames glare through smoke, and rise above the twin peaks, where dance the Corycian nymphs, your votaries, hard by Castalia's stream.

You come from the ivy mantled slopes of Nysa's hills, from the green shore with many-clustered vines; and you hear your name in the streets of Thebes lifted up by immortal voices.

Thebes, of all cities, you hold first in honor, you, and also your mother whom the lightning struck. Now, when all our people bow before a violent plague, come with healing feet over the Parnassian height, over the moaning sea!

O you with whom the stars rejoice as they move, the stars whose breath is fire; O master of the voices of the night; son begotten of Zeus; come to us, O King, with your attendant Bacchantes, who in night-long frenzy dance before you, the Giver of Good Gifts, Bacchus!

(Enter MESSENGER *from the left of the stage.)*

MESSENGER   Citizens of Thebes, the mortal life of man is never assured. Fortune raises and Fortune humbles the lucky or the unlucky from day to day, and no one can foretell what will be from what is. For Creon once was blessed, as I count bliss. He had saved Thebes from its enemies. He was clothed with sole authority in the land; he reigned, the glorious father of princely children. And now—all has been lost. For when a man has had life's pleasures taken from him, I count him as good as dead, a breathing corpse. Heap up riches, if you will, live like a king, but if there is no joy, I would not give the shadow of a shadow for such a life.

CHORUS   What new sorrow has come to our princes?

MESSENGER   Death. And the guilt is on those that live.

CHORUS   Who is the slayer and who the slain? Speak!

MESSENGER   Haemon is dead, his blood spilled by no stranger.

CHORUS   By his father's hand or by his own?

MESSENGER   By his own, in anger with his father for the murder.

CHORUS   O prophet, how true, then, have proved your words!

MESSENGER   So much you have heard. You must decide what to do.

CHORUS   Ah, Eurydice, Creon's unfortunate wife, approaches. Perhaps she comes by chance, or perhaps she has heard the news of her son.

(*Enter* EURYDICE.)

EURYDICE   People of Thebes, I heard what you were saying as I was going forth to salute with prayers the goddess Athena. Just as I was opening the gate, the messages of woe struck my ears. Filled with terror, I sank back into the arms of my handmaids, my senses numbed. Now, say again what you have already said. I shall hear it as one who is no stranger to sorrow.

MESSENGER   Dear lady, I will tell what I saw and leave no word of the truth untold. Why, indeed, should I soothe you with words which would soon be proved false? Truth is always best.

I attended your lord as his guide to the farthest part of the plain, where the body of Polynices, torn by dogs, still lay unhonored. We prayed to Hecate and to Pluto,[9] in mercy to restrain their anger. We washed the body with holy washing and with freshly broken boughs we solemnly burned such relics as there were. Then we raised a high mound of native earth. After that we turned away to enter the maiden's wedding chamber with its rocky couch, the caverned mansion of the bride of Death. From far off, one of us heard loud wailing at the bride's unblessed bower, and came to tell our master Creon.

As the King drew nearer, uncertain sounds of bitter crying floated about him. He groaned. In anguish he muttered: "Wretched that I am, can my foreboding be true? Am I going on the saddest way that I ever went? My son's voice greets me. Go, my servants—hasten, and when you have reached the tomb, passed through the opening where the stones have been wrenched away to the cave's very mouth and look—see if it is Haemon's voice that I know—or if my ear is fooled by the gods."

This search, ordered by our despairing master, we went to make, and in the innermost part of the vault we saw Antigone hanging by the neck. The halter was fashioned from the fine linen thread of her dress. Haemon held his arms about her waist—crying out over the death of his bride, and his father's cruelty, and his own ill-starred love.

But his father, when he saw his son, raised a dreadful cry, and went in and called to him with the voice of despair: "O unhappy son, what have you done? What thoughts possess you? What kind of mischance has made you mad? Come away, my boy! I pray you—I implore!" But the boy glared at him with fierce eyes, spat in his face, and without a word of answer, drew forth his cross-fitted sword. His father fled, and the sword missed. Then, insane with anger, Haemon leaned with all his weight against the blade and drove it half its length into his side. While consciousness was fading, he clasped Antigone to his weak embrace and, gasping, spilled his blood on her pale cheek.

Corpse embracing corpse he lies. He has won his wedding rites, poor youth—not here, but in the halls of Death. He has shown to man that of all curses that plague mankind, ill counsel is the sovereign curse. (EURYDICE *retires into the Palace.*)

CHORUS   What do you make of this? She has left without a word.

MESSENGER   I, too, am startled; yet I feed on the hope that she simply wishes not to vent in public her grief over such sorrowful news. She will perhaps set her handmaids to mourn in privacy. She has had many lessons in woe and may do nothing rash.

CHORUS   I do not know. But to me, at any rate, too much silence seems to bode evil, no less than loud lamenting.

---

[9] Hecate was a goddess of the underworld and Pluto its ruler.

MESSENGER   Well, I will go in, and learn whether in truth she is hiding some rash purpose in the depths of her passionate heart. Yes, you say true: too much silence may have a dangerous meaning. (*Exit* MESSENGER.)

(*Enter* CREON *from the left, with* ATTENDANTS, *carrying in a shroud the body of* HAEMON.)

CHORUS   See, yonder the King himself draws near, bearing that which tells too clear a tale—the work (if one may say so) not of a stranger's madness but of his own misdeeds.

CREON   Woe for the sins of a darkened soul, stubborn sins, shadowed by Death. Look on us—the father who has slain—the son who has perished! Darkest sorrow is mine for the wretched blindness of my stubborn will! Oh, my poor son, you have died in your youth, victim of an ill-timed doom—woe to me! Fled is your spirit, not by your folly but because of mine.

CHORUS   Ah, too late you seem to see the right.

CREON   I have learned the bitter lesson. But then, oh then, some god—I think—struck me from above with heavy weight, and hurled me into the ways of cruelty—overthrowing and trampling on my joy. Bitter woe comes to the labors of man.

(*Enter* MESSENGER *from the Palace.*)

MESSENGER   Sire, you come bearing sorrow; you are soon to look upon more within your Palace.

CREON   What more? What pain is yet to be added?

MESSENGER   Your queen has died, true mother of that corpse. Unhappy lady, her blows are newly dealt.

CREON   O Death, is there no end to your greed? Have you no mercy? You bearer of these evil, bitter words, what do you say? Already I was dead, yet you have struck me anew! What said you, my son? What is this new message—of my wife's death—of slaughter heaped on slaughter! (*The central door of the Palace is opened revealing the corpse of* EURYDICE.)

CHORUS   You can see for yourself—for now nothing is hidden.

CREON   Still another horror! What fate, ah what, can yet await me? I have just lifted my son in my arms, and now another corpse lies before me. Unhappy mother! Unhappy son!

MESSENGER   There at the altar she lay, stabbed with the sharp knife, and as her eyes grew dim she wailed for the noble sacrifice of Megareus, and then for the fate of Haemon who lies there. With her last breath, she invoked a curse upon you, the slayer of your sons.

CREON   O terror! I shake with dread! Is there no one to strike me to the heart with two-edged sword? Miserable, miserable, overwhelmed by anguish!

MESSENGER   Yes, both deaths—your son's, your wife's—are charged to you by her whose corpse you see.

CREON   Her last act—how—how did she it?

MESSENGER   When she had learned the fate of her son, with her own hand she drove the sharp knife home to her heart.

CREON   No man can be found guilty of this but I. Wretched that I am, I own the crime—it was I who murdered you. Take me away, my servants. My life is as death. Lead me away with all speed.

CHORUS   This were best, if best can be found in evil. Swiftness is best when only trouble is before us.

CREON   Let it come, I say. Let it appear, that fairest of fates for me that brings my last day. Yes! best fate of all. Let it come, that never may I look on tomorrow's light.

CHORUS   These things are for the future which is not known. Present tasks claim our care.

CREON   These, at any rate, are my fervent prayers.

CHORUS   Pray no more, for mortals have no escape from what will be.

CREON   Lead me away, I beg you, a rash, foolish man who has unwittingly murdered a son and a wife. I know not where to cast my eyes or where to seek support, for all has gone amiss with everything I have touched, and upon my head a crushing fate has fallen. (*Exit* CREON.)

CHORUS   Wisdom is the crown of happiness and reverence for the gods must be inviolate. The great words of prideful men are punished with great blows, which, in old age, teach the chastened to be wise.

Pronunciation of Proper Names in Antigone

Antigone	Ān-ti′-gō-nē	Labdacus	Lăb′-dă-cŭs
Ares	Ā′-rēz	Laius	Lāy′-ŭs
Bacchantes	Băc-căn′-tēz	Lycurgus	Lȳ-cŭr′-gŭs
Corycian	Cŏr-ĭsh′-yăn	Megareus	Mĕ-gă′-rē-ŭs
Creon	Crē′-ŏn	Menoeceus	Men-ē′-sē-us
Danaë	Dăn′-ā-ē	Niobe	Nī′-ō-bē
Dirce	Dŭr′-sē	Nysa	Nī′-suh
Eleusis	Ĕl-yū′-sis	Oedipus	Ē′-dĭ-pŭs
Eteocles	Ē-tē′-ō-klēz	Phineus	Fĭn′-ē-us
Eurydice	Yū-rĭ′-dĭ-sē	Polynices	Pōlē-nĭ-sēz
Haemon	Hē′-mŏn	Salmydessus	Săl-mĭ-děs′-sus
Hecate	Hĕ-că-tē	Thebes	Thēb′z
Ismene	Ĭz-mē′-nē	Tiresias	Tī-rē′-sē-ăs
Ismenus	Ĭz-mē′-nŭs		

Comments and Questions

1. FIRST IMPRESSIONS. Was the play difficult to understand? Is the action credible? Here first impressions may be misleading, and you may wish to answer two other questions: credible for 2,400 years ago? credible for our time? After analyzing the play more thoroughly, see whether or not you wish to modify your answers.

2. THE FACTS OF THE PLAY. The facts are simple enough, but you should record them as completely as possible. The problem here is to find the precise event that has any bearing on the present action. Does one need to go back farther than the duel between Eteocles and Polynices, which resulted in the deaths of these two brothers of Antigone?

3. EXPOSITION AND ANTECEDENT ACTION. Sophocles, as we have said, depended upon the fact that his audience knew the history of the Theban royal house. He, therefore, allows Ismene to say to Antigone:

Remember how our father perished, amid hate and scorn, when sins, self-revealed, moved him to strike out his eyes with his own hands.

The Greek audience knew that "our father" was Oedipus and that his "awful sin" had been the murder of his father and marriage to his mother. This allusion and the ones that follow in Ismene's speech were simple reminders to the Greeks and did not tell them what they did not already know. The point of course is that the problem of exposition was simplified for the Greek dramatist.

4. SETTING. Greek drama, for the most part, preserved what Aristotle and Renaissance writers on drama identified as the three unities; that is, the unities of time, place, and action. Unity of time required that all the action should be completed in one day; unity of place that the action should occur in one place. *Antigone,* of course, observes these unities. Of how much importance, then, is setting to this play? In what sense does time become of the essence? Consider Creon's actions after he capitulates to the gods. (Compare O'Neill's treatment of time in *Ile.* See Action Line, p. 598.)

5. PLOT. List the sequence of actions that make up the plot. In what way does the plot represent unity of action? What is the essential conflict? Do all actions rise out of this conflict? At what point is the conflict resolved? When, in other words, does Creon realize the terrible implications of his defiance of the gods? What happens after Creon decides to reverse his decrees concerning Polynices and Antigone? Why does Creon bury Polynices before attempting to save Antigone? Explain carefully.

6. CHARACTER. In spite of the title of this play, is Antigone the chief character? Discuss. Although you may find the comparison a curious one, consider the likenesses and differences between Captain Keeney *(Ile)* and Creon. (You may look forward to comparing Creon and Madame Zachanassian in *The Visit,* p. 845.) What are Creon's strengths and weaknesses? Antigone's? Ismene's? Haemon's? Eurydice's? What sort of character does the Chorus have? Consider its wisdom, its doubts, its waverings, its decisions. Can a case be made for identifying the Chorus with public opinion?

7. THE SUMMING PROCESS. What does your analysis add up to? What is the meaning of the play? Is the play concerned only with the question of whether or not Polynices should be buried? Or is it concerned with a conflict between the claims of the state and the claims of the gods? Or does it go beyond even this large issue to an even larger one—man's fate?

How does one get at such questions? Perhaps by asking a few others. Would every man have acted as Creon did? every woman as Antigone? A king other than Creon might have refused burial to both Eteocles and Polynices on the grounds that both were guilty of fratricide. Still someone else in Creon's place might have refused burial to Eteocles and granted it to Polynices on the grounds that Polynices through ridding Thebes of Eteocles had made way for a better man to mount the throne. And what of Antigone? Another daughter might have seen the justice in Creon's action or, like Ismene, might have bent to his will. We are forced to see that because Creon and Antigone acted as they did and not in some other way, they are *individuals responsible for what happened to them.*

Perhaps this conclusion is clear enough, but what of Ismene, Haemon, and Eurydice? What is their guilt? Ismene seems cautious. Is that her weakness or her strength? Haemon is dragged into conflict and destroyed by it. Could he have avoided destruction? Think carefully before you answer. Eurydice seems the most innocent of the bystanders. If she is without fault, how is her suicide to be explained?

If we pull things together now, we may glimpse a vastly disturbing conclusion about man's fate. Creon is guilty of a murderous drive to have his own way. He is crushed. Antigone is stubborn but ranges herself on the side of the gods. She is crushed. Haemon speaks with the voice of reason, stands for principles, but fails. He is crushed. Eurydice, without any part in the struggle, is overwhelmed by it. She is crushed. Ismene, timid and willing to accept what she assumes cannot be changed, survives, but survives without any of the persons she loves.

What is the pattern for this wholesale laying-low of the mighty and the near-mighty? Consider the last lines of the play:

> Wisdom is the crown of happiness and reverence for the gods must be inviolate. The great words of prideful men are punished with great blows, which, in old age, teach the chastened to be wise.

Do these statements account for what has happened to each of the characters?

Many other approaches to this play are possible, but whatever the approach, full meaning is to be realized only after each part of the play has been related to all the other parts.

William Shakespeare (1564–1616)
The Tragedy of Hamlet, Prince of Denmark

A critical essay on *Hamlet* appears on pp. 1130–1142. The play should be read first, then Charlton's comments; then the play should be reviewed. It is also suggested that a first reading of the play be uninterrupted by references to the many footnotes. The gist will be clear. Because, however, Elizabethan English differs from modern English just enough to require some "translation," it will prove useful to check all annotations during the second reading.

DRAMATIS PERSONAE

CLAUDIUS, *King of Denmark*
HAMLET, *son to former King, nephew to Claudius*
POLONIUS, *Lord Chamberlain*
HORATIO, *friend to Hamlet*
LAERTES, *son to Polonius*
Courtiers: VOLTEMAND, CORNELIUS, ROSEN-
   CRANTZ, GUILDENSTERN, OSRIC, A GENTLEMAN
A PRIEST
Officers: MARCELLUS, BERNARDO
FRANCISCO, *a soldier*
REYNALDO, *servant to Polonius*

PLAYERS
TWO CLOWNS, *gravediggers*
FORTINBRAS, *Prince of Norway*
A NORWEGIAN CAPTAIN
ENGLISH AMBASSADORS
GERTRUDE, *Queen of Denmark, Hamlet's mother*
OPHELIA, *daughter to Polonius*
GHOST OF HAMLET'S FATHER
LORDS, LADIES, OFFICERS, SOLDIERS, MESSENGERS, ATTENDANTS

ACT I

Scene I. *Elsinore. A Platform before the Castle.*

Enter two SENTINELS—*first,* FRANCISCO, *who paces up and down at his post; then* BERNARDO, *who approaches him.*

BERNARDO   Who's there?
FRANCISCO   Nay, answer me. Stand and unfold yourself.

Scene I, set in darkness, after midnight

BERNARDO	Long live the King!	
FRANCISCO	Bernardo?	
5	BERNARDO	He.
FRANCISCO	You come most carefully upon your hour.
BERNARDO	'Tis now struck twelve. Get thee to bed, Francisco.
FRANCISCO	For this relief much thanks. 'Tis bitter cold,

And I am sick at heart.

BERNARDO Have you had quiet guard?

10 FRANCISCO   Not a mouse stirring.

BERNARDO Well, good night.

If you do meet Horatio and Marcellus,

The rivals of my watch, bid them make haste.

Enter HORATIO *and* MARCELLUS.

FRANCISCO I think I hear them. Stand, ho! Who is there?

HORATIO Friends to this ground.

15 MARCELLUS   And liegemen to the Dane.

FRANCISCO Give you good night.

MARCELLUS   O, farewell, honest soldier.

Who hath reliev'd you?

FRANCISCO   Bernardo hath my place.

Give you good night.   *Exit.*

MARCELLUS   Holla, Bernardo!

BERNARDO   Say—

What, is Horatio there?

HORATIO   A piece of him.

20 BERNARDO Welcome, Horatio. Welcome, good Marcellus.

MARCELLUS What, has this thing appear'd again to-night?

BERNARDO I have seen nothing.

MARCELLUS Horatio says 'tis but our fantasy,

And will not let belief take hold of him

25 Touching this dreaded sight, twice seen of us.

Therefore I have entreated him along,

With us to watch the minutes of this night,

That, if again this apparition come,

He may approve our eyes and speak to it.

HORATIO Tush, tush, 'twill not appear.

30 BERNARDO   Sit down awhile,

And let us once again assail your ears,

That are so fortified against our story,

What we two nights have seen.

HORATIO   Well, sit we down,

And let us hear Bernardo speak of this.

---

[3] *Long live the King!* (possibly the watchword. Francisco cannot yet see Bernardo clearly.)
[6] *carefully,* punctually   [9] *sick at heart,* depressed (unaccountably)   [13] *rivals,* partners
[14] *ground,* Denmark   [15] *the Dane,* newly crowned Claudius   [19] *A piece of him* (a bit of mild humor, denoting Horatio's lack of enthusiasm for this cold midnight watch)   [23] *fantasy,* imagination   [25] *of us,* by us   [29] *approve our eyes,* agree that we have indeed seen what we have told him we have seen; *speak to it,* accost the "dreaded sight" (something Marcellus and Bernardo had not dared to do)

35 BERNARDO Last night of all,
When yond same star that's westward from the pole
Had made his course t' illume that part of heaven
Where now it burns, Marcellus and myself,
The bell then beating one—

Enter GHOST.

40 MARCELLUS Peace! break thee off! Look where it comes again!
BERNARDO In the same figure, like the King that's dead.
MARCELLUS Thou art a scholar; speak to it, Horatio.
BERNARDO Looks it not like the King? Mark it, Horatio.
HORATIO Most like. It harrows me with fear and wonder.
BERNARDO It would be spoke to.
45 MARCELLUS   Question it, Horatio.
HORATIO What art thou that usurp'st this time of night
Together with that fair and warlike form
In which the majesty of buried Denmark
Did sometimes march? By heaven I charge thee speak!
MARCELLUS It is offended.
50 BERNARDO   See, it stalks away!
HORATIO Stay! Speak, speak! I charge thee speak!

Exit GHOST.

MARCELLUS 'Tis gone and will not answer.
BERNARDO How now, Horatio? You tremble and look pale.
Is not this something more than fantasy?
55 What think you on't?
HORATIO Before my God, I might not this believe
Without the sensible and true avouch
Of mine own eyes.
MARCELLUS   Is it not like the King?
HORATIO As thou art to thyself.
60 Such was the very armour he had on
When he th' ambitious Norway combated.
So frown'd he once when, in an angry parle,
He smote the sledded Polacks on the ice.
'Tis strange.
65 MARCELLUS Thus twice before, and jump at this dead hour,
With martial stalk hath he gone by our watch.
HORATIO In what particular thought to work I know not;
But, in the gross and scope of my opinion,
This bodes some strange eruptions to our state.
70 MARCELLUS Good now, sit down, and tell me he that knows,
Why this same strict and most observant watch

---

[42] *Thou art a scholar,* you are a schooled young man (so you will know how to address this spirit in the proper form).   [44] *harrows,* distresses   [49] *sometimes,* formerly   [62] *angry parle,* loud negotiations (which resulted in a battle between the King of Denmark, Hamlet's father, and "the sledded Polacks")   [65] *jump,* exactly   [68] *gross and scope* (my) general view (imprecise and intuitive)   [70-79] (Marcellus picks up Horatio's vague suggestion and mentions evidences that something of great moment—preparations for imminent war, perhaps—is going on in Denmark.)

So nightly toils the subject of the land,
And why such daily cast of brazen cannon
And foreign mart for implements of war;
75 Why such impress of shipwrights, whose sore task
Does not divide the Sunday from the week.
What might be toward, that this sweaty haste
Doth make the night joint-labourer with the day?
Who is't that can inform me?
HORATIO   That can I.
80 At least, the whisper goes so. Our last king,
Whose image even but now appear'd to us,
Was, as you know, by Fortinbras of Norway,
Thereto prick'd on by a most emulate pride,
Dar'd to the combat; in which our valiant Hamlet
85 (For so this side of our known world esteem'd him)
Did slay this Fortinbras; who, by a seal'd compact,
Well ratified by law and heraldry,
Did forfeit, with his life, all those his lands
Which he stood seiz'd of, to the conqueror;
90 Against the which a moiety competent
Was gaged by our king; which had return'd
To the inheritance of Fortinbras,
Had he been vanquisher, as, by the same comart
And carriage of the article design'd,
95 His fell to Hamlet. Now, sir, young Fortinbras,
Of unimproved mettle hot and full,
Hath in the skirts of Norway, here and there,
Shark'd up a list of lawless resolutes,
For food and diet, to some enterprise
100 That hath a stomach in't; which is no other,
As it doth well appear unto our state,
But to recover of us, by strong hand
And terms compulsatory, those foresaid lands
So by his father lost; and this, I take it,
105 Is the main motive of our preparations,
The source of this our watch, and the chief head
Of this post-haste and romage in the land.
BERNARDO   I think it be no other but e'en so.
Well may it sort that this portentous figure
110 Comes armed through our watch, so like the King
That was and is the question of these wars.
HORATIO   A mote it is to trouble the mind's eye.
In the most high and palmy state of Rome,
A little ere the mightiest Julius fell,

---

⁷⁵ *impress,* conscription   ⁷⁷ *might be toward,* might be about to happen   ⁹⁰ *moiety competent,*
a sufficient portion   ⁹¹ *gaged,* pledged   ⁹³ *comart,* bargain agreed upon   ⁹⁸ *Shark'd up,*
took any war-willing, desperate men, as allegedly sharks indiscriminately gather their prey   ¹⁰⁰ *a*
stomach, valor   ¹⁰⁶ *head,* motive   ¹⁰⁷ *romage,* feverish activity   ^{112–125} (Horatio calls the appearance of the Ghost a portent similar to the horrendous natural events that preceded the murder
of Julius Caesar.)

115   The graves stood tenantless, and the sheeted dead
        Did squeak and gibber in the Roman streets;
        As stars with trains of fire, and dews of blood,
        Disasters in the sun; and the moist star
        Upon whose influence Neptune's empire stands
120   Was sick almost to doomsday with eclipse.
        And even the like precurse of fierce events,
        As harbingers preceding still the fates
        And prologue to the omen coming on,
        Have heaven and earth together demonstrated
125   Unto our climature and countrymen.

(Enter GHOST *again.)*

        But soft! behold! Lo, where it comes again!
        I'll cross it, though it blast me.—Stay, illusion!

(Spreads his arms)

        If thou hast any sound, or use of voice,
        Speak to me.
130   If there be any good thing to be done,
        That may to thee do ease, and grace to me,
        Speak to me.
        If thou art privy to thy country's fate,
        Which happily foreknowing may avoid,
135   O, speak!
        Or if thou hast uphoarded in thy life
        Extorted treasure in the womb of earth
        (For which, they say, you spirits oft walk in death),

(The cock crows.)

        Speak of it! Stay, and speak!—Stop it, Marcellus!
140 MARCELLUS   Shall I strike at it with my partisan?
    HORATIO   Do, if it will not stand.
    BERNARDO   'Tis here!
    HORATIO   'Tis here!
    MARCELLUS   'Tis gone!

(Exit GHOST.*)*

        We do it wrong, being so majestical,
        To offer it the show of violence;
145   For it is as the air, invulnerable,

---

[117] (Some scholars assume that a line before this line has been lost. Why?)   [118] *moist star,* the moon   [119] (The moon controls Neptune's empire, the oceans.)   [122] *harbingers,* officers who precede the king to make arrangements for his care; here forerunners of disaster   [123] *omen,* terrible happening   [126] *soft!,* hush!   [127] *blast,* destroy   [131] *to thee do ease, and grace to me,* bring the ghost relief without disgracing Horatio. (Note the repetition of the imperative, "Speak to me." The implication is that Horatio, if told what to do, will do it—provided the deed be honorable.)   [138] *the cock crows* (a conventional signal to ghosts that they must retire)   [140] *partisan,* a shafted weapon with a broad blade   [143–146] (Marcellus makes the sensible observation that it is a mere "mockery" to try to harm a ghost.)

And our vain blows malicious mockery.
BERNARDO   It was about to speak, when the cock crew.
HORATIO   And then it started, like a guilty thing
    Upon a fearful summons. I have heard
150   The cock, that is the trumpet to the morn,
    Doth with his lofty and shrill sounding throat
    Awake the god of day; and at his warning,
    Whether in sea or fire, in earth or air,
    Th' extravagant and erring spirit hies
155   To his confine; and of the truth herein
    This present object made probation.
MARCELLUS   It faded on the crowing of the cock.
    Some say that ever, 'gainst that season comes
    Wherein our Saviour's birth is celebrated,
160   The bird of dawning singeth all night long;
    And then, they say, no spirit dare stir abroad,
    The nights are wholesome, then no planets strike,
    No fairy takes, nor witch hath power to charm,
    So hallow'd and so gracious is the time.
165 HORATIO   So have I heard and do in part believe it.
    But look, the morn, in russet mantle clad,
    Walks o'er the dew of yon high eastward hill.
    Break we our watch up; and by my advice
    Let us impart what we have seen to-night
170   Unto young Hamlet; for, upon my life,
    This spirit, dumb to us, will speak to him.
    Do you consent we shall acquaint him with it,
    As needful in our loves, fitting our duty?
MARCELLUS   Let's do't, I pray; and I this morning know
175   Where we shall find him most conveniently.

(Exeunt.)

Scene II. *Elsinore. A Room of State in the Castle.*

Flourish. Enter CLAUDIUS, *King of Denmark,* GERTRUDE *the Queen,* HAMLET, POLONIUS, LAERTES, *and his sister* OPHELIA, VOLTEMAND, CORNELIUS, *Lords Attendant.*

KING   Though yet of Hamlet our dear brother's death
    The memory be green, and that it us befitted
    To bear our hearts in grief, and our whole kingdom
    To be contracted in one brow of woe,
5   Yet so far hath discretion fought with nature
    That we with wisest sorrow think on him

---

[154] *extravagant and erring,* wandering out-of-bounds   [156] *made probation,* offered proof
[158] *'gainst,* immediately preceding   [162] *wholesome,* healthful in every respect   [163] *takes,* puts under a spell   [165] *in part believe it,* some (of their lore) I believe. (Later on Hamlet also in part believes but is firmly convinced only by the evidence provided, not by the Ghost, but by the effect of the mousetrap play. See III. ii.)   *Scene II,* morning of the same day   [2] *us,* all Danes
[5] *discretion,* moderation (There can be too much of a noble sentiment, even grief.)   [6] *wisest sorrow,* sorrow held in check (so that affairs of state can go forward)

Together with remembrance of ourselves.
Therefore our sometime sister, now our queen,
Th' imperial jointress to this warlike state,
10 Have we, as 'twere with a defeated joy,
With an auspicious, and a dropping eye,
With mirth in funeral, and with dirge in marriage,
In equal scale weighing delight and dole,
Taken to wife; nor have we herein barr'd
15 Your better wisdoms, which have freely gone
With this affair along. For all, our thanks.
Now follows, that you know, young Fortinbras,
Holding a weak supposal of our worth,
Or thinking by our late dear brother's death
20 Our state to be disjoint and out of frame,
Colleagued with this dream of his advantage,
He hath not fail'd to pester us with message
Importing the surrender of those lands
Lost by his father, with all bands of law,
25 To our most valiant brother. So much for him.
Now for ourself and for this time of meeting.
Thus much the business is: we have here writ
To Norway, uncle of young Fortinbras,
Who, impotent and bedrid, scarcely hears
30 Of this his nephew's purpose, to suppress
His further gait herein, in that the levies,
The lists, and full proportions are all made
Out of his subject; and we here dispatch
You, good Cornelius, and you, Voltemand,
35 For bearers of this greeting to old Norway,
Giving to you no further personal power
To business with the King, more than the scope
Of these dilated articles allow. *(Gives a paper)*
Farewell, and let your haste commend your duty.
40 CORNELIUS, VOLTEMAND   In that, and all things, will we show our duty.
KING   We doubt it nothing. Heartily farewell.

(*Exeunt* VOLTEMAND *and* CORNELIUS.)

And now, Laertes, what's the news with you?
You told us of some suit. What is't, Laertes?
You cannot speak of reason to the Dane
45 And lose your voice. What wouldst thou beg, Laertes,
That shall not be my offer, not thy asking?

---

⁹ *jointress,* co-inheritor (of the Danish throne)   ¹⁰⁻¹⁶ (Claudius is here attempting to justify his quick marriage, a marriage of joy against a backdrop of sorrow over the death of Hamlet's father. He reminds his Council that it had tacitly approved the action.)   ¹⁸ *a weak supposal of our worth,* an underestimate of my ability to rule   ²¹ *Colleagued . . . advantage,* produced a (foolish) dream of superiority   ²⁴ *bands,* sanctions   ³⁸ *dilated,* fully expressed   ⁴⁰ *will we show our duty,* we will do what we are ordered to do. (The subservience of Cornelius and Voltemand shows that Claudius has indeed taken over as a respected king.)   ⁴²⁻⁶³ (Laertes further supports with complete deference the new king, who probably has been helped to the throne by Polonius, Laertes' father.)

The head is not more native to the heart,
The hand more instrumental to the mouth,
Than is the throne of Denmark to thy father.
What wouldst thou have, Laertes?

50 LAERTES   My dread lord,
Your leave and favour to return to France;
From whence though willingly I came to Denmark
To show my duty in your coronation,
Yet now I must confess, that duty done,

55 My thoughts and wishes bend again toward France
And bow them to your gracious leave and pardon.
KING   Have you your father's leave? What says Polonius?
POLONIUS   He hath, my lord, wrung from me my slow leave
By laboursome petition, and at last

60 Upon his will I seal'd my hard consent.
I do beseech you give him leave to go.
KING   Take thy fair hour, Laertes. Time be thine,
And thy best graces spend it at thy will!
But now, my cousin Hamlet, and my son—

65 HAMLET *(Aside)*   A little more than kin, and less than kind!
KING   How is it that the clouds still hang on you?
HAMLET   Not so, my lord. I am too much i' th' sun.
QUEEN   Good Hamlet, cast thy nighted colour off,
And let thine eye look like a friend on Denmark.

70 Do not for ever with thy vailed lids
Seek for thy noble father in the dust.
Thou know'st 'tis common. All that lives must die,
Passing through nature to eternity.
HAMLET   Ay, madam, it is common.
QUEEN   If it be,

75 Why seems it so particular with thee?
HAMLET   Seems, madam? Nay, it is. I know not "seems."
'Tis not alone my inky cloak, good mother,
Nor customary suits of solemn black,
Nor windy suspiration of forc'd breath,

80 No, nor the fruitful river in the eye,
Nor the dejected haviour of the visage,
Together with all forms, moods, shapes of grief,
That can denote me truly. These indeed seem,
For they are actions that a man might play;

85 But I have that within which passeth show—
These but the trappings and the suits of woe.
KING   'Tis sweet and commendable in your nature, Hamlet,

---

51 *leave and favour,* generous permission   56 *leave and pardon,* permission to go back (to France)   62 *fair hour,* youth (and make best use of it)   63 *graces,* qualities (of character)   64 *cousin,* kinsman   65 (Hamlet's first words indicate an intuitive bitterness. He is doubly kin to Claudius—son and nephew—but has no kindly feeling toward his father's successor.)   67 *too much i' th' sun,* in the unwanted forefront of affairs   69 *Denmark,* the King of Denmark   70–73 (Gertrude, a simple soul, counsels with the cliché that "all that lives must die.")   76–86 (Hamlet's outward appearance is but a weak representation of his inward sorrow.)

To give these mourning duties to your father;
But you must know, your father lost a father;
90   That father lost, lost his, and the survivor bound
In filial obligation for some term
To do obsequious sorrow. But to persever
In obstinate condolement is a course
Of impious stubbornness. 'Tis unmanly grief;
95   It shows a will most incorrect to heaven,
A heart unfortified, a mind impatient,
An understanding simple and unschool'd;
For what we know must be, and is as common
As any the most vulgar thing to sense,
100   Why should we in our peevish opposition
Take it to heart? Fie! 'tis a fault to heaven,
A fault against the dead, a fault to nature,
To reason most absurd, whose common theme
Is death of fathers, and who still hath cried,
105   From the first corse till he that died to-day,
"This must be so." We pray you throw to earth
This unprevailing woe, and think of us
As of a father; for let the world take note
You are the most immediate to our throne,
110   And with no less nobility of love
Than that which dearest father bears his son
Do I impart toward you. For your intent
In going back to school in Wittenberg,
It is most retrograde to our desire;
115   And we beseech you, bend you to remain
Here in the cheer and comfort of our eye,
Our chiefest courtier, cousin, and our son.
  QUEEN   Let not thy mother lose her prayers, Hamlet.
I pray thee stay with us, go not to Wittenberg.
120   HAMLET   I shall in all my best obey you, madam.
  KING   Why, 'tis a loving and a fair reply.
Be as ourself in Denmark. Madam, come.
This gentle and unforc'd accord of Hamlet
Sits smiling to my heart; in grace whereof,
125   No jocund health that Denmark drinks to-day
But the great cannon to the clouds shall tell,
And the King's rouse the heaven shall bruit again,
Respeaking earthly thunder. Come away.

(Flourish. Exeunt all but HAMLET.)

  HAMLET   O that this too too solid flesh would melt,
130   Thaw, and resolve itself into a dew!
Or that the Everlasting had not fix'd
His canon 'gainst self-slaughter! O God! God!
How weary, stale, flat, and unprofitable
Seem to me all the uses of this world!
135   Fie on't! ah, fie! 'Tis an unweeded garden

That grows to seed; things rank and gross in nature
Possess it merely. That it should come to this!
But two months dead! Nay, not so much, not two.
So excellent a king, that was to this
140 Hyperion to a satyr; so loving to my mother
That he might not beteem the winds of heaven
Visit her face too roughly. Heaven and earth!
Must I remember? Why, she would hang on him
As if increase of appetite had grown
145 By what it fed on; and yet, within a month—
Let me not think on't! Frailty, thy name is woman!—
A little month, or ere those shoes were old
With which she followed my poor father's body
Like Niobe, all tears—why she, even she
150 (O God! a beast that wants discourse of reason
Would have mourn'd longer) married with my uncle;
My father's brother, but no more like my father
Than I to Hercules. Within a month,
Ere yet the salt of most unrighteous tears
155 Had left the flushing in her galled eyes,
She married. O, most wicked speed, to post
With such dexterity to incestuous sheets!
It is not, nor it cannot come to good.
But break, my heart, for I must hold my tongue!

Enter HORATIO, MARCELLUS, *and* BERNARDO.

HORATIO   Hail to your lordship!
160 HAMLET   I am glad to see you well.
    Horatio!—or I do forget myself.
HORATIO   The same, my lord, and your poor servant ever.
HAMLET   Sir, my good friend—I'll change that name with you.
    And what make you from Wittenberg, Horatio?
165 Marcellus?
MARCELLUS   My good lord!
HAMLET   I am very glad to see you.—(*To* BERNARDO) Good even, sir.—
    But what, in faith, make you from Wittenberg?
HORATIO   A truant disposition, good my lord.
170 HAMLET   I would not hear your enemy say so,
    Nor shall you do my ear that violence
    To make it truster of your own report
    Against yourself. I know you are no truant.
    But what is your affair in Elsinore?
175 We'll teach you to drink deep ere you depart.
HORATIO   My lord, I came to see your father's funeral.
HAMLET   I prithee do not mock me, fellow student.
    I think it was my mother's wedding.
HORATIO   Indeed, my lord, it followed hard upon.

---

140 *Hyperion to a satyr,* the sun god to a creature half human and half goat   141 *beteem,* allow
155 *galled,* irritated (by salty tears)   175 *to drink deep,* to exchange many toasts

180 HAMLET   Thrift, thrift, Horatio! The funeral bak'd meats
   Did coldly furnish forth the marriage tables.
   Would I had met my dearest foe in heaven
   Or ever I had seen that day, Horatio!
   My father—methinks I see my father.
   HORATIO   O, where, my lord?
185 HAMLET   In my mind's eye, Horatio.
   HORATIO   I saw him once. He was a goodly king.
   HAMLET   He was a man, take him for all in all.
   I shall not look upon his like again.
   HORATIO   My lord, I think I saw him yesternight.
190 HAMLET   Saw? who?
   HORATIO   My lord, the King your father.
   HAMLET   The King my father?
   HORATIO   Season your admiration for a while
   With an attent ear, till I may deliver,
   Upon the witness of these gentlemen,
   This marvel to you.
195 HAMLET   For God's love let me hear!
   HORATIO   Two nights together had these gentlemen
   (Marcellus and Bernardo) on their watch
   In the dead vast and middle of the night
   Been thus encount'red. A figure like your father,
200   Armed at point exactly, cap-a-pe,
   Appears before them and with solemn march
   Goes slow and stately by them. Thrice he walk'd
   By their oppress'd and fear-surprised eyes,
   Within his truncheon's length; whilst they distill'd
205   Almost to jelly with the act of fear,
   Stand dumb and speak not to him. This to me
   In dreadful secrecy impart they did,
   And I with them the third night kept the watch;
   Where, as they had deliver'd, both in time,
210   Form of the thing, each word made true and good,
   The apparition comes. I knew your father.
   These hands are not more like.
   HAMLET   But where was this?
   MARCELLUS   My lord, upon the platform where we watch'd.
   HAMLET   Did you not speak to it?
   HORATIO   My lord, I did;
215   But answer made it none. Yet once methought
   It lifted up it head and did address
   Itself to motion, like as it would speak;
   But even then the morning cock crew loud,
   And at the sound it shrunk in haste away
   And vanish'd from our sight.

[182] *dearest foe,* worst enemy [186] *goodly,* good-looking or handsome [192] *Season your admira-*
tion, control your wonderment [198] *the dead vast,* unlimited darkness [200] *at point . . . cap-a-*
pe, completely, from head to foot [204] *truncheon's length,* the distance represented by a short
baton [216] *it head,* its head

220 HAMLET 'Tis very strange.

HORATIO   As I do live, my honour'd lord, 'tis true;
And we did think it writ down in our duty
To let you know of it.

HAMLET   Indeed, indeed, sirs. But this troubles me.
Hold you the watch to-night?

225 BOTH (MARCELLUS *and* BERNARDO)   We do, my lord.

HAMLET   Arm'd, say you?

BOTH   Arm'd, my lord.

HAMLET   From top to toe?

BOTH   My lord, from head to foot.

HAMLET   Then saw you not his face?

230 HORATIO   O, yes, my lord! He wore his beaver up.

HAMLET   What, look'd he frowningly?

HORATIO   A countenance more in sorrow than in anger.

HAMLET   Pale or red?

HORATIO   Nay, very pale.

HAMLET   And fix'd his eyes upon you?

HORATIO   Most constantly.

235 HAMLET   I would I had been there.

HORATIO   It would have much amaz'd you.

HAMLET   Very like, very like. Stay'd it long?

HORATIO   While one with moderate haste might tell a hundred.

BOTH   Longer, longer.

HORATIO   Not when I saw't.

240 HAMLET   His beard was grizzled—no?

HORATIO   It was, as I have seen it in his life,
A sable silver'd.

HAMLET   I will watch to-night.
Perchance 'twill walk again.

HORATIO   I warr'nt it will.

HAMLET   If it assume my noble father's person,
245 I'll speak to it, though hell itself should gape
And bid me hold my peace. I pray you all,
If you have hitherto conceal'd this sight,
Let it be tenable in your silence still;
And whatsoever else shall hap to-night,
250 Give it an understanding but no tongue.
I will requite your loves. So, fare you well.
Upon the platform, 'twixt eleven and twelve,
I'll visit you.

ALL   Our duty to your honour.

HAMLET   Your loves, as mine to you. Farewell.

(*Exeunt all but* HAMLET.)

255 My father's spirit—in arms? All is not well.
I doubt some foul play. Would the night were come!

---

[230] *beaver,* visor   [238] *tell,* count   [244] *assume,* put on (Hamlet has yet no way to be sure the figure is really the ghost of his father.)   [256] *I doubt some foul play,* I suspect some sort of crime has been committed.

Till then sit still, my soul. Foul deeds will rise,
Though all the earth o'erwhelm them, to men's eyes.   *Exit.*

Scene III. *Elsinore. A Room in the House of* POLONIUS.

Enter LAERTES *and* OPHELIA.

LAERTES   My necessaries are embark'd. Farewell.
And, sister, as the winds give benefit
And convoy is assistant, do not sleep,
But let me hear from you.
OPHELIA   Do you doubt that?
5 LAERTES   For Hamlet, and the trifling of his favour,
Hold it a fashion, and a toy in blood;
A violet in the youth of primy nature,
Forward, not permanent—sweet, not lasting,
The perfume and suppliance of a minute;
No more.
OPHELIA   No more but so?
10 LAERTES   Think it no more.
For nature crescent does not grow alone
In thews and bulk; but as this temple waxes
The inward service of the mind and soul
Grows wide withal. Perhaps he loves you now,
15   And now no soil nor cautel doth besmirch
The virtue of his will; but you must fear,
His greatness weigh'd, his will is not his own;
For he himself is subject to his birth.
He may not, as unvalued persons do,
20   Carve for himself, for on his choice depends
The safety and health of this whole state,
And therefore must his choice be circumscrib'd
Unto the voice and yielding of that body
Whereof he is the head. Then if he says he loves you,
25   It fits your wisdom so far to believe it
As he in his particular act and place
May give his saying deed; which is no further
Than the main voice of Denmark goes withal.
Then weigh what loss your honour may sustain
30   If with too credent ear you list his songs,
Or lose your heart, or your chaste treasure open
To his unmast'red importunity.
Fear it, Ophelia, fear it, my dear sister,
And keep you in the rear of your affection,
35   Out of the shot and danger of desire.

Scene III, afternoon of the same day   [3] *convoy,* mail service   [5–10] (Laertes warns his sister not
to take seriously Hamlet's courting, for it is simply the fashion of young princes to flirt. Obviously
Ophelia does not think much of this advice.)   [9] *perfume and suppliance of a minute,* fragrance
pleasant now but soon gone   [11] *nature crescent,* nature moving toward dominance   [15] *cautel,*
deceit   [23] *voice and yielding,* assent (of Denmark)   [30] *credent,* easily believing

The chariest maid is prodigal enough
If she unmask her beauty to the moon.
Virtue itself scapes not calumnious strokes.
The canker galls the infants of the spring
40 Too oft before their buttons be disclos'd,
And in the morn and liquid dew of youth
Contagious blastments are most imminent.
Be wary then; best safety lies in fear.
Youth to itself rebels, though none else near.
45 OPHELIA   I shall th' effect of this good lesson keep
As watchman to my heart. But, good my brother,
Do not as some ungracious pastors do,
Show me the steep and thorny way to heaven,
Whiles, like a puff'd and reckless libertine,
50 Himself the primrose path of dalliance treads
And recks not his own rede.
LAERTES   O, fear me not!

(*Enter* POLONIUS.)

I stay too long. But here my father comes.
A double blessing is a double grace;
Occasion smiles upon a second leave.
55 POLONIUS   Yet here, Laertes? Aboard, aboard, for shame!
The wind sits in the shoulder of your sail,
And you are stay'd for. There—my blessing with thee!
And these few precepts in thy memory
Look thou character. Give thy thoughts no tongue,
60 Nor any unproportion'd thought his act.
Be thou familiar, but by no means vulgar:
Those friends thou hast, and their adoption tried,
Grapple them unto thy soul with hoops of steel;
But do not dull thy palm with entertainment
65 Of each new-hatch'd, unfledg'd comrade. Beware
Of entrance to a quarrel; but being in,
Bear't that th' opposed may beware of thee.
Give every man thine ear, but few thy voice;
Take each man's censure, but reserve thy judgment.
70 Costly thy habit as thy purse can buy,
But not express'd in fancy; rich, not gaudy;
For the apparel oft proclaims the man,
And they in France of the best rank and station
Are most select and generous, chief in that.
75 Neither a borrower nor a lender be;
For loan oft loses both itself and friend,
And borrowing dulls the edge of husbandry.

---

[36] *chariest,* most modest, most careful   [37] *to the moon,* to the man in the moon?   [39] *infants of the spring,* early flowers   [45–51] (Ophelia makes light, effective fun of her brother and punctures his pompous balloon.)   [55–81] (Polonius offers what is, no doubt, sound advice, but is he merely mouthing a series of clichés?)

This above all—to thine own self be true,
And it must follow, as the night the day,
80   Thou canst not then be false to any man.
Farewell. My blessing season this in thee!
LAERTES   Most humbly do I take my leave, my lord.
POLONIUS   The time invites you. Go, your servants tend.
LAERTES   Farewell, Ophelia, and remember well
What I have said to you.
85   OPHELIA   'Tis in my memory lock'd,
And you yourself shall keep the key of it.
LAERTES   Farewell.   *Exit.*
POLONIUS   What is't, Ophelia, he hath said to you?
OPHELIA   So please you, something touching the Lord Hamlet.
90   POLONIUS   Marry, well bethought!
'Tis told me he hath very oft of late
Given private time to you, and you yourself
Have of your audience been most free and bounteous.
If it be so—as so 'tis put on me,
95   And that in way of caution—I must tell you
You do not understand yourself so clearly
As it behooves my daughter and your honour.
What is between you? Give me up the truth.
OPHELIA   He hath, my lord, of late made many tenders
100   Of his affection to me.
POLONIUS   Affection? Pooh! You speak like a green girl,
Unsifted in such perilous circumstance.
Do you believe his tenders, as you call them?
OPHELIA   I do not know, my lord, what I should think.
105   POLONIUS   Marry, I will teach you! Think yourself a baby
That you have ta'en these tenders for true pay,
Which are not sterling. Tender yourself more dearly,
Or (not to crack the wind of the poor phrase,
Running it thus) you'll tender me a fool.
110   OPHELIA   My lord, he hath importun'd me with love
In honourable fashion.
POLONIUS   Ay, fashion you may call it. Go to, go to!
OPHELIA   And hath given countenance to his speech, my lord,
With almost all the holy vows of heaven.
115   POLONIUS   Ay, springes to catch woodcocks! I do know.
When the blood burns, how prodigal the soul
Lends the tongue vows. These blazes, daughter,
Giving more light than heat, extinct in both
Even in their promise, as it is a-making,
120   You must not take for fire. From this time
Be something scanter of your maiden presence.
Set your entreatments at a higher rate

---

[99] *tenders,* assurances   [108] *crack the wind of a poor phrase,* overdo or ride to wheezing a bad
pun   [109]*you'll tender me a fool,* you'll present me with an illegitimate grandchild (and thereby
make a fool of me?)   [115] *springes,* traps

Than a command to parley. For Lord Hamlet,
Believe so much in him, that he is young,
125 And with a larger tether may he walk
Than may be given you. In few, Ophelia,
Do not believe his vows; for they are brokers,
Not of that dye which their investments show,
But mere implorators of unholy suits,
130 Breathing like sanctified and pious bawds,
The better to beguile. This is for all:
I would not, in plain terms, from this time forth
Have you so slander any moment leisure
As to give words or talk with the Lord Hamlet.
135 Look to't, I charge you. Come your ways.
OPHELIA   I shall obey, my lord.   *Exeunt.*

Scene IV. *Elsinore. The Platform before the Castle.*

Enter HAMLET, HORATIO, *and* MARCELLUS.

HAMLET   The air bites shrewdly; it is very cold.
HORATIO   It is a nipping and an eager air.
HAMLET   What hour now?
HORATIO   I think it lacks of twelve.
MARCELLUS   No, it is struck.
5 HORATIO   Indeed! I heard it not. It then draws near the season
Wherein the spirit held his wont to walk.

(A flourish of trumpets, and two pieces go off.)

What does this mean, my lord?
HAMLET   The King doth wake to-night and takes his rouse,
Keeps wassail, and the swagg'ring upspring reels,
10 And, as he drains his draughts of Rhenish down,
The kettledrum and trumpet thus bray out
The triumph of his pledge.
HORATIO   Is it a custom?
HAMLET   Ay, marry, is't;
But to my mind, though I am native here
15 And to the manner born, it is a custom
More honour'd in the breach than the observance.
This heavy-headed revel east and west
Makes us traduc'd and tax'd of other nations;
They clip us drunkards and with swinish phrase
20 Soil our addition; and indeed it takes
From our achievements, though perform'd at height,

---

125 *larger tether,* more leeway to make love (for he is a man, a prince, and as such may take advantage of the double standard.)   127 *brokers,* cheaters (offering false promises to gain a "sale")
Scene IV, after midnight, about 24 hours later than Scene I   6 *spirit* (Horatio is careful not to say
"the ghost of your father.")   9 *swagg'ring upspring,* a lively dance   12 *the triumph of his pledge,*
the lusty feat of swigging down at one gulp liquor drunk as a toast   19 *clip,* name   20 *Soil our
addition,* blemish our reputation

The pith and marrow of our attribute.
So oft it chances in particular men
That, for some vicious mole of nature in them,
25 As in their birth,—wherein they are not guilty,
Since nature cannot choose his origin,—
By the o'ergrowth of some complexion,
Oft breaking down the pales and forts of reason,
Or by some habit that too much o'erleavens
30 The form of plausive manners, that these men
Carrying, I say, the stamp of one defect,
Being nature's livery, or fortune's star,
Their virtues else—be they as pure as grace,
As infinite as man may undergo—
35 Shall in the general censure take corruption
From that particular fault. The dram of e'il
Doth all the noble substance often dout
To his own scandal.

Enter GHOST.

HORATIO   Look, my lord, it comes!
HAMLET Angels and ministers of grace defend us!
40 Be thou a spirit of health or goblin damn'd,
Bring with thee airs from heaven or blasts from hell,
By thy intents wicked or charitable,
Thou com'st in such a questionable shape
That I will speak to thee. I'll call thee Hamlet,
45 King, father, royal Dane. O, answer me!
Let me not burst in ignorance, but tell
Why thy canoniz'd bones, hearsed in death,
Have burst their cerements; why the sepulchre
Wherein we saw thee quietly inurn'd,
50 Hath op'd his ponderous and marble jaws
To cast thee up again. What may this mean
That thou, dead corse, again in complete steel,
Revisits thus the glimpses of the moon,
Making night hideous, and we fools of nature
55 So horridly to shake our disposition
With thoughts beyond the reaches of our souls?
Say, why is this? wherefore? What should we do?

GHOST *beckons* HAMLET.

HORATIO It beckons you to go away with it,
As if it some impartment did desire

23-38 (These lines advance the notion that a man or a nation—no matter how virtuous otherwise—
may be disgraced by one fault, in this case the reputation for carousing.)   43 *questionable shape,*
in a shape (like that of the dead king) to be questioned   47 *canoniz'd,* given church-approved
burial service; *hearsed,* entombed   53 *glimpses,* short views (because of scudding clouds)
54 *fools of nature* (made to act like fools by a nature which denies us access to the supernatural)
59 *impartment,* communication

To you alone.
60 MARCELLUS   Look with what courteous action
It waves you to a more removed ground.
But do not go with it!
HORATIO   No, by no means!
HAMLET   It will not speak. Then will I follow it.
HORATIO   Do not, my lord!
HAMLET   Why, what should be the fear?
65 I do not set my life at a pin's fee;
And for my soul, what can it do to that,
Being a thing immortal as itself?
It waves me forth again. I'll follow it.
HORATIO   What if it tempt you toward the flood, my lord,
70 Or to the dreadful summit of the cliff
That beetles o'er his base into the sea,
And there assume some other, horrible form
Which might deprive your sovereignty of reason
And draw you into madness? Think of it.
75 The very place puts toys of desperation,
Without more motive, into every brain
That looks so many fadoms to the sea
And hears it roar beneath.
HAMLET   It waves me still.
Go on. I'll follow thee.
MARCELLUS   You shall not go, my lord.
80 HAMLET   Hold off your hands!
HORATIO   Be rul'd. You shall not go.
HAMLET   My fate cries out
And makes each petty artere in this body
As hardy as the Nemean lion's nerve.

(GHOST *beckons.*)

Still am I call'd. Unhand me, gentlemen.
85 By heaven, I'll make a ghost of him that lets me!—
I say, away!—Go on. I'll follow thee.

Exeunt GHOST *and* HAMLET.

HORATIO   He waxes desperate with imagination.
MARCELLUS   Let's follow. 'Tis not fit thus to obey him.
HORATIO   Have after. To what issue will this come?
90 MARCELLUS   Something is rotten in the state of Denmark.
HORATIO   Heaven will direct it.
MARCELLUS   Nay, let's follow him.   *Exeunt.*

---

[65] *a pin's fee,* the value of a pin   [75-78] (Elsinore is perched on a crag below which is a rough-water channel which separates Denmark from Sweden. Horatio warns that, once Hamlet is lured to the brink of the crag, the Ghost, which may be a demon, will simply allow the hypnotic effect of height and the roaring sea to cause the Prince to pitch forward to his destruction.)   [81] *My fate cries out,* my destiny is calling   [83] *Nemean lion's nerve,* sinews of the lion of Nemea (the killing of which was one of the twelve labors of Hercules)   [85] *lets me,* tries to stop me

Scene V. *Elsinore. The Castle. Another Part of the Fortifications.*

Enter GHOST *and* HAMLET.

HAMLET   Whither wilt thou lead me? Speak! I'll go no further.
GHOST   Mark me.
HAMLET   I will.
GHOST   My hour is almost come,
  When I to sulph'rous and tormenting flames
  Must render up myself.
HAMLET   Alas, poor ghost!
5 GHOST   Pity me not, but lend thy serious hearing
  To what I shall unfold.
HAMLET   Speak. I am bound to hear.
GHOST   So art thou to revenge, when thou shalt hear.
HAMLET   What?
GHOST   I am thy father's spirit,
10   Doom'd for a certain term to walk the night,
  And for the day confin'd to fast in fires,
  Till the foul crimes done in my days of nature
  Are burnt and purg'd away. But that I am forbid
  To tell the secrets of my prison house,
15   I could a tale unfold whose lightest word
  Would harrow up thy soul, freeze thy young blood,
  Make thy two eyes, like stars, start from their spheres,
  Thy knotted and combined locks to part,
  And each particular hair to stand an end
20   Like quills upon the fretful porpentine.
  But this eternal blazon must not be
  To ears of flesh and blood. List, list, O, list!
  If thou didst ever thy dear father love—
HAMLET   O God!
25 GHOST   Revenge his foul and most unnatural murther.
HAMLET   Murther?
GHOST   Murther most foul, as in the best it is;
  But this most foul, strange, and unnatural.
HAMLET   Haste me to know't, that I, with wings as swift
30   As meditation or the thoughts of love,
  May sweep to my revenge.
GHOST   I find thee apt;
  And duller shouldst thou be than the fat weed
  That rots itself in ease on Lethe wharf,
  Wouldst thou not stir in this. Now, Hamlet, hear.
35   'Tis given out that, sleeping in my orchard,
  A serpent stung me. So the whole ear of Denmark

---

¹ *I'll go no further* (Hamlet does not yet know whether he is being tricked by a demon.)
³ *flames* (of purgatory)   ⁶ *bound,* eager   ¹² *foul crimes* (The elder Hamlet has committed
only the "crime" of living but must expiate just the same his common human failings.)   ¹³⁻²² (No
mortal could bear to be told what purgatory—*prison house,* 14—is like.)   ³³ *Lethe,* river of oblivion in Hades   ³⁵ *orchard,* garden area (of the Palace)

Is by a forged process of my death
Rankly abus'd. But know, thou noble youth,
The serpent that did sting thy father's life
Now wears his crown.
40 HAMLET   O my prophetic soul!
My uncle?
GHOST   Ay, that incestuous, that adulterate beast,
With witchcraft of his wit, with traitorous gifts—
O wicked wit and gifts, that have the power
45 So to seduce!—won to his shameful lust
The will of my most seeming-virtuous queen.
O Hamlet, what a falling-off was there,
From me, whose love was of that dignity
That it went hand in hand even with the vow
50 I made to her in marriage, and to decline
Upon a wretch whose natural gifts were poor
To those of mine!
But virtue, as it never will be mov'd,
Though lewdness court it in a shape of heaven,
55 So lust, though to a radiant angel link'd,
Will sate itself in a celestial bed
And prey on garbage.
But soft! methinks I scent the morning air.
Brief let me be. Sleeping within my orchard,
60 My custom always of the afternoon,
Upon my secure hour thy uncle stole,
With juice of cursed hebona in a vial,
And in the porches of my ears did pour
The leperous distilment; whose effect
65 Holds such an enmity with blood of man
That swift as quicksilver it courses through
The natural gates and alleys of the body,
And with a sudden vigour it doth posset
And curd, like eager droppings into milk,
70 The thin and wholesome blood. So did it mine;
And a most instant tetter bark'd about,
Most lazar-like, with vile and loathsome crust
All my smooth body.
Thus was I, sleeping, by a brother's hand
75 Of life, of crown, of queen, at once dispatch'd;
Cut off even in the blossoms of my sin,
Unhous'led, disappointed, unanel'd,
No reck'ning made, but sent to my account

---

[40] *O my prophetic soul!,* O how right my intuitions! (that some evil caused my father's death)
[42] *adulterate* (suggests that Gertrude had been untrue, but perhaps the Ghost regarded the quick marriage as adultery)   [62] *hebona,* sap of the ebony tree (apparently as poisonous as hemlock)
[68] *posset,* coagulate   [71] *tetter bark'd about,* eczema made the skin resemble the rough bark of a tree   [76] *sin,* sinfulness (see footnote to 12, above)   [77] *Unhous'led, disappointed, unanel'd,* unconfessed, unready, not having received extreme unction

With all my imperfections on my head.
80 HAMLET O, horrible! O, horrible! most horrible!
GHOST If thou hast nature in thee, bear it not.
Let not the royal bed of Denmark be
A couch for luxury and damned incest.
But, howsoever thou pursuest this act,
85 Taint not thy mind, nor let thy soul contrive
Against thy mother aught. Leave her to heaven,
And to those thorns that in her bosom lodge
To prick and sting her. Fare thee well at once.
The glowworm shows the matin to be near
90 And gins to pale his uneffectual fire.
Adieu, adieu, adieu! Remember me. *Exit.*
HAMLET O all you host of heaven! O earth! What else?
And shall I couple hell? Hold, hold, my heart!
And you, my sinews, grow not instant old,
95 But bear me stiffly up. Remember thee?
Ay, thou poor ghost, while memory holds a seat
In this distracted globe. Remember thee?
Yea, from the table of my memory
I'll wipe away all trivial fond records,
100 All saws of books, all forms, all pressures past
That youth and observation copied there,
And thy commandment all alone shall live
Within the book and volume of my brain,
Unmix'd with baser matter. Yes, by heaven!
105 O most pernicious woman!
O villain, villain, smiling, damned villain!
My tables! Meet it is I set it down
That one may smile, and smile, and be a villain;
At least I am sure it may be so in Denmark.

(Writes)

110 So, uncle, there you are. Now to my word:
It is "Adieu, adieu! Remember me."
I have sworn't.
HORATIO *(Within)* My lord, my lord!

Enter HORATIO *and* MARCELLUS.

MARCELLUS Lord Hamlet!
HORATIO Heaven secure him!
HAMLET So be it!
115 MARCELLUS Illo, ho, ho, my lord!
HAMLET Hillo, ho, ho, boy! Come, bird, come.
MARCELLUS How is't, my noble lord?

---

83 *luxury,* lechery 93 *shall I couple hell?,* shall I conspire with hell? (if necessary to gain my revenge) 97 *distracted globe,* (Hamlet's) confused head 100 *saws,* wise sayings 107 *My tables!,* my notebooks 115–116 (Hamlet is reminded by the cry of Marcellus of the falconer's sound in calling back a hawk.)

HORATIO   What news, my lord?

HAMLET   O, wonderful!

HORATIO   Good my lord, tell it.

HAMLET   No, you will reveal it.

HORATIO   Not I, my lord, by heaven!

120 MARCELLUS   Nor I, my lord.

HAMLET   How say you then? Would heart of man once think it?
But you'll be secret?

BOTH   Ay, by heaven, my lord.

HAMLET   There's ne'er a villain dwelling in all Denmark
But he's an arrant knave.

125 HORATIO   There needs no ghost, my lord, come from the grave
To tell us this.

HAMLET   Why, right! You are in the right!
And so, without more circumstance at all,
I hold it fit that we shake hands and part;
You, as your business and desire shall point you,

130 For every man hath business and desire,
Such as it is; and for my own poor part,
Look you, I'll go pray.

HORATIO   These are but wild and whirling words, my lord.

HAMLET   I am sorry they offend you, heartily;
Yes, faith, heartily.

135 HORATIO   There's no offence, my lord.

HAMLET   Yes, by Saint Patrick, but there is, Horatio,
And much offence too. Touching this vision here,
It is an honest ghost, that let me tell you.
For your desire to know what is between us,

140 O'ermaster't as you may. And now, good friends,
As you are friends, scholars, and soldiers,
Give me one poor request.

HORATIO   What is't, my lord? We will.

HAMLET   Never make known what you have seen to-night.

BOTH   My lord, we will not.

HAMLET   Nay, but swear't.

145 HORATIO   In faith,
My lord, not I.

MARCELLUS   Nor I, my lord—in faith.

HAMLET   Upon my sword.

MARCELLUS   We have sworn, my lord, already.

HAMLET   Indeed, upon my sword, indeed.

GHOST *cries under the stage.*

GHOST   Swear.

150 HAMLET   Aha boy, say'st thou so? Art thou there, truepenny?

---

127 *circumstance,* ceremony   138 *an honest ghost,* above-board, nondemonic ghost   147 *Upon my sword* (The blade and the hilt form a cross, so that an oath taken on a sword would be like swearing on a holy instrument.)   150 *truepenny,* good old boy (a slangy term, implying the easy relationship Hamlet—temporarily—has established with the Ghost)

Come on! You hear this fellow in the cellarage.
Consent to swear.
HORATIO   Propose the oath, my lord.
HAMLET   Never to speak of this that you have seen.
Swear by my sword.
155 GHOST *(Beneath)* Swear.
HAMLET   Hic et ubique? Then we'll shift our ground.
Come hither, gentlemen,
And lay your hands again upon my sword.
Never to speak of this that you have heard:
160 Swear by my sword.
GHOST *(Beneath)* Swear by his sword.
HAMLET   Well said, old mole! Canst work i' th' earth so fast?
A worthy pioner! Once more remove, good friends.
HORATIO   O day and night, but this is wondrous strange!
165 HAMLET   And therefore as a stranger give it welcome.
There are more things in heaven and earth, Horatio,
Than are dreamt of in your philosophy.
But come!
Here, as before, never, so help you mercy,
170 How strange or odd soe'er I bear myself
(As I perchance hereafter shall think meet
To put an antic disposition on),
That you, at such times seeing me, never shall,
With arms encumb'red thus, or this headshake,
175 Or by pronouncing of some doubtful phrase,
As "Well, well, we know," or "We could, an if we would,"
Or "If we list to speak," or "There be, an if they might,"
Or such ambiguous giving out, to note
That you know aught of me—this not to do,
180 So grace and mercy at your most need help you,
Swear.
GHOST *(Beneath)* Swear.

They swear.

HAMLET   Rest, rest, perturbed spirit! So, gentlemen,
With all my love I do commend me to you;
185 And what so poor a man as Hamlet is
May do t' express his love and friending to you,
God willing, shall not lack. Let us go in together;
And still your fingers on your lips, I pray.
The time is out of joint. O cursed spite
190 That ever I was born to set it right!
Nay, come, let's go together.   *Exeunt.*

---

[156] *Hic et ubique?*, here and everywhere   [163] *pioner*, a digger in the earth   [167] *philosophy*, scientific attitude (which does not acknowledge the possibility of ghosts)   [172] *antic*, whimsical, feigning madness   [174] *encumb'red*, folded (in a knowing but not telling manner)   [177] *list*, chose   [189] *spite*, imposition (the implication is that unjust powers have saddled Hamlet with a highly unwelcome duty)

ACT II

Scene I. *Elsinore. A Room in the House of* POLONIUS.

Enter POLONIUS *and* REYNALDO.

POLONIUS Give him this money and these notes, Reynaldo.
REYNALDO I will, my lord.
POLONIUS You shall do marvell's wisely, good Reynaldo,
　Before you visit him, to make inquire
　Of his behaviour.
5 REYNALDO　　　　　My lord, I did intend it.
POLONIUS Marry, well said, very well said. Look you, sir,
　Enquire me first what Danskers are in Paris;
　And how, and who, what means, and where they keep,
　What company, at what expense; and finding
10　By this encompassment and drift of question
　That they do know my son, come you more nearer
　Than your particular demands will touch it.
　Take you, as 'twere, some distant knowledge of him;
　As thus, "I know his father and his friends,
15　And in part him." Do you mark this, Reynaldo?
REYNALDO Ay, very well, my lord.
POLONIUS "And in part him, but," you may say, "not well.
　But if't be he I mean, he's very wild
　Addicted so and so"; and there put on him
20　What forgeries you please; marry, none so rank
　As may dishonour him—take heed of that;
　But, sir, such wanton, wild, and usual slips
　As are companions noted and most known
　To youth and liberty.
REYNALDO　　　　　As gaming, my lord.
25 POLONIUS Ay, or drinking, fencing, swearing, quarrelling,
　Drabbing. You may go so far.
REYNALDO My lord, that would dishonour him.
POLONIUS Faith, no, as you may season it in the charge.
　You must not put another scandal on him,
30　That he is open to incontinency.
　That's not my meaning. But breathe his faults so quaintly
　That they may seem the taints of liberty,
　The flash and outbreak of a fiery mind,
　A savageness in unreclaimed blood,
　Of general assault.
35 REYNALDO　　　　　But, my good lord—
POLONIUS Wherefore should you do this?
REYNALDO　　　　　　　　　Ay, my lord,
　I would know that.
POLONIUS　　　　　Marry, sir, here's my drift,

Scene I, Scholars estimate that six to eight weeks elapse between I. v and II. i.   [3] *marvell's,* extraordinarily   [20] *forgeries,* false accusations   [26] *Drabbing,* whoring   [35] *Of general assault,* of common occurrence (in young men)

And I believe it is a fetch of warrant.
You laying these slight sullies on my son
40   As 'twere a thing a little soil'd i' th' working,
Mark you,
Your party in converse, him you would sound,
Having ever seen in the prenominate crimes
The youth you breathe of guilty, be assur'd
45   He closes with you in this consequence:
"Good sir," or so, or "friend," or "gentleman"—
According to the phrase or the addition
Of man and country—
REYNALDO   Very good, my lord.
POLONIUS   And then, sir, does 'a this—'a does—
50   What was I about to say? By the mass, I was
about to say something! Where did I leave?
REYNALDO   At "closes in the consequence," at
"friend or so," and "gentleman."
POLONIUS   At "closes in the consequence"—Ay, marry!
55   He closes thus: "I know the gentleman.
I saw him yesterday, or t'other day,
Or then, or then, with such or such; and, as you say,
There was 'a gaming; there o'ertook in's rouse;
There falling out at tennis"; or perchance,
60   "I saw him enter such a house of sale,"
Videlicet, a brothel, or so forth.
See you now—
Your bait of falsehood takes this carp of truth;
And thus do we of wisdom and of reach,
65   With windlasses and with assays of bias
By indirections find directions out.
So, by my former lecture and advice,
Shall you my son. You have me, have you not?
REYNALDO   My lord, I have.
POLONIUS   God b' wi' ye, fare ye well!
70   REYNALDO   Good my lord!   *Going.*
POLONIUS   Observe his inclination in yourself.
REYNALDO   I shall, my lord.
POLONIUS   And let him ply his music.
REYNALDO   Well, my lord.
POLONIUS   Farewell!   (*Exit* REYNALDO.)

(*Enter* OPHELIA.)

How now, Ophelia? What's the matter?
75   OPHELIA   O my lord, my lord, I have been so affrighted!
POLONIUS   With what, i' th' name of God?
OPHELIA   My lord, as I was sewing in my closet,

---

[38] *a fetch of warrant,* fully justified   [43] *prenominate,* aforementioned   [45] *closes with,* goes
along with   [58] *o'ertook in's rouse,* done in by overdrinking   [61] *Videlicet,* that is, or namely
[65] *windlasses . . . assays of bias,* indirect ways . . . attempts by curved means, as with a bowling
ball   [68] *you have me,* you understand me

Lord Hamlet, with his doublet all unbrac'd,
No hat upon his head, his stockings foul'd,
80   Ungart'red, and down-gyved to his ankle;
Pale as his shirt, his knees knocking each other,
And with a look so piteous in purport
As if he had been loosed out of hell
To speak of horrors—he comes before me.
POLONIUS   Mad for thy love?
85 OPHELIA   My lord, I do not know,
But truly I do fear it.
POLONIUS   What said he?
OPHELIA   He took me by the wrist and held me hard;
Then goes he to the length of all his arm,
And, with his other hand thus o'er his brow,
90   He falls to such perusal of my face
As he would draw it. Long stay'd he so.
At last, a little shaking of mine arm,
And thrice his head thus waving up and down,
He rais'd a sigh so piteous and profound
95   As it did seem to shatter all his bulk
And end his being. That done, he lets me go.
And with his head over his shoulder turn'd
He seem'd to find his way without his eyes,
For out o'doors he went without their help
100   And to the last bended their light on me.
POLONIUS   Come, go with me. I will go seek the King.
This is the very ecstasy of love,
Whose violent property fordoes itself
And leads the will to desperate undertakings
105   As oft as any passion under heaven
That does afflict our natures. I am sorry.
What, have you given him any hard words of late?
OPHELIA   No, my good lord; but, as you did command,
I did repel his letters and denied
His access to me.
110 POLONIUS   That hath made him mad.
I am sorry that with better heed and judgment
I had not quoted him. I fear'd he did but trifle
And meant to wrack thee; but beshrew my jealousy!
By heaven, it is as proper to our age
115   To cast beyond ourselves in our opinions
As it is common for the younger sort
To lack discretion. Come, go we to the King.
This must be known; which, being kept close, might move
More grief to hide than hate to utter love.
120   Come.   *Exeunt.*

---

[78] *unbrac'd,* unlaced   [80] *down-gyved,* drooping   [85] *Mad,* insane   [102] *ecstasy,* excess (to the point of madness)   [112] *quoted,* credited   [113] *wrack,* ruin. *beshrew,* curse   [118] *close,* concealed

Scene II. *Elsinore. A Room in the Castle.*

Flourish. Enter KING *and* QUEEN, ROSENCRANTZ, *and* GUILDENSTERN, *cum aliis.*

KING   Welcome, dear Rosencrantz and Guildenstern.
Moreover that we much did long to see you,
The need we have to use you did provoke
Our hasty sending. Something have you heard
5   Of Hamlet's transformation. So I call it,
Sith nor th' exterior nor the inward man
Resembles that it was. What it should be,
More than his father's death, that thus hath put him
So much from th' understanding of himself,
10   I cannot dream of. I entreat you both
That, being of so young days brought up with him,
And since so neighbour'd to his youth and haviour,
That you vouchsafe your rest here in our court
Some little time; so by your companies
15   To draw him on to pleasures, and to gather
So much as from occasion you may glean,
Whether aught to us unknown afflicts him thus
That, open'd, lies within our remedy.
QUEEN   Good gentlemen, he hath much talk'd of you,
20   And sure I am two men there are not living
To whom he more adheres. If it will please you
To show us so much gentry and good will
As to expend your time with us awhile
For the supply and profit of our hope,
25   Your visitation shall receive such thanks
As fits a king's remembrance.
ROSENCRANTZ   Both your Majesties
Might, by the sovereign power you have of us,
Put your dread pleasures more into command
Than to entreaty.
GUILDENSTERN   But we both obey,
30   And here give up ourselves, in the full bent,
To lay our service at your feet,
To be commanded.
KING   Thanks, Rosencrantz and gentle Guildenstern.
QUEEN   Thanks, Guildenstern and gentle Rosencrantz.
35   And I beseech you instantly to visit
My too much changed son.—Go, some of you,
And bring these gentlemen where Hamlet is.
GUILDENSTERN   Heavens make our presence and our practices
Pleasant and helpful to him!
QUEEN   Ay, amen!

Exeunt ROSENCRANTZ *and* GUILDENSTERN *with some Attendants.*

[13] *vouchsafe your rest,* agree to stay   [22] *gentry,* gentle manliness   [24] *supply and profit,* realization and advancement (accomplishing)

Enter POLONIUS.

40 POLONIUS   Th' ambassadors from Norway, my good lord,
Are joyfully return'd.
KING   Thou still hast been the father of good news.
POLONIUS   Have I, my lord? Assure you, my good liege,
I hold my duty as I hold my soul,
45   Both to my God and to my gracious king;
And I do think—or else this brain of mine
Hunts not the trail of policy so sure
As it hath us'd to do—that I have found
The very cause of Hamlet's lunacy.
50 KING   O, speak of that! That do I long to hear.
POLONIUS   Give first admittance to th' ambassadors.
My news shall be the fruit to that great feast.
KING   Thyself do grace to them, and bring them in.

(*Exit* POLONIUS.)

He tells me, my dear Gertrude, he hath found
55   The head and source of all your son's distemper.
QUEEN   I doubt it is no other but the main,
His father's death and our o'erhasty marriage.
KING   Well, we shall sift him.

(*Enter* POLONIUS, VOLTEMAND, *and* CORNELIUS.)

Welcome, my good friends.
Say, Voltemand, what from our brother Norway?
60 VOLTEMAND   Most fair return of greetings and desires.
Upon our first, he sent out to suppress
His nephew's levies; which to him appear'd
To be a preparation 'gainst the Polack,
But better look'd into, he truly found
65   It was against your Highness; whereat griev'd,
That so his sickness, age, and impotence
Was falsely borne in hand, sends out arrests
On Fortinbras; which he, in brief, obeys,
Receives rebuke from Norway, and, in fine,
70   Makes vow before his uncle never more
To give th' assay of arms against your Majesty.
Whereon old Norway, overcome with joy,
Gives him three thousand crowns in annual fee
And his commission to employ those soldiers,
75   So levied as before, against the Polack;
With an entreaty, herein further shown,

(*Gives a paper*)

That it might please you to give quiet pass

---

[47] *policy,* statecraft (as Polonius understands it)   [56] *doubt,* suspect   [67] *borne in hand,* acted
upon

Through your dominions for this enterprise,
On such regards of safety and allowance
As therein are set down.
 80 KING   It likes us well;
And at our more consider'd time we'll read,
Answer, and think upon this business.
Meantime we thank you for your well-took labour.
Go to your rest; at night we'll feast together.
Most welcome home!   *Exeunt Ambassadors.*
 85 POLONIUS   This business is well ended.
My liege, and madam, to expostulate
What majesty should be, what duty is,
Why day is day, night night, and time is time,
Were nothing but to waste night, day, and time.
 90   Therefore, since brevity is the soul of wit,
And tediousness the limbs and outward flourishes,
I will be brief. Your noble son is mad.
Mad call I it; for, to define true madness,
What is't but to be nothing else but mad?
But let that go.
 95 QUEEN   More matter, with less art.
    POLONIUS   Madam, I swear I use no art at all.
That he is mad, 'tis true: 'tis true 'tis pity;
And pity 'tis 'tis true. A foolish figure!
But farewell it, for I will use no art.
 100 Mad let us grant him then. And now remains
That we find out the cause of this effect—
Or rather say, the cause of this defect,
For this effect defective comes by cause.
Thus it remains, and the remainder thus.
 105 Perpend.
I have a daughter (have while she is mine),
Who in her duty and obedience, mark,
Hath given me this. Now gather, and surmise.

(Reads the letter)

 110   "To the celestial, and my soul's idol,
The most beautified Ophelia."—
That's an ill phrase, a vile phrase; "beautified"
is a vile phrase. But you shall hear. Thus:

(Reads)

   "In her excellent white bosom, these, &c."
   QUEEN   Came this from Hamlet to her?
 115 POLONIUS   Good madam, stay awhile. I will be faithful.

(Reads)

     "Doubt thou the stars are fire;
        Doubt that the sun doth move;

---

[86] *expostulate,* describe   [90] *wit,* wisdom   [105] *Perpend,* listen carefully

        Doubt truth to be a liar;
                But never doubt I love.
120 "O dear Ophelia, I am ill at these numbers;
    I have not art to reckon my groans; but that I
    love thee best, O most best, believe it. Adieu.
    "Thine evermore, most dear lady, whilst this
                machine is to him, HAMLET."
125 This, in obedience, hath my daughter shown me;
    And more above, hath his solicitings,
    As they fell out by time, by means, and place,
    All given to mine ear.
    KING   But how hath she
    Receiv'd his love?
    POLONIUS   What do you think of me?
130 KING   As of a man faithful and honourable.
    POLONIUS   I would fain prove so. But what might you think,
    When I had seen this hot love on the wing
    (As I perceiv'd it, I must tell you that,
    Before my daughter told me), what might you,
135 Or my dear Majesty your queen here, think,
    If I had play'd the desk or table book,
    Or given my heart a winking, mute and dumb,
    Or look'd upon this love with idle sight?
    What might you think? No, I went round to work
140 And my young mistress thus I did bespeak:
    "Lord Hamlet is a prince, out of thy star.
    This must not be." And then I prescripts gave her,
    That she should lock herself from his resort,
    Admit no messengers, receive no tokens.
145 Which done, she took the fruits of my advice,
    And he, repulsed, a short tale to make,
    Fell into a sadness, then into a fast,
    Thence to a watch, thence into a weakness,
    Thence to a lightness, and, by this declension,
150 Into the madness wherein now he raves,
    And all we mourn for.
    KING   Do you think 'tis this?
    QUEEN   It may be, very like.
    POLONIUS   Hath there been such a time—I would fain know that—
    That I have positively said " 'Tis so,"
    When it prov'd otherwise?
155 KING   Not that I know.
    POLONIUS *(Points to his head and shoulder)*
        Take this from this, if this be otherwise.
    If circumstances lead me, I will find
    Where truth is hid, though it were hid indeed

---

124 *machine,* body   126 *above,* besides
(stored information and did not act on it)
148 *watch,* wakefulness
136 *play'd the desk or table book,* filed the matter away
141 *out of thy star,* not included in your destiny

Within the centre.

KING   How may we try it further?

160 POLONIUS   You know sometimes he walks four hours together
Here in the lobby.

QUEEN   So he does indeed.

POLONIUS   At such a time I'll loose my daughter to him.
Be you and I behind an arras then.
Mark the encounter. If he love her not,
165   And be not from his reason fall'n thereon,
Let me be no assistant for a state,
But keep a farm and carters.

KING   We will try it.

Enter HAMLET, *reading on a book.*

QUEEN   But look where sadly the poor wretch comes reading.

POLONIUS   Away, I do beseech you, both away!
170   I'll board him presently. O, give me leave.

(Exeunt KING *and* QUEEN, *with Attendants.)*

How does my good Lord Hamlet?

HAMLET   Well, God-a-mercy.

POLONIUS   Do you know me, my lord?

HAMLET   Excellent well. You are a fishmonger.

175 POLONIUS   Not I, my lord.

HAMLET   Then I would you were so honest a man.

POLONIUS   Honest, my lord?

HAMLET   Ay, sir. To be honest, as this world goes, is to be one man pick'd out of ten
thousand.

180 POLONIUS   That's very true, my lord.

HAMLET   For if the sun breed maggots in a dead dog, being a god kissing carrion—Have
you a daughter?

POLONIUS   I have, my lord.

HAMLET   Let her not walk i' th' sun. Conception is a blessing, but not as your daughter
185   may conceive. Friend, look to't.

POLONIUS *(Aside)*   How say you by that? Still harping on my daughter. Yet he knew me not
at first. He said I was a fishmonger. He is far gone, far gone! And truly in my youth I
suff'red much extremity for love—very near this. I'll speak to him again.—What do
you read, my lord?

190 HAMLET   Words, words, words.

POLONIUS   What is the matter, my lord?

HAMLET   Between who?

POLONIUS   I mean, the matter that you read, my lord.

HAMLET   Slanders, sir; for the satirical rogue says here that old men have grey beards; that
195   their faces are wrinkled; their eyes purging thick amber and plum-tree gum; and
that they have a plentiful lack of wit, together with most weak hams. All which, sir,
though I most powerfully and potently believe, yet I hold it not honesty to have
it thus set down; for you yourself, sir, should be old as I am if, like a crab, you
could go backward.

[170] *board,* accost   [186] *How say you by that?,* What did I tell you!

200 POLONIUS *(Aside)*   Though this be madness, yet there is method in't.—Will you walk out of the air, my lord?

HAMLET   Into my grave?

POLONIUS   Indeed, that is out o' th' air. *(Aside)* How pregnant sometimes his replies are! a happiness that often madness hits on, which reason and sanity could not so prosper-
205 ously be delivered of. I will leave him and suddenly contrive the means of meeting between him and my daughter.—My honourable lord, I will most humbly take my leave of you.

HAMLET   You cannot, sir, take from me anything that I will more willingly part withal—except my life, except my life, except my life.

Enter ROSENCRANTZ *and* GUILDENSTERN.

210 POLONIUS   Fare you well, my lord.

HAMLET   These tedious old fools!

POLONIUS   You go to seek the Lord Hamlet. There he is.

ROSENCRANTZ *(To* POLONIUS*)*   God save you sir!

Exit POLONIUS.

GUILDENSTERN   My honour'd lord!
215 ROSENCRANTZ   My most dear lord!

HAMLET   My excellent good friends! How dost thou, Guildenstern? Ah, Rosencrantz! Good lads, how do ye both?

ROSENCRANTZ   As the indifferent children of the earth.

GUILDENSTERN   Happy in that we are not overhappy. On Fortune's cap we are not the very
220 button.

HAMLET   Nor the soles of her shoe?

ROSENCRANTZ   Neither, my lord.

HAMLET   Then you live about her waist, or in the middle of her favours?

GUILDENSTERN   Faith, her privates we.
225 HAMLET   In the secret parts of Fortune? O, most true! she is a strumpet. What news?

ROSENCRANTZ   None, my lord, but that the world's grown honest.

HAMLET   Then is doomsday near! But your news is not true. Let me question more in particular. What have you, my good friends, deserved at the hands of Fortune that she sends you to prison hither?

230 GUILDENSTERN   Prison, my lord?

HAMLET   Denmark's a prison.

ROSENCRANTZ   Then is the world one.

HAMLET   A goodly one; in which there are many confines, wards, and dungeons, Denmark being one o' th' worst.

235 ROSENCRANTZ   We think not so, my lord.

HAMLET   Why, then 'tis none to you; for there is nothing either good or bad but thinking makes it so. To me it is a prison.

ROSENCRANTZ   Why, then your ambition makes it one. 'Tis too narrow for your mind.

HAMLET   O God, I could be bounded in a nutshell and count myself a king of infinite
240 space, were it not that I have bad dreams.

GUILDENSTERN   Which dreams indeed are ambition; for the very substance of the ambitious is merely the shadow of a dream.

HAMLET   A dream itself is but a shadow.

---

[218]*indifferent children,* ordinary persons

ROSENCRANTZ   Truly, and I hold ambition of so airy and light a quality that it is but a
245   shadow's shadow.

HAMLET   Then are our beggars bodies, and our monarchs and outstretch'd heroes the beggars' shadows. Shall we to th' court? for, by my fay, I cannot reason.

BOTH   We'll wait upon you.

HAMLET   No such matter! I will not sort you with the rest of my servants; for, to speak to
250   you like an honest man, I am most dreadfully attended. But in the beaten way of
friendship, what make you at Elsinore?

ROSENCRANTZ   To visit you, my lord; no other occasion.

HAMLET   Beggar that I am, I am even poor in thanks; but I thank you; and sure, dear
friends, my thanks are too dear a halfpenny. Were you not sent for? Is it your own
255   inclining? Is it a free visitation? Come, deal justly with me. Come, come! Nay, speak.

GUILDENSTERN   What should we say, my lord?

HAMLET   Why, anything—but to th' purpose. You were sent for; and there is a kind of
confession in your looks, which your modesties have not craft enough to colour. I
know the good King and Queen have sent for you.

260   ROSENCRANTZ   To what end, my lord?

HAMLET   That you must teach me. But let me conjure you by the rights of our fellowship,
by the consonancy of our youth, by the obligation of our ever-preserved love, and by
what more dear a better proposer could charge you withal, be even and direct with
me, whether you were sent for or no.

265   ROSENCRANTZ   (*Aside to* GUILDENSTERN)   What say you?

HAMLET   (*Aside*)   Nay then, I have an eye of you.—If you love me, hold not off.

GUILDENSTERN   My lord, we were sent for.

HAMLET   I will tell you why. So shall my anticipation prevent your discovery, and your
secrecy to the King and Queen moult no feather. I have of late—but wherefore I
270   know not—lost all my mirth, forgone all custom of exercises; and indeed, it goes so
heavily with my disposition that this goodly frame, the earth, seems to me a sterile
promontory; this most excellent canopy, the air, look you, this brave o'erhanging
firmament, this majestical roof fretted with golden fire—why, it appeareth no other
thing to me than a foul and pestilent congregation of vapours. What a piece of work
275   is a man! how noble in reason! how infinite in faculties! in form and moving how
express and admirable! in action how like an angel! in apprehension how like a god!
the beauty of the world, the paragon of animals! And yet to me what is this quintes-
sence of dust? Man delights not me—no, nor woman neither, though by your smiling
you seem to say so.

280   ROSENCRANTZ   My lord, there was no such stuff in my thoughts.

HAMLET   Why did you laugh then, when I said "Man delights not me"?

ROSENCRANTZ   To think, my lord, if you delight not in man, what lenten entertainment the
players shall receive from you. We coted them on the way, and hither are they coming
to offer you service.

285   HAMLET   He that plays the king shall be welcome—his Majesty shall have tribute of me; the
adventurous knight shall use his foil and target; the lover shall not sigh gratis; the
humorous man shall end his part in peace; the clown shall make those laugh whose
lungs are tickle o' th' sere; and the lady shall say her mind freely, or the blank verse
shall halt for't. What players are they?

---

[254] *too dear a halfpenny,* not worth a halfpenny   [268] *prevent,* forestall; *discovery,* disclosure   [272] *brave,* magnificent   [282] *lenten,* spare   [283] *coted,* passed   [288] *tickle o' th' sere,* easily amused

290 ROSENCRANTZ   Even those you were wont to take such delight in, the tragedians of the city.
HAMLET   How chances it they travel? Their residence, both in reputation and profit, was better both ways.
ROSENCRANTZ   I think their inhibition comes by the means of the late innovation.
HAMLET   Do they hold the same estimation they did when I was in the city? Are they so
295   follow'd?
ROSENCRANTZ   No indeed are they not.
HAMLET   How comes it? Do they grow rusty?
ROSENCRANTZ   Nay, their endeavour keeps in the wonted pace; but there is, sir, an eyrie of children, little eyases, that cry out on the top of question and are most tyrannically
300   clapp'd for't. These are now the fashion, and so berattle the common stages (so they call them) that many wearing rapiers are afraid of goosequills and dare scarce come thither.
HAMLET   What, are they children? Who maintains 'em? How are they escoted? Will they pursue the quality no longer than they can sing? Will they not say afterwards, if they
305   should grow themselves to common players (as it is most like, if their means are no better), their writers do them wrong to make them exclaim against their own succession.
ROSENCRANTZ   Faith, there has been much to do on both sides; and the nation holds it no sin to tarre them to controversy. There was, for a while, no money bid for argument
310   unless the poet and the player went to cuffs in the question.
HAMLET   Is't possible?
GUILDENSTERN   O, there has been much throwing about of brains.
HAMLET   Do the boys carry it away?
ROSENCRANTZ   Ay, that they do, my lord—Hercules and his load too.
315 HAMLET   It is not very strange; for my uncle is King of Denmark, and those that would make mows at him while my father lived give twenty, forty, fifty, a hundred ducats apiece for his picture in little. 'Sblood, there is something in this more than natural, if philosophy could find it out.

Flourish for the Players.

GUILDENSTERN   There are the players.
320 HAMLET   Gentlemen, you are welcome to Elsinore. Your hands, come! Th' appurtenance of welcome is fashion and ceremony. Let me comply with you in this garb, lest my extent to the players (which I tell you must show fairly outwards) should more appear like entertainment than yours. You are welcome. But my uncle-father and aunt-mother are deceiv'd.
325 GUILDENSTERN   In what, my dear lord?
325 HAMLET   I am but mad north-north-west. When the wind is southerly I know a hawk from a handsaw.

Enter POLONIUS.

POLONIUS   Well be with you, gentlemen!

[293] *inhibition . . . innovation* (decision to leave) . . . new fashion (in play-acting)
[298-299] *eyrie . . . eyases,* covey . . . baby hawks   [299] *tyrannically,* loudly   [300] *berattle the common stages,* berate (make fun of) adult actors   [301] *many wearing rapiers . . . goosequills,* armed adults . . . pens (used to make fun of "common stages" and those who attended them)
[303] *escoted,* financed   [304] *pursue the quality . . . sing?,* continue to act until their voices change?   [309] *tarre,* egg on   [316] *make mows,* make faces

HAMLET   Hark you, Guildenstern—and you too—at each ear a hearer! That great baby you
330   see there is not yet out of his swaddling clouts.

ROSENCRANTZ   Happily he's the second time come to them; for they say an old man is twice
a child.

HAMLET   I will prophesy he comes to tell me of the players. Mark it.—You say right, sir; a
Monday morning; 'twas so indeed.

335 POLONIUS   My lord, I have news to tell you.

HAMLET   My lord, I have news to tell you. When Roscius was an actor in Rome—

POLONIUS   The actors are come hither, my lord.

HAMLET   Buzz, buzz!

POLONIUS   Upon my honour—

340 HAMLET   Then came each actor on his ass—

POLONIUS   The best actors in the world, either for tragedy, comedy, history, pastoral, pas-
toral-comical, historical-pastoral, tragical-historical, tragical-comical-historical-pastoral;
scene individable, or poem unlimited. Seneca cannot be too heavy, nor Plautus too
light. For the law of writ and the liberty, these are the only men.

345 HAMLET   O Jephthah, judge of Israel, what a treasure hadst thou!

POLONIUS   What treasure had he, my lord?

HAMLET   Why,

> "One fair daughter, and no more,
>   The which he loved passing well."

350 POLONIUS *(Aside)*   Still on my daughter.

HAMLET   Am I not i' th' right, old Jephthah?

POLONIUS   If you call me Jephthah, my lord, I have a daughter that I love passing well.

HAMLET   Nay, that follows not.

POLONIUS   What follows then, my lord?

355 HAMLET   Why,

> "As by lot, Got wot,"

and then, you know,

> "It came to pass, as most like it was."

The first row of the pious chanson will show you more; for look where my abridg-
360   ment comes.

(Enter four or five PLAYERS.*)*

You are welcome, masters; welcome, all.—I am glad to see thee well.—Welcome,
good friends.—O, my old friend? Why, thy face is valanc'd since I saw thee last. Com'st
thou to beard me in Denmark?—What, my young lady and mistress? By'r Lady, your
ladyship is nearer to heaven than when I saw you last by the altitude of a chopine.
365   Pray God your voice, like a piece of uncurrent gold, be not crack'd within the ring.—
Masters, you are all welcome. We'll e'en to't like French falconers, fly at anything we

---

[344] *law of writ and the liberty,* the three unities (time, place, and action) and freedom from them
[345] *Jephthah* (subject of a popular song from which Hamlet quotes later)   [359] *row . . . chanson,*
stanza . . . song   [359] *abridgment,* interruption   [362] *valanc'd,* bearded   [363] *young lady* (boy
who acted young women's parts)   [364] *chopine,* short stilt   [365] *not crack'd within
the ring,* not made worthless as a cracked coin (a pun: Hamlet hopes the boy's voice has not
cracked.)

see. We'll have a speech straight. Come, give us a taste of your quality. Come, a passionate speech.

1. PLAYER   What speech, my good lord?

370 HAMLET   I heard thee speak me a speech once, but it was never acted; or if it was, not above once; for the play, I remember, pleas'd not the million, 'twas caviar to the general; but it was (as I receiv'd it, and others, whose judgments in such matters cried in the top of mine) an excellent play, well digested in the scenes, set down with as much modesty as cunning. I remember one said there were no sallets in the lines to

375 make the matter savoury, nor no matter in the phrase that might indict the author of affectation; but call'd it an honest method, as wholesome as sweet, and by very much more handsome than fine. One speech in't I chiefly lov'd. 'Twas Æneas' tale to Dido, and thereabout of it especially where he speaks of Priam's slaughter. If it live in your memory, begin at this line—let me see, let me see:

380   "The rugged Pyrrhus, like th' Hyrcanian beast—"

'Tis not so; it begins with Pyrrhus:

"The rugged Pyrrhus, he whose sable arms,
Black as his purpose, did the night resemble
When he lay couched in the ominous horse,

385 Hath now this dread and black complexion smear'd
With heraldry more dismal. Head to foot
Now is he total gules, horridly trick'd
With blood of fathers, mothers, daughters, sons,
Bak'd and impasted with the parching streets,

390 That lend a tyrannous and a damned light
To their lord's murther. Roasted in wrath and fire,
And thus o'ersized with coagulate gore,
With eyes like carbuncles, the hellish Pyrrhus
Old grandsire Priam seeks."

395 So, proceed you.

POLONIUS   Fore God, my lord, well spoken, with good accent and good discretion.

1. PLAYER   "Anon he finds him,
Striking too short at Greeks. His antique sword,
Rebellious to his arm, lies where it falls,

400 Repugnant to command. Unequal match'd,
Pyrrhus at Priam drives, in rage strikes wide;
But with the whiff and wind of his fell sword
Th' unnerved father falls. Then senseless Ilium,
Seeming to feel this blow, with flaming top

405 Stoops to his base, and with a hideous crash

---

[371] *caviar to the general,* sturgeon eggs (not pleasing) to most people   [372-373] *cried in the top of mine,* outshouted my voice   [374] *modesty . . . cunning,* artistic control . . . skill   [374] *sallets,* salads (presumably spicy)   [376] *honest,* unaffected   [377] *Dido,* mythological Queen of Carthage   [378] *Priam's slaughter,* Trojan king's death (described in Virgil's *Aeneid*)   [380] *Hyrcanian beast* (Hyrcania was a province of the Persian empire.)   [384] *ominous horse* (the wooden horse, a gift to the Trojans, in which the Greek warriors hid and thereby gained entrance to Troy)   [387] *gules . . . trick'd,* red . . . adorned   [392] *o'ersized,* glazed   [400] *repugnant,* refusing (Priam's order to obey)   [402] *the whiff and wing* (the weak old man is blown down by the swish of Pyrrhus' sword.)

Takes prisoner Pyrrhus' ear. For lo! his sword,
Which was declining on the milky head
Of reverend Priam, seem'd i' th' air to stick.
So, as a painted tyrant, Pyrrhus stood,
410 And, like a neutral to his will and matter,
Did nothing.
But, as we often see, against some storm,
A silence in the heavens, the rack stand still,
The bold winds speechless, and the orb below
415 As hush as death—anon the dreadful thunder
Doth rend the region; so, after Pyrrhus' pause,
Aroused vengeance sets him new awork;
And never did the Cyclops' hammers fall
On Mars's armour, forg'd for proof eterne,
420 With less remorse than Pyrrhus' bleeding sword
Now falls on Priam.
Out, out, thou strumpet Fortune! All you Gods,
In general synod take away her power;
Break all the spokes and fellies from her wheel,
425 And bowl the round nave down the hill of heaven,
As low as to the fiends!"

POLONIUS   This is too long.
HAMLET   It shall to the barber's, with your beard.—Prithee say on. He's for a jig or a tale
of bawdry, or he sleeps. Say on; come to Hecuba.

430 1. PLAYER   "But who, O who, had seen the mobled queen—"

HAMLET   "The mobled queen"?
POLONIUS   That's good! "Mobled queen" is good.

1. PLAYER   "Run barefoot up and down, threat'ning the flames
With bisson rheum; a clout upon that head
435 Where late the diadem stood, and for a robe,
About her lank and all o'erteemed loins,
A blanket, in the alarm of fear caught up—
Who this had seen, with tongue in venom steep'd
'Gainst Fortune's state would treason have pronounc'd.
440 But if the gods themselves did see her then,
When she saw Pyrrhus make malicious sport
In mincing with his sword her husband's limbs,
The instant burst of clamour that she made
(Unless things mortal move them not at all)
445 Would have made milch the burning eyes of heaven
And passion in the gods."

POLONIUS   Look, whe'r he has not turn'd his colour, and has tears in's eyes. Prithee no
more!

---

418 *Cyclops* (one-eyed giant, workman for Vulcan, god of armor-making)   423–426 (a request to the gods to destroy the wheel of fickle Fortune)   428 *jig,* short, comic exchange (acted-out jokes)   430 *mobled,* muffled   434 *bisson rheum . . . clout,* blinding tears . . . a cloth   436 *o'erteemed loins,* loins worn out by excessive child-bearing

HAMLET 'Tis well. I'll have thee speak out the rest of this soon.—Good my lord, will you
450 see the players well bestow'd? Do you hear? Let them be well us'd; for they are the
abstract and brief chronicles of the time. After your death you were better have a bad
epitaph than their ill report while you live.

POLONIUS My lord, I will use them according to their desert.

HAMLET God's bodykins, man, much better! Use every man after his desert, and who
455 should scape whipping? Use them after your own honour and dignity. The less they
deserve, the more merit is in your bounty. Take them in.

POLONIUS Come, sirs.

HAMLET Follow him, friends. We'll hear a play to-morrow.

(*Exeunt* POLONIUS *and* PLAYERS *except the* FIRST.)

Dost thou hear me, old friend? Can you play "The Murther of Gonzago"?
460 1. PLAYER Ay, my lord.

HAMLET We'll ha't to-morrow night. You could, for a need, study a speech of some dozen
or sixteen lines which I would set down and insert in't, could you not?

1. PLAYER Ay, my lord.

HAMLET Very well. Follow that lord—and look you mock him not.

(*Exit* FIRST PLAYER.)

465 My good friends, I'll leave you till night. You are welcome to Elsinore.

ROSENCRANTZ Good my lord!

HAMLET Ay, so, God b' wi' ye!

(*Exeunt* ROSENCRANTZ *and* GUILDENSTERN.)

Now I am alone.
O, what a rogue and peasant slave am I!
Is it not monstrous that this player here,
470 But in a fiction, in a dream of passion,
Could force his soul so to his own conceit
That, from her working, all his visage wann'd,
Tears in his eyes, distraction in's aspect,
A broken voice, and his whole function suiting
475 With forms to his conceit? And all for nothing!
For Hecuba!
What's Hecuba to him, or he to Hecuba,
That he should weep for her? What would he do,
Had he the motive and the cue for passion
480 That I have? He would drown the stage with tears
And cleave the general ear with horrid speech;
Make mad the guilty and appal the free,
Confound the ignorant, and amaze indeed
The very faculties of eyes and ears.
485 Yet I,
A dull and muddy-mettled rascal, peak
Like John-a-dreams, unpregnant of my cause,
And can say nothing! No, not for a king,

[476] *Hecuba,* Priam's wife

Upon whose property and most dear life
490 A damn'd defeat was made. Am I a coward?
Who calls me villain? breaks my pate across?
Plucks off my beard and blows it in my face?
Tweaks me by th' nose? gives me the lie i' th' throat
As deep as to the lungs? Who does me this, ha?
495 'Swounds, I should take it! for it cannot be
But I am pigeon-liver'd and lack gall
To make oppression bitter, or ere this
I should have fatted all the region kites,
With this slave's offal. Bloody, bawdy villain!
500 Remorseless, treacherous, lecherous, kindless villain!
O, vengeance!
Why, what an ass am I! This is most brave,
That I, the son of a dear father murther'd,
Prompted to my revenge by heaven and hell,
505 Must (like a whore) unpack my heart with words
And fall a-cursing like a very drab,
A scullion!
Fie upon't! foh! About, my brain! Hum, I have heard
That guilty creatures, sitting at a play,
510 Have by the very cunning of the scene
Been struck so to the soul that presently
They have proclaim'd their malefactions;
For murther, though it have no tongue, will speak
With most miraculous organ. I'll have these players
515 Play something like the murther of my father
Before mine uncle. I'll observe his looks;
I'll tent him to the quick. If he but blench,
I know my course. The spirit that I have seen
May be a devil; and the devil hath power
520 T' assume a pleasing shape; yea, and perhaps
Out of my weakness and my melancholy,
As he is very potent with such spirits,
Abuses me to damn me. I'll have grounds
More relative than this. The play's the thing
525 Wherein I'll catch the conscience of the King.

Exit.

ACT III

Scene I. *Elsinore. A Room in the Castle*

      Enter KING, QUEEN, POLONIUS, OPHELIA, ROSENCRANTZ, GUILDENSTERN, *and* LORDS.

KING   And can you by no drift of circumstance
    Get from him why he puts on this confusion,

---

[504] *by heaven and hell* (Heaven asks vengeance because Claudius deserves punishment; hell eggs on by stirring hatred in Hamlet.)   [508] *about,* get to work   [510] *cunning,* skill (in the acting)   [517] *tent,* watch intently   [1] *by no drift of circumstance,* by no trick of questioning   [2] *puts on this confusion,* dresses (himself) in madness

Grating so harshly all his days of quiet
With turbulent and dangerous lunacy?
5 ROSENCRANTZ He does confess he feels himself distracted,
But from what cause he will by no means speak.
GUILDENSTERN   Nor do we find him forward to be sounded,
But with a crafty madness keeps aloof
When we would bring him on to some confession
Of his true state.
10 QUEEN   Did he receive you well?
ROSENCRANTZ   Most like a gentleman.
GUILDENSTERN   But with much forcing of his disposition.
ROSENCRANTZ   Niggard of question, but of our demands
Most free in his reply.
QUEEN   Did you assay him
15 To any pastime?
ROSENCRANTZ   Madam, it so fell out that certain players
We o'erraught on the way. Of these we told him,
And there did seem in him a kind of joy
To hear of it. They are here about the court,
20 And, as I think, they have already order
This night to play before him.
POLONIUS   'Tis most true;
And he beseech'd me to entreat your Majesties
To hear and see the matter.
KING   With all my heart, and it doth much content me
25 To hear him so inclin'd.
Good gentlemen, give him a further edge
And drive his purpose on to these delights.
ROSENCRANTZ   We shall, my lord.

Exeunt ROSENCRANTZ *and* GUILDENSTERN.

KING   Sweet Gertrude, leave us too;
For we have closely sent for Hamlet hither,
30 That he, as 'twere by accident, may here
Affront Ophelia.
Her father and myself (lawful espials)
Will so bestow ourselves that, seeing unseen,
We may of their encounter frankly judge
35 And gather by him, as he is behav'd,
If't be th' affliction of his love, or no,
That thus he suffers for.
QUEEN   I shall obey you;
And for your part, Ophelia, I do wish
That your good beauties be the happy cause
40 Of Hamlet's wildness. So shall I hope your virtues
Will bring him to his wonted way again,
To both your honours.

---

[13] *demands,* questions   [17] *o'erraught,* overtook   [29] *closely,* privately   [31] *affront,* meet (face to face)   [32] *espials,* eavesdroppers

OPHELIA   Madam, I wish it may.

Exit QUEEN.

POLONIUS   Ophelia, walk you here.—Gracious, so please you,
We will bestow ourselves.—(*To* OPHELIA) Read on this book,
45   That show of such an exercise may colour
Your loneliness.—We are oft to blame in this,
'Tis too much prov'd, that with devotion's visage
And pious action we do sugar o'er
The devil himself.
KING *(Aside)*   O, 'tis too true!
50   How smart a lash that speech doth give my conscience!
The harlot's cheek, beautied with plast'ring art,
Is not more ugly to the thing that helps it
Than is my deed to my most painted word.
O heavy burthen!
55   POLONIUS   I hear him coming. Let's withdraw, my lord.

Exeunt KING *and* POLONIUS.

Enter HAMLET.

HAMLET   To be, or not to be—that is the question:
Whether 'tis nobler in the mind to suffer
The slings and arrows of outrageous fortune
Or to take arms against a sea of troubles,
60   And by opposing end them. To die—to sleep—
No more; and by a sleep to say we end
The heartache, and the thousand natural shocks
That flesh is heir to. 'Tis a consummation
Devoutly to be wish'd. To die—to sleep.
65   To sleep—perchance to dream: ay, there's the rub!
For in that sleep of death what dreams may come
When we have shuffled off this mortal coil,
Must give us pause. There's the respect
That makes calamity of so long life.
70   For who would bear the whips and scorns of time,
Th' oppressor's wrong, the proud man's contumely,
The pangs of despis'd love, the law's delay,
The insolence of office, and the spurns
That patient merit of th' unworthy takes,
75   When he himself might his quietus make
With a bare bodkin? Who would these fardels bear,
To grunt and sweat under a weary life,
But that the dread of something after death—
The undiscover'd country, from whose bourn
80   No traveller returns—puzzles the will,
And makes us rather bear those ills we have
Than fly to others that we know not of?

---

[76] *bodkin,* needle—or perhaps dagger; *fardels,* burdens   [79] *bourn,* borders

Thus conscience does make cowards of us all,
And thus the native hue of resolution
85 Is sicklied o'er with the pale cast of thought,
And enterprises of great pith and moment
With this regard their currents turn awry
And lose the name of action.—Soft you now.
The fair Ophelia!—Nymph, in thy orisons
Be all my sins rememb'red.
90 OPHELIA   Good my lord,
How does your honour for this many a day?
HAMLET I humbly thank you; well, well, well.
OPHELIA My lord, I have remembrances of yours
That I have longed long to re-deliver.
I pray you, now receive them.
95 HAMLET   No, not I!
I never gave you aught.
OPHELIA My honour'd lord, you know right well you did,
And with them words of so sweet breath compos'd
As made the things more rich. Their perfume lost,
100 Take these again; for to the noble mind
Rich gifts wax poor when givers prove unkind.
There, my lord.
HAMLET Ha, ha! Are you honest?
OPHELIA My lord?
105 HAMLET Are you fair?
OPHELIA What means your lordship?
HAMLET That if you be honest and fair, your honesty should admit no discourse to your beauty.
OPHELIA Could beauty, my lord, have better commerce than with honesty?
110 HAMLET Ay, truly; for the power of beauty will sooner transform honesty from what it is to a bawd than the force of honesty can translate beauty into his likeness. This was sometime a paradox, but now the time gives it proof. I did love you once.
OPHELIA Indeed, my lord, you made me believe so.
HAMLET You should not have believ'd me; for virtue cannot so inoculate our old stock but
115 we shall relish of it. I loved you not.
OPHELIA I was the more deceived.
HAMLET Get thee to a nunnery! Why wouldst thou be a breeder of sinners? I am myself indifferent honest, but yet I could accuse me of such things that it were better my mother had not borne me. I am very proud, revengeful, ambitious; with more of-
120 fences at my beck than I have thoughts to put them in, imagination to give them shape, or time to act them in. What should such fellows as I do, crawling between earth and heaven? We are arrant knaves all; believe none of us. Go thy ways to a nunnery. Where's your father?
OPHELIA At home, my lord.
125 HAMLET Let the doors be shut upon him, that he may play the fool nowhere but in's own house. Farewell.
OPHELIA O, help him, you sweet heavens!

---

[89] *orisons*, prayers   [103] *honest*, virginal   [114] *inoculate our old stock*, produce a change in our store (of original sinfulness)

HAMLET If thou dost marry, I'll give thee this plague for thy dowry: be thou as chaste as
ice, as pure as snow, thou shalt not escape calumny. Get thee to a nunnery. Go,
130   farewell. Or if thou wilt needs marry, marry a fool; for wise men know well enough
what monsters you make of them. To a nunnery, go; and quickly too. Farewell.

OPHELIA O heavenly powers, restore him!

HAMLET I have heard of your paintings too, well enough. God hath given you one face,
and you make yourselves another. You jig, you amble, and you lisp; you nickname
135   God's creatures and make your wantonness your ignorance. Go to, I'll no more on't!
it hath made me mad. I say, we will have no moe marriages. Those that are married
already—all but one—shall live; the rest shall keep as they are. To a nunnery, go. *Exit.*

OPHELIA O, what a noble mind is here o'erthrown!
The courtier's, scholar's, soldier's, eye, tongue, sword,
140   Th' expectancy and rose of the fair state,
The glass of fashion and the mould of form,
Th' observ'd of all observers—quite, quite down!
And I, of ladies most deject and wretched,
That suck'd the honey of his music vows,
145   Now see that noble and most sovereign reason,
Like sweet bells jangled, out of tune and harsh;
That unmatch'd form and feature of blown youth
Blasted with ecstasy. O, woe is me
T' have seen what I have seen, see what I see!

Enter KING *and* POLONIUS.

150 KING Love? his affections do not that way tend;
Nor what he spake, though it lack'd form a little,
Was not like madness. There's something in his soul
O'er which his melancholy sits on brood;
And I do doubt the hatch and the disclose
155   Will be some danger; which for to prevent,
I have in quick determination
Thus set it down: he shall with speed to England
For the demand of our neglected tribute.
Haply the seas, and countries different,
160   With variable objects, shall expel
This something-settled matter in his heart,
Whereon his brains still beating puts him thus
From fashion of himself. What think you on't?

POLONIUS It shall do well. But yet do I believe
165   The origin and commencement of his grief
Sprung from neglected love.—How now, Ophelia?
You need not tell us what Lord Hamlet said.
We heard it all.—My lord, do as you please;
But if you hold it fit, after the play
170   Let his queen mother all alone entreat him
To show his grief. Let her be round with him;

---

[128] *plague,* black reputation   [131] *monsters,* cuckolds   [133] *paintings,* rougings   [135] *make your*
wantonness your ignorance, blame your licentiousness on innocence   [147] *blown,* full-blown
[148] *ecstasy,* insanity   [154] *doubt,* fear   [158] *our neglected tribute,* their unpaid debt

And I'll be plac'd, so please you, in the ear
Of all their conference. If she find him not,
To England send him; or confine him where
Your wisdom best shall think.
175 KING   It shall be so.
Madness in great ones must not unwatch'd go.

Exeunt.

Scene II. *Elsinore. A Hall in the Castle.*

Enter HAMLET *and three of the* PLAYERS.

HAMLET   Speak the speech, I pray you, as I pronounc'd it to you, trippingly on the tongue. But if you mouth it, as many of our players do, I had as live the town crier spoke my lines. Nor do not saw the air too much with your hand, thus, but use all gently; for in the very torrent, tempest, and (as I may say) whirlwind of your passion, you must
5   acquire and beget a temperance that may give it smoothness. O, it offends me to the soul to hear a robustious periwig-pated fellow tear a passion to tatters, to very rags, to split the ears of the groundlings, who (for the most part) are capable of nothing but inexplicable dumb shows and noise. I would have such a fellow whipp'd for o'erdoing Termagant. It out-herods Herod. Pray you avoid it.
10 PLAYER   I warrant your honour.
HAMLET   Be not too tame neither, but let your own discretion be your tutor. Suit the action to the word, the word to the action; with this special observance, that you o'erstep not the modesty of nature: for anything so overdone is from the purpose of playing, whose end, both at the first and now, was and is, to hold, as 'twere, the mirror up to
15   nature; to show virtue her own feature, scorn her own image, and the very age and body of the time his form and pressure. Now this overdone, or come tardy off, though it make the unskilful laugh, cannot but make the judicious grieve; the censure of the which one must in your allowance o'erweigh a whole theatre of others. O, there be players that I have seen play, and heard others praise, and that highly (not to speak it
20   profanely), that, neither having the accent of Christians, nor the gait of Christian, pagan, nor man, have so strutted and bellowed that I have thought some of Nature's journeymen had made men, and not made them well, they imitated humanity so abominably.
PLAYER   I hope we have reform'd that indifferently with us, sir.
25 HAMLET   O, reform it altogether! And let those that play your clowns speak no more than is set down for them. For there be of them that will themselves laugh, to set on some quantity of barren spectators to laugh too, though in the mean time some necessary question of the play be then to be considered. That's villanous and shows a most pitiful ambition in the fool that uses it. Go make you ready.

(*Exeunt* PLAYERS.)

(*Enter* POLONIUS, ROSENCRANTZ, *and* GUILDENSTERN.)

30   How now, my lord? Will the King hear this piece of work?
POLONIUS   And the Queen too, and that presently.
HAMLET   Bid the players make haste. (*Exit* POLONIUS.) Will you two help to hasten them?

---

² *live,* lief   ¹⁶ *pressure,* impression   ¹⁷ *unskilful,* those lacking taste   ¹⁷ *the censure of the which one,* the judgment of one (judicious person)   ²⁴ *indifferently,* passably   ³¹ *presently,* immediately

BOTH We will, my lord.

Exeunt they two.

HAMLET What, ho, Horatio!

Enter HORATIO.

35 HORATIO Here, sweet lord, at your service.
HAMLET Horatio, thou art e'en as just a man
As e'er my conversation cop'd withal.
HORATIO O, my dear lord!
HAMLET   Nay, do not think I flatter;
For what advancement may I hope from thee,
40 That no revenue hast but thy good spirits
To feed and clothe thee? Why should the poor be flatter'd?
No, let the candied tongue lick absurd pomp,
And crook the pregnant hinges of the knee
Where thrift may follow fawning. Dost thou hear?
45 Since my dear soul was mistress of her choice
And could of men distinguish, her election
Hath seal'd thee for herself. For thou hast been
As one, in suff'ring all, that suffers nothing;
A man that Fortune's buffets and rewards
50 Hast ta'en with thanks; and blest are those
Whose blood and judgment are so well commingled
That they are not a pipe for Fortune's finger
To sound what stop she please. Give me that man
That is not passion's slave, and I will wear him
55 In my heart's core, ay, in my heart of heart,
As I do thee. Something too much of this!
There is a play to-night before the King.
One scene of it comes near the circumstance,
Which I have told thee, of my father's death.
60 I prithee, when thou seest that act afoot,
Even with the very comment of thy soul
Observe my uncle. If his occulted guilt
Do not itself unkennel in one speech,
It is a damned ghost that we have seen,
65 And my imaginations are as foul
As Vulcan's stithy. Give him heedful note;
For I mine eyes will rivet to his face,
And after we will both our judgments join
In censure of his seeming.
HORATIO   Well, my lord.
70 If he steal aught the whilst this play is playing,
And scape detecting, I will pay the theft.

Sound a flourish. Enter Trumpets and Kettledrums. Danish march. Enter KING, QUEEN, PO-
LONIUS, OPHELIA, ROSENCRANTZ, GUILDENSTERN, *and other* LORDS *attendant, with the* GUARD *carrying torches.*

---

36 *just,* well-balanced   37 *cop'd withal,* had to do with   44 *thrift,* reward

HAMLET   They are coming to the play. I must be idle.
   Get you a place.

KING   How fares our cousin Hamlet?

75 HAMLET   Excellent, i' faith; of the chameleon's dish. I eat the air, promise-cramm'd. You
   cannot feed capons so.

KING   I have nothing with this answer, Hamlet.
   These words are not mine.

HAMLET   No, nor mine now. (*To* POLONIUS) My lord, you play'd once i' th' university, you
80   say?

POLONIUS   That did I, my lord, and was accounted a good actor.

HAMLET   What did you enact?

POLONIUS   I did enact Julius Caesar; I was kill'd i' th' Capitol; Brutus kill'd me.

HAMLET   It was a brute part of him to kill so capital a calf there. Be the players ready?

85 ROSENCRANTZ   Ay, my lord. They stay upon your patience.

QUEEN   Come hither, my dear Hamlet, sit by me.

HAMLET   No, good mother. Here's metal more attractive.

POLONIUS (*To the* KING)   O, ho! do you mark that?

HAMLET   Lady, shall I lie in your lap?

Sits down at OPHELIA's *feet.*

90 OPHELIA   No, my lord.

HAMLET   I mean, my head upon your lap?

OPHELIA   Ay, my lord.

HAMLET   Do you think I meant country matters?

OPHELIA   I think nothing, my lord.

95 HAMLET   That's a fair thought to lie between maids' legs.

OPHELIA   What is, my lord?

HAMLET   Nothing.

OPHELIA   You are merry, my lord.

HAMLET   Who, I?

100 OPHELIA   Ay, my lord.

HAMLET   O God, your only jig-maker! What should a man do but be merry? For look you
   how cheerfully my mother looks, and my father died within 's two hours.

OPHELIA   Nay, 'tis twice two months, my lord.

HAMLET   So long? Nay then, let the devil wear black, for I'll have a suit of sables. O heavens!
105   die two months ago, and not forgotten yet? Then there's hope a great man's memory
   may outlive his life half a year. But, by'r Lady, he must build churches then; or else
   shall he suffer not thinking on, with the hobby-horse, whose epitaph is "For O, for O,
   the hobby-horse is forgot!"

Hautboys play. The dumb show enters.

Enter a KING and a QUEEN very lovingly; the QUEEN embracing him, and he her. She kneels,
and makes show of protestation unto him. He takes her up, and declines his head upon
her neck. He lays him down upon a bank of flowers. She, seeing him asleep, leaves him.
Anon comes in a fellow, takes off his crown, kisses it, pours poison in the sleeper's ears,
and leaves him. The QUEEN returns, finds the KING dead, and makes passionate action. The
POISONER with some three or four MUTES, come in again, seem to condole with her. The

---

[72] *idle,* mad   [75] *chameleon's dish,* air   [101] *jig-maker,* comic song writer   [107] *suffer not*
thinking on, risk not being remembered

dead body is carried away. The POISONER wooes the QUEEN with gifts; she seems harsh and unwilling awhile, but in the end accepts his love.

Exeunt.

OPHELIA   What means this, my lord?
110   HAMLET   Marry, this is miching malhecho; it means mischief.
OPHELIA   Belike this show imports the argument of the play.

Enter PROLOGUE.

HAMLET   We shall know by this fellow. The players cannot keep counsel; they'll tell all.
OPHELIA   Will he tell us what this show meant?
HAMLET   Ay, or any show that you'll show him. Be not asham'd to show, he'll not shame to
115   tell you what it means.
OPHELIA   You are naught, you are naught! I'll mark the play.

PROLOGUE   For us, and for our tragedy,
Here stooping to your clemency,
We beg your hearing patiently.

Exit.

120   HAMLET   Is this a prologue, or the posy of a ring?
OPHELIA   'Tis brief, my lord.
HAMLET   As a woman's love.

Enter two PLAYERS *as* KING *and* QUEEN.

KING   Full thirty times hath Phoebus' cart gone round
Neptune's salt wash and Tellus' orbed ground,
125   And thirty dozen moons with borrowed sheen
About the world have times twelve thirties been,
Since love our hearts, and Hymen did our hands,
Unite comutual in most sacred bands.
QUEEN   So many journeys may the sun and moon
130   Make us again count o'er ere love be done!
But woe is me! you are so sick of late,
So far from cheer and from your former state,
That I distrust you. Yet, though I distrust,
Discomfort you, my lord, it nothing must;
135   For women's fear and love holds quantity,
In neither aught, or in extremity.
Now what my love is, proof hath made you know;
And as my love is siz'd, my fear is so.
Where love is great, the littlest doubts are fear;
140   Where little fears grow great, great love grows there.
KING   Faith, I must leave thee, love, and shortly too;
My operant powers their functions leave to do.
And thou shalt live in this fair world behind,

---

[110] *miching malhecho,* underhanded crime   [112] *keep counsel,* keep a secret   [116] *naught,* naughty   [123] *Phoebus' cart,* the sun's chariot   [124] *Neptune's salt wash,* the ocean; *Tellus' orbed ground,* the earth   [127] *Hymen,* god of marriage   [133] *distrust you,* am concerned about you   [142] *operant powers,* vital force

Honour'd, belov'd, and haply one as kind
For husband shalt thou—
145 QUEEN   O, confound the rest!
Such love must needs be treason in my breast.
In second husband let me be accurst!
None wed the second but who kill'd the first.

HAMLET *(Aside)* Wormwood, wormwood!

150 QUEEN The instances that second marriage move
Are base respects of thrift, but none of love.
A second time I kill my husband dead
When second husband kisses me in bed.
      KING I do believe you think what now you speak;
155 But what we do determine oft we break.
Purpose is but the slave to memory,
Of violent birth, but poor validity;
Which now, like fruit unripe, sticks on the tree,
But fall unshaken when they mellow be.
160 Most necessary 'tis that we forget
To pay ourselves what to ourselves is debt.
What to ourselves in passion we propose,
The passion ending, doth the purpose lose.
The violence of either grief or joy
165 Their own enactures with themselves destroy.
Where joy most revels, grief doth most lament;
Grief joys, joy grieves, on slender accident.
This world is not for aye, nor 'tis not strange
That even our loves should with our fortunes change;
170 For 'tis a question left us yet to prove,
Whether love lead fortune, or else fortune love.
The great man down, you mark his favourite flies,
The poor advanc'd makes friends of enemies;
And hitherto doth love on fortune tend,
175 For who not needs shall never lack a friend,
And who in want a hollow friend doth try,
Directly seasons him his enemy.
But, orderly to end where I begun,
Our wills and fates do so contrary run
180 That our devices still are overthrown;
Our thoughts are ours, their ends none of our own.
So think thou wilt no second husband wed;
But die thy thoughts when thy first lord is dead.
      QUEEN Nor earth to me give food, nor heaven light,
185 Sport and repose lock from me day and night,
To desperation turn my trust and hope,
An anchor's cheer in prison be my scope,
Each opposite that blanks the face of joy
Meet what I would have well, and it destroy,

---

[145] *O, confound the rest!* (Don't mention the possibility of another husband for me!)

190 Both here and hence pursue me lasting strife,
   If, once a widow, ever I be wife!

HAMLET If she should break it now!

KING 'Tis deeply sworn. Sweet, leave me here awhile.
   My spirits grow dull, and fain I would beguile
   The tedious day with sleep.
195 QUEEN   Sleep rock thy brain,

(He sleeps.)

And never come mischance between us twain!

Exit.

HAMLET Madam, how like you this play?
QUEEN The lady doth protest too much, methinks.
HAMLET O, but she'll keep her word.
200 KING Have you heard the argument? Is there no offence in't?
HAMLET No, no! They do but jest, poison in jest; no offence i' th' world.
KING What do you call the play?
HAMLET "The Mousetrap." Marry, how? Tropically. This play is the image of a murther
   done in Vienna. Gonzago is the duke's name; his wife, Baptista. You shall see anon.
205 'Tis a knavish piece of work; but what o' that? Your Majesty, and we that have free
   souls, it touches us not. Let the gall'd jade winch; our withers are unwrung.

(Enter LUCIANUS.*)*

This is one Lucianus, nephew to the King.
OPHELIA You are as good as a chorus, my lord.
HAMLET I could interpret between you and your love, if I could see the puppets dallying.
210 OPHELIA You are keen, my lord, you are keen.
HAMLET It would cost you a groaning to take off my edge.
OPHELIA Still better, and worse.
HAMLET So you must take your husbands.—Begin, murtherer. Pox, leave thy damnable
   faces, and begin! Come, the croaking raven doth bellow for revenge.

215 LUCIANUS Thoughts black, hands apt, drugs fit, and time agreeing;
   Confederate season, else no creature seeing;
   Thou mixture rank, of midnight weeds collected,
   With Hecate's ban thrice blasted, thrice infected,
   Thy natural magic and dire property
220 On wholesome life usurp immediately.

Pours the poison in his ears.

HAMLET He poisons him i' th' garden for's estate. His name's Gonzago. The story is extant,
   and written in very choice Italian. You shall see anon how the murtherer gets the love
   of Gonzago's wife.
OPHELIA The King rises.
225 HAMLET What, frighted with false fire?

---

[203] *Tropically,* figuratively   [206] *gall'd jade winch; our withers are unwrung,* the sore horse may
wince, but this (horse's) neck is not rubbed raw.   [209] *puppets* (Ophelia and her imagined
lover)   [216] *Confederate season,* right moment   [218] *ban,* curse

QUEEN   How fares my lord?
POLONIUS   Give o'er the play.
KING   Give me some light! Away!
ALL   Lights, lights, lights!

Exeunt all but HAMLET *and* HORATIO.

230   HAMLET   Why, let the strucken deer go weep,
        The hart ungalled play;
      For some must watch, while some must sleep:
        Thus runs the world away.
   Would not this, sir, and a forest of feathers—
235   If the rest of my fortunes turn Turk with me—
With two Provincial roses on my raz'd shoes,
Get me a fellowship in a cry of players, sir?
HORATIO   Half a share.
HAMLET   A whole one I!
240   For thou dost know, O Damon dear,
        This realm dismantled was
      Of Jove himself; and now reigns here
        A very, very—pajock.
HORATIO   You might have rhym'd.
245   HAMLET   O good Horatio, I'll take the ghost's word for a thousand pound! Didst perceive?
HORATIO   Very well, my lord.
HAMLET   Upon the talk of the poisoning?
HORATIO   I did very well note him.
HAMLET   Aha! Come, some music! Come, the recorders!
250   For if the King like not the comedy,
   Why then, belike he likes it not, perdy.
   Come, some music!

Enter ROSENCRANTZ *and* GUILDENSTERN.

GUILDENSTERN   Good my lord, vouchsafe me a word with you.
HAMLET   Sir, a whole history.
255   GUILDENSTERN   The King, sir—
HAMLET   Ay, sir, what of him?
GUILDENSTERN   Is in his retirement, marvellous distemper'd.
HAMLET   With drink, sir?
GUILDENSTERN   No, my lord; rather with choler.
260   HAMLET   Your wisdom should show itself more richer to signify this to the doctor; for for
me to put him to his purgation would perhaps plunge him into far more choler.
GUILDENSTERN   Good my lord, put your discourse into some frame, and start not so wildly
from my affair.
HAMLET   I am tame, sir; pronounce.
265   GUILDENSTERN   The Queen, your mother, in most great affliction of spirit hath sent me to
you.
HAMLET   You are welcome.

---

[225] *false fire* (only gunpowder, no bullet)   [231] *hart,* male deer   [234] *this . . . forest of feathers*
(the way the foregoing lines were spoken) . . . player's extravagant costume   [235] *turn Turk,* play
false   [243] *pajock,* peacock   [249] *recorders,* musical instruments   [259] *choler,* bile (a bilious attack)

GUILDENSTERN   Nay, good my lord, this courtesy is not of the right breed. If it shall please you to make me a wholesome answer, I will do your mother's commandment; if not,
270   your pardon and my return shall be the end of my business.

HAMLET   Sir, I cannot.

GUILDENSTERN   What, my lord?

HAMLET   Make you a wholesome answer; my wit's diseas'd. But, sir, such answer as I can make, you shall command; or rather, as you say, my mother. Therefore no more, but
275   to the matter! My mother, you say—

ROSENCRANTZ   Then thus she says: your behavior hath struck her into amazement and admiration.

HAMLET   O wonderful son, that can so stonish a mother! But is there no sequel at the heels of this mother's admiration? Impart.

280   ROSENCRANTZ   She desires to speak with you in her closet ere you go to bed.

HAMLET   We shall obey, were she ten times our mother. Have you any further trade with us?

ROSENCRANTZ   My lord, you once did love me.

HAMLET   And do still, by these pickers and stealers!

285   ROSENCRANTZ   Good my lord, what is your cause of distemper? You do surely bar the door upon your own liberty, if you deny your griefs to your friend.

HAMLET   Sir, I lack advancement.

ROSENCRANTZ   How can that be, when you have the voice of the King himself for your succession in Denmark?

290   HAMLET   Aye, sir, but "while the grass grows"— the proverb is something musty.

(Enter the PLAYERS *with recorders.)*

O, the recorders! Let me see one. To withdraw with you—why do you go about to recover the wind of me, as if you would drive me into a toil?

GUILDENSTERN   O my lord, if my duty be too bold, my love is too unmannerly.

HAMLET   I do not well understand that. Will you play upon this pipe?

295   GUILDENSTERN   My lord, I cannot.

HAMLET   I pray you.

GUILDENSTERN   Believe me, I cannot.

HAMLET   I do beseech you.

GUILDENSTERN   I know no touch of it, my lord.

300   HAMLET   It is as easy as lying. Govern these ventages with your fingers and thumbs, give it breath with your mouth, and it will discourse most eloquent music. Look you, these are the stops.

GUILDENSTERN   But these cannot I command to any utt'rance of harmony. I have not the skill.

305   HAMLET   Why, look you now, how unworthy a thing you make of me! You would play upon me; you would seem to know my stops; you would pluck out the heart of my mystery; you would sound me from my lowest note to the top of my compass; and there is much music, excellent voice, in this little organ, yet cannot you make it speak. 'Sblood, do you think I am easier to be play'd on than a pipe? Call me what instrument you
310   will, though you can fret me, you cannot play upon me.

276–277 *amazement and admiration,* bewilderment and wonder   280 *closet,* bedroom
284 *pickers and stealers,* two hands   286 *liberty,* freedom of action   290 *"while the grass grows"*
(the old saw which ends,"the horse starves")   290 *musty,* lacking in frankness   291–292 *go about
to recover the wind of me,* try to discover my purposes   292 *toil,* trap   300 *ventages,* holes, or
stops, in the instrument   310 *fret,* bar of wire or wood to guide fingering (also, a pun)

(*Enter* POLONIUS.)

God bless you, sir!

POLONIUS   My lord, the Queen would speak with you, and presently.

HAMLET   Do you see yonder cloud that's almost in shape of a camel?

POLONIUS   By th' mass, and 'tis like a camel indeed.

315 HAMLET   Methinks it is like a weasel.

POLONIUS   It is back'd like a weasel.

HAMLET   Or like a whale.

POLONIUS   Very like a whale.

HAMLET   Then will I come to my mother by-and-by.—They fool me to the top of my bent.

320   —I will come by-and-by.

POLONIUS   I will say so.   *Exit.*

HAMLET   "By-and-by" is easily said.—Leave me, friends.

(*Exeunt all but* HAMLET.)

'Tis now the very witching time of night,
When churchyards yawn, and hell itself breathes out
325 Contagion to this world. Now could I drink hot blood
And do such bitter business as the day
Would quake to look on. Soft! now to my mother!
O heart, lose not thy nature; let not ever
The soul of Nero enter this firm bosom.
330 Let me be cruel, not unnatural;
I will speak daggers to her, but use none.
My tongue and soul in this be hypocrites—
How in my words somever she be shent,
To give them seals never, my soul, consent!

Scene III. *A Room in the Castle.*

Enter KING, ROSENCRANTZ, *and* GUILDENSTERN.

KING   I like him not, nor stands it safe with us
To let his madness range. Therefore prepare you;
I your commission will forthwith dispatch,
And he to England shall along with you.
5 The terms of our estate may not endure
Hazard so near us as doth hourly grow
Out of his lunacies.

GUILDENSTERN   We will ourselves provide.
Most holy and religious fear it is
To keep those many many bodies safe
10 That live and feed upon your Majesty.

ROSENCRANTZ   The single and peculiar life is bound
With all the strength and armour of the mind
To keep itself from noyance; but much more
That spirit upon whose weal depends and rests
15 The lives of many. The cesse of majesty

---

[319] *by-and-by*, at once   [329] *Nero* (Roman emperor who murdered his mother)   [333] *shent*, cas-
tigated   [3] *dispatch*, prepare   [11] *peculiar*, individual   [13] *noyance*, harm   [15] *cesse*, demise

Dies not alone, but like a gulf doth draw
What's near it with it. It is a massy wheel,
Fix'd on the summit of the highest mount,
To whose huge spokes ten thousand lesser things
20 Are mortis'd and adjoin'd; which when it falls,
Each small annexment, petty consequence,
Attends the boist'rous ruin. Never alone
Did the king sigh, but with a general groan.
KING   Arm you, I pray you, to this speedy voyage;
25 For we will fetters put upon this fear,
Which now goes too free-footed.
BOTH   We will haste us.

Exeunt GENTLEMEN.

Enter POLONIUS.

POLONIUS   My lord, he's going to his mother's closet.
Behind the arras I'll convey myself
To hear the process. I'll warrant she'll tax him home;
30 And, as you said, and wisely was it said,
'Tis meet that some more audience than a mother,
Since nature makes them partial, should o'erhear
The speech, of vantage. Fare you well, my liege.
I'll call upon you ere you go to bed
And tell you what I know.
35 KING   Thanks, dear my lord.

(*Exit* POLONIUS.)

O, my offence is rank, it smells to heaven;
It hath the primal eldest curse upon't,
A brother's murther! Pray can I not,
Though inclination be as sharp as will.
40 My stronger guilt defeats my strong intent,
And, like a man to double business bound,
I stand in pause where I shall first begin,
And both neglect. What if this cursed hand
Were thicker than itself with brother's blood.
45 Is there not rain enough in the sweet heavens
To wash it white as snow? Whereto serves mercy
But to confront the visage of offence?
And what's in prayer but this twofold force,
To be forestalled ere we come to fall,
50 Or pardon'd being down? Then I'll look up;
My fault is past. But, O, what form of prayer
Can serve my turn? "Forgive me my foul murther"?
That cannot be; since I am still possess'd
Of those effects for which I did the murther—

---

[24] *arm you,* make ready   [29] *tax him home,* scold him thoroughly   [37] *primal eldest curse* (curse upon Cain for murdering his brother Abel)

55   My crown, mine own ambition, and my queen.
     May one be pardon'd and retain th' offence?
     In the corrupted currents of this world
     Offence's gilded hand may shove by justice,
     And oft 'tis seen the wicked prize itself
60   Buys out the law; but 'tis not so above.
     There is no shuffling; there the action lies
     In his true nature, and we ourselves compell'd,
     Even to the teeth and forehead of our faults,
     To give in evidence. What then? What rests?
65   Try what repentance can. What can it not?
     Yet what can it when one cannot repent?
     O wretched state! O bosom black as death!
     O limed soul, that, struggling to be free,
     Art more engag'd! Help, angels! Make assay.
70   Bow, stubborn knees; and heart with strings of steel,
     Be soft as sinews of the new-born babe!
     All may be well.   *He kneels.*

                          Enter HAMLET.

     HAMLET   Now might I do it pat, now he is praying;
     And now I'll do't. And so he goes to heaven,
75   And so am I reveng'd. That would be scann'd.
     A villain kills my father; and for that,
     I, his sole son, do this same villain send
     To heaven.
     Why, this is hire and salary, not revenge!
80   He took my father grossly, full of bread,
     With all his crimes broad blown, as flush as May;
     And how his audit stands, who knows save heaven?
     But in our circumstances and course of thought,
     'Tis heavy with him; and am I then reveng'd,
85   To take him in the purging of his soul,
     When he is fit and season'd for his passage?
     No.
     Up, sword, and know thou a more horrid hent.
     When he is drunk asleep; or in his rage;
90   Or in th' incestuous pleasure of his bed;
     At gaming, swearing, or about some act
     That has no relish of salvation in't—
     Then trip him, that his heels may kick at heaven,
     And that his soul may be as damn'd and black
95   As hell, whereto it goes. My mother stays.
     This physic but prolongs thy sickly days.

                             Exit.

---

[73] *pat,* easily   [75] *scann'd,* examined (thought about)   [80] *full of bread,* filled with earthly satisfactions   [82] *his audit,* judgment of him   [83] *our circumstance,* our restricted, human point of view   [88] *hent,* moment   [96] *physic,* purgation (temporarily getting rid of the decision to kill Claudius)

KING *(Rises)*   My words fly up, my thoughts remain below.
  Words without thoughts never to heaven go.

Exit.

Scene IV. *The* QUEEN's *Closet.*

Enter QUEEN *and* POLONIUS.

POLONIUS   He will come straight. Look you lay home to him.
  Tell him his pranks have been too broad to bear with,
  And that your Grace hath screen'd and stood between
  Much heat and him. I'll silence me even here.
5   Pray you be round with him.
HAMLET *(Within)*   Mother, mother, mother!
QUEEN   I'll warrant you; fear me not. Withdraw; I hear him coming.

POLONIUS *hides behind the arras.*

Enter HAMLET.

HAMLET   Now, mother, what's the matter?
QUEEN   Hamlet, thou hast thy father much offended.
10 HAMLET   Mother, you have my father much offended.
QUEEN   Come, come, you answer with an idle tongue.
HAMLET   Go, go, you question with a wicked tongue.
QUEEN   Why, how now, Hamlet?
HAMLET   What's the matter now?
QUEEN   Have you forgot me?
HAMLET   No, by the rood, not so!
15   You are the Queen, your husband's brother's wife,
  And (would it were not so!) you are my mother.
QUEEN   Nay, then I'll set those to you that can speak.
HAMLET   Come, come, and sit you down. You shall not budge!
  You go not till I set you up a glass
20   Where you may see the inmost part of you.
QUEEN   What wilt thou do? Thou wilt not murther me?
  Help, help, ho!
POLONIUS *(Behind)*   What, ho! help, help, help!
HAMLET *(Draws)*   How now? a rat? Dead for a ducat, dead!

Makes a pass through the arras and kills POLONIUS.

POLONIUS *(Behind)*   O, I am slain!
25 QUEEN   O me, what hast thou done?
HAMLET   Nay, I know not. Is it the King?
QUEEN   O, what a rash and bloody deed is this!
HAMLET   A bloody deed—almost as bad, good mother,
  As kill a king, and marry with his brother.
QUEEN   As kill a king?
30 HAMLET   Ay, lady, it was my word.

---

² *broad,* free-wheeling   ¹⁷*those* (a threat stating that if Hamlet will not listen to his mother, others
with greater power will handle him)

(*Lifts up the arras and sees* POLONIUS)

Thou wretched, rash, intruding fool, farewell!
I took thee for thy better. Take thy fortune.
Thou find'st to be too busy is some danger.
Leave wringing of your hands. Peace! sit you down
35 And let me wring your heart; for so I shall
If it be made of penetrable stuff;
If damned custom have not braz'd it so
That it is proof and bulwark against sense.
QUEEN   What have I done that thou dar'st wag thy tongue
In noise so rude against me?
40 HAMLET   Such an act
That blurs the grace and blush of modesty;
Calls virtue hypocrite; takes off the rose
From the fair forehead of an innocent love,
And sets a blister there; makes marriage vows
45 As false as dicers' oaths. O, such a deed
As from the body of contraction plucks
The very soul, and sweet religion makes
A rhapsody of words! Heaven's face doth glow;
Yea, this solidity and compound mass,
50 With tristful visage; as against the doom,
Is thought-sick at the act.
QUEEN   Ay me, what act,
That roars so loud and thunders in the index?
HAMLET   Look here upon this picture, and on this,
The counterfeit presentment of two brothers.
55 See what a grace was seated on this brow;
Hyperion's curls; the front of Jove himself;
An eye like Mars, to threaten and command;
A station like the herald Mercury
New lighted on a heaven-kissing hill:
60 A combination and a form indeed
Where every god did seem to set his seal
To give the world assurance of a man.
This was your husband. Look you now what follows.
Here is your husband, like a mildew'd ear
65 Blasting his wholesome brother. Have you eyes?
Could you on this fair mountain leave to feed,
And batten on this moor? Ha! have you eyes?
You cannot call it love; for at your age
The heydey in the blood is tame, it's humble,
70 And waits upon the judgment; and what judgment
Would step from this to this? Sense sure you have,
Else could you not have motion; but sure that sense

---

³³ *too busy,* too much a busybody   ⁴⁰ *Such an act,* hasty marriage (Some scholars say the act is adultery, but it is doubtful that the Ghost will be protective of Gertrude if he thought she had had an affair with Claudius.)   ⁴⁴ *blister,* brand   ⁴⁶ *contraction,* marriage vows   ⁴⁸ *glow,* blush with shame   ⁵² *index,* table of contents   ⁵⁸ *station,* posture   ⁶⁷ *batten,* gorge

Is apoplex'd; for madness would not err,
Nor sense to ecstasy was ne'er so thrall'd
75 But it reserv'd some quantity of choice
To serve in such a difference. What devil was't
That thus hath cozen'd you at hoodman-blind?
Eyes without feeling, feeling without sight,
Ears without hands or eyes, smelling sans all,
80 Or but a sickly part of one true sense
Could not so mope.
O shame! where is thy blush? Rebellious hell,
If thou canst mutine in a matron's bones,
To flaming youth let virtue be as wax
85 And melt in her own fire. Proclaim no shame
When the compulsive ardour gives the charge,
Since frost itself as actively doth burn,
And reason panders will.
QUEEN   O Hamlet, speak no more!
Thou turn'st mine eyes into my very soul,
90 And there I see such black and grained spots
As will not leave their tinct.
HAMLET   Nay, but to live
In the rank sweat of an enseamed bed,
Stew'd in corruption, honeying and making love
Over the nasty sty!
QUEEN   O, speak to me no more!
95 These words like daggers enter in mine ears.
No more, sweet Hamlet!
HAMLET   A murtherer and villain!
A slave that is not twentieth part the tithe
Of your precedent lord; a vice of kings;
A cutpurse of the empire and the rule,
100 That from a shelf the precious diadem stole
And put it in his pocket!
QUEEN   No more!

Enter the GHOST *in his nightgown.*

HAMLET   A king of shreds and patches!—
Save me and hover o'er me with your wings,
You heavenly guards! What would your gracious figure?
105 QUEEN   Alas, he's mad!
HAMLET   Do you not come your tardy son to chide,
That, laps'd in time and passion, lets go by
Th' important acting of your dread command?
O, say!
110 GHOST   Do not forget. This visitation
Is but to whet thy almost blunted purpose.
But look, amazement on thy mother sits.

---

[74] *ecstasy,* madness   [77] *cozen'd,* fooled   [79] *sans,* without   [81] *so mope,* be so insensitive
[88] *reason panders will,* reason becomes a slave to ardor   [92] *enseamed,* greasy   [102] *shreds and patches,* disreputable appearance (figurative)

O, step between her and her fighting soul!
Conceit in weakest bodies strongest works.
Speak to her, Hamlet.
115 HAMLET   How is it with you, lady?
QUEEN   Alas, how is't with you,
    That you do bend your eye on vacancy,
    And with th' incorporal air do hold discourse?
    Forth at your eyes your spirits wildly peep;
120   And, as the sleeping soldiers in th' alarm,
    Your bedded hairs, like life in excrements,
    Start up and stand on end. O gentle son,
    Upon the heat and flame of thy distemper
    Sprinkle cool patience! Whereon do you look?
125 HAMLET   On him, on him! Look you how pale he glares!
    His form and cause conjoin'd, preaching to stones,
    Would make them capable.—Do not look upon me,
    Lest with this piteous action you convert
    My stern effects. Then what I have to do
130   Will want true colour—tears perchance for blood.
QUEEN   To whom do you speak this?
HAMLET   Do you see nothing there?
QUEEN   Nothing at all; yet all that is I see.
HAMLET   Nor did you nothing hear?
QUEEN   No, nothing but ourselves.
HAMLET   Why, look you there! Look how it steals away!
135   My father, in his habit as he liv'd!
    Look where he goes even now out at the portal!

                    Exit GHOST.

QUEEN   This is the very coinage of your brain.
    This bodiless creation ecstasy
    Is very cunning in.
HAMLET   Ecstasy?
140   My pulse as yours doth temperately keep time
    And makes as healthful music. It is not madness
    That I have utt'red. Bring me to the test,
    And I the matter will reword; which madness
    Would gambol from. Mother, for love of grace,
145   Lay not that flattering unction to your soul,
    That not your trespass but my madness speaks.
    It will but skin and film the ulcerous place,
    Whiles rank corruption, mining all within,
    Infects unseen. Confess yourself to heaven;
150   Repent what's past; avoid what is to come;
    And do not spread the compost on the weeds
    To make them ranker. Forgive me this my virtue;
    For in the fatness of these pursy times
    Virtue itself of vice must pardon beg—

---

[121] *bedded,* groomed; *excrements,* outgrowths   [144] *gambol from,* skip away from   [153] *pursy,* over-fat

155   Yea, curb and woo for leave to do him good.
        QUEEN   O Hamlet, thou hast cleft my heart in twain.
        HAMLET   O, throw away the worser part of it,
           And live the purer with the other half.
           Good night—but go not to my uncle's bed.
160   Assume a virtue, if you have it not.
           That monster, custom, who all sense doth eat
           Of habits evil, is angel yet in this,
           That to the use of actions fair and good
           He likewise gives a frock or livery,
165   That aptly is put on. Refrain to-night,
           And that shall lend a kind of easiness
           To the next abstinence; the next more easy;
           For use almost can change the stamp of nature,
           And either [master] the devil, or throw him out
170   With wondrous potency. Once more, good night;
           And when you are desirous to be blest,
           I'll blessing beg of you.—For this same lord,
           I do repent; but heaven hath pleas'd it so,
           To punish me with this, and this with me,
175   That I must be their scourge and minister.
           I will bestow him, and will answer well
           The death I gave him. So again, good night.
           I must be cruel, only to be kind;
           Thus bad begins, and worse remains behind.
           One word more, good lady.
180   QUEEN   What shall I do?
        HAMLET   Not this, by no means, that I bid you do:
           Let the bloat King tempt you again to bed;
           Pinch wanton on your cheek; call you his mouse;
           And let him, for a pair of reechy kisses,
185   Or paddling in your neck with his damn'd fingers,
           Make you to ravel all this matter out,
           That I essentially am not in madness,
           But mad in craft. 'Twere good you let him know;
           For who that's but a queen, fair, sober, wise,
190   Would from a paddock, from a bat, a gib,
           Such dear concernings hide? Who would do so?
           No, in despite of sense and secrecy,
           Unpeg the basket on the house's top,
           Let the birds fly, and like the famous ape,
195   To try conclusions, in the basket creep
           And break your own neck down.
        QUEEN   Be thou assur'd, if words be made of breath,
           And breath of life, I have no life to breathe
           What thou hast said to me.
        HAMLET   I must to England; you know that?

---

[172] *this same lord,* Polonius   [179] *worse remains behind* (murder of Claudius is yet to come)
[182] *bloat,* swollen with drink   [184] *reechy,* slobbery

200 QUEEN   Alack,
    I had forgot! 'Tis so concluded on.
  HAMLET   There's letters seal'd; and my two schoolfellows,
    Whom I will trust as I will adders fang'd,
    They bear the mandate; they must sweep my way
205   And marshal me to knavery. Let it work;
    For 'tis the sport to have the enginer
    Hoist with his own petar; and 't shall go hard
    But I will delve one yard below their mines
    And blow them at the moon. O, 'tis most sweet
210   When in one line two crafts directly meet.
    This man shall set me packing.
    I'll lug the guts into the neighbour room.—
    Mother, good night.—Indeed, this counsellor
    Is now most still, most secret, and most grave,
215   Who was in life a foolish prating knave.
    Come, sir, to draw toward an end with you.
    Good night, mother.

            Exit the QUEEN. *Then exit* HAMLET, *tugging in* POLONIUS.

ACT IV

Scene I. *Elsinore. A Room in the Castle*

Enter KING *and* QUEEN, *with* ROSENCRANTZ *and* GUILDENSTERN.

  KING   There's matter in these sighs. These profound heaves
    You must translate; 'tis fit we understand them.
    Where is your son?
  QUEEN   Bestow this place on us a little while.

          (*Exeunt* ROSENCRANTZ *and* GUILDENSTERN.)

5   Ah, mine own lord, what have I seen tonight!
  KING   What, Gertrude? How does Hamlet?
  QUEEN   Mad as the sea and wind when both contend
    Which is the mightier. In his lawless fit,
    Behind the arras hearing something stir,
10   Whips out his rapier, cries "A rat, a rat!"
    And in this brainish apprehension kills
    The unseen good old man.
  KING   O heavy deed!
    It had been so with us, had we been there.
    His liberty is full of threats to all—
15   To you yourself, to us, to every one.
    Alas, how shall this bloody deed be answer'd?
    It will be laid to us, whose providence
    Should have kept short, restrain'd, and out of haunt

---

[207] *Hoist with his own petar,* blown up with his own bomb   [11] *brainish apprehension,* demented
notion   [18] *out of haunt,* away from others

This mad young man. But so much was our love
20 We would not understand what was most fit,
But, like the owner of a foul disease,
To keep it from divulging, let it feed
Even on the pith of life. Where is he gone?
QUEEN To draw apart the body he hath kill'd;
25 O'er whom his very madness, like some ore
Among a mineral of metals base,
Shows itself pure. He weeps for what is done.
KING O Gertrude, come away!
The sun no sooner shall the mountains touch
30 But we will ship him hence; and this vile deed
We must with all our majesty and skill
Both countenance and excuse. Ho, Guildenstern!

(*Enter* ROSENCRANTZ *and* GUILDENSTERN.)

Friends both, go join you with some further aid.
Hamlet in madness hath Polonius slain,
35 And from his mother's closet hath he dragg'd him.
Go seek him out; speak fair, and bring the body
Into the chapel. I pray you haste in this.

(*Exeunt* ROSENCRANTZ *and* GUILDENSTERN.)

Come, Gertrude, we'll call up our wisest friends
And let them know both what we mean to do
40 And what's untimely done. (So haply slander—)
Whose whisper o'er the world's diameter,
As level as the cannon to his blank,
Transports his pois'ned shot—may miss our name
And hit the woundless air.—O, come away!
45 My soul is full of discord and dismay.

Exeunt.

Scene II. *Elsinore. A Passage in the Castle.*

Enter HAMLET.

HAMLET Safely stow'd.
GENTLEMEN *(Within)* Hamlet! Lord Hamlet!
HAMLET But soft! What noise? Who calls on Hamlet? O, here they come.

Enter ROSENCRANTZ *and* GUILDENSTERN.

ROSENCRANTZ What have you done, my lord, with the dead body?
5 HAMLET Compounded it with dust, whereto 'tis kin.
ROSENCRANTZ Tell us where 'tis, that we may take it thence
And bear it to the chapel.
HAMLET Do not believe it.
ROSENCRANTZ Believe what?

[25] *ore,* precious metal [42] *level,* accurate aim; *blank,* target.

10 HAMLET That I can keep your counsel, and not mine own. Besides, to be demanded of a
sponge, what replication should be made by the son of a king?

ROSENCRANTZ Take you me for a sponge, my lord?

HAMLET Ay, sir; that soaks up the King's countenance, his rewards, his authorities. But such
officers do the King best service in the end. He keeps them, like an ape, in the corner
15 of his jaw; first mouth'd, to be last swallowed. When he needs what you have glean'd,
it is but squeezing you and, sponge, you shall be dry again.

ROSENCRANTZ I understand you not, my lord.

HAMLET I am glad of it. A knavish speech sleeps in a foolish ear.

ROSENCRANTZ My lord, you must tell us where the body is and go with us to the King.

20 HAMLET The body is with the King, but the King is not with the body. The King is a thing—

GUILDENSTERN A thing, my lord?

HAMLET Of nothing. Bring me to him. Hide fox, and all after.

Exeunt.

Scene III. *Elsinore. A Room in the Castle.*

Enter KING.

KING I have sent to seek him and to find the body.
How dangerous is it that this man goes loose!
Yet must not we put the strong law on him.
He's lov'd of the distracted multitude,
5 Who like not in their judgment, but their eyes;
And where 'tis so, th' offender's scourge is weigh'd,
But never the offence. To bear all smooth and even,
This sudden sending him away must seem
Deliberate pause. Diseases desperate grown
10 By desperate appliance are reliev'd,
Or not at all.

(*Enter* ROSENCRANTZ.)

How now? What hath befall'n?

ROSENCRANTZ Where the dead body is bestow'd, my lord,
We cannot get from him.

KING   But where is he?

ROSENCRANTZ Without, my lord; guarded, to know your pleasure.

15 KING Bring him before us.

ROSENCRANTZ Ho, Guildenstern! Bring in my lord.

Enter HAMLET *and* GUILDENSTERN *with* ATTENDANTS.

KING Now, Hamlet, where's Polonius?

HAMLET At supper.

KING At supper? Where?

20 HAMLET Not where he eats, but where he is eaten. A certain convocation of politic worms
are e'en at him. Your worm is your only emperor for diet. We fat all creatures else to

---

[10] *counsel,* secrets   [11] *replication,* formal reply   [22] *Hide fox* (reference to the child's game,
hounds and the fox, with Hamlet pretending to be the fox)   [4] *distracted,* fooled   [7] *bear,* manage   [9] *deliberate pause,* the result of thoughtful deliberation

fat us, and we fat ourselves for maggots. Your fat king and your lean beggar is but variable service—two dishes, but to one table. That's the end.

KING Alas, alas!

25 HAMLET A man may fish with the worm that hath eat of a king, and eat of the fish that hath fed of that worm.

KING What dost thou mean by this?

HAMLET Nothing but to show you how a king may go a progress through the guts of a beggar.

30 KING Where is Polonius?

HAMLET In heaven. Send thither to see. If your messenger find him not there, seek him i' th' other place yourself. But indeed, if you find him not within this month, you shall nose him as you go up the stairs into the lobby.

KING Go seek him there. (*To* ATTENDANTS.)

35 HAMLET He will stay till you come.

Exeunt ATTENDANTS.

KING Hamlet, this deed, for thine especial safety,—
Which we do tender as we dearly grieve
For that which thou hast done,—must send thee hence
With fiery quickness. Therefore, prepare thyself.
40 The bark is ready and the wind at help,
Th' associates tend, and everything is bent
For England.

HAMLET For England?

KING Ay, Hamlet.

HAMLET Good.

KING So is it, if thou knew'st our purposes.

HAMLET I see a cherub that sees them. But come, for England! Farewell, dear mother.

45 KING Thy loving father, Hamlet.

HAMLET My mother! Father and mother is man and wife; man and wife is one flesh; and so, my mother. Come, for England! *Exit.*

KING Follow him at foot; tempt him with speed aboard.
Delay it not; I'll have him hence to-night.
50 Away! for everything is seal'd and done
That else leans on th' affair. Pray you make haste.

(*Exeunt* ROSENCRANTZ *and* GUILDENSTERN.)

And, England, if my love thou hold'st at aught,—
As my great power thereof may give thee sense,
Since yet thy cicatrice looks raw and red
55 After the Danish sword, and thy free awe
Pays homage to us,—thou mayst not coldly set
Our sovereign process, which imports at full,
By letters congruing to that effect,
The present death of Hamlet. Do it, England;
60 For like the hectic in my blood he rages,

---

[28] *a progress,* royal visits to estates of noblemen   [44] *I see a cherub,* I see as a cherub (every-thing)   [48] *tempt him,* coax him   [51] *leans on,* pertains to   [56] *coldly set,* be indifferent to   [58] *congruing,* informing   [60] *the hectic,* constant fever

And thou must cure me. Till I know 'tis done,
Howe'er my haps, my joys were ne'er begun.

Exit.

Scene IV. *Near Elsinore.*

Enter FORTINBRAS *with his* ARMY *over the stage.*

FORTINBRAS   Go, Captain, from me greet the Danish king.
Tell him that by his license Fortinbras
Craves the conveyance of a promis'd march
Over his kingdom. You know the rendezvous.
5   If that his Majesty would aught with us,
We shall express our duty in his eye;
And let him know so.
CAPTAIN   I will do't, my lord.
FORTINBRAS   Go softly on.

Exeunt all but the CAPTAIN.

Enter HAMLET, ROSENCRANTZ, GUILDENSTERN, *and others.*

HAMLET   Good sir, whose powers are these?
10   CAPTAIN   They are of Norway, sir.
HAMLET   How purpos'd, sir, I pray you?
CAPTAIN   Against some part of Poland
HAMLET   Who commands them, sir?
CAPTAIN   The nephew to old Norway, Fortinbras.
15   HAMLET   Goes it against the main of Poland, sir,
Or for some frontier?
CAPTAIN   Truly to speak, and with no addition,
We go to gain a little patch of ground
That hath in it no profit but the name.
20   To pay five ducats, five, I would not farm it;
Nor will it yield to Norway or the Pole
A ranker rate, should it be sold in fee.
HAMLET   Why, then the Polack never will defend it.
CAPTAIN   Yes, it is already garrison'd.
25   HAMLET   Two thousand souls and twenty thousand ducats
Will not debate the question of this straw.
This is th' imposthume of much wealth and peace,
That inward breaks, and shows no cause without
Why the man dies.—I humbly thank you, sir.
30   CAPTAIN   God b' wi' you, sir.   *Exit.*
ROSENCRANTZ   Will't please you go, my lord?
HAMLET   I'll be with you straight. Go a little before.

(Exeunt all but HAMLET.)

How all occasions do inform against me

---

[62] *haps,* fortune (what happens to me)   [3] *conveyance,* escort   [8] *softly,* quietly   [22] *a ranker rate,* a higher return   [27] *imposthume,* ulcer (hidden within but damaging)

And spur my dull revenge! What is a man,
35   If his chief good and market of his time
Be but to sleep and feed? A beast, no more.
Sure he that made us with such large discourse,
Looking before and after, gave us not
That capability and godlike reason
40   To fust in us unus'd. Now, whether it be
Bestial oblivion, or some craven scruple
Of thinking too precisely on th' event,—
A thought which, quarter'd, hath but one part wisdom
And ever three parts coward,—I do not know
45   Why yet I live to say "This thing's to do,"
Sith I have cause, and will, and strength, and means
To do't. Examples gross as earth exhort me.
Witness this army of such mass and charge,
Led by a delicate and tender prince,
50   Whose spirit, with divine ambition puff'd,
Makes mouths at the invisible event,
Exposing what is mortal and unsure
To all that fortune, death, and danger dare,
Even for an eggshell. Rightly to be great
55   Is not to stir without great argument,
But greatly to find quarrel in a straw
When honour's at the stake. How stand I then,
That have a father kill'd, a mother stain'd,
Excitements of my reason and my blood,
60   And let all sleep, while to my shame I see
The imminent death of twenty thousand men
That for a fantasy and trick of fame
Go to their graves like beds, fight for a plot
Whereon the numbers cannot try the cause,
65   Which is not tomb enough and continent
To hide the slain? O, from this time forth,
My thoughts be bloody, or be nothing worth!

Exit.

Scene V. *Elsinore. A Room in the Castle.*

Enter HORATIO, QUEEN, *and a* GENTLEMAN.

QUEEN   I will not speak with her.
GENTLEMAN   She is importunate, indeed distract.
Her mood will needs be pitied.
QUEEN   What would she have?
GENTLEMAN   She speaks much of her father; says she hears
5   There's tricks i' th' world, and hems, and beats her heart;
Spurns enviously at straws; speaks things in doubt,

---

[35] *market of his time,* wager for his time   [40] *fust,* become moldy   [62] *a fantasy,* fanciful imagining   [65] *continent,* able to contain   [6] *spurns enviously at straws,* takes offense over small things

That carry but half sense. Her speech is nothing,
Yet the unshaped use of it doth move
The hearers to collection; they aim at it,
10   And botch the words up fit to their own thoughts;
Which, as her winks and nods and gestures yield them,
Indeed would make one think there might be thought,
Though nothing sure, yet much unhappily.
HORATIO   'Twere good she were spoken with; for she may strew
15   Dangerous conjectures in ill-breeding minds.
QUEEN   Let her come in.

                  (*Exit* GENTLEMAN.)

(*Aside*) To my sick soul (as sin's true nature is)
Each toy seems prologue to some great amiss.
So full of artless jealousy is guilt
20   It spills itself in fearing to be spilt.

              Enter OPHELIA *distracted*.

OPHELIA   Where is the beauteous Majesty of Denmark?
QUEEN   How now, Ophelia?
OPHELIA (*Sings*)   How should I your true-love know
      From another one?
25   By his cockle hat and staff
      And his sandal shoon.
QUEEN   Alas, sweet lady, what imports this song?
OPHELIA   Say you? Nay, pray you mark.
(*Sings*)   He is dead and gone, lady,
30   He is dead and gone;
      At his head a grass-green turf,
      At his heels a stone.
    O, ho!
QUEEN   Nay, but Ophelia—
35 OPHELIA   Pray you mark.
(*Sings*)   White his shroud as the mountain snow—

                  Enter KING.

QUEEN   Alas, look here, my lord!
OPHELIA   (*Sings*) Larded all with sweet flowers;
      Which bewept to the grave did not go
40   With true-love showers.
KING   How do you, pretty lady?
OPHELIA   Well, God dild you! They say the owl was a baker's daughter. Lord, we know
    what we are, but know not what we may be. God be at your table!
KING   Conceit upon her father.
45 OPHELIA   Pray let's have no words of this; but when they ask you what it means, say you
this:
(*Sings*)   To-morrow is Saint Valentine's day

---

[9] *collection*, combined interpretations (of Ophelia's ravings)   [15] *ill-breeding*, evilly imagining
[42] *God dild you*, God be good to you   [44] *Conceit upon*, suggested by thoughts of her father

All in the morning betime,
And I a maid at your window,
50   To be your Valentine.
Then up he rose and donn'd his clo'es
And dupp'd the chamber door,
Let in the maid, that out a maid
Never departed more.
55 KING Pretty Ophelia!
OPHELIA Indeed, la, without an oath, I'll make an end on't!
(Sings) By Gis and by Saint Charity,
        Alack, and fie for shame!
Young men will do't if they come to't.
60   By Cock, they are to blame.
Quoth she, "Before you tumbled me,
    You promis'd me to wed."
He answers:
    "So would I 'a' done, by yonder sun,
65   An thou hadst not come to my bed."
KING How long hath she been thus?
OPHELIA I hope all will be well. We must be patient; but I cannot choose but weep to
    think they would lay him i' th' cold ground. My brother shall know of it; and so I
    thank you for your good counsel. Come, my coach! Good night, ladies. Good night,
70   sweet ladies. Good night, good night.   *Exit.*
KING Follow her close; give her good watch, I pray you.

(*Exit* HORATIO.)

O, this is the poison of deep grief; it springs
All from her father's death. O Gertrude, Gertrude,
When sorrows come, they come not single spies,
75 But in battalions! First, her father slain;
Next, your son gone, and he most violent author
Of his own just remove; the people muddied,
Thick and unwholesome in their thoughts and whispers
For good Polonius' death, and we have done but greenly
80 In hugger-mugger to inter him; poor Ophelia
Divided from herself and her fair judgment,
Without the which we are pictures or mere beasts;
Last, and as much containing as all these,
Her brother is in secret come from France;
85 Feeds on his wonder, keeps himself in clouds,
And wants not buzzers to infect his ear
With pestilent speeches of his father's death,
Wherein necessity, of matter beggar'd,
Will nothing stick our person to arraign
90 In ear and ear. O my dear Gertrude, this,

---

[52] *dupp'd,* opened   [57] *By Gis,* by Jesus   [60] *by Cock,* by God   [61] *tumbled,* had intercourse
with   [77] *muddied,* muddled   [79] *greenly,* too innocently   [80] *in hugger-mugger,* without respectful (proper) ceremony   [85] *wonder,* speculation (without action)   [86] *buzzers,* irresponsible gossipers   [89] *stick,* hesitate

Like to a murd'ring piece, in many places
Gives me superfluous death.

A noise within.

QUEEN   Alack, what noise is this?
KING   Where are my Switzers? Let them guard the door.

(*Enter a* MESSENGER.)

What is the matter?
MESSENGER   Save yourself, my lord:
95   The ocean, overpeering of his list,
Eats not the flats with more impetuous haste
Than young Laertes, in a riotous head,
O'erbears your officers. The rabble call him lord;
And, as the world were now but to begin,
100   Antiquity forgot, custom not known,
The ratifiers and props of every word,
They cry "Choose we! Laertes shall be king!"
Caps, hands, and tongues applaud it to the clouds,
"Laertes shall be king! Laertes king!"

A noise within.

105   QUEEN   How cheerfully on the false trail they cry!
O, this is counter, you false Danish dogs!
KING   The doors are broke.

Enter LAERTES *with others.*

LAERTES   Where is this king?—Sirs, stand you all without.
ALL   No, let's come in!
110   LAERTES   I pray you give me leave.
ALL   We will, we will!
LAERTES   I thank you. Keep the door. (*Exeunt his Followers.*) O thou vile king,
Give me my father!
QUEEN   Calmly, good Laertes.
LAERTES   That drop of blood that's calm proclaims me bastard;
115   Cries cuckold to my father; brands the harlot
Even here between the chaste unsmirched brows
Of my true mother.
KING   What is the cause, Laertes,
That thy rebellion looks so giantlike?
Let him go, Gertrude. Do not fear our person.
120   There's such divinity doth hedge a king
That treason can but peep to what it would,
Acts little of his will. Tell me, Laertes,
Why thou art thus incens'd. Let him go, Gertrude.

---

[93] *Switzers,* Swiss guards   [95] *overpeering of his list,* surging over its high-water mark   [101] *the ratifiers and props* (antiquity and custom should determine who should be king, but the rabble ignore old customs)   [106] *counter,* opposite (to the true scent)   [121] *peep to,* look from afar

Speak, man.

LAERTES   Where is my father?

KING   Dead.

125 QUEEN   But not by him!

KING   Let him demand his fill.

LAERTES   How came he dead? I'll not be juggled with:
To hell, allegiance! vows, to the blackest devil!
Conscience and grace, to the profoundest pit!

130 I dare damnation. To this point I stand,
That both the worlds I give to negligence,
Let come what comes; only I'll be reveng'd
Most throughly for my father.

KING   Who shall stay you?

LAERTES   My will, not all the world!

135 And for my means, I'll husband them so well
They shall go far with little.

KING   Good Laertes,
If you desire to know the certainty
Of your dear father's death, is't writ in your revenge
That swoopstake you will draw both friend and foe,

140 Winner and loser?

LAERTES   None but his enemies.

KING   Will you know them then?

LAERTES   To his good friends thus wide I'll ope my arms
And, like the kind life-rend'ring pelican,
Repast them with my blood.

KING   Why, now you speak

145 Like a good child and a true gentleman.
That I am guiltless of your father's death,
And am most sensibly in grief for it,
It shall as level to your judgment pierce
As day does to your eye.
(A noise within)   "Let her come in."

150 LAERTES   How, now? What noise is that?

(Enter OPHELIA.*)*

O heat, dry up my brains! Tears seven times salt
Burn out the sense and virtue of mine eye!
By heaven, thy madness shall be paid by weight
Till our scale turn the beam. O rose of May!

155 Dear maid, kind sister, sweet Ophelia!
O heavens! is't possible a young maid's wits
Should be as mortal as an old man's life?
Nature is fine in love, and where 'tis fine,
It sends some precious instance of itself

160 After the thing it loves.

OPHELIA *(Sings)*

---

[139] *swoopstake,* in one fell swoop   [148] *as level to your judgment pierce,* aim so accurately as to
convince without question

They bore him barefac'd on the bier
    (Hey non nony, nony, hey nony)
And in his grave rain'd many a tear.
Fare you well, my dove!

165 LAERTES   Hadst thou thy wits, and didst persuade revenge
It could not move thus.

OPHELIA   You must sing "A-down a-down, and you call him a-down-a." O, how the wheel becomes it! It is the false steward, that stole his master's daughter.

LAERTES   This nothing's more than matter.

170 OPHELIA   There's rosemary, that's for remembrance. Pray you, love, remember. And there is pansies, that's for thoughts.

LAERTES   A document in madness! Thoughts and remembrance fitted.

OPHELIA   There's fennel for you, and columbines. There's rue for you, and here's some for me. We may call it herb of grace o' Sundays. O, you must wear your rue with a

175 difference! There's a daisy. I would give you some violets, but they wither'd all when my father died. They say he made a good end.

(Sings) For bonny sweet Robin is all my joy.

LAERTES   Thought and affliction, passion, hell itself,
   She turns to favour and to prettiness.

OPHELIA *(Sings)*

180   And will he not come again?
     And will he not come again?
       No, no, he is dead;
       Go to thy deathbed;
     He never will come again.

185   His beard was as white as snow,
     All flaxen was his poll.
       He is gone, he is gone,
       And we cast away moan.
     God 'a' mercy on his soul!

190   And of all Christian souls, I pray God. God b' wi' you.   *Exit.*

LAERTES   Do you see this, O God?

KING   Laertes, I must commune with your grief,
   Or you deny me right. Go but apart,
   Make choice of whom your wisest friends you will,

195   And they shall hear and judge 'twixt you and me.
   If by direct or by collateral hand
   They find us touch'd, we will our kingdom give,
   Our crown, our life, and all that we call ours,
   To you in satisfaction; but if not,

200   Be you content to lend your patience to us,
   And we shall jointly labour with your soul
   To give it due content.

LAERTES   Let this be so.
   His means of death, his obscure funeral—

---

[167] *wheel,* spinning wheel (rhythmic in accompanying the singing of ballads)   [169] *this nothing's more than matter,* this meaninglessness carries more effect than sane speech would.   [173] *fennel* (represents deceit)   [174] *rue* (represents sadness, or ruefulness)

No trophy, sword, nor hatchment o'er his bones,
205   No noble rite nor formal ostenation,—
Cry to be heard, as 'twere from heaven to earth,
That I must call't in question.
KING   So you shall;
And where th' offence is let the great axe fall.
I pray you go with me.

                              Exeunt.

Scene VI. *Elsinore. Another Room in the Castle.*

               Enter HORATIO *and an* ATTENDANT.

HORATIO   What are they that would speak with me?
SERVANT   Seafaring men, sir. They say they have letters for you.
HORATIO   Let them come in.

                     (*Exit* ATTENDANT)

I do not know from what part of the world
5   I should be greeted, if not from Lord Hamlet.

                   (*Enter* SAILORS.)

SAILOR   God bless you, sir.
HORATIO   Let him bless thee too.
SAILOR   'A shall, sir, an't please him. There's a letter for you, sir,—it comes from th' ambas-
sador that was bound for England—if your name be Horatio, as I am let to know it is.

10   HORATIO *(Reads the letter)*   "Horatio, when thou shalt have overlook'd this, give these fellows some means to the King. They have letters for him. Ere we were two days old at
sea, a pirate of very warlike appointment gave us chase. Finding ourselves too slow
of sail, we put on a compelled valour, and in the grapple I boarded them. On the
instant they got clear of our ship; so I alone became their prisoner. They have dealt
15   with me like thieves of mercy; but they knew what they did: I am to do a good turn
for them. Let the King have the letters I have sent, and repair thou to me with as
much speed as thou wouldest fly death. I have words to speak in thine ear will make
thee dumb; yet are they much too light for the bore of the matter. These good fellows
will bring thee where I am. Rosencrantz and Guildenstern hold their course for En-
20   gland. Of them I have much to tell thee. Farewell.
     "He that thou knowest thine, HAMLET."

Come, I will give you way for these your letters,
And do't the speedier that you may direct me
To him from whom you brought them.

                              Exeunt.

Scene VII. *Elsinore. Another Room in the Castle.*

                 Enter KING *and* LAERTES.

KING   Now must your conscience my acquittance seal,
And you must put me in your heart for friend,

---

[204] *hatchment,* gravestone   [208] *the great axe,* vengeance

Sith you have heard, and with a knowing ear,
That he which hath your noble father slain
Pursued my life.
5 LAERTES   It well appears. But tell me
Why you proceeded not against these feats
So crimeful and so capital in nature,
As by your safety, wisdom, all things else,
You mainly were stirr'd up.
   KING   O, for two special reasons,
10 Which may to you, perhaps, seem much unsinew'd,
But yet to me they are strong. The Queen his mother
Lives almost by his looks; and for myself,—
My virtue or my plague, be it either which,—
She's so conjunctive to my life and soul
15 That, as the star moves not but in his sphere,
I could not but by her. The other motive
Why to a public count I might not go
Is the great love the general gender bear him,
Who, dipping all his faults in their affection,
20 Would, like the spring that turneth wood to stone,
Convert his gyves to graces; so that my arrows,
Too slightly timber'd for so loud a wind,
Would have reverted to my bow again,
And not where I had aim'd them.
25 LAERTES   And so have I a noble father lost;
A sister driven into desp'rate terms,
Whose worth, if praises may go back again,
Stood challenger on mount of all the age
For her perfections. But my revenge will come.
30 KING   Break not your sleeps for that. You must not think
That we are made of stuff so flat and dull
That we can let our beard be shook with danger,
And think it pastime. You shortly shall hear more.
I lov'd your father, and we love ourself,
35 And that, I hope, will teach you to imagine—

(Enter a MESSENGER *with letters.)*

How now? What news?
MESSENGER   Letters, my lord, from Hamlet:
This to your Majesty; this to the Queen.
KING   From Hamlet? Who brought them?
MESSENGER   Sailors, my lord, they say; I saw them not.
40 They were given me by Claudio; he receiv'd them
Of him that brought them.
   KING   Laertes, you shall hear them.
Leave us.

(Exit MESSENGER.*)*

---

[10] *much unsinew'd,* without strength   [18] *general gender,* ordinary citizens   [21] *gyves,* fetters

(Reads) "High and Mighty,—You shall know I am set naked on your kingdom. To-morrow shall I beg leave to see your kingly eyes; when I shall (first asking your pardon
45   thereunto) recount the occasion of my sudden and more strange return.   "HAMLET."

What should this mean? Are all the rest come back?
Or is it some abuse, and no such thing?
LAERTES   Know you the hand?
KING   'Tis Hamlet's character, "Naked!"
And in a postscript here, he says "alone."
50   Can you advise me?
LAERTES   I am lost in it, my lord. But let him come!
It warms the very sickness in my heart
That I shall live and tell him to his teeth,
"Thus didest thou."
KING   If it be so, Laertes
55   (As how should it be so? how otherwise?),
Will you be rul'd by me?
LAERTES   Ay, my lord,
So you will not o'errule me to a peace.
KING   To thine own peace. If he be now return'd,
As checking at his voyage, and that he means
60   No more to undertake it, I will work him
To an exploit now ripe in my device,
Under the which he shall not choose but fall;
And for his death no wind of blame shall breathe,
But even his mother shall uncharge the practice
And call it accident.
65 LAERTES   My lord, I will be rul'd;
The rather, if you could devise it so
That I might be the organ.
KING   It falls right.
You have been talk'd of since your travel much,
And that in Hamlet's hearing, for a quality
70   Wherein they say you shine. Your sum of parts
Did not together pluck such envy from him
As did that one; and that, in my regard,
Of the unworthiest siege.
LAERTES   What part is that, my lord?
KING   A very riband in the cap of youth—
75   Yet needful too; for youth no less becomes
The light and careless livery that it wears
Than settled age his sables and his weeds,
Importing health and graveness. Two months since
Here was a gentleman of Normandy.
80   I have seen myself, and serv'd against, the French,
And they can well on horseback; but this gallant
Had witchcraft in't. He grew unto his seat,
And to such wondrous doing brought his horse

---

⁴⁷ *abuse,* trick   ⁶⁴ *uncharge the practice,* accept what happens   ⁷³ *siege,* rank

As had he been incorps'd and demi-natur'd
85　With the brave beast. So far he topp'd my thought
That I, in forgery of shapes and tricks,
Come short of what he did.

LAERTES 　　　　　　　　　A Norman was't?

KING　A Norman.

LAERTES　Upon my life, Lamound.

KING 　　　　　　　　　　The very same.

90　LAERTES　I know him well. He is the brooch indeed
And gem of all the nation.

KING　He made confession of you;
And gave you such a masterly report
For art and exercise in your defence,
95　And for your rapier most especially,
That he cried out 'twould be a sight indeed
If one could match you. The scrimers of their nation
He swore had neither motion, guard, nor eye,
If you oppos'd them. Sir, this report of his
100　Did Hamlet so envenom with his envy
That he could nothing do but wish and beg
Your sudden coming o'er to play with you.
Now, out of this—

LAERTES 　　　　　　　What out of this, my lord?

KING　Laertes, was your father dear to you?
105　Or are you like the painting of a sorrow,
A face without a heart?

LAERTES 　　　　　　　　Why ask you this?

KING　Not that I think you did not love your father;
But that I know love is begun by time,
And that I see, in passages of proof,
110　Time qualifies the spark and fire of it.
There lives within the very flame of love
A kind of wick or snuff that will abate it;
And nothing is at a like goodness still;
For goodness, growing to a plurisy,
115　Dies in his own too-much. That we would do,
We should do when we would; for this "would" changes,
And hath abatements and delays as many
As there are tongues, are hands, are accidents;
And then this "should" is like a spendthrift sigh,
120　That hurts by easing. But to the quick o' th' ulcer!
Hamlet comes back. What would you undertake
To show yourself your father's son in deed
More than in words?

LAERTES 　　　　　　　To cut his throat i' th' church!

KING　No place indeed should murther sanctuarize;
125　Revenge should have no bounds. But, good Laertes,

---

⁸⁴ *incorps'd and demi-natur'd,* a part of the horse and thus a kind of half-man, half-horse
⁹⁷ *scrimers,* fencers 　　¹¹⁴ *plurisy,* overabundance

Will you do this? Keep close within your chamber.
Hamlet return'd shall know you are come home.
We'll put on those shall praise your excellence
And set a double varnish on the fame
130   The Frenchman gave you; bring you in fine together
And wager on your heads. He, being remiss
Most generous, and free from all contriving,
Will not peruse the foils; so that with ease,
Or with a little shuffling, you may choose
135   A sword unbated, and, in a pass of practice,
Requite him for your father.
  LAERTES   I will do't!
And for that purpose I'll anoint my sword.
I bought an unction of a mountebank,
So mortal that, but dip a knife in it,
140   Where it draws blood no cataplasm so rare,
Collected from all simples that have virtue
Under the moon, can save the thing from death
This is but scratch'd withal. I'll touch my point
With this contagion, that, if I gall him slightly,
145   It may be death.
      KING   Let's further think of this,
Weigh what convenience both of time and means
May fit us to our shape. If this should fail,
And that our drift look through our bad performance,
'Twere better not assay'd. Therefore this project
150   Should have a back or second, that might hold
If this did blast in proof. Soft! let me see.
We'll make a solemn wager on your cunnings—
I ha't!
When in your motion you are hot and dry—
155   As make your bouts more violent to that end—
And that he calls for drink, I'll have prepar'd him
A chalice for the nonce; whereon but sipping,
If he by chance escape your venom'd stuck,
Our purpose may hold there.—But stay, what noise?

                    (*Enter* QUEEN.)

160   How now, sweet queen?
  QUEEN One woe doth tread upon another's heel,
    So fast they follow. Your sister's drown'd, Laertes.
  LAERTES Drown'd! O, where?
  QUEEN   There is a willow grows aslant a brook,
165   That shows his hoar leaves in the glassy stream.
There with fantastic garlands did she come
Of crowflowers, nettles, daisies, and long purples

---

[131] *remiss,* easygoing   [134] *shuffling,* trickery   [139] *mountebank,* medicine man
[140] *cataplasm,* poultice   [144] *gall,* break the skin   [151] *blast in proof,* blow up when tested
[157] *for the nonce,* for the occasion   [158] *stuck,* thrust   [167] *long purples,* orchids

That liberal shepherds give a grosser name,
But our cold maids do dead men's fingers call them.
170 There on the pendent boughs her coronet weeds
Clamb'ring to hang, an envious sliver broke,
When down her weedy trophies and herself
Fell in the weeping brook. Her clothes spread wide
And, mermaid-like, awhile they bore her up;
175 Which time she chaunted snatches of old tunes,
As one incapable of her own distress,
Or like a creature native and indued
Unto that element; but long it could not be
Till that her garments, heavy with their drink,
180 Pull'd the poor wretch from her melodious lay
To muddy death.
LAERTES   Alas, then she is drown'd?
QUEEN Drown'd, drown'd.
LAERTES Too much of water hast thou, poor Ophelia,
And therefore I forbid my tears; but yet
185 It is our trick; nature her custom holds,
Let shame say what it will. When these are gone,
The woman will be out. Adieu, my lord.
I have a speech of fire, that fain would blaze
But that this folly douts it.   *Exit.*
KING   Let's follow, Gertrude.
190 How much I had to do to calm his rage!
Now fear I this will give it start again;
Therefore let's follow.
                                   Exeunt.

ACT V

Scene I. *Elsinore. A Churchyard.*

Enter two CLOWNS *with spades and pickaxes.*

CLOWN   Is she to be buried in Christian burial when she wilfully seeks her own salvation?
OTHER   I tell thee she is; therefore make her grave straight. The crowner hath sate on her,
and finds it Christian burial.
CLOWN   How can that be, unless she drown'd herself in her own defence?
5 OTHER   Why, 'tis found so.
CLOWN   It must be *se offendendo;* it cannot be else. For here lies the point: if I drown
myself wittingly, it argues an act; and an act hath three branches—it is to act, to do,
and to perform; argal, she drown'd herself wittingly.
OTHER   Nay, but hear you, Goodman Delver!

---

[168] *liberal,* licentious   [171] *envious,* malicious   [176] *incapable,* unwitting   [187] *woman,* coward   [189] *folly douts,* weeping douses   *Clowns,* rustics (gravediggers)   [2] *crowner,* coroner
[6] *se offendendo,* self-offense (a mistake for *se defendendo,* self-defense)   [8] *argal,* therefore (for
ergo)

10 CLOWN   Give me leave. Here lies the water; good. Here stands the man; good. If the man
go to this water and drown himself, it is, will he nill he, he goes—mark you that. But
if the water come to him and drown him, he drowns not himself. Argal, he that is not
guilty of his own death shortens not his own life.

OTHER   But is this law?

15 CLOWN   Ay, marry, is't—crowner's quest law.

OTHER   Will you ha' the truth an't? If this had not been a gentlewoman, she should have
been buried out o' Christian burial.

CLOWN   Why, there thou say'st! And the more pity that great folk should have count'nance
in this world to drown or hang themselves more than their even-Christen. Come, my

20   spade! There is no ancient gentlemen but gard'ners, ditchers, and grave-makers. They
hold up Adam's profession.

OTHER   Was he a gentleman?

CLOWN   'A was the first that ever bore arms.

OTHER   Why, he had none.

25 CLOWN   What, art a heathen? How dost thou understand the Scripture? The Scripture says
Adam digg'd. Could he dig without arms? I'll put another question to thee. If thou
answerest me not to the purpose, confess thyself—

OTHER   Go to!

CLOWN   What is he that builds stronger than either the mason, the shipwright, or the

30   carpenter?

OTHER   The gallows-maker; for that frame outlives a thousand tenants.

CLOWN   I like thy wit well, in good faith. The gallows does well. But how does it well? It
does well to those that do ill. Now, thou dost ill to say that gallows is built stronger
than the church. Argal, the gallows may do well to thee. To't again, come!

35 OTHER   Who builds stronger than a mason, a shipwright, or a carpenter?

CLOWN   Ay, tell me that, and unyoke.

OTHER   Marry, now I can tell!

CLOWN   To't.

OTHER   Mass, I cannot tell.

Enter HAMLET *and* HORATIO *afar off.*

40 CLOWN   Cudgel thy brains no more about it, for your dull ass will not mend his pace with
beating; and when you are ask'd this question next, say "a grave-maker." The houses
he makes lasts till doomsday. Go, get thee to Yaughan; fetch me a stoup of liquor.

(*Exit* SECOND CLOWN.)

(CLOWN *digs and sings.*)

In youth when I did love, did love
Methought it was very sweet;

45   To contract—O—the time for—a—my behove,
O, methought there—a—was nothing—a—meet.

HAMLET   Has this fellow no feeling of his business, that he sings at grave-making?

HORATIO   Custom hath made it in him a property of easiness.

HAMLET   'Tis e'en so. The hand of little employment hath the daintier sense.

---

[11] *will he nill he,* willy-nilly   [15] *quest,* inquest   [19] *even-Christen,* fellow Christians
[36] *unyoke,* unharness (call it a day)   [42] *Yaughan,* John; *stoup,* large mug   [45] *contract . . . be-*
hove, to shorten time to my benefit   [48] *Custom . . . easiness* (long practice in grave digging
leaves him with an untroubled mind.)

CLOWN *(Sings)*

50   But age with his stealing steps
            Hath clawed me in his clutch,
        And hath shipped me intil the land,
            As if I had never been such.

Throws up a skull.

HAMLET   That skull had a tongue in it, and could sing once. How the knave jowls it to the
55   ground, as if 'twere Cain's jawbone, that did the first murther! This might be the pate
        of a politician, which this ass now o'erreaches; one that would circumvent God, might
        it not?

HORATIO   It might, my lord.

HAMLET   Or of a courtier, which could say "Good morrow, sweet lord! How dost thou,
60   good lord?" This might be my Lord Such-a-one, that prais'd my Lord Such-a-one's
        horse when he meant to beg it—might it not?

HORATIO   Ay, my lord.

HAMLET   Why, e'en so! and now my Lady Worm's, chapless, and knock'd about the mazzard
        with a sexton's spade. Here's fine revolution, an we had the trick to see't. Did these
65   bones cost no more the breeding but to play at loggets with 'em? Mine ache to think o't.

CLOWN *(Sings)*

        A pickaxe and a spade, a spade,
            For and a shrouding sheet;
        O, a pit of clay for to be made
            For such a guest is meet.

Throws up another skull.

70 HAMLET   There's another. Why may not that be the skull of a lawyer? Where be his quidits
        now, his quillets, his cases, his tenures, and his tricks? Why does he suffer this rude
        knave now to knock him about the sconce with a dirty shovel, and will not tell him
        of his action of battery? Hum! This fellow might be in's time a great buyer of land,
        with his statutes, his recognizances, his fines, his double vouchers, his recoveries. Is
75   this the fine of his fines, and the recovery of his recoveries, to have his fine pate full
        of fine dirt? Will his vouchers vouch him no more of his purchases, and double ones
        too, than the length and breadth of a pair of indentures? The very conveyances of his
        lands will scarcely lie in this box; and must th' inheritor himself have no more, ha?

HORATIO   Not a jot more, my lord.

80 HAMLET   Is not parchment made of sheepskins?

HORATIO   Ay, my lord, and of calveskins too.

HAMLET   They are sheep and calves which seek out assurance in that. I will speak to this
        fellow. Whose grave's this, sirrah?

CLOWN   Mine, sir.

85 *(Sings)* O, a pit of clay for to be made
                For such a guest is meet.

HAMLET   I think it be thine indeed for thou liest in't.

---

[51] *clawed,* grabbed   [52] *intil,* into   [54] *jowls,* tosses   [56] *o'erreaches,* acts superior to
[63] *chapless,* without a lower jaw   [63] *mazzard,* head   [65] *loggets,* a game played with small
pieces of wood   [70–71] *quiddits . . . quillets,* tricky definitions . . . quibbles   [72] *sconce,* pate
[75] *fine,* end, result   [77] *indentures,* contracts

CLOWN   You lie out on't, sir, and therefore 'tis not yours. For my part, I do not lie in't, yet
   it is mine.

90 HAMLET   Thou dost lie in't, to be in't and say it is thine. 'Tis for the dead, not for the quick;
   therefore thou liest.

CLOWN   'Tis a quick lie, sir; 'twill away again from me to you.

HAMLET   What man dost thou dig it for?

CLOWN   For no man, sir.

95 HAMLET   What woman then?

CLOWN   For none neither.

HAMLET   Who is to be buried in't?

CLOWN   One that was a woman, sir; but, rest her soul, she's dead.

HAMLET   How absolute the knave is! We must speak by the card, or equivocation will undo
100   us. By the Lord, Horatio, this three years I have taken note of it, the age is grown so
   picked that the toe of the peasant comes so near the heel of the courtier he galls his
   kibe.—How long hast thou been a grave-maker?

CLOWN   Of all the days i' th' year, I came to't that day that our last king Hamlet overcame
   Fortinbras.

105 HAMLET   How long is that since?

CLOWN   Cannot you tell that? Every fool can tell that. It was the very day that young Hamlet
   was born—he that is mad, and sent into England.

HAMLET   Ay, marry, why was he sent into England?

CLOWN   Why, because 'a was mad. 'A shall recover his wits there; or, if 'a do not, 'tis no
110   great matter there.

HAMLET   Why?

CLOWN   'Twill not be seen in him there. There the men are as mad as he.

HAMLET   How came he mad?

CLOWN   Very strangely, they say.

115 HAMLET   How strangely?

CLOWN   Faith, e'en with losing his wits.

HAMLET   Upon what ground?

CLOWN   Why, here in Denmark. I have been sexton here, man and boy, thirty years.

HAMLET   How long will a man lie i' th' earth ere he rot?

120 CLOWN   Faith, if 'a be not rotten before 'a die (as we have many pocky corses now-a-days
   that will scarce hold the laying in), 'a will last you some eight year or nine year. A
   tanner will last you nine year.

HAMLET   Why he more than another?

CLOWN   Why, sir, his hide is so tann'd with his trade that 'a will keep out water a great
125   while; and your water is a sore decayer of your whoreson dead body. Here's a skull
   now. This skull hath lien you i' th' earth three-and-twenty years.

HAMLET   Whose was it?

CLOWN   A whoreson mad fellow's it was. Whose do you think it was?

HAMLET   Nay, I know not.

130 CLOWN   A pestilence on him for a mad rogue! 'A pour'd a flagon of Rhenish on my head
   once. This same skull, sir, was Yorick's skull, the King's jester.

HAMLET   This?

CLOWN   E'en that.

HAMLET   Let me see. *(Takes the skull)* Alas, poor Yorick! I knew him, Horatio. A fellow of

---

⁹⁰ *quick,* alive   ⁹⁹ *by the card,* accurately   ¹⁰⁰⁻¹⁰¹ *so picked,* so refined   ¹⁰¹ *galls his kibe,*
rubs raw the chilblains on his heel

135 infinite jest, of most excellent fancy. He hath borne me on his back a thousand times. And now how abhorred in my imagination it is! My gorge rises at it. Here hung those lips that I have kiss'd I know not how oft. Where be your gibes now? your gambols? your songs? your flashes of merriment that were wont to set the table on a roar? Not one now, to mock your own grinning? Quite chapfall'n? Now get you to my lady's
140 chamber, and tell her, let her paint an inch thick, to this favour she must come. Make her laugh at that. Prithee, Horatio, tell me one thing.

HORATIO   What's that, my lord?

HAMLET   Dost thou think Alexander look'd o' this fashion i' th' earth?

HORATIO   E'en so.

145 HAMLET   And smelt so? Pah!

Puts down the skull.

HORATIO   E'en so, my lord.

HAMLET   To what base uses we may return, Horatio! Why may not imagination trace the noble dust of Alexander till he find it stopping a bunghole?

HORATIO   'Twere to consider too curiously, to consider so.

150 HAMLET   No, faith, not a jot; but to follow him thither with modesty enough, and likelihood to lead it; as thus: Alexander died, Alexander was buried, Alexander returneth into dust; the dust is earth; of earth we make loam; and why of that loam (whereto he was converted) might they not stop a beer barrel?
   Imperious Cæsar, dead and turn'd to clay,
155 Might stop a hole to keep the wind away.
   O, that that earth which kept the world in awe
   Should patch a wall t' expel the winter's flaw!
   But soft! but soft! aside! Here comes the King—

(Enter PRIESTS *with a coffin in funeral procession,* KING, QUEEN, LAERTES, *with* LORDS *attendant.)*

   The Queen, the courtiers. Who is this they follow?
160 And with such maimed rites? This doth betoken
   The corse they follow did with desp'rate hand
   Fordo it own life. 'Twas of some estate.
   Couch we awhile, and mark.

Retires with HORATIO.

LAERTES   What ceremony else?

HAMLET   That is Laertes,
165 A very noble youth. Mark.

LAERTES   What ceremony else?

PRIEST   Her obsequies have been as far enlarg'd
   As we have warranty. Her death was doubtful;
   And, but that great command o'ersways the order,
170 She should in ground unsanctified have lodg'd
   Till the last trumpet. For charitable prayers,
   Shards, flints, and pebbles should be thrown on her.
   Yet here she is allow'd her virgin crants,
   Her maiden strewments, and the bringing home

---

[160] *maimed,* incomplete   [172] *shards,* pieces of broken pottery   [173] *crants,* garland

175   Of bell and burial.

LAERTES   Must there no more be done?

PRIEST   No more be done.

   We should profane the service of the dead

   To sing a requiem and such a rest to her

   As to peace-parted souls.

LAERTES   Lay her i' th' earth;

180   And from her fair and unpolluted flesh

   May violets spring! I tell thee, churlish priest,

   A minist'ring angel shall my sister be

   When thou liest howling.

HAMLET   What, the fair Ophelia?

QUEEN   Sweets to the sweet! Farewell.

(Scatters flowers)

185   I hop'd thou shouldst have been my Hamlet's wife;

   I thought thy bride-bed to have deck'd, sweet maid,

   And not have strew'd thy grave.

LAERTES   O, treble woe

   Fall ten times treble on that cursed head

   Whose wicked deed thy most ingenious sense

190   Depriv'd thee of! Hold off the earth awhile,

   Till I have caught her once more in mine arms.

(Leaps in the grave)

   Now pile your dust upon the quick and dead

   Till of this flat mountain you have made

   T' o'ertop old Pelion or the skyish head

195   Of blue Olympus.

HAMLET *(Comes forward)*   What is he whose grief

   Bears such an emphasis? whose phrase of sorrow

   Conjures the wand'ring stars, and makes them stand

   Like wonder-wounded hearers? This is I,

   Hamlet the Dane.   *Leaps in after Laertes.*

200 LAERTES   The devil take thy soul!

Grapples with him.

HAMLET   Thou pray'st not well.

   I prithee take thy fingers from my throat;

   For, though I am not splenitive and rash,

   Yet have I in me something dangerous,

205   Which let thy wisdom fear. Hold off thy hand!

KING   Pluck them asunder.

QUEEN   Hamlet, Hamlet!

ALL   Gentlemen!

HORATIO   Good my lord, be quiet.

The ATTENDANTS *part them, and they come out of the grave.*

---

[189] *ingenious sense,* keen intellect   [194] *Pelion,* a high mountain (on which giants piled Mt. Ossa)   [198] *conjures,* affects   [203] *splenitive,* easily angered

HAMLET   Why, I will fight with him upon this theme
   Until my eyelids will no longer wag.
210 QUEEN   O my son, what theme?
HAMLET   I lov'd Ophelia. Forty thousand brothers
   Could not (with all their quantity of love)
   Make up my sum. What wilt thou do for her?
KING   O, he is mad, Laertes.
215 QUEEN   For love of God, forbear him!
HAMLET   'Swounds, show me what thou't do.
   Woo't weep? woo't fight? woo't fast? woo't tear thyself?
   Woo't drink up esill? eat a crocodile?
   I'll do't. Dost thou come here to whine?
220 To outface me with leaping in her grave?
   Be buried quick with her, and so will I.
   And if thou prate of mountains, let them throw
   Millions of acres on us, till our ground,
   Singeing his pate against the burning zone,
225 Make Ossa like a wart! Nay, an thou'lt mouth,
   I'll rant as well as thou.
QUEEN   This is mere madness;
   And thus a while the fit will work on him.
   Anon, as patient as the female dove
   When that her golden couplets are disclos'd,
   His silence will sit drooping.
230 HAMLET   Hear you, sir!
   What is the reason that you use me thus?
   I lov'd you ever. But it is no matter.
   Let Hercules himself do what he may,
   The cat will mew, and dog will have his day.

Exit.

235 KING   I pray thee, good Horatio, wait upon him.

(*Exit* HORATIO.)

(*To* LAERTES) Strengthen your patience in our last night's speech.
   We'll put the matter to the present push.—
   Good Gertrude, set some watch over your son.—
   This grave shall have a living monument.
240 An hour of quiet shortly shall we see;
   Till then in patience our proceeding be.

Exeunt.

Scene II. *Elsinore. A Hall in the Castle.*

Enter HAMLET *and* HORATIO.

HAMLET   So much for this, sir; now shall you see the other.
   You do remember all the circumstance?

---

[218] *esill,* vinegar   [224] *burning zone,* celestial area bounded by the Tropics of Cancer and Capricorn   [237] *to the present push,* into immediate action

HORATIO   Remember it, my lord!

HAMLET   Sir, in my heart there was a kind of fighting

5   That would not let me sleep. Methought I lay

Worse than the mutines in the bilboes. Rashly—

And prais'd be rashness for it; let us know,

Our indiscretion sometime serves us well

When our deep plots do pall; and that should learn us

10   There's a divinity that shapes our ends,

Rough-hew them how we will—

HORATIO   That is most certain.

HAMLET   Up from my cabin,

My sea-gown scarf'd about me, in the dark

Grop'd I to find out them; had my desire,

15   Finger'd their packet, and in fine withdrew

To mine own room again; making so bold

(My fears forgetting manners) to unseal

Their grand commission; where I found, Horatio

(O royal knavery!), an exact command,

20   Larded with many several sorts of reasons,

Importing Denmark's health, and England's too,

With, hoo! such bugs and goblins in my life—

That, on the supervise, no leisure bated,

No, not to stay the grinding of the axe,

My head should be struck off.

25   HORATIO   Is't possible?

HAMLET   Here's the commission; read it at more leisure.

But wilt thou hear me how I did proceed?

HORATIO   I beseech you.

HAMLET   Being thus benetted round with villanies,

30   Or I could make a prologue to my brains,

They had begun the play. I sat me down;

Devis'd a new commission; wrote it fair.

I once did hold it, as our statists do,

A baseness to write fair, and labour'd much

35   How to forget that learning; but, sir, now

It did me yeoman's service. Wilt thou know

Th' effect of what I wrote?

HORATIO   Ay, good my lord.

HAMLET   An earnest conjuration from the King,

As England was his faithful tributary,

40   As love between them like the palm might flourish,

As peace should still her wheaten garland wear

And stand a comma 'tween their amities,

And many such-like as's of great charge,

That, on the view and knowing of these contents,

45   Without debatement further, more or less,

---

6 *mutines,* mutineers; *bilboes,* irons (stocks)   7 *rashness,* unreasoned action   9 *deep plots,* carefully planned actions   15 *finger'd,* stole   22 *bugs,* bugbears   23 *on the supervise,* on the reading of the document   30 *or,* ere (before)

He should the bearers put to sudden death,
Not shriving time allow'd.

HORATIO   How was this seal'd?

HAMLET   Why, even in that was heaven ordinant.
I had my father's signet in my purse,
50   Which was the model of that Danish seal;
Folded the writ up in the form of th' other,
Subscrib'd it, gave't th' impression, plac'd it safely,
The changeling never known. Now, the next day
Was our sea-fight; and what to this was sequent
55   Thou know'st already.

HORATIO   So Guildenstern and Rosencrantz go to't.

HAMLET   Why, man, they did make love to this employment!
They are not near my conscience; their defeat
Does by their own insinuation grow.
60   'Tis dangerous when the baser nature comes
Between the pass and fell incensed points
Of mighty opposites.

HORATIO   Why, what a king is this!

HAMLET   Does it not, thinks't thee, stand me now upon
He that hath kill'd my king, and whor'd my mother;
65   Popp'd in between th' election and my hopes;
Thrown out his angle for my proper life,
And with such coz'nage—is't not perfect conscience
To quit him with this arm? And is't not to be damn'd
To let this canker of our nature come
70   In further evil?

HORATIO   It must be shortly known to him from England
What is the issue of the business there.

HAMLET   It will be short; the interim is mine,
And a man's life's no more than to say "one."
75   But I am very sorry, good Horatio,
That to Laertes I forgot myself;
For by the image of my cause I see
The portraiture of his. I'll court his favours.
But sure the bravery of his grief did put me
Into a tow'ring passion.

80 HORATIO   Peace! Who comes here?

Enter young OSRIC, *a courtier*.

OSRIC   Your lordship is right welcome back to Denmark.

HAMLET   I humbly thank you, sir. (*Aside to* HORATIO) Dost know this waterfly?

HORATIO (*Aside to* HAMLET) No, my good lord.

HAMLET (*Aside to* HORATIO)   Thy state is the more gracious; for 'tis a vice to know him
85   He hath much land, and fertile. Let a beast be lord of beasts, and his crib shall stand
at the king's mess. 'Tis a chough; but, as I say, spacious in the possession of dirt.

---

[47] *shriving time,* time for confession and absolution   [48] *ordinant,* helpful   [58] *defeat,* destruction   [59] *their own insinuation,* their own efforts to become involved in the plot   [82] *waterfly,*
gorgeous, flitty creature   [86] *chough,* jackdaw (chatterer)

OSRIC   Sweet lord, if your lordship were at leisure, I should impart a thing to you from his Majesty.

HAMLET   I will receive it, sir, with all diligence of spirit. Put your bonnet to his right use.
90   'Tis for the head.

OSRIC   I thank your lordship, it is very hot.

HAMLET   No, believe me, 'tis very cold; the wind is northerly.

OSRIC   It is indifferent cold, my lord, indeed.

HAMLET   But yet methinks it is very sultry and hot for my complexion.

95   OSRIC   Exceedingly, my lord; it is very sultry, as 'twere—I cannot tell how. But, my lord, his Majesty bade me signify to you that he has laid a great wager on your head. Sir, this is the matter—

HAMLET   I beseech you remember.

HAMLET *moves him to put on his hat.*

OSRIC   Nay, good my lord; for mine ease, in good faith. Sir, here is newly come to court
100   Laertes; believe me, an absolute gentleman, full of most excellent differences, of very soft society and great showing. Indeed, to speak feelingly of him, he is the card or calendar of gentry; for you shall find in him the continent of what part a gentleman would see.

HAMLET   Sir, his definement suffers no perdition in you; though, I know, to divide him
105   inventorially would dozy th' arithmetic of memory, and yet but yaw neither in respect of his quick sail. But, in the verity of extolment, I take him to be a soul of great article, and his infusion of such dearth and rareness as, to make true diction of him, his semblable is his mirror, and who else would trace him, his umbrage, nothing more.

OSRIC   Your lordship speaks most infallibly of him.

110   HAMLET   The concernancy, sir? Why do we wrap the gentleman in our more rawer breath?

OSRIC   Sir?

HORATIO (*Aside to* HAMLET)   Is't not possible to understand in another tongue? You will do't, sir, really.

HAMLET   What imports the nomination of this gentleman?

115   OSRIC   Of Laertes?

HORATIO *(Aside)*   His purse is empty already. All's golden words are spent.

HAMLET   Of him, sir.

OSRIC   I know you are ignorant—

HAMLET   I would you did, sir; yet, in faith, if you did, it would not much approve me. Well,
120   sir?

OSRIC   You are ignorant of what excellence Laertes is—

HAMLET   I dare not confess that, lest I should compare with him in excellence; but to know a man well were to know himself.

OSRIC   I mean, sir, for his weapon; but in the imputation laid on him by them, in his meed
125   he's unfellowed.

HAMLET   What's his weapon?

OSRIC   Rapier and dagger.

HAMLET   That's two of his weapons—but well.

OSRIC   The King, sir, hath wager'd with him six Barbary horses; against the which he has
130   impon'd, as I take it, six French rapiers and poniards, with their assigns, as girdle,

---

100 *differences,* superiorities (that set him apart)   105 *dozy,* confuse   105 *yaw,* steer badly (and drop behind)   107 *his infusion,* his natural quality   108 *semblable,* seeming   108 *umbrage,* shadow   124 *meed,* competence   125 *unfellowed,* nobody can equal   130 *impon'd,* put up

hangers, and so. Three of the carriages, in faith, are very dear to fancy, very responsive to the hilts, most delicate carriages, and of very liberal conceit.

HAMLET   What call you the carriages?

HORATIO (*Aside to* HAMLET)   I knew you must be edified by the margent ere you had done.

135   OSRIC   The carriages, sir, are the hangers.

HAMLET   The phrase would be more germane to the matter if we could carry cannon by our sides. I would it might be hangers till then. But on! Six Barbary horses against six French swords, their assigns, and three liberal-conceited carriages: that's the French bet against the Danish. Why is this all impon'd, as you call it?

140   OSRIC   The King, sir, hath laid that, in a dozen passes between yourself and him, he shall not exceed you three hits; he hath laid on twelve for nine, and it would come to immediate trial if your lordship would vouchsafe the answer.

HAMLET   How if I answer no?

OSRIC   I mean, my lord, the opposition of your person in trial.

145   HAMLET   Sir, I will walk here in the hall. If it please his Majesty, it is the breathing time of day with me. Let the foils be brought, the gentleman willing, and the King hold his purpose, I will win for him if I can; if not, I will gain nothing but my shame and the odd hits.

OSRIC   Shall I redeliver you e'en so?

150   HAMLET   To this effect, sir, after what flourish your nature will.

OSRIC   I commend my duty to your lordship.

HAMLET   Yours, yours. (*Exit* OSRIC.) He does well to commend it himself; there are no tongues else for's turn.

HORATIO   This lapwing runs away with the shell on his head.

155   HAMLET   He did comply with his dug before he suck'd it. Thus has he, and many more of the same bevy that I know the drossy age dotes on, only got the tune of the time and outward habit of encounter—a kind of yesty collection, which carries them through and through the most fann'd and winnowed opinions; and do but blow them to their trial—the bubbles are out.

Enter a LORD.

160   LORD   My lord, his Majesty commended him to you by young Osric, who brings back to him, that you attend him in the hall. He sends to know if your pleasure hold to play with Laertes, or that you will take longer time.

HAMLET   I am constant to my purposes; they follow the King's pleasure. If his fitness speaks, mine is ready; now or whensoever, provided I be so able as now.

165   LORD   The King and Queen and all are coming down.

HAMLET   In happy time.

LORD   The Queen desires you to use some gentle entertainment to Laertes before you fall to play.

HAMLET   She well instructs me

---

¹³² *liberal conceit,* handsomely designed   ¹³⁴ *edified by the margent,* impressed by the marginal note   ^{137–139} (The terms of the wager are made deliberately intricate so that Hamlet will think the duel is regarded by Claudius simply as a sporting event.)   ¹⁴⁵ *breathing time,* time for physical exercise   ¹⁵⁴ *lapwing . . . shell,* this (precocious) bird . . . (gets going before it has lost part of the) shell   ¹⁵⁶ *drossy,* degenerate   ¹⁵⁷ *yesty,* frothy   ¹⁵⁸ *fann'd and winnowed,* sophisticated to the point of absurdity   ¹⁶⁷ *entertainment,* cordiality; *fall to play,* start the fencing

Exit LORD.

170 HORATIO   You will lose this wager, my lord.

HAMLET   I do not think so. Since he went into France I have been in continual practice. I
shall win at the odds. But thou wouldst not think how ill all's here about my heart.
But it is no matter.

HORATIO   Nay, good my lord—

175 HAMLET   It is but foolery; but it is such a kind of gaingiving as would perhaps trouble a
woman.

HORATIO   If your mind dislike anything, obey it. I will forestall their repair hither and say
you are not fit.

HAMLET   Not a whit, we defy augury; there's a special providence in the fall of a sparrow.

180 If it be now, 'tis not to come; if it be not to come, it will be now; if it be not now, yet
it will come: the readiness is all. Since no man knows aught of what he leaves, what
is't to leave betimes? Let be.

Enter KING, QUEEN, LAERTES, OSRIC, *and* LORDS, *with other* ATTENDANTS *with foils and gauntlets.*
A table and flagons of wine on it.

KING   Come, Hamlet, come, and take this hand from me.

The KING *puts* LAERTES' *hand into* HAMLET'S.

HAMLET   Give me your pardon, sir. I have done you wrong;
185 But pardon't, as you are a gentleman.
This presence knows,
And you must needs have heard, how I am punish'd
With sore distraction. What I have done
That might your nature, honour, and exception
190 Roughly awake, I here proclaim was madness.
Was't Hamlet wrong'd Laertes? Never Hamlet.
If Hamlet from himself be ta'en away,
And when he's not himself does wrong Laertes,
Then Hamlet does it not, Hamlet denies it.
195 Who does it, then? His madness. If't be so,
Hamlet is of the faction that is wrong'd;
His madness is poor Hamlet's enemy.
Sir, in this audience,
Let my disclaiming from a purpos'd evil
200 Free me so far in your most generous thoughts
That I have shot my arrow o'er the house
And hurt my brother.

LAERTES   I am satisfied in nature,
Whose motive in this case should stir me most
To my revenge. But in my terms of honour
205 I stand aloof, and will no reconcilement
Till by some elder masters of known honour
I have a voice and precedent of peace
To keep my name ungor'd. But till that time
I do receive your offer'd love like love,
And will not wrong it.

---

175 *gaingiving,* portent or omen   186 *this presence,* the King and Queen   189 *exception,* resentment   206*elder masters,* authorities (on what constitutes a proper defense of one's honor)

210 HAMLET I embrace it freely,
And will this brother's wager frankly play.
Give us the foils. Come on.

LAERTES Come, one for me.

HAMLET I'll be your foil, Laertes. In mine ignorance
Your skill shall, like a star i' th' darkest night
Stick fiery off indeed.

215 LAERTES You mock me, sir.

HAMLET No, by this hand.

KING Give them the foils, young Osric. Cousin Hamlet,
You know the wager?

HAMLET Very well, my lord.
Your Grace has laid the odds o' th' weaker side.

220 KING I do not fear it, I have seen you both;
But since he is better'd, we have therefore odds.

LAERTES This is too heavy; let me see another.

HAMLET This likes me well. These foils have all a length? *Prepare to play.*

OSRIC Ay, my good lord.

225 KING Set me the stoups of wine upon that table.
If Hamlet give the first or second hit,
Or quit in answer of the third exchange,
Let all the battlements their ordnance fire;
The King shall drink to Hamlet's better breath,

230 And in the cup an union shall he throw
Richer than that which four successive kings
In Denmark's crown have worn. Give me the cups;
And let the kettle to the trumpet speak,
The trumpet to the cannoneer without,

235 The cannons to the heavens, the heaven to earth,
"Now the King drinks to Hamlet." Come, begin.
And you the judges, bear a wary eye.

HAMLET Come on, sir.

LAERTES Come, my lord. *They play.*

HAMLET One.

LAERTES No.

HAMLET Judgment!

OSRIC A hit, a very palpable hit.

LAERTES Well, again!

240 KING Stay, give me drink. Hamlet, this pearl is thine;
Here's to thy health.

(Drum; trumpets sound; a piece goes off within.)

Give him the cup.

HAMLET I'll play this bout first; set it by awhile.
Come. *(They play.)* Another hit. What say you?

LAERTES A touch, a touch; I do confess't.

KING Our son shall win.

245 QUEEN He's fat, and scant of breath.
Here, Hamlet, take my napkin, rub thy brows.

---

225 *stoups,* large mugs   230 *an union,* a large, perfect pearl   233 *kettle,* kettledrum   245 *fat,* soft

The Queen carouses to thy fortune, Hamlet.

HAMLET   Good madam!

KING   Gertrude, do not drink.

QUEEN   I will, my lord; I pray you pardon me.   *Drinks.*

250 KING *(Aside)*   It is the poison'd cup; it is too late.

HAMLET   I dare not drink yet, madam; by-and-by.

QUEEN   Come, let me wipe thy face.

LAERTES   My lord, I'll hit him now.

KING   I do not think't.

LAERTES *(Aside)*   And yet it is almost against my conscience.

255 HAMLET   Come for the third, Laertes! You but dally.

I pray you pass with your best violence;

I am afeard you make a wanton of me.

LAERTES   Say you so? Come on.   *Play.*

OSRIC   Nothing neither way.

LAERTES   Have at you now!

LAERTES *wounds* HAMLET; *then, in scuffling, they change rapiers and* HAMLET *wounds* LAERTES.

260 KING   Part them! They are incens'd.

HAMLET   Nay come! again!   *The* QUEEN *falls.*

OSRIC   Look to the Queen there, ho!

HORATIO   They bleed on both sides. How is it, my lord?

OSRIC   How is't, Laertes?

LAERTES   Why, as a woodcock to mine own springe, Osric.

265   I am justly kill'd with mine own treachery.

HAMLET   How does the Queen?

KING   She sounds to see them bleed.

QUEEN   No, no! the drink, the drink! O my dear Hamlet!

The drink, the drink! I am poison'd.   *Dies.*

HAMLET   O villany! Ho! let the door be lock'd. Treachery! Seek it out.

LAERTES *falls.*

270 LAERTES   It is here, Hamlet. Hamlet, thou art slain;

No med'cine in the world can do thee good.

In thee there is not half an hour of life.

The treacherous instrument is in thy hand,

Unbated and envenom'd. The foul practice

275   Hath turn'd itself on me. Lo, here I lie,

Never to rise again. Thy mother's poison'd.

I can no more. The King, the King's to blame.

HAMLET   The point envenom'd too?

Then, venom, to thy work.   *Hurts the* KING.

280 ALL   Treason! treason!

KING   O, yet defend me, friends! I am but hurt.

HAMLET   Here, thou incestuous, murd'rous, damned Dane,

Drink off this potion! Is thy union here?

Follow my mother.   KING *dies.*

---

[257] *make a wanton of me,* treat me too carelessly   [266] *sounds,* swoons

LAERTES He is justly serv'd.
285 It is a poison temper'd by himself.
Exchange forgiveness with me, noble Hamlet.
Mine and my father's death come not upon thee,
Nor thine on me! *Dies.*
HAMLET Heaven make thee free of it! I follow thee.
290 I am dead, Horatio. Wretched queen, adieu!
You that look pale and tremble at this chance,
That are but mutes or audience to this act,
Had I but time (as this fell sergeant, Death,
Is strict in his arrest) O, I could tell you—
295 But let it be. Horatio, I am dead;
Thou liv'st; report me and my cause aright
To the unsatisfied.
HORATIO Never believe it.
I am more an antique Roman than a Dane.
Here's yet some liquor left.
HAMLET As th'art a man,
300 Give me the cup. Let go! By heaven, I'll ha't.
O good Horatio, what a wounded name
(Things standing thus unknown) shall live behind me!
If thou didst ever hold me in thy heart,
Absent thee from felicity awhile,
305 And in this harsh world draw thy breath in pain,
To tell my story.

(March afar off, and shot within)

What warlike noise is this?
OSRIC Young Fortinbras, with conquest come from Poland,
To the ambassadors of England gives
This warlike volley.
HAMLET O, I die, Horatio!
310 The potent poison quite o'ercrows my spirit.
I cannot live to hear the news from England,
But I do prophesy th' election lights
On Fortinbras. He has my dying voice.
So tell him, with th' occurrents, more and less,
315 Which have solicited—the rest is silence. *Dies.*
HORATIO Now cracks a noble heart. Good night, sweet prince,
And flights of angels sing thee to thy rest!

(March within)

Why does the drum come hither?

Enter FORTINBRAS *and* ENGLISH AMBASSADORS, *with* DRUM, COLOURS, *and* ATTENDANTS.

FORTINBRAS Where is this sight?
HORATIO What is it you would see?
320 If aught of woe or wonder, cease your search.

---

[297] *the unsatisfied,* the uninformed

FORTINBRAS   This quarry cries on havoc. O proud Death,
   What feast is toward in thine eternal cell
   That thou so many princes at a shot
   So bloodily hast struck?
AMBASSADOR   The sight is dismal;
325   And our affairs from England come too late.
   The ears are senseless that should give us hearing
   To tell him his commandment is fulfill'd,
   That Rosencrantz and Guildenstern are dead.
   Where should we have our thanks?
HORATIO   Not from his mouth,
330   Had it th' ability of life to thank you.
   He never gave commandment for their death.
   But since, so jump upon this bloody question,
   You from the Polack wars, and you from England,
   Are here arriv'd, give order that these bodies
335   High on a stage be placed to the view;
   And let me speak to th' yet unknowing world
   How these things came about. So shall you hear
   Of carnal, bloody, and unnatural acts;
   Of accidental judgments, casual slaughters;
340   Of deaths put on by cunning and forc'd cause;
   And, in this upshot, purposes mistook
   Fall'n on th'inventors' heads. All this can I
   Truly deliver.
FORTINBRAS   Let us haste to hear it,
   And call the noblest to the audience.
345   For me, with sorrow I embrace my fortune.
   I have some rights of memory in this kingdom,
   Which now to claim my vantage doth invite me.
HORATIO   Of that I shall have also cause to speak,
   And from his mouth whose voice will draw on more.
350   But let this same be presently perform'd,
   Even while men's minds are wild, lest more mischance
   On plots and errors happen.
FORTINBRAS   Let four captains
   Bear Hamlet like a soldier to the stage;
   For he was likely, had he been put on,
355   To have prov'd most royally; and for his passage
   The soldiers' music and the rites of war
   Speak loudly for him.
   Take up the bodies. Such a sight as this
   Becomes the field, but here shows much amiss.
360   Go, bid the soldiers shoot.

Exeunt marching, after the which a peal of ordinance are shot off.

---

[321] *havoc,* massacre   [332] *so jump,* so opportunely

Comments and Questions

T. S. Eliot has observed that in Shakespeare's plays there are "several levels of significance. For the simplest auditors there is the plot, for the more thoughtful the characters and conflict of characters, for the more literary the words and phrasing, for the more musically sensitive the rhythm, and for auditors of greater sensitivity and understanding a meaning which reveals itself gradually." He adds that this classification is not clear-cut and that "the sensitiveness of every auditor is acted upon by all these elements at once, though in different degrees of consciousness" (*The Use of Poetry and the Use of Criticism,* Cambridge, Mass.: Harvard University Press, 1933). The chief point here is that by digging deep into a Shakespearean play one may discover how virtually inexhaustible are the treasures. Explorations into *Hamlet,* one of the richest of plays, will reveal all the layers of interest observed by T. S. Eliot. One may start by looking next at H. B. Charlton's essay on *Hamlet,* p. 1130. After reading Charlton's analysis, one may profitably use the outline for play dissection set forth on pp. 601–603.

    1. The working out of the action in *Hamlet* is intricate, but the initial issue is simple indeed; as Charlton puts it, "A son is called upon to kill his father's murderer." What, then, is the central problem, the problem that allowed Shakespeare to create an absorbing five-act play?

    2. The cause of Hamlet's delay in avenging his father's murder has been the subject of a great deal of the commentary on the play. Give evidence for or against these interpretations of Hamlet's procrastination, as summarized by Charlton: (a) as a man of high moral principle, Hamlet finds killing Claudius an abhorrent act; (b) he begins to doubt the testimony of the ghost and is therefore uncertain of Claudius' guilt; (c) by killing the king he will risk the Danes' retribution; (d) in Freudian terms, his unconscious attraction to his mother (the Oedipal complex) is activated by Claudius' incestuous relationship with Gertrude, producing an inner conflict in Hamlet that renders him incapable of punishing Claudius for fulfilling his own latent desires; (e) he is essentially a scholar and not a man of action; (f) as a philosopher, he thinks only in abstract terms and is indifferent to the real world around him. Which of these explanations is most convincing in light of Hamlet's words and actions? Are there other possible interpretations? Is the complexity of Shakespeare's creation of the character such as to render all rational explanation of Hamlet's motives inadequate? What of his supposed madness? Is it real or merely a device to aid his vengeance against the king?

    3. Examine Hamlet's soliloquies. What do they reveal about his own self-analysis? How does Hamlet see himself? How does he justify his inaction?

    4. What is Hamlet's attitude toward Gertrude? Does it change as the play progresses? What explanation can be given for his callous treatment of his mother? Why is he so harsh toward Ophelia? What lies behind Hamlet's attitude toward women? Discuss Shakespeare's portrayal of Gertrude and Ophelia.

    5. All drama rests upon conflict. The overt conflict here involves Hamlet and Claudius. Yet Hamlet is also torn by an inner conflict. Does Claudius exhibit similar conflicting impulses? Is he purely a villain? Does he have any saving graces? In Hamlet's eyes, Claudius has been guilty of two crimes—murder and incest. Which of these two is most horrifying to Hamlet? Examine closely the passages in which Hamlet speaks of Claudius' crimes.

    6. Shakespeare rarely neglected his minor characters. Discuss his depiction of Polonius, Laertes, and such lesser characters as Rosencrantz, Guildenstern, and Osric.

    7. Compare Hamlet and Antigone as tragic characters. Does one have the feeling that inevitable doom hangs over Hamlet as it did over Antigone? Discuss the differences.

8. Virtually every critic of Shakespeare has attempted to "pluck out the heart" of Hamlet's mystery. Is there a mystery? If so, what is it? What is there about Hamlet as a character that continues to fascinate readers and audiences and that produces so many conflicting explanations of his essential nature?

Molière (Jean-Baptiste Poquelin)
(1622–1673)
The Physician in Spite of Himself

CHARACTERS (in order of appearance)

SGANARELLE, *Martine's husband*
MARTINE, *Sganarelle's wife*
M. ROBERT, *Sganarelle's neighbour*
VALÈRE, *Géronte's servant*
LUCAS, *Jacqueline's husband*
GÉRONTE, *Lucinde's father*

JACQUELINE, *Lucas's wife*
LÉANDRE, *Lucinde's lover*
THIBAUT, *peasant*
PERRIN, *Thibaut's son*
LUCINDE, *Géronte's daughter, in love with Léandre*

ACT I. *A Forest.*

Scene I. SGANARELLE, MARTINE *appearing on the stage, quarrelling.*

SGANARELLE   No; I tell you that I will do nothing of the kind. It is for me to speak, and to be master.

MARTINE   And I tell you that I will have you live as I like, and that I am not married to you to put up with your freaks.

SGANARELLE   Oh! what a nuisance it is to have a wife! Aristotle is perfectly right in saying that a woman is worse than a devil.

MARTINE   Look at the clever man with his silly Aristotle!

SGANARELLE   Yes, clever indeed. Find me another faggot-binder who can argue upon things as I can, who has served a famous physician for six years, and who, when only a boy, knew his grammar by heart!

MARTINE   Plague on the arrant fool.

SGANARELLE   Plague on the slut!

MARTINE   Cursed be the hour and the day when I took it into my head to say yes.

SGANARELLE   Cursed be the cuckold of a notary that made me sign my own ruination.

MARTINE   Certainly it well becomes you to complain on that score. Ought you not rather to thank Heaven every minute of the day that you have me for a wife? Did you deserve to marry a woman like me?

SGANARELLE   It is true you did me too much honour, and I had great occasion to be satisfied with my wedding-night. Zounds! do not make me open my mouth too wide: I might say certain things . . .

MARTINE   Well! What could you say?

SGANARELLE   Enough; let us drop the subject. It is enough that we know what we know, and that you were very lucky to meet with me.

MARTINE   What do you call very lucky to meet with you? A fellow who will drive me to the hospital—a debauched, deceitful wretch, who gobbles up every farthing I have got!

SGANARELLE   That is a lie: I drink part of it.

MARTINE   Who sells piecemeal every stick of furniture in the house!

SGANARELLE   That is living upon one's means.

MARTINE   Who has taken the very bed from under me!

SGANARELLE   You will get up all the earlier.

MARTINE   In short, who does not leave me a stick in the whole house.

SGANARELLE   There will be less trouble in moving.

MARTINE   And who from morning to night does nothing but gamble and guzzle.

SGANARELLE   That is done in order not get to in the dumps.

MARTINE   And what am I to do all the while with my family?

SGANARELLE   Whatever you like.

MARTINE   I have got four poor children on my hands.

SGANARELLE   Put them down.

MARTINE   Who keep asking me every moment for bread.

SGANARELLE   Whip them. When I have had enough to eat and to drink, every one in the house ought to be satisfied.

MARTINE   And do you mean to tell me, you sot, that things can always go on so?

SGANARELLE   Wife, let us proceed gently, if you please.

MARTINE   That I am to bear forever with your insolence and your debauchery?

SGANARELLE   Do not let us get into a passion, wife.

MARTINE   And that I do not know the way to bring you back to your duty?

SGANARELLE   Wife, you know that I am not very patient, and that my arm is somewhat heavy.

MARTINE   I laugh at your threats.

SGANARELLE   My sweet wife, my pet, your skin is itching as usual.

MARTINE   I will let you see that I am not afraid of you.

SGANARELLE   My dearest rib, you have set your heart upon a thrashing.

MARTINE   Do you think that I am frightened at your talk?

SGANARELLE   Sweet object of my affections, I shall box your ears for you.

MARTINE   Drunkard!

SGANARELLE   I shall thrash you.

MARTINE   Wine-cask!

SGANARELLE   I shall pummel you.

MARTINE   Infamous wretch!

SGANARELLE   I shall curry your skin for you.

MARTINE   Wretch! villain! deceiver! cur! scoundrel! gallows-bird! churl! rogue! scamp! thief! . . .

SGANARELLE   You will have it, will you? *(Takes a stick and beats her)*

MARTINE   *(shrieking)*   Help! help! help! help!

SGANARELLE   That is the best way of quieting you.

Scene II. M. ROBERT, SGANARELLE, MARTINE.

M. ROBERT   Hulloa, hulloa, hulloa! Fie! What is this? What a disgraceful thing! Plague take the scamp to beat his wife so.

MARTINE *(her arms akimbo, speaks to* M. ROBERT, *and makes him draw back; at last she gives him a slap on the face.)*   I like him to beat me, I do.

M. ROBERT   If that is the case, I consent with all my heart.

MARTINE   What are you interfering with?

M. ROBERT   I am wrong.

MARTINE   Is it any of your business?

M. ROBERT   You are right.

MARTINE   Just look at this impertinent fellow, who wishes to hinder husbands from beating their wives!

M. ROBERT   I apologize.

MARTINE   What have you got to say to it?

M. ROBERT   Nothing.

MARTINE   Is it for you to poke your nose into it?

M. ROBERT   No.

MARTINE   Mind your own business.

M. ROBERT   I shall not say another word.

MARTINE   It pleases me to be beaten.

M. ROBERT   Agreed.

MARTINE   It does not hurt you.

M. ROBERT   That is true.

MARTINE   And you are a fool to interfere with what does not concern you.

M. ROBERT   Neighbour, I ask your pardon with all my heart. Go on, thrash and beat your wife as much as you like; I shall help you, if you wish it. *(He goes towards* SGANARELLE, *who also speaks to him, makes him draw back, and beats him with the stick he has been using.)*

SGANARELLE   I do not wish it.

M. ROBERT   Ah! that is a different thing.

SGANARELLE   I will beat her if I like; and I will not beat her if I do not like.

M. ROBERT   Very good.

SGANARELLE   She is my wife, and not yours.

M. ROBERT   Undoubtedly.

SGANARELLE   It is not for you to order me about.

M. ROBERT   Just so.

SGANARELLE   I do not want your help.

M. ROBERT   Exactly so.

SGANARELLE   And it is like your impertinence to meddle with other people's business. Remember that Cicero says that between the tree and the finger you should not put the bark. *(He drives him away, then comes back to his wife, and says to her, squeezing her hand.)*

Scene III. SGANARELLE, MARTINE.

SGANARELLE   Come, let us make it up. Shake hands.

MARTINE   Yes, after having beaten me thus!

SGANARELLE   Never mind that. Shake hands.

MARTINE   I will not.

SGANARELLE   Eh?

MARTINE   No.

SGANARELLE   Come, wife!

MARTINE   I shall not.

SGANARELLE   Come, I tell you.

MARTINE   I will do nothing of the kind.

SGANARELLE   Come, come, come.

MARTINE   No; I will be angry.

SGANARELLE   Bah! it is a trifle. Do.

MARTINE   Leave me alone.

SGANARELLE   Shake hands, I tell you.

MARTINE   You have treated me too ill.

SGANARELLE   Well! I beg your pardon; put your hand there.

MARTINE   I forgive you *(Aside, softly);* but I shall make you pay for it.

SGANARELLE   You are silly to take notice of it; these are trifles that are necessary now and then to keep up good feeling; and five or six strokes of a cudgel between people who love each other, only brighten the affections. There now! I am going to the wood, and I promise you that you shall have more than a hundred faggots to-day.

Scene IV. MARTINE, *alone.*

Go, my lad, whatever look I may put on, I shall not forget to pay you out; and I am dying to hit upon something to punish you for the blows you gave me. I know well enough that a wife has always the means of being avenged upon her husband; but that is too delicate a punishment for my hangdog; I want a revenge that shall strike home a little more, or it will not pay me for the insult which I have received.

Scene V. VALÈRE, LUCAS, MARTINE.

LUCAS (*to* VALÈRE, *without seeing* MARTINE)   I'll be blowed but we have undertaken a curious errand; and I do not know, for my part, what we shall get by it.

VALÈRE (*to* LUCAS, *without seeing* MARTINE)   What is the use of grumbling, good foster-father? We are bound to do as our master tells us; and, besides, we have both of us some interest in the health of his daughter, our mistress; for her marriage, which is put off through her illness, will no doubt bring us in something. Horace, who is generous, is the most likely to succeed among her suitors; and although she has shown some inclination for a certain Léandre, you know well enough that her father would never consent to receive him for his son-in-law.

MARTINE (*musing on one side, thinking herself alone)*   Can I not find out some way of avenging myself?

LUCAS (*to* VALÈRE)   But what an idea has he taken into his head, since the doctors are quite at a loss.

VALÈRE (*to* LUCAS)   You may sometimes find by dint of seeking, what cannot be found at once; and often in the most unlikely spots you may . . .

MARTINE (*still thinking herself alone)*   Yes; I must pay him out, no matter at what cost. Those cudgel blows lie heavy on my stomach; I cannot digest them; and . . . *(She is saying all this musingly, and as she moves, she comes in contact with the two men.)* Ah, gentlemen, I beg your pardon, I did not notice you, and was puzzling my brain about something that perplexes me.

VALÈRE   Every one has his troubles in this world, and we also are looking for something that we should be very glad to find.

MARTINE   Is it something in which I can assist you?

VALÈRE   Perhaps. We are endeavouring to meet with some clever man, some special physician, who could give some relief to our master's daughter, seized with an illness which has at once deprived her of the use of her tongue. Several physicians have already exhausted all their knowledge on her behalf; but sometimes one may find people with wonderful secrets, and certain peculiar remedies, who very often succeed where others have failed; and that is the sort of man we are looking for.

MARTINE *(softly and aside)*   Ah! This is an inspiration from Heaven to revenge myself on my rascal. *(Aloud)*   You could never have addressed yourselves to any one more able to find what you want; and we have a man here, the most wonderful fellow in the world for desperate maladies.

VALÈRE   Ah! for mercy's sake, where can we meet with him?

MARTINE   You will find him just now in that little spot yonder, where he is amusing himself in cutting wood.

LUCAS   A doctor who cuts wood!

VALÈRE   Who is amusing himself in gathering some simples, you mean to say?

MARTINE   No; he is a strange fellow who takes delight in this; a fantastic, eccentric, whimsical man, whom you would never take to be what he really is. He goes about dressed in a most extraordinary fashion, pretends sometimes to be very ignorant, keeps his knowledge to himself, and dislikes nothing so much every day as using the marvellous talents which God has given him for the healing art.

VALÈRE   It is a wonderful thing that all these great men have always some whim, some slight grain of madness mixed with their learning.

MARTINE   The madness of this man is greater than can be imagined, for sometimes he has to be beaten before he will own his ability; and I warn you beforehand that you will not succeed, that he will never own that he is a physician, unless you take each a stick, and compel him, by dint of blows, to admit at last what he will conceal at first. It is thus that we act when we have need of him.

VALÈRE   What a strange delusion!

MARTINE   That is true; but after that, you shall see that he works wonders.

VALÈRE   What is his name?

MARTINE   His name is Sganarelle. But it is very easy to recognise him. He is a man with a large black beard, and wears a ruff, and a yellow and green coat.

LUCAS   A yellow and green coat! He is then a parrot-doctor?

VALÈRE   But is it really true that he is as clever as you say?

MARTINE   As clever. He is a man who works miracles. About six months ago, a woman was given up by all the other physicians; she was considered dead at least six hours, and they were going to bury her, when they dragged by force the man we are speaking of to her bedside. Having seen her, he poured a small drop of something into her mouth; and at that very instant she rose from her bed, and began immediately to walk in her room as if nothing had happened.

LUCAS   Ah!

VALÈRE   It must have been a drop of liquid gold.

MARTINE   Possibly so. Not more than three weeks ago, a young child, twelve years old, fell from the top of the belfry, and smashed his head, arms, and legs on the stones. No sooner took they our man to it, than he rubbed the whole body with a certain ointment, which he knows how to prepare; and the child immediately rose on its legs, and ran away to play at chuck-farthing.

LUCAS   Hah!

VALÈRE   This man must have the universal cure-all.

MARTINE   Who doubts it?

LUCAS   Odds-bobs! that is the very man we want. Let us go quickly and fetch him.

VALÈRE   We thank you for the service you have rendered us.

MARTINE   But do not fail to remember the warning I have given you.

LUCAS   Hey! Zooks! leave it to us. If he wants nothing but a thrashing, we will gain our point.

VALÈRE (*to* LUCAS)   We are very glad to have met with this woman; and I conceive the best hopes in the world from it.

Scene VI. SGANARELLE, VALÈRE, LUCAS.

SGANARELLE (*singing behind the scene*)   La, la, la . . .

VALÈRE   I hear someone singing and cutting wood.

SGANARELLE (*coming on, with a bottle in his hand, without perceiving* VALÈRE *or* LUCAS)   La, la, la. . . . Really I have done enough to deserve a drink. Let us take a little breath. *(He drinks.)* This wood is as salt as the very devil. *(Sings)*

> *What pleasure's so sweet as the bottle can give,*
> *What music's so good as thy little gull-gull!*
> *My fate might be envied by all on the earth*
> *Were my dear jolly flask but constantly full.*
> *Say why, my sweet bottle, I pray thee, say why*
> *Since, full you're delightful, you ever are dry?*

Come! Zounds! we must take care not to get the blues.

VALÈRE (*softly to* LUCAS)   This is the very man.

LUCAS (*softly to* VALÈRE)   I think you are right, and that we have just hit upon him.

VALÈRE   Let us look a little closer.

SGANARELLE (*hugging the bottle*)   Ah! you little rogue! I love you, my pretty dear! *(He sings; but perceiving* LUCAS *and* VALÈRE, *who are examining him, he lowers his voice.)* My fate . . . might be envied . . . by all . . . on the earth. *(Seeing that they examine him more closely.)* Whom the deuce do these people want?

VALÈRE (*to* LUCAS)   It is surely he.

LUCAS (*to* VALÈRE)   There he is, exactly as he has been described to us.

SGANARELLE (*aside. At this point he puts down his bottle; and when* VALÈRE *stoops down to bow to him, he thinks that it is in order to snatch it away, and puts it on the other side. As* LUCAS *is doing the same thing as* VALÈRE, SGANARELLE *takes it up again, and hugs it to his breast, with various grimaces which make a great deal of by-play.)*   They are consulting each other, while looking at me. What can be their intentions!

VALÈRE   Sir, is not your name Sganarelle?

SGANARELLE   Hey! What!

VALÈRE   I ask you if your name is not Sganarelle.

SGANARELLE (*turning first to* VALÈRE, *then to* LUCAS)   Yes, and no. It depends on what you want with him.

VALÈRE   We want nothing with him, but to offer him our utmost civilities.

SGANARELLE   In that case my name is Sganarelle.

VALÈRE   We are delighted to see you, Sir. We have been recommended to you for what we are in search of; and we have come to implore your help, of which we are in want.

SGANARELLE   If it be anything, gentlemen, that belongs to my little trade, I am quite ready to oblige you.

VALÈRE   You are too kind to us, Sir. But put your hat on, Sir, if you please; the sun might hurt you.

LUCAS   Pray, Sir, put it on.

SGANARELLE *(aside)*   What a deal of ceremony these people use. *(He puts his hat on.)*

VALÈRE   You must not think it strange, Sir, that we have addressed ourselves to you. Clever people are always much sought after, and we have been informed of your capacity.

SGANARELLE   It is true, gentlemen, that I am the best hand in the world at making faggots.

VALÈRE   Oh! Sir . . .

SGANARELLE   I spare no pains, and make them in a fashion that leaves nothing to be desired.

VALÈRE   That is not the question we have come about, Sir.

SGANARELLE   But I charge a hundred and ten sous the hundred.

VALÈRE   Let us not speak about that, if you please.

SGANARELLE   I pledge you my word that I could not sell them for less.

VALÈRE   We know what is what, Sir.

SGANARELLE   If you know what is what, you know that I charge that price.

VALÈRE   This is a joke, Sir, but . . .

SGANARELLE   It is no joke at all, I cannot bate a farthing.

VALÈRE   Let us talk differently, please.

SGANARELLE   You may find some elsewhere for less; there be faggots and faggots; but for those which I make . . .

VALÈRE   Let us change the conversation, pray, Sir.

SGANARELLE   I take my oath that you shall not have them for less, not a fraction.

VALÈRE   Fie! Fie!

SGANARELLE   No, upon my word, you shall have to pay that price. I am speaking frankly, and I am not the man to overcharge.

VALÈRE   Ought a gentleman like you, Sir, to amuse himself with those clumsy pretences, to lower himself to talk thus? Ought so learned a man, such a famous physician as you are, wish to disguise himself in the eyes of the world and keep buried his great talents?

SGANARELLE *(aside)*   He is mad.

VALÈRE   Pray, Sir, do not dissemble with us.

SGANARELLE   What do you mean?

LUCAS   All this beating about the bush is useless. We know what we know.

SGANARELLE   What do you know? What do you want with me? For whom do you take me?

VALÈRE   For what you are, a great physician.

SGANARELLE   Physician yourself; I am not one, and I have never been one.

VALÈRE *(aside)*   Now the fit is on him. *(Aloud)* Sir, do not deny things any longer, and do not, if you please, make us have recourse to unpleasant extremities.

SGANARELLE   Have recourse to what?

VALÈRE   To certain things that we should be sorry for.

SGANARELLE   Zounds! Have recourse to whatever you like. I am not a physician, and do not understand what you mean.

VALÈRE *(aside)*   Well, I perceive that we shall have to apply the remedy. *(Aloud)* Once more, Sir, I pray you to confess what you are.

LUCAS   Odds-bobs, do not talk any more nonsense; and confess plainly that you are a physician.

SGANARELLE *(aside)*   I am getting in a rage.

VALÈRE   What is the good of denying what all the world knows?

LUCAS   Why all these funny falsehoods? What is the good of it?

SGANARELLE   One word is as good as a thousand, gentlemen. I tell you that I am not a physician.

VALÈRE You are not a physician?

SGANARELLE No.

LUCAS You are not a physician?

SGANARELLE No, I tell you.

VALÈRE Since you will have it so, we must make up our minds to do it. *(They each take a stick, and thrash him.)*

SGANARELLE Hold! hold! hold, gentlemen! I will be anything you like.

VALÈRE Why, Sir, do you oblige us to use this violence?

LUCAS Why do you make us take the trouble of giving you a beating?

VALÈRE I assure you that I regret it with all my heart.

LUCAS Upon my word I am sorry for it, too.

SGANARELLE What the devil does it all mean, gentlemen? For pity's sake, is it a joke, or are you both gone out of your minds, to wish to make me out a physician?

VALÈRE What! you do not give in yet, and you still deny being a physician?

SGANARELLE The devil take me if I am one!

LUCAS Are you not a physician?

SGANARELLE No, plague choke me! *(They begin to thrash him again.)* Hold! hold! Well, gentlemen, yes, since you will have it so, I am a physician, I am a physician—an apothecary into the bargain, if you like. I prefer saying yes to everything to being knocked about so.

VALÈRE Ah! that is right, Sir; I am delighted to see you so reasonable.

LUCAS It does my heart good to hear you speak in this way.

VALÈRE I beg your pardon with all my heart.

LUCAS I hope you will forgive me for the liberty I have taken.

SGANARELLE *(aside)* Bless my soul! Am I perhaps myself mistaken, and have I become a physician without being aware of it?

VALÈRE You shall not regret, Sir, having shown us what you are; and you shall certainly be satisfied.

SGANARELLE But, tell me, gentlemen, may you not be yourselves mistaken? Is it quite certain that I am a physician?

LUCAS Yes, upon my word!

SGANARELLE Really and truly?

VALÈRE Undoubtedly.

SGANARELLE The devil take me if I knew it!

VALÈRE Nonsense! You are the cleverest physician in the world.

SGANARELLE Ha, ha!

LUCAS A physician who has cured I do not know how many complaints.

SGANARELLE The dickens I have!

VALÈRE A woman was thought dead for six hours; she was ready to be buried when you, with a drop of something, brought her to again, and made her walk at once about the room.

SGANARELLE The deuce I did!

LUCAS A child of twelve fell from the top of the belfry, by which he had his head, his legs, and his arms smashed; and you, with I do not know what ointment, made him immediately get up on his feet, and off he ran to play chuck-farthing.

SGANARELLE The deuce I did!

VALÈRE In short, Sir, you will be satisfied with us, and you shall earn whatever you like, if you allow us to take you where we intend.

SGANARELLE I shall earn whatever I like?

VALÈRE Yes.

SGANARELLE   In that case I am a physician: there is no doubt of it. I had forgotten it; but I recollect it now. What is the matter? Where am I to go?

VALÈRE   We will conduct you. The matter is to see a girl who has lost her speech.

SGANARELLE   Indeed! I have not found it.

VALÈRE (*softly to* LUCAS)   How he loves his joke! (*To* SGANARELLE) Come along, Sir!

SGANARELLE   Without a physician's gown!

VALÈRE   We will get one.

SGANARELLE (*presenting his bottle to* VALÈRE)   You carry this: I put my juleps in there. (*Turning round to* LUCAS *and spitting on the ground*) And you, stamp on this, by order of the physician.

LUCAS   Odds sniggers! this is a physician I like. I think he will do, for he is a comical fellow.

ACT II. *A Room in* GÉRONTE'S *House.*

Scene I.   GÉRONTE, VALÈRE, LUCAS, JACQUELINE.

VALERE   Yes, Sir, I think you will be satisfied; we have brought the greatest physician in the world with us.

LUCAS   Oh! Zooks! this one beats everything; all the others are not worthy to hold the candle to him.

VALÈRE   He is a man who has performed some marvellous cures.

LUCAS   Who has put dead people on their legs again.

VALÈRE   He is somewhat whimsical, as I have told you; and at times there are moments when his senses wander, and he does not seem what he really is.

LUCAS   Yes, he loves a joke, and one would say sometimes that he has got a screw loose somewhere.

VALÈRE   But in reality he is quite scientific; and very often he says things quite beyond anyone's comprehension.

LUCAS   When he sets about it, he talks as finely as if he were reading a book.

VALÈRE   He has already a great reputation hereabout, and everybody comes to consult him.

GÉRONTE   I am very anxious to see him; send him to me quickly.

VALÈRE   I am going to fetch him.

Scene II.   GÉRONTE, JACQUELINE, LUCAS.

JACQUELINE   Upon my word, Sir, this one will do just the same as all the rest. I think it will be six of the one and half-a-dozen of the others; and the best medicine to give to your daughter would, in my opinion, be a handsome strapping husband, for whom she could have some love.

GÉRONTE   Lord bless my soul, nurse dear, you are meddling with many things.

LUCAS   Hold your tongue, mother Jacqueline; it is not for you to poke your nose there.

JACQUELINE   I tell you, and a dozen more of you, that all these physicians do her no good; that your daughter wants something else than rhubarb and senna, and that a husband is a plaster which cures all girls' complaints.

GÉRONTE   Would any one have her in her present state, with that affliction on her? and when I intended her to marry, has she not opposed my wishes?

JACQUELINE   No wonder. You wished to give her a man whom she does not like. Why did you not give her to Monsieur Léandre, who takes her fancy? She would have been very obedient, and I vouch for it that he will take her as she is, if you but give her to him.

GÉRONTE   Léandre is not the man we want; he has not got a fortune like the other.

JACQUELINE   He has got an uncle who is so rich, and he is the heir.

GÉRONTE   All these expectations seem to me but moonshine. Brag is a good dog, but Holdfast is a better; and we run a great risk in waiting for dead men's shoes. Death is not always at the beck and call of gentlemen heirs; and while the grass grows, the cow starves.

JACQUELINE   That is all well and good, but I have always heard that in marriage, as in everything else, happiness excels riches. Fathers and mothers have this cursed habit of asking always, "How much has he got?" and "How much has she got?" And gaffer Peter has married his Simonette to that lout Thomas, because he has got a few more vineyards than young Robin, for whom the girl had a fancy; and now the poor creature is as yellow as a guinea, and has not looked like herself ever since. That is a good example for you, Sir. After all, folks have but their pleasure in this world; and I would sooner give my daughter a husband whom she likes than have all the riches in the country.

GÉRONTE   Bless, me, nurse, how you chatter! Hold your tongue, let me beg of you; you take too much upon yourself, and you will spoil your milk.

LUCAS *(slapping* GÉRONTE'S *shoulder at every word)*   Indeed, be silent; you are too saucy. The master does not want your speeches, and he knows what he is about. All you have got to do is to suckle your baby, without arguing so much. Our master is the girl's father, and he is good and clever enough to know what she wants.

GÉRONTE   Gently, gently.

LUCAS *(still slapping* GÉRONTE'S *shoulder)*   I wish to show her her place, and teach her the respect due to you, Sir.

GÉRONTE   Very well. But it does not need all this gesticulating.

Scene III. VALÈRE, SGANARELLE, GÉRONTE, LUCAS, JACQUELINE.

VALÈRE   Look out, Sir, here is our physician coming.

GÉRONTE *(to* SGANARELLE*)*   I am delighted to see you, Sir, at my house, and we have very great need of you.

SGANARELLE *(in a physician's gown with a very pointed cap)*   Hippocrates says . . . that we should both put our hats on.

GÉRONTE   Hippocrates says that?

SGANARELLE   Yes.

GÉRONTE   In which chapter, if you please?

SGANARELLE   In his chapter . . . on hats.

GÉRONTE   Since Hippocrates says so, we must obey.

SGANARELLE   Doctor, having heard of the marvellous things. . .

GÉRONTE   To whom are you speaking, pray?

SGANARELLE   To you.

GÉRONTE   I am not a physician.

SGANARELLE   You are not a physician?

GÉRONTE   Indeed I am not.

SGANARELLE   Really?

GÉRONTE   Really. (SGANARELLE *takes a stick and thrashes* GÉRONTE.) Oh! Oh! Oh!

SGANARELLE   Now you are a physician, I have never taken any other degree.

GÉRONTE (*to* VALÈRE)   What a devil of a fellow you have brought me here!

VALÈRE   Did I tell you that he was a funny sort of a physician?

GÉRONTE   Yes; but I shall send him about his business with his fun.

LUCAS   Do not take any notice of it, Sir. It is only his joking.

GÉRONTE   The joking does not suit me.

SGANARELLE   Sir, I beg your pardon for the liberty I have taken.

GÉRONTE   I am your humble servant, Sir.

SGANARELLE   I am sorry. . .

GÉRONTE   It is nothing.

SGANARELLE   For the cudgelling I . . .

GÉRONTE   There is no harm done.

SGANARELLE   Which I have had the honour to give you.

GÉRONTE   Do not say any more about it, Sir. I have a daughter who is suffering from a strange complaint.

SGANARELLE   I am delighted, Sir, that your daughter has need of my skill; and I wish, with all my heart, that you stood in the same need of it, you and all your family, in order to show you my wish to serve you.

GÉRONTE   I am obliged to you for these kind feelings.

SGANARELLE   I assure you that I am speaking from my very heart.

GÉRONTE   You really do me too much honour.

SGANARELLE   What is your daughter's name?

GÉRONTE   Lucinde.

SGANARELLE   Lucinde! Ah! a pretty name to physic! Lucinde!

GÉRONTE   I will just see what she is doing.

SGANARELLE   Who is that tall woman?

GÉRONTE   She is my baby's nurse.

Scene IV. SGANARELLE, JACQUELINE, LUCAS.

SGANARELLE *(aside)*   The deuce! that is a fine piece of household furniture. *(Aloud)* Ah, nurse! Charming nurse! my physic is the very humble slave of your nurseship, and I should like to be the fortunate little nursling to suck the milk of your good graces. *(He puts his hand on her bosom.)* All my nostrums, all my skill, all my cleverness, is at your service; and . . .

LUCAS   By your leave, M. Doctor; leave my wife alone, I pray you.

SGANARELLE   What! is she your wife?

LUCAS   Yes.

SGANARELLE   Oh! indeed! I did not know that, but I am very glad of it for the love of both. *(He pretends to embrace LUCAS, but embraces the nurse.)*

LUCAS *(pulling SGANARELLE away, and placing himself between him and his wife)* Gently, if you please.

SGANARELLE   I assure you that I am delighted that you should be united together. I congratulate her upon having such a husband as you; and I congratulate you upon having a wife so handsome, so discreet, and so well shaped as she is. *(He pretends once more to embrace LUCAS, who holds out his arms; he slips under them and embraces the nurse.)*

LUCAS *(pulling him away again)*   Do not pay so many compliments, I beg of you.

SGANARELLE   Shall I not rejoice with you about such a lovely harmony?

LUCAS   With me as much as you like; but a truce to compliments with my wife.

SGANARELLE   I have both your happiness equally at heart; and if I embrace you to show my delight in you, I embrace her to show my delight in her. *(Same by-play)*

LUCAS *(pulling him away for the third time)*   Odds boddikins, Doctor, what capers you cut!

Scene V. GÉRONTE, SGANARELLE, LUCAS, JACQUELINE.

GÉRONTE   My daughter will be here directly, Sir.

SGANARELLE   I am awaiting her, Sir, with all my physic.

GÉRONTE   Where is it?

SGANARELLE *(touching his forehead)*   In there.

GÉRONTE   That is good.

SGANARELLE   But as I feel much interested in your family, I should like to test the milk of your nurse, and examine her breasts. (*He draws close to* JACQUELINE.)

LUCAS *(pulling him away, and swinging him round)*   Nothing of the sort, nothing of the sort. I do not wish it.

SGANARELLE   It is the physician's duty to see the breasts of the nurse.

LUCAS   Duty or no duty, I will not have it.

SGANARELLE   Have you the audacity to contradict a physician? Out with you.

LUCAS   I do not care a straw about a physician.

SGANARELLE *(looking askance at him)*   I will give you a fever.

JACQUELINE *(taking* LUCAS *by the arm, and swinging him around also)*   Get out of the way. Am I not big enough to take my own part, if he does anything to me which he ought not to do?

LUCAS   I will not have him touch you, I will not.

SGANARELLE   For shame you rascal, to be jealous of your wife.

GÉRONTE   Here comes my daughter.

Scene VI. LUCINDE, GÉRONTE, SGANARELLE, VALÈRE, LUCAS, JACQUELINE.

SGANARELLE   Is this the patient?

GÉRONTE   Yes, I have but one daughter; and I would never get over it if she were to die.

SGANARELLE   Do not let her do anything of the kind. She must not die without a prescription of the physician.

GÉRONTE   A chair here!

SGANARELLE *(seated between* GÉRONTE *and* LUCINDE)   This is not at all an unpleasant patient, and I am of the opinion that she would not be at all amiss for a man in very good health.

GÉRONTE   You have made her laugh, Sir.

SGANARELLE   So much the better. It is the best sign in the world when a physician makes the patient laugh. (*To* LUCINDE) Well, what is the matter? What ails you? What is it you feel?

LUCINDE *(replies by motions, by putting her hands to her mouth, her head, and under her chin)*   Ha, hi, ho, ha!

SGANARELLE   What do you say?

LUCINDE *(continues the same motions)*   Ha, hi, ho, ha, ha, hi, ho!

SGANARELLE   What is that?

LUCINDE   Ha, hi, ho!

SGANARELLE *(imitating her)*   Ha, hi, ho, ha, ha! I do not understand you. What sort of language do you call that?

GÉRONTE That is just where her complaint lies, Sir. She has become dumb, without our having been able till now to discover the cause. This accident has obliged us to postpone her marriage.

SGANARELLE And why so?

GÉRONTE He whom she is going to marry wishes to wait for her recovery to conclude the marriage.

SGANARELLE And who is this fool that does not want his wife to be dumb? Would to Heaven that mine had that complaint! I should take particular care not to have her cured.

GÉRONTE To the point, Sir. We beseech you to use all your skill to cure her of this affliction.

SGANARELLE Do not make yourself uneasy. But tell me, does this pain oppress her much?

GÉRONTE Yes, Sir.

SGANARELLE So much the better. Is the suffering very acute?

GÉRONTE Very acute.

SGANARELLE That is right. Does she go to . . . you know where?

GÉRONTE Yes.

SGANARELLE Freely?

GÉRONTE That I know nothing about.

SGANARELLE Is the matter healthy?

GÉRONTE I do not understand these things.

SGANARELLE *(turning to the patient)* Give me your hand. (*To* GÉRONTE) The pulse tells me that your daughter is dumb.

GÉRONTE Sir, that is what is the matter with her; ah! yes, you have found it out at the first touch.

SGANARELLE Of course!

JACQUELINE See how he has guessed her complaint.

SGANARELLE We great physicians, we know matters at once. An ignoramus would have been nonplussed, and would have told you: it is this, that, or the other; but I hit the nail on the head from the very first, and I tell you that your daughter is dumb.

GÉRONTE Yes; but I should like you to tell me whence it arises.

SGANARELLE Nothing is easier; it arises from loss of speech.

GÉRONTE Very good. But the reason of her having lost her speech, pray?

SGANARELLE Our best authorities will tell you that it is because there is an impediment in the action of her tongue.

GÉRONTE But, once more, your opinion upon this impediment in the action of her tongue.

SGANARELLE Aristotle on this subject says . . . a great many clever things.

GÉRONTE I dare say.

SGANARELLE Ah! He was a great man!

GÉRONTE No doubt.

SGANARELLE Yes, a very great man. (*Holding out his arm, and putting a finger of the other hand in the bend*) A man who was, by this, much greater than I. But to come back to our argument: I hold that this impediment in the action of her tongue is caused by certain humours, which among us learned men, we call peccant humours; peccant—that is to say . . . peccant humours; inasmuch as the vapours formed by the exhalations of the influences which rise in the very region of diseases, coming, . . . as we may say to. . . . Do you understand Latin?

GÉRONTE Not in the least.

SGANARELLE *(suddenly rising)* You do not understand Latin?

GÉRONTE   No.

SGANARELLE   (*assuming various comic attitudes*) *Cabricias arci thuram, catalamus, singulariter, nominativo, bœc musa,* the muse, *bonus, bona, bonum. Deus sanctus, estne oratio latinas? Etiam.* Yes. *Quare?* Why? *Quia substantivo et adjectivum, concordat in generi, numerum, et casus.*

GÉRONTE   Ah! Why did I not study?

JACQUELINE   What a clever man!

LUCAS   Yes, it is so beautiful that I do not understand a word of it.

SGANARELLE   Thus these vapours which I speak of, passing from the left side, where the liver is, to the right side, where we find the heart, it so happens that the lungs, which in Latin we call *armyan,* having communication with the brain, which in Greek we style *nasmus,* by means of *vena cava,* which in Hebrew, is termed *cubile,* meet in their course the said vapours, which fill the ventricles of the omoplata; and because the said vapours . . . now understand well this argument, pray . . . and because these said vapours are endowed with a certain malignity . . . listen well to this, I beseech you.

GÉRONTE   Yes.

SGANARELLE   Are endowed with a certain malignity which is caused . . . pay attention here, if you please.

GÉRONTE   I do.

SGANARELLE   Which is caused by the acridity of these humours engendered in the concavity of the diaphragm, it happens that these vapours . . . *Ossabandus, nequeis, nequer, potarinum, puipsa milus.* That is exactly the reason that your daughter is dumb.

JACQUELINE   Ah! How well this gentleman explains all this

LUCAS   Why does not my tongue wag as well as his?

GÉRONTE   It is undoubtedly impossible to argue better. There is but one thing that I cannot exactly make out: that is the whereabouts of the liver and the heart. It appears to me that you place them differently from where they are; that the heart is on the left side, and the liver on the right.

SGANARELLE   Yes; this was formerly; but we have changed all that, and we now-a-days practice the medical art on an entirely new system.

GÉRONTE   I did not know that, and I pray you pardon my ignorance.

SGANARELLE   There is no harm done; and you are not obliged to be so clever as we are.

GÉRONTE   Certainly not. But what think you, Sir, ought to be done for this complaint?

SGANARELLE   What do I think ought to be done?

GÉRONTE   Yes.

SGANARELLE   My advice is to put her to bed again, and make her, as a remedy, take plenty of bread soaked in wine.

GÉRONTE   Why so, Sir?

SGANARELLE   Because there is in bread and wine mixed together a sympathetic virtue which produces speech. Do you not see that they give nothing else to parrots, and that, by eating it, they learn to speak?

GÉRONTE   That is true. Oh! the great man! Quick, plenty of bread and wine.

SGANARELLE   I shall come back to-night to see how the patient is getting on

Scene VII. GÉRONTE, SGANARELLE, JACQUELINE.

SGANARELLE   (*to* JACQUELINE)   Stop a little, you. (*To* GÉRONTE)   Sir, I must give some medicine to your nurse.

JACQUELINE   To me, Sir? I am as well as can be.

SGANARELLE   So much the worse, nurse, so much the worse. This excess of health is dangerous, and it would not be amiss to bleed you a little gently, and to administer some little soothing injection.

GÉRONTE   But, my dear Sir, that is a method which I cannot understand. Why bleed folks when they are not ill?

SGANARELLE   It does not matter, the method is salutary; and as we drink for the thirst to come, so must we bleed for the disease to come.

JACQUELINE *(going)*   I do not care a fig for all this, and I will not have my body made an apothecary's shop.

SGANARELLE   You object to my remedies; but we shall know how to bring you to reason.

Scene VIII. GÉRONTE, SGANARELLE.

SGANARELLE   I wish you good day.

GÉRONTE   Stay a moment, if you please.

SGANARELLE   What are you going to do?

GÉRONTE   Give you your fee, Sir.

SGANARELLE *(putting his hands behind him, from under his gown, while* GÉRONTE *opens his purse)*   I shall not accept it, Sir.

GÉRONTE   Sir.

SGANARELLE   Not at all.

GÉRONTE   One moment.

SGANARELLE   On one consideration.

GÉRONTE   Pray!

SGANARELLE   You are jesting.

GÉRONTE   That is settled.

SGANARELLE   I shall do nothing of the kind.

GÉRONTE   What!

SGANARELLE   I do not practise for money's sake.

GÉRONTE   I am convinced of that.

SGANARELLE *(after having taken the money)*   Are they good weight?

GÉRONTE   Yes, Sir.

SGANARELLE   I am not a mercenary physician.

GÉRONTE   I am well aware of it.

SGANARELLE   I am not actuated by interest.

GÉRONTE   I do not for a moment think so.

SGANARELLE *(alone, looking at the money he has received)*   Upon my word, this does not promise badly; and provided . . .

Scene IX. LÉANDRE, SGANARELLE.

LÉANDRE   I have been waiting some time for you, Sir, and I have come to beg your assistance.

SGANARELLE *(feeling his pulse)*   That is a very bad pulse.

LÉANDRE   I am not ill, Sir; and it is not for that I am come to you.

SGANARELLE   If you are not ill, why the devil do you not tell me so?

LÉANDRE   No. To tell you the matter in a few words, my name is Léandre. I am in love with Lucinde to whom you have just paid a visit; and as all access to her is denied to me, through the ill-temper of her father, I venture to beseech you to serve me in my love affair, and to assist me in a stratagem that I have invented, so as to say a few words to her, on which my whole life and happiness absolutely depend.

SGANARELLE *(in apparent anger)* Whom do you take me for? How dare you address yourself to me to assist you in your love affair, and to wish me to lower the dignity of a physician by an affair of that kind!

LÉANDRE Do not make a noise, Sir!

SGANARELLE *(driving him back)* I will make a noise. You are an impertinent fellow.

LÉANDRE Ah! gently, Sir.

SGANARELLE An ill-mannered jackanapes.

LÉANDRE Pray!

SGANARELLE I will teach you that I am not the kind of man you take me for, and that it is the greatest insolence . . .

LÉANDRE *(taking out a purse)* Sir . . .

SGANARELLE To wish to employ me . . . *(Taking the purse)* I am not speaking about you, for you are a gentleman; and I should be delighted to be of any use to you; but there are certain impertinent people in this world who take folks for what they are not; and I tell you candidly that this puts me in a passion.

LÉANDRE I ask your pardon, Sir, for the liberty I have . . .

SGANARELLE You are jesting. What is the affair in question?

LÉANDRE You must know then, Sir, that this disease which you wish to cure is a feigned complaint. The physicians have argued about it, as they ought to do, and they have not failed to give it as their opinion—this one, that it arose from the brain; that one, from the intestines; another, from the spleen; another, again, from the liver; but the fact is that love is its real cause, and that Lucinde has only invented this illness in order to free herself from a marriage with which she has been harassed. But for fear that we may be seen together, let us retire; and I will tell you as we go along, what I wish you to do.

SGANARELLE Come along, then, Sir. You have inspired me with an inconceivable interest in your love; and if all my medical science does not fail me, the patient shall either die or be yours.

ACT III. *A Place Near* GÉRONTE'S *House.*

Scene I. LÉANDRE, SGANARELLE.

LÉANDRE I think that I am not at all badly got up for an apothecary; and as her father has scarcely ever seen me, this change of dress and wig is likely enough, I think, to disguise me.

SGANARELLE There is no doubt of it.

LÉANDRE Only I should like to know five or six big medical words to leaven my conversation with, and to give me the air of a learned man.

SGANARELLE Go along, go along; it is not at all necessary. The dress is sufficient; and I know no more about it than you do.

LÉANDRE How is that!

SGANARELLE The devil take me if I understand anything about medicine! You are a gentleman, and I do not mind confiding in you, as you have confided in me.

LÉANDRE What! Then you are not really . . .

SGANARELLE No, I tell you. They have made me a physician in the teeth of my protests. I have never attempted to be so learned as that; and all my studies did not go farther than the lowest class at school. I do not know how the idea has come to them; but when

I saw that in spite of everything they would have it that I was a physician, I made up my mind to be so at somebody's expense. You would not believe, however, how this error has spread, and how everyone is possessed, and believes me to be a learned man. They come seeking me on all sides; and if things go on in this way, I am resolved to stick to the profession all my life. I find that it is the best trade of all; for, whether we manage well or ill, we are paid just the same. Bad workmanship never recoils on us; and we cut the material we have to work with pretty much as we like. A shoemaker, in making a pair of shoes, cannot spoil a scrap of leather without having to bear the loss; but in our business we may spoil a man without its costing us a farthing. The blunders are never put down to us, and it is always the fault of the fellow who dies. The best of this profession is, that there is the greatest honesty and discretion among the dead; for you never find them complain of the physician who has killed them.

LÉANDRE   It is true that the dead are very honourable in that respect.

SGANARELLE *(seeing some people advancing towards him)*   There come some people, who seem anxious to consult me. (*To* LÉANDRE) Go and wait for me near the house of your ladylove.

Scene II. THIBAUT, PERRIN, SGANARELLE.

THIBAUT   Sir, we come to look for you, my son Perrin and myself.

SGANARELLE   What is the matter?

THIBAUT   His poor mother, whose name is Perrette, has been on a bed of sickness for the last six months.

SGANARELLE *(holding out his hand as if to receive money)*   What would you have me do to her?

THIBAUT   I would like you to give me some little doctor's stuff to cure her.

SGANARELLE   We must first see what is the matter with her.

THIBAUT   She is ill with the hypocrisy, Sir.

SGANARELLE   With the hypocrisy?

THIBAUT   Yes; I mean she is swollen everywhere. They say that there is a lot of seriosities in her inside, and that her liver, her belly, or her spleen, as you would call it, instead of making blood makes nothing but water. She has, every other day, the quotiguian fever, with lassitude and pains in the muscles of her legs. We can hear in her throat phlegms that are ready to choke her, and she is often taken with syncoles and conversions, so that we think she is going off the hooks. We have got in our village an apothecary— with respect be it said—who has given her, I do not know how much stuff; and it has cost me more than a dozen good crowns in clysters, saving your presence, in apostumes which he has made her swallow, in infections of hyacinth, and in cordial potions. But all this, as people say, was nothing but an ointment of fiddle-faddle. He wanted to give her a certain drug called ametile wine; but I was downright afeard that this would send her to the other world altogether; because they tell me that those big physicians kill, I do not know how many, with that new-fangled potion.

SGANARELLE *(still holding out his hand, and moving it about to show that he wants money)*   Let us come to the point, friend, let us come to the point.

THIBAUT   The point is, Sir, that we have come to beg of you to tell us what we must do.

SGANARELLE   I do not understand you at all.

PERRIN   My mother is ill, Sir, and here are two crowns which we have brought you to give us some stuff.

SGANARELLE   Ah! you I do understand. There is a lad who speaks clearly, and explains himself as he should. You say that your mother is ill with the dropsy; that she is swollen all over her body; that she has a fever, with pains in the legs; that she sometimes is taken with syncopes and convulsions, that is to say with fainting fits.

PERRIN   Indeed, Sir! that is just it.

SGANARELLE   I understand you at once. Your father does not know what he says. And now you ask me for a remedy?

PERRIN   Yes sir.

SGANARELLE   A remedy to cure her?

PERRIN   That is just what I mean.

SGANARELLE   Take this then. It is a piece of cheese which you must make her take.

PERRIN   A piece of cheese, Sir?

SGANARELLE   Yes; it is a kind of prepared cheese, in which there is gold, coral, and pearls, and a great many other precious things.

PERRIN   I am very much obliged to you, Sir, and I shall go and make her take it directly.

SGANARELLE   Go, and if she dies, do not fail to bury her in the best style you can.

Scene III. *The scene changes, and represents, as in the Second Act, a room in* GÉRONTE'S *house.* JACQUELINE, SGANARELLE, LUCAS, *at the far end of the stage.*

SGANARELLE   Here is the pretty nurse. Ah! you darling nurse, I am delighted at this meeting; and the sight of you is like rhubarb, cassia, and senna to me, which purges all melancholy from my mind.

JACQUELINE   Upon my word, M. Physician, it is no good talking to me in that style, and I do not understand your Latin at all.

SGANARELLE   Get ill, nurse, I beg of you; get ill for my sake. I shall have all the pleasure in the world of curing you.

JACQUELINE   I am your humble servant; I would much rather not be cured.

SGANARELLE   How I grieve for you, beautiful nurse, in having such a jealous and troublesome husband.

JACQUELINE   What am I to do, Sir? It is as a penance for my sins; and where the goat is tied down she must browse.

SGANARELLE   What! Such a clod-hopper as that! a fellow who is always watching you, and will let no one speak to you!

JACQUELINE   Alas! you have seen nothing yet; and that is only a small sample of his bad temper.

SGANARELLE   Is it possible? and can a man have so mean a spirit as to ill-use a woman like you? Ah! I know some, sweet nurse, and who are not very far off, who would only be too glad to kiss your little feet! Why should such a handsome woman have fallen into such hands! and a mere animal, a brute, a stupid, a fool. . . . Excuse me, nurse, for speaking in that way of your husband.

JACQUELINE   Oh! Sir, I know full well that he deserves all these names.

SGANARELLE   Undoubtedly, nurse, he deserves them; and he also deserves that you should plant something on his head to punish him for his suspicions.

JACQUELINE   It is true enough that if I had not his interest so much at heart, he would drive me to do some strange things.

SGANARELLE   Indeed it would just serve him right if you were to revenge yourself upon him with some one. The fellow richly deserves it all, I tell you, and if I were fortunate enough, fair nurse, to be chosen by you . . . *(While* SGANARELLE *is holding out his arms to embrace* JACQUELINE, LUCAS *passes his head under them, and comes between the two.*

SGANARELLE *and* JACQUELINE *stare at* LUCAS, *and depart on opposite sides, but the doctor does so in a very comic manner.)*

Scene IV. GÉRONTE, LUCAS.

GÉRONTE   I say, Lucas, have not you seen our physician here?

LUCAS   Indeed I have seen him, by all the devils, and my wife, too.

GÉRONTE   Where can he be?

LUCAS   I do not know; but I wish he were with the devil.

GÉRONTE   Just go and see what my daughter is doing.

Scene V. SGANARELLE, LÉANDRE, GÉRONTE.

GÉRONTE   I was just inquiring after you, Sir.

SGANARELLE   I have just been amusing myself in your court with expelling the superfluity of drink. How is the patient?

GÉRONTE   Somewhat worse since your remedy.

SGANARELLE   So much the better; it shows that it takes effect.

GÉRONTE   Yes; but while it is taking effect, I am afraid it will choke her.

SGANARELLE   Do not make yourself uneasy; I have some remedies that will make it all right! and I will wait until she is at death's door.

GÉRONTE *(pointing to* LÉANDRE.) Who is this man that is with you?

SGANARELLE *(intimates by motions of his hands that it is an apothecary)*   It is . . .

GÉRONTE   What?

SGANARELLE   He who . . .

GÉRONTE   Oh!

SGANARELLE   Who . . .

GÉRONTE   I understand.

SGANARELLE   Your daughter will want him.

Scene VI. LUCINDE, GÉRONTE, LÉANDRE, JACQUELINE, SGANARELLE.

JACQUELINE   Here is your daughter, Sir, who wishes to stretch her limbs a little.

SGANARELLE   That will do her good. Go to her, M. Apothecary, and feel her pulse, so that I may consult with you presently about her complaint. *(At this point he draws* GÉRONTE *to one end of the stage, and putting one arm upon his shoulder, he places his under under his chin, with which he makes him turn towards him, each time that* GÉRONTE *wants to look at what is passing between his daughter and the apothecary, while he holds the following discourse with him.)* Sir, it is a great and subtle question among physicians to know whether women or men are more easily cured. I pray you to listen to this, if you please. Some say "no," others say "yes": I say both "yes" and "no"; inasmuch as the incongruity of the opaque humours, which are found in the natural temperament of women, causes the brutal part to struggle for the mastery over the sensitive, we find that the conflict of their opinion depends on the oblique motion of the circle of the moon; and as the sun, which darts its beams on the concavity of the earth, meets . . .

LUCINDE *(to* LÉANDRE) No; I am not at all likely to change my feelings.

GÉRONTE   Hark! my daughter speaks! O great virtue of the remedy! O excellent physician! How deeply am I obliged to you, Sir, for this marvellous cure! And what can I do for you after such a service?

SGANARELLE *(strutting about the stage, fanning himself with his hat)*   This case has given me some trouble.

LUCINDE   Yes, father, I have recovered my speech; but I have recovered it to tell you that I will never have any other husband than Léandre, and that it is in vain for you to wish to give me to Horace.

GÉRONTE   But . . .

LUCINDE   Nothing will shake the resolution I have taken.

GÉRONTE   What . . .

LUCINDE   All your fine arguments will be in vain.

GÉRONTE   If . . .

LUCINDE   All your talking will be of no use.

GÉRONTE   I . . .

LUCINDE   I have made up my mind about the matter.

GÉRONTE   But . . .

LUCINDE   No paternal authority can compel me to marry against my will.

GÉRONTE   I have . . .

LUCINDE   You may try as much as you like.

GÉRONTE   It . . .

LUCINDE   My heart cannot submit to this tyranny.

GÉRONTE   The . . .

LUCINDE   And I will sooner go into a convent than marry a man I do not love.

GÉRONTE   But . . .

LUCINDE *(in a loud voice)*   No. By no means. It is of no use. You waste your time. I shall do nothing of the kind. I am fully determined.

GÉRONTE   Ah! what a torrent of words! One cannot hold out against it. (*To* SGANARELLE) I beseech you, Sir, to make her dumb again.

SGANARELLE   That is impossible. All that I can do in your behalf is to make you deaf, if you like.

GÉRONTE   I thank you. (*To* LUCINDE) Do you think . . .

LUCINDE   No; all your reasoning will not have the slightest effect upon me.

GÉRONTE   You shall marry Horace this very evening.

LUCINDE   I would sooner marry death itself.

SGANARELLE (*to* GÉRONTE) Stop, for Heaven's sake! stop. Let me doctor this matter; it is a disease that has got hold of her, and I know the remedy to apply to it.

GÉRONTE   Is it possible, indeed, Sir, that you can cure this disease of the mind also?

SGANARELLE   Yes; let me manage it. I have remedies for everything; and our apothecary will serve us capitally for this cure. (*To* LÉANDRE) A word with you. You perceive that the passion she has for this Léandre is altogether against the wishes of the father; that there is no time to lose; that the humours are very acrimonious; and that it becomes necessary to find speedily a remedy for this complaint, which may get worse by delay. As for myself, I see but one, which is a dose of purgative flight, mixed, as it should be, with two drachms of matrimonium, made up into pills. She may, perhaps, make some difficulty about taking this remedy; but as you are a clever man in your profession, you must induce her to consent to it, and make her swallow the thing as best you can. Go and take a little turn in the garden with her to prepare the humours, while I converse here with her father; but, above all, lose not a moment. Apply the remedy quick! apply the specific!

Scene VII. GÉRONTE, SGANARELLE.

GÉRONTE   What drugs are those you have just mentioned, Sir? It seems to me that I never heard of them before.

SGANARELLE   They are drugs which are used only in urgent cases.

GÉRONTE   Did you ever see such insolence as hers?

SGANARELLE   Daughters are a little headstrong at times.

GÉRONTE   You would not believe how she is infatuated with this Léandre.

SGANARELLE   The heat of the blood produces those things in young people.

GÉRONTE   As for me, the moment I discovered the violence of this passion, I took care to keep my daughter under lock and key.

SGANARELLE   You have acted wisely.

GÉRONTE   And I have prevented the slightest communication between them.

SGANARELLE   Just so.

GÉRONTE   They would have committed some folly, if they had been permitted to see each other.

SGANARELLE   Undoubtedly.

GÉRONTE   And I think she would have been the girl to run away with him.

SGANARELLE   You have argued very prudently.

GÉRONTE   I was informed that he tried every means to get speech of her.

SGANARELLE   The rascal!

GÉRONTE   But he will waste his time.

SGANARELLE   Aye! Aye!

GÉRONTE   And I will effectually prevent him from seeing her.

SGANARELLE   He has no fool to deal with, and you know some tricks of which he is ignorant. One must get up very early to catch you asleep.

Scene VIII. LUCAS, GÉRONTE, SGANARELLE.

LUCAS   Odds-bobs, Sir, here is a pretty to do. Your daughter has fled with her Léandre. It was he that played the apothecary, and this is the physician who has performed this nice operation.

GÉRONTE   What! to murder me in this manner! Quick, fetch a magistrate, and take care that he does not get away. Ah villain! I will have you punished by the law.

LUCAS   I am afraid, Master Doctor, that you will be hanged. Do not stir a step, I tell you.

Scene IX. MARTINE, SGANARELLE, LUCAS.

MARTINE (*to* LUCAS)   Good gracious! what a difficulty I have had to find this place! Just tell me what has become of the physician I recommended to you?

LUCAS   Here he is; just going to be hanged.

MARTINE   What! my husband hanged! Alas, and for what?

LUCAS   He has helped some one to run away with master's daughter.

MARTINE   Alas, my dear husband, is it true that you are going to be hanged?

SGANARELLE   Judge for yourself. Ah!

MARTINE   And must you be made an end of in the presence of such a crowd.

SGANARELLE   What am I to do?

MARTINE   If you had only finished cutting our wood, I should be somewhat consoled.

SGANARELLE   Leave me, you break my heart.

MARTINE   No, I will remain to encourage you to die; and I will not leave you until I have seen you hanged.

SGANARELLE   Ah!

Scene X. GÉRONTE, SGANARELLE, MARTINE.

GÉRONTE (*to* SGANARELLE) The magistrate will be here directly, and we shall put you in a place of safety where they will be answerable for you.

SGANARELLE *(on his knees, hat in hand)* Alas! will not a few strokes with a cudgel do instead?

GÉRONTE No; no; the law shall decide. But what do I see?

Scene XI. GÉRONTE, LÉANDRE, LUCINDE, SGANARELLE, LUCAS, MARTINE.

LÉANDRE Sir, I appear before you as Léandre, and am come to restore Lucinde to your authority. We intended to run away, and get married; but this design has given away to a more honourable proceeding. I will not presume to steal away your daughter, and it is from your hands alone that I will obtain her. I must at the same time acquaint you, that I have just now received some letters informing me of the death of my uncle, and that he has left me heir to all his property.

GÉRONTE Really, Sir, your virtue is worthy of my utmost consideration, and I give you my daughter with the greatest pleasure in the world.

SGANARELLE *(aside)* The physician has had a narrow escape!

MARTINE Since you are not going to be hanged, you may thank me for being a physician; for I have procured you this honour.

SGANARELLE Yes, it is you who procured me, I do not know how many thwacks with a cudgel.

LÉANDRE (*to* SGANARELLE) The result has proved too happy to harbour any resentment.

SGANARELLE Be it so. (*To* MARTINE) I forgive you the blows on account of the dignity to which you have elevated me; but prepare yourself henceforth to behave with great respect towards a man of my consequence; and consider that the anger of a physician is more to be dreaded than people imagine.

Comments and Questions

This play, along with many others by Molière, represents the laughing theater at its best. It is all sunlight and no shadows. For this reason, serious analysis may seem out of place. The greatness of the art, however, has challenged critics for three hundred years, and serious analysis does help one to enter more fully into the pure fun; to laugh again at what he has laughed at before.

1. You may have been mildly puzzled by the many scenes. What occurs when a new scene is indicated? How does Molière's practice in this respect differ from modern practice? Compare, for example, the scenes in *Ghosts,* next.

2. The facts of the play are preposterous. What are the literal facts? How does each bit of action grow out of the preceding action?

3. How does the plot involving Sganarelle and Martine encompass the plot involving Léandre, Lucinde, and Géronte? Outline both plots.

4. Discuss the by-play, that is, the action that the author indicates for the actors through stage directions. How much of the play's effect must depend upon the ability and agility of the actors? Compare *The Sunshine Boys,* p. 930. Consider particularly the scene in which Sganarelle makes advances to Jacqueline in the presence of Lucas, her husband (see II. iv).

5. Point out the passages in which Molière satirizes practitioners of medicine. Is the satire directed as much at the gullibility of people as at physicians? Is any of the satire still applicable today? Discuss.

Henrik Ibsen   (1828–1906)
Ghosts

CHARACTERS

MRS. ALVING (HELEN), *widow of Captain Alving, late Chamberlain to the King*

OSWALD ALVING, *her son, a painter*

PASTOR MANDERS

JACOB ENGSTRAND, *a carpenter*

REGINA ENGSTRAND, *Mrs. Alving's maid*

The action takes place at Mrs. Alving's country house, beside one of the large fiords in western Norway.

ACT I

A spacious garden-room, with one door to the left, and two doors to the right. In the middle of the room a round table, with chairs about it. On the table lie books, periodicals, and newspapers. In the foreground to the left a window, and by it a small sofa, with a work-table in front of it. In the background, the room is continued into a somewhat narrower conservatory, which is shut in by glass walls with large panes. In the right-hand wall of the conservatory is a door leading down into the garden. Through the glass wall one catches a glimpse of a gloomy fiord-landscape, veiled by steady rain.

ENGSTRAND, the carpenter, stands by the garden door. His left leg is somewhat bent; he has a clump of wood under the sole of his boot. REGINA, *with an empty garden syringe in her hand, hinders him from advancing.*

REGINA *(in a low voice)*   What do you want? Stop where you are. You're positively dripping.

ENGSTRAND   It's the Lord's own rain, my girl.

REGINA   It's the devil's rain, *I* say.

ENGSTRAND   Lord! how you talk, Regina. *(Limps a few steps forward into the room)* What I wanted to say was this—

REGINA   Don't clatter so with that foot of yours, I tell you! The young master's asleep upstairs.

ENGSTRAND   Asleep? In the middle of the day?

REGINA   It's no business of yours.

ENGSTRAND   I was out on the loose last night—

REGINA   I can quite believe that.

ENGSTRAND   Yes, we're weak vessels, we poor mortals, my girl—

REGINA   So it seems.

ENGSTRAND   —and temptations are manifold in this world, you see; but all the same, I was hard at work, God knows, at half-past five this morning.

REGINA   Very well; only be off now. I won't stop here and have *rendezvous*[1] with you.

ENGSTRAND   What is it you won't have?

REGINA   I won't have any one find you here; so just you go about your business.

ENGSTRAND *(advances a step or two)*   Blest if I go before I've had a talk with you. This afternoon I shall have finished my work at the school-house, and then I shall take to-night's boat and be off home to the town.

REGINA *(mutters)*   A pleasant journey to you.

ENGSTRAND   Thank you, my child. To-morrow the Asylum's to be opened, and then there'll be fine doings, no doubt, and plenty of intoxicating drink going, you know. And nobody shall say of Jacob Engstrand that he can't keep out of temptation's way.

REGINA   Oh!

ENGSTRAND   You see, there are to be any number of swells here to-morrow. Pastor Manders is expected from town, too.

REGINA   He's coming to-day.

ENGSTRAND   There, you see! And I should be cursedly sorry if he found out anything to my disadvantage, don't you understand?

REGINA   Oh! is that your game?

ENGSTRAND   Is what my game?

REGINA *(looking hard at him)*   What trick are you going to play on Pastor Manders?

ENGSTRAND   Hush! hush! Are you crazy? Do *I* want to play any trick on Pastor Manders? Oh no! Pastor Manders has been far too kind to me for that. But I just wanted to say, you know—that I mean to set off home again tonight.

REGINA   The sooner the better, say I.

ENGSTRAND   Yes, but I want to take you with me, Regina.

REGINA *(open-mouthed)*   You want me—? What are you talking about?

ENGSTRAND   I want to take you home, I say.

REGINA *(scornfully)*   Never in this world shall you get me home with you.

ENGSTRAND   We'll see about that.

REGINA   Yes, you may be sure we'll see about it! I, who have been brought up by a lady like Mrs. Alving! I, who am treated almost as a daughter here! Is it me you want to go home with you?—to a house like yours? For shame!

ENGSTRAND   What the devil do you mean? Do you set yourself up against your father, girl?

REGINA *(mutters without looking at him)*   You've said often enough I was no child of yours.

ENGSTRAND   Stuff! Why should you trouble about that?

REGINA   Haven't you many a time sworn at me and called me a—? *Fi donc!*

ENGSTRAND   Curse me, now, if ever I used such an ugly word.

REGINA   Oh! I know quite well what word you used.

ENGSTRAND   Well, but that was only when I was a bit on, don't you know? Hm! Temptations are manifold in this world, Regina.

---

[1] This and other French words used by Regina are in that language in the original.

REGINA   Ugh!

ENGSTRAND   And besides, it was when your mother rode her high horse. I had to find something to twit her with, my child. She was always setting up for a fine lady. *(Mimics)* "Let me go, Engstrand; let me be. Remember I've been three years in Chamberlain Alving's family at Rosenvold." *(Laughs)* Mercy on us! She could never forget that the Captain was made a Chamberlain while she was in service here.

REGINA   Poor mother! you very soon worried her into her grave.

ENGSTRAND *(turns on his heel)*   Oh, of course! I'm to be blamed for everything.

REGINA *(turns away; half aloud)*   Ugh! And that leg too!

ENGSTRAND   What do you say, girl?

REGINA   *Pied de mouton.*

ENGSTRAND   Is that English, eh?

REGINA   Yes.

ENGSTRAND   Oh, ah; you've picked up some learning out here; and that may come in useful now, Regina.

REGINA *(after a short silence)*   What do you want with me in town?

ENGSTRAND   Can you ask what a father wants with his only child? Am I not a lonely and forsaken widower?

REGINA   Oh! don't try on any nonsense like that! Why do you want me?

ENGSTRAND   Well, let me tell you, I've been thinking of starting a new line of business.

REGINA *(contemptuously)*   You've tried that often enough, and never done any good.

ENGSTRAND   Yes, but this time you shall see, Regina! Devil take me—

REGINA *(stamps)*   Don't swear!

ENGSTRAND   Hush, hush; you're right enough there, my girl. What I wanted to say was just this—I've laid by a very tidy pile from this Orphanage job.

REGINA   Have you? That's a good thing for you.

ENGSTRAND   What can a man spend his ha'pence on here in the country?

REGINA   Well, what then?

ENGSTRAND   Why, you see, I thought of putting the money into some paying speculation. I thought of a sort of sailors' tavern—

REGINA   Horrid!

ENGSTRAND   A regular high-class affair, of course; not a mere pigstye for common sailors. No! damn it! it would be for captains and mates, and—and—all those swells, you know.

REGINA   And I was to—?

ENGSTRAND   You were to help, to be sure. Only for appearance' sake, you understand. Devil a bit of hard work shall you have, my girl. You shall do exactly what you like.

REGINA   Oh, indeed!

ENGSTRAND   But there must be a petticoat in the house; that's as clear as daylight. For I want to have it a little lively in the evenings, with singing and dancing, and so forth. You must remember they're weary wanderers on the ocean of life. *(Nearer)* Now don't be stupid and stand in your own light, Regina. What can become of you out here? Your mistress has given you a lot of learning; but what good is it to you? You're to look after the children at the new Orphanage, I hear. Is that the sort of thing for you, eh? Are you so desperately bent upon wearing yourself out for the sake of the dirty brats?

REGINA   No; if things go as I want them to, then—well, there's no saying—there's no saying.

ENGSTRAND   What do you mean by "there's no saying"?

REGINA   Never you mind. How much money have you saved up here?

ENGSTRAND   What with one thing and another, a matter of seven or eight hundred crowns.[2]

REGINA   That's not so bad.

ENGSTRAND   It's enough to make a start with, my girl.

REGINA   Aren't you thinking of giving me any?

ENGSTRAND   No, I'm damned if I am!

REGINA   Not even of sending me a scrap of stuff for a new dress?

ENGSTRAND   If you'll come to town with me, you can get dresses enough.

REGINA   Pooh! I can do that on my own account if I want to.

ENGSTRAND   No, a father's guiding hand is what you want, Regina. Now, I've my eye on a capital house in Little Harbour Street. It won't need much ready-money, and it could be a sort of sailors' home, you know.

REGINA   But I will *not* live with you. I have nothing whatever to do with you. Be off!

ENGSTRAND   You wouldn't remain long with me, my girl. No such luck! If you knew how to play your cards, such a fine girl as you've grown in the last year or two—

REGINA   Well?

ENGSTRAND   You'd soon get hold of some mate—or perhaps even a captain—

REGINA   I won't marry any one of that sort. Sailors have no *savoir vivre.*

ENGSTRAND   What haven't they got?

REGINA   I know what sailors are, I tell you. They're not the sort of people to marry.

ENGSTRAND   Then never mind about marrying them. You can make it pay all the same. *(More confidentially)* He—the Englishman—the man with the yacht—he gave three hundred dollars, he did; and she wasn't a bit handsomer than you.

REGINA *(going towards him)*   Out you go!

ENGSTRAND *(falling back)*   Come, come! You're not going to strike me, I hope.

REGINA   Yes, if you begin to talk about mother I shall strike you. Get away with you, I say. *(Drives him back towards the garden door)* And don't bang the doors. Young Mr. Alving—

ENGSTRAND   He's asleep; I know. It's curious how you're taken up about young Mr. Alving—*(More softly)* Oho! it surely can't be he that—?

REGINA   Be off at once! You're crazy, I tell you! No, not that way. There comes Pastor Manders. Down the kitchen stairs with you.

ENGSTRAND *(towards the right)*   Yes, yes, I'm going. But just you talk to him that's coming there. He's the man to tell you what a child owes its father. For I am your father all the same, you know. I can prove it from the church-register.

He goes out through the second door to the right, which REGINA *has opened, and fastens again after him.* REGINA *glances hastily at herself in the mirror, dusts herself with her pocket handkerchief, and settles her collar; then she busies herself with the flowers.* PASTOR MANDERS, *in an overcoat, with an umbrella, and with a small travelling-bag on a strap over his shoulder, comes through the garden door into the conservatory.*

MANDERS   Good morning, Miss Engstrand.

REGINA *(turning round, surprised and pleased)*   No, really! Good morning, Pastor Manders. Is the steamer in already?

MANDERS   It's just in. *(Enters the sitting-room)* Terrible weather we've been having lately.

---

[2] A "krone" was equal to approximately twenty-seven cents.

REGINA *(follows him)* It's such blessed weather for the country, sir.

MANDERS Yes, you're quite right. We townspeople think too little about that. *(He begins to take off his overcoat.)*

REGINA Oh, mayn't I help you? There! Why, how wet it is! I'll just hang it up in the hall. And your umbrella, too—I'll open it and let it dry.

She goes out with the things through the second door on the right. PASTOR MANDERS *takes off his travelling-bag and lays it and his hat on a chair. Meanwhile* REGINA *comes in again.*

MANDERS Ah! it's a comfort to get safe under cover. Everything going on well here?

REGINA Yes, thank you, sir.

MANDERS You have your hands full, I suppose, in preparation for to-morrow?

REGINA Yes, there's plenty to do, of course.

MANDERS And Mrs. Alving is at home, I trust?

REGINA Oh dear, yes. She's just upstairs looking after the young master's chocolate.

MANDERS Yes, by-the-bye—I heard down at the pier that Oswald had arrived.

REGINA Yes, he came the day before yesterday. We didn't expect him before to-day.

MANDERS Quite strong and well, I hope?

REGINA Yes, thank you, quite; but dreadfully tired with the journey. He has made one rush all the way from Paris. I believe he came the whole way in one train. He's sleeping a little now, I think; so perhaps we'd better talk a little quietly.

MANDERS Hush!—as quietly as you please.

REGINA *(arranging an arm-chair beside the table)* Now, do sit down, Pastor Manders, and make yourself comfortable. *(He sits down; she puts a footstool under his feet.)* There! are you comfortable now, sir?

MANDERS Thanks, thanks. I'm most comfortable. *(Looks at her)* Do you know, Miss Engstrand, I positively believe you've grown since I last saw you.

REGINA Do you think so, sir? Mrs. Alving says my figure has developed too.

MANDERS Developed? Well, perhaps a little; just enough. *(Short pause)*

REGINA Shall I tell Mrs. Alving you are here?

MANDERS Thanks, thanks, there's no hurry, my dear child. By-the-bye, Regina, my good girl, just tell me: how is your father getting on out here?

REGINA Oh, thank you, he's getting on well enough.

MANDERS He called upon me last time he was in town.

REGINA Did he, indeed? He's always so glad of a chance of talking to you, sir.

MANDERS And you often look in upon him at his work, I daresay?

REGINA I? Oh, of course, when I have time, I—

MANDERS Your father is not a man of strong character, Miss Engstrand. He stands terribly in need of a guiding hand.

REGINA Oh, yes; I daresay he does.

MANDERS He needs to have some one near him whom he cares for, and whose judgment he respects. He frankly admitted that when he last came to see me.

REGINA Yes, he mentioned something of the sort to me. But I don't know whether Mrs. Alving can spare me; especially now that we've got the new Orphanage to attend to. And then I should be so sorry to leave Mrs. Alving; she has always been so kind to me.

MANDERS But a daughter's duty, my good girl—Of course we must first get your mistress' consent.

REGINA But I don't know whether it would be quite proper for me, at my age, to keep house for a single man.

MANDERS What! My dear Miss Engstrand! When the man is your own father!

REGINA Yes, that may be; but all the same—Now if it were in a thoroughly respectable house, and with a real gentleman—

MANDERS But, my dear Regina—

REGINA —one I could love and respect, and be a daughter to—

MANDERS Yes, but my dear, good child—

REGINA Then I should be glad to go to town. It's very lonely out here; you know yourself, sir, what it is to be alone in the world. And I can assure you I'm both quick and willing. Don't you know of any such place for me, sir?

MANDERS I? No, certainly not.

REGINA But, dear, dear sir, do remember me if—

MANDERS *(rising)* Yes, yes, certainly, Miss Engstrand.

REGINA For if I—

MANDERS Will you be so good as to fetch your mistress?

REGINA I will, at once, sir. *(She goes out to the left.)*

MANDERS *(paces the room two or three times, stands a moment in the background with his hands behind his back, and looks out over the garden. Then he returns to the table, takes up a book, and looks at the title-page; starts, and looks at several)* Hm—indeed!

MRS. ALVING *enters by the door on the left; she is followed by* REGINA, *who immediately goes out by the first door on the right.*

MRS. ALVING *(holds out her hand)* Welcome, my dear Pastor.

MANDERS How do you do, Mrs. Alving? Here I am as I promised.

MRS. ALVING Always punctual to the minute.

MANDERS You may believe it wasn't so easy for me to get away. With all the Boards and Committees I belong to—

MRS. ALVING That makes it all the kinder of you to come so early. Now we can get through our business before dinner. But where's your luggage?

MANDERS *(quickly)* I left it down at the inn. I shall sleep there to-night.

MRS. ALVING *(suppressing a smile)* Are you really not to be persuaded, even now, to pass the night under my roof?

MANDERS No, no, Mrs. Alving; many thanks. I shall stay down there as usual. It's so convenient for starting again.

MRS. ALVING Well, you must have your own way. But I really should have thought we two old people—

MANDERS Now you're making fun of me. Ah! you're naturally in great spirits to-day—what between to-morrow's festival and Oswald's return.

MRS. ALVING Yes; you can think what a delight it is to me! It's more than two years since he was home last. And now he has promised to stay with me all winter.

MANDERS Has he really? That's very nice and dutiful of him. For I can well believe that life in Rome and Paris has far more attractions.

MRS. ALVING True. But here he has his mother, you see. My own darling boy, he hasn't forgotten his old mother!

MANDERS It would be grievous indeed, if absence and absorption in art and that sort of thing were to blunt his natural feelings.

MRS. ALVING Yes, you may well say so. But there's nothing of that sort to fear in him. I'm quite curious to see whether you'll know him again. He'll be down presently; he's upstairs just now, resting a little on the sofa. But do sit down, my dear Pastor.

MANDERS Thank you. Are you quite at liberty—?

MRS. ALVING Certainly. *(She sits by the table.)*

MANDERS   Very well. Then you shall see—*(He goes to the chair where his travelling-bag lies, takes out a packet of papers, sits down on the opposite side of the table, and tries to find a clear space for the papers.)* Now, to begin with, here is—*(Breaking off)*—Tell me, Mrs. Alving, how do these books come here?

MRS. ALVING   These books? They are books I am reading.

MANDERS   Do you read this sort of literature?

MRS. ALVING   Certainly I do.

MANDERS   Do you feel better or happier for reading of this kind?

MRS. ALVING   I feel, so to speak, more secure.

MANDERS   That's strange. How do you mean?

MRS. ALVING   Well, I seem to find explanation and confirmation of all sorts of things I myself have been thinking. For that's the wonderful part of it, Pastor Manders, there's really nothing new in those books, nothing but what most people think and believe. Only most people either don't formulate it to themselves, or else keep quiet about it.

MANDERS   Great heavens! Do you really believe that most people—?

MRS. ALVING   I do, indeed.

MANDERS   But surely not in this country? Not here, among us?

MRS. ALVING   Yes, certainly, among us too.

MANDERS   Well, I really must say—!

MRS. ALVING   For the rest, what do you object to in these books?

MANDERS   Object to in them? You surely don't suppose that I have nothing to do but study such productions as these?

MRS. ALVING   That is to say, you know nothing of what you are condemning.

MANDERS   I have read enough *about* these writings to disapprove of them.

MRS. ALVING   Yes; but your own opinion—

MANDERS   My dear Mrs. Alving, there are many occasions in life when one must rely upon others. Things are so ordered in this world; and it's well that they are. How could society get on otherwise?

MRS. ALVING   Well, I daresay you're right there.

MANDERS   Besides, I of course don't deny that there may be much that is interesting in such books. Nor can I blame you for wishing to keep up with the intellectual movements that are said to be going on in the great world, where you have let your son pass so much of his life. But—

MRS. ALVING   But?

MANDERS   *(lowering his voice)*   But one shouldn't talk about it, Mrs. Alving. One is certainly not bound to account to everybody for what one reads and thinks within one's own four walls.

MRS. ALVING   Of course not; I quite think so.

MANDERS   Only think, now, how you are bound to consider the interests of this Orphanage which you decided on founding at a time when you thought very differently on spiritual matters—so far as I can judge.

MRS. ALVING   Oh yes; I quite admit that. But it was about the Orphanage—

MANDERS   It was about the Orphanage we were to speak; yes. All I say is: prudence, my dear lady! And now we'll get to business. *(Opens the packet, and takes out a number of papers)* Do you see these?

MRS. ALVING   The documents?

MANDERS   All—and in perfect order. I can tell you it was hard work to get them in time. I had put on strong pressure. The authorities are almost painfully scrupulous when you want them to come to the point. But here they are at last. *(Looks through the bundle)* See! here is the formal deed of gift of the parcel of ground known as Solvik in the Manor of Rosenvold, with all the newly-constructed buildings, schoolrooms, master's house, and chapel. And here is the legal fiat for the endowment and for the Regulations of the Institution. Will you look at them? *(Reads)* "Regulation for the Children's Home to be known as 'Captain Alving's Foundation.' "

MRS. ALVING *(looks long at the paper)*   So there it is.

MANDERS   I have chosen the designation "Captain" rather than "Chamberlain." "Captain" looks less pretentious.

MRS. ALVING   Oh, yes; just as you think best.

MANDERS   And here you have the Bank Account of the capital lying at interest to cover the current expenses of the Orphanage.

MRS. ALVING   Thank you; but please keep it—it will be more convenient.

MANDERS   With pleasure. I think we will leave the money in the Bank for the present. The interest is certainly not what we could wish—four per cent, and six months' notice of withdrawal. If a good mortgage could be found later on—of course it must be a first mortgage and an undoubted security—then we could consider the matter.

MRS. ALVING   Certainly, my dear Pastor Manders. You are the best judge in these things.

MANDERS   I will keep my eyes open at any rate. But now there's one thing more which I have several times been intending to ask you.

MRS. ALVING   And what's that?

MANDERS   Shall the Orphanage buildings be insured or not?

MRS. ALVING   Of course they must be insured.

MANDERS   Well, stop a minute, Mrs. Alving. Let us look into the matter a little more closely.

MRS. ALVING   I have everything insured; buildings and movables and stock and crops.

MANDERS   Of course you have—on your own estate. And so have I—of course. But here, you see, it's quite another matter. The Orphanage is to be consecrated, as it were, to a higher purpose.

MRS. ALVING   Yes, but that's no reason—

MANDERS   For my own part, I should not see the smallest impropriety in guarding against all contingencies—

MRS. ALVING   No, I should think not.

MANDERS   But what is the general feeling in the neighbourhood? You, of course, know better than I.

MRS. ALVING   Hm—the general feeling—

MANDERS   Is there any considerable number of people—really responsible people—who might be scandalised?

MRS. ALVING   What do you mean by "really responsible people"?

MANDERS   Well, I mean people in such independent and influential positions that one cannot help allowing some weight to their opinions.

MRS. ALVING   There are several people of that sort here, who would very likely be shocked if—

MANDERS   There, you see! In town we have many such people. Think of all my colleague's adherents! People would be only too ready to interpret our action as a sign that neither you nor I had the right faith in a Higher Providence.

MRS. ALVING   But for your own part, my dear Pastor, you can at least tell yourself that—

MANDERS   Yes, I know—I know; my conscience would be quite easy, that is true enough. But nevertheless we should not escape grave misinterpretation; and that might very likely react unfavourably upon the Orphanage.

MRS. ALVING   Well, in that case, then—

MANDERS   Nor can I lose sight of the difficult—I may even say painful—position *I* might perhaps get into. In the leading circles of the town people are much taken up about this Orphanage. It is, of course, founded partly for the benefit of the town, as well; and it is to be hoped it will, to a considerable extent, result in lightening our Poor Rates. Now, as I have been your adviser, and have had the business matters in my hands, I cannot but fear that I may have to bear the brunt of fanaticism.

MRS. ALVING   Oh, you mustn't run the risk of that.

MANDERS   To say nothing of the attacks that would assuredly be made upon me in certain papers and periodicals, which—

MRS. ALVING   Enough, my dear Pastor Manders. That consideration is quite decisive.

MANDERS   Then you do not wish the Orphanage insured?

MRS. ALVING   No. We'll let it alone.

MANDERS *(leaning back in his chair)*   But if a disaster were to happen?—one can never tell. Would you be able to make good the damage?

MRS. ALVING   No; I tell you plainly I should do nothing of the kind.

MANDERS   Then I must tell you, Mrs. Alving, we are taking no small responsibility upon ourselves.

MRS. ALVING   Do you think we can do otherwise?

MANDERS   No, that's just the thing; we really cannot do otherwise. We must not expose ourselves to misinterpretation; and we have no right whatever to give offence to our neighbours.

MRS. ALVING   You, as a clergyman, certainly should not.

MANDERS   I really think, too, we may trust that such an institution has fortune on its side; in fact, that it stands under a Special Providence.

MRS. ALVING   Let us hope so, Pastor Manders.

MANDERS   Then we'll let the matter alone.

MRS. ALVING   Yes, certainly.

MANDERS   Very well. Just as you think best. *(Makes a note)* Then—no insurance.

MRS. ALVING   It's rather curious that you should just happen to mention the matter to-day.

MANDERS   I have often thought of asking you about it—

MRS. ALVING   —for we very nearly had a fire down there yesterday.

MANDERS   You don't say so!

MRS. ALVING   Oh, it was of no importance. A heap of shavings had caught fire in the carpenter's workshop.

MANDERS   Where Engstrand works?

MRS. ALVING   Yes. They say he's often very careless with matches.

MANDERS   He has so many things in his head, that man—so many temptations. Thank God, he's now striving to lead a decent life, I hear.

MRS. ALVING   Indeed! Who says so?

MANDERS   He himself assures me of it. And he's certainly a capital workman.

MRS. ALVING   Oh, yes; so long as he's sober.

MANDERS   Yes, that's a sad weakness. But he's often driven to it by his bad leg, he says. Last time he was in town I was really touched by him. He came and thanked me so warmly for having got him work here, so that he might be near Regina.

MRS. ALVING   He doesn't see much of *her*.

MANDERS   Oh, yes; he has a talk with her every day. He told me so himself.

MRS. ALVING   Well, it may be so.

MANDERS   He feels so acutely that he needs some one to hold him back when temptation comes. That's what I can't help liking about Jacob Engstrand; he comes to you helplessly, accusing himself and confessing his own weakness. The last time he was talking to me—Believe me, Mrs. Alving, supposing it were a real necessity for him to have Regina home again—

MRS. ALVING *(rising hastily)* Regina!

MANDERS —you must not set yourself against it.

MRS. ALVING Indeed I shall set myself against it! And besides—Regina is to have a position in the Orphanage.

MANDERS But, after all, remember he's her father—

MRS. ALVING Oh! I know best what sort of a father he has been to her. No! she shall never go to him with my goodwill.

MANDERS *(rising)* My dear lady, don't take the matter so warmly. You misjudge Engstrand sadly. You seem to be quite terrified—

MRS. ALVING *(more quietly)* It makes no difference. I have taken Regina into my house, and there she shall stay. *(Listens)* Hush, my dear Mr. Manders; don't say any more about it. *(Her face lights up with gladness.)* Listen! there's Oswald coming downstairs. Now we'll think of no one but him.

OSWALD ALVING, *in a light overcoat, hat in hand and smoking a large meerschaum, enters through the door on the left; he stops in the doorway.*

OSWALD Oh! I beg your pardon; I thought you were in the study. *(Comes forward)* Good-morning, Pastor Manders.

MANDERS *(staring)* Ah—! How strange—!

MRS. ALVING Well now, what do you think of him, Mr. Manders?

MANDERS I—I—can it really be—?

OSWALD Yes, it's really the Prodigal Son, sir.

MANDERS *(protesting)* My dear young friend—!

OSWALD Well, then, the Reclaimed Son.

MRS. ALVING Oswald remembers how much you were opposed to his becoming a painter.

MANDERS To our human eyes many a step seems dubious which afterwards proves—*(Wrings his hand)* Anyhow, welcome, welcome home. Why, my dear Oswald—I suppose I may call you by your Christian name?

OSWALD What else should you call me?

MANDERS Very good. What I wanted to say was this, my dear Oswald—you mustn't believe that I utterly condemn the artist's calling. I have no doubt there are many who can keep their inner self unharmed in that profession, as in any other.

OSWALD Let us hope so.

MRS. ALVING *(beaming with delight)* I know one who has kept both his inner and outer self unharmed. Just look at him, Mr. Manders.

OSWALD *(moves restlessly about the room)* Yes, yes, my dear mother; let's say no more about it.

MANDERS Why, certainly—that's undeniable. And you have begun to make a name for yourself already. The newspapers have often spoken of you, most favourably. By-the-bye, just lately they haven't mentioned you so often, I fancy.

OSWALD *(up in the conservatory)* I haven't been able to paint so much lately.

MRS. ALVING Even a painter needs a little rest now and then.

MANDERS I can quite believe it. And meanwhile he can be gathering his forces for some great work.

OSWALD Yes—Mother, will dinner soon be ready?

MRS. ALVING In less than half-an-hour. He has a capital appetite, thank God.

MANDERS And a taste for tobacco, too.

OSWALD   I found my father's pipe in my room, and so—

MANDERS   Aha! then that accounts for it.

MRS. ALVING   For what?

MANDERS   When Oswald stood there, in the doorway, with the pipe in his mouth, I could have sworn I saw his father, large as life.

OSWALD   No, really?

MRS. ALVING   Oh! how can you say so? Oswald takes after me.

MANDERS   Yes, but there's an expression about the corners of the mouth—something about the lips that remind one exactly of Alving; at any rate, now that he's smoking.

MRS. ALVING   Not in the least. Oswald has rather a clerical curve about his mouth, I think.

MANDERS   Yes, yes; some of my colleagues have much the same expression.

MRS. ALVING   But put your pipe away, my dear boy; I won't have smoking in here.

OSWALD *(does so)*   By all means. I only wanted to try it; for I once smoked it when I was a child.

MRS. ALVING   You?

OSWALD   Yes. I was quite small at the time. I recollect I came up to father's room one evening when he was in great spirits.

MRS. ALVING   Oh, you can't recollect anything of these times.

OSWALD   Yes, I recollect distinctly. He took me up on his knees, and gave me the pipe. "Smoke, boy," he said; "smoke away, boy." And I smoked as hard as I could, until I felt I was growing quite pale, and the perspiration stood in great drops on my forehead. Then he burst out laughing heartily—

MANDERS   That was most extraordinary.

MRS. ALVING   My dear friend, it's only something Oswald has dreamt.

OSWALD   No, mother, I assure you I didn't dream it. For—don't you remember *this?*—you came and carried me out into the nursery. Then I was sick, and I saw you were crying.—Did father often play such pranks?

MANDERS   In his youth he overflowed with the joy of life—[3]

OSWALD   And yet he managed to do so much in the world; so much that was good and useful; and he died so young, too.

MANDERS   Yes, you have inherited the name of an active and worthy man, my dear Oswald Alving. No doubt it will be an incentive to you—

OSWALD   It ought to, indeed.

MANDERS   It was good of you to come home for the ceremony in his honour.

OSWALD   I could do no less for my father.

MRS. ALVING   And I am to keep him so long! That's the best of all.

MANDERS   You're going to pass the winter at home, I hear.

OSWALD   My stay is indefinite, sir. But, oh! how delightful it is to be at home again!

MRS. ALVING *(beaming)*   Yes, isn't it?

MANDERS *(looking sympathetically at him)*   You went out into the world early, my dear Oswald.

OSWALD   I did. I sometimes wonder whether it wasn't *too* early.

MRS. ALVING   Oh, not at all. A healthy lad is all the better for it; especially when he's an only child. He oughtn't to hang on at home with his mother and father and get spoilt.

MANDERS   It's a very difficult question, Mrs. Alving. A child's proper place is, and must be, the home of his fathers.

OSWALD   There I quite agree with you, Pastor Manders.

---

[3] "Var en særdeles livsglad mand"—literally, "was a man who took the greatest pleasure in life," *la joie de vivre*—an expression which frequently recurs in this play.

MANDERS   Only look at your own son—there's no reason why we shouldn't say it in his presence—what has the consequence been for him? He's six or seven and twenty, and has never had the opportunity of learning what home life really is.

OSWALD   I beg your pardon, Pastor; there you're quite mistaken.

MANDERS   Indeed? I thought you had lived almost exclusively in artistic circles.

OSWALD   So I have.

MANDERS   And chiefly among the younger artists.

OSWALD   Yes, certainly.

MANDERS   But I thought few of these young fellows could afford to set up house and support a family.

OSWALD   There are many who can't afford to marry, sir.

MANDERS   Yes, that's just what I say.

OSWALD   But they can have a home for all that. And several of them have, as a matter of fact; and very pleasant, comfortable homes they are, too.

(MRS. ALVING *follows with breathless interest; nods, but says nothing.*)

MANDERS   But I am not talking of bachelors' quarters. By a "home" I understand the home of a family, where a man lives with his wife and children.

OSWALD   Yes; or with his children and his children's mother.

MANDERS *(starts; clasps his hands)*   But, good heavens—!

OSWALD   Well?

MANDERS   Lives with—his children's mother!

OSWALD   Yes. Would you have him turn his children's mother out of doors?

MANDERS   Then it's illicit relations you are talking of! Irregular marriages, as people call them!

OSWALD   I have never noticed anything particularly irregular about the life these people lead.

MANDERS   But how is it possible that a—a young man or young woman with any decent principles can endure to live in that way?—in the eyes of all the world!

OSWALD   What are they to do? A poor young artist—a poor girl—it costs a lot to get married. What are they to do?

MANDERS   What are they to do? Let me tell you, Mr. Alving, what they ought to do. They ought to exercise self-restraint from the first; that's what they ought to do.

OSWALD   Such talk won't go far with warm-blooded young people, over head and ears in love.

MRS. ALVING   No, it wouldn't go far.

MANDERS *(continuing)*   How can the authorities tolerate such things? Allow them to go on in the light of day? (*To* MRS. ALVING) Had I not cause to be deeply concerned about your son? In circles where open immorality prevails, and has even a sort of prestige—!

OSWALD   Let me tell you, sir, that I have been a constant Sunday-guest in one or two such irregular homes—

MANDERS   On Sunday of all days!

OSWALD   Isn't that the day to enjoy oneself? Well, never have I heard an offensive word, and still less have I witnessed anything that could be called immoral. No; do you not know when and where I have come across immorality in artistic circles?

MANDERS   No, thank heaven, I don't!

OSWALD   Well, then, allow me to inform you. I have met with it when one or other of our pattern husbands and fathers has come to Paris to have a look around on his own account, and has done the artists the honour of visiting their humble haunts. *They* knew what was what. These gentlemen could tell us all about places and things we had never dreamt of.

MANDERS What! Do you mean to say that respectable men from home here would—?

OSWALD Have you never heard these respectable men, when they got home again, talking about the way in which immorality was running rampant abroad?

MANDERS Yes, of course.

MRS. ALVING I have too.

OSWALD Well, you may take their word for it. They know what they're talking about! *(Presses his hands to his head)* Oh! that that great, free, glorious life out there should be defiled in such a way!

MRS. ALVING You mustn't get excited, Oswald. You will do yourself harm.

OSWALD Yes; you're quite right, mother. It's not good for me. You see, I'm wretchedly worn out. I'll go for a little turn before dinner. Excuse me, Pastor; I know you can't take my point of view; but I couldn't help speaking out.

(He goes out through the second door to the right.)

MRS. ALVING My poor boy!

MANDERS You may well say so. Then that's what he has come to!

(MRS. ALVING looks at him silently.)

MANDERS *(walking up and down)* He called himself the Prodigal Son—alas! alas!

(MRS. ALVING continues looking at him.)

MANDERS And what do you say to all this?

MRS. ALVING I say that Oswald was right in every word.

MANDERS *(stands still)* Right! Right! In such principles?

MRS. ALVING Here, in my loneliness, I have come to the same way of thinking, Pastor Manders. But I've never dared to say anything. Well! now my boy shall speak for me.

MANDERS You are much to be pitied, Mrs. Alving. But now I must speak seriously to you. And now it is no longer your business manager and adviser, your own and your late husband's early friend, who stands before you. It is the priest—the priest who stood before you in the moment of your life when you had gone most astray.

MRS. ALVING And what has the priest to say to me?

MANDERS I will first stir up your memory a little. The time is well chosen. To-morrow will be the tenth anniversary of your husband's death. To-morrow the memorial in his honour will be unveiled. To-morrow I shall have to speak to the whole assembled multitude. But to-day I will speak to you alone.

MRS. ALVING Very well, Pastor Manders. Speak.

MANDERS Do you remember that after less than a year of married life you stood on the verge of an abyss? That you forsook your house and home? That you fled from your husband? Yes, Mrs. Alving—fled, fled, and refused to return to him, however much he begged and prayed you?

MRS. ALVING Have you forgotten how infinitely miserable I was in that first year?

MANDERS It is only the spirit of rebellion that craves for happiness in this life. What right have we human beings to happiness? No, we have to do our duty! And your duty was to hold firmly to the man you had once chosen and to whom you were bound by a holy tie.

MRS. ALVING You know very well what sort of life Alving was leading—what excesses he was guilty of.

MANDERS I know very well what rumours there were about him, and I am the last to approve the life he led in his young days, if report did not wrong him. But a wife is not to be her husband's judge. It was your duty to bear with humility the cross which a Higher

Power had, for your own good, laid upon you. But instead of that you rebelliously throw away the cross, desert the backslider whom you should have supported, go and risk your good name and reputation and—nearly succeed in ruining other people's reputation into the bargain.

MRS. ALVING   Other people's? One other person's, you mean.

MANDERS   It was incredibly reckless of you to seek refuge with me

MRS. ALVING   With our clergyman? With our intimate friend?

MANDERS   Just on that account. Yes, you may thank God that I possessed the necessary firmness; that I dissuaded you from your wild designs; and that it was vouchsafed me to lead you back to the path of duty, and home to your lawful husband.

MRS. ALVING   Yes, Pastor Manders, it was certainly your work.

MANDERS   I was but a poor instrument in a Higher Hand. And what a blessing has it not been to you, all the days of your life, that I got you to resume the yoke of duty and obedience! Did not everything happen as I foretold? Did not Alving turn his back on his errors, as a man should? Did he not live with you from that time, lovingly and blamelessly, all his days? Did he not become a benefactor to the whole district? And did he not raise you up to him so that you little by little became his assistant in all his undertakings? And a capital assistant, too—Oh! I know, Mrs. Alving, that praise is due to you. But now I come to the next great error in your life.

MRS. ALVING   What do you mean?

MANDERS   Just as you once disowned a wife's duty, so you have since disowned a mother's.

MRS. ALVING   Ah!

MANDERS   You have been all your life under the dominion of a pestilent spirit of self-will. All your efforts have been bent towards emancipation and lawlessness. You have never known how to endure any bond. Everything that has weighed upon you in life you have cast away without care or conscience, like a burden you could throw off at will. It did not please you to be a wife any longer, and you left your husband. You found it troublesome to be a mother, and you sent your child forth among strangers.

MRS. ALVING   Yes. That is true. I did so.

MANDERS   And thus you have become a stranger to him.

MRS. ALVING   No! No! I am not.

MANDERS   Yes, you are; and must be. And how have you got him back again? Bethink yourself well, Mrs. Alving. You have sinned greatly against your husband;—that you recognise by raising yonder memorial to him. Recognise now, also, how you have sinned against your son. There may be time to lead him back from the paths of error. Turn back yourself, and save what may yet be saved in him. For *(With uplifted forefinger)* verily, Mrs. Alving, you are a guilt-laden mother!—This I have thought it my duty to say to you. *(Silence)*

MRS. ALVING *(slowly and with self-control)*   You have now spoken out, Pastor Manders; and to-morrow you are to speak publicly in memory of my husband. I shall not speak to-morrow. But I will speak frankly to you, as you have spoken to me.

MANDERS   To be sure; you will plead excuses for your conduct—

MRS. ALVING   No. I will only narrate.

MANDERS   Well?

MRS. ALVING   All that you have just said about me and my husband and our life after you had brought me back to the path of duty—as you called it—about all that you know nothing from personal observation. From that moment you, who had been our intimate friend, never set foot in our house again.

MANDERS   You and your husband left the town immediately after.

MRS. ALVING   Yes; and in my husband's lifetime you never came to see us. It was business that forced you to visit me when you undertook the affairs of the Orphanage.

MANDERS *(softly and uncertainly)* Helen—if that is meant as a reproach, I would beg you to bear in mind—

MRS. ALVING —the regard you owed to your position, yes; and that I was a runaway wife. One can never be too careful with such unprincipled creatures.

MANDERS My dear—Mrs. Alving, you know that is an absurd exaggeration—

MRS. ALVING Well well, suppose it is. My point is that your judgment as to my married life is founded upon nothing but current gossip.

MANDERS Well, I admit that. What then?

MRS. ALVING Well, then, Mr. Manders—I will tell you the truth. I have sworn to myself that one day you should know it—you alone!

MANDERS What is the truth, then?

MRS. ALVING The truth is that my husband died just as dissolute as he had lived all his days.

MANDERS *(feeling after a chair)* What do you say?

MRS. ALVING After nineteen years of marriage, as dissolute—in his desires at any rate—as he was before you married us.

MANDERS And those—those wild oats, those irregularities, those excesses, if you like, you call "a dissolute life"?

MRS. ALVING Our doctor used the expression.

MANDERS I don't understand you.

MRS. ALVING You need not.

MANDERS It almost makes me dizzy. Your whole married life, the seeming union of all these years, was nothing more than a hidden abyss!

MRS. ALVING Nothing more. Now you know it.

MANDERS This is—it will take me long to accustom myself to the thought. I can't grasp it! I can't realise it! But how was it possible to—? How could such a state of things be kept dark?

MRS. ALVING That has been my ceaseless struggle, day after day. After Oswald's birth, I thought Alving seemed to be a little better. But it didn't last long. And then I had to struggle twice as hard, fighting for life or death, so that nobody should know what sort of a man my child's father was. And you know what power Alving had of winning people's hearts. Nobody seemed able to believe anything but good of him. He was one of those people whose life does not bite upon their reputation. But at last, Mr. Manders—for you must know the whole story—the most repulsive thing of all happened.

MANDERS More repulsive than the rest?

MRS. ALVING I had gone on bearing with him, although I knew very well the secrets of his life out of doors. But when he brought the scandal within our own walls—

MANDERS Impossible! Here!

MRS. ALVING Yes; here in our own house. It was there *(Pointing towards the first door on the right)* in the dining room, that I first got to know of it. I was busy with something in there, and the door was standing ajar. I heard our house-maid come up from the garden, with water for those flowers.

MANDERS Well—?

MRS. ALVING Soon after I heard Alving come too. I heard him say something softly to her. And then I heard—*(With a short laugh)*—oh! it still sounds in my ears, so hateful and yet so ludicrous—I heard my own servant-maid whisper, "Let me go, Mr. Alving! Let me be."

MANDERS What unseemly levity on his part! But it cannot have been more than levity, Mrs. Alving; believe me, it cannot.

MRS. ALVING   I soon knew what to believe. Mr. Alving had his way with the girl; and that connection had consequences, Mr. Manders.

MANDERS *(as though petrified)*   Such things in this house! in this house!

MRS. ALVING   I had borne a great deal in this house. To keep him at home in the evenings—and at night—I had to make myself his boon companion in his secret orgies up in his room. There I have had to sit alone with him, to clink glasses and drink with him, and to listen to his ribald, silly talk. I have had to fight with him to get him dragged to bed—

MANDERS *(moved)*   And you were able to bear all that?

MRS. ALVING   I had to bear it for my little boy's sake. But when the last insult was added; when my own servant-maid—Then I swore to myself: This shall come to an end. And so I took the reins into my own hand—the whole control over him and everything else. For now I had a weapon against him, you see; he dared not oppose me. It was then I sent Oswald from home. He was in his seventh year, and was beginning to observe and ask questions, as children do. That I could not bear. It seemed to me the child must be poisoned by merely breathing the air of this polluted house. That was why I sent him away. And now you can see, too, why he was never allowed to set foot inside his home so long as his father lived. No one knows what it has cost me.

MANDERS   You have indeed had a life of trial.

MRS. ALVING   I could never have borne it if I hadn't had my work. For I may truly say that I have worked! All those additions to the estate—all the improvements—all the useful appliances, that won Alving such general praise—do you suppose *he* had energy for anything of the sort?—he who lay all day on the sofa and read an old court guide! No; this I will tell you too: it was I who urged him on when he had his better intervals; it was I who had to drag the whole load when he relapsed into his evil ways, or sank into querulous wretchedness.

MANDERS   And to that man you raise a memorial?

MRS. ALVING   There you see the power of an evil conscience.

MANDERS   Evil—? What do you mean?

MRS. ALVING   It always seemed to me impossible but that the truth must come out and be believed. So the Asylum was to deaden all rumours and banish doubt.

MANDERS   In that you have certainly not missed your aim, Mrs. Alving.

MRS. ALVING   And besides, I had one other reason. I did not wish that Oswald, my own boy, should inherit anything whatever from his father.

MANDERS   Then it is Alving's fortune that—?

MRS. ALVING   Yes. The sums I have spent upon the Orphanage, year by year, make up the amount—I have reckoned it up precisely—the amount which made Lieutenant Alving a good match in his day.

MANDERS   I don't quite understand—

MRS. ALVING   It was my purchase-money. I do not choose that that money should pass into Oswald's hands. My son shall have everything from me—everything. (OSWALD ALVING *enters through the second door to the right; he has taken off his hat and overcoat in the hall.* MRS. ALVING *goes towards him.*) Are you back again already? my dear, dear boy!

OSWALD   Yes. What can a fellow do out of doors in this eternal rain? But I hear dinner's ready. That's capital!

REGINA *(with a parcel, from the dining-room)*   A parcel has come for you, Mrs. Alving. *(Hands it to her.)*

MRS. ALVING *(with a glance at* MR. MANDERS*)*   No doubt copies of the ode for tomorrow's ceremony.

MANDERS   Hm—

REGINA   And dinner is ready.

MRS. ALVING   Very well. We'll come directly. I'll just—*(Begins to open the parcel.)*

REGINA *(to* OSWALD*)*   Would Mr. Alving like red or white wine?

OSWALD   Both, if you please.

REGINA   *Bien.* Very well, sir. *(She goes into the dining-room.)*

OSWALD   I may as well help to uncork it. *(He also goes into the dining-room, the door of which swings half open behind him.)*

MRS. ALVING *(who has opened the parcel)*   Yes, as I thought. Here is the Ceremonial Ode, Pastor Manders.

MANDERS *(with folded hands)*   With what countenance I'm to deliver my discourse tomorrow—!

MRS. ALVING   Oh! you'll get through it somehow.

MANDERS *(softly, so as not to be heard in the dining-room)*   Yes; it would not do to provoke scandal.

MRS. ALVING *(under her breath, but firmly)*   No. But then this long, hateful comedy will be ended. From the day after to-morrow it shall be for me as though he who is dead had never lived in this house. No one shall be here but my boy and his mother. *(From within the dining-room comes the noise of a chair overturned, and at the same moment is heard:)*

REGINA *(sharply, but whispering)*   Oswald! take care! are you mad? Let me go!

MRS. ALVING *(starts in terror)*   Ah!

She stares wildly towards the half-opened door. OSWALD *is heard coughing and humming. A bottle is uncorked.*

MANDERS *(excited)*   What in the world is the matter? What is it, Mrs. Alving?

MRS. ALVING *(hoarsely)*   Ghosts! The couple from the conservatory—risen again!

MANDERS   What! Is it possible! Regina—? Is she—?

MRS. ALVING   Yes. Come. Not another word!

(She seizes MR. MANDERS *by the arm, and walks unsteadily towards the dining-room.)*

ACT II

The same room. The mist still lies heavy over the landscape. MANDERS *and* MRS. ALVING *enter from the dining-room.*

MRS. ALVING *(still in the doorway)*   Hearty appetite, Mr. Manders. *(Turns back towards the dining-room)* Aren't you coming too, Oswald?

OSWALD *(from within)*   No, thank you. I think I shall go out a little.

MRS. ALVING   Yes, do. The weather seems brighter now. *(She shuts the dining-room door, goes to the hall door, and calls:)* Regina!

REGINA *(outside)*   Yes, Mrs. Alving.

MRS. ALVING   Go down to the laundry, and help with the garlands.

REGINA   I'll go directly, Mrs. Alving.

*(*MRS. ALVING *assures herself that* REGINA *goes; then shuts the door.)*

MANDERS   I suppose he can't overhear us in there?

MRS. ALVING   Not when the door is shut. Besides, he's just going out.

MANDERS   I'm still quite upset. I can't think how I could get down a morsel of dinner.

MRS. ALVING *(controlling her nervousness, walks up and down)*   No more can I. But what's to be done now?

MANDERS   Yes; what's to be done? Upon my honour, I don't know. I'm so utterly without experience in matters of this sort.

MRS. ALVING   I'm quite convinced that, so far, no mischief has been done.

MANDERS   No; heaven forbid! But it's an unseemly state of things, nevertheless.

MRS. ALVING   The whole thing is an idle fancy of Oswald's; you may be sure of that.

MANDERS   Well, as I say, I'm not accustomed to affairs of the kind. But I should certainly think—

MRS. ALVING   Out of the house she must go, and that immediately. That's as clear as daylight.

MANDERS   Yes, of course she must.

MRS. ALVING   But where to? It would not be right to—

MANDERS   Where to? Home to her father, of course.

MRS. ALVING   To whom did you say?

MANDERS   To her—But then Engstrand is not—? Good God, Mrs. Alving, it's impossible! You must be mistaken after all.

MRS. ALVING   Alas! I'm mistaken in nothing. Johanna confessed all to me, and Alving could not deny it. So there was nothing to be done but to get the matter hushed up.

MANDERS   No, you could do nothing else.

MRS. ALVING   The girl left our service at once, and got a good sum of money to hold her tongue for the time. The rest she managed for herself when she got into the town. She renewed her old acquaintance with Engstrand, no doubt gave him to understand how much money she had received, and told him some tale about a foreigner who put in here with a yacht that summer. So she and Engstrand got married in hot haste. Why, you married them yourself.

MANDERS   But then how to account for—? I recollect distinctly Engstrand coming to give notice of the marriage. He was broken down with contrition, and reproached himself so bitterly for the misbehaviour he and his sweetheart had been guilty of.

MRS. ALVING   Yes; of course he had to take the blame upon himself.

MANDERS   But such a piece of duplicity on his part! And towards me too! I never could have believed it of Jacob Engstrand. I shan't fail to give him a serious talking to; he may be sure of that. And then the immorality of such a connection! For money! How much did the girl receive?

MRS. ALVING   Three hundred dollars.

MANDERS   There! think of that! for a miserable three hundred dollars to go and marry a fallen woman!

MRS. ALVING   Then what have you to say of me? I went and married a fallen man.

MANDERS   But—good heavens!—what are you talking about? A fallen man?

MRS. ALVING   Do you think Alving was any purer when I went with him to the altar than Johanna was when Engstrand married her?

MANDERS   Well, but there's a world of difference between the two cases—

MRS. ALVING   Not so much difference after all, except in the price—a wretched three hundred dollars and a whole fortune.

MANDERS   How can you compare the two cases? You had taken counsel with your own heart and with your friends.

MRS. ALVING *(without looking at him)*   I thought you understood where what you call my heart had strayed to at the time.

MANDERS *(distantly)*   Had I understood anything of the kind, I should not have continued a daily guest in your husband's house.

MRS. ALVING   Well, the fact remains that with myself I took no counsel whatever.

MANDERS   Well then, with your nearest relatives—as your duty bade you—with your mother and both your aunts.

MRS. ALVING   Yes, that's true. Those three cast up the account for me. Oh! it's marvellous how clearly they made out that it would be downright madness to refuse such an offer. If mother could only see me now, and know what all that grandeur has come to!

MANDERS   Nobody can be held responsible for the result. This, at least, remains clear; your marriage was in accordance with law and order.

MRS. ALVING *(at the window)*   Oh! that perpetual law and order! I often think that's what does all the mischief here in the world.

MANDERS   Mrs. Alving, that is a sinful way of talking.

MRS. ALVING   Well, I can't help it; I can endure all this constraint and cowardice no longer. It's too much for me. I must work my way out to freedom.

MANDERS   What do you mean by that?

MRS. ALVING *(drumming on the window-sill)*   I ought never to have concealed the facts of Alving's life. But at that time I was afraid to do anything else—afraid on my own account. I was such a coward.

MANDERS   A coward?

MRS. ALVING   If people had come to know anything, they would have said—"Poor man! with a runaway wife, no wonder he kicks over the traces."

MANDERS   Such remarks might have been made with a certain show of right.

MRS. ALVING *(looking steadily at him)*   If I were what I ought to be, I should go to Oswald and say, "Listen, my boy; your father was self-indulgent and vicious—"

MANDERS   Merciful heavens—!

MRS. ALVING   —and then I should tell him all I have told you—every word of it.

MANDERS   The idea is shocking, Mrs. Alving.

MRS. ALVING   Yes; I know that. I know that very well. I'm shocked at it myself. *(Goes away from the window)* I'm such a coward.

MANDERS   You call it "cowardice" to do your plain duty? Have you forgotten that a son should love and honour his father and mother?

MRS. ALVING   Don't let us talk in such general terms. Let us ask: should Oswald love and honour Chamberlain Alving?

MANDERS   Is there no voice in your mother's heart that forbids you to destroy your son's ideals?

MRS. ALVING   But what about the truth?

MANDERS   But what about the ideals?

MRS. ALVING   Oh! Ideals! Ideals! If only I weren't such a coward!

MANDERS   Do not despise ideals, Mrs. Alving; they will avenge themselves cruelly. Take Oswald's case; he, unfortunately, seems to have few enough ideals as it is; but I can see that his father stands before him as an ideal.

MRS. ALVING   You're right there.

MANDERS   And this habit of mind you have yourself implanted and fostered by your letters.

MRS. ALVING   Yes; in my superstitious awe for Duty and Decency I lied to my boy, year after year. Oh! what a coward, what a coward I've been!

MANDERS   You have established a happy illusion in your son's heart, Mrs. Alving, and assuredly you ought not to undervalue it.

MRS. ALVING   Hm; who knows whether it's so happy after all—? But, at any rate, I won't have any goings-on with Regina. He shan't go and ruin the poor girl.

MANDERS   No; good God! that would be dreadful!

MRS. ALVING   If I knew he was in earnest, and that it would be for his happiness—

MANDERS   What? What then?

MRS. ALVING   But it couldn't be; for I'm sorry to say Regina is not a girl to make him happy.

MANDERS   Well, what then? What do you mean?

MRS. ALVING   If I weren't such a pitiful coward I would say to him, "Marry her, or make what arrangement you please, only let us have nothing underhand about it."

MANDERS   Good heavens, would you let them *marry!* Anything so dreadful—! so unheard of—!

MRS. ALVING   Do you really mean "unheard of"? Frankly, Pastor Manders, do you suppose that throughout the country there aren't plenty of married couples as closely akin as they?

MANDERS   I don't in the least understand you.

MRS. ALVING   Oh yes, indeed you do.

MANDERS   Ah, you are thinking of the possibility that—Yes, alas! family life is certainly not always so pure as it ought to be. But in such a case as you point to, one can never know—at least with any certainty. Here, on the other hand—that you, a mother, can think of letting your son—!

MRS. ALVING   But I can't—I wouldn't for anything in the world; that's precisely what I am saying.

MANDERS   No, because you are a "coward," as you put it. But if you were not a "coward," then—? Good God! a connection so shocking.

MRS. ALVING   So far as that goes, they say we're all sprung from connections of that sort. And who is it that arranged the world so, Pastor Manders?

MANDERS   Questions of that kind I must decline to discuss with you, Mrs. Alving; you are far from being in the right frame of mind for them. But that you dare to call your scruples "cowardly"—!

MRS. ALVING   Let me tell you what I mean. I am timid and half-hearted because I cannot get rid of the Ghosts that haunt me.

MANDERS   What do you say haunts you?

MRS. ALVING   Ghosts! When I heard Regina and Oswald in there, I seemed to see Ghosts before me. I almost think we're all of us Ghosts, Pastor Manders. It's not only what we have inherited from our father and mother that "walks" in us. It's all sorts of dead ideas, and lifeless old beliefs, and so forth. They have no vitality, but they cling to us all the same, and we can't get rid of them. Whenever I take up a newspaper, I seem to see Ghosts gliding between the lines. There must be Ghosts all the country over, as thick as the sand of the sea. And then we are, one and all, so pitifully afraid of the light.

MANDERS   Ah! here we have the fruits of your reading! And pretty fruits they are, upon my word! Oh! those horrible, revolutionary, free-thinking books!

MRS. ALVING   You are mistaken, my dear Pastor. It was you yourself who set me thinking; and I thank you for it with all my heart.

MANDERS   I?

MRS. ALVING   Yes—when you forced me under the yoke you called Duty and Obligation; when you praised as right and proper what my whole soul rebelled against as something loathsome. It was then that I began to look into the seams of your doctrine. I wanted only to pick at a single knot; but when I had got that undone, the whole thing ravelled out. And then I understood that it was all machine-sewn.

MANDERS *(softly, with emotion)*   And was that the upshot of my life's hardest battle?

MRS. ALVING   Call it rather your most pitiful defeat.

MANDERS   It was my greatest victory, Helen—the victory over myself.

MRS. ALVING   It was a crime against us both.

MANDERS   When you went astray, and came to me crying, "Here I am; take me!" I commanded you, saying, "Woman, go home to your lawful husband." Was that a crime?

MRS. ALVING   Yes, I think so.

MANDERS   We two do not understand each other.

MRS. ALVING   Not now, at any rate.

MANDERS   Never—never in my most secret thoughts have I regarded you otherwise than as another's wife.

MRS. ALVING   Oh!—indeed?

MANDERS   Helen—!

MRS. ALVING   People so easily forget their past selves.

MANDERS   I do not. I am what I always was.

MRS. ALVING *(changing the subject)*   Well, well, well; don't let us talk of old times any longer. You are now over head and ears in Commissions and Boards of Direction, and I am fighting my battle with Ghosts both within me and without.

MANDERS   Those without I shall help you to lay. After all the shocking things I've heard from you today, I cannot in conscience permit an unprotected girl to remain in your house.

MRS. ALVING   Don't you think the best plan would be to get her provided for?—I mean, by a good marriage.

MANDERS   No doubt. I think it would be desirable for her in every respect. Regina is now at the age when— Of course I don't know much about these things, but—

MRS. ALVING   Regina matured very early.

MANDERS   Yes, did she not? I have an impression that she was remarkably well developed, physically, when I prepared her for confirmation. But in the meantime, she must go home, under her father's eye.—Ah! but Engstrand is not— That he—that *he*—could so hide the truth from me!

(A knock at the door into the hall)

MRS. ALVING   Who can that be? Come in!

ENGSTRAND *(in his Sunday clothes, in the doorway)*   I beg your pardon humbly, but—

MANDERS   Ah! Hm—

MRS. ALVING   Is that you, Engstrand?

ENGSTRAND   —there was none of the servants about, so I took the great liberty of just knocking.

MRS. ALVING   Oh! very well. Come in. Do you want to speak to me?

ENGSTRAND *(comes in)*   No, I'm greatly obliged to you; it was with his Reverence I wanted to have a word or two.

MANDERS *(walking up and down the room)*   Hm—indeed! You want to speak to me, do you?

ENGSTRAND   Yes, I should like so much to—

MANDERS *(stops in front of him)*   Well; may I ask what you want?

ENGSTRAND   Well, it was just this, your Reverence; we've been paid off down yonder—my grateful thanks to you, ma'am—and now everything's finished. I've been thinking it would be but right and proper if we, that have been working so honestly together all this time—well, I was thinking we ought to end up with a little prayer-meeting tonight.

MANDERS   A prayer-meeting? Down at the Orphanage?

ENGSTRAND   Oh, if your Reverence doesn't think it proper—

MANDERS   Oh yes! I do; but—hm—

ENGSTRAND   I've been in the habit of offering up a little prayer in the evenings, myself.

MRS. ALVING   Have you?

ENGSTRAND   Yes, every now and then—just a little exercise, you might call it. But I'm a poor, common man, and have little enough gift, God help me! and so I thought, as the Reverend Mr. Manders happened to be here, I'd—

MANDERS Well, you see, Engstrand, I must first ask you a question. Are you in the right frame of mind for such a meeting? Do you feel your conscience clear and at ease?

ENGSTRAND Oh! God help us, your Reverence! we'd better not talk about conscience.

MANDERS Yes, that's just what we must talk about. What have you to answer?

ENGSTRAND Why—one's conscience—it can be bad enough now and then.

MANDERS Ah, you admit that. Then will you make a clean breast of it, and tell the truth about Regina?

MRS. ALVING *(quickly)* Mr. Manders!

MANDERS *(reassuringly)* Just let me—

ENGSTRAND About Regina! Lord! how you frighten me! *(Looks at* MRS. ALVING*)* There's nothing wrong about Regina, is there?

MANDERS We'll hope not. But I mean, what is the truth about you and Regina? You pass for her father, eh!

ENGSTRAND *(uncertain)* Well—hm—your Reverence knows all about me and poor Johanna.

MANDERS Come, no more prevarication! Your wife told Mrs. Alving the whole story before quitting her service.

ENGSTRAND Well, then, may—! Now, did she really?

MANDERS So you're found out, Engstrand.

ENGSTRAND And she swore and took her Bible oath—

MANDERS Did she take her Bible oath?

ENGSTRAND No; she only swore; but she did it so earnestly.

MANDERS And you have hidden the truth from me all these years? Hidden it from me! from me, who have trusted you without reserve, in everything.

ENGSTRAND Well, I can't deny it.

MANDERS Have I deserved this of you, Engstrand? Haven't I always been ready to help you in word and deed, so far as it stood in my power? Answer me. Have I not?

ENGSTRAND It would have been a poor look-out for me many a time but for the Reverend Mr. Manders.

MANDERS And you reward me thus! You cause me to enter falsehoods in the Church Register, and you withhold from me, year after year, the explanations you owed alike to me and to truth. Your conduct has been wholly inexcusable, Engstrand; and from this time forward all is over between us.

ENGSTRAND *(with a sigh)* Yes! I suppose it must be.

MANDERS How can you possibly justify yourself?

ENGSTRAND How could I think she'd gone and made bad worse by talking about it? Will your Reverence just fancy yourself in the same trouble as poor Johanna—

MANDERS I!

ENGSTRAND Lord bless you! I don't mean just exactly the same. But I mean, if your Reverence had anything to be ashamed of in the eyes of the world, as the saying is— We men oughtn't to judge a poor woman too hardly, your Reverence.

MANDERS I am not doing so. It's you I am reproaching.

ENGSTRAND Might I make so bold as to ask your Reverence a bit of a question?

MANDERS Yes, ask away.

ENGSTRAND Isn't it right and proper for a man to raise up the fallen?

MANDERS Most certainly it is.

ENGSTRAND And isnt a man bound to keep his sacred word?

MANDERS Why, of course he is; but—

ENGSTRAND When Johanna had got into trouble through that Englishman—or it might have been an American or a Russian, as they call them—well, you see, she came down into the town. Poor thing! she'd sent me about my business once or twice before: for she couldn't bear the sight of anything but what was handsome; and I'd got this damaged leg. Your Reverence recollects how I ventured up into a dancing-saloon, where seafaring people carried on with drink and devilry, as the saying goes. And then, when I was for giving them a bit of an admonition to lead a new life—

MRS. ALVING *(at the window)* Hm—

MANDERS I know all about that, Engstrand; the ruffians threw you downstairs. You've told me of the affair already.

ENGSTRAND I'm not puffed up about it, your Reverence. But what I wanted to say was, that then she came and confessed all to me, with weeping and gnashing of teeth, I can tell your Reverence I was sore at heart to hear it.

MANDERS Were you indeed, Engstrand? Well, go on.

ENGSTRAND So I said to her, "The American, he's sailing about on the boundless sea. And as for you, Johanna," said I, "you've committed a grievous sin and you're a fallen creature. But Jacob Engstrand," said I, "he's got two good legs to stand upon, *he* has—" You know, your Reverence, I was speaking figurative-like.

MANDERS I understand quite well. Go on.

ENGSTRAND Well, that was how I raised her up and made an honest woman of her, so that folks shouldn't get to know how she'd gone astray with foreigners.

MANDERS All that was very good of you. Only I can't approve of your stooping to take money—

ENGSTRAND Money? I? Not a farthing!

MANDERS *(inquiringly to* MRS. ALVING*)* But—

ENGSTRAND Oh, wait a minute!—now I recollect. Johanna had a trifle of money. But I would have nothing to do with it. "No," said I, "that's mammon; that's the wages of sin. This dirty gold—or notes, or whatever it was—we'll just fling that back to the American," said I. But he was gone and away, over the stormy sea, your Reverence.

MANDERS Was he really, my good fellow?

ENGSTRAND Ay, sir. So Johanna and I, we agreed that the money should go to the child's education; and so it did, and I can account for every blessed farthing of it.

MANDERS Why, this alters the case considerably.

ENGSTRAND That's just how it stands, your Reverence. And I make so bold as to say I've been an honest father to Regina, so far as my poor strength went; for I'm but a poor creature, worse luck!

MANDERS Well, well, my good fellow—

ENGSTRAND But I may make bold to say that I've brought up the child, and lived kindly with poor Johanna, and ruled over my own house, as the Scripture has it. But I could never think of going up to your Reverence and puffing myself up and boasting because I too had done some good in the world. No, sir; when anything of that sort happens to Jacob Engstrand, he holds his tongue about it. It doesn't happen so very often, I daresay. And when I do come to see your Reverence, I find a mortal deal to say about what's wicked and weak. For I do say—as I was saying just now—one's conscience isn't always as clean as it might be.

MANDERS Give me your hand, Jacob Engstrand.

ENGSTRAND Oh, Lord! your Reverence—

MANDERS Come, no nonsense. *(Wrings his hand)* There we are!

ENGSTRAND And if I might humbly beg your Reverence's pardon—

MANDERS You? On the contrary, it's I who ought to beg your pardon—

ENGSTRAND Lord, no, sir!

MANDERS Yes, certainly. And I do it with all my heart. Forgive me for misunderstanding you. And I wish I could give you some proof of my hearty regret, and of my good-will towards you—

ENGSTRAND   Would your Reverence?

MANDERS   With the greatest pleasure.

ENGSTRAND   Well then, there's the very opportunity now. With the money I've saved here, I was thinking I might set up a Sailors' Home down in the town.

MRS. ALVING   *You?*

ENGSTRAND   Yes; it too might be a sort of Orphanage, in a manner of speaking. There are many temptations for seafaring folk ashore. But in this Home of mine, a man might feel as under a father's eye, I was thinking.

MANDERS   What do you say to this, Mrs. Alving?

ENGSTRAND   It isn't much I've got to start with, the Lord help me! But if I could only find a helping hand, why—

MANDERS   Yes, yes; we'll look into the matter. I entirely approve of your plan. But now, go before me and make everything ready, and get the candles lighted, so as to give the place an air of festivity. And then we'll pass an edifying hour together, my good fellow; for now I quite believe you're in the right frame of mind.

ENGSTRAND   Yes, I trust I am. And so I'll say good-bye, ma'am, and thank you kindly; and take good care of Regina for me—*(Wipes a tear from his eye)*—poor Johanna's child; hm, it's an odd thing, now; but it's just as if she'd grown into the very apple of my eye. It is indeed.

(He bows and goes out through the hall.)

MANDERS   Well, what do you say of that man now, Mrs. Alving? That threw a totally different light on matters, didn't it?

MRS. ALVING   Yes, it certainly did.

MANDERS   It only shows how excessively careful one must be in judging one's fellow-creatures. But it's a great joy to ascertain that one has been mistaken. Don't you think so?

MRS. ALVING   I think you are, and will always be, a great baby, Manders.

MANDERS   I?

MRS. ALVING *(laying her two hands upon his shoulders)*   And I say that I've half a mind to put my arms round your neck, and kiss you.

MANDERS *(stepping hastily back)*   No, no! God bless me! What an idea!

MRS. ALVING *(with a smile)*   Oh! you needn't be afraid of me.

MANDERS *(by the table)*   You have sometimes such an exaggerated way of expressing yourself. Now, I'll just collect all the documents, and put them in my bag. *(He does so.)* There, now. And now, good-bye for the present. Keep your eyes open when Oswald comes back. I shall look in again later.

(He takes his hat and goes out through the hall door.)

MRS. ALVING *(sighs, looks for a moment out of the window, sets the room in order a little, and is about to go into the dining-room, but stops at the door with a half-suppressed cry)*   Oswald, are you still at table?

OSWALD *(in the dining-room)*   I'm only finishing my cigar.

MRS. ALVING   I thought you'd gone for a little walk.

OSWALD   In such weather as this? *(A glass clinks.* MRS. ALVING *leaves the door open, and sits down with her knitting on the sofa by the window.)*   Wasn't that Pastor Manders that went out just now?

MRS. ALVING   Yes; he went down to the Orphanage.

OSWALD   Hm. *(The glass and decanter clink again.)*

MRS. ALVING *(with a troubled glance)*   Dear Oswald, you should take care of that liqueur. It's strong.

OSWALD   It keeps out the damp.

MRS. ALVING   Wouldn't you rather come in to me?

OSWALD   I mayn't smoke in there.

MRS. ALVING   You know quite well you may smoke cigars.

OSWALD   Oh! all right then; I'll come in. Just a tiny drop more first! There! *(He comes into the room with his cigar, and shuts the door after him. A short silence)* Where's Manders gone to?

MRS. ALVING   I've just told you; he went down to the Orphanage.

OSWALD   Oh, ah; so you did.

MRS. ALVING   You shouldn't sit so long at table after dinner, Oswald.

OSWALD *(holding his cigar behind him)*   But I find it so pleasant, mother. *(Strokes and pets her)* Just think what it is for me to come home and sit at mother's own table, in mother's room, and eat mother's delicious dinners.

MRS. ALVING   My dear, dear boy!

OSWALD *(somewhat impatiently walks about and smokes)*   And what else can I do with myself here? I can't set to work at anything.

MRS. ALVING   Why can't you?

OSWALD   In such weather as this? Without a single ray of sunlight the whole day? *(Walks up the room)* Oh! not to be able to work!

MRS. ALVING   Perhaps it was not quite wise of you to come home?

OSWALD   Oh, yes, mother; I had to.

MRS. ALVING   Why? I would ten times rather forego the joy of having you here than—

OSWALD *(stops beside the table)*   Now just tell me, mother; does it really make you so very happy to have me home again?

MRS. ALVING   Does it make me happy!

OSWALD *(crumpling up a newspaper)*   I should have thought it must be pretty much the same to you whether I was in existence or not.

MRS. ALVING   Have you the heart to say that to your mother, Oswald?

OSWALD   But you've got on very well without me all this time.

MRS. ALVING   Yes; I've got on without you. That's true.

A silence. Twilight gradually falls. OSWALD *walks to and fro across the room. He has laid his cigar down.*

OSWALD *(stops beside* MRS. ALVING*)*   Mother, may I sit on the sofa beside you?

MRS. ALVING *(makes room for him)*   Yes do, my dear boy.

OSWALD *(sits down)*   Now I'm going to tell you something, mother.

MRS. ALVING *(anxiously)*   Well?

OSWALD *(looks fixedly before him)*   For I can't go on hiding it any longer.

MRS. ALVING   Hiding what? What is it?

OSWALD *(as before)*   I could never bring myself to write to you about it; and since I've come home—

MRS. ALVING *(seizes him by the arm)*   Oswald, what *is* the matter?

OSWALD *(as before)*   Both yesterday and today I've tried to put the thoughts away from me—to get free from them; but it won't do.

MRS. ALVING *(rising)*   Now you must speak out, Oswald.

OSWALD *(draws her down to the sofa again)*   Sit still; and then I'll try to tell you. I complained of fatigue after my journey—

MRS. ALVING   Well, what then?

OSWALD   But it isn't that that's the matter with me; it isn't any ordinary fatigue—

MRS. ALVING *(tries to jump up)* You're not ill, Oswald?

OSWALD *(draws her down again)* Do sit still, mother. Only take it quietly. I'm not downright ill, either; not what's commonly called "ill." *(Clasps his hands above his head)* Mother, my mind is broken down—ruined—I shall never be able to work again. *(With his hands before his face, he buries his head in her lap, and breaks into bitter sobbing.)*

MRS. ALVING *(white and trembling)* Oswald! Look at me! No, no; it isn't true.

OSWALD *(looks up with despair in his eyes)* Never to be able to work again! Never! never! It will be like living death! Mother, can you imagine anything so horrible?

MRS. ALVING My poor boy! How has this horrible thing come over you?

OSWALD *(sits upright)* That's just what I can't possibly grasp or understand. I've never led a dissipated life—never, in any respect. You mustn't believe that of me, mother. I've never done that.

MRS. ALVING I'm sure you haven't, Oswald.

OSWALD And yet this has come over me just the same—this awful misfortune!

MRS. ALVING Oh, but it will pass away, my dear, blessed boy. It's nothing but over-work. Trust me, I am right.

OSWALD *(sadly)* I thought so too at first; but it isn't so.

MRS. ALVING Tell me the whole story from beginning to end.

OSWALD Well, I will.

MRS. ALVING When did you first notice it?

OSWALD It was directly after I had been home last time, and had got back to Paris again. I began to feel the most violent pains in my head chiefly in the back of my head, I thought. It was as though a tight iron ring was being screwed round my neck and up-wards.

MRS. ALVING Well, and then?

OSWALD At first I thought it was nothing but the ordinary headache I had been so plagued with when I was growing up—

MRS. ALVING Yes, yes—

OSWALD But it wasn't that. I soon found that out. I couldn't work. I wanted to begin upon a big new picture, but my powers seemed to fail me; all my strength was crippled; I couldn't form any definite images; everything swam before me—whirling round and round. Oh! it was an awful state! At last I sent for a doctor, and from him I learned the truth.

MRS. ALVING How do you mean?

OSWALD He was one of the first doctors in Paris. I told him my symptoms, and then he set to work asking me a heap of questions which I thought had nothing to do with the matter. I couldn't imagine what the man was after—

MRS. ALVING Well?

OSWALD At last he said: "You have been worm-eaten from your birth." He used that very word—*vermoulu.*

MRS. ALVING *(breathlessly)* What did he mean by that?

OSWALD I didn't understand either, and begged him to explain himself more clearly. And then the old cynic said—*(Clenching his fist)* Oh—!

MRS. ALVING What did he say?

OSWALD He said, "The sins of the fathers are visited upon the children."

MRS. ALVING *(rising slowly)* The sins of the fathers—!

OSWALD I very nearly struck him in the face—

MRS. ALVING *(walks away across the floor)* The sins of the fathers—

OSWALD *(smiles sadly)* Yes; what do you think of that? Of course I assured him that such a thing was out of the question. But do you think he gave in? No, he stuck to it; and it was only when I produced your letters and translated the passages relating to father—

MRS . ALVING   But then?

OSWALD   Then of course he was bound to admit that he was on the wrong track; and so I got to know the truth—the incomprehensible truth! I ought to have held aloof from my bright and happy life among my comrades. It had been too much for my strength. So I had brought it upon myself!

MRS. ALVING   Oswald! Oh, no, don't believe it!

OSWALD   No other explanation was possible, he said. That's the awful part of it. Incurably ruined for life—by my own heedlessness! All that I meant to have done in the world—I never dare think of again—I'm not *able* to think of it. Oh! if I could but live over again, and undo all I've done! *(He buries his face in the sofa.* MRS. ALVING *wrings her hands and walks, in silent struggle, backwards and forwards.* OSWALD, *after a while, looks up and remains resting upon his elbow.)* If it had only been something inherited, something one wasn't responsible for! But this! To have thrown away so shamefully, thoughtlessly, recklessly, one's own happiness, one's own health, everything in the world—one's future, one's very life!

MRS. ALVING   No, no, my dear, darling boy! It's impossible. *(Bends over him)* Things are not so desperate as you think.

OSWALD   Oh! you don't know— *(Springs up)* And then, mother, to cause you all this sorrow! Many a time I've almost wished and hoped that at bottom you didn't care so very much about me.

MRS. ALVING   I, Oswald? My only boy! You are all I have in the world! The only thing I care about!

OSWALD *(seizes both her hands and kisses them)*   Yes, mother dear, I see it well enough. When I'm at home, I see it, of course; and that's the hardest part for me. But now you know the whole story, and now we won't talk any more about it to-day. I daren't think of it for long together. *(Goes up the room)* Get me something to drink, mother.

MRS. ALVING   Drink? What do you want to drink now?

OSWALD   Oh! anything you like. You have some cold punch in the house.

MRS. ALVING   Yes, but my dear Oswald—

OSWALD   Don't refuse me, mother. Do be nice, now! I must have something to wash down all these gnawing thoughts. *(Goes into the conservatory)* And then—it's so dark here! (MRS. ALVING *pulls a bell-rope on the right.)* And this ceaseless rain! It may go on week after week for months together. Never to get a glimpse of the sun! I can't recollect ever having seen the sun shine all the times I've been at home.

MRS. ALVING   Oswald, you're thinking of going away from me.

OSWALD   Hm—*(Drawing a deep breath)*—I'm not thinking of anything. I can't think of anything. *(In a low voice)* I let thinking alone.

REGINA *(from the dining-room)*   Did you ring, ma'am?

MRS. ALVING   Yes; let us have the lamp in.

REGINA   I will, directly. It's ready lighted. *(Goes out)*

MRS. ALVING *(goes across to* OSWALD)   Oswald, be frank with me.

OSWALD   Well, so I am, mother. *(Goes to the table)* I think I've told you enough.

(REGINA *brings the lamp and sets it upon the table.)*

MRS. ALVING   Regina, you might fetch us a half-bottle of champagne.

OSWALD *(puts his arm round* MRS. ALVING's *neck)*   That's just what I wanted. I knew mother wouldn't let her boy be thirsty.

MRS. ALVING   My own, poor, darling Oswald, how could I deny you anything now?

OSWALD *(eagerly)*   Is that true, mother? Do you mean it?

MRS. ALVING   How? What?

OSWALD   That you couldn't deny me anything.

MRS. ALVING My dear Oswald—

OSWALD Hush!

REGINA *(brings a tray with a half-bottle of champagne and two glasses, which she sets on the table)* Shall I open it?

OSWALD No, thanks. I'll do it myself.

(REGINA *goes out again.*)

MRS. ALVING *(sits down by the table)* What was it you meant, I mustn't deny you?

OSWALD *(busy opening the bottle)* First let's have a glass—or two.

(The cork pops; he pours wine into one glass, and is about to pour it into the other.)

MRS. ALVING *(holding her hand over it)* Thanks; not for me.

OSWALD Oh! won't you? Then I will!

(He empties the glass, fills, and empties it again; then he sits down by the table.)

MRS. ALVING *(in expectation)* Well?

OSWALD *(without looking at her)* Tell me—I thought you and Pastor Manders seemed so odd—so quiet—at dinner to-day.

MRS. ALVING Did you notice it?

OSWALD Yes. Hm—*(After a short silence)* Tell me: what do you think of Regina?

MRS. ALVING What do I think?

OSWALD Yes; isn't she splendid?

MRS. ALVING My dear Oswald, you don't know her as I do—

OSWALD Well?

MRS. ALVING Regina, unfortunately, was allowed to stay at home too long. I ought to have taken her earlier in my house.

OSWALD Yes, but isn't she splendid to look at, mother?

(He fills his glass.)

MRS. ALVING Regina has many serious faults.

OSWALD Oh, what does it matter?

(He drinks again.)

MRS. ALVING But I'm fond of her, nevertheless, and I'm responsible for her. I wouldn't for all the world have any harm happen to her.

OSWALD *(springs up)* Mother! Regina is my only salvation.

MRS. ALVING *(rising)* What do you mean by that?

OSWALD I can't go on bearing all this anguish of mind alone.

MRS. ALVING Haven't you got your mother to share it with you?

OSWALD Yes, that's what I thought; and so I came home to you. But that won't do. I see it won't do. I can't endure my life here.

MRS. ALVING Oswald!

OSWALD I must live differently, mother. That's why I must leave you. I won't have you looking on at it.

MRS. ALVING My unhappy boy! But, Oswald, while you're so ill as this—

OSWALD If it were only the illness, I should stay with you, mother, you may be sure; for you are the best friend I have in the world.

MRS. ALVING Yes, indeed I am, Oswald; am I not?

OSWALD *(wanders restlessly about)* But it's all the torment, the remorse; and besides that, the great, killing dread. Oh! that awful dread!

MRS. ALVING *(walking after him)* Dread? What dread? What do you mean?

OSWALD   Oh, you mustn't ask me any more! I don't know. I can't describe it. (MRS. ALVING *goes over to the right and pulls the bell.*) What is it you want?

MRS. ALVING   I want my boy to be happy—that's what I want. He shan't go on racking his brains. *(To* REGINA, *who comes in at the door)* More champagne—a whole bottle. (REGINA *goes.*)

OSWALD   Mother!

MRS. ALVING   Do you think we don't know how to live here at home?

OSWALD   Isn't she splendid to look at? How beautifully she's built! And so thoroughly healthy!

MRS. ALVING *(sits by the table)*   Sit down, Oswald; let us talk quietly together.

OSWALD *(sits)*   I daresay you don't know, mother, that I owe Regina some reparation.

MRS. ALVING   You?

OSWALD   For a bit of thoughtlessness, or whatever you like to call it—very innocent, anyhow. When I was home last time—

MRS. ALVING   Well?

OSWALD   She used often to ask me about Paris, and I used to tell her one thing and another. Then I recollect I happened to say to her one day, "Wouldn't you like to go there yourself?"

MRS. ALVING   Well?

OSWALD   I saw her face flush, and then she said, "Yes, I should like it of all things." "Ah, well," I replied, "it might perhaps be managed"—or something like that.

MRS. ALVING   And then?

OSWALD   Of course I'd forgotten the whole thing; but the day before yesterday I happened to ask her whether she was glad I was to stay at home so long—

MRS. ALVING   Yes?

OSWALD   And then she looked so strangely at me and asked, "But what's to become of my trip to Paris?"

MRS. ALVING   Her trip!

OSWALD   And so I got out of her that she had taken the thing seriously; that she had been thinking of me the whole time, and had set to work to learn French—

MRS. ALVING   So that was why she did it!

OSWALD   Mother! when I saw that fresh, lovely, splendid girl standing there before me—till then I had hardly noticed her—but when she stood there as though with open arms ready to receive me—

MRS. ALVING   Oswald!

OSWALD   —then it flashed upon me that my salvation lay in her; for I saw that she was full of the joy of life.[4]

MRS. ALVING *(starts)*   The joy of life? Can there be salvation in that?

REGINA *(from the dining-room, with a bottle of champagne)*   I'm sorry to have been so long, but I had to go to the cellar. *(Puts the bottle on the table)*

OSWALD   And now fetch another glass.

REGINA *(looks at him in surprise)*   There is Mrs. Alving's glass, Mr. Alving.

OSWALD   Yes, fetch one for yourself, Regina. (REGINA *starts and gives a lightning-like side glance at* MRS. ALVING.) Why do you wait?

REGINA *(softly and hesitatingly)*   Is it Mrs. Alving's wish?

MRS. ALVING   Fetch the glass, Regina.

(REGINA *goes out into the dining-room.*)

---

[4] Livsglæde—"la joie de vivre"

OSWALD *(follows her with his eyes)*   Have you noticed how she walks?—so firmly and lightly!

MRS. ALVING   It can never be, Oswald!

OSWALD   It's a settled thing. Can't you see that? It's no use saying anything against it. (REGINA *enters with an empty glass, which she keeps in her hand.*) Sit down, Regina.

(REGINA *looks inquiringly at* MRS. ALVING.)

MRS. ALVING   Sit down. (REGINA *sits on a chair by the dining-room door, still holding the empty glass in her hand.*) Oswald, what were you saying about the joy of life?

OSWALD   Ah! the joy of life, mother—that's a thing you don't know much about in these parts. I've never felt it here.

MRS. ALVING   Not when you're with me?

OSWALD   Not when I'm at home. But you don't understand that.

MRS. ALVING   Yes, yes; I think I almost understand it—now.

OSWALD   And then, too, the joy of work! At bottom, it's the same thing. But that, too, you know nothing about.

MRS. ALVING   Perhaps you're right, Oswald; tell me more about it.

OSWALD   Well, I only mean that here people are brought up to believe that work is a curse and a punishment for sin, and that life is something miserable, something we want to be done with, the sooner the better.

MRS. ALVING   "A vale of tears," yes; and we take care to make it one.

OSWALD   But in the great world people won't hear of such things. There, nobody really believes such doctrines any longer. There, you feel it bliss and ecstasy merely to draw the breath of life. Mother, have you noticed that everything I've painted has turned upon the joy of life?—always, always upon the joy of life?—light and sunshine and glorious air and faces radiant with happiness. That's why I'm afraid of remaining at home with you.

MRS. ALVING   Afraid? What are you afraid of here, with me?

OSWALD   I'm afraid lest all my instincts should be warped into ugliness.

MRS. ALVING *(looks steadily at him)*   Do you think that would be the way of it?

OSWALD   I know it. You may live the same life here as there, and yet it won't be the same life.

MRS. ALVING *(who has been listening eagerly, rises, her eyes big with thought, and says)*   Now I see the connection.

OSWALD   What is it you see?

MRS. ALVING   I see it now for the first time. And now I can speak.

OSWALD *(rising)*   Mother, I don't understand you.

REGINA *(who has also risen)*   Perhaps I ought to go?

MRS. ALVING   No. Stay here. Now I can speak. Now, my boy, you shall know the whole truth. And then you can choose. Oswald! Regina!

OSWALD   Hush! Here's Manders—

MANDERS *(comes in by the hall door)*   There! We've had a most edifying time down there.

OSWALD   So have we.

MANDERS   We must stand by Engstrand and his Sailors' Home. Regina must go to him and help him—

REGINA   No thank you, sir.

MANDERS *(noticing her for the first time)*   What? You here? and with a glass in your hand!

REGINA *(hastily putting the glass down) Pardon!*

OSWALD   Regina is going with me, Mr. Manders.

MANDERS   Going with you!

OSWALD   Yes; as my wife—if she wishes it.

MANDERS   But, good God—

REGINA   I can't help it, sir.

OSWALD   Or she'll stay here, if I stay.

REGINA *(involuntarily)*   Here!

MANDERS   I am thunderstruck at your conduct, Mrs. Alving.

MRS. ALVING   They will do neither one thing nor the other; for now I can speak out
plainly.

MANDERS   You surely won't do that. No, no, no!

MRS. ALVING   Yes, I can speak and I will. And no ideal shall suffer after all.

OSWALD   Mother! What on earth are you hiding from me?

REGINA *(listening)*   Oh, ma'am! listen! Don't you hear shouts outside?

(She goes into the conservatory and looks out.)

OSWALD *(at the window on the left)*   What's going on? Where does that light come
from?

REGINA *(cries out)*   The Orphanage is on fire!

MRS. ALVING *(rushing to the window)*   On fire?

MANDERS   On fire! Impossible! I've just come from there.

OSWALD   Where's my hat? Oh, never mind it—Father's Orphanage!

(He rushes out through the garden door.)

MRS. ALVING   My shawl, Regina! It's blazing!

MANDERS   Terrible! Mrs. Alving, it's a judgment upon this abode of sin.

MRS. ALVING   Yes, of course. Come, Regina.

(She and REGINA *hasten out through the hall.)*

MANDERS *(clasps his hands together)*   And uninsured, too.

(He goes out the same way.)

ACT III

*The room as before. All the doors stand open. The lamp is still burning on the table. It is
dark out of doors; there is just a faint glow from the conflagration in the background at
the left.*

MRS. ALVING, *with a shawl over her head, stands in conservatory and looks out.* REGINA, *also
with a shawl on, stands a little behind her.*

MRS. ALVING   All burnt!—burnt to the ground!

REGINA   The basement is still burning.

MRS. ALVING   How is it Oswald doesn't come home? There's nothing to be saved.

REGINA   Would you like me to take down his hat to him?

MRS. ALVING   Hasn't he even got his hat on?

REGINA *(pointing to the hall)*   No; there it hangs.

MRS. ALVING   Let it be. He must come up now. I'll go and look for him myself.

(She goes out through the garden door.)

MANDERS *(comes in from the hall)*   Isn't Mrs. Alving here?

REGINA   She's just gone down the garden.

MANDERS   This is the most terrible night I ever went through.

REGINA   Yes; isn't it a dreadful misfortune, sir?

MANDERS   Oh, don't talk about it! I can hardly bear to think of it.

REGINA   How *can* it have happened?

MANDERS   Don't ask me, Regina! How should *I* know? Do *you* too—? Isn't it enough that your father—?

REGINA   What about him?

MANDERS   Oh! he has driven me clean out of my mind—

ENGSTRAND *(comes through the hall)*   Your Reverence!

MANDERS *(turns round in terror)*   Are you after me here, too?

ENGSTRAND   Yes, strike me dead, but I must—Oh, Lord! what am I saying? It's an awfully ugly business, your Reverence.

MANDERS *(walks to and fro)*   Alas! alas!

REGINA   What's the matter?

ENGSTRAND   Why, it all came of that prayer-meeting, you see. *(Softly)* The bird's limed, my girl. *(Aloud)* And to think that it's my fault that it's his Reverence's fault!

MANDERS   But I assure you, Engstrand—

ENGSTRAND   There wasn't another soul except your Reverence that ever touched the candles down there.

MANDERS *(stops)*   Ah! so you declare. But I certainly can't recollect that I ever had a candle in my hand.

ENGSTRAND   And I saw as clear as daylight how your Reverence took the candle and snuffed it with your fingers, and threw away the snuff among the shavings.

MANDERS   And you stood and looked on?

ENGSTRAND   Yes; I saw it as plain as a pikestaff.

MANDERS   It's quite beyond my comprehension. Besides, it's never been my habit to snuff candles with my fingers.

ENGSTRAND   And very risky it looked, that it did! But is there so much harm done after all, your Reverence?

MANDERS *(walks restlessly to and fro)*   Oh, don't ask me!

ENGSTRAND *(walks with him)*   And your Reverence hadn't insured it, neither?

MANDERS *(continuing to walk up and down)*   No, no, no; you've heard that already.

ENGSTRAND *(following him)*   Not insured! And then to go right down and set light to the whole thing. Lord! Lord! what a misfortune!

MANDERS *(wipes the sweat from his forehead)*   Ay, you may well say that, Engstrand.

ENGSTRAND   And to think that such a thing should happen to a benevolent institution, that was to have been a blessing both to town and country, as the saying is! The newspapers won't handle your Reverence very gently, I expect.

MANDERS   No; that's just what I'm thinking of. That's almost the worst of it. All the malignant attacks and accusations—! Oh! it's terrible only to imagine it.

MRS. ALVING *(comes in from the garden)*   He can't be got away from the fire.

MANDERS   Ah! there you are, Mrs. Alving!

MRS. ALVING   So you've escaped your Inaugural Address, Pastor Manders.

MANDERS   Oh! I should so gladly—

MRS. ALVING *(in an undertone)*   It's all for the best. That Orphanage would have done no good to anybody.

MANDERS   Do you think not?

MRS. ALVING   Do you think it would?

MANDERS   It's a terrible misfortune, all the same.

MRS. ALVING   Let us speak plainly of it, as a piece of business. Are you waiting for Mr. Manders, Engstrand?

ENGSTRAND *(at the hall door)*   Ay, ma'am; indeed I am.

MRS. ALVING   Then sit down meanwhile.

ENGSTRAND   Thank you, ma'am; I'd rather stand.

MRS. ALVING *(to MANDERS)*   I suppose you're going by the steamer?

MANDERS   Yes; it starts in an hour.

MRS. ALVING   Be so good as to take all the papers with you. I won't hear another word about this affair. I have other things to think about.

MANDERS   Mrs. Alving—

MRS. ALVING   Later on I shall send you a Power of Attorney to settle everything as you please.

MANDERS   That I shall very readily undertake. The original destination of the endowment must now be completely changed, alas!

MRS. ALVING   Of course it must.

MANDERS   I think, first of all, I shall arrange that the Solvik property shall pass to the parish. The land is by no means without value. It can always be turned to account for some purpose or other. And the interest of the money in the Bank I could, perhaps, best apply for the benefit of some undertaking that has proved itself a blessing to the town.

MRS. ALVING   Do just as you please. The whole matter is now completely indifferent to me.

ENGSTRAND   Give a thought to my Sailors' Home, your Reverence.

MANDERS   Yes, that's not a bad suggestion. That must be considered.

ENGSTRAND   Oh, devil take considering—I beg your pardon!

MANDERS *(with a sigh)*   And I'm sorry to say I don't know how long I shall be able to retain control of these things—whether public opinion may not compel me to retire. It entirely depends upon the result of the official inquiry into the fire—

MRS. ALVING   What are you talking about?

MANDERS   And the result can by no means be foretold.

ENGSTRAND *(comes close to him)*   Ay, but it can though. For here stands Jacob Engstrand.

MANDERS   Well, well, but—?

ENGSTRAND *(more softly)*   And Jacob Engstrand isn't the man to desert a noble benefactor in the hour of need, as the saying is.

MANDERS   Yes, but my good fellow—how—?

ENGSTRAND   Jacob Engstrand may be likened to a guardian angel, he may, your Reverence.

MANDERS   No, no; I can't accept that.

ENGSTRAND   Oh! you will though, all the same. I know a man that's taken others' sins upon himself before now, I do.

MANDERS   Jacob! *(Wrings his hand)* You are a rare character. Well, you shall be helped with your Sailors' Home. That you may rely upon. (ENGSTRAND *tries to thank him, but cannot for emotion.* MR. MANDERS *hangs his travelling-bag over his shoulder.*) And now let's be off. We two go together.

ENGSTRAND *(at the dining-room door, softly to REGINA)*   You come along too, girl. You shall live as snug as the yolk in an egg.

REGINA *(tosses her head)*   Merci!

(She goes out into the hall and fetches MANDERS's overcoat.)

MANDERS   Good-bye, Mrs. Alving! and may the spirit of Law and Order descend upon this house, and that quickly.

MRS. ALVING   Good-bye, Manders.

She goes up towards the conservatory, as she sees OSWALD *coming in through the garden door.*

ENGSTRAND *(while he and* REGINA *help* MANDERS *to get his coat on)*   Good-bye, my child. And if any trouble should come to you, you know where Jacob Engstrand is to be found. *(Softly)* Little Harbour Street, hm—! *(To* MRS. ALVING *and* OSWALD*)* And the refuge for wandering mariners shall be called "Captain Alving's Home," that it shall! And if I'm spared to carry on that house in my own way, I venture to promise that it shall be worthy of his memory.

MANDERS *(in the doorway)*   Hm-hm!—Now come, my dear Engstrand. Good-bye! Good-bye!

(He and ENGSTRAND *go out through the hall.)*

OSWALD *(goes towards the table)*   What house was he talking about?

MRS. ALVING   Oh, a kind of Home that he and Manders want to set up.

OSWALD   It will burn down like the other.

MRS. ALVING   What makes you think so?

OSWALD   Everything will burn. All that recalls father's memory is doomed. Here am I, too, burning down.

*(*REGINA *starts and looks at him.)*

MRS. ALVING   Oswald! you oughtn't to have remained so long down there, my poor boy!

OSWALD *(sits down by the table)*   I almost think you're right.

MRS. ALVING   Let me dry your face, Oswald; you're quite wet.

(She dries his face with her pocket-handkerchief.)

OSWALD *(stares indifferently in front of him)*   Thanks, mother.

MRS. ALVING   Aren't you tired, Oswald? Would you like to sleep?

OSWALD *(nervously)*   No, no—I can't sleep. I never sleep. I only pretend to. *(Sadly)* That will come soon enough.

MRS. ALVING *(looking sorrowfully at him)*   Yes, you really are ill, my blessed boy.

REGINA *(eagerly)*   Is Mr. Alving ill?

OSWALD *(impatiently)*   Oh, do shut all the doors! This killing dread—

MRS. ALVING   Shut the doors, Regina.

REGINA *shuts them and remains standing by the hall door.* MRS. ALVING *takes her shawl off.* REGINA *does the same.* MRS. ALVING *draws a chair across to* OSWALD'S, *and sits by him.*

MRS. ALVING   There now! I'm going to sit beside you—

OSWALD   Ah! do. And Regina shall stay here, too. Regina shall be with me always. You'll come to the rescue, Regina, won't you?

REGINA   I don't understand—

MRS. ALVING   To the rescue?

OSWALD   Yes—in the hour of need.

MRS. ALVING   Oswald, have you not your mother to come to the rescue?

OSWALD   You? *(Smiles)* No, mother; *that* rescue you will never bring me. *(Laughs sadly)* You! ha ha! *(Looks earnestly at her)* Though, after all, it lies nearest to you. *(Impetuously)* Why don't you say "thou"[1] to me, Regina? Why don't you call me "Oswald"?

REGINA *(softly)*   I don't think Mrs. Alving would like it.

[1] "Sige du" = Fr. *tutoyer*

MRS. ALVING   You shall soon have leave to do it. And sit over here beside us, won't you?

(REGINA *sits down quietly and hesitatingly at the other side of the table.*)

MRS. ALVING   And now, my poor suffering boy, I'm going to take the burden off your mind—

OSWALD   You, mother?

MRS. ALVING   —all the gnawing remorse and self-reproach you speak of.

OSWALD   And you think you can do that?

MRS. ALVING   Yes, now I can, Oswald. You spoke of the joy of life; and at that word a new light burst for me over my life and all it has contained.

OSWALD *(shakes his head)*   I don't understand you.

MRS. ALVING   You ought to have known your father when he was a young lieutenant. He was brimming over with the joy of life!

OSWALD   Yes, I know he was.

MRS. ALVING   It was like a breezy day only to look at him. And what exuberant strength and vitality there was in him!

OSWALD   Well—?

MRS. ALVING   Well then, child of joy as he was—for he *was* like a child at that time— he had to live here at home in a half-grown town, which had no joys to offer him—only dissipations. He had no object in life—only an official position. He had no work into which he could throw himself heart and soul; he had only business. He had not a single comrade that knew what the joy of life meant—only loungers and boon-companions—

OSWALD   Mother!

MRS. ALVING   So the inevitable happened.

OSWALD   The inevitable?

MRS. ALVING   You said yourself, this evening, what would happen to you if you stayed at home.

OSWALD   Do you mean to say that father—?

MRS. ALVING   Your poor father found no outlet for the overpowering joy of life that was in him. And I brought no brightness into his home.

OSWALD   Not even you?

MRS. ALVING   They had taught me a lot about duties and so on, which I had taken to be true. Everything was marked out into duties—into my duties, and his duties, and—I'm afraid I made home intolerable for your poor father, Oswald.

OSWALD   Why did you never write me anything about all this?

MRS. ALVING   I have never before seen it in such a light that I could speak of it to you, his son.

OSWALD   In what light did you see it then?

MRS. ALVING *(slowly)*   I saw only this one thing, that your father was a broken-down man before you were born.

OSWALD *(softly)*   Ah!

(*He rises and walks away to the window.*)

MRS. ALVING   And then, day after day, I dwelt on the one thought that by rights Regina should be at home in this house—just like my own boy.

OSWALD *(turning round quickly)*   Regina!

REGINA *(springs up and asks, with bated breath)*   I?

MRS. ALVING   Yes, now you know it, both of you.

OSWALD   Regina!

REGINA *(to herself)*   So mother was that kind of woman, after all.

MRS. ALVING   Your mother had many good qualities, Regina.

REGINA   Yes, but she was one of that sort, all the same. Oh! I've often suspected it; but—And now, if you please, ma'am, may I be allowed to go away at once?

MRS. ALVING   Do you really wish it, Regina?

REGINA   Yes, indeed I do.

MRS. ALVING   Of course you can do as you like; but—

OSWALD *(goes toward* REGINA*)*   Go away now? Isn't this your home?

REGINA   *Merci,* Mr. Alving!—or now, I suppose, I may say Oswald. But I can tell you this wasn't what I expected.

MRS. ALVING   Regina, I have not been frank with you—

REGINA   No, that you haven't, indeed. If I'd known that Oswald was ill, why—And now, too, that it can never come to anything serious between us—I really can't stop out here in the country and wear myself out nursing sick people.

OSWALD   Not even one who is so near to you?

REGINA   No, that I can't. A poor girl must make the best of her young days, or she'll be left out in the cold before she knows where she is. And I, too, have the joy of life in me, Mrs. Alving.

MRS. ALVING   Yes, I see you have. But don't throw yourself away, Regina.

REGINA   Oh! what must be, must be. If Oswald takes after his father, I take after my mother, I daresay. May I ask, ma'am, if Mr. Manders knows all this about me?

MRS. ALVING   Mr. Manders knows all about it.

REGINA *(puts on her shawl hastily)*   Well then, I'd better make haste and get away by this steamer. Pastor Manders is so nice to deal with; and I certainly think I've as much right to a little of that money as he has—that brute of a carpenter.

MRS. ALVING   You're heartily welcome to it, Regina.

REGINA *(looks hard at her)*   I think you might have brought me up as a gentleman's daughter, ma'am; it would have suited me better. *(Tosses her head)* But it's done now—it doesn't matter! *(With a bitter side glance at the corked bottle)* All the same, I may come to drink champagne with gentlefolks yet.

MRS. ALVING   And if you ever need a home, Regina, come to me.

REGINA   No, thank you, ma'am. Mr. Manders will look after me, I know. And if the worst comes to the worst, I know of one house where I've every right to a place.

MRS. ALVING   Where is that?

REGINA   "Captain Alving's Home."

MRS. ALVING   Regina—now I see it—you're going to your ruin.

REGINA   Oh, stuff! Good-bye.

(She nods and goes out through the hall.)

OSWALD *(stands at the window and looks out)*   Is she gone?

MRS. ALVING   Yes.

OSWALD *(murmuring aside to himself)*   I think it's a great mistake, all this.

MRS. ALVING *(goes behind him and lays her hands on his shoulders)*   Oswald, my dear boy; has it shaken you very much?

OSWALD *(turns his face towards her)*   All that about father, do you mean?

MRS. ALVING   Yes, about your unhappy father. I'm so afraid it may have been too much for you.

OSWALD   Why should you fancy that? Of course it came upon me as a great surprise; but, after all, it can't matter much to me.

MRS. ALVING *(draws her hands away)*   Can't matter! That your father was so infinitely miserable!

OSWALD   Of course I can pity him as I would anybody else; but—

MRS. ALVING   Nothing more? Your own father!

OSWALD *(impatiently)*   Oh, there! "father," "father"! I never knew anything of father. I don't remember anything about him except that he once made me sick.

MRS. ALVING   That's a terrible way to speak! Should a son not love his father, all the same?

OSWALD   When a son has nothing to thank his father for? has never known him? Do you really cling to that old superstition?—you who are so enlightened in other ways?

MRS. ALVING   Is it only a superstition—?

OSWALD   Yes; can't you see it, mother? It's one of those notions that are current in the world, and so—

MRS. ALVING *(deeply moved)*   Ghosts!

OSWALD *(crossing the room)*   Yes; you may well call them Ghosts.

MRS. ALVING *(wildly)*   Oswald!—then you don't love me, either!

OSWALD   You I know, at any rate.

MRS. ALVING   Yes, you know me; but is that all?

OSWALD   And of course I know how fond you are of me, and I can't but be grateful to you. And you can be so very useful to me, now that I'm ill.

MRS. ALVING   Yes, can't I, Oswald? Oh! I could almost bless the illness that has driven you home to me. For I can see very plainly you are not mine; I have to win you.

OSWALD *(impatiently)*   Yes, yes, yes; all these are just so many phrases. You must recollect I'm a sick man, mother. I can't be much taken up with other people; I have enough to do thinking about myself.

MRS. ALVING *(in a low voice)*   I shall be patient and easily satisfied.

OSWALD   And cheerful too, mother.

MRS. ALVING   Yes, my dear boy, you're quite right. *(Goes towards him)* Have I relieved you of all remorse and self-reproach now?

OSWALD   Yes, you have. But who's to relieve me of the dread?

MRS. ALVING   The dread?

OSWALD *(walks across the room)*   Regina could have been got to do it.

MRS. ALVING   I don't understand you. What is all this about dread—and Regina?

OSWALD   Is it very late, mother?

MRS. ALVING   It's early morning. *(She looks out through the conservatory.)* The day is dawning over the hills; and the weather is fine, Oswald. In a little while you shall see the sun.

OSWALD   I'm glad of that. Oh! I may still have much to rejoice in and live for—

MRS. ALVING   Yes, much—much, indeed!

OSWALD   Even if I can't work—

MRS. ALVING   Oh! you'll soon be able to work again, my dear boy, now that you haven't got all those gnawing and depressing thoughts to brood over any longer.

OSWALD   Yes, I'm glad you were able to rid me of all those fancies; and when I've got one thing more arranged—*(Sits on the sofa)* Now we'll have a little talk, mother.

MRS. ALVING   Yes, let us.

(She pushes an arm-chair towards the sofa, and sits down close to him.)

OSWALD   And meantime the sun will be rising. And then you'll know all. And then I shan't have that dread any longer.

MRS. ALVING   What am I to know?

OSWALD *(not listening to her)*   Mother, didn't you say, a little while ago, that there was nothing in the world you wouldn't do for me, if I asked you?

MRS. ALVING   Yes, to be sure I said it.

OSWALD And you'll stick to it, mother?

MRS. ALVING You may rely on that, my dear and only boy! I have nothing in the world to live for but you alone.

OSWALD All right, then; now you shall hear. Mother, you have a strong, steadfast mind, I know. Now you're to sit quite still when you hear it.

MRS. ALVING What dreadful thing can it be—?

OSWALD You're not to scream out. Do you hear? Do you promise me that? We'll sit and talk about it quite quietly. Promise me, mother?

MRS. ALVING Yes, yes; I promise. Only speak.

OSWALD Well, you must know that all this fatigue, and my inability to think of work—all that is not the illness itself—

MRS. ALVING Then what is the illness itself?

OSWALD The disease I have as my birthright *(He points to his forehead and adds very softly)*—is seated here.

MRS. ALVING *(almost voiceless)* Oswald! No, no!

OSWALD Don't scream. I can't bear it. Yes, it's seated here—waiting. And it may break out any day—at any moment.

MRS. ALVING Oh! what horror!

OSWALD Now, do be quiet. That's how it stands with me—

MRS. ALVING *(jumps up)* It's not true, Oswald. It's impossible. It can't be so.

OSWALD I have had one attack down there already. It was soon over. But when I got to know what had been the matter with me, then the dread came upon me raging and tearing; and so I set off home to you as fast as I could.

MRS. ALVING Then this is the dread—?

OSWALD Yes, for it's so indescribably loathsome, you know. Oh! if it had only been an ordinary mortal disease—! For I'm not so afraid of death—though I should like to live as long as I can.

MRS. ALVING Yes, yes, Oswald, you must!

OSWALD But this is so unutterably loathsome! To become a little baby again. To have to be fed! To have to—Oh, it's not to be spoken of!

MRS. ALVING The child has his mother to nurse him.

OSWALD *(jumps up)* No, never; that's just what I won't have. I can't endure to think that perhaps I should lie in that state for many years—get old and grey. And in the meantime you might die and leave me. *(Sits in* MRS. ALVING'S *chair)* For the doctor said it wouldn't necessarily prove fatal at once. He called it a sort of softening of the brain—or something of the kind. *(Smiles sadly)* I think that expression sounds so nice. It always sets me thinking of cherry-coloured velvet—something soft and delicate to stroke.

MRS. ALVING *(screams)* Oswald!

OSWALD *(springs up and paces the room)* And now you have taken Regina from me. If I'd only had her! She would come to the rescue, I know.

MRS. ALVING *(goes to him)* What do you mean by that, my darling boy? Is there any help in the world that I wouldn't give you?

OSWALD When I got over my attack in Paris, the doctor told me that when it came again—and it will come again—there would be no more hope.

MRS. ALVING He was heartless enough to—

OSWALD I demanded it of him. I told him I had preparations to make. *(He smiles cunningly.)* And so I had. *(He takes a little box from his inner breast pocket and opens it.)* Mother, do you see this?

MRS. ALVING What is that?

OSWALD Morphia.

MRS. ALVING *(looks horrified at him)*   Oswald—my boy!

OSWALD   I've scraped together twelve pilules—

MRS. ALVING *(snatches at it)*   Give me the box, Oswald.

OSWALD   Not yet, mother.

(He hides the box again in his pocket.)

MRS. ALVING   I shall never survive this!

OSWALD   It must be survived. Now if I'd had Regina here, I should have told her how things stood with me, and begged her to come to the rescue at the last. She would have done it. I'm certain she would.

MRS. ALVING   Never!

OSWALD   When the horror had come upon me, and she saw me lying there helpless, like a little new-born baby, impotent, lost, hopeless, past all saving—

MRS. ALVING   Never in all the world would Regina have done this.

OSWALD   Regina would have done it. Regina was so splendidly light-hearted. And she would soon have wearied of nursing an invalid like me—

MRS. ALVING   Then heaven be praised that Regina is not here.

OSWALD   Well then, it's you that must come to the rescue, mother.

MRS. ALVING *(screams aloud)*   I!

OSWALD   Who is nearer to it than you?

MRS. ALVING   I! your mother!

OSWALD   For that very reason.

MRS. ALVING   I, who gave you life!

OSWALD   I never asked you for life. And what sort of a life have you given me? I won't have it. You shall take it back again.

MRS. ALVING   Help! Help!

(She runs out into the hall.)

OSWALD *(going after her)*   Don't leave me. Where are you going?

MRS. ALVING *(in the hall)*   To fetch the doctor, Oswald. Let me go.

OSWALD *(also outside)*   You shall not go. And no one shall come in. *(The locking of a door is heard.)*

MRS. ALVING *(comes in again)*   Oswald—Oswald!—my child!

OSWALD *(follows her)*   Have you a mother's heart for me, and yet can see me suffer from this unutterable dread?

MRS. ALVING *(after a moment's silence, commands herself, and says)*   Here's my hand upon it.

OSWALD   Will you—?

MRS. ALVING   If it's ever necessary. But it will never be necessary. No, no; it's impossible.

OSWALD   Well, let us hope so, and let us live together as long as we can. Thank you, mother.

He seats himself in the arm-chair which MRS. ALVING *has moved to the sofa. Day is breaking. The lamp is still burning on the table.*

MRS. ALVING *(drawing near cautiously)*   Do you feel calm now?

OSWALD   Yes.

MRS. ALVING *(bending over him)*   It has been a dreadful fancy of yours, Oswald— nothing but a fancy. All this excitement has been too much for you. But now you shall have a long rest; at home with your mother, my own blessed boy. Everything you point to you shall have, just as when you were a little child. There now. That crisis is over now. You see how easily it passed. Oh! I was sure it would—And do you see, Oswald, what a lovely day we're going to have? Brilliant sunshine! Now you'll really be able to see your home.

She goes to the table and puts the lamp out. Sunrise. The glacier and the snow-peaks in the background glow in the morning light.

OSWALD *(sits in the arm-chair with his back towards the landscape, without moving. Suddenly he says)*   Mother, give me the sun.

MRS. ALVING *(by the table, starts and looks at him)*   What do you say?

OSWALD *(repeats, in a dull, toneless voice)*   The sun. The sun.

MRS. ALVING *(goes to him)*   Oswald, what's the matter with you? (OSWALD *seems to shrink together in the chair; all his muscles relax; his face is expressionless, his eyes have a glassy stare.* MRS. ALVING *is quivering with terror.)* What is this? *(Shrieks)* Oswald, what's the matter with you? *(Falls on her knees beside him and shakes him)* Oswald, Oswald! look at me! Don't you know me?

OSWALD *(tonelessly as before)*   The sun. The sun.

MRS. ALVING *(springs up in despair, entwines her hands in her hair and shrieks)*   I can't bear it! *(Whispers, as though petrified)* I can't bear it! Never! *(Suddenly)* Where has he got them? *(Fumbles hastily in his breast)* Here! *(Shrinks back a few steps and screams)* No; no; no! Yes!—No; no!

She stands a few steps from him with her hands twisted in her hair, and stares at him in speechless terror.

OSWALD *(sits motionless as before and says)*   The sun. The sun.

Comments and Questions

Ibsen is regarded as the father of realistic drama. *Ghosts* qualifies as realistic on one level, but perhaps not on another. The characters are surely ordinary people who talk ordinary prose, not poetry, and who do nothing to shake the world. No Hamlet here, no Antigone. What happens no doubt became the subject of gossip in a small Norwegian community. Yet the play itself did disturb Europe vastly, did, along with Ibsen's other plays, open a new way to write drama.

Is the realism complete? All the action takes place in "a spacious garden-room." The play begins at mid-morning of one day and ends, less than twenty-four hours later, at sunrise of the next day. During that short time, everything comes to a head, a series of climaxes in the lives of *all* the characters. In observing the Greek unities of time, place, and action, Ibsen puts something of a strain on one's willing suspension of disbelief, particularly since the one new event of the play—the burning of the Orphanage—also occurs on this fateful night. "Fateful" is the word, for by adhering to the unities, the playwright called attention to a destiny not decreed by the gods but just as inexorably by genetics.

1. Realism requires that there be no heroes, no villains. Is there a villain in this play? Is there a hero?

2. A writer of rare thrift, Ibsen makes each speech count and yet manages to maintain the casualness of offhand conversation. Because of the economy and naturalness of the dialogue, it is necessary to make an especially careful summary of the plain facts before attempting to assess the meaning of the whole play. Revelations come thick and fast, all designed to set straight misinterpretations of past events and misconceptions of the sort of man Captain Alving was. Is the Captain, though long dead, a key character?

3. Is there a single thesis to this play? If so, what is it? Are there subordinate theses? What about the role of Mrs. Alving as a woman who submitted to a male's dominance and, then, too late, rebelled?

4. This is a play of reversals. Describe the reversals that occur in each of the characters. A reversal happens when two individuals radically change positions. Consider these relationships: Pastor Manders—Jacob Engstrand; Mrs. Alving—Regina; Oswald—Regina; Pastor Manders—Mrs. Alving.

5. Pastor Manders professes to be shocked by what Mrs. Alving has been reading. We are not told the specific titles of the offending books. We may, however, deduce the nature of the material. What was the subject matter? Would it bother anyone today? Note that Manders admits that he has not read the books; he has only heard about them and read what others have said about them. Does this admission invalidate the Pastor's opinions? Discuss.

6. Joseph Wood Krutch in "The Tragic Fallacy" compares *Hamlet* and *Ghosts*. (See p. 1112.) He summarizes in this fashion: "We can believe in Oswald but we cannot believe in Hamlet, and a light has gone out in the universe. Shakespeare justifies the ways of God to man, but in Ibsen there is no such happy end and with him tragedy, so called, has become merely an expression of our despair at finding that such justification is no longer possible." Discuss the implications of Krutch's comparison.

7. Aristotle contended that great tragedy produces in viewers a sense of elation, not of depression. For example, we do not despair when Hamlet dies. We are uplifted. We do despair when Oswald sinks into imbecility, for what happens to him, observes Krutch, "is trivial and meaningless." Is the conclusion of the play ultimately meaningless? How could one argue against Krutch's view of the play?

August Strindberg   (1849–1912)
Miss Julie*
A Naturalistic Tragedy

(Translated by Elizabeth Sprigge)

AUTHOR'S FOREWORD

Theatre has long seemed to me—in common with much other art—a *Biblia Pauperum,* a Bible in pictures for those who cannot read what is written or printed; and I see the playwright as a lay preacher peddling the ideas of his time in popular form, popular enough for the middle-classes, mainstay of theatre audiences, to grasp the gist of the matter without troubling their brains too much. For this reason theatre has always been an elementary school for the young, the semi-educated, and for women who still have a primitive

---

* See A. Alvarez's essay "August Strindberg," p. 1143.

capacity for deceiving themselves and letting themselves be deceived—who, that is to say, are susceptible to illusion and to suggestion from the author. I have therefore thought it not unlikely that in these days, when that rudimentary and immature thought-process operating through fantasy appears to be developing into reflection, research and analysis, that theatre, like religion, might be discarded as an outworn form for whose appreciation we lack the necessary conditions. This opinion is confirmed by the major crisis still prevailing in the theatres of Europe, and still more by the fact that in those countries of culture, producing the greatest thinkers of the age, namely England and Germany, drama—like other fine arts—is dead.

Some countries, it is true, have attempted to create a new drama by using the old forms with up-to-date contents, but not only has there been insufficient time for these new ideas to be popularized, so that the audience can grasp them, but also people have been so wrought up by the taking of sides that pure, disinterested appreciation has become impossible. One's deepest impressions are upset when an applauding or a hissing majority dominates as forcefully and openly as it can in the theatre. Moreover, as no new form has been devised for these new contents, the new wine has burst the old bottles.

In this play I have not tried to do anything new, for this cannot be done, but only to modernize the form to meet the demands which may, I think, be made on this art today. To this end I chose—or surrendered myself to—a theme which claims to be outside the controversial issues of today, since questions of social climbing or falling, of higher or lower, better or worse, of man and woman, are, have been, and will be of lasting interest. When I took this theme from a true story told me some years ago, which made a deep impression, I saw it as a subject for tragedy, for as yet it is tragic to see one favored by fortune go under, and still more to see a family heritage die out, although a time may come when we have grown so developed and enlightened that we shall view with indifference life's spectacle, now seeming so brutal, cynical, and heartless. Then we shall have dispensed with those inferior, unreliable instruments of thought called feelings, which become harmful and superfluous as reasoning develops.

The fact that my heroine rouses pity is soley due to weakness; we cannot resist fear of the same fate overtaking us. The hyper-sensitive spectator may, it is true, go beyond this kind of pity, while the man with belief in the future may actually demand some suggestion for remedying the evil—in other words some kind of policy. But, to begin with, there is no such thing as absolute evil; the downfall of one family is the good fortune of another, which thereby gets a chance to rise, and, fortune being only comparative, the alternation of rising and falling is one of life's principal charms. Also, to the man of policy, who wants to remedy the painful fact that the bird of prey devours the dove, and lice the bird of prey, I should like to put the question: why should it be remedied? Life is not so mathematically idiotic as only to permit the big to eat the small; it happens just as often that the bee kills the lion or at least drives it mad.

That my tragedy depresses many people is their own fault. When we have grown strong as pioneers of the French revolution, we shall be happy and relieved to see the national parks cleared of ancient rotting trees which have stood too long in the way of others equally entitled to a period of growth—as relieved as we are when an uncurable invalid dies.

My tragedy "The Father" was recently criticized for being too sad—as if one wants cheerful tragedies! Everybody is clamoring for this supposed "joy of life," and theatre managers demand farces, as if the joy of life consisted in being ridiculous and portraying all human beings as suffering from St. Vitus's dance or total idiocy. I myself find the joy of life in its strong and cruel struggles, and my pleasure in learning, in adding to my knowledge. For this reason I have chosen for this play an unusual situation, but an instructive one—an exception, that is to say, but a great exception, one proving the rule, which will no doubt annoy all lovers of the commonplace. What will offend simple minds is that my plot is not simple, nor its point of view single. In real life an action—this, by the way, is a somewhat new discovery—is generally caused by a whole series of motives, more or less fundamental, but as a rule the spectator chooses just one of these—the one which his mind can most easily grasp or that does most credit to his intelligence. A suicide is committed. Business troubles, says the man of affairs. Unrequited love, say the women. Sickness, says the invalid. Despair, says the down-and-out. But it is possible that the motive lay in all or none of these directions, or that the dead man concealed his actual motive by revealing quite another, likely to reflect more to his glory.

I see Miss Julie's tragic fate to be the result of many circumstances: the mother's character, the father's mistaken upbringing of the girl, her own nature, and the influence of her fiancé on a weak, degenerate mind. Also, more directly, the festive mood of Midsummer Eve, her father's absence, her monthly indisposition, her preoccupation with animals, the excitement of dancing, the magic of dusk, the strongly aphrodisiac influence of flowers, and finally the chance that drives the couple into a room alone—to which must be added the urgency of the excited man.

My treatment of the theme, moreover, is neither exclusively physiological nor psychological. I have not put the blame wholly on the inheritance from her mother, nor on her physical condition at the time, nor on immorality. I have not even preached a moral sermon; in the absence of a priest I leave this to the cook.

I congratulate myself on this multiplicity of motives as being up-to-date, and if others have done the same thing before me, then I congratulate myself on not being alone in my "paradoxes," as all innovations are called.

In regard to the drawing of the characters, I have made my people somewhat "characterless" for the following reasons. In the course of time the word character has assumed manifold meanings. It must have originally signified the dominating trait of the soul-complex, and this was confused with temperament. Later it became the middle-class term for the automaton, one whose nature had become fixed or who had adapted himself to a particular rôle in life. In fact a person who had ceased to grow was called a character, while one continuing to develop—the skillful navigator of life's river, sailing not with sheets set fast, but veering before the wind to luff again—was called characterless, in a derogatory sense, of course, because he was so hard to catch, classify, and keep track of. This middle-class conception of the immobility of the soul was transferred to the stage where the middle-class has always ruled. A character came to signify a man fixed and finished: one who invariably appeared either drunk or jocular or melancholy, and characterization required nothing more than a physical defect such as a clubfoot, a wooden leg, a red nose; or the fellow might be made to repeat some such phrase as: "That's capital!" or: "Barkis is willin'!" This simple way of regarding human beings still survives in the great Molière. Harpagon is nothing but a miser, although Harpagon might have been not only a miser, but also a first-rate financier, an excellent father, and a good citizen. Worse still, his "failing" is a distinct advantage to his son-in-law and his daughter, who are his heirs, and who therefore cannot criticize him, even if they have to wait a while to get to bed. I do not believe, therefore, in simple stage characters; and the summary judgments of authors—this man is stupid, that one brutal, this jealous, that stingy, and so forth—should be challenged by the Naturalists who know the richness of the soul-complex and realize that vice has a reverse side very much like virtue.

Because they are modern characters, living in a period of transition more feverishly hysterical than its predecessor at least, I have drawn my figures vacillating, disintegrated, a blend of old and new. Nor does it seem to me unlikely that, through newspapers and conversations, modern ideas may have filtered down to the level of the domestic servant.

My souls (characters) are conglomerations of past and present stages of civilization, bits from books and newspapers, scraps of humanity, rags and tatters of fine clothing, patched together as is the human soul. And I have added a little evolutionary history by making the weaker steal and repeat the words of the stronger, and by making the characters borrow ideas or "suggestions" from one another.

Miss Julie is a modern character, not that the half-woman, the man-hater, has not existed always, but because now that she has been discovered she has stepped to the front and begun to make a noise. The half-woman is a type who thrusts herself forward, selling herself nowadays for power, decorations, distinctions, diplomas, as formerly for money. The type implies degeneration; it is not a good type and it does not endure; but it can unfortunately transmit its misery, and degenerate men seem instinctively to choose their mates from among such women, and so they breed, producing offspring of indeterminate sex to whom life is torture. But fortunately they perish, either because they cannot come to terms with reality, or because their repressed instincts break out uncontrollably, or again because their hopes of catching up with men are shattered. The type is tragic, revealing a desperate fight against nature, tragic too in its Romantic inheritance now dissipated by Naturalism, which wants nothing but happiness—and for happiness strong and sound species are required.

But Miss Julie is also a relic of the old warrior nobility now giving way to the new nobility of nerve and brain. She is a victim of the discord which a mother's "crime" has produced in a family, a victim too of the day's complaisance, of circumstances, of her own defective constitution, all of which are equivalent to the Fate or Universal Law of former days. The Naturalist has abolished guilt with God, but the consequences of the action—punishment, imprisonment or the fear of it—he cannot abolish, for the simple reason that they remain whether he is acquitted or not. An injured fellow-being is not so complacent as outsiders, who have not been injured, can afford to be. Even if the father had felt impelled to take no vengeance, the daughter would have taken vengeance on herself, as she does here, from that innate or acquired sense of honor which the upper-classes inherit—whether from Barbarism or Aryan forebears, or from the chivalry of the Middle Ages, who knows? It is a very beautiful thing, but it has become a danger nowadays to the preservation of the race. It is the nobleman's *hara-kiri,* the Japanese law of inner conscience which compels him to cut his own stomach open at the insult of another, and which survives in modified form in the duel, a privilege of the nobility. And so the valet Jean lives on, but Miss Julie cannot live without honor. This is the thrall's advantage over the nobleman, that he lacks this fatal preoccupation with honor. And in all of us Aryans there is something of the nobleman, or the Don Quixote, which makes us sympathize with the man who commits suicide because he has done something ignoble and lost his honor. And we are noblemen enough to suffer at the sight of fallen greatness littering the earth like a corpse—yes, even if the fallen rise again and make restitution by honorable deeds. Jean, the valet, is a race-builder, a man of marked characteristics. He was a laborer's son who has educated himself towards becoming a gentleman. He has learnt easily, through his well-developed senses (smell, taste, vision)—and he also has a sense of beauty. He has already bettered himself, and is thick-skinned enough to have no scruples about using other people's services. He is already foreign to his associates, despising them as part of the life he has turned his back on, yet also fearing and fleeing from them because they know his secrets, pry into his plans, watch his rise with envy, and look forward with pleasure to his fall. Hence his dual, indeterminate character, vacillating between love of the heights and hatred of those who have already achieved them. He is, he says himself, an aristocrat; he has learned the secrets of good society. He is polished, but vulgar within; he already wears his tails with taste, but there is no guarantee of his personal cleanliness.

He has some respect for his young lady, but he is frightened of Kristin, who knows his dangerous secrets, and he is sufficiently callous not to allow the night's events to wreck his plans for the future. Having both the slave's brutality and the master's lack of squeamishness, he can see blood without fainting and take disaster by the horns. Consequently he emerges from the battle unscathed, and probably ends his days as a hotelkeeper. And even if *he* does not become a Rumanian Count, his son will doubtless go to the university and perhaps become a county attorney.

The light which Jean sheds on a lower-class conception of life, life seen from below, is on the whole illuminating—when he speaks the truth, which is not often, for he says what is favorable to himself rather than what is true. When Miss Julie suggests that the lower-classes must be oppressed by the attitude of their superiors, Jean naturally agrees, as his object is to gain her sympathy; but when he perceives the advantage of separating himself from the common herd, he at once takes back his words.

It is not because Jean is now rising that he has the upper hand of Miss Julie, but because he is a man. Sexually he is the aristocrat because of his virility, his keener senses, and his capacity for taking the initiative. His inferiority is mainly due to the social environment in which he lives, and he can probably shed it with his valet's livery.

The slave mentality expresses itself in his worship of the Count (the boots), and his religious superstition; but he worships the Count chiefly because he holds that higher position for which Jean himself is striving. And this worship remains even when he has won the daugher of the house and seen how empty is that lovely shell.

I do not believe that a love relationship in the "higher" sense could exist between two individuals of such different quality, but I have made Miss Julie imagine that she is in love, so as to lessen her sense of guilt, and I let Jean suppose that if his social position were altered he would truly love her. I think love is like the hyacinth which has to strike roots in darkness *before* it can produce a vigorous flower. In this case it shoots up quickly, blossoms and goes to seed all at the same time, which is why the plant dies so soon.

As for Kristin, she is a female slave, full of servility and sluggishness acquired in front of the kitchen fire, and stuffed full of morality and religion, which are her cloak and scapegoat. She goes to church as a quick and easy way of unloading her household thefts on to Jesus and taking on a fresh cargo of guiltlessness. For the rest she is a minor character, and I have therefore sketched her in the same manner as the Pastor and the Doctor in "The Father," where I wanted ordinary human beings, as are most country pastors and provincial doctors. If these minor characters seem abstract to some people this is due to the fact that ordinary people are to a certain extent abstract in pursuit of their work; that is to say, they are without individuality, showing, while working, only one side of themselves. And as long as the spectator does not feel a need to see them from other sides, there is nothing wrong with my abstract presentation.

In regard to the dialogue, I have departed somewhat from tradition by not making my characters catechists who ask stupid questions in order to elicit a smart reply. I have avoided the symmetrical, mathematical construction of French dialogue, and let people's minds work irregularly, as they do in real life where, during a conversation, no topic is drained to the dregs, and one mind finds in another a chance cog to engage in. So too the dialogue wanders, gathering in the opening scenes material which is later picked up, worked over, repeated, expounded and developed like the theme in a musical composition.

The plot speaks for itself, and as it really only concerns two people, I have concentrated on these, introducing only one minor character, the cook, and keeping the unhappy spirit of the father above and behind the action. I have done this because it seems to me that the psychological process is what interests people most today. Our inquisitive souls are no longer satisfied with seeing a thing happen; we must also know how it happens. We want to see the wires themselves, to watch the machinery, to examine the box with the false bottom, to take hold of the magic ring in order to find the join, and look at the cards to see how they are marked.

In this connection I have had in view the documentary novels of the Goncourt brothers, which appeal to me more than any other modern literature.

As far as the technical side of the work is concerned I have made the experiment of abolishing the division into acts. This is because I have come to the conclusion that our capacity for illusion is disturbed by the intervals, during which the audience has time to reflect and escape from the suggestive influence of the author-hypnotist. My play will probably take an hour and a half, and as one can listen to a lecture, a sermon, or a parliamentary debate for as long as that or longer, I do not think a theatrical performance will be fatiguing in the same length of time. As early as 1872, in one of my first dramatic attempts, "The Outlaw," I tried this concentrated form, although with scant success. The play was written in five acts, and only when finished did I become aware of the restless, disjointed effect that it produced. The script was burnt and from the ashes rose a single well-knit act—fifty pages of print, playable in one hour. The form of the present play is, therefore, not new, but it appears to be my own, and changing tastes may make it timely. My hope is one day to have an audience educated enough to sit through a whole evening's entertainment in one act, but one would have to try this out to see. Meanwhile, in order to provide respite for the audience and the players, without allowing the audience to escape from the illusion, I have introduced three art forms: monologue, mime, and ballet. These are all part of drama, having their origins in classic tragedy, monody having become monologue and the chorus, ballet.

Monologue is now condemned by our realists as unnatural, but if one provides motives for it one makes it natural, and then can use it to advantage. It is, surely, natural for a public speaker to walk up and down the room practicing his speech, natural for an actor to read his part aloud, for a servant girl to talk to her cat, a mother to prattle to her child, an old maid to chatter to her parrot, and a sleeper to talk in his sleep. And in order that the actor may have a chance, for once, of working independently, free from the author's direction, it is better that the monologue should not be written, but only indicated. For since it is of small importance what is said in one's sleep or to the parrot or to the cat—none of it influences the action—a talented actor, identifying himself with the atmosphere and the situation, may improvise better than the author, who cannot calculate ahead how much may be said or how long taken without waking the audience from the illusion.

Some Italian theatres have, as we know, returned to improvisation, thereby producing actors who are creative, although within the bounds set by the author. This may well be a step forward, or even the beginning of a new art-form worthy to be called *productive*.

In places where monologue would be unnatural I have used mime, leaving here an even wider scope for the actor's imagination, and more chance for him to win independent laurels. But so as not to try the audience beyond endurance, I have introduced music—fully justified by the Midsummer Eve dance—to exercise its powers of persuasion during the dumb show. But I beg the musical director to consider carefully his choice of compositions, so that conflicting moods are not induced by selections from the current operetta or dance show, or by folk-tunes of too local a character.

The ballet I have introduced cannot be replaced by the usual kind of "crowd-scene," for such scenes are too badly played—a lot of grinning idiots seizing the opportunity to show off and thus destroying the illusion. And as peasants cannot improvise their taunts, but use ready-made phrases with a double meaning. I have not composed their lampoon, but taken a little-known song and dance which I myself noted down in the Stockholm district. The words are not quite to the point, but this too is intentional, for the cunning, i.e. weakness, of the slave prevents him from direct attack. Nor can there be clowning in a serious action, or coarse joking in a situation which nails the lid on a family coffin.

As regards the scenery, I have borrowed from impressionist painting its asymmetry and its economy; thus, I think, strengthening the illusion. For the fact that one does not see the whole room and all the furniture leaves scope for conjecture—that is to say imagination is roused and complements what is seen. I have succeeded too in getting rid of those tiresome exits through doors, since scenery doors are made of canvas, and rock at the slightest touch. They cannot even express the wrath of an irate head of the family who, after a bad dinner, goes out slamming the door behind him, "so that the whole house shakes." On the stage it rocks. I have also kept to a single set, both in order to let the characters develop in their métier and to break away from overdecoration. When one has only one set, one may expect it to be realistic; but as a matter of fact nothing is harder than to get a stage room that looks something like a room, however easily the scene painter can produce flaming volcanoes and water-falls. Presumably the walls must be of canvas; but it seems about time to dispense with painted shelves and cooking utensils. We are asked to accept so many stage conventions that we might at least be spared the pain of painted pots and pans.

I have set the back wall and the table diagonally so that the actors may play full-face and in half-profile when they are sitting opposite one another at the table. In the opera *Aïda* I saw a diagonal background, which led the eye to unfamiliar perspectives and did not look like mere reaction against boring straight lines.

Another much needed innovation is the abolition of foot-lights. This lighting from below is said to have the purpose of making the actors' faces fatter. But why, I ask, should all actors have fat faces? Does not this under-lighting flatten out all the subtlety of the lower part of the face, specially the jaw, falsify the shape of the nose and throw shadows up over the eyes? Even if this were not so, one thing is certain: that the lights hurt the performers' eyes, so that the full play of their expression is lost. The foot-lights strike part of the retina usually protected—except in sailors who have to watch sunlight on water—and therefore one seldom sees anything other than a crude rolling of the eyes, either sideways or up towards the gallery, showing their whites. Perhaps this too causes that tiresome blinking of the eyelashes, especially by actresses. And when anyone on the stage wants to speak with his eyes, the only thing he can do is to look straight at the audience, with whom he or she then gets into direct communication, outside the framework of the set—a habit called, rightly or wrongly, "greeting one's friends."

Would not sufficiently strong side-lighting, with some kind of reflectors, add to the actor's powers of expression by allowing him to use the face's greatest asset:—the play of the eyes?

I have few illusions about getting the actors to play *to* the audience instead of *with* it, although this is what I want. That I shall see an actor's back throughout a critical scene is beyond my dreams, but I do wish crucial scenes could be played, not in front of the prompter's box, like duets expecting applause, but in the place required by the action. So, no revolutions, but just some small modifications, for to make the stage into a real room with the fourth wall missing would be too upsetting altogether.

I dare not hope that the actresses will listen to what I have to say about make-up, for they would rather be beautiful than life-like, but the actor might consider whether it is to his advantage to create an abstract character with grease-paints, and cover his face with it like a mask. Take the case of a man who draws a choleric charcoal line between his eyes and then, in this fixed state of wrath, has to smile at some repartee. What a frightful grimace the result is! And equally, how is that false forehead, smooth as a billiard ball, to wrinkle when the old man loses his temper?

In a modern psychological drama, where the subtlest reactions of a character need to be mirrored in the face rather than expressed by sound and gesture, it would be worthwhile experimenting with powerful side-lighting on a small stage and a cast without make-up, or at least with the minimum.

If, in addition, we could abolish the visible orchestra, with its distracting lamps and its faces turned toward the audience; if we could have the stalls raised so that the spectators' eyes were higher than the players' knees; if we could get rid of the boxes (the center of my target), with their tittering diners and supper-parties, and have total darkness in the auditorium during the performance; and if, first and foremost, we could have a *small* stage and a *small* house, then perhaps a new dramatic art might arise, and theatre once more become a place of entertainment for educated people. While waiting for such a theatre we may as well go on writing so as to stock that repertory of the future.

I have made an attempt! If it has failed, there is time enough to try again!

CHARACTERS

MISS JULIE, *aged 25*   KRISTIN, *the cook, aged 35*
JEAN, *the valet, aged 30*

SCENE: *The large kitchen of a Swedish manor house in a country district in the 1880's.*
Midsummmer Eve.
The kitchen has three doors, two small ones into JEAN'S *and* KRISTIN'S *bedrooms, and a large, glass-fronted double one, opening on to a courtyard. This is the only way to the rest of the house.*
Through these glass doors can be seen part of a fountain with a cupid, lilac bushes in flower and the tops of some Lombardy poplars. On one wall are shelves edged with scalloped paper on which are kitchen utensils of copper, iron and tin.
To the left is the corner of a large tiled range and part of its chimney-hood, to the right the end of the servants' dinner table with chairs beside it.
The stove is decorated with birch boughs, the floor strewn with twigs of juniper. On the end of the table is a large Japanese spice jar full of lilac.
There are also an ice-box, a scullery table and a sink.
Above the double door hangs a big old-fashioned bell; near it is a speaking-tube.
A fiddle can be heard from the dance in the barn near-by.
KRISTIN *is standing at the stove, frying something in a pan. She wears a light-colored cotton dress and a big apron.*
JEAN *enters, wearing livery and carrying a pair of large riding-boots with spurs, which he puts in a conspicuous place.*

JEAN   Miss Julie's crazy again tonight, absolutely crazy.
KRISTIN   Oh, so you're back, are you?
JEAN   When I'd taken the Count to the station, I came back and dropped in at the Barn for a dance. And who did I see there but our young lady leading off with the gamekeeper. But the moment she sets eyes on me, up she rushes and invites me to waltz with her. And how she waltzed—I've never seen anything like it! She's crazy.
KRISTIN   Always has been, but never so bad as this last fortnight since the engagement was broken off.

JEAN   Yes, that was a pretty business, to be sure. He's a decent enough chap, too, even if he isn't rich. Oh, but they're choosy! *(Sits down at the end of the table)* In any case, it's a bit odd that our young—er—lady would rather stay at home with yokels than go with her father to visit her relations.

KRISTIN   Perhaps she feels a bit awkward, after that bust-up with her fiancé.

JEAN   Maybe. That chap had some guts though. Do you know the sort of thing that was going on, Kristin? I saw it with my own eyes, though I didn't let on I had.

KRISTIN   You saw them . . .?

JEAN   Didn't I just! Came across the pair of them one evening in the stable-yard. Miss Julie was doing what she called "training" him. Know what that was? Making him jump over her riding-whip—the way you teach a dog. He did it twice and got a cut each time for his pains, but when it came to the third go, he snatched the whip out of her hand and broke it into smithereens. And then he cleared off.

KRISTIN   What goings on! I never did!

JEAN   Well, that's how it was with that little affair . . . Now, what have you got for me, Kristin? Something tasty?

KRISTIN   *(serving from the pan to his plate)*   Well, it's just a little bit of kidney I cut off their joint.

JEAN   *(smelling it)*   Fine! That's my special *délice. (feels the plate)* But you might have warmed the plate.

KRISTIN   When you choose to be finicky you're worse than the Count himself. *(Pulls his hair affectionately)*

JEAN   *(crossly)*   Stop pulling my hair. You know how sensitive I am.

KRISTIN   There, there! It's only love, you know. (JEAN *eats.* KRISTIN *brings a bottle of beer.)*

JEAN   Beer on Midsummer Eve? No thanks! I've got something better than that. *(From a drawer in the table brings out a bottle of red wine with a yellow seal)* Yellow seal, see! Now get me a glass. You use a glass with a stem of course when you're drinking it straight.

KRISTIN   *(giving him a wine-glass)*   Lord help the woman who gets you for a husband, you old fusser! *(She puts the beer in the ice-box and sets a small saucepan on the stove.)*

JEAN   Nonsense! You'll be glad enough to get a fellow as smart as me. And I don't think it's done you any harm, people calling me your fiancé. *(Tastes the wine)* Good. Very good indeed. But not quite warmed enough. *(Warms the glass in his hand)* We bought this in Dijon. Four francs the liter without the bottle, and duty on top of that. What are you cooking now? It stinks.

KRISTIN   Some bloody muck Miss Julie wants for Diana.

JEAN   You should be more refined in your speech, Kristin. But why should you spend a holiday cooking for that bitch? Is she sick or what?

KRISTIN   Yes, she's sick. She sneaked out with the pug at the lodge and got in the usual mess. And that, you know, Miss Julie won't have.

JEAN   Miss Julie's too high-and-mighty in some respects, and not enough in others, just like her mother before her. The Countess was more at home in the kitchen and cowsheds than anywhere else, but would she ever go driving with only one horse? She went round with her cuffs filthy, but she had to have the coronet on the cuff-links. Our young lady—to come back to her—hasn't any proper respect for herself or her position. I mean she isn't refined. In the Barn just now she dragged the gamekeeper away from Anna and made him dance with her—no waiting to be asked. We wouldn't do a thing like that. But that's what happens when the gentry try to behave like the common people—they become common . . . Still, she's a fine girl. Smashing! What shoulders! And what—er—etcetera!

KRISTIN   Oh come off it! I know what Clara says, and she dresses her.

JEAN   Clara? Pooh, you're all jealous! But I've been out riding with her . . . and as for her dancing!

KRISTIN   Listen, Jean. You will dance with me, won't you, as soon as I'm through.

JEAN   Of course I will.

KRISTIN   Promise?

JEAN   Promise? When I say I'll do a thing I do it. Well, thanks for the supper. It was a real treat. *(Corks the bottle.)*

(JULIE *appears in the doorway, speaking to someone outside.*)

JULIE   I'll be back in a moment. Don't wait.

(JEAN *slips the bottle into the drawer and rises respectfully.* JULIE *enters and joins* KRISTIN *at the stove.*)

Well, have you made it? (KRISTIN *signs that* JEAN *is near them.*)

JEAN *(gallantly)*   Have you ladies got some secret?

JULIE *(flipping his face with her handkerchief)*   You're very inquisitive.

JEAN   What a delicious smell! Violets.

JULIE *(coquettishly)*   Impertinence! Are you an expert of scent too? I must say you know how to dance. Now don't look. Go away. *(The music of a schottische begins.)*

JEAN *(with impudent politeness)*   Is it some witches' brew you're cooking on Midsummer Eve? Something to tell your stars by, so you can see your future?

JULIE *(sharply)*   If you could see that you'd have good eyes (*To* KRISTIN) Put it in a bottle and cork it tight. Come and dance this schottische with me, Jean.

JEAN *(hesitating)*   I don't want to be rude, but I've promised to dance this one with Kristin.

JULIE   Well, she can have another, can't you, Kristin? You'll lend me Jean, won't you?

KRISTIN *(bottling)*   It's nothing to do with me. When you're so condescending, Miss, it's not his place to say no. Go on, Jean, and thank Miss Julie for the honor.

JEAN   Frankly speaking, Miss, and no offense meant, I wonder if it's wise for you to dance twice running with the same partner, specially as those people are so ready to jump to conclusions.

JULIE *(flaring up)*   What did you say? What sort of conclusions? What do you mean?

JEAN *(meekly)*   As you choose not to understand, Miss Julie, I'll have to speak more plainly. It looks bad to show a preference for one of your retainers when they're all hoping for the same unusual favor.

JULIE   Show a preference! The very idea! I'm surprised at you. I'm doing the people an honor by attending their ball when I'm mistress of the house, but if I'm really going to dance, I mean to have a partner who can lead and doesn't make me look ridiculous.

JEAN   If those are your orders, Miss, I'm at your service.

JULIE *(gently)*   Don't take it as an order. To-night we're all just people enjoying a party. There's no question of class. So now give me your arm. Don't worry, Kristin. I shan't steal your sweetheart.

(JEAN *gives* JULIE *his arm and leads her out.*)

(Left alone, KRISTIN *plays her scene in an unhurried, natural way, humming to the tune of the schottische, played on a distant violin. She clears* JEAN'S *place, washes up and puts things away, then takes off her apron, brings out a small mirror from a drawer, props it against the jar of lilac, lights a candle, warms a small pair of tongs and curls her fringe. She goes to the door and listens, then turning back to the table finds* MISS JULIE'S *handkerchief. She smells it, then meditatively smooths it out and folds it.*)

(Enter JEAN.)

JEAN   She really *is* crazy. What a way to dance! With people standing grinning at her too from behind the doors. What's got into her, Kristin?

KRISTIN   Oh, it's just her time coming on. She's always queer then. Are you going to dance with me now?

JEAN   Then you're not wild with me for cutting that one.

KRISTIN   You know I'm not—for a little thing like that. Besides, I know my place.

JEAN   *(putting his arm round her waist)*   You're a sensible girl, Kristin, and you'll make a very good wife . . .

(Enter JULIE, *unpleasantly surprised.)*

JULIE   *(with forced gaiety)*   You're a fine beau—running away from your partner.

JEAN   Not away, Miss Julie, but as you see back to the one I deserted.

JULIE *(changing her tone)*   You really can dance, you know. But why are you wearing your livery on a holiday? Take it off at once.

JEAN   Then I must ask you to go away for a moment, Miss. My black coat's here. *(Indicates it hanging on the door to his room.)*

JULIE   Are you so shy of me—just over changing a coat? Go into your room then— or stay here and I'll turn my back.

JEAN   Excuse me then, Miss. *(He goes to his room and is partly visible as he changes his coat.)*

JULIE   Tell me, Kristin, is Jean your fiancé? You seem very intimate.

KRISTIN   My fiancé? Yes, if you like. We call it that.

JULIE   Call it?

KRISTIN   Well, you've had a fiancé yourself, Miss, and . . .

JULIE   But we really were engaged.

KRISTIN   All the same it didn't come to anything.

(JEAN *returns in his black coat.*)

JULIE   *Très gentil, Monsieur Jean. Très gentil.*[1]

JEAN   *Vous voulez plaisanter, Madame.*

JULIE   *Et vous voulez parler français.* Where did you learn it?

JEAN   In Switzerland, when I was steward at one of the biggest hotels in Lucerne.

JULIE   You look quite the gentleman in that get-up. Charming. *(Sits at the table.)*

JEAN   Oh, you're just flattering me!

JULIE *(annoyed)*   Flattering you?

JEAN   I'm too modest to believe you would pay real compliments to a man like me, so I must take it you are exaggerating—that this is what's known as flattery.

JULIE   Where on earth did you learn to make speeches like that? Perhaps you've been to the theater a lot.

JEAN   That's right. And traveled a lot too.

JULIE   But you come from this neighborhood, don't you?

JEAN   Yes, my father was a laborer on the next estate—the District Attorney's place. I often used to see you, Miss Julie, when you were little, though you never noticed me.

---

[1]   JULIE Very nice, Monsieur Jean, very nice.
JEAN You like to joke, Madame.
JULIE And you like to speak French.

JULIE   Did you really?

JEAN   Yes. One time specially I remember . . . but I can't tell you about that.

JULIE   Oh do! Why not? This is just the time.

JEAN   No, I really can't now. Another time perhaps.

JULIE   Another time means never. What harm in now?

JEAN   No harm, but I'd rather not. *(Points to* KRISTIN, *now fast asleep)* Look at her.

JULIE   She'll make a charming wife, won't she? I wonder if she snores.

JEAN   No, she doesn't, but she talks in her sleep.

JULIE *(cynically)*   How do you know she talks in her sleep?

JEAN *(brazenly)*   I've heard her. *(Pause. They look at one another.)*

JULIE   Why don't you sit down?

JEAN   I can't take such a liberty in your presence.

JULIE   Supposing I order you to.

JEAN   I'll obey.

JULIE   Then sit down. No, wait a minute. Will you get me a drink first?

JEAN   I don't know what's in the ice-box. Only beer, I expect.

JULIE   There's no only about it. My taste is so simple I prefer it to wine.

*(*JEAN *takes a bottle from the ice-box, fetches a glass and plate and serves the beer.)*

JEAN   At your service.

JULIE   Thank you. Won't you have some yourself?

JEAN   I'm not really a beer-drinker, but if it's an order . . .

JULIE   Order? I should have thought it was ordinary manners to keep your partner company.

JEAN   That's a good way of putting it. *(He opens another bottle and fetches a glass.)*

JULIE   Now drink my health. *(He hesitates.)* I believe the man really is shy.

*(*JEAN *kneels and raises his glass with mock ceremony.)*

JEAN   To the health of my lady!

JULIE   Bravo! Now kiss my shoe and everything will be perfect. *(He hesitates, then boldly takes hold of her foot and lightly kisses it.)* Splendid. You ought to have been an actor.

JEAN *(rising)*   We can't go on like this, Miss Julie. Someone might come in and see us.

JULIE   Why would that matter?

JEAN   For the simple reason that they'd talk. And if you knew the way their tongues were wagging out there just now, you . . .

JULIE   What were they saying? Tell me. Sit down.

JEAN *(sitting)*   No offense meant, Miss, but . . . well, their language wasn't nice, and they were hinting . . . oh, you know quite well what. You're not a child, and if a lady's seen drinking alone at night with a man—and a servant at that—then . . .

JULIE   Then what? Besides, we're not alone. Kristin's here.

JEAN   Yes, asleep.

JULIE   I'll wake her up. *(Rises)* Kristin, are you asleep? *(*KRISTIN *mumbles in her sleep.)* Kristin! Goodness, how she sleeps!

KRISTIN *(in her sleep)*   The Count's boots are cleaned—put the coffee on—yes, yes, at once . . . *(Mumbles incoherently.)*

JULIE *(tweaking her nose)*   Wake up, can't you!

JEAN *(sharply)*   Let her sleep.

JULIE   What?

JEAN   When you've been standing at the stove all day you're likely to be tired at night. And sleep should be respected.

JULIE *(changing her tone)*   What a nice idea. It does you credit. Thank you for it. *(Holds out her hand to him)* Now come out and pick some lilac for me. *(During the following* KRISTIN *goes sleepily in to her bedroom.)*

JEAN   Out with you, Miss Julie?

JULIE Yes.

JEAN   It wouldn't do. It really wouldn't.

JULIE I don't know what you mean. You can't possibly imagine that . . .

JEAN   I don't, but others do.

JULIE What? That I'm in love with the valet?

JEAN   I'm not a conceited man, but such a thing's been known to happen, and to these rustics nothing's sacred.

JULIE You, I take it, are an aristocrat.

JEAN   Yes, I am.

JULIE And I am coming down in the world.

JEAN   Don't come down, Miss Julie. Take my advice. No one will believe you came down of your own accord. They'll all say you fell.

JULIE I have a higher opinion of our people than you. Come and put it to the test. Come on. *(Gazes into his eyes.)*

JEAN   You're very strange, you know.

JULIE Perhaps I am, but so are you. For that matter everything is strange. Life, human beings, everything, just scum drifting about on the water until it sinks—down and down. That reminds me of a dream I sometimes have, in which I'm on top of a pillar and can't see any way of getting down. When I look down I'm dizzy; I have to get down but I haven't the courage to jump. I can't stay there and I long to fall, but I don't fall. There's no respite. There can't be any peace at all for me until I'm down, right down on the ground. And if I did get to the ground I'd want to be under the ground . . . Have you ever felt like that?

JEAN   No. In my dream I'm lying under a great tree in a dark wood. I want to get up, up to the top of it, and look out over the bright landscape where the sun is shining and rob that high nest of its golden eggs. And I climb and climb, but the trunk is so thick and smooth and it's so far to the first branch. But I know if I can once reach that first branch I'll go to the top just as if I'm on a ladder. I haven't reached it yet, but I shall get there, even if only in my dreams.

JULIE Here I am chattering about dreams with you. Come on. Only into the park. *(She takes his arm and they go toward the door.)*

JEAN   We must sleep on nine midsummer flowers to-night; then our dreams will come true, Miss Julie. *(They turn at the door. He has a hand to his eye.)*

JULIE Have you got something in your eye? Let me see.

JEAN   Oh, it's nothing. Just a speck of dust. It'll be gone in a minute.

JULIE My sleeve must have rubbed against you. Sit down and let me see to it. *(Takes him by the arm and makes him sit down, bends his head back and tries to get the speck out with the corner of her handkerchief)* Keep still now, quite still. *(Slaps his hand)* Do as I tell you. Why, I believe you're trembling, big, strong man though you are! *(Feels his biceps)* What muscles!

JEAN   *(warning)*   Miss Julie!

JULIE Yes, Monsieur Jean?

JEAN   *Attention. Je ne suis qu'un homme.*[2]

---

[2] Careful. I'm only a man.

JULIE   Will you stay still! There now. It's out. Kiss my hand and say thank you.

JEAN *(rising)*   Miss Julie, listen. Kristin's gone to bed now. Will you listen?

JULIE   Kiss my hand first.

JEAN   Very well, but you'll have only yourself to blame.

JULIE   For what?

JEAN   For what! Are you still a child at twenty-five? Don't you know it's dangerous to play with fire?

JULIE   Not for me. I'm insured.

JEAN *(bluntly)*   No, you're not. And even if you are, there's still stuff here to kindle a flame.

JULIE   Meaning yourself?

JEAN   Yes. Not because I'm me, but because I'm a man and young and . . .

JULIE   And good-looking? What incredible conceit! A Don Juan perhaps? Or a Joseph? Good Lord, I do believe you are a Joseph!

JEAN   Do you?

JULIE   I'm rather afraid so.

(JEAN *goes boldly up and tries to put his arms round her and kiss her. She boxes his ears.*)

How dare you!

JEAN   Was that in earnest or a joke?

JULIE   In earnest.

JEAN   Then what went before was in earnest too. You take your games too seriously and that's dangerous. Anyhow I'm tired of playing now and beg leave to return to my work. The Count will want his boots first thing and it's past midnight now.

JULIE   Put those boots down.

JEAN   No. This is my work, which it's my duty to do. But I never undertook to be your play-fellow and I never will be. I consider myself too good for that.

JULIE   You're proud.

JEAN   In some ways—not all.

JULIE   Have you ever been in love?

JEAN   We don't put it that way, but I've been gone on quite a few girls. And once I went sick because I couldn't have the one I wanted. Sick, I mean, like those princes in the Arabian Nights who couldn't eat or drink for love.

JULIE   Who was she? *(No answer)* Who was she?

JEAN   You can't force me to tell you that.

JULIE   If I ask as an equal, ask as a—friend? Who was she?

JEAN   You.

JULIE *(sitting)*   How absurd!

JEAN   Yes, ludicrous if you like. That's the story I wouldn't tell you before, see, but now I will . . . Do you know what the world looks like from below? No, you don't. No more than the hawks and falcons do whose backs one hardly ever sees because they're always soaring up aloft. I lived in a laborer's hovel with seven other children and a pig, out in the gray fields where there isn't a single tree. But from the window I could see the wall round the Count's park with apple-trees above it. That was the Garden of Eden, guarded by many terrible angels with flaming swords. All the same I and the other boys managed to get to the tree of life. Does all this make you despise me?

JULIE   Goodness, all boys steal apples!

JEAN   You say that now, but all the same you do despise me. However, one time I went into the Garden of Eden with my mother to weed the onion beds. Close to the kitchen garden there was a Turkish pavilion hung all over with jasmine and honeysuckle. I hadn't any idea what it was used for, but I'd never seen such a beautiful building. People used to go in and then come out again, and one day the door was left open. I crept up and saw the walls covered with pictures of kings and emperors, and the windows had red curtains with fringes—you know now what the place was, don't you? I . . . *(Breaks off a piece of lilac and holds it for* JULIE *to smell. As he talks, she takes it from him.)* I had never been inside the manor, never seen anything but the church, and this was more beautiful. No matter where my thoughts went, they always came back—to that place. The longing went on growing in me to enjoy it fully, just once. *Enfin,*[3] I sneaked in, gazed and admired. Then I heard someone coming. There was only one way out for the gentry, but for me there was another and I had no choice but to take it. (JULIE *drops the lilac on the table.)* Then I took to my heels, plunged through the raspberry canes, dashed across the strawberry beds and found myself on the rose terrace. There I saw a pink dress and a pair of white stockings—it was you. I crawled into a weed pile and lay there right under it among prickly thistles and damp rank earth. I watched you walking among the roses and said to myself: "If it's true that a thief can get to heaven and be with the angels, it's pretty strange that a laborer's child here on God's earth mayn't come in the park and play with the Count's daughter."

JULIE *(sentimentally)*   Do you think all poor children feel the way you did?

JEAN *(taken aback, then rallying)*   *All* poor children? . . . Yes, of course they do. Of course.

JULIE   It must be terrible to be poor.

JEAN *(with exaggerated distress)*   Oh yes, Miss Julie, yes. A dog may lie on the Countess's sofa, a horse may have his nose stroked by a young lady, but a servant . . . *(Change of tone)* well, yes, now and then you meet one with guts enough to rise in the world, but how often? Anyhow, do you know what I did? Jumped in the millstream with my clothes on, was pulled out and got a hiding. But the next Sunday, when Father and all the rest went to Granny's, I managed to get left behind. Then I washed with soap and hot water, put my best clothes on and went to church so as to see you. I did see you and went home determined to die. But I wanted to die beautifully and peacefully, without any pain. Then I remembered it was dangerous to sleep under an elder bush. We had a big one in full bloom, so I stripped it and climbed into the oats-bin with the flowers. Have you ever noticed how smooth oats are? Soft to touch as human skin . . . Well, I closed the lid and shut my eyes, fell asleep, and when they woke me I was very ill. But I didn't die, as you see. What I meant by all that I don't know. There was no hope of winning you—you were simply a symbol of the hopelessness of ever getting out of the class I was born in.

JULIE   You put things very well, you know. Did you go to school?

JEAN   For a while. But I've read a lot of novels and been to the theater. Besides, I've heard educated folk talking—that's what's taught me most.

JULIE   Do you stand round listening to what we're saying?

JEAN   Yes, of course. And I've heard quite a bit too! On the carriage box or rowing the boat. Once I heard you, Miss Julie, and one of your young lady friends . . .

JULIE   Oh! Whatever did you hear?

JEAN   Well, it wouldn't be nice to repeat it. And I must say I was pretty startled. I couldn't think where you had learnt such words. Perhaps, at bottom, there isn't as much difference between people as one's led to believe.

JULIE   How dare you! We don't behave as you do when we're engaged.

JEAN *(looking hard at her)*   Are you sure? It's no use making out so innocent to me.

JULIE   The man I gave my love to was a scoundrel.

JEAN   That's what you always say—afterward.

---

[3] Well

JULIE   Always?

JEAN   I think it must be always. I've heard the expression several times in similar circumstances.

JULIE   What circumstances?

JEAN   Like those in question. The last time . . .

JULIE *(rising)*   Stop. I don't want to hear any more.

JEAN   Nor did *she*—curiously enough. May I go to bed now please?

JULIE *(gently)*   Go to bed on Midsummer Eve?

JEAN   Yes. Dancing with that crowd doesn't really amuse me.

JULIE   Get the key of the boathouse and row me out on the lake. I want to see the sun rise.

JEAN   Would that be wise?

JULIE   You sound as though you're frightened for your reputation.

JEAN   Why not? I don't want to be made a fool of, nor to be sent packing without references when I'm trying to better myself. Besides, I have Kristin to consider.

JULIE   So now it's Kristin.

JEAN   Yes, but it's you I'm thinking about too. Take my advice and go to bed.

JULIE   Am I to take orders from you?

JEAN   Just this once for your own sake. Please. It's very late and sleepiness goes to one's head and makes one rash. Go to bed. What's more, if my ears don't deceive me, I hear people coming this way. They'll be looking for me, and if they find us here, you're done for.

(*The* CHORUS *approaches, singing. During the following dialogue the song is heard in snatches, and in full when the peasants enter.*)

Out of the wood two women came,
Tridiri-ralla, tridiri-ra.
The feet of one were bare and cold,
Tridiri-ralla-la.

The other talked of bags of gold,
Tridiri-ralla, tridiri-ra.
But neither had a sou to her name,
Tridiri-ralla-la.

The bridal wreath I give to you,
Tridiri-ralla, tridiri-ra.
But to another I'll be true,
Tridiri-ralla-la.

JULIE   I know our people and I love them, just as they do me. Let them come. You'll see.

JEAN   No, Miss Julie, they don't love you. They take your food, then spit at it. You must believe me. Listen to them, just listen to what they're singing . . . No, don't listen.

JULIE *(listening)*   What are they singing?

JEAN   They're mocking—you and me.

JULIE   Oh no! How horrible! What cowards!

JEAN   A pack like that's always cowardly. But against such odds there's nothing we can do but run away.

JULIE   Run away? Where to? We can't get out and we can't go into Kristin's room.

JEAN   Into mine then. Necessity knows no rules. And you can trust me. I really am your true and devoted friend.

August Strindberg

JULIE   But supposing . . . supposing they were to look for you in there?

JEAN   I'll bolt the door, and if they try to break in I'll shoot. Come on. *(Pleading)* Please come.

JULIE *(tensely)*   Do you promise . . .?

JEAN   I swear!

(JULIE *goes quickly into his room and he excitedly follows her.*)

Led by the fiddler, the peasants enter in festive attire with flowers in their hats. They put a barrel of beer and a keg of spirits, garlanded with leaves, on the table, fetch glasses and begin to carouse. The scene becomes a ballet. They form a ring and dance and sing and mime; "Out of the wood two women came." Finally they go out, still singing. JULIE *comes in alone. She looks at the havoc in the kitchen, wrings her hands, then takes out her powder puff and powders her face.*

(JEAN *enters in high spirits.*)

JEAN   Now you see! And you heard, didn't you? Do you think it's possible for us to stay here?

JULIE   No, I don't. But what can we do?

JEAN   Run away. Far away. Take a journey.

JULIE   Journey? But where to?

JEAN   Switzerland. The Italian lakes. Ever been there?

JULIE   No. Is it nice?

JEAN   Ah! Eternal summer, oranges, evergreens . . . ah!

JULIE   But what would we do there?

JEAN   I'll start a hotel. First-class accommodation and first-class customers.

JULIE   Hotel?

JEAN   There's life for you. New faces all the time, new languages—no time for nerves or worries, no need to look for something to do—work rolling up of its own accord. Bells ringing night and day, trains whistling, buses coming and going, and all the time gold pieces rolling on to the counter. There's life for you!

JULIE   For *you*. And I?

JEAN   Mistress of the house, ornament of the firm. With your looks, and your style . . . oh, it's bound to be a success! Terrific! You'll sit like a queen in the office and set your slaves in motion by pressing an electric button. The guests will file past your throne and nervously lay their treasure on your table. You've no idea the way people tremble when they get their bills. I'll salt the bills and you'll sugar them with your sweetest smiles. Ah, let's get away from here! *(Produces a time-table)* At once, by the next train. We shall be at Malmö at six-thirty, Hamburg eight-forty next morning, Frankfurt-Basle the following day, and Como by the St. Gotthard Pass in—let's see—three days. Three days!

JULIE   That's all very well. But Jean, you must give me courage. Tell me you love me. Come and take me in your arms.

JEAN *(reluctantly)*   I'd like to, but I daren't. Not again in this house. I love you— that goes without saying. You can't doubt that, Miss Julie, can you?

JULIE *(shyly, very feminine)*   Miss? Call me Julie. There aren't any barriers between us now. Call me Julie.

JEAN *(uneasily)*   I can't. As long as we're in this house, there *are* barriers between us. There's the past and there's the Count. I've never been so servile to anyone as I am to him. I've only got to see his gloves on a chair to feel small. I've only to hear his bell and I shy like a horse. Even now, when I look at his boots, standing there so proud and stiff, I feel my back beginning to bend. *(Kicks the boots)* It's those old, narrow-minded notions drummed into us as children . . . but they can soon be forgotten. You've only got to get to another country, a republic, and people will bend themselves double before my porter's livery. Yes, double they'll bend themselves, but I shan't. I wasn't born to bend. I've got guts, I've got character, and once I reach that first branch, you'll watch me climb. Today I'm valet, next year I'll be proprietor, in ten years I'll have made a fortune, and then I'll go to Rumania, get myself decorated and I may, I only say *may,* mind you, end up as a Count.

JULIE *(sadly)*   That would be very nice.

JEAN   You see in Rumania one can buy a title, and then you'll be a Countess after all. My Countess.

JULIE   What do I care about all that? I'm putting those things behind me. Tell me you love me, because if you don't . . . if you don't, what am I?

JEAN   I'll tell you a thousand times over—later. But not here. No sentimentality now or everything will be lost. We must consider this thing calmly like reasonable people. *(Takes a cigar, cuts and lights it)* You sit down there and I'll sit here and we'll talk as if nothing has happened.

JULIE   My God, have you no feelings at all?

JEAN   Nobody has more. But I know how to control them.

JULIE   A short time ago you were kissing my shoe. And now . . .

JEAN *(harshly)*   Yes, that was then. Now we have something else to think about.

JULIE   Don't speak to me so brutally.

JEAN   I'm not. Just sensibly. One folly's been committed, don't let's have more. The Count will be back at any moment and we've got to settle our future before that. Now, what do you think of my plans? Do you approve?

JULIE   It seems a very good idea—but just one thing. Such a big undertaking would need a lot of capital. Have you got any?

JEAN *(chewing his cigar)*   I certainly have. I've got my professional skill, my wide experience, and my knowledge of foreign languages. That's capital worth having, it seems to me.

JULIE   But it won't buy even one railway ticket.

JEAN   Quite true. That's why I need a backer to advance some ready cash.

JULIE   How could you get that at a moment's notice?

JEAN   You must get it, if you want to be my partner.

JULIE   I can't. I haven't any money of my own. *(Pause.)*

JEAN   Then the whole thing's off.

JULIE   And . . . ?

JEAN   We go on as we are.

JULIE   Do you think I'm going to stay under this roof as your mistress? With everyone pointing at me. Do you think I can face my father after this? No. Take me away from here, away from this shame, this humiliation. Oh my God, what have I done? My God, my God! *(Weeps)*

JEAN   So that's the tune now, is it? What have you done? Same as many before you.

JULIE *(hysterically)*   And now you despise me. I'm falling, I'm falling.

JEAN   Fall as far as me and I'll lift you up again.

JULIE   Why was I so terribly attracted to you? The weak to the strong, the falling to the rising? Or was it love? Is that love? Do you know what love is?

JEAN   Do I? You bet I do. Do you think I never had a girl before?

JULIE   The things you say, the things you think!

JEAN   That's what life's taught me, and that's what I am. It's no good getting hysterical or giving yourself airs. We're both in the same boat now. Here, my dear girl, let me give you a glass of something special. *(Opens the drawer, takes out the bottle of wine and fills two used glasses.)*

JULIE   Where did you get that wine?

JEAN   From the cellar.

JULIE   My father's burgundy.

JEAN   Why not, for his son-in-law?

JULIE   And I drink beer.

JEAN   That only shows your taste's not so good as mine.

JULIE   Thief!

JEAN   Are you going to tell on me?

JULIE   Oh God! The accomplice of a petty thief! Was I blind drunk? Have I dreamt this whole night? Midsummer Eve, the night for innocent merrymaking.

JEAN   Innocent, eh?

JULIE   Is anyone on earth as wretched as I am now?

JEAN   Why should *you* be? After such a conquest. What about Kristin in there? Don't you think she has any feelings?

JULIE   I did think so, but I don't any longer. No. A menial is a menial . . .

JEAN   And a whore is a whore.

JULIE *(falling to her knees, her hands clasped)*   O God in heaven, put an end to my miserable life! Lift me out of his filth in which I'm sinking. Save me! Save me!

JEAN   I must admit I'm sorry for you. When I was in the onion bed and saw you up there among the roses, I . . . yes, I'll tell you now . . . I had the same dirty thoughts as all boys.

JULIE   You, who wanted to die because of me?

JEAN   In the oats-bin? That was just talk.

JULIE   Lies, you mean.

JEAN *(getting sleepy)*   More or less. I think I read a story in some paper about a chimney-sweep who shut himself up in a chest full of lilac because he'd been summonsed for not supporting some brat . . .

JULIE   So this is what you're like.

JEAN   I had to think up something. It's always the fancy stuff that catches the women.

JULIE   Beast!

JEAN   *Merde!*

JULIE   Now you have seen the falcon's back.

JEAN   Not exactly its *back.*

JULIE   I was to be the first branch.

JEAN   But the branch was rotten.

JULIE   I was to be a hotel sign.

JEAN   And I the hotel.

JULIE   Sit at your counter, attract your clients and cook their accounts.

JEAN   I'd have done that myself.

JULIE   That any human being can be so steeped in filth!

JEAN   Clean it up then.

JULIE   Menial! Lackey! Stand up when I speak to you.

JEAN   Menial's whore, lackey's harlot, shut your mouth and get out of here! Are you the one to lecture me for being coarse? Nobody of my kind would ever be as coarse as you were tonight. Do you think any servant girl would throw herself at a man that way? Have you ever seen a girl of my class asking for it like that? I haven't. Only animals and prostitutes.

JULIE *(broken)* Go on. Hit me, trample on me—it's all I deserve. I'm rotten. But help me! If there's any way out at all, help me.

JEAN *(more gently)* I'm not denying myself a share in the honor of seducing you, but do you think anybody in my place would have dared look in your direction if you yourself hadn't asked for it? I'm still amazed. . . .

JULIE   And proud.

JEAN   Why not? Though I must admit the victory was too easy to make me lose my head.

JULIE   Go on hitting me.

JEAN *(rising)* No. On the contrary I apologize for what I've said. I don't hit a person who's down—least of all a woman. I can't deny there's a certain satisfaction in finding that what dazzled one below was just moonshine, that that falcon's back is gray after all, that there's powder on the lovely cheek, that polished nails can have black tips, that the handkerchief is dirty although it smells of scent. On the other hand it hurts to find that what I was struggling to reach wasn't high and isn't real. It hurts to see you fallen so low you're far lower than your own cook. Hurts like when you see the last flowers of summer lashed to pieces by rain and turned to mud.

JULIE   You're talking as if you're already my superior.

JEAN   I am. I might make you a Countess, but you could never make me a Count, you know.

JULIE   But I am the child of a Count, and you could never be that.

JEAN   True, but I might be the father of Counts if . . .

JULIE   You're a thief. I'm not.

JEAN   There are worse things than being a thief—much lower. Besides, when I'm in a place I regard myself as a member of the family to some extent, as one of the children. You don't call it stealing when children pinch a berry from overladen bushes. *(His passion is roused again.)* Miss Julie, you're a glorious woman, far too good for a man like me. You were carried away by some kind of madness, and now you're trying to cover up your mistake by persuading yourself you're in love with me. You're not, although you may find me physically attractive, which means your love's no better than mine. But I wouldn't be satisfied with being nothing but an animal for you, and I could never make you love me.

JULIE   Are you sure?

JEAN   You think there's a chance? Of my loving you, yes, of course. You're beautiful, refined *(Takes her hand),* educated, and you can be nice when you want to be. The fire you kindle in a man isn't likely to go out. *(Puts his arm round her)* You're like mulled wine, full of spices, and your kisses . . . *(He tries to pull her to him, but she breaks away.)*

JULIE   Let go of me! You won't win me that way.

JEAN   Not that way, how then? Not by kisses and fine speeches, not by planning the future and saving you from shame? How then?

JULIE   How? How? I don't know. There isn't any way. I loathe you—loathe you as I loathe rats, but I can't escape from you.

JEAN   Escape with me.

JULIE *(pulling herself together)* Escape? Yes, we must escape. But I'm so tired. Give me a glass of wine. *(He pours it out. She looks at her watch.)* First we must talk. We still have a little time. *(Empties the glass and holds it out for more.)*

JEAN   Don't drink like that. You'll get tipsy.

JULIE   What's that matter?

JEAN   What's it matter? It's vulgar to get drunk. Well, what have you got to say?

JULIE   We've got to run away, but we must talk first—or rather, I must, for so far you've done all the talking. You've told me about your life, now I want to tell you about mine, so that we really know each other before we begin this journey together.

JEAN   Wait. Excuse my saying so, but don't you think you may be sorry afterward if you give away your secrets to me?

JULIE   Aren't you my friend?

JEAN   On the whole. But don't rely on me.

JULIE   You can't mean that. But anyway everyone knows my secrets. Listen. My mother wasn't well-born; she came of quite humble people, and was brought up with all those new ideas of sex-equality and women's rights and so on. She thought marriage was quite wrong. So when my father proposed to her, she said she would never become his *wife* . . . but in the end she did. I came into the world, as far as I can make out, against my mother's will, and I was left to run wild, but I had to do all the things a boy does—to prove women are as good as men. I had to wear boys' clothes; I was taught to handle horses—and I wasn't allowed in the dairy. She made me groom and harness and go out hunting; I even had to try to plough. All the men on the estate were given the women's jobs, and the women the men's, until the whole place went to rack and ruin and we were the laughing-stock of the neighborhood. At last my father seemed to have come to his senses and rebelled. He changed everything and ran the place his own way. My mother got ill—I don't know what was the matter with her, but she used to have strange attacks and hide herself in the attic or the garden. Sometimes she stayed out all night. Then came the great fire which you have heard people talking about. The house and the stables and the barns—the whole place burnt to the ground. In very suspicious circumstances. Because the accident happened the very day the insurance had to be renewed, and my father had sent the new premium, but through some carelessness of the messenger it arrived too late. *(Refills her glass and drinks.)*

JEAN   Don't drink any more.

JULIE   Oh, what does it matter? We were destitute and had to sleep in the carriages. My father didn't know how to get money to rebuild, and then my mother suggested he should borrow from an old friend of hers, a local brick manufacturer. My father got the loan and, to his surprise, without having to pay interest. So the place was rebuilt. *(Drinks)* Do you know who set fire to it?

JEAN   Your lady mother.

JULIE   Do you know who the brick manufacturer was?

JEAN   Your mother's lover?

JULIE   Do you know whose the money was?

JEAN   Wait . . . no, I don't know that.

JULIE   It was my mother's.

JEAN   In other words the Count's, unless there was a settlement.

JULIE   There wasn't any settlement. My mother had a little money of her own which she didn't want my father to control, so she invested it with her—friend.

JEAN   Who grabbed it.

JULIE   Exactly. He appropriated it. My father came to know all this. He couldn't bring an action, couldn't pay his wife's lover, nor prove it was his wife's money. That was my mother's revenge because he made himself master in his own house. He nearly shot himself then—at least there's a rumor he tried and didn't bring it off. So he went on living, and my mother had to pay dearly for what she'd done. Imagine what those five years were like for me. My natural sympathies were with my father, yet I took my mother's side, because I didn't know the facts. I'd learnt from her to hate and distrust men—you know how she loathed the whole male sex. And I swore to her I'd never become the slave of any man.

JEAN   And so you got engaged to that attorney.

JULIE   So that he should be my slave.

JEAN   But he wouldn't be.

JULIE   Oh yes, he wanted to be, but he didn't have the chance. I got bored with him.

JEAN   Is that what I saw—in the stable-yard?

JULIE   What did you see?

JEAN   What I saw was him breaking off the engagement.

JULIE   That's a lie. It was I who broke it off. Did he say it was him? The cad.

JEAN   He's not a cad. Do you hate men, Miss Julie?

JULIE   Yes . . . most of the time. But when that weakness comes, oh . . . the shame!

JEAN   Then do you hate me?

JULIE   Beyond words. I'd gladly have you killed like an animal.

JEAN   Quick as you'd shoot a mad dog, eh?

JULIE   Yes.

JEAN   But there's nothing here to shoot with—and there isn't a dog. So what do we do now?

JULIE   Go abroad.

JEAN   To make each other miserable for the rest of our lives?

JULIE   No, to enjoy ourselves for a day or two, for a week, for as long as enjoyment lasts, and then—to die . . .

JEAN   Die? How silly! I think I would be far better to start a hotel.

JULIE *(without listening)*   . . . die on the shores of Lake Como, where the sun always shines and at Christmas time there are green trees and glowing oranges.

JEAN   Lake Como's a rainy hole and I didn't see any oranges outside the shops. But it's a good place for tourists. Plenty of villas to be rented by—er—honeymoon couples. Profitable business that. Know why? Because they all sign a lease for six months and all leave after three weeks.

JULIE *(naïvely)*   After three weeks? Why?

JEAN   They quarrel, of course. But the rent has to be paid just the same. And then it's let again. So it goes on and on, for there's plenty of love although it doesn't last long.

JULIE   You don't want to die with me?

JEAN   I don't want to die at all. For one thing I like living and for another I consider suicide's a sin against the Creator who gave us life.

JULIE   You believe in God—*you?*

JEAN   Yes, of course. And I go to church every Sunday. Look here, I'm tired of all this. I'm going to bed.

JULIE   Indeed! And do you think I'm going to leave things like this? Don't you know what you owe the woman you've ruined?

JEAN *(taking out his purse and throwing a silver coin on the table)*   There you are. I don't want to be in anybody's debt.

JULIE *(pretending not to notice the insult)*   Don't you know what the law is?

JEAN   There's no law unfortunately that punishes a woman for seducing a man.

JULIE   But can you see anything for it but to go abroad, get married and then divorce?

JEAN   What if I refuse this misalliance?

JULIE   Misalliance?

JEAN   Yes, for me. I'm better bred than you, see! Nobody in my family committed arson.

JULIE   How do you know?

JEAN   Well, you can't prove otherwise, because we haven't any family records outside the Registrar's office. But I've seen your family tree in that book on the drawing-room table. Do you know who the founder of your family was? A miller who let his wife sleep with the King one night during the Danish war. I haven't any ancestors like that. I haven't any ancestors at all, but I might become one.

JULIE   This is what I get for confiding in someone so low, for sacrificing my family honor . . .

JEAN   Dishonor! Well, I told you so. One shouldn't drink, because then one talks. And one shouldn't talk.

JULIE   Oh, how ashamed I am, how bitterly ashamed! If at least you loved me!

JEAN   Look here—for the last time—what do you want? Am I to burst into tears? Am I to jump over your riding whip? Shall I kiss you and carry you off to Lake Como for three weeks, after which . . . What am I to do? What do you want? This is getting unbearable, but that's what comes of playing around with women. Miss Julie, I can see how miserable you are; I know you're going through hell, but I don't understand you. We don't have scenes like this; we don't go in for hating each other. We make love for fun in our spare time, but we haven't all day and all night for it like you. I think you must be ill. I'm sure you're ill.

JULIE   Then you must be kind to me. You sound almost human now.

JEAN   Well, be human yourself. You spit at me, then won't let me wipe it off—on you.

JULIE   Help me, help me! Tell me what to do, where to go.

JEAN   Jesus, as if I knew!

JULIE   I've been mad, raving mad, but there must be a way out.

JEAN   Stay here and keep quiet. Nobody knows anything.

JULIE   I can't. People do know. Kristin knows.

JEAN   They don't know and they wouldn't believe such a thing.

JULIE *(hesitating)*   But—it might happen again.

JEAN   That's true.

JULIE   And there might be—consequences.

JEAN *(in panic)*   Consequences! Fool that I am I never thought of that. Yes, there's nothing for it but to go. At once. I can't come with you. That would be a complete giveaway. You must go alone—abroad—anywhere.

JULIE   Alone? Where to? I can't.

JEAN   You must. And before the Count gets back. If you stay, we know what will happen. Once you've sinned you feel you might as well go on, as the harm's done. Then you get more and more reckless and in the end you're found out. No. You must go abroad. Then write to the Count and tell him everything, except that it was me. He'll never guess that—and I don't think he'll want to.

JULIE   I'll go if you come with me.

JEAN   Are you crazy, woman? "Miss Julie elopes with valet." Next day it would be in the headlines, and the Count would never live it down.

JULIE   I can't go. I can't stay. I'm so tired, so completely worn out. Give me orders. Set me going. I can't think any more, can't act . . .

JEAN   You see what weaklings you are. Why do you give yourselves airs and turn up your noses as if you're the lords of creation? Very well, I'll give you your orders. Go upstairs and dress. Get money for the journey and come down here again.

JULIE *(softly)*   Come up with me.

JEAN   To your room? Now you've gone crazy again. *(Hesitates a moment)* No! Go along at once. *(Takes her hand and pulls her to the door.)*

JULIE *(as she goes)*   Speak kindly to me, Jean.

JEAN   Orders always sound unkind. Now you know. Now you know.

(Left alone, JEAN *sighs with relief, sits down at the table, takes out a note-book and pencil and adds up figures, now and then aloud. Dawn begins to break.* KRISTIN *enters dressed for church, carrying his white dickey and tie.)*

KRISTIN Lord Jesus, look at the state the place is in! What have you been up to? *(Turns out the lamp.)*

JEAN Oh, Miss Julie invited the crowd in. Did you sleep through it? Didn't you hear anything?

KRISTIN I slept like a log.

JEAN And dressed for church already.

KRISTIN Yes, you promised to come to Communion with me today.

JEAN Why, so I did. And you've got my bib and tucker, I see. Come on then. *(Sits.*

KRISTIN *begins to put his things on. Pause. Sleepily)* What's the lesson today?

KRISTIN It's about the beheading of John the Baptist, I think.

JEAN That's sure to be horribly long. Hi, you're choking me! Oh Lord, I'm so sleepy, so sleepy!

KRISTIN Yes, what have you been doing up all night? You look absolutely green.

JEAN Just sitting here talking with Miss Julie.

KRISTIN She doesn't know what's proper, that one. *(Pause.)*

JEAN I say, Kristin.

KRISTIN What?

JEAN It's queer really, isn't it, when you come to think of it? Her.

KRISTIN What's queer?

JEAN The whole thing. *(Pause.)*

KRISTIN *(looking at the half-filled glasses on the table)* Have you been drinking together too?

JEAN Yes.

KRISTIN More shame you. Look me straight in the face.

JEAN Yes.

KRISTIN Is it possible? Is it possible?

JEAN *(after a moment)* Yes, it is.

KRISTIN Oh! This I would never have believed. How low!

JEAN You're not jealous of her, surely?

KRISTIN No, I'm not. If it had been Clara or Sophie I'd have scratched your eyes out. But not of her. I don't know why; that's how it is though. But it's disgusting.

JEAN You're angry with her then.

KRISTIN No. With you. It was wicked of you, very very wicked. Poor girl. And, mark my words, I won't stay here any longer now—in a place where one can't respect one's employers.

JEAN Why should one respect them?

KRISTIN You should know since you're so smart. But you don't want to stay in the service of people who aren't respectable, do you? I wouldn't demean myself.

JEAN But it's rather a comfort to find out they're no better than us.

KRISTIN I don't think so. If they're no better there's nothing for us to live up to. Oh and think of the Count! Think of him. He's been through so much already. No, I won't stay in the place any longer. A fellow like you too! If it had been that attorney now or somebody of her own class . . .

JEAN Why, what's wrong with . . .

KRISTIN Oh, you're all right in your own way, but when all's said and done there is a difference between one class and another. No, this is something I'll never be able to stomach. That our young lady who was so proud and so down on men you'd never believe she'd let one come near her should go and give herself to one like you. She who wanted to have poor Diana shot for running after the lodgekeeper's pug. No. I must say . . . ! Well, I won't stay here any longer. On the twenty-fourth of October I quit.

JEAN And then?

KRISTIN Well, since you mention it, it's about time you began to look around, if we're ever going to get married.

JEAN But what am I to look for? I shan't get a place like this when I'm married.

KRISTIN I know you won't. But you might get a job as porter or caretaker in some public institution. Government rations are small but sure, and there's a pension for the widow and children.

JEAN That's all very fine, but it's not in my line to start thinking at once about dying for my wife and children. I must say I had rather bigger ideas.

KRISTIN You and your ideas! You've got obligations too, and you'd better start thinking about them.

JEAN Don't *you* start pestering me about obligations. I've had enough of that. *(Listens to a sound upstairs)* Anyway we've plenty of time to work things out. Go and get ready now and we'll be off to church.

KRISTIN Who's that walking about upstairs?

JEAN Don't know . . . unless it's Clara.

KRISTIN *(going)* You don't think the Count could have come back without our hearing him?

JEAN *(scared)* The Count? No, he can't have. He'd have rung for me.

KRISTIN God help us! I've never known such goings on. *(Exit.)*

(The sun has now risen and is shining on the tree-tops. The light gradually changes until it slants in through the windows. JEAN *goes to the door and beckons.* JULIE *enters in traveling clothes, carrying a small bird-cage covered with a cloth which she puts on a chair.)*

JULIE I'm ready.

JEAN Hush! Kristin's up.

JULIE *(in a very nervous state)* Does she suspect anything?

JEAN Not a thing. But, my God, what a sight you are!

JULIE Sight? What do you mean?

JEAN You're white as a corpse and—pardon me—your face is dirty.

JULIE Let me wash then. *(Goes to the sink and washes her face and hands)* There. Give me a towel. Oh! The sun is rising!

JEAN And that breaks the spell.

JULIE Yes. The spell of Midsummer Eve . . . But listen, Jean. Come with me. I've got the money.

JEAN *(skeptically)* Enough?

JULIE Enough to start with. Come with me. I can't travel alone today. It's Midsummer Day, remember. I'd be packed into a suffocating train among crowds of people who'd all stare at me. And it would stop at every station while I yearned for wings. No, I can't do that, I simply can't. There will be memories too; memories of Midsummer Days when I was little. The leafy church—birch and lilac—the gaily spread dinner table, relatives, friends—evening in the park—dancing and music and flowers and fun. Oh, however far you run away—there'll always be memories in the baggage car—and remorse and guilt.

JEAN I will come with you, but quickly now then, before it's too late. At once.

JULIE Put on your things. *(Picks up the cage.)*

JEAN No luggage, mind. That would give us away.

JULIE No, only what we can take with us in the carriage.

JEAN *(fetching his hat)* What on earth have you got there? What is it?

JULIE   Only my greenfinch. I don't want to leave it behind.

JEAN   Well, I'll be damned! We're to take a bird-cage along, are we? You're crazy. Put that cage down.

JULIE   It's the only thing I'm taking from my home. The only living creature who cares for me since Diana went off like that. Don't be cruel. Let me take it.

JEAN   Put that cage down, I tell you—and don't talk so loud. Kristin will hear.

JULIE   No, I won't leave it in strange hands. I'd rather you killed it.

JEAN   Give the little beast here then and I'll wring its neck.

JULIE   But don't hurt it, don't . . . no, I can't.

JEAN   Give it here. I *can.*

JULIE   *(taking the bird out of the cage and kissing it)*   Dear little Serena, must you die and leave your mistress?

JEAN   Please don't make a scene. It's *your* life and future we're worrying about. Come on, quick now!

(He snatches the bird from her, puts it on a board and picks up a chopper. JULIE *turns away.)*

You should have learnt how to kill chickens instead of target-shooting. Then you wouldn't faint at a drop of blood.

JULIE *(screaming)*   Kill me too! Kill me! You who can butcher an innocent creature without a quiver. Oh, how I hate you, how I loathe you! There is blood between us now. I curse the hour I first saw you. I curse the hour I was conceived in my mother's womb.

JEAN   What's the use of cursing. Let's go.

JULIE *(going to the chopping-block as if drawn against her will)*   No, I won't go yet. I can't . . . I must look. Listen! There's a carriage. *(Listens without taking her eyes off the board and chopper)* You don't think I can bear the sight of blood. You think I'm so weak. Oh, how I should like to see your blood and your brains on a chopping-block! I'd like to see the whole of your sex swimming like that in a sea of blood. I think I could drink out of your skull, bathe my feet in your broken breast and eat your heart roasted whole. You think I'm weak. You think I love you, that my womb yearned for your seed and I want to carry your offspring under my heart and nourish it with my blood. You think I want to bear your child and take your name. By the way, what is your name? I've never heard your surname. I don't suppose you've got one. I should be "Mrs. Hovel" or "Madam Dunghill." You dog wearing my collar, you lackey with my crest on your buttons! I share you with my cook; I'm my own servant's rival! Oh! Oh! Oh! . . . You think I'm a coward and will run away. No, now I'm going to stay—and let the storm break. My father will come back . . . find his desk broken open . . . his money gone. Then he'll ring that bell—twice for the valet—and then he'll send for the police . . . and I shall tell everything. Everything. Oh how wonderful to make an end of it all—a real end! He has a stroke and dies and that's the end of all of us. Just peace and quietness . . . eternal rest. The coat of arms broken on the coffin and the Count's line extinct . . . But the valet's line goes on in an orphanage, wins laurels in the gutter and ends in jail.

JEAN   There speaks the noble blood! Bravo, Miss Julie. But now, don't let the cat out of the bag.

*(*KRISTIN *enters dressed for church, carrying a prayer-book.* JULIE *rushes to her and flings herself into her arms for protection.)*

JULIE   Help me, Kristin! Protect me from this man!

KRISTIN *(unmoved and cold)*   What goings-on for a feast day morning! *(Sees the board)* And what a filthy mess. What's it all about? Why are you screaming and carrying on so?

JULIE   Kristin, you're a woman and my friend. Beware of that scoundrel!

JEAN *(embarrassed)*   While you ladies are talking things over, I'll go and shave. *(Slips into his room.)*

JULIE   You must understand. You must listen to me.

KRISTIN   I certainly don't understand such loose ways. Where are you off to in those traveling clothes? And he had his hat on, didn't he, eh?

JULIE   Listen, Kristin. Listen, I'll tell you everything.

KRISTIN   I don't want to know anything.

JULIE   You must listen.

KRISTIN   What to? Your nonsense with Jean? I don't care a rap about that; it's nothing to do with me. But if you're thinking of getting him to run off with you, we'll soon put a stop to that.

JULIE *(very nervously)*   Please try to be calm, Kristin, and listen. I can't stay here, nor can Jean—so we must go abroad.

KRISTIN   Hm, hm!

JULIE *(brightening)*   But you see, I've had an idea. Supposing we all three go—abroad—to Switzerland and start a hotel together . . . I've got some money, you see . . . and Jean and I could run the whole thing—and I thought you would take charge of the kitchen. Wouldn't that be splendid? Say yes, do. If you come with us everything will be fine. Oh do say yes! *(Puts her arms round* KRISTIN.*)*

KRISTIN *(coolly thinking)*   Hm, hm.

JULIE *(presto tempo)*   You've never traveled, Kristin. You should go abroad and see the world. You've no idea how nice it is traveling by train—new faces all the time and new countries. On our way through Hamburg we'll go to the zoo—you'll love that—and we'll go to the theater and the opera too . . . and when we get to Munich there'll be the museums, dear, and pictures by Rubens and Raphael—the great painters, you know . . . You've heard of Munich, haven't you? Where King Ludwig lived—you know, the king who went mad. . . . We'll see his castles—some of his castles are still just like in fairy-tales . . . and from there it's not far to Switzerland—and the Alps. Think of the Alps, Kristin dear, covered with snow in the middle of summer . . . and there are oranges there and trees that are green the whole year round . . .

(JEAN *is seen in the door of his room, sharpening his razor on a strop which he holds with his teeth and his left hand. He listens to the talk with satisfaction and now and then nods approval.* JULIE *continues, tempo prestissimo.)*

And then we'll get a hotel . . . and I'll sit at the desk, while Jean receives the guests and goes out marketing and writes letters . . . There's life for you! Trains whistling, buses driving up, bells ringing upstairs and downstairs . . . and I shall make out the bills—and I shall cook them too . . . you've no idea how nervous travelers are when it comes to paying their bills. And you—you'll sit like a queen in the kitchen . . . of course there won't be any standing at the stove for you. You'll always have to be nicely dressed and ready to be seen, and with your looks—no, I'm not flattering you—one fine day you'll catch yourself a husband . . . some rich Englishman, I shouldn't wonder—they're the ones who are easy *(Slowing down)* to catch . . . and then we'll get rich and build ourselves a villa on Lake Como . . . of course it rains there a little now and then—but *(Dully)* the sun must shine there too sometimes—even though it seems gloomy—and if not—then we can come home again—come back—*(Pause)*—here—or somewhere else . . .

KRISTIN   Look here, Miss Julie, do you believe all that yourself?

JULIE *(exhausted)*   Do I believe it?

KRISTIN   Yes.

JULIE *(wearily)*   I don't know. I don't believe anything any more. *(Sinks down on the bench; her head in her arms on the table)* Nothing. Nothing at all.

KRISTIN (*turning to* JEAN) So you meant to beat it, did you?

JEAN (*disconcerted, putting the razor on the table*) Beat it? What are you talking about? You've heard Miss Julie's plan, and though she's tired now with being up all night, it's a perfectly sound plan.

KRISTIN Oh, is it? If you thought I'd work for that . . .

JEAN (*interrupting*) Kindly use decent language in front of your mistress. Do you hear?

KRISTIN Mistress?

JEAN Yes.

KRISTIN Well, well, just listen to that!

JEAN Yes, it would be a good thing if you did listen and talked less. Miss Julie is your mistress and what's made you lose your respect for her now ought to make you feel the same about yourself.

KRISTIN I've always had enough self-respect—

JEAN To despise other people.

KRISTIN —not to go below my own station. Has the Count's cook ever gone with the groom or the swine-herd? Tell me that.

JEAN No, you were lucky enough to have a high-class chap for your beau.

KRISTIN High-class all right—selling the oats out of the Count's stable.

JEAN You're a fine one to talk—taking a commission on the groceries and bribes from the butcher.

KRISTIN What the devil . . . ?

JEAN And now you can't feel any respect for your employers. You, you!

KRISTIN Are you coming to church with me? I should think you need a good sermon after your fine deeds.

JEAN No, I'm not going to church today. You can go alone and confess your own sins.

KRISTIN Yes, I'll do that and bring back enough forgiveness to cover yours too. The Saviour suffered and died on the cross for all our sins, and if we go to Him with faith and a penitent heart, He takes all our sins upon Himself.

JEAN Even grocery thefts?

JULIE Do you believe that, Kristin?

KRISTIN That is my living faith, as sure as I stand here. The faith I learnt as a child and have kept ever since, Miss Julie. "But where sin abounded, grace did much more abound."

JULIE Oh, if I had your faith! Oh, if . . .

KRISTIN But you see you can't have it without God's special grace, and it's not given to all to have that.

JULIE Who is it given to then?

KRISTIN That's the great secret of the workings of grace, Miss Julie. God is no respecter of persons, and with Him the last shall be first . . .

JULIE Then I suppose He does respect the last.

KRISTIN (*continuing*) . . . and it is easier for a camel to go through the eye of a needle than for a rich man to enter into the kingdom of God. That's how it is, Miss Julie. Now I'm going—alone, and on my way I shall tell the groom not to let any of the horses out, in case anyone should want to leave before the Count gets back. Good-by.

(Exit.)

JEAN What a devil! And all on account of a greenfinch.

JULIE (*wearily*) Never mind the greenfinch. Do you see any way out of this, any end to it?

JEAN *(pondering)* No.

JULIE If you were in my place, what would you do?

JEAN In your place? Wait a bit. If I was a woman—a lady of rank who had—fallen. I don't know. Yes, I do know now.

JULIE *(picking up the razor and making a gesture)* This?

JEAN Yes. But *I* wouldn't do it, you know. There's a difference between us.

JULIE Because you're a man and I'm a woman? What is the difference?

JEAN The usual difference—between man and woman.

JULIE *(holding the razor)* I'd like to. But I can't. My father couldn't either, that time he wanted to.

JEAN No, he didn't want to. He had to be revenged first.

JULIE And now my mother is revenged again, through me.

JEAN Didn't you ever love your father, Miss Julie?

JULIE Deeply, but I must have hated him too—unconsciously. And he let me be brought up to despise my own sex, to be half woman, half man. Whose fault is what's happened? My father's, my mother's, or my own? My own? I haven't anything that's my own. I haven't one single thought that I didn't get from my father, one emotion that didn't come from my mother, and as for this last idea—about all people being equal—I got that from him, my fiancé—that's why I call him a cad. How can it be my fault? Push the responsibility on to Jesus, like Kristin does? No, I'm too proud and—thanks to my father's teaching—too intelligent. As for all that about a rich person not being able to get into heaven, it's just a lie, but Kristin, who has money in the savings-bank, will certainly not get in. Whose fault is it? What does it matter whose fault it is? In any case I must take the blame and bear the consequences.

JEAN Yes, but . . . *(There are two sharp rings on the bell.* JULIE *jumps to her feet.* JEAN *changes into his livery.)* The Count is back. Supposing Kristin . . . *(Goes to the speaking-tube, presses it and listens.)*

JULIE Has he been to his desk yet?

JEAN This is Jean, sir. *(Listens)* Yes, sir. *(Listens)* Yes, sir, very good, sir. *(Listens)* At once, sir? *(Listens)* Very good, sir. In half an hour.

JULIE *(in panic)* What did he say? My God, what did he say?

JEAN He ordered his boots and his coffee in half an hour.

JULIE Then there's half an hour . . . Oh, I'm so tired! I can't do anything. Can't be sorry, can't run away, can't stay, can't live—can't die. Help me. Order me, and I'll obey like a dog. Do me this last service—save my honor, save his name. You know what I ought to do, but haven't the strength to do. Use your strength and order me to do it.

JEAN I don't know why—I can't now—I don't understand . . . It's just as if this coat made me—I can't give you orders—and now that the Count has spoken to me—I can't quite explain, but . . . well, that devil of a lackey is bending my back again. I believe if the Count came down now and ordered me to cut my throat, I'd do it on the spot.

JULIE Then pretend you're him and I'm you. You did some fine acting before, when you knelt to me and played the aristocrat. Or . . . Have you ever seen a hypnotist at the theater? *(He nods.)* He says to the person "Take the broom," and he takes it. He says "Sweep," and he sweeps . . .

JEAN But the person has to be asleep.

JULIE *(as if in a trance)* I am asleep already . . . the whole room has turned to smoke—and you look like a stove—a stove like a man in black with a tall hat—your eyes are glowing like coals when the fire is low—and your face is a white patch like ashes. *(The sunlight has now reached the floor and lights up* JEAN.*)* How nice and warm it is! *(She holds out her hands as though warming them at a fire.)* And so light—and so peaceful.

JEAN *(putting the razor in her hand)*   Here is the broom. Go now while it's light—out to the barn—and . . . *(Whispers in her ear.)*

JULIE *(waking)*   Thank you. I am going now—to rest. But just tell me that even the first can receive the gift of grace.

JEAN   The first? No, I can't tell you that. But wait . . . Miss Julie, I've got it! You aren't one of the first any longer. You're one of the last.

JULIE   That's true. I'm one of the very last. I *am* the last. Oh! . . . But now I can't go. Tell me again to go.

JEAN   No, I can't now either. I can't.

JULIE   And the first shall be last.

JEAN   Don't think, don't think. You're taking my strength away too and making me a coward. What's that? I thought I saw the bell move . . . To be so frightened of a bell! Yes, but it's not just a bell. There's somebody behind it—a hand moving it—and something else moving the hand—and if you stop your ears—if you stop your ears—yes, then it rings louder than ever. Rings and rings until you answer—and then it's too late. Then the police come and . . . and . . *(The bell rings twice loudly.* JEAN *flinches, then straightens himself up.)* It's horrible. But there's no other way to end it . . . Go!

(JULIE *walks firmly out through the door.*)

(Curtain.)

Comments and Questions

Modern drama got its start in Scandinavia more than one hundred years ago. Ibsen is its acknowledged father; Strindberg, a notable disciple who carried on and added to Ibsen's dramatic innovations. Both writers embraced what they themselves labeled naturalism, a term closely akin to realism. Characters were to represent ordinary human beings influenced by heredity and environment, inescapably selfish, and were to be analyzed with scientific precision.

Strindberg's carefully thought-out Foreword to *Miss Julie* sets forth what a realistic drama should do. Perhaps one should read the play first, then the Foreword to see how the author's convictions have been translated into art.

1. Strindberg calls *Miss Julie* a "Naturalistic Tragedy." This description suggests a departure from classical tragedy. Many differences will be apparent if one compares Strindberg's play with *Antigone* or with *Hamlet.* What are the major differences?

2. Strindberg gained a reputation as a misogynist, a hater of women. Does this attitude show itself in *Miss Julie?* If so, how? If so, does the play suffer? Discuss.

3. What is the central conflict? Does this conflict contain more than one element?

4. List the innovations in staging that the author calls for in the Foreword. Which ones have become routine in today's theaters? Are sets, for example, still flimsy? What has happened to theater lighting?

5. Strindberg says that Jean, the valet, seldom speaks the truth. Can you identify the speeches that probably represent what he really feels and believes?

6. Why does the author place the main action downstairs in the kitchen rather than, say, upstairs in the drawing-room?

7. Are there symbols in the play? Consider, for example, Kristin's stove and the Count's riding-boots.

8. Compare in detail *Ghosts* and *Miss Julie.*

John Millington Synge (1871–1909)
The Playboy of the Western World

PREFACE

In writing *The Playboy of the Western World,* as in my other plays, I have used one or two words only that I have not heard among the country people of Ireland, or spoken in my own nursery before I could read the newspapers. A certain number of the phrases I employ I have heard also from herds and fishermen along the coast from Kerry to Mayo, or from beggar-women and ballad-singers nearer Dublin; and I am glad to acknowledge how much I owe to the folk-imagination of these fine people. Anyone who has lived in real intimacy with the Irish peasantry will know that the wildest sayings and ideas in this play are tame indeed, compared with the fancies one may hear in any little hillside cabin in Geesala, or Carraroe, or Dingle Bay. All art is a collaboration; and there is little doubt that in the happy ages of literature, striking and beautiful phrases were as ready to the story-teller's or the playwright's hand, as the rich cloaks and dresses of his time. It is probable that when the Elizabethan dramatist took his ink-horn and sat down to his work he used many phrases that he had just heard, as he sat at dinner, from his mother or his children. In Ireland, those of us who know the people have the same privilege. When I was writing *The Shadow of the Glen,* some years ago, I got more aid than any learning could have given me from a chink in the floor of the old Wicklow house where I was staying, that let me hear what was being said by the servant girls in the kitchen. This matter, I think, is of importance, for in countries where the imagination of the people, and the language they use, is rich and living, it is possible for a writer to be rich and copious in his words, and at the same time to give the reality, which is the root of all poetry, in a comprehensive and natural form. In the modern literature of towns, however, richness is found only in sonnets, or prose poems, or in one or two elaborate books that are far away from the profound and common interests of life. One has, on one side, Mallarmé and Huysmans producing this literature; and on the other, Ibsen and Zola dealing with the reality of life in joyless and pallid words. On the stage one must have reality, and one must have joy; and that is why the intellectual modern drama has failed, and people have grown sick of the false joy of the musical comedy, that has been given them in place of the rich joy found only in what is superb and wild in reality. In a good play every speech should be as fully flavoured as a nut or apple, and such speeches cannot be written by anyone who works among people who have shut their lips on poetry. In Ireland, for a few years more, we have a popular imagination that is fiery and magnificent, and tender; so that those of us who wish to write start with a chance that is not given to writers in places where the springtime of the local life has been forgotten, and the harvest is a memory only, and the straw has been turned into bricks.

                                                                          J.M.S.

January 21, 1907

CHARACTERS

CHRISTOPHER MAHON

OLD MAHON, *his father, a squatter*

MICHAEL JAMES FLAHERTY, called MICHAEL JAMES, *a publican*

MARGARET FLAHERTY, called PEGEEN MIKE, *his daughter*

SHAWN KEOGH, *her cousin, a young farmer*

WIDOW QUIN, *a woman of about thirty*

PHILLY CULLEN and JIMMY FARRELL, *small farmers*   A BELLMAN *or Town Crier*
SARA TANSEY, SUSAN BRADY, HONOR BLAKE, *and*   SOME PEASANTS
  NELLY, *village girls*

The action takes place near a village, on a wild coast of Mayo.[1] *The first Act passes on an evening of autumn, the other two Acts on the following day.*

ACT I

SCENE: *Country public-house or shebeen, very rough and untidy. There is a sort of counter on the right with shelves, holding many bottles and jugs, just seen above it. Empty barrels stand near the counter. At back, a little to left of counter, there is a door into the open air, then, more to the left, there is a settle with shelves above it, with more jugs, and a table beneath a window. At the left there is a large open fire place, with turf fire, and a small door into inner room.* PEGEEN, *a wild-looking but fine girl of about twenty, is writing at table. She is dressed in the usual peasant dress.*

PEGEEN *(slowly as she writes)* Six yards of stuff for to make a yellow gown. A pair of lace boots with lengthy heels on them and brassy eyes. A hat is suited for a wedding-day. A fine tooth comb. To be sent with three barrels of porter in Jimmy Farrell's creel cart on the evening of the coming Fair to Mister Michael James Flaherty. With the best compliments of this season. Margaret Flaherty.

SHAWN KEOGH *(a fat and fair young man comes in as she signs, looks round awkwardly, when he sees she is alone.)* Where's himself?

PEGEEN *(without looking at him)* He's coming. *(She directs the letter.)* To Master Sheamus Mulroy, Wine and Spirit Dealer, Castlebar.

SHAWN *(uneasily)* I didn't see him on the road.

PEGEEN How would you see him *(Licks stamp and puts it on letter)* and it dark night this half hour gone by?

SHAWN *(turning toward the door again)* I stood a while outside wondering would I have a right to pass on or to walk in and see you, Pegeen Mike, *(Comes to fire)* and I could hear the cows breathing, and sighing in the stillness of the air, and not a step moving any place from this gate to the bridge.

PEGEEN *(putting letter in envelope)* It's above at the cross-roads he is, meeting Philly Cullen; and a couple more are going along with him to Kate Cassidy's wake.

SHAWN *(looking at her blankly)* And he's going that length in the dark night?

PEGEEN *(impatiently)* He is surely, and leaving me lonesome on the scruff of the hill. *(She gets up and puts envelope on dresser, then winds clock.)* Isn't it long the nights are now, Shawn Keogh, to be leaving a poor girl with her own self counting the hours to the dawn of day?

SHAWN *(with awkward humour)* If it is, when we're wedded in a short while you'll

[1] The county of Mayo is located in the northwest of Ireland, exposed to the Atlantic Ocean. Most of the communities and areas mentioned throughout the play can be located on a standard map of Ireland.

have no call to complain, for I've little will to be walking off to wakes or weddings in the darkness of the night.

PEGEEN *(with rather scornful good humour)* You're making mighty certain, Shaneen, that I'll wed you now.

SHAWN Aren't we after making a good bargain, the way we're only waiting these days on Father Reilly's dispensation[2] from the bishops, or the Court of Rome?

PEGEEN *(looking at him teasingly, washing up at dresser)* It's a wonder, Shaneen, the Holy Father'd be taking notice of the likes of you; for if I was him I wouldn't bother with this place where you'll meet none but Red Linahan, has a squint in his eye, and Patcheen is lame in his heel, or the mad Mulrannies were driven from California and they lost in their wits. We're a queer lot these times to go troubling the Holy Father on his sacred seat.

SHAWN *(scandalized)* If we are, we're as good this place as another, maybe, and as good these times as we were for ever.

PEGEEN *(with scorn)* As good, is it? Where now will you meet the like of Daneen Sullivan knocked the eye from a peeler,[3] or Marcus Quin, God rest him, got six months for maiming ewes, and he a great warrant to tell stories of holy Ireland till he'd have the old women shedding down tears about their feet. Where will you find the like of them, I'm saying?

SHAWN *(timidly)* If you don't, it's a good job, maybe; for *(With peculiar emphasis on the words)* Father Reilly has small conceit to have that kind walking around and talking to the girls.

PEGEEN *(impatiently, throwing water from basin out of the door)* Stop tormenting me with Father Reilly *(Imitating his voice)* when I'm asking only what way I'll pass these twelve hours of dark, and not take my death with the fear. *(Looking out of door.)*

SHAWN *(timidly)* Would I fetch you the Widow Quin, maybe?

PEGEEN Is it the like of that murderer? You'll not, surely.

SHAWN *(going to her, soothingly)* Then I'm thinking himself will stop along with you when he sees you taking on, for it'll be a long night-time with great darkness, and I'm after feeling a kind of fellow above in the furzy ditch, groaning wicked like a maddening dog, the way it's good cause you have, maybe, to be fearing now.

PEGEEN *(turning on him sharply)* What's that? Is it a man you seen?

SHAWN *(retreating)* I couldn't see him at all; but I heard him groaning out, and breaking his heart. It should have been a young man from his words speaking.

PEGEEN *(going after him)* And you never went near to see was he hurted or what ailed him at all?

SHAWN I did not, Pegeen Mike. It was a dark, lonesome place to be hearing the like of him.

PEGEEN Well, you're a daring fellow, and if they find his corpse stretched above in the dews of dawn, what'll you say then to the peelers, or the Justice of the Peace?

SHAWN *(thunderstruck)* I wasn't thinking of that. For the love of God, Pegeen Mike, don't let on I was speaking of him. Don't tell your father and the men is coming above; for if they heard that story, they'd have great blabbing this night at the wake.

PEGEEN I'll maybe tell them, and I'll maybe not.

SHAWN They are coming at the door. Will you whisht, I'm saying?

PEGEEN Whisht yourself. *(She goes behind counter.* MICHAEL JAMES, *fat jovial publican, comes in followed by* PHILLY CULLEN, *who is thin and mistrusting, and* JIMMY FARRELL, *who is fat and amorous, about forty-five.)*

---

[2] A papal dispensation was required to permit marriage between cousins.   [3] A policeman.

MEN *(together)*   God bless you. The blessing of God on this place.

PEGEEN   God bless you kindly.

MICHAEL *(to men who go to the counter)*   Sit down now, and take your rest. *(Crosses to* SHAWN *at the fire)* And how is it you are, Shawn Keogh? Are you coming over the sands to Kate Cassidy's wake?

SHAWN   I am not, Michael James. I'm going home the short cut to my bed.

PEGEEN *(speaking across the counter)*   He's right too, and have you no shame, Michael James, to be quitting off for the whole night, and leaving myself lonesome in the shop?

MICHAEL *(good-humouredly)*   Isn't it the same whether I go for the whole night or a part only? and I'm thinking it's a queer daughter you are if you'd have me crossing backward through the Stooks[4] of the Dead Women, with a drop taken.

PEGEEN   If I am a queer daughter, it's a queer father'd be leaving me lonesome these twelve hours of dark, and I piling the turf with the dogs barking, and the calves mooing, and my own teeth rattling with the fear.

JIMMY *(flatteringly)*   What is there to hurt you, and you a fine, hardy girl would knock the head of any two men in the place?

PEGEEN *(working herself up)*   Isn't there the harvest boys with their tongues red for drink, and the ten tinkers is camped in the east glen, and the thousand militia—bad cess to them!—walking idle through the land. There's lots surely to hurt me, and I won't stop alone in it, let himself do what he will.

MICHAEL   If you're that afeard, let Shawn Keogh stop along with you. It's the will of God, I'm thinking, himself should be seeing to you now.

(They all turn on SHAWN *)*

SHAWN *(in horrified confusion)*   I would and welcome, Michael James, but I'm afeard of Father Reilly; and what at all would the Holy Father and the Cardinals of Rome be saying if they heard I did the like of that?

MICHAEL *(with contempt)*   God help you! Can't you sit in by the hearth with the light lit and herself beyond in the room? You'll do that surely, for I've heard tell there's a queer fellow above, going mad or getting his death, maybe, in the gripe of the ditch, so she'd be safer this night with a person here.

SHAWN *(with plaintive despair)*   I'm afeard of Father Reilly, I'm saying. Let you not be tempting me, and we near married itself.

PHILLY *(with cold contempt)*   Lock him in the west room. He'll stay then and have no sin to be telling to the priest.

MICHAEL *(to* SHAWN, *getting between him and the door)*   Go up now.

SHAWN *(at the top of his voice)*   Don't stop me, Michael James. Let me out of the door, I'm saying, for the love of the Almighty God. Let me out. *(Trying to dodge past him)* Let me out of it, and may God grant you His indulgence in the hour of need.

MICHAEL *(loudly)*   Stop your noising, and sit down by the hearth. *(Gives him a push and goes to counter laughing.)*

SHAWN *(turning back, wringing his hands)*   Oh, Father Reilly and the saints of God, where will I hide myself today? Oh, St. Joseph, and St. Patrick, and St. Brigid, and St. James, have mercy on me now! (SHAWN *turns round, sees door clear, and makes a rush for it.*)

MICHAEL *(catching him by the coat-tail)*   You'd be going, is it?

SHAWN *(screaming)*   Leave me go, Michael James, leave me go, you old Pagan, leave me go, or I'll get the curse of the priests on you, and of the scarlet-coated bishops of the

---

[4] Stacked sheaves of wheat; apparently superstition was attached to a field where grain was stacked.

courts of Rome. *(With a sudden movement he pulls himself out of his coat, and disappears out of the door, leaving his coat in* MICHAEL's *hands.)*

MICHAEL *(turning round, and holding up coat)*   Well, there's the coat of a Christian man. Oh, there's sainted glory this day in the lonesome west; and by the will of God I've got you a decent man, Pegeen, you'll have no call to be spying after if you've a score of young girls, maybe, weeding in your fields.

PEGEEN *(taking up the defence of her property)*   What right have you to be making game of a poor fellow for minding the priest, when it's your own the fault is, not paying a penny pot-boy to stand along with me and give me courage in the doing of my work? *(She snaps the coat away from him, and goes behind counter with it.)*

MICHAEL *(taken aback)*   Where would I get a pot-boy? Would you have me send the bellman screaming in the streets of Castlebar?

SHAWN *(opening the door a chink and putting in his head, in a small voice)*   Michael James!

MICHAEL *(imitating him)*   What ails you?

SHAWN   The queer dying fellow's beyond looking over the ditch. He's come up, I'm thinking, stealing your hens. *(Looks over his shoulder)* God help me, he's following me now, *(He runs into room.)* and if he's heard what I said, he'll be having my life, and I going home lonesome in the darkness of the night.

(For a perceptible moment they watch the door with curiosity. Someone coughs outside. Then CHRISTY MAHON, *a slight young man, comes in very tired and frightened and dirty.)*

CHRISTY *(in a small voice)*   God save all here!

MEN   God save you kindly.

CHRISTY *(going to the counter)*   I'd trouble you for a glass of porter, woman of the house. *(He puts down coin.)*

PEGEEN *(serving him)*   You're one of the tinkers, young fellow, is beyond camped in the glen?

CHRISTY   I am not; but I'm destroyed walking.

MICHAEL *(patronizingly)*   Let you come up then to the fire. You're looking famished with the cold.

CHRISTY   God reward you. *(He takes up his glass and goes a little way across to the left, then stops and looks about him.)* Is it often the polis do be coming into this place, master of the house?

MICHAEL   If you'd come in better hours, you'd have seen "Licensed for the sale of Beer and Spirits, to be consumed on the premises," written in white letters above the door, and what would the polis want spying on me, and not a decent house within four miles, the way every living Christian is a bona fide,[5] saving one widow alone?

CHRISTY *(with relief)*   It's a safe house, so. *(He goes over to the fire, sighing and moaning. Then he sits down, putting his glass beside him and begins gnawing a turnip, too miserable to feel the others staring at him with curiosity.)*

MICHAEL *(going after him)*   Is it yourself is fearing the polis? You're wanting, maybe?

CHRISTY   There's many wanting.

MICHAEL   Many surely, with the broken harvest and the ended wars. *(He picks up some stockings, etc., that are near the fire, and carries them away furtively.)* It should be larceny, I'm thinking.

CHRISTY *(dolefully)*   I had it in my mind it was a different word and a bigger.

---

[5] A person could be served drinks outside regular tavern hours if he had slept over three miles away on the previous night.

PEGEEN There's a queer lad. Were you never slapped in school, young fellow, that you don't know the name of your deed?

CHRISTY *(bashfully)* I'm slow at learning, a middling scholar only.

MICHAEL If you're a dunce itself, you'd have a right to know that larceny's robbing and stealing. Is it for the like of that you're wanting?

CHRISTY *(with a flash of family pride)* And I the son of a strong farmer *(With a sudden qualm)*, God rest his soul, could have bought up the whole of your old house awhile since, from the butt of his tail-pocket, and not have missed the weight of it gone.

MICHAEL *(impressed)* If it's not stealing, it's maybe something big.

CHRISTY *(flattered)* Aye; it's maybe something big.

JIMMY He's a wicked-looking young fellow. Maybe he followed after a young woman on a lonesome night.

CHRISTY *(shocked)* Oh, the saints forbid, mister; I was all times a decent lad.

PHILLY *(turning on* JIMMY*)* You're a silly man, Jimmy Farrell. He said his father was a farmer a while since, and there's himself now in a poor state. Maybe the land was grabbed from him, and he did what any decent man would do.

MICHAEL *(to* CHRISTY, *mysteriously)* Was it bailiffs?

CHRISTY The divil a one.[6]

MICHAEL Agents?

CHRISTY The divil a one.

MICHAEL Landlords?

CHRISTY *(peevishly)* Ah, not at all, I'm saying. You'd see the like of them stories on any little paper of a Munster town. But I'm not calling to mind any person, gentle, simple, judge or jury, did the like of me.

(They all draw nearer with delighted curiosity.)

PHILLY Well, that lad's a puzzle-the-world.

JIMMY He'd beat Dan Davies' circus, or the holy missioners making sermons on the villainy of man. Try him again, Philly.

PHILLY Did you strike golden guineas out of solder, young fellow, or shilling coins itself?

CHRISTY I did not, mister, not sixpence nor a farthing coin.

JIMMY Did you marry three wives maybe? I'm told there's a sprinkling have done that among the holy Luthers of the preaching north.

CHRISTY *(shyly)* I never married with one, let alone with a couple or three.

PHILLY Maybe he went fighting for the Boers, the like of the man beyond, was judged to be hanged, quartered and drawn. Were you off east, young fellow, fighting bloody wars for Kruger and the freedom of the Boers?

CHRISTY I never left my own parish till Tuesday was a week.

PEGEEN *(coming from counter)* He's done nothing, so. *(To* CHRISTY*)* If you didn't commit murder or a bad, nasty thing, or false coining, or robbery, or butchery, or the like of them, there isn't anything that would be worth your troubling for to run from now. You did nothing at all.

CHRISTY *(his feelings hurt)* That's an unkindly thing to be saying to a poor orphaned traveller, has a prison behind him, and hanging before, and hell's gap gaping below.

PEGEEN *(with a sign to the men to be quiet)* You're only saying it. You did nothing at all. A soft lad the like of you wouldn't slit the windpipe of a screeching sow.

CHRISTY *(offended)* You're not speaking the truth.

---

[6] Not a one.

PEGEEN *(in mock rage)*   Not speaking the truth, is it? Would you have me knock the head off you with the butt of the broom?

CHRISTY *(twisting round on her with a sharp cry of horror)*   Don't strike me. I killed my poor father, Tuesday was a week, for doing the like of that.

PEGEEN *(with blank amazement)*   Is it killed your father?

CHRISTY *(subsiding)*   With the help of God I did surely, and that the Holy Immaculate Mother may intercede for his soul.

PHILLY *(retreating with* JIMMY)   There's a daring fellow.

JIMMY   Oh, glory be to God!

MICHAEL *(with great respect)*   That was a hanging crime, mister honey. You should have had good reason for doing the like of that.

CHRISTY *(in a very reasonable tone)*   He was a dirty man, God forgive him, and he getting old and crusty, the way I couldn't put up with him at all.

PEGEEN   And you shot him dead?

CHRISTY *(shaking his head)*   I never used weapons. I've no license, and I'm a law-fearing man.

MICHAEL   It was with a hilted knife maybe? I'm told, in the big world it's bloody knives they use.

CHRISTY *(loudly, scandalized)*   Do you take me for a slaughter-boy?

PEGEEN   You never hanged him, the way Jimmy Farrell hanged his dog from the license,[7] and had it screeching and wriggling three hours at the butt of a string, and himself swearing it was a dead dog, and the peelers swearing it had life?

CHRISTY   I did not then. I just riz the loy[8] and let fall the edge of it on the ridge of his skull, and he went down at my feet like an empty sack, and never let a grunt or groan from him at all.

MICHAEL *(making a sign to* PEGEEN *to fill* CHRISTY'S *glass)*   And what way weren't you hanged, mister? Did you bury him then?

CHRISTY *(considering)*   Aye. I buried him then. Wasn't I digging spuds in the field?

MICHAEL   And the peelers never followed after you the eleven days that you're out?

CHRISTY *(shaking his head)*   Never a one of them, and I walking forward facing hog, dog, or divil on the highway of the road.

PHILLY *(nodding wisely)*   It's only with a common week-day kind of a murderer them lads would be trusting their carcase, and that man should be a great terror when his temper's roused.

MICHAEL   He should then. *(To* CHRISTY) And where was it, mister honey, that you did the deed?

CHRISTY *(looking at him with suspicion)*   Oh, a distant place, master of the house, a windy corner of high, distant hills.

PHILLY *(nodding with approval)*   He's a close man, and he's right, surely.

PEGEEN   That's be a lad with the sense of Solomon to have for a pot-boy, Michael James, if it's the truth you're seeking one at all.

PHILLY   The peelers is fearing him, and if you'd that lad in the house there isn't one of them would come smelling around if the dogs itself were lapping poteen[9] from the dung-pit of the yard.

JIMMY   Bravery's a treasure in a lonesome place, and a lad would kill his father, I'm thinking, would face a foxy divil with a pitch-pike on the flags of hell.

PEGEEN   It's the truth they're saying, and if I'd that lad in the house, I wouldn't be fearing the looséd kharki cut-throats,[10] or the walking dead.

---

[7] Because he had no license for the dog.   [8] A narrow spade widely used in Ireland for digging peat.   [9] It was illegal to distill or sell this strong whiskey.   [10] British soldiers.

CHRISTY *(swelling with surprise and triumph)*   Well, glory be to God!

MICHAEL *(with deference)*   Would you think well to stop here and be pot-boy, mister honey, if we gave you good wages, and didn't destroy you with the weight of work?

SHAWN *(coming forward uneasily)*   That'd be a queer kind to bring into a decent quiet household with the like of Pegeen Mike.

PEGEEN *(very sharply)*   Will you whisht? Who's speaking to you?

SHAWN *(retreating)*   A bloody-handed murderer the like of . . .

PEGEEN *(snapping at him)*   Whisht I am saying; we'll take no fooling from your like at all. *(To* CHRISTY *with a honeyed voice)* And you, young fellow, you'd have a right to stop, I'm thinking, for we'd do our all and utmost to content your needs.

CHRISTY *(overcome with wonder)*   And I'd be safe in this place from the searching law?

MICHAEL   You would, surely. If they're not fearing you, itself, the peelers in this place is decent droughty poor fellows, wouldn't touch a cur dog and not give warning in the dead of night.

PEGEEN *(very kindly and persuasively)*   Let you stop a short while anyhow. Aren't you destroyed walking with your feet in bleeding blisters, and your whole skin needing washing like a Wicklow sheep?

CHRISTY *(looking round with satisfaction)*   It's a nice room, and if it's not humbugging me you are, I'm thinking that I'll surely stay.

JIMMY *(jumps up)*   Now, by the grace of God, herself will be safe this night, with a man killed his father holding danger from the door, and let you come on, Michael James, or they'll have the best stuff drunk at the wake.

MICHAEL *(going to the door with men)*   And begging your pardon, mister, what name will we call you, for we'd like to know?

CHRISTY   Christopher Mahon.

MICHAEL   Well, God bless you, Christy, and a good rest till we meet again when the sun'll be rising to the noon of day.

CHRISTY   God bless you all.

MEN   God bless you.

(They go out except SHAWN, *who lingers at door.)*

SHAWN *(to* PEGEEN*)*   Are you wanting me to stop along with you and keep you from harm?

PEGEEN *(gruffly)*   Didn't you say you were fearing Father Reilly?

SHAWN   There'd be no harm staying now, I'm thinking, and himself in it too.

PEGEEN   You wouldn't stay when there was need for you, and let you step off nimble this time when there's none.

SHAWN   Didn't I say it was Father Reilly . . .

PEGEEN   Go on, then, to Father Reilly *(In a jeering tone),* and let him put you in the holy brotherhoods, and leave that lad to me.

SHAWN   If I meet the Widow Quin . . .

PEGEEN   Go on, I'm saying, and don't be waking this place with your noise. *(She hustles him out and bolts the door.)* That lad would wear the spirits from the saints of peace. *(Bustles about, then takes off her apron and pins it up in the window as a blind.* CHRISTY *watching her timidly. Then she comes to him and speaks with bland good-humour.)* Let you stretch out now by the fire, young fellow. You should be destroyed travelling.

CHRISTY *(shyly again, drawing off his boots)*   I'm tired, surely, walking wild eleven days, and waking fearful in the night. *(He holds up one of his feet, feeling his blisters, and looking at them with compassion.)*

PEGEEN *(standing beside him, watching him with delight)*   You should have had great people in your family, I'm thinking, with the little, small feet you have, and you with a kind of a quality name, the like of what you'd find on the great powers and potentates of France and Spain.

CHRISTY *(with pride)*   We were great surely, with wide and windy acres of rich Munster land.

PEGEEN   Wasn't I telling you, and you a fine, handsome young fellow with a noble brow?

CHRISTY *(with a flash of delighted surprise)*   Is it me?

PEGEEN   Aye. Did you never hear that from the young girls where you come from in the west or south?

CHRISTY *(with venom)*   I did not then. Oh, they're bloody liars in the naked parish where I grew a man.

PEGEEN   If they are itself, you've heard it these days, I'm thinking, and you walking the world telling out your story to young girls or old.

CHRISTY   I've told my story no place till this night, Pegeen Mike, and it's foolish I was here, maybe, to be talking free, but you're decent people, I'm thinking, and yourself a kindly woman, the way I wasn't fearing you at all.

PEGEEN *(filling a sack with straw)*   You've said the like of that, maybe, in every cot and cabin where you've met a young girl on your way.

CHRISTY *(going over to her, gradually raising his voice)*   I've said it nowhere till this night, I'm telling you, for I've seen none the like of you the eleven long days I am walking the world, looking over a low ditch or a high ditch on my north or my south, into stony scattered fields, or scribes[11] of bog, where you'd see young, limber girls, and fine prancing women making laughter with the men.

PEGEEN   If you weren't destroyed travelling, you'd have as much talk and streeleen,[12] I'm thinking, as Owen Roe O'Sullivan[13] or the poets of the Dingle Bay, and I've heard all times it's the poets are your like, fine fiery fellows with great rages when their temper's roused.

CHRISTY *(drawing a little nearer to her)*   You're a power of rings, God bless you, and would there be any offence if I was asking are you single now?

PEGEEN   What would I want wedding so young?

CHRISTY *(with relief)*   We're alike, so.

PEGEEN *(she puts sack on settle and beats it up)*   I never killed my father. I'd be afeard to do that, except I was the like of yourself with blind rages tearing me within, for I'm thinking you should have had great tussling when the end was come.

CHRISTY *(expanding with delight at the first confidential talk he has ever had with a woman)*   We had not then. It was a hard woman was come over the hill, and if he was always a crusty kind when he'd a hard woman setting him on, not the divil himself or his four fathers could put up with him at all.

PEGEEN *(with curiosity)*   And isn't it a great wonder that one wasn't fearing you?

CHRISTY *(very confidentially)*   Up to the day I killed my father, there wasn't a person in Ireland knew the kind I was, and I there drinking, waking, eating, sleeping, a quiet, simple, poor fellow with no man giving me heed.

PEGEEN *(getting a quilt out of the cupboard and putting it on the sack)*   It was the girls were giving you heed maybe, and I'm thinking it's most conceit[14] you'd have to be gaming with their like.

---

[11] Wide expanses.   [12] Charmingly irresponsible, swaggering chatter; palaver.   [13] O'Sullivan (d. 1784) and other Jacobite poets from Munster in southern Ireland were strolling poets whose songs and deeds would excite Pegeen's imagination.   [14] Desire, inclination.

CHRISTY *(shaking his head, with simplicity)* Not the girls itself, and I won't tell you a lie. There wasn't anyone heeding me in that place saving only the dumb beasts of the field. *(He sits down at fire.)*

PEGEEN *(with disappointment)* And I thinking you should have been living the like of a king of Norway or the Eastern world. *(She comes and sits beside him after placing bread and mug of milk on the table.)*

CHRISTY *(laughing piteously)* The like of a king, is it? And I after toiling, moiling, digging, dodging from the dawn till dusk with never a sight of joy or sport saving only when I'd be abroad in the dark night poaching rabbits on hills, for I was a divil to poach, God forgive me *(Very naïvely)*, and I near got six months for going with a dung fork and stabbing a fish.

PEGEEN And it's that you'd call sport, is it, to be abroad in the darkness with yourself alone?

CHRISTY I did, God help me, and there I'd be as happy as the sunshine of St. Martin's Day, watching the light passing the north or the patches of fog, till I'd hear a rabbit starting to screech and I'd go running in the furze. Then when I'd my full share I'd come walking down where you'd see the ducks and geese stretched sleeping on the highway of the road, and before I'd pass the dunghill, I'd hear himself snoring out, a loud lonesome snore he'd be making all times, the while he was sleeping, and he a man'd be raging all times, the while he was waking, like a gaudy officer you'd hear cursing and damning and swearing oaths.

PEGEEN Providence and Mercy, spare us all!

CHRISTY It's that you'd say surely if you seen him and he after drinking for weeks, rising up in the red dawn, or before it maybe, and going out into the yard as naked as an ash tree in the moon of May, and shying clods against the visage of the stars till he'd put the fear of death into the banbhs[15] and the screeching sows.

PEGEEN I'd be well-nigh afeard of that lad myself, I'm thinking. And there was no one in it but the two of you alone?

CHRISTY The divil a one, though he'd sons and daughters walking all great states and territories of the world, and not a one of them, to this day, but would say their seven curses on him, and they rousing up to let a cough or sneeze, maybe, in the deadness of the night.

PEGEEN *(nodding her head)* Well, you should have been a queer lot. I never cursed my father the like of that, though I'm twenty and more years of age.

CHRISTY Then you'd have cursed mine, I'm telling you, and he a man never gave peace to any, saving when he'd get two months or three, or be locked in the asylums for battering peelers or assaulting men *(With depression)* the way it was a bitter life he led me till I did up a Tuesday and halve his skull.

PEGEEN *(putting her hand on his shoulder)* Well, you'll have peace in this place, Christy Mahon, and none to trouble you, and it's near time a fine lad like you should have your good share of the earth.

CHRISTY It's time surely, and I a seemly fellow with great strength in me and bravery of . . .

(Someone knocks.)

CHRISTY *(clinging to PEGEEN)* Oh, glory! it's late for knocking, and this last while I'm in terror of the peelers, and the walking dead.

(Knocking again.)

---

[15] Young pigs; sucklings.

PEGEEN   Who's there?

VOICE *(outside)*   Me.

PEGEEN   Who's me?

VOICE   The Widow Quin.

PEGEEN *(jumping up and giving him the bread and milk)*   Go on now with your supper, and let on to be sleepy, for if she found you were such a warrant to talk, she's be stringing gabble till the dawn of day. *(He takes bread and sits shyly with his back to the door.)*

PEGEEN *(opening door, with temper)*   What ails you, or what is it you're wanting at this hour of the night?

WIDOW QUIN *(coming in a step and peering at* CHRISTY*)*   I'm after meeting Shawn Keogh and Father Reilly below, who told me of your curiosity man, and they fearing by this time he was maybe roaring, romping on your hands with drink.

PEGEEN *(pointing to* CHRISTY*)*   Look now is he roaring and he stretched away drowsy with his supper and his mug of milk. Walk down and tell that to Father Reilly and to Shaneen Keogh.

WIDOW QUIN *(coming forward)*   I'll not see them again, for I've their word to lead that lad forward for to lodge with me.

PEGEEN *(in blank amazement)*   This night, is it?

WIDOW QUIN *(going over.)*   This night. "It isn't fitting," says the priesteen, "to have his likeness lodging with an orphaned girl." *(To* CHRISTY*)* God save you, mister!

CHRISTY *(shyly)*   God save you kindly.

WIDOW QUIN *(looking at him with half-amazed curiosity)*   Well, aren't you a little smiling fellow? It should have been great and bitter torments did rouse your spirits to a deed of blood.

CHRISTY *(doubtfully)*   It should, maybe.

WIDOW QUIN   It's more than "maybe" I'm saying, and it'd soften my heart to see you sitting so simple with your cup and cake, and you fitter to be saying your catechism than slaying your da.

PEGEEN *(at counter, washing glasses)*   There's talking when any'd see he's fit to be holding his head high with the wonders of the world. Walk on from this, for I'll not have him tormented and he destroyed travelling since Tuesday was a week.

WIDOW QUIN *(peaceably)*   We'll be walking surely when his supper's done, and you'll find we're great company, young fellow, when it's of the like of you and me you'd hear the penny poets singing in an August Fair.

CHRISTY *(innocently)*   Did you kill your father?

PEGEEN *(contemptuously)*   She did not. She hit himself[16] with a worm pick, and the rusted poison did corrode his blood the way he never overed it, and died after. That was a sneaky kind of murder did win small glory with the boys itself. *(She crosses to* CHRISTY's *left.)*

WIDOW QUIN *(with good-humour)*   If it didn't, maybe all knows a widow woman has buried her children and destroyed her man is a wiser comrade for a young lad than a girl, the like of you, who'd go helter-skeltering after any man would let you a wink upon the road.

PEGEEN *(breaking out into wild rage)*   And you'll say that, Widow Quin, and you gasping with the rage you had racing the hill beyond to look on his face.

WIDOW QUIN *(laughing derisively)*   Me, is it? Well, Father Reilly has cuteness to divide

[16] Her husband.

you now. *(She pulls* CHRISTY *up.)*   There's great temptation in a man did slay his da, and we'd best be going, young fellow; so rise up and come with me.

PEGEEN *(seizing his arm)*   He'll not stir. He's pot-boy in this place, and I'll not have him stolen off and kidnabbed while himself's abroad.

WIDOW QUIN   It'd be a crazy pot-boy'd lodge him in the shebeen where he works by day, so you'd have a right to come on, young fellow, till you see my little houseen, a perch[17] off on the rising hill.

PEGEEN   Wait till morning, Christy Mahon. Wait till you lay eyes on her leaky thatch is growing more pasture for her buck goat than her square of fields, and she without a tramp itself to keep in order her place at all.

WIDOW QUIN   When you see me contriving in my little gardens, Christy Mahon, you'll swear the Lord God formed me to be living lone, and that there isn't my match in Mayo for thatching, or mowing, or shearing sheep.

PEGEEN *(with noisy scorn)*   It's true the Lord God formed you to contrive indeed. Doesn't the world know you reared a black lamb at your own breast, so that the Lord Bishop of Connaught felt the elements of a Christian, and he eating it after in a kidney stew? Doesn't the world know you've been seen shaving the foxy skipper from France for a threepenny bit, and a sop of grass tobacco would wring the liver from a mountain goat you'd meet leaping the hills?

WIDOW QUIN *(with amusement)*   Do you hear her now, young fellow? Do you hear the way she'll be rating at your own self when a week is by?

PEGEEN *(to* CHRISTY*)*   Don't heed her. Tell her to go into her pigsty and not plague us here.

WIDOW QUIN   I'm going; but he'll come with me.

PEGEEN *(shaking him)*   Are you dumb, young fellow?

CHRISTY *(timidly, to* WIDOW QUIN*)*   God increase you; but I'm pot-boy in this place, and it's here I'd liefer stay.

PEGEEN *(triumphantly)*   Now you have heard him, and go on from this.

WIDOW QUIN *(looking round the room)*   It's lonesome this hour crossing the hill, and if he won't come along with me, I'd have a right maybe to stop this night with your-selves. Let me stretch out on the settle, Pegeen Mike; and himself can lie by the hearth.

PEGEEN *(short and fiercely)*   Faith, I won't. Quit off or I will send you now.

WIDOW QUIN *(gathering her shawl up)*   Well, it's a terror to be aged a score.[18] *(To* CHRISTY*)* God bless you now, young fellow, and let you be wary, or there's right torment will await you here if you go romancing with her like, and she waiting only, as they bade me say, on a sheepskin parchment to be wed with Shawn Keogh of Killakeen.

CHRISTY *(going to* PEGEEN *as she bolts the door)*   What's that she's after saying?

PEGEEN   Lies and blather, you've no call to mind. Well, isn't Shawn Keogh an impu-dent fellow to send up spying on me? Wait till I lay hands on him. Let him wait, I'm saying.

CHRISTY   And you're not wedding him at all?

PEGEEN   I wouldn't wed him if a bishop came walking for to join us here.

CHRISTY   That God in glory may be thanked for that.

PEGEEN   There's your bed now. I've put a quilt upon you I'm after quilting a while since with my own two hands, and you'd best stretch out now for your sleep, and may God give you a good rest till I call you in the morning when the cocks will crow.

CHRISTY *(as she goes to inner room)*   May God and Mary and St. Patrick bless you and reward you, for your kindly talk. *(She shuts the door behind her. He settles his bed*

---

[17] Short distance.   [18] She's a terror for a 20-year-old girl!

slowly, feeling the quilt with immense satisfaction.) Well, it's a clean bed and soft with it, and it's great luck and company I've won me in the end of time—two fine women fighting for the likes of me—till I'm thinking this night wasn't I a foolish fellow not to kill my father in the years gone by.

(Curtain.)

ACT II

SCENE: *As before. Brilliant morning light.* CHRISTY, *looking bright and cheerful, is cleaning a girl's boots.*

CHRISTY *(to himself, counting jugs on dresser)* Half a hundred beyond. Ten there. A score that's above. Eighty jugs. Six cups and a broken one. Two plates. A power of glasses. Bottles, a school-master'd be hard set to count, and enough in them, I'm thinking, to drunken all the wealth and wisdom of the County Clare. *(He puts down the boot carefully.)* There's her boots now, nice and decent for her evening use, and isn't it grand brushes she has? *(He puts them down and goes by degrees to the looking-glass.)* Well, this'd be a fine place to be my whole life talking out with swearing Christians, in place of my old dogs and cat, and I stalking around, smoking my pipe and drinking my fill, and never a day's work but drawing a cork an odd time, or wiping a glass, or rinsing out a shiny tumbler for a decent man. *(He takes the looking-glass from the wall and puts it on the back of a chair; then sits down in front of it and begins washing his face.)* Didn't I know rightly I was handsome, though it was the divil's own mirror we had beyond, would twist a squint across an angel's brow; and I'll be growing fine from this day, the way I'll have a soft lovely skin on me and won't be the like of the clumsy young fellows do be ploughing all times in the earth and dung. *(He starts.)* Is she coming again? *(He looks out.)* Stranger girls. God help me, where'll I hide myself away and my long neck naked to the world? *(He looks out.)* I'd best go to the room maybe till I'm dressed again. *(He gathers up his coat and the looking-glass, and runs into the inner room. The door is pushed open, and* SUSAN BRADY *looks in, and knocks on door.)*

SUSAN There's nobody in it. *(Knocks again.)*

NELLY *(pushing her in and following her with* HONOR BLAKE *and* SARA TANSEY*)* It'd be early for them both to be out walking the hill.

SUSAN I'm thinking Shawn Keogh was making game of us and there's no such man in it at all.

HONOR *(pointing to straw and quilt)* Look at that. He's been sleeping there in the night. Well, it'll be a hard case[1] if he's gone off now, the way we'll never set our eyes on a man killed his father, and we after rising early and destroying ourselves running fast on the hill.

NELLY Are you thinking them's his boots?

SARA *(taking them up)* If they are, there should be his father's track on them. Did you never read in the papers the way murdered men do bleed and drip?

SUSAN Is that blood there, Sara Tansey?

SARA *(smelling it)* That's bog water, I'm thinking, but it's his own they are surely, for I never seen the like of them for whity mud, and red mud, and turf on them, and the fine sands of the sea. That man's been walking, I'm telling you. *(She goes down right, putting on one of his boots.)*

SUSAN *(going to window)* Maybe he's stolen off to Belmullet with the boots of Mi-

---

[1] Bad luck for us.

chael James, and you'd have a right so to follow after him, Sara Tansey, and you the one yoked the ass cart and drove ten miles to set your eyes on the man bit the yellow lady's nostril on the northern shore. *(She looks out.)*

SARA *(running to window with one boot on)* Don't be talking, and we fooled today. *(Putting on other boot)* There's a pair do fit me well, and I'll be keeping them for walking to the priest, when you'd be ashamed this place, going up winter and summer with nothing worth while to confess at all.

HONOR *(who has been listening at the door)* Whisht! there's someone inside the room. *(She pushes door a chink open.)* It's a man.

*(*SARA *kicks off boots and puts them where they were. They all stand in a line looking through chink.)*

SARA   I'll call him. Mister! Mister! *(He puts in his head.)* Is Pegeen within?

CHRISTY *(coming in as meek as a mouse, with the looking-glass held behind his back)* She's above on the cnuceen,[2] seeking the nanny goats, the way she'd have a sup of goat's milk for to colour my tea.

SARA   And asking your pardon, is it you's the man killed his father?

CHRISTY *(sidling toward the nail where the glass was hanging)* I am, God help me!

SARA *(taking eggs she has brought)* Then my thousand welcomes to you, and I've run up with a brace of duck's eggs for your food today. Pegeen's ducks is no use, but these are the real rich sort. Hold out your hand and you'll see it's no lie I'm telling you.

CHRISTY *(coming forward shyly, and holding out his left hand)* They're a great and weighty size.

SUSAN   And I run up with a pat of butter, for it'd be a poor thing to have you eating your spuds dry, and you after running a great way since you did destroy your da.

CHRISTY   Thank you kindly.

HONOR   And I brought you a little cut of cake, for you should have a thin stomach on you, and you that length walking the world.

NELLY   And I brought you a little laying pullet—boiled and all she is—was crushed at the fall of night by the curate's car. Feel the fat of that breast, mister.

CHRISTY   It's bursting, surely. *(He feels it with the back of his hand, in which he holds the presents.)*

SARA   Will you pinch it? Is your right hand too sacred for to use at all? *(She slips round behind him.)* It's a glass he has. Well, I never seen to this day a man with a looking-glass held to his back. Them that kills their fathers is a vain lot surely.

(Girls giggle.)

CHRISTY *(smiling innocently and piling presents on glass)* I'm very thankful to you all today . . .

WIDOW QUIN *(coming in quickly, at door)* Sara Tansey, Susan Brady, Honor Blake! What in glory has you here at this hour of day?

GIRLS *(giggling)* That's the man killed his father.

WIDOW QUIN *(coming to them)* I know well it's the man; and I'm after putting him down in the sports below for racing, leaping, pitching, and the Lord knows what.

SARA *(exuberantly)* That's right, Widow Quin. I'll bet my dowry that he'll lick the world.

WIDOW QUIN   If you will, you'd have a right to have him fresh and nourished in place of nursing a feast.[3] *(Taking presents)* Are you fasting or fed, young fellow?

---

[2] Small hill.   [3] Needing to be fed.

CHRISTY   Fasting, if you please.

WIDOW QUIN *(loudly)*   Well, you're the lot. Stir up now and give him his breakfast. *(To* CHRISTY*)* Come here to me *(She puts him on bench beside her while the girls make tea and get his breakfast.)* and let you tell us your story before Pegeen will come, in place of grinning your ears off like the moon of May.

CHRISTY *(beginning to be pleased)*   It's a long story; you'd be destroyed listening.

WIDOW QUIN   Don't be letting on to be shy, a fine, gamey, treacherous lad the like of you. Was it in your house beyond you cracked his skull?

CHRISTY *(shy but flattered)*   It was not. We were digging spuds in his cold, sloping, stony, divil's patch of a field.

WIDOW QUIN   And you went asking money of him, or making talk of getting a wife would drive him from his farm?

CHRISTY   I did not, then; but there I was, digging and digging, and "You squinting idiot," says he, "let you walk down now and tell the priest you'll wed the Widow Casey in a score of days."

WIDOW QUIN   And what kind was she?

CHRISTY *(with horror)*   A walking terror from beyond the hills, and she two score and five years, and two hundredweights and five pounds in the weighing scales, with a limping leg on her, and a blinded eye, and she a woman of noted misbehavior with the old and young.

GIRLS *(clustering round him, serving him)*   Glory be.

WIDOW QUIN   And what did he want driving you to wed with her? *(She takes a bit of the chicken.)*

CHRISTY *(eating with growing satisfaction)*   He was letting on I was wanting a protector from the harshness of the world, and he without a thought the whole while but how he'd have her hut to live in and her gold to drink.

WIDOW QUIN   There's maybe worse than a dry hearth and a widow woman and your glass at night. So you hit him then?

CHRISTY *(getting almost excited)*   I did not. "I won't wed her," says I, "when all know she did suckle me for six weeks when I came into the world, and she a hag this day with a tongue on her has the crows and seabirds scattered, the way they wouldn't cast a shadow on her garden with the dread of her curse."

WIDOW QUIN *(teasingly)*   That one should be right company.

SARA *(eagerly)*   Don't mind her. Did you kill him then?

CHRISTY   "She's too good for the like of you," says he, "and go on now or I'll flatten you out like a crawling beast has passed under a dray." "You will not if I can help it," says I. "Go on," says he, "or I'll have the divil making garters of your limbs tonight." "You will not if I can help it," says I. *(He sits up, brandishing his mug.)*

SARA   You were right surely.

CHRISTY *(impressively)*   With that the sun came out between the cloud and the hill, and it shining green in my face. "God have mercy on your soul," says he, lifting a scythe; "or on your own," says I, raising the loy.

SUSAN   That's a grand story.

HONOR   He tells it lovely.

CHRISTY *(flattered and confident, waving bone)*   He gave a drive with the scythe, and I gave a lep to the east. Then I turned around with my back to the north, and I hit a blow on the ridge of his skull, laid him stretched out, and he split to the knob of his gullet. *(He raises the chicken bone to his Adam's apple.)*

GIRLS *(together.)*   Well, you're a marvel! Oh, God bless you! You're the lad surely!

SUSAN   I'm thinking the Lord God sent him this road to make a second husband to the Widow Quin, and she with a great yearning to be wedded, though all dread her here. Lift him on her knee, Sara Tansey.

WIDOW QUIN   Don't tease him.

SARA *(going over to dresser and counter very quickly, and getting two glasses and porter)*   You're heroes surely, and let you drink a supeen with your arms linked like the outlandish lovers in the sailor's song. *(She links their arms and gives them the glasses.)* There now. Drink a health to the wonders of the western world, the pirates, preachers, poteen-makers, with the jobbing jockies;[4] parching peelers, and the juries fill their stomachs selling judgments of the English law. *(Brandishing the bottle.)*

WIDOW QUIN   That's a right toast, Sara Tansey. Now, Christy.

(They drink with their arms linked, he drinking with his left hand, she with her right. As they are drinking, PEGEEN MIKE *comes in with a milk can and stands aghast. They all spring away from* CHRISTY. *He goes down left.* WIDOW QUIN *remains seated.)*

PEGEEN *(angrily, to* SARA*)*   What is it you're wanting?

SARA *(twisting her apron)*   An ounce of tobacco.

PEGEEN   Have you tuppence?

SARA   I've forgotten my purse.

PEGEEN   Then you'd best be getting it and not fooling us here. *(To the* WIDOW QUIN, *with more elaborate scorn)* And what is it you're wanting, Widow Quin?

WIDOW QUIN *(insolently)*   A penn'orth of starch.

PEGEEN *(breaking out)*   And you without a white shift or a shirt in your whole family since the drying of the flood. I've no starch for the like of you, and let you walk on now to Killamuck.

WIDOW QUIN *(turning to* CHRISTY, *as she goes out with the girls)*   Well, you're mighty huffy this day, Pegeen Mike, and, you young fellow, let you not forget the sports and racing when the noon is by.

(They go out.)

PEGEEN *(imperiously)*   Fling out that rubbish and put them cups away. (CHRISTY *tidies away in great haste.*) Shove in the bench by the wall. *(He does so.)* And hang that glass on the nail. What disturbed it at all?

CHRISTY *(very meekly)*   I was making myself decent only, and this a fine country for young lovely girls.

PEGEEN *(sharply)*   Whisht your talking of girls. *(Goes to counter, right.)*

CHRISTY   Wouldn't any wish to be decent in a place . . .

PEGEEN   Whisht I'm saying.

CHRISTY *(looks at her face for a moment with great misgivings, then as a last effort, takes up a loy, and goes toward her, with feigned assurance)*   It was with a loy the like of that I killed my father.

PEGEEN *(still sharply)*   You've told me that story six times since the dawn of day.

CHRISTY *(reproachfully)*   It's a queer thing you wouldn't care to be hearing it and them girls after walking four miles to be listening to me now.

PEGEEN *(turning around astonished)*   Four miles!

CHRISTY *(apologetically)*   Didn't himself say there were only four bona fides living in the place?

PEGEEN   It's bona fides by the road they are, but that lot came over the river lepping the stones. It's not three perches when you go like that, and I was down this morning

---

[4] Petty crooks or poteen-peddlers.

looking on the papers the post-boy does have in his bag. *(With meaning and emphasis)* For there was great news this day, Christopher Mahon. *(She goes into room left.)*

CHRISTY *(suspiciously)* Is it news of my murder?

PEGEEN *(inside)* Murder, indeed.

CHRISTY *(loudly)* A murdered da?

PEGEEN *(coming in again and crossing right)* There was not, but a story filled half a page of the hanging of a man. Ah, that should be a fearful end, young fellow, and it worst of all for a man who destroyed his da, for the like of him would get small mercies, and when it's dead he is, they'd put him in a narrow grave, with cheap sacking wrapping him round, and pour down quicklime on his head, the way you'd see a woman pouring any frish-frash[5] from a cup.

CHRISTY *(very miserably)* Oh, God help me. Are you thinking I'm safe? You were saying at the fall of night, I was shut of jeopardy and I here with yourselves.

PEGEEN *(severely)* You'll be shut of jeopardy in no place if you go talking with a pack of wild girls the like of them do be walking abroad with the peelers, talking whispers at the fall of night.

CHRISTY *(with terror)* And you're thinking they'd tell?

PEGEEN *(with mock sympathy)* Who knows, God help you.

CHRISTY *(loudly)* What joy would they have to bring hanging to the likes of me?

PEGEEN It's queer joys they have, and who knows the thing they'd do, if it'd make the green stones cry itself to think of you swaying and swiggling at the butt of a rope, and you with a fine, stout neck, God bless you! the way you'd be a half an hour, in great anguish, getting your death.

CHRISTY *(getting his boots and putting them on)* If there's that terror of them, it'd be best, maybe, I went on wandering like Esau or Cain and Abel on the sides of Neifin or the Erris plain.

PEGEEN *(beginning to play with him)* It would, maybe, for I've heard the Circuit Judges this place is a heartless crew.

CHRISTY *(bitterly)* It's more than Judges this place is a heartless crew. *(Looking up at her)* And isn't it a poor thing to be starting again and I a lonesome fellow will be looking out on women and girls the way the needy fallen spirits do be looking on the Lord?

PEGEEN What call have you to be that lonesome when there's poor girls walking Mayo in their thousands now?

CHRISTY *(grimly)* It's well you know what call I have. It's well you know it's a lonesome thing to be passing small towns with the lights shining sideways when the night is down, or going in strange places with a dog noising before you and a dog noising behind, or drawn to the cities where you'd hear a voice kissing and talking deep love in every shadow of the ditch, and you passing on with an empty, hungry stomach failing from your heart.

PEGEEN I'm thinking you're an odd man, Christy Mahon. The oddest walking fellow I ever set my eyes on to this hour today.

CHRISTY What would any be but odd men and they living lonesome in the world?

PEGEEN I'm not odd, and I'm my whole life with my father only.

CHRISTY *(with infinite admiration)* How would a lovely handsome woman the like of you be lonesome when all men should be thronging around to hear the sweetness of your voice, and the little infant children should be pestering your steps I'm thinking, and you walking the roads.

---

[5] Slops, dregs.

PEGEEN　I'm hard set to know what way a coaxing fellow the like of yourself should be lonesome either.

CHRISTY　Coaxing?

PEGEEN　Would you have me think a man never talked with the girls would have the words you've spoken today? It's only letting on you are to be lonesome, the way you'd get around me now.

CHRISTY　I wish to God I was letting on; but I was lonesome all times, and born lonesome, I'm thinking, as the moon of dawn. *(Going to door.)*

PEGEEN *(puzzled by his talk)*　Well, it's a story I'm not understanding at all why you'd be worse than another, Christy Mahon, and you a fine lad with the great savagery to destroy your da.

CHRISTY　It's little I'm understanding myself, saving only that my heart's scalded this day, and I am going off stretching out the earth between us, the way I'll not be waking near you another dawn of the year till the two of us do arise to hope or judgment with the saints of God, and now I'd best be going with my wattle in my hand, for hanging is a poor thing *(Turning to go)*, and it's little welcome only is left me in this house today.

PEGEEN *(sharply)*　Christy! *(He turns round.)* Come here to me. *(He goes toward her.)* Lay down that switch and throw some sods on the fire. You're pot-boy in this place, and I'll not have you mitch[6] off from us now.

CHRISTY　You were saying I'd be hanged if I stay.

PEGEEN *(quite kindly at last)*　I'm after going down and reading the fearful crimes of Ireland for two weeks or three, and there wasn't a word of your murder. *(Getting up and going over to the counter)* They've likely not found the body. You're safe so with ourselves.

CHRISTY *(astonished, slowly)*　It's making game of me you were *(Following her with fearful joy)*, and I can stay so, working at your side, and I not lonesome from this mortal day.

PEGEEN　What's to hinder you from staying, except the widow woman or the young girls would inveigle you off?

CHRISTY *(with rapture)*　And I'll have your words from this day filling my ears, and that look is come upon you meeting my two eyes, and I watching you loafing around in the warm sun, or rinsing your ankles when the night is come.

PEGEEN *(kindly, but a little embarrassed)*　I'm thinking you'll be a loyal young lad to have working around, and if you vexed me a while since with your leaguing with the girls, I wouldn't give a thraneen[7] for a lad hadn't a mighty spirit in him and a gamey heart.

(SHAWN KEOGH *runs in carrying a cleeve*[8] *on his back, followed by the* WIDOW QUIN.)

SHAWN *(to* PEGEEN*)*　I was passing below, and I seen your mountainy sheep eating cabbages in Jimmy's field. Run up or they'll be bursting surely.

PEGEEN　Oh, God mend them! *(She puts a shawl over her head and runs out.)*

CHRISTY *(looking from one to the other, still in high spirit)*　I'd best go to her aid maybe. I'm handy with ewes.

WIDOW QUIN *(closing the door)*　She can do that much, and there is Shaneen has long speeches for to tell you now. *(She sits down with an amused smile.)*

SHAWN *(taking something from his pocket and offering it to* CHRISTY*)*　Do you see that, mister?

CHRISTY *(looking at it)*　The half of a ticket to the Western States![9]

SHAWN *(trembling with anxiety)*　I'll give it to you and my new hat *(Pulling it out of*

---

[6] Sneak.　　[7] Worthless token.　　[8] Basket.　　[9] The United States.

hamper); and my breeches with the double seat *(Pulling it off);* and my new coat is woven from the blackest shearings for three miles around *(Giving him the coat);* I'll give you the whole of them, and my blessing, and the blessing of Father Reilly itself, maybe, if you'll quit from this and leave us in the peace we had till last night at the fall of dark.

CHRISTY *(with a new arrogance)* And for what is it you're wanting to get shut of me?

SHAWN *(looking to the* WIDOW *for help)* I'm a poor scholar with middling faculties to coin a lie, so I'll tell you the truth, Christy Mahon. I'm wedding with Pegeen beyond, and I don't think well of having a clever fearless man the like of you dwelling in her house.

CHRISTY *(almost pugnaciously)* And you'd be using bribery for to banish me?

SHAWN *(in an imploring voice)* Let you not take it badly, mister honey, isn't beyond the best place for you where you'll have golden chains and shiny coats and you riding upon hunters with the ladies of the land. *(He makes an eager sign to the* WIDOW QUIN *to come to help him.)*

WIDOW QUIN *(coming over)* It's true for him, and you'd best quit off and not have that poor girl setting her mind on you, for there's Shaneen thinks she wouldn't suit you though all is saying that she'll wed you now.

*(*CHRISTY *beams with delight.)*

SHAWN *(in terrified earnest)* She wouldn't suit you, and she with the divil's own temper the way you'd be strangling one another in a score of days. *(He makes the movement of strangling with his hands.)* It's the like of me only that she's fit for, a quiet simple fellow wouldn't raise a hand upon her if she scratched itself.

WIDOW QUIN *(putting* SHAWN's *hat on* CHRISTY) Fit them clothes on you anyhow, young fellow, and he'd maybe loan them to you for the sports. *(Pushing him toward inner door)* Fit them on and you can give your answer when you have them tried.

CHRISTY *(beaming, delighted with the clothes)* I will then. I'd like herself to see me in them tweeds and hat. *(He goes into room and shuts the door.)*

SHAWN *(in great anxiety)* He'd like herself to see them. He'll not leave us, Widow Quin. He's a score of divils in him the way it's well nigh certain he will wed Pegeen.

WIDOW QUIN *(jeeringly)* It's true all girls are fond of courage and do hate the like of you.

SHAWN *(walking about in desperation)* Oh, Widow Quin, what'll I be doing now? I'd inform again him, but he'd burst from Kilmainham[10] and he'd be sure and certain to destroy me. If I wasn't so God-fearing, I'd near have courage to come behind him and run a pike into his side. Oh, it's a hard case to be an orphan and not to have your father that you're used to, and you'd easy kill and make youself a hero in the sight of all. *(Coming up to her)* Oh, Widow Quin, will you find me some contrivance when I've promised you a ewe?

WIDOW QUIN A ewe's a small thing, but what would you give me if I did wed him and did save you so?

SHAWN *(with astonishment)* You?

WIDOW QUIN Aye. Would you give me the red cow you have and the mountainy ram, and the right of way across your rye path, and a load of dung at Michaelmas, and turbary[11] upon the western hill?

SHAWN *(radiant with hope)* I would surely, and I'd give you the wedding-ring I have, and the loan of a new suit, the way you'd have him decent on the wedding-day. I'd give

---

[10] Penitentiary in Dublin.   [11] The right to dig turf or peat on another's land, or the piece of land itself. Widow Quin seems most interested in the right.

you two kids for your dinner, and a gallon of poteen, and I'd call the piper on the long car to your wedding from Crossmolina or from Ballina. I'd give you . . .

WIDOW QUIN   That'll do so, and let you whisht, for he's coming now again.

(CHRISTY *comes in very natty in the new clothes.* WIDOW QUIN *goes to him admiringly.*)

WIDOW QUIN   If you seen yourself now, I'm thinking you'd be too proud to speak to us at all, and it'd be a pity surely to have your like sailing from Mayo to the Western World.

CHRISTY *(as proud as a peacock)*   I'm not going. If this is a poor place itself, I'll make myself contented to be lodging here.

(WIDOW QUIN *makes a sign to* SHAWN *to leave them.*)

SHAWN   Well, I'm going measuring the racecourse while the tide is low, so I'll leave you the garments and my blessing for the sports today. God bless you! *(He wriggles out.)*

WIDOW QUIN *(admiring* CHRISTY*)*   Well, you're mighty spruce, young fellow. Sit down now while you're quiet till you talk with me.

CHRISTY *(swaggering)*   I'm going abroad on the hillside for to seek Pegeen.

WIDOW QUIN   You'll have time and plenty for to seek Pegeen, and you heard me saying at the fall of night the two of us should be great company.

CHRISTY   From this out I'll have no want of company when all sorts is bringing me their food and clothing, *(He swaggers to the door, tightening his belt.)* the way they'd set their eyes upon a gallant orphan cleft his father with one blow to the breeches belt. *(He opens door, then staggers back.)* Saints of glory! Holy angels from the throne of light!

WIDOW QUIN *(going over)*   What ails you?

CHRISTY   It's the walking spirit of my murdered da!

WIDOW QUIN *(looking out)*   Is it that tramper?

CHRISTY *(wildly)*   Where'll I hide my poor body from that ghost of hell?

(The door is pushed open, and old MAHON *appears on threshold.* CHRISTY *darts in behind door.)*

WIDOW QUIN *(in great amusement)*   God save you, my poor man.

MAHON *(gruffly)*   Did you see a young lad passing this way in the early morning or the fall of night?

WIDOW QUIN   You're a queer kind to walk in not saluting at all.

MAHON   Did you see the young lad?

WIDOW QUIN *(stiffly)*   What kind was he?

MAHON   An ugly young streeler[12] with a murderous gob[13] on him, and a little switch in his hand. I met a tramper seen him coming this way at the fall of night.

WIDOW QUIN   There's harvest hundreds do be passing these days for the Sligo boat. For what is it you're wanting him, my poor man?

MAHON   I want to destroy him for breaking the head on me with the clout of a loy. *(He takes off a big hat, and shows his head in a mass of bandages and plaster, with some pride.)* It was he did that, and amn't I a great wonder to think I've traced him ten days with that rent in my crown?

WIDOW QUIN *(taking his head in both hands and examining it with extreme delight)* That was a great blow. And who hit you? A robber maybe?

MAHON   It was my own son hit me, and he the divil a robber, or anything else, but a dirty, stuttering lout.

WIDOW QUIN *(letting go his skull and wiping her hands in her apron)*   You'd best be wary of a mortified[14] scalp, I think they call it, lepping around with that wound in the

---

[12] Stroller, vagrant.   [13] Face.   [14] Poisoned, perhaps gangrenous; dying.

splendour of the sun. It was a bad blow surely, and you should have vexed him fearful to make him strike that gash in his da.

MAHON   Is it me?

WIDOW QUIN *(amusing herself)*   Aye. And isn't it a great shame when the old and hardened do torment the young?

MAHON *(raging)*   Torment him, is it? And I after holding out with the patience of a martyred saint till there's nothing but destruction on, and I'm driven out in my old age with none to aid me.

WIDOW QUIN *(greatly amused)*   It's a sacred wonder the way that wickedness will spoil a man.

MAHON   My wickedness, is it? Amn't I after saying it is himself has me destroyed, and he a lier on walls, a talker of folly, a man you'd see stretched the half of the day in the brown ferns with his belly to the sun.

WIDOW QUIN   Not working at all?

MAHON   The divil a work, or if he did itself, you'd see him raising up a haystack like the stalk of a rush, or driving our last cow till he broke her leg at the hip, and when he wasn't at that he'd be fooling over little birds he had—finches and felts[15]—or making mugs at his own self in the bit of a glass we had hung on the wall.

WIDOW QUIN *(looking at* CHRISTY*)*   What way was he so foolish? It was running wild after the girls maybe?

MAHON *(with a shout of derision)*   Running wild, is it? If he seen a red petticoat coming swinging over the hill, he'd be off to hide in the sticks, and you'd see him shooting out his sheep's eyes between the little twigs and the leaves, and his two ears rising like a hare looking out through a gap. Girls, indeed!

WIDOW QUIN   It was drink maybe?

MAHON   And he a poor fellow would get drunk on the smell of a pint. He'd a queer rotten stomach, I'm telling you, and when I gave him three pulls from my pipe a while since, he was taken with contortions till I had to send him in the ass cart to the females' nurse.

WIDOW QUIN *(clasping her hands)*   Well, I never till this day heard tell of a man the like of that!

MAHON   I'd take a mighty oath you didn't surely, and wasn't he the laughing joke of every female woman where four baronies meet, the way the girls would stop their weeding if they seen him coming the road to let a roar at him, and call him the looney of Mahon's.

WIDOW QUIN   I'd give the world and all to see the like of him. What kind was he?

MAHON   A small low fellow.

WIDOW QUIN   And dark?

MAHON   Dark and dirty.

WIDOW QUIN *(considering)*   I'm thinking I seen him.

MAHON *(eagerly)*   An ugly young blackguard.

WIDOW QUIN   A hideous, fearful villain, and the spit of you.

MAHON   What way is he fled?

WIDOW QUIN   Gone over the hills to catch a coasting steamer to the north or south.

MAHON   Could I pull up on him now?

WIDOW QUIN   If you'll cross the sands below where the tide is out, you'll be in it as soon as himself, for he had to go round ten miles by the top of the bay. *(She points to the door.)* Strike down by the head beyond and then follow on the roadway to the north and east.

---

[15] Thrushes.

(MAHON *goes abruptly.*)

WIDOW QUIN *(shouting after him)*   Let you give him a good vengeance when you come up with him, but don't put yourself in the power of the law, for it'd be a poor thing to see a judge in his black cap reading out his sentence on a civil warrior the like of you. *(She swings the door to and looks at* CHRISTY, *who is cowering in terror, for a moment, then she bursts into a laugh.)* Well, you're the walking Playboy[16] of the Western World, and that's the poor man you had divided to his breeches belt.

CHRISTY *(looking out: then, to her)*   What'll Pegeen say when she hears that story? What'll she be saying to me now?

WIDOW QUIN   She'll knock the head of you, I'm thinking, and drive you from the door. God help her to be taking you for a wonder, and you a little schemer making up the story you destroyed your da.

CHRISTY *(turning to the door, nearly speechless with rage, half to himself)*   To be letting on he was dead, and coming back to his life, and following after me like an old weasel tracing a rat, and coming in here laying desolation between my own self and the fine women of Ireland, and he a kind of carcase that you'd fling upon the sea . . .

WIDOW QUIN *(more soberly)*   There's talking for a man's one only son.

CHRISTY *(breaking out)*   His one son, is it? May I meet him with one tooth and it aching, and one eye to be seeing seven and seventy divils in the twists of the road, and one old timber leg on him to limp into the scalding grave. *(Looking out)* There he is now crossing the strands, and that the Lord God would send a high wave to wash him from the world.

WIDOW QUIN *(scandalized)*   Have you no shame? *(Putting her hand on his shoulder and turning him round)* What ails you? Near crying, is it?

CHRISTY *(in despair and grief)*   Amn't I after seeing the lovelight of the star of knowledge shining from her brow, and hearing words would put you thinking on the holy Brigid speaking to the infant saints, and now she'll be turning again, and speaking hard words to me, like an old woman with a spavindy[17] ass she'd have, urging on a hill.

WIDOW QUIN   There's poetry talk for a girl you'd see itching and scratching, and she with a stale stink of poteen on her from selling in the shop.

CHRISTY *(impatiently)*   It's her like is fitted to be handling merchandise in the heavens above, and what'll I be doing now, I ask you, and I a kind of wonder was jilted by the heavens when a day was by.

(There is a distant noise of girls' voices. WIDOW QUIN *looks from window and comes to him, hurriedly.)*

WIDOW QUIN   You'll be doing like myself, I'm thinking, when I did destroy my man, for I'm above many's the day, odd times in great spirits, abroad in the sunshine, darning a stocking or stitching a shift; and odd times again looking out on the schooners, hookers, trawlers is sailing the sea, and I thinking on the gallant hairy fellows are drifting beyond, and myself long years living alone.

CHRISTY *(interested)*   You're like me, so.

WIDOW QUIN   I am your like, and it's for that I'm taking a fancy to you, and I with my little houseen above where there'd be myself to tend you, and none to ask were you a murderer or what at all.

CHRISTY   And what would I be doing if I left Pegeen?

WIDOW QUIN   I've nice jobs you could be doing, gathering shells to make a whitewash for our hut within, building up a little goose-house, or stretching a new skin on an

---

[16] Here used in the sense of *hoaxer* or *big talker*.   [17] Lame.

old curragh I have, and if my hut is far from all sides, it's there you'll meet the wisest old men, I tell you, at the corner of my wheel, and it's there yourself and me will have great times whispering and hugging. . . .

VOICES *(outside, calling far away)*   Christy! Christy Mahon! Christy!

CHRISTY   Is it Pegeen Mike?

WIDOW QUIN   It's the young girls, I'm thinking, coming to bring you to the sports below, and what is it you'll have me to tell them now?

CHRISTY   Aid me for to win Pegeen. It's herself only that I'm seeking now. (WIDOW QUIN *gets up and goes to window.*) Aid me for to win her, and I'll be asking God to stretch a hand to you in the hour of death, and lead you short cuts through the Meadows of Ease, and up the floor of Heaven to the Footstool of the Virgin's Son.

WIDOW QUIN   There's praying.

VOICES *(nearer)*   Christy! Christy Mahon!

CHRISTY *(with agitation)*   They're coming. Will you swear to aid and save me for the love of Christ?

WIDOW QUIN *(looks at him for a moment)*   If I aid you, will you swear to give me a right of way I want, and a mountainy ram, and a load of dung at Michaelmas, the time that you'll be master here?

CHRISTY   I will, by the elements and stars of night.

WIDOW QUIN   Then we'll not say a word of the old fellow, the way Pegeen won't know your story till the end of time.

CHRISTY   And if he chances to return again?

WIDOW QUIN   We'll swear he's a maniac and not your da. I could take an oath I seen him raving on the sands today.

(Girls run in.)

SUSAN   Come on to the sports below. Pegeen says you're to come.

SARA TANSEY   The lepping's beginning, and we've a jockey's suit to fit upon you for the mule race on the sands below.

HONOR   Come on, will you?

CHRISTY   I will then if Pegeen's beyond.

SARA TANSEY   She's in the boreen[18] making game of Shaneen Keogh.

CHRISTY   Then I'll be going to her now. *(He runs out followed by the girls.)*

WIDOW QUIN   Well, if the worst comes in the end of all, it'll be great game to see there's none to pity him but a widow woman, the like of me, has buried her children and destroyed her man. *(She goes out.)*

(Curtain.)

ACT III

SCENE: *As before. Later in the day.* JIMMY *comes in, slightly drunk.*

JIMMY *(calls)*   Pegeen! *(Crosses to inner door)* Pegeen Mike! *(comes back again into the room)* Pegeen! (PHILLY *comes in in the same state.*) (*To* PHILLY) Did you see herself?

PHILLY   I did not; but I sent Shawn Keogh with the ass cart for to bear him home. *(Trying cupboards which are locked)* Well, isn't he a nasty man to get into such staggers at

---

[18] Lane, country road.

a morning wake? and isn't herself the divil's daughter for locking, and she so fussy after that young gaffer, you might take your death with drought and none to heed you?

JIMMY   It's little wonder she'd be fussy, and he after bringing bankrupt ruin on the roulette man, and the trick-o'-the-loop man, and breaking the nose of the cockshot-man, and winning all in the sports below, racing, lepping, dancing, and the Lord knows what! He's right luck, I'm telling you.

PHILLY   If he has, he'll be rightly hobbled yet, and he not able to say ten words without making a brag of the way he killed his father, and the great blow he hit with the loy.

JIMMY   A man can't hang by his own informing, and his father should be rotten by now.

(Old MAHON *passes window slowly.)*

PHILLY   Supposing a man's digging spuds in that field with a long spade, and supposing he flings up the two halves of that skull, what'll be said then in the papers and the courts of law?

JIMMY   They'd say it was an old Dane, maybe, was drowned in the flood. *(Old* MAHON *comes in and sits down near door listening.)* Did you never hear tell of the skulls they have in the city of Dublin, ranged out like blue jugs in a cabin of Connaught?

PHILLY   And you believe that?

JIMMY *(pugnaciously)*   Didn't a lad see them and he after coming from harvesting in the Liverpool boat? "They have them there," says he, "making a show of the great people there was one time walking the world. White skulls and black skulls and yellow skulls, and some with full teeth, and some haven't only but one."

PHILLY   It was no lie, maybe, for when I was a young lad there was a graveyard beyond the house with the remnants of a man who had thighs as long as your arm. He was a horrid man, I'm telling you, and there was many a fine Sunday I'd put him together for fun, and he with shiny bones, you wouldn't meet the like of these days in the cities of the world.

MAHON *(getting up)*   You wouldn't, is it? Lay your eyes on that skull, and tell me where and when there was another the like of it, is splintered only from the blow of a loy.

PHILLY   Glory be to God! And who hit you at all?

MAHON *(triumphantly)*   It was my own son hit me. Would you believe that?

JIMMY   Well, there's wonders hidden in the heart of man!

PHILLY *(suspiciously)*   And what way was it done?

MAHON *(wandering about the room)*   I'm after walking hundreds and long scores of miles, winning clean beds and the fill of my belly four times in the day, and I doing nothing but telling stories of that naked truth. *(He comes to them a little aggressively.)* Give me a supeen and I'll tell you now.

(WIDOW QUIN *comes in and stands aghast behind him. He is facing* JIMMY *and* PHILLY, *who are on the left.)*

JIMMY   Ask herself beyond. She's the stuff hidden in her shawl.

WIDOW QUIN *(coming to* MAHON *quickly)*   You here, is it? You didn't go far at all?

MAHON   I seen the coasting steamer passing, and I got a drought upon me and a cramping leg, so I said, "The divil go along with him," and turned again. *(Looking under her shawl)* And let you give me a supeen, for I'm destroyed travelling since Tuesday was a week.

WIDOW QUIN *(getting a glass, in a cajoling tone)*   Sit down then by the fire and take your ease for a space. You've a right to be destroyed indeed, with your walking, and fighting, and facing the sun. *(Giving him poteen from a stone jar she has brought in)* There now is a drink for you, and may it be to your happiness and length of life.

MAHON *(taking glass greedily and sitting down by fire)*   God increase you!

WIDOW QUIN *(taking men to the right stealthily)*   Do you know what? That man's raving from his wound today, for I met him a while since telling a rambling tale of a tinker had him destroyed. Then he heard of Christy's deed, and he up and says it was his son had cracked his skull. O, isn't madness a fright, for he'll go killing someone yet, and he thinking it's the man has struck him so?

JIMMY *(entirely convinced)*   It's a fright, surely. I knew a party was kicked in the head by a red mare, and he went killing horses a great while, till he eat the insides of a clock and died after.

PHILLY *(with suspicion)*   Did he see Christy?

WIDOW QUIN   He didn't. *(With a warning gesture)* Let you not be putting him in mind of him, or you'll be likely summoned if there's murder done. *(Looking round at* MAHON*)* Whisht! He's listening. Wait now till you hear me taking him easy and unravelling all. *(She goes to* MAHON.) And what way are you feeling, mister? Are you in contentment now?

MAHON *(slightly emotional from his drink)*   I'm poorly only, for it's a hard story the way I'm left today, when it was I did tend him from his hour of birth, and he a dunce never reached his second book, the way he'd come from school, many's the day, with his legs lamed under him, and he blackened with his beatings like a tinker's ass. It's a hard story, I'm saying, the way some do have their next and nighest raising up a hand of murder on them, and some is lonesome getting their death with lamentation in the dead of night.

WIDOW QUIN *(not knowing what to say)*   To hear you talking so quiet, who'd know you were the same fellow we seen pass today?

MAHON   I'm the same surely. The wrack and ruin of three score years; and it's a terror to live that length, I tell you, and to have your sons going to the dogs against you, and you wore out scolding them, and skelping them, and God knows what.

PHILLY *(to* JIMMY)   He's not raving. *(To* WIDOW QUIN) Will you ask him what kind was his son?

WIDOW QUIN *(to* MAHON, *with a peculiar look)*   Was your son that hit you a lad of one year and a score maybe, a great hand at racing and lepping and licking the world?

MAHON *(turning on her with a roar of rage)*   Didn't you hear me say he was the fool of men, the way from this out he'll know the orphan's lot with old and young making game of him and they swearing, raging, kicking at him like a mangy cur.

(A great burst of cheering outside, some way off.)

MAHON *(putting his hands to his ears)*   What in the name of God do they want roaring below?

WIDOW QUIN *(with the shade of a smile)*   They're cheering a young lad, the champion Playboy of the Western World.

(More cheering.)

MAHON *(going to window)*   It'd split my heart to hear them, and I with pulses in my brain-pan for a week gone by. Is it racing they are?

JIMMY *(looking from door)*   It is then. They are mounting him for the mule race will be run upon the sands. That's the playboy on the winkered mule.

MAHON *(puzzled)*   That lad, is it? If you said it was a fool he was, I'd have laid a mighty oath he was the likeness of my wandering son. *(Uneasily, putting his hand to his head)* Faith, I'm thinking I'll go walking for to view the race.

WIDOW QUIN *(stopping him, sharply)*   You will not. You'd best take the road to Belmullet, and not be dilly-dallying in this place where there isn't a spot you could sleep.

PHILLY *(coming forward)*   Don't mind her. Mount there on the bench and you'll have a view of the whole. They're hurrying before the tide will rise, and it'd be near over if you went down the pathway through the crags below.

MAHON *(mounts on bench,* WIDOW QUIN *beside him)* That's a right view again the edge of the sea. They're coming now from the point. He's leading. Who is he at all?

WIDOW QUIN He's the champion of the world, I tell you, and there isn't a hop'orth isn't falling lucky to his hands today.

PHILLY *(looking out, interested in the race)* Look at that. They're pressing him now.

JIMMY He'll win it yet.

PHILLY Take your time, Jimmy Farrell. It's too soon to say.

WIDOW QUIN *(shouting)* Watch him taking the gate. There's riding.

JIMMY *(cheering)* More power to the young lad!

MAHON He's passing the third.

JIMMY He'll lick them yet!

WIDOW QUIN He'd lick them if he was running races with a score itself.

MAHON Look at the mule he has, kicking the stars.

WIDOW QUIN There was a lep! *(Catching hold of* MAHON *in her excitement)* He's fallen! He's mounted again! Faith, he's passing them all!

JIMMY Look at him skelping her!

PHILLY And the mountain girls hooshing him on!

JIMMY It's the last turn! The post's cleared for them now!

MAHON Look at the narrow place. He'll be into the bogs! *(With a yell)* Good rider! He's through it again!

JIMMY He's neck and neck!

MAHON Good boy to him! Flames, but he's in!

(Great cheering, in which all join.)

MAHON *(with hesitation)* What's that? They're raising him up. They're coming this way. *(With a roar of rage and astonishment)* It's Christy! by the stars of God! I'd know his way of spitting and he astride the moon.

(He jumps down and makes for the door, but WIDOW QUIN *catches him and pulls him back.)*

WIDOW QUIN Stay quiet, will you. That's not your son. *(To* JIMMY*)* Stop him, or you'll get a month for the abetting of manslaughter and be fined as well.

JIMMY I'll hold him.

MAHON *(struggling)* Let me out! Let me out, the lot of you! till I have my vengeance on his head today.

WIDOW QUIN *(shaking him, vehemently)* That's not your son. That's a man is going to make a marriage with the daughter of this house, a place with fine trade, with a license, and with poteen too.

MAHON *(amazed)* That man marrying a decent and a moneyed girl! Is it mad yous are? Is it in a crazy-house for females that I'm landed now?

WIDOW QUIN It's mad yourself is with the blow upon your head. That lad is the wonder of the Western World.

MAHON I seen it's my son.

WIDOW QUIN You seen that you're mad. *(Cheering outside)* Do you hear them cheering him in the zig-zags of the road? Aren't you after saying that your son's a fool, and how would they be cheering a true idiot born?

MAHON *(getting distressed)* It's maybe out of reason that that man's himself. *(Cheering again)* There's none surely will go cheering him. Oh, I'm raving with a madness that would fright the world! *(He sits down with his hand to his head.)* There was one time I seen ten scarlet divils letting on they'd cork my spirit in a gallon can; and one time I seen rats as big as badgers sucking the life blood from the butt of my lug;[1] but I never till this day confused that dribbling idiot with a likely man. I'm destroyed surely.

WIDOW QUIN   And who'd wonder when it's your brain-pan that is gaping now?

MAHON   Then the blight of the sacred drought upon myself and him, for I never went mad to this day, and I not three weeks with the Limerick girls drinking myself silly, and parlatic[2] from the dusk to dawn. *(To* WIDOW QUIN, *suddenly)* Is my visage astray?

WIDOW QUIN   It is then. You're a sniggering maniac, a child could see.

MAHON *(getting up more cheerfully)*   Then I'd best be going to the union[3] beyond, and there'll be a welcome before me, I tell you *(With great pride),* and I a terrible and fearful case, the way that there I was one time, screeching in a straitened waistcoat, with seven doctors writing out my sayings a printed book. Would you believe that?

WIDOW QUIN   If you're a wonder itself, you'd best be hasty, for them lads caught a maniac one time and pelted the poor creature till he ran out, raving and foaming, and was drowned in the sea.

MAHON *(with philosophy)*   It's true mankind is the divil when your head's astray. Let me out now and I'll slip down the boreen, and not see them so.

WIDOW QUIN *(showing him out)*   That's it. Run to the right, and not a one will see.

(He runs off.)

PHILLY *(wisely)*   You're at some gaming, Widow Quin; but I'll walk after him and give him his dinner and a time to rest, and I'll see then if he's raving or as sane as you.

WIDOW QUIN *(annoyed)*   If you go near that lad, let you be wary of your head, I'm saying. Didn't you hear him telling he was crazed at times?

PHILLY   I heard him telling a power; and I'm thinking we'll have right sport, before night will fall. *(He goes out.)*

JIMMY   Well, Philly's a conceited and foolish man. How could that madman have his senses and his brain-pan slit? I'll go after them and see him turn on Philly now.

(He goes; WIDOW QUIN *hides poteen behind counter. Then hubbub outside.)*

VOICES   There you are! Good jumper! Grand lepper! Darlint boy! He's the racer! Bear him on, will you!

*(*CHRISTY *comes in, in jockey's dress, with* PEGEEN MIKE, SARA, *and other girls, and men.)*

PEGEEN *(to crowd)*   Go on now and don't destroy him and he drenching with sweat. Go along, I'm saying, and have your tug-of-warring till he's dried his skin.

CROWD   Here's his prizes! A bagpipes! A fiddle was played by a poet in the years gone by! A flat and three-thorned blackthorn would lick the scholars out of Dublin town!

CHRISTY *(taking prizes from the men)*   Thank you kindly, the lot of you. But you'd say it was little only I did this day if you'd seen me a while since striking my one single blow.

TOWN CRIER *(outside, ringing a bell)*   Take notice, last event of this day! Tug-of-warring on the green below! Come on, the lot of you! Great achievements for all Mayo men!

PEGEEN   Go on, and leave him for to rest and dry. Go on, I tell you, for he'll do no more. *(She hustles crowd out;* WIDOW QUIN *following them.)*

MEN *(going)*   Come on, then. Good luck for the while!

PEGEEN *(radiantly, wiping his face with her shawl)*   Well, you're the lad, and you'll

---

[1] Lobe of my ear.   [2] Paralyzed; Mahon's version of *paralytic.*   [3] A workhouse and hospital for the unemployed.

have great times from this out when you could win that wealth of prizes, and you sweating in the heat of noon!

CHRISTY *(looking at her with delight)* I'll have great times if I win the crowning prize I'm seeking now, and that's your promise that you'll wed me in a fortnight, when our banns is called.

PEGEEN *(backing away from him)* You're right daring to go ask me that, when all knows you'll be starting to some girl in your own townland, when your father's rotten in four months, or five.

CHRISTY *(indignantly)* Starting from you, is it? *(He follows her.)* I will not, then, and when the airs is warming in four months, or five, it's then yourself and me should be pacing Neifin in the dews of night, the times sweet smells do be rising, and you'd see a little shiny new moon, maybe, sinking on the hills.

PEGEEN *(looking at him playfully)* And it's that kind of a poacher's love you'd make, Christy Mahon, on the sides of Neifin, when the night is down?

CHRISTY It's little you'll think if my love's a poacher's, or an earl's itself, when you'll feel my two hands stretched around you, and I squeezing kisses on your puckered lips, till I'd feel a kind of pity for the Lord God in all ages sitting lonesome in his golden chair.

PEGEEN That'll be right fun, Christy Mahon, and any girl would walk her heart out before she'd meet a young man was your like for eloquence, or talk, at all.

CHRISTY *(encouraged)* Let you wait, to hear me talking, till we're astray in Erris, when Good Friday's by, drinking a sup from a well, and making mighty kisses with our wetted mouths, or gaming in a gap of sunshine, with yourself stretched back unto your necklace, in the flowers of the earth.

PEGEEN *(in a lower voice, moved by his tone)* I'd be nice so, is it?

CHRISTY *(with rapture)* If the mitred bishops seen you that time, they'd be the like of the holy prophets, I'm thinking, do be straining the bars of Paradise to lay eyes on the Lady Helen of Troy, and she abroad, pacing back and forward, with a nosegay in her golden shawl.

PEGEEN *(with real tenderness)* And what is it I have, Christy Mahon, to make me fitting entertainment for the like of you, that has such poet's talking, and such bravery of heart?

CHRISTY *(in a low voice)* Isn't there the light of seven heavens in your heart alone, the way you'll be an angel's lamp to me from this out, and I abroad in the darkness, spearing salmons in the Owen, or the Carrowmore?

PEGEEN If I was your wife, I'd be along with you those nights, Christy Mahon, the way you'd see I was a great hand at coaxing bailiffs, or coining funny nicknames for the stars of night.

CHRISTY You, is it? Taking your death in the hailstones, or in the fogs of dawn.

PEGEEN Yourself and me would shelter easy in a narrow bush *(With a qualm of dread)*, but we're only talking, maybe, for this would be a poor, thatched place to hold a fine lad is the like of you.

CHRISTY *(putting his arm around her)* If I wasn't a good Christian, it's on my naked knees I'd be saying my prayers and paters to every jackstraw you have roofing your head, and every stony pebble is paving the laneway to your door.

PEGEEN *(radiantly)* If that's the truth, I'll be burning candles from this out to the miracles of God that have brought you from the south today, and I, with my gowns bought ready, the way that I can wed you, and not wait at all.

CHRISTY It's miracles, and that's the truth. Me there toiling a long while, and walking a long while, not knowing at all I was drawing all times nearer to this holy day.

PEGEEN And myself, a girl, was tempted often to go sailing the seas till I'd marry a

Jew-man, with ten kegs of gold, and I not knowing at all there was the like of you drawing nearer, like the stars of God.

CHRISTY And to think I'm long years hearing women talking that talk, to all bloody fools, and this the first time I've heard the like of your voice talking sweetly for my own delight.

PEGEEN And to think it's me is talking sweetly, Christy Mahon, and I the fright of seven townlands for my biting tongue. Well, the heart's a wonder; and, I'm thinking, there won't be our like in Mayo, for gallant lovers, from this hour, today. *(Drunken singing is heard outside.)* There's my father coming from the wake, and when he's had his sleep we'll tell him, for he's peaceful then. *(They separate.)*

MICHAEL *(singing outside)*

> The jailor and the turnkey
>   They quickly ran us down,
> And brought us back as prisoners
>   Once more to Cavan town.

(He comes in supported by SHAWN.*)*

> There we lay bewailing
>   All in a prison bound. . . .

(He sees CHRISTY. *Goes and shakes him drunkenly by the hand, while* PEGEEN *and* SHAWN *talk on the left.)*

MICHAEL *(to* CHRISTY*)* The blessing of God and the holy angels on your head, young fellow. I hear tell you're after winning all in the sports below; and wasn't it a shame I didn't bear you along with me to Kate Cassidy's wake, a fine, stout lad, the like of you, for you'd never see the match of it for flows of drink, the way when we sunk her bones at noonday in her narrow grave, there were five men, aye, and six men, stretched out retching speechless on the holy stones.

CHRISTY *(uneasily, watching* PEGEEN*)* Is that the truth?

MICHAEL It is then, and aren't you a louty schemer to go burying your poor father unbeknownst when you'd a right to throw him on the crupper of a Kerry mule and drive him westwards, like holy Joseph in the days gone by, the way we could have given him a decent burial, and not have him rotting beyond, and not a Christian drinking a smart drop to the glory of his soul?

CHRISTY *(gruffly)* It's well enough he's lying, for the likes of him.

MICHAEL *(slapping him on the back)* Well, aren't you a hardened slayer? It'll be a poor thing for the household man where you go sniffing for a female wife; and *(Pointing to* SHAWN*)* look beyond at that shy and decent Christian I have chosen for my daughter's hand, and I after getting the gilded dispensation this day for to wed them now.

CHRISTY And you'll be wedding them this day, is it?

MICHAEL *(drawing himself up)* Aye. Are you thinking, if I'm drunk itself, I'd leave my daughter living single with a little frisky rascal is the like of you?

PEGEEN *(breaking away from* SHAWN*)* Is it the truth the dispensation's come?

MICHAEL *(triumphantly)* Father Reilly's after reading it in gallous[4] Latin, and "It's come in the nick of time," says he; "so I'll wed them in a hurry, dreading that young gaffer who'd capsize the stars."

PEGEEN *(fiercely)* He's missed his nick of time, for it's that lad, Christy Mahon, that I'm wedding now.

---

[4] Fine-sounding, over-acted.

MICHAEL (*loudly with horror*)   You'd be making him a son to me, and he wet and crusted with his father's blood?

PEGEEN   Aye. Wouldn't it be a bitter thing for a girl to go marrying the like of Shaneen, and he a middling kind of a scarecrow, with no savagery or fine words in him at all?

MICHAEL (*gasping and sinking on a chair*)   Oh, aren't you a heathen daughter to go shaking the fat of my heart, and I swamped and drownded with the weight of drink? Would you have them turning on me the way that I'd be roaring to the dawn of day with the wind upon my heart? Have you not a word to aid me, Shaneen? Are you not jealous at all?

SHAWN (*in great misery*)   I'd be afeard to be jealous of a man did slay his da.

PEGEEN   Well, it'd be a poor thing to go marrying your like. I'm seeing there's a world of peril for an orphan girl, and isn't it a great blessing I didn't wed you, before himself came walking from the west or south?

SHAWN   It's a queer story you'd go picking a dirty tramp up from the highways of the world.

PEGEEN (*playfully*)   And you think you're a likely beau to go straying along with, the shiny Sundays of the opening year, when it's sooner on a bullock's liver you'd put a poor girl thinking than on the lily or the rose?

SHAWN   And have you no mind of my weight of passion, and the holy dispensation, and the drift of heifers I am giving, and the golden ring?

PEGEEN   I'm thinking you're too fine for the like of me, Shawn Keogh of Killakeen, and let you go off till you'd find a radiant lady with droves of bullocks on the plains of Meath, and herself bedizened in the diamond jewelries of Pharaoh's ma. That'd be your match, Shaneen. So God save you now! (*She retreats behind* CHRISTY.)

SHAWN   Won't you hear me telling you . . .?

CHRISTY (*with ferocity*)   Take yourself from this, young fellow, or I'll maybe add a murder to my deeds today.

MICHAEL (*springing up with a shriek*)   Murder is it? Is it mad yous are? Would you go making murder in this place, and it piled with poteen for our drink tonight? Go on to the foreshore if it's fighting you want, where the rising tide will wash all traces from the memory of man. (*Pushing* SHAWN *toward* CHRISTY.)

SHAWN (*shaking himself free, and getting behind* MICHAEL)   I'll not fight him, Michael James. I'd liefer live a bachelor, simmering in passions to the end of time, than face a lepping savage the like of him has descended from the Lord knows where. Strike him yourself, Michael James, or you'll lose my drift of heifers and my blue bull from Sneem.

MICHAEL   Is it me fight him, when it's father-slaying he's bred to now? (*Pushing* SHAWN) Go on, you fool, and fight him now.

SHAWN (*coming forward a little*)   Will I strike him with my hand?

MICHAEL   Take the loy is on your western side.

SHAWN   I'd be afeard of the gallows if I struck him with that.

CHRISTY (*taking up the loy*)   Then I'll make you face the gallows or quit off from this.

(SHAWN *flies out of the door.*)

CHRISTY   Well, fine weather be after him (*Going to* MICHAEL, *coaxingly*) and I'm thinking you wouldn't wish to have that quaking blackguard in your house at all. Let you give us your blessing and hear her swear her faith to me, for I'm mounted on the springtide of the stars of luck, the way it'll be good for any to have me in the house.

PEGEEN (*at the other side of* MICHAEL)   Bless us now, for I swear to God I'll wed him, and I'll not renege.

MICHAEL (*standing up in the centre, holding on to both of them*)   It's the will of God,

I'm thinking, that all should win an easy or a cruel end, and it's the will of God that all should rear up lengthy families for the nurture of the earth. What's a single man, I ask you, eating a bit in one house and drinking a sup in another, and he with no place of his own, like an old braying jackass strayed upon the rocks? (*To* CHRISTY) It's many would be in dread to bring your like into their house for to end them, maybe, with a sudden end; but I'm a decent man of Ireland, and I liefer face the grave untimely and I seeing a score of grandsons growing up little gallant swearers by the name of God, than go peopling my bedside with puny weeds the like of what you'd breed, I'm thinking, out of Shaneen Keogh. (*He joins their hands.*) A daring fellow is the jewel of the world, and a man did split his father's middle with a single clout, should have the bravery of ten, so may God and Mary and St. Patrick bless you, and increase you from this mortal day.

CHRISTY AND PEGEEN   Amen, O Lord!

(*Hubbub outside.*)

(Old MAHON *rushes in, followed by all the crowd, and* WIDOW QUIN. *He makes a rush at* CHRISTY, *knocks him down, and begins to beat him.*)

PEGEEN (*dragging back his arm*)   Stop that, will you? Who are you at all?

MAHON   His father, God forgive me!

PEGEEN (*drawing back*)   Is it rose from the dead?

MAHON   Do you think I look so easy quenched with the tap of a loy? (*Beats* CHRISTY *again.*)

PEGEEN (*glaring at* CHRISTY)   And it's lies you told, letting on you had him slitted, and you nothing at all.

CHRISTY (*catching* MAHON's *stick*)   He's not my father. He's a raving maniac would scare the world. (*Pointing to* WIDOW QUIN) Herself knows it is true.

CROWD   You're fooling Pegeen! The Widow Quin seen him this day, and you likely knew! You're a liar!

CHRISTY (*dumbfounded*)   It's himself was a liar, lying stretched out with an open head on him, letting on he was dead.

MAHON   Weren't you off racing the hills before I got my breath with the start I had seeing you turn on me at all?

PEGEEN   And to think of the coaxing glory we had given him, and he after doing nothing but hitting a soft blow and chasing northward in a sweat of fear. Quit off from this.

CHRISTY (*piteously*)   You've seen my doings this day, and let you save me from the old man; for why would you.be in such a scorch of haste to spur me to destruction now?

PEGEEN   It's there your treachery is spurring me, till I'm hard set to think you're the one I'm after lacing in my heart-strings half-an-hour gone by. (*To* MAHON) Take him on from this, for I think bad the world should see me raging for a Munster liar, and the fool of men.

MAHON   Rise up now to retribution, and come on with me.

CROWD (*jeeringly*)   There's the playboy! There's the lad thought he'd rule the roost in Mayo. Slate[5] him now, mister.

CHRISTY (*getting up in shy terror*)   What is it drives you to torment me here, when I'd asked the thunders of the might of God to blast me if I ever did hurt to any saving only that one single blow.

MAHON (*loudly*)   If you didn't, you're a poor good-for-nothing, and isn't it by the like of you the sins of the whole world are committed?

CHRISTY (*raising his hands*)   In the name of the Almighty God. . . .

[5] Let him have it; give him a good scolding.

MAHON Leave troubling the Lord God. Would you have him sending down droughts, and fevers, and the old hen and the cholera morbus?

CHRISTY *(to* WIDOW QUIN) Will you come between us and protect me now?

WIDOW QUIN I've tried a lot, God help me, and my share is done.

CHRISTY *(looking round in desperation)* And I must go back into my torment is it, or run off like a vagabond straying through the unions[6] with the dusts of August making mudstains in the gullet of my throat, or the winds of March blowing on me till I'd take an oath I felt them making whistles of my ribs within?

SARA Ask Pegeen to aid you. Her like does often change.

CHRISTY I will not then, for there's torment in the splendour of her like, and she a girl any moon of midnight would take pride to meet, facing southwards on the heaths of Keel. But what did I want crawling forward to scorch my understanding at her flaming brow?

PEGEEN *(to* MAHON, *vehemently, fearing she will break into tears)* Take him on from this or I'll set the young lads to destroy him here.

MAHON *(going to him, shaking his stick)* Come on now if you wouldn't have the company to see you skelped.

PEGEEN *(half laughing, through her tears)* That's it, now the world will see him pandied[7], and he an ugly liar was playing off the hero, and the fright of men.

CHRISTY *(to* MAHON, *very sharply)* Leave me go!

CROWD That's it. Now, Christy. If them two set fighting, it will lick the world.

MAHON *(making a grab at* CHRISTY) Come here to me.

CHRISTY *(more threateningly)* Leave me go, I'm saying.

MAHON I will maybe, when your legs is limping, and your back is blue.

CROWD Keep it up, the two of you. I'll back the old one. Now the playboy.

CHRISTY *(in low and intense voice)* Shut your yelling, for if you're after making a mighty man of me this day by the power of a lie, you're setting me now to think if it's a poor thing to be lonesome, it's worse maybe to go mixing with the fools of earth.

(MAHON *makes a movement toward him.*)

CHRISTY *(almost shouting)* Keep off . . . lest I do show a blow unto the lot of you would set the guardian angels winking in the clouds above. *(He swings round with a sudden rapid movement and picks up a loy.)*

CROWD *(half frightened, half amused)* He's going mad! Mind yourselves! Run from the idiot!

CHRISTY If I am an idiot, I'm after hearing my voice this day saying words would raise the topknot on a poet in a merchant's town. I've won your racing, your lepping, and . . .

MAHON Shut your gullet and come on with me.

CHRISTY I'm going, but I'll stretch you first.

(He runs at old MAHON *with the loy, chases him out of the door, followed by crowd and* WIDOW QUIN. *There is a great noise outside, then a yell, and dead silence for a moment.* CHRISTY *comes in, half dazed, and goes to fire.)*

WIDOW QUIN *(coming in, hurriedly, and going to him)* They're turning again you. Come on, or you'll be hanged, indeed.

CHRISTY I'm thinking, from this out, Pegeen'll be giving me praises the same as in the hours gone by.

WIDOW QUIN *(impatiently)* Come by the backdoor. I'd think bad to have you stifled on the gallows tree.

---

[6] Wandering from one parish workhouse to another.   [7] Beaten and exposed.

CHRISTY *(indignantly)*   I will not, then. What good'd be my life-time, if I left Pegeen?

WIDOW QUIN   Come on, and you'll be no worse than you were last night; and you with a double murder this time to be telling to the girls.

CHRISTY   I'll not leave Pegeen Mike.

WIDOW QUIN *(impatiently)*   Isn't there the match of her in every parish public, from Binghamstown unto the plain of Meath? Come on, I tell you, and I'll find you finer sweet-hearts at each waning moon.

CHRISTY   It's Pegeen I'm seeking only, and what'd I care if you brought me a drift of chosen females, standing in their shifts itself, maybe, from this place to the Eastern World?

SARA *(runs in, pulling off one of her petticoats)*   They're going to hang him. *(Holding out petticoat and shawl)* Fit these upon him, and let him run off to the east.

WIDOW QUIN   He's raving now; but we'll fit them on him, and I'll take him, in the ferry, to the Achill boat.

CHRISTY *(struggling feebly)*   Leave me go, will you? When I'm thinking of my luck today, for she will wed me surely, and I a proven hero in the end of all.

(They try to fasten petticoat round him.)

WIDOW QUIN   Take his left hand, and we'll pull him now. Come on, young fellow.

CHRISTY *(suddenly starting up)*   You'll be taking me from her? You're jealous, is it, of her wedding me? Go on from this. *(He snatches up a stool, and threatens them with it.)*

WIDOW QUIN *(going)*   It's in the mad-house they should put him, not in jail, at all. We'll go by the back-door, to call the doctor, and we'll save him so.

(She goes out, with SARA, *through inner room. Men crowd in the doorway.* CHRISTY *sits down again by the fire.)*

MICHAEL. *(in a terrified whisper)*   Is the old lad killed surely?

PHILLY   I'm after feeling the last gasps quitting his heart.

(They peer in at CHRISTY.*)*

MICHAEL *(with a rope)*   Look at the way he is. Twist a hangman's knot on it, and slip it over his head, while he's not minding at all.

PHILLY   Let you take it, Shaneen. You're the soberest of all that's here.

SHAWN   Is it me to go near him, and he the wickedest and worst with me? Let you take it, Pegeen Mike.

PEGEEN   Come on, so.

(She goes forward with the others, and they drop the double hitch over his head.)

CHRISTY   What ails you?

SHAWN *(triumphantly, as they pull the rope tight on his arms)*   Come on to the peel-ers, till they stretch you now.

CHRISTY   Me!

MICHAEL   If we took pity on you, the Lord God would, maybe, bring us ruin from the law today, so you'd best come easy, for hanging is an easy and a speedy end.

CHRISTY   I'll not stir. *(To* PEGEEN*)*   And what is it you'll say to me, and I after doing it this time in the face of all?

PEGEEN   I'll say, a strange man is a marvel, with his mighty talk; but what's a squabble in your backyard, and the blow of a loy, have taught me that there's a great gap between a gallous story and a dirty deed. *(To* MEN*)* Take him on from this, or the lot of us will be likely put on trial for his deed today.

CHRISTY *(with horror in his voice)*   And it's yourself will send me off, to have a horny-fingered hangman hitching his bloody slipknots at the butt of my ear.

MEN *(pulling rope)*   Come on, will you?

(He is pulled down on the floor.)

CHRISTY *(twisting his legs round the table)*   Cut the rope, Pegeen, and I'll quit the lot of you, and live from this out, like the madmen of Keel, eating muck and green weeds, on the faces of the cliffs.

PEGEEN   And leave us to hang, is it, for a saucy liar, the like of you? (*To* MEN) Take him on, out from this.

SHAWN   Pull a twist on his neck, and squeeze him so.

PHILLY   Twist yourself. Sure he cannot hurt you, if you keep your distance from his teeth alone.

SHAWN   I'm afeard of him. (*To* PEGEEN) Lift a lighted sod, will you, and scorch his leg.

PEGEEN *(blowing the fire, with a bellows)*   Leave go now, young fellow, or I'll scorch your shins.

CHRISTY   You're blowing for to torture me. *(His voice rising and growing stronger)* That's your kind, is it? Then let the lot of you be wary, for, if I've to face the gallows, I'll have a gay march down, I tell you, and shed the blood of some of you before I die.

SHAWN *(in terror)*   Keep a good hold, Philly. Be wary, for the love of God. For I'm thinking he would liefest wreak his pains on me.

CHRISTY *(almost gaily)*   If I do lay my hands on you, it's the way you'll be at the fall of night, hanging as a scarecrow for the fowls of hell. Ah, you'll have a gallous jaunt I'm saying, coaching out through Limbo with my father's ghost.

SHAWN *(to* PEGEEN)   Make haste, will you? Oh, isn't he a holy terror, and isn't it true for Father Reilly, that all drink's a curse that has the lot of you so shaky and uncertain now?

CHRISTY   If I can wring a neck among you, I'll have a royal judgment looking on the trembling jury in the courts of law. And won't there be crying out in Mayo the day I'm stretched upon the rope with ladies in their silks and satins snivelling in their lacy kerchiefs, and they rhyming songs and ballads on the terror of my fate? *(He squirms round on the floor and bites* SHAWN's *leg.)*

SHAWN *(shrieking)*   My leg's bit on me. He's the like of a mad dog, I'm thinking, the way that I will surely die.

CHRISTY *(delighted with himself)*   You will then, the way you can shake out hell's flags of welcome for my coming in two weeks or three, for I'm thinking Satan hasn't many have killed their da in Kerry, and in Mayo too.

(Old MAHON *comes in behind on all fours and looks on unnoticed.)*

MEN *(to* PEGEEN)   Bring the sod, will you?

PEGEEN *(coming over)*   God help him so. *(Burns his leg.)*

CHRISTY *(kicking and screaming)*   O, glory be to God!

(He kicks loose from the table, and they all drag him toward the door.)

JIMMY *(seeing old* MAHON)   Will you look what's come in?

(They all drop CHRISTY *and run left.)*

CHRISTY *(scrambling on his knees face to face with old* MAHON)   Are you coming to be killed a third time, or what ails you now?

MAHON   For what is it they have you tied?

CHRISTY   They're taking me to the peelers to have me hanged for slaying you.

MICHAEL *(apologetically)*   It is the will of God that all should guard their little cabins from the treachery of law, and what would my daughter be doing if I was ruined or was hanged itself?

MAHON *(grimly, loosening* CHRISTY)   It's little I care if you put a bag on her back, and went picking cockles till the hour of death; but my son and myself will be going our own way, and we'll have great times from this out telling stories of the villainy of Mayo, and the fools is here. *(To* CHRISTY, *who is freed)* Come on now.

CHRISTY   Go with you, is it? I will then, like a gallant captain with his heathen slave. Go on now and I'll see you from this day stewing my oatmeal and washing my spuds, for I'm master of all fights from now. *(Pushing* MAHON) Go on, I'm saying.

MAHON   Is it me?

CHRISTY   Not a word out of you. Go on from this.

MAHON *(walking out and looking back at* CHRISTY *over his shoulder)*   Glory be to God! *(With a broad smile)* I am crazy again! *(Goes.)*

CHRISTY   Ten thousand blessings upon all that's here, for you've turned me a likely gaffer in the end of all, the way I'll go romancing through a romping lifetime from this hour to the dawning of the judgment day. *(He goes out.)*

MICHAEL   By the will of God, we'll have peace now for our drinks. Will you draw the porter, Pegeen?

SHAWN *(going up to her)*   It's a miracle Father Reilly can wed us in the end of all, and we'll have none to trouble us when his vicious bite is healed.

PEGEEN *(hitting him a box on the ear)*   Quit my sight. *(Putting her shawl over her head and breaking out into wild lamentations)* Oh, my grief, I've lost him surely. I've lost the only Playboy of the Western World.

(Curtain.)

Comments and Questions

Synge's play presents a view of Ireland, a close look at a paradoxical people whose every-day speech has the lilt of poetry and whose everyday actions show a fondness for violence. The playwright in his Preface emphasizes the importance of "striking and beautiful phrases" but does not try to explain the hero-worship accorded a supposed murderer.

1. "All art is a collaboration," Synge observes. What does he mean? He goes on to speculate that in Elizabethan times a dramatist could draw on the speech of the common people for his effective lines. Does *Hamlet* contain such lines? Consider Act V, Scene i.

2. Synge disapproves of Ibsen who, he says, deals "with the reality of life in joyless and pallid words." Does the dialogue in *Ghosts* bear out this criticism? Is there a possible contradiction in the Irish dramatist's dictum that "on the stage one must have reality and one must have joy"? Discuss.

3. "The playboy of the western world"—what does this expansive epithet denote and connote? Recall where the play takes place. The play is filled with hyperboles. Cite some examples.

4. Christy's character changes once, again, and still one more time. Do we see him as he really is at the end of the play? Have events modified him in a significant way? Discuss.

5. Pegeen rejects her suitor, Shawn, because he has "no savagery or fine words in him at all." Discuss the values exhibited by the characters of the play.

6. Synge states in the Preface that "in countries where the imagination of the people, and the language they use, is rich and living, it is possible for a writer to be rich and copious in his words, and at the same time to give the reality, which is the root of all poetry, in a comprehensive and natural form." The implication is that the play is able to blend the realistic and the poetic by relying on the imaginative speech of the Irish. Is the play successful in striking a balance between poetic language and a realistic depiction of ordinary life? How important to the success of the play is the colloquial language (as opposed, say, to plot and characterization)?

7. *The Playboy of the Western World* had its first performance in Dublin on January 26, 1907. All went well for two acts, then suddenly the audience began to hiss, yell, and catcall. Bedlam continued until the curtain was drawn, ending the play before it was over. The reason for the outburst? A line spoken by Christy: "a drift of chosen females, standing in their shifts itself." That line was a shocker in 1907 Ireland. Is there anything about the play that would be shocking to a modern audience? What about the central premise of the play—that a man becomes a hero for supposedly murdering his father? After reading in *Hamlet* of a son who loses his life in avenging his father's murder, what are we to make of Christy? What does the comparison say about the differences between tragedy and comedy or between the different levels of society depicted in the two plays? Discuss also the contrasts in setting, action, language, and character.

Friedrich Duerrenmatt   (1921–   )
The Visit

(Adapted by Maurice Valency)

CHARACTERS *(In order of appearance)*

HOFBAUER, *first man*	SECOND GRANDCHILD
HELMESBERGER, *second man*	MIKE
WECHSLER, *third man*	MAX
VOGEL, *fourth man*	FIRST BLIND MAN
PAINTER	SECOND BLIND MAN
STATION MASTER	ATHLETE
BURGOMASTER	FRAU BURGOMASTER
TEACHER	FRAU SCHILL
PASTOR	DAUGHTER
ANTON SCHILL	SON
CLAIRE ZACHANASSIAN	DOCTOR NÜSSLIN
CONDUCTOR	FRAU BLOCK, *first woman*
PEDRO CABRAL	TRUCK DRIVER
BOBBY	REPORTER
POLICEMAN	TOWNSMAN
FIRST GRANDCHILD	

The action of the play takes place in and around the little town of Güllen, somewhere in Europe.

There are three acts.

ACT 1

A railway-crossing bell starts ringing. Then is heard the distant sound of a locomotive whistle. The curtain rises.

The scene represents, in the simplest possible manner, a little town somewhere in Central Europe. The time is the present. The town is shabby and ruined, as if the plague had passed there. Its name, Güllen, is inscribed on the shabby signboard which adorns the façade of the railway station. This edifice is summarily indicated by a length of rusty iron paling, a platform parallel to the proscenium, beyond which one imagines the rails to be, and a baggage truck standing by a wall on which a torn timetable, marked "Fahrplan," is affixed by three nails. In the station wall is a door with a sign: "Eintritt Verboten."[1] This leads to the STATION MASTER'S *office.*

Left of the station is a little house of gray stucco, formerly whitewashed. It has a tile roof, badly in need of repair. Some shreds of travel posters still adhere to the windowless walls. A shingle hanging over the entrance, left, reads: "Männer."[2] On the other side of the shingle reads: "Damen."[3] Along the wall of the little house there is a wooden bench, backless, on which four men are lounging cheerlessly, shabbily dressed, with cracked shoes. A fifth man is busied with paintpot and brush. He is kneeling on the ground, painting a strip of canvas with the words: "Welcome, Clara."

The warning signal rings uninterruptedly. The sound of the approaching train comes closer and closer. The STATION MASTER *issues from his office, advances to the center of the platform and salutes.*

The train is heard thundering past in a direction parallel to the footlights, and is lost in the distance. The men on the bench follow its passing with a slow movement of their heads, from left to right.

> FIRST MAN   The "Emperor." Hamburg-Naples.
> SECOND MAN   Then comes the "Diplomat."
> THIRD MAN   Then the "Banker."
> FOURTH MAN   And at eleven twenty-seven the "Flying Dutchman." Venice-Stockholm.
> FIRST MAN   Our only pleasure—watching trains.

(The station bell rings again. The STATION MASTER *comes out of his office and salutes another train. The men follow its course, right to left.)*

> FOURTH MAN   Once upon a time the "Emperor" and the "Flying Dutchman" used to stop here in Güllen. So did the "Diplomat," the "Banker," and the "Silver Comet."

---

[1] Entrance forbidden.   [2] Men.   [3] Ladies.

SECOND MAN   Now it's only the local from Kaffigen and the twelve-forty from Kalberstadt.

THIRD MAN   The fact is, we're ruined.

FIRST MAN   What with the Wagonworks shut down . . .

SECOND MAN   The Foundry finished . . .

FOURTH MAN   The Golden Eagle Pencil Factory all washed up . . .

FIRST MAN   It's life on the dole.

SECOND MAN   Did you say life?

THIRD MAN   We're rotting.

FIRST MAN   Starving.

SECOND MAN   Crumbling.

FOURTH MAN   The whole damn town.

(The station bell rings.)

THIRD MAN   Once we were a center of industry.

PAINTER   A cradle of culture.

FOURTH MAN   One of the best little towns in the country.

FIRST MAN   In the world.

SECOND MAN   Here Goethe slept.

FOURTH MAN   Brahms composed a quartet.

THIRD MAN   Here Berthold Schwarz invented gunpowder.[4]

PAINTER   And I once got first prize at the Dresden Exhibition of Contemporary Art.
What am I doing now? Painting signs.

(The station bell rings. The STATION MASTER *comes out. He throws away a cigarette butt. The
men scramble for it.)*

FIRST MAN   Well, anyway, Madame Zachanassian will help us.

FOURTH MAN   If she comes . . .

THIRD MAN   If she comes.

SECOND MAN   Last week she was in France. She gave them a hospital.

FIRST MAN   In Rome she founded a free public nursery.

THIRD MAN   In Leuthenaw, a bird sanctuary.

PAINTER   They say she got Picasso to design her car.

FIRST MAN   Where does she get all that money?

SECOND MAN   An oil company, a shipping line, three banks and five railways—

FOURTH MAN   And the biggest string of geisha houses in Japan.

(From the direction of the town come the BURGOMASTER, *the* PASTOR, *the* TEACHER *and* ANTON
SCHILL. *The* BURGOMASTER, *the* TEACHER *and* SCHILL *are men in their fifties. The* PASTOR *is ten
years younger. All four are dressed shabbily and are sad-looking. The* BURGOMASTER *looks
official.* SCHILL *is tall and handsome, but graying and worn; nevertheless a man of considerable charm and presence. He walks directly to the little house and disappears into it.)*

PAINTER   Any news, Burgomaster? Is she coming?

ALL   Yes, is she coming?

BURGOMASTER   She's coming. The telegram has been confirmed. Our distinguished
guest will arrive on the twelve-forty from Kalberstadt. Everyone must be ready.

TEACHER   The mixed choir is ready. So is the children's chorus.

---

[4] Berthold Schwarz was a German monk who lived in the fourteenth century. The invention of gunpowder has been attributed to him and to many others.

BURGOMASTER   And the church bell, Pastor?

PASTOR   The church bell will ring. As soon as the new bell ropes are fitted. The man is working on them now.

BURGOMASTER   The town band will be drawn up in the market place and the Athletic Association will form a human pyramid in her honor—the top man will hold the wreath with her initials. Then lunch at the Golden Apostle. I shall say a few words.

TEACHER   Of course.

BURGOMASTER   I had thought of illuminating the town hall and the cathedral, but we can't afford the lamps.

PAINTER   Burgomaster—what do you think of this?

(He shows the banner.)

BURGOMASTER *(calls)*   Schill! Schill!

TEACHER   Schill!

(SCHILL *comes out of the little house.)*

SCHILL   Yes, right away. Right away.

BURGOMASTER   This is more in your line. What do you think of this?

SCHILL *(looks at the sign)*   No, no, no. That certainly won't do, Burgomaster. It's much too intimate. It shouldn't read: "Welcome, Clara." It should read: "Welcome Madame . . ."

TEACHER   Zachanassian.

BURGOMASTER   Zachanassian.

SCHILL   Zachanassian.

PAINTER   But she's Clara to us.

FIRST MAN   Clara Wäscher.

SECOND MAN   Born here.

THIRD MAN   Her father was a carpenter. He built this.

(All turn and stare at the little house.)

SCHILL   All the same . . .

PAINTER   If I . . .

BURGOMASTER   No, no, no. He's right. You'll have to change it.

PAINTER   Oh, well, I'll tell you what I'll do. I'll leave this and I'll put "Welcome, Madame Zachanassian" on the other side. Then if things go well, we can always turn it around.

BURGOMASTER   Good idea. *(To* SCHILL*)* Yes?

SCHILL   Well, anyway, it's safer. Everything depends on the first impression.

(The train bell is heard. Two clangs. The PAINTER *turns the banner over and goes to work.)*

FIRST MAN   Hear that? The "Flying Dutchman" has just passed through Leuthenau.

FOURTH MAN   Eleven twenty.

BURGOMASTER   Gentlemen, you know that the millionairess is our only hope.

PASTOR   Under God.

BURGOMASTER   Under God. Naturally. Schill, we depend entirely on you.

SCHILL   Yes, I know. You keep telling me.

BURGOMASTER   After all, you're the only one who really knew her.

SCHILL   Yes, I knew her.

PASTOR   You were really quite close to one another, I hear, in those days.

SCHILL   Close? Yes, we were close, there's no denying it. We were in love. I was young—good-looking, so they said—and Clara—you know, I can still see her in the great barn coming toward me—like a light out of the darkness. And in the Konradsweil Forest she'd come running to meet me—barefooted—her beautiful red hair streaming behind her. Like a witch. I was in love with her, all right. But you know how it is when you're twenty.

PASTOR What happened?

SCHILL *(shrugs)* Life came between us.

BURGOMASTER You must give me some points about her for my speech.

(He takes out his notebook.)

SCHILL I think I can help you there.

TEACHER Well, I've gone through the school records. And the young lady's marks were, I'm afraid to say, absolutely dreadful. Even in deportment. The only subject in which she was even remotely passable was natural history.

BURGOMASTER Good in natural history. That's fine. Give me a pencil.

(He makes a note.)

SCHILL She was an outdoor girl. Wild. Once, I remember, they arrested a tramp, and she threw stones at the policeman. She hated injustice passionately.

BURGOMASTER Strong sense of justice. Excellent.

SCHILL And generous . . .

ALL Generous?

SCHILL Generous to a fault. Whatever little she had, she shared—so good-heartedly. I remember once she stole a bag of potatoes to give to a poor widow.

BURGOMASTER *(writing in notebook)* Wonderful generosity—

TEACHER Generosity.

BURGOMASTER That, gentlemen, is something I must not fail to make a point of.

SCHILL And such a sense of humor. I remember once when the oldest man in town fell and broke his leg, she said, "Oh, dear, now they'll have to shoot him."

BURGOMASTER Well, I've got enough. The rest, my friend, is up to you.

(He puts the notebook away.)

SCHILL Yes, I know, but it's not so easy. After all, to part a woman like that from her millions—

BURGOMASTER Exactly. Millions. We have to think in big terms here.

TEACHER If she's thinking of buying us off with a nursery school—

ALL Nursery school!

PASTOR Don't accept.

TEACHER Hold out.

SCHILL I'm not so sure that I can do it. You know, she may have forgotten me completely.

BURGOMASTER *(He exchanges a look with the TEACHER and the PASTOR.)* Schill, for many years you have been our most popular citizen. The most respected and the best loved.

SCHILL Why, thank you . . .

BURGOMASTER And therefore I must tell you—last week I sounded out the political opposition, and they agreed. In the spring you will be elected to succeed me as Burgomaster. By unanimous vote.

(The others clap their hands in approval.)

SCHILL But, my dear Burgomaster—!

BURGOMASTER It's true.

TEACHER I'm a witness. I was at the meeting.

SCHILL This is—naturally, I'm terribly flattered—It's a completely unexpected honor.

BURGOMASTER You deserve it.

SCHILL Burgomaster! Well, well—! *(Briskly)* Gentlemen, to business. The first chance I get, of course, I shall discuss our miserable position with Clara.

TEACHER But tactfully, tactfully—

SCHILL What do you take me for? We must feel our way. Everything must be correct. Psychologically correct. For example, here at the railway station, a single blunder, one false note, could be disastrous.

BURGOMASTER He's absolutely right. The first impression colors all the rest. Madame Zachanassian sets foot on her native soil for the first time in many years. She sees our love and she sees our misery. She remembers her youth, her friends. The tears well up into her eyes. Her childhood companions throng about her. I will naturally not present myself like this, but in my black coat with my top hat. Next to me, my wife. Before me, my two grandchildren all in white, with roses. My God, if it only comes off as I see it! If only it comes off. *(The station bell begins ringing.)* Oh, my God! Quick! We must get dressed.

FIRST MAN It's not her train. It's only the "Flying Dutchman."

PASTOR *(calmly)* We have still two hours before she arrives.

SCHILL For God's sake, don't let's lose our heads. We still have a full two hours.

BURGOMASTER Who's losing their heads? *(To FIRST and SECOND MAN)* When her train comes, you two, Helmesberger and Vogel, will hold up the banner with "Welcome Madame Zachanassian." The rest will applaud.

THIRD MAN Bravo!

(He applauds.)

BURGOMASTER But, please, one thing—no wild cheering like last year with the government relief committee. It made no impression at all and we still haven't received any loan. What we need is a feeling of genuine sincerity. That's how we greet with full hearts our beloved sister who has been away from us so long. Be sincerely moved, my friends, that's the secret; be sincere. Remember you're not dealing with a child. Next a few brief words from me. Then the church bell will start pealing—

PASTOR If he can fix the ropes in time.

(The station bell rings.)

BURGOMASTER —Then the mixed choir moves in. And then—

TEACHER We'll form a line down here.

BURGOMASTER Then the rest of us will form in two lines leading from the station—

(He is interrupted by the thunder of the approaching train. The men crane their heads to see it pass. The STATION MASTER advances to the platform and salutes. There is a sudden shriek of air brakes. The train screams to a stop. The four men jump up in consternation.)

PAINTER But the "Flying Dutchman" never stops!

FIRST MAN It's stopping.

SECOND MAN In Güllen!

THIRD MAN In the poorest—

FIRST MAN The dreariest—

SECOND MAN The lousiest—

FOURTH MAN The most God-forsaken hole between Venice and Stockholm.

STATION MASTER It cannot stop!

(The train noises stop. There is only the panting of the engine.)

PAINTER It's stopped!

(The STATION MASTER *runs out.)*

OFFSTAGE VOICES What's happened? Is there an accident?

(A hubbub of offstage voices, as if the passengers on the invisible train were alighting.)

CLAIRE *(offstage)*   Is this Güllen?
CONDUCTOR *(offstage)*   Here, here, what's going on?
CLAIRE *(offstage)*   Who the hell are you?
CONDUCTOR *(offstage)*   But you pulled the emergency cord, madame!
CLAIRE *(offstage)*   I always pull the emergency cord.
STATION MASTER *(offstage)*   I must ask you what's going on here.
CLAIRE *(offstage)*   And who the hell are you?
STATION MASTER *(offstage)*   I'm the Station Master, madame, and I must ask you—
CLAIRE *(enters)*   No!

(From the right CLAIRE ZACHANASSIAN *appears. She is an extraordinary woman. She is in her fifties, red-haired, remarkably dressed, with a face as impassive as that of an ancient idol, beautiful still, and with a singular grace of movement and manner. She is simple and unaffected, yet she has the haughtiness of a world power. The entire effect is striking to the point of the unbelievable. Behind her comes her fiancé,* PEDRO CABRAL, *tall, young, very handsome, and completely equipped for fishing, with creel and net, and with a rod case in his hand. An excited* CONDUCTOR *follows.)*

CONDUCTOR But, madame, I must insist! You have stopped the "Flying Dutchman." I must have an explanation.
CLAIRE Nonsense. Pedro.
PEDRO Yes, my love?
CLAIRE This is Güllen. Nothing has changed. I recognize it all. There's the forest of Konradsweil. There's a brook in it full of trout, where you can fish. And there's the roof of the great barn. Ha! God! What a miserable blot on the map.

(She crosses the stage and goes off with PEDRO.)*

SCHILL My God! Clara!
TEACHER Claire Zachanassian!
ALL Claire Zachanassian!
BURGOMASTER And the town band? The town band! Where is it?
TEACHER The mixed choir! The mixed choir!
PASTOR The church bell! The church bell!
BURGOMASTER *(to the* FIRST MAN*)*   Quick! My dress coat. My top hat. My grandchildren. Run! Run! *(*FIRST MAN *runs off. The* BURGOMASTER *shouts after him.)* And don't forget my wife!

(General panic. The THIRD MAN *and* FOURTH MAN *hold up the banner, on which only part of the name has been painted: "Welcome Mad—"* CLAIRE *and* PEDRO *reenter, right.)*

CONDUCTOR *(mastering himself with an effort)*   Madame. The train is waiting. The entire international railway schedule has been disrupted. I await your explanation.
CLAIRE You're a very foolish man. I wish to visit this town. Did you expect me to jump off a moving train?
CONDUCTOR *(stupefied)*   You stopped the "Flying Dutchman" because you wished to visit the town?

CLAIRE Naturally.

CONDUCTOR *(inarticulate)* Madame!

STATION MASTER Madame, if you wished to visit the town, the twelve-forty from Kalberstadt was entirely at your service. Arrival in Güllen, one seventeen.

CLAIRE The local that stops at Loken, Beisenbach, and Leuthenau? Do you expect me to waste three-quarters of an hour chugging dismally through this wilderness?

CONDUCTOR Madame, you shall pay for this!

CLAIRE Bobby, give him a thousand marks.

(BOBBY, *her butler, a man in his seventies, wearing dark glasses, opens his wallet. The townspeople gasp.*)

CONDUCTOR *(taking the money in amazement)* But, madame!

CLAIRE And three thousand for the Railway Widows' Relief Fund.

CONDUCTOR *(with the money in his hands)* But we have no such fund, madame.

CLAIRE Now you have.

(*The* BURGOMASTER *pushes his way forward.*)

BURGOMASTER *(He whispers to the* CONDUCTOR *and* TEACHER.*)* The lady is Madame Claire Zachanassian!

CONDUCTOR Claire Zachanassian? Oh, my God! But that's naturally quite different. Needless to say, we would have stopped the train if we'd had the slightest idea. (*He hands the money back to* BOBBY.) Here, please. I couldn't dream of it. Four thousand. My God!

CLAIRE Keep it. Don't fuss.

CONDUCTOR Would you like the train to wait, madame, while you visit the town? The administration will be delighted. The cathedral porch. The town hall—

CLAIRE You may take the train away. I don't need it any more.

STATION MASTER All aboard!

(*He puts his whistle to his lips.* PEDRO *stops him.*)

PEDRO But the press, my angel. They don't know anything about this. They're still in the dining car.

CLAIRE Let them stay there. I don't want the press in Güllen at the moment. Later they will come by themselves. (*To* STATION MASTER) And now what are you waiting for?

STATION MASTER All aboard!

(*The* STATION MASTER *blows a long blast on his whistle. The train leaves. Meanwhile, the* FIRST MAN *has brought the* BURGOMASTER'S *dress coat and top hat. The* BURGOMASTER *puts on the coat, then advances slowly and solemnly.*)

CONDUCTOR I trust madame will not speak of this to the administration. It was a pure misunderstanding.

(*He salutes and runs for the train as it starts moving.*)

BURGOMASTER *(bows)* Gracious lady, as Burgomaster of the town of Güllen, I have the honor—

(*The rest of the speech is lost in the roar of the departing train. He continues speaking and gesturing, and at last bows amid applause as the train noises end.*)

CLAIRE Thank you, Mr. Burgomaster.

(She glances at the beaming faces, and lastly at SCHILL, *whom she does not recognize. She turns upstage.)*

SCHILL Clara!

CLAIRE *(turns and stares)* Anton?

SCHILL Yes. It's good that you've come back.

CLAIRE Yes. I've waited for this moment. All my life. Ever since I left Güllen.

SCHILL *(a little embarrassed)* That is very kind of you to say, Clara.

CLAIRE And have you thought about me?

SCHILL Naturally. Always. You know that.

CLAIRE Those were happy times we spent together.

SCHILL Unforgettable.

(He smiles reassuringly at the BURGOMASTER.*)*

CLAIRE Call me by the name you used to call me.

SCHILL *(whispers)* My kitten.

CLAIRE What?

SCHILL *(louder)* My kitten.

CLAIRE And what else?

SCHILL Little witch.

CLAIRE I used to call you my black panther. You're gray now, and soft.

SCHILL But you are still the same, little witch.

CLAIRE I am the same? *(She laughs.)* Oh, no, my black panther, I am not at all the same.

SCHILL *(gallantly)* In my eyes you are. I see no difference.

CLAIRE Would you like to meet my fiancé? Pedro Cabral. He owns an enormous plantation in Brazil.

SCHILL A pleasure.

CLAIRE We're to be married soon.

SCHILL Congratulations.

CLAIRE He will be my eighth husband. (PEDRO *stands by himself downstage, right.*) Pedro, come here and show your face. Come along, darling—come here! Don't sulk. Say hello.

PEDRO Hello.

CLAIRE A man of few words! Isn't he charming? A diplomat. He's interested only in fishing. Isn't he handsome, in his Latin way? You'd swear he was a Brazilian. But he's not— he's a Greek. His father was a White Russian. We were betrothed by a Bulgarian priest. We plan to be married in a few days here in the cathedral.

BURGOMASTER Here in the cathedral? What an honor for us!

CLAIRE No. It was my dream, when I was seventeen, to be married in Güllen cathedral. The dreams of youth are sacred, don't you think so, Anton?

SCHILL Yes, of course.

CLAIRE Yes, of course. I think so, too. Now I would like to look at the town. *(The mixed choir arrives, breathless, wearing ordinary clothes with green sashes.)* What's all this? Go away. *(She laughs.)* Ha! Ha! Ha!

TEACHER Dear lady—*(He steps forward, having put on a sash also.)* Dear lady, as Rector of the high school and a devotee of that noble muse, Music, I take pleasure in presenting the Güllen mixed choir.

CLAIRE How do you do?

TEACHER Who will sing for you an ancient folk song of the region, with specially amended words—if you will deign to listen.

CLAIRE Very well. Fire away.

(The TEACHER *blows a pitch pipe. The mixed choir begins to sing the ancient folk song with the amended words. Just then the station bell starts ringing. The song is drowned in the roar of the passing express. The* STATION MASTER *salutes. When the train has passed, there is applause.)*

BURGOMASTER The church bell! The church bell! Where's the church bell?

(The PASTOR *shrugs helplessly.)*

CLAIRE Thank you, Professor. They sang beautifully. The big little blond bass—no, not that one—the one with the big Adam's apple—was most impressive. *(The* TEACHER *bows. The* POLICEMAN *pushes his way professionally through the mixed choir and comes to attention in front of* CLAIRE ZACHANASSIAN.*)* Now, who are you?

POLICEMAN *(clicks heels)* Police Chief Schultz. At your service.

CLAIRE *(She looks him up and down.)* I have no need of you at the moment. But I think there will be work for you by and by. Tell me, do you know how to close an eye from time to time?

POLICEMAN How else could I get along in my profession?

CLAIRE You might practice closing both.

SCHILL *(laughs)* What a sense of humor, eh?

BURGOMASTER *(puts on the top hat)* Permit me to present my grandchildren, gracious lady. Hermine and Adolphine. There's only my wife still to come.

(He wipes the perspiration from his brow, and replaces the hat. The little girls present the roses with elaborate curtsies.)

CLAIRE Thank you, my dears. Congratulations, Burgomaster. Extraordinary children.

(She plants the roses in PEDRO'S *arms. The* BURGOMASTER *secretly passes his top hat to the* PASTOR, *who puts it on.)*

BURGOMASTER Our pastor, madame.

(The PASTOR *takes off the hat and bows.)*

CLAIRE Ah. The pastor. How do you do? Do you give consolation to the dying?

PASTOR *(a bit puzzled)* That is part of my ministry, yes.

CLAIRE And to those who are condemned to death?

PASTOR Capital punishment has been abolished in this country, madame.

CLAIRE I see. Well, it could be restored, I suppose.

(The PASTOR *hands back the hat. He shrugs his shoulders in confusion.)*

SCHILL *(laughs)* What an original sense of humor!

(All laugh, a little blankly.)

CLAIRE Well, I can't sit here all day—I should like to see the town.

(The BURGOMASTER *offers his arm.)*

BURGOMASTER May I have the honor, gracious lady?

CLAIRE Thank you, but these legs are not what they were. This one was broken in five places.

SCHILL *(full of concern)*   My kitten!

CLAIRE   When my airplane bumped into a mountain in Afghanistan. All the others were killed. Even the pilot. But as you see, I survived. I don't fly any more.

SCHILL   But you're as strong as ever now.

CLAIRE   Stronger.

BURGOMASTER   Never fear, gracious lady. The town doctor has a car.

CLAIRE   I never ride in motors.

BURGOMASTER   You never ride in motors?

CLAIRE   Not since my Ferrari crashed in Hong Kong.

SCHILL   But how do you travel, then, little witch? On a broom?

CLAIRE   Mike—Max! *(She claps her hands. Two huge bodyguards come in, left, carrying a sedan chair. She sits in it.)* I travel this way—a bit antiquated, of course. But perfectly safe. Ha! Ha! Aren't they magnificent? Mike and Max. I bought them in America. They were in jail, condemned to the chair. I had them pardoned. Now they're condemned to my chair. I paid fifty thousand dollars apiece for them. You couldn't get them now for twice the sum. The sedan chair comes from the Louvre. I fancied it so much that the President of France gave it to me. The French are so impulsive, don't you think so, Anton? Go!

(MIKE *and* MAX *start to carry her off.)*

BURGOMASTER   You wish to visit the cathedral? And the old town hall?

CLAIRE   No. The great barn. And the forest of Konradsweil. I wish to go with Anton and visit our old haunts once again.

THE PASTOR   Very touching.

CLAIRE *(to the butler)*   Will you send my luggage and the coffin to the Golden Apostle?

BURGOMASTER   The coffin?

CLAIRE   Yes. I brought one with me. Go!

TEACHER   Hip-hip—

ALL   Hurrah! Hip-hip, hurrah! Hurrah!

(They bear off in the direction of the town. The townspeople burst into cheers. The church bell rings.)

BURGOMASTER   Ah, thank God—the bell at last.

(The POLICEMAN *is about to follow the others, when the two* BLIND MEN *appear. They are not young, yet they seem childish—a strange effect. Though they are of different height and features, they are dressed exactly alike, and so create the effect of being twins. They walk slowly, feeling their way. Their voices, when they speak, are curiously high and flutelike, and they have a curious trick of repetition of phrases.)*

FIRST BLIND MAN   We're in—

BOTH BLIND MEN   Güllen.

FIRST BLIND MAN   We breathe—

SECOND BLIND MAN   We breathe—

BOTH BLIND MEN   We breathe the air, the air of Güllen.

POLICEMAN *(startled)*   Who are you?

FIRST BLIND MAN   We belong to the lady.

SECOND BLIND MAN   We belong to the lady. She calls us—

FIRST BLIND MAN   Kobby.

SECOND BLIND MAN   And Lobby.

POLICEMAN   Madame Zachanassian is staying at the Golden Apostle.

FIRST BLIND MAN We're blind.

SECOND BLIND MAN We're blind.

POLICEMAN Blind? Come along with me, then. I'll take you there.

FIRST BLIND MAN Thank you, Mr. Policeman.

SECOND BLIND MAN Thanks very much.

POLICEMAN Hey! How do you know I'm a policeman, if you're blind?

BOTH BLIND MEN By your voice. By your voice.

FIRST BLIND MAN All policemen sound the same.

POLICEMAN You've had a lot to do with the police, have you, little men?

FIRST BLIND MAN Men he calls us!

BOTH BLIND MEN Men!

POLICEMAN What are you then?

BOTH BLIND MEN You'll see. You'll see.

(The POLICEMAN *claps his hands suddenly. The* BLIND MEN *turn sharply toward the sound. The* POLICEMAN *is convinced they are blind.)*

POLICEMAN What's your trade?

BOTH BLIND MEN We have no trade.

SECOND BLIND MAN We play music.

FIRST BLIND MAN We sing.

SECOND BLIND MAN We amuse the lady.

FIRST BLIND MAN We look after the beast.

SECOND BLIND MAN We feed it.

FIRST BLIND MAN We stroke it.

SECOND BLIND MAN We take it for walks.

POLICEMAN What beast?

BOTH BLIND MEN You'll see—you'll see.

SECOND BLIND MAN We give it raw meat.

FIRST BLIND MAN And she gives us chicken and wine.

SECOND BLIND MAN Every day—

BOTH BLIND MEN Every day.

POLICEMAN Rich people have strange tastes.

BOTH BLIND MEN Strange tastes—strange tastes.

(The POLICEMAN *puts on his helmet.)*

POLICEMAN Come along, I'll take you to the lady.

(The two BLIND MEN *turn and walk off.)*

BOTH BLIND MEN We know the way—we know the way.

(The station and the little house vanish. A sign representing the Golden Apostle descends. The scene dissolves into the interior of the inn. The Golden Apostle is seen to be in the last stages of decay. The walls are cracked and moldering, and the plaster is falling from the ancient lath. A table represents the café of the inn. The BURGOMASTER *and the* TEACHER *sit at this table, drinking a glass together. A procession of townspeople, carrying many pieces of luggage, passes. Then comes a coffin, and, last, a large box covered with a canvas. They cross the stage from right to left.)*

BURGOMASTER Trunks. Suitcases. Boxes. *(He looks up apprehensively at the ceiling.)* The floor will never bear the weight. *(As the large covered box is carried in, he peers under the canvas, then draws back.)* Good God!

TEACHER Why, what's in it?

BURGOMASTER A live panther. *(They laugh. The* BURGOMASTER *lifts his glass solemnly.)* Your health, Professor. Let's hope she puts the Foundry back on its feet.

TEACHER *(lifts his glass)* And the Wagonworks.

BURGOMASTER And the Golden Eagle Pencil Factory. Once that starts moving, everything else will go. *Prosit.*[5]

(They touch glasses and drink.)

TEACHER What does she need a panther for?

BURGOMASTER Don't ask me. The whole thing is too much for me. The Pastor had to go home and lie down.

TEACHER *(sets down his glass)* If you want to know the truth, she frightens me.

BURGOMASTER *(nods gravely)* She's a strange one.

TEACHER You understand, Burgomaster, a man who for twenty-two years has been correcting the Latin compositions of the students of Güllen is not unaccustomed to surprises. I have seen things to make one's hair stand on end. But when this woman suddenly appeared on the platform, a shudder tore through me. It was as though out of the clear sky all at once a fury descended upon us, beating its black wings—

(The POLICEMAN *comes in. He mops his face.)*

POLICEMAN Ah! Now the old place is livening up a bit!

BURGOMASTER Ah, Schultz, come and join us.

POLICEMAN Thank you. *(He calls.)* Beer!

BURGOMASTER Well, what's the news from the front?

POLICEMAN I'm just back from Schill's barn. My God! What a scene! She had us all tiptoeing around in the straw as if we were in church. Nobody dared to speak above a whisper. And the way she carried on! I was so embarrassed I let them go to the forest by themselves.

BURGOMASTER Does the fiancé go with them?

POLICEMAN With his fishing rod and his landing net. In full marching order. *(He calls again.)* Beer!

BURGOMASTER That will be her seventh husband.

TEACHER Her eighth.

BURGOMASTER But what does she expect to find in the Konradsweil forest?

POLICEMAN The same thing she expected to find in the old barn, I suppose. The—the—

TEACHER The ashes of her youthful love.

POLICEMAN Exactly.

TEACHER It's poetry.

POLICEMAN Poetry.

TEACHER Sheer poetry! It makes one think of Shakespeare, of Wagner. Of Romeo and Juliet.

(The SECOND MAN *comes in as a waiter. The* POLICEMAN *is served his beer.)*

BURGOMASTER Yes, you're right. *(Solemnly)* Gentlemen, I would like to propose a toast. To our great and good friend, Anton Schill, who is even now working on our behalf.

POLICEMAN Yes! He's really working.

BURGOMASTER Gentlemen, to the best-loved citizen of this town. My successor, Anton Schill!

---

[5] Your health.

(They raise their glasses. At this point an unearthly scream is heard. It is the black panther howling offstage. The sign of the Golden Apostle rises out of sight. The lights go down. The inn vanishes. Only the wooden bench, on which the four men were lounging in the opening scene, is left on the stage, downstage right. The procession comes on upstage. The two bodyguards carry in CLAIRE's *sedan chair. Next to it walks* SCHILL. PEDRO *walks behind, with his fishing rod. Last come the two* BLIND MEN *and the butler.* CLAIRE *alights.)*

CLAIRE   Stop! Take my chair off somewhere else. I'm tired of looking at you. *(The bodyguards and the sedan chair go off.)* Pedro darling, your brook is just a little further along down that path. Listen. You can hear it from here. Bobby, take him and show him where it is.

BOTH BLIND MEN   We'll show him the way—we'll show him the way.

(They go off, left. PEDRO *follows.* BOBBY *walks off, right.)*

CLAIRE   Look, Anton. Our tree. There's the heart you carved in the bark long ago.
SCHILL   Yes. It's still there.
CLAIRE   How it has grown! The trunk is black and wrinkled. Why, its limbs are twice what they were. Some of them have died.
SCHILL   It's aged. But it's there.
CLAIRE   Like everything else. *(She crosses, examining other trees.)* Oh, how tall they are. How long it is since I walked here, barefoot over the pine needles and the damp leaves! Look, Anton. A fawn.
SCHILL   Yes, a fawn. It's the season.
CLAIRE   I thought everything would be changed. But it's all just as we left it. This is the seat we sat on years ago. Under these branches you kissed me. And over there under the hawthorn, where the moss is soft and green, we would lie in each other's arms. It is all as it used to be. Only we have changed.
SCHILL   Not so much, little witch. I remember the first night we spent together, you ran away and I chased you till I was quite breathless—
CLAIRE   Yes.
SCHILL   Then I was angry and I was going home, when suddenly I heard you call and I looked up, and there you were sitting in a tree, laughing down at me.
CLAIRE   No. It was in the great barn. I was in the hayloft.
SCHILL   Were you?
CLAIRE   Yes. What else do you remember?
SCHILL   I remember the morning we went swimming by the waterfall, and afterwards we were lying together on the big rock in the sun, when suddenly we heard footsteps and we just had time to snatch up our clothes and run behind the bushes when the old pastor appeared and scolded you for not being in school.
CLAIRE   No. It was the schoolmaster who found us. It was Sunday and I was supposed to be in church.
SCHILL   Really?
CLAIRE   Yes. Tell me more.
SCHILL   I remember the time your father beat you, and you showed me the cuts on your back, and I swore I'd kill him. And the next day I dropped a tile from a roof top and split his head open.
CLAIRE   You missed him.
SCHILL   No!
CLAIRE   You hit old Mr. Reiner.
SCHILL   Did I?

CLAIRE Yes. I was seventeen. And you were not yet twenty. You were so handsome. You were the best-looking boy in town.

(The two BLIND MEN *begin playing mandolin music offstage, very softly.)*

SCHILL And you were the prettiest girl.

CLAIRE We were made for each other.

SCHILL So we were.

CLAIRE But you married Mathilde Blumhard and her store, and I married old Zachanassian and his oil wells. He found me in a whorehouse in Hamburg. It was my hair that entangled him, the old golden beetle.

SCHILL Clara!

CLAIRE *(She claps her hands.)* Bobby! A cigar.

(BOBBY *appears with a leather case. He selects a cigar, puts it in a holder, lights it, and presents it to* CLAIRE.)

SCHILL My kitten smokes cigars!

CLAIRE Yes. I adore them. Would you care for one?

SCHILL Yes, please. I've never smoked one of those.

CLAIRE It's a taste I acquired from old Zachanassian. Among other things. He was a real connoisseur.

SCHILL We used to sit on this bench once, you and I, and smoke cigarettes. Do you remember?

CLAIRE Yes. I remember.

SCHILL The cigarettes I bought from Mathilde.

CLAIRE No. She gave them to you for nothing.

SCHILL Clara—don't be angry with me for marrying Mathilde.

CLAIRE She had money.

SCHILL But what a lucky thing for you that I did!

CLAIRE Oh?

SCHILL You were so young, so beautiful. You deserved a far better fate than to settle in this wretched town without any future.

CLAIRE Yes?

SCHILL If you had stayed in Güllen and married me, your life would have been wasted, like mine.

CLAIRE Oh?

SCHILL Look at me. A wretched shopkeeper in a bankrupt town!

CLAIRE But you have your family.

SCHILL My family! Never for a moment do they let me forget my failure, my poverty.

CLAIRE Mathilde has not made you happy?

SCHILL *(shrugs)* What does it matter?

CLAIRE And the children?

SCHILL *(shakes his head)* They're so completely materialistic. You know, they have no interest whatever in higher things.

CLAIRE How sad for you.

(A moment's pause, during which only the faint tinkling of the music is heard.)

SCHILL Yes. You know, since you went away my life has passed by like a stupid dream. I've hardly once been out of this town. A trip to a lake years ago. It rained all the time. And once five days in Berlin. That's all.

CLAIRE The world is much the same everywhere.

SCHILL   At least you've seen it.

CLAIRE   Yes. I've seen it.

SCHILL   You've lived in it.

CLAIRE   I've lived in it. The world and I have been on very intimate terms.

SCHILL   Now that you've come back, perhaps things will change.

CLAIRE   Naturally. I certainly won't leave my native town in this condition.

SCHILL   It will take millions to put us on our feet again.

CLAIRE   I have millions.

SCHILL   One, two, three.

CLAIRE   Why not?

SCHILL   You mean—you will help us?

CLAIRE   Yes.

(A woodpecker is heard in the distance.)

SCHILL   I knew it—I knew it. I told them you were generous. I told them you were good. Oh, my kitten, my kitten.

(He takes her hand. She turns her head away and listens.)

CLAIRE   Listen! A woodpecker.

SCHILL   It's all just the way it was in the days when we were young and full of courage. The sun high above the pines. White clouds, piling up on one another. And the cry of the cuckoo in the distance. And the wind rustling the leaves, like the sound of surf on a beach. Just as it was years ago. If only we could roll back time and be together always.

CLAIRE   Is that your wish?

SCHILL   Yes. You left me, but you never left my heart. *(He raises her hand to his lips.)* The same soft little hand.

CLAIRE   No, not quite the same. It was crushed in the plane accident. But they mended it. They mend everything nowadays.

SCHILL   Crushed? You wouldn't know it. See, another fawn.

CLAIRE   The old wood is alive with memories.

*(*PEDRO* appears, right, with a fish in his hand.)*

PEDRO   See what I've caught, darling. See? A pike. Over two kilos.

(The BLIND MEN *appear onstage.)*

BOTH BLIND MEN *(clapping their hands)*   A pike! A pike! Hurrah! Hurrah!

(As the BLIND MEN *clap their hands,* CLAIRE *and* SCHILL *exit, and the scene dissolves. The clapping of hands is taken up on all sides. The townspeople wheel in the walls of the café. A brass band strikes up a march tune. The door of the Golden Apostle descends. The townspeople bring in tables and set them with ragged tablecloths, cracked china, and glassware. There is a table in the center, upstage, flanked by two tables perpendicular to it, right and left. The* PASTOR *and the* BURGOMASTER *come in.* SCHILL *enters. Other townspeople filter in, left and right. One, the* ATHLETE, *is in gymnastic costume. The applause continues.)*

BURGOMASTER   She's coming! (CLAIRE *enters upstage, center, followed by* BOBBY.) The applause is meant for you, gracious lady.

CLAIRE   The band deserves it more than I. They blow from the heart. And the human pyramid was beautiful. You, show me your muscles. *(The* ATHLETE *kneels before her.)* Superb. Wonderful arms, powerful hands. Have you ever strangled a man with them?

ATHLETE   Strangled?

CLAIRE   Yes. It's perfectly simple. A little pressure in the proper place, and the rest goes by itself. As in politics.

(The BURGOMASTER'S *wife comes up, simpering.)*

BURGOMASTER *(presents her)*   Permit me to present my wife, Madame Zachanassian.
CLAIRE   Annette Dummermuth. The head of our class.
BURGOMASTER *(He presents another sour-looking woman.)*   Frau Schill.
CLAIRE   Mathilde Blumhard. I remember the way you used to follow Anton with your eyes, from behind the shop door. You've grown a little thin and dry, my poor Mathilde.
SCHILL   My daughter, Ottilie.
CLAIRE   Your daughter . . .
SCHILL   My son, Karl.
CLAIRE   Your son. Two of them!

(The town DOCTOR *comes in, right. He is a man of fifty, strong and stocky, with bristly black hair, a mustache, and a saber cut on his cheek. He is wearing an old cutaway.)*

DOCTOR   Well, well, my old Mercedes got me here in time after all!
BURGOMASTER   Dr. Nüsslin, the town physician. Madame Zachanassian.
DOCTOR   Deeply honored, madame.

(He kisses her hand. CLAIRE *studies him.)*

CLAIRE   It is you who signs the death certificates?
DOCTOR   Death certificates?
CLAIRE   When someone dies.
DOCTOR   Why certainly. That is one of my duties.
CLAIRE   And when the heart dies, what do you put down? Heart failure?
SCHILL *(laughing)*   What a golden sense of humor!
DOCTOR   Bit grim, wouldn't you say?
SCHILL *(whispers)*   Not at all, not at all. She's promised us a million.
BURGOMASTER *(turns his head)*   What?
SCHILL   A million!
ALL *(whisper)*   A million!

*(*CLAIRE *turns toward them.)*

CLAIRE   Burgomaster.
BURGOMASTER   Yes?
CLAIRE   I'm hungry. *(The girls and the waiter fill glasses and bring food. There is a general stir. All take their places at the tables.)* Are you going to make a speech?

(The BURGOMASTER *bows,* CLAIRE *sits next to the* BURGOMASTER. *The* BURGOMASTER *rises, tapping his knife on his glass. He is radiant with good will. All applaud.)*

BURGOMASTER   Gracious lady and friends. Gracious lady, it is now many years since you first left your native town of Güllen, which was founded by the Elector Hasso and which nestles in the green slope between the forest of Konradsweil and the beautiful valley of Pückenried. Much has taken place in this time, much that is evil.
TEACHER   That's true.
BURGOMASTER   The world is not what it was; it has become harsh and bitter, and we too have had our share of harshness and bitterness. But in all this time, dear lady, we have never forgotten our little Clara. *(Applause)* Many years ago you brightened the town with your pretty face as a child, and now once again you brighten it with your presence. *(Polite applause)* We haven't forgotten you, and we haven't forgotten your family. Your mother,

beautiful and robust even in her old age—*(He looks for his notes on the table.)*—although unfortunately taken from us in the bloom of her youth by an infirmity of the lungs. Your respected father, Siegfried Wäscher, the builder, an example of whose work next to our railway station is often visited—(SCHILL *covers his face.*)—that is to say, admired—a lasting monument of local design and local workmanship. And you, gracious lady, whom we remember as a golden-haired—*(He looks at her.)*—little red-headed sprite romping about our peaceful streets—on your way to school—which of us does not treasure your memory? *(He pokes nervously at his notebook.)* We will remember your scholarly attainments—

TEACHER   Yes.

BURGOMASTER   Natural history . . . Extraordinary sense of justice . . . And, above all, your supreme generosity. *(Great applause)* We shall never forget how you once spent the whole of your little savings to buy a sack of potatoes for a poor starving widow who was in need of food. Gracious lady, ladies and gentlemen, today our little Clara has become the world-famous Claire Zachanassian who has founded hospitals, soup kitchens, charitable institutes, art projects, libraries, nurseries, and schools, and now that she has at last once more returned to the town of her birth, sadly fallen as it is, I say in the name of all her loving friends who have sorely missed her: Long live our Clara!

ALL   Long live our Clara!

(Cheers. Music. Fanfare. Applause. CLAIRE *rises.)*

CLAIRE   Mr. Burgomaster. Fellow townsmen. I am greatly moved by the nature of your welcome and the disinterested joy which you have manifested on the occasion of my visit to my native town. I was not quite the child the Burgomaster described in his gracious address . . .

BURGOMASTER   Too modest, madame.

CLAIRE   In school I was beaten—

TEACHER   Not by me.

CLAIRE   And the sack of potatoes which I presented to Widow Boll, I stole with the help of Anton Schill, not to save the old trull from starvation, but so that for once I might sleep with Anton in a real bed instead of under the trees of the forest. *(The townspeople look grave, embarrassed.)* Nevertheless, I shall try to deserve your good opinion. In memory of the seventeen years I spent among you, I am prepared to hand over as a gift to the town of Güllen the sum of one billion marks. Five hundred million to the town, and five hundred million to be divided per capita among the citizens.

(There is a moment of dead silence.)

BURGOMASTER   A billion marks?

CLAIRE   On one condition.

(Suddenly a movement of uncontrollable joy breaks out. People jump on chairs, dance about, yell excitedly. The ATHLETE *turns handsprings in front of the speaker's table.)*

SCHILL   Oh, Clara, you astonishing, incredible, magnificent woman! What a heart! What a gesture! Oh—my little witch!

(He kisses her hand.)

BURGOMASTER *(holds up his arms for order)*   Quiet! Quiet, please! On one condition, the gracious lady said. Now, madame, may we know what that condition is?

CLAIRE   I will tell you. In exchange for my billion marks, I want justice.

(Silence.)

BURGOMASTER Justice, madam?

CLAIRE I wish to buy justice.

BURGOMASTER But justice cannot be bought, madame.

CLAIRE Everything can be bought.

BURGOMASTER I don't understand at all.

CLAIRE Bobby, step forward.

(The butler goes to the center of the stage. He takes off his dark glasses and turns his face with a solemn air.)

BOBBY Does anyone here present recognize me?

FRAU SCHILL Hofer! Hofer!

ALL Who? What's that?

TEACHER Not Chief Magistrate Hofer?

BOBBY Exactly. Chief Magistrate Hofer. When Madame Zachanassian was a girl, I was presiding judge at the criminal court of Güllen. I served there until twenty-five years ago, when Madame Zachanassian offered me the opportunity of entering her service as butler. I accepted. You may consider it a strange employment for a member of the magistracy, but the salary—

(CLAIRE *bangs the mallet on the table.*)

CLAIRE Come to the point.

BOBBY You have heard Madame Zachanassian's offer. She will give you a billion marks—when you have undone the injustice that she suffered at your hands here in Güllen as a girl.

(All murmur.)

BURGOMASTER Injustice at our hands? Impossible!

BOBBY Anton Schill . . .

SCHILL Yes?

BOBBY Kindly stand.

(SCHILL *rises. He smiles, as if puzzled. He shrugs.*)

SCHILL Yes?

BOBBY In those days, a bastardy case was tried before me. Madame Claire Zacha-nassian, at that time called Clara Wäscher, charged you with being the father of her illegit-imate child. *(Silence)* You denied the charge. And produced two witnesses in your support.

SCHILL That's ancient history. An absurd business. We were children. Who remem-bers?

CLAIRE Where are the blind men?

BOTH BLIND MEN Here we are. Here we are.

(MIKE *and* MAX *push them forward.*)

BOBBY You recognize these men, Anton Schill?

SCHILL I never saw them before in my life. What are they?

BOTH BLIND MEN We've changed. We've changed.

BOBBY What were your names in your former life?

FIRST BLIND MAN I was Jacob Hueblein. Jacob Hueblein.

SECOND BLIND MAN I was Ludwig Sparr. Ludwig Sparr.

BOBBY (to SCHILL) Well?

SCHILL These names mean nothing to me.

BOBBY   Jacob Hueblein and Ludwig Sparr, do you recognize the defendant?

FIRST BLIND MAN   We're blind.

SECOND BLIND MAN   We're blind.

SCHILL   Ha-ha-ha!

BOBBY   By his voice?

BOTH BLIND MEN   By his voice. By his voice.

BOBBY   At that trial, I was the judge. And you?

BOTH BLIND MEN   We were the witnesses.

BOBBY   And what did you testify on that occasion?

FIRST BLIND MAN   That we had slept with Clara Wäscher.

SECOND BLIND MAN   Both of us. Many times.

BOBBY   And was it true?

FIRST BLIND MAN   No.

SECOND BLIND MAN   We swore falsely.

FIRST BLIND MAN   Anton Schill bribed us.

SECOND BLIND MAN   He bribed us.

BOBBY   With what?

BOTH BLIND MEN   With a bottle of schnapps.

BOBBY   And now tell the people what happened to you. *(They hesitate and whimper.)* Speak!

FIRST BLIND MAN *(in a low voice)*   She tracked us down.

BOBBY   Madame Zachanassian tracked them down. Jacob Hueblein was found in Canada. Ludwig Sparr in Australia. And when she found you, what did she do to you?

SECOND BLIND MAN   She handed us over to Mike and Max.

BOBBY   And what did Mike and Max do to you?

FIRST BLIND MAN   They made us what you see.

(The BLIND MEN *cover their faces.* MIKE *and* MAX *push them off.)*

BOBBY   And there you have it. We are all present in Güllen once again. The plaintiff. The defendant. The two false witnesses. The judge. Many years have passed. Does the plaintiff have anything further to add?

CLAIRE   There is nothing to add.

BOBBY   And the defendant?

SCHILL   Why are you doing this? It was all dead and buried.

BOBBY   What happened to the child that was born?

CLAIRE *(in a low voice)*   It lived a year.

BOBBY   And what happened to you?

CLAIRE   I became a whore.

BOBBY   Why?

CLAIRE   The judgment of the court left me no alternative. No one would trust me. No one would give me work.

BOBBY   So. And now, what is the nature of the reparation you demand?

CLAIRE   I want the life of Anton Schill.

*(*FRAU SCHILL *springs to Anton's side. She puts her arms around him. The children rush to him. He breaks away.)*

FRAU SCHILL   Anton! No! No!

SCHILL   No— No— She's joking. That happened long ago. That's all forgotten.

CLAIRE   Nothing is forgotten. Neither the mornings in the forest, nor the nights in the great barn, nor the bedroom in the cottage, nor your treachery at the end. You said this morning that you wished that time might be rolled back. Very well—I have rolled it back. And now it is I who will buy justice. You bought it with a bottle of schnapps. I am willing to pay one billion marks.

(The BURGOMASTER *stands up, very pale and dignified.)*

BURGOMASTER Madame Zachanassian, we are not in the jungle. We are in Europe. We may be poor, but we are not heathens. In the name of the town of Güllen, I decline your offer. In the name of humanity. We shall never accept.

(All applaud wildly. The applause turns into a sinister rhythmic beat. As CLAIRE *rises, it dies away. She looks at the crowd, then at the* BURGOMASTER.*)*

CLAIRE Thank you, Burgomaster. *(She stares at him a long moment.)* I can wait.

(She turns and walks off.)

(Curtain.)

ACT II

The façade of the Golden Apostle, with a balcony on which chairs and a table are set out. To the right of the inn is a sign which reads: "ANTON SCHILL, HANDLUNG."[1] *Under the sign the shop is represented by a broken counter. Behind the counter are some shelves with tobacco, cigarettes, and liquor bottles. There are two milk cans. The shop door is imaginary, but each entrance is indicated by a doorbell with a tinny sound.*

It is early morning.

SCHILL *is sweeping the shop. The son has a pan and brush and also sweeps. The* DAUGHTER *is dusting. They are singing "The Happy Wanderer."*

SCHILL Karl—

*(*KARL *crosses with a dustpan.* SCHILL *sweeps dust into the pan. The doorbell rings. The* THIRD MAN *appears, carrying a crate of eggs.)*

THIRD MAN 'Morning.
SCHILL Ah, good morning, Wechsler.
THIRD MAN Twelve dozen eggs, medium brown. Right?
SCHILL Take them, Karl. *(The* SON *puts the crate in a corner.)* Did they deliver the milk yet?
SON Before you came down.
THIRD MAN Eggs are going up again, Herr Schill. First of the month.

(He gives SCHILL *a slip to sign.)*

SCHILL What? Again? And who's going to buy them?
THIRD MAN Fifty pfennig a dozen.
SCHILL I'll have to cancel my order, that's all.
THIRD MAN That's up to you, Herr Schill.

*(*SCHILL *signs the slip.)*

SCHILL There's nothing else to do. *(He hands back the slip.)* And how's the family?

---

[1] "Anton Schill, Merchandise."

THIRD MAN   Oh, scraping along. Maybe now things will get better.

SCHILL   Maybe.

THIRD MAN *(going)* 'Morning.

SCHILL   Close the door. Don't let the flies in. *(The children resume their singing.)* Now, listen to me, children. I have a little piece of good news for you. I didn't mean to speak of it yet awhile, but well, why not? Who do you suppose is going to be the next Burgomaster? Eh? *(They look up at him.)* Yes, in spite of everything. It's settled. It's official. What an honor for the family, eh? Especially at a time like this. To say nothing of the salary and the rest of it.

SON   Burgomaster!

SCHILL   Burgomaster. *(The* SON *shakes him warmly by the hand. The* DAUGHTER *kisses him.)* You see, you don't have to be entirely ashamed of your father. *(Silence)* Is your mother coming down to breakfast soon?

DAUGHTER   Mother's tired. She's going to stay upstairs.

SCHILL   You have a good mother, at least. There you are lucky. Oh, well, if she wants to rest, let her rest. We'll have breakfast together, the three of us. I'll fry some eggs and open a tin of the American ham. This morning we're going to breakfast like kings.

SON   I'd like to, only—I can't.

SCHILL   You've got to eat, you know.

SON   I've got to run down to the station. One of the laborers is sick. They said they could use me.

SCHILL   You want to work on the rails in all this heat? That's no work for a son of mine.

SON   Look, Father, we can use the money.

SCHILL   Well, if you feel you have to.

(The SON *goes to the door. The* DAUGHTER *moves toward* SCHILL.)

DAUGHTER   I'm sorry, Father. I have to go too.

SCHILL   You too? And where is the young lady going, if I may be so bold?

DAUGHTER   There may be something for me at the employment agency.

SCHILL   Employment agency?

DAUGHTER   It's important to get there early.

SCHILL   All right. I'll have something nice for you when you get home.

SON *and* DAUGHTER *(salute)*   Good day, Burgomaster.

(The SON *and* DAUGHTER *go out. The* FIRST MAN *comes into* SCHILL's *shop. Mandolin and guitar music are heard offstage.)*

SCHILL   Good morning, Hofbauer.

FIRST MAN   Cigarettes. (SCHILL *takes a pack from the shelf.*) Not those. I'll have the green today.

SCHILL   They cost more.

FIRST MAN   Put it in the book.

SCHILL   What?

FIRST MAN   Charge it.

SCHILL   Well, all right, I'll make an exception this time—seeing it's you, Hofbauer.

(SCHILL *writes in his cash book.*)

FIRST MAN *(opening the pack of cigarettes)*   Who's that playing out there?

SCHILL   The two blind men.

FIRST MAN   They play well.

SCHILL To hell with them.

FIRST MAN They make you nervous? (SCHILL *shrugs. The* FIRST MAN *lights a cigarette.*) She's getting ready for the wedding, I hear.

SCHILL Yes. So they say.

(Enter the FIRST *and* SECOND WOMAN. *They cross to the counter.)*

FIRST WOMAN Good morning, good morning.

SECOND WOMAN Good morning.

FIRST MAN Good morning.

SCHILL Good morning, ladies.

FIRST WOMAN Good morning, Herr Schill.

SECOND WOMAN Good morning.

FIRST WOMAN Milk please, Herr Schill.

SCHILL Milk.

SECOND WOMAN And milk for me too.

SCHILL A liter of milk each. Right away.

FIRST WOMAN Whole milk, please, Herr Schill.

SCHILL Whole milk?

SECOND WOMAN Yes. Whole milk, please.

SCHILL Whole milk, I can only give you half a liter each of whole milk.

FIRST WOMAN All right.

SCHILL Half a liter of whole milk here, and half a liter of whole milk here. There you are.

FIRST WOMAN And butter please, a quarter kilo.

SCHILL Butter, I haven't any butter. I can give you some very nice lard?

FIRST WOMAN No. Butter.

SCHILL Goose fat? *(The* FIRST WOMAN *shakes her head.)* Chicken fat?

FIRST WOMAN Butter.

SCHILL Butter. Now, wait a minute, though. I have a tin of imported butter here somewhere. Ah. There you are. No, sorry, she asked first, but I can order some for you from Kalkerstadt tomorrow.

SECOND WOMAN And white bread.

SCHILL White bread.

(He takes a loaf and a knife.)

SECOND WOMAN The whole loaf.

SCHILL But a whole loaf would cost . . .

SECOND WOMAN Charge it.

SCHILL Charge it?

FIRST WOMAN And a package of milk chocolate.

SCHILL Package of milk chocolate—right away.

SECOND WOMAN One for me, too, Herr Schill.

SCHILL And a package of milk chocolate for you, too.

FIRST WOMAN We'll eat it here, if you don't mind.

SCHILL Yes, please do.

SECOND WOMAN It's so cool at the back of the shop.

SCHILL Charge it?

WOMEN Of course.

SCHILL All for one, one for all.

(The SECOND MAN *enters.)*

SECOND MAN   Good morning.

THE TWO WOMEN   Good morning.

SCHILL   Good morning, Helmesberger.

SECOND MAN   It's going to be a hot day.

SCHILL   Phew!

SECOND MAN   How's business?

SCHILL   Fabulous. For a while no one came, and now all of a sudden I'm running a luxury trade.

SECOND MAN   Good!

SCHILL   Oh, I'll never forget the way you all stood by me at the Golden Apostle in spite of your need, in spite of everything. That was the finest hour of my life.

FIRST MAN   We're not heathens, you know.

SECOND MAN   We're behind you, my boy; the whole town's behind you.

FIRST MAN   As firm as a rock.

FIRST WOMAN *(munching her chocolate)*   As firm as a rock, Herr Schill.

BOTH WOMEN   As firm as a rock.

SECOND MAN   There's no denying it—you're the most popular man in town.

FIRST MAN   The most important.

SECOND MAN   And in the spring, God willing, you will be our Burgomaster.

FIRST MAN   Sure as a gun.

ALL   Sure as a gun.

(Enter PEDRO *with fishing equipment and a fish in his landing net.)*

PEDRO   Would you please weigh my fish for me?

SCHILL *(weighs it)*   Two kilos.

PEDRO   Is that all?

SCHILL   Two kilos exactly.

PEDRO   Two kilos!

(He gives SCHILL *a tip and exits.)*

SECOND WOMAN   The fiancé.

FIRST WOMAN   They're to be married this week. It will be a tremendous wedding.

SECOND WOMAN   I saw his picture in the paper.

FIRST WOMAN *(sighs)*   Ah, what a man!

SECOND MAN   Give me a bottle of schnapps.

SCHILL   The usual?

SECOND MAN   No, cognac.

SCHILL   Cognac? But cognac costs twenty-two marks fifty.

SECOND MAN   We all have to splurge a little now and again—

SCHILL   Here you are. Three Star.

SECOND MAN   And a package of pipe tobacco.

SCHILL   Black or blond?

SECOND MAN   English.

SCHILL   English! But that makes twenty-three marks eighty.

SECOND MAN   Chalk it up.

SCHILL   Now, look. I'll make an exception this week. Only, you will have to pay me the moment your unemployment check comes in. I don't want to be kept waiting. *(Suddenly)* Helmesberger, are those new shoes you're wearing?

SECOND MAN   Yes, what about it?

SCHILL You too, Hofbauer. Yellow shoes! Brand new!

FIRST MAN So?

SCHILL *(to the women)* And you. You all have new shoes! New shoes!

FIRST WOMAN A person can't walk around forever in the same old shoes.

SECOND WOMAN Shoes wear out.

SCHILL And the money. Where does the money come from?

FIRST WOMAN We got them on credit, Herr Schill.

SECOND WOMAN On credit.

SCHILL On credit? And where all of a sudden do you get credit?

SECOND MAN Everybody gives credit now.

FIRST WOMAN You gave us credit yourself.

SCHILL And what are you going to pay with? Eh? *(They are all silent.* SCHILL *advances upon them threateningly.)* With what? Eh? With what? With what?

(Suddenly he understands. He takes his apron off quickly, flings it on the counter, gets his jacket, and walks off with an air of determination. Now the shop sign vanishes. The shelves are pushed off. The lights go up on the balcony of the Golden Apostle, and the balcony unit itself moves forward into the optical center. CLAIRE *and* BOBBY *step out on the balcony.* CLAIRE *sits down.* BOBBY *serves coffee.)*

CLAIRE A lovely autumn morning. A silver haze on the streets and a violet sky above. Count Holk would have liked this. Remember him, Bobby? My third husband?

BOBBY Yes, madame.

CLAIRE Horrible man!

BOBBY Yes, madame.

CLAIRE Where is Monsieur Pedro? Is he up yet?

BOBBY Yes, madame. He's fishing.

CLAIRE Already? What a singular passion!

(PEDRO *comes in with the fish.)*

PEDRO Good morning, my love.

CLAIRE Pedro! There you are.

PEDRO Look, my darling. Four kilos!

CLAIRE A jewel! I'll have it grilled for your lunch. Give it to Bobby.

PEDRO Ah—it is so wonderful here! I like your little town.

CLAIRE Oh, do you?

PEDRO Yes. These people, they are all so—what is the word?

CLAIRE Simple, honest, hard-working, decent.

PEDRO But, my angel, you are a mind reader. That's just what I was going to say—however did you guess?

CLAIRE I know them.

PEDRO Yet when we arrived it was all so dirty, so—what is the word?

CLAIRE Shabby.

PEDRO Exactly. But now everywhere you go, you see them busy as bees, cleaning their streets—

CLAIRE Repairing their houses, sweeping—dusting—hanging new curtains in the windows—singing as they work.

PEDRO But you astonishing, wonderful woman! You can't see all that from here.

CLAIRE I know them. And in their gardens—I am sure that in their gardens they are manuring the soil for the spring.

PEDRO   My angel, you know everything. This morning on my way fishing I said to myself, look at them all manuring their gardens. It is extraordinary—and it's all because of you. Your return has given them a new—what is the word?

CLAIRE   Lease on life?

PEDRO   Precisely.

CLAIRE   The town was dying, it's true. But a town doesn't have to die. I think they realize that now. People die, not towns. Bobby! (BOBBY *appears.*) A cigar.

(The lights fade on the balcony, which moves back upstage. Somewhat to the right, a sign descends. It reads: "Polizei." The POLICEMAN *pushes a desk under it. This, with the bench, becomes the police station. He places a bottle of beer and a glass on the desk, and goes to hang up his coat offstage. The telephone rings.)*

POLICEMAN   Schultz speaking. Yes, we have a couple of rooms for the night. No, not for rent. This is not the hotel. This is the Güllen police station.

(He laughs and hangs up. SCHILL *comes in. He is evidently nervous.)*

SCHILL   Schultz.

POLICEMAN   Hello, Schill. Come in. Sit down. Beer?

SCHILL   Please.

(He drinks thirstily.)

POLICEMAN   What can I do for you?

SCHILL   I want you to arrest Madame Zachanassian.

POLICEMAN   Eh?

SCHILL   I said I want you to arrest Madame Zachanassian.

POLICEMAN   What the hell are you talking about?

SCHILL   I ask you to arrest this woman at once.

POLICEMAN   What offense has the lady committed?

SCHILL   You know perfectly well. She offered a billion marks—

POLICEMAN   And you want her arrested for that?

(He pours beer into his glass.)

SCHILL   Schultz! It's your duty.

POLICEMAN   Extraordinary! Extraordinary idea!

(He drinks his beer.)

SCHILL   I'm speaking to you as your next Burgomaster.

POLICEMAN   Schill, that's true. The lady offered us a billion marks. But that doesn't entitle us to take police action against her.

SCHILL   Why not?

POLICEMAN   In order to be arrested, a person must first commit a crime.

SCHILL   Incitement to murder.

POLICEMAN   Incitement to murder is a crime. I agree.

SCHILL   Well?

POLICEMAN   And such a proposal—if serious—constitutes an assault.

SCHILL   That's what I mean.

POLICEMAN   But her offer can't be serious.

SCHILL   Why?

POLICEMAN   The price is too high. In a case like yours, one pays a thousand marks, at the most two thousand. But not a billion! That's ridiculous. And even if she meant it, that would only prove she was out of her mind. And that's not a matter for the police.

SCHILL Whether she's out of her mind or not, the danger to me is the same. That's obvious.

POLICEMAN Look, Schill, you show us where anyone threatens your life in any way— say, for instance, a man points a gun at you—and we'll be there in a flash.

SCHILL *(gets up)* So I'm to wait till someone points a gun at me?

POLICEMAN Pull yourself together, Schill. We're all for you in this town.

SCHILL I wish I could believe it.

POLICEMAN You don't believe it?

SCHILL No. No, I don't. All of a sudden my customers are buying white bread, whole milk, butter, imported tobacco. What does it mean?

POLICEMAN It means business is picking up.

SCHILL Helmesberger lives on the dole; he hasn't earned anything in five years. To-day he bought French cognac.

POLICEMAN I'll have to try your cognac one of these days.

SCHILL And shoes. They all have new shoes.

POLICEMAN And what have you got against new shoes? I'm wearing a new pair myself.

(He holds out his foot.)

SCHILL You too?

POLICEMAN Why not?

(He pours out the rest of his beer.)

SCHILL Is that Pilsen you're drinking now?

POLICEMAN It's the only thing.

SCHILL You used to drink the local beer.

POLICEMAN Hogwash.

(Radio music is heard offstage.)

SCHILL Listen. You hear?

POLICEMAN "The Merry Widow." Yes.

SCHILL No. It's a radio.

POLICEMAN That's Bergholzer's radio.

SCHILL Bergholzer!

POLICEMAN You're right. He should close his window when he plays it. I'll make a note to speak to him.

(He makes a note in his notebook.)

SCHILL And how can Bergholzer pay for a radio?

POLICEMAN That's his business.

SCHILL And you, Schultz, with your new shoes and your imported beer—how are you going to pay for them?

POLICEMAN That's my business. *(His telephone rings. He picks it up.)* Police Station, Güllen. What? What? Where? Where? How? Right, we'll deal with it.

(He hangs up.)

SCHILL *(He speaks during the* POLICEMAN'S *telephone conversation.)* Schultz, listen. No. Schultz, please—listen to me. Don't you see they're all . . . Listen, please. Look,

They're all running up debts. And out of these debts comes this sudden prosperity. And out of this prosperity comes the absolute need to kill me.

POLICEMAN *(putting on his jacket)*   You're imagining things.

SCHILL   All she has to do is to sit on her balcony and wait.

POLICEMAN   Don't be a child.

SCHILL   You're all waiting.

POLICEMAN *(snaps a loaded clip into the magazine of a rifle)*   Look, Schill, you can relax. The police are here for your protection. They know their job. Let anyone, any time, make the slightest threat to your life, and all you have to do is let us know. We'll do the rest . . . Now, don't worry.

SCHILL   No, I won't.

POLICEMAN   And don't upset yourself. All right?

SCHILL   Yes. I won't. *(Then suddenly, in a low tone)* You have a new gold tooth in your mouth!

POLICEMAN   What are you talking about?

SCHILL *(taking the* POLICEMAN's *head in his hands, and forcing his lips open)*   A brand new, shining gold tooth.

POLICEMAN *(breaks away and involuntarily levels the gun at* SCHILL*)*   Are you crazy? Look, I've no time to waste. Madame Zachanassian's panther's broken loose.

SCHILL   Panther?

POLICEMAN   Yes, it's at large. I've got to hunt it down.

SCHILL   You're not hunting a panther and you know it. It's me you're hunting!

(The POLICEMAN *clicks on the safety and lowers the gun.)*

POLICEMAN   Schill! Take my advice. Go home. Lock the door. Keep out of everyone's way. That way you'll be safe. Cheer up! Good times are just around the corner!

(The lights dim in this area and light up on the balcony. PEDRO *is lounging in a chair.* CLAIRE *is smoking.)*

PEDRO   Oh, this little town oppresses me.

CLAIRE   Oh, does it? So you've changed your mind?

PEDRO   It is true, I find it charming, delightful—

CLAIRE   Picturesque.

PEDRO   Yes. After all, it's the place where you were born. But it is too quiet for me. Too provincial. Too much like all small towns everywhere. These people—look at them. They fear nothing, they desire nothing, they strive for nothing. They have everything they want. They are asleep.

CLAIRE   Perhaps one day they will come to life again.

PEDRO   My God—do I have to wait for that?

CLAIRE   Yes, you do. Why don't you go back to your fishing?

PEDRO   I think I will.

*(*PEDRO *turns to go.)*

CLAIRE   Pedro.

PEDRO   Yes, my love?

CLAIRE   Telephone the president of Hambro's Bank.[2] Ask him to transfer a billion marks to my current account.

PEDRO   A billion? Yes, my love.

---

[2] One of the principal banks of England.

The Visit **873**

(He goes. The lights fade on the balcony. A sign is flown in. It reads: "Rathaus."[3] The THIRD MAN *crosses the stage, right to left, wheeling a new television set on a hand truck. The counter of* SCHILL'S *shop is transformed into the* BURGOMASTER'S *office. The* BURGOMASTER *comes in. He takes a revolver from his pocket, examines it and sets it down on the desk. He sits down and starts writing.* SCHILL *knocks.)*

BURGOMASTER Come in.
SCHILL I must have a word with you, Burgomaster.
BURGOMASTER Ah, Schill. Sit down, my friend.
SCHILL Man to man. As your successor.
BURGOMASTER But of course. Naturally.

*(*SCHILL *remains standing. He looks at the revolver.)*

SCHILL Is that a gun?
BURGOMASTER Madame Zachanassian's black panther's broken loose. It's been seen near the cathedral. It's as well to be prepared.
SCHILL Oh, yes. Of course.
BURGOMASTER I've sent out a call for all able-bodied men with firearms. The streets have been cleared. The children have been kept in school. We don't want any accidents.
SCHILL *(suspiciously)* You're making quite a thing of it.
BURGOMASTER *(shrugs)* Naturally. A panther is a dangerous beast. Well? What's on your mind? Speak out. We're old friends.
SCHILL That's a good cigar you're smoking, Burgomaster.
BURGOMASTER Yes. Havana.
SCHILL You used to smoke something else.
BURGOMASTER Fortuna.
SCHILL Cheaper.
BURGOMASTER Too strong.
SCHILL A new tie? Silk?
BURGOMASTER Yes. Do you like it?
SCHILL And have you also bought new shoes?
BURGOMASTER *(brings his feet out from under the desk)* Why, yes. I ordered a new pair from Kalberstadt. Extraordinary! However did you guess?
SCHILL That's why I'm here.

(The THIRD MAN *knocks.)*

BURGOMASTER Come in.
THIRD MAN The new typewriter, sir.
BURGOMASTER Put it on the table. *(The* THIRD MAN *sets it down and goes.)* What's the matter with you? My dear fellow, aren't you well?
SCHILL It's you who don't seem well, Burgomaster.
BURGOMASTER What do you mean?
SCHILL You look pale.
BURGOMASTER I?
SCHILL Your hands are trembling. *(The* BURGOMASTER *involuntarily hides his hands.)* Are you frightened?
BURGOMASTER What have I to be afraid of?
SCHILL Perhaps this sudden prosperity alarms you.

---

[3] City Hall.

BURGOMASTER   Is prosperity a crime?

SCHILL   That depends on how you pay for it.

BURGOMASTER   You'll have to forgive me, Schill, but I really haven't the slightest idea what you're talking about. Am I supposed to feel like a criminal every time I order a new typewriter?

SCHILL   Do you?

BURGOMASTER   Well, I hope you haven't come here to talk about a new typewriter. Now, what was it you wanted?

SCHILL   I have come to claim the protection of the authorities.

BURGOMASTER   Ei! Against whom?

SCHILL   You know against whom.

BURGOMASTER   You don't trust us?

SCHILL   That woman has put a price on my head.

BURGOMASTER   If you don't feel safe, why don't you go to the police?

SCHILL   I have just come from the police.

BURGOMASTER   And?

SCHILL   The chief has a new gold tooth in his mouth.

BURGOMASTER   A new—? Oh, Schill, really! You're forgetting. This is Güllen, the town of humane traditions. Goethe slept here. Brahms composed a quartet. You must have faith in us. This is a law-abiding community.

SCHILL   Then arrest this woman who wants to have me killed.

BURGOMASTER   Look here, Schill. God knows the lady has every right to be angry with you. What you did there wasn't very pretty. You forced two decent lads to perjure themselves and had a young girl thrown out on the streets.

SCHILL   That young girl owns half the world.

(A moment's silence.)

BURGOMASTER   Very well, then, we'll speak frankly.

SCHILL   That's why I'm here.

BURGOMASTER   Man to man, just as you said. *(He clears his throat.)* Now—after what you did, you have no moral right to say a word against this lady. And I advise you not to try. Also—I regret to have to tell you this—there is no longer any question of your being elected Burgomaster.

SCHILL   Is that official?

BURGOMASTER   Official.

SCHILL   I see.

BURGOMASTER   The man who is chosen to exercise the high post of Burgomaster must have, obviously, certain moral qualifications. Qualifications which, unhappily, you no longer possess. Naturally, you may count on the esteem and friendship of the town, just as before. That goes without saying. The best thing will be to spread the mantle of silence over the whole miserable business.

SCHILL   So I'm to remain silent while they arrange my murder?

(The BURGOMASTER gets up.)

BURGOMASTER   *(suddenly noble)*   Now, who is arranging your murder? Give me the names and I will investigate the case at once. Unrelentingly. Well? The names?

SCHILL   You.

BURGOMASTER   I resent this. Do you think we want to kill you for money?

SCHILL   No. You don't want to kill me. But you want to have me killed.

(The lights go down. The stage is filled with men prowling about with rifles, as if they were stalking a quarry. In the interval the POLICEMAN's *bench and the* BURGOMASTER's *desk are shifted somewhat, so that they will compose the setting for the sacristy. The stage empties. The lights come up on the balcony.* CLAIRE *appears.)*

CLAIRE   Bobby, what's going on here? What are all these men doing with guns? Whom are they hunting?

BOBBY   The black panther has escaped, madame.

CLAIRE   Who let him out?

BOBBY   Kobby and Lobby, madame.

CLAIRE   How excited they are! There may be shooting?

BOBBY   It is possible, madame.

(The lights fade on the balcony. The sacristan comes in. He arranges the set, and puts the altar cloth on the altar. Then SCHILL *comes on. He is looking for the* PASTOR. *The* PASTOR *enters, left. He is wearing his gown and carrying a rifle.)*

SCHILL   Sorry to disturb you, Pastor.

PASTOR   God's house is open to all. *(He sees that* SCHILL *is staring at the gun.)* Oh, the gun? That's because of the panther. It's best to be prepared.

SCHILL   Pastor, help me.

PASTOR   Of course. Sit down. *(He puts the rifle on the bench.)* What's the trouble?

SCHILL *(sits on the bench)*   I'm frightened.

PASTOR   Frightened? Of what?

SCHILL   Of everyone. They're hunting me down like a beast.

PASTOR   Have no fear of man, Schill. Fear God. Fear not the death of the body. Fear the death of the soul. Zip up my gown behind, Sacristan.

SCHILL   I'm afraid, Pastor.

PASTOR   Put your trust in heaven, my friend.

SCHILL   You see, I'm not well. I shake. I have such pains around the heart. I sweat.

PASTOR   I know. You're passing through a profound psychic experience.

SCHILL   I'm going through hell.

PASTOR   The hell you are going through exists only within yourself. Many years ago you betrayed a girl shamefully, for money. Now you think that we shall sell you just as you sold her. No, my friend, you are projecting your guilt upon others. It's quite natural. But remember, the root of our torment lies always within ourselves, in our hearts, in our sins. When you have understood this, you can conquer the fears that oppress you; you have weapons with which to destroy them.

SCHILL   Siemethofer has bought a new washing machine.

PASTOR   Don't worry about the washing machine. Worry about your immortal soul.

SCHILL   Stockers has a television set.

PASTOR   There is also great comfort in prayer. Sacristan, the bands. (SCHILL *crosses to the altar and kneels. The sacristan ties on the* PASTOR's *bands.)* Examine your conscience, Schill. Repent. Otherwise your fears will consume you. Believe me, this is the only way. We have no other. *(The church bell begins to peal.* SCHILL *seems relieved.)* Now I must leave you. I have a baptism. You may stay as long as you like. Sacristan, the Bible, Liturgy, and Psalter. The child is beginning to cry. I can hear it from here. It is frightened. Let us make haste to give it the only security which this world affords.

SCHILL   A new bell?

PASTOR   Yes. It's tone is marvelous, don't you think? Full. Sonorous.

SCHILL *(steps back in horror)*   A new bell! You too, Pastor? You too?

(The PASTOR *clasps his hands in horror. Then he takes* SCHILL *into his arms.)*

PASTOR   Oh, God, God forgive me. We are poor, weak things, all of us. Do not tempt us further into the hell in which you are burning. Go Schill, my friend, go my brother, go while there is time.

(The PASTOR *goes.* SCHILL *picks up the rifle with a gesture of desperation. He goes out with it. As the lights fade, men appear with guns. Two shots are fired in the darkness. The lights come up on the balcony, which moves forward.)*

CLAIRE   Bobby! What was that shooting? Have they caught the panther?
BOBBY   He is dead, madame.
CLAIRE   There were two shots.
BOBBY   The panther is dead, madame.
CLAIRE   I loved him. *(Waves* BOBBY *away)* I shall miss him.

(The TEACHER *comes in with two little girls, singing. They stop under the balcony.)*

TEACHER   Gracious lady, be so good as to accept our heartfelt condolences. Your beautiful panther is no more. Believe me, we are deeply pained that so tragic an event should mar your visit here. But what could we do? The panther was savage, a beast. To him our human laws could not apply. There was no other way—(SCHILL *appears with the gun. He looks dangerous. The girls run off, frightened. The* TEACHER *follows the girls.)* Children—children—children!

CLAIRE   Anton, why are you frightening the children?

(He works the bolt, loading the chamber, and raises the gun slowly.)

SCHILL   Go away, Claire—I warn you. Go away.
CLAIRE   How strange it is, Anton! How clearly it comes back to me! The day we saw one another for the first time, do you remember? I was on a balcony then. It was a day like today, a day in autumn without a breath of wind, warm as it is now—only lately I am always cold. You stood down there and stared at me without moving. I was embarrassed. I didn't know what to do. I wanted to go back into the darkness of the room, where it was safe, but I couldn't. You stared up at me darkly, almost angrily, as if you wished to hurt me, but your eyes were full of passion. (SCHILL *begins to lower the rifle involuntarily.)* Then, I don't know why, I left the balcony and I came down and stood in the street beside you. You didn't greet me, you didn't say a word, but you took my hand and we walked together out of the town into the fields, and behind us came Kobby and Lobby, like two dogs, sniveling and giggling and snarling. Suddenly you picked up a stone and hurled it at them, and they ran yelping back into the town, and we were alone. (SCHILL *has lowered the rifle completely. He moves forward toward her, as close as he can come.)* That was the beginning, and everything else had to follow. There is no escape.

(She goes in and closes the shutters. SCHILL *stands immobile. The* TEACHER *tiptoes in. He stares at* SCHILL, *who doesn't see him. Then he beckons to the children.)*

TEACHER   Come, children, sing. Sing.

(They begin singing. He creeps behind SCHILL *and snatches away the rifle.* SCHILL *turns sharply. The* PASTOR *comes in.)*

PASTOR   Go, Schill—go!

*(SCHILL *goes out. The children continue singing, moving across the stage and off. The Golden Apostle vanishes. The crossing bell is heard. The scene dissolves into the railway-*

station setting, as in Act One. But there are certain changes. The timetable marked "Fahr-plan" is now new, the frame freshly painted. There is a new travel poster on the station wall. It has a yellow sun and the words: "Reist in den Süden."[4] On the other side of the Fahrplan is another poster with the words: "Die Passionsspiele Oberammergau."[5] The sound of passing trains covers the scene change. SCHILL *appears with an old valise in his hand, dressed in a shabby trench coat, his hat on his head. He looks about with a furtive air, walking slowly to the platform. Slowly, as if by chance, the townspeople enter, from all sides.* SCHILL *hesitates, stops.)*

BURGOMASTER *(from upstage, center)*　Good evening, Schill.

SCHILL　Good evening.

POLICEMAN　Good evening.

SCHILL　Good evening.

PAINTER *(enters)*　Good evening.

SCHILL　Good evening.

DOCTOR　Good evening.

SCHILL　Good evening.

BURGOMASTER　So you're taking a little trip?

SCHILL　Yes. A little trip.

POLICEMAN　May one ask where to?

SCHILL　I don't know.

PAINTER　Don't know?

SCHILL　To Kalberstadt.

BURGOMASTER *(with disbelief, pointing to the valise)*　Kalberstadt?

SCHILL　After that—somewhere else.

PAINTER　Ah. After that somewhere else.

(The FOURTH MAN *walks in.)*

SCHILL　I thought maybe Australia.

BURGOMASTER　Australia!

ALL　Australia!

SCHILL　I'll raise the money somehow.

BURGOMASTER　But why Australia?

POLICEMAN　What would you be doing in Australia?

SCHILL　One can't always live in the same town, year in, year out.

PAINTER　But Australia—

DOCTOR　It's a risky trip for a man of your age.

BURGOMASTER　One of the lady's little men ran off to Australia . . .

ALL　Yes.

POLICEMAN　You'll be much safer here.

PAINTER　Much!

*(*SCHILL *looks about him in anguish, like a beast at bay.)*

SCHILL *(low voice.)*　I wrote a letter to the administration at Kaffigen.

BURGOMASTER　Yes? And?

(They are all intent on the answer.)

SCHILL　They didn't answer.

[4] Travel in the South.　　[5] The Oberammergau Passion Play, portraying the suffering and death of Jesus, is performed in the south German village every ten years.

(All laugh.)

DOCTOR   Do you mean to say you don't trust old friends? That's not very flattering, you know.

BURGOMASTER   No one's going to do you any harm here.

DOCTOR   No harm here.

SCHILL   They didn't answer because our postmaster held up my letter.

PAINTER   Our postmaster? What an idea.

BURGOMASTER   The postmaster is a member of the town council.

POLICEMAN   A man of the utmost integrity.

DOCTOR   He doesn't hold up letters. What an idea!

STATION MASTER *(announces)*   Local to Kalberstadt!

(The townspeople all cross down to see the train arrive. Then they turn, with their backs to the audience, in a line across the stage. SCHILL *cannot get through to reach the train.)*

SCHILL *(in a low voice)*   What are you all doing here? What do you want of me?

BURGOMASTER   We don't like to see you go.

DOCTOR   We've come to see you off.

(The sound of the approaching train grows louder.)

SCHILL   I didn't ask you to come.

POLICEMAN   But we have come.

DOCTOR   As old friends.

ALL   As old friends.

(The STATION MASTER *holds up his paddle. The train stops with a screech of brakes. We hear the engine panting offstage.)*

VOICE *(offstage)*   Güllen!

BURGOMASTER   A pleasant journey.

DOCTOR   And long life!

PAINTER   And good luck in Australia!

ALL   Yes, good luck in Australia.

(They press around him jovially. He stands motionless and pale.)

SCHILL   Why are you crowding me?

POLICEMAN   What's the matter now?

(The STATION MASTER *blows a long blast on his whistle.)*

SCHILL   Give me room.

DOCTOR   But you have plenty of room.

(They all move away from him.)

POLICEMAN   Better get aboard, Schill.

SCHILL   I see. I see. One of you is going to push me under the wheels.

POLICEMAN   Oh, nonsense. Go on, get aboard.

SCHILL   Get away from me, all of you.

BURGOMASTER   I don't know what you want. Just get on the train.

SCHILL   No. One of you will push me under.

DOCTOR   You're being ridiculous. Now, go on, get on the train.

SCHILL   Why are you all so near me?

DOCTOR   The man's gone mad.

STATION MASTER   'Board!

> (*He blows his whistle. The engine bell clangs. The train starts.*)

BURGOMASTER   Get aboard, man. Quick.

(*The following speeches are spoken all together until the train noises fade away.*)

DOCTOR   The train's starting.

ALL   Get aboard, man. Get aboard. The train's starting.

SCHILL   If I try to get aboard, one of you will hold me back.

ALL   No, no.

BURGOMASTER   Get on the train.

SCHILL   (*in terror, crouches against the wall of the* STATION MASTER's *office*)   No—no—no. No. (*He falls on his knees. The others crowd around him. He cowers on the ground, abjectly. The train sounds fade away.*) Oh, no—no—don't push me, don't push me!

POLICEMAN   There. It's gone off without you.

(*Slowly they leave him. He raises himself up to a sitting position, still trembling. A* TRUCK DRIVER *enters with an empty can.*)

TRUCK DRIVER   Do you know where I can get some water? My truck's boiling over. (SCHILL *points to the station office.*) Thanks. (*He enters the office, gets the water and comes out. By this time,* SCHILL *is erect.*) Missed your train?

SCHILL   Yes.

TRUCK DRIVER   To Kalberstadt?

SCHILL   Yes.

TRUCK DRIVER   Well, come with me. I'm going that way.

SCHILL   This is my town. This is my home. (*With strange new dignity*) No, thank you. I've changed my mind. I'm staying.

TRUCK DRIVER   (*shrugs*)   All right.

> (*He goes out.* SCHILL *picks up his bag, looks right and left, and slowly walks off.*)

> (*Curtain*)

ACT III

Music is heard. Then the curtain rises on the interior of the old barn, a dim, cavernous structure. Bars of light fall across the shadowy forms, shafts of sunlight from the holes and cracks in the walls and roof. Overhead hang old rags, decaying sacks, great cobwebs. Extreme left is a ladder leading to the loft. Near it, an old haycart. Left, CLAIRE ZACHANASSIAN *is sitting in her gilded sedan chair, motionless, in her magnificent bridal gown and veil. Near the chair stands an old keg.*

BOBBY   (*comes in, treading carefully*)   The doctor and the teacher from the high school to see you, madame.

CLAIRE   (*impassive*)   Show them in.

(BOBBY *ushers them in as if they were entering a hall of state. The two grope their way through the litter. At last they find the lady, and bow. They are both well dressed in new clothes, but are very dusty.*)

BOBBY   Dr. Nüsslin and Professor Müller.

DOCTOR   Madame.

CLAIRE   You look dusty, gentlemen.

DOCTOR *(dusts himself off vigorously)*   Oh, forgive us. We had to climb over an old carriage.

TEACHER   Our respects.

DOCTOR   A fabulous wedding.

TEACHER   Beautiful occasion.

CLAIRE   It's stifling here. But I love this old barn. The smell of hay and old straw and axle grease—it is the scent of my youth. Sit down. All this rubbish—the haycart, the old carriage, the cask, even the pitchfork—it was all here when I was a girl.

TEACHER   Remarkable place.

(He mops his brow.)

CLAIRE   I thought the pastor's text was very appropriate. The lesson a trifle long.

TEACHER   1 Corinthians 13.[1]

CLAIRE   Your choristers sang beautifully, Professor.

TEACHER   Bach. From the *St. Matthew Passion*.

DOCTOR   Güllen has never seen such magnificence! The flowers! The jewels! And the people.

TEACHER   The theatrical world, the world of finance, the world of art, the world of science . . .

CLAIRE   All these worlds are now back in their Cadillacs, speeding toward the capital for the wedding reception. But I'm sure you didn't come here to talk about them.

DOCTOR   Dear lady, we should not intrude on your valuable time. Your husband must be waiting impatiently.

CLAIRE   No, no, I've packed him off to Brazil.

DOCTOR   To Brazil, madame?

CLAIRE   Yes. For his honeymoon.

TEACHER *and* DOCTOR   Oh! But your wedding guests?

CLAIRE   I've planned a delightful dinner for them. They'll never miss me. Now what was it you wished to talk about?

TEACHER   About Anton Schill, madame.

CLAIRE   Is he dead?

TEACHER   Madame, we may be poor. But we have our principles.

CLAIRE   I see. Then what do you want?

TEACHER *(He mops his brow again.)*   The fact is, madame, in anticipation of your well-known munificence, that is, feeling that you would give the town some sort of gift, we have all been buying things. Necessities . . .

DOCTOR   With money we don't have.

(The TEACHER blows his nose.)

CLAIRE   You've run into debt?

DOCTOR   Up to here.

CLAIRE   In spite of your principles?

TEACHER   We're human, madame.

CLAIRE   I see.

---

[1] See 1 Corinthians 13:13: "But now abideth faith, hope, love, these three; and the greatest of these is love."

TEACHER   We have been poor for a long time. A long, long time.

DOCTOR *(He rises.)*   The question is, how are we going to pay?

CLAIRE   You already know.

TEACHER *(courageously)*   I beg you, Madame Zachanassian, put yourself in our position for a moment. For twenty-two years I've been cudgeling my brains to plant a few seeds of knowledge in this wilderness. And all this time, my gallant colleague, Dr. Nüsslin, has been rattling around in his ancient Mercedes, from patient to patient, trying to keep these wretches alive. Why? Why have we spent our lives in this miserable hole? For money? Hardly. The pay is ridiculous.

DOCTOR   And yet, the professor here has declined an offer to head the high school in Kalberstadt.

TEACHER   And Dr. Nüsslin has refused an important post at the University of Erlangen. Madame, the simple fact is, we love our town. We were born here. It is our life.

DOCTOR   That's true.

TEACHER   What has kept us going all these years is the hope that one day the community will prosper again as it did in the days when we were young.

CLAIRE   Good.

TEACHER   Madame, there is no reason for our poverty. We suffer here from a mysterious blight. We have factories. They stand idle. There is oil in the valley of Pückenried.

DOCTOR   There is copper under the Konradsweil Forest. There is power in our streams, in our waterfalls.

TEACHER   We are not poor, madame. If we had credit, if we had confidence, the factories would open, orders and commissions would pour in. And our economy would bloom together with our cultural life. We would become once again like the towns around us, healthy and prosperous.

DOCTOR   If the Wagonworks were put on its feet again—

TEACHER   The Foundry.

DOCTOR   The Golden Eagle Pencil Factory.

TEACHER   Buy these plants, madame. Put them in operation once more, and I swear to you, Güllen will flourish and it will bless you. We don't need a billion marks. Ten million, properly invested, would give us back our life, and incidentally return to the investor an excellent dividend. Save us, madame. Save us, and we will not only bless you, we will make money for you.

CLAIRE   I don't need money.

DOCTOR   Madame, we are not asking for charity. This is business.

CLAIRE   It's a good idea . . .

DOCTOR   Dear lady! I knew you wouldn't let us down.

CLAIRE   But it's out of the question. I cannot buy the Wagonworks. I already own them.

DOCTOR   The Wagonworks?

TEACHER   And the Foundry?

CLAIRE   And the Foundry.

DOCTOR   And the Golden Eagle Pencil Factory?

CLAIRE   Everything. The valley of Pückenried with its oil, the forest of Konradsweil with its ore, the barn, the town, the streets, the houses, the shops, everything. I had my agents buy up this rubbish over the years, bit by bit, piece by piece, until I had it all. Your hopes were an illusion, your vision empty, your self-sacrifice a stupidity, your whole life completely senseless.

TEACHER   Then the mysterious blight—

CLAIRE   The mysterious blight was I.

DOCTOR   But this is monstrous!

CLAIRE   Monstrous. I was seventeen when I left this town. It was winter. I was dressed in a sailor suit and my red braids hung down my back. I was in my seventh month. As I walked down the street to the station, the boys whistled after me, and someone threw something. I sat freezing in my seat in the Hamburg Express. But before the roof of the great barn was lost behind the trees, I had made up my mind that one day I would come back . . .

TEACHER   But, madame—

CLAIRE *(She smiles.)*   And now I have. *(She claps her hands.)* Mike. Max. Take me back to the Golden Apostle. I've been here long enough.

(MIKE *and* MAX *start to pick up the sedan chair. The* TEACHER *pushes* MIKE *away.)*

TEACHER   Madame. One moment. Please. I see it all now. I had thought of you as an avenging fury, a Medea, a Clytemnestra—but I was wrong. You are a warm-hearted woman who has suffered a terrible injustice, and now you have returned and taught us an unforgettable lesson. You have stripped us bare. But now that we stand before you naked, I know you will set aside these thoughts of vengeance. If we made you suffer, you too have put us through the fire. Have mercy, madame.

CLAIRE   When I have had justice. Mike!

(She signals to MIKE *and* MAX *to pick up the sedan chair. They cross the stage. The* TEACHER *bars the way.)*

TEACHER   But, madame, one injustice cannot cure another. What good will it do to force us into crime? Horror succeeds horror, shame is piled on shame. It settles nothing.

CLAIRE   It settles everything.

(They move upstage toward the exit. The TEACHER *follows.)*

TEACHER   Madame, this lesson you have taught us will never be forgotten. We will hand it down from father to son. It will be a monument more lasting than any vengeance. Whatever we have been, in the future we shall be better because of you. You have pushed us to the extreme. Now forgive us. Show us the way to a better life. Have pity, madame—pity. That is the highest justice.

(The sedan chair stops.)

CLAIRE   The highest justice has no pity. It is bright and pure and clear. The world made me into a whore; now I make the world into a brothel. Those who wish to go down, may go down. Those who wish to dance with me, may dance with me. *(To her porters)* Go.

(She is carried off. The lights black out. Downstage, right, appears SCHILL's *shop. It has a new sign, a new counter. The doorbell, when it rings, has an impressive sound.* FRAU SCHILL *stands behind the counter in a new dress. The* FIRST MAN *enters, left. He is dressed as a prosperous butcher, a few bloodstains on his snowy apron, a gold watch chain across his open vest.)*

FIRST MAN   What a wedding! I'll swear the whole town was there. Cigarettes.

FRAU SCHILL   Clara is entitled to a little happiness after all. I'm happy for her. Green or white?

FIRST MAN   Turkish. The bridesmaids! Dancers and opera singers. And the dresses! Down to here.

FRAU SCHILL   It's the fashion nowadays.

FIRST MAN   Reporters! Photographers! From all over the world! *(In a low voice)* They will be here any minute.

FRAU SCHILL   What have reporters to do with us? We are simple people, Herr Hofbauer. There is nothing for them here.

FIRST MAN   They're questioning everybody. They're asking everything. *(The* FIRST MAN *lights a cigarette. He looks up at the ceiling.)* Footsteps.

FRAU SCHILL   He's pacing the room. Up and down. Day and night.

FIRST MAN   Haven't seen him all week.

FRAU SCHILL   He never goes out.

FIRST MAN   It's his conscience. That was pretty mean, the way he treated poor Madame Zachanassian.

FRAU SCHILL   That's true. I feel very badly about it myself.

FIRST MAN   To ruin a young girl like that—God doesn't forgive it. (FRAU SCHILL *nods solemnly with pursed lips. The butcher gives her a level glance.*) Look, I hope he'll have sense enough to keep his mouth shut in front of the reporters.

FRAU SCHILL   I certainly hope so.

FIRST MAN   You know his character.

FRAU SCHILL   Only too well, Herr Hofbauer.

FIRST MAN   If he tries to throw dirt at our Clara and tell a lot of lies, how she tried to get us to kill him, which anyway she never meant—

FRAU SCHILL   Of course not.

FIRST MAN   —Then we'll really have to do something! And not because of the money—*(He spits.)* But out of ordinary human decency. God knows Madame Zachanassian has suffered enough through him already.

FRAU SCHILL   She has indeed.

(The TEACHER *comes in. He is not quite sober.)*

TEACHER *(looks about the shop)*   Has the press been here yet?

FIRST MAN   No.

TEACHER   It's not my custom, as you know, Frau Schill—but I wonder if I could have a strong alcoholic drink?

FRAU SCHILL   It's an honor to serve you, Herr Professor. I have a good Steinhäger.[2] Would you like to try a glass?

TEACHER   A very small glass.

(FRAU SCHILL *serves bottle and glass. The* TEACHER *tosses off a glass.*)

FRAU SCHILL   Your hand is shaking, Herr Professor.

TEACHER   To tell the truth, I have been drinking a little already.

FRAU SCHILL   Have another glass. It will do you good.

(He accepts another glass.)

TEACHER   Is that he up there, walking?

FRAU SCHILL   Up and down. Up and down.

FIRST MAN   It's God punishing him.

(The PAINTER *comes in with the* SON *and the* DAUGHTER.)

PAINTER   Careful! A reporter just asked us the way to this shop.

FIRST MAN   I hope you didn't tell him.

---

[2] A kind of gin.

PAINTER   I told him we were strangers here.

(They all laugh. The door opens. The SECOND MAN *darts into the shop.)*

SECOND MAN   Look out, everybody! The press! They are across the street in your shop, Hofbauer.

FIRST MAN   My boy will know how to deal with them.

SECOND MAN   Make sure Schill doesn't come down, Hofbauer.

FIRST MAN   Leave that to me.

(They group themselves about the shop.)

TEACHER   Listen to me, all of you. When the reporters come I'm going to speak to them. I'm going to make a statement. A statement to the world on behalf of myself as Rector of Güllen High School and on behalf of you all, for all your sakes.

PAINTER   What are you going to say?

TEACHER   I shall tell the truth about Claire Zachanassian.

FRAU SCHILL   You're drunk, Herr Professor; you should be ashamed of yourself.

TEACHER   I should be ashamed? You should all be ashamed!

SON   Shut your trap. You're drunk.

DAUGHTER   Please, Professor—

TEACHER   Girl, you disappoint me. It is your place to speak. But you are silent and you force your old teacher to raise his voice. I am going to speak the truth. It is my duty and I am not afraid. The world may not wish to listen, but no one can silence me. I'm not going to wait—I'm going over to Hofbauer's shop now.

ALL   No, you're not. Stop him. Stop him.

(They all spring at the TEACHER. *He defends himself. At this moment,* SCHILL *appears through the door upstage. In contrast to the others, he is dressed shabbily in an old black jacket, his best.)*

SCHILL   What's going on in my shop? *(The townsmen let go of the* TEACHER *and turn to stare at* SCHILL.) What's the trouble, Professor?

TEACHER   Schill, I am speaking out at last! I am going to tell the press everything.

SCHILL   Be quiet, Professor.

TEACHER   What did you say?

SCHILL   Be quiet.

TEACHER   You want me to be quiet?

SCHILL   Please.

TEACHER   But, Schill, if I keep quiet, if you miss this opportunity—they're over in Hofbauer's shop now . . .

SCHILL   Please.

TEACHER   As you wish. If you too are on their side, I have no more to say.

(The doorbell jingles. A REPORTER *comes in.)*

REPORTER   Herr Schill.

SCHILL   Er—no. Herr Schill's gone to Kalberstadt for the day.

REPORTER   Oh, thank you. Good day.

(He goes out.)

PAINTER *(mops his brow)*   Whew! Close shave.

(He follows the REPORTER *out.)*

SECOND MAN (*walking up to* SCHILL)   That was pretty smart of you to keep your mouth shut. You know what to expect if you don't.

(He goes.)

FIRST MAN   Give me a Havana. *(*SCHILL *serves him.)* Charge it. You bastard!

(He goes. SCHILL *opens his account book.)*

FRAU SCHILL   Come along, children—

(FRAU SCHILL, *the* SON *and the* DAUGHTER *go off, upstage.*)

TEACHER   They're going to kill you. I've known it all along, and you too, you must have known it. The need is too strong, the temptation too great. And now perhaps I too will join against you. I belong to them and, like them, I can feel myself hardening into something that is not human—not beautiful.

SCHILL   It can't be helped.

TEACHER   Pull yourself together, man. Speak to the reporters; you've no time to lose.

(SCHILL *looks up from his account book.*)

SCHILL   No. I'm not going to fight any more.

TEACHER   Are you so frightened that you don't dare open your mouth?

SCHILL   I made Claire what she is, I made myself what I am. What should I do? Should I pretend that I'm innocent?

TEACHER   No, you can't. You are as guilty as hell.

SCHILL   Yes.

TEACHER   You are a bastard.

SCHILL   Yes.

TEACHER   But that does not justify your murder. (SCHILL *looks at him.*) I wish I could believe that for what they're doing—for what they're going to do—they will suffer for the rest of their lives. But it's not true. In a little while they will have justified everything and forgotten everything.

SCHILL   Of course.

TEACHER   Your name will never again be mentioned in this town. That's how it will be.

SCHILL   I don't hold it against you.

TEACHER   But I do. I will hold it against myself all my life. That's why—

(The doorbell jingles. The BURGOMASTER *comes in. The* TEACHER *stares at him, then goes out without another word.)*

BURGOMASTER   Good afternoon, Schill. Don't let me disturb you. I've just dropped in for a moment.

SCHILL   I'm just finishing my accounts for the week.

(A moment's pause.)

BURGOMASTER   The town council meets tonight. At the Golden Apostle. In the auditorium.

SCHILL   I'll be there.

BURGOMASTER   The whole town will be there. Your case will be discussed and final action taken. You've put us in a pretty tight spot, you know.

SCHILL   Yes. I'm sorry.

BURGOMASTER   The lady's offer will be rejected.

SCHILL   Possibly.

BURGOMASTER   Of course I may be wrong.

SCHILL   Of course.

BURGOMASTER   In that case—are you prepared to accept the judgment of the town? The meeting will be covered by the press, you know.

SCHILL   By the press?

BURGOMASTER   Yes, and the radio and the newsreel. It's a very ticklish situation. Not only for you—believe me, it's even worse for us. What with the wedding, and all the publicity, we've become famous. All of a sudden our ancient democratic institutions have become of interest to the world.

SCHILL   Are you going to make the lady's condition public?

BURGOMASTER   No, no, of course not. Not directly. We will have to put the matter to a vote—that is unavoidable. But only those involved will understand.

SCHILL   I see.

BURGOMASTER   As far as the press is concerned, you are simply the intermediary between us and Madame Zachanassian. I have whitewashed you completely.

SCHILL   That is very generous of you.

BURGOMASTER   Frankly, it's not for your sake, but for the sake of your family. They are honest and decent people.

SCHILL   Oh—

BURGOMASTER   So far we've all played fair. You've kept your mouth shut and so have we. Now can we continue to depend on you? Because if you have any idea of opening your mouth at tonight's meeting, there won't be any meeting.

SCHILL   I'm glad to hear an open threat at last.

BURGOMASTER   We are not threatening you. You are threatening us. If you speak, you force us to act—in advance.

SCHILL   That won't be necessary.

BURGOMASTER   So if the town decides against you?

SCHILL   I will accept their decision.

BURGOMASTER   Good. *(A moment's pause)* I'm delighted to see there is still a spark of decency left in you. But—wouldn't it be better if we didn't have to call a meeting at all? *(He pauses. He takes a gun from his pocket and puts it on the counter.)* I've brought you this.

SCHILL   Thank you.

BURGOMASTER   It's loaded.

SCHILL   I don't need a gun.

BURGOMASTER *(He clears his throat.)*   You see? We could tell the lady that we had condemned you in secret session and you had anticipated our decision. I've lost a lot of sleep getting to this point, believe me.

SCHILL   I believe you.

BURGOMASTER   Frankly, in your place, I myself would prefer to take the path of honor. Get it over with, once and for all. Don't you agree? For the sake of your friends! For the sake of our children, your own children—you have a daughter, a son—Schill, you know our need, our misery.

SCHILL   You've put me through hell, you and your town. You were my friends, you smiled and reassured me. But day by day I saw you change—your shoes, your ties, your suits—your hearts. If you had been honest with me then, perhaps I would feel differently toward you now. I might even use that gun you brought me. For the sake of my friends. But now I have conquered my fear. Alone. It was hard, but it's done. And now you will have to judge me. And I will accept your judgment. For me that will be justice. How it will be for you, I don't know. *(He turns away.)* You may kill me if you like. I won't complain, I won't protest, I won't defend myself. But I won't do your job for you either.

BURGOMASTER *(takes up his gun)*   There it is. You've had your chance and you won't take it. Too bad. *(He takes out a cigarette.)* I suppose it's more than we can expect of a man like you. (SCHILL *lights the* BURGOMASTER'S *cigarette.*) Good day.

SCHILL   Good day. *(The* BURGOMASTER *goes.* FRAU SCHILL *comes in, dressed in a fur coat. The* DAUGHTER *is in a new red dress. The* SON *has a new sports jacket.)* What a beautiful coat, Mathilde!

FRAU SCHILL   Real fur. You like it?

SCHILL   Should I? What a lovely dress, Ottilie!

DAUGHTER   *C'est très chic, n'est-ce pas?*[3]

SCHILL   What?

FRAU SCHILL   Ottilie is taking a course in French.

SCHILL   Very useful. Karl—whose autombile is that out there at the curb?

SON   Oh, it's only an Opel. They're not expensive.

SCHILL   You bought yourself a car?

SON   On credit. Easiest thing in the world.

FRAU SCHILL   Everyone's buying on credit now, Anton. These fears of yours are ridiculous. You'll see. Clara has a good heart. She only means to teach you a lesson.

DAUGHTER   She means to teach you a lesson, that's all.

SON   It's high time you got the point, Father.

SCHILL   I get the point. *(The church bells start ringing.)* Listen. The bells of Güllen. Do you hear?

SON   Yes, we have four bells now. It sounds quite good.

DAUGHTER   Just like *Gray's Elegy.*

SCHILL   What?

FRAU SCHILL   Ottilie is taking a course in English literature.

SCHILL   Congratulations! It's Sunday. I should very much like to take a ride in your car. Our car.

SON   You want to ride in the car?

SCHILL   Why not? I want to ride through the Konradsweil Forest. I want to see the town where I've lived all my life.

FRAU SCHILL   I don't think that will look very nice for any of us.

SCHILL   No—perhaps not. Well, I'll go for a walk by myself.

FRAU SCHILL   Then take us to Kalberstadt, Karl, and we'll go to a cinema.

SCHILL   A cinema? It's a good idea.

FRAU SCHILL   See you soon, Anton.

SCHILL   Good-bye, Ottilie. Good-bye, Karl. Good-bye, Mathilde.

FAMILY   Good-bye.

(They go out.)

SCHILL   Good-bye. *(The shop sign flies off. The lights black out. They come up at once on the forest scene.)* Autumn. Even the forest has turned to gold.

(SCHILL *wanders down to the bench in the forest. He sits.* CLAIRE'S *voice is heard.*)

CLAIRE *(offstage)*   Stop. Wait here. (CLAIRE *comes in. She gazes slowly up at the trees, kicks at some leaves. Then she walks slowly down center. She stops before a tree, glances up the trunk.)* Bark-borers. The old tree is dying.

---

[3] It's very smart, isn't it?

(She catches sight of SCHILL.*)*

SCHILL   Clara.

CLAIRE   How pleasant to see you here. I was visiting my forest. May I sit by you?

SCHILL   Oh, yes. Please do. *(She sits next to him.)* I've just been saying good-bye to my family. They've gone to the cinema. Karl has bought himself a car.

CLAIRE   How nice.

SCHILL   Ottilie is taking French lessons. And a course in English literature.

CLAIRE   You see? They're beginning to take an interest in higher things.

SCHILL   Listen. A finch. You hear?

CLAIRE   Yes, it's a finch. And a cuckoo in the distance. Would you like some music?

SCHILL   Oh, yes. That would be very nice.

CLAIRE   Anything special?

SCHILL   "Deep in the Forest."

CLAIRE   Your favorite song. They know it.

(She raises her hand. Offstage, the mandolin and guitar play the tune softly.)

SCHILL   We had a child?

CLAIRE   Yes.

SCHILL   Boy or girl?

CLAIRE   Girl.

SCHILL   What name did you give her?

CLAIRE   I called her Genevieve.

SCHILL   That's a very pretty name.

CLAIRE   Yes.

SCHILL   What was she like?

CLAIRE   I saw her only once. When she was born. Then they took her away from me.

SCHILL   Her eyes?

CLAIRE   They weren't open yet.

SCHILL   And her hair?

CLAIRE   Black, I think. It's usually black at first.

SCHILL   Yes, of course. Where did she die, Clara?

CLAIRE   In some family. I've forgotten their name. Meningitis, they said. The officials wrote me a letter.

SCHILL   Oh, I'm so very sorry, Clara.

CLAIRE   I've told you about our child. Now tell me about myself.

SCHILL   About yourself?

CLAIRE   Yes. How I was when I was seventeen in the days when you loved me.

SCHILL   I remember one day you waited for me in the great barn. I had to look all over the place for you. At last I found you lying in the haycart with nothing on and a long straw between your lips . . .

CLAIRE   Yes. I was pretty in those days.

SCHILL   You were beautiful, Clara.

CLAIRE   You were strong. The time you fought with those two railwaymen who were following me, I wiped the blood from your face with my red petticoat. *(The music ends.)* They've stopped.

SCHILL   Tell them to play "Thoughts of Home."

CLAIRE   They know that too.

(The music plays.)

SCHILL   Here we are, Clara, sitting together in our forest for the last time. The town council meets tonight. They will condemn me to death, and one of them will kill me. I don't know who and I don't know where. Clara, I only know that in a little while a useless life will come to an end.

(He bows his head on her bosom. She takes him in her arms.)

CLAIRE *(tenderly)*   I shall take you in your coffin to Capri. You will have your tomb in the park of my villa, where I can see you from my bedroom window. White marble and onyx in a grove of green cypress. With a beautiful view of the Mediterranean.

SCHILL   I've always wanted to see it.

CLAIRE   Your love for me died years ago, Anton. But my love for you would not die. It turned into something strong, like the hidden roots of the forest; something evil, like white mushrooms that grow unseen in the darkness. And slowly it reached out for your life. Now I have you. You are mine. Alone. At last, and forever, a peaceful ghost in a silent house.

(The music ends.)

SCHILL   The song is over.

CLAIRE   Adieu, Anton.

(CLAIRE *kisses* ANTON, *a long kiss. Then she rises.*)

SCHILL   Adieu.

(She goes. SCHILL *remains sitting on the bench. A row of lamps descends from the flies. The townsmen come in from both sides, each bearing his chair. A table and chairs are set upstage, center. On both sides sit the townspeople. The* POLICEMAN, *in a new uniform, sits on the bench behind* SCHILL. *All the townsmen are in new Sunday clothes. Around them are technicians of all sorts, with lights, cameras, and other equipment. The townswomen are absent. They do not vote. The* BURGOMASTER *takes his place at the table, center. The* DOCTOR *and the* PASTOR *sit at the same table, at his right, and the* TEACHER *in his academic gown, at his left.)*

BURGOMASTER *(At a sign from the radio technician, he pounds the floor with his wand of office.)*   Fellow citizens of Güllen, I call this meeting to order. The agenda: there is only one matter before us. I have the honor to announce officially that Madame Claire Zachanassian, daughter of our beloved citizen, the famous architect Siegfried Wäscher, has decided to make a gift to the town of one billion marks. Five hundred million to the town, five hundred million to be divided per capita among the citizens. After certain necessary preliminaries, a vote will be taken, and you, as citizens of Güllen, will signify your will by a show of hands. Has anyone any objection to this mode of procedure? The pastor? *(Silence)* The police? *(Silence)* The town health official? *(Silence)* The Rector of Güllen High School? *(Silence)* The political opposition? *(Silence)* I shall then proceed to the vote— *(The* TEACHER *rises. The* BURGOMASTER *turns in surprise and irritation.)* You wish to speak?

TEACHER   Yes.

BURGOMASTER   Very well.

(He takes his seat. The TEACHER *advances. The movie camera starts running.)*

TEACHER   Fellow townsmen. *(The photographer flashes a bulb in his face.)* Fellow townsmen. We all know that by means of this gift, Madame Claire Zachanassian intends to attain a certain object. What is this object? To enrich the town of her youth, yes. But more than that, she desires by means of this gift to reestablish justice among us. This desire expressed by our benefactress raises an all-important question. Is it true that our community harbors in its soul such a burden of guilt?

BURGOMASTER   Yes! True!

SECOND MAN   Crimes are concealed among us.

THIRD MAN *(He jumps up.)*   Sins!

FOURTH MAN *(He jumps up also.)*   Perjuries!

PAINTER   Justice!

TOWNSMEN   Justice! Justice!

TEACHER   Citizens of Güllen, this, then, is the simple fact of the case. We have participated in an injustice. I thoroughly recognize the material advantages which this gift opens to us—I do not overlook the fact that it is poverty which is the root of all this bitterness and evil. Nevertheless, there is no question here of money.

TOWNSMEN   No! no!

TEACHER   Here there is no question of our prosperity as a community, or our well-being as individuals—The question is—must be—whether or not we wish to live according to the principles of justice, those principles for which our forefathers lived and fought and for which they died, those principles which form the soul of our Western culture.

TOWNSMEN   Hear! Hear!

(Applause.)

TEACHER *(desperately, realizing that he is fighting a losing battle, and on the verge of hysteria)*   Wealth has meaning only when benevolence comes of it, but only he who hungers for grace will receive grace. Do you feel this hunger, my fellow citizens, this hunger of the spirit, or do you feel only that other profane hunger, the hunger of the body? That is the question which I, as Rector of your high school, now propound to you. Only if you can no longer tolerate the presence of evil among you, only if you can in no circumstances endure a world in which injustice exists, are you worthy to receive Madame Zachanassian's billion and fulfill the condition bound up with this gift. If not—*(Wild applause. He gestures desperately for silence.)* If not, then God have mercy on us!

(The townsmen crowd around him, ambiguously, in a mood somewhat between threat and congratulation. He takes his seat, utterly crushed, exhausted by his effort. The BURGOMASTER *advances and takes charge once again. Order is restored.)*

BURGOMASTER   Anton Schill—*(The* POLICEMAN *gives* SCHILL *a shove.* SCHILL *gets up.)* Anton Schill, it is through you that this gift is offered to the town. Are you willing that this offer should be accepted?

*(*SCHILL *mumbles something.)*

RADIO REPORTER *(steps to his side)*   You'll have to speak up a little, Herr Schill.

SCHILL   Yes.

BURGOMASTER   Will you respect our decision in the matter before us?

SCHILL   I will respect your decision.

BURGOMASTER   Then I proceed to the vote. All those who are in accord with the terms on which this gift is offered will signify the same by raising their right hands. *(After a moment, the* POLICEMAN *raises his hand. Then one by one the others. Last of all, very slowly, the* TEACHER.*)* All against? The offer is accepted. I now solemnly call upon you, fellow townsmen, to declare in the face of all the world that you take this action, not out of love for worldly gain . . .

TOWNSMEN *(in chorus)*   Not out of love for worldly gain . . .

BURGOMASTER   But out of love for the right.

TOWNSMEN   But out of love for the right.

BURGOMASTER *(holds up his hand, as if taking an oath)*   We join together, now, as brothers . . .

TOWNSMEN *(hold up their hands)*   We join together, now, as brothers . . .

BURGOMASTER   To purify our town of guilt . . .

TOWNSMEN   To purify our town of guilt . . .

BURGOMASTER   And to reaffirm our faith . . .

TOWNSMEN   And to reaffirm our faith . . .

BURGOMASTER   In the eternal power of justice.

TOWNSMEN   In the eternal power of justice.

(The lights go off suddenly.)

SCHILL *(a scream)*   Oh, God!

VOICE   I'm sorry, Herr Burgomaster. We seem to have blown a fuse. *(The lights go on.)* Ah—there we are. Would you mind doing that last bit again?

BURGOMASTER   Again?

THE CAMERAMAN *(walks forward)*   Yes, for the newsreel.

BURGOMASTER   Oh, the newsreel. Certainly.

THE CAMERAMAN   Ready now? Right.

BURGOMASTER   And to reaffirm our faith . . .

TOWNSMEN   And to reaffirm our faith . . .

BURGOMASTER   In the eternal power of justice.

TOWNSMEN   In the eternal power of justice.

THE CAMERAMAN *(to his assistant)*   It was better before, when he screamed "Oh, God."

(The assistant shrugs.)

BURGOMASTER   Fellow citizens of Güllen, I declare this meeting adjourned. The ladies and gentlemen of the press will find refreshments served downstairs, with the compliments of the town council. The exits lead directly to the restaurant.

THE CAMERAMAN   Thank you.

(The newsmen go off with alacrity. The townsmen remain on the stage. SCHILL *gets up.)*

POLICEMAN *(pushes* SCHILL *down)*   Sit down.

SCHILL   Is it to be now?

POLICEMAN   Naturally, now.

SCHILL   I thought it might be best to have it at my house.

POLICEMAN   It will be here.

BURGOMASTER   Lower the lights. *(The lights dim.)* Are they all gone?

VOICE   All gone.

BURGOMASTER   The gallery?

SECOND VOICE   Empty.

BURGOMASTER   Lock the doors.

THE VOICE   Locked here.

SECOND VOICE   Locked here.

BURGOMASTER   Form a lane. *(The men form a lane. At the end stands the* ATHLETE *in elegant white slacks, a red scarf around his singlet.)* Pastor. Will you be so good?

(The PASTOR *walks slowly to* SCHILL.*)*

PASTOR   Anton Schill, your heavy hour has come.

SCHILL   May I have a cigarette?
PASTOR   Cigarette, Burgomaster.
BURGOMASTER   Of course. With pleasure. And a good one.

(He gives his case to the PASTOR, who offers it to SCHILL. The POLICEMAN lights the cigarette. The PASTOR returns the case.)

PASTOR   In the words of the prophet Amos—
SCHILL   Please—

(He shakes his head.)

PASTOR   You're no longer afraid?
SCHILL   No. I'm not afraid.
PASTOR   I will pray for you.
SCHILL   Pray for us all.

(The PASTOR bows his head.)

BURGOMASTER   Anton Schill, stand up!

(SCHILL *hesitates.)*

POLICEMAN   Stand up, you swine!
BURGOMASTER   Schultz, please.
POLICEMAN   I'm sorry. I was carried away.

(SCHILL *gives the cigarette to the* POLICEMAN. *Then he walks slowly to the center of the stage and turns his back on the audience.)*

Enter the lane.

(SCHILL *hesitates a moment. He goes slowly into the lane of silent men. The* ATHLETE *stares at him from the opposite end.* SCHILL *looks in turn at the hard faces of those who surround him, and sinks slowly to his knees. The lane contracts silently into a knot as the men close in and crouch over. Complete silence. The knot of men pulls back slowly, coming down-stage. Then it opens. Only the* DOCTOR *is left in the center of the stage, kneeling by the corpse, over which the* TEACHER's *gown has been spread. The* DOCTOR *rises and takes off his stethoscope.)*

PASTOR   Is it all over?
DOCTOR   Heart failure.
BURGOMASTER   Died of joy.
ALL   Died of joy.

(The townsmen turn their backs on the corpse and at once light cigarettes. A cloud of smoke rises over them. From the left comes CLAIRE ZACHANASSIAN, *dressed in black, followed by* BOBBY. *She sees the corpse. Then she walks slowly to center stage and looks down at the body of* SCHILL.)*

CLAIRE   Uncover him. (BOBBY *uncovers* SCHILL's *face. She stares at it a long moment. She sighs.)* Cover his face.

(BOBBY *covers it.* CLAIRE *goes out, up center.* BOBBY *takes the check from his wallet, holds it out peremptorily to the* BURGOMASTER, *who walks over from the knot of silent men. He holds out his hand for the check. The lights fade. At once the warning bell is heard, and the scene dissolves into the setting of the railway station. The gradual transformation of the shabby town into a thing of elegance and beauty is now accomplished. The railway station glitters with neon lights and is surrounded with garlands, bright posters, and flags. The townsfolk, men and women, now in brand new clothes, form themselves into a group in front of the station. The sound of the approaching train grows louder. The train stops.)*

STATION MASTER   Güllen-Rome Express. All aboard, please. *(The church bells start pealing. Men appear with trunks and boxes, a procession which duplicates that of the lady's arrival, but in inverse order. Then come the* TWO BLIND MEN, *then* BOBBY, *and* MIKE *and* MAX *carrying the coffin. Lastly* CLAIRE. *She is dressed in modish black. Her head is high, her face as impassive as that of an ancient idol. The procession crosses the stage and goes off. The people bow in silence as the coffin passes. When* CLAIRE *and her retinue have boarded the train, the* STATION MASTER *blows a long blast.)* 'Bo—ard!

(He holds up his paddle. The train starts and moves off slowly, picking up speed. The crowd turns slowly, gazing after the departing train in complete silence. The train sounds fade.)

(The curtain falls slowly.)

Comments and Questions

Duerrenmatt has said that "Claire Zachanassian represents neither justice nor the Marshall Plan nor even the Apocalypse; let her be only what she is: the richest woman in the world, whose fortune has put her in a position to act like the heroine of a Greek tragedy: absolute, cruel, something like Medea." It is possible, of course, to read this play as straight melodrama, as a kind of dark fairy tale with an unacceptable ending. The most literal-minded person, however, would feel uneasy in accepting Claire and the other characters in this play as individuals without allegorical significance.

   1. What evidence may be adduced to identify Claire with justice? In what ways does this identification break down? What was the Marshall Plan? Why might readers at the time of the Marshall Plan have been tempted to see traces of a political allegory in the play? Can Claire be equated with the Apocalypse? In what way does this suggested identification break down almost at once? Because none of these identifications fits perfectly, one may be tempted to try others. Is the play about the corrupting influence of wealth, human greed, the fragility of the social structure, sin and retribution? Which interpretation takes into account most completely all the elements of the play?

   2. What about Anton Schill? Is the play as much his as it is Claire's, or is it more? Explain. Can a case be made for his being the only *individual* in the play? Consider the villagers. Consider Claire's entourage. What may one conclude about these groups? Also, what is the dramatic purpose of Claire's wedding? Why does the author have the world's great flock to Güllen for this affair?

   3. Claire's entourage is a human menagerie plus a black panther. The whole village of Güllen is slowly disciplined, tamed, and corrupted. How does this view of human frailties fit the tenets of the Theater of the Absurd? See Martin Esslin's "The Absurdity of the Absurd," page 1120.

   4. Camus' *Caligula*, the next play, presents a ruler with absolute power. Compare Caligula and Claire Zachanassian. The statement that power corrupts and absolute power corrupts absolutely may be applied to the inordinately rich woman in *The Visit* and to the Roman Emperor. Is there a difference, however, in the way these two protagonists exert their authority? Is Claire corrupted by what she does? Or is she chiefly a corrupter? The same questions may be asked about Caligula. What motivates Claire? Caligula?

5. Compare the use of symbols in *The Visit* with their use in *Miss Julie*.

6. Captain Keeney in *Ile* is, within his tiny sphere, master. Compare what happened to him with what happens to Claire and Caligula.

Albert Camus   (1913–1960)
Caligula

(Translated by Stuart Gilbert)

Caligula (Gaius Caesar) was born twelve years after the birth of Christ and assassinated twenty-nine years later. As a child he was the darling of the Roman legionnaires, by whom he was given the name Caligula, which means Little Boots. At age twenty-five he succeeded Tiberius as Emperor with absolute power. Almost at once he began what has been called a reign of terror without parallel in history. His favorite banquet entertainments took the form of bloody executions, sometimes of criminals, frequently of innocent, respectable citizens. His was government by whim. Once when he could not find the enemy army (Germans), he dressed half his own men as the enemy and pursued them with the other half. He built an ivory stable with a golden manger for his favorite horse and made the animal a Consul.

Camus' play interprets this historical character in Absurdist terms. (See Esslin's "The Absurdity of the Absurd," p. 1120.) It has been said that "Insanity . . . is in general suspect as a fictional device" (see p. 979). Does Camus regard the actions of his Caligula as those of a madman? (See excerpts from Suetonius' biography of Caligula, p. 1050.)

CHARACTERS

CALIGULA	LEPIDUS
CÆSONIA	INTENDANT
HELICON	MEREIA
SCIPIO	MUCIUS
CHEREA	MUCIUS' WIFE
THE OLD PATRICIAN	PATRICIANS, KNIGHTS, POETS, GUARDS, SERVANTS
METELLUS	

ACT I

A number of patricians, one a very old man, are gathered in a state room of the imperial palace. They are showing signs of nervousness.

FIRST PATRICIAN   Still no news.

THE OLD PATRICIAN   None last night, none this morning.

SECOND PATRICIAN   Three days without news. Strange indeed!

THE OLD PATRICIAN   Our messengers go out, our messengers return. And always they shake their heads and say: "Nothing."

SECOND PATRICIAN   They've combed the whole countryside. What more can be done?

FIRST PATRICIAN   We can only wait. It's no use meeting trouble halfway. Perhaps he'll return as abruptly as he left us.

THE OLD PATRICIAN   When I saw him leaving the palace, I noticed a queer look in his eyes.

FIRST PATRICIAN   Yes, so did I. In fact I asked him what was amiss.

SECOND PATRICIAN   Did he answer?

FIRST PATRICIAN   One word: "Nothing."

(A short silence. HELICON enters. He is munching onions.)

SECOND PATRICIAN *(in the same nervous tone)*   It's all very perturbing.

FIRST PATRICIAN   Oh, come now! All young fellows are like that.

THE OLD PATRICIAN   You're right there. They take things hard. But time smooths everything out.

SECOND PATRICIAN   Do you really think so?

THE OLD PATRICIAN   Of course. For one girl dead, a dozen living ones.

HELICON   Ah? So you think that there's a girl behind it?

FIRST PATRICIAN   What else should there be? Anyhow—thank goodness!—grief never lasts forever. Is any one of us here capable of mourning a loss for more than a year on end?

SECOND PATRICIAN   Not I, anyhow.

FIRST PATRICIAN   No one can do that.

THE OLD PATRICIAN   Life would be intolerable if one could.

FIRST PATRICIAN   Quite so. Take my case. I lost my wife last year. I shed many tears, and then I forgot. Even now I feel a pang of grief at times. But, happily, it doesn't amount to much.

THE OLD PATRICIAN   Yes, Nature's a great healer.

(CHEREA enters.)

FIRST PATRICIAN   Well . . . ?

CHEREA   Still nothing.

HELICON   Come, gentlemen! There's no need for consternation.

FIRST PATRICIAN   I agree.

HELICON   Worrying won't mend matters—and it's lunchtime.

THE OLD PATRICIAN   That's so. We mustn't drop the prey for the shadow.

CHEREA   I don't like the look of things. But all was going too smoothly. As an emperor, he was perfection's self.

SECOND PATRICIAN   Yes, exactly the emperor we wanted; conscientious and inexperienced.

FIRST PATRICIAN   But what's come over you? There's no reason for all these lamentations. We've no ground for assuming he will change. Let's say he loved Drusilla. Only natural; she was his sister. Or say his love for her was something more than brotherly; shocking enough, I grant you. But it's really going too far, setting all Rome in a turmoil because the girl has died.

CHEREA Maybe. But, as I said, I don't like the look of things; this escapade alarms me.

THE OLD PATRICIAN Yes, there's never smoke without fire.

FIRST PATRICIAN In any case, the interests of the State should prevent his making a public tragedy of . . . of, let's say, a regrettable attachment. No doubt such things happen; but the less said the better.

HELICON How can you be sure Drusilla is the cause of all this trouble?

SECOND PATRICIAN Who else should it be?

HELICON Nobody at all, quite likely. When there's a host of explanations to choose from, why pick on the stupidest, most obvious one?

(Young SCIPIO *enters.* CHEREA *goes toward him.)*

CHEREA Well?

SCIPIO Still nothing. Except that some peasants think they saw him last night not far from Rome, rushing through the storm.

(CHEREA *comes back to the patricians,* SCIPIO *following him.*)

CHEREA That makes three days, Scipio, doesn't it?

SCIPIO Yes . . . I was there, following him as I usually do. He went up to Drusilla's body. He stroked it with two fingers, and seemed lost in thought for a long while. Then he swung round and walked out, calmly enough. . . . And ever since we've been hunting for him—in vain.

CHEREA *(shaking his head)* That young man was too fond of literature.

SECOND PATRICIAN Oh, at his age, you know . . .

CHEREA At his age, perhaps; but not in his position. An artistic emperor is an anomaly. I grant you we've had one or two; misfits happen in the best of empires. But the others had the good taste to remember they were public servants.

FIRST PATRICIAN It made things run more smoothly.

THE OLD PATRICIAN One man, one job—that's how it should be.

SCIPIO What can we do, Cherea?

CHEREA Nothing.

SECOND PATRICIAN We can only wait. If he doesn't return, a successor will have to be found. Between ourselves—there's no shortage of candidates.

FIRST PATRICIAN No, but there's a shortage of the right sort.

CHEREA Suppose he comes back in an ugly mood?

FIRST PATRICIAN Oh, he's a mere boy; we'll make him see reason.

CHEREA And what if he declines to see it?

FIRST PATRICIAN *(laughing)* In that case, my friend, don't forget I once wrote a manual of revolutions. You'll find all the rules there.

CHEREA I'll look it up—if things come to that. But I'd rather be left to my books.

SCIPIO If you'll excuse me. . . .

(Goes out.)

CHEREA He's offended.

THE OLD PATRICIAN Scipio is young, and young people always hang together.

HELICON Scipio doesn't count, anyhow.

(Enter a member of the imperial bodyguard.)

THE GUARDMAN   Caligula has been seen in the palace gardens.

(All leave the room. The stage is empty for some moments. Then CALIGULA *enters stealthily from the left. His legs are caked with mud, his garments dirty; his hair is wet, his look distraught. He brings his hand to his mouth several times. Then he approaches a mirror, stopping abruptly when he catches sight of his reflected self. After muttering some unintelligible words, he sits down on the right, letting his arms hang limp between his knees.* HELICON *enters, left. On seeing* CALIGULA, *he stops at the far end of the stage and contemplates him in silence.* CALIGULA *turns and sees him. A short silence.)*

HELICON *(across the stage)*   Good morning, Caius.

CALIGULA *(in quite an ordinary tone)*   Good morning, Helicon.

(A short silence)

HELICON   You're looking tired.

CALIGULA   I've walked a lot.

HELICON   Yes, you've been away for quite a while.

(Another short silence.)

CALIGULA   It was hard to find.

HELICON   What was hard to find?

CALIGULA   What I was after.

HELICON   Meaning?

CALIGULA *(in the same matter-of-fact tone)*   The moon.

HELICON   What?

CALIGULA   Yes, I wanted the moon.

HELICON   Ah. . . . *(Another silence.* HELICON *approaches* CALIGULA.*)* And why did you want it?

CALIGULA   Well . . . it's one of the things I haven't got.

HELICON   I see. And now—have you fixed it up to your satisfaction?

CALIGULA   No. I couldn't get it.

HELICON   Too bad!

CALIGULA   Yes, and that's why I'm tired. *(Pauses; then)* Helicon!

HELICON   Yes, Caius?

CALIGULA   No doubt, you think I'm crazy.

HELICON   As you know well, I never think.

CALIGULA   Ah, yes. . . . Now, listen! I'm not mad; in fact I've never felt so lucid. What happened to me is quite simple; I suddenly felt a desire for the impossible. That's all. *(Pauses)* Things as they are, in my opinion, are far from satisfactory.

HELICON   Many people share your opinion.

CALIGULA   That is so. But in the past I didn't realize it. *Now* I know. *(Still in the same matter-of-fact tone)* Really, this world of ours, the scheme of things as they call it, is quite intolerable. That's why I want the moon, or happiness, or eternal life—something, in fact, that may sound crazy, but which isn't of this world.

HELICON   That's sound enough in theory. Only, in practice one can't carry it through to its conclusion.

CALIGULA *(rising to his feet, but still with perfect calmness)*   You're wrong there. It's just because no one *dares* to follow up his ideas to the end that nothing is achieved. All that's needed, I should say, is to be logical right through, at all costs. *(He studies* HELICON's *face.)* I can see, too, what you're thinking. What a fuss over a woman's death! But that's not it. True enough, I seem to remember that a woman died some days ago; a woman whom

I loved. But love, what is it? A side issue. And I swear to you her death is not the point; it's no more than the symbol of a truth that makes the moon essential to me. A childishly simple, obvious, almost silly truth, but one that's hard to come by and heavy to endure.

HELICON   May I know what it is, this truth that you've discovered?

CALIGULA *(his eyes averted, in a toneless voice)*   Men die; and they are not happy.

HELICON *(after a short pause)*   Anyhow, Caligula, it's a truth with which one comes to terms, without much trouble. Only look at the people over there. This truth of yours doesn't prevent them from enjoying their meal.

CALIGULA *(with sudden violence)*   All it proves is that I'm surrounded by lies and self-deception. But I've had enough of that; I wish men to live by the light of truth. And I've the power to make them do so. For I know what they need and haven't got. They're without understanding and they need a teacher; someone who knows what he's talking about.

HELICON   Don't take offense, Caius, if I give you a word of advice. . . . But that can wait. First, you should have some rest.

CALIGULA *(sitting down; his voice is gentle again)*   That's not possible, Helicon. I shall never rest again.

HELICON   But—why?

CALIGULA   If I sleep, who'll give me the moon?

HELICON *(after a short silence)*   That's true.

CALIGULA *(rising to his feet again, with an effort)*   Listen, Helicon . . . I hear footsteps, voices. Say nothing—and forget you've seen me.

HELICON   I understand.

CALIGULA *(looking back, as he moves toward the door)*   And please help me, from now on.

HELICON   I've no reason not to do so, Caius. But I know very few things, and few things interest me. In what way can I help you?

CALIGULA   In the way of . . . the impossible.

HELICON   I'll do my best.

(CALIGULA *goes out.* SCIPIO *and* CÆSONIA *enter hurriedly.*)

SCIPIO   No one! Haven't you seen him?

HELICON   No.

CÆSONIA   Tell me, Helicon. Are you quite sure he didn't say anything to you before he went away?

HELICON   I'm not a sharer of his secrets, I'm his public. A mere onlooker. It's more prudent.

CÆSONIA   Please don't talk like that.

HELICON   My dear Cæsonia, Caius is an idealist as we all know. He follows his bent, and no one can foresee where it will take him. . . . But, if you'll excuse me, I'll go to lunch.

(Exit HELICON.)

CÆSONIA *(sinking wearily onto a divan)*   One of the palace guards saw him go by. But all Rome sees Caligula everywhere. And Caligula, of course, sees nothing but his own idea.

SCIPIO   What idea?

CÆSONIA   How can I tell, Scipio?

SCIPIO   Are you thinking of Drusilla?

CÆSONIA Perhaps. One thing is sure; he loved her. And it's a cruel thing to have someone die today whom only yesterday you were holding in your arms.

SCIPIO *(timidly)* And you . . . ?

CÆSONIA Oh, I'm the old, trusted mistress. That's my role.

SCIPIO Cæsonia, we must save him.

CÆSONIA So you, too, love him?

SCIPIO Yes. He's been very good to me. He encouraged me; I shall never forget some of the things he said. He told me life isn't easy, but it has consolations: religion, art, and the love one inspires in others. He often told me that the only mistake one makes in life is to cause others suffering. He tried to be a just man.

CÆSONIA *(rising)* He's only a child. *(She goes to the glass and scans herself.)* The only god I've ever had is my body, and now I shall pray this god of mine to give Caius back to me.

(CALIGULA enters. On seeing CÆSONIA and SCIPIO he hesitates, and takes a backward step. At the same moment several men enter from the opposite side of the room: patricians and the INTENDANT of the palace. They stop short when they see CALIGULA. CÆSONIA turns. She and SCIPIO hurry toward CALIGULA, who checks them with a gesture.)

INTENDANT *(in a rather quavering voice)* We . . . we've been looking for you, Cæsar, high and low.

CALIGULA *(in a changed, harsh tone)* So I see.

INTENDANT We . . . I mean . . .

CALIGULA *(roughly)* What do you want?

INTENDANT We were feeling anxious, Cæsar.

CALIGULA *(going toward him)* What business had you to feel anxious?

INTENDANT Well . . . er . . . *(He has an inspiration.)* Well, as you know, there are points to be settled in connection with the Treasury.

CALIGULA *(bursting into laughter)* Ah, yes. The Treasury! That's so. The Treasury's of prime importance.

INTENDANT Yes, indeed.

CALIGULA *(still laughing, to CÆSONIA)* Don't you agree, my dear? The Treasury is all-important.

CÆSONIA No, Caligula. It's a secondary matter.

CALIGULA That only shows your ignorance. We are extremely interested in our Treasury. Everything's important: our fiscal system, public morals, foreign policy, army equipment, and agrarian laws. Everything's of cardinal importance, I assure you. And everything's on an equal footing: the grandeur of Rome and your attacks of arthritis. . . . Well, well, I'm going to apply my mind to all that. And, to begin with . . . Now listen well, Intendant.

INTENDANT We are listening, sir.

(The patricians come forward.)

CALIGULA You're our loyal subjects, are you not?

INTENDANT *(in a reproachful tone)* Oh, Cæsar . . . !

CALIGULA Well, I've something to propose to you. We're going to make a complete change in our economic system. In two moves. Drastic and abrupt. I'll explain, Intendant . . . when the patricians have left. *(The patricians go out. CALIGULA seats himself beside CÆSONIA, with his arm around her waist.)* Now mark my words. The first move's this. Every patrician, everyone in the Empire who has any capital—small or large, it's all the same thing—is ordered to disinherit his children and make a new will leaving his money to the State.

INTENDANT But Cæsar . . .

CALIGULA I've not yet given you leave to speak. As the need arises, we shall have these people die; a list will be drawn up by us fixing the order of their deaths. When the fancy takes us, we may modify that order. And, of course, we shall step into their money.

CÆSONIA *(freeing herself)* But—what's come over you?

CALIGULA *(imperturbably)* Obviously the order of their going has no importance. Or, rather, all these executions have an equal importance—from which it follows that none has any. Really all those fellows are on a par, one's as guilty as another. *(To the* INTENDANT, *peremptorily)* You are to promulgate this edict without a moment's delay and see it's carried out forthwith. The wills are to be signed by residents in Rome this evening; within a month at the latest by persons in the provinces. Send out your messengers.

INTENDANT Caesar, I wonder if you realize . . .

CALIGULA Do I realize . . . ? Now, listen well, you fool! If the Treasury has paramount importance, human life has none. That should be obvious to you. People who think like you are bound to admit the logic of my edict, and since money is the only thing that counts, should set no value on their lives or anyone else's. I have resolved to be logical, and I have the power to enforce my will. Presently you'll see what logic's going to cost you! I shall eliminate contradictions and contradictors. If necessary, I'll begin with you.

INTENDANT Caesar, my good will can be relied on, that I swear.

CALIGULA And mine, too; that I guarantee. Just see how ready I am to adopt your point of view, and give the Treasury the first place in my program. Really you should be grateful to me; I'm playing into your hand, and with your own cards. *(He pauses, before continuing in a flat, unemotional tone.)* In any case there is a touch of genius in the simplicity of my plan—which clinches the matter. I give you three seconds in which to remove yourself. One . . .

(The INTENDANT *hurries out.)*

CÆSONIA I can't believe it's you! But it was just a joke, wasn't it?—all you said to him.

CALIGULA Not quite that, Cæsonia. Let's say, a lesson in statesmanship.

SCIPIO But, Caius, it's . . . it's impossible!

CALIGULA That's the whole point.

SCIPIO I don't follow.

CALIGULA I repeat—that is my point. I'm exploiting the impossible. Or, more accurately, it's a question of making the impossible possible.

SCIPIO But that game may lead to—to anything! It's a lunatic's pastime.

CALIGULA No, Scipio. An emperor's vocation. *(He lets himself sink back wearily among the cushions.)* Ah, my dears, at last I've come to see the uses of supremacy. It gives impossibilities a run. From this day on, so long as life is mine, my freedom has no frontier.

CÆSONIA *(sadly)* I doubt if this discovery of yours will make us any happier.

CALIGULA So do I. But, I suppose, we'll have to live it through.

*(*CHEREA *enters.)*

CHEREA I have just heard of your return. I trust your health is all it should be.

CALIGULA My health is duly grateful. *(A pause, then, abruptly)* Leave us, Cherea. I don't want to see you.

CHEREA Really, Caius, I'm amazed . . .

CALIGULA There's nothing to be amazed at. I don't like literary men, and I can't bear lies.

CHEREA If we lie, it's often without knowing it. I plead Not Guilty.

CALIGULA Lies are never guiltless. And yours attribute importance to people and to things. That's what I cannot forgive you.

CHEREA And yet—since this world is the only one we have, why not plead its cause?

CALIGULA Your pleading comes too late, the verdict's given. . . . This world has no importance; once a man realizes that, he wins his freedom. *(He has risen to his feet.)* And that is why I hate you, you and your kind; because you are not free. You see in me the one free man in the whole Roman Empire. You should be glad to have at last among you an emperor who points the way to freedom. Leave me, Cherea; and you, too, Scipio, go— for what is friendship? Go, both of you, and spread the news in Rome that freedom has been given her at last, and with the gift begins a great probation.

(They go out. CALIGULA *has turned away, hiding his eyes.)*

CÆSONIA Crying?

CALIGULA Yes, Cæsonia.

CÆSONIA But, after all, what's changed in your life? You may have loved Drusilla, but you loved many others—myself included—at the same time. Surely that wasn't enough to set you roaming the countryside for three days and nights and bring you back with this . . . this cruel look on your face?

CALIGULA *(swinging round on her)* What nonsense is this? Why drag in Drusilla? Do you imagine love's the only thing that can make a man shed tears?

CÆSONIA I'm sorry, Caius. Only I was trying to understand.

CALIGULA Men weep because . . . the world's all wrong. *(She comes toward him.)* No Cæsonia. *(She draws back.)* But stay beside me.

CÆSONIA I'll do whatever you wish. *(Sits down)* At my age one knows that life's a sad business. But why deliberately set out to make it worse?

CALIGULA No, it's no good; you can't understand. But what matter? Perhaps I'll find a way out. Only, I feel a curious stirring within me, as if undreamed of things were forcing their way up into the light—and I'm helpless against them. *(He moves closer to her.)* Oh, Cæsonia, I knew that men felt anguish, but I didn't know what that word anguish meant. Like everyone else I fancied it was a sickness of the mind—no more. But no, it's my body that's in pain. Pain everywhere, in my chest, in my legs and arms. Even my skin is raw, my head is buzzing. I feel like vomiting. But worst of all is this queer taste in my mouth. Not blood, or death, or fever, but a mixture of all three. I've only to stir my tongue, and the world goes black, and everyone looks . . . horrible. How hard, how cruel it is, this process of becoming a man!

CÆSONIA What you need, my dear, is a good, long sleep. Let yourself relax, and above all stop thinking. I'll stay by you while you sleep. And when you wake, you'll find the world's got back its savor. Then you must use your power to good effect—for loving better what you still find lovable. For the possible, too, deserves to be given a chance.

CALIGULA Ah but for that I'd need to sleep, to let myself go—and that's impossible.

CÆSONIA So one always thinks when one is overtired. A time comes when one's hand is firm again.

CALIGULA But one must know where to place it. And what's the use to me of a firm hand, what use is the amazing power that's mine, if I can't have the sun set in the east, if I can't reduce the sum of suffering and make an end of death? No, Cæsonia, it's all one whether I sleep or keep awake, if I've no power to tamper with the scheme of things.

CÆSONIA But that's madness, sheer madness. It's wanting to be a god on earth.

CALIGULA So you, too, think I'm mad. And yet—what is a god that I should wish to be his equal? No, it's something higher, far above the gods, that I'm aiming at, longing for with all my heart and soul. I am taking over a kingdom where the impossible is king.

CÆSONIA You can't prevent the sky from being the sky, or a fresh young face from aging, or a man's heart from growing cold.

CALIGULA *(with rising excitement)* I want . . . I want to drown the sky in the sea, to infuse ugliness with beauty, to wring a laugh from pain.

CÆSONIA *(facing him with an imploring gesture)* There's good and bad, high and low, justice and injustice. And I swear to you these will never change.

CALIGULA *(in the same tone)* And I'm resolved to change them . . . . I shall make this age of ours a kingly gift—the gift of equality. And when all is leveled out, when the impossible has come to earth and the moon is in my hands—then, perhaps, I shall be transfigured and the world renewed; then men will die no more and at last be happy.

CÆSONIA *(with a little cry)* And love? Surely you won't go back on love!

CALIGULA *(in a wild burst of anger)* Love, Cæsonia! *(He grips her shoulders and shakes her.)* I've learned the truth about love; it's nothing, nothing! That fellow was quite right—you heard what he said, didn't you?—it's only the Treasury that counts. The fountainhead of all. Ah, now at last I'm going to live, really *live*. And living, my dear, is the opposite of loving. I know what I'm talking about—and I invite you to the most gorgeous of shows, a sight for gods to gloat on, a whole world called to judgment. But for that I must have a crowd—spectators, victims, criminals, hundreds and thousands of them. *(He rushes to the gong and begins hammering on it, faster and faster.)* Let the accused come forward. I want my criminals, and they all are criminals. *(Still striking the gong)* Bring in the condemned men. I must have my public. Judges, witnesses, accused—all sentenced to death without a hearing. Yes, Cæsonia, I'll show them something they have never seen before, the one free man in the Roman Empire. *(To the clangor of the gong the palace has been gradually filling with noises; the clash of arms, voices, footsteps slow or hurried, coming nearer, growing louder. Some soldiers enter, and leave hastily.)* And you, Cæsonia, shall obey me. You must stand by me to the end. It will be marvelous, you'll see. Swear to stand by me, Cæsonia.

CÆSONIA *(wildly, between two gong strokes)* I needn't swear. You know I love you.

CALIGULA *(in the same tone)* You'll do all I tell you.

CÆSONIA All, all, Caligula—but do, please stop. . . .

CALIGULA *(still striking the gong)* You will be cruel.

CÆSONIA *(sobbing)* Cruel.

CALIGULA *(still beating the gong)* Cold and ruthless.

CÆSONIA Ruthless.

CALIGULA And you will suffer, too.

CÆSONIA Yes, yes—oh, no, please . . . I'm—I'm going mad, I think! *(Some patricians enter, followed by members of the palace staff. All look bewildered and perturbed.* CALIGULA *bangs the gong for the last time, raises his mallet, swings round and summons them in a shrill, half-crazy voice.)*

CALIGULA Come here. All of you. Nearer. Nearer still. *(He is quivering with impatience.)* Your Emperor commands you to come nearer. *(They come forward, pale with terror.)* Quickly. And you, Cæsonia, come beside me. *(He takes her hand, leads her to the mirror, and with a wild sweep of his mallet effaces a reflection on its surface. Then gives a sudden laugh.)* All gone. You see, my dear? An end of memories; no more masks. Nothing, nobody left. Nobody? No, that's not true. Look, Cæsonia. Come here, all of you, and look . . .

(He plants himself in front of the mirror in a grotesque attitude.)

CÆSONIA *(staring, horrified, at the mirror)* Caligula! (CALIGULA *lays a finger on the glass. His gaze steadies abruptly and when he speaks his voice has a new, proud ardor.)*
CALIGULA Yes . . . Caligula.

(Curtain.)

ACT II

Three years later.
A room in CHEREA'S *house, where the patricians meet in secret.*

FIRST PATRICIAN It's outrageous, the way he's treating us.
THE OLD PATRICIAN He calls me "darling"! In public, mind you—just to make a laughingstock of me. Death's too good for him.
FIRST PATRICIAN And fancy making us run beside his litter when he goes into the country.
SECOND PATRICIAN He says the exercise will do us good.
THE OLD PATRICIAN Conduct like that is quite inexcusable.
THIRD PATRICIAN You're right. That's precisely the sort of thing one can't forgive.
FIRST PATRICIAN He confiscated your property, Patricius. He killed your father, Scipio. He's taken your wife from you, Octavius, and forced her to work in his public brothel. He has killed your son, Lepidus. I ask you, gentlemen, can you endure this? I, anyhow, have made up my mind. I know the risks, but I also know this life of abject fear is quite unbearable. Worse than death, in fact. Yes, as I said, my mind's made up.
SCIPIO He made my mind up for me when he had my father put to death.
FIRST PATRICIAN Well? Can you still hesitate?
A KNIGHT No. We're with you. He's transferred our stalls at the Circus to the public, and egged us on to fight with the rabble—just to have a pretext for punishing us, of course.
THE OLD PATRICIAN He's a coward.
SECOND PATRICIAN A bully.
THIRD PATRICIAN A buffoon.
THE OLD PATRICIAN He's impotent—that's his trouble, I should say.

(A scene of wild confusion follows, weapons are brandished, a table is overturned, and there is a general rush toward the door. Just at this moment CHEREA *strolls in, composed as usual, and checks their onrush.)*
CHEREA What's all this about? Where are you going?
A PATRICIAN To the palace.
CHEREA Ah, yes. And I can guess why. But do you think you'll be allowed to enter?
THE PATRICIAN There's no question of asking leave.
CHEREA Lepidus, would you kindly shut that door? *(The door is shut.* CHEREA *goes to the overturned table and seats himself on a corner of it. The others turn toward him.)* It's not so simple as you think, my friends. You're afraid, but fear can't take the place of courage and deliberation. In short, you're acting too hastily.
A KNIGHT If you're not with us, go. But keep your mouth shut.
CHEREA I suspect I'm with you. But make no mistake. Not for the same reasons.
A VOICE That's enough idle talk.
CHEREA *(standing up)* I agree. Let's get down to facts. But, first, let me make myself clear. Though I am *with* you, I'm not *for* you. That, indeed, is why I think you're going about it the wrong way. You haven't taken your enemy's measure; that's obvious, since you

attribute petty motives to him. But there's nothing petty about Caligula, and you're riding for a fall. You'd be better placed to fight him if you would try to see him as he really is.

A VOICE   We see him as he is—a crazy tyrant.

CHEREA   No. We've had experience of mad emperors. But this one isn't mad enough. And what I loathe in him is this: that he knows what he wants.

FIRST PATRICIAN   And we, too, know it; he wants to murder us all.

CHEREA   You're wrong. Our deaths are only a side issue. He's putting his power at the service of a loftier, deadlier passion; and it imperils everything we hold most sacred. True, it's not the first time Rome has seen a man wielding unlimited power; but it's the first time he sets no limit to his use of it, and counts mankind, and the world we know, for nothing. That's what appalls me in Caligula; that's what I want to fight. To lose one's life is no great matter; when the time comes I'll have the courage to lose mine. But what's intolerable is to see one's life being drained of meaning, to be told there's no reason for existing. A man can't live without some reason for living.

FIRST PATRICIAN   Revenge is a good reason.

CHEREA   Yes, and I propose to share it with you. But I'd have you know that it's not on your account, or to help you to avenge your petty humiliations. No, if I join forces with you, it's to combat a big idea—an ideal, if you like—whose triumph would mean the end of everything. I can endure your being made a mock of, but I cannot endure Caligula's carrying out his theories to the end. He is converting his philosophy into corpses and— unfortunately for us—it's a philosophy that's logical from start to finish. And where one can't refute, one strikes.

A VOICE   Yes. We must *act.*

CHEREA   We must take action, I agree. But a frontal attack's quite useless when one is fighting an imperial madman in the full flush of his power. You can take arms against a vulgar tyrant, but cunning is needed to fight down disinterested malice. You can only urge it on to follow its bent, and bide your time until its logic founders in sheer lunacy. As you see, I prefer to be quite frank, and I warn you I'll be with you only for a time. Afterward, I shall do nothing to advance your interests; all I wish is to regain some peace of mind in a world that has regained a meaning. What spurs me on is not ambition but fear, my very reasonable fear of that inhuman vision in which my life means no more than a speck of dust.

FIRST PATRICIAN *(approaching him)*   I have an inkling of what you mean, Cherea. Anyhow, the great thing is that you, too, feel that the whole fabric of society is threatened. You, gentlemen, agree with me, I take it, that our ruling motive is of a moral order. Family life is breaking down, men are losing their respect for honest work, a wave of immorality is sweeping the country. Who of us can be deaf to the appeal of our ancestral piety in its hour of danger? Fellow conspirators, will you tolerate a state of things in which patricians are forced to run, like slaves, beside the Emperor's litter?

THE OLD PATRICIAN   Will you allow them to be addressed as "darling"?

A VOICE   And have their wives snatched from them?

ANOTHER VOICE   And their money?

ALL TOGETHER   No!

FIRST PATRICIAN   Cherea, your advice is good, and you did well to calm our passion. The time is not yet ripe for action; the masses would still be against us. Will you join us in watching for the best moment to strike—and strike hard?

CHEREA   Yes—and meanwhile let Caligula follow his dream. Or, rather, let's actively encourage him to carry out his wildest plans. Let's put method into his madness. And then, at last, a day will come when he's alone, a lonely man in an empire of the dead and kinsmen of the dead.

*(A general uproar. Trumpet calls outside. Then silence, but for whispers of a name: "*CALI-GULA!*"* CALIGULA *enters with* CÆSONIA, *followed by* HELICON *and some soldiers. Pantomime.* CALIGULA *halts and gazes at the conspirators. Without a word he moves from one to the other, straightens a buckle on one man's shoulder, steps back to contemplate another, sweeps them with his gaze, then draws his hand over his eyes and walks out, still without a word.)*

CÆSONIA *(ironically, pointing to the disorder of the room)*   Were you having a fight?

CHEREA   Yes, we were fighting.

CÆSONIA *(in the same tone)*   Really? Might I know what you were fighting about?

CHEREA   About . . . nothing in particular.

CÆSONIA   Ah? Then it isn't true.

CHEREA   What isn't true?

CÆSONIA   You were *not* fighting.

CHEREA   Have it your own way. We weren't fighting.

CÆSONIA *(smiling)*   Perhaps you'd do better to tidy up the place. Caligula hates untidiness.

HELICON *(to the* OLD PATRICIAN*)*   You'll end by making him do something out of character.

THE OLD PATRICIAN   Pardon . . . I don't follow. What have we done to him?

HELICON   Nothing. Just nothing. It's fantastic being futile to that point; enough to get on anybody's nerves. Try to put yourselves in Caligula's place. *(A short pause)* I see; doing a bit of plotting, weren't you now?

THE OLD PATRICIAN   Really, that's too absurd. I hope Caligula doesn't imagine

HELICON   He doesn't imagine. He *knows*. But, I suppose, at bottom, he rather wants it. . . . Well, we'd better set to tidying up.

(All get busy. CALIGULA *enters and watches them.)*

CALIGULA *(to the* OLD PATRICIAN*)*   Good day, darling. *(To the others)* Gentlemen, I'm on my way to an execution. But I thought I'd drop in at your place, Cherea, for a light meal. I've given orders to have food brought here for all of us. But send for your wives first. *(A short silence)* Rufius should thank his stars that I've been seized with hunger. *(Confidentially)* Rufius, I may tell you, is the knight who's going to be executed. *(Another short silence)* What's this? None of you asks me why I've sentenced him to death? *(No one speaks. Meanwhile slaves lay the table and bring food.)* Good for you! I see you're growing quite intelligent. *(He nibbles an olive.)* It has dawned on you that a man needn't have done anything for him to die. *(He stops eating and gazes at his guests with a twinkle in his eye.)* Soldiers, I am proud of you. *(Three or four women enter.)* Good! Let's take our places. Anyhow. No order of precedence today. *(All are seated.)* There's no denying it, that fellow Rufius is in luck. But I wonder if he appreciates this short reprieve. A few hours gained on death, why, they're worth their weight in gold! *(He begins eating; the others follow suit. It becomes clear that* CALIGULA's *table manners are deplorable. There is no need for him to flick his olive stones onto his neighbors' plates, or to spit out bits of gristle over the dish, or to pick his teeth with his nails, or to scratch his head furiously. However, he indulges in these practices throughout the meal, without the least compunction. At one moment he stops eating, stares at* LEPIDUS, *one of the guests, and says roughly)* You're looking grumpy, Lepidus. I wonder, can it be because I had your son killed?

LEPIDUS *(thickly)*   Certainly not, Caius. Quite the contrary.

CALIGULA *(beaming at him)*   "Quite the contrary!" It's always nice to see a face that hides the secrets of the heart. Your face is sad. But what about your heart? Quite the contrary—isn't that so, Lepidus?

LEPIDUS *(doggedly)*   Quite the contrary, Cæsar.

CALIGULA *(more and more enjoying the situation)*   Really, Lepidus, there's no one I like better than you. Now let's have a laugh together, my dear friend. Tell me a funny story.

LEPIDUS *(who has overrated his endurance)*   Please . . .

CALIGULA   Good! Very good! Then it's I who'll tell the story. But you'll laugh, won't you, Lepidus? *(With a glint of malice)* If only for the sake of your other son. *(Smiling again)* In any case, as you've just told us, you're not in a bad humor. *(He takes a drink, then says in the tone of a teacher prompting a pupil.)* Quite . . . quite the . . .

LEPIDUS *(wearily)*   Quite the contrary, Cæsar.

CALIGULA   Splendid! *(Drinks again)* Now listen. *(In a gentle, faraway tone)* Once upon a time there was a poor young emperor whom nobody loved. He loved Lepidus, and to root out of his heart his love for Lepidus, he had his youngest son killed. *(In a brisker tone)* Needless to say, there's not a word of truth in it. Still it's a funny story, eh? But you're not laughing. Nobody's laughing. Now listen! *(In a burst of anger)* I insist on everybody's laughing. You, Lepidus, shall lead the chorus. Stand up, every one of you, and laugh. *(He thumps the table.)* Do you hear what I say? I wish to see you laughing, all of you. *(All rise to their feet. During this scene all the players,* CALIGULA *and* CÆSONIA *excepted, behave like marionettes in a puppet play.* CALIGULA *sinks back on his couch, beaming with delight, and bursts into a fit of laughter.)* Oh, Cæsonia! Just look at them! The game is up; honor, respectability, the wisdom of the nations, gone with the wind! The wind of fear has blown them all away. Fear, Cæsonia—don't you agree?—is a noble emotion, pure and simple, self-sufficient, like no other; it draws its patent of nobility straight from the guts. *(He strikes his forehead and drinks again. In a friendly tone)* Well, well, let's change the subject. What have you to say, Cherea? You've been very silent.

CHEREA   I'm quite ready to speak, Caius. When you give me leave.

CALIGULA   Excellent. Then—keep silent. I'd rather have a word from our friend Mucius.

MUCIUS *(reluctantly)*   As you will, Caius.

CALIGULA   Then tell us something about your wife. And begin by sending her to this place, on my right. (MUCIUS' WIFE *seats herself beside* CALIGULA.) Well, Mucius? We're waiting.

MUCIUS *(hardly knowing what he says)*   My wife . . . but . . . I'm very fond of her.

(General laughter.)

CALIGULA   Why, of course, my friend, of course. But how ordinary of you! So unoriginal! *(He is leaning toward her, tickling her shoulder playfully with his tongue.)* By the way, when I came in just now, you were hatching a plot, weren't you? A nice bloody little plot?

OLD PATRICIAN   Oh, Caius, how can you . . . ?

CALIGULA   It doesn't matter in the least, my pet. Old age will be served. I won't take it seriously. Not one of you has the spunk for a heroic act. . . . Ah, it's just come to my mind, I have some affairs of state to settle. But, first, let the imperious desires that nature creates in us have their way.

He rises and leads MUCIUS' WIFE *into an adjoining room.* MUCIUS *starts up from his seat.*

CÆSONIA *(amiably)*   Please, Mucius. Will you pour me out another glass of this excellent wine. (MUCIUS *complies; his movement of revolt is quelled. Everyone looks embarrassed. Chairs creak noisily. The ensuing conversation is in a strained tone.* CÆSONIA *turns to* CHEREA.) Now, Cherea, suppose you tell me why you people were fighting just now?

CHEREA *(coolly)*   With pleasure, my dear Cæsonia. Our quarrel arose from a discussion whether poetry should be bloodthirsty or not.

CÆSONIA   An interesting problem. Somewhat beyond my feminine comprehension, of course. Still it surprises me that your passion for art should make you come to blows.

CHEREA *(in the same rather stilted tone)*   That I can well understand. But I remember Caligula's telling me the other day that all true passion has a spice of cruelty.

CÆSONIA *(helping herself from the dish in front of her)*   There's truth in that. Don't you agree, gentlemen?

THE OLD PATRICIAN   Ah, yes. Caligula has a rare insight into the secret places of the heart.

FIRST PATRICIAN   And how eloquently he spoke just now of courage!

SECOND PATRICIAN   Really, he should put his ideas into writing. They would be most instructive.

CHEREA   And, what's more, it would keep him busy. It's obvious he needs something to occupy his leisure.

CÆSONIA *(still eating)*   You'll be pleased to hear that Caligula shares your views; he's working on a book. Quite a big one, I believe.

(CALIGULA *enters, accompanied by* MUCIUS' WIFE.)

CALIGULA   Mucius, I return your wife, with many thanks. But excuse me, I've some orders to give.

(He hurries out. MUCIUS *has gone pale and risen to his feet.)*

CÆSONIA *(to* MUCIUS, *who is standing)*   This book of his will certainly rank among our Latin Classics. Are you listening, Mucius?

MUCIUS *(His eyes still fixed on the door by which* CALIGULA *went out.)*   Yes. And what's the book about, Cæsonia?

CÆSONIA *(indifferently)*   Oh, it's above my head, you know.

CHEREA   May we assume it deals with the murderous power of poetry?

CÆSONIA   Yes, something of that sort, I understand.

THE OLD PATRICIAN *(cheerfully)*   Well anyhow, as our friend Cherea said, it will keep him busy.

CÆSONIA   Yes, my love. But I'm afraid there's one thing you won't like quite so much about this book, and that's its title.

CHEREA   What is it?

CAESONIA   *Cold Steel.*

(CALIGULA *hurries in.*)

CALIGULA   Excuse me, but I've some urgent public work in hand. *(To the* INTENDANT) Intendant, you are to close the public granaries. I have signed a decree to that effect; you will find it in my study.

INTENDANT   But, sire . . .

CALIGULA   Famine begins tomorrow.

INTENDANT   But . . . but heaven knows what may happen—perhaps a revolution.

CALIGULA *(firmly and deliberately)*   I repeat; famine begins tomorrow. We all know what famine means—a national catastrophe. Well, tomorrow there will be a catastrophe, and I shall end it when I choose. After all, I haven't so many ways of proving I am free. One is always free at someone else's expense. Absurd perhaps, but so it is. *(With a keen glance at* MUCIUS) Apply this principle to your jealousy—and you'll understand better. *(In a meditative tone)* Still, what an ugly thing is jealousy! A disease of vanity and the imagination. One pictures one's wife . . . (MUCIUS *clenches his fists and opens his mouth to speak. Before he can get a word out,* CALIGULA *cuts in.)* Now, gentlemen, let's go on with our meal. . . . Do you know, we've been doing quite a lot of work, with Helicon's assistance? Putting the final touches to a little monograph on execution—about which you will have much to say.

HELICON   Assuming we ask your opinion.

CALIGULA   Why not be generous, Helicon, and let them into our little secrets? Come now, give them a sample. Section Three, first paragraph.

HELICON *(standing, declaims in a droning voice)*   "Execution relieves and liberates. It is universal, tonic, just in precept and in practice. A man dies because he is guilty. A man is guilty because he is one of Caligula's subjects. Now all men are Caligula's subjects. *Ergo,* all man are guilty and shall die. It is only a matter of time and patience."

CALIGULA *(laughing)*   There's logic for you, don't you agree? That bit about patience was rather neat, wasn't it? Allow me to tell you, that's the quality I most admire in you . . . your patience. Now, gentlemen, you can disperse. Cherea doesn't need your presence any longer. Cæsonia, I wish you to stay. You too, Lepidus. Also our old friend Mereia. I want to have a little talk with you about our National Brothel. It's not functioning too well; in fact, I'm quite concerned about it.

(The others file out slowly. CALIGULA *follows* MUCIUS *with his eyes.)*

CHEREA   At your orders, Caius. But what's the trouble? Is the staff unsatisfactory?

CALIGULA   No, but the takings are falling off.

MEREIA   Then you should raise the entrance fee.

CALIGULA   There, Mereia, you missed a golden opportunity of keeping your mouth shut. You're too old to be interested in the subject, and I don't want your opinion.

MEREIA   Then why ask me to stay?

CALIGULA   Because, presently, I may require some cool, dispassionate advice.

*(*MEREIA *moves away.)*

CHEREA   If you wish to hear my views on the subject, Caius, I'd say, neither coolly nor dispassionately, that it would be a blunder to raise the scale of charges.

CALIGULA   Obviously. What's needed is a bigger turnover. I've explained my plan of campaign to Cæsonia, and she will tell you all about it. As for me, I've had too much wine, I'm feeling sleepy.

(He lies down and closes his eyes.)

CÆSONIA   It's very simple. Caligula is creating a new order of merit.

CHEREA   Sorry, I don't see the connection.

CÆSONIA   No? But there is one. It will be called the Badge of Civic Merit and awarded to those who have patronized Caligula's National Brothel most assiduously.

CHEREA   A brilliant idea!

CÆSONIA   I agree. Oh, I forgot to mention that the badge will be conferred each month, after checking the admission tickets. Any citizen who has not obtained the badge within twelve months will be exiled, or executed.

CHEREA   Why "or executed"?

CÆSONIA   Because Caligula says it doesn't matter which—but it's important he should have the right of choosing.

CHEREA   Bravo! The Public Treasury will wipe out its deficit in no time.

*(*CALIGULA *has half opened his eyes and is watching old* MEREIA *who, standing in a corner, has produced a small flask and is sipping its contents.)*

CALIGULA *(still lying on the couch)*   What's that you're drinking, Mereia?

MEREIA   It's for my asthma, Caius.

CALIGULA (*rises, and thrusting the others aside, goes up to* MEREIA *and sniffs his mouth*)   No, it's an antidote.

MEREIA   What an idea, Caius! You must be joking. I have choking fits at night and I've been in the doctor's hands for months.

CALIGULA   So you're afraid of being poisoned?

MEREIA   My asthma . . .

CALIGULA   No. Why beat about the bush? You're afraid I'll poison you. You suspect me. You're keeping an eye on me.

MEREIA   Good heavens, no!

CALIGULA   You suspect me. I'm not to be trusted, eh?

MEREIA   Caius!

CALIGULA (*roughly*)   Answer! (*In a cool, judicial tone*) If you take an antidote, it follows that you credit me with the intention of poisoning you. Q.E.D.

MEREIA   Yes . . . I mean . . . no!

CALIGULA   And thinking I intend to poison you, you take steps to frustrate my plan.

(*He falls silent. Meanwhile* CÆSONIA *and* CHEREA *have moved away, backstage.* LEPIDUS *is watching the speakers with an air of consternation.*)

That makes two crimes, Mereia, and a dilemma from which you can't escape. *Either* I have no wish to cause your death; in which case you are unjustly suspecting me, your emperor. *Or else* I desire your death; in which case, vermin that you are, you're trying to thwart my will. (*Another silence.* CALIGULA *contemplates the old man gloatingly.*) Well, Mereia, what have you to say to my logic?

MEREIA   It . . . it's sound enough, Caius. Only it doesn't apply to the case.

CALIGULA   A third crime. You take me for a fool. Now sit down and listen carefully. (*To* LEPIDUS) Let everyone sit down. (*To* MEREIA) Of these three crimes only one does you honor; the second one—because by crediting me with a certain wish and presuming to oppose it you are deliberately defying me. You are a rebel, a leader of revolt. And that needs courage. (*Sadly*) I've a great liking for you, Mereia. And that is why you'll be condemned for crime number two, and not for either of the others. You shall die nobly, a rebel's death. (*While he talks* MEREIA *is shrinking together on his chair.*) Don't thank me. It's quite natural. Here. (*Holds out a phial. His tone is amiable.*) Drink this poison. (MEREIA *shakes his head. He is sobbing violently.* CALIGULA *shows signs of impatience.*) Don't waste time. Take it. (MEREIA *makes a feeble attempt to escape. But* CALIGULA *with a wild leap is on him, catches him in the center of the stage and after a brief struggle pins him down on a low couch. He forces the phial between his lips and smashes it with a blow of his fist. After some convulsive movements* MEREIA *dies. His face is streaming with blood and tears.* CALIGULA *rises, wipes his hands absent-mindedly, then hands* MEREIA'S *flask to* CÆSONIA.) What was it? An antidote?

CÆSONIA (*calmly*)   No, Caligula. A remedy for asthma.

(*A short silence.*)

CALIGULA (*gazing down at* MEREIA)   No matter. It all comes to the same thing in the end. A little sooner, a little later. . . .

(*He goes out hurriedly, still wiping his hands.*)

LEPIDUS (*in a horrified tone*)   What . . . what shall we do?

CÆSONIA (*coolly*)   Remove that body to begin with, I should say. It's rather a beastly sight.

(CHEREA *and* LEPIDUS *drag the body into the wings.*)

LEPIDUS (*to* CHEREA)   We must act quickly.

CHEREA   We'll need to be two hundred.

(*Young* SCIPIO *enters. Seeing* CÆSONIA, *he makes as if to leave.*)

CÆSONIA   Come.

SCIPIO   What do you want?

CÆSONIA   Come nearer. (*She pushes up his chin and looks him in the eyes. A short silence. Then, in a calm, unemotional voice*) He killed your father, didn't he?

SCIPIO   Yes.

CÆSONIA   Do you hate him?

SCIPIO   Yes.

CÆSONIA   And you'd like to kill him?

SCIPIO   Yes.

CÆSONIA (*withdrawing her hand*)   But—why tell me this?

SCIPIO   Because I fear nobody. Killing him or being killed—either way out will do. And anyhow you won't betray me.

CÆSONIA   That's so. I won't betray you. But I want to tell you something—or, rather, I'd like to speak to what is best in you.

SCIPIO   What's best in me is—my hatred.

CÆSONIA   Please listen carefully to what I'm going to say. It may sound hard to grasp, but it's as clear as daylight, really. And it's something that would bring about the one real revolution in this world of ours, if people would only take it in.

SCIPIO   Yes? What is it?

CÆSONIA   Wait! Try to call up a picture of your father's death, of the agony on his face as they were tearing out his tongue. Think of the blood streaming from his mouth, and recall his screams, like a tortured animal's.

SCIPIO   Yes.

CÆSONIA   And now think of Caligula.

SCIPIO (*his voice rough with hatred*)   Yes.

CÆSONIA   Now listen. *Try to understand him.*

(*She goes out, leaving* SCIPIO *gaping after her in bewilderment.* HELICON *enters.*)

HELICON   Caligula will be here in a moment. Suppose you go for your meal, young poet?

SCIPIO   Helicon, help me.

HELICON   Too dangerous, my lamb. And poetry means nothing to me.

SCIPIO   You can help me. You know . . . so many things.

HELICON   I know that the days go by—and growing boys should have their meals on time . . . I know, too, that you could kill Caligula . . . and he wouldn't greatly mind it.

(HELICON *goes out.* CALIGULA *enters.*)

CALIGULA   Ah, it's you, Scipio. (*He pauses. One has the impression that he is somewhat embarrassed.*) It's quite a long time since I saw you last. (*Slowly approaches* SCIPIO) What have you been up to? Writing more poems, I suppose. Might I see your latest composition?

SCIPIO (*likewise ill at ease, torn between hatred and some less defined emotion*) Yes, Cæsar, I've written some more poems.

CALIGULA   On what subject?

SCIPIO   Oh, on nothing in particular. Well, on Nature in a way.

CALIGULA   A fine theme. And a vast one. And what has Nature done for you?

SCIPIO (*pulling himself together, in a somewhat truculent tone*)   It consoles me for not being Cæsar.

CALIGULA   Really? And do you think Nature could console me for being Cæsar?

SCIPIO *(in the same tone)*   Why not? Nature has healed worse wounds than that.

CALIGULA *(in a curiously young, unaffected voice)*   Wounds, you said? There was anger in your voice. Because I put your father to death? . . . That word you used—if you only knew how apt it is! My wounds! *(In a different tone)* Well, well, there's nothing like hatred for developing the intelligence.

SCIPIO *(stiffly)*   I answered your question about Nature.

*(*CALIGULA *sits down, gazes at* SCIPIO, *then brusquely grips his wrists and forces him to stand up. He takes the young man's face between his hands.)*

CALIGULA   Recite your poem to me, please.

SCIPIO   No, please, don't ask me that.

CALIGULA   Why not?

SCIPIO   I haven't got it on me.

CALIGULA   Can't you remember it?

SCIPIO   No.

CALIGULA   Anyhow you can tell me what it's about.

SCIPIO *(still hostile; reluctantly)*   I spoke of a . . . a certain harmony . . .

CALIGULA *(breaking in; in a pensive voice)*   . . . between one's feet and the earth.

SCIPIO *(looking surprised)*   Yes, it's almost that . . . and it tells of the wavy outline of the Roman hills and the sudden thrill of peace that twilight brings to them . . .

CALIGULA   And the cries of swifts winding through the green dusk.

SCIPIO *(yielding more and more to his emotion)*   Yes, yes! And that fantastic moment when the sky all flushed with red and gold swings round and shows its other side, spangled with stars.

CALIGULA   And the faint smell of smoke and trees and streams that mingles with the rising mist.

SCIPIO *(in a sort of ecstasy)*   Yes, and the chirr of crickets, the coolness veining the warm air, the rumble of carts and the farmers' shouts, dogs barking . . .

CALIGULA   And the roads drowned in shadow winding through the olive groves . . .

SCIPIO   Yes, yes. That's it, exactly. . . . But how did you know?

CALIGULA *(drawing* SCIPIO *to his breast)*   I wonder! Perhaps because the same eternal truths appeal to us both.

SCIPIO *(quivering with excitement, burying his head on* CALIGULA'S *breast)*   Anyhow, what does it matter! All I know is that everything I feel or think of turns to love.

CALIGULA *(stroking his hair)*   That, Scipio, is a privilege of noble hearts—and how I wish I could share your . . . your limpidity! But my appetite for life's too keen; Nature can never sate it. You belong to quite another world, and you can't understand. You are single-minded for good; and I am single-minded—for evil.

SCIPIO   I *do* understand.

CALIGULA   No. There's something deep down in me—an abyss of silence, a pool of stagnant water, rotting weeds. *(With an abrupt change of manner)* Your poem sounds very good indeed, but, if you really want my opinion. . . .

SCIPIO *(his head on* CALIGULA'S *breast, murmurs)*   Yes?

CALIGULA   All that's a bit . . . anemic.

SCIPIO *(recoiling abruptly, as if stung by a serpent, and gazing, horrified, at* CALIGULA, *he cries hoarsely)*   Oh, you brute! You loathsome brute! You've fooled me again. I know! You were playing a trick on me, weren't you? And now you're gloating over your success.

CALIGULA *(with a hint of sadness)*   There's truth in what you say. I *was* playing a part.

SCIPIO *(in the same indignant tone)*   What a foul, black heart you have! And how all that wickedness and hatred must make you suffer!

CALIGULA *(gently)*   That's enough.

SCIPIO   How I loathe you! And how I pity you!

CALIGULA *(angrily)*   Enough, I tell you.

SCIPIO   And how horrible a loneliness like yours must be!

CALIGULA *(in a rush of anger, gripping the boy by the collar, and shaking him)* Loneliness! What do *you* know of it? Only the loneliness of poets and weaklings. You prate of loneliness, but you don't realize that one is *never* alone. Always we are attended by the same load of the future and the past. Those we have killed are always with us. But *they* are no great trouble. It's those we have loved, those who loved us and whom we did not love; regrets, desires, bitterness and sweetness, whores and gods, the celestial gang! Always, always with us! *(He releases* SCIPIO *and moves back to his former place.)* Alone! Ah, if only in this loneliness, this ghoul-haunted wilderness of mine, I could know, but for a moment, real solitude, real silence, the throbbing stillness of a tree! *(Sitting down, in an access of fatigue.)* Solitude? No, Scipio, mine is full of gnashings of teeth, hideous with jarring sounds and voices. And when I am with the women I make mine and darkness falls on us and I think, now my body's had its fill, that I can feel myself my own at last, poised between death and life—ah, then my solitude is fouled by the stale smell of pleasure from the woman sprawling at my side.

(A long silence. CALIGULA *seems weary and despondent.* SCIPIO *moves behind him and approaches hesitantly. He slowly stretches out a hand toward him, from behind, and lays it on his shoulder. Without looking round,* CALIGULA *places his hand on* SCIPIO's.)

SCIPIO   All men have a secret solace. It helps them to endure, and they turn to it when life has wearied them beyond enduring.

CALIGULA   Yes, Scipio.

SCIPIO   Have you nothing of the kind in your life, no refuge, no mood that makes the tears well up, no consolation?

CALIGULA   Yes, I have something of the kind.

SCIPIO   What is it?

CALIGULA *(very quietly)*   Scorn.

(Curtain.)

ACT III

A room in the imperial palace.

Before the curtain rises a rhythmic clash of cymbals and the thudding of a drum have been coming from the stage, and when it goes up we see a curtained-off booth, with a small proscenium in front, such as strolling players use at country fairs. On the little stage are CÆSONIA *and* HELICON, *flanked by cymbal players. Seated on benches, with their backs to the audience, are some patricians and young* SCIPIO.

HELICON *(in the tone of a showman at a fair)*   Walk up! Walk up! *(A clash of cymbals)* Once more the gods have come to earth. They have assumed the human form of our heaven-born emperor, known to men as Caligula. Draw near, mortals of common clay; a holy miracle is taking place before your eyes. By a divine dispensation peculiar to Caligula's hallowed reign, the secrets of the gods will be revealed to you. *(Cymbals.)*

CÆSONIA   Come, gentlemen. Come and adore him—and don't forget to give your alms. Today heaven and its mysteries are on show, at a price to suit every pocket.

HELICON   For all to see, the secrets of Olympus, revelations in high places, featuring gods in undress, their little plots and pranks. Step this way! The whole truth about your gods! *(Cymbals.)*

CÆSONIA Adore him, and give your alms. Come near, gentlemen. The show's beginning.

(Cymbals. Slaves are placing various objects on the platform.)

HELICON An epoch-making reproduction of the life celestial, warranted authentic in every detail. For the first time the pomp and splendor of the gods are presented to the Roman public. You will relish our novel, breathtaking effects: flashes of lightning *(Slaves light Greek fires.)*, peals of thunder *(They roll a barrel filled with stones.)*, the divine event on its triumphal way. Now watch with all your eyes.

(He draws aside the curtain. Grotesquely attired as Venus, CALIGULA *beams down on them from a pedestal.)*

CALIGULA *(amiably)* I'm Venus today.

CÆSONIA Now for the adoration. Bow down. *(All but* SCIPIO *bend their heads.)* And repeat after me the litany of Venus called Caligula. "Our Lady of pangs and pleasures . . ."

THE PATRICIANS "Our Lady of pangs and pleasures . . ."

CÆSONIA "Born of the waves, bitter and bright with seafoam . . ."

THE PATRICIANS "Born of the waves, bitter and bright with seafoam . . ."

CÆSONIA "O Queen whose gifts are laughter and regrets . . ."

THE PATRICIANS "O Queen whose gifts are laughter and regrets . . ."

CÆSONIA "Rancors and raptures . . ."

THE PATRICIANS "Rancors and raptures . . ."

CÆSONIA "Teach us the indifference that kindles love anew . . ."

THE PATRICIANS "Teach us the indifference that kindles love anew . . ."

CÆSONIA "Make known to us the truth about this world—which is that it has none . . ."

THE PATRICIANS "Make known to us the truth about this world—which is that it has none . . ."

CÆSONIA "And grant us strength to live up to this verity of verities."

THE PATRICIANS "And grant us strength to live up to this verity of verities."

CÆSONIA Now, pause.

THE PATRICIANS Now, pause.

CÆSONIA *(after a short silence)* "Bestow your gifts on us, and shed on our faces the light of your impartial cruelty, your wanton hatred; unfold above our eyes your arms laden with flowers and murders . . ."

THE PATRICIANS ". . . your arms laden with flowers and murders."

CÆSONIA "Welcome your wandering children home, to the bleak sanctuary of your heartless, thankless love. Give us your passions without object, your griefs devoid of reason, your raptures that lead nowhere . . ."

THE PATRICIANS ". . . your raptures that lead nowhere . . ."

CÆSONIA *(raising her voice)* "O Queen, so empty yet so ardent, inhuman yet so earthly, make us drunk with the wine of your equivalence, and surfeit us forever in the brackish darkness of your heart."

THE PATRICIANS "Make us drunk with the wine of your equivalence, and surfeit us forever in the brackish darkness of your heart." *(When the patricians have said the last response,* CALIGULA, *who until now has been quite motionless, snorts and rises.)*

CALIGULA *(in a stentorian voice)* Granted, my children. Your prayer is heard. *(He squats cross-legged on the pedestal. One by one the patricians make obeisance, deposit their alms, and line up on the right. The last, in his flurry, forgets to make an offering.* CALIGULA *bounds to his feet.)* Steady! Steady on! Come here, my lad. Worship's very well, but alms-giving is better. Thank you. We are appeased. Ah, if the gods had no wealth other than the love you mortals give them, they'd be as poor as poor Caligula. Now, gentlemen, you may go, and spread abroad the glad tidings of the miracle you've been allowed to witness. You have seen Venus, seen her godhead with your fleshly eyes, and Venus herself has spoken to you. Go, most favored gentlemen. *(The patricians begin to move away.)* Just a moment. When you leave, mind you take the exit on your left. I have posted sentries in the others, with orders to kill you.

(The patricians file out hastily, in some disorder. The slaves and musicians leave the stage.)

HELICON *(pointing a threatening finger at* SCIPIO) Naughty boy, you've been playing the anarchist again.

SCIPIO *(to* CALIGULA) You spoke blasphemy, Caius.

CALIGULA Blasphemy? What's that?

SCIPIO You're befouling heaven, after bloodying the earth.

HELICON How this youngster loves big words!

(He stretches himself on a couch.)

CÆSONIA *(composedly)* You should watch your tongue, my lad. At this moment men are dying in Rome for saying much less.

SCIPIO Maybe—but I've resolved to tell Caligula the truth.

CÆSONIA Listen to him, Caligula! That was the one thing missing in your Empire—a bold young moralist.

CALIGULA *(giving* SCIPIO *a curious glance)* Do you really believe in the gods, Scipio?

SCIPIO No.

CALIGULA Then I fail to follow. If you don't believe, why be so keen to scent out blasphemy?

SCIPIO One may deny something without feeling called on to besmirch it, or deprive others of the right of believing in it.

CALIGULA But that's humility, the real thing, unless I'm much mistaken. Ah, my dear Scipio, how glad I am on your behalf—and a trifle envious, too. Humility's the one emotion I may never feel.

SCIPIO It's not I you're envious of; it's the gods.

CALIGULA If you don't mind, that will remain our secret—the great enigma of our reign. Really, you know, there's only one thing for which I might be blamed today—and that's this small advance I've made upon the path of freedom. For someone who loves power the rivalry of the gods is rather irksome. Well, I've proved to these imaginary gods that any man, without previous training, if he applies his mind to it, can play their absurd parts to perfection.

SCIPIO That, Caius, is what I meant by blasphemy.

CALIGULA No, Scipio, it's clear-sightedness. I've merely realized that there's only one way of getting even with the gods. All that's needed is to be as cruel as they.

SCIPIO All that's needed is to play the tyrant.

CALIGULA Tell me, my young friend. What exactly *is* a tyrant?

SCIPIO A blind soul.

CALIGULA That's a moot point. I should say the real tyrant is a man who sacrifices a whole nation to his ideal or his ambition. But I have no ideal, and there's nothing left for me to covet by way of power or glory. If I use this power of mine, it's to compensate.

SCIPIO For what?

CALIGULA For the hatred and stupidity of the gods.

SCIPIO Hatred does not compensate for hatred. Power is no solution. Personally I know only one way of countering the hostility of the world we live in.

CALIGULA   Yes? And what is it?

SCIPIO   Poverty.

CALIGULA *(bending over his feet and scrutinizing his toes)*   I must try that, too.

SCIPIO   Meanwhile many men round you are dying.

CALIGULA   Oh, come! Not so many as all that. Do you know how many wars I've refused to embark on?

SCIPIO   No.

CALIGULA   Three. And do you know why I refused?

SCIPIO   Because the grandeur of Rome means nothing to you.

CALIGULA   No. Because I respect human life.

SCIPIO   You're joking, Caius.

CALIGULA   Or, anyhow, I respect it more than I respect military triumphs. But it's a fact that I don't respect it more than I respect my own life. And if I find killing easy, it's because dying isn't hard for me. No, the more I think about it, the surer I feel that I'm no tyrant.

SCIPIO   What does it matter, if it costs us quite as dear as if you were one?

CALIGULA *(with a hint of petulance)*   If you had the least head for figures you'd know that the smallest war a tyrant—however level-headed he might be—indulged in would cost you a thousand times more than all my vagaries (shall we call them?) put together.

SCIPIO   Possibly. But at least there'd be *some* sense behind a war; it would be under-standable—and to understand makes up for much.

CALIGULA   There's no understanding fate; therefore I choose to play the part of fate. I wear the foolish, unintelligible face of a professional god. And that is what the men who were here with you have learned to adore.

SCIPIO   That, too, Caius, is blasphemy.

CALIGULA   No, Scipio, it's dramatic art. The great mistake you people make is not to take the drama seriously enough. If you did, you'd know that any man can play lead in the divine comedy and become a god. All he needs do is to harden his heart.

SCIPIO   You may be right, Caius. But I rather think you've done everything that was needed to rouse up against you a legion of human gods, ruthless as yourself, who will drown in blood your godhead of a day.

CÆSONIA   Really, Scipio!

CALIGULA *(peremptorily)*   No, don't stop him, Cæsonia. Yes, Scipio, you spoke truer than you knew; I've done everything needed to that end. I find it hard to picture the event you speak of—but I sometimes dream it. And in all those faces surging up out of the angry darkness, convulsed with fear and hatred, I see, and I rejoice to see, the only god I've worshipped on this earth; foul and craven as the human heart. *(Irritably)* Now go. I've had enough of you, more than enough. *(In a different tone)* I really must attend to my toenails; they're not nearly red enough, and I've no time to waste. *(All go, with the exception of* HELICON. *He hovers round* CALIGULA, *who is busy examining his toes.)* Helicon!

HELICON   Yes?

CALIGULA   Getting on with your task?

HELICON   What task?

CALIGULA   You know . . . the moon.

HELICON   Ah yes, the moon. . . . It's a matter of time and patience. But I'd like to have a word with you.

CALIGULA   I might have patience; only I have not much time. So you must make haste.

HELICON   I said I'd do my utmost. But, first, I have something to tell you. Very seri-ous news.

CALIGULA *(as if he has not heard)*   Mind you, I've had her already.

HELICON   Whom?

CALIGULA The moon.

HELICON Yes, yes. . . . Now listen, please. Do you know there's a plot being hatched against your life?

CALIGULA What's more, I had her thoroughly. Only two or three times, to be sure. Still, I had her all right.

HELICON For the last hour I've been trying to tell you about it, only—

CALIGULA It was last summer. I'd been gazing at her so long, and stroking her so often on the marble pillars in the gardens that evidently she'd come to understand.

HELICON Please stop trifling, Caius. Even if you refuse to listen, it's my duty to tell you this. And if you shut your ears, it can't be helped.

CALIGULA *(applying red polish to his toenails)* This varnish is no good at all. But, to come back to the moon—it was a cloudless August night. (HELICON *looks sulkily away, and keeps silence.*) She was coy, to begin with. I'd gone to bed. First she was blood-red, low on the horizon. Then she began rising, quicker and quicker, growing brighter and brighter all the while. And the higher she climbed, the paler she grew, till she was like a milky pool in a dark wood rustling with stars. Slowly, shyly she approached, through the warm night air, soft, light as gossamer, naked in beauty. She crossed the threshold of my room, glided to my bed, poured herself into it, and flooded me with her smiles and sheen. . . . No, really this new varnish is a failure. . . . So you see, Helicon, I can say, without boasting, that I've had her.

HELICON Now will you listen, and learn the danger that's threatening you?

CALIGULA *(ceasing to fiddle with his toes, and gazing at him fixedly)* All I want, Helicon, is—the moon. For the rest, I've always known what will kill me. I haven't yet exhausted all that is to keep me living. That's why I want the moon. And you must not return till you have secured her for me.

HELICON Very well. . . . Now I'll do my duty and tell you what I've learned. There's a plot against you. Cherea is the ringleader. I came across this tablet which tells you all you need to know. See, I put it here.

(He places the tablet on one of the seats and moves away.)

CALIGULA Where are you off to, Helicon?

HELICON *(from the threshold)* To get the moon for you.

(There is a mouselike scratching at the opposite door. CALIGULA *swings round and sees the* OLD PATRICIAN.*)*

THE OLD PATRICIAN *(timidly)* May I, Caius . . .

CALIGULA *(impatiently)* Come in! Come in! *(Gazes at him)* So, my pet, you've returned to have another look at Venus.

THE OLD PATRICIAN Well . . . no. It's not quite that. Ssh! Oh, sorry, Caius! I only wanted to say . . . You know I'm very, very devoted to you—and my one desire is to end my days in peace.

CALIGULA Be quick, man. Get it out!

THE OLD PATRICIAN Well, it's . . . it's like this. *(Hurriedly)* It's terribly serious, that's what I meant to say.

CALIGULA No, it isn't serious.

THE OLD PATRICIAN But—I don't follow. *What* isn't serious?

CALIGULA But what are we talking about, my love?

THE OLD PATRICIAN *(glancing nervously round the room)* I mean to say . . . *(Wriggles, shuffles, then bursts out with it)* There's a plot afoot, against you.

CALIGULA There! You see. Just as I said; it isn't serious.

THE OLD PATRICIAN But, Caius, they mean to kill you.

CALIGULA *(approaching him and grasping his shoulders)* Do you know why I can't believe you?

THE OLD PATRICIAN *(raising an arm, as if to take an oath)* The gods bear witness, Caius, that . . .

CALIGULA *(gently but firmly pressing him back toward the door)* Don't swear. I particularly ask you not to swear. Listen, instead. Suppose it were true, what you are telling me—I'd have to assume you were betraying your friends, isn't that so?

THE OLD PATRICIAN *(flustered)* Well, Caius, considering the deep affection I have for you . . .

CALIGULA *(in the same tone as before)* And I cannot assume *that*. I've always loathed baseness of that sort so profoundly that I could never restrain myself from having a betrayer put to death. But I know the man you are, my worthy friend. And I'm convinced you neither wish to play the traitor nor to die.

THE OLD PATRICIAN Certainly not, Caius. Most certainly not.

CALIGULA So you see I was right in refusing to believe you. You wouldn't stoop to baseness, would you?

THE OLD PATRICIAN Oh, no, indeed!

CALIGULA Nor betray your friends?

THE OLD PATRICIAN I need hardly tell you that, Caius.

CALIGULA Therefore it follows that there isn't any plot. It was just a joke—between ourselves, rather a silly joke—what you've just been telling me, eh?

THE OLD PATRICIAN *(feebly)* Yes, yes. A joke, merely a joke.

CALIGULA Good. So now we know where we are. Nobody wants to kill me.

THE OLD PATRICIAN Nobody. That's it. Nobody at all.

CALIGULA *(drawing a deep breath; in measured tones)* Then—leave me, sweetheart. A man of honor is an animal so rare in the present-day world that I couldn't bear the sight of one too long. I must be left alone to relish this unique experience. *(For some moments he gazes, without moving, at the tablet. He picks it up and reads it. Then, again, draws a deep breath. Then summons a palace guard.)*

CALIGULA Bring Cherea to me. *(The man starts to leave.)* Wait! *(The man halts.)* Treat him politely. *(The man goes out. CALIGULA falls to pacing the room. After a while he approaches the mirror.)* You decided to be logical, didn't you, poor simpleton? Logic for ever! The question now is: Where will that take you? *(Ironically)* Suppose the moon were brought here, everything would be different. That was the idea, wasn't it? Then the impossible would become possible, in a flash the Great Change come, and all things be transfigured. After all, why shouldn't Helicon bring it off? One night, perhaps, he'll catch her sleeping in a lake, and carry her here, trapped in a glistening net, all slimy with weeds and water, like a pale bloated fish drawn from the depths. Why not, Caligula? Why not, indeed? *(He casts a glance round the room.)* Fewer and fewer people round me; I wonder why. *(Addressing the mirror, in a muffled voice)* Too many dead, too many dead—that makes an emptiness. . . . No, even if the moon were mine, I could not retrace my way. Even were those dead men thrilling again under the sun's caress, the murders wouldn't go back underground for that. *(Angrily)* Logic, Caligula; follow where logic leads. Power to the uttermost; willfulness without end. Ah, I'm the only man on earth to know the secret—that power can never be complete without a total self-surrender to the dark impulse of one's destiny. No, there's no return. I must go on and on, until the consummation.

(CHEREA enters. CALIGULA is slumped in his chair, the cloak drawn tightly round him.)

CHEREA You sent for me, Caius?

CALIGULA *(languidly)*   Yes, Cherea.

(A short silence.)

CHEREA   Have you anything particular to tell me?
CALIGULA   No, Cherea.

(Another silence.)

CHEREA *(with a hint of petulance)*   Are you sure you really need my presence?
CALIGULA   Absolutely sure, Cherea. *(Another silence. Then, as if suddenly recollecting himself)* I'm sorry for seeming so inhospitable. I was following up my thoughts, and—Now do sit down, we'll have a friendly little chat. I'm in a mood for some intelligent conversation. (CHEREA *sits down. For the first time since the play began,* CALIGULA *gives the impression of being his natural self.*) Do you think, Cherea, that it's possible for two men of much the same temperament and equal pride to talk to each other with complete frankness—if only once in their lives? Can they strip themselves naked, so to speak, and shed their prejudices, their private interests, the lies by which they live?

CHEREA   Yes, Caius, I think it possible. But I don't think you'd be capable of it.

CALIGULA   You're right. I only wished to know if you agreed with me. So let's wear our masks, and muster up our lies. And we'll talk as fencers fight, padded on all the vital parts. Tell me, Cherea, why don't you like me?

CHEREA   Because there's nothing likable about you, Caius. Because such feelings can't be had to order. And because I understand you far too well. One cannot like an aspect of oneself which one always tries to keep concealed.

CALIGULA   But why is it you hate me?

CHEREA   There, Caius, you're mistaken. I do not hate you. I regard you as noxious and cruel, vain and selfish. But I cannot hate you, because I don't think you are happy. And I cannot scorn you, because I know you are no coward.

CALIGULA   Then why wish to kill me?

CHEREA   I've told you why; because I regard you as noxious, a constant menace. I like, and need, to feel secure. So do most men. They resent living in a world where the most preposterous fancy may at any moment become a reality, and the absurd transfix their lives, like a dagger in the heart. I feel as they do; I refuse to live in a topsy-turvy world. I want to know where I stand, and to stand secure.

CALIGULA   Security and logic don't go together.

CHEREA   Quite true. My plan of life may not be logical, but at least it's sound.

CALIGULA   Go on.

CHEREA   There's no more to say. I'll be no party to your logic. I've a very different notion of my duties as a man. And I know that the majority of your subjects share my view. You outrage their deepest feelings. It's only natural that you should . . . disappear.

CALIGULA   I see your point, and it's legitimate enough. For most men, I grant you, it's obvious. But *you*, I should have thought, would have known better. You're an intelligent man, and given intelligence, one has a choice; either to pay its price or to disown it. Why do you shirk the issue and neither disown it nor consent to pay its price?

CHEREA   Because what I want is to live, and to be happy. Neither, to my mind, is possible if one pushes the absurd to its logical conclusions. As you see, I'm quite an ordinary sort of man. True, there are moments when, to feel free of them, I desire the death of those I love, or I hanker after women from whom the ties of family or friendship debar me. Were logic everything, I'd kill or fornicate on such occasions. But I consider that these passing fancies have no great importance. If everyone set to gratifying them, the world would be impossible to live in, and happiness, too, would go by the board. And these, I repeat, are the things that count, for me.

CALIGULA So, I take it, you believe in some higher principle?

CHEREA Certainly I believe that some actions are—shall I say?—more praiseworthy than others.

CALIGULA And *I* believe that all are on an equal footing.

CHEREA I know it, Caius, and that's why I don't hate you. I understand, and, to a point, agree with you. But you're pernicious, and you've got to go.

CALIGULA True enough. But why risk your life by telling me this?

CHEREA Because others will take my place, and because I don't like lying.

(A short silence.)

CALIGULA Cherea!

CHEREA Yes, Caius?

CALIGULA Do you think that two men of similar temperament and equal pride can, if only once in their lives, open their hearts to each other?

CHEREA That, I believe, is what we've just been doing.

CALIGULA Yes, Cherea. But you thought I was incapable of it.

CHEREA I was wrong, Caius. I admit it, and I thank you. Now I await your sentence.

CALIGULA My sentence? Ah, I see. *(Producing the tablet from under his cloak)* You know what this is, Cherea?

CHEREA I knew you had it.

CALIGULA *(passionately)* You knew I had it! So your frankness was all a piece of play acting. The two friends did *not* open their hearts to each other. Well, well! It's no great matter. Now we can stop playing at sincerity, and resume life on the old footing. But first I'll ask you to make just one more effort; to bear with my caprices and my tactlessness a little longer. Listen well, Cherea. This tablet is the one and only piece of evidence against you.

CHEREA Caius, I'd rather go. I'm sick and tired of all these antics. I know them only too well, and I've had enough. Let me go, please.

CALIGULA *(in the same tense, passionate voice)* No, stay. This tablet is the only evidence. Is that clear?

CHEREA Evidence? I never knew you needed evidence to send a man to his death.

CALIGULA That's true. Still, for once I wish to contradict myself. Nobody can object to that. It's so pleasant to contradict oneself occasionally; so restful. And I need rest, Cherea.

CHEREA I don't follow . . . and, frankly, I've no taste for these subtleties.

CALIGULA I know, Cherea, I know. You're not like me; you're an ordinary man, sound in mind and body. And naturally you've no desire for the extraordinary. *(With a burst of laughter)* You want to live and to be happy. That's all!

CHEREA I think, Caius, we'd better leave it at that. . . . Can I go?

CALIGULA Not yet. A little patience, if you don't mind—I shall not keep you long. You see this thing—this piece of evidence? I choose to assume that I can't sentence you to death without it. That's my idea . . . and my repose. Well! See what becomes of evidence in an emperor's hands. *(He holds the tablet to a torch.* CHEREA *approaches. The torch is between them. The tablet begins to melt.)* You see, conspirator! The tablet's melting, and as it melts a look of innocence is dawning on your face. What a handsome forehead you have, Cherea! And how rare, how beautiful a sight is an innocent man! Admire my power. Even the gods cannot restore innocence without first punishing the culprit. But your emperor needs only a torch flame to absolve you and give you a new lease of hope. So carry on, Cherea; follow out the noble precepts we've been hearing, wherever they may take you. Meanwhile your emperor awaits his repose. It's his way of living and being happy.

(CHEREA *stares, dumbfounded, at* CALIGULA. *He makes a vague gesture, seems to understand, opens his mouth to speak—and walks abruptly away. Smiling, holding the tablet to the flame,* CALIGULA *follows the receding figure with his gaze.*)

(Curtain.)

ACT IV

A room in the imperial palace.

The stage is in semidarkness. CHEREA *and* SCIPIO *enter.* CHEREA *crosses to the right, then comes back left to* SCIPIO.

SCIPIO *(sulkily)*   What do you want of me?

CHEREA   There's no time to lose. And we must know our minds, we must be resolute.

SCIPIO   Who says I'm not resolute?

CHEREA   You didn't attend our meeting yesterday.

SCIPIO *(looking away)*   That's so, Cherea.

CHEREA   Scipio, I am older than you, and I'm not in the habit of asking others' help. But, I won't deny it, I need you now. This murder needs honorable men to sponsor it. Among all these wounded vanities and sordid fears, our motives only, yours and mine, are disinterested. Of course I know that, if you leave us, we can count on your silence. But that is not the point. What I want is—for you to stay with us.

SCIPIO   I understand. But I can't, oh, no, I *cannot* do as you wish.

CHEREA   So you are with him?

SCIPIO   No. But I cannot be against him. *(Pauses; then in muffled voice)* Even if I killed him, my heart would still be with him.

CHEREA   And yet—he killed your father!

SCIPIO   Yes—and that's how it all began. But that, too, is how it ends.

CHEREA   He denies what you believe in. He tramples on all that you hold sacred.

SCIPIO   I know, Cherea. And yet something inside me is akin to him. The same fire burns in both our hearts.

CHEREA   There are times when a man must make his choice. As for me, I have silenced in my heart all that might be akin to him.

SCIPIO   But—I—I cannot make a choice. I have my own sorrow, but I suffer with him, too; I share his pain. I understand all—that is my trouble.

CHEREA   So that's it. You have chosen to take his side.

SCIPIO *(passionately)*   No, Cherea. I beg you, don't think that. I can never, never again take anybody's side.

CHEREA *(affectionately; approaching* SCIPIO)   Do you know, I hate him even more for having made of you—what he has made.

SCIPIO   Yes, he has taught me to expect everything of life.

CHEREA   No, he has taught you despair. And to have instilled despair into a young heart is fouler than the foulest of the crimes he has committed up to now. I assure you, *that* alone would justify me in killing him out of hand.

(He goes toward the door. HELICON *enters.)*

HELICON   I've been hunting for you high and low, Cherea. Caligula's giving a little party here, for his personal friends only. Naturally he expects you to attend it. *(To* SCIPIO*)* You, my boy, aren't wanted. Off you go!

SCIPIO *(looking back at* CHEREA *as he goes out)*   Cherea.

CHEREA *(gently)*   Yes, Scipio?

SCIPIO   Try to understand.

CHEREA *(in the same gentle tone)*   No, Scipio.

*(*SCIPIO *and* HELICON *go out. A clash of arms in the wings. Two soldiers enter at right, escorting the* OLD PATRICIAN *and the* FIRST PATRICIAN, *who show signs of alarm.)*

FIRST PATRICIAN *(to one of the soldiers, in a tone which he vainly tries to steady)*   But . . . but what *can* he want with us at this hour of the night?

SOLDIER   Sit there. *(Points to the chairs on the right)*

FIRST PATRICIAN   If it's only to have us killed—like so many others—why all these preliminaries?

SOLDIER   Sit down, you old mule.

THE OLD PATRICIAN   Better do as he says. It's clear he doesn't know anything.

SOLDIER   Yes, darling, quite clear. *(Goes out.)*

FIRST PATRICIAN   We should have acted sooner; I always said so. Now we're in for the torture chamber.

(The SOLDIER *comes back with* CHEREA, *then goes out.)*

CHEREA *(seating himself. He shows no sign of apprehension.)*   Any idea what's happening?

FIRST PATRICIAN AND THE OLD PATRICIAN *(speaking together)*   He's found out about the conspiracy.

CHEREA   Yes? And then?

THE OLD PATRICIAN *(shuddering)*   The torture chamber for us all.

CHEREA *(still unperturbed)*   I remember that Caligula once gave eighty-one thousand sesterces to a slave who, though he was tortured nearly to death, wouldn't confess to a theft he had committed.

FIRST PATRICIAN   A lot of consolation that is—for us!

CHEREA   Anyhow, it shows that he appreciates courage. You ought to keep that in mind. *(To the* OLD PATRICIAN*)* Would you very much mind not chattering with your teeth? It's a noise I particularly dislike.

THE OLD PATRICIAN   I'm sorry, but—

FIRST PATRICIAN   Enough trifling! Our lives are at stake.

CHEREA *(coolly)*   Do you know Caligula's favorite remark?

THE OLD PATRICIAN *(on the verge of tears)*   Yes. He says to the executioner: "Kill him slowly, so that he feels what dying's like!"

CHEREA   No, there's a better one. After an execution he yawns, and says quite seriously: "What I admire most is my imperturbability."

FIRST PATRICIAN   Do you hear . . . ?

(A clanking of weapons is heard off stage.)

CHEREA   That remark betrays a weakness in his make-up.

THE OLD PATRICIAN   Would you be kind enough to stop philosophizing? It's something I particularly dislike.

(A slave enters and deposits a sheaf of knives on a seat.)

CHEREA *(who has not noticed him)*   Still, there's no denying it's remarkable, the effect this man has on all with whom he comes in contact. He forces one to think. There's nothing like insecurity for stimulating the brain. That, of course, is why he's so much hated.

THE OLD PATRICIAN *(pointing a trembling finger)*   Look!

CHEREA *(noticing the knives, in a slightly altered tone)*   Perhaps you were right.

FIRST PATRICIAN   Yes, waiting was a mistake. We should have acted at once.

CHEREA   I agree. Wisdom's come too late.

THE OLD PATRICIAN   But it's . . . it's crazy. I don't want to die.

(He rises and begins to edge away. Two soldiers appear, and, after slapping his face, force him back onto his seat. The FIRST PATRICIAN *squirms in his chair.* CHEREA *utters some inaudible words. Suddenly a queer music begins behind the curtain at the back of the stage; a thrumming and tinkling of zithers and cymbals. The patricians gaze at each other in silence. Outlined on the illuminated curtain, in shadow play,* CALIGULA *appears, makes some grotesque dance movements, and retreats from view. He is wearing ballet dancer's skirts and his head is garlanded with flowers. A moment later a* SOLDIER *announces gravely:* "Gentlemen, the performance is over." *Meanwhile* CÆSONIA *has entered soundlessly behind the watching patricians. She speaks in an ordinary voice, but nonetheless they give a start on hearing it.)*

CÆSONIA   Caligula has instructed me to tell you that, whereas in the past he always summoned you for affairs of state, today he invited you to share with him an artistic emotion. *(A short pause. Then she continues in the same tone.)* He added, I may say, that anyone who has not shared in it will be beheaded. *(They keep silent.)* I apologize for insisting, but I must ask you if you found that dance beautiful.

FIRST PATRICIAN *(after a brief hesitation)*   Yes, Cæsonia. It was beautiful.

THE OLD PATRICIAN *(effusively)*   Lovely! Lovely!

CÆSONIA   And you, Cherea?

CHEREA *(icily)*   It was . . . very high art.

CÆSONIA   Good. Now I can describe your artistic emotions to Caligula.

*(*CÆSONIA *goes out.)*

CHEREA   And now we must act quickly. You two stay here. Before the night is out there'll be a hundred of us.

(He goes out.)

THE OLD PATRICIAN   No, no. *You* stay. Let me go, instead. *(Sniffs the air)* It smells of death here.

FIRST PATRICIAN   And of lies. *(Sadly)* I said that dance was beautiful!

THE OLD PATRICIAN *(conciliatingly)*   And so it was, in a way. Most original.

(Some patricians and knights enter hurriedly.)

SECOND PATRICIAN   What's afoot? Do you know anything? The Emperor's summoned us here.

THE OLD PATRICIAN *(absent-mindedly)*   For the dance, maybe.

SECOND PATRICIAN   What dance?

THE OLD PATRICIAN   Well, I mean . . . er . . . the artistic emotion.

THIRD PATRICIAN   I've been told Caligula's very ill.

FIRST PATRICIAN   He's a sick man, yes . . .

THIRD PATRICIAN   What's he suffering from? *(In a joyful tone)* By God, is he going to die?

FIRST PATRICIAN   I doubt it. His disease is fatal—to others only.

THE OLD PATRICIAN   That's one way of putting it.

SECOND PATRICIAN   Quite so. But hasn't he some other disease less serious, and more to our advantage?

FIRST PATRICIAN   No. That malady of his excludes all others.

(He goes out. CÆSONIA *enters. A short silence.)*

CÆSONIA *(in a casual tone)*   If you want to know, Caligula has stomach trouble. Just now he vomited blood.

(The patricians crowd round her.)

SECOND PATRICIAN   O mighty gods, I vow, if he recovers, to pay the Treasury two hundred thousand sesterces as a token of my joy.

THIRD PATRICIAN *(with exaggerated eagerness)*   O Jupiter, take my life in place of his!

*(*CALIGULA *has entered, and is listening.)*

CALIGULA *(going up to the* SECOND PATRICIAN*)*   I accept your offer, Lucius. And I thank you. My Treasurer will call on you tomorrow. *(Goes to the* THIRD PATRICIAN *and embraces him)* You can't imagine how touched I am. *(A short silence; then, tenderly)* So you love me, Cassius, as much as that?

THIRD PATRICIAN *(emotionally)*   Oh, Cæsar, there's nothing, nothing I wouldn't sacrifice for your sake.

CALIGULA *(embracing him again)*   Ah, Cassius, this is really too much; I don't deserve all this love. (CASSIUS *makes a protesting gesture.)* No, no, really I don't! I'm not worthy of it. *(He beckons to two soldiers.)* Take him away. *(Gently, to* CASSIUS*)* Go, dear friend, and remember that Caligula has lost his heart to you.

THIRD PATRICIAN *(vaguely uneasy)*   But—where are they taking me?

CALIGULA   Why, to your death, of course. Your generous offer was accepted, and I feel better already. Even that nasty taste of blood in my mouth has gone. You've cured me, Cassius. It's been miraculous, and how proud you must feel of having worked the miracle by laying your life down for your friend—especially when that friend's none other than Caligula! So now you see me quite myself again, and ready for a festive night.

THIRD PATRICIAN *(shrieking, as he is dragged away)*   No! No! I don't want to die. You can't be serious!

CALIGULA *(in a thoughtful voice, between the shrieks)*   Soon the sea roads will be golden with mimosas. The women will wear their lightest dresses. And the sky! Ah, Cassius, what a blaze of clean, swift sunshine! The smiles of life. (CASSIUS *is near the door.* CALIGULA *gives him a gentle push. Suddenly his tone grows serious.)* Life, my friend, is something to be cherished. Had you cherished it enough, you wouldn't have gambled it away so rashly. (CASSIUS *is led off.* CALIGULA *returns to the table.)* The loser must pay. There's no alternative. *(A short silence)* Come, Cæsonia. *(He turns to the others.)* By the way, an idea has just waylaid me, and it's such an apt one that I want to share it with you. Until now my reign has been too happy. There's been no world-wide plague, no religious persecution, not even a rebellion—nothing in fact to make us memorable. And that, I'd have you know, is why I try to remedy the stinginess of fate. I mean—I don't know if you've followed me— that, well *(He gives a little laugh.)*, it's I who replace the epidemics that we've missed. *(In a different tone)* That's enough. I see Cherea's coming. Your turn, Cæsonia. (CALIGULA *goes out.* CHEREA *and the* FIRST PATRICIAN *enter.* CÆSONIA *hurries toward* CHEREA.*)*

CÆSONIA   Caligula is dead.

(She turns her head, as if to hide her tears; her eyes are fixed on the others, who keep silence. Everyone looks horrified, but for different reasons.)

FIRST PATRICIAN   You . . . you're *sure* this dreadful thing has happened? It seems incredible. Only a short while ago he was dancing.

CÆSONIA   Quite so—and the effort was too much for him. *(CHEREA moves hastily from one man to the other. No one speaks.)* You've nothing to say, Cherea?

CHEREA *(in a low voice)*   It's a great misfortune for us all, Cæsonia.

(CALIGULA bursts in violently and goes up to CHEREA.)

CALIGULA   Well played, Cherea. *(He spins round and stares at the others. Petulantly)* Too bad! It didn't come off. *(To* CÆSONIA) Don't forget what I told you.

(CALIGULA goes out. CÆSONIA stares after him without speaking.)

THE OLD PATRICIAN *(hoping against hope)*   Is he ill, Cæsonia?

CÆSONIA *(with a hostile look)*   No, my pet. But what you don't know is that the man never has more than two hours' sleep and spends the best part of the night roaming about the corridors in his palace. Another thing you don't know—and you've never given a thought to—is what may pass in this man's mind in those deadly hours between midnight and sunrise. Is he ill? No, not ill—unless you invent a name and medicine for the black ulcers that fester in his soul.

CHEREA *(seemingly affected by her words)*   You're right, Cæsonia. We all know that Caius . . .

CÆSONIA *(breaking in emotionally)*   Yes, you know it—in your fashion. But, like all those who have none, you can't abide anyone who has too much soul. Healthy people loathe invalids. Happy people hate the sad. Too much soul! That's what bites you, isn't it? You prefer to label it a disease; that way all the dolts are justified and pleased. *(In a changed tone)* Tell me, Cherea. Has love ever meant anything to you?

CHEREA *(himself again)*   I'm afraid we're too old now, Cæsonia, to learn the art of lovemaking. And anyhow it's highly doubtful if Caligula will give us time to do so.

CÆSONIA *(who has recovered her composure)*   True enough. *(She sits down.)* Oh, I was forgetting. . . . Caligula asked me to impart some news to you. You know, perhaps, that it's a red-letter day today, consecrated to art.

THE OLD PATRICIAN   According to the calendar?

CÆSONIA   No, according to Caligula. He's convoked some poets. He will ask them to improvise a poem on a set theme. And he particularly wants those of you who are poets to take part in the competition. He specially mentioned young Scipio and Metellus.

METELLUS   But we're not ready.

CÆSONIA *(in a level tone, as if she has not heard him)*   Needless to say there are prizes. There will be penalties, too. *(Looks of consternation)* Between ourselves, the penalties won't be so very terrible.

(CALIGULA enters, looking gloomier than ever.)

CALIGULA   All ready?

CÆSONIA   Yes. *(To a soldier)* Bring in the poets.

(Enter, two by two, a dozen poets, keeping step; they line up on the right of the stage.)

CALIGULA   And the others?

CÆSONIA   Metellus! Scipio!

(They cross the stage and take their stand beside the poets. CALIGULA *seats himself, backstage on the left, with* CÆSONIA *and the patricians. A short silence.)*

CALIGULA   Subject: death. Time limit: one minute.

(The poets scribble feverishly on their tablets.)

THE OLD PATRICIAN   Who will compose the jury?

CALIGULA   I. Isn't that enough?

THE OLD PATRICIAN   Oh, yes, indeed. Quite enough.

CHEREA   Won't you take part in the competition, Caius?

CALIGULA   Unnecessary. I made my poem on that theme long ago.

THE OLD PATRICIAN *(eagerly)*   Where can one get a copy of it?

CALIGULA   No need to get a copy. I recite it every day, after my fashion. *(*CÆSONIA *eyes him nervously.* CALIGULA *rounds on her almost savagely.)* Is there anything in my appearance that displeases you?

CÆSONIA *(gently)*   I'm sorry. . . .

CALIGULA   No meekness, please. For heaven's sake, no meekness. You're exasperating enough as it is, but if you start being humble . . . *(*CÆSONIA *slowly moves away.* CALIGULA *turns to* CHEREA.*)* I continue. It's the only poem I have made. And it's proof that I'm the only true artist Rome has known—the only one, believe me—to match his inspiration with his deeds.

CHEREA   That's only a matter of having the power.

CALIGULA   Quite true. Other artists create to compensate for their lack of power. I don't need to make a work of art; I *live* it. *(Roughly.)* Well, poets, are you ready?

METELLUS   I think so.

THE OTHERS   Yes.

CALIGULA   Good. Now listen carefully. You are to fall out of line and come forward one by one. I'll whistle. Number One will start reading his poem. When I whistle, he must stop, and the next begin. And so on. The winner, naturally, will be the one whose poem hasn't been cut short by the whistle. Get ready. *(Turning to* CHEREA, *he whispers.)* You see, organization's needed for everything, even for art.

(Blows his whistle.)

FIRST POET   Death, when beyond thy darkling shore . . .

A blast of the whistle. The poet steps briskly to the left. The others will follow the same procedure. These movements should be made with mechanical precision.

SECOND POET   In their dim cave, the Fatal Sisters Three . . .

(Whistle.)

THIRD POET   Come to me death, beloved . . .

(A shrill blast of the whistle. The FOURTH POET *steps forward and strikes a dramatic posture. The whistle goes before he has opened his mouth.)*

FIFTH POET   When I was in my happy infancy . . .

CALIGULA *(yelling)*   Stop that! What earthly connection has a blockhead's happy infancy with the theme I set? The connection! Tell me the connection!

FIFTH POET   But, Caius, I've only just begun, and . . .

(Shrill blast.)

SIXTH POET *(in a high-pitched voice)*   Ruthless, he goes his hidden ways . . .

(Whistle.)

SEVENTH POET *(mysteriously)*   Oh, long, abstruse orison . . .

(Whistle, broken off as SCIPIO *comes forward without a tablet.)*

CALIGULA   You haven't a tablet?

SCIPIO   I do not need one.

CALIGULA   Well, let's hear you. *(He chews at his whistle.)*

SCIPIO *(Standing very near* CALIGULA, *he recites listlessly, without looking at him.)*

> Pursuit of happiness that purifies the heart,
> Skies rippling with light,
> O wild, sweet, festal joys, frenzy without hope!

CALIGULA *(gently)*   Stop, please. The others needn't compete. *(To* SCIPIO) You're very young to understand so well the lessons we can learn from death.

SCIPIO *(gazing straight at* CALIGULA)   I was very young to lose my father.

CALIGULA *(turning hastily)*   Fall in, the rest of you. No, really a sham poet is too dreadful an infliction. Until now I'd thought of enrolling you as my allies; I sometimes pictured a gallant band of poets defending me in the last ditch. Another illusion gone! I shall have to relegate you to my enemies. So now the poets are against me—and that looks much like the end of all. March out in good order. As you go past you are to lick your tablets so as to efface the atrocities you scrawled on them. Attention! Forward! *(He blows his whistle in short rhythmic jerks. Keeping step, the poets file out by the right, tonguing their immortal tablets.* CALIGULA *adds in a lower tone)* Now leave me, everyone.

(In the doorway, as they are going out, CHEREA *touches the* FIRST PATRICIAN's *shoulder, and speaks in his ear.)*

CHEREA   Now's our opportunity.

*(*SCIPIO*, who has overheard, halts on the threshold and walks back to* CALIGULA.)

CALIGULA *(acidly)*   Can't you leave me in peace—as your father's doing?

SCIPIO   No, Caius, all that serves no purpose now. For now I know, I *know* that you have made your choice.

CALIGULA   Won't you leave me in peace!

SCIPIO   Yes, you shall have your wish; I am going to leave you, for I think I've come to understand you. There's no way out left to us, neither to you nor to me—who am like you in so many ways. I shall go away, far away, and try to discover the meaning of it all. *(He gazes at* CALIGULA *for some moments. Then, with a rush of emotion)* Good-by, dear Caius. When all is ended, remember that I loved you. *(He goes out.* CALIGULA *makes a vague gesture. Then, almost savagely, he pulls himself together and takes some steps toward* CÆ-SONIA.)

CÆSONIA   What did he say?

CALIGULA   Nothing you'd understand.

CÆSONIA   What are you thinking about?

CALIGULA   About him. And about you, too. But it amounts to the same thing.

CÆSONIA   What is the matter?

CALIGULA *(staring at her)*   Scipio has gone. I am through with his friendship. But you, I wonder why you are still here. . . .

CÆSONIA   Why, because you're fond of me.

CALIGULA   No. But I think I'd understand—if I had you killed.

CÆSONIA   Yes, that would be a solution. Do so, then. . . . But why, oh, why can't you relax, if only for a moment, and live freely, without constraint?

CALIGULA   I have been doing that for several years; in fact I've made a practice of it.

CÆSONIA   I don't mean that sort of freedom. I mean—Oh, don't you realize what it can be to live and love quite simply, naturally, in . . . in purity of heart?

CALIGULA   This purity of heart you talk of—every man acquires it, in his own way. Mine has been to follow the essential to the end. . . . Still all that needn't prevent me from putting you to death. *(Laughs)* It would round off my career so well, the perfect climax. *(He rises and swings the mirror round toward himself. Then he walks in a circle, letting his arms hang limp, almost without gestures; there is something feral in his gait as he continues speaking.)* How strange! When I don't kill, I feel alone. The living don't suffice to people my world and dispel my boredom. I have an impression of an enormous void when you and the others are here, and my eyes see nothing but empty air. No, I'm at ease only in the company of my dead. *(He takes his stand facing the audience, leaning a little forward. He has forgotten* CÆSONIA's *presence.)* Only the dead are real. They are of my kind. I see them waiting for me, straining toward me. And I have long talks with this man or that, who screamed to me for mercy and whose tongue I had cut out.

CÆSONIA   Come. Lie down beside me. Put your head on my knees. (CALIGULA *does so.*) That's better, isn't it? Now rest. How quiet it is here!

CALIGULA   Quiet? You exaggerate, my dear. Listen! *(Distant metallic tinklings, as of swords or armor)* Do you hear those thousands of small sounds all around us, hatred stalking its prey? *(Murmuring voices, footsteps.)*

CÆSONIA   Nobody would dare. . . .

CALIGULA   Yes, stupidity.

CÆSONIA   Stupidity doesn't kill. It makes men slow to act.

CALIGULA   It can be murderous, Cæsonia. A fool stops at nothing when he thinks his dignity offended. No, it's not the men whose sons or fathers I have killed who'll murder me. *They,* anyhow, have understood. They're with me, they have the same taste in their mouths. But the others—those I made a laughingstock of—I've no defense against their wounded vanity.

CÆSONIA *(passionately)*   We will defend you. There are many of us left who love you.

CALIGULA   Fewer every day. It's not surprising. I've done all that was needed to that end. And then—let's be fair—it's not only stupidity that's against me. There's the courage and the simple faith of men who ask to be happy.

CÆSONIA *(in the same tone)*   No, *they* will not kill you. Or, if they tried, fire would come down from heaven and blast them, before they laid a hand on you.

CALIGULA   From heaven! There is no heaven, my poor dear woman! *(He sits down.)* But why this sudden access of devotion? It wasn't provided for in our agreement, if I remember rightly.

CÆSONIA *(who has risen from the couch and is pacing the room)*   Don't you understand? Hasn't it been enough to see you killing others, without my knowing you'll be killed as well? Isn't it enough to feel you hard and cruel, seething with bitterness, when I hold you in my arms; to breathe a reek of murder when you lie on me? Day after day I see all that's human in you dying out, little by little. *(She turns toward him.)* Oh, I know. I know I'm getting old, my beauty on the wane. But it's you only I'm concerned for now; so much so that I've ceased troubling whether you love me. I only want you to get well, quite well again. You're still a boy, really; you've a whole life ahead of you. And, tell me, what greater thing can you want than a whole life?

CALIGULA *(rising, looks at her fixedly)*   You've been with me a long time now, a very long time.

CÆSONIA Yes . . . But you'll keep me, won't you?

CALIGULA I don't know. I only know that, if you're with me still, it's because of all those nights we've had together, nights of fierce, joyless pleasure; it's because you alone know me as I am. *(He takes her in his arms, bending her head back a little with his right hand.)* I'm twenty-nine. Not a great age really. But today when none the less my life seems so long, so crowded with scraps and shreds of my past selves, so complete in fact, you remain the last witness. And I can't avoid a sort of shameful tenderness for the old woman that you soon will be.

CÆSONIA Tell me that you mean to keep me with you.

CALIGULA I don't know. All I know—and it's the most terrible thing of all—is that this shameful tenderness is the one sincere emotion that my life has given up to now. *(CÆSONIA frees herself from his arms. CALIGULA follows her. She presses her back to his chest and he puts his arms round her.)* Wouldn't it be better that the last witness should disappear?

CÆSONIA That has no importance. All I know is: I'm happy. What you've just said has made me very happy. But why can't I share my happiness with you?

CALIGULA Who says I'm unhappy?

CÆSONIA Happiness is kind. It doesn't thrive on bloodshed.

CALIGULA Then there must be two kinds of happiness, and I've chosen the murderous kind. For I *am* happy. There was a time when I thought I'd reached the extremity of pain. But, no, one can go farther yet. Beyond the frontier of pain lies a splendid, sterile happiness. Look at me. *(She turns toward him.)* It makes me laugh, Cæsonia, when I think how for years and years all Rome carefully avoided uttering Drusilla's name. Well, all Rome was mistaken. Love isn't enough for me; I realized it then. And I realize it again today, when I look at you. To love someone means that one's willing to grow old beside that person. That sort of love is right outside my range. Drusilla old would have been far worse than Drusilla dead. Most people imagine that a man suffers because out of the blue death snatches away the woman he loves. But his real suffering is less futile; it comes from the discovery that grief, too, cannot last. Even grief is vanity.

You see, I had no excuses, nor the shadow of a real love, neither bitterness nor profound regret. Nothing to plead in my defense! But today—you see me still freer than I have been for years; freed as I am from memories and illusion. *(He laughs bitterly.)* I know now that nothing, *nothing* lasts. Think what that knowledge means! There have been just two or three of us in history who really achieved this freedom, this crazy happiness. Well Cæsonia, you have seen out a most unusual drama. It's time the curtain fell, for you.

(He stands behind her again, linking his forearm round CÆSONIA's neck.)

CÆSONIA *(terrified)* No, it's impossible! How can you call it happiness, this terrifying freedom?

CALIGULA *(gradually tightening his grip on CÆSONIA's throat)* Happiness it is, Cæsonia; I know what I'm saying. But for this freedom I'd have been a contented man. Thanks to it, I have won the godlike enlightenment of the solitary. *(His exaltation grows as little by little he strangles CÆSONIA, who puts up no resistance, but holds her hands half opened, like a suppliant's, before her. Bending his head, he goes on speaking, into her ear.)* I live, I kill, I exercise the rapturous power of a destroyer, compared with which the power of a creator is merest child's play. And this, *this* is happiness; this and nothing else—this intolerable release, devastating scorn, blood, hatred all around me; the glorious isolation of a man who all his life long nurses and gloats over the ineffable joy of the unpunished murderer; the ruthless logic that crushes out human lives *(He laughs.)*, that's crushing yours out, Cæsonia, so as to perfect at last the utter loneliness that is my heart's desire.

CÆSONIA *(struggling feebly)*   Oh, Caius . . .

CALIGULA *(more and more excitedly)*   No. No sentiment. I must have done with it, for the time is short. My time is very short, dear Cæsonia. (CÆSONIA *is gasping, dying.* CALIGULA *drags her to the bed and lets her fall on it. He stares wildly at her; his voice grows harsh and grating.*) You, too, were guilty. But killing is not the solution. *(He spins round and gazes crazily at the mirror.)* Caligula! You, too; you, too, are guilty. Then what of it— a little more, a little less? Yet who can condemn me in this world where there is no judge, where nobody is innocent? *(He brings his eyes close to his reflected face. He sounds genuinely distressed.)* You see, my poor friend. Helicon has failed you. I won't have the moon. Never, never, never! But how bitter it is to know all, and to have to go through to the consummation! Listen! That was a sound of weapons. Innocence arming for the fray—and innocence will triumph. Why am I not in their place, among them? And I'm afraid. That's cruelest of all, after despising others, to find oneself as cowardly as they. Still, no matter. Fear, too, has an end. Soon I shall attain that emptiness beyond all understanding, in which the heart has rest. *(He steps back a few paces, then returns to the mirror. He seems calmer. When he speaks again his voice is steadier, less shrill.)*

Yet, really, it's quite simple. If I'd had the moon, if love were enough, all might have been different. But where could I quench this thirst? What human heart, what god, would have for me the depth of a great lake? *(Kneeling, weeping)* There's nothing in this world, or in the other, made to my stature. And yet I know, and you, too, know *(Still weeping, he stretches out his arms toward the mirror.)* that all I need is for the impossible to be. The impossible! I've searched for it at the confines of the world, in the secret places of my heart. I've stretched out my hands *(His voice rises to a scream.);* see, I stretch you my hands, but it's always you I find, you only, confronting me, and I've come to hate you. I have chosen a wrong path, a path that leads to nothing. My freedom isn't the right one . . . Nothing, nothing yet. Oh, how oppressive is this darkness! Helicon has not come; we shall be forever guilty. The air tonight is heavy as the sum of human sorrows. *(A clash of arms and whisperings are heard in the wings.* CALIGULA *rises, picks up a stool, and returns to the mirror, breathing heavily. He contemplates himself, makes a slight leap forward, and, watching the symmetrical movement of his reflected self, hurls the stool at it, screaming.)* To history, Caligula! Go down to history! *(The mirror breaks and at the same moment armed conspirators rush in.* CALIGULA *swings round to face them with a mad laugh.* SCIPIO *and* CHEREA, *who are in front, fling themselves at him and stab his face with their daggers.* CALIGULA's *laughter turns to gasps. All strike him, hurriedly, confusedly. In a last gasp, laughing and choking,* CALIGULA *shrieks.)* I'm still alive!

(Curtain.)

Comments and Questions

See Comments and Questions for *The Visit,* page 893.

The basic tenet of absurdism is that life is meaningless. Krutch in his essay "The Tragic Fallacy" (p. 1112) contends that if indeed life has no meaning, there can be no tragedy, certainly none in the make-believe world of plays. Camus shows us a character intent upon finding substance in his life, a character free to do this completely on his own terms. Has Camus ruled out tragedy by having his protagonist find that life is nothing? Others may be boxed in by conventional morality, by fears and scruples, by hopes and aspirations, by a thousand and one pushing and pulling influences, but not Caligula. He was free—or was he?

1. "Freedom's just another word for nothin' left to lose," so sings the Me of "Me and Bobby McGee," (p. 344). How would Caligula restate that observation? Consider Caligula's words to Cherea: "This world has no importance; once a man realizes that, he wins his freedom."

2. Although Caligula acts on whim, is there a pattern to his actions? If so, what is it?

3. Some say that Camus' play is simply a vehicle for examining ideas, that it is nothing more than a dramatized philosophical essay. Others regard the play as a chronicle of a human being agonizing in the inner recesses of his disturbed mind. Is Caligula a puppet on Camus' strings or a character as, say, Hamlet is a character?

4. Interpret Caligula's last words: "I'm still alive!"

5. Are any of the minor characters of consequence in the working out of the plot? If so, which ones, and in what way?

Neil Simon (1927–   )
The Sunshine Boys

CHARACTERS

WILLIE CLARK	EDDIE
BEN SILVERMAN	NURSE
AL LEWIS	REGISTERED NURSE
PATIENT	

The action takes place in New York City.

ACT I. *Scene I: A small apartment in an old hotel on upper Broadway in the mid-Eighties. It is an early afternoon in mid-winter. Scene II: The following Monday, late morning.* ACT II. *Scene I: A Manhattan television studio. Scene II: The same as* ACT I. *It is two weeks later, late afternoon.*

ACT I
Scene I

The scene is a two-room apartment in an old hotel on upper Broadway, in the mid-Eighties. It's rather a depressing place. There is a bed, a bureau, a small dining table with two chairs, an old leather chair that faces a TV set on a cheap, metal stand. There is a small kitchen to one side—partitioned off from the living room by a curtain—a small bathroom on the other. A window looks out over Broadway. It is early afternoon, midwinter.

At rise, the TV is on, and the banal dialogue of a soap opera drones on. In the leather chair sits WILLIE CLARK, *in slippers, pajamas and an old bathrobe.* WILLIE *is in his seventies. He watches the program but is constantly dozing off, then catching himself and watching for a few more minutes at a time. The set drones on and* WILLIE *dozes off. The tea kettle on the stove in the kitchen comes to a boil and whistles.* WILLIE'S *head perks up at the sound; he reaches over and picks up the telephone.*

WILLIE *(into the phone)*   Hello? . . . Who's this?

(The whistle continues from the kettle, and WILLIE *looks over in that direction. He hangs up the phone and does not seem embarrassed or even aware of his own absentmindedness. He simply crosses into the kitchen and turns off the flame under the kettle.)*

VOICE FROM TV   We'll be back with *Storm Warning* after this brief message from Lipton Tea.

WILLIE   Don't worry, I'm not going anywhere.

(He puts a tea ball into a mug and pours the boiling water in. Then he goes over to the dining table in the living room, takes a spoon, dips into a jar of honey, and pours it into his tea. He glances over at the TV set, which has just played the Lipton Tea commercial.)

VOICE FROM TV   And now for Part Three of today's *Storm Warning.*

WILLIE   What happened to Part Two? I missed Part Two? *(He drinks his tea as Part Three continues and the banal dialogue drones on.* WILLIE *listens as he shuffles toward his chair. The TV set, which is away from the wall, has an electric plug running from it, along the ground and into the wall.* WILLIE, *who never seems to look where he's going, comes up against the cord with his foot, inadvertently pulling the cord out of its socket in the wall. The TV set immediately dies.* WILLIE *sits, then looks at the set. Obviously, no picture. He gets up and fiddles with the dials. How could his best friend desert him at a time like this? He hits the set on the top with his hand.)* What's the matter with you? *(He hits the set again and twists the knobs futilely, never thinking for a moment it might be something as simple as the plug. He slaps the picture tube.)* Come on, for Pete's sakes, what are you doing there? *(He stares at it in disbelief. He kicks the stand on which it rests. Then he crosses to the phone, and picks it up.)* Hello? . . . Sandy? . . . Let me have Sandy . . . Sandy? . . . My television's dead . . . My television . . . Is this Sandy? . . . My television died . . . No, not Willie. Mr. Clark to you, please . . . Never mind the jokes, wise guy, it's not funny . . . Send up somebody to fix my dead television . . . I didn't touch nothing . . . Nothing. I'm telling you . . . It's a crappy set . . . You live in a crappy hotel, you get a crappy television . . . The what? . . . The plug? . . . What plug? . . . Wait a minute. *(He lays the phone down, crosses to behind the set, bends down, picks up the plug and looks at it. He goes back to the telephone. Into the phone)* Hello? . . . It's not the plug. It's something else. I'll fix it myself. *(He hangs up, goes over to the wall plug and plugs it in. The set goes back on.)* He tells me the plug . . . When he calls me Mr. Clark then I'll tell him it was the plug. *(He sits and picks up his cup of tea.)* The hell with all of 'em. *(There is a knock on the door.* WILLIE *looks at the wall on the opposite side of the room.)* Bang all you want, I'm not turning it off. I'm lucky it works.

(There is a pause; then a knock on the front door again, this time accompanied by a male voice.)

BEN'S VOICE   Uncle Willie? It's me. Ben.

(WILLIE *turns and looks at the front door, not acknowledging that he was mistaken about the knocking on the other wall.*)

WILLIE   Who's that?

BEN'S VOICE   Ben.

WILLIE   Ben? Is that you?

BEN'S VOICE   Yes, Uncle Willie, it's Ben. Open the door.

WILLIE   Wait a minute. *(He rises, crosses to the door, tripping over the TV cord again, disconnecting the set. He starts to unlatch the door, but has trouble manipulating it. His fingers are not too manipulative.)* Wait a minute . . . *(He is having great difficulty with it.)* . . . Wait a minute.

BEN'S VOICE   Is anything wrong?

WILLIE *(still trying)*   Wait a minute. *(He tries forcing it.)*

BEN'S VOICE   What's the matter?

WILLIE   I'm locked in. The lock is broken, I'm locked in. Go down and tell the boy, Sandy. Tell Sandy that Mr. Clark is locked in.

BEN'S VOICE   What is it, the latch?

WILLIE   It's the latch. It's broken, I'm locked in. Go tell the boy Sandy, they'll get somebody.

BEN'S VOICE   That happened last week. Don't try to force it. Just slide it out. (WILLIE *stares at the latch.*) Uncle Willie, do you hear me? Don't force it. Slide it out.

WILLIE *(fiddling with the latch)*   Wait a minute. *(Carefully, he slides it open.)* It's open. Never mind, I did it myself.

(*He opens the door.* BEN SILVERMAN, *a well dressed man in his early thirties, enters. He is wearing a topcoat and carrying a shopping bag from Bloomingdale's, filled to the brim with assorted foodstuffs and a copy of the weekly* Variety.)

BEN   You probably have to oil it.

WILLIE   I don't have to oil nothing. The hell with 'em.

(BEN *hangs up his coat in the closet.*)

BEN *(crosses to the table with the shopping bag)*   You feeling all right?

WILLIE   What is this, Wednesday?

BEN *(puzzled)*   Certainly. Don't I always come on Wednesdays?

WILLIE   But this is Wednesday today?

BEN *(puts his bag down)*   Yes, of course. Haven't you been out?

WILLIE   When?

BEN   Today. Yesterday. This week. You haven't been out all week?

WILLIE *(crossing to him)*   Sunday. I was out Sunday. I went to the park Sunday.

(BEN *hands* WILLIE *the* Variety. WILLIE *tucks it under his arm and starts to look through the shopping bag.*)

BEN   What are you looking for?

WILLIE *(going through the bag)*   My *Variety.*

BEN   I just gave it to you. It's under your arm.

WILLIE *(looks under his arm)*   Why do you put it there? He puts it under my arm.

BEN *(starts taking items out of the bag)*   Have you been eating properly? No corned beef sandwiches, I hope.

The Sunshine Boys

933

WILLIE *(opens to the back section)* Is this today's?

BEN Certainly it's today's. *Variety* comes out on Wednesday, doesn't it? And today is Wednesday.

WILLIE I'm just asking, don't get so excited. (BEN *shakes his head in consternation.*) . . . Because I already read last Wednesday's.

BEN *(takes more items out)* I got you six different kinds of soups. All low-sodium, salt-free. All very good for you . . . Are you listening?

WILLIE *(his head in the paper)* I'm listening. You got six lousy-tasting soups . . . Did you see this?

BEN What?

WILLIE What I'm looking at. Did you see this?

BEN How do I know what you're looking at?

WILLIE Two new musicals went into rehearsals today and I didn't even get an audition. Why didn't I get an audition?

BEN Because there were no parts for you. One of them is a young rock musical and the other show is all black.

WILLIE What's the matter, I can't do black? I did black in 1928. And when I did black, you understood the words, not like today.

BEN I'm sorry, you're not the kind of black they're looking for. *(He shivers.)* Geez, it's cold in here. You know it's freezing in here? Don't they ever send up any heat?

WILLIE *(has turned a page)* How do you like that? Sol Burton died.

BEN Who?

WILLIE Sol Burton. The songwriter. Eighty-nine years old, went like that, from nothing.

BEN Why didn't you put on a sweater?

WILLIE I knew him very well . . . A terrible person. Mean, mean. He should rest in peace, but he was a mean person. His best friends didn't like him.

BEN *(goes to the bureau for a sweater)* Why is it so cold in here?

WILLIE You know what kind of songs he wrote? . . . The worst. The worst songs ever written were written by Sol Burton. *(He sings.)* "Lady, Lady, be my baby . . ." Did you ever hear anything so rotten? Baby he rhymes with lady . . . No wonder he's dead.

(He turns the page.)

BEN This radiator is ice-cold. Look, Uncle Willie, I'm not going to let you live here any more. You've got to let me find you another place . . . I've been asking you for seven years now. You're going to get sick.

WILLIE *(still looking at* Variety*)* Tom Jones is gonna get a hundred thousand dollars a week in Las Vegas. When Lewis and I were headlining at the Palace, the *Palace* didn't cost a hundred thousand dollars.

BEN That was forty years ago. And forty years ago this hotel was twenty years old. They should tear it down. They take advantge of all you people in here because they know you don't want to move.

(WILLIE crosses to the table and looks into the shopping bag.)

WILLIE No cigars?

BEN *(making notes on his memo pad)* You're not supposed to have cigars.

WILLIE Where's the cigars?

BEN You know the doctor told you you're not supposed to smoke cigars any more. I didn't bring any.

WILLIE   Gimme the cigars.
BEN   What cigars? I just said I don't have them. Will you forget the cigars?
WILLIE   Where are they, in the bag?
BEN   On the bottom. I just brought three. It's the last time I'm doing it.
WILLIE   *(takes out a bag with three cigars)*   How's your family? The children all right?

(He removes one cigar.)

BEN   Suddenly you're interested in my family? It's not going to work, Uncle Willie. I'm not bringing you any more cigars.
WILLIE   I just want to know how the children are.
BEN   The children are fine. They're wonderful, thank you.
WILLIE   Good. Next time bring the big cigars.

(He puts two cigars in the breast pocket of his bathrobe and the other one in his mouth. He crosses into the kitchen looking for a light.)

BEN   You don't even know their names. What are the names of my children?
WILLIE   Millie and Sidney.
BEN   Amanda and Michael.
WILLIE   What's the matter, you didn't like Millie and Sidney?
BEN   I was *never* going to name them Millie and Sidney. You forgot, so you made something up. You forget everything. I'll bet you didn't drink the milk from last week. I'll bet it's still in the refrigerator. *(Crosses quickly, and opens the refrigerator and looks in)* There's the milk from last week.
WILLIE   *(comes out of the kitchen, still looking for a light)*   Do they know who I am?
BEN   *(looking through the refrigerator)*   Who?
WILLIE   Amanda and Sidney.
BEN   Amanda and Michael. That you were a big star in vaudeville? They're three years old, Uncle Willie, you think they remember vaudeville? *I* never saw vaudeville . . . This refrigerator won't last another two days.
WILLIE   Did you tell them six times on *The Ed Sullivan Show*?

(He sits, tries a cigarette lighter. It's broken.)

BEN   They never heard of Ed Sullivan. Uncle Willie, they're three years old. They don't follow show business. *(Comes back into the living room and sees* WILLIE *with the cigar in his mouth)* What are you doing? You're not going to smoke that now. You promised me you'd only smoke one after dinner.
WILLIE   Am I smoking it? Do you see smoke coming from the cigar?
BEN   But you've got it in your mouth.
WILLIE   I'm rehearsing . . . After dinner I'll do the show.
BEN   *(crossing back into the kitchen)*   I'm in the most aggravating business in the whole world and I never get aggravated until I come here.

(He opens the cupboards and looks in.)

WILLIE   *(looking around)*   So don't come. I got Social Security.
BEN   You think that's funny? I don't think that's funny, Uncle Willie.
WILLIE   *(thumbing through* Variety)   If you had a sense of humor, you'd think it was funny.
BEN   *(angrily, through gritted teeth)*   I have a *terrific* sense of humor.
WILLIE   Like your father—he laughed once in 1932.

BEN   I can't talk to you.

WILLIE   Why, they're funny today? Tell me who you think is funny today, and I'll show you where he's not funny.

BEN   Let's not get into that, huh? I've got to get back to the office. Just promise me you'll have a decent lunch today.

WILLIE   If I were to tell a joke and got a laugh from you, I'd throw it out.

BEN   How can I laugh when I see you like this, Uncle Willie? You sit in your pajamas all day in a freezing apartment watching soap operas on a thirty-five-dollar television set that doesn't have a horizontal hold. The picture just keeps rolling from top to bottom—pretty soon your eyes are gonna roll around your head . . . You never eat anything. You never go out because you don't know how to work the lock on the door. Remember when you locked yourself in the bathroom overnight? It's a lucky thing you keep bread in there, you would have starved . . . And you wonder why I worry.

WILLIE   Calvin Coolidge, that's your kind of humor.

BEN   Look, Uncle Willie, promise me you'll eat decently.

WILLIE   I'll eat decently. I'll wear a blue suit, a white shirt and black shoes.

BEN   And if you're waiting for a laugh, you're not going to get one from me.

WILLIE   Who could live that long? Get me a job instead of a laugh.

BEN   *(sighs, exasperatedly)*   You know I've been trying, Uncle Willie. It's not easy. There's not much in town. Most of the work is commercials and . . . well, you know, we've had a little trouble in that area.

WILLIE   The potato chips? The potato chips wasn't my fault.

BEN   Forget the potato chips.

WILLIE   What about the Shick Injector? Didn't I audition funny on the Shick Injector?

BEN   You were very funny but your hand was shaking. And you can't show a man shaving with a shaky hand.

WILLIE   Why couldn't you get me on the Alka-Seltzer? That's my kind of comedy. I got a terrific face for an upset stomach.

BEN   I've submitted you twenty times.

WILLIE   What's the matter with twenty-one?

BEN   Because the word is out in the business that you can't remember the lines, and they're simply not interested.

WILLIE   *(That hurt.)*   I couldn't remember the lines? I COULDN'T REMEMBER THE LINES? I don't remember that.

BEN   For the Frito-Lays potato chips. I sent you over to the studio, you couldn't even remember the address.

WILLIE   Don't tell me I didn't remember the lines. The lines I remembered beautifully. The name of the potato chip I couldn't remember . . . What was it?

BEN   Frito-Lays.

WILLIE   Say it again.

BEN   Frito-Lays.

WILLIE   I still can't remember it—because it's not funny. If it's funny, I remember it. Alka-Seltzer is funny. You say "Alka-Seltzer," you get a laugh. The other word is not funny. What is it?

BEN   Frito-Lays.

WILLIE   Maybe in *Mexico* that's funny, not here. Fifty-seven years I'm in this business, you learn a few things. You know what makes an audience laugh. Do you know which words are funny and which words are *not* funny?

BEN   You told me a hundred times, Uncle Willie. Words with a "K" in it are funny.

WILLIE   Words with a "K" in it are funny. You didn't know that, did you? If it doesn't have a "K," it's not funny. I'll tell you which words always get a laugh.

(He is about to count on his fingers.)

BEN   Chicken.

WILLIE   Chicken is funny.

BEN   Pickle.

WILLIE   Pickle is funny.

BEN   Cupcake.

WILLIE   Cupcake is funny . . . Tomato is *not* funny. Roast beef is *not* funny.

BEN   But cookie is funny.

WILLIE   But cookie is funny.

BEN   Uncle Willie, you've explained that to me ever since I was a little boy.

WILLIE   Cucumber is funny.

BEN *(falling in again)*   Car keys.

WILLIE   Car keys is funny.

BEN   Cleveland.

WILLIE   Cleveland is funny . . . Maryland is *not* funny.

BEN   Listen, I have to get back to the office, Uncle Willie, but there's something I'd like to talk to you about first. I got a call yesterday from C.B.S.

WILLIE   Casey Stengel, that's a funny name; Robert Taylor is not funny.

BEN *(sighs exasperatedly)*   Why don't you listen to me?

WILLIE   I heard. You got a call from N.B.C.

BEN   C.B.S.

WILLIE   Whatever.

BEN   C.B.S. is doing a big special next month. An hour and a half variety show. They're going to have some of the biggest names in the history of show business. They're trying to get Flip Wilson to host the show.

WILLIE   Him I like. He gives me a laugh. With the dress and the little giggle and the red wig. That's a funny boy . . . What's the boy's name again?

BEN   Flip Wilson. And it doesn't have a K.

WILLIE   But he's *black,* with a "K." You see what I mean?

BEN *(looks to heaven for help; it doesn't come.)*   I do, I do. The theme of this variety show—

WILLIE   What's the theme of the show?

BEN   *The theme of the show* is the history of comedy dating from the early Greek times, through the days of vaudeville, right up to today's stars.

WILLIE   Why couldn't you get me on this show?

BEN   I *got* you on the show.

WILLIE   Alone?

BEN   With Lewis.

WILLIE *(turns away)*   You ain't got me on the show.

BEN   Let me finish.

WILLIE   You're finished. It's no.

BEN   Can't you wait until I'm through before you say "no"? Can't we discuss it for a minute?

WILLIE   I'm busy.

BEN   Doing what?

WILLIE   Saying "no."

BEN   You can have the courtesy of hearing me out. They begged me at C.B.S. *Begged* me.

WILLIE   Talk faster, because you're coming up to another "no."

BEN   They said to me the history of comedy in the United States would not be complete unless they included one of the greatest teams ever to come out of vaudeville, Lewis and Clark, The Sunshine Boys. The vice-president of C.B.S. said this to me on the phone.

WILLIE   The vice-president said this?

BEN   Yes. He is the greatest Lewis and Clark fan in this country. He knows by heart every one of your old routines.

WILLIE   Then let *him* go on with that bastard.

BEN   It's one shot. You would just have to do it one night, one of the old sketches. They'll pay ten thousand dollars for the team. That's top money for these shows, I promise you. Five thousand dollars apiece. And that's more money than you've earned in two years.

WILLIE   I don't need money. I live alone. I got two nice suits, I don't have a pussycat, I'm very happy.

BEN   You're *not* happy. You're miserable.

WILLIE   *I'm happy!* I just *look* miserable!

BEN   You're dying to go to work again. You call me six times a day in the office. I can't see over my desk for all your messages.

WILLIE   Call me back sometime, you won't get so many messages.

BEN   I call you every day of the week. I'm up here every Wednesday, rain or shine, winter or summer, flu or diphtheria.

WILLIE   What are you, a mailman? You're a nephew. I don't ask you to come. You're my brother's son, you've been very nice to me. I appreciate it, but I've never asked you for anything . . . except a job. You're a good boy but a stinking agent.

BEN   I'M A GOOD AGENT? Damn it, don't say that to me, Uncle Willie, I'm a *goddamn good agent!*

WILLIE   What are you screaming for? What is it, such a wonderful thing to be a good agent?

BEN *(holds his chest)*   I'm getting chest pains. You give me chest pains, Uncle Willie.

WILLIE   It's *my* fault you get excited?

BEN   Yes, it's *your* fault! I only get chest pains on Wednesdays.

WILLIE   So come on Tuesdays.

BEN *(starts for the door)*   I'm going. I don't even want to discuss this with you any more. You're impossible to talk to. FORGET THE VARIETY SHOW!

(He starts for the door.)

WILLIE   I forgot it.

BEN *(stops)*   I'm not coming back any more. I'm not bringing you your *Variety* or your cigars or your low-sodium soups—do you understand, Uncle Willie? I'm not bringing you anything any more.

WILLIE   Good. Take care of yourself. Say hello to Millie and Phyllis.

BEN *(breathing heavily)*   Why won't you do this for me? I'm not asking you to be partners again. If you two don't get along, all right. But this is just for one night. One last show. Once you get an exposure like that, Alka-Seltzer will come begging to *me* to sign you up. Jesus, how is it going to look if I go back to the office and tell them I couldn't make a deal with my own uncle?

WILLIE   My personal opinion? Lousy!

BEN *(falls into a chair, exhausted)*   Do you really hate Al Lewis that much?

WILLIE *(looks away)*   I don't discuss Al Lewis any more.

BEN *(gets up)*   We *have* to discuss him, because C.B.S. is waiting for an answer today, and if we turn them down, I want to have a pretty good reason why. You haven't seen him in—what? ten years now.

WILLIE *(takes a long time before answering)*   Eleven years!

BEN *(amazed)*   You mean to tell me you haven't *spoken* to him in eleven years?

WILLIE   I haven't *seen* him in eleven years. I haven't *spoken* to him in twelve years.

BEN   You mean you saw him for a whole year that you didn't speak to him?

WILLIE   It wasn't easy. I had to sneak around backstage a lot.

BEN   But you spoke to him onstage.

WILLIE   Not to *him*. If he played a gypsy, I spoke to the gypsy. If he played a lunatic, I spoke to the lunatic. But that bastard I didn't speak to.

BEN   I can't believe that.

WILLIE   You don't believe it? I can show you witnesses who *saw* me never speaking to him.

BEN   It's been eleven years, Uncle Willie. Hasn't time changed anything for you?

WILLIE   Yes. I hate him eleven years more.

BEN   Why?

WILLIE   Why? . . . You never met him?

BEN   Sure I met him. I was fifteen years old. I met him once at benefit at Madison Square Garden and once backstage at some television show. He seemed nice enough to me.

WILLIE   That's only twice. You had to meet him three times to hate him.

BEN   Uncle Willie, could I make a suggestion?

WILLIE   He used to give me the finger.

BEN   The what?

WILLIE   The finger! The finger! He would poke me in the chest with the finger. *(He crosses to* BEN *and demonstrates on him by poking a finger in* BEN'S *chest every time he makes a point.)* He would say, "*Listen,* Doctor." *(Pokes finger)* "I'm *telling* you, Doctor." *(Pokes finger)* "You know what I *mean,* Doctor." *(Pokes finger;* BEN *rubs his chest in pain.)* Hurts, doesn't it? How'd you like it for forty-three years? I got a black and blue hole in my chest. My wife to her dying day thought it was a tattoo. I haven't worked with him in eleven years, it's just beginning to fade away . . . The man had the sharpest finger in show business.

BEN   If you work with him again, I promise you I'll buy you a thick padded under-shirt.

WILLIE   You think I never did that? One night I put a steel plate under my shirt. He gave me the finger, he had it in a splint for a month.

BEN   Something else must have happened you're not telling me about. You don't work with a person for forty-three years without some bond of affection remaining.

WILLIE   You wanna hear other things? He used to spit in my face. Onstage *the man would spit in my face!*

BEN   Not on purpose.

WILLIE *(turns away)*   He tells me "not on purpose" . . . If there was some way I could have saved the spit, I would show it to you.

BEN   You mean he would just stand there and spit in your face?

WILLIE   What do you think, he's stupid? He worked it into the act. He would stand with his nose on top of my nose and purposely only say words that begin with a "T." *(As he demonstrates, he spits.)* "Tootsie Roll." *(Spit)* "Tinker Toy." "Typing on the typewriter."

(Spits. BEN *wipes his face.)* Some nights I thought I would drown! I don't know where he got it all from . . . I think he would drink all day and save it up for the night.

BEN   I'll put it in the contract. If he spits at you, he won't get paid.

WILLIE   If he can get another chance to spit at me, he wouldn't *want* to get paid.

BEN   Then will you answer me one question? If it was all that bad, why did you stick together for forty-three years?

WILLIE *(turns; looks at him)*   Because he was terrific. There'll never be another one like him . . . Nobody could time a joke the way he could time a joke. Nobody could say a line the way he said it. I knew what he was thinking, he knew what I was thinking. One person, that's what we were . . . No, no. Al Lewis was the best. The *best!* You understand?

BEN   I understand.

WILLIE   As an actor, no one could touch him. As a human being, no one *wanted* to touch him.

BEN *(sighs)*   So what do I tell C.B.S.? No deal because Al Lewis spits?

WILLIE   You know when the last time was we worked together?

BEN   Eleven years ago on *The Ed Sullivan Show.*

WILLIE   Eleven years ago on *The Ed Sullivan Show.* July twenty-seventh. He wouldn't put us on in the winter when people were watching, but never mind. We did The Doctor and the Tax Examination. You never saw that, did you?

BEN   No, but I heard it's wonderful.

WILLIE   What about a "classic"? A *classic!* A *dead* person watching that sketch would laugh. We did it maybe eight thousand times, it never missed . . . *That* night it missed. Something was wrong with him, he was rushing, his timing was off, his mind was some-place else. I thought he was sick. Still, we got terrific applause. Five times Ed Sullivan said, "How about that?" We got back into the dressing room, he took off his make-up, put on his clothes, and said to me, "Willie, if it's all the same to you, I'm retiring." I said, "What do you mean, retiring? It's not even nine o'clock. Let's have something to eat." He said, "I'm not retiring for the night. I'm retiring for what's left of my life." And he puts on his hat, walks out of the theater, becomes a stockbroker and I'm left with an act where I ask questions and there's no one there to answer. Never saw the man again to this day. Oh, he called me, I wouldn't answer. He wrote me, I tore it up. He sent me telegrams, they're probably still under the door.

BEN   Well, Uncle Willie, with all due respect, you really weren't getting that much work any more. Maybe he was getting tired of doing the same thing for forty-three years. I mean a man has a right to retire when he wants, doesn't he?

WILLIE   Not him. Don't forget, when he retired himself, he retired me too. And god-damn it, I wasn't ready yet. Now suddenly maybe he needs five thousand dollars, and he wants to come crawling back, the hell with him. I'm a single now . . .

BEN   I spoke to Al Lewis on the phone last night. He doesn't even care about the money. He just wants to do the show for old times' sake. For his grandchildren who never saw him.

WILLIE   Sure. He probably retired broke from the stock market. I guarantee you *those* high-class people never got a spit in the face once.

BEN   Did you know his wife died two years ago? He's living with his daughter now, somewhere in New Jersey. He doesn't do anything any more. He's got very bad arthritis, he's got asthma, he's got poor blood circulation—

WILLIE   I'll send him a pump. He'll outlive *you,* believe me.

BEN   He wants very much to do this show, Willie.

WILLIE   With arthritis? Forget it. Instead of a finger, he'll poke me with a cane.

BEN   C.B.S. wants you to do the doctor sketch. Lewis told me he could get on a stage tonight and do that sketch letter perfect. He doesn't even have to rehearse it.

WILLIE   I don't even want to discuss it . . . And in the second place, I would definitely not do it without a rehearsal.

BEN   All right, then will you agree to this? Just rehearse with him one day. If it doesn't work out, we'll call it off.

WILLIE   I don't trust him. I think he's been planning this for eleven years. We rehearse all week and then he walks out on me just before the show.

BEN   Let me call him on the phone. *(Going over to the phone)* Let me set up a rehearsal time for Monday.

WILLIE   WAIT A MINUTE! I got to think about this.

BEN   We don't have that much time. C.B.S. is waiting to hear.

WILLIE   What's their rush? What are they, going out of business?

BEN *(picks up the phone)*   I'm dialing. I'm dialing him, Uncle Willie, okay?

WILLIE   Sixty-forty—I get six thousand, he gets four thousand . . . What the hell can he buy in New Jersey anyway?

BEN *(holding the phone)*   I can't do that, Uncle Willie . . . God, I hope this works out.

WILLIE   Tell him I'm against it. I want him to know. I'll do it with an "against it."

BEN   It's ringing.

WILLIE   And he's got to come here. I'm not going there, you understand?

BEN   He's got to be home. I told him I would call about one.

WILLIE   Sure. You know what he's doing? He's practicing spitting.

BEN *(into the phone)*   Hello? . . . Mr. Lewis? . . . Ben Silverman . . . Yes, fine, thanks . . . I'm here with him now.

WILLIE   Willie Clark. The one he left on *The Ed Sullivan Show*. Ask him if remembers.

BEN   It's okay, Mr. Lewis . . . Uncle Willie said yes.

WILLIE   With an "against it." Don't forget the "against it."

BEN   No, he's very anxious to do it.

WILLIE *(jumping up in anger)*   WHO'S ANXIOUS? I'M AGAINST IT! TELL HIM, you lousy nephew.

BEN   Can you come here for rehearsal on Monday? . . . Oh, that'll be swell . . . In the morning. *(To* WILLIE*)* About eleven o'clock? How long is the drive. About two hours?

WILLIE   Make it nine o'clock.

BEN   Be reasonable, Willie. *(Into the phone)* Eleven o'clock is fine, Mr. Lewis . . . Can you give me your address, please, so I can send you the contracts? *(He takes a pen out of his pocket and writes in his notebook.)* One-one-nine, South Pleasant Drive . . .

WILLIE   Tell him if he starts with the spitting or poking, I'm taking him to court. I'll have a man on the show watching. Tell him.

BEN   West Davenport, New Jersey . . . Oh-nine-seven-seven-oh-four . . .

WILLIE   I don't want any— *(Spitting)*—"*T*oy *t*elephones *t*apping on *t*in *t*urtles." Tell him. Tell him.

(Curtain.)

Scene II

It is the following Monday, a few minutes before eleven in the morning.

The stage is empty. Suddenly the bathroom door opens and WILLIE *emerges. He is still wear-*

ing his slippers and the same pajamas, but instead of his bathrobe, he has made a conces-
sion to the occasion. He is wearing a double-breasted blue suit-jacket, buttoned, and he is
putting a handkerchief in his pocket. He looks in the mirror, and brushes back his hair. He
shuffles over to the window and looks out.

There is a knock on the door. WILLIE *turns and stares at it. He doesn't move. There is*
another knock, and then we hear BEN's *voice.*

BEN'S VOICE   Uncle Willie. It's Ben.

WILLIE   Ben? Is that you?

BEN'S VOICE   Yes. Open up. (WILLIE *starts toward the door, then stops.*)

WILLIE   You're alone or he's with you?

BEN'S VOICE   I'm alone.

WILLIE *(nods)*   Wait a minute. *(The latch is locked again, and again he has trouble*
getting it open.) Wait a minute.

BEN'S VOICE   Slide it, don't push it.

WILLIE   Wait a minute. I'll push it.

BEN'S VOICE   DON'T PUSH IT! SLIDE IT!

WILLIE   Wait a minute. *(He gets the lock open and opens the door.* BEN *walks in.)*
You're supposed to slide it.

BEN   I rushed like crazy. I didn't want him getting here before me. Did he call or
anything?

WILLIE   Where's the *Variety?*

BEN *(taking off his coat)*   It's Monday, not Wednesday. Didn't you know it was
Monday?

WILLIE   I remembered, but I forgot.

BEN   What are you wearing? What is that? You look half-dressed.

WILLIE   Why, for him I should get *all* dressed?

BEN   Are you all right? Are you nervous or anything?

WILLIE   Why should *I* be nervous? *He* should be nervous. I don't get nervous.

BEN   Good.

WILLIE   Listen, I changed my mind. I'm not doing it.

BEN   *What?*

WILLIE   Don't get so upset. Everything is the same as before, except I'm not doing it.

BEN   When did you decide this?

WILLIE   I decided it when you asked me.

BEN   No, you didn't. You told me you *would* do it.

WILLIE   Well, it was a bad decision. This time I made a good one.

BEN   Well, I'm sorry, you have to do it. I've already told C.B.S. that you would be
rehearsing this week and, more important, that man is on his way over here now and I'm
not going to tell him that you called it off.

WILLIE   We'll leave him a note outside the door.

BEN   We're not leaving any notes. That's why I came here this morning, I was afraid
you would try something like this. I'm going to stay until I think you're both acting like
civilized human beings, and then when you're ready to rehearse, I'm going to leave you
alone. Is that understood?

WILLIE   I'm sick. I woke up sick today.

BEN   No, you're not.

WILLIE   What are you, a doctor? You're an agent. I'm telling you I'm sick.

BEN   What's wrong?

WILLIE   I think I got hepatitis.

BEN   You don't even know what hepatitis is.

WILLIE   If you got it, what's the difference?

BEN   There's nothing wrong with you except a good case of the nerves. You're not backing out, Willie. I don't care what kind of excuse you make, you're going to go through with this. You promised me you would give it at least one day.

WILLIE   I'll pick another day.

BEN   TODAY! You're going to meet with him and rehearse with him TODAY. Now *stop* and just behave yourself.

WILLIE   What do you mean, "behave yourself"? Who do you think you're talking to, Susan and Jackie?

BEN   *Amanda* and Jackie!—Michael! I wish I were. I can reason with them. And now I'm getting chest pains on Monday.

WILLIE   Anyway, he's late. He's purposely coming late to aggravate me.

BEN *(looking out the window)*   He's not late. It's two minutes after eleven.

WILLIE   So what is he, early? He's *late!*

BEN   You're *looking* to start trouble, I can tell.

WILLIE   I was up and dressed at eight o'clock, don't tell me.

BEN   Why didn't you shave?

WILLIE   Get me the Shick commercial, I'll shave. *(He looks in the mirror.)* I really think I got hepatitis. Look how green I look.

BEN   You don't get green from hepatitis. You get yellow.

WILLIE   Maybe I got a very bad case.

BEN *(looks at his watch)*   Now you got me nervous. I wonder if I should call him? Maybe he's sick.

WILLIE *(glares at him)*   You believe *he's* sick, but me you won't believe . . . Why don't you become *his* nephew:

(Suddenly there is a knock on the door. WILLIE *freezes and stares at it.)*

BEN   That's him. You want me to get it—

WILLIE   Get what? I didn't hear anything.

BEN *(starts toward the door)*   All right, now take it easy. Please just behave yourself and give this a chance. Promise me you'll give it a chance.

WILLIE *(starts for the kitchen)*   I'll give it every possible chance in the world . . . But it's not gonna work.

BEN   Where are you going?

WILLIE   To make tea. I feel like some hot tea. *(He crosses into the kitchen and closes the curtain. Starts to fill up the kettle with water.)*

BEN *(panicky)*   NOW? NOW? (BEN *looks at him, exasperated; a knock on the door again and* BEN *crosses to it and opens it.* AL LEWIS *stands there. He is also about seventy years old and is dressed in his best blue suit, hat, scarf, and carries a walking stick. He was probably quite a gay blade in his day, but time has slowed him down somewhat. Our first impression is that he is soft-spoken and pleasant—and a little nervous.)* Mr. Lewis, how do you do? I'm Ben Silverman.

*(*BEN*, nervous, extends his hand.)*

AL   How are you? Hello. It's nice to see you. *(His eyes dart around looking for* WILLIE. *He doesn't see him yet.)* How do you do? . . . Hello . . . Hello . . . How are you?

BEN   We met before, a long time ago. My father took me backstage, I forget the theater. It must have been fifteen, twenty years ago.

AL I remember . . . Certainly . . . It was backstage . . . Maybe fifteen, twenty years ago . . . I forget the theater.

BEN That's right.

AL Sure, I remember.

(He has walked into the room and shoots a glance toward the kitchen. WILLIE *doesn't look up from his tea-making.)*

BEN Please sit down. Uncle Willie's making some tea.

AL Thank you very much.

(He sits on the edge of the table.)

BEN *(trying hard to make conversation)* Er . . . Did you have any trouble getting in from Jersey?

AL My daughter drove me in. She has a car.

BEN Oh, that's nice.

AL A 1972 Chrysler . . . black . . .

BEN Yes, the Chrysler's a wonderful car.

AL The big one . . . the Imperial.

BEN I know. I drove it.

AL My daughter's car?

BEN No, the big Chrysler Imperial. I rented one in California.

AL *(nods)* No, she owns.

BEN I understand . . . Do you come into New York often?

AL Today's the first time in two years.

BEN Really? Well, how did you find it?

AL My daughter drove.

BEN No, I mean, do you find the city different in the two years since you've been here?

AL It's not my New York.

BEN No, I suppose it's not. *(He shoots a glance toward the kitchen.* WILLIE *still hasn't looked in.)* Hey, listen, I'm really very excited about all this. Well, for that matter, everyone in the industry is.

AL *(nods, noncommittally)* Well, we'll see. *(He looks around the room, scrutinizing it.)*

BEN *(He calls out toward the kitchen.)* Uncle Willie, how we doing? *(No answer. Embarrassed, to* AL*)* I guess it's not boiling yet . . . Oh, listen, I'd like to arrange to have a car pick you up and take you home after you're through rehearsing.

AL My daughter's going to pick me up.

BEN Oh, I see. What time did you say? Four? Five?

AL She's going to call me every hour.

BEN Right . . .

(Suddenly WILLIE *sticks his head out of the kitchen, but looks at* BEN *and not at* AL*.)*

WILLIE One tea or two teas?

BEN Oh, here he is. Well, Uncle Willie, I guess it's been a long time since you two—

WILLIE One tea or two teas?

BEN Oh. Er, nothing for me, thanks. I'm just about leaving. Mr. Lewis? Some tea?

AL *(doesn't look toward* WILLIE*)* Tea would be nice, thank you.

BEN *(to* WILLIE*)* Just the one, Uncle Willie.

WILLIE   You're sure? I got two tea balls. I could dunk again.

BEN *(looks at his watch)*   No, I've got to get back to the office. Honestly.

WILLIE *(nods)*   Mm-hmm. One tea.

(On his way back in, he darts a look at LEWIS, *then goes back into the kitchen. He pulls the curtain shut.)*

BEN *(to* LEWIS*)*   Well, er . . . Do you have any questions you want to ask about the show? About the studio or rehearsals or the air date? Is there anything on your mind that I could help you with?

AL   Like what?

BEN   Like, er, the studio? Or the rehearsals? Or air date? Things like that?

AL   You got the props?

BEN   Which props are those?

AL   The props. For the doctor sketch. You gotta have props.

BEN   Oh, props. Certainly. What do you need? I'll tell them.

(Takes out a pad; writes.)

AL   You need a desk. A telephone. A pointer. A blackboard. A piece of white chalk, a piece of red chalk. A skeleton, not too tall, a stethoscope, a thermometer, an "ahh" stick—

BEN   What's an "ahh" stick?

AL   To put in your mouth to say "ahh."

BEN   Oh, right, an "ahh" stick.

AL   A look stick, a bottle of pills—

BEN   A look stick? What's a look stick?

AL   A stick to look in the ears. With cotton on the end.

BEN   Right. A look stick.

AL   A bottle of pills. Big ones, like for a horse.

BEN *(makes a circle with his two fingers)*   About this big?

AL   That's for a pony. *(Makes a circle using the fingers of both hands)* For a horse is like this. Some bandages, cotton, and eye chart—

BEN   Wait a minute, you're going too fast.

AL *(slowly)*   A-desk . . . *a*-telephone . . . *a*-pointer . . .

BEN   No, I got all that—after the cotton and eye chart.

AL   A man's suit. Size forty. Like the one I'm wearing.

BEN   Also in blue?

AL   What do I need two blue suits—Get me a brown.

BEN   A brown suit. Is that all?

AL   That's all.

WILLIE *(from the kitchen, without looking in)*   A piece of liver.

AL   That's all, plus a piece of liver.

BEN   What kind of liver?

AL   Regular calves' liver. From the butcher.

BEN   Like how much? A pound?

AL   A little laugh is a pound. A big laugh is two pounds. Three pounds with a lot of blood'll bring the house down.

BEN   Is that it?

AL   That's it. And a blonde.

BEN   You mean a woman—

AL   You know a blonde nurse that's a man? . . . Big! As big as you can find. With a big chest—a forty-five, a fifty—and a nice bottom.

BEN   You mean a sexy girl with a full, round, rear end?

AL *(spreads hands apart)*   About like this. *(Makes a smaller behind with his hands)* This is too small. *(Makes a bigger one)* And this is too big. *(Goes back to the original one)* Like this is perfect.

BEN   I know what you mean.

AL   If you can bring me pictures, I'll pick out one.

BEN   There's a million girls like that around.

AL   The one we had was the best. I would call her, but she's maybe fifty-five, sixty.

BEN   No, no. I'll get a girl. Anything else?

AL   Not for me.

BEN   Uncle Willie?

WILLIE *(from the kitchen)*   I wasn't listening.

BEN   Well, if either of you thinks of anything, just call me. *(Looks at his watch again)* Eleven-fifteen—I've got to go. *(He gets up.)* Uncle Willie, I'm going. *(He crosses to* LEWIS *and extends his hand.)* Mr. Lewis, I can't express to you enough how happy I am, and speaking for the millions of young people in this country who never had the opportunity of seeing Lewis and Clark work, I just want to say "thank you." To both of you. *(Calls out)* To *both of you,* Uncle Willie.

AL *(nods)*   I hope they won't be disappointed.

BEN   Oh, they won't.

AL   I know they won't. I'm just saying it.

BEN *(crosses to the kitchen)*   Goodbye, Uncle Willie. I'm going.

WILLIE   I'll show you the elevator.

BEN   I *know* where it is. I'll call you tonight. I just want to say that this is a very happy moment for me. To see you both together again, reunited . . . The two kings of comedy. *(Big smile)* I'm sure it must be *very exciting* for the both of you, isn't it? *(No answer. They both just stare at him.)* Well, it looks like we're off to a great start. I'll call you later . . . Goodbye.

(He leaves and closes the door. They are alone. WILLIE *carries the two teas to the dining table, where the sugar bowl is. He pours himself a teaspoonful of sugar.)*

WILLIE *(without looking in* AL'S *direction)*   Sugar?

AL *(doesn't turn)*   If you got.

WILLIE *(nods)*   I got sugar. *(He bangs the sugar bowl down in front of* AL, *crosses with his own tea to his leather chair and sits. And then the two drink tea . . . silently and interminably. They blow, they sip, they blow, they sip and they sit. Finally)* You like a cracker?

AL *(sips)*   What kind of cracker?

WILLIE   Graham, chocolate, coconut, whatever you want.

AL   Maybe just a plain cracker.

WILLIE   I don't have plain crackers. I got graham, chocolate, and coconut.

AL   All right, a graham cracker.

WILLIE *(without turning, points into the kitchen)*   They're in the kitchen, in the closet.

*(*AL *looks over at him, a little surprised at his uncordiality. He nods in acknowledgment.)*

AL   Maybe later.

(They both sip their tea.)

WILLIE *(long pause)*   I was sorry to hear about Lillian.

AL   Thank you.

WILLIE   She was a nice woman. I always liked Lillian.

AL   Thank you.

WILLIE   And how about you?

AL   Thank God, knock wood—*(Raps knuckles on his cane)*—perfect.

WILLIE   I heard different. I heard your blood didn't circulate.

AL   Not true. My blood circulates . . . I'm not saying *everywhere,* but it circulates.

WILLIE   Is that why you use the cane?

AL   It's not a cane. It's a walking stick . . . Maybe once in a great while it's a cane.

WILLIE   I've been lucky, thank God. I'm in the pink.

AL   I was looking. For a minute I thought you were having a flush.

WILLIE *(sips his tea)*   You know Sol Burton died?

AL   Go on . . . Who's Sol Burton?

WILLIE   You don't remember Sol Burton?

AL *(thinks)*   Oh, yes. The manager from the Belasco.

WILLIE   That was Sol Bernstein.

AL   Not Sol Bernstein. Sol *Burton* was the manager from the Belasco.

WILLIE   Sol *Bernstein* was the manager from the Belasco, and it wasn't the Belasco, it was the Morosco.

AL   Sid *Weinstein* was the manager from the Morosco. Sol *Burton* was the manager from the Belasco. Sol *Bernstein* I don't know *who* the hell was.

WILLIE   How can you remember anything if your blood doesn't circulate?

AL   It circulates in my *head.* It doesn't circulate in my *feet.*

(He stomps his foot on the floor a few times.)

WILLIE   Is anything coming down?

AL   Wait a minute. Wasn't Sid Weinstein the songwriter?

WILLIE   No for chrissakes! That's SOL BURTON!

AL   Who wrote "Lady, lady, be my baby"?

WILLIE   That's what I'm telling you! Sol Burton, the lousy songwriter.

AL   Oh, *that* Sol Burton . . . He died?

WILLIE   Last week.

AL   Where?

WILLIE *(points)*   In *Variety.*

AL   Sure, now I remember . . . And how is Sol Bernstein?

WILLIE   I didn't read anything.

AL   Good. I always liked Sol Bernstein. *(They quietly sip their tea.* AL *looks around the room.)* So-o-o . . . this is where you live now?

WILLIE   Didn't I always live here?

AL *(looks again)*   Not in here. You lived in the big suite.

WILLIE   This *is* the big suite . . . Now it's five small suites.

*(*AL *nods, understanding.)*

AL *(looks around)*   That's what they do today. Anything to squeeze a dollar. What do they charge now for a small suite?

WILLIE   The same as they used to charge for the big suite.

*(*AL *nods, understanding.)*

AL   I have a very nice room with my daughter in New Jersey. I have my own bathroom. They don't bother me, I don't bother them.

WILLIE   What is it, in the country?

AL   Certainly it's in the country. Where do you think New Jersey is, in the city?

WILLIE *(shrugs)*   New Jersey is what I see from the bench on Riverside Drive. What have they got, a private house?

AL   Certainly it's a private house. It's some big place. Three quarters of an acre. They got their own trees, their own bushes, a nice little swimming pool for the kids they blow up in the summertime, a big swing in the back, a little dog house, a rock garden—

WILLIE   A what?

AL   A rock garden.

WILLIE   What do you mean, a rock garden? You mean for rocks?

AL   You never saw a rock garden?

WILLIE   And I'm not that anxious.

AL   It's beautiful. A Chinaman made it. Someday you'll take a bus and you'll come out and I'll show you.

WILLIE   I should drive all the way out to New Jersey on a bus to see a rock garden?

AL   You don't even know what I'm talking about. You have to live in the country to appreciate it. I never thought it was possible I could be so happy in the country.

WILLIE   You don't mind it's so quiet?

AL *(looks at him)*   They got noise in New Jersey. But it's a quiet noise. Birds . . . drizzling . . . Not like here with the buses and trucks and screaming and yelling.

WILLIE   Well, it's different for you. You like the country better because you're retired. You can sit on a porch, look at a tree, watch a bush growing. You're still not active like me. You got a different temperament, you're a slow person.

AL   I'm a slow person?

WILLIE   You're here fifteen minutes, you still got a whole cup of tea. I'm finished already.

AL   That's right. You're finished, and I'm still enjoying it. That was always the difference with us.

WILLIE   You're wrong. I can get up and make a *second* cup of tea and enjoy it twice as much as you. I like a busy life. That's why I love the city. I gotta be near a phone. I never know when a picture's gonna come up, a musical, a commercial . . .

AL   When did you do a picture?

WILLIE   They're negotiating.

AL   When did you do a musical?

WILLIE   They're talking.

AL   When did you do a commercial?

WILLIE   All the time. I did one last week.

AL   For what?

WILLIE   For, er, for the . . . what's it, the potato chips.

AL   What potato chips?

WILLIE   The big one. The crispy potato chips . . . er . . . you know.

AL   What do I know? I don't eat potato chips.

WILLIE   Well, what's the difference what the name is?

AL   They hire you to sell potato chips and you can't remember the name?

WILLIE   Did you remember Sol Burton?

AL *(shrugs)*   I'm not selling Sol Burton.

WILLIE   Listen, I don't want to argue with you.

AL   I didn't come from New Jersey to argue.

(They sit quietly for a few seconds. AL sips his tea; WILLIE looks at his empty cup.)

WILLIE *(finally)*   So-o-o . . . What do you think? . . . You want to do the doctor sketch?

AL *(thinks)*   Well, listen, it's very good money. It's only a few days' work, I can be back in New Jersey. If you feel you'd like to do it, then my feeling is I'm agreeable.

WILLIE   And my feeling they told you.

AL   What?

WILLIE   They didn't tell you? My feeling is I'm against it.

AL   You're against it?

WILLIE   Right. But I'll do it if you want to.

AL   I don't want to do it if you're against it. If you're against it, don't do it.

WILLIE   What do you care if I'm against it as long as we're doing it? I just want you to know *why* I'm doing it.

AL   Don't do me any favors.

WILLIE   Who's doing you a favor? I'm doing my nephew a favor. It'll be good for him in the business if we do it.

AL   You're sure?

WILLIE   Certainly I'm sure. It's a big break for a kid like that to get big stars like us.

AL   That's different. In that case, I'm against it too but I'll do it.

WILLIE *(nods)*   As long as we understand each other.

AL   And I want to be sure you know I'm not doing it for the money. The money goes to my grandchildren.

WILLIE   The whole thing?

AL   The whole thing. But not now. Only if I die. If I don't die, it'll be· for my old age.

WILLIE   The same with me.

AL   The same with me.

AL   You don't have grandchildren.

WILLIE   My *nephew's* children. Sidney and Marvin.

AL *(nods)*   Very good.

WILLIE   Okay . . . So-o-o, you wanna rehearse?

AL   You're not against rehearsing?

WILLIE   Why should I be against rehearsing? I'm only against doing the show. Rehearsing is important.

AL   All right, let's rehearse. Why don't we move the furniture, and we'll make the set.

(They both get up and start to move the furniture around. First each one takes a single chair and moves it into a certain position. Then they both take a table and jointly move it away. Then they each take the chair the other one had moved before, and move it into a different place. Every time one moves something somewhere, the other moves it into a different spot. Finally WILLIE becomes aware that they are getting nowhere.)

WILLIE   Wait a minute, wait a minute. What the hell are we doing here?

AL   I'm fixing up the set, I don't know what you're doing.

WILLIE   You're fixing up the set?

AL   That's right.

WILLIE   You're fixing up the set for the doctor sketch?

(AL looks at him for a long time without saying a word. It suddenly becomes clear to him.)

AL   Oh, the *doctor* sketch?

(He then starts to pick up a chair and move it into another position. WILLIE *does the same with another chair. They both move the table . . . and then they repeat what they did before. Every time one moves a chair, the other one moves the same chair to a different position.* WILLIE *stops and looks again.)*

WILLIE   Wait a minute! Wait a minute! We're doing the same goddamn thing. Are you fixing up for the doctor sketch or are you redecorating my apartment?

AL   I'm fixing up for the doctor sketch. If you'd leave what I'm doing alone, we'd be finished.

WILLIE   We'd be finished, but we'd be wrong.

AL   Not for the doctor sketch. I know what I'm doing. I did this sketch for forty-three years.

WILLIE   And where was I all that time, taking a smoke? Who did you think did it with you for forty-three years? That was *me,* mister.

AL   Don't call me mister, you know my name. I never liked it when you called me mister.

WILLIE   It's not a dirty word.

AL   It is when you say it.

WILLIE   Forgive me, *sir.*

AL   Let's please, for Pete's sakes, fix up for the doctor sketch.

WILLIE   You think *you* know how to do it? You fix it up.

AL   It'll be my pleasure. (WILLIE *stands aside and watches with arms folded as* AL *proceeds to move table and chairs and stools until he arranges them exactly the way he wants them. Then he stands back and folds his arms the same way.)* There! That's the doctor sketch!

WILLIE *(smiles arrogantly)*   For how much money?

AL   I don't want to bet you.

WILLIE   You're afraid to lose?

AL   I'm afraid to *win.* You don't even have enough to buy a box of plain crackers.

WILLIE   —Don't be so afraid you're gonna win—because you're gonna lose! That's not the doctor sketch. That's the gypsy chiropractor sketch.

AL   You're positive?

WILLIE   I'm *more* than positive. I'm *sure.*

AL   All right. Show me the doctor sketch.

WILLIE *(looks at him confidently, then goes to a chair, picks it up and moves it to the left about four inches, if that much. Then he folds his arms over his chest.)*   There, *that's* the doctor sketch!

AL *(looks at him)*   You know what you are, Willie? You're a lapalooza.

WILLIE *(nods)*   If I'm a lapalooza, you're a mister.

AL   Let's please rehearse the sketch.

WILLIE   All right, go outside. I'm in the office.

AL   You gonna do the part with the nurse first?

WILLIE   You see a nurse here? How can I rehearse with a nurse that's not here?

AL   I'm just asking a question. I'm not allowed to ask questions?

WILLIE   Ask whatever you want. But try to make them intelligent questions.

AL   I beg your pardon. I usually ask the kind of question to the kind of person I'm talking to . . . You get my drift?

WILLIE   I get it, mister.

AL   All right. Let's skip over the nurse. We'll start from where I come in.

WILLIE   All right, from where you come in. First go out.

AL *(takes a few steps toward the door, stops and turns)*   All right, I'm outside. *(Pantomimes with his fist, knocking on a door)* Knock, knock, knock! I was looking for the doctor.

WILLIE   Wait a minute. You're not outside.

AL   Certainly I'm outside.

WILLIE   If you were outside, you couldn't see me, could you?

AL   No.

WILLIE   Can you see me?

AL   Yes.

WILLIE   So you're not outside. Go *all* the way outside. What the hell kind of a rehearsal is this?

AL   It's a rehearsing rehearsal. Can't you make believe I'm all the way out in the hall?

WILLIE   I could also make believe you were still in New Jersey, but you're not. You're here. Let's have a professional rehearsal, for chrissakes. We ain't got a nurse, but we got a door. Let's use what we got.

AL *(sighs deeply)*   Listen, we're not gonna stop for every little thing, are we? I don't know how many years I got left, I don't wanna spend it rehearsing.

WILLIE   We're not gonna stop for the little things. We're gonna stop for the big things . . . The door is a big thing.

AL   All right, I'll go through the door, I'll come in, and then we'll run through the sketch once or twice, and that'll be it for today. All right?

WILLIE   Right . . . Unless another big thing comes up.

AL *(glares at him)*   All right, I'm going out. I'll be right back in. *(He crosses to the door, opens it, stops and turns.)* If I'm outside and my daughter calls, tell her to pick me up in an hour.

(He goes out and closes the door behind him.)

WILLIE *(mumbles, half to himself)*   She can pick you up *now* for all I care. *(He puts his hands behind his back, clasps them, and paces back and forth. He calls out.)* All right! Knock, knock, knock!

AL *(from outside)*   Knock, knock, knock!

WILLIE *(screams)*   *Don't say it,* for God's sakes, *do it!* *(To himself)* He probably went *crazy* in the country.

AL *(from outside)*   You ready?

WILLIE *(yells)*   I'm ready. Knock, knock, knock! (AL *knocks three times on the door.)* Come in. *(We see and hear the doorknob jiggle, but it doesn't open. This is repeated.)* All right, come in already.

AL *(from outside)*   It doesn't open—it's stuck.

WILLIE *(wearily.)*   All right, wait a minute. *(He shuffles over to the door and puts his hand on the knob and pulls. It doesn't open.)* Wait a minute.

(He tries again, to no avail.)

AL *(from outside)*   What's the matter?

WILLIE   Wait a minute.

(He pulls harder, to no avail.)

AL   Is it locked?

WILLIE   It's not locked. Wait a minute. *(He tries again; it doesn't open.)* It's locked. You better get somebody. Call the boy downstairs. Sandy. Tell him it's locked.

AL *(from outside)*   Let me try it again.

WILLIE   What are you wasting time? Call the boy. Tell him it's locked.

(AL tries it again, turning it in the other direction, and the door opens. They stand there face-to-face.)

AL   I fixed it.

WILLIE *(glares at him)*   You didn't fix it. You just don't know how to open a door.

AL   Did my daughter call?

WILLIE   You know, I think you went crazy in the country.

AL   You want to stand here and insult me, or do you want to rehearse the sketch?

WILLIE   I would like to do *both,* but we ain't got the time . . . Let's forget the door. Stand in here and say "Knock, knock, knock."

AL *(AL comes in and closes the door. Sarcastically)*   I hope I can get *out* again.

WILLIE   I hope so too. *(He places his hands behind his back and paces.)* All right. "Knock, knock, knock."

AL *(pantomimes with his fist)*   Knock, knock, knock.

WILLIE *(singsong)*   Enter!

AL *(stops and looks at him)*   What do you mean "Enter"? *(He does it in the same singsong way.)* What happened to "Come in"?

WILLIE   It's the same thing, isn't it? "Enter" or "Come in." What's the difference, as long as you're in?

AL   The difference is we've done this sketch twelve thousand times, and you've always said "Come in," and suddenly today it's "Enter." Why today, after all these years, do you suddenly change it to "Enter"?

WILLIE *(shrugs)*   I'm trying to freshen up the act.

AL   Who asked you to freshen up the act? They asked for the doctor sketch, didn't they? The doctor sketch starts with "Come in," not "Enter." You wanna freshen up something, put some flowers in here.

WILLIE   It's a new generation today. This is not 1934, you know.

AL   No kidding? I didn't get today's paper.

WILLIE   What's bad about "Enter" instead of "Come in"?

AL   Because it's different. You know why we've been doing it the same way for forty-three years? Because it's good.

WILLIE   And you know why we don't do it any more? Because we've been doing it the same way for forty-three years.

AL   So, if we're not doing it any more, why are we changing it?

WILLIE   Can I make a comment, nothing personal? I think you've been sitting on a New Jersey porch too long.

AL   What does that mean?

WILLIE   That means I think you've been sitting on a New Jersey porch too long. From my window, I see everything that goes on in the world. I see old people, I see young people, nice people, bad people, I see holdups, drug addicts, ambulances, car crashes, jumpers from buildings—I see everything. You see a lawn mower and a milkman.

AL *(looks at him for a long moment)*   And that's why you want to say "Enter" instead of "Come in"?

WILLIE   Are you listening to me?

AL *(looks around)*   Why, there's someone else in the room?

WILLIE You don't know the first thing that's going on today?

AL All right, what's going on today?

WILLIE Did you ever hear the expression "That's where it is"? Well, this is where it is, and that's where I am.

AL I see . . . Did you ever hear the expression "You don't know what the hell you're talking about"? It comes right in front of the *other* expression "You *never* knew what the hell you were talking about."

WILLIE *I* wasn't the one who retired. You know why you retired? Because you were tired. You were getting old-fashioned. I was still new-fashioned, and I'll *always* be.

AL I see. That's why you're in such demand. That's why you're such a "hot" property today. That's why you do movies you don't do, that's why you're in musicals you're not in, and that's why you make commercials you don't make—because you can't even remember them to *make* them.

WILLIE You know what I *do* remember? I remember what a pain in the ass you are to work with, that's what I remember.

AL That's right. And when you worked with this pain in the ass, you lived in a *five*-room suite. Now you live in a *one*-room suite . . . And you're still wearing the same goddamn pajamas you wore in the five-room suite.

WILLIE I don't have to take this crap from you.

AL You're lucky you're getting it. No one else wants to give it to you.

WILLIE I don't want to argue with you. After you say "Knock, knock, knock," I'm saying "Enter," and if you don't like it you don't have to come in.

AL You can't say nothing without my permission. I own fifty percent of this act.

WILLIE Then say *your* fifty percent. I'm saying "Enter" in my fifty percent.

AL If you say "Enter" after "Knock, knock, knock" . . . I'm coming in all right. But not alone. I'm bringing a lawyer with me.

WILLIE Where? From New Jersey? You're lucky if a *cow* comes with you.

AL Against *you* in court, I could *win* with a cow.

(He enunciates each point by poking WILLIE *in the chest.)*

WILLIE *(slaps his hand away)* The *finger?* You're starting with the finger again?

(He runs into the kitchen and comes out brandishing a knife.)

AL I'll tell you the truth now. I didn't retire. I *escaped.*

WILLIE *(wielding the knife)* The next time you give me the finger, say goodbye to the finger.

AL *(hiding behind a chair)* Listen, I got a terrific idea. Instead of working together again, let's never work together again. You're crazy.

WILLIE I'm crazy, heh? I'M CRAZY!

AL Keep saying it until you believe it.

WILLIE I may be crazy, but you're *senile!* You know what that is?

AL I'm not giving you any straight lines.

WILLIE Crazy is when you got a couple of parts that go wrong. Senile is when you went the hell out of business. That's you, mister. *(The phone rings.* AL *moves toward the phone.)* Get away from that phone. *(He drives the knife into the table.* AL *backs away in shock.* WILLIE *picks up the phone.)* Hello?

AL Is that my daughter?

WILLIE Hello . . . How are you?

AL Is that my daughter? Is that her?

WILLIE *(to* AL*)* Will you shut up? Will you be quiet? Can't you see I'm talking? Don't you see me on the phone with a person? For God's sakes, behave like a human being for five seconds, will you? WILL YOU BEHAVE FOR FIVE SECONDS LIKE A HUMAN BEING? *(Into the phone)* Hello? . . . Yes . . . Just a minute. *(To* AL*)* It's your daughter.

(He sits, opens up Variety.*)*

AL *(takes the phone, turns his back to* WILLIE, *speaks low)* Hello . . . Hello, sweet-heart . . . No . . . No . . . I can't talk now . . . I said I can't talk now . . . Because he's a crazy bedbug, that's why.

WILLIE *(jumps up)* Mister is no good but bedbug is all right?? *(Yells into the phone)* Your father is sick! Come and get your sick father!

AL *(turns to him)* Don't you see me on the phone with a person? Will you please be quiet, for God's sakes! *(Back into the phone)* Listen, I want you to pick me up now . . . I don't want to discuss it. Pick me up now. In front of the hotel. Don't park too close, it's filthy here . . . I *know* what I promised. Don't argue with me. I'm putting on my coat. I'll wait in the street—I'll probably get mugged . . . All right, just a minute. *(He hands the phone to* WILLIE.*)* She'd like to talk to you for a second.

WILLIE Who is it?

AL *(glares at him)* Mrs. Eleanor Roosevelt . . . What do you mean, who is it? Didn't you just say it's my daughter?

WILLIE I know it's your daughter. I forgot her name.

AL Doris.

WILLIE What does she want?

AL *(yells)* Am I Doris? She'll tell you.

WILLIE *(takes the phone)* Hello? . . . Hello, dear, this is Willie Clark . . . Unpleas-antness? There was no unpleasantness . . . There was stupidity maybe but no unpleasant-ness . . .

AL Tell her I'm getting into my coat. *(He is putting his coat on.)* Tell her I got one sleeve on.

WILLIE *(into the phone)* I was hoping it would work out too . . . I bent over back-wards and forwards. He didn't even bend sideways . . .

AL I got the other sleeve on . . . Tell her I'm up to my hat and then I'm out the door.

WILLIE It's a question of one word, darling. "Enter!" . . . "Enter"—that's all it comes down to.

AL *(puts his hat on)* The hat is on. I'm bundled up, tell her.

WILLIE *(into the phone)* Yes . . . Yes, I will . . . I'll tell him myself. I promise . . . Goodbye, Dorothy. *(He hangs up.)* I told her we'll give it one more chance.

AL Not if you say "Enter." "Come in," I'll stay. "Enter," I go.

WILLIE Ask me "Knock, knock, knock."

AL Don't fool around with me. I got enough pains in my neck. Are you going to say "Come in"?

WILLIE Ask me "Knock, knock, knock"!

AL I know you, you bastard!

WILLIE ASK ME "KNOCK, KNOCK, KNOCK"!

AL KNOCK, KNOCK, KNOCK!

WILLIE *(grinding it in)* EN-TERRR!

AL BEDBUG! CRAZY BEDBUG!

(He starts to run out.)

WILLIE *(big smile)* ENNN-TERRRRR!

(The curtain starts down.)

AL *(heading for the door)*   LUNATIC BASTARD!
WILLIE   ENNN-TERRRR!

(Curtain.)

ACT II

Scene I

The scene is a doctor's office or, rather, an obvious stage "flat" representation of a doctor's office. It has an old desk and chair, a telephone, a cabinet filled with medicine bottles, a human skeleton hanging on a stand, a blackboard with chalk and pointer, an eye chart on the wall.

Overhead television lights surround the top of the set. Two boom microphones extend from either end of the set over the office.

At rise, the set is not fully lit. A thin, frail man in a hat and business suit sits in the chair next to the doctor's desk, patiently waiting.

VOICE OF TV DIRECTOR *(over the loudspeaker)*   Eddie! *EDDIE!*

(EDDIE, a young assistant TV director with headset and speaker, trailing wires and carrying a clipboard, steps out on the set. He speaks through his mike.)

EDDIE   Yeah, Phil?
VOICE OF TV DIRECTOR   Any chance of doing this today?
EDDIE *(shrugs)*   We're all set here, Phil. We're just waiting on the actors.
VOICE OF TV DIRECTOR   What the hell is happening?
EDDIE   I don't know. There's a problem with the makeup. Mr. Clark wants a Number Seven amber or something.
VOICE OF TV DIRECTOR   Well, get it for him.
EDDIE   Where? They stopped making it thirty-four years ago.
VOICE OF TV DIRECTOR   Christ!
EDDIE   And Mr. Lewis says the "ahh" sticks are too short.
VOICE OF TV DIRECTOR   The what?
EDDIE   The "ahh" sticks. Don't ask me. I'm still trying to figure out what a "look" stick is.
VOICE OF TV DIRECTOR   What the hell are we making, *Nicholas and Alexandra?* Tell them it's just a dress rehearsal. We'll worry about the props later. Let's get moving, Eddie. Christ Almighty.

(WILLIE'S nephew BEN appears onstage. He talks up into the overhead mike.)

BEN   Mr. Schaefer . . . Mr. Schaefer, I'm awfully sorry about the delay. Mr. Lewis and Mr. Clark have had a few technical problems backstage.
VOICE OF TV DIRECTOR   Yeah, well, we've had it all week . . . I'm afraid we're running out of time here. I've got twelve goddamned other numbers to get through today.
BEN   I'll get them right out. There's no problem.
VOICE OF TV DIRECTOR   Tell them I want to run straight through, no stopping. They can clean up whatever they want afterwards.
BEN   Absolutely.
VOICE OF TV DIRECTOR   I haven't seen past "Knock, knock, knock"—"Come in" since Tuesday.

BEN (*looks offstage*)   Right. There they are. (*Into the mike*) We're ready, Mr. Schaefer. I'll tell them we're going to go straight through, no stopping. Thank you very much.

(BEN *exits very quickly.*)

VOICE OF TV DIRECTOR   All right, Eddie, bring in the curtains.
EDDIE   What?
VOICE OF TV DIRECTOR   Bring in the curtains. Let's run it from the top with the voice over.
EDDIE (*calls up*)   Let's have the curtains.

(*The curtains come in.*)

VOICE OF TV DIRECTOR   Voice over!
ANNOUNCER   The golden age of comedy reached its zenith during a fabulous and glorious era known as Vaudeville—Fanny Brice, W. C. Fields, Eddie Cantor, Ed Wynn, Will Rogers and a host of other greats fill its Hall of Fame. There are two other names that belong on this list, but they can never be listed separately. They are more than a team. They are two comic shining lights that beam as one. For, Lewis without Clark is like laughter without joy. We are privileged to present tonight, in their first public performance in over eleven years, for half a century known as "The Sunshine Boys"—Mr. Al Lewis and Mr. Willie Clark, in their beloved scene, "The Doctor Will See You Now."

(*The curtain rises, and the set is fully lit. The frail man in the hat is sitting on the chair as* WILLIE, *the doctor, dressed in a floor-length white doctor's jacket, a mirror attached to his head and a stethoscope around his neck is looking into the* PATIENT's *mouth, holding his tongue down with an "ahh" stick.*)

WILLIE   Open wider and say "Ahh."
PATIENT   Ahh.
WILLIE   Wider.
PATIENT   *Ahhh!*
WILLIE (*moves with his back to the audience*)   A little wider.
PATIENT   Ahhh!
WILLIE (*steps away*)   Your throat is all right, but you're gonna have some trouble with your stomach.
PATIENT   How come?
WILLIE   You just swallowed the stick.

(*The* PATIENT *feels his stomach.*)

PATIENT   Is that bad?
WILLIE   It's terrible. I only got two left.
PATIENT   What about getting the stick out?
WILLIE   What am I, a tree surgeon? . . . All right, for another ten dollars, I'll take it out.
PATIENT   That's robbery.
WILLIE   Then forget it. Keep the stick.
PATIENT   No, no I'll pay. Take the stick out.
WILLIE   Come back tomorrow. On Thursdays I do woodwork. (*The* PATIENT *gets up and crosses to the door, then exits.* WILLIE *calls out*) Oh, Nurse! Nursey!

(*The* NURSE *enters. She is a tall, voluptuous and over-stacked blonde in a tight dress.*)

NURSE   Did you want me, Doctor?

WILLIE *(he looks at her, knowingly)* Why do you think I hired you? . . . What's your name again?

NURSE Miss MacKintosh. You know, like the apples.

WILLIE *(nods)* The name I forgot, the apples I remembered . . . Look in my appointment book, see who's next.

NURSE It's a Mr. Kornheiser.

WILLIE Maybe you're wrong. Look in the book. It's better that way.

(She crosses to the desk and bends way over as she looks through the appointment book. Her firm, round rear end faces us and WILLIE. WILLIE *shakes his head from side to side in wonderful contemplation.)*

NURSE *(still down)* No, I was right.

WILLIE So was I.

NURSE *(straightens up and turns around)* It's Mr. Kornheiser.

WILLIE Are you sure? Spell it.

NURSE *(turns, bends and gives us the same wonderful view again)* K-o-r-n-h-e-i-s-e-r!

(She turns and straightens up.)

WILLIE *(nods)* What's the first name?

NURSE *(turns, bends)* Walter.

WILLIE Stay down for the middle name.

NURSE *(remains down)* Benjamin.

WILLIE Don't move and give me the whole thing.

NURSE *(still rear end up, reading)* Walter Benjamin Kornheiser.

(She turns and straightens up.)

WILLIE Oh, boy. From now on I only want to see patients with long names.

NURSE Is there anything else you want?

WILLIE Yeah. Call a carpenter and have him make my desk lower.

(The NURSE *walks sexily right up to* WILLIE *and stands with her chest practically on his, breathing and heaving.)*

NURSE *(pouting)* Yes, Doctor.

WILLIE *(wipes his brow)* Whew, it's hot in here. Did you turn the steam on?

NURSE *(sexily)* No, Doctor.

WILLIE In that case, take a five-dollar raise. Send in the next patient before *I'm* the next patient.

NURSE Yes, Doctor. *(She coughs.)* Excuse me, I think I have a chest cold.

WILLIE Looks more like an epidemic to me.

NURSE Yes, Doctor. *(She wriggles her way to the door.)* Is there anything else you can think of?

WILLIE I can *think* of it, but I'm not so sure I can *do* it.

NURSE Well, if I *can* help you, Doctor, that's what the nurse is for.

(She exits and closes the door with an enticing look.)

WILLIE I'm glad I didn't go to law school. *(Then we hear three knocks on the door. "Knock, knock, knock.")* Aha. That must be my next patient. *(Calls out)* Come in! *(The door starts to open.)*—and enter!

(AL *steps in and glares angrily at* WILLIE. *He is in a business suit, wears a wig, and carries a cheap attaché case.*)

AL   I'm looking for the doctor.

WILLIE   Are you sick?

AL   Are *you* the doctor?

WILLIE   Yes.

AL   I'm not *that* sick.

WILLIE   What's your name, please?

AL   Kornheiser. Walter Benjamin Kornheiser. You want me to spell it?

WILLIE   Never mind. I got a better speller than you . . . *(Takes a tongue depressor from his pocket)* Sit down and open your mouth, please.

AL   There's nothing wrong with my mouth.

WILLIE   Then just sit down.

AL   There's nothing wrong with that either.

WILLIE   Then what are you doing here?

AL   I came to examine you.

WILLIE   I think you got everything backwards.

AL   It's possible. I dressed in a hurry this morning.

WILLIE   You mean you came here for me to examine *you.*

AL   No, I came here for me to examine *you.* I'm a tax collector.

WILLIE *(nods)*   That's nice. I'm a stamp collector. What do you do for a living?

AL   I find out how much money people make.

WILLIE   Oh, a busybody. Make an appointment with the nurse.

AL   I did. I'm seeing her Friday night . . .

WILLIE *(jumps up and down angrily)*   Don't fool around with my nurse. DON'T FOOL AROUND WITH MY NURSE! She's a nice girl. She's a *Virginian!*

AL   A what?

WILLIE   A *Virginian.* That's where she's from.

AL   Well, she ain't going *back,* I can tell you that. *(He sits, opens the attaché case.)* I got some questions to ask you.

WILLIE   I'm too busy to answer questions. I'm a doctor. If you wanna see me, you gotta be a patient.

AL   But I'm not sick.

WILLIE   Don't worry. We'll find something.

AL   All right, you examine me and I'll examine you . . . *(Takes out a tax form as* WILLIE *wields the tongue depressor)* The first question is, How much money did you make last year?

WILLIE   Last year I made—

(*He moves his lips mouthing a sum, but it's not audible.*)

AL   I didn't hear that.

WILLIE   Oh. Hard of hearing. I knew we'd find something. Did you ever have any childhood diseases?

AL   Not lately.

WILLIE   Father living or deceased?

AL   Both.

WILLIE   What do you mean, both?

AL   First he was living, now he's deceased.

WILLIE   What did your father die from?

AL   My mother . . . Now it's my turn. Are you married?

WILLIE   I'm looking.

AL   Looking to get married?

WILLIE   No, looking to get out.

(He looks in AL's *ear with a flashlight.)*

AL   What are you doing?

WILLIE   I'm examining your lower intestines.

AL   So why do you look in the ear?

WILLIE   If I got a choice of two places to look, I'll take this one.

AL *(consulting his form)*   Never mind. Do you own a car?

WILLIE   Certainly I own a car. Why?

AL   If you use it for medical purposes, you can deduct it from your taxes. What kind of car do you own?

WILLIE   An ambulance.

AL   Do you own a house?

WILLIE   Can I deduct it?

AL   Only if you use it for medical purposes. Where do you live?

WILLIE   In Mount Sinai Hospital . . . Open your shirt, I want to listen to your heart-beat.

AL *(unbuttons two buttons on his shirt)*   Will this take long?

WILLIE   Not if I hear something. *(He puts his ear to* AL's *chest and listens.)* Uh-huh. I hear something . . . You're all right.

AL   Aren't you going to listen with the stethoscope?

WILLIE   Oh, sure. I didn't know you wanted a thorough examination. *(Puts the stethoscope to his ears and listens to* AL's *chest)* Oh, boy. Ohh, boyyyy! You know what you got?

AL   What?

WILLIE   A filthy undershirt.

AL   Never mind that. Am I in good health?

WILLIE   Not unless you change your undershirt.

AL   What is this, a doctor's office or a laundry? I bet you never went to medical school.

WILLIE *(jumping up and down again)*   What are you talkin'? . . . WHAT ARE YOU TALKIN'? . . . I went to Columbia Medical School.

AL   Did you pass?

WILLIE   Certainly.

AL   Well, you should have gone *in!*

WILLIE   Never mind . . . I'm gonna examine your eyes now.

AL   They're perfect. I got twenty-twenty eyes.

WILLIE   That's too much. All you need is one and one. Look at that chart on the wall. Now put your left hand over your left eye and your right hand over your right eye. (AL *does so.*) Now tell me what you see.

AL   I don't see nothing.

WILLIE   Don't panic, I can cure you . . . Take your hands away. (AL *does.*) Can you see now?

AL   Certainly I can see now.

WILLIE   You know, I fixed over two thousand people like that.

AL   It's a miracle.

WILLIE   Thank you.

AL   A miracle you're not in jail . . . What do you charge for a visit?

WILLIE   A dollar.

AL   A dollar? That's very cheap for an examination.

WILLIE   It's not an examination. It's just a visit. "Hello and Goodbye" . . . "Hello and How Are You?" is ten dollars.

AL   If you ask me, you're a quack.

WILLIE   If I was a duck I would ask you . . . Now roll up your sleeve, I wanna take some blood.

AL   I can't do it.

WILLIE   Why not?

AL   If I see blood, I get sick.

WILLIE   Do what I do. Don't look.

AL   I'm sorry. I'm not giving blood. I'm anemic.

WILLIE   What's anemic?

AL   You're a doctor and you don't know what anemic means?

WILLIE   That's because I'm a specialist.

AL   What do you specialize in?

WILLIE   Everything but anemic.

AL   Listen, can I continue my examination?

WILLIE   You continue yours, and I'll continue mine. All right, cross your legs. *(He hits* AL's *knee with a small hammer.)* Does it hurt if I hit you with the hammer?

AL   Yes.

WILLIE   Good. From now on, try not to get hit with a hammer. *(He throws the hammer over his shoulder. He takes a specimen bottle from the cabinet and returns.)* You see this bottle?

AL   Yes.

WILLIE   You know what you're supposed to do with this bottle?

AL   I think so.

WILLIE   You *think* so or you *know* so? If you're not sure, let me know. The girl doesn't come in to clean today.

AL   What do you want me to do?

WILLIE   I want you to go in this bottle.

AL   I haven't got time. I have to go over your books.

WILLIE   *The hell you will!*

AL   If I don't go over your books, the *government* will come in here and go over your books.

WILLIE   Don't they have a place in Washington?

AL   Certainly, but they have to go where the books are.

WILLIE   The whole government?

AL   No, just the Treasury Department.

WILLIE   That's a relief.

AL   I'm glad you're relieved.

WILLIE   I wish *you* were before you came in here.

(The door opens and the big-chested NURSE *steps in.)*

NURSE   Oh, Doctor. Doctor Klockenmeyer.

WILLIE   Yes.

NURSE   Mrs. Kolodny is on the phone. She wants you to rush right over and deliver her baby.

WILLIE   I'm busy now. Tell her I'll mail it to her in the morning.

NURSE   Yes, Doctor.

(She exits and closes the door.)

AL   Where did you find a couple of nurses like that?

WILLIE   She was standing on Forty-third and Forty-fourth Street . . . Let me see your tongue, please.

AL   I don't want to.

*(*WILLIE *squeezes* AL*'s throat, and his tongue comes out.)*

WILLIE   Open the mouth . . . How long have you had that white coat on your tongue?

AL   Since January. In the spring I put on a gray sports jacket.

WILLIE   Now hold your tongue with your fingers and say "shish kabob."

AL *(holds his tongue with his fingers)* Thickabob.

WILLIE   Again.

AL   Thickabob.

WILLIE   I have bad news for you.

AL   What is it?

WILLIE   If you do that in a restaurant, you'll never get shish kabob.

AL *(stands with his face close to* WILLIE*'s)*   Never mind that. What about your *t*axes?

(On the "T," he spits a little.)

WILLIE *(wipes his face)*   The what?

AL   The *t*axes. It's *t*ime *t*o pay your *t*axes to the *T*reasury.

(All the "T's" are quite fluid. WILLIE *wipes his face and glares angrily at* AL*.)*

WILLIE   I'm warning you, don't start in with me.

AL   What are you talking about?

WILLIE   You know what I'm talking about. *(Illustrates)* "It's *t*ime *t*o pay the *t*axes." You're speaking with spitting again.

AL   I said the right line, didn't I? If it comes out juicy, I can't help that.

WILLIE *(quite angry)*   It doesn't come out juicy unless you squeeze the "T's." I'm warning you, don't squeeze them on me.

*(*VOICE OF TV DIRECTOR *is heard over the loudspeaker.)*

VOICE OF TV DIRECTOR   Okay, let's hold it a second. Mr. Clark, I'm having trouble with the dialogue. I don't find those last few lines in the script.

WILLIE *(shouts up)*   It's not in the script, it's in *his mouth.*

AL *(talking up into the mike)*   I said the right line. Look in the script, you'll find it there.

WILLIE *(shouting)*   You'll find the words, you won't find the spit. The spit's his own idea. He's doing it on *purpose!*

AL   I don't spit on purpose. I spit on accident. I've *always* spitted on accident. It's not possible to say that line without spitting a little.

WILLIE *(addressing all his remarks to the unseen director)*   *I* can say it. *(He says the line with great delicacy, especially on the "T's".)* "It's *t*ime *t*o pay your *t*axes to the *T*rea-sury." *(Back to his normal inflection)* There wasn't a spit in my entire mouth. Why doesn't he say it like *that?*

AL   What am I, an Englishman? I'm talking the same as I've talked for forty-three years.

VOICE OF TV DIRECTOR   Gentlemen, can we argue this point after the dress rehearsal and go on with the sketch?

WILLIE   I'm not going to stand here and get a shower in the face. If you want me to go on, either take out the line or get me an umbrella.

VOICE OF TV DIRECTOR   Can we *please* go on? With all due respect, gentlemen, we have twelve other scenes to rehearse and we cannot spend all day on personal squabbles . . .

WILLIE   I'll go on, but I'm moving to a safer spot.

VOICE OF TV DIRECTOR   Don't worry about the moves, we'll pick you up on camera. Now, let's skip over this spot and pick it up on "I hope you don't have what Mr. Melnick had." (WILLIE *moves away from* AL.) All right, Mr. Clark, whenever you're ready.

WILLIE   (*waits a minute, then goes back into the doctor character*)   I hope you don't have what Mr. Melnick had.

AL   What did Mr. Melnick have?

WILLIE   (*points to standing skeleton*)   Ask him yourself, he's standing right there.

AL   That's Mr. Melnick?

WILLIE   It could be *Mrs.* Melnick. Without high heels, I can't tell.

AL   If he's dead, why do you leave him standing in the office?

WILLIE   He's still got one more appointment with me.

AL   (*crosses to him*)   You know what you are? You're a charlatan! (*As* AL *says that line, he punctuates each word by poking* WILLIE *in the chest with his finger. It does not go unnoticed by* WILLIE.) Do you know what a charlatan is?

(More pokes.)

WILLIE   It's a city in North Carolina. And if you're gonna poke me again like that, you're gonna end up in Poughkeepsie.

VOICE OF TV DIRECTOR   (*over the loudspeaker*)   Hold it, hold it. Where does it say, "You're going to end up in Poughkeepsie"?

WILLIE   (*furious*)   Where does it say he can poke me in the chest? He's doing it on purpose. He *always* did it on purpose, just to get my goat.

AL   (*looking up to the mike*)   I didn't poke him, I tapped him. A light little tap, it wouldn't hurt a baby.

WILLIE   Maybe a baby elephant. I *knew* I was going to get poked. First comes the spitting, then comes the poking. I know his routine already.

AL   (*to the mike*)   Excuse me. I'm sorry we're holding up the rehearsal, but we have a serious problem on our hands. The man I'm working with is a lunatic.

WILLIE   (*almost in a rage*)   *I'm* a lunatic, heh? He breaks my chest and spits in my face and calls *me* a lunatic! I'm gonna tell you something now I never told you in my entire life. I hate your guts.

AL   You told it to me on Monday.

WILLIE   Then I'm telling it to you again.

VOICE OF TV DIRECTOR   Listen, gentlemen, I really don't see any point in going on with this rehearsal.

AL   I don't see any point in going on with this *show*. This man is persecuting me. For eleven years he's been waiting to get back at me, only I'm not gonna give him the chance.

(The assistant director, EDDIE, *walks out in an attempt to make peace.)*

WILLIE   (*half-hysterical*)   I knew it! I knew it! He planned it! He's been setting me up for eleven years just to walk out on me again.

EDDIE *(trying to be gentle)*   All right, Mr. Clark, let's settle down. Why don't we all go into the dressing room and talk this out?

AL   I didn't want to do it in the first place.

WILLIE *(apoplectic)*   Liar! Liar! His daughter *begged* me on the phone. She *begged* me!

(BEN rushes out to restrain WILLIE.)

BEN   Uncle Willie, please, that's enough. Come back to the dressing room.

EDDIE   Gentlemen, we need the stage. Can we please do this over on the side?

AL *(to the assistant director)*   The man is hysterical, you can see for yourself. He's been doing this to me all week long.

(He starts taking off the wig and suit jacket.)

WILLIE   Begged me. She begged me. His own daughter begged me.

BEN   Uncle Willie, stop it, please.

AL *(to the others)*   I'm sorry we caused everyone so much trouble. I should have stayed in New Jersey in the first place. *(On his way out; to the assistant director)* He pulled a knife on me last week. In his own apartment he pulled a knife on me. A crazy man.

(He is gone.)

WILLIE   I don't need you. I *never* needed you. You were nothing when I found you, and that's what you are today.

BEN   Come on, Willie. *(Out front)* I'm sorry about this, Mr. Schaefer.

WILLIE   He thinks I can't get work without him. Maybe *his* career is over, but not mine. Maybe he's finished, but not me. You hear? not me! NOT M—

(He clutches his chest.)

BEN *(turns and sees him stagger)*   Grab him, quick! (EDDIE *rushes to* WILLIE, *but it's too late*—WILLIE *falls to the floor.* BEN *rushes to his side.)* All right, take it easy, Uncle Willie, just lie there. *(To* EDDIE*)* Get a doctor, please hurry.

(A bit actor and the NURSE *rush onstage behind* BEN.*)*

WILLIE *(breathing hard)*   I don't need a doctor. Don't get a doctor, I don't trust them.

BEN   Don't talk, Willie, you're all right. *(To the* NURSE*)* Somebody get a blanket, please.

WILLIE *(breathing fast)*   Don't tell him. Don't tell him I fell down. I don't want to give him the satisfaction.

BEN   Of course, I won't tell him, Willie. There's nothing to tell. You're going to be all right.

WILLIE   Frito-Lays . . . That's the name of the potato chip . . . You see? I remembered . . . I remembered the name! Frito-Lays.

(BEN is holding WILLIE's hand as the lights dim. The curtain falls on the scene. In the dark, we hear the voice of the ANNOUNCER.)

ANNOUNCER   The golden age of comedy reached its zenith during a fabulous and glorious era known as Vaudeville—Fanny Brice, W. C. Fields, Eddie Cantor, Ed Wynn, Will Rogers and a host of other greats fill its Hall of Fame. There are two other names that belong on this list, but they can never be listed separately. They are more than a team. They are two comic shining lights that beam as one. For, Lewis without Clark is like laughter without joy. When these two greats retired, a comic style disappeared from the American scene that will never see its likes again . . . Here, then, in a sketch taped nearly eleven years ago on *The Ed Sullivan Show,* are Lewis and Clark in their classic scene, "The Doctor Will See You Now."

(*We hear* WILLIE's *voice and that of the first* PATIENT.)

WILLIE   Open wider and say "Ahh."

PATIENT   Ahh.

WILLIE   Wider.

PATIENT   Ahh.

WILLIE   A little wider.

PATIENT   Ahhh!

WILLIE   Your throat is all right, but you're gonna have some trouble with your stomach.

PATIENT   How come?

WILLIE   You just swallowed the stick.

Scene II

The curtain rises. The scene is WILLIE's *hotel room, two weeks later. It is late afternoon,* WILLIE *is in his favorite pajamas in bed, propped up on the pillows, his head hanging down, asleep.*

The television is droning away—another daytime serial. A black REGISTERED NURSE *in uniform, a sweater draped over her shoulders, and her glasses on a chain around her neck, is sitting in a chair watching the television. She is eating from a big box of chocolates. Two very large vases of flowers are on the bureau.* WILLIE's *head bobs a few times; then he opens his eyes.*

WILLIE   What time is it?

NURSE   *(turns off the TV and glances at her watch)*   Ten to one.

WILLIE   Ten to one? . . . Who are you?

NURSE   Don't give me that. You now who I am.

WILLIE   You're the same nurse from yesterday?

NURSE   I'm the same nurse from every day for two weeks now. Don't play your games with me.

WILLIE   I can't even chew a piece of bread, who's gonna play games? . . . Why'd you turn off the television?

NURSE   It's either watching that or watching you sleep—either one ain't too interesting.

WILLIE   I'm sorry. I'll try to sleep more entertaining . . . What's today, Tuesday?

NURSE   Wednesday.

(*She bites into a piece of chocolate.*)

WILLIE   How could this be Wednesday? I went to sleep on Monday.

NURSE   Haven't we already seen Mike Douglas twice this week?

WILLIE   Once.

NURSE   Twice.

WILLIE *(reluctantly)*   All right, twice . . . I don't even remember. I was all right yesterday?

NURSE   We are doing very well.

WILLIE   We are? When did *you* get sick?

NURSE *(deadly serious, no smile)*   That's funny. That is really funny, Mr. Clark. Soon as I get home tonight I'm gonna bust out laughing.

WILLIE You keep eating my candy like that, you're gonna bust out a lot sooner.

NURSE Well, *you* can't eat it and there's no sense throwing it out. I'm just storing up energy for the winter.

WILLIE Maybe you'll find time in between the nougat and the peppermint to take my pulse.

NURSE I took it. It's a little better today.

WILLIE When did you take my pulse?

NURSE When you were sleeping.

WILLIE *Everybody's* pulse is good when they're sleeping. You take a pulse when a person is up. Thirty dollars a day, she takes a sleeping pulse. I'll tell you the truth, I don't think you know what you're doing . . . and I'm not a prejudiced person.

NURSE Well, *I* am: I don't like sick people who tell registered nurses how to do their job. You want your tea now?

WILLIE I don't want to interrupt your candy.

NURSE And don't get fresh with me. You can get fresh with your nephew, but you can't get fresh with me. Maybe *he* has to take it, but I'm not a blood relative.

WILLIE That's for sure.

NURSE That's even funnier than the other one. My *whole* evening's gonna be taken up tonight with nothing but laughing.

WILLIE I don't even eat candy. Finish the whole box. When you're through, I hope you eat the flowers too.

NURSE You know why I don't get angry at anything you say to me?

WILLIE I give up. Why?

NURSE Because I have a good sense of humor. I am *known* for my good sense of humor. That's why I can take anything you say to me.

WILLIE If you nurse as good as your sense of humor, I won't make it to Thursday . . . Who called?

NURSE No one.

WILLIE I thought I heard the phone.

NURSE *(gets up)* No one called. *(She crosses and puffs up his pillow.)* Did you have a nice nap?

WILLIE It was a nap, nothing special . . . Don't puff up the pillows, please. *(He swats her hands away.)* It takes me a day and a night to get them the way I like them, and then you puff them up.

NURSE Oh, woke up a little grouchy, didn't we?

WILLIE Stop making yourself a partner all the time. I woke up grouchy. Don't make the bed, please. I'm still sleeping in it. Don't make a bed with a person in it.

NURSE Can't stand to have people do things for you, can you? If you just want someone to sit here and watch you, you're better off getting a dog, Mr. Clark. I'll suggest that to your nephew.

WILLIE Am I complaining? I'm only asking for two things. Don't take my pulse when I'm sleeping and don't make my bed when I'm in it. Do it the other way around and then we're in business.

NURSE It doesn't bother me to do nothing as long as I'm getting paid for it.

(She sits.)

WILLIE *(a pause)* I'm hungry.

NURSE You want your junket?

WILLIE Forget it. I'm not hungry. *(She reads.)* Tell me something, how old is a woman like you?

NURSE   That is none of your business.

WILLIE   I'm not asking for business.

NURSE   I am fifty-four years young.

WILLIE   Is that so? . . . You're married?

NURSE   My husband passed away four years ago.

WILLIE   Oh . . . You were the nurse?

NURSE   No, I was not the nurse . . . You could use some sleep and I could use some quiet.

(She gets up.)

WILLIE   You know something? For a fifty-four-year-old registered widow, you're an attractive woman.

(He tries to pat her. She swings at him.)

NURSE   And don't try that with me!

WILLIE   Who's trying anything?

NURSE   You are. You're getting fresh in a way I don't like.

WILLIE   What are you worried about? I can't even put on my slippers by myself.

NURSE   I'm not worried about your slippers. And don't play on my sympathy. I don't have any, and I ain't expecting any coming in, in the near future.

WILLIE   Listen, how about a nice alcohol rub?

NURSE   I just gave you one.

WILLIE   No, I'll give *you* one.

NURSE   I know you just say things like that to agitate me. You like to agitate people, don't you? Well, I am not an agitatable person.

WILLIE   You're right. I think I'd be better off with the dog.

NURSE   How did your poor wife stand a man like you?

WILLIE   Who told you about my poor wife?

NURSE   Your poor nephew . . . Did you ever think of getting married again?

(She takes his pulse.)

WILLIE   What is this, a proposal?

NURSE   *(laughs)*   Not from me . . . I am *not* thinking of getting married again . . . Besides, you're just not my type.

WILLIE   Why? It's a question of religion?

NURSE   It's a question of age. You'd wear me out in no time.

WILLIE   You think I can't support you? I've got Medicare.

NURSE   You never stop, do you?

WILLIE   When I stop, I won't be here.

NURSE   Well, that's where you're gonna be unless you learn to slow up a little.

WILLIE   Slow up? I moved two inches in three weeks, she tells me slow up.

NURSE   I mean, if you're considering getting well again, you have to stop worrying about telephone calls and messages, and especially about when you're going back to work.

WILLIE   I'm an actor—I have to act. It's my profession.

NURSE   Your profession right now is being a sick person. And if you're gonna act anywhere, it's gonna be from a sick bed.

WILLIE   Maybe I can get a job on Marcus Welby.

NURSE   You can turn everything I say into a vaudeville routine if you want, but I'm gonna give you a piece of advice, Mr. Clark . . .

WILLIE   What?

NURSE   The world is full of sick people. And there just ain't enough doctors or nurses to go around to take care of all these sick people. And all the doctors and all the nurses can do just so much, Mr. Clark. But God, in His Infinite Wisdom, has said He will help those who help themselves.

WILLIE   *(looks at her)*   So? What's the advice?

NURSE   *Stop bugging me!*

WILLIE   All right, I'll stop bugging you . . . I don't even know what the hell it means.

NURSE   That's better. Now you're my type again.

(The doorbell rings. The NURSE *crosses to the door.)*

WILLIE   Here comes today's candy.

(She opens the door. BEN *enters with packages.)*

BEN   Hello. How is he?

NURSE   Fine. I think we're gonna get married.

BEN   Hey, Uncle Willie, you look terrific.

WILLIE   You got my *Variety?*

BEN   *(goes over to him, and hands him* Variety)   I also got about two hundred get-well telegrams from just about every star in show business—Lucille Ball, Milton Berle, Bob Hope, the mayor. It'll take you nine months just to answer them.

WILLIE   What about a commercial? Did you hear from Alka-Seltzer?

BEN   We have plenty of time to talk about that . . . Miss O'Neill, did you have your lunch yet?

NURSE   Not yet.

WILLIE   She just finished two pounds of appetizers.

BEN   Why don't you go out, take an hour or so? I'll be here for a while.

NURSE   Thank you. I could use some fresh air. *(Gets her coat; to* WILLIE)   Now, when I'm gone, I don't want you getting all agitated again, you hear?

WILLIE   I hear, I hear. Stop bugging me.

NURSE   And don't get up to go to the bathroom. Use the you-know-what.

WILLIE   *(without looking up from his* Variety)   And if not, I'll do it you-know-where.

(The NURSE *exits.)*

BEN   *(pulling up a chair next to the bed)*   Never mind, she's a very good nurse.

WILLIE   *(looks in the paper)*   Oh boy, Bernie Eisenstein died.

BEN   Who?

WILLIE   Bernie Eisenstein. Remember the dance team "Ramona and Rodriguez"? Bernie Eisenstein was Rodriguez. . . . He would have been seventy-eight in August.

BEN   *(sighs)*   Uncle Willie, could you put down *Variety* for a second?

WILLIE   *(still reading)*   Did you bring a cigar?

BEN   Uncle Willie, you realize you've had a heart attack, don't you? . . . You've been getting away with it for years—the cigars, the corned beef sandwiches, the tension, the temper tantrums. You can't do it any more, Willie. Your heart's just not going to take it.

WILLIE   This is the good news you rushed up with? For this we could have skipped a Wednesday.

BEN   *(a pause)*   I talked to the doctor this morning . . . and I'm going to have to be very frank and honest with you, Willie . . . You've got to retire. I mean give it up. Show business is out.

WILLIE   Until when?

BEN   Until *ever!* Your blood pressure is abnormally high, your heart is weak—if you tried to work again you would kill yourself.

WILLIE   All right, let me think it over.

BEN   *Think what over?* There's nothing to think over. You can't work any more, there's no decision to be made. Can't you understand that?

WILLIE   You decide for Ben Silverman, I'll decide for Willie Clark.

BEN   No, *I'll* decide for Willie Clark. I am your closest and *only* living relative, and I am responsible for your welfare . . . You can't live here any more, Willie. Not alone . . . And I can't afford to keep this nurse on permanently. Right now she's making more than I am. Anyway she already gave me her notice. She's leaving Monday. She's going to Buffalo to work for a very wealthy family.

WILLIE   Maybe she'll take me. I always did well in Buffalo.

BEN   Come on, Willie, face the facts. We have to do something, and we have to do it quickly.

WILLIE   I can't think about it today. I'm tired, I'm going to take a nap.

(He closes his eyes and drops his head to the side on the pillow.)

BEN   You want to hear my suggestion?

WILLIE   I'm napping. Don't you see my eyes closed?

BEN   I'd like you to move in with me and Helen and the kids. We have the small spare room in the back, I think you would be very comfortable . . . Uncle Willie, did you hear what I said?

WILLIE   What's the second suggestion?

BEN   What's the matter with the first?

WILLIE   It's not as good as the second.

BEN   I haven't made any yet.

WILLIE   It's still better than the first. Forget it.

BEN   Why?

WILLIE   I don't like your kids. They're noisy. The little one hit me in the head with a baseball bat.

BEN   And I've also seen you talk to them for hours on end about vaudeville and had the time of your life. Right?

WILLIE   If I stopped talking, they would hit me with the bat. No offense, but I'm not living with your children. If you get rid of them, then we'll talk . . .

BEN   I know the reason you won't come. Because Al Lewis lives with his family, and you're just trying to prove some stupid point about being independent.

WILLIE   What's the second suggestion?

BEN   *(a long sigh)*   All right . . . Now don't jump when I say this, because it's not as bad as it sounds.

WILLIE   Say it.

BEN   There's the Actors' Home in New Brunswick—

WILLIE   It's as bad as it sounds.

BEN   You're wrong. I drove out there last Sunday and they showed me around the whole place. I couldn't believe how beautiful it was.

WILLIE   You went out there? You didn't have the decency to wait until I turned down living with you first?

BEN   I just went out to investigate, that's all. No commitments.

WILLIE   The Old Actors' Home: the first booking you got me in ten years.

BEN   It's on a lake, it's got twenty-five acres of beautiful grounds, it's an old converted mansion with a big porch . . .

WILLIE   I knew it. You got me on a porch in New Jersey. He put you up to this, didn't he?

BEN   You don't have to sit on the porch. There's a million activities there. They put on shows every Friday and Saturday night. I mean, it's all old actors—what could be better for you?

WILLIE   Why New Jersey? I hate New Jersey . . . I'm sorry they ever finished the George Washington Bridge.

BEN   I couldn't get over how many old actors were there that I knew and remembered. I thought they were all dead.

WILLIE   Some recommendation. A house in the swamps with forgotten people.

BEN   They're not forgotten. They're well taken care of . . . Uncle Willie, I promise you, if you spend one day there that you're not happy, you can come back and move in with me.

WILLIE   That's my choice—New Jersey or the baseball bat.

BEN   All right, I feel a lot better about everything.

WILLIE   And what about you?

BEN   What do you mean what about me?

WILLIE   *(a pause; looks away)*   I won't see you no more?

BEN   Certainly you'll see me. As often as I can . . . Did you think I wouldn't come to visit you, Uncle Willie?

WILLIE   Well, you know . . . People don't go out to New Jersey unless they have to.

BEN   Uncle Willie, I'll be there every week. *With* the *Variety.* I'll even bring Helen and the kids.

WILLIE   *Don't bring the kids!* Why do you think I'm going to the home for?

BEN   You know, this is the first moment since I've known you, that you've treated me like a nephew and not an agent. It's like a whole new relationship.

WILLIE   I hope this one works out better than the other one.

BEN   I've been waiting for this for fifteen years. You just wouldn't ever let me get close, Uncle Willie.

WILLIE   If you kiss me, I call off the whole thing.

BEN   No kiss, I promise . . . Now there's just one other thing I'd like you to do for me.

WILLIE   With my luck it's a benefit.

BEN   In a way it is a benefit. But not for any organization. It's for another human being.

WILLIE   What are you talking about?

BEN   Al Lewis wants to come and see you.

WILLIE   If you wanted to kill me, why didn't you bring the cigars?

BEN   He's been heartsick ever since this happened.

WILLIE   What do you think I've been? What is this, the mumps?

BEN   You know what I mean . . . He calls me twice a day to see how you are. He's worried to death.

WILLIE   Tonight tell him I'm worse.

BEN   He's not well himself, Willie. He's got diabetes, hardening of the arteries, his eyes are getting very bad . . .

WILLIE   He sees good enough to spit in my face.

BEN   He's lost seven pounds since you were in the hospital. Who do you think's been sending all the candy and flowers every day? He keeps signing other people's names because he knows otherwise you'd throw them out.

WILLIE   They're *his* flowers? Throw 'em out.

BEN   Uncle Willie, I've never asked you to do a personal favor for me as long as I've known you. But this is important—for me, and for you, for Al Lewis. He won't even stay. He just wants to come up and say hello . . .

WILLIE Hello, heh?

BEN That's all.

WILLIE And if he pokes me in the chest with the finger, I'm a dead man. That's murder, you know.

BEN Come on, Willie. Give us all a break.

WILLIE Well, if he wants to come up, I won't stop him. But I can't promise a "hello." I may be taking a nap.

BEN *(starts toward the phone)* I knew I could count on you, Willie. He's going to be very happy.

(He picks up the phone.)

WILLIE You don't have to call him from here. Why should I pay sixty cents for him to come say hello?

BEN *(He dials "O.")* It's not going to cost you sixty cents. *(To the operator)* Hello. Would you tell the boy at the desk to send Mr. Lewis up to Mr. Clark's room, please? Thank you.

(He hangs up.)

WILLIE *(as near to shouting as he can get)* You mean he's here now in the hotel?

BEN He's been with me all morning. I knew it would be all right.

WILLIE First you commit me to the Old Man's Home, bring that bastard here and *then* you ask me?

BEN *(all smiles)* I'm sorry. I apologize. Never speak to me again . . . But just promise you'll be decent to Al Lewis.

WILLIE I'll be wonderful to him. In my will, I'll leave him *you!*

(He starts to get out of bed.)

BEN What are you doing? You're not supposed to be out of bed.

WILLIE You think I'm going to give him the satisfaction of seeing me laying in bed like a sick person? I'm gonna sit in my chair and I'm gonna look healthier than he does.

(He tries weakly to get on his slippers.)

BEN The doctor said you're not to get out of bed for *anything*.

WILLIE Lewis coming to apologize to Clark is not anything. To me, this is worth another heart attack. Get my coat from the closet.

BEN *(starting for the closet)* All right, but just walk slowly, will you, please?

(He opens the closet.)

WILLIE And then I want you to move my chair all the way back. I want that son-of-a-bitch to have a long walk.

BEN *(takes out a bathrobe from the closet)* Here, put this on.

WILLIE Not the bathrobe, the jacket. The blue sports jacket. This is gonna be a *formal* apology.

BEN *(puts back the bathrobe and takes out the blue sports jacket)* He's not coming to apologize. He's just coming to say hello.

WILLIE If he doesn't apologize, I'll drop dead in the chair for spite. And you can tell him that.

(BEN helps him into the blue sports jacket over the pajamas.)

BEN Now I'm sorry I started in with this.

WILLIE   That's funny. Because now I'm starting to feel good. *(Buttons the jacket)* Push the chair back. All the way.

(BEN *picks up the chair and carries it to the far side of the room.*)

BEN   I thought I was bringing you two together.

WILLIE *(He shuffles over to the chair.* BEN *helps him to sit.)*   Put a pillow underneath. Make it two pillows. When I sit, I wanna look down on him.

(BEN *puts a pillow under* WILLIE.)

BEN   This is the last time. I'm never going to butt into your lives again.

WILLIE   The only thing that could have made today better is if it was raining. I would love to see him apologize dripping wet. *(And then come three knocks on the door: "Knock, knock, knock.")* Aha! This is it! . . . *This* was worth getting sick for! Come on, knock again. *(Points his finger in the air, his crowning moment.* AL *knocks again.) En-terrr!*

(BEN *crosses to the door and opens it.* AL LEWIS *timidly steps in, with his hat in his hand.* WILLIE *immediately drops his head to his side, closes his eye and snores, feigning a nap.*)

AL *(whispers)*   Oh, he's sleeping. I could come back later.

BEN *(also whispers)*   No, that's all right. He must be dozing. Come on in. (AL *steps in and* BEN *closes the door.)* Can I take your hat?

AL   No, I'd like to hold on to something, if you don't mind.

(BEN *crosses over to* WILLIE, *who is still dozing. He bends over and speaks softly in* WILLIE's *ear.*)

BEN   Uncle Willie. There's someone here to see you.

WILLIE *(opens his eyes, stirs)*   Heh? What?

BEN   Look who's here to see you, Uncle Willie.

WILLIE *(squints)*   I don't have my glasses. Who's that?

AL   It's me, Willie, Al . . . Al Lewis.

WILLIE *(squints harder)*   Al Lewis? You're so far away . . . Walk all the way over here. (AL *sheepishly makes the trek across the room with hat in hand. He squints again.)* Oh, *that* Al Lewis.

AL   I don't want to disturb you, Willie. I know you're resting.

WILLIE   That's all right. I was just reading my telegrams from Lucille Ball and Bob Hope.

AL   Oh, that's nice . . . *(Turns, looks at the vase)* Oh, look at the beautiful flowers.

WILLIE   I'm throwing them out. I don't like the smell. People send them to me every day with boxes of cheap candy. They mean well.

AL *(nods)*   They certainly do . . . Well, I just came up to see how you're doing. I don't want to take up your time. I just wanted to say hello . . . So "hello"—and goodbye.

(He starts to put on his hat to go.)

WILLIE   Wait a minute. You got a few minutes before my next nap. Sit down and talk for a while.

AL   You're sure it's okay?

WILLIE   I'm sure you got a lot more to say than just "hello" . . . Would you like some tea?

AL   I would love some.

WILLIE   Go in the kitchen and make it.

BEN   I've got a better idea. I'll go down and have the kitchen send up a tray. If I call room service it'll take forever.

(He starts for the door.)

WILLIE *(to* BEN*)*   You're going? You don't want to hear what Al has to say?

BEN   I don't think it's necessary. I'll be back in ten minutes. *(At the door)* It's good to see you, Mr. Lewis . . . It's good to see the *both* of you.

(He nods, then exits, closing the door. There is an awkward silence between the two men for a moment.)

AL *(finally)*   He's a nice boy.

WILLIE   He's the best . . . Not too bright, but a good boy.

AL *(nods)*   You've got everything you need here?

WILLIE   What could I need here?

AL   Some books? Some magazines?

WILLIE   No, I got plenty to do. I got all my fan mail to answer.

AL   You get fan mail?

WILLIE   Don't you?

AL   I don't even get jury duty.

WILLIE   Sure, plenty of people still remember . . . *(He coughs.)* Excuse me.

AL   You're sure it's all right for you to talk like this?

WILLIE   I'm not talking. I'm just answering. *You're* talking. *(There is a long pause.)* Why? Is there something special you wanted to talk about?

AL   Like what?

WILLIE   What do I know like what? How should I know what's on your mind? Do I know why you can't sleep at night?

AL   Who said I don't sleep at night! I sleep beautifully.

WILLIE   Funny, to me you look tired. A little troubled. Like a person who had something on his conscience, what do I know?

AL   I have nothing on my conscience.

WILLIE *(a pause)*   Are you sure you looked good?

AL   I have *nothing* on my conscience. The only thing I feel badly about is that you got sick.

WILLIE   Thank you. *I accept your apology!*

AL   What apology? Who apologized? I just said I'm sorry you got sick.

WILLIE   Who do you think *made* me sick?

AL   Who? *You* did, that's who! Not me. You yelled and screamed and carried on like a lunatic until you made yourself sick . . . and for that I'm sorry.

WILLIE   All right, as long as you're sorry for something.

AL   I'm also sorry that people are starving in India, but I am not going to apologize. I didn't do it.

WILLIE   I didn't accuse you of India. I'm just saying you're responsible for making me sick, and since you've come up here to apologize, I am gentleman enough to accept it.

AL   Don't be such a gentleman, because there's nothing to accept.

WILLIE   You're the one who came up here with your hat in your hand, not me.

AL   It's a twenty-five dollar hat, what was I gonna do, fold it up in my pocket?

WILLIE   If you didn't come to apologize, why did you send me the candy and flowers?

AL   I sent you candy and flowers?

WILLIE   Yes. Because it was on your conscience and *that's* why you couldn't sleep at night and *that's* why you came up here with your hat in your hand to apologize, only *this* time I'm not a gentleman any more and I *don't accept the apology!* How do you like that?

(AL *stares at* WILLIE.)

AL   I knew there was gonna be trouble when you said "Enter" instead of "Come in."

WILLIE   There's no trouble. The trouble is over. I got what I want and now I'm happy.

AL   What did you get? You got "no apology" from me, which you didn't accept.

WILLIE   I don't want to discuss it any more, I just had a heart attack.

(AL *stares at* WILLIE *silently.*)

AL *(calmly)*   You know something, Willie. I don't think we get along too good.

WILLIE   Well, listen, everybody has their ups and downs.

AL   In forty-three years, we had maybe one "up" . . . To tell you the truth, I can't take the "downs" any more.

WILLIE   To be honest with you, for the first time I feel a little tired myself. In a way this heart attack was good for me. I needed the rest.

AL   So what are you going to do now?

WILLIE   Well, my nephew made me two very good offers today.

AL   Is that right?

WILLIE   I think I'm gonna take the second one.

AL   Are you in any condition to work again?

WILLIE   Well, it wouldn't be too strenuous . . . Mostly take it easy, maybe do a show on Saturday night, something like that.

AL   Is that so? Where, in New York?

WILLIE   No, no. Out of town . . .

AL   Isn't that wonderful.

WILLIE   Well, you know me, I gotta keep busy . . . What's with you?

AL   Oh, I'm very happy. My daughter's having another baby. They're gonna need my room, and I don't want to be a burden on them. . . . So we talked it over, and I decided I'm gonna move to the Actors' Home in New Brunswick.

WILLIE *(He sinks back onto his pillow, his head falls over to one side, and he sighs deeply.)*   Ohh, God. I got the finger again.

AL   What's the matter? You all right? Why are you holding your chest? You got pains?

WILLIE   Not yet. But I'm expecting.

AL *(nervously)*   Can I get you anything? Should I call the doctor?

WILLIE   It wouldn't help.

AL   It wouldn't hurt.

(The realization that they slipped accidentally into an old vaudeville joke causes WILLIE *to smile.)*

WILLIE   "It wouldn't hurt" . . . How many times have we done that joke?

AL   It always worked . . . Even from you I just got a laugh.

WILLIE   You're a funny man, Al . . . You're a pain in the ass, but you're a funny man.

AL   You know what your trouble was, Willie? You always took the jokes too seriously. They were just jokes. We did comedy on the stage for forty-three years, I don't think you enjoyed it once.

WILLIE   If I was there to enjoy it, I would buy a ticket.

AL   Well, maybe now you can start enjoying it . . . If you're not too busy, maybe you'll come over one day to the Actors' Home and visit me.

WILLIE   You can count on it.

AL   I feel a lot better now that I've talked to you . . . Maybe you'd like to rest now, take a nap.

WILLIE   I think so . . . Keep talking to me, I'll fall asleep.

AL *(looks around)*   What's new in *Variety?*

WILLIE   Bernie Eisenstein died.

AL   Go on. Bernie Eisenstein? The house doctor at the Palace?

WILLIE   That was Sam Hesseltine. Bernie Eisenstein was "Ramona and Rodriguez."

AL   Jackie Aaronson was Ramona and Rodriguez. Bernie Eisenstein was the house doctor at the Palace. Sam Hesseltine was Sophie Tucker's agent.

WILLIE   Don't argue with me, I'm sick.

AL   I know. But why should I get sick too? *(The curtain starts to fall.* WILLIE *moans.)* Bernie Eisenstein was the house doctor when we played for the first time with Sophie Tucker, and that's when we met Sam Hesseltine . . . Jackie Aaronson wasn't Rodriguez yet . . . He was "DeMarco and Lopez" . . . Lopez died, and DeMarco went into real estate, so Jackie became Rodriguez . . .

(Curtain.)

(Curtain Call.)

AL   Don't you remember Big John McCafferey? The Irishman? He owned the Biltmore Theater in Pittsburgh? And the Adams Theater in Syracuse? Always wore a two-pound diamond ring on his finger? He was the one who used to take out Mary Donatto, the cute little Italian girl from the Follies. Well, she used to go with Abe Berkowitz who was then the booker for the Orpheum circuit and Big John hated his guts because of the time when Harry Richman . . .

Comments and Questions

Neil Simon is the most successful and prolific writer of light comedy in America today. Few, however, have taken Simon seriously. He writes by formula, his critics say, and besides, he only makes audiences laugh. His defenders reply that if tragedy requires belief in human beings as consequential (see Krutch's "The Tragic Fallacy," p. 1112), so does comedy, perhaps even more, for laughter is people believing. The conflict of Willie and Al is obviously exploited for its comic potential, but the play is not unmindful of the plight of the two aging vaudevillians, living in the past, reading the obituaries in *Variety*, and looking ahead to the Actors' Home in New Brunswick.

1. If *The Sunshine Boys* is clearly not a "serious" dramatic work in the manner of the other modern plays represented here, it is a well-made popular play that satisfies many of our expectations of good comedy. In "Some Prefatory Words on Comedy" (p. 1126), Louis Kronenberger notes several universal elements of the genre. Discuss the four quoted below as they apply to *The Sunshine Boys*: (a) ". . . comedy is concerned with human imperfection. . . ." (b) "Comedy is criticism . . . because it exposes human beings for what they are in contrast to what they profess to be." (c) ". . . most comedy is born of ignorance or false knowledge; is based on misunderstanding." (d) ". . . it will not be mere circumstance or coincidence, but qualities of character that block the way. Envy proves an obstruction, or arrogance; or a too great tendency to be suspicious or to take offense." To what extent, for example, does the play depend on the difference between what the characters are and what they profess to be? Is the humor of the play based on misunderstanding, or does it follow from qualities of character—envy, arrogance, and a too great tendency to take offense?

2. Are the amusing lines simply wisecracks imposed on the characters by the author, or do they fit the *individuals* who speak them? Consider Willie in particular.

3. Compare *The Sunshine Boys* and Molière's *The Physician in Spite of Himself* (p. 718). The plots are quite different, but what about the stage business in both plays? How much of the fun grows out of physical actions of the characters?

4. Comment on the overt irony of the title.

5. Humor has been the subject of many heavy treatises. Willie and Al know nothing about theory but much about the art of provoking laughter. Examine their specific observations on what is funny and what is not.

6. It is said that humor and pathos are close kin. Is there any pathos in the play?

Biography

No one can write a man's life but himself.
ROUSSEAU

Preliminaries

The Biographical Urge

The biographical urge is best illustrated by our daily habit of probing into the health, habits, and affairs of others. We ask many questions that we could summarize as one demand: "Bring me up to date on your biography." Askers frequently await eagerly their chance to be answerers. We have here, therefore, a pleasant arrangement through which we can partly satisfy our natural desire to talk about ourselves and to hear others talk about themselves. Perhaps the question of where idle talk about others (gossip) leaves off and serious talk about others (biography) begins is a matter of motivation. In any event, there is a great deal of entertaining talk, gossip or not, in the best biographies from earliest to latest times.

We want first of all and perhaps last of all to find out about ourselves, but in order to do this, we soon realize that we must find out as much as possible about others. We are essentially lonely. We live exclusively with ourselves, but only rarely do we like this arrangement of life. Much of our effort is expended in an attempt to live sociably—to break through to other persons. Yet the most sociable, outgoing persons collect in a lifetime not more than a few hundred acquaintances out of perhaps several billion persons theoretically available to them. Of the acquaintances, only a few become intimates. If, therefore, people wish any real quantitative extension of themselves, any considerable relief for their isolation, they cannot depend upon their limited sphere of social activity.

Individuals may, of course, sit out their lives contemplating their navels. They contemplate some form, or forms, of art to relieve their boredom with themselves and to remove some of the uncertainty about themselves. All arts, because they are communicative, are attacks on the loneliness of the individual. Literature makes the most direct attack, and biography pinpoints it.

"That's just a tale," we may say, and the teller may protest, "No, it's not. It really happened." We like what "really happened." We are real, and our first taste is to hear about real persons like or unlike ourselves. If they are like ourselves, we enjoy the recognition of the likeness; we feel greater confidence in what we may have only suspected from self-examination to be true. If they are unlike ourselves, we enjoy the strangeness of the differences; we are extended. After much pondering over the lives of others, we come to understand the force of John Donne's insistence on the oneness of man:

> No man is an Island, entire of itself; every man is a piece of the *Continent,* a part of the *main,* if a *Clod* be washed away by the *Sea, Europe* is the less, as well as if a *Promontory* were, as well as if a Manor of thy *friends* or of *thine own* were, any man's *death* diminishes *me,* because I am involved in *Mankind;* and therefore never send to know for whom the *bell* tolls; it tolls for *thee. (Devotions upon Emergent Occasions,* 1624, No. XVII.)

We are indeed involved in humankind, deeply and intricately involved; and if a death—any death—diminishes us, a life—any life—increases us. Biographical writings seek to suspend oblivion for certain individuals, and one has but to imagine a world without any life-records to realize how shrunken and parochial such a world would be.

The Importance of Facts

Biography, like science, begins with fact. It presents specifics about individuals and is not required to illustrate representative truth. It is concerned with heredity and environment, with ancestry, birth, education, marriage, escapades, failures, and triumphs. At one level, facts exclude biographers and make of them mere recorders. They must respect verified dates and occurrences and, if they use them, must set them down as they are. Here then is an important difference between nonfictional and fictional forms of literature: in nonfiction writers deal with facts but do not create them; in fiction, writers may create the facts with which they deal. It is possible to challenge a fictional fact on the ground that it does not jibe with comparable nonfictional facts. A biographical fact, once proved, is simply incontrovertible and is not subject to either belief or disbelief. It *is.*

Does the sort of interest one has in a narrative depend upon whether it is truth or fiction? Here is one way to test for an answer. Consider the following bare account:

> A family consisting of a father, mother, daughter, and son live together. The father, though fairly well off, neglects the family. The son is subject to mental disorders.

His sister, ten years his senior and apparently more normal, one day in a sudden fit of insanity kills her mother with a table-knife. The brother becomes his sister's guardian and cares for her, with no recurrence of his own malady, until his death thirty-eight years later. Toward the end of his life his sister's mental disturbances become more frequent and of longer duration. After the brother's death, the sister lives on for thirteen years without further mental troubles.

Does it make any difference whether we are here dealing with fact or fiction, with what really happened or with what has been made up? If the facts were invented, we would give the author a chance to make these facts probable. We would not care very much what names the characters were given but would care a great deal about the handling of what seems to be the big scene—the murder of the mother—and the explanation of how a man could be mad and then sane and a woman could be sane, then mad, then sane again. Although we know that sudden murders do occur and that temporary insanity is a common defense for such murders, we tend not to believe in them in fiction. Insanity itself is in general suspect as a fictional device. If there is method in the madness, we see that as super-shrewdness and accept it—at least in Hamlet—but insist that nothing important in a story shall hinge on an insane (irresponsible) action.

We can see the difference immediately if the facts, as stated, are true. If the father, mother, daughter, and son are real people, we want to know at once *who* they are—what are their names? Suppose the answer is that these people are Mr. and Mrs. John Doe and Mary and Charles Doe. Accounts of such persons might appear in a psychiatrist's casebook or perhaps in the records of the hearing for murder. Our interest would center chiefly in the queerness of the case, and the names, as in a fictional account, would matter less. If, however, these people are famous *for other reasons*, if instead of Mr. and Mrs. John Doe, the father and mother are Mr. and Mrs. John Lamb; the daughter, Mary Lamb; and the key figure, Charles Lamb, our interest gains a new perspective.

Biographers may seek a logical motivation for Mary Lamb's brutal action, but if they fail to find it, the fact remains, and they must accept it, just as we must. Herein lies the truth of the observation that fact *is* stranger than fiction. Fact is stranger than good fiction or good drama dares to be, for facts stubbornly remain even when their logic is not apparent. (See "The Apprenticeship of a Mass Murderer," p. 1041.)

What to Do with the Facts: Three Problems

Every life moves in an unbroken sequence from birth to death. Every action follows a previous action; every thought, a previous thought in uninterrupted series. Let us suppose that a man of considerable interest to the public had a life span of fifty-two years, or, deducting time out for sleep, 303,680 waking hours. Something went on during each of those hours; all were significant in making up the total account of this man. The ideal biographer writing the ideal biography should know those hours, all of them. Of course, the ideal biographer never does. If the subject is Shakespeare—who lived fifty-two years—this biographer has no problem of selection at all and can put down with three drops of ink—though a barrel may be used—all that is surely known of this man from Stratford. A hampering lack of facts, then, may be, and frequently is, one of the biographer's problems.

The second problem, a reverse of the first, is that too many facts may prove an embarrassment. Queen Victoria lived for eighty-two years, and there are probably more records available for any one year of her life than have been found for all of Shakespeare's fifty-two years. It is staggering to imagine the lofty mountain of facts already accumulated about Queen Elizabeth II. Of course, biographers are better off with abundance than with famine, but their problems as artists are greatly increased. The essence of art is selection, the removal of the superfluous so that a convincing portrait remains. All the selections that follow illustrate this point.

The third problem is an ethical one and exists whenever the facts are in adequate supply. It amounts to this: What shall be done with facts that may throw a bad light on an essentially good individual or a good light on an essentially evil individual? Suppose it could be determined—it seldom can—that a person is nine-tenths saint and one-tenth sinner. One biographer might make such a person all saint; another, with somewhat less justification, all scoundrel. The first biographer may have observed, as Somerset Maugham says, that "people turn away with dismay when candid biographers reveal the truth about famous persons." But the second biographer, the debunker, may also tilt the balance too far and produce false weight. We shall note with what skill Boswell, who idolized Samuel Johnson, handled the problem of keeping his great hero in perspective.

Facts Are Not Enough

If we regard facts as the bony structure of biography, we must next look for the flesh and blood. The facts about Charles and Mary Lamb, as given above, are momentarily arresting but tell only *what* happened. The questions of *when, where,* and *why* are not answered. More important, interpretive details are lacking, flesh for the bones. Let us look for a moment at a plain statement of fact: "Richard Rodgers wrote the music for 'Bali Ha'i' in five minutes." This, or something like it, was doubtless one of Lincoln Barnett's notes when he sat down to write a close-up of the composer Richard Rodgers. From the following anecdote, we may see how appropriate is the word *close-up*.

> To others who may labor for hours to evolve a usable phrase, the fluency with which music wells from Rodgers is profoundly discouraging. "He could write music to the telephone book," a friend once remarked. Where it may take Hammerstein two or three weeks to complete a single set of lyrics that satisfy his rigorous poetic standards, Rodgers often exudes his loveliest melodies in a matter of minutes. Asked to describe their methods of collaboration, Hammerstein once said: "I simply hand him a lyric and get out of the way." One evening a few weeks before *South Pacific* was due to enter rehearsal, several observers had an opportunity to witness this system of operation. Rodgers was dining with a few friends at the home of Joshua Logan, the director and playwright. Coffee had just been served when Hammerstein arrived, happily waving the completed lyrics to the final song that remained to be written for the show. It was "Bali Ha'i." Rodgers quickly scanned the typewritten verses. Then pushing his demitasse to one side, he took out a pencil, drew a staff on the

paper Hammerstein had given him, and without visible hesitation began writing down notes. Five minutes later he laid down his pencil. The melody for "Bali Ha'i," which a few weeks hence was to be whistled across the land, was done. Not a note or an accent had to be changed after those first few minutes of swift creation. (*Writing on Life: Sixteen Close-Ups,* New York, 1951, pp 293–294.)

What has happened to the plain fact? Obviously there are many more words in the anecdote: 11 for the plain fact and 240 for the anecdote. Of what use are these additional words? The fact was already clear; the extra words do not make it clearer. The anecdote does not seek out and illuminate a hidden meaning, for apparently there is no hidden meaning. Yet we certainly *feel* that the anecdote gave us a kind of pleasure that the plain statement did not. By discovering the source of this pleasure, we reveal a basic truth about all literature: *literature does not merely tell; it shows.* Although far removed from the actual experience, the reader participates in the recounting of the experience. In the anecdote, it is as though the author, operating a camera on a moving crane, had taken the first picture of the subject at a distance and then had moved steadily closer until the eye of the camera hovered over the composer's shoulder as he wrote his music. The plain fact *told* us something: the anecdote *showed* us something.

The Anecdote

What it is   An anecdote, as we have seen, is a moment of biography, the shortest form of a complete narrative. In it something of interest happens. "I was at a lawn party and shook hands with the host, who said, 'I'm glad to see you.' " Is this an anecdote? Something happens, but is it interesting? It could be, of course, but much depends on which lawn and which host. "I was at a party on the White House lawn and shook hands with the President, who said, 'I'm glad to see you.' " Further details would *show* us this meeting with the President and the result would be a satisfactory anecdote.

Its uses   An anecdote may be told for its own sake, for one of its requirements is the ability to stand on its own merits. Nevertheless, it normally is used to illustrate some sort of generalization, to *show* what the generalization means. Anecdotes, even when they may not be true, make broad statements memorable. Generalization: George Washington was always truthful. Anecdote: the cherry tree episode. Generalization: Richard Rodgers is a rapid composer. Anecdote: the composition of "Bali Ha'i." Generalization: Memory softens past agonies. Anecdote: "Episode near Munich" (see p. 988).

Generalizations such as those just cited are subject to comment and perhaps to argument. Biographical sketches frequently resemble the essay in that they support generalizations that invite discussion and, in some instances, argument. "The Oxford Method" (p. 990) does more than report the meeting between a student and an Oxford tutor. Many of the sketches that follow are really dramatized essays. They are related, on the one hand, to short stories and, on the other, to essays. As essays, they provide some excellent topics for discussion, written or oral.

Quotations   A decided characteristic of biographical writing is the frequent use of direct quotation. Writers of autobiography in particular are prone to tell their experiences through dialogue. Rather than tell their readers about the experience, they prefer to show it to them, to let them hear the actual words that were spoken. (Why does the autobiographer feel a greater freedom in the use of dialogue than a biographer may feel?) To bring the reader into the presence of people talking is a technique almost as important to the autobiographer as to the novelist or the writer of short stories. Direct quotations can often, for example, add authority or credibility to a point, just as they can provide dramatic interest and color.

Allusion   An allusion is a passing or casual reference. In "The Oxford Method," Logan Pearsall Smith refers in passing to "Socratic irony" and does not elaborate because he assumes that the reader knows what the phrase means. We mention allusion here, not because it is a distinctive feature of biographical writing (it is not), but because readers can find it baffling. The passing references in the anecdotal selections are few and not very difficult; you can prepare for your later reading by examining these allusions and learning to solve them.

Its technique

    1. Point of view. The position from which an experience is seen is the point of view. All the following anecdotes are autobiographical with the exception of those taken from Boswell's *Life of Johnson,* and one might assume that autobiography would, by definition, have a fixed point of view. When authors are writing about themselves, it is from their point of view that the incidents are told. This statement is true but not the whole truth. Rousseau indicates the difficulty in separating fact from fiction. Autobiographers are frequently older individuals trying to recapture experiences of their youth. If our bodies completely change every seven years, as we are told they do, then the older individual is really trying to recover an experience that happened to someone else. The older individual may adopt any one of numerous possible points of view. You may see what the possibilities are by comparing "A Cub Pilot's Experience" (p. 1009) and "Christmas" (p. 1002).

    2. Timing. In conversation, good timing is the ability to come to the point before someone tells you to. In literature, it is the ability to come to the point before the readers wish they could tell the writer to. When we say that literary artists try to measure out exactly the right number of words, in the right sequence, to achieve their purpose, we are talking about timing. It is clear that the anecdote about the composition of "Bali Ha'i" shows resistance to some tempting side excursions. For example, the author might have said more about Oscar Hammerstein II or Joshua Logan, both important individuals in the theater. He might have described Logan's home, the other guests, or even the dinner. By resisting such temptations, the author achieved effective timing.

    3. Fusion of fact and form. Facts are the basis of all selections in this section, but as we have said before, facts are not enough. Some facts, of course, are unalterable and can be put down in one way only. Most of the information that we carry about in our heads in the form of memory is definitely alterable; that is, it may be put down in many different ways, and *how* it is put down will largely determine its meaning. The basic question for all writers is this: how can I make my material mean to the reader what it means to me? Three closely related processes are involved in the answer to this question: *selection, arrangement,* and *choice of words.* It is through these processes that fact and form are blended or fused. Once the selecting, arranging, and wording have been settled, the result is unique. For better or for worse, the wedding is permanent. This does not mean that all marriages between What and How were made in heaven. It does mean that, so long as authors do not literally destroy what they have written or revise it into another union, What and How are dependent on each other. For purposes of analysis, however, we may talk about content and form separately even though we know that they are really one.

Jean Jacques Rousseau   (1712–1778)
The Principle of Autobiography*

No one can write a man's life but himself. The character of his inner being, his real life, is known only to himself; but, in writing it, he disguises it; under the name of his life, he makes an apology; he shows himself as he wishes to be seen, but not at all as he is. The sincerest persons are truthful at most in what they say, but they lie by their reticences, and that of which they say nothing so changes that which they pretend to confess, that in uttering only a part of the truth they say nothing. I put Montaigne at the head of these falsely-sincere persons who wish to deceive in telling the truth. He shows himself with his faults, but he gives himself none but amiable ones; there is no man who has not odious ones. Montaigne paints his likeness, but it is a profile. Who knows whether some scar on the cheek, or an eye put out, on the side which he conceals from us, would not have totally changed the physiognomy? . . .

If I wish to produce a work written with care, like the others, I shall not paint, I shall rouge myself. It is with my portrait that I am here concerned, and not with a book. I am going to work, so to speak, in the darkroom; there is no other art necessary than to follow exactly the traits which I see marked. I form my resolution then about the style as about the things. I shall not try at all to render it uniform; I shall write always that which comes to me, I shall change it, without scruple, according to my humour; I shall speak of everything as I feel it, as I see it, without care, without constraint, without being embarrassed by the medley. In yielding myself at once to the memory of the impression received and to the present sentiment, I shall doubly paint the state of my soul, namely, at the moment when the event happened to me and the moment when I describe it; my style,

*From a rough draft of the introduction to Rousseau's *Confessions,* as quoted by Sainte-Beuve in his essay "Rousseau," first published in 1851.

unequal and natural, sometimes rapid and sometimes diffuse, sometimes wise and sometimes foolish, sometimes grave and sometimes gay, will itself make a part of my history.
Finally, whatever may be the way in which this book may be written, it will be always, by
its object, a book precious for philosophers; it is, I repeat, an illustrative piece for the
study of the human heart, and it is the only one that exists.

Comments and Questions

Rousseau's fierce pride in writing with utmost frankness about himself is evident. The
difficulty of writing in this manner is equally evident.

1. Why does Rousseau speculate that Montaigne, A French essayist, is a "falsely-
sincere" person? (See the next two selections.) How does Rousseau define "sincere"? What
is basic to his conception of honest self-portrayal? What, probably, would his comment be
on Floyd Dell's "Christmas" (p. 1002)?

2. What is meant to be conveyed by the words "rouge myself"? And the clause: "I
shall doubly paint the state of my soul"?

3. Rousseau thought his *Confessions* would always be valuable to philosophers. Why?

Michel Eyquem Sieur de Montaigne
(1533-1592)
The Author to the Reader

It has been said that Montaigne's *Essays* contain his biography. This observation is
true enough if one is content with a psychological portrait, for this inventor of the informal essay constantly analyzes himself, sometimes with genuine, sometimes with
mock modesty. We offer here only glimpses of the man Rousseau regarded as "falsely-
sincere" (see p. 983).

Reader thou hast here an honest book; it doth at the outset forewarn thee that, in
contriving the same, I have proposed to myself no other than a domestic and private end:
I have had no consideration at all either to thy service or to my glory. My powers are not
capable of any such design. I have dedicated it to the particular commodity of my kinsfolk
and friends, so that, having lost me (which they must do shortly), they may therein recover
some traits of my conditions and humors, and by that means preserve more whole, and
more life-like, the knowledge they had of me. Had my intention been to seek the world's
favor, I should surely have adorned myself with borrowed beauties: I desire therein to be
viewed as I appear in mine own genuine, simple, and ordinary manner, without study and
artifice: for it is myself I paint. My defects are therein to be read to the life, and my
imperfections and my natural form, so far as public reverence hath permitted me. If I had

lived among those nations, which (they say) yet dwell under the sweet liberty of nature's primitive laws, I assure thee I would most willingly have painted myself quite fully and quite naked. Thus, reader, myself am the matter of my book: there's no reason thou shouldst employ thy leisure about so frivolous and vain a subject. Therefore, farewell.

Michel Eyquem Sieur de Montaigne
(1533-1592)
From Of the Education of Children

I never yet saw that father, but let his son be never so decrepit or deformed, would not, notwithstanding, own him: not, nevertheless, if he were not totally besotted, and blinded with his paternal affection, that he did not well enough discern his defects: but that with all defaults, he was still his. Just so, I see better than any other, that all I write here are but the idle reveries of a man that has only nibbled upon the outward crust of sciences in his nonage, and only retained a general and formless image of them; who has got a little snatch of everything, and nothing of the whole, *à la Françoise*. For I know, in general, that there is such a thing as physic, as jurisprudence: four parts in mathematics, and roughly, what all these aim and point at; and peradventure, I yet know farther, what sciences in general pretend unto, in order to the service of our life: but to dive farther than that, and to have cudgelled my brains in the study of Aristotle, the monarch of all modern learning, or particularly addicted myself to any one science, I have never done it; neither is there any one art of which I am able to draw the first lineaments and dead color; insomuch that there is not a boy of the lowest form in a school, that may not pretend to be wiser than I, who am not able to examine him in his first lesson, which, if I am at any time forced upon, I am necessitated, in my own defense, to ask him, unaptly enough, some universal questions, such as may serve to try his natural understanding; a lesson as strange and unknown to him, as his is to me.

I never seriously settled myself to the reading any book of solid learning but Plutarch and Seneca; and there, like the Danaides, I eternally fill, and it as constantly runs out; something of which drops upon this paper, but little or nothing stays with me. History is my particular game as to matter of reading, or else poetry, for which I have particular kindness and esteem: for, as Cleanthes said, as the voice, forced through the narrow passage of a trumpet, comes out more forcible and shrill; so methinks, a sentence pressed within the harmony of verse, darts out more briskly upon the understanding, and strikes my ear and apprehension with a smarter and more pleasing effect. As to the natural parts I have, of which this is the essay, I find them to bow under the burden; my fancy and judgment do but grope in the dark, tripping and stumbling in the way, and when I have gone as far as I can, I am in no degree satisfied; I discover still a new and greater extent of land before me, with a troubled and imperfect sight and wrapped up in clouds, that I am not able to penetrate. And taking upon me to write indifferently of whatever comes into my head, and therein making use of nothing but my own proper and natural means, if it befall me, as oft-times it does, accidentally to meet in any good author, the same heads and commonplaces upon which I have attempted to write (as I did but just now in Plutarch's "Discourse of the Force of Imagination"), to see myself so weak and so forlorn, so heavy and so flat, in comparison of those better writers, I at once pity or despise myself. Yet do I please myself with this, that my opinions have often the honor and good fortune to jump with theirs, and that I go in the same path, though at a very great distance, and can say, "Ah, that is so." I am farther satisfied to find, that I have a quality, which every one is not blessed withal, which is, to discern the vast difference betwixt them and me; and notwithstanding all that, suffer my own inventions, low and feeble as they are, to run on in their career, without mending or plastering up the defects that this comparison has laid open to my own view. And, in plain truth, a man had need of a good strong back to keep pace with these people. The indiscreet scribblers of our times, who, amongst their laborious nothings, insert whole sections and pages out of ancient authors, with a design, by that means, to illustrate their own writings, do quite contrary; for this infinite dissimilitude of ornaments renders the complexion of their own compositions so sallow and deformed, that they lose much more than they get. . . .

Questions

1. What does Montaigne mean by the phrases "universal questions" and "natural understanding"? Consider the sort of questions children ask and the bases for such questions.

2. How appropriate is the simile "like the Danaides"? (Any good dictionary will tell you the plight of Danaus's daughters.)

3. Discuss Montaigne's metaphor describing the effect of poetry upon him. Does he define well what good poetry ought to do?

W. Somerset Maugham (1874-1965)
Brandy

My second adventure was droll. I was being driven round the country by a woman who had been doing a great deal, as had a few charitable English and American women, to alleviate the lot of the unfortunate refugees, and latish in the afternoon I remarked that I must think about getting a room in some hotel for the night.

"You needn't bother about that," she said. "I have some distant cousins in this part of the country who'll be glad to put you up. They're very simple provincial people, but they're quite nice, and they'll give you a good dinner."

"That's very kind of them," I said.

She did not volunteer their name, and it did not occur to me to ask it. I gathered from what she said that they were poor relations who lived very modestly, so I was surprised when at nightfall we drove into a town and stopped at a house that in the darkness seemed quite imposing. We were received by a shortish, fat man with a red, homely face.

He was dressed in dark, somewhat ill-fitting clothes and looked the typical French bourgeois. He showed me to a warm and comfortably furnished room, and I was glad to see that there was a bathroom. He told me that dinner was at half past seven. I took a bath and, as I was very tired, had a nap. At the appointed hour I went downstairs and found my way to a living room in which a bright fire of logs was blazing. My host was sitting there and he offered me a glass of sherry. I sank into a large armchair.

5   "Did you find a bottle of brandy in your room?" he asked me.

"I didn't look," I said.

"I always keep a bottle of brandy in every bedroom in the house, even the children's rooms. They never touch it, but I like to know it's there."

I thought this an odd notion, but said nothing. Presently my driver of the day came in with a thin, dark woman to whom I was introduced. She was my host's sister, but I did not catch her name. I gathered from the conversation that my host was a bachelor and that she was staying with him with her two daughters, her husband being mobilized, for the duration of the war. We went in to dinner and found waiting for us two girls of perhaps fourteen and fifteen with a prim governess. We were waited on by an ancient butler and a maid. My host said: "I've opened for you my last magnum of claret, a Chateau Larose, 1874."

I had never seen a magnum of claret before, and I was impressed. It was delicious. For a poor relation I thought my host was doing very well. The food was excellent, real French country cooking, copious, slightly on the heavy side perhaps, and very rich, but extremely succulent. One dish was so good that I was forced to remark on it.

"I'm glad you like that," said my host, "Everything in this house is cooked in brandy."

I began to think it was a very strange house indeed, and I wished I knew who on earth this hospitable person was. We finished dinner and had coffee. Then the butler brought some large glasses and an immense bottle of brandy. I had done myself very well with the claret, I was among strangers, and thought it wise not to take any more alcohol, so when it was offered to me I refused.

"What," cried my host, throwing himself back in his chair, "have you come to spend the night in the house of Martell and you refuse a glass of brandy?"

I had been dining in the house of the greatest brandy merchant in the world.

Comments and Questions

In the telling of this little incident, we know from almost the beginning that the author is deliberately creating mild suspense. Nearly the entire interest of the experience depends on withholding, until the right moment, a name that he could have given to us at once. *Timing* here is all important. We are treated to a series of small surprises: the "simple provincial people" live in a house that "seemed quite imposing"; brandy is everywhere, even in "the children's rooms"; governess, butler, maid, magnum of claret, fine food—all are part of the careful build-up. At precisely the right moment the point of the incident is made clear.

1. If this were a fictional episode, would the author have told it the same way? See "Preliminaries" in the fiction division.

2. Is one's interest in this episode dependent on the importance of the person whose name is revealed at the end? If one is not impressed by brandy merchants, would that fact reduce one's interest in the episode? Is any person sufficiently significant who for any reason qualifies as "greatest . . . in the world"? Discuss.

Leo Rosten (1908–   )
Episode near Munich: A Lost Address

"The things that are hardest to bear are sweetest to remember," wrote Seneca. What nonsense. How kindly memory represses the anguished moments of the past. Life would be unbearable were we unable to forget.

The other night, some friends were talking about the war (I mean the big war, called II), and suddenly, with the sharpness of a knife thrust, I remembered something pushed into the cellars of my mind long ago. It is not easy for me to write about it even now.

It was 1945, just after the Nazis collapsed. I was on a special mission. We were driving from Augsburg to Munich—"Tex," my GI driver; Major O'Neill; and myself, a civilian in officer's uniform, with lofty colonel rank.

It had been raining for two days—a harsh, very cold rain. We swept around a wide curve in the road, and I saw a figure far ahead, marching toward us, head down, shoulders hunched. It wore no hat, no coat. As we came closer, I saw it was a young man. He was soaking wet. The rain dripped off his hair. His shirt stuck to his wet skin. A rucksack was half slung across his back.

5   I had seen hundreds of people plodding down the roads of France and Germany this way: alone, in groups, silent, beaten, stunned. But there was a curious jauntiness in this boy's pace. I told Tex to stop.

The boy slowed down warily, but when he spotted the U.S. Army star on our car, his face lit up. "Hollo, *Amerikaner!*"

"Hello. *Wie weit ist München?*" I asked.

"München? Ja. Oh—thirty kilometers, sir." He spoke in Yiddish. *"Aber,* I am no German! No! Look." He was jabbing at a red-cloth triangle sewed onto his shirt: it was the badge Jews had been forced to wear. He rolled up a wet sleeve: I saw blue numbers tattooed on his forearm.

"Get in," I told the boy. He clambered in next to Tex.

"Which camp were you in?"

"Buchenwald."

"Where are you going?"

He pointed to the West.

"Where?"

He shrugged. "To France, maybe. Holland. Anywhere. Then, I hope, America. Everyone wants to go to America. I have a relative there! An aunt. My mother's sister. I never saw her, you understand, because she left Poland before I was born, but my mother got letters from her before the war . . . I would like to get word to my aunt. About me. Being alive, I mean. She's the only member of our family still alive. I just want her to know. That's all. If someone was glad I survived—well, that would make a difference."

"What's he saying?" O'Neill asked me. I told him.

He fumbled for a cigarette. O'Neill was the toughest-looking Irishman you ever saw, and he wore a shoulder holster with a fearful .45 bulging in it. The pistol had given me great comfort until I learned that "Buzz," a PR joker, was afraid to load it. ("Scares hell out of you *un*-loaded, right?" He certainly was right.)

"Your aunt," I said to the boy. "What's her name?"

"I don't know. She married."

"Do you know her address?"

"Her address." The boy sighed. "That's the trouble. I don't remember. I had her whole name and address in a little notebook. But when they took us to Buchenwald they lined us all up in the snow and told us to undress—naked, absolutely naked. I had that little notebook in my pocket, with my aunt's name and address in it, and I took the notebook out of my pocket as I took all my clothes off, but one of the Nazi guards grabbed the book out of my hands and threw it on the pile of other things. I asked him if he wouldn't please let me keep just one page. He hit me with his gun and knocked me down. Then all the men were herded into a room; they tatooed numbers on our arms."

"What's he saying?" O'Neill asked.

I told him.

"Oh, Jesus."

"I never really knew my *uncle's* name," the boy said. "I just figured it was in the notebook. . . . And the address—how many times, in the camp, I tried to remember it! But all I could bring back was that it was in New York, and the street was a number, and it had four numbers. Every night, before I'd fall asleep, I tried to bring that address back to my mind. . . . All I want is for my aunt to know. It's nice to think one person in the world is glad I got out alive. . . ."

"Isn't there any part of the address you remember?"

He frowned. "I think the street was Two—and the numbers began one eight. That's all I could remember."

I did not know what to say. I asked, "Did you report this to the Americans?"

"Oh, yes. The Displaced Persons authorities, the Red Cross—they were all nice. They filled out forms. . . . But what could they do? What can anyone do?"

We gave him a poncho, some soap, chocolate, K rations, and cigarettes. The boy made a half-hearted gesture of refusal, but O'Neill told him not to be a damned fool. The boy stuffed the things into his rucksack. "The cigarettes are very valuable," he said. "I can trade them." He slipped the poncho over his head and burst into a grin. "This is wonderful!"

I wrote my name and APO number on a slip of paper. "Look, if you ever do remember any more—about your aunt or uncle's address—write me. Or ask one of our soldiers. They'll do it."

"If I could only remember," he said.

He got out of the car and started down the road to the West. Once he turned to wave to us, and I saw that he was wolfing the chocolate.

"Goddamn it, Parks!" O'Neill suddenly shouted at Tex. "What the hell you waiting for? Get the lead out of your ass! Move it! *Move!*"

Soon we splashed through some miserable village, and O'Neill stuck his head out of the window and kept yelling, "*Schwein!* Sonsabitches! Dirty, rotten murderers! Murderers, mur-der-ers!"

In Munich we got drunk quite quickly. All Buzz O'Neill did was curse and shout obscenities I can hear even now.

Comments and Questions

There are many aphorisms by poets great and obscure on the subject of memory. Examples:

> No greater grief than to remember days
> Of joy, when misery is at hand.
>   *Dante*

> Sorrows remembered sweeten present joy.
> *Robert Pollok*

Rosten says that Seneca's generalization is nonsense, then narrates an anecdote to prove his point. Is this an instance in which the exception (Rosten's experience) tests the rule (Seneca's observation)? Have you endured something in the past that time has mellowed and made palatable?

1. What one word is the key to this episode?

2. This one word has connotations for Rosten and particularly for Major O'Neill. What are the connotations and how do they account for the Major's berserk behavior?

Logan Pearsall Smith (1865–1946)
The Oxford Method

The Oxford school of *Litterae humaniores*—or "Greats" as it is called—seems to my mature judgment the best scheme of education that I have ever heard of. It is based upon an accurate knowledge of Greek and Latin texts, especially the texts of Plato and Aristotle and Thucydides and Tacitus, and the subjects studied in it are the eternal problems of thought, of conduct, and of social organization. These are discussed, not by means of contemporary catchwords, but by translating them back into another world and another language. Nor could anything be more profitable from the pupil's point of view than the way in which this scheme of education was carried on. The student would prepare a paper on some special subject, and go with it, generally alone, and read it to his tutor, who would then discuss it and criticize it at length; or a group of two or three would meet in the tutor's room for a kind of Socratic discussion of some special point. These discussions were carried on much in the spirit of the Socratic dialogues; and the Socratic irony and assumed ignorance of the instructors, their deferential questions, as if the pupil were the teacher and they the learners, was a method which I found it hard at first to understand.

I remember, for instance, in reading a paper to Nettleship, I mentioned the distinction between form and matter. "Excuse me for interrupting you," Nettleship said, "but this distinction you make, though it is no doubt most important, is one that I find a little difficult to grasp. If it is not troubling you too much, it would be a real kindness if you would try to explain it to me."

"Oh, it's quite simple," I answered patronizingly. "There's the idea, say, in a poem, and there's the way in which it is expressed."

Nettleship still seemed puzzled. "Could you give me an instance?" he pleaded.

5   "Oh, nothing easier." I answered. "Take the lines, for instance, when Lovelace says,

> I could not love thee, Dear, so much,
> Loved I not Honour more.[1]

Now he might have said, 'I couldn't be nearly so fond of you, my dear, if I didn't care still

---

[1] See p. 450 for the poem.

more for my reputation.' The form, you see, is very different in both these sentences, but the subject of them—what they mean—is exactly the same."

Nettleship seemed greatly discouraged.

"I'm afraid," he said, "I can't see that the meaning of the two sentences is the same. I'm afraid I'm very stupid; but to me they seem to say quite different things."

He was, I thought, curiously stupid; but in my patient attempt to make my meaning clearer to him a dim suspicion began to waken in me that perhaps it was not Nettleship but myself who was playing the part of the fool in this dialogue.

Comments and Questions

1. How is the method of this anecdote similar to the method of "Brandy"? How is it different?

2. We are told that the Oxford method involves "a kind of Socratic discussion" between the student and the tutor, and then we are shown such a discussion. On the basis of what you find in the anecdote, how would you define a Socratic discussion?

3. What possible advantage does this Oxford method have over the teaching methods practiced in American universities? What advantage do you see in approaching "the eternal problems of thought, of conduct, and of social organization" through the works of Greek philosophers and Greek and Roman historians?

4. The young scholar and the tutor discuss the relation of form and matter. Show how their observations throw light on what has been said about this problem in "Preliminaries" in the biography division (see pp. 976 ff.).

5. How well does the young scholar succeed in his prose paraphrase of the lines from Lovelace? What is the intent of his tutor's questions? What pertinence does the discussion have to the study of poetry? Compare "Preliminaries" in the poetry division (pp. 296 ff.). If form and substance in poetry are inseparable, can a poem be paraphrased? Discuss.

James Boswell   (1740–1795)
Passages from *The Life of Johnson*

Sufficiently Uncouth

He (Dr. Johnson) received me very courteously; but, it must be confessed, that his apartment, and furniture, and morning dress, were sufficiently uncouth. His brown suit of clothes looked very rusty: he had on a little old shrivelled unpowdered wig, which was too small for his head; his shirtneck and knees of his breeches were loose; his black worsted stockings ill drawn up; and he had a pair of unbuckled shoes by way of slippers. But all these slovenly particularities were forgotten the moment that he began to talk.

I Mind My Belly Very Studiously

At supper this night he talked of good eating with uncommon satisfaction. "Some people (said he), have a foolish way of not minding, or pretending not to mind, what they eat. For my part, I mind my belly very studiously, and very carefully; for I look upon it, that he who does not mind his belly, will hardly mind anything else." He now appeared to me *Jean Bull philosophe,* and he was for the moment, not only serious but vehement. Yet I have heard him, upon other occasions, talk with great contempt of people who were anxious to gratify their palates; and the 206th number of his *Rambler* is a masterly essay against gulosity. His practice, indeed, I must acknowledge, may be considered as casting the balance of his different opinions upon this subject; for I never knew any man who relished good eating more than he did. When at table, he was totally absorbed in the business of the moment; his looks seemed riveted to his plate; nor would he, unless when in very high company, say one word, or even pay the least attention to what was said by others, till he had satisfied his appetite: which was so fierce, and indulged with such intenseness, that while in the act of eating, the veins of his forehead swelled, and generally a strong perspiration was visible. To those whose sensations were delicate, this could not but be disgusting; and it was doubtless not very suitable to the character of a philosopher, who should be distinguished by self-command. But it must be owned, that Johnson, though he could be rigidly *abstemious,* was not a *temperate* man either in eating or drinking. He could refrain, but he could not use moderately. He told me, that he had fasted two days without inconvenience, and that he had never been hungry but once. They who beheld with wonder how much he ate upon all occasions, when his dinner was to his taste, could not easily conceive what he must have meant by hunger.

Comments and Questions

1. Why does Boswell refer to Johnson as *Jean Bull philosophe?* Since this is simply the French for *John Bull as philosopher,* why did Boswell choose the French form? Review the subject of discussion, food, and you will see why. Context here would be all that could explain this allusion.

2. Does this excerpt sound as though it came from a journal? Explain.

A Good-Humoured Fellow

As a curious instance how little a man knows, or wishes to know his own character in the world, or, rather as a convincing proof that Johnson's roughness was only external; and did not proceed from his heart, I insert the following dialogue. JOHNSON. "It is wonderful, Sir, how rare a quality good humour is in life. We meet with very few good-humoured men." I mentioned four of our friends, none of whom he would allow to be good-humored. One was *acid,* another was *muddy,* and to the others he had objections which have escaped me. Then, shaking his head and stretching himself at ease in the coach, and smiling with much complacency, he turned to me and said, "I look upon *myself* as a good-humoured fellow." The epithet *fellow,* applied to the great Lexicographer, the stately Moralist, the Masterly Critic, as if he had been *Sam* Johnson, a mere pleasant companion, was highly diverting; and this light notion of himself struck me with wonder. I answered, also smiling, "No, no, Sir; that will *not* do. You are good-natured, but not good-humoured: you are irascible. You have not patience with folly and absurdity. I believe you would pardon them, if there were time to deprecate your vengeance; but punishment follows so quick after sentence, that they cannot escape."

Vinous Flights

Johnson and I supped this evening at the Crown and Anchor tavern, in company with Sir Joshua Reynolds, Mr. Langton, Mr. Nairne, now one of the Scotch Judges, with the title of Lord Dunsinan, and my very worthy friend, Sir William Forbes, or Pitsligo.

We discussed the question, whether drinking improved conversation and benevolence. "No, Sir, before dinner men meet with great inequality of understanding; and those who are conscious of their inferiority have the modesty not to talk. When they have drunk wine, every man feels himself happy, and loses that modesty, and grows impudent and vociferous; but he is not improved: he is only not sensible of his defects." Sir Joshua said the Doctor was talking of the effects of excess in wine; but that a moderate glass enlivened the mind, by giving a proper circulation to the blood. "I am, (said he,) in very good spirits, when I get up in the morning. By dinner-time I am exhausted; wine puts me into the same state as when I got up: and I am sure that moderate drinking makes people talk better." JOHNSON. "No, Sir; wine gives not light, gay, ideal hilarity; but tumultuous, noisy, clamorous merriment. I have heard none of those drunken,—nay, drunken is a coarse word,—none of those *vinous* flights." SIR JOSHUA. "Because you have sat by, quite sober, and felt an envy of the happiness of those who were drinking." JOHNSON. "Perhaps, contempt.—And, Sir, it is not necessary to be drunk one's self, to relish the wit of drunkenness. Do we not judge of the drunken wit of the dialogue between Iago and Cassio, the most excellent of its kind, when we are quite sober? Wit is wit, by whatever means it is produced; and, if good, will appear so at all times. I admit that the spirits are raised by drinking, as by the common participation of any pleasure: cockfighting, or bearbaiting, will raise the spirits of a company, as drinking does, though surely they will not improve conversation. I also admit, that there are some sluggish men who are improved by drinking; as there are fruits which are not good till they are rotten. There are such men, but they are medlars. I indeed allow that there have been a few men of talents who were improved by drinking; but I maintain that I am right about the effects of drinking in general: and let it be considered, that there is no position, however false in its universality, which is not true of some particular man."

Questions

From the context, can you guess what *medlars* are? (If the clause "There are such men" refers to the statement "There are some sluggish men who are improved by drinking," then to what statement does the word *medlars* refer?)

A Desire of Knowledge

On Saturday, July 30, Dr. Johnson and I took a sculler at the Temple stairs, and set out for Greenwich. I asked him if he really thought a knowledge of the Greek and Latin languages an essential requisite to a good education. JOHNSON. "Most certainly, Sir; for those who know them have a very great advantage over those who do not. Nay, Sir, it is wonderful what a difference learning makes upon people even in the common intercourse of life, which does not appear to be much connected with it." "And yet, (said I) people go through the world very well, and carry on the business of life to good advantage, without learning." JOHNSON. "Why, Sir, that may be true in cases where learning cannot possibly be of use; for instance, this boy rows us as well without learning, as if he could sing the song of Orpheus to the Argonauts, who were the first sailors." He then called to the boy. "What would you give, my lad, to know about the Argonauts?" "Sir, (said the boy) I would give what I have." Johnson was much pleased with his answer, and we gave him a double fare.

Dr. Johnson then turning to me, "Sir (said he) a desire of knowledge is the natural feeling of mankind; and every human being, whose mind is not debauched, will be willing to give all that he has, to get knowledge."

Comments and Questions

1. Allusions that refer to Greek or Roman culture are called *classical*. There are classical allusions in two of the preceding selections. In which ones?

2. Classical allusions normally disturb and sometimes baffle modern readers. Often, however, references to myth, as here in the naming of Orpheus and the Argonauts, are sufficiently self-explanatory. For the plain sense of this passage, it is enough to know what Johnson tells: that Orpheus was a singer and the Argonauts the first sailors. But, as we have said before, allusions are intended to light up the text. Johnson and Boswell on the Thames river, far from the land and age of myth, take from that remote time a reference appropriate to their conversation. Two centuries later, we listen to their talk but understand it fully only if we understand the casual references. Look up *Orpheus* and *Argonauts* in your desk dictionary, and see what extra light is then thrown on this anecdote

A Propensity to Paltry Saving
The heterogeneous composition of human nature was remarkably exemplified in Johnson. His liberality in giving his money to persons in distress was extraordinary. Yet there lurked about him a propensity to paltry saving. One day I owned to him, that "I was occasionally troubled with a fit of *narrowness.*" "Why, Sir, (said he,) so am I. *But I do not tell it.*" He has now and then borrowed a shilling of me; and when I asked him for it again, seemed to be rather out of humor. A droll little circumstance once occurred: As if he meant to reprimand my minute exactness as a creditor, he thus addressed me;— "Boswell, *lend* me sixpence—*not to be repaid.*"

Clear Your Mind of Cant
I have no minute of any interview with Johnson till Thursday, May 15th, when I find what follows: BOSWELL. "I wish much to be in Parliament, Sir." JOHNSON. "Why, Sir, unless you come resolved to support any administration, you would be the worse for being in Parliament, because you would be obliged to live more expensively." BOSWELL. "Perhaps, Sir, I should be the less happy for being in Parliament. I never would sell my vote, and I should be vexed if things went wrong." JOHNSON. "That's cant, Sir. It would not vex you more in the house than in the gallery; public affairs vex no man." BOSWELL. "Have not they vexed yourself a little, Sir? Have not you been vexed by all the turbulence of this reign, and by that absurd vote of the House of Commons, 'That the influence of the Crown has increased, is increasing, and ought to be diminished'?" JOHNSON. "Sir, I have never slept an hour less, nor eat an ounce less meat. I would have knocked the factious dogs on the head, to be sure; but I was *not vexed.*" BOSWELL. "I declare, Sir, upon my honour, I did imagine I was vexed, and took a pride in it; but it *was*, perhaps, cant; for I own I neither eat less, nor slept less." JOHNSON. "My dear friend, clear your *mind* of cant. You may *talk* as other people do; you may say to a man, 'Sir, I am your most humble servant.' You are *not* his most humble servant. You may say, 'These are bad times; it is a melancholy thing to be reserved to such times.' You don't mind the times. You tell a man, 'I am sorry you had such bad weather the last day of your journey, and were so much wet. You don't care sixpence whether he is wet or dry. You may *talk* in this manner; it is a mode of talking in Society: but don't *think* foolishly."

Comments and Questions

1. Neither Johnson nor Boswell defines the word *cant,* but from what it is made to describe, can you define it?

2. If Johnson "would have knocked the factious dogs on the head" and yet was not vexed, what was he?

3. Johnson's political opinions are made clearer in passages quoted below, but there is a broad hint of his political beliefs here. What is the hint?

The Dignity of Danger

We talked of war. JOHNSON. "Every man thinks meanly of himself for not having been a soldier, or not having been at sea." BOSWELL. "Lord Mansfield does not." JOHNSON. "Sir, if Lord Mansfield were in a company of General Officers and Admirals who have been in service, he would shrink; he'd wish to creep under the table." BOSWELL. "No; he'd think he could *try* them all." JOHNSON. "Yes, if he could catch them: but they'd try him much sooner. No, Sir: were Socrates and Charles the Twelfth of Sweden both present in any company, and Socrates to say, 'Follow me, and hear a lecture in philosophy'; and Charles, laying his hand on his sword, to say, 'Follow me, and dethrone the Czar'; a man would be ashamed to follow Socrates. Sir, the impression is universal: yet it is strange. As to the sailor, when you look down from the quarter-deck to the space below, you see the utmost extremity of human misery: such crowding, such filth, such stench!" BOSWELL. "Yet sailors are happy." JOHNSON. "They are happy as brutes are happy, with a piece of fresh meat, with the grossest sensuality. But, Sir, the profession of soldiers and sailors has the dignity of danger. Mankind reverence those who have got over fear, which is so general a weakness."

Comments and Questions

1. As in the passages above, there are here several self-revealing allusions. Few but specialists in the eighteenth century would know anything about Lord Mansfield but, by the information given and a bit of reasoning, any reader can sufficiently identify him. See if you can do so.

2. Is Johnson's use of the word *try* a pun? Explain.

3. Do you agree with Johnson's contention about soldiers and sailors?

Dismal Apprehensions

When we were alone, I introduced the subject of death, and endeavored to maintain that the fear of it might be got over. I told him that David Hume said to me, he was no more uneasy to think that he should *not be* after his life, than that he *had not been* before he began to exist. JOHNSON. "Sir, if he really thinks so, his perceptions are disturbed; he is mad; if he does not think so, he lies. He may tell you he holds his finger in the flame of a candle without feeling pain; would you believe him? When he dies, he at least gives up all he has." BOSWELL. "Foote, Sir, told me, that when he was very ill he was not afraid to die." JOHNSON. "It is not true, Sir. Hold a pistol to Foote's breast, or to Hume's breast and threaten to kill them, and you'll see how they behave." BOSWELL. "But may we not fortify our minds for the approach of death?"—Here I am sensible I was in the wrong, to bring before his view what he ever looked upon with horror; for although when in a celestial frame of mind in his *Vanity of Human Wishes,* he has supposed death to be "kind Nature's signal for retreat," from this state of being to "a happier seat," his thoughts upon this awful change were in general full of dismal apprehensions. His mind resembled the vast amphitheatre, the Coliseum at Rome. In the centre stood his judgment, which like a mighty gladiator, combated those apprehensions that, like the wild beasts of the Arena, were all about in cells, ready to be let out upon him. After a conflict, he drives them back into their dens; but not killing them, they were still assailing him. To my question, whether we might not fortify our minds for the approach of death, he answered, in a passion, "No, Sir, let it alone. It matters not how a man dies, but how he lives. The act of dying is not of importance, it lasts so short a time." He added (with an earnest look), "A man knows it must be so, and submits. It will do him no good to whine."

I attempted to continue the conversation. He was so provoked, that he said: "Give us no more of this"; and was thrown into such a state of agitation, that he expressed himself in a way that alarmed and distressed me; showed an impatience that I should leave him, and when I was going away, called to me sternly, "Don't let us meet to-morrow."

I went home exceedingly uneasy. All the harsh observations which I had ever heard made upon his character, crowded into my mind, and I seemed to myself like the man who had put his head into the lion's mouth a great many times with perfect safety, but at last had it bit off.

That Celebrated Letter

When the *Dictionary* was on the eve of publication, Lord Chesterfield, who, it is said, had flattered himself with the expectation that Johnson would dedicate the work to him, attempted, in a courtly manner, to soothe and insinuate himself with the Sage, conscious, as it should seem, of the cold indifference with which he had treated its learned author; and further attempted to conciliate him, by writing two papers in *The World,* in recommendation of the work; and it must be confessed, that they contain some studied compliments, so finely turned, that if there had been no previous offense, it is probable that Johnson would have been highly delighted. Praise, in general, was pleasing to him; but by praise from a man of rank and elegant accomplishments, he was peculiarly gratified.

This courtly device failed of its effect. Johnson, who thought that "all was false and hollow," despised the honeyed words, and was even indignant that Lord Chesterfield should, for a moment, imagine, that he could be the dupe of such an artifice. His expression to me concerning Lord Chesterfield, upon this occasion, was, "Sir, after making great professions, he had, for many years, taken no notice of me; but when my *Dictionary* was coming out, he fell a scribbling in *The World* about it. Upon which, I wrote him a letter expressed in civil terms, but such as might show him that I did not mind what he said or wrote, and that I had done with him."

This is that celebrated letter of which so much has been said, and about which curiosity has been so long excited, without being gratified. I for many years solicited Johnson to favor me with a copy of it, that so excellent a composition might not be lost to posterity. He delayed from time to time to give it to me; till at last in 1781, when we were on a visit at Mr. Dilly's, at Southhill, in Bedfordshire, he was pleased to dictate it to me from memory. He afterwards found among his papers a copy of it, which he had dictated to Mr. Baretti, with its title and corrections, in his own handwriting. This he gave to Mr. Langton; adding that if it were to come into print, he wished it to be from that copy. By Mr. Langton's kindness, I am enabled to enrich my work with a perfect transcript of what the world has so eagerly desired to see.

"To the Right Honorable the Earl of Chesterfield

"My Lord,   *February 7, 1755.*

"I have been lately informed, by the proprietor of the *World,* that two papers, in which my *Dictionary* is recommended to the public, were written by your Lordship. To be so distinguished, is an honor, which, being very little accustomed to favors from the great, I know not well how to receive, or in what terms to acknowledge.

"When, upon some slight encouragement, I first visited your Lordship, I was over-powered, like the rest of mankind, by the enchantment of your address, and could not forbear to wish that I might boast myself *Le vainqueur du vainqueur de la terre;*[1]—that I might obtain that regard for which I saw the world contending; but I found my attendance so little encouraged, that neither pride nor modesty would suffer me to continue it. When I had once addressed your Lordship in public, I had exhausted all the art of pleasing which a retired and uncourtly scholar can possess. I had done all that I could; and no man is well pleased to have his all neglected, be it ever so little.

5   "Seven years, my Lord, have now passed, since I waited in your outward rooms, or was repulsed from your door; during which time I have been pushing on my work through difficulties, of which it is useless to complain, and have brought it, at last, to the verge of publication, without one act of assistance, one word of encouragement, or one smile of favor. Such treatment I did not expect, for I never had a Patron before.

"The shepherd in Virgil grew at last acquainted with Love, and found him a native of the rocks.

"Is not a Patron, my Lord, one who looks with unconcern on a man struggling for life in the water, and when he has reached ground, encumbers him with help? The notice which you have been pleased to take of my labors, had it been early, had been kind; but it has been delayed till I am indifferent, and cannot enjoy it; till I am solitary, and cannot impart it; till I am known, and do not want it. I hope it is no very cynical asperity, not to confess obligations where no benefit has been received, or to be unwilling that the Public should consider me as owing that to a Patron, which Providence has enabled me to do for myself.

"Having carried on my work thus far with so little obligation to any favorer of learning, I shall not be disappointed though I should conclude it, if less be possible, with less; for I have been long wakened from that dream of hope, in which I once boasted myself with so much exultation,

"My Lord,
"Your Lordship's most humble,
"Most obedient servant,
"Sam. Johnson."

Comments and Questions

Boswell and others forgave or overlooked Johnson's uncouthness, but it is doubtful that the most elegant man of the century ever could have done so. In a letter to his son, Lord Chesterfield recommended "a genteel, easy manner and carriage, wholly free from those odd tricks, ill habits, and awkwardnesses, which even many very worthy and sensible people have in their behavior." He added: "I have known many a man, from his awkwardness, give people such a dislike of him at first, that all his merit could not get the better of it afterwards." Johnson was doubtless a worthy, sensible man of merit but not "wholly free from those odd tricks, ill habits, and awkwardnesses" which Lord Chesterfield found so distasteful. Johnson, for his part, had great respect for noblemen but more respect for his own integrity.

1. Explain the reference, in paragraph four of Johnson's letter, to the "shepherd in Virgil." Does one need to know this story more fully in order to understand the allusion?

[1] The conqueror of the conqueror of the world.

2. Does any part of this letter contain a touch of sarcasm?

3. In the next-to-last paragraph, what does Johnson mean by the statement, "but it has been delayed . . . till I am solitary, and cannot impart it"?

4. What was "that dream of hope" referred to in the last paragraph?

The Spirit of Contradiction

Notwithstanding the high veneration which I entertained for Dr. Johnson, I was sensible that he was sometimes a little actuated by the spirit of contradiction, and by means of that I hoped I should gain my point. I was persuaded that if I should come upon him with a direct proposal, "Sir, will you dine in company with Jack Wilkes?" he would have flown into a passion, and probably would have answered, "Dine with Jack Wilkes, Sir! I'd as soon dine with Jack Ketch." I therefore, while we were sitting quietly by ourselves at his house in an evening, took occasion to open my plan thus: "Mr. Dilly, Sir, sends his respectful compliments to you, and would be happy if you would do him the honor to dine with him on Wednesday next along with me, as I must soon go to Scotland." JOHNSON. "Sir, I am obliged to Mr. Dilly. I will wait upon him—" BOSWELL. "Provided, Sir, I suppose, that the company which he is to have, is agreeable to you." JOHNSON. "What do you mean, Sir? What do you take me for? Do you think I am so ignorant of the world, as to imagine that I am to prescribe to a gentleman what company he is to have at his table?" BOSWELL. "I beg your pardon, Sir, for wishing to prevent you from meeting people whom you might not like. Perhaps he may have some of what he calls his patriotic friends with him." JOHNSON. "Well, Sir, and what then? What care *I* for his *patriotic friends?* Poh!" BOSWELL. "I should not be surprised to find Jack Wilkes there." JOHNSON. "And if Jack Wilkes *should* be there, what is that to *me*, Sir? My dear friend, let us have no more of this. I am sorry to be angry with you; but really it is treating me strangely to talk to me as if I could not meet any company whatever, occasionally." BOSWELL. "Pray, forgive me, Sir, I meant well. But you shall meet whoever comes, for me." Thus I secured him, and told Dilly that he would find him very well pleased to be one of his guests on the day appointed.

Comments and Questions

1. Jack Ketch was a name for the public hangman. How much do we find out about Jack Wilkes?

2. By inference, how much do we find out about Johnson's politics?

The Levelling Doctrine

He again insisted on the duty of maintaining subordination of rank. "Sir, I would no more deprive a nobleman of his respect, than of his money. I consider myself as acting a part in the great system of society, and I do to others as I would have them do to me. I would behave to a nobleman as I should expect he would behave to me, were I a nobleman and he Sam Johnson. Sir, there is one Mrs. Macaulay in this town, a great republican. One day when I was at her house, I put on a very grave countenance, and said to her, 'Madam, I am now become a convert to your way of thinking. I am convinced that all mankind are upon an equal footing; and to give you an unquestionable proof, Madam, that I am in earnest, here is a very sensible, civil, well-behaved fellow-citizen, your footman; I desire that he may be allowed to sit down and dine with us.' I thus, Sir, showed her the absurdity of the levelling doctrine. She has never liked me since. Sir, your levellers wish to level *down* as far as themselves; but they cannot bear levelling *up* to themselves. They would all have some people under them; why not then have some people above them?" I mentioned a certain author who disgusted me by his forwardness, and by showing no deference to noblemen into whose company he was admitted. JOHNSON. "Suppose a shoemaker should claim an equality with him, as he does with a lord; how he would stare. 'Why, Sir, do you stare? (says the shoemaker,) I do great service to society. 'Tis true I am paid for doing it; but so are you, Sir: and I am sorry to say it, paid better than I am, for doing something not so necessary, for mankind could do better without your books, than without my shoes.' Thus, Sir, there would be a perpetual struggle for precedence, were there no fixed invariable rules for the distinction of rank, which creates no jealousy, as it is allowed to be accidental."

Questions

1. Is there anything *reasonable* in Johnson's doctrine? If noble birth is an accident— as obviously it is—on what can respect be based? Is Johnson simply approving the *orderliness* of his society?

2. Do you think that Mrs. Macaulay should have called Johnson's bluff and invited the footman to dinner? If she had done so, what do you think Johnson would have done? Would a present-day Mrs. Macaulay act differently?

3. How far have we progressed toward leveling the humps out of society and reducing all to a flat plain? Is it true, as someone has said: "Mount Olympus is still there, and as one set of gods tumbles, the ones who pushed them off take their places"?

The Subject of Toleration

I introduced the subject of toleration. JOHNSON. "Every society has a right to preserve public peace and order, and therefore has a good right to prohibit the propagation of opinions which have a dangerous tendency. To say the *magistrate* has this right, is using an inadequate word: it is the *society* for which the magistrate is agent. He may be morally or theologically wrong in restraining the propagation of opinions which he thinks dangerous, but he is politically right." MAYO. "I am of opinion, Sir, that every man is entitled to liberty of conscience in religion; and that the magistrate cannot restrain the right." JOHNSON. "Sir, I agree with you. Every man has a right of liberty of conscience, and with that the magistrate cannot interfere. People confound liberty of thinking with liberty of talking; nay, with liberty of preaching. Every man has a physical right to think as he pleases; for it cannot be discovered how he thinks. He has not a moral right, for he ought to inform himself, and think justly. But, Sir, no member of society has a right to *teach* any doctrine contrary to what the society holds to be true. The magistrate, I say, may be wrong in what he thinks; but while he thinks himself right, he may and ought to enforce what he thinks." MAYO. "Then Sir, we are to remain always in error, and truth never can prevail; and the magistrate was right in persecuting the first Christians." JOHNSON. "Sir, the only method by which religious truth can be established is by martyrdom. The magistrate has a right to enforce what he thinks; and he who is conscious of the truth has a right to suffer. I am afraid there is no other way of ascertaining the truth but by persecution on the one hand and enduring it on the other." GOLDSMITH. "But how is a man to act, Sir? Though firmly convinced of the truth of his doctrine, may he not think it wrong to expose himself to persecution? Has he a right to do so? Is it not, as it were, committing voluntary suicide?" JOHNSON. "Sir, as to voluntary suicide, as you call it, there are twenty thousand men in an army who will go without scruple to be shot at, and mount a breach for five-pence a day." GOLDSMITH. "But have they a moral right to do this?" JOHNSON. "Nay, Sir, if you will not take the universal opinion of mankind, I have nothing to say. If mankind cannot defend their own way of thinking, I cannot defend it. Sir, if a man is in doubt whether it would be better to expose himself to martyrdom or not, he should not do it. He must be convinced that he has a delegation from heaven." GOLDSMITH. "I would consider whether there were a greater chance of good or evil upon the whole. If I see a man who had fallen into a well, I would wish to help him out: but if there is a greater probability that he shall pull me in, than that I shall pull him out, I would not attempt it. So were I to go to Turkey, I might wish to convert the Grand Signor to the Christian faith; but when I considered that I should probably be put to death without effectuating my purpose in any degree, I should keep myself quiet." JOHNSON. "Sir, you must consider that we have perfect and imperfect obligations. Perfect obligations, which are generally not to do something, are clear and positive: as, 'thou shalt not kill.' But charity, for instance, is not definable by limits. It is a duty to give to the poor; but no man can say how much another should give to the poor, or when a man has given too little to save his soul. In the same manner it is a duty to instruct the ignorant, and of consequence to convert infidels to Christianity; but no man in the common course of things is obliged to carry this to such a degree as to incur the danger of martyrdom, as no man is obliged to strip himself to the shirt in order to give charity. I have said that a man must be persuaded that he has a particular delegation from heaven." GOLDSMITH. "How is this to be known? Our first reformers, who were burnt for not believing bread and wine to be Christ—" JOHNSON (interrupting him). "Sir, they were not burnt for not believing bread and wine to be Christ, but for insulting those who did believe it. And, Sir, when the first reformers began, they did not intend to be martyred: as many of them ran away as could." BOSWELL. "But, Sir, there was your countryman, Elwal, who you told me challenged King George with his black-guards, and his red-guards." JOHNSON. "My countryman, Elwal, Sir, should have been put in the stocks; a proper pulpit for him; and he'd have had a numerous audience. A man who preaches in the stocks will always have hearers enough." BOSWELL. "But Elwal thought himself in the right." JOHNSON. "We are not providing for mad people; there are places for them in the neighborhood" (meaning Moorfields). MAYO. "But, Sir, is it not very hard that I should not be allowed to teach my children what I believe to be the truth?" JOHNSON. "Why, Sir, you might contrive to teach your children *extrà scandalum;* but, Sir, the magistrate, if he knows it, has a right to restrain you. Suppose you teach your children to be thieves?" MAYO. "This is making a joke of the subject." JOHNSON. "Nay, Sir, take it thus:—that you teach them the community of goods; for which there are as many plausible arguments as for most erroneous doctrines. You teach them that all things at first were in common, and that no man had a right to anything but as he laid his hands upon it; and that this still is, or ought to be, the rule amongst mankind. Here, Sir, you sap a great principle in society,—property. And don't you think the magistrate would have a right to prevent you? Or, suppose you should teach your children the notion of the Adamites, and they should run naked into the streets, would not the magistrate have a right to flog 'em into their doublets?" MAYO. "I think the magistrate has no right to interfere till there is some overt act." BOSWELL. "So, Sir, though he sees an enemy to the state charging a blunderbuss, he is not to interfere till it is fired off?" MAYO. "He must be sure of its direction against the state." JOHNSON. "The magistrate is to judge of that—He has no right to restrain your thinking, because the evil centers in yourself. If a man were sitting at this table, and chopping off his fingers, the magistrate, as guardian of the community, has no authority to restrain him, however he might do it from kindness as a parent.—Though, indeed, upon more consideration, I think he may; as it is probable, that he who is chopping off his own fingers, may soon proceed to chop off those of other people. If I think it right to steal Mr. Dilly's plate, I am a bad man; but he can say nothing to me. If I make an open declaration that I think so, he will keep me out of his house. If I put forth my hand, I shall be sent to Newgate. This is the gradation of thinking, preaching, and acting: if a man thinks erroneously, he may keep his thoughts to himself, and nobody will trouble him; if he preaches erroneous doctrine, society may expel him; if he acts in consequence of it, the law takes place, and he is hanged." MAYO. "But, Sir, ought not Christians to have liberty of conscience?" JOHNSON. "I have already told you so, Sir. You are coming back to where you were." BOSWELL. "Dr. Mayo is always taking a return post-chaise, and going the stage over again. He has it at half price." JOHNSON. "Dr. Mayo, like other champions for unlimited toleration, has got a set of words. Sir, it is no matter, politically, whether the magistrate be right or wrong. Suppose a club were to be formed, to drink confusion to King George the Third, and a happy restoration to Charles the Third, this would be very bad with respect to the state; but every member of that club must either conform to its rules, or be turned out of it. Old Baxter, I remember, maintains, that the magistrate should 'tolerate all things that are tolerable.' This is no good definition of toleration upon any principle; but it shows that he thought some things were not tolerable." TOPLADY. "Sir, you have untwisted this difficult subject with great dexterity."

During this argument, Goldsmith sat in restless agitation, from a wish to get in and *shine.* Finding himself excluded, he had taken his hat to go away, but remained for some time with it in his hand, like a gamester, who at the close of a long night, lingers for a little while, to see if he can have a favourable opening to finish with success. Once when he was beginning to speak, he found himself overpowered by the loud voice of Johnson, who was at the opposite end of the table, and did not perceive Goldsmith's attempt. Thus disappointed of his wish to obtain the attention of the company, Goldsmith in a passion threw down his hat, looking angrily at Johnson, and exclaiming in a bitter tone, *"Take it."* When Toplady was going to speak, Johnson uttered some sound, which led Goldsmith to think that he was beginning again, and taking the words from Toplady. Upon which, he seized this opportunity of venting his own envy and spleen, under the pretext of supporting another person: "Sir (said he to Johnson), the gentleman has heard you patiently for an hour; pray allow us now to hear him." JOHNSON (sternly). "Sir, I was not interrupting the gentleman. I was only giving him a signal of my attention. Sir, you are impertinent." Goldsmith made no reply, but continued in the company for some time.

Comments and Questions

1. If freedom of thought is not subject to control, is it a true freedom? (Is one condition of liberty that it could be taken away?)

2. This animated conversation of eighteenth-century individuals brings forcibly to mind current arguments, perhaps even more animated. Do you see some parallels?

3. Is Goldsmith on the track when he mentions "voluntary suicide"? Are both Goldsmith and Johnson, perhaps for the sake of argument, misusing the word *suicide*?

4. Is Johnson's argument sound about "perfect and imperfect obligations"? Do human beings recognize the injunction against killing as absolute? And what progress have people made toward reducing "charity" to a science? Is there any such thing as "the universal opinion of mankind"?

5. Do you agree that Johnson "untwisted" the difficult subject of toleration "with great dexterity"?

6. At the end are your sympathies with Goldsmith or with Johnson?

Questions on the Passages as a Whole

1. Suppose some holocaust had destroyed all we know of Boswell and Johnson except what we have in the passages quoted here. What would your estimate of the two men be? What would it be of other persons who appear briefly: Goldsmith, Sir Joshua Reynolds, Dr. Mayo?

2. There are three sharply defined attitudes toward Boswell: (1) that he attained literary eminence because he was "a great fool" (Macaulay); (2) that he attained literary eminence because, in spite of being a great fool, he had "an open loving heart" (Carlyle); (3) that he attained literary eminence because he was *not* a great fool but possibly a better man than Johnson. We have only glimpses of Boswell in the passages quoted here, but what do you make of those glimpses? What can be said about his sense of humor? His originality? His reasoning? His understanding of psychology—particularly Johnson's? Now look at a different side of him. What are his qualities as a reporter? As a literary artist? Is he simply one or the other or a blend of both?

3. There seems little doubt that without Boswell's *Life,* Johnson would have sunk into obscurity, for most of his writings have not stood up well. The *Life* has delayed obscurity indefinitely. One should remember, however, that Johnson created the original fascination; Boswell did not make it up. What is that fascination? His rightness in all his arguments? His club-wielding tactics in conversation? His tact or lack of it? The fact that he had a strong opinion on every subject and was willing, eager, to state it? His kindness? generosity? manliness? What combination of reasons accounts for our still whiffing with pleasure the Johnsonian ether?

4. One technical point: Which of the passages quoted would you classify as anecdotes?

Floyd Dell   (1887–1969)
Christmas

Memories of childhood are strange things. The obscurity of the past opens a little lighted space—a scene, unconnected with anything else. One must figure out when it happened. There may be anomalies in the scene, which need explanation. Sometimes the scenes are tiny fragments only. Again they are long dramas. Having once been remembered, they can be lived through again in every moment, with a detailed experiencing of movement and sensation and thought. One can start the scene in one's mind and see it all through again. Exactly so it was—clearer in memory than something that happened yesterday, though it was forty years ago. And, oddly enough, if there is some detail skipped over, lost out of the memory picture, no repetition of the remembering process will supply it—the gap is always there.

That fall, before it was discovered that the soles of both my shoes were worn clear through, I still went to Sunday school. And one time the Sunday-school superintendent made a speech to all the classes. He said that these were hard times, and that many poor children weren't getting enough to eat. It was the first time that I had heard about it. He asked everybody to bring some food for the poor children next Sunday. I felt very sorry for the poor children.

Also little envelopes were distributed to all the classes. Each little boy and girl was to bring money for the poor, next Sunday. The pretty Sunday-school teacher explained that we were to write our names, or have our parents write them, up in the left-hand corner of the little envelopes. . . . I told my mother all about it when I came home. And my mother gave me, the next Sunday, a small bag of potatoes to carry to Sunday school. I supposed the poor children's mothers would make potato soup out of them. . . . Potato soup was good. My father, who was quite a joker, would always say, as if he were surprised, "Ah! I see we have some nourishing soup today!" It was so good that we had it every day. My father was at home all day long and every day, now; and I liked that, even if he was grumpy as he sat reading Grant's *Memoirs.* I had my parents all to myself, too; the others were away. My oldest brother was in Quincy, and memory does not reveal where the others were: perhaps with relatives in the country.

Taking my small bag of potatoes to Sunday school, I looked around for ·the poor children; I was disappointed not to see them. I had heard about poor children in stories. But I was told just to put my contribution with the others on the big table in the side room.

5   I had brought with me the little yellow envelope, with some money in it and sealed up. My mother wouldn't tell me how much money she had put in it, but it felt like several dimes. Only she wouldn't let me write my name on the envelope. I had learned to write my name, and I was proud of being able to do it. But my mother said firmly, *no*, I must *not* write my name on the envelope; she didn't tell me why. On the way to Sunday school I had pressed the envelope against the coins until I could tell what they were; they weren't dimes but pennies.

When I handed in my envelope, my Sunday-school teacher noticed that my name wasn't on it, and she gave me a pencil; I could write my own name, she said. So I did. But I was confused because my mother had said not to; and when I came home, I confessed what I had done. She looked distressed. "I told you not to!" she said. But she didn't explain why. . . .

I didn't go back to school that fall. My mother said it was because I was sick. I did have a cold the week that school opened; I had been playing in the gutters and had got my feet wet, because there were holes in my shoes. My father cut insoles out of cardboard, and I wore those in my shoes. As long as I had to stay in the house anyway, they were all right.

I stayed cooped up in the house, without any companionship. We didn't take a Sunday paper any more, but the *Barry Adage* came every week in the mails; and though I did not read small print, I could see the Santa Clauses and holly wreaths in the advertisements.

There was a calendar in the kitchen. The red days were Sundays and holidays; and that red 25 was Christmas. (It was on a Monday, and the two red figures would come right together in 1893; but this represents research in the *World Almanac*, not memory.) I knew when Sunday was, because I could look out of the window and see the neighbor's children, all dressed up, going to Sunday school. I knew just when Christmas was going to be.

But there was something queer! My father and mother didn't say a word about Christmas. And once, when I spoke of it, there was a strange silence; so I didn't say anything more about it. But I wondered, and was troubled. Why didn't they say anything about it? Was what I had said I wanted (memory refuses to supply that detail) too expensive?

I wasn't arrogant and talkative now. I was silent and frightened. What was the matter?

Why didn't my father and mother say anything about Christmas? As the day approached, my chest grew tighter with anxiety.

Now it was the day before Christmas. I couldn't be mistaken. But not a word about it from my father and mother. I waited in painful bewilderment all day. I had supper with them, and was allowed to sit up for an hour. I was waiting for them to say something. "It's time for you to go to bed," my mother said gently. I *had* to say something.

"This is Christmas Eve, isn't it?" I asked, as if I didn't know. My father and mother looked at one another. Then my mother looked away. Her face was pale and stony. My father cleared his throat, and his face took on a joking look. He pretended he hadn't known it was Christmas Eve, because he hadn't been reading the papers. He said he would go downtown and find out.

My mother got up and walked out of the room. I didn't want my father to have to keep on being funny about it, so I got up and went to bed. I went by myself without having a light. I undressed in the dark and crawled into bed.

I was numb. As if I had been hit by something. It was hard to breathe. I ached all through. I was stunned—with finding out the truth.

My body knew before my mind quite did. In a minute, when I could think, my mind would know. And as the pain in my body ebbed, the pain in my mind began. I *knew*. I couldn't put it into words yet. But I knew why I had taken only a little bag of potatoes to Sunday school that fall. I knew why there had been only pennies in my little yellow envelope. I knew why I hadn't gone to school that fall—why I hadn't any new shoes—why we had been living on potato soup all winter. All these things, and others, many others, fitted themselves together in my mind, and meant something.

Then the words came into my mind and I whispered them into the darkness.

"We're poor!"

That was it. I was one of those poor children I had been sorry for, when I heard about them in Sunday school. My mother hadn't told me. My father was out of work, and we hadn't any money. That was why there wasn't going to be any Christmas at our house.

Then I remembered something that made me squirm with shame—a boast. (Memory will not yield this up. Had I said to some nice little boy, "I'm going to be President of the United States"? Or to a nice little girl: "I'll marry you when I grow up"? It was some boast as horribly shameful to remember.)

"We're poor." There in bed in the dark, I whispered it over and over to myself. I was making myself get used to it. (Or—just torturing myself, as one pressed the tongue against a sore tooth? No, memory says not like that—but to keep myself from every being such a fool again: suffering now, to keep this awful thing from ever happening again. Memory is clear on that; it was more like pulling the tooth, to get it over with—never mind the pain, this will be the end!)

It wasn't so bad, now that I knew. *I just hadn't known!* I had thought all sorts of foolish things; that I was going to Ann Arbor—going to be a lawyer—going to make speeches in the Square, going to be President! Now I knew better.

I had wanted (something) for Christmas. I didn't want it, now. I didn't want anything.

I lay there in the dark, feeling the cold emotion of renunciation. (The tendrils of desire unfold their clasp on the outer world of objects, withdraw, shrivel up. Wishes shrivel up, turn black, die. It is like that.)

It hurt. But nothing would ever hurt again. I would never let myself want anything again.

I lay there stretched out straight and stiff in the dark, my fists clenched hard upon Nothing. . . .

In the morning it had been like a nightmare that is not clearly remembered—that one wishes to forget. Though I hadn't hung up any stocking, there was one hanging at the foot of my bed. A bag of popcorn, and lead pencil, for me. They had done the best they could, now they realized that I knew about Christmas. But they needn't have thought they had to. I didn't want anything.

Comments

Try to imagine what would happen to the effect of this account if it were told differently. Here is a sample of a different telling of the first paragraph:

> That autumn I still trudged manfully off to Sunday school even though my little shoes had long since seen their best days. On one memorable Sabbath, the Sunday-school superintendent made a very moving speech to all the classes. It wrung our little hearts when he reminded us that because of the difficult times many poverty-stricken children actually were not getting enough good wholesome food to fill their empty little stomachs. It was heartrending, and I was so innocent that I had never realized before that such conditions existed. Then we were told to help the poor little boys and girls by bringing them some food the next Sunday. I was filled with childish pity as I thought of those less fortunate (I imagined!) than myself.

If one compares this version with the original, two observations may be made: (1) *truth* itself may depend on *how* something is said; (2) direct attempts to make a reader *feel* are self-defeating.

Let us examine for a moment this first observation. Floyd Dell was recalling events and feelings from a distance of years. His problem was to see and feel as a young boy had seen and felt. As a man his feelings towards what happened to the boy were doubtless quite different, but he rigorously excludes these mature emotions. Here, then, truth depends not entirely on *what* is said but also on *how* it is said. In the second version of the first paragraph, a false note is struck at once with the word *autumn,* and this sort of falseness continues throughout the paragraph in words and phrases that you can easily pick out.

We can restate the second observation this way: the greater the inherent emotional content of a situation, the less welcome are words that label it as emotional. A child's disappointment at Christmas time is a situation of this sort. Any direct attempt at drawing tears would result in sloppy sentimentality and no tears. Floyd Dell knew this pitfall and avoided it by sticking to a simple, straightforward account. As a result the pathos of the piece is powerful and authentic.

We have in "Christmas" our best example so far of the fusion of content and form, matter and manner. "Exactly so it was," says the author, and the matter-manner of the telling convinces us that so it was. This sort of fusion is characteristic of poetry, particularly lyric poetry (see "Preliminaries" in the poetry division). All forms of literature seek this fusion; the great works always attain it.

Dylan Thomas   (1914–1953)
Memories of Christmas

One Christmas was so much like another, in those years, around the sea town corner now, and out of all sound except the distant speaking of the voices I sometimes hear a moment before sleep, that I can never remember whether it snowed for six days and six nights when I was twelve or whether it snowed for twelve days and twelve nights when I was six; or whether the ice broke and the skating grocer vanished like a snow man through a white trap-door on that same Christmas Day that the mince-pies finished Uncle Arnold and we tobogganed down the seaward hill, all the afternoon, on the best tea-tray, and Mrs. Griffiths complained, and we threw a snowball at her niece, and my hands burned so, with the heat and the cold, when I held them in front of the fire, that I cried for twenty minutes and then had some jelly.

All the Christmases roll down the hill towards the Welsh-speaking sea, like a snow-ball growing whiter and bigger and rounder, like a cold and headlong moon bundling down the sky that was our street; and they stop at the rim of the ice-edged, fish-freezing waves, and I plunge my hands in the snow and bring out whatever I can find; holly or robins or pudding, squabbles and carols and oranges and tin whistles, and the fire in the front room, and bang go the crackers, and holy, holy, holy, ring the bells, and the glass bells shaking on the tree, and Mother Goose, and Struwelpeter—oh! the baby-burning flames and the clacking scissorman!—Billy Bunter and Black Beauty, Little Women and boys who have three helpings, Alice and Mrs. Potter's badgers, penknives, teddy-bears—named after a Mr. Theodore Bear, their inventor, or father, who died recently in the United States—mouth-organs, tin-soldiers, and blanc-mange, and Auntie Bessie playing "Pop Goes the Weasel" and "Nuts in May" and "Oranges and Lemons" on the untuned piano in the parlour all through the thimble-hiding musical-chairing blindman's-buffing party at the end of the never-to-be-forgotten day at the end of the unremembered year.

In goes my hand into that wool-white bell-tongued ball of holidays resting at the margin of the carol-singing sea, and out come Mrs. Prothero and the firemen.

It was on the afternoon of the day of Christmas Eve, and I was in Mrs. Prothero's garden, waiting for cats, with her son Jim. It was snowing. It was always snowing at Christmas; December, in my memory, is white as Lapland, though there were no reindeers. But there were cats. Patient, cold and callous, our hands wrapped in socks, we waited to snow-ball the cats. Sleek and long as jaguars and terrible-whiskered, spitting and snarling they would slink and sidle over the white back-garden walls, and the lynx-eyed hunters, Jim and I, fur-capped and moccasined trappers from Hudson's Bay off Eversley Road, would hurl our deadly snowballs at the green of their eyes. The wise cats never appeared. We were so still, Eskimo-footed arctic marksmen in the muffling silence of the eternal snows—eternal, ever since Wednesday—that we never heard Mrs. Prothero's first cry from her igloo at the bottom of the garden. Or, if we heard it at all, it was, to us, like the far-off challenge of our enemy and prey, the neighbour's Polar Cat. But soon the voice grew louder. "Fire!" cried Mrs. Prothero, and she beat the dinner-gong. And we ran down the garden, with the snowballs in our arms, towards the house, and smoke, indeed, was pouring out of the dining-room, and the gong was bombilating, and Mrs. Prothero was announcing ruin like a town-crier in Pompeii. This was better than all the cats in Wales standing on the wall in a row. We bounded into the house, laden with snowballs, and stopped at the open door of the smoke-filled room. Something was burning all right; perhaps it was Mr. Prothero, who always slept there after midday dinner with a newspaper over his face; but he was standing in the middle of the room, saying "A fine Christmas!" and smacking at the smoke with a slipper.

5   "Call the fire-brigade," cried Mrs. Prothero as she beat the gong.

"They won't be there," said Mr. Prothero. "It's Christmas."

There was no fire to be seen, only clouds of smoke and Mr. Prothero standing in the middle of them, waving his slipper as though he were conducting.

"Do something," he said.

And we threw all our snowballs into the smoke—I think we missed Mr. Prothero— and ran out of the house to the telephone-box.

"Let's call the police as well," Jim said.

"And the ambulance."

"And Ernie Jenkins, he likes fires."

But we only called the fire-brigade, and soon the fire-engine came and three tall men in helmets brought a hose into the house and Mr. Prothero got out just in time before they turned it on. Nobody could have had a noisier Christmas Eve. And when the firemen turned off the hose and were standing in the wet and smoky room, Jim's aunt, Miss Prothero, came downstairs and peered in at them. Jim and I waited, very quietly, to hear what she would say to them. She said the right thing, always. She looked at the three tall firemen in their shining helmets, standing among the smoke and cinders and dissolving snowballs, and she said: "Would you like something to read?"

Now out of that bright white snowball of Christmas gone comes the stocking, the stocking of stockings, that hung at the foot of the bed with the arm of a golliwog dangling over the top and small bells ringing in the toes. There was a company, gallant and scarlet but never nice to taste though I always tried when very young, of belted and busbied and musketed lead soldiers so soon to lose their heads and legs in the wars on the table kitchen after the tea-things, the mince-pies, and the cakes that I helped to make by stoning the raisins and eating them, had been cleared away; and a bag of moist and many-coloured jelly-babies and a folded flag and a false nose and a tram-conductor's cap and a machine that punched tickets and rang a bell; never a catapult; once, by a mistake that no one could explain, a little hatchet; and a rubber buffalo, or it may have been a horse, with a yellow head and haphazard legs; and a celluloid duck that made, when you pressed it, a most unducklike noise, a mewing moo that an ambitious cat might make who wishes to be a cow; and a painting-book in which I could make the grass, the trees, the sea, and the animals any colour I pleased: and still the dazzling sky-blue sheep are grazing in the red field under a flight of rainbow-beaked and pea-green birds.

Christmas morning was always over before you could say Jack Frost. And look! suddenly the pudding was burning! Bang the gong and call the fire-brigade and the book-loving firemen! Someone found the silver three-penny-bit with a currant on it; and the someone was always Uncle Arnold. The motto in my cracker read:

> Let's all have fun this Christmas Day,
> Let's play and sing and shout hooray!

and the grownups turned their eyes towards the ceiling, and Aunt Bessie, who had already been frightened, twice, by a clock-work mouse, whimpered at the sideboard and had some elderberry wine. And someone put a glass bowl full of nuts on the littered table, and my uncle said, as he said once every year: "I've got a shoe-nut here. Fetch me a shoe-horn to open it, boy."

And dinner was ended.

And I remembered that on the afternoon of Christmas Day, when the others sat around the fire and told each other that this was nothing, no, nothing, to the great snowbound and turkey-proud yule-log-crackling holly-berry-bedizened and kissing-under-the-mistletoe Christmas when *they* were children. I would go out, school-capped and gloved and mufflered, with my bright new boots squeaking, into the white world on to the seaward hill, to call on Jim and Dan and Jack and to walk with them through the silent snowscape of our town.

We went padding through the streets, leaving huge deep footprints in the snow, on the hidden pavements.

"I bet people'll think there's been hippoes."

20   "What would you do if you saw a hippo coming down Terrace Road?"

"I'd go like this, bang! I'd throw him over the railings and roll him down the hill and then I'd tickle him under the ear and he'd wag his tail . . . "

"What would you do if you saw *two* hippoes . . . ?"

Iron-flanked and bellowing he-hippoes clanked and blundered and battered through the scudding snow towards us as we passed by Mr. Daniel's house.

"Let's post Mr. Daniel a letter through his letter box."

25   "Let's write 'Mr. Daniel looks like a spaniel' all over his lawn."

"Look," Jack said, "I'm eating snow-pie."

"What's it taste like?"

"Like snow-pie," Jack said.

Or we walked on the white shore.

30   "Can the fishes see it's snowing?"

"They think it's the sky falling down."

The silent one-clouded heavens drifted on to the sea.

"All the old dogs have gone."

Dogs of a hundred mingled makes yapped in the summer at the sea-rim and yelped at the trespassing mountains of the waves.

35   "I bet St. Bernards would like it now."

And we were snowblind travellers lost on the north hills, and the dewlapped dogs, with brandy-flasks round their necks, ambled and shambled up to us, baying "Excelsior."

We returned home through the desolate poor sea-facing streets where only a few children fumbled with bare red fingers in the thick wheel-rutted snow and cat-called after us, their voices fading away, as we trudged uphill, into the cries of the dock-birds and the hooters of ships out in the white and whirling bay.

Bring out the tall tales now that we told by the fire as we roasted chestnuts and the gaslight bubbled low. Ghosts with their heads under their arms trailed their chains and said "whooo" like owls in the long nights when I dared not look over my shoulder; wild beasts lurked in the cubby-hole under the stairs where the gas-meter ticked. "Once upon a time, " Jim said, "there were three boys, just like us, who got lost in the dark in the snow, near Bethesda Chapel, and this is what happened to them. . . . " It was the most dreadful happening I had ever heard.

And I remember that we went singing carols once, a night or two before Christmas Eve, when there wasn't the shaving of a moon to light the secret, white-flying street. At the end of a long road was a drive that led to a large house, and we stumbled up the darkness of the drive that night, each one of us afraid, each one holding a stone in his hand in case, and all of us too brave to say a word. The wind made through the drive-trees noises as of old and unpleasant and maybe web-footed men wheezing in caves. We reached the black bulk of the house.

40   "What shall we give them?" Dan whispered.

" 'Hark the Herald'? 'Christmas Comes but Once a Year'?"

"No," Jack said: "We'll sing 'Good King Wenceslas.' I'll count three."

One, two, three, and we began to sing, our voices high and seemingly distant in the snow-felted darkness round the house that was occupied by nobody we knew. We stood close together, near the dark door.

> Good King Wenceslas looked out
> On the Feast of Stephen.

And then a small, dry voice, like the voice of someone who has not spoken for a long time, suddenly joined our singing: a small, dry voice from the other side of the door: a small dry voice through the keyhole. And when we stopped running we were outside *our* house; the front room was lovely and bright; the gramophone was playing; we saw the red and white balloons hanging from the gas-brackets; uncles and aunts sat by the fire; I thought I smelt our supper being fried in the kitchen. Everything was good again, and Christmas shone through all the familiar town.

45 "Perhaps it was a ghost," Jim said.
"Perhaps it was trolls," Dan said, who was always reading.
"Let's go in and see if there's any jelly left," Jack said.
And we did that.

Comments and Questions

1. What is the effect of the breathless opening paragraphs? When one thinks back to earlier experiences, how do the impressions register, in orderly or in chaotic fashion?

2. Note the structure of this piece. Obviously memories of many Christmases are racing through the author's mind, but how is the impression of a single Christmas achieved?

3. Compare the mood and tone of this piece with Floyd Dell's "Christmas" (p. 1002).

Mark Twain (Samuel L. Clemens)
(1835–1910)
A Cub Pilot's Experience

. . . The *Paul Jones* was now bound for St. Louis. I planned a siege against my pilot, and at the end of three hard days he surrendered. He agreed to teach me the Mississippi River from New Orleans to St. Louis for five hundred dollars, payable out of the first wages I should receive after graduating. I entered upon the small enterprise of "learning" twelve or thirteen hundred miles of the great Mississippi River with the easy confidence of my time of life. If I had really known what I was about to require of my faculties, I should not have had the courage to begin. I supposed that all a pilot had to do was to keep his boat in the river, and I did not consider that that could be much of a trick, since it was so wide.

The boat backed out from New Orleans at four in the afternoon, and it was "our watch" until eight. Mr. Bixby, my chief, "straightened her up," ploughed her along past the sterns of the other boats that lay at the Levee, and then said, "Here, take her; shave those steamships as close as you'd peel an apple." I took the wheel, and my heart-beat fluttered up into the hundreds; for it seemed to me that we were about to scrape the side off every ship in the line, we were so close. I held my breath and began to claw the boat away from the danger; and I had my own opinion of the pilot who had known no better than to get us into such peril, but I was too wise to express it. In half a minute I had a wide margin of safety intervening between the *Paul Jones* and the ships; and within ten seconds more I was set aside in disgrace, and Mr. Bixby was going into danger again and flaying me alive with abuse of my cowardice. I was stung, but I was obliged to admire the easy confidence with which my chief loafed from side to side of his wheel, and trimmed the ships so closely that disaster seemed ceaselessly imminent. When he had cooled a little he told me that the easy water was close ashore and the current outside, and therefore we must hug the bank, upstream, to get the benefit of the former, and stay well out, down-stream, to take advantage of the latter. In my own mind I resolved to be a down-stream pilot and leave the up-streaming to people dead to prudence.

Now and then Mr. Bixby called my attention to certain things. Said he, "This is Six-Mile Point." I assented. It was pleasant enough information but I could not see the bearing of it. I was not conscious that it was a matter of any interest to me. Another time he said, "This is Nine-Mile Point." Later he said, "This is Twelve-Mile Point." They were all about level with the water's edge; they all looked about alike to me; they were monotonously unpicturesque. I hoped Mr. Bixby would change the subject. But no; he would crowd up around a point, hugging the shore with affection, and then say: "The slack water ends here, abreast this bunch of China-trees; now we cross over." So he crossed over. He gave me the wheel once or twice, but I had no luck. I either came near chipping off the edge of a sugar plantation, or I yawed too far from shore, and so dropped back into disgrace again and got abused.

The watch was ended at last, and we took supper and went to bed. At midnight the glare of a lantern shone in my eyes, and the night watchman said: "Come, turn out!"

5   And then he left. I could not understand this extraordinary procedure; so I presently gave up trying to, and dozed off to sleep. Pretty soon the watchman was back again, and this time he was gruff. I was annoyed. I said:

"What do you want to come bothering around here in the middle of the night for? Now, as like as not, I'll not get to sleep again tonight."

The watchman said:

"Well, if this ain't good, I'm blessed."

The "off-watch" was just turning in, and I heard some brutal laughter from them, and such remarks as "Hello, watchman! ain't the new cub turned out yet? He's delicate, likely. Give him some sugar in a rag, and send for the chambermaid to sing 'Rock-a-by Baby' to him."

10   About this time Mr. Bixby appeared on the scene. Something like a minute later I was climbing the pilothouse steps with some of my clothes on and the rest in my arms. Mr. Bixby was close behind, commenting. Here was something fresh—this thing of getting up in the middle of the night to go to work. It was a detail in piloting that had never occurred to me at all. I knew that boats ran all night, but somehow I had never happened to reflect that somebody had to get up out of a warm bed to run them. I began to fear that piloting was not quite so romantic as I had imagined it was; there was something very real and worklike about this new phase of it.

It was a rather dingy night, although a fair number of stars were out. The big mate was at the wheel, and he had the old tub pointed at a star and was holding her straight up the middle of the river. The shores on either hand were not much more than half a mile apart, but they seemed wonderfully far away and ever so vague and indistinct. The mate said:

"We've got to land at Jones's plantation, sir."

The vengeful spirit in me exulted. I said to myself, "I wish you joy of your job, Mr. Bixby; you'll have a good time finding Mr. Jones's plantation such a night as this; and I hope you never *will* find it as long as you live."

Mr. Bixby said to the mate:

15 "Upper end of the plantation, or the lower?"

"Upper."

"I can't do it. The stumps there are out of the water at this stage. It's no great distance to the lower, and you'll have to get along with that."

"All right, sir. If Jones don't like it, he'll have to lump it, I reckon."

And then the mate left. My exultation began to cool and my wonder to come up. Here was a man who not only proposed to find this plantation on such a night, but to find either end of it you preferred. I dreadfully wanted to ask a question, but I was carrying about as many short answers as my cargo-room would admit of, so I held my peace. All I desired to ask Mr. Bixby was the simple question whether he was ass enough to really imagine he was going to find that plantation on a night when all plantations were exactly alike and all of the same color. But I held in. I used to have fine inspirations of prudence in those days.

20 Mr. Bixby made for the shore and soon was scraping it, just the same as if it had been daylight. And not only that, but singing: "Father in heaven, the day is declining," etc. It seemed to me that I had put my life in the keeping of a peculiarly reckless outcast. Presently he turned on me and said:

"What's the name of the first point above New Orleans?"

I was gratified to be able to answer promptly, and I did. I said I didn't know.

"Don't *know?*"

This manner jolted me. I was down at the foot again, in a moment. But I had to say just what I had said before.

25 "Well, you're a smart one!" said Mr. Bixby. "What's the name of the *next* point?"

Once more I didn't know.

"Well, this beats anything. Tell me the name of *any* point or place I told you."

I studied a while and decided that I couldn't.

"Look here! What do you start out from, above Twelve-Mile Point, to cross over?"

30 "I—I—don't know."

"You—you—don't know?" mimicking my drawling manner of speech. "What *do* you know?"

"I—I—nothing, for certain."

"By the great Caesar's ghost, I believe you! You're the stupidest dunderhead I ever saw or ever heard of, so help me Moses! The idea of *you* being a pilot—*you!* Why, you don't know enough to pilot a cow down a lane."

Oh, but his wrath was up! He was a nervous man, and he shuffled from one side of his wheel to the other as if the floor was hot. He would boil a while to himself, and then overflow and scald me again.

35 "Look here! What do you suppose I told you the names of those points for?"

I tremblingly considered a moment, and then the devil of temptation provoked me to say:

"Well—to—to—be entertaining, I thought."

This was a red rag to the bull. He raged and stormed so (he was crossing the river at the time) that I judged it made him blind, because he ran over the steering-oar of a trading-scow. Of course the traders sent up a volley of red-hot profanity. Never was a man so grateful as Mr. Bixby was; because he was brimful, and here were subjects who could *talk back.* He threw open a window, thrust his head out, and such an irruption followed as I never had heard before. The fainter and farther away the scowmen's curses drifted, the higher Mr. Bixby lifted his voice and the weightier his adjectives grew. When he closed the window he was empty. You could have drawn a seine through his system and not caught curses enough to disturb your mother with. Presently he said to me in the gentlest way:

"My boy, you must get a little memorandum-book; and every time I tell you a thing, put it down right away. There's only one way to be a pilot, and that is to get this entire river by heart. You have to know it just like A B C."

40   This was a dismal revelation to me; for my memory was never loaded with anything but blank cartridges. However, I did not feel discouraged long. I judged that it was best to make some allowances, for doubtless Mr. Bixby was "stretching." Presently he pulled a rope and struck a few strokes on the big bell. The stars were all gone now, and the night was as black as ink. I could hear the wheels churn along the bank, but I was not entirely certain that I could see the shore. The voice of the invisible watchman called up from the hurricane-deck:

"What's this, sir?"

"Jones's plantation."

I said to myself, "I wish I might venture to offer a small bet that it isn't." But I did not chirp. I only waited to see. Mr. Bixby handled the engine-bells, and in due time the boat's nose came to the land, a torch glowed from the forecastle, a man skipped ashore, a darky's voice on the bank said, "Gimme de k'yarpetbag, Mass' Jones," and the next moment we were standing up the river again, all serene. I reflected deeply a while and then said— but not aloud—"Well, the finding of that plantation was the luckiest accident that ever happened; but it couldn't happen again in a hundred years." And I fully believed it *was* an accident, too.

By the time we had gone seven or eight hundred miles up the river, I had learned to be a tolerably plucky upstream steersman, in daylight, and before we reached St. Louis I had made a trifle of progress in night-work, but only a trifle. I had a note-book that fairly bristled with the names of towns, "points," bars, islands, bends, reaches, etc., but the information was to be found only in the note-book—none of it was in my head. It made my heart ache to think I had only got half the river set down; for as our watch was four hours off and four hours on, day and night, there was a long four-hour gap in my book for every time I had slept since the voyage began.

45   My chief was presently hired to go on a big New Orleans boat, and I packed my satchel and went with him. She was a grand affair. When I stood in her pilot-house I was so far above the water that I seemed perched on a mountain; and her decks stretched so far away, fore and aft, below me, that I wondered how I could ever have considered the little *Paul Jones* a large craft. There were other differences, too. The *Paul Jones's* pilot- house was a cheap, dingy, battered rattletrap, cramped for room; but here was a sump- tuous glass temple; room enough to have a dance in; showy red and gold window curtains; an imposing sofa; leather cushions and a back to the high bench where visiting pilots sit, to spin yarns and "look at the river"; bright, fanciful "cuspidores," instead of a broad wooden box filled with sawdust; nice new oilcloth on the floor; a hospitable big stove for winter; a wheel as high as my head, costly with inlaid work; a wire tiller-rope; bright brass knobs for the bells; and a tidy, white-aproned black "texas-tender," to bring up tarts and ices and coffee during mid-watch, day and night. Now this was "something like"; and so I began to take heart once more to believe that piloting was a romantic sort of occupation after all. The moment we were under way I began to prowl about the great steamer and

fill myself with joy. She was as clean and as dainty as a drawing-room; when I looked down her long, gilded saloon, it was like gazing through a splendid tunnel; she had an oil-picture, by some gifted signpainter, on every stateroom door; she glittered with no end of prism-fringed chandeliers; the clerk's office was elegant, the bar was marvellous, and the barkeeper had been barbered and upholstered at incredible cost. The boiler-deck (*i.e.,* the second story of the boat, so to speak) was as spacious as a church, it seemed to me; so with the forecastle; and there was no pitiful handful of deck-hands, firemen, and roustabouts down there, but a whole battalion of men. The fires were fiercely glaring from a long row of furnaces, and over them were eight huge boilers! This was unutterable pomp. The mighty engines—but enough of this. I had never felt so fine before. And when I found that the regiment of natty servants respectfully "sir'd" me, my satisfaction was complete.

Comments and Questions

1. Characterize Mr. Bixby. Was he an expert teacher? Describe his methods.

2. What attitude does Mark Twain, the cub pilot, take toward his experience? Is this the source of humor that pervades the account? Discuss. Cite several examples of obvious exaggeration.

Robert Drake (1930–   )
Amazing Grace

I didn't much want to go with Daddy and Mamma out to Salem Church that Sunday. They were going to have dinner on the ground after preaching, and then after that the Barlow County Singing Convention was going to meet. I was twelve years old, and it looked like to me that I never was going to get away from the country. Every Sunday afternoon we had to go out to Uncle Jim and Aunt Mary's at Maple Grove, where Pa Drake used to live. Pa had been dead for several years, but it looked like Daddy and Mamma didn't know how to quit going. And every time we had to sit around and listen to all those old tales about when the Drake boys were growing up and all the fun they used to have with their neighbors like the Powells and the Sweats.

Pa Drake had come from Virginia after the war and married Grandma, who had been a Sanders, and I think his folks always thought he had married beneath himself. But Daddy used to tell Mamma and she told *me* that they would all have starved to death if it hadn't been for Grandma. Pa had been raised with slaves to wait on him and had gone off to school and learned to read Latin and Greek before he went off to the War, and I reckon he wasn't ever about to learn how to do anything else.

But, anyhow, it looked like everybody in my family was from the country and wasn't ever going to be anywhere else. None of them had ever been off to college because they didn't have any money for *anything,* much less education. They just all went to school out at Maple Grove a few months every year and went to church every Sunday, and that was about as far as any of them got, except Uncle Buford; and he finished high school because Daddy quit school to let him go.

But I was bound and determined that wasn't going to happen to me. I was going to get all the education in the world so I never would have to be ashamed of saying *seen* and *done* and *taken,* and I was going to go places and do things. They needn't to think they were going to keep *me* in Barlow County all my life. I had already had a big argument with Daddy, though, because I said I wanted to go to school at Harvard, which was supposed to be the best school in the whole country. But Daddy said no, sir, I wasn't going to get above my raising and go up there to school with a lot of Yankees that all loved the Negroes so much; I was going to school in the South and like it. It made me mad because I thought he just couldn't stand for me to go off and do things nobody in the whole Drake family had ever done before.

5   Well, anyhow, somebody in the Salem community had asked us out that Sunday, so about ten o'clock we got in the car and drove off. It was laying-by time, after all the weeds had been chopped out of the cotton, and the cotton was growing like wildfire all along the road. But it was hot as a fox, and I wasn't looking forward to the prospect of eating off the ground with all those ants and worms crawling all over the food and you, too.

It didn't take us long to get out to Salem; it was only about five miles out from Woodville. The church, which was a Baptist church, sat back off the road under some great big oak trees, and people had parked all over the yard without any system at all. They just drove up and stopped wherever they got ready. Most of the cars were old and broken-down looking, and there were a lot of pick-up trucks, too. Daddy was always talking about how poor farmers were and what a hard time they had, so I was used to them looking pretty run-down. But what made me kind of tired was the way Daddy seemed to *enjoy* talking about how bad off they were, like there might be something good about having to work so hard and never having any money and never going anywhere and doing anything. For my part, I just couldn't wait to go to New York and see all the museums and theaters and famous people and everything that was going on. But nothing ever happened to any of the Drakes; they just went on year after year as slow as Christmas.

There were still a lot of people in the cars, like couples courting and women nursing babies and changing their diapers right there in your face. But then they began getting out to go in the church, and they were all laughing and hollering like they hadn't seen each other in a thousand years. I thought it was all pretty disgusting and common. It didn't look like any of them had any refinement, and I didn't see how Daddy could be so crazy about them. But he was. He was always talking about some old man out in the country who probably didn't know how to read and write and saying, "He's one of the best men that ever had on a pair of pants"; or he would mention some old woman that was ugly as homemade sin and say, "Yes, I know she's so cross-eyed, when she cries, the tears run down her back, but she's one of the best women you ever saw." That kind of thing worried me because it looked like you had to be ugly and ignorant in order to be good, just like if you really enjoyed something, like going to the picture show, it was probably a bad influence on you. Or at least that was the way a lot of people acted.

The sermon was a pretty regulation Baptist kind with lots of emphasis on whether you were a wise or a foolish virgin and whether you would be ready if Jesus should come tonight. It looked like to me I had more and more things to worry about all the time. It wasn't enough for you to worry about whether or not you were going to get all A's on your report card so you could go to the picture show on school nights and whether you had practiced your hour on the piano every day. Then, on top of all that, you had to worry about going to Heaven and all. It looked like some people just couldn't be satisifed.

So I was pretty glad when church was over and it was time to eat, even if we were going to eat off the ground. The women went on out in the yard and started unloading the food from the cars and spreading their white Sunday tablecloths out under the big oak trees. There was lots of fried chicken and country ham and sliced tomatoes and stuffed eggs and all kinds of cake and pie. And somebody had gone into Woodville right after church to get the ice for the iced tea. Then everybody got a paper plate and started going around and helping himself to everything. When we started around, Mamma whispered to me that we had to take some of everything so as not to hurt anybody's feelings. That was another thing you had to worry about—whether or not you were going to hurt somebody's feelings. But it didn't look like to me anybody was sitting up late at night worrying about whether or not he had hurt *my* feelings.

10   We went around helping ourselves to everything and trying to eat a little on the side. A cross-eyed woman with buckteeth and dyed hair came up to Mamma and said, "Have you had any of my *cormel* cake?" And Mamma said, "Why, it's Cousin Lucy Belle Sanders, isn't it? No, indeed, I must get some of your caramel cake right away." It seemed like it was always people like that that we had to be kin to, and you always had to be nice to them when you didn't really want to. I used to wonder sometimes whether it would hurt you as much to be nice to people with straight eyes and straight teeth; but then, of course, when they were like that, you didn't have to worry about being *nice* to them in the first place.

Brother Jernigan, the preacher, was stepping around, speaking to all the ladies and eating enough to kill a mule. It looked like I hadn't ever seen a preacher yet that wasn't a big eater and a big man with the ladies; it looked like that just sort of *went* with preaching. And *they* always acted like they had it coming to them just for getting up there once a week and making you wonder about whether or not you were worrying about all the things you should. But they didn't seem to worry much about anything themselves. I reckoned it was sort of like the ravens feeding Elijah or doctors never getting sick or something.

About two o'clock when everybody was full as he could be and all the babies had gone to sleep, everybody began to get up off the ground and brush themselves off and put away the food and everything before the singing convention started. There was going to be a Bette Davis movie on that afternoon at the Dixie Theater in Woodville, and I begged Daddy to let us go on back home so I could see it. But he said, "Now, Robert, we're not going to eat and run like that. That would be just plain ordinary." I didn't like it, but I had to stop and think. It never had occurred to me before that I could be ordinary; it was uneducated people out in the country that were ordinary. I didn't exactly know what to make of it, so I followed Mamma and Daddy on into the church without saying anything.

The church was just like an oven, and you could tell that a lot of those people in there weren't any too familiar with soap and water. The place was jam-packed, and there didn't seem to be a breath of air stirring anywhere. The singing convention met only about four times a year, so they were always pretty sure to have a good crowd on hand. People came from all over the county to hear the different solos and quartets and things from every community. Daddy said, though, that they used to meet more often; it was just one more old thing that was dying out.

Everybody got real quiet, and then the Boyd's Landing Quartet got up to sing. They were supposed to be the best quartet in the county; and Daddy said that Mr. Tom Newman, who sang bass, had a voice like distant thunder. They started off with "Alas, and did my Savior bleed?" which was another one of those hymns where you had to low-rate yourself and say you were a worm. ("Would He devote that sacred head for such a worm as I?") It was just like everything else; you never could enjoy anything without thinking maybe you didn't have any right to and were probably going to have to pay for it some day.

15   I looked at Mamma to see how she was holding out, but she and Daddy were sitting there looking like they couldn't think of anywhere else in the world they would rather be

than right there. So I decided I might as well make up my mind to sit there all afternoon, but I sure hoped God was taking notice of how good I was being and was putting it down by my name in the Lamb's Book of Life or wherever He kept all His records.

Finally, after they had sung "Near-o my God to Thee" (they always pronounced "nearer" that way out in the country) and "On Jordan's stormy banks I stand," they got to "Amazing Grace." That was the first hymn I had ever learned; my nurse, Louella, had taught it to me when I was five years old. And it was written by John Newton, who was a con-verted slave trader. So I followed right along with the Quartet in my mind.

The first verse went:

> "Amazing grace! how sweet the sound,
> That saved a wretch like me!
> I once was lost, but now am found,
> Was blind, but now I see."

There you were calling yourself a wretch again, and yet there was supposed to be some-thing sweet about it. I looked around at all those people; and I could see, from the way they looked so far off from the world, so calm and peaceful, that they all thought there was something sweet about being a wretch, too. But why was it so sweet to be a wretch? If it was good to be a wretch, it might also be good to live out in the country and have nothing but lamps for light and have dinner on the ground. Did it mean that God didn't really care whether you said *taken* or got all A's on your report card or lived at Salem or in New York, and that maybe He sort of enjoyed some people saying *taken* and living out in the country, and that maybe He didn't really care whether or not you were worrying about Jesus coming tonight? Was grace maybe something like rain that just fell anyhow and didn't care where it was falling and that was why it was so amazing?

I looked around at Daddy, and his eyes were full—just like they always got whenever he talked about Grandma and Pa or whenever he told me he loved Mamma even more now than he did when they were married or whenever he said he wanted me to have all the opportunities he had never had. Then the Quartet went on to another verse and sang:

> " 'Twas grace that taught my heart to fear,
> And grace my fears relieved;
> How precious did that grace appear,
>   The hour I first believed!"

I was sitting there thinking that grace must be about the most wonderful thing going if it could do all that and that that must have been the way John Newton felt when he wrote that hymn, when, all of a sudden, Daddy put his arm around me and whispered, "Son, you just don't know how much Daddy loves you." And then, right there, in front of all those people, I just reached up and hugged him around the neck.

Comments and Questions

1. The movement of this piece seems to be casual, as though the narrator were simply offering impressions of "dinner on the ground after preaching." Is the selection of details really haphazard, or are the details highly controlled?

2. What is the basic dissatisfaction of the twelve-year-old boy toward his parents, his relatives, and the whole situation of his home town? How does this attitude give point to the unrestrained gesture at the end of the episode?

William E. Cole   (1904–1979)
Living and Dying in Shady Valley

The Shady Valley my great-great-grandfather Jesse Cole knew and the one I knew as a child must have been greatly different. His community had 100 souls, mine had 750. His community had a single combination log church and schoolhouse only a fourth mile from where he lived. The lake in the middle of the swamp was much larger in his day. The paths across the mountains in those days had been changed to narrow roads for hauling goods, timber, and lumber in my day. We also had a railroad now.

The geographic locality was the same—12 miles northeast from Mountain City in Johnson County, the tip end of the county making up the eastern end of the sled runner shape of the state of Tennessee, and 22 miles southeast of Bristol, Tennessee-Virginia. In Jesse's day, Bristol was an important trading place, the site of an old fort, and in my time a principal trading center for a dozen counties in Eastern Tennessee, Southwest Virginia, and Western North Carolina. As in Jesse Cole's time, the Iron Mountain had to be crossed to get to Mountain City, the county seat, and the Holston Mountain and the Holston River had to be negotiated to get to Bristol. When I was small, the river had no bridge. If it was at flood stage or too high to ford, one camped in his wagon beside the river until it went down.

The mountain roads were narrow, steep, and rocky. The first automobiles were not driven in the Valley because the roads were too rough. The common mode of travel was to walk, ride bareback, or go by wagon or buggy. The county had a single high school which I attended for three years, boarded in the dormitory, walked the 12 miles home on Friday after school, and walked back to school on Sunday afternoon. People going from the Valley to Bristol would sometimes walk across the Holston Mountain to the Holston River where they would catch a narrow gauge, logging train into Bristol. This train had a combined baggage and passenger car attached to the log and lumber cars.

Shady Valley then was a mosaic of interesting places. These somehow fitted together into a pattern of stimulus and response which made the Valley an interesting place in which to grow up, and in which to be, whatever one's stage in the life cycle. At the turn of the twentieth century, rural communities in Appalachia and the South had four social institutions—families, churches, one and two teacher schools, and country stores.

5   I started going to the store alone in 1908 when I was four years old. The store was a half mile from home, and the road was muddy in winter. My folks had bought me a little red wagon which I sometimes pulled to the store. I learned early that if I pecked on the glass showcase where the candy was stored, Uncle Lewis Garland would give me a piece of candy. The store ledger shows that three cents worth of candy "by Earle" was charged to dad's account by me on April 8, 1908. I was not yet four years old.

Being a company store, J. W. Broce and Company made wide use of "due bills," a form of paper script. The company would also give "orders" to the store. The bearer would trade out some amount and receive a due bill or cash for the balance. A person who had a charge account at the store, and whose credit was good, could write an order to the store to let the bearer have a designated amount of goods and the merchant would charge this to the store account of the issuer.

In no small way the charge accounts reflect the standard of living and style of life of the customers and the composition of families. Some families were known as "big spenders," actually spending modest amounts, but large in response to what they made or had.

In the language of some, they lived out of the store. Some families, my own for example, were almost completely self-sufficient, buying little at the store. My family grew its own fruits and vegetables. My dad would kill a dozen hogs. We would eat the hams, fry some of the shoulder meat, cook with some of the bacon, locally called "middling," and sell the remainder to people who came to our house for corn, eggs, and meat. If the store ran out of bacon, my dad would sell a side or a shoulder of pork to the store.

Customers paid their accounts at the store in many ways. Some did not pay at all but this was unusual. In one instance, not unique, one family, very poor by any standards, had a page of charges and no credits. The family had two mentally deranged children whom they kept chained to their beds until they were grown, at which time they were moved to the mental hospital in Knoxville. The keepers of the store knew what people could pay and what they could not pay. I have a feeling this family was carried at the store's expense. Customers would often "chip in" to help a family pay for funeral expenses or to meet some other emergency expense. There is in the ledger an item of $26 for "funeral supplies" for a man whose identity I cannot establish. He appeared not to belong to any family. Some ten people contributed to liquidating this bill, some paying as little as 25 cents.

The store plan was simple. A single large floor formed the basis for a large rectangular room attractively ceiled with planed poplar boards. The rows of counters set out three feet from the wall, and the shelves which lined the wall gave the merchant room to "wait on the trade." Some of the store's shelves were attractively filled with bolts of cloth and piece goods. The boards in the counter tops had shrunk some since being installed. More than one person had had their boils lanced by a kindly customer who would have the ailing person put his boil over a crack in the counter while he put his knife blade into the crack from under the counter and, carefully gauging the distance, would slit the boil. The keeper of the store was also adept at this minor surgery.

10   Near a window at the back of the store was the merchant's "office," with an old oak roll top desk, with lots of pigeon holes half filled with papers. The desk was behind the counter but near to the public. A large potbelly stove doubled as a source of heat and as an incinerator. Around the store were a half dozen durable hickory bottomed chairs. In winter the stove area served as a social center as did the front porch in summer. Ample Brown's Mule tobacco boxes served as cuspidores for the tobacco chewers and snuff dippers, mostly men, as few women loitered around the store. The store was no small segment of a man's world in upper Shady Valley.

An extra unheated room in the back of the store was the meat room. It was used largely for storing "sides" or "squares" of bacon, called locally "sowbelly" or fatback, or just "meat." The meat was heavily salted and arrived at the store sewed in burlap. From time to time, locally slaughtered pork or beef was sold by the store.

A large room along one side of the store's main floor was used for storing flour, meal, wheat bran, or chop as it was called, salt, wire, heavier hardware, tarpaper roofing, which was beginning to replace handmade wooden shingles and boards, and cheap, fragile pink-tinted building paper, which came in four-foot rolls and was held on to walls and ceilings by metal discs through which a nail was driven. Poor families used it to cover the walls of their rooms, replacing paper from magazines and newspapers which had been attached to the walls with a flour paste as "wallpaper" to keep the cold out. Newspapers and magazines were often passed from family to family for reading and later wound up on the walls of some houses for wallpaper.

The store had an ample porch or unloading platform in front. This faced the east and provided shade in the afternoon. In spring, summer and fall it was a favorite place for the "loafers" to "set," tell stories, and argue. The store, a house with outbuildings, and the school, were on five acres in the middle of my father's farm. His farming activity, being highly visible to people on the store porch, was always a favorite topic of conversation. Out of respect for the law, the front door of the store was liberally used for official notices generally placed there by the county sheriff, the local constable, the tax assessor, or the county trustee.

As a rule, women and children came and traded but did not tarry long at the store. I spent as much time there as my parents would permit. Women were scarce at the store in winter. Those who "set" were not the *le haute société* of Shady Valley. A few female "characters" lingered to be teased by the men. On the whole the store was a male hangout. The presence of women inhibited both argument, news, and the telling of racy stories and jokes.

15   In different parts of the South country stores had different functions. For the most part, whatever their location, country stores were community institutions as were their proprietors. Many merchants were confidants to people who had problems, many of them economic and having to do with farming or timbering. Country stores were sources of credit long before banks were established. They were also sources of credit to people who did not have access to banks. They constituted a local market for many farm products and were, therefore, an important factor in the development and maintenance of the family farm. My family often sold meat, butter, eggs, corn, oats, hay, straw, hides, tallow, and lard to the J. W. Broce Company, sometimes by order from the store to a customer or sometimes directly to the store for resale.

As one went the three hundred yards from the store to the lumber yard, the odors changed. The meat room at the store smelled of bacon, salt, and brined fish. New clothes and shoes gave a newness odor to the store. Near the candy counter one could detect the mingled smells of peppermint, birch, liquorice, and chocolate.

The frequency, multiplicity, and intensity of sights, sounds, and smells tend to condition us to them and somewhat immunize us to their effects. But the smell of fresh timber, wood, and tanbark on the lumber yards was unforgettable. The best of the odors were of spruce, chestnut, oak, and pine. The lumber yard smells were almost as good as those of our spruce and pine woodland on a damp morning where we often played and tracked opossums to their dens. The community in 1908 or 1912 was simple but the sounds and the smells were good.

Our barns were oases of smells. Within each were islands of smells. The horses, the sheep, the cows, new calves, lambs, and pigs had their own "this is us" odors. The work horses added a distinctive smell of hard labor. The corn crib smelled heavily of mice, corn being odorless, while the granary had the smell of dry wheat, oats, rats, and mice.

A job that I always hated was to hold small male pigs between my legs with their rears pointed upward and away from the sun, while my dad castrated them. Their piercing squeals registered intense pain. Dad would invariably say that their squeals were changed to sounds of "ruint, ruint" when we released them.

20   Shady Valley is a deep valley surrounded by mountains, some of them over 4,000 feet high. The isolation of the valley, and the closeness of the mountains, caused sounds to be unforgettable. One could hear the whistle of the steam engines powering the sawmills on the mountains and the hum of the circular saws cutting their way through chestnut, oak, spruce, and maple logs.

The swamp lay in the middle of the valley. Its sounds changed with the seasons. It was quiet in the winter. Only the bark of an occasional dog running a rabbit or a fox or the hoot of an owl in the evening disturbed its silence. In the spring the swamp came to life. As the days warmed, the frogs of many kinds began to croak. Then came the migrating redwing blackbirds which moved into the swamp to mate and nest there. There were thousands of them. These were followed by a half dozen other species of birds. Whatever the season, as I lay in bed the hoot of the owls would send a chill up my spine.

In the summer, redwing blackbirds, grackles, a variety of warblers, and noisesome blue jays dominated the swamp. It was a cathedral and symphony of song. In the fields were quail, meadowlarks, crows, kildeers, mockingbirds, and robins. Downy and hairy woodpeckers and yellow-breasted sapsuckers were common in the orchards and in the swamp and woods. The pileated woodpeckers were there but more elusive and not so common. In the evening there were lots of martins and chimney swifts. Occasionally one would come down a chimney and would be found attached to the curtain in a room.

After supper, when the winds blew over the Holston Mountain from the West, I would often stand at the back of our yard overlooking the swamp and hear the trains switching in Bristol or the whistles of the great trains running up and down the main line between Washington and the South. The sounds created in me a deep feeling of loneliness and desire to be where the action was.

A sound that was unique disappeared as my dad reached his sixties. My mother's heart attack in 1930 probably had something to do with it. Prior to then my dad would get up at four o'clock in the morning and walk a quarter of a mile to the big barn to do his feeding and milking. All the way there he would sing at the top of his voice. Families living a mile away could hear Uncle Will's voice and would use him as an alarm clock. What dad sang no one in the Valley knew. What he lacked in clarity he made up for in volume. We never asked him why he sang. I always felt that this was his way of expressing his happiness for being alive and living and working in Shady Valley. There was a church in the middle of our farm. One of dad's neighbors said he was singing in church there one Sunday morning, and that his cattle came up to the fence around the church yard and bawled for him. This he denied.

25　　　　Until the federal government acquired most of the mountain land in Shady Valley, forming part of the Cherokee National Forest, the mountains were frequently burned over, especially when they were dry in the spring and fall. At night the flaming forests and sounds of burning and falling timbers were awesome. There were no resources for fighting the fires. Tracts would burn out or burn until the rains came. From our back yard we would watch the fires with concern and a feeling of helplessness and listen to the great dead trees falling into their fiery graves.

From about the age of eight when I could handle a 22 or 32 calibre rifle, I hunted the swamp, occasionally killing a rabbit, a "chicken" hawk, a crow which picked up corn, a blackbird, or a little red squirrel, locally called a "boomer," and only found at high altitudes in Appalachia. There were lots of these in our woods and swamp. At times they would come from the swamp to eat corn from our corn cribs.

With rifle and muzzle loader shotgun, my friend Bill Pennington and I roamed the swamp. Bill lived on the edge of it. We fished the creek for suckers, bullheads, chubs, and an occasional brook trout. Brook trout had been native to the mountain area but had been largely killed out by the release of sawdust into the stream and later by the release of washings from ore.

Bill Pennington and I could cross the swamp at two or three places. We roamed it and made bows and arrows from laurel. We ate teaberries, blackberries, and muscadine grapes in season. Whatever we did we always held in awe the swamp's darkness, its great trees, the wild life and the constancy and change of it.

As death often comes to good things, it came to the swamp. It came in two great strokes. First, in the depression a decision was made by the county civil works administration, the WPA, to survey the creek, straighten bends in it, and blast out certain rock reefs that were keeping the water level from lowering. This move didn't destroy the swamp, only reduced the size of it. Then, the Soil Conservation Corps decided to ditch the creek and build a supporting earth dam at the upper end of the Valley, to hold and gradually release flood water. Now most of the land has been timbered and may be cultivated. It is held by half a dozen people. Call it progress if you will. I don't. Only a handful of farmers benefited from the SCS operation. An interesting swamp was destroyed. One of the worst floods the Valley has had took place after the project was completed.

30   Mountain people have a strong attachment to place—to streams, mountains and lakes, and to hunting and fishing. Often they have almost a clanlike feeling for family and kin. Isolation, large families, kin networks, and dependence upon one another account in part for this attachment. One Saturday an old neighbor, a real mountain man, died. On Sunday the rains came and covered the low water bridges so the preacher couldn't get there to conduct the funeral. The saddened wife called on his neighbor, also a mountain man and a friend of her husband, to "say a few words." The neighbor had never spoken in public before, but he knew and loved old Zeb Taylor, the deceased. He got up with his black wool hat in his hands and in sadness said: "Poor old Zeb he's dead. He had good coon dogs and he run 'em. He had good game chickens and he fit 'em; he had good corn licker and he drunk it. Such is the Kingdom of Heaven, Amen," and sat down.

Stories about death, some sad some amusing, were common. One mother asked that the new dress on her dead daughter be removed before she was buried and replaced by an old dress her daughter had worn, so her living sister might have the new one. One man, who had a small farm on the side of the mountain, asked that when he died he be buried standing up vertically in his coffin so that he might look out over the Valley. With pick and shovel a seven-foot vertical grave was too difficult to construct, so he was buried in a horizontal grave.

We had a delightful, hardworking, hunchback man in the community. When he died they strapped him to an ironing board to straighten him out so he would fit into the homemade coffin. Rigor mortis set in and the tie-down straps broke and he sat up on the ironing board startling Preacher Phipps, who was kneeling on the floor praying beside the body. An onlooker declared that Phipps said, "Lay down there Billy or damn you I'll kill you."

My dad told a story of a funeral in a small church for a hunchback who sat up in the coffin. Everyone, scared, headed for the outside. One old lady asked another what the preacher said when he came through the door. He said, said the lady, "Damn a church with only one door."

At funerals, preachers generally spoke kindly of the person and sometimes overdid it. In such an instance a widow at her husband's funeral grew increasingly apprehensive at the glowing remarks the preacher was making about her somewhat ornery husband. She admonished one of his kids, "Johnny, will you go over there and look in that coffin to see if that's your pappy the preacher is talking about."

35   Mountain preachers as a rule would use a funeral occasion not just to inventory the merits of the dead but to admonish the living to lead better lives. They particularly aimed their remarks at the sinners, reminding them that death is inevitable and often sudden.

The first traumatic experience I can remember was when Grandmother Cole died. She was born Sarah A. Shoun in Doe Valley, across the Iron Mountain, some six miles from home, on January 2, 1829. She died on July 13, 1909 just before my fifth birthday. She had married my grandfather, Washington Cole, on June 8, 1854. They had eight children, two of whom died in infancy. Granddad had died in 1870, leaving grandmother widowed for thirty-nine years. She had five boys and a daughter to care for. She lived with our family at the old home place, a portion of which had been owned by Jesse Cole and other ancestors.

Although grandmother was eighty years old, we were not prepared for her death.

She had had few illnesses of consequence. On the day she died, she got up early in the morning, ate her breakfast and then she suddenly felt sick and lay down and died. She was industrious and had always worked hard. She was good to us children and always had time for us. She was a bit stooped, a characteristic of the Coles as they get old. She wore long dresses, some of them homespun from the loom in our loom house. She always wore a long starched apron and pulled her hair back over her head and fastened it in a bun on the back of her head.

I knew nothing of the meaning of death although I knew my mother had lost her parents and sister soon after I was born. I only knew I would miss grandmother and I was sad for my brother and sister and my parents.

A neighbor cared for me while grandmother was buried. From a window in the end of our living room I could see people on the top of the hill a fourth of a mile from the house when grandmother was being buried in the Cole cemetery. Her body was hauled there in my dad's wagon. At the funeral the preacher very fittingly said of her: "Hers was a noble, devoted life."

40   When I was small, we did not have an undertaker in the county. People had to be buried fairly soon after death. It was a custom to put mint under a bed or coffin when a person lay a corpse. This was to counteract any body odors. Persons who had died of cancer, tuberculosis, locally called consumption, or who had died from injuries involving gangrene appeared to be the worst. Mint was placed under grandmother's bed as she lay a corpse. Even today, when I smell mint, I think of death.

A first principle is to keep alive. A second is to try to be physically adequate. We call it healthy. We had a doctor—Dr. J. C. Hutchinson. He had been invited to come to the Valley by one of the lumber companies. The company had assured him that a doctor would be needed, that Shady Valley would be a good place to practice, and that there would be opportunity to supplement his income through the operation of a store and from the buying and selling of timber and lumber. Also, he later became postmaster and operated the post office from a room in his store.

"Doc," as he was called, had a good rural reputation as a doctor of wounds and as an obstetrician and "baby doctor." He had some success with fevers—both typhoid and pneumonia. Some patients felt he was too generous and easy with the use of calomel. He walked with a limp from an old leg injury. Babies were delivered in the home by Doc, and by one of three or so midwives or by Dr. Jody Proffitt, who came from Doe Valley six miles away, across the Iron Mountain when called. Dr. Smythe or Dr. Butler would come from the county seat twelve miles away for six to ten dollars.

All rode horses into the Valley. Dr. Jody Proffitt rolled some of his own pills and packaged many of his own powders. He carried his supplies in saddle bags thrown across his horse. Jody was a tall, absent-minded, kindly man. He practiced medicine until he was 92 years of age. One time my mother asked Jody the sex of a baby he had delivered. He said, "Sally, I'll be darned if I haven't forgotten, but I'm pretty sure it's either a boy or a girl."

Our community, for those who spent their lives there, was a kind of a cradle to the grave arrangement. The store had soft flannel and soft cloth to diaper a baby and keep it warm. There were booties and socks and cheap shoes for baby's feet. For the dead, there were "going away clothes" at the store, usually grey or black. Neither caskets nor their metal parts were stocked. These were obtained from the hardware dealer a dozen miles away. For the poorest people only the screws for the top of the casket, or coffin, and handles were obtained. The store had cotton and fine cloth for lining the casket. A funeral kit was the "Belknap Funeral Kit" sold to hardware stores by salesmen from the wholesale Belknap Hardware Company in Louisville. Plaques with the Belknap kit might vary according to the age or sex of the deceased. A favorite was "At rest." The plaques were interchangeable and were designed to fit the deceased and the occasion.

45   At the store there was usually an assessment of the dead. The discussion often turned into a kind of country store Judgment Day. Uncle Jim Wright, patriarch that he was, often led the discussion. The how and why of dying emerged from the discussions, along with the circumstances of one's dying, what he or she had left, and whether or not they would be missed. How the living would adjust and what would happen to the farm or home were usual topics for speculation.

A number of people kept dry lumber in their barns suitable for caskets. My dad kept both white pine and poplar boards suitable for either wagon beds or caskets in his barn loft. It was free if used for caskets. On the day of death, citizens would gather at the graveyard to dig the grave; others would gather at someone's place to plane the boards, stain and varnish them, and pad and line the casket. One man on horseback would be dispatched across the mountain to get the "silver" trimmings. Ladies would gather at the home of the deceased with food or to help with food preparation and the chores and to take care of the children. Other neighbors would sit up with the corpse throughout the night. The living knew the people who died and deaths were sad occasions. The people were close to the sick and knew what was going on. Spirits would rise or decline as the ill recovered or worsened in condition. Sometimes the sick person would want a squirrel or a rabbit or a chicken to eat and a member of the family or a neighbor would be dispatched to obtain it. Some lingered and suffered so long that death was a happy relief to everyone. Some fought death for reasons one never knew and were generally never told. Death was accepted as normal, inevitable, and according to the will of God. Neither the young nor the old were shielded from it. The preacher talked about it and the people experienced it. Mothers, fathers, and neighbors welcomed the newborn into this world and fondled them, while mountain men with strong arms and shoulders carried the dead away from the living into the graveyards.

Comments and Questions

1. In this selection a distinguished sociologist recreates the Appalachian mountain community of his own boyhood some sixty to seventy years earlier. The piece is an engaging and informative combination, in places a skillful blend, of personal memory and objective, descriptive sociology. Point out some passages that predominantly reflect the intimacy of personal recollection, and cite others that exhibit a greater distance between the writer and his materials. Are there notable stylistic differences between the two groups of passages you have identified (consider diction, syntax, sentence structure and type, perspective)? What other differences can you note in content, apparent sources of information or in response generated in you by passages from the different groupings?

2. Cole describes hearing distant train whistles as a boy and wanting "to be where the action was." In the preceding selection, the narrator recalls, "I was twelve years old, and it looked like to me that I never was going to get away from the country." Yet each author here circles back compulsively to his origins. Why? Are there indications in the pieces themselves?

3. How would you compare other aspects of the Drake and Cole selections? How are specific instances of emotion and humor revealing of character or community in each selection? How do the selections differ in sentence structure, language, imagery, consistency of expression by the narrator himself? Would it be accurate to say that the first piece is primarily an imaginative or creative rendering of memory and the second is primarily a sociological one? Support your answer by defining *creative* and *sociological* and by comparing specific aspects of the two selections.

4. Describe the community attitude toward death in Shady Valley. How does Cole convey to his reader a sense of the origins and progressive development of that attitude in this selection?

5. What parallels can you draw between the various means of depicting death here and in Tolstoy's "Three Deaths" (p. 287)? How are those means functional? How do they contribute to theme in each selection? Characterize and compare the relationship between life and death in the two (and you might want to consider Porter's "The Grave," p. 109; and Tennyson's "Tears, Idle Tears," p. 472, in this connection).

Frederick Douglass   (c. 1817–1895)
A Child's Reasoning

The incidents related in the foregoing chapter[1] led me thus early to inquire into the origin and nature of slavery. Why am I a slave? Why are some people slaves and others masters? These were perplexing questions and very troublesome to my childhood. I was very early told by some one that *"God up in the sky"* had made all things, and had made black people to be slaves and white people to be masters. I was told too that God was good, and that He knew what was best for everybody. This was, however, less satisfactory than the first statement. It came point blank against all my notions of goodness. The case of Aunt Esther[2] was in my mind. Besides, I could not tell how anybody could know that God made black people to be slaves. Then I found, too, that there were puzzling exceptions to this theory of slavery, in the fact that all black people were not slaves, and all white people were not masters.

An incident occurred about this time that made a deep impression on my mind. My Aunt Jennie and one of the men slaves of Captain Anthony ran away. A great noise was made about it. Old master was furious. He said he would follow them and catch them and bring them back, but he never did, and somebody told me that Uncle Noah and Aunt Jennie had gone to the free states and were free. Besides this occurrence, which brought much light to my mind on the subject, there were several slaves on Mr. Lloyd's place who remembered being brought from Africa. There were others who told me that their fathers and mothers were stolen from Africa.

This to me was important knowledge, but not such as to make me feel very easy in my slave condition. The success of Aunt Jennie and Uncle Noah in getting away from slavery was, I think, the first fact that made me seriously think of escape for myself. I could

---

[1] Chapter 4 of *Life and Times of Frederick Douglass,* revised edition of 1892.   [2] The little boy had witnessed "old master," as the slave owner was called, brutally whipping the bared back of his Aunt Esther.

not have been more than seven or eight years old at the time of this occurrence, but young as I was, I was already, in spirit and purpose, a fugitive from slavery.

Up to the time of the brutal treatment of my Aunt Esther, already narrated, and the shocking plight in which I had seen my cousin from Tuckahoe, my attention had not been especially directed to the grosser and more revolting features of slavery. I had, of course, heard of whippings and savage mutilations of slaves by brutal overseers, but happily for me I had always been out of the way of such occurrences. My play time was spent outside of the corn and tobacco fields, where the overseers and slaves were brought together and in conflict. But after the case of my Aunt Esther I saw others of the same disgusting and shocking nature. The one of these which agitated and distressed me most was the whipping of a woman, not belonging to my old master, but to Col. Lloyd. The charge against her was very common and very indefinite, namely, *"impudence."* This crime could be committed by a slave in a hundred different ways, and depended much upon the temper and caprice of the overseer as to whether it was committed at all. He could create the offense whenever it pleased him. A look, a word, a gesture, accidental or intentional, never failed to be taken as impudence when he was in the right mood for such an offense. In this case there were all the necessary conditions for the commission of the crime charged. The offender was nearly white, to begin with; she was the wife of a favorite hand on board of Mr. Lloyd's sloop, and was, besides, the mother of five sprightly children. Vigorous and spirited woman that she was, a wife and a mother, with a predominating share of the blood of the master running in her veins, Nellie (for that was her name) had all the qualities essential to impudence to a slave overseer. My attention was called to the scene of the castigation by the loud screams and curses that proceeded from the direction of it. When I came near the parties engaged in the struggle the overseer had hold of Nellie, endeavoring with his whole strength to drag her to a tree against her resistance. Both his and her faces were bleeding, for the woman was doing her best. Three of her children were present, and though quite small (from seven to ten years old, I should think), they gallantly took the side of their mother against the overseer, and pelted him well with stones and epithets. Amid the screams of the children, "Let my mammy go! Let my mammy go!" the hoarse voice of the maddened overseer was heard in terrible oaths that he would teach her how to give a white man *impudence.* The blood on his face and on hers attested her skill in the use of her nails, and his dogged determination to conquer. His purpose was to tie her up to a tree and give her, in slaveholding parlance, a "genteel flogging," and he evidently had not expected the stern and protracted resistance he was meeting, or the strength and skill needed to its execution. There were times when she seemed likely to get the better of the brute, but he finally overpowered her and succeeded in getting her arms firmly tied to the tree towards which he had been dragging her. The victim was now at the mercy of his merciless lash. What followed I need not here describe. The cries of the now helpless woman, while undergoing the terrible infliction, were mingled with the hoarse curses of the overseer and the wild cries of her distracted children. When the poor woman was untied her back was covered with blood. She was whipped, terribly whipped, but she was not subdued, and continued to denounce the overseer and to pour upon him every vile epithet of which she could think.

5   Such floggings are seldom repeated on the same persons by overseers. They prefer to whip those who are the most easily whipped. The doctrine that submission to violence is the best cure for violence did not hold good as between slaves and overseers. He was whipped oftener who was whipped easiest. That slave who had the courage to stand up for himself against the overseer, although he might have many hard stripes at first, became while legally a slave virtually a freeman. "You can shoot me," said a slave to Rigby Hopkins, "but you can't whip me," and the result was he was neither whipped nor shot. I do not

know that Mr. Sevier ever attempted to whip Nellie again. He probably never did, for he was taken sick not long after and died. It was commonly said that his deathbed was a wretched one, and that, the ruling passion being strong in death, he died flourishing the slave whip and with horrid oaths upon his lips. This deathbed scene may only be the imaginings of the slaves. One thing is certain, that when he was in health his profanity was enough to chill the blood of an ordinary man. Nature, or habit, had given to his face an expression of uncommon savageness. Tobacco and rage had ground his teeth short, and nearly every sentence that he uttered was commenced or completed with an oath. Hated for his cruelty, despised for his cowardice, he went to his grave lamented by nobody on the place outside of his own house, if, indeed, he was even lamented there.

In Mr. James Hopkins, the succeeding overseer, we had a different and a better man, as good perhaps as any man could be in the position of a slave overseer. Though he sometimes wielded the lash, it was evident that he took no pleasure in it and did it with much reluctance. He stayed but a short time here, and his removal from the position was much regretted by the slaves generally. Of the sucessor of Mr. Hopkins I shall have something to say at another time and in another place.

For the present we will attend to a further description of the businesslike aspect of Col. Lloyd's "Great House" farm. There was always much bustle and noise here on the two days at the end of each month, for then the slaves belonging to the different branches of this great estate assembled here by their representatives to obtain their monthly allowances of cornmeal and pork. These were gala days for the slaves of the outlying farms, and there was much rivalry among them as to who should be elected to go up to the Great House farm for the "Allowances," and indeed to attend to any other business at this great place, to them the capital of a little nation. Its beauty and grandeur, its immense wealth, its numerous population, and the fact that uncles Harry, Peter, and Jake, the sailors on board the sloop, usually kept on sale trinkets which they bought in Baltimore to sell to their less fortunate fellow-servants, made a visit to the Great House farm a high privilege, and eagerly sought. It was valued, too, as a mark of distinction and confidence, but probably the chief motive among the competitors for the office was the opportunity it afforded to shake off the monotony of the field and to get beyond the overseer's eye and lash. Once on the road with an oxteam and seated on the tongue of the cart, with no overseer to look after him, one felt comparatively free.

Slaves were expected to sing as well as to work. A silent slave was not liked, either by masters or overseers. "Make a noise there! Make a noise there!" and "bear a hand," were words usually addressed to slaves when they were silent. This, and the natural disposition of the Negro to make a noise in the world, may account for the almost constant singing among them when at their work. There was generally more or less singing among the teamsters, at all times. It was a means of telling the overseer, in the distance, where they were and what they were about. But on the allowance days those commissioned to the Great House farm were peculiarly vocal. While on the way they would make the grand old woods for miles around reverberate with their wild and plaintive notes. They were indeed both merry and sad. Child as I was, these wild songs greatly depressed my spirits. Nowhere outside of dear old Ireland, in the days of want and famine, have I heard sounds so mournful.

In all these slave songs there was some expression of praise of the Great House farm—something that would please the pride of the Lloyds.

> I am going to the Great House farm,
>   O, yea! O, yea! O, yea!
> My old master is a good old master,
>   O, yea! O, yea! O, yea!

10   These words would be sung over and over again, with others, improvised as they went along—jargon, perhaps, to the reader, but full of meaning to the singers. I have sometimes thought that the mere hearing of these songs would have done more to impress the good people of the North with the soul-crushing character of slavery than whole volumes exposing the physical cruelties of the slave system, for the heart has no language like song. Many years ago, when recollecting my experience in this respect, I wrote of these slave songs in the following strain:

"I did not, when a slave, fully understand the deep meaning of those rude and apparently incoherent songs. I was, myself, within the circle, so that I could then neither hear nor see as those without might see and hear. They breathed the prayer and complaint of souls overflowing with the bitterest anguish. They depressed my spirits and filled my heart with ineffable sadness."

The remark in the olden time was not unfrequently made, that slaves were the most contented and happy laborers in the world, and the dancing and singing were referred to in proof of this alleged fact; but it was a great mistake to suppose them happy because they sometimes made those joyful noises. The songs of the slaves represented their sorrows, rather than their joys. Like tears, they were a relief to aching hearts. It is not inconsistent with the constitution of the human mind that it avails itself of one and the same method for expressing opposite emotions. Sorrow and desolation have their songs, as well as joy and peace.

It was the boast of slaveholders that their slaves enjoyed more of the physical comforts of life than the peasantry of any country in the world. My experience contradicts this. The men and the women slaves on Col. Lloyd's farm received, as their monthly allowance of food, eight pounds of pickled pork, or its equivalent in fish. The pork was often tainted, and the fish were of the poorest quality. With their pork or fish, they had given them one bushel of Indian meal, unbolted, of which quite fifteen per cent was more fit for pigs than for men. With this, one pint of salt was given, and this was the entire monthly allowance of a full-grown slave, working constantly in the open field from morning till night every day in the month except Sunday. There is no kind of work which really requires a better supply of food to prevent physical exhaustion than the field-work of a slave. The yearly allowance of clothing was not more ample than the supply of food. It consisted of two tow-linen shirts, one pair of trousers of the same coarse material, for summer, and a woolen pair of trousers and a woolen jacket for winter, with one pair of yarn stockings and a pair of shoes of the coarsest description. Children under ten years old had neither shoes, stockings, jackets, nor trousers. They had two coarse tow-linen shirts per year, and when these were worn out they went naked till the next allowance day—and this was the condition of the little girls as well as of the boys.

As to beds, they had none. One coarse blanket was given them, and this only to the men and women. The children stuck themselves in holes and corners about the quarters, often in the corners of huge chimneys, with their feet in the ashes to keep them warm. The want of beds, however, was not considered a great privation by the field hands. Time to sleep was of far greater importance. For when the day's work was done most of these had their washing, mending, and cooking to do, and having few or no facilities for doing such things, very many of their needed sleeping hours were consumed in necessary preparations for the labors of the coming day. The sleeping apartments, if they could have been properly called such, had little regard to comfort or decency. Old and young, male and female, married and single, dropped down upon the common clay floor, each covering up with his or her blanket, their only protection from cold or exposure. The night, however, was shortened at both ends. The slaves worked often as long as they could see, and were late in cooking and mending for the coming day, and at the first gray streak of the morning they were summoned to the field by the overseer's horn. They were whipped for over-sleeping more than for any other fault. Neither age nor sex found any favor. The overseer stood at the quarter door, armed with stick and whip, ready to deal heavy blows upon any who might be a little behind time. When the horn was blown there was a rush for the door, for the hindermost one was sure to get a blow from the overseer. Young mothers who worked in the field were allowed an hour about ten o'clock in the morning to go home to nurse their children. This was when they were not required to take them to the field with them, and leave them upon "turning row," or in the corner of the fences.

15   As a general rule the slaves did not come to their quarters to take their meals, but took their ashcake (called thus because baked in the ashes) and piece of pork, or their salt herrings, where they were at work.

But let us now leave the rough usage of the field, where vulgar coarseness and brutal cruelty flourished as rank as weeds in the tropics and where a vile wretch, in the shape of a man, rides, walks, and struts about, with whip in hand, dealing heavy blows and leaving deep gashes on the flesh of men and women, and turn our attention to the less repulsive slave life as it existed in the home of my childhood. Some idea of the splendor of that place sixty years ago has already been given. The contrast between the condition of the slaves and that of their masters was marvelously sharp and striking. There were pride, pomp, and luxury on the one hand, servility, dejection, and misery on the other.

Comments and Questions

Douglass looms large today as a black who overcame great obstacles. Many tributes are paid to him, such as Robert Hayden's "Frederick Douglass," page 527.

1. This selection was taken from *Life and Times of Frederick Douglass* (chapter 5). It is, therefore, only a small segment of a long autobiography, a work that centers in the person of one man but that, just as importantly, exposes the reality of a slave-owning society. Does the author succeed in his attempt to make his readers *feel* the condition of being a field-hand slave? Note the stateliness of the prose. Note also the use of adjectives: *brutal, shocking, revolting, savage, terrible,* and the like. Do these words evoke the re-sponse Douglass was seeking? Compare the style of Floyd Dell in "Christmas," page 1002.

2. Memories of childhood have also been the basis of the five pieces preceding this one. All six authors display distinctive styles. If style is the individual, what may be con-cluded about Dell, Thomas, Clemens, Drake, Cole, and Douglass?

3. Chapter 7 of Douglass's autobiography is called "Luxuries of the Great House." It throws into sharp contrast the lives of the slave owners and their slaves; yet the obser-vation is made that "the poor slave, on his hard pine plank, scantily covered with his thin blanket, slept more soundly than the feverish voluptuary who reclined upon his downy pillow." Comment.

James Anthony Froude (1818–1894)
The Execution of a Queen

The point of view in all the preceding selections, even in the passages from the *Life of Johnson*, has been from the inside looking out, with each biographer his own interpreter. In "The Execution of a Queen" Froude acts as a detached observer, the skillful artist who swings the camera close to his subject and gives us an intimate view of the last hours of Mary, Queen of Scots.

Her last night was a busy one. As she said to herself, there was much to be done and the time was short. A few lines to the King of France were dated two hours after midnight. They were to insist for the last time that she was innocent of the conspiracy, that she was dying for religion, and for having asserted her right to the crown; and to beg that out of the sum which he owed her, her servants' wages might be paid and masses provided for her soul. After this she slept for three or four hours, and then rose and with the most elaborate care prepared to encounter the end.

At eight in the morning the provost-marshal knocked at the outer door which communicated with her suite of apartments. It was locked and no one answered, and he went back in some trepidation lest the fears might prove true which had been entertained the preceding evening. On his returning with the sheriff, however, a few minutes later, the door was open, and they were confronted with the tall majestic figure of Mary Stuart standing before them in splendour. The plain gray dress had been exchanged for a robe of black satin; her jacket was of black satin also, looped and slashed and trimmed with velvet. Her false hair was arranged studiously with a coif, and over her head and falling down over her back was a white veil of delicate lawn. A crucifix of gold hung over her neck. In her hand she held a crucifix of ivory, and a number of jewelled pater-nosters was attached to her girdle. Led by two of Paulet's gentlemen, the sheriff walking before her, she passed to the chamber of presence in which she had been tried, where Shrewsbury, Kent, Paulet, Drury, and others were waiting to receive her. Andrew Melville, Sir Robert's brother, who had been master of her household, was kneeling in tears. "Melville," she said, "you should rather rejoice than weep that the end of my troubles is come. Tell my friends I die a true Catholic. Commend me to my son. Tell him I have done nothing to prejudice his kingdom of Scotland, and so, good Melville, farewell." She kissed him, and turning asked for her chaplain Du Preau. He was not present. There had been a fear of some religious melodrama which it was thought well to avoid. Her ladies, who had attempted to follow her, had been kept back also. She could not afford to leave the account of her death to be reported by enemies and Puritans, and she required assistance for the scene which she meditated. Missing them she asked the reason of their absence, and said she wished them to see her die. Kent said he feared they might scream or faint, or attempt perhaps to dip their handkerchiefs in her blood. She undertook that they should be quiet and obedient. "The queen," she said, "would never deny her so slight a request"; and when Kent still hesitated, she added with tears, "You know I am cousin to your queen, of the blood of Henry VII, a married Queen of France, and anointed Queen of Scotland."

It was impossible to refuse. She was allowed to take six of her own people with her, and select them herself. She chose her physician Burgoyne, Andrew Melville, the apothecary Gorion, and her surgeon, with two ladies, Elizabeth Kennedy, and Curle's young wife Barbara Mowbray, whose child she had baptized.

Allons donc, she then said—"Let us go," and passing out attended by the earls, and leaning on the arm of an officer of the guard, she descended the great staircase to the hall. The news had spread far through the country. Thousands of people were collected outside the walls. About three hundred knights and gentlemen of the county had been admitted to witness the execution. The tables and forms had been removed, and a great wood fire was blazing in the chimney. At the upper end of the hall, above the fireplace, but near it, stood the scaffold, twelve feet square and two feet and a half high. It was covered with black cloth; a low rail ran around it covered with black cloth also, and the sheriff's guard of halberdiers were ranged on the floor below on the four sides to keep off the crowd. On the scaffold was the block, black like the rest; a square black cushion was placed behind it, and behind the cushion a black chair; on the right were two other chairs for the earls. The ax leaned against the rail, and two masked figures stood like mutes on either side at the back. The Queen of Scots as she swept in seemed as if coming to take part in some solemn pageant. Not a muscle of her face could be seen to quiver; she ascended the scaffold with absolute composure, looked round her smiling, and sat down. Shrewsbury and Kent followed and took their places, the sheriff stood at her left hand, and Beale then mounted a platform and read the warrant aloud.

5   In all the assembly Mary Stuart appeared the person least interested in the words which were consigning her to death.

"Madam," said Lord Shrewsbury to her, when the reading was ended, "you hear what we are commanded to do."

"You will do your duty," she answered, and rose as if to kneel and pray.

The Dean of Peterborough, Dr. Fletcher, approached the rail. "Madam," he began, with a low obeisance, "the queen's most excellent majesty"—thrice he commenced his sentence, wanting words to pursue it. When he repeated the words a fourth time, she cut him short.

"Mr. Dean," she said, "I am a Catholic, and must die a Catholic. It is useless to attempt to move me, and your prayers will avail me but little."

10   "Change your opinion, madam," he cried, his tongue being loosed at last; "repent of your sins, settle your faith in Christ, by him to be saved."

"Trouble not yourself further, Mr. Dean," she answered; "I am settled in my own faith, for which I mean to shed my blood."

"I am sorry, madam," said Shrewsbury, "to see you so addicted to popery."

"That image of Christ you hold there," said Kent, "will not profit you if he be not engraved in your heart."

She did not reply, and turning her back on Fletcher, knelt for her own devotions.

15   He had been evidently instructed to impair the Catholic complexion of the scene, and the Queen of Scots was determined that he should not succeed. When she knelt he commenced an extempore prayer in which the assembly joined. As his voice was sounded out in the hall she raised her own, reciting with powerful deep-chested tones the penitential psalms in Latin, introducing English sentences at intervals that the audience might know what she was saying, and praying with especial distinctness for her Holy Father the Pope.

From time to time, with conspicuous vehemence, she struck the crucifix against her bosom, and then, as the Dean gave up the struggle, leaving her Latin, she prayed in English wholly, still clear and loud. She prayed for the Church which she had been ready to betray, for her son whom she had disinherited, for the queen whom she had endeavoured to murder. She prayed God to avert his wrath from England, that England which she had sent a last message to Philip to beseech him to invade. She forgave her enemies, whom she had invited Philip not to forget, and then, praying to the saints to intercede for her with Christ, and kissing the crucifix and crossing her own breast, "Even as thy arms, O Jesus," she cried, "were spread upon the cross, so receive me into thy mercy and forgive my sins."

With these words she rose; the black mutes stepped forward, and in the usual form begged her forgiveness.

"I forgive you," she said, "for now I hope you shall end all my troubles." They offered their help in arranging her dress. "Truly, my lords," she said with a smile to the earls, "I never had such grooms waiting on me before." Her ladies were allowed to come up upon the scaffold to assist her; for the work to be done was considerable, and had been prepared with no common thought.

She laid her crucifix on her chair. The chief executioner took it as a perquisite, but was ordered instantly to lay it down. The lawn veil was lifted carefully off, not to disturb the hair, and was hung upon the rail. The black robe was next removed. Below it was a petticoat of crimson velvet. The black jacket followed, and under the jacket was a body of crimson satin. One of her ladies handed her a pair of crimson sleeves, with which she hastily covered her arms; and thus she stood on the black scaffold with the black figures all around her, blood-red from head to foot.

20   Her reasons for adopting so extraordinary a costume must be left to conjecture. It is only certain that is must have been carefully studied, and that the pictorial effect must have been appalling.

The women, whose firmness had hitherto borne the trial, began now to give way, spasmodic sobs bursting from them which they could not check. *Ne criez vous,* she said, *j'ay promis pour vous.* Struggling bravely, they crossed their breasts again and again, she crossing them in turn and bidding them pray for her. Then she knelt on the cushion. Barbara Mowbray bound her eyes with a handkerchief. *Adieu,* she said, smiling for the last time and waving her hand to them *Adieu, au revoir.* They stepped back from off the scaffold and left her alone. On her knees she repeated the psalm, *In te, Domine, confido,* "In Thee, O Lord, have I put my trust." Her shoulders being exposed, two scars became visible, one on either side, and the earls being now a little behind her, Kent pointed to them with his white wand and looked inquiringly at his companion. Shrewsbury whispered that they were the remains of two abcesses from which she had suffered while living with him at Sheffield.

When the psalm was finished she felt for the block, and laying down her head she muttered: *In manus, Domine tuas, commendo animam meam.* The hard wood seemed to hurt her, for she placed her hands under her neck. The executioners gently removed them, lest they should deaden the blow, and then one of them holding her slightly, the other raised the ax and struck. The scene had been too trying even for the practised headsman of the Tower. His arm wandered. The blow fell on the knot of the handkerchief, and scarcely broke the skin. She neither spoke nor moved. He struck again, this time effectively. The head hung by a shred of skin, which he divided without withdrawing the ax; and at once a metamorphosis was witnessed, strange as was ever wrought by wand of fabled enchanter. The coif fell off and the false plaits. The laboured illusion vanished. The lady who had knelt before the block was in the maturity of grace and loveliness. The executioner, when he raised the head, as usual, to show it to the crowd, exposed the withered features of a grizzled, wrinkled old woman.

"So perish all enemies of the queen," said the Dean of Peterborough. A loud Amen rose over the hall. "Such end," said the Earl of Kent, rising and standing over the body, "to the queen's and the Gospels' enemies."

Orders had been given that everything which she had worn should be immediately destroyed, that no relics should be carried off to work imaginary miracles. Sentinels stood at the doors who allowed no one to pass out without permission; and after the first pause, the earls still keeping their places, the body was stripped. It then appeared that a favourite lapdog had followed its mistress unperceived, and was concealed under her clothes; when discovered it gave a short cry, and seated itself between the head and the neck, from which the blood was still flowing. It was carried away and carefully washed, and then beads, Paternoster, handkerchief—each particle of dress which the blood had touched, with the cloth on the block and on the scaffold, was burned in the hall fire in the presence of the crowd. The scaffold itself was next removed: a brief account of the execution was drawn up, with which Henry Talbot, Lord Shrewsbury's son, was sent to London, and then everyone was dismissed. Silence settled down on Fotheringay, and the last scene of the life of Mary Stuart, in which tragedy and melodrama were so strangely intermingled, was over. . . .

Comments and Questions

1. What is the essential conflict in this episode? What purpose does the Queen hope to realize through her careful preparation for the execution scene?

2. Explain the metamorphosis "strange as was ever wrought by wand of fabled enchanter."

3. In what way is this account like fiction? How does it differ from fiction?

4. Much is made by some modern critics of what is called "aesthetic distance." Although this phrase is more fully discussed elsewhere (see p. 14), it may be briefly defined here as describing the distance an author thinks appropriate for separating the reader from an action. It is assumed that some scenes can be fully responded to only if the emotional aspects of the scene are tightly controlled. Several questions in this connection arise when one considers "The Execution of a Queen." In general should historians as opposed to, say, novelists be concerned with aesthetic distance? Discuss. Specifically, is Froude justified in writing the paragraph, third from the end of the selection, in which the actual execution is described? Even more specifically, should he have written the sentence beginning: "The head hung by a shred of skin. . ."?

Sylvia Plath   (1932–1963)
"The last thing I wanted was infinite security. . . ."

Although all autobiography is inevitably fictionalized to some extent, the following selection is frankly a hybrid of fiction and fact. The essential truth of Sylvia Plath's "confessions," however, cannot be doubted. She admitted that in *The Bell Jar*, from which this excerpt (chapter 7) has been taken, "many people close to her" were only "slightly disguised." In her own words: "I've tried to picture my world and the people in it as seen through the distorting lens of a bell jar" (quoted in Lois Ames' "A Biographical Note," which appeared in the first American edition of *The Bell Jar*, New York: Harper & Row, 1971).

Of course, Constantin was much too short, but in his own way he was handsome, with light brown hair and dark blue eyes and a lively, challenging expression. He could almost have been an American, he was so tan and had such good teeth, but I could tell straight away that he wasn't. He had what no American man I've ever met has had, and that's intuition.

From the start Constantin guessed I wasn't any protégé of Mrs. Willard's. I raised an eyebrow here and dropped a dry little laugh there, and pretty soon we were both openly raking Mrs. Willard over the coals and I thought, "This Constantin won't mind if I'm too tall and don't know enough languages and haven't been to Europe, he'll see through all that stuff to what I really am."

Constantin drove me to the UN in his old green convertible with cracked, comfortable brown leather seats and the top down. He told me his tan came from playing tennis, and when we were sitting there side by side flying down the streets in the open sun he took my hand and squeezed it, and I felt happier than I had been since I was about nine and running along the hot white beaches with my father the summer before he died.

And while Constantin and I sat in one of those hushed plush auditoriums in the UN, next to a stern muscular Russian girl with no makeup who was a simultaneous interpreter like Constantin, I thought how strange it had never occurred to me before that I was only purely happy until I was nine years old.

5   After that—in spite of the Girl Scouts and the piano lessons and the water-color lessons and the dancing lessons and the sailing camp, all of which my mother scrimped to give me, and college, with crewing in the mist before breakfast and blackbottom pies and the little new firecrackers of ideas going off every day—I had never been really happy again.

I stared through the Russian girl in her double-breasted gray suit, rattling off idiom after idiom in her own unknowable tongue—which Constantin said was the most difficult part because the Russians didn't have the same idioms as our idioms—and I wished with all my heart I could crawl into her and spend the rest of my life barking out one idiom after another. It mightn't make me any happier, but it would be one more little pebble of efficiency among all the other pebbles.

Then Constantin and the Russian girl interpreter and the whole bunch of black and white and yellow men arguing down there behind their labeled microphones seemed to move off at a distance. I saw their mouths going up and down without a sound, as if they were sitting on the deck of a departing ship, stranding me in the middle of a huge silence.

I started adding up all the things I couldn't do.

I began with cooking.

10   My grandmother and my mother were such good cooks that I left everything to them. They were always trying to teach me one dish or another, but I would just look on and say, "Yes, yes, I see," while the instructions slid through my head like water, and then I'd always spoil what I did so nobody would ask me to do it again.

I remember Jody, my best and only girlfriend at college in my freshman year, making me scrambled eggs at her house one morning. They tasted unusual, and when I asked her if she had put in anything extra, she said cheese and garlic salt. I asked who told her to do that, and she said nobody, she just thought it up. But then, she was practical and a sociology major.

I didn't know shorthand either.

This meant I couldn't get a good job after college. My mother kept telling me nobody wanted a plain English major. But an English major who knew shorthand was something else again. Everybody would want her. She would be in demand among all the up-and-coming young men and she would transcribe letter after thrilling letter.

The trouble was, I hated the idea of serving men in any way. I wanted to dictate my own thrilling letters. Besides, those little shorthand symbols in the book my mother showed me seemed just as bad as let *t* equal time and let *s* equal the total distance.

15   My list grew longer.

I was a terrible dancer. I couldn't carry a tune. I had no sense of balance, and when we had to walk down a narrow board with our hands out and a book on our heads in gym class I always fell over. I couldn't ride a horse or ski, the two things I wanted to do most, because they cost too much money. I couldn't speak German or read Hebrew or write Chinese. I didn't even know where most of the old out-of-the-way countries the UN men in front of me represented fitted in on the map.

For the first time in my life, sitting there in the soundproof heart of the UN building between Constantin who could play tennis as well as simultaneously interpret and the Russian girl who knew so many idioms, I felt dreadfully inadequate. The trouble was, I had been inadequate all along. I simply hadn't thought about it.

The one thing I was good at was winning scholarships and prizes, and that era was coming to an end.

I felt like a racehorse in a world without racetracks or a champion college footballer suddenly confronted by Wall Street and a business suit, his days of glory shrunk to a little gold cup on his mantel with a date engraved on it like the date on a tombstone.

20   I saw my life branching out before me like the green fig tree in the story.

From the tip of every branch, like a fat purple fig, a wonderful future beckoned and winked. One fig was a husband and a happy home and children, and another fig was a famous poet, and another fig was a brilliant professor, and another fig was Ee Gee, the amazing editor, and another fig was Europe and Africa and South America, and another fig was Constantin and Socrates and Attila and a pack of other lovers with queer names and offbeat professions, and another fig was an Olympic lady crew champion, and beyond and above these figs were many more figs I couldn't quite make out.

I saw myself sitting in the crotch of this fig tree, starving to death, just because I couldn't make up my mind which of the figs I would choose. I wanted each and every one of them, but choosing one meant losing all the rest, and, as I sat there, unable to decide, the figs began to wrinkle and go black, and, one by one, they plopped to the ground at my feet.

Constantin's restaurant smelt of herbs and spices and sour cream. All the time I had been in New York I had never found such a restaurant. I only found those Heavenly Hamburger places, where they serve giant hamburgers and soup-of-the-day and four kinds of fancy cake at a very clean counter facing a long glarey mirror.

To reach this restaurant we had to climb down seven dimly lit steps into a sort of cellar.

25   Travel posters plastered the smoke-dark walls, like so many picture windows overlooking Swiss lakes and Japanese mountains and African velds, and thick, dusty bottle-candles, that seemed for centuries to have wept their colored waxes red over blue over green in a fine, three-dimensional lace, cast a circle of light round each table where the faces floated, flushed and flamelike themselves.

I don't know what I ate, but I felt immensely better after the first mouthful. It occurred to me that my vision of the fig tree and all the fat figs that withered and fell to earth might well have arisen from the profound void of an empty stomach.

Constantin kept refilling our glasses with a sweet Greek wine that tasted of pine bark, and I found myself telling him how I was going to learn German and go to Europe and be a war correspondent like Maggie Higgins.

I felt so fine by the time we came to the yogurt and strawberry jam that I decided I would let Constantin seduce me.

Ever since Buddy Willard had told me about that waitress I had been thinking I ought to go out and sleep with somebody myself. Sleeping with Buddy wouldn't count, though, because he would still be one person ahead of me, it would have to be with somebody else.

30   The only boy I ever actually discussed going to bed with was a bitter, hawk-nosed Southerner from Yale, who came to college one weekend only to find his date had eloped with a taxi driver the day before. As the girl had lived in my house and I was the only one home that particular night, it was my job to cheer him up.

At the local coffee shop, hunched in one of the secretive, high-backed booths with hundreds of people's names gouged into the wood, we drank cup after cup of black coffee and talked frankly about sex.

This boy—his name was Eric—said he thought it disgusting the way all the girls at my college stood around on the porches under the lights and in the bushes in plain view, necking madly before the one o'clock curfew, so everybody passing by could see them. A million years of evolution, Eric said bitterly, and what are we? Animals.

Then Eric told me how he had slept with his first woman.

He went to a Southern prep school that specialized in building all-round gentlemen, and by the time you graduated it was an unwritten rule that you had to have known a woman. Known in the Biblical sense, Eric said.

35   So one Saturday Eric and a few of his classmates took a bus into the nearest city and visited a notorious whorehouse. Eric's whore hadn't even taken off her dress. She was a fat, middle-aged woman with dyed red hair and suspiciously thick lips and rat-colored skin and she wouldn't turn off the light, so he had had her under a fly-spotted twenty-five watt bulb, and it was nothing like it was cracked up to be. It was boring as going to the toilet.

I said maybe if you loved a woman it wouldn't seem so boring, but Eric said it would be spoiled by thinking this woman too was just an animal like the rest, so if he loved anybody he would never go to bed with her. He'd go to a whore if he had to and keep the woman he loved free of all that dirty business.

It had crossed my mind at the time that Eric might be a good person to go to bed with, since he had already done it and, unlike the usual run of boys, didn't seem dirty-minded or silly when he talked about it. But then Eric wrote me a letter saying he thought he might really be able to love me, I was so intelligent and cynical and yet had such a kind face, surprisingly like his older sister's; so I knew it was no use, I was the type he would never go to bed with, and wrote him I was unfortunately about to marry a child-hood sweetheart.

The more I thought about it the better I liked the idea of being seduced by a simultaneous interpreter in New York City. Constantin seemed mature and considerate in every way. There were no people I knew he would want to brag to about it, the way college boys bragged about sleeping with girls in the backs of cars to their roommates or their friends on the basketball team. And there would be a pleasant irony in sleeping with a man Mrs. Willard had introduced me to, as if she were, in a roundabout way, to blame for it.

When Constantin asked if I would like to come up to his apartment to hear some balalaika records I smiled to myself. My mother had always told me never under any circumstances to go with a man to a man's rooms after an evening out, it could mean only one thing.

40   "I am very fond of balalaika music," I said.

Constantin's room had a balcony, and the balcony overlooked the river, and we could hear the hooing of the tugs down in the darkness. I felt moved and tender and perfectly certain about what I was going to do.

I knew I might have a baby, but that thought hung far and dim in the distance and didn't trouble me at all. There was no one hundred per cent sure way not to have a baby, it said in an article my mother cut out of the *Reader's Digest* and mailed to me at college. This article was written by a married woman lawyer with children and called "In Defense of Chastity."

It gave all the reasons a girl shouldn't sleep with anybody but her husband and then only after they were married.

The main point of the article was that a man's world is different from a woman's world and a man's emotions are different from a woman's emotions and only marriage can bring the two worlds and the two different sets of emotions together properly. My mother said this was something a girl didn't know about till it was too late, so she had to take the advice of people who were already experts, like a married woman.

45   This woman lawyer said the best men wanted to be pure for their wives, and even if they weren't pure, they wanted to be the ones to teach their wives about sex. Of course they would try to persuade a girl to have sex and say they would marry her later, but as soon as she gave in, they would lose all respect for her and start saying that if she did that with them she would do that with other men and they would end up by making her life miserable.

The woman finished her article by saying better be safe than sorry and besides, there was no sure way of not getting stuck with a baby and then you'd really be in a pickle.

Now the one thing this article didn't seem to me to consider was how a girl felt.

It might be nice to be pure and then to marry a pure man, but what if he suddenly confessed he wasn't pure after we were married, the way Buddy Willard had? I couldn't stand the idea of a woman having to have a single pure life and a man being able to have a double life, one pure and one not.

Finally I decided that if it was so difficult to find a red-blooded intelligent man who was still pure by the time he was twenty-one I might as well forget about staying pure myself and marry somebody who wasn't pure either. Then when he started to make my life miserable I could make his miserable as well.

50   When I was nineteen, pureness was the great issue.

Instead of the world being divided up into Catholics and Protestants or Republicans and Democrats or white men and black men or even men and women, I saw the world divided into people who had slept with somebody and people who hadn't, and this seemed the only really significant difference between one person and another.

I thought a spectacular change would come over me the day I crossed the boundary line.

I thought it would be the way I'd feel if I ever visited Europe. I'd come home, and if I looked closely into the mirror I'd be able to make out a little white Alp at the back of my eye. Now I thought that if I looked into the mirror tomorrow I'd see a doll-size Constantin sitting in my eye and smiling out at me.

Well, for about an hour we lounged on Constantin's balcony in two separate slingback chairs with the victrola playing and the balalaika records stacked between us. A faint milky light diffused from the street lights or the half moon or the cars or the stars, I couldn't tell what, but apart from holding my hand Constantin showed no desire to seduce me whatsoever.

55   I asked if he was engaged or had any special girlfriend, thinking maybe that's what was the matter, but he said no, he made a point of keeping clear of such attachments.

At last I felt a powerful drowsiness drifting through my veins from all the pine-bark wine I had drunk.

"I think I'll go in and lie down," I said.

I strolled casually into the bedroom and stooped over to nudge off my shoes. The clean bed bobbed before me like a safe boat. I stretched full length and shut my eyes. Then I heard Constantin sigh and come in from the balcony. One by one his shoes clonked on to the floor, and he lay down by my side.

I looked at him secretly from under a fall of hair.

60   He was lying on his back, his hands under his head, staring at the ceiling. The starched white sleeves of his shirt, rolled up to the elbows, glimmered eerily in the half dark and his tan skin seemed almost black. I thought he must be the most beautiful man I'd ever seen.

I thought if only I had a keen, shapely bone structure to my face or could discuss politics shrewdly or was a famous writer Constantin might find me interesting enough to sleep with.

And then I wondered if as soon as he came to like me he would sink into ordinariness, and if as soon as he came to love me I would find fault after fault, the way I did with Buddy Willard and the boys before him.

The same thing happened over and over:

I would catch sight of some flawless man off in the distance, but as soon as he moved closer I immediately saw he wouldn't do at all.

65   That's one of the reasons I never wanted to get married. The last thing I wanted was infinite security and to be the place an arrow shoots off from. I wanted change and excitement and to shoot off in all directions myself, like the colored arrows from a Fourth of July rocket.

I woke to the sound of rain.

It was pitch dark. After a while I deciphered the faint outlines of an unfamiliar window. Every so often a beam of light appeared out of thin air, traversed the wall like a ghostly, exploratory finger, and slid off into nothing again.

Then I heard the sound of somebody breathing.

At first I thought it was only myself, and that I was lying in the dark in my hotel room after being poisoned. I held my breath, but the breathing kept on.

70   A green eye glowed on the bed beside me. It was divided into quarters like a compass. I reached out slowly and closed my hand on it. I lifted it up. With it came an arm, heavy as a dead man's, but warm with sleep.

Constantin's watch said three o'clock.

He was lying in his shirt and trousers and stocking feet just as I had left him when I dropped asleep, and as my eyes grew used to the darkness I made out his pale eyelids and his straight nose and his tolerant, shapely mouth, but they seemed insubstantial, as if drawn on fog. For a few minutes I leaned over, studying him. I had never fallen asleep beside a man before.

I tried to imagine what it would be like if Constantin were my husband.

It would mean getting up at seven and cooking him eggs and bacon and toast and coffee and dawdling about in my nightgown and curlers after he'd left for work to wash up the dirty plates and make the bed, and then when he came home after a lively, fascinating day he'd expect a big dinner, and I'd spend the evening washing up even more dirty plates till I fell into bed, utterly exhausted.

75 This seemed a dreary and wasted life for a girl with fifteen years of straight A's, but I knew that's what marriage was like, because cook and clean and wash was just what Buddy Willard's mother did from morning till night, and she was the wife of a university professor and had been a private school teacher herself.

Once when I visited Buddy I found Mrs. Willard braiding a rug out of strips of wool from Mr. Willard's old suits. She'd spent weeks on that rug, and I had admired the tweedy browns and greens and blues patterning the braid, but after Mrs. Willard was through, instead of hanging the rug on the wall the way I would have done, she put it down in place of her kitchen mat, and in a few days it was soiled and dull and indistinguishable from any mat you could buy for under a dollar in the five and ten.

And I knew that in spite of all the roses and kisses and restaurant dinners a man showered on a woman before he married her, what he secretly wanted when the wedding service ended was for her to flatten out underneath his feet like Mrs. Willard's kitchen mat.

Hadn't my own mother told me that as soon as she and my father left Reno on their honeymoon—my father had been married before, so he needed a divorce—my father said to her, "Whew, that's a relief, now we can stop pretending and be ourselves"?—and from that day on my mother never had a minute's peace.

I also remembered Buddy Willard saying in a sinister, knowing way that after I had children I would feel differently, I wouldn't want to write poems any more. So I began to think maybe it was true that when you were married and had children it was like being brainwashed, and afterward you went about numb as a slave in some private, totalitarian state.

80 As I stared down at Constantin the way you stare down at a bright, unattainable pebble at the bottom of deep well, his eyelids lifted and he looked through me, and his eyes were full of love. I watched dumbly as a shutter of recognition clicked across the blur of tenderness and the wide pupils went glossy and depthless as patent leather.

Constantin sat up, yawning. "What time is it?"

"Three," I said in a flat voice. "I better go home. I have to be at work first thing in the morning."

"I'll drive you."

As we sat back to back on our separate sides of the bed fumbling with our shoes in the horrid cheerful white light of the bed lamp, I sensed Constantin turn round. "Is your hair always like that?"

85 "Like what?"

He didn't answer but reached over and put his hand at the root of my hair and ran his fingers out slowly to the tip ends like a comb. A little electric shock flared through me and I sat quite still. Ever since I was small I loved feeling somebody comb my hair. It made me go all sleepy and peaceful.

"Ah, I know what it is," Constantin said. "You've just washed it."

And he bent to lace up his tennis shoes.

An hour later I lay in my hotel bed, listening to the rain. It didn't even sound like rain, it sounded like a tap running. The ache in the middle of my left shin bone came to life, and I abandoned any hope of sleep before seven, when my radio-alarm clock would rouse me with its hearty renderings of Sousa.

90 Every time it rained the old leg-break seemed to remember itself, and what it remembered was a dull hurt.

Then I thought, "Buddy Willard made me break that leg."

Then I thought, "No, I broke it myself. I broke it on purpose to pay myself back for being such a heel."

Comments and Questions

1. One notes an adolescent lighthearted frankness in the author's recounting of her experiences. A quite different mood pervades Plath's poems. Read "Two Views of a Cadaver Room" and "Suicide off Egg Rock," page 558, and compare the mood in these poems with the mood in the prose sketch.

2. Explain the metaphor of the figs. How does Plath, later in the chapter, make fun of the dark implications of the withering figs?

3. Lamb observed that all people fall into only two classes: borrowers and lenders. (See "The Two Races of Men," p. 1067.) Into what two classes does Plath, at nineteen, divide humankind?

4. Plath is something of a heroine to the women's liberationists of today. Locate the passages in this selection that qualify her for this rôle. Locate others that do not.

Biography: Sketches

Biography in Three Lengths

The biographical sketch stands somewhere between encyclopedia accounts and full-length biographies. It is an expansion of the first and a distillation of the second. The encyclopedist works strictly by formula and within rigid space limitations, presenting highly selective, straight facts in chronological order, with a few details and little comment. Somewhat more informative than tombstone biography, the encyclopedia's compilation serves the same sort of need that a map of routes through a city does in a travel book. Encyclopedists may safely assume the interest of the reader and do nothing to stimulate it. Their one job is to include facts relating to the highlights of the subject's career: dates of birth and death, education, chief claim to fame, marital status, homes, travels, with perhaps a word about reputation yesterday and today, and the names of one or two authoritative books on the subject. The encyclopedist is a reporter, not an artist.

Writers of full-length biography are necessarily artists. They may be good or poor, but they cannot escape most of the problems that the creative artist has to solve. Unlike encyclopedists but like creative writers, they cannot assume continuing interest on the part of readers. They must select and arrange their materials, which may be vast. More important, they must interpret and account for the pattern of their subject's life. Sometimes the biographer digs out the facts *and* writes the biography. Boswell, for example, was a searcher, researcher, and biographer and was great at all three. Many biographies are simply a reworking of known facts which are decked out in a new style, in a different arrangement, with a shifted emphasis—all of which constitute a new interpretation. Often these biographies are fat tomes, as long as, or longer than, novels.

The personal sketch has something of the same relation to full-length biography that the short story has to the novel. Differences, however, are greater than the surface similarities. The purpose of the sketcher is to provide a quickly readable, entertaining account. To achieve this goal, the sketcher, too, writes by for-mula—the formula of the artist, not the compiler. This formula consists of what may be called tricks of the trade—methods carefully worked out and tested by which the writer expects to seize and hold the attention of the reader. The writer assumes that the reader already knows something about the person being por-trayed: the person's chief claim to fame, approximate dates, and perhaps other facts. The writer's main task is to provide a focus, a way of looking at the subject. Writers give information, but it is incidental to interpretation. They handle the facts so much as an essayist would that the term "biographical essay" could be accurately applied to most of these sketches.

Sketches of the Quick and the Dead

Portraits of living persons involve special difficulties, not the least of which is the restraining influence of the libel laws. For this reason, the sketch from life may give the appearance of a retouched photograph with all the wrinkles missing. Information may be abundant; it may include, and frequently does, personal con-tact between the subject and the sketcher. At such close range, however, accurate focusing is difficult, the problem of interpretation great. We have included one unretouched photograph of a living person, Charles Manson, mass-murderer. The account is starkly factual, notes, so to speak, for a biographer.

Camus based his play *Caligula* (see p. 894) on material provided by the Roman historian Suetonius. Biographical techniques have been greatly refined since Suetonius, particularly in the area of interpretation. The historian now not only provides facts; great historians also interpret. In this instance, Camus does the interpreting. We have strung together excerpts from Suetonius's account (see p. 1050), some of the materials from which the French writer fashioned his play.

Guide Questions Basic to Analyses of Biographical Sketches

Even though "The Apprenticeship of a Mass Murderer" and the excerpts from the life of Caligula are very crude biography, like more artistic life-narratives they may be analyzed through responses to these specific questions:

How is the beginning handled?
Is a controlling idea for the whole sketch indicated?
At what point, if at all, does the chronological account of the life begin?
What parts of the narrative would you call interpretative?
How much quoted material is used and for what purpose?
Are all allusions familiar?
How is the ending handled?

Vincent Bugliosi (1934–   )
and Curt Gentry (1931–   )
The Apprenticeship of a Mass Murderer

The following selection demonstrates the validity of the adage that truth is often stranger than fiction. Here are the skeletal facts in what became known as the Tate murder case:

1. Charles Manson, whose career preceding the murders is sketched below, was known to many of his followers (the Family) as superhuman, as, indeed, Jesus Christ.

2. This Son of Man, or Manson, had specific visions of a race war in which blacks would be pitted against whites. (In the Sixties a war of this sort seemed at least remotely possible to many besides Manson.)

3. The vision was supported, Manson was sure, by the Beatles, the English singers, in some of their lyrics, particularly in a song called "Helter-Skelter," a phrase that Manson interpreted to mean the uprising of blacks.

4. Although blacks in the Sixties had burned Watts in Los Angeles and ghettos in other American cities, the showdown between blacks and whites was not shaping up fast enough to suit Manson. He would speed it up by terrorizing whites and leading them to believe that blacks were responsible for the terror. Whites would strike back, and bloody confrontation would result.

5. Confident that the blacks would win, Manson planned to hide himself and his Family in the Bottomless Pit, an imagined location in Death Valley.

6. After the victory, blacks would prove incapable of running society. Manson would then reappear as the Messiah and take over.

Fantastic? Yes. But on Saturday, August 9, 1969, Manson set his plan in motion. He dispatched four of his disciples, three girls and one man, to the isolated home of Sharon Tate with simple instructions to kill everyone they found at that location. They found two men and two women, one of the women (Sharon Tate) eight months pregnant. They butchered all four. They also shot to death a boy who happened along at the wrong time. The next day, the killers found out from the newspapers the names of their victims. The next night, Manson himself participated in the mutilation and murder of two more chance-chosen whites, the LaBiancas.

So that blacks would be suspected of committing these atrocities, the word PIG, an epithet used by black militants to describe any white man or woman, was printed in Sharon Tate's blood on the wall of the actress's home, and DEATH TO PIGS on the wall of the LaBianca apartment, along with the curious phrase HEALTER SKELTER. Those two words, even with the misspelling, when traced and interpreted became as clear as a signature, the signature of Charles Manson. (For a full account of this horror story, see *Helter Skelter,* by Vincent Bugliosi and Curt Gentry, W. W. Norton and Company, New York, 1974. This is the hardback edition; a paperback is available from Bantam Books. Vincent Bugliosi, deputy district attorney for Los Angeles, was chiefly responsible for piecing together the many parts of this intricate puzzle, particularly for ferreting out the motives.)

Charles Manson was born "no name Maddox" on November 12, 1934, in Cincinnati, Ohio, the illegitimate son of a sixteen-year-old girl named Kathleen Maddox.[1]

Though Manson himself would later state that his mother was a teen-age prostitute, other relatives say she was simply "loose." One remarked, "She ran around a lot, drank, got in trouble." Whatever the case, she lived with a succession of men. One, a much older man named William Manson, whom she married, was around just long enough to provide a surname for the youth.

The identity of Charles Manson's father was something of a mystery. In 1936 Kathleen filed a bastardy suit in Boyd County, Kentucky, against one "Colonel Scott,"[2] a resident of Ashland, Kentucky. On April 19, 1937, the court awarded her a judgment of $25, plus $5 a month for the support of "Charles Milles Manson." Though it was an "agreed judgment," Colonel Scott apparently didn't honor it, for as late as 1940 Kathleen was attempting to file an attachment on his wages. Most accounts state that Colonel Scott died in 1954; though this has never been officially verified, Manson himself apparently believed it. He also stated on numerous occasions that he never met his father.

According to her own relatives, Kathleen would leave the child with obliging neighbors for an hour, then disappear for days or weeks. Usually his grandmother or maternal aunt would have to claim him. Most of his early years were spent with one or the other, in West Virginia, Kentucky or Ohio.

5   In 1939 Kathleen and her brother Luther robbed a Charleston, West Virginia, service station, knocking out the attendant with Coke bottles. They were sentenced to five years in the state penitentiary for armed robbery. While his mother was in prison, Manson lived with his aunt and uncle in McMechen, West Virginia. Manson would later tell his counselor at the National Training School for Boys that his uncle and aunt had "some marital difficulty until they became interested in religion and became very extreme."

A very strict aunt, who thought all pleasures sinful but who gave him love. A promiscuous mother, who let him do anything he wanted, just so long as he didn't bother her. The youth was caught in a tug-of-war between the two.

Paroled in 1942, Kathleen reclaimed Charles, then eight. The next several years were a blur of run-down hotel rooms and newly introduced "uncles," most of whom, like his mother, drank heavily. In 1947 she tried to have him put in a foster home, but, none being available, the court sent him to the Gibault School for Boys, a caretaking institution in Terre Haute, Indiana. He was twelve years old.

According to school records, he made a "poor institutional adjustment" and "his attitude toward schooling was at best only fair." Though "during the short lapses when Charles was pleasant and feeling happy he presented a likable boy," he had "a tendency toward moodiness and a persecution complex . . ." He remained at Gibault ten months, then ran away, returning to his mother.

She didn't want him, and he ran away again. Burglarizing a grocery store, he stole enough money to rent a room. He then broke into several other stores, stealing, among other things, a bicycle. Caught during a burglary, he was placed in the juvenile center in Indianapolis. He escaped the next day. When he was apprehended, the court—erroneously informed that he was Catholic—made arrangements through a local priest to have him accepted at Father Flanagan's Boys Town.

10   He didn't make its distinguished alumni list. Four days after his arrival, he and an-

---

[1] As with almost everything else written about Manson's early years, even his date of birth is usually given erroneously, although for an understandable reason. Unable to remember her child's birthday, the mother changed it to November 11, which was Armistice Day and an easier date to remember.
[2] His first name remains unknown. Even in official records he is referred to as "Colonel Scott."

other boy, Blackie Nielson, stole a car and fled to the home of Blackie's uncle in Peoria, Illinois. En route they committed two armed robberies—one a grocery store, the other a gambling casino. Among criminals, as in the law itself, a distinction is made between non-violent and violent crimes. Manson had "graduated," commiting his first armed robbery at age thirteen.

The uncle was glad to see them. Both boys were small enough to slip through skylights. A week after their arrival in Peoria, the pair broke into a grocery store and stole $1,500. For their efforts, the uncle gave them $150. Two weeks later they tried a repeat, but this time they were caught. Both talked, implicating the uncle. Still only thirteen, Charles Manson was sent to the Indiana School for Boys at Plainfield.

He remained there three years, running away a total of eighteen times. According to his teachers, "He professed no trust in anyone" and "did good work only for those from whom he figured he could obtain something."

In February 1951, Charles Manson and two other sixteen-year-olds escaped and headed for California. For transportation they stole cars. For support they burglarized gas stations—Manson would later estimate they hit fifteen or twenty—before, just outside Beaver, Utah, a roadblock set up for a robbery suspect netted them instead.

In taking a stolen vehicle across a state line, the youths had broken a federal law, the Dyer Act. This was the beginning of a pattern for Charles Manson of committing federal crimes, which carry far stiffer sentences than local or state offenses.

15   On March 9, 1951, Manson was ordered confined to the National Training School for Boys, in Washington, D.C., until reaching his majority.

Detailed records were kept on Charles Manson during the time he was there.[3] On arrival, he was given a battery of aptitude and intelligence tests. Manson's IQ was 109. Though he had completed four years of school, he remained illiterate. Intelligence, mechanical aptitude, manual dexterity: all average. Subject liked best: music. Observed his first case worker, with considerable understatement, "Charles is a sixteen-year-old boy who has an unfavorable family life, if it can be called family life at all." He was, the case worker concluded, aggressively antisocial.

One month after his arrival: "This boy tries to give the impression that he is trying hard to adjust although he actually is not putting forth any effort in this respect . . . I feel in time he will try to be a wheel in the cottage."

After three months: "Manson has become somewhat of an 'institution politician.' He does just enough work to get by on . . . Restless and moody most of the time, the boy would rather spend his class time entertaining his friends." The report concluded: "It appears that this boy is a very emotionally upset youth who is definitely in need of some psychiatric orientation."

Manson was anxious to be transferred to Natural Bridge Honor Camp, a minimum security institution. Because of his run-away record, school officials felt the opposite—i.e., transfer to a reformatory-type institution—was in order, but they decided to withhold decision until after the boy had been examined by a psychiatrist.

20   On June 29, 1951, Charles Manson was examined by a Dr. Block. The psychiatrist noted "the marked degree of rejection, instability, and psychic trauma" in Manson's background. His sense of inferiority in relation to his mother was so pronounced, Block said, that he constantly felt it necessary "to suppress any thoughts about her." Because of his diminutive stature, his illegitimacy, and the lack of parental love, "he is constantly striving for status with the other boys." To attain this, Manson had "developed certain facile techniques for dealing with people. These for the most part consist of a good sense of humor"

---

[3] I would not obtain the results of these until much later; however, portions are quoted here.

and an "ability to ingratiate himself . . . This could add up to a fairly 'slick' institutionalized youth, but one is left with the feeling that behind all this lies an extremely sensitive boy who has not yet given up in terms of securing some kind of love and affection from the world."

Though the doctor observed that Manson was "quite unable to accept any kind of authoritative direction," he found that he "accepted with alacrity the offer of psychiatric interviews."

If he found this suspicious, the doctor did not indicate it in his report. For the next three months he gave Manson individual psychotherapy. It may be presumed that Charles Manson also worked on the doctor, for in his October 1 report Dr. Block was convinced that what Manson most required were experiences which would build up his self-confidence. In short, he needed to be trusted. The doctor recommended the transfer.

It would appear that Charles Manson had conned his first psychiatrist. Though the school authorities considered him at best a "calculated risk," they accepted the doctor's recommendation, and on October 24, 1951, he was transferred to Natural Bridge Camp.

That November he turned seventeen. Shortly after his birthday he was visited by his aunt, who told the authorities that she would supply a home and employment for him if he was released. He was due for a parole hearing in February 1952, and, with her offer, his chances looked good. Instead, less than a month before the hearing, he took a razor blade and held it against another boy's throat while he sodomized him.

25   As a result of the offense, he lost ninety-seven days good-time and, on January 18, 1952, he was transferred to the Federal Reformatory at Petersburg, Virginia. He was considered "dangerous," one official observing, "He shouldn't be trusted across the street." By August he had committed eight serious disciplinary offenses, three involving homosexual acts. His progress report, if it could be called that, stated, "Manson definitely has homosexual and assaultive tendencies." He was classified "safe only under supervision." For the protection of himself as well as others, the authorities decided to transfer him to a more secure institution, the Federal Reformatory at Chillicothe, Ohio. He was sent there on September 22, 1952.

From the Chillicothe files: "Associates with trouble makers . . . seems to be the unpredictable type of inmate who will require supervision both at work and in quarters . . . In spite of his age, he is criminally sophisticated . . . regarded as grossly unsuited for retention in an open reformatory type institution such as Chillicothe . . ." This from a report written less than a month after his transfer there.

Then, suddenly, Manson changed. For the rest of the year there were no serious disciplinary offenses. Except for minor infractions of the rules, and a consistently "poor attitude toward authority," his good conduct continued into 1953. A progress report that October noted: "Manson has shown a marked improvement in his general attitude and cooperation with officers and is also showing an active interest in the educational program . . . He is especially proud of the fact that he raised his [educational level from lower fourth to upper seventh grade] and that he can now read most material and use simple arithmetic."

Because of his educational advancement and his good work habits in the transportation unit, where he repaired and maintained vehicles belonging to the institution, on January 1, 1954, he was given a Meritorious Service Award. Far more important to Charles Manson, on May 8, 1954, he was granted parole. He was nineteen.

One of the conditions of his parole was that he live with his aunt and uncle in McMechen. He did, for a time, then, when his mother moved to nearby Wheeling, he joined her. They seemed drawn together, yet unable to stand each other for any length of time.

30   Since fourteen, Charles Manson's only sexual contacts had been homosexual. Shortly after his release he met a seventeen-year-old McMechen girl, Rosalie Jean Willis, a waitress in the local hospital. They were married in January 1955. For support Manson worked as a busboy, service-station helper, parking-lot attendant. He also boosted cars. He would later admit to stealing six. He appeared to have learned nothing; he took at least two across state lines. One, stolen in Wheeling, West Virginia, he abandoned in Fort Lauderdale, Florida. The second, a 1951 Mercury, he drove from Bridgeport, Ohio, to Los Angeles in July 1955, accompanied by his now pregnant wife. Manson had finally made it to the Golden State. He was arrested less than three months later, and admitted both Dyer Act violations. Taken to federal court, he pleaded guilty to the theft of the Mercury, and asked for psychiatric help, stating, "I was released from Chillicothe in 1954 and, having been confined for nine years, I was badly in need of psychiatric treatment. I was mentally confused and stole a car as a means of mental release from the confused state of mind that I was in."

The judge requested a psychiatric report. Manson was examined on October 26, 1955, by Dr. Edwin McNiel. He gave the psychiatrist a much abbreviated version of his past, stating that he was first sent to an institution "for being mean to my mother." Of his wife, Manson said, "She is the best wife a guy could want. I didn't realize how good she was until I got in here. I beat her at times. She writes to me all the time. She is going to have a baby."

He also told McNiel that "he spent so much time in institutions that he never really learned much of what 'real life on the outside was all about.' He said that now he has a wife and is about to become a father it has become important to him to try to be on the outside and be with his wife. He said she is the only one he has ever cared about in his life."

Dr. McNiel observed: "It is evident that he has an unstable personality and that his environmental influences throughout most of his life have not been good . . . In my opinion this boy is a poor risk for probation; on the other hand, he has spent nine years in institutions with apparently little benefit except to take him out of circulation. With the incentive of a wife and probable fatherhood, it is possible that he might be able to straighten himself out. I would, therefore, respectfully recommend to the court that probation be considered in this case under careful supervision." Accepting the suggestion, on November 7, 1955, the court gave Manson five years probation.

There remained the Florida charge. Though his chances of getting probation on it were excellent, before the hearing he skipped. A warrant was issued for his arrest. He was picked up in Indianapolis on March 14, 1956, and returned to Los Angeles. His probation was revoked, and he was sentenced to three years imprisonment at Terminal Island, San Pedro, California. By the time Charles Manson, Jr., was born, his father was back in jail.

35   "This inmate will no doubt be in serious difficulty soon," wrote the orientation officer. "He is young, small, baby-faced, and unable to control himself . . ."

Given another battery of tests, Manson received average marks in all categories except "word meaning," where he had a high score. His IQ was now 121. With some perception, when it came to his work assignment Manson requested "a small detail where he is not with too many men. He states he has a tendency to cut up and misbehave if he is around a gang . . ."

Rosalie moved in with his mother, now living in Los Angeles, and during his first year at Terminal Island she visited him every week, his mother somewhat less frequently.

"Manson's work habits and attitudes range from good to poor," noted his March 1957 progress report. "However, as the time of his parole hearing approaches, his work performance report has jumped from good to excellent, showing that he is capable of a good adjustment if he wants to."

His parole hearing was set for April 22. In March his wife's visits ceased. Manson's mother told him Rosalie was living with another man. In early April he was transferred to the Coast Guard unit, under minimal custody. On April 10 he was found in the Coast Guard parking lot, dressed in civilian clothes, wiring the ignition of a car. Subsequently indicted for attempted escape, he pleaded guilty, and an extra five years probation was tacked onto the end of his current sentence. On April 22 the parole request was denied.

Rosalie filed for divorce not long after this, the divorce becoming final in 1958. She retained custody of Charles, Jr., remarried, and had no further contact with Manson or his mother.

40   April 1958, annual review: His work performance was "sporadic," his behavior continued to be "erratic and moody." Almost without exception, he would let down anyone who went to bat for him, the report noted. "For example, he was selected to attend the current Dale Carnegie Course, being passed over a number of other applicants because it was felt that this course might be beneficial in his case and he urgently desired enrollment. After attending a few sessions and apparently making excellent progress, he quit in a mood of petulance and has since engaged in no educational activity."

Manson was called "an almost classic text book case of the correctional institutional inmate . . . His is a very difficult case and it is impossible to predict his future adjustment with any degree of accuracy."

He was released September 30, 1958, on five years parole.

By November, Manson had found a new occupation: pimping. His teacher was Frank Peters, a Malibu bartender and known procurer, with whom he was living.

Unknown to Manson, he was under surveillance by the FBI, and had been since his release from prison. The federal agents, who were looking for a fugitive who had once lived with Peters, told Manson's parole officer that his "first string" consisted of a sixteen-year-old girl named Judy, whom he had personally "turned out"; as additional support, he was getting money from "Fat Flo," an unattractive Pasadena girl who had wealthy parents.

45   His parole officer called him in for a talk. Manson denied he was pimping; said he was no longer living with Peters; promised never to see Judy again; but stated that he wished to continue his relationship with Flo, "for money and sex." After all, he said, he had "been in a long time." After the interview the parole officer wrote: "This certainly is a very shaky probationer and it seems just a matter of time before he gets in further trouble."

On May 1, 1959, Manson was arrested attempting to cash a forged U.S. Treasury check for $37.50 in Ralph's, a Los Angeles supermarket. According to the arresting officers, Manson told them he had stolen the check from a mailbox. Two more federal offenses.

LAPD turned Manson over to Secret Service agents for questioning. What then happened was somewhat embarrassing. "Unfortunately for them," read a report of the incident, "the check itself has disappeared; they feel certain subject took it off table and swallowed it when they momentarily turned their backs." The charges remained, however.

In mid-June an attractive nineteen-year-old girl named Leona called on Manson's parole officer and told him she was pregnant by Charlie. The parole officer was skeptical and wanted to see a medical report. He also began checking her background.

With the aid of an attorney, Manson obtained a deal: if he would plead guilty to forging the check, the mail theft charge would be dropped. The judge ordered a psychiatric examination, and Dr. McNiel examined Manson a second time.

50   When Manson appeared in court on September 28, 1959, Dr. McNiel, the U.S. Attor-

ney's Office, and the probation department *all* recommended against probation. Leona also appeared and made a tearful plea in Manson's behalf. They were deeply in love, she told the judge, and would marry if Charlie were freed. Though it was proved that Leona had lied about being pregnant, and that she had an arrest record as a prostitute under the name Candy Stevens, the judge, evidently moved by Leona's plea and Manson's promise to make good, gave the defendant a ten-year sentence, then suspended it and placed him on probation.

Manson returned to pimping and breaking federal laws.

By December he had been arrested by LAPD twice: for grand theft auto and the use of stolen credit cards. Both charges were dismissed for lack of evidence. That month he also took Leona-aka-Candy and a girl named Elizabeth from Needles, California, to Lordsburg, New Mexico, for purposes of prostitution, violating the Mann Act, still another federal beef.

Held briefly, questioned, then released, he was given the impression that he had "beat the rap." He must have suspected that the investigation was continuing, however. Possibly to prevent Leona from testifying against him, he did marry her, though he didn't inform his probation officer of this. He remained free throughout January 1960, while the FBI prepared its case.

Late in February, Manson's probation officer was visited by an irate parent, Ralph Samuels, from Detroit. Samuels' daughter Jo Anne, nineteen, had come to California in response to an ad for an airline stewardess school, only to learn, after paying her tuition, that the school was a fraud. She had $700 in savings, however, and together with another disillusioned student, Beth Beldon, had rented an apartment in Hollywood. About November 1959, Jo Anne had the misfortune to meet Charles Manson, who introduced himself, complete with printed card, as "President, 3-Star-Enterprises, Nite Club, Radio and TV Productions." Manson conned her into investing her savings in his nonexistent company; drugged and raped her roommate; and got Jo Anne pregnant. It was an ectopic pregnancy, the fetus growing in one of the Fallopian tubes, and she nearly died.

55   The probation officer could offer little more than a sympathetic ear, however, for Charles Manson had disappeared. A bench warrant was issued, and on April 28 a federal grand jury indicted him on the Mann Act violation. He was arrested June 1 in Laredo, Texas, after police picked up one of his girls on a prostitution charge, and brought back to Los Angeles, where, on June 23, 1960, the court ruled he had violated his probation and ordered him returned to prison to serve out his ten-year sentence. The judge observed: "If there ever was a man who demonstrated himself completely unfit for probation, he is it." This was the same judge who had granted him probation the previous September.

The Mann Act charge was later dropped. For a full year Manson remained in the Los Angeles County Jail, while appealing the revocation. The appeal was denied, and in July 1961 he was sent to the United States Penitentiary at McNeil Island, Washington. He was twenty-six.

According to staff evaluation, Manson had become something of an actor: "He hides his loneliness, resentment, and hostility behind a façade of superficial ingratiation . . . An energetic, young-appearing person whose verbalization flows quite easily, he gestures profusely and can dramatize situations to hold the listener's attention." Then a statement which, in one form or another, was to reappear often in his prison records, and, much later, in post-prison interviews: "He has commented that institutions have become his way of life and that he receives security in institutions which is not available to him in the outside world."

Manson gave as his claimed religion "Scientologist," stating that he "has never settled upon a religious formula for his beliefs and is presently seeking an answer to his question in the new mental health cult known as Scientology."

Scientology, an outgrowth of science-fiction writer L. Ron Hubbard's Dianetics, was just coming into vogue at this time. Manson's teacher, i.e., "auditor," was another convict, Lanier Rayner. Manson would later claim that while in prison he achieved Scientology's highest level, "theta clear."[4]

60   Although Manson remained interested in Scientology much longer than he did in any other subject except music, it appears that, like the Dale Carnegie course, he stuck with it only as long as his enthusiasm lasted, then dropped it, extracting and retaining a number of terms and phrases ("auditing," "cease to exist," "coming to Now") and some concepts (karma, reincarnation, etc.) which, perhaps fittingly, Scientology had borrowed in the first place.

He was still interested in Scientology when his annual progress report was written that September. Furthermore, according to the report, that interest "has led him to make a semi-professional evaluation of his personality which strangely enough is quite consistent with the evaluations made by previous social studies. He appears to have developed a certain amount of insight into his problems through his study of this discipline. Manson is making progress for the first time in his life."

The report also noted that Manson "is active in softball, basketball and croquet" and "is a member of the Drama Club and the Self Improvement Group." He had become "somewhat of a fanatic at practicing the guitar."[5]

He held one fairly responsible job eleven months, the longest he held any prison assignment, before being caught with contraband in his cell and reassigned to janitorial work.

The annual report that September took a close, hard look at the twenty-eight-year-old convict:

65   "Charles Manson has a tremendous drive to call attention to himself. Generally he is unable to succeed in positive acts, therefore he often resorts to negative behavior to satisfy this drive. In his effort to 'find' himself, Manson peruses different religious philosophies, e.g., Scientology and Buddhism; however, he never remains long enough with any given teachings to reap meaningful benefits. Even these attempts and his cries for help represent a desire for attention, with only superficial meaning. Manson has had more than the usual amount of staff attention, yet there is little indication of change in his demeanor. In view of his deep-seated personality problems . . . continuation of institutional treatment is recommended."

On October 1, 1963, prison officials were informed, "according to court papers received in this institution, that Manson was married to a Leona Manson in 1959 in the State of California, and that the marriage was terminated by divorce on April 10, 1963, in Denver, Colorado, on grounds of mental cruelty and conviction of a felony. One child, Charles Luther Manson, is alleged to have been of this union."

This is the only reference, in any of Manson's records, to his second marriage and second child.

Manson's annual review of September 1964 revealed a clear conduct record, but little else encouraging. "His past pattern of employment instability continues . . . seems to

---

[4] In one of his pamphlets, Hubbard defined a "clear" as "one who has straightened up this lifetime." It is rather hard to see how this might apply to Charles Manson.   [5] He in fact requested a transfer to Leavenworth, considered a much tougher institution, because "he claimed he would be allowed to practice his guitar more often." The request was denied.

have an intense need to call attention to himself . . . remains emotionally insecure and tends to involve himself in various fanatical interests."

Those "fanatical interests" weren't identified in the prison reports, but at least are known. In addition to Scientology and his guitar, there was now a third. In January 1964 "I Want to Hold Your Hand" became the No. 1 song on U.S. record charts. With the New York arrival of the "four Liverpool lads" the following month, the United States experienced, later than Great Britain but with no less intensity, the phenomenon known as Beatlemania. According to former inmates at McNeil, Manson's interest in the Beatles was almost an obsession. It didn't necessarily follow that he was a fan. There was more than a little jealousy in his reaction. He told numerous people that, given the chance, he could be much bigger than the Beatles. One person he told this to was Alvin Karpis, lone survivor of the Ma Barker gang. Manson had struck up a friendship with the aging gangster after learning he could play the steel guitar. Karpis taught Manson how. Again an observable pattern. Manson managed to get something from almost everyone with whom he associated.

70   May 1966: "Manson continues to maintain a clear conduct record . . . Recently he has been spending most of his free time writing songs, accumulating about 80 or 90 of them during the past year, which he ultimately hopes to sell following release . . . He also plays the guitar and drums, and is hopeful that he can secure employment as a guitar player or as a drummer or singer . . .

"He shall need a great deal of help in the transition from institution to the free world."

In June 1966, Charles Manson was returned to Terminal Island for release purposes.

August 1966: "Manson is about to complete his ten-year term. He has a pattern of criminal behavior and confinement that dates to his teen years. This pattern is one of instability whether in free society or a structured institutional community. Little can be expected in the way of change in his attitude, behavior, or mode of conduct . . ." The last report noted that Manson had no further interest in academic or vocational training; that he was no longer an advocate of Scientology; that "he has come to worship his guitar and music"; and, finally, "He has no plans for release as he says he has nowhere to go."

The morning Charles Manson was to be freed, he begged the authorities to let him remain in prison. Prison had become his home, he told them. He didn't think he could adjust to the world outside.

75   His request was denied. He was released at 8:15 A.M. on March 21, 1967, and given transportation to Los Angeles. That same day he requested and received permission to go to San Francisco. It was there, in the Haight-Ashbury section, that spring, that the Family was born.

Charles Manson was thirty-two years old. Over seventeen of those years—more than half his life—had been spent in institutions. In those seventeen years, Manson had only been examined by a psychiatrist three times, and then very superficially.

I was surprised, in studying Manson's record, to find no sustained history of violence—armed robbery age thirteen, homosexual rape age seventeen, wife beating age twenty, that was it. I was more than surprised, I was amazed at the number of federal offenses. Probably ninety-nine out of one hundred criminals never see the inside of a federal court. Yet here was Manson, described as "criminally sophisticated," violating the Dyer Act, the Mann Act, stealing from the mails, forging a government check, and so on. Had Manson been convicted of comparable offenses in state courts, he probably would have served *less than five years* instead of over seventeen.

Why? I could only guess. Perhaps, as he said before his reluctant release from Terminal Island, prison was the only home he had. It was also possible that, consciously or unconsciously, he sought out those offenses that carried the most severe punishments. A third speculation—and I wasn't overlooking the possibility that it could be a combination of all three—was a need, amounting almost to a compulsion, to challenge the strongest authority.

I was a long way from understanding Charles Manson. Though I could see patterns in his conduct, which might be clues to his future actions, a great deal was missing.

80   Burglar, car thief, forger, pimp—was this the portrait of a mass murderer? . . .

Comments and Questions

At this writing, Manson and members of his Family remain in prison, although they were first eligible for parole in 1978. Before the death penalty was abolished in California, society would have acted to end the careers of those found guilty of committing first-degree murders.

1. What are the arguments for and against the right of the State to inflict the death penalty? Does this sketch affect how you stand on this issue?

2. Is there a way to explain the fanatical devotion of Manson's followers? May a clue be found in the fact that evil men in the very intensity of their evil may attract the support of those seeking direction for their own evil tendencies? Compare the hypnotic power of Hitler, greatly admired by Manson, over a whole nation. Discuss.

3. What has been quoted from *Helter Skelter* is not literature. However, might not this account provide the raw material for a novel or a play? Consider what Shakespeare did to turn a bloody tragedy into *Hamlet* (p. 626), and what Camus did to turn the historical Caligula (below) into the play *Caligula* (p. 894).

Suetonius   (c. 70–c. 140)
From Gaius Caligula

Caligula became Emperor in the year 37 A.D. "By thus gaining the throne," Suetonius observes, "he fulfilled the highest hopes of the Roman people." As a consequence of this trust, "full and absolute power was at once put into his hands by the unanimous consent of the senate and of the mob." During the early part of his reign, generous and benign acts brought him the accolade of "Greatest and Best of the Caesars." The honeymoon was short. As the passages below reveal, a dramatic change took place as the darling of the people began his reign of terror. (See the forenote to Camus' *Caligula* and the play itself, p. 894.)

. . . So much for Caligula as emperor; we must now tell of his career as a monster.

After he had assumed various complimentary names . . . chancing to overhear some kings who had come to Rome to pay their respects to him, disputing at dinner about the nobility of their descent, he cried:

Let there be one Lord, one King.

And he came near assuming a crown at once and changing the semblance of a principate into the form of a monarchy. But on being reminded that he had risen above the elevation both of princes and kings, he began from that time on to lay claim to divine majesty; for after giving orders that such statues of the gods as were especially famous for their sanctity or their artistic merit, including that of Jupiter of Olympia, should be brought from Greece, in order to remove their heads and put his own in their place, he built out a part of the Palace as far as the Forum, and making the temple of Castor and Pollux its vestibule, he often took his place between the divine brethren, and exhibited himself there to be worshipped by those who presented themselves; and some hailed him as Jupiter Latiaris. He also set up a special temple to his own godhead, with priests and with victims of the choicest kind. In this temple was a life-sized statue of the emperor in gold, which was dressed each day in clothing such as he wore himself. The richest citizens used all their influence to secure the priesthoods of his cult and bid high for the honour. The victims were flamingoes, peacocks, woodcocks, guinea-hens, and pheasants, offered day by day each after its own kind. At night he used constantly to invite the full and radiant moon to his embraces and his bed, while in the daytime he would talk confidentially with Jupiter Capitolinus, now whispering and then in turn putting his ear to the mouth of the god, now in louder and even angry language; for he was heard to make the threat: "Lift me up, or I'll lift thee." . . .

He lived in habitual incest with all his sisters, and at a large banquet he placed each of them in turn below him, while his wife reclined above. Of these he is believed to have violated Drusilla when he was still a minor, and even to have been caught lying with her by his grandmother Antonia, at whose house they were brought up in company. Afterwards, when she was the wife of Lucius Cassius Longinus, an ex-consul, he took her from him and openly treated her as his lawful wife; and when ill, he made her heir to his property and the throne. When she died, he appointed a season of public mourning, during which it was a capital offence to laugh, bathe, or dine in company with one's parents, wife, or children. He was so beside himself with grief that suddenly fleeing the city by night and traversing Campania, he went to Syracuse and hurriedly returned from there without cutting his hair or shaving his beard. And he never afterwards took oath about matters of the highest moment, even before the assembly of the people or in the presence of the soldiers, except by the godhead of Drusilla. The rest of his sisters he did not love with so great affection, nor honour so highly, but often prostituted them to his favorites; so that he was the readier at the trial of Aemilius Lepidus to condemn them, as adulteresses and privy to the conspiracies against him; and he not only made public letters in the handwriting of all of them, procured by fraud and seduction, but also dedicated to Mars the Avenger, with an explanatory inscription, three swords designed to take his life. . . .

He seldom had anyone put to death except by numerous slight wounds, his constant order, which soon became well-known, being: "Strike so that he may feel that he is dying." When a different man than he had intended had been killed, through a mistake in the names, he said that the victim too had deserved the same fate. He often uttered the familiar line of the tragic poet:

Let them hate me, so they but fear me.

5   . . . He even used openly to deplore the state of his times, because they had been marked by no public disasters, saying that the rule of Augustus had been made famous by the Varus massacre, and that of Tiberius by the collapse of the amphitheatre at Fidenae, while his own was threatened with oblivion because of its prosperity; and every now and then he wished for the destruction of his armies, for famine, pestilence, fires, or a great earthquake. . . .

At one of his more sumptuous banquets he suddenly burst into a fit of laughter, and when the consuls, who were reclining next him, politely inquired at what he was laughing, he replied: "What do you suppose, except that at a single nod of mine both of you could have your throats cut on the spot?"

As a sample of his humor, he took his place beside a statue of Jupiter, and asked the tragic actor Apelles which of the two seemed to him the greater, and when he hesitated, Caligula had him flayed with whips, extolling his voice from time to time, when the wretch begged for mercy, as passing sweet even in his groans. Whenever he kissed the neck of his wife or sweetheart, he would say: "Off comes this beautiful head whenever I give the word." He even used to threaten now and then that he would resort to torture if necessary, to find out from his dear Caesonia why he loved her so passionately. . . .

He respected neither his own chastity nor that of anyone else. He is said to have had unnatural relations with Marcus Lepidus, the pantomimic actor Mnester, and certain hostages. Valerius Catullus, a young man of a consular family, publicly proclaimed that he had violated the emperor and worn himself out in commerce with him. To say nothing of his incest with his sisters and his notorious passion for the concubine Pyrallis, there was scarcely any woman of rank whom he did not approach. These as a rule he invited to dinner with their husbands, and as they passed by the foot of his couch, he would inspect them critically and deliberately, as if buying slaves, even putting out his hand and lifting up the face of anyone who looked down in modesty; then as often as the fancy took him he would leave the room, sending for the one who pleased him best, and returning soon afterward with evident signs of what had occurred, he would openly commend or criticize his partner, recounting her charms or defects and commenting on her conduct. To some he personally sent a bill of divorce in the name of their absent husbands, and had it entered in the public records. . . .

He was very tall and extremely pale, with a huge body, but very thin neck and legs. His eyes and temples were hollow, his forehead broad and grim, his hair thin and entirely gone on the top of his head, though his body was hairy. Because of this to look upon him from a higher place as he passed by, or for any reason whatever to mention a goat, was treated as a capital offence. While his face was naturally forbidding and ugly, he purposely made it even more savage, practising all kinds of terrible and fearsome expressions before a mirror.

10   He was sound neither of body nor mind. As a boy he was troubled with the falling sickness, and while in his youth he had some endurance, yet at times because of sudden faintness he was hardly able to walk, to stand up, to collect his thoughts, or to hold up his head. He himself realized his mental infirmity, and thought at times of going into retirement and clearing his brain. It is thought that his wife Caesonia gave him a drug intended for a love potion, which however had the effect of driving him mad. He was especially tormented with sleeplessness; for he never rested more than three hours at night, and even for that length of time he did not sleep quietly, but was terrified by strange appari-

tions, once for example dreaming that the spirit of the Ocean talked with him. Therefore weary of lying in bed wide awake during the greater part of the night, he would now sit upon his couch, and now wander through the long colonnades, crying out from time to time for daylight and longing for its coming.

I think I may fairly attribute to mental weakness the existence of two exactly opposite faults in the same person, extreme assurance and, on the other hand, excessive timorousness. For this man, who so utterly despised the gods, was wont at the slightest thunder and lightning to shut his eyes, to muffle up his head, and if they increased, to leap from his bed and hide under it. In his journey through Sicily, though he made all manner of fun of the miracles in various places, he suddenly fled from Messana by night, panic-stricken by the smoke and roaring from Aetna's crater. Full of threats as he was also against the barbarians, when he was riding in a chariot through a narrow defile on the far side of the Rhine, and someone said that there would be no slight panic if the enemy should appear anywhere, he immediately mounted a horse and hastily returned to the bridges. Finding them crowded with camp servants and baggage, in his impatience of any delay he was passed along from hand to hand over the men's heads. Soon after, hearing of an uprising in Germany, he made preparations to flee from the city and equipped fleets for the purpose, finding comfort only in the thought that the provinces across the sea would at any rate be left him, in case the enemy should be victorious and take possession of the summits of the Alps, as the Cimbri, or even of the city, as the Senones had once done. And it was this, I think, that later inspired his assassins with the idea of pretending to the riotous soldiers that he had laid hands on himself in terror at the report of a defeat.

In his clothing, his shoes, and the rest of his attire he did not follow the usage of his country and his fellow-citizens; not always even that of his sex, or in fact, that of an ordinary mortal. He often appeared in public in embroidered cloaks covered with precious stones, with a long-sleeved tunic and bracelets; sometimes in silk and in a woman's robe; now in slippers or buskins, again in boots, such as the emperor's body-guard wear, and at times in the low shoes which are used by females. But oftentimes, he exhibited himself with a golden beard, holding in his hand a thunderbolt, a trident, or a caduceus, emblems of the gods, and even in the garb of Venus. He frequently wore the dress of a triumphing general, even before his campaign, and sometimes the breastplate of Alexander the Great, which he had taken from his sarcophagus.

As regards liberal studies, he gave little attention to literature but a great deal to oratory, and he was as ready of speech and eloquent as you please, especially if he had occasion to make a charge against anyone. For when he was angry, he had an abundant flow of words and thoughts, and his voice and delivery were such that for very excitement he could not stand still and he was clearly heard by those at a distance. . . .

On the ninth day before the Kalends of February at about the seventh hour he hesitated whether or not to get up for luncheon, since his stomach was still disordered from excess of food on the day before, but at length he came out at the persuasion of his friends. In the covered passage through which he had to pass, some boys of good birth, who had been summoned from Asia to appear on the stage, were rehearsing their parts, and he stopped to watch and encourage them; and had not the leader of the troop complained that he had a chill, he would have returned and had the performance given at once. From this point there are two versions of the story: some say that as he was talking with the boys, Chaerea came up behind and gave him a deep cut in the neck, having first cried, "Do your duty," and that then the tribune Cornelius Sabinus, who was the other conspirator and faced Gaius, stabbed him in the breast. Others say that Sabinus, after getting rid of the crowd through centurions who were in the plot, asked for the watch-word, as soldiers do, and that when Gaius gave him "Jupiter," he cried "So be it," and as

Gaius looked around, he split his jawbone with a blow of his sword. As he lay upon the ground and with writhing limbs called out that he still lived, the others dispatched him with thirty wounds; for the general signal was "Strike again." Some even thrust their swords through his privates. At the beginning of the disturbance his bearers ran to his aid with their poles, and presently the Germans of his body-guard, and they slew several of his assassins, as well as some inoffensive senators.

15 He lived twenty-nine years and ruled three years, ten months and eight days. . . .

Gibbon, Edward

from *The Columbia Encyclopedia*

Gibbon, Edward (gĭ' bun), 1737–1794, English historian, author of the monumental *Decline and Fall of the Roman Empire.* His childhood was sickly, and he had little formal education but read enormously and omnivorously. He went at 15 to Magdalen College, Oxford, but was forced to leave because of his conversion to Roman Catholicism. His father sent him (1753) to Lausanne, where he was formally reconverted to Protestantism. Actually he became a sceptic and later greatly offended the pious by his famous chapters of historical criticism of Christianity in his great work. In Lausanne he fell in love with the penniless daughter of a pastor, Suzanne Curchod (who was later to be the great intellectual, Mme. Necker). The two were engaged to be married, but Gibbon's father refused to consent. Gibbon "sighed as a lover" but "obeyed as a son" and gave up the match. He left Lausanne in 1758. It was on a visit to Rome that he conceived the idea of his magnificent and panoramic history. This appeared as *The History of the Decline and Fall of the Roman Empire* (6 vols., 1776–88), and won immediate acclaim, despite some harsh criticism. Gibbon himself was assured of the greatness of his work, which is, indeed, one of the most-read historical works of modern times. Gibbon himself, was not, however, accorded much personal admiration. He moved in the high circles of society and was a member of the literary circle of Samuel Johnson, but he was personally unprepossessing. Short (under 5 ft.), bulbously fat, always dressed in ornate and vivid clothes that flattered his vanity but not his appearance, and affected in manner and speech, he was a figure of ridicule. The salons buzzed with stories mocking him. He entered upon a short and highly inglorious political career, serving as a member of Parliament from 1774 to 1783. He violently opposed the American Revolution, though later he was to look with favor on the more radical French Revolution. In 1783 he withdrew to Lausanne, where he completed his great work. One of the fascinating things about Gibbon is the disparity between his personal character and his work, a disparity not resolved by his own *Memoirs of His Life and Writings,* commonly called the *Autobiography,* which first appeared in the edition of his miscellaneous works by Lord Sheffield in 1796. The autobiography is, however, one of the most subtle and interesting works of its kind in English. An edition of Gibbon's original six drafts appeared as *The Autobiographies* in 1896. Editions of the *Decline and Fall* are legion. The modern standard edition is that of J. B. Bury (7 vols., 1896–1900). A bibliography of the works of Gibbon by Jane E. Norton appeared in 1941. See biography by D. M. Low (1937).

Lytton Strachey (1880–1932)
Gibbon

Happiness is the word that immediately rises to the mind at the thought of Edward Gibbon: and happiness in its widest connotation—including good fortune as well as enjoyment. Good fortune, indeed, followed him from the cradle to the grave in the most tactful way possible; occasionally it appeared to fail him, but its absence always turned out to be a blessing in disguise. Out of a family of seven he alone had the luck to survive—but only with difficulty; and the maladies of his childhood opened his mind to the pleasures of study and literature. His mother died; but her place was taken by a devoted aunt, whose care brought him through the dangerous years of adolescence to a vigorous manhood. His misadventures at Oxford saved him from becoming a don. His exile to Lausanne, by giving him a command of the French language, initiated him into European culture, and at the same time enabled him to lay the foundations of his scholarship. His father married again; but his stepmother remained childless and became one of his dearest friends. He fell in love; the match was forbidden; and he escaped the dubious joys of domestic life with the future Madame Necker. While he was allowed to travel on the Continent, it seemed doubtful for some time whether his father would have the resources or the generosity to send him over the Alps into Italy. His fate hung in the balance; but at last his father produced the necessary five hundred pounds, and, in the autumn of 1764 Rome saw her historian. His father died at exactly the right moment, and left him exactly the right amount of money. At the age of thirty-three Gibbon found himself his own master, with a fortune just sufficient to support him as an English gentleman of leisure and fashion. For ten years he lived in London, a member of Parliament, a place-man, and a diner-out, and during those ten years he produced the first three volumes of his History. After that he lost his place, failed to obtain another, and, finding his income unequal to his expenses, returned to Lausanne, where he took up his residence in the house of a friend, overlooking the Lake of Geneva. It was the final step in his career, and no less fortunate than all the others. In Lausanne he was rich once more, he was famous, he enjoyed a delightful combination of retirement and society. Before another ten years were out he had completed his History; and in ease, dignity, and absolute satisfaction his work in this world was accomplished.

One sees in such a life an epitome of the blessings of the eighteenth century—the wonderul μηδὲν ἄγαν [nothing in excess] of that most balmy time—the rich fruit ripening slowly on the sunwarmed wall, and coming inevitably to its delicious perfection. It is difficult to imagine, at any other period in history, such a combination of varied qualities, so beautifully balanced—the profound scholar who was also a brilliant man of the world—the votary of cosmopolitan culture, who never for a moment ceased to be a supremely English "character." The ten years of Gibbon's life in London afford an astonishing spectacle of interacting energies. By what strange power did he succeed in producing a masterpiece of enormous erudition and perfect form, while he was leading the gay life of a man about town, spending his evenings at White's or Boodle's or the Club, attending Parliament, oscillating between his house in Bentineck Street, his country cottage at Hampton Court, and his little establishment at Brighton, spending his summers in Bath or Paris, and even, at odd moments, doing a little work at the Board of Trade, to show that his place was not entirely a sinecure? Such a triumph could only have been achieved by the sweet reasonableness of the eighteenth century. "Monsieur Gibbon n'est point mon homme," said Rousseau. Decidedly! The prophet of the coming age of sentiment and romance could have nothing in common with such a nature. It was not that the historian was a mere frigid observer of the golden mean—far from it. He was full of fire and feeling. His youth had been at moments riotous—night after night he had reeled hallooing down St. James's Street. Old age did not diminish the natural warmth of his affections; the beautiful letter—a model of its kind—written on the death of his aunt, in his fiftieth year, is a proof of it. But the fire and the feeling were controlled and co-ordinated. Boswell was a Rousseauite, one of the first of the Romantics, an inveterate sentimentalist and nothing could be more complete than the contrast between his career and Gibbon's. He, too, achieved a glorious triumph; but it was by dint of the sheer force of native genius asserting itself over the extravagance and disorder of an agitated life—a life which, after a desperate struggle, seemed to end at last in darkness and shipwreck. With Gibbon there was never any struggle: everything came naturally to him—learning and dissipation, industry and indolence, affection and scepticism—in the correct proportions; and he enjoyed himself up to the very end.

To complete the picture one must notice another antithesis: the wit, the genius, the massive intellect, were housed in a physical mould that was ridiculous. A little figure, extraordinarily rotund, met the eye, surmounted by a top-heavy head, with a button nose, planted amid a vast expanse of cheek and ear, and chin upon chin rolling downward. Nor was this appearance only; the odd shape reflected something in the inner man. Mr. Gibbon, it was noticed, was always slightly over-dressed; his favourite wear was flowered velvet. He was a little vain, a little pompous; at the first moment one almost laughed; then one forgot everything under the fascination of that even flow of admirably intelligent, exquisitely turned, and most amusing sentences. Among all his other merits this obviously ludicrous egotism took its place. The astonishing creature was able to make a virtue of absurdity. Without that touch of nature he would have run the risk of being too much of a good thing; as it was there was no such danger; he was preposterous and a human being.

It is not difficult to envisage the character and figure; what seems strange, and remote, and hard to grasp is the connection between this individual and the decline and fall of the Roman Empire. The paradox, indeed, is so complete as to be almost romantic. At a given moment—October 15, 1764—at a given place—the Capitoline Hill, outside the church of Aracoeli—the impact occurred between the serried centuries of Rome and Edward Gibbon. His life, his work, his fame, his place in the history of civilization, followed from that circumstance. The point of his achievement lay precisely in the extreme improbability of it. The utter incongruity of those combining elements produced the masterpiece—the gigantic ruin of Europe through a thousand years, mirrored in the mind of an eighteenth-century English gentleman.

5   How was the miracle accomplished? Needless to say, Gibbon was a great artist—one of those rare spirits, with whom a vital and penetrating imagination and a supreme capacity for general conceptions express themselves instinctively in an appropriate form. That the question has ever been not only asked but seriously debated, whether History was an art, is certainly one of the curiosities of human ineptitude. What else can it possibly be? It is obvious that History is not a science: it is obvious that History is not the accumulation of facts, but the relation of them. Only the pedantry of incomplete academic persons could have given birth to such a monstrous supposition. Facts relating to the past, when they are collected without art, are compilations; and compilations, no doubt, may be useful; but they are no more History than butter, eggs, salt and herbs are an omelette. That Gibbon was a great artist, therefore, is implied in the statement that he was a great historian; but what is interesting is the particular nature of his artistry. His whole genius was preëminently classical; order, lucidity, balance, precision—the great classical qualities—dominate

his work; and his History is chiefly remarkable as one of the supreme monuments of Classic Art in European literature.

L'ordre est ce qu'il y a de plus rare dans les opérations de l'esprit.[1] Gibbon's work is a magnificent illustration of the splendid dictum of Fénelon. He brought order out of the enormous chaos of his subject—a truly stupendous achievement! With characteristic good fortune, indeed, the material with which he had to cope was still just not too voluminous to be digested by a single extremely competent mind. In the following century even a Gibbon would have collapsed under the accumulated mass of knowledge at his disposal. As it was, by dint of a superb constructive vision, a serene self-confidence, a very acute judgment, and an astonishing facility in the manipulation of material, he was able to dominate the known facts. To dominate, nothing more; anything else would have been foreign to his purpose. He was a classicist; and his object was not comprehension but illumination. He drove a straight, firm road through the vast unexplored forest of Roman history; his readers could follow with easy pleasure along the wonderful way; they might glance, as far as their eyes could reach, into the entangled recesses on either side of them; but they were not invited to stop, or wander, or camp out, or make friends with the natives; they must be content to look and to pass on.

It is clear that Gibbon's central problem was the one of exclusion: how much, and what, was he to leave out? This was largely a question of scale—always one of the major difficulties in literary composition—and it appears from several passages in the Autobiographies that Gibbon paid particular attention to it. Incidentally, it may be observed that the six Autobiographies were not so much excursions in egotism—though no doubt it is true that Gibbon was not without a certain fondness for what he himself called "the most disgusting of the pronouns"—as exercises on the theme of scale. Every variety of compression and expansion is visible among those remarkable pages; but apparently, since the manuscripts were left in an unfinished state, Gibbon still felt, after the sixth attempt, that he had not discovered the right solution. Even with the scale of the History he was not altogether satisfied; the chapters on Christianity, he thought, might, with further labour, have been considerably reduced. But, even more fundamental than the element of scale, there was something else that in reality, conditioned the whole treatment of his material, the whole scope and nature of his History; and that was the style in which it was written. The style once fixed, everything else followed. Gibbon was well aware of this. He wrote his first chapter three times over, his second and third twice; then at last he was satisfied, and after that he wrote on without a hitch. In particular the problem of exclusion was solved. Gibbon's style is probably the most exclusive in literature. By its very nature it bars out a great multitude of human energies. It makes sympathy impossible, it takes no cognizance of passion, it turns its back upon religion with a withering smile. But that was just what was wanted. Classic beauty came instead. By the penetrating influence of style—automatically, inevitably—lucidity, balance and precision were everywhere introduced; and the miracle of order was established over the chaos of a thousand years.

Of course, the Romantics raised a protest. "Gibbon's style," said Coleridge, "is detestable; but," he added, "it is not the worst thing about him." Critics of the later nineteenth century were less consistent. They admired Gibbon for everything except his style, imagining that his History would have been much improved if it had been written in some other way; they did not see that, if it had been written in any other way, it would have ceased to exist; just as St. Paul's would cease to exist if it were rebuilt in Gothic. Obsessed by the colour and movement of romantic prose, they were blind to the subtlety, the clarity, the continuous strength of Gibbon's writing. Gibbon could turn a bold phrase with the

[1] Order is what is rarest in the workings of the mind.

best of them—"the fat slumbers of the Church," for instance—if he wanted to; but he very rarely wanted to; such effects would have disturbed the easy, close-knit, homogeneous surface of his work. His use of words is, in fact, extremely delicate. When, describing St. Simeon Stylites on his pillar, he speaks of "this last and lofty station," he succeeds, with the least possible emphasis, merely by the combination of those two alliterative epithets with that particular substantive, in making the whole affair ridiculous. One can almost see his shoulders shrug. The nineteenth century found him pompous; they did not relish the irony beneath the pomp. He produces some of his most delightful effects by rhythm alone. In the *Vindication*—a work which deserves to be better known, for it shows us Gibbon, as one sees him nowhere else, really letting himself go—there is an admirable example of this. "I still think," he says, in reply to a criticism by Dr. Randolph, "I still think that an hundred Bishops, with Athanasius at their head, were as competent judges of the discipline of the fourth century, as even the Lady Margaret's Professor of Divinity in the University of Oxford." Gibbon's irony, no doubt, is the salt of his work; but, like all irony, it is the product of style. It was not for nothing that he read through every year the *Lettres Provinciales* of Pascal. From this point of view it is interesting to compare him with Voltaire. The irony of the great Frenchman was a flashing sword—extreme, virulent, deadly—a terrific instrument of propaganda. Gibbon uses the weapon with far more delicacy; he carves his enemy "as a dish fit for the Gods"; his mocking is aloof, almost indifferent, and perhaps, in the long run, for that very reason, even more effective.

At every period of his life Gibbon is a pleasant thing to contemplate, but perhaps most pleasant of all in the closing weeks of it, during his last visit to England. He had hurried home from Lausanne to join his friend Lord Sheffield, whose wife had died suddenly, and who, he felt, was in need of his company. The journey was no small proof of his affectionate nature; old age was approaching; he was corpulent, gouty, and accustomed to every comfort; and the war of the French Revolution was raging in the districts through which he had to pass. But he did not hesitate; and after skirting the belligerent armies in his chaise, arrived safely in England. After visiting Lord Sheffield he proceeded to Bath, to stay with his stepmother. The amazing little figure, now almost spherical, bowled along the Bath Road in the highest state of exhilaration. "I am always," he told his friend, "so much delighted and improved with this union of ease and motion, that, were not the expense enormous, I would travel every year some hundred miles, more especially in England." Mrs. Gibbon, a very old lady, but still full of vitality, worshipped her stepson, and the two spent ten days together, talking, almost always *tête-à-tête,* for ten hours a day. Then the historian went off to Althorpe, where he spent a happy morning with Lord Spencer, looking at early editions of Cicero. And so back to London. In London a little trouble arose. A protuberance in the lower part of his person, which, owing to years of characteristic *insouciance,* had grown to extraordinary proportions, required attention; an operation was necessary; but it went off well, and there seemed to be no danger. Once more Mr. Gibbon dined out. Once more he was seen, in his accustomed attitude, with advanced forefinger, addressing the company, and rapping his snuff box at the close of each particularly pointed phrase. But illness came on again—nothing very serious. The great man lay in bed discussing how much longer he would live—he was fifty-six—ten years, twelve years, or perhaps twenty. He ate some chicken and drank three glasses of madeira. Life seemed almost as charming as usual. Next morning, getting out of bed for a necessary moment, *"Je suis plus adroit,"*[2] he said with his odd smile to his French valet. Back in bed again, he muttered something more, a little incoherently, lay back among the pillows, dozed, half-woke, dozed again, and became unconscious—forever.

---

[2] "I am more active."

Comments and Questions

1. How much interpretive comment is offered in the *Encyclopedia* account of Gibbon?

2. Note Strachey's first paragraph. Besides length, what does it have in common with the *Encyclopedia* account? In what ways does it differ? Which provides more factual information? How does purpose account for this difference? Which is more interpretive?

3. What controls the selection of details in the *Encyclopedia* account? What controls Strachey's account? What controls Strachey's selection of details?

4. Show what happens in Strachey's "Gibbon" to each of the facts included in the *Encyclopedia* account. Does Strachey make use of all the facts? How do you account for specific omissions? Does he ever tell when Gibbon was born? What facts does he use that are not even summarized by the encyclopedist? Do these facts pertain chiefly to Gibbon's personal or to his professional life?

5. Consider Strachey's style. Style is a "characteristic mode of expression," which may be partly identified by answering certain questions. What is the pattern of the sketch as a whole? What are the main divisions? In what way does Strachey avoid monotony in his sentences? Consider any sequence of ten sentences, and record what you find as to length and arrangement. Does each sentence move the sketch forward, or do some of the sentences simply restate what has already been said? What comment can you make about word choice? Could you determine from the context the meanings of words you did not know? Could you do the same for the allusions? Are there many allusions? Are there many figures of speech? Are the transitions smoothly achieved? Consider, for example, the movement from paragraph to paragraph. Can you point to any memorable phrases, sentences, or passages? Now, after answering all these questions, how would you summarize your impression of Strachey's style?

6. Follow up some of Strachey's casual references to Gibbon's activities or to those of his contemporaries. What were the "misadventures at Oxford"? What kind of person was Madame Necker that Strachey should have referred to "the dubious joy of domestic life" with her? Compare Gibbon and Boswell; Gibbon and Rousseau. (Strachey has written sketches of both Boswell and Rousseau.)

7. How much quoted material does Strachey use? For what purposes?

8. In what way does the last paragraph of the sketch offer a final comment on Strachey's thesis concerning Gibbon? Why does the author go into more detail at this point than he does elsewhere?

A model biographical profile: Strachey's "Gibbon"   Strachey says of Gibbon: his "central problem was one of exclusion: how much, and what, was he to leave out?" This is precisely Strachey's own problem and that of any artist. One can imagine Gibbon's biographer in deep thought, pondering the vast accumulation of facts about the great historian. What one controlling idea would best organize the available data? No doubt many possibilities presented themselves. All but one had to be rejected. The one chosen had to be least vulnerable to exceptions, the one under which could be arrayed the events of a lifetime. Strachey found the key in the words "happiness in its widest connotation."

The danger in this technique is oversimplification, the temptation to force all the data into one pattern. Does Strachey always escape this danger? Consider Gibbon's thwarted love affair. It was lucky, says the biographer, that a father's good sense allowed his son to avoid "the dubious joys of domestic life with the future Madame Necker." Is this comment a rationalization?

Exclusions settled, key words selected, Strachey's next step was to begin writing. The beginning of a good profile should be exciting, like the start of a school term, the kickoff at a football game, the rise of a curtain at a play, or the first line of a poem. Strachey's first sentence is mildly startling, for happiness is not the lot of many geniuses. The reader is interested in proofs, and the author begins to list them. In the process, Strachey offers many generalizations and always provides illustrations to support them. Generalization: Gibbon was a great stylist; examples of effective style follow.

Thus, Strachey's "Gibbon" is a model of consistency. The beginning dictates both middle and ending, all acting together to give the reader a living portrait.

Essays

The essay is one damn thing after another, but in a sequence that in some miraculous way develops a central theme and relates it to the rest of human experience.
ALDOUS HUXLEY

Preliminaries

The essay as a form stands astride the line dividing literature as a tool and literature as an interpretive art. Essayists are chiefly interested in the interpretation of facts. They may wish to report a fact, explain it, correct a previous misinterpretation of it, or merely express an opinion concerning a fact. To further their effects, they may use at will the devices and techniques associated with biography, fiction, poetry, or drama. This borrowing of devices is a sort of literary fair play because biographers, fiction writers, poets, and dramatists use as needed the devices of the essay.

 Of all the forms of literature the essay is in its method the least complex. Anyone who can put pen to paper can compose an essay of a sort, something that very likely would be nearer the form attempted than would be the result of a similar effort to produce a poem, a play, or even a short story. The papers or themes written as high school or college exercises are in the tradition of the essay. So you are probably aware of the form's general characteristics. As a review of these characteristics, let us examine excerpts from two very different essays: Thomas Henry Huxley's "The Nature of an Hypothesis" and Charles Lamb's "The Two Races of Men." First we shall observe the qualities of the essay as revealed

1063

in Huxley. Next we shall see how these qualities are repeated, modified, or added to in Lamb.

The Serious Approach

"The Nature of an Hypothesis" is an excerpt but will serve to illustrate the features of a serious essay written for a practical purpose. Before we read Huxley, let us look at the word "hypothesis" as a dictionary might define it:

> *hypothesis:* a supposition or unproved theory which may be provisionally accepted to explain or account for a group of facts; *a working hypothesis* provides a basis for continued investigation.

Does Huxley say anything more than this in the following paragraphs?

Thomas Henry Huxley (1825–1895)
The Nature of an Hypothesis

When our means of observation of any natural fact fail to carry us beyond a certain point it is perfectly legitimate, and often extremely useful, to make a supposition as to what we should see, if we could carry direct observation a step farther. A supposition of this kind is called an *hypothesis,* and the value of any hypothesis depends upon the extent to which reasoning upon the assumption that it is true enables us to account for the phenomena with which it is concerned.

Thus, if a person is standing close behind you, and you suddenly feel a blow on your back, you have no direct evidence of the cause of the blow; and if you two were alone, you could not possibly attain any; but you immediately suppose that this person has struck you. Now that is an hypothesis, and it is a legitimate hypothesis, first, because it explains the fact; and, secondly, because no other explanation is probable; probable meaning in the ordinary course of nature. If your companion declared that you fancied you felt a blow, or that some invisible spirit struck you, you would probably decline to accept his explanation of the fact. You would say that both the hypotheses by which he professed to explain the phenomenon were extremely improbable or in other words, that in the ordinary course of nature fancies of this kind do not occur, nor spirits strike blows. In fact his hypotheses would be illegitimate, and yours would be legitimate; and, in all probability, you would act upon your own. In daily life nine-tenths of our actions are based upon suppositions or hypotheses, and our success or failure in practical affairs depends upon the legitimacy of these hypotheses. You believe a man on the hypothesis that he is always truthful; you give him pecuniary credit on the hypothesis that he is solvent.

Thus, everybody invents, and, indeed, is compelled to invent, hypotheses in order to account for phenomena of the cause of which he has no direct evidence; and they are just as legitimate and necessary in science as in common life. Only the scientific reasoner must be careful to remember that which is sometimes forgotten in daily life, that an hypothesis must be regarded as a means and not as an end; that we may cherish it so long as it helps us to explain the order of nature; and that we are bound to throw it away without hesitation as soon as it is shown to be inconsistent with any part of that order.

Telling and showing   What has Huxley done to bring his definition within the scope of interpretive literature and within the compass of the essay form? In his first paragraph he *tells* us why suppositions are necessary; he *tells* us that a supposition is a hypothesis; he *tells* us that a hypothesis is valuable if it helps to account for other phenomena. If he had continued in this vein, he would have produced good, scientific prose, as lucid and exact as dictionary prose but more spacious. The cool tone of this paragraph is only slightly warmed by the use of the personal pronouns *our, us,* and *we*. All the remaining words are as impersonal as ciphers.

Now see what happens in the second paragraph. Persons appear. A little scene is suggested. *You,* the reader, are in the scene. What happens, happens to you. Huxley has gone straight to drama for his device, and in doing so has temporarily abandoned *telling* for *showing*. An action has brought an abstraction—the word *hypothesis*—to life. This is the way of interpretive literature.

Focus   Why, having borrowed from drama, did not Huxley create a full scene, complete with dialogue? Something like this:

> *(You are standing, abstracted, looking off into space, when you feel a sudden blow on your back. You whirl and come face to face with the only other occupant of the room.)*
>
> *You:* What's the idea?
> *Other Occupant:* Idea of what?
> *You:* Idea of hitting me, that's what!
> *O.O.:* Who hit you?
> *You:* You hit me. Don't say you didn't.
> *O.O.:* Prove it.
> *You:* Why, you, you . . . I ought to . . .
> *O.O.:* Don't get excited. You're imagining things. Probably nobody hit you.
> *You:* Imagining, my eye! I felt the blow—right there—between the shoulder blades.
> *O.O.:* Right there? Well, maybe a spirit struck you.

And so on. If Huxley had so indulged himself, what would have happened to the focus on the word *hypothesis?* Clearly there was need for just so much drama and no more, for Huxley was intent upon making his definition memorable and not in creating a diversion. We have here revealed one fairly constant characteristic of the essay: it is chiefly aimed at explaining and uses sparingly the devices of showing as a means to that end.

Tone and purpose   We can see that Huxley is not simply toying with an idea. He is serious. He is genuinely concerned that we shall understand what he is talking about. In the third paragraph he indicates why he, a scientist and a spokesman for science, wishes to have the conception of a hypothesis understood. "Everybody invents . . . hypotheses," he says, "and they are just as legitimate and necessary in science as in common life." Here is his central point. Because his point is a serious one and because he has treated it seriously, we call the result a formal essay.

Such essays, furthermore, are called formal because they are impersonal. Like a lecturer who turns a globe to indicate its shape, Huxley shows us the form of a hypothesis. We look at the object, not at the lecturer. We may admire the clarity of the lecturer's mind and ability to use the right words in the right places, but our attention is where the lecturer wants it to be: on the subject.

Directness   The essay is more direct than any other form of literature, except perhaps biography. In "Quality" Galsworthy tells us a story but not its meaning. In *Ile* O'Neill tells a story in the form of a play, but he leaves it to us to find the meaning. If we fail to find the meaning of either of these works, the narrative or the plot remains. If we read an essay and fail to understand it, to know what it means, virtually nothing remains. Essayists, therefore, are seldom coy. They are intent upon revealing their meaning as directly as possible.

This directness is frequently apparent in the title chosen: "The Nature of an Hypothesis"; "The Literature of Knowledge and the Literature of Power." Essayists like the flat, aphoristic statement: "Truth is mysterious, elusive, ever to be won anew" (Albert Camus, "Nobel Prize Acceptance Speech"). They define or partly define whenever necessary and as they go along: "A poem has many levels of meaning and none of them is prose" (Stephen Spender, "On Teaching Modern Poetry").

What effect does the direct approach have on the appeal of the essay? Clearly it is farthest removed from the appeal of poetry, which depends upon indirection and which exercises both our understanding and our feelings. The essay appeals almost exclusively to the understanding and feeds most directly our desire to know.

Incompleteness   We gain from T. H. Huxley a clear but limited notion of the qualities and uses of hypotheses. He could have used many more examples. He could have developed a single hypothesis and carried it through its various stages from first observations through all the phases of testing, modifying, testing again, and so on to the establishment of a theory or perhaps a law. Why did not Huxley do this? For one thing he was writing for a general audience, not for scientists. He accepted the limitations of this fact and in so doing accepted the limiting scope of the essay. The essay, even when the subject itself is relatively narrow, does not pretend to completeness.

Is incompleteness characteristic of all forms of literature? In a sense it is. The plot structures of short stories have been described as open or closed (see "Preliminaries" in the fiction division, p. 10). The closed story is rounded at the end and is in a technical sense complete, for all the questions *posed by the author* of the particular story have been answered. No story, however, carries a comment upon itself, and no comments of readers and critics ever exhaust the story's implications. In this sense and others, then, any piece of writing is incomplete.

The essay, however, is by definition *an attempt,* a tentative examination of a single subject. In short, it offers a word, but far from the last word, on a given topic.

The Light Approach

We turn now to the opening paragraphs of another essay written with a different purpose and to a quite different effect from Huxley's. Before we examine Lamb's remarks on "The Two Races of Men," let us see how a dictionary defines the word "race":

> *race:* any of the major biological divisions of mankind, distinguished by color and texture of hair, color of skin and eyes, stature, bodily proportions, etc.: many ethnologists now consider that there are only three primary divisions, the Caucasian (loosely, *white race*), Negroid (loosely, *black race*) and Mongoloid (loosely, *yellow race*), each with various subdivisions.

Does Lamb say anything resembling this definition in his remarks on races?

Charles Lamb (1775–1834)
The Two Races of Men

The human species, according to the best theory I can form of it, is composed of two distinct races, *the men who borrow, and the men who lend.* To these two original diversities may be reduced all those impertinent classifications of Gothic and Celtic tribes, white men, black men, red men. All the dwellers upon earth, "Parthians, and Medes, and Elamites," flock hither, and do naturally fall in with one or other of these primary distinctions. The infinite superiority of the former, which I choose to designate as the *great race,* is discernible in their figure, port, and a certain instinctive sovereignty. The latter are born degraded. "He shall serve his brethren." There is something in the air of one of this cast, lean and suspicious; contrasting with the open, trusting, generous manners of the other.

Observe who have been the greatest borrowers of all ages—Alcibiades—Falstaff—Sir Richard Steele—our late incomparable Brinsley—what a family likeness in all four!

What a careless, even deportment hath your borrower! what rosy gills! what a beautiful reliance on Providence doth he manifest,—taking no more thought than lilies! What contempt for money, accounting it (yours and mine especially) no better than dross! What a liberal confounding of those pedantic distinctions of *meum* and *tuum!* or rather what a noble simplification of language (beyond Tooke), resolving these supposed opposites into one clear, intelligible pronoun adjective!—What near approaches doth he make to the primitive *community,*—to the extent of one half of the principle at least.

He is the true taxer who "calleth all the world up to be taxed"; and the distance is as vast between him and *one of us,* as subsisted between the Augustan Majesty and the poorest obolary Jew that paid it tribute-pittance at Jerusalem!—His exactions, too, have such a cheerful, voluntary air! So far removed from your sour parochial or state-gatherers,—those ink-horn varlets, who carry their want of welcome in their faces! He cometh to you with a smile, and troubleth you with no receipt; confining himself to no set season. Every day is his Candlemas, or his Feast of Holy Michael. He applieth the *lene tormentum* of a pleasant look to your purse,—which to that gentle warmth expands her silken leaves, as naturally as the cloak of the traveller, for which sun and wind contended! He is the true Propontic which never ebbeth! The sea which taketh handsomely at each man's hand. In vain the victim, whom he delighteth to honour, struggles with destiny; he is in the net. Lend therefore cheerfully, O man ordained to lend—that thou lose not in the end, with thy worldly penny, the reversion promised. Combine not preposterously in thine own person the penalties of Lazarus and of Dives!—but, when thou seest the proper authority coming, meet it smilingly, as it were half-way. Come, a handsome sacrifice! See how light *he* makes of it! Strain not courtesies with a noble enemy.

The Range of the Essay Form

We have recognized that Huxley was seriously intent upon making clear the nature of a hypothesis. Is Lamb equally serious in his attempt to make clear the distinction between his two "races"? Does his explanation bear any resemblance to the dictionary definition of the word race? He begins solemnly enough:

> The human species, according to the best theory I can form of it, is composed of two distinct races. . . .

These could be the first words of a treatise on ethnology (the science of races). Here in these sober words—except for the unscientific first person—we have the authentic tone of a serious speculation. Indeed, after reading Huxley, we anticipate an upcoming hypothesis. When Lamb tells us that the two races are *"the men who borrow and the men who lend,"* the matter-of-fact tone remains, but we know that the fact itself—the scientific substance—is not there. Yet Lamb, after announcing his theory, proceeds as if his speculation were so reasonable as to be self-evident. He waves aside all the "impertinent classifications" that have preceded his revelation. Having disposed of these impertinencies, he turns to the contrasts between his races. In the second paragraph he continues the "scientific approach." "Observe," he advises, and names four exemplars of the great race of borrowers. We note Falstaff in his list, a dramatic creation mingling with three historical characters. We know now, if we did not know immediately, that Lamb's intent is only superficially similar to Huxley's. And if we miss the ironic tone of Lamb's essay, we miss all the fun.

Yet both essayists depend chiefly upon telling rather than showing and use illustrations to highlight their main contention. Both maintain a focus on a single topic, although Lamb's beam of light wavers more than does Huxley's. Even the structure of the two excerpts is similar, as one may see by comparing the first two paragraphs of the two selections. In the matter of directness, Lamb seems as intent on driving home his point as is Huxley. And both essayists appeal to the understanding and hardly at all to the emotions.

All these points of similarity are matters of technique. In essence the selections are as different as beavers and squirrels, both of which are rodents. Huxley has the businesslike efficiency of the beaver; Lamb the frisky, darting playfulness of the squirrel. Both get their business done. The excerpts from these two writers suggest the range of the essay, from the practical and serious to the fanciful and playful. We would not wish the range to be less wide.

Allusions

Huxley entertained us, perhaps, but that was not his chief purpose. Entertainment is apparently Lamb's chief purpose. It is certain that he is only mildly concerned that even his main contention be accepted. We do learn something about human nature from him, or, if we do not learn, we are at least pleasantly reminded of something we already know. From our own experience we can testify to at least the limited validity of Lamb's thesis concerning rosy borrowers and submissive lenders. Even here, however, Lamb is only playing with an idea based upon random observation.

Because it was Lamb's purpose to amuse, his far-ranging allusions are devices for achieving his purpose. We may muse for a moment over the "family likeness" among the four great borrowers: an Athenian general (Alcibiades), a man with personal talent, enough to levy tribute on friend and foe alike; the fat, lovable rascal (Falstaff), who forgave Mistress Quickly for his own offense so that she might feel free to lend him more; the lighthearted moralist (Sir Richard Steele) who plundered the dour lender, Addison; the gay and irresponsible playwright (Richard Brinsley Sheridan) who spent affably other persons' money. The family likeness is evident, and it is a pleasure to recognize it. From paragraph 3 onward, Lamb frisks through a fast sequence of allusions and suggestions. When he exclaims, "what rosy gills!" a picture flashes before us of glowing confidence, good health, and something of the solemn rightness of a fish's countenance. Just this touch of an allusion—"Taking no more thought than the lilies!"—opens our memories: "Consider the lilies of the field, how they grow; they toil not, neither do they spin: And yet I say unto you, That even Solomon in all his glory was not arrayed like one of these." Through this allusion Lamb allows us *to show* ourselves the very substance of the borrower. For the remainder of this paragraph and on through the next, Lamb uses allusion after allusion to complete his picture.

Two sorts of pleasure may be found in allusions: recognition and application. Of course, if recognition fails, there is no opportunity for pleasure here— but some for annoyance. The second pleasure may be had, however, if one will look up the allusion and then apply what is found to the context. The habit of investigating allusions is a good one to cultivate as one of the pleasantest and most purposeful ways to extend one's knowledge.

Values

If Lamb has not given us dependable information or even a separation of fictional from historical characters, if he has not been serious and practical, are we to conclude that what he has written is trivial and of less value than the sort of essay

Huxley wrote? Most readers would say in answer to this question that both writers have been expert in carrying out their respective purposes and that these samples of their work are to be weighed on different scales. Huxley's essay should be compared with one of comparably serious intentions, with, for example, Aldous Huxley's "Music at Night" (p. 1074). One needs to come even closer than this for a valid comparison at all points—to an essay with similar subject matter. Lamb's essay should be compared with other essays written in a light and playful vein, with, for example, Thurber's "The Unicorn in the Garden" below. The point is that we do not need to make exclusive choices and forego Huxley if we like Lamb or forego Lamb if we like Huxley. Both have much to offer, just as the whole varied range of literature, from its most useful to its most fanciful forms, has much to offer.

James Thurber (1894–1961)
The Unicorn in the Garden

Once upon a sunny morning a man who sat in a breakfast nook looked up from his scrambled eggs to see a white unicorn with a gold horn quietly cropping the roses in the garden. The man went up to the bedroom where his wife was still asleep and woke her. "There's a unicorn in the garden," he said. "Eating roses." She opened one unfriendly eye and looked at him. "The unicorn is a mythical beast," she said, and turned her back on him. The man walked slowly downstairs and out into the garden. The unicorn was still there; he was now browsing among the tulips. "Here, unicorn," said the man, and he pulled up a lily and gave it to him. The unicorn ate it gravely. With a high heart, because there was a unicorn in his garden, the man went upstairs and roused his wife again. "The unicorn," he said, "ate a lily." His wife sat up in bed and looked at him, coldly. "You are a booby," she said, "and I am going to have you put in the booby-hatch." The man, who had never liked the words "booby" and "booby-hatch," and who liked them even less on a shining morning when there was a unicorn in the garden, thought for a moment. "We'll see about that," he said. He walked over to the door. "He has a golden horn in the middle of his forehead," he told her. Then he went back to the garden to watch the unicorn; but the unicorn had gone away. The man sat down among the roses and went to sleep.

As soon as the husband had gone out of the house, the wife got up and dressed as fast as she could. She was very excited and there was a gloat in her eye. She telephoned the police and she telephoned a psychiatrist; she told them to hurry to her house and bring a strait-jacket. When the police and the psychiatrist arrived they sat down in chairs and looked at her, with great interest. "My husband," she said, "saw a unicorn this morning." The police looked at the psychiatrist and the psychiatrist looked at the police. "He told me it ate a lily," she said. The psychiatrist looked at the police and the police looked at the psychiatrist. "He told me it had a golden horn in the middle of its forehead," she said. At a solemn signal from the psychiatrist, the police leaped from their chairs and seized the wife. They had a hard time subduing her, for she put up a terrific struggle, but they finally subdued her. Just as they got her into the strait-jacket, the husband came back into the house.

"Did you tell your wife you saw a unicorn?" asked the police. "Of course not," said the husband. "The unicorn is a mythical beast." "That's all I wanted to know," said the psychiatrist. "Take her away. I'm sorry, sir, but your wife is as crazy as a jay bird." So they took her away, cursing and screaming, and shut her up in an institution. The husband lived happily ever after.

Moral: Don't count your boobies until they are hatched.

Comments and Questions

1. Is this an essay? Think carefully, then justify your answer. (You may wish to compare Thurber's purpose with Galsworthy's in "Quality," pp. 4 ff. Is "Quality" a short story?)

2. This is a tightly knit piece in which every word counts. Note the matter-of-fact opening sentence. How can a man look "up from his scrambled eggs" and see "a white unicorn with a golden horn"? Why "scrambled eggs"? What is significant about the wife's being "still asleep"? Why does the husband not like "the words 'booby' and 'booby-hatch' "? Has he heard them before? What is the effect of the figure of speech: "There was a gloat in her eye"?

3. By suggestion, Thurber allows the reader to do at least three things: characterize the wife, characterize the husband, and judge the marriage. Do all three, with supporting evidence from the fable.

4. Lamb divides all the human race into borrowers and lenders. (See "The Two Races of Men," p. 1067.) Thurber makes a simple division, too. What is it?

Thomas De Quincey (1785–1859)
The Literature of Knowledge and the Literature of Power[1]

In that great social organ which, collectively, we call literature, there may be distinguished two separate offices, that may blend and often *do* so, but capable, severally, of a severe insulation, and naturally fitted for reciprocal repulsion. There is, first, the literature of *knowledge,* and, secondly, the literature of *power.* The function of the first is to *teach;* the function of the second is to *move:* the first is a rudder; the second an oar or a sail. The first speaks to the *mere* discursive understanding; the second speaks ultimately, it may

[1] From *The Poetry of Pope,* 1848.

happen, to the higher understanding, or reason, but always *through* affections of pleasure and sympathy. Remotely it may travel towards an object seated in what Lord Bacon calls *dry* light; but proximately it does and must operate—else it ceases to be a literature of *power*—on and through that *humid* light which clothes itself in the mists and glittering *iris* of human passions, desires, and genial emotions. Men have so little reflected on the higher functions of literature as to find it a paradox if one should describe it as a mean or subordinate purpose of books to give information. But this is a paradox only in the sense which makes it honorable to be paradoxical. Whenever we talk in ordinary language of seeking information or gaining knowledge, we understand the words as connected with something of absolute novelty. But it is the grandeur of all truth which *can* occupy a very high place in human interests that it is never absolutely novel to the meanest of minds: it exists eternally, by way of germ or latent principle, in the lowest as in the highest, needing to be developed but never to be planted. To be capable of transplantation is the immediate criterion of a truth that ranges on a lower scale. Besides which, there is a rarer thing than truth, namely *power,* or deep sympathy with truth. What is the effect, for instance, upon society, of children? By the pity, by the tenderness, and by the peculiar modes of admiration, which connect themselves with the helplessness, with the innocence, and with the simplicity of children, not only are the primal affections strengthened and continually renewed, but the qualities which are dearest in the sight of heaven—the frailty, for instance, which appeals to forbearance, the innocence which symbolizes the heavenly, and the simplicity which is most alien from the worldly—are kept up in perpetual remembrance, and their ideals are continually refreshed. A purpose of the same nature is answered by the higher literature, viz., the literature of power. What do you learn from *Paradise Lost*? Nothing at all. What do you learn from a cookery-book? Something new, something that you did not know before, in every paragraph. But would you therefore put the wretched cookery-book on a higher level of estimation than the divine poem? What you owe to Milton is not any knowledge, of which a million separate items are still but a million of advancing steps on the same earthly level; what you owe is *power,* that is, exercise and expansion to your own latent capacity of sympathy with the infinite, where every pulse and each separate influx is a step upwards, a step ascending as upon a Jacob's ladder from earth to mysterious altitudes above the earth. *All* the steps of knowledge, from first to last, carry you further on the same plane, but could never raise you one foot above your ancient level of earth; whereas the very *first* step in power is a flight, is an ascending movement into another element where earth is forgotten.

Were it not that human sensibilities are ventilated and continually called out into exercise by the great phenomena of infancy, or of real life as it moves through chance and change, or of literature as it recombines these elements in the mimicries of poetry, romance, etc., it is certain that, like any animal power or muscular energy falling into disuse, all such sensibilities would gradually droop and dwindle. It is in relation to these great *moral* capacities of man that the literature of power, as contradistinguished from that of knowledge, lives and has its field of action. It is concerned with what is highest in man; for the Scriptures themselves never condescended to deal by suggestion or co-operation with the mere discursive understanding: when speaking of man in his intellectual capacity, the Scriptures speak, not of the understanding, but of *"the understanding heart,"* making the heart,—that is, the great *intuitive* (or nondiscursive) organ, to be the interchangeable formula for man in his highest state of capacity for the infinite. Tragedy, romance, fairy tale, or epopee, all alike restore to man's mind the ideals of justice, of hope, of truth, of mercy, of retribution, which else (left to the support of daily life in its realities) would languish for want of sufficient illustration. What is meant, for instance, by *poetic justice*? It does not mean a justice that differs by its object from the ordinary justice of human jurisprudence, for then it must be confessedly a very bad kind of justice; but it means a justice that differs from common forensic justice by the degree in which it *attains* its object, a justice that is more omnipotent over its own ends, as dealing, not with the refractory elements of earthly life, but with the elements of its own creation and with materials flexible to its own purest preconceptions. It is certain that, were it not for the literature of power, these ideals would often remain amongst us as mere arid notional forms; whereas, by the creative forces of man put forth in literature, they gain a vernal life of restoration and germinate into vital activities. The commonist novel, by moving in alliance with human fears and hopes, with human instincts of wrong and right, sustains and quickens those affections. Calling them into action, it rescues them from torpor. And hence the pre-eminency, over all authors that merely *teach,* of the meanest that moves, or that teaches, if at all, indirectly *by* moving. The very highest work that has ever existed in the literature of knowledge is but a provisional work, a book upon trial and sufferance, and *quamdiu bene se gesserit* [as long as it bore itself well]. Let its teaching be even partially revised, let it be but expanded, nay, even let its teaching be but placed in a better order, and instantly it is superseded. Whereas the feeblest works in the literature of power, surviving at all, survive as finished and unalterable among men. For instance, the *Principia* of Sir Isaac Newton was a book *militant* on earth from the first. In all stages of its progress it would have to fight for its existence: first, as regards absolute truth; secondly, when that combat was over, as regards its form, or mode of presenting the truth. And as soon as a La Place, or anybody else, builds higher upon the foundations laid by this book, effectually he throws it out of the sunshine into decay and darkness; by weapons won from this book he superannuates and destroys this book, so that soon the name of Newton remains as a mere *nominis umbra* [shadow of a name], but his book, as a living power, has transmigrated into other forms. Now, on the contrary, the *Iliad,* the *Prometheus* of Æschylus, the *Othello* or *King Lear,* the *Hamlet* or *Macbeth,* and the *Paradise Lost* are not militant but triumphant forever, as long as the languages exist in which they speak or can be taught to speak. They never *can* transmigrate into new incarnations. To reproduce these in new forms or variations, even if in some things they should be improved, would be to plagiarize. A good steam-engine is properly superseded by a better. But one lovely pastoral valley is not superseded by another, nor a statue of Praxiteles by a statue of Michelangelo. These things are separated, not by imparity, but by disparity. They are not thought of as unequal under the same standard, but as different in *kind,* and, if otherwise equal, as equal under a different standard. Human works of immortal beauty and works of nature in one respect stand on the same footing: they never absolutely repeat each other, never approach so near as not to differ; and they differ not as better and worse, or simply by more and less; they differ by undecipherable and incommunicable differences, that cannot be caught by mimicries, that cannot be reflected in the mirror of copies, that cannot become ponderable in the scales of vulgar comparison.

Comments and Questions

   1. Why does De Quincey call literature a "social organ"? Does this suggest that the fundamental function of literature is communication? Discuss.

   2. At one point the author calls the literature of knowledge a "rudder" and then adds further on that it is "a mean or subordinate purpose of books to give information." Does there seem to be a contradiction here? Discuss carefully.

   3. Explain: "all truth . . . exists eternally, by way of germ or latent principle, in the lowest as in the highest, needing to be developed but never to be planted." Compare Emerson: "To believe your own thought, to believe that what is true for you in your private heart is true for all men,—that is genius." Now, contrast Ciardi, who has his Poet ask of the Citizen: "The point is why *should* I write for you?" (See "Dialogue with the Audience," p. 1105.)

4. How does De Quincey use children to illustrate the function of the literature of power?

5. Define *poetic justice*. Compare your definition with De Quincey's.

6. Explain the term "militant" as applied to the literature of knowledge, and contrast with the word "triumphant" as applied to the literature of power.

Aldous Huxley   (1894–1963)
Music at Night

Moonless, this June night is all the more alive with stars. Its darkness is perfumed with faint gusts from the blossoming lime trees, with the smell of wetted earth and the invisible greenness of the vines. There is silence; but a silence that breathes with the soft breathing of the sea, and the thin shrill noise of a cricket, insistently, incessantly harps on the fact of its own deep perfection. Far away, the passage of a train is like a long caress, moving gently, with an inexorable gentleness, across the warm living body of the night.

Music, you say; it would be a good night for music. But I have music here in a box, shut up, like one of those bottled djinns in the *Arabian Nights,* and ready at a touch to break out of its prison. I make the necessary mechanical magic, and suddenly, by some miraculously appropriate coincidence (for I had selected the record in the dark, without knowing what music the machine would play), suddenly the introduction to the *Benedictus* in Beethoven's *Missa Solemnis* begins to trace its patterns on the moonless sky.

The *Benedictus.* Blessed and blessing, this music is in some sort the equivalent of the night, of the deep and living darkness, into which, now in a single jet, now in a fine interweaving of melodies, now in pulsing and almost solid clots of harmonious sound, it pours itself, stanchlessly pours itself, like time, like the rising and falling, falling trajectories of a life. It is the equivalent of the night in another mode of being, as an essence is the equivalent of the flowers, from which it is distilled.

There is, at least there sometimes seems to be, a certain blessedness lying at the heart of things, a mysterious blessedness, of whose existence occasional accidents or providences (for me, this night is one of them) make us obscurely, or it may be intensely, but always fleetingly, alas, always only for a few brief moments aware. In the *Benedictus* Beethoven gives expression to this awareness of blessedness. His music is the equivalent of this Mediterranean night, or rather of the blessedness at the heart of the night, of the blessedness as it would be if it could be sifted clear of irrelevance and accident, refined and separated out into its quintessential purity.

5   "*Benedictus, benedictus . . .* " One after another the voices take up the theme pro-

pounded by the orchestra and lovingly meditated through a long and exquisite solo (for the blessedness reveals itself most often to the solitary spirit) by a single violin. *"Benedictus, benedictus . . . "* And then, suddenly, the music dies; the flying djinn has been rebottled. With a stupid insect-like insistence, a steel point rasps and rasps the silence.

At school, when they taught us what was technically known as English, they used to tell us to "express in our own words" some passage from whatever play of Shakespeare was at the moment being rammed, with all its annotations—particularly the annotations—down our reluctant throats. So there we would sit, a row of inky urchins, laboriously translating "now silken dalliance in the wardrobe lies" into "now smart silk clothes lie in the wardrobe," or "To be or not to be" into "I wonder whether I ought to commit suicide or not." When we had finished, we would hand in our papers, and the presiding pedagogue would give us marks more or less according to the accuracy with which "our own words" had "expressed" the meaning of the Bard.

He ought, of course, to have given us naught all round with a hundred lines to himself for ever having set us the silly exercise. Nobody's "own words," except those of Shakespeare himself, can possibly "express" what Shakespeare meant. The substance of a work of art is inseparable from its form; its truth and its beauty are two and yet, mysteriously, one. The verbal expression of even a metaphysic or a system of ethics is very nearly as much of a work of art as a love poem. The philosophy of Plato expressed in the "own words" of Jowett is not the philosophy of Plato; nor in the "own words" of, say, Billy Sunday, is the teaching of St. Paul St. Paul's teaching.

"Our own words" are inadequate even to express the meaning of other words; how much more inadequate, when it is a matter of rendering meanings which have their original expression in terms of music or one of the visual arts! What, for example, does music "say"? You can buy at almost any concert an analytical programme that will tell you exactly. Much too exactly; that is the trouble. Every analyst has his own version. Imagine Pharaoh's dream interpreted successively by Joseph, by the Egyptian soothsayers, by Freud, by Rivers, by Adler, by Jung, by Wohlgemuth: it would "say" a great many different things. Not nearly so many, however, as the Fifth Symphony has been made to say in the verbiage of its analysts. Not nearly so many as the Virgin of the Rocks and the Sistine Madonna have no less lyrically said.

Annoyed by the verbiage and this absurd multiplicity of attributed "meanings," some critics have protested that music and painting signify nothing but themselves; that the only things they "say" are things, for example, about modulations and fugues, about colour values and three-dimensional forms. That they say anything about human destiny or the universe at large is a notion which these purists dismiss as merely nonsensical.

10   If the purists were right, then we should have to regard painters and musicians as monsters. For it is strictly impossible to be a human being and not to have views of some kind about the universe at large, very difficult to be a human being and not to express those views, at any rate by implication. Now, it is a matter of observation that painters and musicians are *not* monsters. Therefore . . . The conclusion follows, unescapably.

It is not only in programme music and problem pictures that composers and painters express their views about the universe. The purest and most abstract artistic creations can be, in their own peculiar language, as eloquent in this respect as the most deliberately tendentious.

Compare, for example, a Virgin by Piero della Francesca with a Virgin by Tura. Two Madonnas—and the current symbolical conventions are observed by both artists. The difference, the enormous difference between the two pictures is a purely pictorial difference, a difference in the forms and their arrangement, in the disposition of the lines and planes and masses. To any one in the least sensitive to the eloquence of pure form, the two Madonnas say utterly different things about the world.

Piero's composition is a welding together of smooth and beautifully balanced solidities. Everything in his universe is endowed with a kind of supernatural substantiality, is much more "there" than any object of the actual world could possibly be. And how sublimely rational, in the noblest, the most humane acceptation of the world, how orderedly philosophical is the landscape, are all the inhabitants of this world! It is the creation of a god who "ever plays the geometer."

What does she say, this Madonna from San Sepolcro? If I have not wholly mistranslated the eloquence of Piero's forms, she is telling us of the greatness of the human spirit, of its power to rise above circumstance and dominate fate. If you were to ask her, "How shall I be saved?" "By Reason," she would probably answer. And, anticipating Milton, "Not only, not mainly upon the Cross," she would say, "is Paradise regained, but in those deserts of utter solitude where man puts forth the strength of his reason to resist the fiend." This particular mother of Christ is probably not a Christian.

15 Turn now to Tura's picture. It is fashioned out of a substance that is like the living embodiment of flame—flame-flesh, alive and sensitive and suffering. His surfaces writhe away from the eye, as though shrinking, as though in pain. The lines flow intricately with something of that disquieting and, you feel, magical calligraphy, which characterizes certain Tibetan paintings. Look closely; feel your way into the picture, into the painter's thoughts and intuitions and emotions. This man was naked and at the mercy of destiny. To be able to proclaim the spirit's stoical independence, you must be able to raise your head above the flux of things; this man was sunk in it, overwhelmed. He could introduce no order into his world; it remained for him a mysterious chaos, fantastically marbled with patches, now of purest heaven, now of the most excruciating hell. A beautiful and terrifying world, is this Madonna's verdict; a world like the incarnation, the material projection, of Ophelia's madness. There are no certainties in it but suffering and occasional happiness. And as for salvation, who knows the way of salvation? There may perhaps be miracles, and there is always hope.

The limits of criticism are very quickly reached. When he has said "in his own words" as much, or rather as little, as "own words" can say, the critic can only refer his readers to the original work of art: let them go and see for themselves. Those who overstep the limit are either rather stupid, vain people, who love their "own words" and imagine that they can say in them more than "own words" are able in the nature of things to express. Or else they are intelligent people who happen to be philosophers or literary artists and who find it convenient to make the criticism of other men's work a jumping-off place for their own creativity.

What is true of painting is equally true of music. Music "says" things about the world, but in specifically musical terms. Any attempt to reproduce these musical statements "in our own words" is necessarily doomed to failure. We cannot isolate the truth contained in a piece of music; for it is a beauty-truth and inseparable from its partner. The best we can do is to indicate in the most general terms the nature of the musical beauty-truth under consideration and to refer curious truth-seekers to the original. Thus, the introduction to the *Benedictus* in the *Missa Solemnis* is a statement about the blessedness that is at the heart of things. But this is about as far as "own words" will take us. If we were to start describing in our "own words" exactly what Beethoven felt about this blessedness, how he conceived it, what he thought its nature to be, we should very soon find ourselves writing lyrical nonsense in the style of the analytical programme makers. Only music, and only Beethoven's music, and only this particular music of Beethoven, can tell us with any precision what Beethoven's conception of the blessedness at the heart of things actually was. If we want to know, we must listen—on a still June night, by preference, with the breathing of the invisible sea for background to the music and the scent of lime trees drifting through the darkness, like some exquisite soft harmony apprehended by another sense.

Comments and Questions

1. Note the structure of this essay. How does the author move from his lyrical tribute to Beethoven into his central statement? Then, at the end, how does he enforce what he has said by a return to Beethoven's music at night?

2. "The substance of a work is inseparable from its form." If this is strictly true, what becomes of the notion that music, painting, poetry—all art forms—can be interpreted?

3. You might wish to look at the two pictures—Piero della Francesca's Virgin and Tura's Virgin—and compare your response to these paintings with Huxley's interpretations. This procedure would be following the author's advice to readers: "let them go and see for themselves."

4. Compare this essay with Malcolm Cowley's "Criticism: A Many-Windowed House," which follows.

Malcolm Cowley   (1898–   )
Criticism:
A Many-Windowed House

1   Although I have been a literary critic for more than forty years, I must confess that I have not devoted much time to the basic theories of my profession. Partly, that oversight is due to indolence, but it is also the result of what might be called an incest taboo: I have tried to avoid critical endogamy and inbreeding. Instead of dealing critically with the critical critics of criticism, I have preferred to be a critic of poems and novels, or at most a literary historian. More recently, however, I have defied the taboo by reviewing several big critical works, and I have been dismayed to find that many of them were so badly written as to reveal a sort of esthetic deafness, that some of them were contemptuous of writers and writing—except as the raw material of critical works—and that most of them were episodes in the battle among critical systems, one or another of which we were being cannonaded into accepting as the only true critical faith.

2   When I tried to compare the systems in order to find a faith for myself, it seemed to me that each of them led to a different but equally specialized and partial standard for judging works of art. Thus, for historical critics the best book is the one that either sums up a historical movement or else has directly influenced history. For biographical critics it is the one most intimately connected with the author's life. For psychoanalytical critics it is the one that reveals how the author sublimated his antisocial desires. For expressionist critics of the Crocean school, the standard is sincerity and spontaneity of expression. For moral critics—who were dominant in this country as late as the 1920's—the best books are those which embody philosophical truths or inculcate the highest moral lessons. For political critics they are the books that advance a political cause, and this, during the 1930's, was usually that of international revolution. Each of these standards is inescapable, being derived from the method itself. Often the critic says, "I do not judge, I merely explain," yet the standard is revealed, if nowhere else, in his choice of books for explication.

3   In the 1960's all those standards have fallen into critical disfavor. The presently accepted system of approaching works of art is one that attempts to purify criticism by purging it of everything that might be regarded as an extraneous element or, to use the fashionable word, as a fallacy. Out go the historical fallacy, the social fallacy, the moral fallacy, the personal fallacy, the genetic fallacy, the effective fallacy. Out goes the author's life; out goes his social background; out goes the audience for which he wrote; out goes the political meaning of his work; out goes its moral effect. What is supposed to remain after this cathartic process is the work itself, as pure act without antecedents or relevance or results; simply the words in their naked glory. They are the purified subject of the system known as textual or integral criticism, or less exactly—since the term has several meanings—as the "new" criticism.

4   Like all other systems, this one involves a standard of judgment derived from the method itself. Let me quote from an essay by John V. Hagopian, who is one of the ablest of the new critics. "The critic's duty," he says—and of course there is no question of the critic's or the reader's pleasure—"is to determine as nearly as he can what feeling-qualities are embodied in the form-content of the work, how they are embodied there, and how well. . . . He has no other task; evaluations of historical significance, autobiographical expression, moral goodness, or philosophical truths are purely gratuitous for criticism, even though"—a generous concession—"they may be valuable to other disciplines of the humanities." Then, after this rejection of other standards, Mr. Hagopian offers an effective but still, it seems to me, oversimplified standard of his own. "Given two literary works," he says, "which are equally successful in resolving an artistic problem, the critics can choose the more important one by determining which has integrated the greatest amount of complexity."

5   To put Mr. Hagopian's statement in slightly different words, the critic pretends that every work of literature is completely autonomous, and then judges it by the complexity of its inner relations. He could find worse standards. The new or integral system of evaluating works has yielded some precious illuminations and has proved to be an effective method of teaching literature. It does, however, involve a disturbing amount of make-believe. Let's pretend that the poem or story was written at no particular date in no particular country. Let's pretend that it has no relation with any other work by the same author, or with any tendencies prevailing among a group of authors. Let's pretend that it can be interpreted and judged with no material except the text itself, and perhaps a few commentaries by other textual critics.

6   All those pretenses are hard to maintain. Literature is not a pure art like music, or a relatively pure art like painting and sculpture. Its medium is not abstract like tones and colors, not inorganic like metal and stone. Instead it uses language, which is a social creation, changing with the society that created it. The study of any author's language carries us straight into history, institutions, moral questions, personal stratagems, and all the other esthetic impurities or fallacies that many new critics are trying to expunge.

7   Nor is that the only reason why these critics cannot be consistently applying their
own standard of judgment. As soon as they admit that a given work of literature was not
self-produced but had an author—as soon as they admit that he wrote other works, some
of which preceded and some followed the work in question—they are violating the purity
of their method and are becoming, if ever so faintly, biographical critics. As soon as they
admit that the work may have been affected by other authors, or may have exerted an
effect on them, they are becoming historical. As soon as they admit that the work was
written for an audience, they are deviating into sociology. As soon as they admit that it had
or might have had an effect on the conduct of that audience, they have to introduce moral
notions; there is no escaping them. As soon as they discuss or even hint at the author's
intentions, they are becoming psychological. Criticism too is a literary art, and like other
forms of literature it is impure by definition.

8   Some critics have looked for a way out of this dilemma by denying that criticism is
an art and by claiming a place for it among the sciences. In order to make it a science,
however, they have to subject it to another process of purgation. This time they have to
remove all its subjective elements, including the critic's feelings about the work and also
including the author of the work, whose mere presence may be a source of nonconformity
to scientific laws. Why not simply abolish the author—or if he can't be abolished, why not
rule him out of consideration?

9   That radical but, in the circumstances, necessary step was taken some years ago by
professors W. K. Wimsatt, Jr., and M. C. Beardsley. In an essay called "The Intentional
Fallacy" they asserted that "The design or intention of the author is neither available nor
desirable as a standard for judging the success of a work of art." They admitted that the
psychology of composition was sometimes a valid and useful study, but they described it
as "an art separate from criticism . . . an individual and private culture, yoga, or system of
self-development which the young poet would do well to notice, but different from"—and
I italicize their words—*"the public science of evaluating poems."*

10   Now "public" implies that the critic should be objective and impersonal. "Science"
implies that he administers a body of universal laws, the truth of which can be demonstrated by quantitative measurements. "Of evaluating poems" implies that judgment or
evaluation is the critic's essential task. Each of these implications, it seems to me, is based
on a radical misconception of what the critic is able or entitled to do.

11   Since his judgment of a work starts with his own reaction to it, he cannot, in practice,
be purely impersonal. He is not entitled to speak of criticism as a science. As Paul Valéry
said many years ago, "There are sciences of exact things, and arts of inexact things." The
best of criticism is inexact. In these days, however, everybody wants to be a scientist and
move in the air of terrified respect that surrounds the men who split the atom. Every
school of the humanities wants to share in the huge endowments of the new physics
laboratories and cancer-research institutes. Inevitably some of the humanists begin to
speak of their work in scientific language, as if it were performed with micrometric gauges,
electronic computers, and balance pans in a vacuum. But there will never be a science of
taste or of belief or of the arts of language. There will only be critics who talk like scientists
and some of whom end by achieving the wooden arrogance of minor critics in the eighteenth century, who also thought they were expounding the laws of universal and unchanging wisdom.

12   Evaluating poems and novels is not the central task of a critic. Rather than judgment
that task is interpretation and definition. The first question for a critic to answer is not
"How good is this poem?" but simply "What *is* this poem, in structure, in style, in meaning,
and in its effect on the reader?" Judgment is the end of the critical process, but if the work
has been defined and interpreted correctly, then judgment often follows as a matter of

course. For example, if one defines a certain novel as "A rapid sequence of events that offers no opportunity to develop the characters in depth," one does not have to add that it is a minor work of fiction.

13   In deciding what a novel or poem *is,* we cannot accept the author's testimony as final, knowing as we do that authors often intend one thing and end by producing another. We think of all the authors who intended masterpieces, as compared with the small number of masterpieces, and we also think of Mark Twain, who intended a boy's book and brought forth an epic. Nevertheless, if the author has offered his testimony—in letters, in outlines, in journals, in public statements—it is probative evidence and we cannot simply throw it out of court. If we fail to consider it we may, like many recent critics, fall into the opposite or unintentional fallacy by substituting our own story, our own creation, our own fantasy for the book that was actually written by the author.

14   Some years ago Stanley Edgar Hyman, always a lively critic, wrote a long and favorable review of a book called *The Disguises of Love,* by Robie Macauley. He presented it as a novel in which "accounts of homosexual relations are disguised as accounts of heterosexual relations," since, the reviewer explained, owing to American prudishness "our authors have no choice but to metamorphose gender." Therefore the heroine's name, Frances feminine, should be altered to Francis masculine by any discerning reader. In the following issue of the *Hudson Review* the author protested against this distortion of his meaning. No homosexuality was involved or implied in the story. Frances feminine was Frances completely female.

15   The reviewer was not in the least disconcerted. He answered in part, "I am sorry that Mr. Macauley, for whatever reason, prefers not to have written the interesting and complicated novel I read and tried to describe, and prefers instead to have written the poor thin novel he describes. . . . Mr. Macauley is not the first novelist to have builded better than he knows or will admit; nor will he, probably, be the last." And then this manifesto, from Mr. Hyman, of complete critical independence: "I am not prepared," he said, "to be scared out of a critical reading of a novel by the author's waspish insistence that it is not *his* reading."

16   Authors haven't much chance with critics who throw their evidence out of court as insubstantial, immaterial, and incompetent. What Stanley Hyman did for a single book (not without a gleam of mischief in his style), Leslie A. Fiedler has done solemnly for American fiction in general. In a work almost as long as Parrington's *Main Currents in American Thought,* he has proclaimed that all our great novelists were sexually immature, that their work represented an escape from a female-dominated world into male companionship, and that *The Last of the Mohicans, Moby-Dick* and *Huckleberry Finn* are almost identical fables of homosexual miscegenation. Mr. Fiedler's book is a final exploit of criticism cut loose from its moorings and sailing across the moon like a Halloween witch on her broomstick.

17   Although it seems impossibly far from Mr. Wimsatt's sober and quasi-scientific type of criticism, still it results from the same doctrine, namely, that an author's intentions should be utterly disregarded. The effect of the doctrine is to deprive the author of all property in his work from the moment it is printed. It becomes the property of everybody and nobody, but it doesn't long remain in that situation. Soon it is seized upon by critics, who claim the privilege of reinterpreting and in fact rewriting it into something the author cannot recognize. If the author protests, the critic feels entitled to jeer at his "waspish insistence." The critic rules supreme, and his next step—which Mr. Fiedler and others have taken—is to present the author as an immature neurotic whom the critic, disguised as a psychoanalyst, is not even attempting to cure, but is merely exposing to public shame.

18   I do not propose to offer still another system of criticism to set against those I have questioned. But since this paper started as a confession, I had better state a few of my own beliefs.

19   First of all I believe that a definition of criticism should be as simple and short as possible. Mightn't it be enough to say that it is *writing which deals with works of art?* Any narrower definition would restrict the liberty of the critic and might also restrict his usefulness.

20   I believe that criticism should be approached as one of the literary arts. The word "literary" implies that it should be written in the language of English literature and not, like a great deal of recent criticism, in some variety of philosophical or social-scientific jargon. When a critic's language is awkward, involved, and inaccurate, we are entitled to question his ability to recognize good prose. As for the word "arts," it implies that criticism is not a science based on exact measurement. If it is going to be persuasive, however, it had better include a great deal of objectively verifiable information.

21   I do not believe that it is one of the major literary arts. The major arts are poetry, fiction, drama, and also nonfictional or documentary writing so long as this last is regarded as a field for exercise of the interpretive imagination. Without those major arts, literary criticism would have no subject matter and would cease to exist. Therefore a critic cannot afford to be arrogant. He is dealing in most cases with better works than he has proved his capability of writing.

22   I believe that the first of his functions is to select works of art worth writing about, with special emphasis on works that are new, not much discussed, or widely misunderstood. Incidentally, this task is neglected by academic critics, most of whom prefer to write about books already regarded as canonical. His second function is to describe or analyze or reinterpret the chosen works, as a basis for judgments which can often be merely implied. In practice his problem may be to explain why he enjoys a particular book, and perhaps to find new reasons for enjoying it, so as to deepen his readers' capacity for appreciation.

23   In practice, again, I always start and end with the text itself, and I am willing to accept the notion of the textual or integral critics that the principal value of a work lies in the complexity and unity of its internal relations. But I also try to start with a sort of innocence, that is, with a lack of preconceptions about what I might or might not discover. To preserve the innocence, I try not to read the so-called secondary or critical sources until my own discoveries, if any, have been made.

24   What I read after the text itself are other texts by the same author. It is a mistake to approach each work as if it were an absolutely separate production, a unique artifact, the last and only relic of a buried civilization. Why not approach it as the author does? It seems to me that any author of magnitude has his eye on something larger than the individual story or poem or novel. He wants each of these to be as good as possible, and self-subsistent, but he also wants it to serve as a chapter or aspect of the larger work that is his lifetime production, his *oeuvre.* This larger work is also part of the critic's subject matter.

25   In this fashion the author's biography comes into the picture, and so do his notebooks and letters. They aren't part of the text to be criticized, but often they help us to find in it what we might otherwise have missed, and they serve as a warning against indulging in fantasies about the text or deforming it into a Gothic fable of love, death, and homoeroticism. We should read not to impose our meanings on a work, but to see what we can find.

26   Innocence is the keynote, and ignorance that tries to become knowledge by asking questions. We know, for example, that Melville spent about a year on *Moby-Dick,* and that he rewrote the book from a lost early version concerned chiefly with the whaling industry. We also know that he wrote *Pierre* in about six weeks, working at top speed while on the edge of a nervous breakdown. That of course, is biographical knowledge, but aren't we justified in using it? Aren't critics losing their sense of proportion when they discuss

both books, the masterpiece and the nightmare, in the same terms, especially if those terms make the nightmare seem more important than the masterpiece? Aren't they wrong to look for the same sort of symbols in *Pierre* that Joyce put into *Finnegans Wake,* on which we know that he slaved for ten years?

27   Innocence is the keynote, but not innocence that refrains from learning about an author's life on the ground that such knowledge would destroy the purity of one's critical method. A truly innocent search might lead us into studies of the society in which an author lived, if they were necessary to explain his meaning. Or again, remembering as we should that a novel or a poem is not merely a structure of words but also a device for producing a certain effect on an audience, as if it were a motionless machine for creating perpetual motion—remembering this, we might try to find the nature of the particular audience for which it was written. That would be deviating into the sociological or affective fallacy, but still it might be a useful and stimulating piece of, yes, critical research.

28   I believe, in short, that criticism is a house with many windows.

Comments and Questions

We note the suggestion of the author's theme in the opening sentence:

> Although I have been a literary critic for more than forty years, I must confess that I have not devoted much time to the basic theories of my profession.

We assume that this essay will consider basic theories of criticism and will include a statement of the theory preferred by the author. The *tone,* sober, serious but not stodgy, is clearly different from the lightheartedness of the essays by Lamb (p. 1067), or by Thurber (p. 1070). The author writes to convince.

For our part as readers, we have three tasks to perform in reading argumentative essays: (1) we must understand what is said; (2) we must judge the truth of what is said; (3) we must adopt or reject, in whole or in part, what is said. (Indifference would constitute a kind of rejection.) In reading "The Two Races of Men" and similar essays, we perform the first two of these tasks but feel no call to perform the third. We say of such essays that we understand them, that they are true—or partly true—but beyond that we are not asked to go. Cowley clearly wishes us to go all the way, to convince us that his is the reasonable approach to critical theorizing.

Structure analyzed   Cowley emphasizes a device to make his purpose clear and effective: the device of *obvious structure.* In the first paragraph, he explains why he has not written on this subject before and why he is writing on it now. Paragraph 2 ticks off the "different but equally specialized" systems of criticism, and paragraph 3 defines "the new criticism," which has tended to cast into disfavor all formerly accepted systems. To give authority to his own definition of the new criticism, the author in paragraph 4 quotes from "one of the ablest of the new critics." It is now clear that Mr. Cowley will contend with the tenets of one system called the new criticism.

After acknowledging in paragraph 5 that some virtues in integral cricism exist, the author proceeds in the remainder of this paragraph and on through paragraphs 6 and 7 to expose the weaknesses of the system. Paragraph 8 reduces the new criticism to an absurdity or at least to an untenable position. In the next four paragraphs (9 through 12) the author shows how two new critics had tried to escape from this position by identifying criticism as a science, not an art. He contends that criticism cannot be a science, for it cannot escape the personal in either the writer or the critic. He adds that evaluation grows out of analysis and is "not the central task of a critic."

In paragraph 13 Cowley cites the new critical principle that authors are to be ignored as interpreters of their own works. Paragraphs 14 through 17 illustrate what happens when critics behave as though authors do not exist, as though their works are disembodied.

From paragraph 18 to the end of the essay, Cowley states his own critical credo, which he summarizes in the final sentence.

Now we may see the skeletal structure of the whole essay:

I. Statement of reasons for writing on this subject (paragraph 1).
II. Identification of topics not to be treated and the one that will be treated (paragraphs 2–4).
III. The negative: analysis and running refutation of points the author considers invalid (paragraphs 5–17.)
IV. The positive: what the author subscribes to as valid (paragraphs 18–28).

This is one pattern for the serious, argumentative essay. Not all essays will include these four parts, and few will preserve the same order, but most essays written with a sober purpose will necessarily adopt a pattern similar to this one.

Why are serious essayists strongly concerned with logical structure? Perhaps more than any other writers they wish to be precisely understood. Unless they are clearly understood, the truth of what they say cannot be judged. And if the truth cannot be judged, the position recommended would remain meaningless.

Because logical structure aids clarity, it does not necessarily follow that a clear argument is a true argument. A clear, wrong argument, however, is more serviceable than a fuzzy, wrong argument. We may be able to do something about the first and merely be baffled by the second. Being clearly wrong is the next best thing to being clearly right. Logical structure and lucid statement are the essayist's best devices for being effective.

1. Examine the structure of "The Two Races of Men" (p. 1067) and account for the way it differs from the pattern of Cowley's essay. In what way are these essays alike?

2. What stimulated the author to examine his own critical tenets? Discuss.

3. Define "integral criticism," and list the arguments in favor of this approach to literature. What approach does Cowley recommend?

4. This essay was written when the "new" criticism was at its height. The new criticism is no longer new, but its influence survives in the way literature is read and taught in the classroom. Regardless of what critical theory is dominant at any one time, are the basic issues of criticism always the same? What are the essential questions about approaches to literature which this essay raises?

5. Do you agree that authors' interpretations of their own work should not influence the reader's interpretation? Robert Frost has said that his poem "Stopping by Woods on a Snowy Evening" does not suggest a death wish on the part of the speaker (see p. 303 n.). Should this contention be heeded?

Albert Camus   (1913–1960)
Nobel Prize Acceptance Speech

(Translated by Justin O'Brien)

Upon receiving the distinction with which your free academy has seen fit to honor me, I measured the extent to which that reward exceeded my personal deserts, and this only increased my gratitude. Every man and, even more understandably, every artist, wants recognition. I want it too. But it was not possible for me to learn of your decision without comparing its repercussions with whatever merits I really have. How could a man still almost young, possessed only of his doubts and of a work still in progress, accustomed to living in the isolation of work or the seclusion of friendship—how could he have failed to feel a sort of panic upon learning of a choice that suddenly focused a harsh spotlight on him alone and reduced to himself? And in what spirit could he receive that honor at a moment when other European writers, often the greatest among them, are reduced to silence, and at a time when his native land is experiencing prolonged suffering?

I felt that shock and that perplexity. I could recover my peace of mind, in short, only by adapting myself to an overgenerous fate. And inasmuch as I could not measure up to it through my own merits, I could think of no other help than what has always comforted me throughout life, even in the most adverse circumstances: the idea I entertain of my art and of the writer's role. Please allow me to express my gratitude and friendship by telling you, as simply as I can, just what that idea is.

I cannot live as a person without my art. And yet I have never set that art above everything else. It is essential to me, on the contrary, because it excludes no one and allows me to live, just as I am, on a footing with all. To me art is not a solitary delight. It is a means of stirring the greatest number of men by providing them with a privileged image of our common joys and woes. Hence it forces the artist not to isolate himself; it subjects him to the humblest and most universal truth. And the man who, as often happens, chose the path of art because he was aware of his difference soon learns that he can nourish his art, and his difference, solely by admitting his resemblance to all. The artist fashions himself in that ceaseless oscillation from himself to others, midway between the beauty he cannot do without and the community from which he cannot tear himself. This is why true artists scorn nothing. They force themselves to understand instead of judging. And if they are to take sides in this world, they can do so only with a society in which, according to Nietzsche's profound words, the judge will yield to the creator, whether he be a worker or an intellectual.

By the same token, the writer's function is not without arduous duties. By definition, he cannot serve today those who make history; he must serve those who are subject to it. Otherwise he is alone and deprived of his art. All the armies of tyranny with their millions of men cannot people his solitude—even, and especially, if he is willing to fall into step with them. But the silence of an unknown prisoner subjected to humiliations at the other end of the world is enough to tear the writer from exile, at least whenever he manages, amid the privileges of freedom, not to forget that silence but to give it voice by means of art.

5   No one of us is great enough for such a vocation. Yet in all the circumstances of his life, unknown or momentarily famous, bound by tyranny or temporarily free to express himself, the writer can recapture the feeling of a living community that will justify him.

But only if he accepts as completely as possible the two trusts that constitute the nobility of his calling: the service of truth and the service of freedom. Because his vocation is to unite the greatest possible number of men, it cannot countenance falsehood and slavery, which breed solitudes wherever they prevail. Whatever our personal frailties may be, the nobility of our calling will always be rooted in two commitments difficult to observe: refusal to lie about what we know and resistance to oppression.

For more than twenty years of absolutely insane history, lost hopelessly like all those of my age in the convulsions of the epoch, I derived comfort from the vague impression that writing was an honor today because the act itself obligated a man, obligated him to more than just writing. It obligated me in particular, such as I was, with whatever strength I possessed, to bear—along with all the others living the same history—the tribulation and hope we shared. Those men born at the beginning of World War I, who had reached the age of twenty just as Hitler was seizing power and the first revolutionary trials were taking place, who then had to complete their education by facing up to war in Spain, World War II, the regime of concentration camps, a Europe of torture and prisons, must today bring their children and their works to maturity in a world threatened with nuclear destruction. No one, I suppose, can expect them to be optimistic. I even go so far as to feel that, without ceasing to struggle against those who through an excess of despair insisted upon their right to dishonor and hurled themselves into the current nihilisms, we must understand their error. Nonetheless, most of us in my country and in Europe rejected that nihilism and strove to find some form of legitimacy. We had to fashion for ourselves an art of living in times of catastrophe in order to be reborn before fighting openly against the death instinct at work in our history.

Probably every generation sees itself as charged with remaking the world. Mine, however, knows that it will not remake the world. But its task is perhaps even greater, for it consists in keeping the world from destroying itself. As the heir of a corrupt history that blends blighted revolutions, misguided techniques, dead gods, and worn-out ideologies, in which second-rate powers can destroy everything today but are unable to win anyone over and in which intelligence has stooped to becoming the servant of hatred and oppression, that generation, starting from nothing but its own negations, has had to re-establish both within and without itself a little of what constitutes the dignity of life and death. Faced with a world threatened with disintegration, in which our grand inquisitors may set up once and for all the kingdoms of death, that generation knows that, in a sort of mad race against time, it ought to re-establish among nations a peace not based on slavery, to reconcile labor and culture again, and to reconstruct with all men an Ark of the Covenant. Perhaps it can never accomplish that vast undertaking, but most certainly throughout the world it has already accepted the double challenge of truth and liberty and, on occasion, has shown that it can lay down its life without hatred. That generation deserves to be acclaimed and encouraged wherever it happens to be, and especially wherever it is sacrificing itself. And to it, confident of your wholehearted agreement, I should like to transfer the honor you have just done me.

At the same time, after having extolled the nobility of the writer's calling, I should have taken the writer down a peg, showing him as he is, with no other rights than those he shares wtih his fellow fighters: vulnerable but stubborn, unjust and eager for justice, constructing his work without shame or pride within sight of all, constantly torn between pain and beauty, and devoted to extracting from his dual nature the creations he obstinately strives to raise up in the destructive fluctuation of history. Who, after that, could expect of him ready-made solutions and fine moral codes? Truth is mysterious, elusive, ever to be won anew. Liberty is dangerous, as hard to get along with as it is exciting. We must progress toward those two objectives, painfully but resolutely, sure in advance that we shall weaken and flinch on such a long road. Consequently, what writer would dare, with a clear conscience, to become a preacher of virtue? As for me, I must say once more that I am far from all that. I have never been able to forget the sunlight, the delight in life, the freedom in which I grew up. But although that nostalgia explains many of my mistakes and shortcomings, it doubtless helped me to understand my calling, and it still helps me to stand implicitly beside all those silent men who, throughout the world, endure the life that has been made for them only because they remember or fleetingly re-experience free moments of happiness.

Reduced in this way to what I am in reality, to my limits and to my liabilities, as well as to my difficult faith, I feel freer to show you in conclusion the extent and generosity of the distinction you have just granted me, freer likewise to tell you that I should like to receive it as a tribute paid to all those who, sharing the same fight, have received no reward, but on the contrary have known only woe and persecution. It remains for me then to thank you from the bottom of my heart and to make you publicly, as a personal token of gratitude, the same age-old promise of allegiance that every true artist, every day, makes to himself, in silence.

Comments and Questions

1. Comment on the statement that "true artists scorn nothing." Does Camus assign a special meaning to the word *scorn*? What special dilemma for the artist does Camus recognize as resulting from current world unrest?

2. Discuss what Camus calls "the death instinct at work in our history." Cite examples of what Camus may have had in mind.

Ralph Ellison   (1914–   )
Brave Words for a Startling Occasion

First, as I express my gratitude for this honor which you have bestowed on me, let me say that I take it that you are rewarding my efforts rather than my not quite fully achieved attempt at a major novel. Indeed, if I were asked in all seriousness just what I considered to be the chief significance of *Invisible Man* as a fiction, I would reply: Its experimental attitude, and its attempt to return to the mood of personal moral responsibility for democracy which typified the best of our nineteenth-century fiction. That my first novel should win this most coveted prize must certainly indicate that there is a crisis in the American novel. You as critics have told us so, and current fiction sales would indicate that the reading public agrees. Certainly the younger novelists concur. The explosive nature of events mocks our brightest efforts. And the very "facts" which the naturalists assumed would make us free have lost the power to protect us from despair. Controversy now rages over just what aspects of American experience are suitable for novelistic treatment. The prestige of the theorists of the so-called novel of manners has been challenged. Thus after a long period of stability we find our assumptions concerning the novel being called into question. And though I was only vaguely aware, it was this growing crisis which shaped the writing of *Invisible Man.*

After the usual apprenticeship of imitation and seeking with delight to examine my experience through the discipline of the novel, I became gradually aware that the forms of so many of the works which impressed me were too restricted to contain the experience which I knew. The diversity of American life with its extreme fluidity and openness seemed too vital and alive to be caught for more than the briefest instant in the tight well-made Jamesian novel, which was, for all its artistic perfection, too concerned with "good taste" and stable areas. Nor could I safely use the forms of the "hard-boiled" novel, with its dedication to physical violence, social cynicism and understatement. Understatement depends, after all, upon commonly held assumptions and my minority status rendered all such assumptions questionable. There was also a problem of language, and even dialogue, which, with its hard-boiled stance and its monosyllabic utterance, is one of the shining achievements of twentieth-century American writing. For despite the notion that its rhythms were those of everyday speech, I found that when compared with the rich babel of idiomatic expression around me, a language full of imagery and gesture and rhetorical canniness, it was embarrassingly austere. Our speech I found resounding with an alive language swirling with over three hundred years of American living, a mixture of the folk, the Biblical, the scientific and the political. Slangy in one stance, academic in another, loaded poetically with imagery at one moment, mathematically bare of imagery in the next. As for the rather rigid concepts of reality which informed a number of the works which impressed me and to which I owe a great deal, I was forced to conclude that reality was far more mysterious and uncertain, and more exciting, and still, despite its raw violence and capriciousness, more promising. To attempt to express that American experience which has carried one back and forth and up and down the land and across, and across again the great river, from freight train to Pullman car, from contact with slavery to contact with a world of advanced scholarship, art and science, is simply to burst such neatly understated forms of the novel asunder.

A novel whose range was both broader and deeper was needed. And in my search I found myself turning to our classical nineteenth-century novelists. I felt that except for the work of William Faulkner something vital had gone out of American prose after Mark Twain. I came to believe that the writers of that period took a much greater responsibility for the condition of democracy and, indeed, their works were imaginative projections of the conflicts within the human heart which arose when the sacred principles of the Constitution and the Bill of Rights clashed with the practical exigencies of human greed and fear, hate and love. Naturally I was attracted to these writers as a Negro. Whatever they thought of my people per se, in their imaginative economy the Negro symbolized both the man lowest down and the mysterious, underground aspect of human personality. In a sense the Negro was the gauge of the human condition as it waxed and waned in our democracy. These writers were willing to confront the broad complexities of American life and we are the richer for their having done so.

Thus to see America with an awareness of its rich diversity and its almost magical fluidity and freedom, I was forced to conceive of a novel unburdened by the narrow naturalism which has led, after so many triumphs, to the final and unrelieved despair which marks so much of our current fiction. I was to dream of a prose which was flexible, and swift as American change is swift, confronting the inequalities and brutalities of our society forthrightly, but yet thrusting forth its images of hope, human fraternity and individual self-realization. It would use the richness of our speech, the idiomatic expression and the rhetorical flourishes from past periods which are still alive among us. And despite my personal failures, there must be possible a fiction which, leaving sociology to the scientists, can arrive at the truth about the human condition, here and now, with all the bright magic of a fairy tale.

5   What has been missing from so much experimental writing has been the passionate will to dominate reality as well as the laws of art. This will is the true source of the experimental attitude. We who struggle with form and with America should remember Eidothea's advice to Menelaus when in the *Odyssey* he and his friends are seeking their way home. She tells him to seize her father, Proteus, and to hold him fast "however he may struggle and fight. He will turn into all sorts of shapes to try you," she says, "into all the creatures that live and move upon the earth, into water, into blazing fire; but you must hold him fast and press him all the harder. When he is himself, and questions you in the same shape that he was when you saw him in his bed, let the old man go; and then, sir, ask which god it is who is angry, and how you shall make your way homewards over the fish-giving sea."

For the novelist, Proteus stands for both America and the inheritance of illusion through which all men must fight to achieve reality; the offended god stands for our sins against those principles we all hold sacred. The way home we seek is that condition of man's being at home in the world, which is called love, and which we term democracy. Our task then is always to challenge the apparent forms of reality—that is, the fixed manners and values of the few, and to struggle with it until it reveals its mad, vari-implicated chaos, its false faces, and on until it surrenders its insight, its truth. We are fortunate as American writers in that with our variety of racial and national traditions, idioms and manners, we are yet one. On its profoundest level American experience is of a whole. Its truth lies in its diversity and swiftness of change. Through forging forms of the novel worthy of it, we achieve not only the promise of our lives, but we anticipate the resolution of those world problems of humanity which for a moment seem to those who are in awe of statistics completely insoluble.

Whenever we as Americans have faced serious crises we have returned to fundamentals; this, in brief, is what I have tried to do.

Comments and Questions

The occasion referred to in the title was a dinner at which Ralph Ellison received the National Book Award for his novel *Invisible Man.*

1. Speeches that respond to an award, particularly one for literary merit, are usually both personal and reflective. Compare this short speech with Camus' (p. 1084), equally short. Note the similarity in the opening sentences, models of modesty both. Camus' speech has no title. Explain Ellison's.

2. What does Ellison mean by "personal moral responsibility for democracy"? He ascribes this sort of responsibility to nineteenth-century fiction writers. Can you tell whether he is talking about American or British novelists?

3. Reread "Preliminaries" in the fiction division particularly the paragraph headed "The Meaning of the Story: The Parts and the Whole" (p. 17). According to both Camus and Ellison, is there a place for writers of fiction as pure entertainment? Do any of the short stories presented in this book qualify as simply pleasant narratives? "Roman Fever" (p. 32), perhaps?

Barbara Farris Graves (1938–)
and Donald J. McBain (1945–)
Electric Orphic Circuit

1

Don't listen to evil rumors; poetry is alive and well. While it is true that the era of T. S. Eliot, Ezra Pound, and Wallace Stevens is over, and that some poets (and critics) are floundering in the wake of these giants, nevertheless more poetry is being written, read, spoken, sung, listened to, and generally appreciated today than perhaps at any time before. And more *kinds* of poetry. A reader looking for recently published poetry can step inside a bookstore and find anything from the word and picture games of John Lennon to the sprawling cosmic chants of Allen Ginsberg to the soft, semiconfessional sonnets of Robert Lowell. Indeed, the post–World War II period has witnessed a parade of variously ephemeral poetic forms, styles, cliques, schools, and movements. Some of these have been highly innovative; some have returned to or developed past traditions. It is difficult to determine whether any have forged new major directions.

In the past decade, forces have gathered to generate a movement whose poets are united often by life style and personal philosophy but principally by the form in which they create—songs, the lyric form. As precursor, prophet, central figure, and sage, Bob Dylan has managed so far to span the movement; at least he saw it through its incipient period, the decade of the sixties. Certainly, he was the first popular songwriter in quite some time to be considered as a poet, although his right to this title has been battered back and forth by all the people who enjoy that sort of thing. People whose poetic backgrounds range from amateur to aesthete have reacted to the phenomenon that Dylan helped to set in motion and that his verse represents. Some have demeaned it for its illiteracy. Some have said that he is only a songwriter and not a poet, and that his art form is outside the realm of modern poetry. Others have proclaimed him the first poet laureate of mass media. Such divergent critical reactions, however, sometimes indicate more about the particular commentators or about the cultural divergences in our society than they do about either Dylan's verse or the movement.

Nevertheless, the movement has made inroads, even in academic circles. Significantly, the high schools were the first to teach current songs in English classes, though usually smuggled into the course by either a hip or a desperate teacher rather than as part of the regular curriculum. More recently, college poetry courses and texts have been including song lyrics, and some schools have offered seminars in "rock" poetry. This must mean the movement has arrived. The questions arise, though: Will it be a major direction?

Is it new? Poet Allen Ginsberg, himself not completely accepted in the more highbrow academic strata, in a recent anthology called *Naked Poetry,* offered a key to the phenomenon:

> . . . But young minstrels have now arisen on the airwaves whose poetic forms outwardly resemble antique verse including regular stanzas, refrains and rhymes: Dylan and Donovan and some fragments of the Rolling Stones because they *think* not only in words but also in music simultaneously have out of the necessities of their own space-age media and electric machinery tunes evolved a natural use of— a personal realistic imaginative rhymed verse. Principle of composition here is, however, unlike antique literary form, primarily spontaneous and improvised (in the studio if need be at the last minute) and prophetic in character in that tune and language are invoked shamanistically on the spot from the unconscious. The new ear is not dead only for eye-page, it's connected with a voice improvising, with hesitancies aloud, a living musician's ear. The old library poets had lost their voices; natural voice was rediscovered, and now natural song for physical voice. Oddly, this fits Pound's paradigm tracing the degeneration of Poesy from the Greek dance-foot-chorus thru minstrel song thru 1900 abstract voiceless pages. So now returned to song and song forms we yet anticipate inspired Creators like Shiva Krishna Chaitanya. . . .
>
> Allen Ginsberg, "Some Metamorphoses of Personal Prosody," in *Naked Poetry: Recent American Poetry in Open Forms,* eds. Stephen Berg and Robert Mezey, New York: Bobbs-Merrill Co., Inc., 1969, p. 221.

"Returned to song and song forms": Ginsberg's words suggest a kind of cyclical pattern, one whose first "revolution" is just now being achieved. It is worthwhile to investigate this idea as an introduction to this book. Hopefully, our investigation will enable us to put these anthologized songs in a historical perspective that dates further back than the rockabilly days of Bill Haley and his Comets, and to establish inroads for further study in this area. In considering an evolutionary cycle of poetry, and specifically lyric poetry, there are four periods that demand our attention—the origins of poetry, the Greek lyric, the Renaissance, and the modern electric lyric. Although evolution is a continuous process, these are recognizable stages and focal points of the development of poetry as it meets us today.

2

The arts of poetry and music had a common origin in primitive song, in what the Greeks were later to call "lyric." These early songs probably consisted of many different kinds—work songs, love songs, lullabies, laments. Song, however, is essentially a public art. Historians, anthropologists, and linguists continue to speculate on the specific date and form of the first actual lyric. However, it is generally agreed on and sustained by the earliest findings of lyric poetry that the lyric grew out of ritualistic patterns surrounding primitive religious ceremonies, and was usually an expression of some kind of mystical experience that the poet was undergoing.

5   Certain key characteristics, then, should be noted concerning what can be considered the genesis of our poetry. The first is that words and music were conceived as a fused unit, evolving perhaps from spontaneous cries around the ceremonial fires, to chants, and eventually to the story-lyric or ballad. The poet, throughout this development, thought "not only in words but in music simultaneously." Second, since the poet was originally associated with mysticism and magic, poetry was rooted in the realm of the supernatural and

the divine. Third, the emphasis was on performance; many of the songs were improvised "shamanistically on the spot from the unconscious." Finally, the entire group participated in the performance, echoing and answering the single voice (this function developed into the Greek "chorus" and, in our modern lyrical poetry, we see its remnant in the refrain, an atrophied, surrogate form of audience participation). Hence the beginnings, and perhaps the essence of poetry, can be found in the primitive lyric, a form that was intense, spontaneous, visceral, communal, magical, mystical . . . and music.

In the Greek period the lyric grew in number and complexity, developing into a profusion of types, such as the triumph, the dirge, the dance-song, the hymn, the processional, and culminating in the fully developed ode with its divisions of strophe and antistrophe. It was also at this time that the term "lyric" first came into use. The Greeks who were Aristotle's contemporaries made three fundamental distinctions. Elegiac and iambic poems were chanted; melic or lyric poems were sung by one voice to musical accompaniment (the lyre), and choric was for several voices. Notice that the distinctions were based on external differences and not subject matter. Eventually, "lyric" became a general name for any poem that was composed for singing, and the meaning did not change until the Renaissance.

In the lyric there is a basic tension between words and music. Although both are temporal forms, always throwing the attention forward, because words have semantic properties, we are tempted (at some times more than others) to stop and think about them; meanwhile the song's melody and rhythm continue to hurtle us on. In addition, there is a basic division in the function of these two components of the lyric. Some critics maintain that the words convey ideas and the music conveys emotion. Others differentiate between the intellectual appeal of music and that of poetry, saying that the former is more related to structure and the latter to content. Whatever the differences of critical opinion as to what the separate functions are, the tension caused by their separateness is generally agreed upon. The ideal lyric profits from this tension, keeping a balance between the weight of the two.

In the primitive lyric the problem of conflict did not exist, since (as we mentioned earlier), the two forms were thought of as a fused unit, and within that unit they not only complemented each other but depended on each other for survival. As each art became more developed, however, the problem of rivalry arose. Words became music in themselves, music attempted to express ideas on its own—one began to outshine the other in virtuosity. In almost all lyric periods, one or the other form has been to some degree subordinated. During the Greek era, for example, in the odes of Pindar and Bacchylides, the music was obviously subordinated to the words. The Elizabethan period, the great age of English lyricism, was a time when, at least in the early part, words and music were written in careful consideration of each other, either by the same artist or by joint contribution of the poet and composer. But the Renaissance brought with it a separation that has lasted for centuries and that has created the hybrid form known as lyrical poetry.

Several events combined in the Renaissance to produce breaches that affected the entire fabric of society and culture and, in turn, the lyric. In the latter part of the Elizabethan period the once nearly symbiotic relationship between poetry and music grew apart. During the late Middle Ages, music had become more sophisticated and was finally able to stand on its own. We can see a marked evolution in the difference between the simple music of the early Elizabethan lutanist, in which the composer was chiefly concerned with conveying the poet's meaning, and the complex patterns of the later madrigals, which were concerned chiefly with the music and which often drowned the words in complicated fugal progressions. So too with poetry. The poet grew weary of the rhyme, the refrain, the end stops, the exact stanza form of the lyric. All these things had once stimulated his art; now he felt shackled by them. Poetry too was becoming more sophisticated and profound. The complex analogies of metaphysical verse required an intellectual analysis, but the temporal experience of song prohibits such lingering. John Donne's poetry, for example, demands reading and rereading. This bring us to a crucial point.

10   The invention of printing completely altered life in the Renaissance and in each succeeding age. It created the literate society, brought us out of the Dark Ages (the ages of magic, by the way), and spread uniformed knowledge and culture across the world. Marshall McLuhan, in *Understanding Media,* and more exhaustively in *The Gutenberg Galaxy,* explained the changes that the medium of print itself effected because of the kind of perspective it demanded (and still demands) from its audience.

Let's review the points that most concern our topic. First, printed, mass-produced books encouraged individualism and the fixed, personal, detached point of view. A book is an artifact. A person can open it or shut it. He can take it to his room to read (indeed, printing even changed architecture, demanding that houses have separate, closed-off rooms that one could go to in order to read his book). Since under normal circumstances books are read individually and privately, the reader's response is individual and private. Thus the communal quality of poetry was lost.

Also the medium is "hot"; it provides a large amount of specific information—information that can be reread as often as desired—thereby precluding the involvement that an oral form required, eliminating the sense of mystery necessary for the survival of magic, urging in, eventually, the Age of Reason. The linear form encouraged linear perspective and linear thought, which nurtured logic and scientific methodology. The line, which was segmented into separate words and separate letters, encouraged fragmentation. The mechanical age was now prepared for, with all its assembly lines and wheels and gadgets.

Since print dictated that poetry be seen and not heard, poets began suiting their work to a visual rather than an auditory medium. Because of its strict pattern and traditionally conventional content, poetry written for music is usually monotonous to read. The rhyme and refrain become wearisome. Sometimes a verbal rhythm seems lopsided when read, although it is even when put to the appropriate music. The poet Dryden once complained, "I have been obliged to cramp my verses, and make them rugged to the reader, that they may be harmonious to the hearer." And so, as a result of all these conflicts, the sister arts went their separate ways. Consequently, although poets continued to be more or less knowledgeable about music, their knowledge resulted more from social contacts than from any close ties between the arts. Moreover, the gulf between them grew wider with time.

The advent of printing intensified another oncoming divorce. The minstrel was shoved out of his position as a disseminator of verse, as poems of all kinds became readily available in print. Also we begin to see a definite split during this period between high and low art, or between art and folk. In the realm of the lyric, there was a growing distinction between the art or literary lyric and the folk lyric. From the close of the Renaissance the folk lyric continued to flourish on its own, however, through the days of the broadsheets and chapbooks, through the Victorian street ballads, the vaudeville and Broadway music halls, to the pop songs of our time. Its illiteracy has always been preserved; the folk lyric has been virtually unaffected by the literary fashion of the day. Usually, however, somewhat more influence has been felt the other way. Sophisticated poets from Swift to Eliot have at times borrowed the street manner for their poems.

15   The art lyric traveled another path. Except for Dryden, after the early seventeenth century no major English poet until Robert Burns spent a large part of his poetic efforts writing songs that were intended for singing. Although poets continued to create many poems that were called "songs" and odes to music (plenty of them in the eighteenth

century), most poets were not interested in its possibilities for poetry. Moreover, few poets besides Milton, Ireland's Thom Moore, and Gerard Manley Hopkins could claim any solid musical training. Moore and Burns, both excellent lyricists, stand out in the English poetic tradition, which was veering further and further away from song. The neoclassic couplet, for example, was about the most unsuitable verse for music in the history of poetry. And, finally, the decline in drama also influenced the lyric's decline, since so many of the best songs had been written for the stage. In 1798, *Lyrical Ballads*,[1] though attempting to return poetry to "real" speech, never approached bringing it back to song. The lyric had become the lyric*al*. The subject and tone defined the poem. The term "lyric" no longer referred specifically to a song-poem, but rather to a particular kind of poetry that was, as the poet William Wordsworth defined it, "emotion recollected in tranquillity."

To emphasize the essential features of a strain that has undoubtedly influenced the writers represented here, let's take additional liberties with time and space. The following have played important roles in the completion of a lyric cycle.

William Blake renewed the concept of the poet as magic-maker, as shaman. His association of the poem with a mystical experience recurs in the works of such spiritual-minded poets as Hopkins, Baudelaire, Yeats, and Rilke. Also, Blake's "Songs of Innocence and Experience" (for which he reputedly had composed melodies that he sang to himself), in their blending of a simple, lyrical surface with deeper levels of mystery, allegory, and archetype, were ideal models for many of our current lyrics. Compare Blake's "Songs," for example, with Dylan's songs on his *John Wesley Harding* album.

Edgar Allan Poe, in his subordination of thought to the music of his words, and in his concept and use of the grotesque, had a considerable influence on all of modern poetry. Much of his influence was directly absorbed and then rebounded by the *fin de siècle* French symbolist poets, especially Mallarmé and Valéry, who consciously aspired to produce in poetry the pure and absolute qualities of music.

The French surrealists, for whom André Breton was a chief spokesman, liberated the unconscious in poetry and for poetry. Among themselves they tried experiments invoking the creative unconscious in the spontaneous "automatic poem," and seeking to collect their creative consciousness in the communal "group poem."

20 During the twenties in America and elsewhere there was much experimental activity in poetry. E. E. Cummings was in the vanguard of this activity, and in his verse we can see the seeds of two divergent strains in poetry. His concern with the formal and spatial arrangement of words (and parts of words) on the page helped to precipitate the concrete movement. Much of this poetry is not merely dependent on but is restricted to a visual orientation. Hence Ginsberg's reference to "abstract voiceless page."

On the other hand, Cummings was very much concerned with the oral form. Many of his visual patterns were aids to oral delivery, and he even made commercial recordings of his own poetry, as many poets have done since. These recordings gave him an infinitely greater listening audience, just as the invention of printing gave the Renaissance poet an infinitely greater reading audience. The differences between the two kinds of audience, as we have mentioned earlier, are significant. And it was the new electric technology that helped to create a new audience or rather, to recreate the audience in its primitive form.

The media of records, radio, television, and film have redirected our orientation toward the spoken and sung word. For example, electronic amplification is one factor in making rock concerts the huge communal gatherings that they are, since it enables the sound to be carried over large areas. These concerts are often recorded and filmed, so they can be replayed to other group audiences. The impact of these new media, and the

---

[1] By Wordsworth and Coleridge.

involvement they demand, is total and continuous. Many observers feel that they are re-placing the printed word, that society has become (or at least is still in the process of becoming) postliterate and thereby postliterary. Electric circuitry, McLuhan tells us, has become modern society's central nervous system. We share via radio and television the everyday experiences of our African and Asian brothers. We are rapidly becoming, in a sense, all members of the same tribe, living in a "global village."

The new media made poets more interested in public readings. In America, the beat movement of the fifties accelerated this interest; readings developed into true communal experiences, complete with chanting and incantations. And once again, the emphasis was on performance, with poems often improvised and spontaneous. Kenneth Patchen and others tried experiments—live and on radio and records—with poetry read to a jazz back-ground, and although the relationship between the two forms was at best contrapuntal, the effort was another major step toward the final fusion and return to song and song forms. As certain jazz forms are heavy influences on current rock music, the beats are the immediate poetic forbears of the current lyric movement.

Pop art has provided another kind of fusion. The pop revolution has proved to be a great cultural equalizer. Be it music, movies, painting, sculpture, or commercial art, pop has consistently shattered traditional boundaries between the sophisticated and the mun-dane, the art and the folk, the classical and the camp. A Dylan song called "Tombstone Blues" has Ma Rainey and Beethoven composing a song together. "Bob Dylan's 115th Dream" mixes various literary, historical and mythological sources in an absurd modern account of the discovery of America. The Beatles' songs and their bankbooks offer collec-tive proof that there need be no distinction between art and public entertainment. Nor is there as much need for conscious cross-fertilization between sophisticated poetry and folk song, nor between culture and subcultures, as the global village becomes a tighter and tighter unit.

25   Dylan's work in the sixties heralded poetry's return to song and song forms. His songs were ingenious combinations of blues, rhythms, surreal imagery, topical protest, fatalistic existentialism, a huge repertory of poetic devices; and colorful verbal idiom. His impact on the pop music scene is undeniable; he made so many musicians conscious of infusing their songs with poetry. But equally important, he has made a growing number of poets aware of the new possibilities of poetry and music together. A milieu, nurtured in the sixties, is now established. Leonard Cohen, already a successful novelist and linear poet, is writing songs and recording them personally. Ed Sanders and Tuli Kupferberg of the Fugs, both linear poets, both incorporate their verses into song, as did Richard Fariña. These poets are by no means ignorant of the literary tradition, but neither do they have to *borrow* the street idiom. Poets and musicians meet in Liverpool, in New York, in San Francisco, and blend their wares.

A significant number of the lyric writers whose works appear in this book[2] have written their own music and performed their own songs. Donovan is perhaps the best current example of both the primitive mystic poet and the early Renaissance minstrel poet. And he and Dylan and the others are reaching (through the electric circuits) millions of young people, some of whom are budding bards themselves. In his excellent study of the lyric, *The Lyric Impulse,* C. Day Lewis commented on this contemporary phenomenon:

> The mantle of the bard has fallen upon the shoulders of the pop singer—from
> which it is frequently torn off by a raving horde of his fans and distributed among

---

[2] By the authors of this essay, *Lyric Voices, Approaches to the Poetry of Contemporary Song,* New York: John Wiley & Sons, Inc., 1972.

them as souvenirs. Nothing new in this. The first pop singer, Orpheus, was torn in pieces by Maenads. And dare we feel superior about these rabid manifestations? Do they not indicate a psychological need, a spontaneity of emotion, which the higher levels of art in the West are today ignoring?

C. Day Lewis, *The Lyric Impulse,* Cambridge, Mass.: Harvard University Press, 1965, p. 2.

3

The minstrel has returned; his stringed instrument is now electric, and without traveling he can be heard across the world. And he will be heard—by everyone—since the human ear is not equipped with earlids.

Thus a cycle seems to be reaching completion. We are now in a position to consider again the questions raised earlier: Will the current lyric movement be a major direction? Is it new? In view of the increasingly large dimensions of the lyric movement, there can be no doubt that it is, by sheer force of numbers, a major trend. The return to the roots of poetry demonstrated by the reemergence of the singer-poets makes this movement, in an even more significant sense, a major direction.

But as these two questions are answered, two further problems can be anticipated concerning the proposed cyclical theory, and so it must be clarified. One, we cannot say that *all* poetry is returning to song; as long as people continue to speak, there will be spoken poetry. As T. S. Eliot once warned, if poetry departs too far from common speech, it can wither and die of abstraction. We can propose, however, that the lyric movement is a major direction. And this brings up the second problem.

30   If the mainstream of poetry is returning to lyric form, and the lyric is by tradition a light, simple song, then what happens to poetry that is by nature sophisticated, complex, and profound? We spoke earlier of the tension between the forward-moving musical pace and the words whose meanings must sometimes be pondered. To preserve the balance, the lyric has traditionally been light and simple in meaning and thereby fast-moving. Although most current lyrics continue to be light, several important songs point toward a new kind of lyric. Dylan's "All Along the Watchtower" is one example. The song has a simple narrative surface that moves along quickly but, in the style of Blake, it uses symbol, allegory, and archetype to suggest more profound meanings. Songs like Phil Ochs' "Crucifixion," Carl Oglesby's "Black Panther," Fariña's "Celebration for a Grey Day," and Dylan's "Sad-Eyed Lady of the Lowlands" are examples of a somewhat different type. These songs, with their intricate image patterns, their many-sided symbols and levels of meaning, are "heavy." They do not offer a contrast to the "higher levels of art."

And yet they are rapid. In each song the music keeps us moving toward the conclusion. We cannot linger on the "meaning"; lingering is for later. In this electric age, things happen allatonce, and, sometimes, if we are to survive, we must let them happen and reflect on them later. So with the films of Fellini and Godard, so with the Joshua Light Show, so with "Sad-Eyed Lady of the Lowlands."

Still another possible explanation of the "heavy" lyric bears consideration. It may be that the electronic media are gradually conditioning us to the ability to respond to many different stimuli on many levels. As we continue to experience the perceptual expansion that the electronic media stimulate, it is possible that our ability to function simultaneously on the perceptual and intellectual levels will increase. Modern film techniques overwhelm us with a rapid series of visual images, while contemporary songs bombard us with an infinitely complex fusion of visual, auditory, and kinetic images and intellectual ideas.

These modern orphic voices are plugging us in to the times we actually live in.

Comments and Questions

1. Explain the title of the essay.

2. What theory do the authors advance for the common origin of poetry and music? How do they account for the eventual separation of poetry from music?

3. The authors recognize four periods in the "evolutionary cycle of . . . lyric poetry." Examine the four. How does each fit into the argument of the essay?

4. What distinction is drawn between the art lyric and the folk lyric?

5. Why, according to the authors, was the emergence of singer-poets like Bob Dylan a "return to the roots of poetry"?

6. See pages 341–355 for examples of the kind of contemporary song lyrics alluded to in the essay. See the index for poems by some of the poets discussed.

Stephen Spender (1909–   )
On Teaching Modern Poetry

A poem has many levels of meaning, and none of them is prose. Are some of these "righter" than others? Is it altogether "wrong" to think that a poem may be paraphrased? Can an appreciation of poetry be acquired? Does poetry have educational value for the student who is incapable of a complete experience of poetry but who can acquire a limited appreciation which may not seem to survive his years at school or college? This last question, which the reader may be inclined to answer with an immediate "No" is, in practice, not so easy to answer. For students who may never completely understand a poem, can often understand other things through the discussion of poetry. Those who prefer discussing poetry to reading poems, look to poetry for an illumination of some of the problems of living. One cannot afford to dismiss this as irrelevant when one is taking into consideration the whole picture of the education of an individual. Many people look to poetry today as an illumination of religious and philosophic problems. Although poetry is not and cannot be a substitute for religion and philosophy, nevertheless, it may lead people to think seriously about such things. It may lead them through poetry and out of it into their real interest or vocation.

Probably most modern critics would agree that a poem *means* the sum of everything which it *is,* in language used to suggest not just thought but also imagery and sound. It means a thought which can be paraphrased in prose, plus the sound of the words in which this thought is expressed and which add as much to the thought as color does to drawing in a painting, plus the imagery which becomes a sensory experience to the reader as he reads from line to line, plus the energy of the metre, plus the poet's taste or palate in words, plus even such things as the punctuation and spacing of the poem upon the printed page. All these things become an *experience* which the poem is and means.[1]

[1] The point of view expressed in this paragraph, especially in the first sentence, is demonstrated in some detail in "Preliminaries" in the poetry division, pp. 299 ff.

Most contemporary critics, as I say, would agree about this. On the whole, the tendency today is to judge the poem by the sacred order of the irreplaceable line, and not by the generalized reducible opinions and attitudes of the poet within his poem. This modern appreciation of the concreteness and texture of art is surely one of the characteristics of intellectual life in the twentieth century which we can consider to be an advance of the nineteenth.

Yet, if we do not feel the need to translate poetry into prose, nevertheless the need to explain and annotate it seems to remain. Why else those books explaining the philosophy of T. S. Eliot's *Four Quartets* or of Rilke's *Duino Elegies?* It is all very well for Mr. Robert Graves to declare that his poems are written only for poets, implying that all poems should be that and that only. But evidently, despite the modern purist desire not to lose the poem in the prose translation, poetry expresses complicated ideas and attitudes. This inevitably leads us on from a discussion of the best order of the best words to that of the ideas behind them. Robert Graves may be right in thinking that poetry should be for poets only. But despite his protestations, the overwhelming mass of contemporary criticism of poetry assumes that poetry is written for a reading public who are not just poets: or at least that there is a content of poetry which exists, as it were, apart from the pure esthetic experience which can only be communicated to people who think poetically, as the poet himself thinks.

5   The teacher of poetry finds that although it is important to stress that poetry *is,* it is also true that poetry is about things. To a certain type of student the "about" ness will always be more important than the "is" ness: and perhaps this student may learn more from having poetry explained to him than the one who understands poetry intuitively and who therefore scarcely requires to be taught.

The teacher is not a poet teaching poets, nor even a literary critic concerned only with readers whose interest in poetry is "pure." He has to accept, I think, that the interest of most students in poetry, however serious it may be, will not be for the sake of that which is essentially the poetry in poetry. At the same time, poetry itself is ambiguous, and that which it is about is inseparably bound up with that which it is. If a critic as austere as Mr. T. S. Eliot can argue that a poet as pure as Blake is not a great poet because he has a "homemade philosophy," that means that one approach to Blake is certainly by way of his philosophy. And if many of Blake's readers never get beyond his philosophy to the center of his imagination, that does not mean that they have entirely missed the poetry in Blake: because Blake's thought, which can perhaps be paraphrased, nevertheless remains a part of his poetry. What a poem is about, even if it can be expressed in critics' prose, does take us some way toward understanding that which it is.

Many students undoubtedly try to *use* poetry to help them develop attitudes towards things other than poetry. Sarah Lawrence College provided me with several examples of such a utilitarian attitude. One student, K., had difficulty with certain modern poems at the beginning of the course, because she disapproved of the views which the poets appeared to her to be expressing in their poems; for example, the pessimism of Thomas Hardy, the mysticism of T. S. Eliot, and the insistence on sexuality of D. H. Lawrence. She thought that poetry should in some way express ideas which contributed to the betterment of human society.

Perhaps I should have argued with K. that poetry had nothing to do with the views of poets and still less to do with improving the lot of humanity. But I only partly did this. I also argued against her views in themselves, quite apart from their relevance to poetry. I tried to point out that the search for a meaning in life, even if it seems to neglect the exigencies of social welfare, is not escapism. The result of allowing her to discuss aspects of poetry, such as the opinions and personalities of poets, which seemed on the face of it to have little to do with their work, was that she did, in the course of a year, develop powers of appreciation which I had not thought possible. A block to her appreciation was removed. She learned tolerance through tolerating poets. Having acquired a certain tolerance she experienced a certain release in her imaginative life which brought her to an appreciation of poetry for its own sake. Her prejudices were not just irrelevant: they were barriers which had to be removed before she could understand poetry at all. Her criticism of every poem—that it said something with which she disagreed—implied conviction that poetry ought to have a social message with which she did agree. It would have been useless to say that what a poem *said* was irrelevant to the poetry, because to her the saying something was what really mattered, and ultimately her objection was to the expression of any attitudes of mind which she did not consider socially responsible. To say to her that Thomas Hardy's pessimism was irrelevant to his poetry would only be a way of making her think that Hardy not only had the wrong opinions but also attempted to evade responsibility for them. Therefore it seemed best to accept her view that poetry was about opinions which she could not tolerate and to point out that those opinions, within the contexts in which they were expressed, might have a value which she could come to appreciate. When she had learned to tolerate these opinions she was well on the way to understanding the freedom of the imagination of the poet in his poetry. On the other hand, so long as she could not tolerate what she considered antisocial opinions, she would not tolerate the life of the imagination.

10   K., it transpired, was using poetry as a means of liberating herself from a narrow application of her social conscience to every situation. Her case was not rare. There is a fairly widespread tendency amongst students today to label a great deal of their reading "escapist," for the most superficial reasons. To them all the poetry of Walter de la Mare is "escapist," Mr. T. S. Eliot is not "escapist" in *The Waste Land* but becomes so in the *Four Quartets,* Mr. W. H. Auden has recently become an "escapist," D. H. Lawrence is escaping from social reality into "personal relationships and mysticism," and so on. Such readers seem to expect that it is the duty of literature to confront them with a social reality, which, in fact, they rarely face themselves in their lives. They wish poets to stop being what is called escapists and become scapegoats, punished and punishing in their work for all the ills of society. One might reasonably argue that if literature did do this, it might indeed be providing a facile escape in imagination from problems which people ought to be facing in their living. In fact, there is a case to be made for saying that people should be social realists in their lives but not in their literature. For living should certainly be pre-occupied with improving conditions, but literature should be concerned with enlarging our ideas of a significance beyond the paraphernalia of living. Without such a significance, improved conditions themselves become a burden. There must be a goal beyond the goal of social improvement—to give significance to better conditions of living when they have been achieved.

In an ideal world I suppose that living would be involved in problems of living, and that literature would be concerned with values which transcend living. It is these values which ultimately give living itself a purpose. Of course, as long as we do not live in an ideal world, some writers will insist on the necessity of using writing as a means of describing the problems of social reality and, if they are so inspired, they will be right to do so. But to call this kind of literature "realistic" and any other kind "escapist" is to sacrifice the pursuit of permanent values for immediate and pressing ones: and there is danger of the sense of that which endures being lost in the exigencies of the present.

If there is any such thing as "escapism" in poetry, it is the tendency of poets sometimes to assert that experiences contained in certain poems have some kind of consoling application to other experiences of a different nature. That a sunset, a rose, or a landscape can be evoked in language which compensates for poverty, social injustice, or war, is obviously a false proposition. To maintain it is to escape from the greater evil into the lesser prettiness. Poets, even in such a poet as Keats, have occasionally misled themselves and their readers in writing about poetry as though it were a housing project for happy dreamers. The mistake perhaps arises from confusing the objective standards by which poetry is made and judged with the subjective experience it provides. For the fact is that poetry is an art employing an objective medium and technique for the purpose of communicating the subjective insight of the poet to the subjective sensibility of the reader. It can express and communicate an experience which may be of great value to the individual reader, perhaps even providing him with a philosphy and helping him in his life. But this kind of individual experience conveyed from one individual to another by means of the objective medium of art, arises only as a possible rather irrelevant reaction of the reader to the subject matter of the poem. Poetry cannot preach social values as effectively as journalism or propaganda or systematized thought, even though it may indirectly have a social effect. Poetry does not provide a kind of reality which can either, on the one hand, console readers for the ills of society, or, on the other, by being "realistic," make people face up to social problems. All poetry may do, as an incidental effect of its use of language, is to provide the reader with an experience which will affect him according to the laws of his own nature. The propagandist view that poetry can save society is just as irrelevant to the nature of poetry as the one that it can provide an escape from the ills of the modern age.

I have dwelt on "escapism" so long because one of the chief prejudices the teacher of students of poetry today has to fight is indicated by the word "escapist." However, I think the teacher should be sympathetic to the student who wants to know how poetry will be useful to him. After all, utility itself, in connection with poetry, is a somewhat complex concept, and there is every reason to consider it. For one thing, poetry is useful to anyone who appreciates it, in enabling him to enter into complex states of mind which should help him to understand his own nature and that of other people. The reader of a poem has the illusion, through the sensuous use of language, of being in the presence of the event which is the occasion of the poem. The subject of a poem is an event individually experienced; its method (sensuous language) creates the form which is the universal form of all experience for everyone of every event. The reader of a poem is made aware that the experience of every event by every individual is a unique occasion in the universe, and that at the same time, this uniqueness is the universal mode of experiencing all events. Poetry makes one realize that one is alone, and complex; and that to be alone is universal.

The fact that one cannot establish the value of the experience of a poem in a hierarchy of utilitarian values, does not mean that poetry is not useful. On the contrary, one can insist that poetry is of use to the individual who appreciates it, even while one may refuse to measure that utility. The teacher who thinks it is part of his integrity, or of the integrity of his subject, to refuse to admit the utility of spiritual values, may be in the position of offering art to his pupils in the form of significantly formed stones, when they are asking for bread. He should ask himself seriously whether there is not a sense in which poetry is indeed bread for those who can understand it, and even, to a lesser extent, to those who partially misunderstand it.

15   Poetry, as has often been said, reveals the familiar as unfamiliar. The inspiration of the poet is the moment in which he becomes aware of unfamiliarity. The unfamiliarity, the newness of things, the uniqueness of every contact of a mind with an event, is, indeed, everything. But there are certain experiences in life which are always unfamiliar for everyone, and these form a vast subject matter for poetry, the unfamiliarity of the unfamiliar. Such subjects are death, love, infinity, the idea of God, the smallness of man in relation to the vastness of the universe, the unknown. Religion, philosophy, and morals are also con-

cerned with these fundamentals of the human condition, and it is here that the experiencing of life in poetry brings the poetic experience close to the reasoned processes of philosophers, theologians, and moralists. Thus the teaching of poetry leads the student to a discussion of conditions of human life, where man is alone with the strangeness of his situation in time and space.

Poets can only express their experiences in terms of other experiences, which men have experienced with their senses. Sensuous language means that the poet creates his poem from words which have associations, and these associations are of the experience of things with the senses. A love poem can only be expressed in words which have associations with actual loving, and in the same way a religious poem can only be created in the language of religious experience—however remote this may seem. For this reason, the teacher will find that a great deal of discussion of poetry in class will consist of inquiring into the connection between the poet's experience and his poem. Is the poet sincere? Did he really feel this? are questions often asked by students. When poetry goes beyond personal experience to the experience of belief, we are brought up against a more difficult question of sincerity. Can the poet really believe this? Does he know God? Can he believe in immortality? We are soon confronted with problems of tradition and belief which may seem far removed from a particular poem, but which may really be essential to an understanding of it.

Amongst our contemporaries today one finds that directly a poet ceases to write of some immediate human experience of an occasional nature, for which purposes he can draw on the simple associative language of the physical senses, one is up against the difficulty that a shared language of religious or philosophical experience, with associations which are as easily recognized as those of the senses, does not exist. In reading poetry such as T. S. Eliot's *Four Quartets* with students, one finds that for many of them there is no sensuous language associated with ideas of eternity. God, immortality, heaven, hell, and so on. Eliot's world is for them a world of abstract speculation, his language never, or almost never strikes the note of an experience of eternity in their own minds. Naturally they think of Eliot's preoccupations as "escapism," because they are about an experience of which they know nothing.

If one wishes to teach such students to appreciate the *Four Quartets* the only way to do so seems to be to build up by intellectual arguments the associations with experience on which the poetry is based. One can show that each of the four poems in the *Four Quartets* is connected with real places which have historic associations with certain disciplines of living dependent on certain metaphysical beliefs. One can discuss the use to which Eliot has deliberately put the influence of Dante in his poem, and one can discuss the time-philosophy and the theological ideas of the *Four Quartets*. All this will not give the student the immediate contact with the metaphysical searching which is as much the sensuous experience of this poetry as the color grey is sensuous experience in the line:

Towards what shores what grey rocks and what islands.

Consider such lines as:

All manner of things shall be well
When the tongues of flame are infolded
Into the crowned knot of fire
And the fire and the rose are one.

Here it is far easier to make the student understand the Dantesque imagery than the sensuous mystical perception of the life of the individual within eternity. Can one understand such writing without having had, consciously or unconsciously, a mystical experience which foreshadows the condition described? This is a baffling question for the teacher. All he can reasonably hope to do is make the student understand the traditional belief within which Eliot's recent poetry exists, and to argue against the view of the student who thinks that mystical experience is "escapist."

Teachers of Latin within the system of a classical education have always taught much poetry, partly because this branch of classical literature is supremely excellent, partly because the language of poetry taught the greatest mastery of all the uses of the language, and partly also because within poetry there exist all the ideas of Roman civilization. These reasons for teaching poetry remain in force today. Insistence on the esthetic aspect should not conceal from us that poetry remains the most instructive of the arts, being rooted in myth, being supremely the exercise by the poet of the historic sense within the tradition of literature, and involving often discussion of general ideas.

20   The most important thing to teach about modern poetry is that modern poetry is simply poetry, expressing what poets have tried to express at all times, but within modern conditions. The problem of the poet has always been to express inward experience in imagery and sound which communicate the significance of this experience to others. He can only communicate to other minds what is significant to him by involving an outward event symbolizing a significance which corresponds to his inner state of mind. If he is an Elizabethan, certain of his inner experiences may have a significance recognized by others when he attaches to these experiences the symbolism of the rose, the crown, or the cross. For a modern man who, as a human being, has an inner experience exactly similar to that of the Elizabethan, the symbol which corresponds to his experience will be one chosen from modern life, if it is to communicate itself in a way which will awaken the living experience of our time to his contemporaries. To select rose, crown, or cross would be for him to detach his experience from the present and place it in a literary past.

Our expansive, restless, materialist, explosive age does not easily provide us in our environment with outward symbols for inner states of mind. For our outer world has little accessible language of symbols to which we can attach the experiences of our lives. Instead of our minds being able to invade it with their inwardness, it invades us with its outward-ness, almost persuading us that not the inner life of man, but non-human, geographical and mechanical events are all that is significant in the universe. However, the fact remains that a man's problem is that everything for him is a mental event in his own mind. This includes the whole extent of the universe, and all the achievements of scientists and generals. The external world is man's inner world and his problem is to organize this inner world within his own mind.

Therefore the eternal problem of poetry—to express inner experiences in terms of outer things—remains, although the apparent unresponsiveness of outer things in the modern world makes this appear difficult. Man has learned, invented, and organized his modern world. It is an object of his awareness, inventiveness, and will. He is not an object of it. Therefore the machine and the spatial distances which appear to impose their vast-ness on him are the material of his own inner spiritual life. Within his mind they are symbols. Perhaps they are symbols of the apparent powerlessness of his inner life. But his sanity depends on his mastering within himself what he has discovered and invented in his outer world. He has power to imagine the inner mastery of his own situation. Modern poetry is an aspect of the struggle to restore the balance of our inner with our outer world.

In view of this, it is a peculiarity of American education that it makes a division of literature into "creative," "critical," and "reading" functions. Some students will tell you that they expect to learn to write creatively, others to criticize, and others to read. An extreme example of this oversimple approach was given to me by a student who told me that I could not expect her to be interested in any of the poets she read: because she wished to learn to write poetry, not to read it. This was exceptional, but three other students whom I taught were only really interested in those poets whom they considered useful to them in their own writing.

The creative writing classes in the United States must be considered a very interesting educational experiment, but their advantages must be weighed against several disadvantages. One disadvantage is that they tend to divide literary studies into creative and non-creative. If this means also that the student thinks of writing as being an activity which has little to do with reading, or which has the effect of limiting the writer's reading to that which helps him in his own creative work, here is a further disadvantage. For one only has to read the lives of writers to see that an avaricious habit of reading everything that comes his way is the atmosphere in which most writers have developed and lived.

25   There is certainly a good deal in the writing of poetry which can be taught. Readers of the prose passages in Dante's *Vita Nuova* will see that Dante considered himself a member of a school who were inventing and propagating a particular style of poetry. Baudelaire, Mallarmé, and several other poets have considered the teaching of poetry as a theoretical possibility. At the beginning of this century the imagists held views about the writing of poetry, such as that the poet must concentrate entirely on producing a perfectly clear image, and that this can be taught and learned.

Poetry is written in various forms, and there is no doubt that these can be taught, just as musical technique can be. The parallel with music exists in theory, but actually it does not quite work out in practice. Music is concerned with notes measured in time. A sequence of notes producing the same tune can be invented to produce a slow or fast effect simply by lengthening the duration of each note, or variations can be made by sustaining some notes and quickening others, within the rhythm. Thus a musician can take a tune and produce a great many variations on it without altering the original idea. However, poetry uses words and not notes. A poet cannot alter the speed and mood of an idea simply by adding syllables and emphatic pauses with the ease which is possible to the composer. Thus the idea which in poetry corresponds to tune can only be created in one set of words in which meaning is inseparable from the form in which it is expressed. A poet is not like a composer in search for freedom of expression which he can achieve among a great variety of forms: he is in search for the few forms which correspond most exactly to that which he wishes to say. When he has discovered those forms, he interests himself in no others, except insofar as he is feeling his way towards those which may further his later development. Form in poetry is inseparable from thought: and the only form which the poet needs is that in which he can think. Thus from Walt Whitman, down to T. S. Eliot, one can think of dozens of poets who know far less in general about poetic forms than is taught in the creative writing courses: they are masters of their own particular forms, and probably even avoid thinking in other ones, through an instinctive discipline.

A sonnet, for example, is a poetic form for thinking a thought which is a sonnet. If a poet had no potentiality for thinking in sonnets, to write them may actually confuse him and prevent him from attaining so soon the form which is uniquely his. The poet W. B. Yeats once told me that he had learned to write in an overliterary poetic tradition and that he had spent his life trying to write poems in a simpler manner. To a lesser talent, nothing might seem simpler than Yeats's problem. All he had to do was to leave out some rhymes and prune away his imagery, one might think. But the ornament, the over-poetic style had become his poetic thought, and when he struggled to express ideas which were too bare and harsh for this form, he had great difficulty in adapting his style to his later subject-matter.

Thus, to teach students to write in a variety of poetic techniques would be a doubtful benefit. What one can do, perhaps, is criticize their work, with a view to helping them to discover their own form, teach them to relate as widely as possible the poetry of others to what they themselves are trying to do, teach them to think concretely and with their senses, and develop in their minds a sense of purpose independent of the literary market and literary fashions.

Young writers often forget that a poem should be as well written as a letter or diary or any other piece of prose, that is to say, as well written, considered simply as writing, as they can possibly make it. Perhaps the most reasonable method of writing a poem is first of all to write down rapidly those impressions, that rhythm, that shape which makes it seem a poetic experience, without regard to other considerations. But the second or third stage of writing should certainly be to take out the "bad writing," that is to say, the redundancies, the bad grammar, the linguistic inversions, and write the sense of the poem as well and clearly as possible. A teacher can certainly be of help here, because a good deal of potentially good poetry is lost under sheer bad writing.

30   A poet discovers his own formal qualities through learning to analyze the qualities of his own sensibility. He must know whether, for example, his gifts are predominantly of the eye or the ear. The visual writer cannot afford to sacrifice his eye to his ear: a preoccupation with rules of rhyme and strict metre could disintegrate the concentration on the image which is necessary to develop his gift.

In relating his own work to that of other poets, the student has to learn to avoid two dangers which have destroyed many talents: on the one hand, the danger of being absorbed into a greater talent; on the other, the danger of shutting out the greater talent for fear of being absorbed. One has to learn to relate one's own work to that of others and to learn from this relation by using other work for purposes of criticizing one's own, or sometimes for interpreting the work of other poets in terms of one's own talent. The relation of Keats to Shakespeare, or, in our own time, of Eliot to Dante, is each a classic example of the power of a poet to interpret within his own sensibility the achievement of a past poet. Here it seems to me that the teacher should be of considerable help to the student. For example, I think it would be a good exercise for students to make free translations of poems in a foreign language, interpreting the particular significance for them of a poem which appeals to them into terms of their own technique and sensibility. They should seek in such free renderings, not for accuracy, but to create in their own language the general effect which appeals to them in the foreign poem.

Of course far and away the most important quality of a poet is his power of thinking sensuously in words. The test of sensuous thought is not the occasional striking image or well-sounding line, but the power as it were to *follow through* with the senses, just as in a game a player may have a perception of a whole sequence of moves following from one move, which affect him physically, as though he were at one moment feeling the muscular changes required by all these moves expanding through his blood and muscles. The power of the verbal eye to see the transformation from line to line of the image and sound in a poem: this is the central excitement of poetry, it is the real life, and everything else is fabrication. The teacher cannot of course teach sensuous energy: still less can he explain how this can clothe itself in vital words. But he can at least be an efficient guide; for it is in confused imagery, mixed metaphor, abstract expressions, that by far the greatest number of mistakes are made by poets. If he is able to see with intensity, even for the duration of a phrase or a line, there is the possibility of development. If he is able to understand the necessity of a certain consistency, a poetic logic in the development of imagery and sound, then he may well be capable of poetry.

Too often in schools of creative writing, the student's eye is directed towards the market of magazines and reviews. Perhaps it would be too idealistic to say that creative writing courses should be directed against rather than towards the standards of editorial offices; but at least it may be said that as far as possible independence from such standards should be taught. The period during a student's life when he is writing only for teachers and friends, is not only in itself one of liberty, but it should represent a freedom which he is able to value afterwards, and to which he should always return. In a sense a writer should always remain a student, should be writing only for himself and his friend. But if, when he is a student, he is already considered to be writing for publication, this standard is destroyed in his own mind. Therefore teachers should encourage students to indulge in that kind of writing which cannot be published: for example, the writing of journals and experiments, perhaps even of erotic and obscene poems. The habit of writing for the wastepaper basket is the most valuable one that a writer can acquire.

Despite the creative writing courses, teaching students to read poems seems more useful than teaching them to write them, for various reasons. Although the true readers of poetry are perhaps as rare as the poets themselves, the reading of poetry does lead to many other things. Poetry is, after all, a nerve center of the consciousness of a civilization, with responses to many of the important situations in that civilization. The reading of poetry within an education therefore justifies itself as a discipline of the humanities. Learning to write poetry is an interesting experiment and in some years' time a survey of the results of this education will be interesting. Perhaps it will be found that in place of the creative writing courses there should be a far greater emphasis on writing in all literary courses. It would seem that a very valuable development of the American experiment would be if the conception of written work in all English courses were extended considerably beyond the essay, to include poems and stories.

35   To sum up: the teacher of poetry has always to remember that he is not only a poet teaching poets or even a critic insisting on the purest and fullest appreciation. He is really filling several roles, of which these two are the easiest and perhaps not the most important, since writers and readers with a true vocation will probably find it without him.

His most important role is to teach poetry as a discipline of the imagination; a discipline which reveals the complexity of the experience of the individual human being isolated in time and place within the universe and experiencing everything at every moment of his life, as no one before or since has experienced or will ever experience it; which, when it has revealed this terrifying uniqueness and complexity, shows how the unique, which is also the universal form of experiencing, can be related through the understanding of poetry to the experiences of other men who have been able to express a similar sense of their isolation within time and space, at other times and other places; which shows that complexity and awareness only become creative when they can be disciplined within a formal pattern.

The student who is unable to attain complete appreciation can learn a great deal from the discipline of poetry. Modern poetry can teach above all that the poetic problem is the same, at all times, though it has to express itself in different forms; the same, because the problem of the poet is to relate his inner significant experiences to the outward world which impresses itself on him. The world of modern phenomena is as much a product of man's spiritual condition as the world in the past has been and the world in the future will be.

Comments and Questions

1. Spender, in his second paragraph, declares that "a poem *means* the sum of everything which it *is*. . . ." Then he breaks up this possible sum into how many parts?

Examine these parts and apply them to a poem that you like. (You may want to choose from the section on poetry.) After discussing the parts, have you yet said anything about the poetic *experience?* Do you think this experience is of such complex impact that it can be realized only intuitively?

2. In what way does this essay support the view that limited appreciation of poetry is better than none at all?

3. What do you understand by the word "escapism"? How has Spender forwarded his definition of poetry by denying that it is escapist? At one point Spender has implied that a poet's pessimism—Hardy's, for example—is not relevant to his poems as poems; elsewhere, he emphasizes the importance of a poet's sincerity. How does he reconcile these statements?

4. Comment on these significant passages:

> Poetry makes one realize that one is alone, and complex; and that to be alone is universal.

> Poetry . . . reveals the familiar as unfamiliar. . . . poetry remains the most instructive of the arts. . . .

> Form in poetry is inseparable from thought: and the only form which the poet needs is that in which he can think.

John Ciardi (1916–   )
Dialogue with the Audience

"I'm not exactly illiterate," says the Citizen. "I'm a pretty fair historian. I can read Freud—at least some of him—without being entirely in the dark. But I get nowhere with this modern poetry. I've given up trying."

The Poet has heard it all before, but the Citizen obviously wants to talk about it. The Poet, as a matter of fact, rather likes the Citizen. Maybe, the Poet thinks, if I can peg the talk to something specific it won't just ramble on aimlessly and forever. Aloud he says: "Just for the fun of it—who is the last particular poet you gave up on?"

"It was Wallace Stevens," says the Citizen. "I read your review of the *Collected Poems* and I shelled out $7.50 for it on your say-so." He reaches up to a shelf and hauls down the book. "Here it is," he says, tossing it on the table, "a big fat collection of unintelligibility."

"Sorry," says the Poet, "no refunds, if that's what you're getting at. But do me a favor: show me a specific poem that you take to be unintelligible."

5   The Citizen stares. "Do you mean to say you understand every poem in this book?"

The Poet shakes his head. "Far from it. I don't even understand White House news releases. But I like Stevens better."

"Without knowing what it is you like?"

"Let's keep the talk as specific as we can. I've asked you to cite a poem: turn around is fair play—find a poem called 'Asides on the Oboe.' Here, take this passage:

The obsolete fiction of the wide river in
An empty land; the gods that Boucher killed;
And the metal heroes that time granulates—
The philosophers' man alone still walks in dew,
Still by the sea-side mutters milky lines
Concerning an immaculate imagery.
If you say on the hautboy man is not enough,
Can never stand as god, is ever wrong
In the end, however naked, tall, there is still
The impossible possible philosophers' man,
The man who has had the time to think enough,
The central man, the human globe, responsive
As a mirror with a voice, the man of glass,
Who in a million diamonds sums us up."

"Let me get it straight," says the Citizen. "Is this an example of a passage you do understand, or of one you don't?"

"As a matter of fact, it's an example of both," says the Poet. "Suppose I were to say I found it elusive, yet clear—would that make any sense? I can't unravel it detail by detail. I encounter areas of obscurity in it. Yet the total force of the passage is both unmistakable and moving, and just beyond every momentary obscurity I keep emerging into areas of immediate clarity."

"No, in a word. It makes no sense to me."

"Well, what do you mean by sense? Stevens does not write for factual-information sense. Why should he? He picks up a theme and orchestrates it. His 'sense' is a structure. The reader must keep that total structure in mind in order to grasp Stevens's kind of sense. He does not, moreover, 'mean' any one thing, but rather all the possibilities of all the relationships he is orchestrating."

"Clear as Navy coffee," says the Citizen. "Am I supposed to swallow it?"

"You do in music," says the Poet, glancing at the Citizen's collection of recordings, "why not in poetry?"

"Because, among other things, words have meanings."

"They have," says the Poet, "but far more meanings than anyone thinks about in reading factual prose. A word is not a meaning but a complex of meanings consisting of all its possibilities: its ability to identify something, the image it releases in making that identification, its sound, its history, its association-in-context with the other words of the passage. Good poets use *more* of the word than most readers are used to."

"Yes," says the Citizen, who is proud of being a fair-minded person, "I suppose that *is* true."

"But not only is the individual word a complex. It is used in a phrase that is itself a complex of complexes. And the phrase is in turn used in the complex of the total poem's structure."

"So a poem is a complex of complexes of complexes," says the Citizen, half-indignant now. "I'm beginning to get a complex myself."

"No," says the Poet, "that's a complex you've always had. You are used to words basically as denotations in statements intended or purporting to intend to convey facts. You have the 'practicality complex' and your basic symptom is 'why doesn't he say it straight'?"

"Well, why doesn't he?"

"As a matter of fact he does at times—even in your terms. Take the line, 'The man

who has had the time to think enough.' How much 'straighter' could he make the phrase
of that line?"

"I can agree there," says the Citizen. "But what about 'milky lines'? Why does he
have to say it on 'the hautboy'? And what's all that about a mirror with a voice?"

"One at a time," says the Poet. "The 'milky lines' is one of those details I remain
unsure of. I suspect that Stevens was thinking of the seas as a kind of mother-of-life and
that he used 'milky' in that connection. If my guess is right that makes 'milky lines' mean
something like lines fed by the essential life fluid of all-mothering nature.' But that is only
a guess and I have no way of verifying it. In fact, some of what follows in the poem—not
in this passage—troubles my guess. That is one of the obscurities I feel in the passage.
One I feel and *welcome,* may I say.

25   "The hautboy, on the other hand, is a straightforward Stevens signature, a part of his
personal idiom, like his blue-guitar. The hautboy is the kind of detail that reveals itself
immediately as you get to know more about the way the poet writes. For the time being I
can only suggest that you take the hautboy to be one of the instruments of art. On that
instrument of artifice, Stevens must make the 'fiction' (always a special term in his writing)
that can replace the 'obsolete fiction' of the gods. In Stevens, the rituals of art constantly
take the place of the rituals of religion—themselves richly obscure.

    "As for the 'mirror with voice,'—there I have to charge you with petulant misread-
ing. Stevens has established the context of his statement clearly enough for any willing
reader, and it is no reading at all to ignore the context. What he is saying is roughly 'that
it is *as if* the responsive man were a mirror with a voice reflecting all of us in a heightened
way, *as if* summing us up in the million-diamond-reflection of his artifice.' I am satisfied
that the gist of it is about that, though I confess I am uncertain about it later when the
poem becomes unmistakably Leibnizian. At that later point, I conclude I don't know Leib-
niz well enough to guess out Stevens's sense of him. I am left puzzled. But I am also left
considerably richer. Certainly, I should be willing to read a much longer and much more
obscure poem than this if only to meet that man 'who has had the time to think enough.'
I want him in my mind."

    "Yes," says the Citizen, "I can go along with some of that. Even with most of it. But
why must he be so elusive about it?"

    The Poet smiles. "We're back to the business of 'saying it straight' again. I suggest,
first, that the thought itself is elusive. And, second, that it's a kind of thinking you're not
used to, partly because you have not read enough Stevens to catch the flavor of his thinking, and partly because you're not really a reader of poetry and never have been."

    The Citizen draws himself up. "Now I don't know about that," he says. "I took quite
a lot of English courses in school and . . ."

30   "And you haven't read as many as three books of new poems a year since then."

    "Well," says the Citizen more slowly, "I guess you have me there. Maybe if I were a
more practised reader I'd see more. But isn't some of it the poets' fault? Why do they make
it so hard for a man to read them? I'm no genius, but I'm reasonably intelligent."

    "And rational," suggests the Poet.

    "Certainly. What's wrong with rationality?"

    "Ask yourself that question as you read through an issue of the *Reader's Digest*
sometime," says the Poet. "Or let me ask you how rationally you got married? Or by what
sequence of syllogisms you begot your children? Or what Certified Public Accountant
writes the scripts of your dreamlife?"

35   The Poet is talking fast now, warming to his most fundamental sermon. "We all
contain elements of rationality, but we're all much more than those elements. A poet thinks
with his senses, his nerve endings, his whole body. He looks at his thought physically, and

he looks from many directions at once. He *feels* what he thinks, and he feels it most in the act of making a poetic structure of it. Just as a composer feels himself into his musical structure. There is no auditing of rationalities in that process; there is, rather, the accomplishment into form of some part of a whole life."

The Citizen is being fair-minded again. "I can't grasp entirely your way of putting things," he says after a while, "but I can get a glimpse of what I think you're saying— especially when I try to feel it in terms of what a composer does inside his music." He rubs his jaw. "I don't know. There are too many ideas in it that are new to me. I suppose if you say so . . ."

"The last time you started supposing on my say-so it cost you $7.50," says the Poet. "Suppose me nothing on my say-so: I refuse to be trusted by any man who can trust himself, and I doubly refuse to be trusted by a man who can't trust himself. Make up your own mind on the basis of what makes sense in itself."

"That's just the trouble," says the Citizen. "You make it sound sensible enough, but then I turn to a poem and I just can't get my hooks into it."

"That's just what I started to ask you in the beginning. There's the book: give me a for-instance."

40   "I remember one queer thing called 'Bantams in Pine-Woods,'" says the Citizen, thumbing the pages. "I swear I spent a day trying to make sense of the first two lines. Here they are."

> Chieftain Iffucan of Azcan in caftan
> Of tan with henna hackles, halt!

"What's the problem?" says the Poet.

"No problem," says the Citizen. "Just gibberish. What the devil is all this henna-hackled Iffucan of Azcan trashcan stuff?"

"Ah!" says the Poet, "I see. To tell you the truth I hadn't ever thought of those lines as a difficulty: they're having such fun with themselves—all those lovely exaggerated sound-sequences and that big spoofing tone."

"Is all that—whatever it is—enough excuse for writing nonsense-syllables?"

45   "Ask Lewis Carroll," says the Poet. "But the fact is they're not nonsense syllables. Note the title. A bantam may certainly be taken as a pretentious and pompous bird strutting around in his half-pint ego as if he owned the world, and refusing to be dwarfed even by pine woods . . ."

"I'm still lost in the Azcan ashcan. And at this point I've had enough of your symbol-threading."

"But the Azcan business is a fact from the world," says the Poet. "Have you ever looked into a pedigree book? I assume this to be a purebred bantam and that he is registered as Chieftain Iffucan of Azcan. Stevens begins by reporting the fact, obviously relishing its pretentiousness. 'Caftan' is his first 'poetic' addition. But note this: a caftan is a garment that hangs down just about the way the leg-feathers of a bantam do. The detail is physically right. And the sound of the word itself is exactly right for the sound-sequence Stevens builds. That's always a sign of the poet—the ability to do more than one thing at once and to have his choices come out equally right on all levels."

The Citizen sits thoughtfully, turning it over in his mind. The Poet, watching the Citizen, once more has the impression of a painful fair-mindedness at work. Somehow that sense depresses him. He has a vision of the Citizen laboring to be open-minded and forever lost to the real life of the poem.

"I have to conclude that you're right," says the Citizen. "But I also know I could never have seen it that way. And I still don't understand the poem."

50   "Nor do I, completely," confesses the Poet. "But what of it? I don't understand 'Kubla Khan' nor 'Tiger, Tiger.' Not in detail. But I can certainly experience them as poems. I can, to put it metaphorically, identify their emotional frequencies and the areas into which they transmit."

     The Citizen is not satisfied. "I'm still thinking of this Iffucan of Azcan business. There I bogged down on a detail I did not recognize. And perhaps I'll never be any better at identifying odd details. But what about the poem that comes right after it? This one 'Anecdote of the Jar.' Now there is a poem I spent a lot of time on and although I understand every word and every sentence, I'm blessed if I know what Stevens is talking about." He reads it over:

> I placed a jar in Tennessee,
> And round it was, upon a hill.
> It made the slovenly wilderness
> Surround that hill.
>
> The wilderness rose up to it,
> And sprawled around, no longer wild.
> The jar was round upon the ground
> And tall and of a port in air.
>
> It took dominion everywhere.
> The jar was gray and bare.
> It did not give of bird or bush,
> Like nothing else in Tennessee.

     The Citizen finishes reading and looks up. "I was bothered at first by 'port,'" he says, "but I checked the word in the dictionary and I think I see what he's doing with it. But how am I supposed to understand 'It made the slovenly wilderness surround that hill'? How can a jar make a wilderness surround a hill? The wilderness was already surrounding the hill, and long before Stevens and his jar came along."

     "In a sense, yes," says the Poet, "but only in the most usual prose-sense. Poetry constantly makes over that usual sense of things. The jar is a made-form; as such it stands for all artifice. The wilderness is nature as-it-happens, the opposite of made-form. But to 'surround' is 'to take position around a center.' And what is formless has no center. It is human artifice, the assertion of human artifice, that puts a center to the wilderness. Because the wilderness is formless it still 'sprawls' but now it sprawls 'up to' the jar. It approaches form, that is, and therefore it 'is no longer wild.'"

     "Wait a minute," says the Citizen, "aren't you the one who is doing the paraphrasing now?"

55   "Yes, surely. I have no quarrel with paraphrase: only with paraphrase as a substitute for the poem. I am not trying to say 'this is what the poem comes to.' Far from it. I am trying to point out the symbolic areas in which the poem moves. The two poles of Stevens's thought seem clearly enough to be 'artifice' and 'formless nature.' Why shouldn't those poles be identified? But the poles are not the poem. The poem is much better seen as those poles plus the force-field they create."

     "That does it!" says the Citizen and slams the book shut. "Symbolic areas, force fields, artifice versus formless-nature—what is all this jargon? Didn't you write once that a poem is an emotion or nothing?"

     "I certainly did."

     "Then tell me how on earth I am supposed to get an emotion from this sort of haywire theorizing?"

The Poet smiles sadly. "I'm about ready to grant you that all criticism is in fact haywire, but would you grant me that criticism is not the poem? At that, one can still rig a weather-vane out of haywire, and that vane can point to the weather. The poem is not the vane, nor is it the haywire from which the vane is improvised: the poem is the weather that is pointed-to.

60 "Stevens, as it happens, had very strong feelings about form versus the formless. Those feelings crowd all his poems. They are fundamental to his very sense of reality. His emotions, to be sure, are intellectual things. If you refuse to think a sense of esthetic-reality as opposed to some other more common ideas of reality is worth an emotion, you are breaking no law but Stevens is obviously not for you. And that, I find myself thinking, is your loss rather than his."

"Maybe so," says the Citizen, but now he is sitting up as if squared for battle. "I'll even say he is obviously not for me. Who *is* he for? I'm the one who brought up Stevens, and I'll grant he may be a special case. But Stevens is not the only one who is obviously not for me. Who *are* you modern poets for? Is there no such thing as an audience?"

This charge, too, is a familiar one to the Poet. "You've fired a lot of questions," he says, "and a full answer would call for a long sermon. Let me try the short form.

"What is the idea of 'the audience'? Is it enough to argue 'I have bought this book of poems and therefore I have certain audience-rights'? I think, first, one must distinguish between two ideas of 'the audience.'

"One idea may be called the horizontal audience and the other the vertical audience. The horizontal audience consists of everybody who is alive at this moment. The vertical audience consists of everyone, vertically through time, who will ever read a given poem.

65 "Isn't it immediately obvious that Stevens can only 'be for' a tiny percentage of the horizontal audience? Even Frost, who is the most seemingly-clear and the most widely loved of our good poets, certainly does not reach more than a small percentage of the total population, or even of that part of the population that thinks of itself as literate—as at least literate enough to buy a best-seller. The fact is that no horizontal audience since the age of folk-poetry has been much interested in good poetry. And you may be sure that a few spokesmen sounding off in the name of that horizontal audience are not going to persuade the poets.

"All good poets write for the vertical audience. The vertical audience for Dante, for example, is now six centuries old. And it is growing. If the human race has any luck at all, part of Dante's audience is still thousands of years short of being born.

"Now try a flight of fancy. Imagine that you held an election tomorrow and asked the horizontal audience to vote for Dante as opposed to Eddie Guest. Guest would certainly swamp Dante in such an election. More people in the horizontal audience have read Guest and even, God save the mark, been moved by him—if only to their own inanition. But moved, nevertheless. And we're a democracy, aren't we? The majority rules: bless the majority?

"Not in art. Not horizontally at least. The verdict in art is vertical. Take the idea of majority vote a step further. Imagine that you held the same election on Judgment Day, calling for a total vote of the human race down through time. Can you fail to believe that Dante would then swamp Eddie Guest plus all the horizontalists from Robert Service to Carl Sandburg?

"The point is that the horizontal audience always outnumbers the vertical at any one moment, but that the vertical audience for good poetry always outnumbers the horizontal in time-enough. And not only for the greatest poets. Andrew Marvell is certainly a minor poet, but given time enough, more people certainly will have read 'To His Coy Mistress' than will ever have subscribed to *Time, Life,* and *Fortune.* Compared to what a good poem can do, Luce is a piker at getting circulation."

70   "Impressive, if true," says the Citizen, "but how does any given poet get his divine sense of this vertical audience?"

"By his own ideal projection of his own best sense of himself. It's as simple as that," says the Poet. "He may be wrong, but he has nothing else to go by. And there is one thing more: all good poets are difficult when their work is new. And their work always becomes less difficult as their total shape becomes more and more visible. As that shape impresses itself upon time, one begins to know how to relate the parts to their total. Even Keats and Shelley confounded their contemporary critics as 'too difficult' and 'not for me.' "

The Citizen throws his hands up. "All right, all right: I've been out-talked. But who *does* write for me?"

The Poet spread his hands palms out. "Keats and Shelley—now that they have lost their first difficulty."

"And are dead enough?" says the Citizen. "Well, may be. But why is it so impossible for *you* to think about writing for me? I'm willing to give it a try."

75   The Poet shrugs. "The sort of try you gave Stevens? But no matter. The point is why *should* I write for you?—you're going to be dead the next time anyone looks. We all are for that matter. But not the poem. Not if it's made right. If I make it for you I have to take the chance that it will die with you. I'm not sure you're that good an investment. Besides which, I have to invest in myself. If we happen to share some of the same sense of poetry, it may work out that I do happen to write for you. But that would be a happy bonus at best. I still cannot think of you as a main investment—not till you show a better 'vertical-sense.' "

"We who are about to die," says the Citizen, "salute the poems we cannot grasp. Is that it?"

"Like nothing else in Tennessee," says the Poet bowing.

Comments and Questions

In "Preliminaries" in the poetry section (p. 299), we have stated that understanding is basic to one's enjoyment of a poem—or of any work of art. We have suggested that readers are wise to fix in their minds the literal statement of a poem as a necessary basis for realizing or comprehending all the poem has to offer. We have insisted that a poem is a whole and that a part should never be taken for the whole. If these things be true, it follows that areas of obscurity make it impossible to be sure—or even reasonably sure—what a poem is. Frustration results and frustration is uncomfortable.

1. How does Mr. Ciardi view this matter of alleged obscurity in modern poetry? He mentions "momentary obscurity" and "areas of immediate clarity." He seems pleased to be able to explain certain lines and also pleased when he cannot. Of the phrase "milky lines," he is "unsure" but says he welcomes such uncertainty. A bit later he says, "I am left puzzled. But I am left considerably richer." Does Mr. Ciardi make clear where this enrichment comes from? Discuss.

2. What does the phrase "personal idiom" mean?

3. Would you say Mr. Ciardi is trying to make the point that there are poets and that everybody else is not-a-poet? Discuss.

4. Explain the distinction made between the *horizontal* and the *vertical audience.* Comment on this use of words. For what the author intends, could these terms be reversed? Discuss the statement: "All good poets write for the vertical audience." List some "good poets" and try to determine what seems to have been their attitude towards the horizontal audience. You may wish to consider Shakespeare, Pope, Byron, Tennyson, Browning, Frost, T. S. Eliot, among many others.

5. Mr. Ciardi's Poet: "The point is why *should* I write for you [the Citizen]?" Perhaps you will wish to answer this question.

6. Make a careful comparison of Spender's "On Teaching Modern Poetry," p. 1096 and this essay of Ciardi's.

Joseph Wood Krutch   (1893–1970)
The Tragic Fallacy

. . . Tragedy, said Aristotle, is the "imitation of noble actions," and though it is some twenty-five hundred years since the dictum was uttered there is only one respect in which we are inclined to modify it. To us "imitation" seems a rather naïve word to apply to that process by which observation is turned into art, and we seek one which would define or at least imply the nature of that interposition of the personality of the artist between the object and the beholder which constitutes his function and by means of which he transmits a modified version, rather than a mere imitation, of the thing which he has contemplated.

In the search for this word the aestheticians of romanticism invented the term "expression" to describe the artistic purpose to which apparent imitation was subservient. Psychologists, on the other hand, feeling that the artistic process was primarily one by which reality is modified in such a way as to render it more acceptable to the desires of the artist, employed various terms in the effort to describe that distortion which the wish may produce in vision. And though many of the newer critics reject both romanticism and psychology, even they insist upon the fundamental fact that in art we are concerned, not with mere imitation but with the imposition of some form upon the material which it would not have if it were merely copied as a camera copies.

Tragedy is not, then, as Aristotle said, the *imitation* of noble actions, for, indeed, no one knows what a *noble* action is or whether or not such a thing as nobility exists in nature apart from the mind of man. Certainly the action of Achilles in dragging the dead body of Hector around the walls of Troy and under the eyes of Andromache, who had begged to be allowed to give it decent burial, is not to us a noble action, though it was such to Homer, who made it the subject of a noble passage in a noble poem. Certainly, too, the same action might conceivably be made the subject of a tragedy and the subject of a farce, depending upon the way in which it was treated; so that to say that tragedy is the *imitation* of a *noble* action is to be guilty of assuming, first, that art and photography are the same and, second, that there may be something inherently noble in an act as distinguished from the motives which prompted it or from the point of view from which it is regarded.

And yet, nevertheless, the idea of nobility is inseparable from the idea of tragedy, which cannot exist without it. If tragedy is not the imitation or even the modified representation of noble actions it is certainly a representation of actions *considered* as noble, and herein lies its essential nature, since no man can conceive it unless he is capable of believing in the greatness and importance of man. Its action is usually, if not always, calamitous, because it is only in calamity that the human spirit has the opportunity to reveal itself triumphant over the outward universe which fails to conquer it; but this calamity in tragedy is only a means to an end and the essential thing which distinguishes real tragedy from those distressing modern works sometimes called by its name is the fact that it is in the former alone that the artist has found himself capable of considering and of making us consider that his people and his actions have that amplitude and importance which make them noble. Tragedy arises then when, as in Periclean Greece or Elizabethan England, a people fully aware of the calamities of life is nevertheless serenely confident of the greatness of man, whose mighty passions and supreme fortitude are revealed when one of these calamities overtakes him.

5   To those who mistakenly think of it as something gloomy or depressing, who are incapable of recognizing the elation which its celebration of human greatness inspires, and who, therefore, confuse it with things merely miserable or pathetic, it must be a paradox that the happiest, most vigorous, and most confident ages which the world has ever known—the Periclean and the Elizabethan—should be exactly those which created and which most relished the mightiest tragedies; but the paradox is, of course, resolved by the fact that tragedy is essentially an expression, not of despair, but of the triumph over despair and of confidence in the value of human life. If Shakespeare himself ever had that "dark period" which his critics and biographers have imagined for him, it was at least no darkness like that bleak and arid despair which sometimes settles over modern spirits. In the midst of it he created both the elemental grandeur of Othello and the pensive majesty of Hamlet and, holding them up to his contemporaries, he said in the words of his own Miranda, "Oh, rare new world that hath *such* creatures in it."

All works of art which deserve their name have a happy end. This is indeed the thing which constitutes them art and through which they perform their function. Whatever the character of the events, fortunate or unfortunate, which they recount, they so mold or arrange or interpret them that we accept gladly the conclusion which they reach and would not have it otherwise. They may conduct us into the realm of pure fancy where wish and fact are identical and the world is remade exactly after the fashion of the heart's desire or they may yield some greater or less allegiance to fact; but they must always reconcile us in one way or another to the representation which they make and the distinctions between the genres are simply the distinctions between the means by which this reconciliation is effected.

Comedy laughs the minor mishaps of its characters away; drama solves all the difficulties which it allows to arise; and melodrama, separating good from evil by simple lines, distributes its rewards and punishments in accordance with the principles of a naïve justice which satisfies the simple souls of its audience, which are neither philosophical enough to question its primitive ethics nor critical enough to object to the way in which its neat events violate the laws of probability. Tragedy, the greatest and the most difficult of the arts, can adopt none of these methods; and yet it must reach its own happy end in its own way. Though its conclusion must be, by its premise, outwardly calamitous, though it must speak to those who know that the good man is cut off and that the fairest things arc the first to perish, yet it must leave them, as *Othello* does, content that this is so. We must be and we are glad that Juliet dies and glad that Lear is turned out into the storm.

Milton set out, he said, to justify the ways of God to man, and his phrase, if it be interpreted broadly enough, may be taken as describing the function of all art, which must, in some way or other, make the life which it seems to represent satisfactory to those who see its reflection in the magic mirror, and it must gratify or at least reconcile the desires of the beholder, not necessarily, as the naïver exponents of Freudian psychology maintain, by gratifying individual and often eccentric wishes, but at least by satisfying the universally human desire to find in the world some justice, some meaning, or, at the very least, some recognizable order. Hence it is that every real tragedy, however tremendous it may be, is an affirmation of faith in life, a declaration that even if God is not in his Heaven, then at least Man is in his world.

We accept gladly the outward defeats which it describes for the sake of the inward victories which it reveals. Juliet died, but not before she had shown how great and resplendent a thing love could be; Othello plunged the dagger into his own breast, but not before he had revealed that greatness of soul which makes his death seem unimportant. Had he died in the instant when he struck the blow, had he perished still believing that the world was as completely black as he saw it before the innocence of Desdemona was revealed to him, then, for him at least, the world would have been merely damnable, but Shakespeare kept him alive long enough to allow him to learn his error and hence to die, not in despair, but in the full acceptance of the tragic reconciliation to life. Perhaps it would be pleasanter if men could believe what the child is taught—that the good are happy and that things turn out as they should—but it is far more important to be able to believe, as Shakespeare did, that however much things in the outward world may go awry, man has, nevertheless, spendors of his own and that, in a word, Love and Honor and Glory are not words but realities.

10   Thus for the great ages tragedy is not an expression of despair but the means by which they saved themselves from it. It is a profession of faith, and a sort of religion; a way of looking at life by virtue of which it is robbed of its pain. The sturdy soul of the tragic author seizes upon suffering and uses it only as a means by which joy may be wrung out of existence, but it is not to be forgotten that he is enabled to do so only because of his belief in the greatness of human nature and because, though he has lost the child's faith in life, he has not lost his far more important faith in human nature. A tragic writer does not have to believe in God, but he must believe in man.

And if, then, the Tragic Spirit is in reality the product of a religious faith in which, sometimes at least, faith in the greatness of God is replaced by faith in the greatness of man, it serves, of course, to perform the function of religion, to make life tolerable for those who participate in its beneficent illusion. It purges the souls of those who might otherwise despair and it makes endurable the realization that the events of the outward world do not correspond with the desires of the heart, and thus, in its own particular way, it does what all religions do, for it gives a rationality, a meaning, and a justification to the universe. But if it has the strength it has also the weakness of all faiths, since it may—nay, it must—be ultimately lost as reality, encroaching further and further into the realm of imagination, leaving less and less room in which the imagination can build its refuge.

It is, indeed, only at a certain stage in the development of the realistic intelligence of a people that the tragic faith can exist. A naïver people may have, as the ancient men of the north had, a body of legends which are essentially tragic, or it may have only (and need only) its happy and childlike mythology which arrives inevitably at its happy end, where the only ones who suffer "deserve" to do so and in which, therefore, life is represented as directly and easily acceptable. A too sophisticated society on the other hand— one which, like ours, has outgrown not merely the simple optimism of the child but also that vigorous, one might almost say adolescent, faith in the nobility of man which marks a Sophocles or a Shakespeare—has neither fairy tales to assure it that all is always right in the end nor tragedies to make it believe that it rises superior in soul to the outward calamities which befall it.

Distrusting its thought, despising its passions, realizing its impotent unimportance in the universe, it can tell itself no stories except those which make it still more acutely aware of its trivial miseries. When its heroes (sad misnomer for the pitiful creatures who people contemporary fiction) are struck down it is not, like Oedipus, by the gods that they are struck but only, like Oswald Alving, by syphilis, for they know that the gods, even if they existed, would not trouble with them, and they cannot attribute to themselves in art an importance in which they do not believe. Their so-called tragedies do not and cannot end with one of those splendid calamities which in Shakespeare seem to reverberate through the universe, because they cannot believe that the universe trembles when their love is, like Romeo's, cut off or when the place where they (small as they are) have gathered up their trivial treasure is, like Othello's sanctuary, defiled. Instead, mean misery piles on mean misery, petty misfortune follows petty misfortune, and despair becomes intolerable because it is no longer even significant or important.

Ibsen once made one of his characters say that he did not read much because he found reading "irrelevant," and the adjective was brilliantly chosen because it held implications even beyond those of which Ibsen was consciously aware. What is it that made the classics irrelevant to him and to us? Is it not just exactly those to him impossible premises which make tragedy what it is, those assumptions that the soul of man is great, that the universe (together with whatever gods may be) concerns itself with him and that he is, in a word, noble? Ibsen turned to village politics for exactly the same reason that his contemporaries and his successors have, each in his own way, sought out some aspect of the common man and his common life—because, that is to say, here was at least something small enough for him to be able to believe.

15 Bearing this fact in mind, let us compare a modern "tragedy" with one of the great works of a happy age, not in order to judge of their relative technical merits but in order to determine to what extent the former deserves its name by achieving a tragic solution capable of purging the soul or of reconciling the emotions to the life which it pictures. And in order to make the comparison as fruitful as possible let us choose *Hamlet* on the one hand and on the other a play like *Ghosts* which was not only written by perhaps the most powerful as well as the most typical of modern writers but which is, in addition, the one of his works which seems most nearly to escape that triviality which cannot be entirely escaped by anyone who feels, as all contemporary minds do, that man is relatively trivial.

In *Hamlet* a prince ("in understanding, how like a god!") has thrust upon him from the unseen world a duty to redress a wrong which concerns not merely him, his mother, and his uncle, but the moral order of the universe. Erasing all trivial fond records from his mind, abandoning at once both his studies and his romance because it has been his good fortune to be called upon to take part in an action of cosmic importance, he plunges (at first) not into action but into thought, weighing the claims which are made upon him and contemplating the grandiose complexities of the universe. And when the time comes at last for him to die he dies, not as a failure, but as a success. Not only has the universe regained the balance which had been upset by what *seemed* the monstrous crime of the guilty pair ("there is nothing either good nor ill but thinking makes it so"), but in the process by which that readjustment is made a mighty mind has been given the opportunity, first to contemplate the magnificent scheme of which it is a part and then to demonstrate the greatness of its spirit by playing a rôle in the grand style which it called for. We do not need to despair in *such* a world if it has *such* creatures in it.

Turn now to *Ghosts*—look upon this picture and upon that. A young man has inherited syphilis from his father. Struck by a to him mysterious malady he returns to his northern village, learns the hopeless truth about himself, and persuades his mother to poison him. The incidents prove, perhaps, that pastors should not endeavor to keep a husband and wife together unless they know what they are doing. But what a world is this in which a great writer can deduce nothing more than that from his greatest work and how are we to be purged or reconciled when we see it acted? Not only is the failure utter, but it is trivial and meaningless as well.

Yet the journey from Elsinore to Skien is precisely the journey which the human spirit has made, exchanging in the process princes for invalids and gods for disease. We say, as Ibsen would say, that the problems of Oswald Alving are more "relevant" to our life than the problems of Hamlet, that the play in which he appears is more "real" than the other more glamorous one, but it is exactly because we find it so that we are condemned. We can believe in Oswald but we cannot believe in Hamlet, and a light has gone out in the universe. Shakespeare justifies the ways of God to man, but in Ibsen there is no such happy end and with him tragedy, so called, has become merely an expression of our despair at finding that such justification is no longer possible.

Modern critics have sometimes been puzzled to account for the fact that the concern of ancient tragedy is almost exclusively with kings and courts. They have been tempted to accuse even Aristotle of a certain naïveté in assuming (as he seems to assume) that the "nobility" of which he speaks as necessary to a tragedy implies a nobility of rank as well as of soul, and they have sometimes regretted that Shakespeare did not devote himself more than he did to the serious consideration of those common woes of the common man which subsequent writers have exploited with increasing pertinacity. Yet the tendency to lay the scene of a tragedy at the court of a king is not the result of any arbitrary convention but of the fact that the tragic writers believed easily in greatness just as we believe easily in meanness. To Shakespeare, robes and crowns and jewels are the garments most appropriate to man because they are the fitting outward manifestation of his inward majesty, but to us they seem absurd because the man who bears them has, in our estimation, so pitifully shrunk. We do not write about kings because we do not believe that any man is worthy to be one and we do not write about courts because hovels seem to us to be dwellings more appropriate to the creatures who inhabit them. Any modern attempt to dress characters in robes ends only by making us aware of a comic incongruity and any modern attempt to furnish them with a language resplendent like Shakespeare's ends only in bombast.

20   True tragedy capable of performing its function and of purging the soul by reconciling man to his woes can exist only by virtue of a certain pathetic fallacy far more inclusive than that to which the name is commonly given. The romantics, feeble descendants of the tragic writers to whom they are linked by their effort to see life and nature in grandiose terms, loved to imagine that the sea or the sky had a way of according itself with their moods, of storming when they stormed and smiling when they smiled. But the tragic spirit sustains itself by an assumption much more far-reaching and no more justified. Man as it sees him lives in a world which he may not dominate but which is always aware of him. Occupying the exact center of a universe which would have no meaning except for him and being so little below the angels that, if he believes in God, he has no hesitation in imagining Him formed as he is formed and crowned with a crown like that which he or one of his fellows wears, he assumes that each of his acts reverberates through the universe. His passions are important to him because he believes them important throughout all time and all space; the very fact that he can sin (no modern can) means that this universe is watching his acts; and though he may perish, a God leans out from infinity to strike him down. And it is exactly because an Ibsen cannot think of man in any such terms as these that his persons have so shrunk and that his "tragedy" has lost that power which real tragedy always has of making that infinitely ambitious creature called man content to accept his misery if only he can be made to feel great enough and important enough. An Oswald is not a Hamlet chiefly because he has lost that tie with the natural and supernat-

ural world which the latter had. No ghost will leave the other world to warn or encourage him, there is no virtue and no vice which he can possibly have which can be really important, and when he dies neither his death nor the manner of it will be, outside the circle of two or three people as unnecessary as himself, any more important than that of a rat behind the arras.

Perhaps we may dub the illusion upon which the tragic spirit is nourished the Tragic, as opposed to the Pathetic, Fallacy, but fallacy though it is, upon its existence depends not merely the writing of tragedy but the existence of that religious feeling of which tragedy is an expression and by means of which a people aware of the dissonances of life manages nevertheless to hear them as harmony. Without it neither man nor his passions can seem great enough or important enough to justify the sufferings which they entail, and literature, expressing the mood of a people, begins to despair where once it had exulted. Like the belief in love and like most of the other mighty illusions by means of which human life has been given a value, the Tragic Fallacy depends ultimately upon the assumption which man so readily makes that something outside his own being, some "spirit not himself"—be it God, Nature, or that still vaguer thing called a Moral Order—joins him in the emphasis which he places upon this or that and confirms him in his feeling that his passions and his opinions are important. When his instinctive faith in that correspondence between the outer and the inner world fades, his grasp upon the faith that sustained him fades also, and Love or Tragedy or what not ceases to be the reality which it was because he is never strong enough in his own insignificant self to stand alone in a universe which snubs him with its indifference.

In both the modern and the ancient worlds tragedy was dead long before writers were aware of the fact. Seneca wrote his frigid melodramas under the impression that he was following in the footsteps of Sophocles, and Dryden probably thought that his *All for Love* was an improvement upon Shakespeare, but in time we awoke to the fact that no amount of rhetorical bombast could conceal the fact that grandeur was not to be counterfeited when the belief in its possibility was dead, and turning from the hero to the common man we inaugurated the era of realism. For us no choice remains except that between mere rhetoric and the frank consideration of our fellow men, who may be the highest of the anthropoids but who are certainly too far below the angels to imagine either that these angels can concern themselves with them or that they can catch any glimpse of even the soles of angelic feet. We can no longer tell tales of the fall of noble men because we do not believe that noble men exist. The best that we can achieve is pathos and the most that we can do is to feel sorry for ourselves. Man has put off his royal robes and it is only in sceptered pomp that tragedy can come sweeping by.

Nietzsche was the last of the great philosophers to attempt a tragic justification of life. His central and famous dogma—"Life is good *because* it is painful"—sums up in a few words the desperate and almost meaningless paradox to which he was driven in his effort to reduce to rational terms the far more imaginative conception which is everywhere present but everywhere unanalyzed in a Sophocles or a Shakespeare and by means of which they rise triumphant over the manifold miseries of life. But the very fact that Nietzsche could not even attempt to state in any except intellectual terms an attitude which is primarily unintellectual and to which, indeed, intellectual analysis is inevitably fatal is proof of the distance which he had been carried (by the rationalizing tendencies of the human mind) from the possibility of the tragic solution which he sought; and the confused, half-insane violence of his work will reveal, by the contrast which it affords with the serenity of the tragic writers whom he admired, how great was his failure.

Fundamentally this failure was, moreover, conditioned by exactly the same thing which has conditioned the failure of all modern attempts to achieve what he attempted—by the fact, that is to say, that tragedy must have a hero if it is not to be merely an accusation against, instead of a justification of, the world in which it occurs. Tragedy is, as Aristotle said, an imitation of noble actions, and Nietzsche, for all his enthusiasm for the Greek tragic writers, was palsied by the universally modern incapacity to conceive man as noble. Out of this dilemma, out of his need to find a hero who could give to life as he saw it the only possible justification, was born the idea of the Superman, but the Superman is, after all, only a hypothetical being, destined to become what man actually was in the eyes of the great tragic writers—a creature (as Hamlet said) "how infinite in capacities, in understanding how like a god." Thus Nietzsche lived half in the past through his literary enthusiasms and half in the future through his grandiose dreams, but for all his professed determination to justify existence he was not more able than the rest of us to find the present acceptable. Life, he said in effect, is not a Tragedy now but perhaps it will be when the Ape-man has been transformed into a hero (the *Übermensch*), and trying to find that sufficient, he went mad.

25   He failed, as all moderns must fail when they attempt, like him, to embrace the tragic spirit as a religious faith, because the resurgence of that faith is not an intellectual but a vital phenomenon, something not achieved by taking thought but born, on the contrary, out of an instinctive confidence in life which is nearer to the animal's unquestioning allegiance to the scheme of nature than it is to that critical intelligence characteristic of a fully developed humanism. And like other faiths it is not to be recaptured merely by reaching an intellectual conviction that it would be desirable to do so.

Modern psychology has discovered (or at least strongly emphasized) the fact that under certain conditions desire produces belief, and having discovered also that the more primitive a given mentality the more completely are its opinions determined by its wishes, modern psychology has concluded that the best mind is that which most resists the tendency to believe a thing simply because it would be pleasant or advantageous to do so. But justified as this conclusion may be from the intellectual point of view, it fails to take into account the fact that in a universe as badly adapted as this one to human as distinguished from animal needs, this ability to will a belief may bestow an enormous vital advantage as it did, for instance, in the case at present under discussion where it made possible for Shakespeare the compensations of a tragic faith completely inaccessible to Nietzsche. Pure intelligence, incapable of being influenced by desire and therefore also incapable of choosing one opinion rather than another simply because the one chosen is the more fruitful or beneficent, is doubtless a relatively perfect instrument for the pursuit of truth, but the question (likely, it would seem, to be answered in the negative) is simply whether or not the spirit of man can endure the literal and inhuman truth.

Certain ages and simple people have conceived of the action which passes upon the stage of the universe as of something in the nature of a Divine Comedy, as something, that is to say, which will reach its end with the words "and they lived happily ever after." Others, less naïve and therefore more aware of those maladjustments whose reality, at least so far as outward events are concerned, they could not escape, have imposed upon it another artistic form and called it a Divine Tragedy, accepting its catastrophe as we accept the catastrophe of an *Othello,* because of its grandeur. But a Tragedy, Divine or otherwise, must, it may again be repeated, have a hero, and from the universe as we see it both the Glory of God and the Glory of Man have departed. Our cosmos may be farcical or it may be pathetic but it has not the dignity of tragedy and we cannot accept it as such.

Yet our need for the consolations of tragedy has not passed with the passing of our ability to conceive it. Indeed, the dissonances which it was tragedy's function to resolve grow more insistent instead of diminishing. Our passions, our disappointments, and our sufferings remain important to us though important to nothing else and they thrust themselves upon us with an urgency which makes it impossible for us to dismiss them as the mere trivialities which, so our intellects tell us, they are. And yet, in the absence of tragic faith or the possibility of achieving it, we have no way in which we may succeed in giving them the dignity which would not only render them tolerable but transform them as they were transformed by the great ages into joys. The death of tragedy is, like the death of love, one of those emotional fatalities as the result of which the human as distinguished from the natural world grows more and more a desert.

Poetry, said Santayana in his famous phrase, is "religion which is no longer believed," but it depends, nevertheless, upon its power to revive in us a sort of temporary or provisional credence and the nearer it can come to producing an illusion of belief the greater is its power as poetry. Once the Tragic Spirit was a living faith and out of it tragedies were written. Today these great expressions of a great faith have declined, not merely into poetry, but into a kind of poetry whose premises are so far from any we can really accept that we can only partially and dimly grasp its meaning.

30   We read but we do not write tragedies. The tragic solution of the problem of existence, the reconciliation to life by means of the tragic spirit is, that is to say, now only a fiction surviving in art. When that art itself has become, as it probably will, completely meaningless, when we have ceased not only to write but to *read* tragic works, then it will be lost and in all real senses forgotten, since the devolution from Religion to Art to Document will be complete.

Comments and Questions

Krutch's essay examines, in the light of twentieth-century shabbiness of spirit, Aristotle's definition of tragedy as "the imitation of noble actions." "The Tragic Fallacy" was written before the theater of the absurd came into being and is both an explication of traditional dramatic values and an accounting for the modern neglect of those values. The essay may be profitably read in conjunction with Martin Esslin's "The Absurdity of the Absurd," next, because the human spiritual incapability, pinpointed by Krutch, may be seen to have reached its logical conclusion: the meaningless absurd.

1. If one recalls *Antigone* (p. 606) and *Hamlet* (p. 626), it is obvious that Sophocles and Shakespeare believed in the greatness and importance of human beings. What of Ibsen, the playwright Krutch attacks? What does the author of *Ghosts* (p. 740) believe about humanity?

2. Consider the falling away of confidence in the worth of humankind by examining this sequence of characters: Hamlet (p. 626), Oswald Alving (*Ghosts,* p. 740), the townspeople of Güllen (*The Visit,* p. 845), and Caligula (*Caligula,* p. 894).

3. What may be made of the statement that "no modern man can" sin? Why not? Discuss.

4. At what point does Krutch make clear what he means by the *tragic fallacy?* Does the author contend that we are, in fact, worthy of tragedy or simply that we are lost without this illusion?

5. Comment on the final statement of this essay: "the devolution from Religion to Art to Document will be complete."

6. See "Comments and Questions" following Kronenberger's "Some Prefatory Words on Comedy" (p. 1126) for a comparison of the two essays. After reading Kronenberger's essay, discuss the relationship of tragedy and comedy. How do the two modes of drama differ, for example, in their basic assumptions about such matters as flaws of character, justice and retribution, the individual versus society?

Martin Esslin   (1918–   )
The Absurdity of the Absurd

In every art form today the effect of a dissonant world is manifest, but in no form so palpably as in drama. With Ibsen, drama first became realistic; then with his successors the settings against which ordinary people exposed their ordinary problems became ultrarealistic. As Krutch has observed, society, as interpreted by many twentieth-century playwrights, is disillusioned, "distrusting its thought, despising its passions, realizing its impotent unimportance in the universe" and accepts, as a consequence, "no stories except those which make it more acutely aware of its trivial miseries." (See "The Tragic Fallacy," p. 1112.)

Since Krutch made the foregoing observation, triviality has become absurdity. Martin Esslin in the following essay gives a perceptive account of the movement.

On November 19, 1957, a group of worried actors were preparing to face their audience. The actors were members of the company of the San Francisco Actors' Workshop. The audience consisted of fourteen hundred convicts at the San Quentin penitentiary. No live play had been performed at San Quentin since Sarah Bernhardt appeared there in 1913. Now, forty-four years later, the play that had been chosen, largely because no woman appeared in it, was Samuel Beckett's *Waiting for Godot*.

No wonder the actors and Herbert Blau, the director, were apprehensive. How were they to face one of the toughest audiences in the world with a highly obscure, intellectual play that had produced near riots among a good many highly sophisticated audiences in Western Europe? Herbert Blau decided to prepare the San Quentin audience for what was to come. He stepped onto the stage and addressed the packed, darkened North Dining Hall—a sea of flickering matches that the convicts tossed over their shoulders after lighting their cigarettes. Blau compared the play to a piece of jazz music "to which one must listen for whatever one may find in it." In the same way, he hoped, there would be some meaning, some personal significance for each member of the audience in *Waiting for Godot*.

The curtain parted. The play began. And what had bewildered the sophisticated audiences of Paris, London, and New York was immediately grasped by an audience of convicts. As the writer of "Memos of a First-Nighter" put it in the columns of the prison paper, the *San Quentin News:*

> The trio of muscle-men, biceps overflowing, . . . parked all 642 lbs on the aisle and waited for the girls and funny stuff. When this didn't appear they audibly fumed and audibly decided to wait until the house lights dimmed before escaping. They made one error. They listened and looked two minutes too long—and stayed. Left at the end. All shook . . .

Or as the writer of the lead story of the same paper reported, under the headline, "San Francisco Group Leaves S.Q. Audience Waiting for Godot":

> From the moment Robin Wagner's thoughtful and limbolike set was dressed with light, until the last futile and expectant handclasp was hesitantly activated between the two searching vagrants, the San Francisco company had its audience of captives in its collective hand. . . . Those that had felt a less controversial vehicle should be attempted as a first play here had their fears allayed a short five minutes after the Samuel Beckett piece began to unfold.

A reporter from the San Francisco *Chronicle* who was present noted that the convicts did not find it difficult to understand the play. One prisoner told him, "Godot is society." Said another: "He's the outside." A teacher at the prison was quoted as saying, "They know what is meant by waiting . . . and they knew if Godot finally came, he would only be a disappointment." The leading article of the prison paper showed how clearly the writer had understood the meaning of the play:

> It was an expression, symbolic in order to avoid all personal error, by an author who expected each member of his audience to draw his own conclusions, make his own errors. It asked nothing in point, it forced no dramatized moral on the viewer, it held out no specific hope. . . . We're still waiting for Godot, and shall continue to wait. When the scenery gets too drab and the action too slow, we'll call each other names and swear to part forever—but then, there's no place to go!

It is said that Godot himself, as well as turns of phrase and characters from the play, have since become a permanent part of the private language, the institutional mythology of San Quentin.

5   Why did a play of the supposedly esoteric avant-garde make so immediate and so deep an impact on an audience of convicts? Because it confronted them with a situation in some ways analogous to their own? Perhaps. Or perhaps because they were unsophisticated enough to come to the theatre without any preconceived notions and ready-made expectations, so that they avoided the mistake that trapped so many established critics who condemned the play for its lack of plot, development, characterization, suspense, or plain common sense. Certainly the prisoners of San Quentin could not be suspected of the sin of intellectual snobbery, for which a sizable proportion of the audiences of *Waiting for Godot* have often been reproached; of pretending to like a play they did not even begin to understand, just to appear in the know.

The reception of *Waiting for Godot* at San Quentin, and the wide acclaim plays by Ionesco, Adamov, Pinter, and others have received, testify that these plays, which are so often superciliously dismissed as nonsense or mystification, *have* something to say and *can* be understood. Most of the incomprehension with which plays of this type are still being received by critics and theatrical reviewers, most of the bewilderment they have caused and to which they still give rise, come from the fact that they are part of a new, and still developing stage convention that has not yet been generally understood and has hardly ever been defined. Inevitably, plays written in this new convention will, when judged by the standards and criteria of another, be regarded as impertinent and outrageous impostures. If a good play must have a cleverly constructed story, these have no story or plot to speak of; if a good play is judged by subtlety of characterization and motivation, these are often without recognizable characters and present the audience with almost mechanical puppets; if a good play has to have a fully explained theme, which is neatly exposed and finally solved, these often have neither a beginning nor an end; if a good play is to hold the mirror up to nature and portray the manners and mannerisms of the age in finely observed sketches, these seem often to be reflections of dreams and nightmares; if a good play relies on witty repartee and pointed dialogue, these often consist of incoherent babblings.

But the plays we are concerned with here pursue ends quite different from those of the conventional play and therefore use quite different methods. They can be judged only by the standards of the Theatre of the Absurd, which it is the purpose of this book to define and clarify.

It must be stressed, however, that the dramatists whose work is here presented and discussed under the generic heading of the Theatre of the Absurd do not form part of any self-proclaimed or self-conscious school or movement. On the contrary, each of the writers in question is an individual who regards himself as a lone outsider, cut off and isolated in his private world. Each has his own personal approach to both subject matter and form; his own roots, sources, and background. If they also, very clearly and in spite of themselves, have a good deal in common, it is because their work most sensitively mirrors and reflects the preoccupations and anxieties, the emotions and thinking of an important segment of their contemporaries in the Western world.

This is not to say that their works are representative of mass attitudes. It is an oversimplification to assume that any age presents a homogeneous pattern. Ours being, more than most others, an age of transition, it displays a bewilderingly stratified picture: medieval beliefs still held and overlaid by eighteenth-century rationalism and mid-nineteenth-century Marxism, rocked by sudden volcanic eruptions of prehistoric fanaticisms and primitive tribal cults. Each of these components of the cultural pattern of the age finds its characteristic artistic expression. The Theatre of the Absurd, however, can be seen as the reflection of what seems the attitude most genuinely representative of our own time's contribution.

10   The hallmark of this attitude is its sense that the certitudes and unshakable basic assumptions of former ages have been swept away, that they have been tested and found wanting, that they have been discredited as cheap and somewhat childish illusions. The decline of religious faith was masked until the end of the Second World War by the substitute religions of faith in progress, nationalism, and various totalitarian fallacies. All this was shattered by the war. By 1942, Albert Camus was calmly putting the question why, since life had lost all meaning, man should not seek escape in suicide. In one of the great, seminal heart-searchings of our time, *The Myth of Sisyphus,* Camus tried to diagnose the human situation in a world of shattered beliefs:

> A world that can be explained by reasoning, however faulty, is a familiar world. But in a universe that is suddenly deprived of illusions and of light, man feels a stranger. His is an irremediable exile, because he is deprived of memories of a lost homeland as much as he lacks the hope of a promised land to come. This divorce between man and his life, the actor and his setting, truly constitutes the feeling of Absurdity.

"Absurd" originally means "out of harmony," in a musical context. Hence its dictionary definition: "out of harmony with reason or propriety; incongruous, unreasonable, illogical." In common usage in the English-speaking world, "absurd" may simply mean "ridiculous." But this is not the sense in which Camus uses the word, and in which it is used when we speak of the Theatre of the Absurd. In an essay on Kafka, Ionesco defined his understanding of the term as follows: "Absurd is that which is devoid of purpose. . . . Cut off from his religious, metaphysical, and transcendental roots, man is lost; all his actions become senseless, absurd, useless."

This sense of metaphysical anguish at the absurdity of the human condition is, broadly speaking, the theme of the plays of Beckett, Adamov, Ionesco, Genet, and the other writers discussed in this book. But it is not merely the subject matter that defines what is here called the Theatre of the Absurd. A similar sense of the senselessness of life, of the inevitable devaluation of ideals, purity, and purpose, is also the theme of much of the work of dramatists like Giraudoux, Anouilh, Salacrou, Sartre, and Camus himself. Yet these writers differ from the dramatists of the Absurd in an important respect: They present their sense of the irrationality of the human condition in the form of highly lucid and logically constructed reasoning, while the Theatre of the Absurd strives to express its sense of the senselessness of the human condition and the inadequacy of the rational approach by the open abandonment of rational devices and discursive thought. While Sartre or Camus express the new content in the old convention, the Theatre of the Absurd goes a step further in trying to achieve a unity between its basic assumptions and the form in which these are expressed. In some senses, the *theatre* of Sartre and Camus is less adequate as an expression of the *philosophy* of Sartre and Camus—in artistic, as distinct from philosophic, terms—than the Theatre of the Absurd.

If Camus argues that in our disillusioned age the world has ceased to make sense, he does so in the elegantly rationalistic and discursive style of an eighteenth-century moralist, in well-constructed and polished plays. If Sartre argues that existence comes before essence and that human personality can be reduced to pure potentiality and the freedom to choose itself anew at any moment, he presents his ideas in plays based on brilliantly drawn characters who remain wholly consistent and thus reflect the old convention that each human being has a core of immutable, unchanging essence—in fact, an immortal soul. And the beautiful phrasing and argumentative brilliance of both Sartre and Camus in their relentless probing still, by implication, proclaim a tacit conviction that logical discourse can offer valid solutions, that the analysis of language will lead to the uncovering of basic concepts—Platonic ideas.

This is an inner contradiction that the dramatists of the Absurd are trying, by instinct and intuition rather than by conscious effort, to overcome and resolve. The Theatre of the Absurd has renounced arguing *about* the absurdity of the human condition; it merely *presents* it in being—that is, in terms of concrete stage images of the absurdity of existence. This is the difference between the approach of the philosopher and that of the poet; the difference, to take an example from another sphere, between the *idea* of God in the works of Thomas Aquinas or Spinoza and the *intuition* of God in those of St. John of the Cross or Meister Eckhart—the difference between theory and experience.

15   It is this striving for an integration between the subject matter and the form in which it is expressed that separates the Theatre of the Absurd from the Existentialist theatre.

The Theatre of the Absurd must also be distinguished from another important, and parallel, trend in the contemporary French theatre, which is equally preoccupied with the absurdity and uncertainty of the 'human condition: the "poetic avant-garde" theatre of dramatists like Michel de Ghelderode, Jacques Audiberti, Georges Neveux, and, in the younger generation, Georges Schehadé, Henri Pichette, and Jean Vauthier, to name only some of its most important exponents. This is an even more difficult dividing line to draw, for the two approaches overlap a good deal. The "poetic avant-garde" relies on fantasy and dream reality as much as the Theatre of the Absurd does; it also disregards such traditional axioms as that of the basic unity and consistency of each character or the need for a plot. Yet basically the "poetic avant-garde" represents a different mood; it is more lyrical, and far less violent and grotesque. Even more important is its different attitude toward language: the "poetic avant-garde" relies to a far greater extent on consciously "poetic" speech; it aspires to plays that are in effect poems, images composed of a rich web of verbal associations.

The Theatre of the Absurd, on the other hand, tends toward a radical devaluation of language, toward a poetry that is to emerge from the concrete and objectified images of the stage itself. The element of language still plays an important, yet subordinate, part in this conception, but what *happens* on the stage transcends, and often contradicts, the *words* spoken by the characters. In Ionesco's *The Chairs,* for example, the poetic content of a powerfully poetic play does not lie in the banal words that are uttered but in the fact that they are spoken to an ever-growing number of empty chairs.

The Theatre of the Absurd is thus part of the "anti-literary" movement of our time, which has found its expression in abstract painting, with its rejection of "literary" elements in pictures; or in the "new novel" in France, with its reliance on the description of objects and its rejection of empathy and anthropomorphism. It is no coincidence that, like all these movements and so many of the efforts to create new forms of expression in all the arts, the Theatre of the Absurd should be centered in Paris.

This does not mean that the Theatre of the Absurd is essentially French. It is broadly based on ancient strands of the Western tradition and has its exponents in Britain, Spain, Italy, Germany, Switzerland, and the United States as well as in France. Moreover, its leading practitoners who live in Paris and write in French are not themselves Frenchmen.

As a powerhouse of the modern movement, Paris is an international rather than a merely French center: it acts as a magnet attracting artists of all nationalities who are in search of freedom to work and to live nonconformist lives unhampered by the need to look over their shoulder to see whether their neighbors are shocked. That is the secret of Paris as the capital of the world's individualists: here, in a world of cafés and small hotels, it is possible to live easily and unmolested.

20   That is why a cosmopolitan of uncertain origin like Apollinaire; Spaniards like Picasso or Juan Gris; Russians like Kandinsky and Chagall; Rumanians like Tzara and Brancusi; Americans like Gertrude Stein, Hemingway, and E. E. Cummings; an Irishman like Joyce; and many others from the four corners of the world could come together in Paris and shape the modern movement in the arts and literature. The Theatre of the Absurd springs from the same tradition and is nourished from the same roots: An Irishman, Samuel Beckett; a Rumanian, Eugène Ionesco; a Russian of Armenian origin, Arthur Adamov, not only found in Paris the atmosphere that allowed them to experiment in freedom, they also found there the opportunities to get their work produced in theatres.

The standards of staging and production in the smaller theatres of Paris are often criticized as slapdash and perfunctory; that may indeed sometimes be the case; yet the fact remains that there is no other place in the world where so many first-rate men of the theatre can be found who are adventurous and intelligent enough to champion the experimental work of new playwrights and to help them acquire a mastery of stage technique— from Lugné-Poë, Copeau, and Dullin to Jean-Louis Barrault, Jean Vilar, Roger Blin, Nicolas Bataille, Jacques Mauclair, Sylvain Dhomme, Jean-Marie Serreau, and a host of others whose names are indissolubly linked with the rise of much that is best in the contemporary theatre.

Equally important, Paris also has a highly intelligent theatregoing public, which is receptive, thoughtful, and as able as it is eager to absorb new ideas. Which does not mean that the first productions of some of the more startling manifestations of the Theatre of the Absurd did not provoke hostile demonstrations or, at first, play to empty houses. What matters is that these scandals were the expression of passionate concern and interest, and that even the emptiest houses contained enthusiasts articulate enough to proclaim loudly and effectively the merits of the original experiments they had witnessed.

Yet in spite of these favorable circumstances, inherent in the fertile cultural climate of Paris, the success of the Theatre of the Absurd, achieved within a short span of time, remains one of the most astonishing aspects of this astonishing phenomenon of our age. That plays so strange and puzzling, so clearly devoid of the traditional attractions of the well-made drama, should within less than a decade have reached the stages of the world from Finland to Japan, from Norway to the Argentine, and that they should have stimulated a large body of work in a similar convention, are in themselves powerful and entirely empirical tests of the importance of the Theatre of the Absurd.

The study of this phenomenon as literature, as stage technique, and as a manifestation of the thinking of its age must proceed from the examination of the works themselves. Only then can they be seen as part of an old tradition that may at times have been submerged but one that can be traced back to antiquity, and only after the movement of today has been placed within its historical context can an attempt be made to assess its significance and to establish its importance and the part it has to play within the pattern of contemporary thought.

25   A public conditioned to an accepted convention tends to receive the impact of artistic experiences through a filter of critical standards, of predetermined expectations and terms of reference, which is the natural result of the schooling of its taste and faculty of perception. This framework of values, admirably efficient in itself, produces only bewildering results when it is faced with a completely new and revolutionary convention—a tug of war ensues between impressions that have undoubtedly been received and critical preconceptions that clearly exclude the possibility that any such impressions could have been felt. Hence the storms of frustration and indignation always caused by works in a new convention.

It is the purpose of this book to provide a framework of reference that will show the works of the Theatre of the Absurd within their own convention so that their relevance and force can emerge as clearly to the reader as *Waiting for Godot* did to the convicts of San Quentin.

Comments and Questions

1. If the absurdists, "very clearly and in spite of themselves, have a good deal in common, it is because their work most sensitively mirrors and reflects the preoccupations and anxieties, the emotions and thinking of an important segment of their contemporaries in the Western world." Compare this statement with the quotation from Krutch in the forenote to Esslin's essay.

2. Although Albert Camus argues that the world has ceased to make sense, Esslin states that works by Camus such as *Caligula* (p. 894) do not belong, strictly speaking, to the theater of the absurd. Why not? What distinction does Esslin draw between the *philosophy* of absurdity and the *theater* of absurdity? Does Duerrenmatt's *The Visit* (p. 845) qualify as an absurdist play according to Esslin's definition? Why or why not?

3. Esslin observes that absurdist plays are "anti-literary," really antidrama. Is there a paradox in this comment? Try to resolve it.

Louis Kronenberger (1904–1980)
Some Prefatory Words on Comedy

Comedy is not just a happy as opposed to an unhappy ending, but a way of surveying life so that happy endings must prevail. But it is not to be confused, on that account, with optimism, any more than a happy ending is to be confused with happiness. Comedy is much more reasonably associated with pessimism—with at any rate a belief in the small-ness that survives as against the greatness that is scarred or destroyed. In mortal affairs it is tragedy, like forgiveness, that seems divine; and comedy, like error, that is human. . . .

Comedy appeals to the laughter, which is in part at least the malice, in us; for com-edy is concerned with human imperfection, with people's failure to measure up either to the world's or to their own conception of excellence. All tragedy is idealistic and says in effect, "The pity of it"—that owing to this fault of circumstance or that flaw of character, a man who is essentially good does evil, a man who is essentially great is toppled from the heights. But all comedy tends to be skeptical and says in effect, "The absurdity of it"—that in spite of his fine talk or noble resolutions, a man is the mere creature of pettiness and vanity and folly. Tragedy is always lamenting the Achilles tendon, the destructive flaw in man; but comedy, in a sense, is always looking for it. Not cheaply, out of malevolence or cynicism; but rather because even at his greatest, man offers some touch of the fatuous and small, just as a murderer, even at his cleverest, usually makes some fatal slip. In tragedy men aspire to more than they can achieve; in comedy, they pretend to more.

The difference, again, between the two is the very question of difference. A great tragic hero—an Oedipus or Lear—strikes us as tremendously far removed from common humanity. But comedy, stripping off the war-paint and the feathers, the college degrees or the military medals, shows how very like at bottom the hero is to everybody else. Tragedy cannot flourish without giving its characters a kind of aura of poetry, or idealism, or doom; comedy scarcely functions till the aura has been dispelled. And as it thrives on a revelation of the true rather than the trumped-up motive, as it is in one way sustained by imposture, so in another it is sustained by incongruity. Here is the celebrated philosopher cursing the universe because he has mislaid a book. Here are all those who, like King Canute, would bid the clock go backward or the waves stand still. Here is not only the cheat, but the victim who but for his own dishonest desires could never be cheated.

Comedy, in brief, is criticism. If through laughing at others we purge ourselves of certain spiteful and ungenerous instincts—as through tragedy we achieve a higher and more publicized catharsis—that is not quite the whole of it. Comedy need not be hostile to idealism; it need only show how far human beings fall short of the ideal. The higher comedy mounts, the airier and more brilliant its forms, the more are we aware of man's capacity for being foolish or self-deluded or complacent; in the very highest comedy, such as the finale of Mozart's *Marriage of Figaro,* we are in a very paradise of self-deceptions and misunderstandings and cross-purposes. At the heart of high comedy there is always a strain of melancholy, as round the edges there is all gaiety and ebullience and glitter; and Schiller was perhaps right in regarding high comedy as the greatest of all literary forms.

5   Comedy is criticism, then, because it exposes human beings for what they are in contrast to what they profess to be. How much idealism, it asks, shall we find entirely free from self-love? How much beneficence is born of guilt, how much affection is produced by flattery? At its most severe, doubtless, comedy is not just skeptical but cynical; and asks many of the same questions, returning many of the same answers, as that prince—or at

any rate duke—of cynics, La Rochefoucauld. "Pride," La Rochefoucauld remarked, "does not wish to owe, and vanity does not wish to pay." Or again: "To establish oneself in the world, one does all one can to seem established there." Of these and many similar maxims, a play or story might easily be written; from each much cold and worldly comedy, or harsh and worldly farce, might be contrived. But comedy need not be so harsh, and seldom is: though it can be harsher still, can be—as in Ben Johnson—gloating and sardonic. But always it is the enemy, not of virtue or idealism, but of hypocrisy and pretense; and what it does in literature is very much, I suppose, what experience does for most of us in life: it knocks the bloom off the peach, the gilt off the gingerbread.

But though the comic spirit is, in Meredith's phrase, "humanely malign," it is also kindly and even companionable, in the sense that it brings men together as fellow-fools and sinners, and is not only criticism but understanding. Comedy is always jarring us with the evidence that we are no better than other people, and always comforting us with the knowledge that most other people are no better than we are. It makes us more critical but it leaves us more tolerant; and to that extent it performs a very notable social function. Its whole character, indeed—quite aside from that point—is rather social than individual.

The social basis rests in the very subject-matter of comedy—in all that has to do with one's life as part of a group; with one's wish to charm or persuade or deceive or dazzle others. Thus no exhibitionist can exist in solitude, no hypocrite or poseur can work without an audience. There are indeed so many social situations that engender comedy that many of them are notably hackneyed. There are all kinds of classic family jokes—the mother-in-law joke preëminently; but equally the rich-uncle theme, or the country cousin, or the visiting relative who forgets to leave, or the one that proffers advice, or the one that prophesies disaster. Right in the home there is the precocious brat or the moping adolescent; there are countless varieties of comic servants; and there is finally the question, though it perhaps belongs in a different category, of who heads the family—the husband or the wife.

The idea of husband and wife more likely belongs with the social aspects of sex, with the War Between the Sexes as it is fought out in the drawing room. As a purely sexual conflict, this war would not be social; but by the same token it would not be comedy. The question whether man really makes the decisions—including the decision to marry—or is merely permitted to think he does, is, whatever the answer, thoroughly social in nature. Or there is the business of how men and women perform in society for one another's benefit: being the fearless protector or the clinging vine, the woman who always understands or the man who is never understood. We have social comedy again when we pit one nationality as well as one sex against another, when the American puritan is ensnared by a continental siren, or when the suitor is German and humorless, and the besought one is French and amused. There is still another social aspect when we add a third person to the situation, a mistress as well as a wife, or a lover as well as a husband; or—for the situation need not be illicit, it need only be triangular—when the wife's old beau or the husband's old flame reappears on the scene. Or there is the man who does not know which of two sisters, or two heiresses, or two widows to marry; or the girl which of a half dozen suitors.

Comedy, indeed, must gain admittance into any part of the world—including prisons and sickrooms and funerals—where people are thrown together. Any institution involving hierarchies and rivalries—for example, a university—is a perfect hotbed of it. There will be everybody's relation to the President or the President's wife; or the President's relation to the President's wife; or to his trustees; all the struggles for precedence and the problems of protocol; the progressives on the faculty and the die-hards; the wives who can't help looking dowdy, the wives who suppose they look chic. For obviously any institution, whether a college or a department store, an artist colony or a country club, provides a cross-section of social types and traits, and brings us face to face with a hundred things out of which comedy is distilled: ambition and pride, arrogance and obsequiousness; a too-slavish following or a too-emphatic flouting of convention; all the stratagems men use in order to outwit or get their way.

10   And of course comedy becomes purely social in that best known and perhaps best liked of all its higher forms—the comedy of manners. Here we have hardly less than a picture of society itself; here the men and women are but parts of a general whole, and what survives—if we have it from the past—is likely to be known as the Restoration Scene, or Regency London, or Victorian Family Life. Here the drawing room is not merely the setting of the play or novel, but the subject and even the hero; here enter all the prejudices, the traditions, the taboos, the aspirations, the absurdities, the snobberies, of a group. The group, to constitute itself one, must partake of a common background and accept a similar view of life: though there will usually exist some outsider, some rebel, some nonconformist who, as the case may be, is ringing the doorbell or shattering the window panes; trying desperately to get in or desperately to get out; bending the knee or thumbing his nose. Or the comedy of manners will contrast one social milieu with another—the urban and the rustic, the capital and the provinces, Philistia and Bohemia, America and Europe. And in the comedy of manners, ignorance of good form has much the same value that, in straight drama, ignorance of some vital fact has.

And with ignorance of one kind or another we begin coming close to the very mainspring of comedy, or at any rate of comedy in action. For most comedy is born of ignorance or false knowledge; is based on misunderstanding. (Obviously not knowing the truth—though here one might add "until it is too late"—applies to much tragedy also.) At the level of ordinary farce or romantic comedy, the lovers are estranged until a quarter of eleven because the young man misunderstood why the young lady was walking with Sir Robert in the garden. At a higher level, it will not be mere circumstance or coincidence, but qualities of character that block the way. Envy proves an obstruction, or arrogance; or a too-great tendency to be suspicious or to take offense. In *Pride and Prejudice* the very title makes this clear. In Jane Austen's finest novel, *Emma,* there is every variety of misunderstanding, but the greatest misunderstanding of all, and the one that leads to so many of the others, is Emma's concerning her own nature. Emma—so high-handed and so wrongheaded, so often reasonable and so seldom right—is herself a wonderfully modulated comic character. And what matters is not so much the realistic consequences of her mistakes as the assured and benevolent air with which she commits them. And now moving higher still, to Meredith's *The Egoist,* we see self-deluded character constituting, really, the whole book. Sir Willoughby Patterne is the supreme example of self-centeredness in literature—the man who, in his absorption with the creature he is and the role he plays and the impression he makes, can care about nobody else. He tramples on the emotions and even the liberties of all who come his way, only cherishing such people so far as they cherish or pay homage to him. He is stunned by what seems to him *their* selfishness when, appalled by his, they walk out or turn away. And as we watch Meredith's great demonstration of human egoism, as we see with what comic flourishes and farcical leaps and wild extravagant motions it proceeds—as we smile and even laugh—we become increasingly uncomfortable. The more monstrous Sir Willoughby seems, the more we realize that in some sense this man is ourselves. If no one ever misunderstood his own nature worse, no one has ever pointed a moral better. Comedy at its greatest is criticism indeed; is nothing less, in fact, than a form of moral enlightenment.

The Egoist is sometimes declared to be comedy in name only, to be at bottom tragic. I would myself disagree—Meredith carries his theme to so extreme a length as to transform his hero from a man into a sort of sublime caricature, and gives him a purely comic intensity, an intensity quite disproportionate to what it is intense about. If just this is the "tragedy" of most human beings, it must yet serve to expose rather than exalt them; otherwise what shall we call genuine tragedy when we encounter it? Malvolio in *Twelfth Night,* who has also been looked upon as tragic, comes somewhat closer to being so. For pretension with him does partake a little of aspiration; his vanity, moreover, is stung because he is a servant, and stimulated by the mischievousness of others. But Malvolio, like Sir Willoughby, is really too trivial for tragedy, as he is also too priggish. What happens to him seems painful rather than tragic; it is not quite our modern idea of fun.

And this brings up the point that though Comedy has its permanent subject-matter and even its body of laws, it is liable, like everything else, to changes in fashion and taste, to differences of sensibility. One generation's pleasure is the next generation's embarrassment: much that the Victorians shuddered at merely makes us laugh, much that they laughed at might well make us shudder. One always reacts—and quite fortunately—from the vantage-point of one's own age; and it is probably a mistake, and certainly a waste of breath, to be arrogant or snobbish or moral about what amuses or does not amuse one: we may fancy we are less callous than our grandfathers and only be less callous about different things. The cuckold was clearly, in Restoration comedy, a figure to hoot at. Simply for being cuckolded we do not today find a man so comic, or even comic at all: though the moment we add an extra element to his role, such as his elation over cuckolding others, he becomes a comic figure for us. To what extent sex itself is a comic theme must naturally vary with the morality of a particular age: there are times when it seems shocking for a man ever to have a mistress; there are times when it seems even more shocking for a man never to have one. Right in the same age, what is considered virtue by the parson may be termed repression by the psychiatrist; and in such an age, which is usually one of moral transition, we may well find conflicting comedy values. The pendulum-swing of taste always makes it hard for people to know what they really like: if they are in revolt against gentility, they are likely to confuse what is funny with what is merely bold or obscene; if they are converts to gentility, they will be too much outraged by the indecent to inquire whether it is funny. There is nothing at which the Comic Spirit must smile more than our fickle and inconstant notions as to what constitutes comedy. We need not always look back to Shakespeare's drearier clowns as an instance of how tastes change: sometimes we need only attend a revival of what convulsed us ten years before.

Comments and Questions

In "The Tragic Fallacy" (p. 1112), Joseph Wood Krutch attempts to counter the assumption that tragedy is something gloomy or depressing. He argues, on the contrary, that tragedy is essentially an expression of the triumph over despair; that it has, in its own terms, a happy ending. In a similar manner, Kronenberger here opposes the assumption that comedy is *merely* a happy ending. Comedy, he finds, is more closely associated with pessimism than with optimism. In looking at the two essays together, we might almost feel that tragedy and comedy, at least as they are commonly perceived, have switched places. A comparison of the two essays may, in fact, force us to reexamine our perceptions of tragedy and comedy and aid us in making some fundamental distinctions between them.

1. Would Kronenberger agree with Krutch's statement that "comedy laughs the minor mishaps of its characters away"? Does that appear to trivialize comedy, which Kronenberger argues is "concerned with human imperfections, with people's failure to measure up either to the world's or to their own conception of excellence"?

2. Kronenberger states that tragedy is idealistic; comedy, skeptical. How might that distinction be illustrated in a comparison of such works as *Antigone* or *Hamlet* on the one hand and *The Physician in Spite of Himself* or *The Sunshine Boys* on the other?

3. In what sense is comedy "criticism," as Kronenberger suggests? Why is comedy harsher than tragedy in its critique of human nature?

4. Why does the basis of comedy rest so firmly on "one's life as part of a group"?

5. Kronenberger points out that comedy is notoriously subject to changes in fashion and taste. What amuses one generation may leave the next one cold. Is tragedy subject to the same shift in sensibility? Is it more difficult for a modern audience to appreciate another generation's comedy than to respond to its tragedy? Are there further implications in comedy's susceptibility to social change? Does tragedy transcend manners and social fashion in a way that comedy cannot?

H. B. Charlton   (1890–1961)
Hamlet

Ostensibly the plot of *Hamlet* is simple. A son is called upon to kill his father's murderer. The son was wellnigh the perfect pattern of manhood, rich in the qualities which make for excellence in the full life of one who in himself is scholar, soldier and courtier. The murdered father, moreover, was dearly loved, one of so much worthiness that the earth seldom has produced his like. The murderer was not only wicked with the common wickedness of murderers; the man he murdered was his brother, and he took to himself not only the murdered man's crown but also his widow. The situation appears even extravagantly simple. The moment the son hears of the murder, he resolves that with "wings as swift as meditation, or the thoughts of love" he will sweep to his revenge. There appears to be no reason on earth why he should not, and could not, do it in the next moment. Yet the whole stuff of the play is that he did not and could not do so. He fails until in the end by an unpremeditated stroke, he kills his uncle by his own last human act. Why then did he fail? What is the inevitability of his doom?

He fails because he is himself, Hamlet, and because the particular circumstance which he is called upon to encounter proves itself to be precisely of the sort which a man such as he cannot surmount. It is obvious that even in this statement of the situation there are elements belonging to the mysteries of life which the drama leaves in their own inscrutable darkness. Why, for instance, was Hamlet the sort of man he was, and why did he chance to be born with such an uncle and in times so very much out of joint? These are questions for all who seek a complete metaphysic; but they are neither raised nor answered in the play: they are *data,* even as in the *Iphigenia* of Euripides certain preliminary acceptances of given conditions are, in the view of Aristotle, to be fully approved: "the fact that the oracle for some reason ordered him [her brother] to go there, is outside the general plan of the play; the purpose, again, of his coming is outside the action proper."[1] Shakespeare takes it for granted as his starting-point that Hamlet is the sort of man he is,

[1] *Poetics* XVII. 3.

and that he was born to such circumstances as those in which we see him move. Round that smaller orb which engrosses Shakespeare's dramatic genius, his poetic imagination throws the sense of more ultimate mysteries, the speculative possibilities undreamed of by philosophy, and the vast dubieties of "thoughts which wander through eternity." But for his human purpose, the play is the thing: and the play is a revelation of how Hamlet, being the man he is, founders on the circumstances which he is called upon to face.

What, then, is there in Hamlet's nature to bring about this disaster? Why does he not kill his uncle forthwith? Teased by the problem, men have propounded many solutions, all of them abstractly possible, and many of them partly warranted by some trait or another in Hamlet's character. Let us look at some of these suggestions.

First of them: Hamlet is clearly a man of fine moral susceptibilities, so exquisite in his sense of right that questions such as that of chastity, and even of the purity of second marriage, touch him profoundly. He is disgusted wellnigh to frenzy by the thought of impurity. Hence, it is held, he was bound to find killing, though the killing of a villain, an immoral deed: still more, he was bound to find the act of killing a loathsome experience from which his sensitiveness would recoil. But though these are qualities commonly associated with to-day's men of fine moral fibre, they are not in themselves, not even now, a necessary adjunct of high morality; how, otherwise, would our war-heroes be fitted into a high moral system? Moreover, the association of these qualities with fineness of soul is of very recent growth: no human sentiment has spread so fruitfully as has the one we call humanitarianism, but its modern form is largely a product of the eighteenth century and after; witness the crusades for penal and social reforms in the last two centuries. In Shakespeare's day, however, a man could be hanged for pilfering, even for wandering without visible means of subsistence. And certainly Hamlet has no squeamishness at the sight of blood, and no abstract compunctions about the taking of life. "Now could I drink hot blood," he says in one of his passions; and a skilled fencer is no more likely to swoon on seeing blood than is a surgeon. Or hear how he talks about the body of Polonius, a body which would still have been alive had not Hamlet just made it a corpse. "I'll lug the guts into the neighbour room." Here, at least, is no anti-vivisectionist's utterance. Nor is Hamlet's mind preoccupied with the sanctity of individual life. He has killed Polonius, not of intent, but by mistake; and Polonius was once to have been his father-in-law. Yet how easily, complacently, and even callously, he puts the incident aside:

> Thou wretched, rash, intruding fool, farewell!
> I took thee for thy better: take thy fortune;
> Thou find'st to be too busy is some danger.[2]

Further, when he plans the death of Rosencrantz and Guildenstern, there is positive gloating in his anticipation of the condign punishment—execution, in fact—which, by his contrivance, is in store for them:

> For 'tis the sport to have the enginer
> Hoist with his own petar: and 't shall go hard
> But I will delve one yard below their mines
> And blow them at the moon.[3]

Perhaps even more incompatible with Hamlet's alleged humanitarian recoil from bloodshed is his soliloquy, as, passing by the king at prayer, he contemplates killing him, and then desists:

---

[2] *Hamlet* III. iv. 31. All succeeding references are to *Hamlet*.   [3] III. iv. 206.

> Now might I do it pat, now he is praying;
> And now I'll do't. And so he goes to heaven;
> And so am I revenged. That would be scann'd.[4]

To kill the king in such circumstances, he decides, would be to do the king a favor, "hire and salary," not revenge. And he is eager to defer the killing until its consequences will be fraught with the direst horrors:

> Am I then revenged,
> To take him in the purging of his soul,
> When he is fit and season'd for his passage?
> No!
> Up, sword; and know thou a more horrid hent;
> When he is drunk asleep, or in his rage,
> Or in the incestuous pleasure of his bed;
> At gaming, swearing, or about some act
> That has no relish of salvation in 't;
> Then trip him, that his heels may kick at heaven,
> And that his soul may be as damn'd and black
> As hell, whereto it goes.[5]

In the face of these instances, it would seem wrong to detect modern sentiments and susceptibilities about bloodshed in the constraints which obstruct Hamlet's achievement of his object.

5   Perhaps the intrusion of a present-day point of view is also responsible for the notion that Hamlet is seriously withheld by a growing feeling of some insufficiency in the evidence on which he has pledged himself to avenge his father's murder. He begins really to distrust the testimony of the ghost, we are asked to believe; and, naturally, the suggestion is easily taken in an age like ours which is eminently sceptical about the supernatural. But does Hamlet ever seriously question the ghost's authenticity and the reliability of its intimations? Nominally he does, of course: but are these genuine doubts or are they excuses in the sense that they are his attempts to rationalize his delay after it has occurred?

One thing is certain. When Hamlet sees and listens to the ghost, there is not even the faintest hint of possible deception. He takes the spectre for what it really is, the spirit of his dead father. Moreover, the tale which the ghost tells him fits exactly into his instinctive sense of the wickedness of his uncle. "O, my prophetic soul, my uncle!"[6] is his immediate conviction of the truth of the ghost's evidence. He does not mean that he suspected his uncle of murder; he means that he has always felt that his uncle was a villain, and now the tale of the murder provides him with particular confirmation. Hamlet's acceptance of the ghost is instantaneous and absolute: and in the relative calm following the exacting encounter, he assures his friends, "It is an honest ghost." The first intimation from Hamlet that he is apparently wavering in this confidence comes only after the lapse of considerable time, and therefore when Hamlet must feel self-reproach at his tardiness. The time-lapse is made clear by the introduction of seemingly extraneous incidents. Laertes has gone back to Paris, and Polonius is sending his "spy" there to see how Laertes is settling down. More striking, there is the dull drawn-out tale of the dispute between Denmark and Norway; a dramatically tedious scene is occupied by the instructions to the emissaries. These envoys have now fulfilled their mission and have returned to Denmark. Some time, therefore, some months, it would seem, have elapsed, and Hamlet's uncle still

---

[4] III. iii. 73.   [5] III. iii. 84.   [6] I. v. 40.

lives. Hamlet surely must needs justify his delay to his own soul. One can almost watch the plea of distrust in the ghost thrusting itself as an excuse into his mind. Chance has brought the players to the court. As Hamlet meets them, his former intellectual interests immediately reassert themselves: he becomes first-nighter and amateur dramatic critic again. There is green-room talk, and an actor or two is asked to go over a familiar speech. At the end, Hamlet asks the troupe to have ready for the morrow a murder play, into which he will insert some dozen or sixteen lines. Of course, the murder is in his mind, and a few lines easily added to a murder play will sharpen its application and will make the murderer writhe. But there is no hint yet that such writhing is being planned for anything more than to submit a murderer to some of the torments which he deserves. Indeed, the moment the players leave Hamlet, he reproaches himself bitterly for a rogue and peasant slave, since a merely fictitious grief can force a player to more passion than real grief seems able to arouse in Hamlet himself. What, thinks Hamlet, what would such a man do,

> Had he the motive and the cue for passion
> That I have?[7]

That is, he accepts entirely the ghost's tale of his uncle's villainy. Indeed he continues to reprove his inexplicable delay. "Am I a coward?" and in bitter scorn of his own apparent inaction, he heaps contempt upon himself:

> 'Swounds, I should take it: for it cannot be
> But I am pigeon-liver'd and lack gall
> To make oppression bitter, or ere this
> I should have fatted all the region kites
> With this slave's offal.

In the heat of his searing self-analysis, he repeats the indictment of his uncle with complete confiction:

> bloody, bawdy villain!
> Remorseless, treacherous, lecherous, kindless villain!

It is at that very moment that he first invents a purpose for the play which he has already planned for the morrow. He knows, of course, that instead of dabbling in theatricals, he should be sharpening his sword: and so he tells himself—and us—that the play is really a necessary part of his main plot:

> I have heard
> That guilty creatures sitting at a play
> Have by the very cunning of the scene
> Been struck so to the soul that presently
> They have proclaim'd their malefactions;
> For murder, though it have no tongue, will speak
> With most miraculous organ. I'll have these players
> Play something like the murder of my father
> Before mine uncle: I'll observe his looks;
> I'll tent him to the quick: if he but blench,
> I know my course. The spirit that I have seen
> May be the devil: and the devil hath power

---

[7] II. ii. 479.

> To assume a pleasing shape; yea, and perhaps
> Out of my weakness and my melancholy,
> As he is very potent with such spirits,
> Abuses me to damn me: I'll have grounds
> More relative than this: the play's the thing,
> Wherein I'll catch the conscience of the king.[8]

But the plea is specious, too palpable; it is Hamlet excusing himself for dissipating his energies and side-tracking his duty, for the execution of which he had so passionately reiterated the full and entire grounds a moment before. Moreover, how real can the need for confirmation of the ghost's story be when though the plan to provide it is spectacularly successful, the success is not followed by the slightest overt move to complete the alleged scheme? "If he but blench, I know my course." But he knew it already; and the additional item of credit now obtained, like his previous knowledge, leaves him passive.

Further, if the play within the play was devised by Hamlet to give him a really necessary confirmation of the ghost's evidence, why is this the moment he chooses to utter his profoundest expression of despair, "To be, or not to be, that is the question"? For, if his difficulty is what he says it is, this surely is the moment when the strings are all in his own hands. He has by chance found an occasion for an appropriate play, and, as the king's ready acceptance of the invitation to attend shows, he can be morally certain that the test will take place; and so, if one supposes him to need confirmation, within a trice he will really know. Yet this very situation finds him in the depths of despair. Can he really have needed the play within the play? The point is of some importance, because in the 1603 Quarto of *Hamlet*, this "To be, or not to be" speech occurs before Hamlet has devised the incriminating play. In the 1604 and later versions, the speech comes where we now read it. I know no more convincing argument that the 1604 Quarto is a master-dramatist's revision of his own first draft of a play.

Characteristic, too, is the nature of his alleged misgivings: they turn on the function and the nature of devils in general—"the devil hath power to assume a pleasing shape." But no stretch of words could describe Hamlet's encounter with the ghost as an appointment with "a pleasing shape." As we shall see, his account is as philosophically valid and as particularly inept as are so many of his generalizations. The fact is patent. He knew it was an honest ghost; he knew that its tale was true; and, not having fulfilled his promise to act on it, his moral nature could only be contented by plausible excuses.

Similarly one might go over other alleged explanations of Hamlet's inaction. There is the flat suggestion that he was restrained by material difficulties: he did not know how the Danes would look on his uncle's death, and he did not know how he could plan his *coup*. But these need not take up our time. Hamlet could rely on the people's approval of almost anything which he might choose to do; even Laertes had no trouble in rousing their suspicion of the new king. Moreover, no elaborate *coup* was needed; one stroke of the sword was all that was necessary; and, as we have seen, when Hamlet foregoes the opportunity, it is not for fear of the people's disapproval, it is because to kill the king at prayers would despatch him to heaven and not to the hell which he deserves. He never doubted that he had cause and will and strength and means to do it.

More difficult to set aside is the Freudian or the semi- or pseudo-Freudian explanation that a mother- or a sex-complex is the primary cause of Hamlet's delay. But the difficulty is one of terminology, not one of substance. The Elizabethans believed that a

[8] II. ii. 508.

man could love his mother without being in love with her or without unconsciously lusting for her. Hamlet's filial love for his mother is certainly a main cause of estrangement from the people who inhabit the world in which he lives, the world in which he must build his own soul. Certainly, too, her "o'er hasty" remarriage shatters the pillars of his moral universe. He has lived in an ideal world, that is, a world fashioned in his own idea, a world in which chastity is a main prop: and when he finds that, of all the women in his world, it is his own mother who seems unaware of this mainstay of the moral order, the structure topples over him. The only way to preserve purity is for womankind to seclude themselves from men: "get thee to a nunnery"; and Ophelia becomes a potential source of contagion. "Why wouldst thou be a breeder of sinners?" But sterility is a denial of life; as a moral injunction it is the tragic negation of morality. It is, however, only the young imaginative idealist's intellectual world which is fractured: but so far that is Hamlet's main, if not his only, world.

Consider, for instance, the difference in depth between his first soliloquy, "O, that this too too solid flesh," and the later one, "To be, or not to be." Both are contemplations of suicide. But what immeasurable difference between the constraining sanctions! When Hamlet speaks the first soliloquy, all that he knows to his own grief is that his father has died and that his mother has married again o'er-hastily. Neither he nor anybody else has any suspicion that murder, and murder most foul and most unnatural, has been done. His father has died from natural causes. But this death and, still more, his mother's remarriage, have reduced Hamlet's ideal universe to chaos. His rich and exquisitely sensitive nature, the observed of all observers, has suffered a shock which starts it reeling. A father dead, and untimely dead, though in itself a common experience, may prompt some sceptical scrutiny of divine providence; but worse still, a mother so soon married again seems to reveal an even more immediate despair; for here, not the divine but the human will seems to be working without moral sensibility. Yet the seat of the sorrow is nothing near so deep in human experience as is that which Hamlet utters when later he knows that his father has been murdered by his uncle.

In the first soliloquy, "O that this too too solid flesh," Hamlet is not so much actively contemplating suicide as passively longing to be dead. And the respect which makes it unthinkable to resort to self-slaughter is that the Everlasting has set his canon against it. In a way there is something of a pose in Hamlet's gesture: as if a young poet peering into the waters of a pool should long for the eternal quiet of its depths, but should be kept to the bank for fear that the water might be too cold. How much deeper in human nature are the constraints which withhold the Hamlet of the "To be, or not to be" soliloquy! No merely intellectual recognition of a theological injunction, but a primitive fear of the unknown after-world. "What dreams may come when we have shuffled off this mortal coil." The first speech is that of a sensitive soul in spiritual discomfort, the second is that of a man in profound despair. The discovery of the murder of his father by his uncle, of an act of uttermost human sacrilege, drives him to abysses of grief deeper than those occasioned by his mother's frailty. Something more human, more overt and intelligible than the Freudian hypothesis is the main stress of Hamlet's tragic incapacitation.

So far our explorations of the source of Hamlet's doom have been negative; mere statements of the inadequacy of suggested causes of it. But cannot something positive be propounded? Why cannot Hamlet perform the simple and righteous act of killing his uncle? The root of the trouble is generally agreed. He is too much, "sicklied o'er with the pale cast of thought." That's the respect which makes calamity of life; he thinks too much, and conscience, that is (in the use of the word here), persistent rumination, makes cowards of us all:

> some craven scruple
> Of thinking too precisely on the event,
> A thought which, quarter'd, hath but one part wisdom
> And ever three parts coward.[9]

He is, we are told, a philosopher, and the habit of thinking unfits him for the practical needs of doing: and, of course, popular opinion will easily take it that a thinker is a dreamer, and a dreamer is incapable of ready and effective action. But, is this easy assumption sufficient to explain Hamlet's failure? Moreover, if it be true, is it not a proposition which must give us pause, especially those of us who as teachers are mainly bent on encouraging the younger world to think? If thought is but a snare, to what then shall we turn? Thinking, in itself, is surely what we all take to be the world's greatest need: if in itself it is an incapacitating and unpractical activity, then the sooner our schools and our universities are abolished the better.

Nor will it do to say that Hamlet fails, not because he thinks, but because he thinks too much. In one sense, if thought is what will save the world, there cannot be too much of it. In another, if all that is meant is that Hamlet thinks too often, then clearly this is no matter for tragedy: it is merely a question of a revised time-table, more time to be allocated for field sports and other nonintellectual forms of activity.

What is wrong is not that Hamlet thinks or thinks too much or too often, but that his way of thinking frustrates the object of thought. It is the kind of distortion to which cerebration is liable when it is fired by a temperamental emotionalism and guided by an easily excited imagination. The emotion thrusts one factor of the thinker's experience into especial prominence, and the imagination freely builds a speculative universe in which this prominence is a fundamental pillar. Hence, the business of thinking overreaches itself. The mind's function to construct an intellectual pattern of reality becomes merely a capacity to build abstract patterns, and the relation of these patterns to reality is misapprehended, if not discounted entirely. In the main, this way of thinking constructs a cosmic picture which only serves to give apparent validity to what the feeling of the person and of the moment makes most immediately significant. But examples will help to make the effect of it apparent. They will be better, because more certainly characteristic of the more normal working of Hamlet's mind, if they are taken from scenes before Hamlet is given the additional shock of discovery that his uncle is a murderer and has murdered his father. There are sufficient of them in his first soliloquy.

The scene of it is worth recalling to establish other qualities of Hamlet which are easily overlooked. He is the hero: and in our backward rumination when we have come to know him, unconsciously we idealize his earlier appearances. But in this first episode, he is not an altogether attractive person. The Court is in session: he is in the royal train, but not a part of it. In manner, in dress and in place, he is staging his contemptuous aloofness from it. He stands apart, taking no share in the social formalities of the occasion, and he draws attention to his aloofness by an extravagant garb of mourning and by excessive display of the conventional gestures of grief. He is swathed in elaborate black: his "inky cloak," on top of his "customary suits of solemn black" in full funereal fashion prescribed by the sixteenth-century mortician, his incessantly repeated sighs, his perpetual flow of tears, his fixed deflection of gaze: these are trappings and suits of conventional woe whose emphasis reflects suspicion of insincerity on their wearer, or at least, until a relative judgment is possible, mark him as liable to such suspicion. Nor is this possibility

[9] IV. iv. 40.

of a Pharisaic isolation weakened by memory of his only other words, his earlier sardonic interjections and his affectedly humorous comments on the king's greeting.

Hence, when he soliloquizes, our willingness to sympathize with a son whose father has died and whose mother has hastily married again is suspended by our suspicion of the son's leaning to morbidity. His words appear to justify suspicion to the full:

> O, that this too too solid flesh would melt,
> Thaw and resolve itself into a dew!
> Or that the Everlasting had not fix'd
> His canon 'gainst self-slaughter![10]

We have seen that the utterance of a wish for death in such a phrase lacks the convincing urgency of the constraints expressed in the incalculable fears of the "To be, or not to be" speech. His imagination goes on to explore illimitable stretches of despair; "weary" and "stale" and "flat" and "unprofitable" are the suggestions by which it deprives the uses of the world of all their value. "Things rank and gross in nature possess it merely." Yet the absoluteness of this denunciation prompts our question. Hamlet has hitherto enjoyed a privileged life, and the good things of the world, material and spiritual, have been fully and freely at his disposal: but the passionate sorrow of the moment blots these out of his intellectual picture of the universe. His next remarks let us see how such obliviousness and its consequently distorted sense of reality are natural to Hamlet's mode of speculation. "But two months dead." Much will happen to these two months as Hamlet fits them into their place in his scheme of things; the fact that as a lapse of time they are in themselves a part of physical nature, unalterable and absolute, will be completely forgotten. "That it should come to this": Hamlet's desperate anger heats his mind. "But two months dead"— an incredibly short span wherein such things should have happened. "Nay, not so much, not two." The notion of a real measure of time, and of its unthinkable brevity for such occasion, is caught up by Hamlet's imagination, still further excited by intermitted recollection of the overwhelming difference between the dead husband and his successor, "Hyperion to a satyr." So the nearly two months is seized by the mind, not as a physical fact, but as a concept of brevity, just as thought habitually converts minutes into moments; and the concept is translated into imaginative symbols which will provide the framework of Hamlet's intellectual cosmology. "A little month," little, that is, not objectively in relation to other months, but little in relation to the moral idea of propriety. As his imagination lashes his anger, other symbols still further hide the natural measure of a month:

> Or 'ere those shoes were old
> With which she follow'd my poor father's body;

the slip of the time-scheme here is perhaps not easily assessable, since we have no exact information as to how long a queen's shoes are held to be wearable. But the final symbolic expression for this "little month,"

> Ere yet the salt of most unrighteous tears
> Had left the flushing in her galled eyes,

can be estimated more readily, for the world knows how long it takes to remove signs of weeping from the complexion. A month, a real objective month, has been imaginatively caught up and is then imaginatively retranslated into objective reality as an hour. The sequence of ideas and the structure of the argument in the whole speech are symbolic of

[10] I. ii. 129.

what Hamlet's mind perpetually does. With the philosopher's genius for intellectual creation, it fashions an image of the universe, but in the fashioning patently distorts
fundamental elements of that universe. The world, as his mind builds it, ceases to be a
representation of the world as it is.

This very soliloquy includes another striking instance of similar intellectual transformation. As he remembers his mother's lapse, his passion prompts the general
condemnation, "Frailty, thy name is woman." As far as one knows, Hamlet, of all the
women in the world, has known but two, his mother and Ophelia. His mother has unexpectedly proved "frail," but, in the Elizabethan sense of the word, Ophelia is entirely free
of such charge. Yet the generalization: all women are frail. Again, the mind's picture of life
is a distortion of real life, of even so much or so little of it as Hamlet really knew.

This does not mean, of course, that Hamlet's thinking is generally or regularly so
prone to fallacious conclusions. His philosophic grasp of much of life's riddle is sure and
permanent: and imagination has prompted his discoveries. But when the thought springs
from a particular incident which moves his own feelings to new depths, imagination leads
his speculations awry. Into the fate of man at large he has a deep and broad view: he holds
the macrocosm more securely than the microcosm of his own personal experience. Hence
the magnificent appeal of the most famous of all the speeches in the play, "To be, or not
to be." Here is a purely philosophical or speculative statement of the general tragedy of
man. The problem is a universal, not a particular, one:

> Whether 'tis nobler in the mind to suffer
> The slings and arrows of outrageous fortune,
> Or to take arms against a sea of troubles,
> And by opposing end them?[11]

That is, it is not really a question of whether Hamlet shall commit suicide, but whether all
men ought not to do so. For Hamlet is a metaphysician, not a psychologist; he is speculative, but not essentially introspective. The ills of life are the "heartache and the thousand
natural shocks that flesh is heir to," all men's flesh, and not Hamlet's in particular. Indeed,
when he recites his examples of man's outrageous fortune, there is scarcely one of them
by which he himself has been especially afflicted: "the oppressor's wrong, the proud man's
contumely, the insolence of office and the spurns that patient merit of the unworthy
take"—these are almost everybody's troubles more than they are Hamlet's: and the "pangs
of despised love" are no part at all of his relation to Ophelia. Naturally, although the whole
problem is seen generally and impersonally, Hamlet's own personality affects his sense of
relative values. The major ill—"what dreams may come when we have shuffled off this
mortal coil"—is only major to such as Hamlet, though even this peculiar sentiment is only
a particular form of the universal dread of something after death, something unpredictable
in the limitless range of conjectural agonies. How completely Hamlet's mind is engrossed
in the general philosophic problem is superbly revealed by the most familiar lines in the
whole speech:

> The undiscover'd country from whose bourn
> No traveller returns.

The phrase has dwelt familiarly on the tongues of men as an indubitable miracle of poetic
utterance, and such indeed it is. Hamlet is putting into words his sense of the after-world.
He fastens on two of the aspects which belong to it in the minds and sentiments of mankind at large, namely, our complete isolation from it, "from whose bourn no traveller

---

[11] III. i. 57.

returns," and our entire ignorance of its particular nature, "the undiscover'd country." But choosing these as the symbols by which to suggest the afterworld he gathers to the general sense a host of other appropriate associations: our intuitive feeling about the after-world is made more conscious and intelligible. The phrase is, in fact, a statement of the after-world which at some, or at many, or at all moments is true for everybody. But the amazing thing is that what makes it impress all of us, its general truth, is a quality which it cannot have for Hamlet. For mankind at large the after-world is the undiscovered country from whose bourn no traveller returns: and the philosopher Hamlet is absorbed in this general truth so completely that he forgets that for him the general truth is a particular error. A traveller *has* returned to him from the after-world, a ghost, the ghost, moreover, of his dead father, to tell a tale setting his hair on end and completely changing the rest of his life. Yet, philosophizing, he climbs to the world of ideas, of abstract truths; and forgets for the moment the most outstanding experience in his own life.

This flair of Hamlet's for abstract thinking is perpetually liable to make him momentarily indifferent to the concrete world about him. Another speech spoken before his mind is doubly strained by knowledge of the murder will show us how the natural functioning of his brain works. The situation is exciting. A ghost has been seen by Hamlet's friends. They have informed Hamlet that his father's spirit in arms has twice appeared at midnight. Hamlet is agog with excitement. The three of them plan to be in wait for the ghost: they are here on the battlements at midnight. "The air bites shrewdly," "very cold," "a nipping and an eager air," "it has struck twelve"—the whole atmosphere is one of strained excited nerves: suddenly, as they peer in hushed expectation, the silence is broken by the blast of cannon. It is a situation not likely, one would think, to soothe nerves on edge. Horatio, normally calmest of men, is rattled: "What does this mean, my lord?" asking questions more from discomposure than from desire to have repeated what he surely knows. Yet at this very moment, of all moments the most inopportune, unexpected and inappropriate, Hamlet solemnly embarks on a regular professorial disquisition about the nature of habit and its influence on moral character: "So, oft it chances in particular men": a characteristic academic text from the chair of philosophy. The discourse which ensues is typically philosophic in form. It glances round all the related contingencies, seeking to build them into a generalization. As tentative propositions are put forward, the philosopher's mind turns momentarily aside to put their implications into line with the general argument. The very syntax of this speech, with its interrupted and broken structure, is Hamlet's brain in action under our eyes. And again he is so enthralled in its operations that when the ghost does appear, his attention to it has to be called, "Look, my lord, it comes."

But this abstraction is not in itself ominous. When he does see the ghost, he is fully capable of meeting the situation which is immediately presented, and, despite his friends' fear, he follows the ghost without hesitation. So he hears the terrible story. Murder had been suspected by nobody, not even by Hamlet. Now he finds villainy blacker than he had known, villainy infecting both his mother and his uncle. He dedicates himself passionately and immediately to obey the ghost's call to revenge. Nothing, he says, will ever cause him to forget:

> Remember thee!
> Ay, thou poor ghost, while memory holds a seat
> In this distracted globe [12]

Yet the words he continues to utter arouse our misgivings: they do not seem part of a promising project for sweeping to revenge with wings as swift as meditation:

---

[12] I. v. 95.

> Yea, from the table of my memory
> I'll wipe away all trivial fond records,
> All saws of books, all forms, all pressures past,
> That youth and observation copied there.

He is, of course, talking metaphorically; the "table of his memory" is the memorandum book, and whilst it is not inappropriate to symbolize memory by such figure, it is disturbing to connect the recollection of the task which Hamlet must perform with the need to jot it down against forgetfulness even in a metaphorical diary. Disturbance grows as the metaphor usurps reality. Hamlet in his excitement is driven by his imagination; its "table," "book and volume," have become palpable, and subconsciously Hamlet is impelled to take out his actual notebook:

> My tables,—meet it is I set it down.

The action is ominous, and would be even if Hamlet should set down his determination to kill his uncle within a week. But more ominous is what he does set down:

> That one may smile, and smile, and be a villain;

—a mere truism, given, too, the conventional philosophical safeguard by qualification,

> At least I'm sure it may be so in Denmark.

It is absolutely clear, then, that Hamlet's habit of mind will in some way or another complicate his procedure. His tendency to abstraction, his proneness to let imagination stimulate and direct his intellectual voyagings beyond the reaches of the soul, his liability to set the mind awork before the body takes its appropriate complementary posture: these may recurrently obstruct a ready response in action. But in themselves they will not induce a general paralysis: and, in fact, Hamlet is normally very ready to act. As soon as he has seen the ghost, he is planning a means to kill the king, though, characteristically, his mind is apter to long-term plans than to ready improvisations. He tells his friends that he may perchance find it convenient to put an antic disposition on. But there are other significant occasions when his deeds are those of the quick resolute actor rather than of the halting, undetermined hesitator. When pirates attack the vessel on which he is sailing to England, he is the first to jump aboard as they grapple. On an earlier occasion, when he sees a stirring behind the arras, he draws at once and kills Polonius: and it is no explanation to say that this was purely instinctive, for it is obvious that he has suspected eavesdropping and, presumably, has determined beforehand on the proper response. When, towards the end, he comes on Ophelia's funeral, he acts with almost a madman's precipitancy, and jumps into the grave; and though it is a frenzied display, it is not one of a man whose sinews have atrophied in general paralysis. It is, indeed, a very significant action. It has energy, deliberateness, and the application of force on circumstances in the world about him: and these qualities are what distinguish action from mere reflex activities. But its significance for the tragedy is this: it is the wrong action for the actual world in which Hamlet must live; it is proper only to the ideal world (that is, the picture of the world which he has built in his own mind) in which he now lives without knowing that it is a distorted image of reality. If his ideal world were a valid intellectual projection of the real world, his action would be apt and effective. A crucial illustration of this is provided by his treatment of Ophelia.

Nothing is more difficult to reconcile with our impulse to sympathize with Hamlet than are his dealings with Ophelia. However docile she may be to her father (and that has not always been regarded as a sign of weakness; moreover, she stands up triumphantly to her preachifying brother), she cannot hide her love for Hamlet from us. She is not forth-coming in the way of the modern girl, nor even as naturally wise as Shakespeare's comic heroines. But is this a moral defect? And can anybody suppose for a moment that it justifies Hamlet's abominable treatment of her? It is not so much that he determines to break with her. It is the manner of the breaking. He talks to her, at best, as a salvationist preacher would reprove a woman of the street, and then as a roué who is being cynical with an associate in looseness. His remarks are disgusting and even revolting; they offend because they are preposterously out of place, for Ophelia is in no wise deserving of such inepti-tudes. But if frailty (that is, immorality) is woman's name, if Ophelia, because a woman, is therefore necessarily frail, then of course everything fits. The serious advice, "get thee to a nunnery," is the only way to save the world; and the smut of the wise-cracks in the play-within-the-play scene is a proper garb. But, of course, these hypotheses are pure fiction. They are real only in Hamlet's "ideal" world, and it is only in that world that his actions would be appropriate. The other and the real world, the one in which he must live and act and succeed or fail, is a different one; and we have seen how Hamlet came to create his ideal world and then to mistake it for a true intellectual projection of the real one.

This, it would appear, is the way of Hamlet's tragedy. His supreme gift for philo-sophic thought allows him to know the universe better than the little world of which he is bodily a part. But his acts must be in this physical world: and his mind has distorted for him the particular objects of his actual environment. So he cannot act properly within it: or rather, towards those parts of it which the stress of his feeling and the heat of his imagination have made especially liable to intellectual distortion, he cannot oppose the right response. He can kill a Rosencrantz, but not his villainous uncle. Yet though the paralysis is localized at first, it tends to be progressive. The world of action, or the world in which outward act is alone possible, becomes increasingly different from the world as his mind conceives it. Yet the mind increasingly imposes its own picture on him as abso-lute. The end is despair. The will to act in the one necessary direction it first frustrated and then gradually atrophied. Worst of all, the recognition of the will's impotence is ac-cepted as spiritual resignation; and the resignation is not seen as the moral abnegation, the *gran rifiuto,* which it certainly is; on the contrary, it is phrased as if it were the calm attainment of a higher benignity, whereas it is nothing more than a fatalist's surrender of his personal responsibility. That is the nadir of Hamlet's fall. The temper of Hamlet's con-verse with Horatio in the graveyard, the placidity of his comments on disinterred bones, his reminiscent ruminations on Yorick's skull, and his assumed hilarity in tracking Alex-ander's progress till the loam whereto he is converted serves to stop a beer-barrel—these are traits of his final frame of mind and they indicate no ascent to the serenity of philo-sophic calm. They are only processes which reconcile him to his last stage of failure. His increasing nonchalance, he confesses to Horatio, is really part of his falling off. "Thou wouldst not think how ill all's here about my heart." And his gesture of noble defiance is no firm confession of trust in a benign Providence: it is merely the courage of despair:

> We defy augury: there's a special providence in the fall of a sparrow. . . .
> If it be not now, yet it will come: the readiness is all: since no man has aught of
> what he leaves, what is't to leave betimes?[13]

This is absolute abdication: if Hamlet's duty is to be done, Providence will occasion its doing, as indeed Providence does in the heat of the fencing match when chance discloses more villainy, and stings Hamlet into a reflex retaliation. But Hamlet has failed. That is the tragedy.

---

[13] V. ii. 179.

In his own world, Hamlet, this noble mind, has been o'erthrown. But as he has moved on to his undoing, his generous nature, instinctively averse from all contriving, has linked the whole audience with the general gender in great love and veneration for him. Yet when his doom overtakes him, there is neither from him nor from the audience any cry of resentment; no anger against the gods, no challenging of the providence that shapes our ends. The rest is silence. The play done, however, and the deep impression of it remaining, the mind of man remits this *Hamlet*-experience to the cumulative mass of spiritual data which is piling up within it through every channel and every mode of consciousness. *Hamlet* is added to the vast medley of other imprints which every act of our living stamps on our spiritual retina: and the mind strives to find some clue to a form in the enigma, some shape in an apparent confusion, a pattern which, giving full force to tragedy, will not compel despair. . . .

Comments and Questions

Hamlet begins on page 626. See Comments and Questions at the end of the play.

The sheer bulk of *Hamlet* criticism is overwhelming. It has been estimated, with some exaggeration, that one could spend a lifetime reading about the Prince of Denmark. Just as every serious male actor wants to act Hamlet, so also do hundreds of serious critics want to interpret the play. No critic so far has satisfied everyone, though some come closer than do others. Charlton looks at the play without blinking and concludes early in his discussion (paragraph 2) that "there are elements belonging to the mysteries of life which the drama leaves in their own inscrutable darkness."

Hamlet acts or fails to act because he is Hamlet and not someone else. He is not Everyman. Macbeth would surely have had no hesitancy in sweeping to his revenge, nor would Othello. But Iago could not have fooled Hamlet, nor would a Lady Macbeth have been able to egg him on to get rid of Claudius. The point then is that this great play gains its power—and its baffling quality—from its protagonist's uniqueness.

1. If what has been said above is true, what becomes of the criterion that chief characters in imaginative works should represent universals? Discuss.

2. Examine Hamlet's varied relationships: with his father, his father's ghost, Polonius, Ophelia, Laertes, his mother, Horatio, Osric, Rosencrantz and Guildenstern, and, of course, Claudius. How do these relationships, when taken together, define Hamlet's character?

3. List the points in Charlton's essay with which you agree, those, that is, that you think are supported by the play. Do you take exception to some of the critic's conclusions? If so, cite your reasons for disagreeing.

A. Alvarez (1929–)
August Strindberg*

The fiftieth anniversary of Strindberg's death misfired in 1962. Elizabeth Sprigge's lovingly prepared translation of twelve of his plays does not seem to have been ready in time. All we got here was *Inferno,* the record of his breakdown after he separated from his second wife, which is fascinating as a case-history but a non-starter as a work of art. The Royal Shakespeare Company's contribution was a burlesque of his quite good one-acter, *Playing with Fire.* And that was that.

Yet it was typical. Strindberg has nearly always had the wrong kind of success and the wrong kind of failure: both have been scandalous, noisy, racked. He seems only to have been able to stomach public acclaim provided it was accompanied by a proportionate public fury. He was, from the start, a tortured man who exploited his tortures, who chronicled his appalling autobiography as it happened, and wrote to hurt. He was as self-destructive as he was paranoid; conversely, he pitied himself as much as he persecuted himself. He had a flair for disastrous marriages and melodramatic affairs. He quarrelled with everyone—particularly his friends—and had his first collection of stories prosecuted for blasphemy. He fancied himself as an alchemist and dabbled in theosophy and occultism. At his worst, he seems preoccupied by his own sinfulness, his "passions" and the sweet smell of decadence.

But these last *fin de siècle* mannerisms are a mere irritation on the surface of his work. Eliot once remarked that the odd thing about the British writers of the Nineties—Wilde, Dowson, Lionel Johnson—was that they suffered so much and wrote so superficially. They were protected, he thought, by their histrionics. Strindberg lacked that extra thickness of skin. Instead, his genius was directly related to the rawness of his nerves. The state of mind he so meticulously described in *Inferno* is, in the technical sense, psychotic; he shows, I am told, all the symptoms of a paranoid schizophrenic. More simply, he commanded neither the defences nor the sense of reality to keep him in the manageable realm of neurosis. Yet it was from precisely this failing that his power and his curiously contemporary air come. In painting, Expressionism may have gone a long way beyond Edvard Munch, whom Strindberg knew in Paris during his *Inferno* period. On the stage, however, it is still catching up with Strindberg.

He seems to have invented what now passes for the *avant-garde* theatre, and a great deal of what we take for granted in the cinema. As early as the foreword to *Miss Julie* he had set about the reform of the stage. He wanted to get rid of the footlights, the distractions of orchestra and intervals, the boxes "with their tittering diners and supper-parties," and the heavy encumbrances of elaborate sets. In their place he wanted a fluid stage—of the kind, presumably, which Svoboda has perfected in Prague—and acting fluid enough to include improvisation, ballet and mime; also a fluidity of writing, to avoid

> the symmetrical, mathematical construction of French dialogue, and let people's minds work irregularly, as they do in real life where, during a conversation, no topic is drained to the dregs, and one mind finds in another a chance cog to engage in.

* From August Strindberg, *Twelve Plays,* translated by Elizabeth Sprigge, London: Constable, 1963; *Inferno,* translated by Mary Sandbach, London: Hutchinson, 1962.

Above all, he was after "a *small* stage and a *small* house" and "total darkness in the auditorium." It sounds like the usual attack on the conventionality, complacency and philistinism of the socialite theatre. But it has little to do with the naturalist programme of Ibsen. Strindberg's brand of realism was more like that of the cinema, where the darkness and the looming black and white images are closer not to life but to dreams.

5   This fits with Strindberg's preoccupation as an artist. He was continually trying to cut through the polished surface of ideas and manners to examine the springs of action. "We want," he wrote, "to see the wires themselves, to watch the machinery." Perhaps Beckett works in the same way. But he is more limited, more negative; the essence of his people is their isolation, and their most passionate relationship is with Nothingness. Strindberg, on the other hand, was too close to Ibsen to be able to abstract his obsessions so tidily. And the obsessions themselves were all concerned with the destructive complexity of his feelings for women.

He is the master of sexual ambivalence and uncertainty. Pathologically jealous, he was a sensualist who yearned always for "masculine virginity." He courted rejection and reacted savagely to any positive show of love. It is as though he were unable to get over the fact that women have their own sexual desires. That is the chief offence of Miss Julie, of Henriette in *Crime and Crime* and of Alice in *The Dance of Death.* It seemed to open to him menacing perspectives of feminism, lesbianism and a whole world in which embattled women usurped the rights of men. His perfect heroines were all virginal, suffering, bodiless: Swanwhite, Eleanor in *Easter,* Indra's Daughter in *A Dream Play,* and the Girl in his masterpiece, *The Ghost Sonata.* All of his heroes, meanwhile, suffered maternal agonies of tenderness for their children, shared even their wives' labour pains and were passionately involved with their wives' former husbands or lovers. The result is an endless and unresolved sense of outrage. His couples destroy each other in acts of what, in *Creditors,* he calls "pure cannibalism." In his works there are no solutions, only at times a grudging acceptance of the horror of the other person's individuality. His talent lay in catching that note of human violence in constricted surroundings. In comparison with his chamber plays, the more ambitious open-scene poetic quests, like *To Damascus* and *The Great Highway,* are diffuse and unconvincing. His genius needed the domestic prison for the full expression of its ferocity. He was the inventor of marital Expressionism.

The core of Expressionism is in an impossible intensity of feeling which lies just behind the work of art but which is never quite expressed by it. You are constantly forced back from the work to its creator. In his famous essay on *Hamlet,* Eliot wrote:

> The only way of expressing emotion in the form of art is by finding an "objective correlative"; in other words, a set of objects, a situation, a chain of events which shall be the formula of that *particular* emotion; such that when the external facts, which must terminate in sensory experience, are given, the emotion is immediately invoked. . . . Hamlet (the man) is dominated by an emotion which is inexpressible, because it is in *excess* of the facts as they appear.

By this reckoning, *Hamlet* is the first Expressionist play. But what is an exception with Shakespeare is the rule with Strindberg. *The Father,* for example, begins with the bullying, insistently masculine hero trapped in a houseful of women and in a heartless, mutually destructive marriage. The situation has all the makings of a piece of Ibsen-like claustrophobia. Then it explodes. His wife has only to drop two hints—that he is mad and that their daughter is not his, both legitimate manoeuvres in the style of battle they are fighting—and he promptly becomes insane. For despite appearances, the madness was already there, though neither in the situation nor in anything you are told of the Captain's character. Instead, it existed in Strindberg's own mind, as a permanent background of horrified anxiety. To understand the play you must understand Strindberg: his history of break-downs, excesses and frenzies; his love-hatred for his first wife and the man he had taken her from, and for his icy father who had married the housekeeper directly his own first wife died, when Strindberg was at puberty. The play calls for a kind of Method reading, just as it calls for Method acting. The words, in order to make sense of the actions they go with, must imply intensities which they do not in fact define. This is the opposite of Shake-speare's way, where the feelings develop with and through the language, the images releasing layer after layer of meaning. In Strindberg's chamber plays the language and the feeling are always a little apart.

He seems to have been aware of the split. It was, I think, in the hope of mending it that he tried to break down the conventions of his contemporary stage and turned more and more to poetic drama. As he said in the note to *A Dream Play:*

> The Author has sought to reproduce the disconnected but apparently logical form of a dream. Anything can happen; everything is possible and probable. Time and space do not exist . . . And since on the whole, there is more pain than plea-sure in the dream, a tone of melancholy, and of compassion for all living things, runs through the swaying narrative.

This is a stage further on from the theatre he postulated in the foreword to *Miss Julie.* In that play Strindberg himself is divided equally between Miss Julie and Jean; in *A Dream Play* he is deliberately fragmented through all the characters. He used the dream conven-tion as a way through to the emotions. The feelings experienced in dreams are both more intense and more direct than any experienced in waking life. So by creating in his "sway-ing narrative" the condition of dreams, he was able to tap the roots of his obsessions without feeling constricted by that reality which, in his sickness, he was never properly able to face.

Yet the pure dream plays lack the power of his earlier, more firmly localized works. He needed the "objective correlative" of domesticity to fix that tension between love as he felt it should be and marriage as he knew it was. He was possessed by the idea of marriage. But only in *The Ghost Sonata* did he manage to reconcile its constrictions with the imagi-native freedom of his dream narrative. The result was a kind of acted-out, personified poetry. "Not reality," as he says in *A Dream Play,* "but more than reality. Not dreams but waking dreams."

Comments and Questions

Strindberg's Foreword to *Miss Julie* begins on page 780; the play, on page 787; the Com-ments and Questions, on page 809. See also Ibsen's *Ghosts,* page 740, and the Comments and Questions that follow that play.

Wallace L. Anderson   (1917–   )
An Analysis of "Mr. Flood's Party"[1]

An old man living alone on the outskirts of Tilbury Town has gone into town to fill his jug with liquor. Returning home, he stops along the road and invites himself to have a drink. He accepts the invitation several times until the bottle is empty, after which presumably he makes his way back to his "forsaken upland hermitage." "Turned down for alcoholic reasons" by *Collier's,* "Mr. Flood's Party" was first published in the *Nation,* November 24, 1920. The origin of the poem goes back twenty-five years to the time when Robinson was working on his prose sketches. Harry de Forest Smith had told him of an interesting character that he knew. "I am going to take a change of air," Robinson wrote Smith, "and write a little thing to be called 'Saturday,' of which you will be indirectly the father, as it is founded on the amiable portrait of one Mr. Hutchings in bed with a pint of rum and a pile of dime novels." Mr. Flood is one of Robinson's original "scattered lives," wonderfully transmuted over the years.

"Mr. Flood's Party" is in some ways much like "Miniver Cheevy" and "Richard Cory." It is a character sketch, a miniature drama with hints and suggestions of the past; its tone is a blend of irony, humor, and pathos. Yet it is, if not more sober, at least more serious, and a finer poem. It is more richly conceived and executed, and it contains two worlds, a world of illusion and a world of reality. A longer poem with a more complex stanza pattern and a heightened use of language, its theme fully informs the poem: it is dramatically represented by Mr. Flood and given emotional and intellectual depth by means of interrelated allusions and images focused on a central symbol. The theme is the transience of life; the central symbol is the jug. Both the theme and the symbolic import of the jug are announced in the line "The bird is on the wing, the poet says," though only the theme, implicit in the image, is immediately apparent. Its relationship to the jug goes back to its source in the *Rubáiyát of Omar Khayyám:*

> Come, fill the Cup, and in the fire of Spring
> Your winter-garment of Repentance fling:
>   The Bird of Time has but a little way
> To flutter—and the Bird is on the Wing.
>
> Whether at Naishapur or Babylon,
> Whether the Cup with sweet or bitter run,
>   The Wine of Life keeps oozing drop by drop,
> The Leaves of Life keep falling one by one.

The transience symbols coupled with the eat-drink-and-be-merry philosophy of the *Rubáiyát* prepare the way for Mr. Flood's party but also intensify the poignance and sharpen the irony. In stanza three, the passage referring to "Roland's ghost winding a silent horn" is the richest in the poem, both in language and in suggestion. It serves a multiple function. The likening of Mr. Flood with lifted jug to Roland, the most courageous of Charlemagne's knights, blowing his magic horn presents a vivid picture, made both striking and humorous by the incongruity. At the same time, however, it is a means of adding pathos and dignity to the figure of Mr. Flood, for there are some similarities. By the time that Roland blew his horn the last time, all his friends were dead; like Mr. Flood he reminisced about

---

[1] "Mr. Flood's Party" appears on p. 494.

the past, and his eyes were dim. Moreover, he had fought valiantly and endured to the end, and these attributes of courage and endurance are transferred to Mr. Flood. The expression "enduring to the end" has a double reference behind it: it calls to mind the words of Jesus when he sent forth his disciples, "He that endureth to the end shall be saved," a statement that Browning said was the theme of his "Childe Roland to the Dark Tower Came." The Roland allusion is even more subtle. The comparison is not to Roland blowing his horn in broad daylight and surrounded by the newly dead, but to the *ghost* of Roland, and the horn he is winding is a "silent horn." Roland, the last to die, is seeking his phantom friends. So is Mr. Flood. Lighted by the harvest moon glinting on the "valiant armor" of Roland-Flood, this is a world of the past, dim and mute. Fusion of figure and scene is complete. "Amid the silver loneliness/Of night" Mr. Flood creates his own illusory world with his jug.

The significance of the jug symbol, foreshadowed by the *Rubáiyát* and Roland references, becomes clear in an extended simile at the mid and focal point of the poem:

> Then, as a mother lays her sleeping child
> Down tenderly, fearing it may awake,
> He set the jug down slowly at his feet
> With trembling care, knowing that most things break.

The interplay of similarities and dissimilarities in the relationship of *mother:child* and *Mr. Flood:jug* is too delicate and suggestive to be pinned down and spoiled by detailed analysis. Suffice it to say here that in the child the future is contained; in the jug, the past. Memories flood in as Eben drinks, and he lives once more, temporarily secure, among "friends of other days," who "had honored him," opened their doors to him, and welcomed him home. Two moons also keep him company, one real and one illusory. A last drink and the singing of "Auld Lang Syne," with its "auld acquaintance" and "cup o' kindness," and the party is over. And with a shock we and Mr. Flood are back in the harsh world of reality which frames the poem and his present and fleeting life:

> There was not much that was ahead of him,
> And there was nothing in the town below.

The loneliness of an old man, the passing of time; Eben Flood, ebb and flood. There is no comment, and none is needed.

Comments and Questions

There are many short poems in the poetry section of this book, all inviting analysis. Mr. Anderson's sensitive explication of Robinson's poem is a good model of how to ferret out the meaning of any poem.

1. The first three sentences of this analysis state the literal facts of the poem. What does the remainder of the paragraph do?

2. Compare "Mr. Flood's Party" and "Miniver Cheevy," page 407. Are Mr. Flood and Miniver Cheevy both "lost souls"? Discuss.

3. At one point, Mr. Anderson says that some imaginative suggestions may be "spoiled by detailed analysis." Does this restriction pose a problem? See "Ars Poetica," page 382, particularly the last two controversial lines:

> A poem should not mean
> But be.

Robert Frost   (1874–1963)
The Figure A Poem Makes

Abstraction is an old story with the philosophers, but it has been like a new toy in the hands of the artists of our day. Why can't we have any one quality of poetry we choose by itself? We can have in thought. Then it will go hard if we can't in practice. Our lives for it.

Granted no one but a humanist much cares how sound a poem is if it is only *a* sound. The sound is the gold in the ore. Then we will have the sound out alone and dispense with the inessential. We do till we make the discovery that the object in writing poetry is to make all poems sound as different as possible from each other, and the resources for that of vowels, consonants, punctuation, syntax, words, sentences, meter are not enough. We need the help of context—meaning—subject matter. That is the greatest help toward variety. All that can be done with words is soon told. So also with meters—particularly in our language where there are virtually but two, strict iambic and loose iambic. The ancients with many were still poor if they depended on meters for all tune. It is painful to watch our sprung-rhythmists straining at the point of omitting one short from a foot for relief from monotony. The possibilities for tune from the dramatic tones of meaning struck across the rigidity of a limited meter are endless. And we are back in poetry as merely one more art of having something to say, sound or unsound. Probably better if sound, because deeper and from wider experience.

Then there is this wildness whereof it is spoken. Granted again that it has an equal claim with sound to being a poem's better half. If it is a wild tune, it is a poem. Our problem then is, as modern abstractionists, to have the wildness pure; to be wild with nothing to be wild about. We bring up as aberrationists, giving way to undirected associations and kicking ourselves from one chance suggestion to another in all directions as of a hot afternoon in the life of a grasshopper. Theme alone can steady us down. Just as the first mystery was how a poem could have a tune in such a straightness as meter, so the second mystery is how a poem can have wildness and at the same time a subject that shall be fulfilled.

It should be of the pleasure of a poem itself to tell how it can. The figure a poem makes. It begins in delight and ends in wisdom. The figure is the same as for love. No one can really hold that the ecstasy should be static and stand still in one place. It begins in delight, it inclines to the impulse, it assumes direction with the first line laid down, it runs a course of lucky events, and ends in a clarification of life—not necessarily a great clarification, such as sects and cults are founded on, but in a momentary stay against confusion. It has denouement. It has an outcome that though unforeseen was pre-destined from the first image of the original mood—and indeed from the very mood. It is but a trick poem and no poem at all if the best of it was thought of first and saved for the last. It finds its own name as it goes and discovers the best waiting for it in some final phrase at once wise and sad—the happy-sad blend of the drinking song.

5   No tears in the writer, no tears in the reader. No surprise for the writer, no surprise for the reader. For me the initial delight is in the surprise of remembering something I didn't know I knew. I am in a place, in a situation, as if I had materialized from cloud or risen out of the ground. There is a glad recognition of the long lost and the rest follows. Step by step the wonder of unexpected supply keeps growing. The impressions most useful to my purpose seem always those I was unaware of and so made no note of at the time when taken, and the conclusion is come to that like giants we are always hurling

experience ahead of us to pave the future with against the day when we may want to strike a line of purpose across it for somewhere. The line will have the more charm for not being mechanically straight. We enjoy the straight crookedness of a good walking stick. Modern instruments of precision are being used to make things crooked as if by eye and hand in the old days.

I tell how there may be a better wildness of logic than of inconsequence. But the logic is backward, in retrospect, after the act. It must be more felt than seen ahead like prophecy. It must be a revelation, or a series of revelations, as much for the poet as for the reader. For it to be that there must have been the greatest freedom of the material to move about in it and to establish relations in it regardless of time and space, previous relation, and everything but affinity. We prate of freedom. We call our schools free because we are not free to stay away from them till we are sixteen years of age. I have given up my democratic prejudices and now willingly set the lower classes free to be completely taken care of by the upper classes. Political freedom is nothing to me. I bestow it right and left. All I would keep for myself is the freedom of my material—the condition of body and mind now and then to summons aptly from the vast chaos of all I have lived through.

Scholars and artists thrown together are often annoyed at the puzzle of where they differ. Both work from knowledge; but I suspect they differ most importantly in the way their knowledge is come by. Scholars get theirs with conscientious thoroughness along projected lines of logic; poets theirs cavalierly and as it happens in and out of books. They stick to nothing deliberately, but let what will stick to them like burrs where they walk in the fields. No acquirement is on assignment, or even self-assignment. Knowledge of the second kind is much more available in the wild free ways of wit and art. A schoolboy may be defined as one who can tell you what he knows in the order in which he learned it. The artist must value himself as he snatches a thing from some previous order in time and space into a new order with not so much as a ligature clinging to it of the old place where it was organic.

More than once I should have lost my soul to radicalism if it had been the originality it was mistaken for by its young converts. Originality and initiative are what I ask for my country. For myself the orginality need be no more than the freshness of a poem run in the way I have described: from delight to wisdom. The figure is the same as for love. Like a piece of ice on a hot stove the poem must ride on its own melting. A poem may be worked over once it is in being, but may not be worried into being. Its most precious quality will remain its having run itself and carried away the poet with it. Read it a hundred times: it will forever keep its freshness as a metal keeps its fragrance. It can never lose its sense of a meaning that once unfolded by surprise as it went.

Comments and Questions

"The Figure a Poem Makes" contains several of Frost's best-known statements on poetry. It is not, however, an essay that yields its meaning easily, and its logic is not that of the typical formal essay. The structure of the essay has the whimsical direction characteristic of Frost's poems, and it constantly surprises us with new turns and twists. Perhaps the essay itself best describes its method. Note these observations on writing from the essay, and discuss them in terms of Frost's manner of arranging his thoughts on poetry:

> No surprise for the writer, no surprise for the reader.

> The line will have the more charm for not being mechanically straight. We enjoy the straight crookedness of a good walking stick.

> It must be more felt than seen ahead like prophecy. It must be a revelation, or a series of revelations. . . .For it to be that there must have been the greatest freedom of the material to move about in it. . . .

Frost is speaking of the artist, but he writes here as the artist and not as the scholar. Notice his distinction between the two in regard to knowledge: "Scholars get theirs with conscientious thoroughness along projected lines of logic; poets theirs cavalierly as it happens in and out of books. They stick to nothing deliberately, but let what will stick to them like burrs when they walk in the fields."

1. To what extent does the essay use the devices we customarily expect in poetry? Discuss Frost's use of metaphor and imagery in the essay.

2. What view of "pure" poetry is Frost objecting to at the beginning of the essay? Why are "vowels, consonants, punctuation, syntax, words, sentences, meter" not enough? Why do poets need meaning, context, subject matter? "Theme alone can steady us down," he says. Why, in Frost's view, do poets need to be steadied down?

3. What are the two mysteries of poetry that the essay addresses?

4. Discuss Frost's view of poetry as "a clarification of life." His most often quoted definition of poetry is as a "momentary stay against confusion." What are some of the implications of this attitude toward the function of poetry? Do the Frost poems represented here satisfy this definition? (See the Index for selections by Frost.) Discuss, for example, "After Apple-Picking" (p. 571) as a "momentary stay against confusion."

5. Frost says that a poem "may be worked over once it is in being, but may not be worried into being." What does he mean? What is implied here about the act of creativity?

Samuel Taylor Coleridge   (1772–1834)
What Is Poetry?*

A poem contains the same elements as a prose composition; the difference therefore must consist in a different combination of them, in consequence of a different object proposed. According to the difference of the object will be the difference of the combination. It is possible, that the object may be merely to facilitate the recollection of any given facts or observations by artificial arrangement; and the composition will be a poem, merely because it is distinguished from prose by metre, or by rhyme, or by both conjointly. In this, the lowest sense, a man might attribute the name of a poem to the well known enumeration of the days in the several months;

> Thirty days hath September,
> April, June, and November, &c.

and others of the same class and purpose. And as a particular pleasure is found in anticipating the recurrence of sounds and quantities, all compositions that have this charm superadded, whatever be their contents, *may* be entitled poems.

* Excerpts from Chapter XIV of *Biographia Literaria* (1817).

So much for the superficial *form*. A difference of object and contents supplies an additional ground of distinction. The immediate purpose may be the communication of truths; either of truth absolute and demonstrable, as in works of science; or of facts experienced and recorded, as in history. Pleasure, and that of the highest and most permanent kind, may *result* from the *attainment* of the end; but it is not itself the immediate end. In other works [including poetry] the communication of pleasure may be the immediate purpose. . . .

But the communication of pleasure may be the immediate object of a work not metrically composed; and that object may have been in a high degree attained, as in novels and romances. Would then the mere superaddition of metre, with or without rhyme, entitle *these* to the name of poems? The answer is, that nothing can permanently please, which does not contain in itself the reason why it is so, and not otherwise. If metre be superadded, all other parts must be made consonant with it. They must be such, as to justify the perpetual and distinct attention to each part, which an exact correspondent recurrence of accent and sound are calculated to excite. The final definition then, so deduced, may be thus worded. A poem is that species of composition, which is opposed to works of science, by proposing for its *immediate* object pleasure, not truth; and from all other species (having *this* object in common with it) it is discriminated by proposing to itself such delight from the *whole,* as is compatible with a distinct gratification from each component *part.*

Controversy is not seldom excited in consequence of the disputants attaching each a different meaning to the same word . . . . But if the definition sought for be that of a *legitimate* poem, I answer, it must be one, the parts of which mutually support and explain each other; all in their proportion harmonizing with, and supporting the purpose and known influences of metrical arrangement. The philosophic critics of all ages coincide with the ultimate judgement of all countries, in equally denying the praises of a just poem, on the one hand, to a series of striking lines or distichs, each of which absorbing the whole attention of the reader to itself disjoins it from its context, and makes it a separate whole, instead of an harmonizing part; and on the other hand, to an unsustained composition, from which the reader collects rapidly the general result unattracted by the component parts. The reader should be carried forward, not merely or chiefly by the mechanical impulse of curiosity, or by a restless desire to arrive at the final solution; but by the pleasureable activity of mind excited by the attractions of the journey itself. Like the motion of a serpent, which the Egyptians made the emblem of intellectual power; or like the path of sound through the air; at every step he pauses and half recedes, and from the retrogressive movement collects the force which again carries him onward. *Præcipitandus est liber spiritus,*[1] says Petronius Arbiter most happily. The epithet, *liber,* here balances the preceding verb; and it is not easy to conceive more meaning condensed in fewer words.

5 But if this should be admitted as a satisfactory character of a poem, we have still to seek for a definition of poetry. . . . What is poetry? is so nearly the same question with, what is a poet? that the answer to the one is involved in the solution of the other. For it is a distinction resulting from the poetic genius itself, which sustains and modifies the images, thoughts, and emotions of the poet's own mind. The poet, described in *ideal* perfection, brings the whole soul of man into activity, with the subordination of its faculties to each other, according to their relative worth and dignity. He diffuses a tone, and spirit of unity, that blends, and (as it were) *fuses,* each into each, by that synthetic and magical power, to which we have exclusively appropriated the name of imagination. This power,

---

[1] The free spirit should be urged forward.

first put in action by the will and understanding, and retained under their irremissive, though gentle and unnoticed, controul *(laxis effertur habenis[2])* reveals itself in the balance or reconciliation of opposite or discordant qualities: of sameness, with difference; of the general, with the concrete; the idea, with the image; the individual, with the representative; the sense of novelty and freshness, with old and familiar objects; a more than usual state of emotion, with more than usual order; judgement ever awake and steady self-possession, with enthusiasm and feeling profound or vehement; and while it blends and harmonizes the natural and the artificial, still subordinates art to nature; the manner to the matter; and our admiration of the poet to our sympathy with the poetry.

Comments and Questions

1. In this passage Coleridge expresses the fundamental principle of his (and much twentieth-century) poetic theory and practice, that the essence of poetry lies in its achievement of imaginative unity through "the balance or reconciliation of opposite or discordant qualities." What imagery can you pull from Frost's essay above which suggests a very similar emphasis on such a reconciliation? What other comparisons in perspective seem worth making between these two practicing poets at some hundred years' distance from each other? To what extent is that hundred years significant in making such comparisons?

2. Elsewhere, in defending Shakespeare from the charge of being only a crude and irregular genius, Coleridge similarly insists on the poetic dramatist's apparent combination of individual genius with a necessary sense of order and purpose: "The spirit of poetry, like all other living powers, must of necessity circumscribe itself by rules, were it only to unite power with beauty. It must embody in order to reveal itself; but a living body is of necessity an organized one . . . ."[3] How would you relate those remarks and Coleridge's comments above to Blake's "The Tiger" (p. 396), a poem at once expressing essential requirements for living a vital life and for creating a genuine poem? How do the dominant qualities of the tiger relate to that theme and to the remarks of both Coleridge and Frost?

3. In connection with Coleridge's emphasis on both intense emotion and more than usual order and control in poetry, it might be helpful to think in terms, say, of a scream on the one hand and a sentence expressing strong feelings on the other. In the second instance, one would have both feeling and (necessarily) order. What are some other potentials that the sentence would offer that the scream alone could not? Remember that a scream is a noise, a sentence is language or, in a sense, organized noise.

4. What relationship do you see between Coleridge's principle of a reconciliation of opposites and the figurative method and theme of his poem "Kubla Khan" (p. 459)? Before answering, you might want to ponder Coleridge's conversational remark (from *Table Talk*) made in his later years that he could write as good poetry as ever if he were free from irritations and in the "hearing of fine music, which has a sensible effect in harmonizing my thoughts, and in animating, and as it were, lubricating my inventive faculty."

[2] Is carried along with loose reins.

[3] For this and other reconstructions from Coleridge's lectures on Shakespeare, see Thomas M. Raysor, *Coleridge's Shakesperian Criticism,* 2 vols., Cambridge, Mass.: Harvard University Press, 1930.

Grover Smith (1923–   )
A Critique of T. S. Eliot's "The Love Song of J. Alfred Prufrock"*

Eliot's Prufrock is a tragic figure. Negligible to others, he suffers in a hell of defeated idealism, tortured by unappeasable desires. He dare not risk the disappointment of seeking actual love, which, if he found it and had energy for it, still could not satisfy him. The plight of this hesitant, inhibited man, an aging dreamer trapped in decayed, shabby-genteel surroundings, aware of beauty and faced with sordidness, mirrors the plight of the sensitive in the presence of the dull. Prufrock, however, has a tragic flaw, which he discloses in the poem: through timidity he is incapable of action. In contrast with the lady in the "Portrait," who feels that she might come alive with lilacs in the spring, he has descended, because of his very idealism, into a winter of passivity. To pursue the tragical analogy, one might call Prufrock's idealism the "curse" which co-operates with his flaw to make him wretched. Alone, neither curse nor flaw would be dangerous; together, they destroy him. Prufrock's responsiveness to ideal values is something theoretically good in itself, an appanage of virtue; yet it partakes of impiety, for it is sentimental instead of ethical. His values are inherited from the romantic-love tradition, a cult of the unreal and consequently of the inapprehensible. But since he is consciously unheroic, as a comparison of his own with Hamlet's dilemma convinces him, Prufrock should seem comic rather than tragic did not precisely his awareness, his sense of proportion, counter laughter with a virtual admission that his case makes much ado about nothing. A comic discovery would set all to rights; Prufrock's discovery of his flaw,

> I have seen the eternal Footman hold my coat, and snicker,
> And in short, I was afraid,

reminds one that no problem is trifling to the man it grieves and that the more ridiculous its revelation would seem to others, the more it may distress him.

The drama of the poem is presented through soliloquy, the action being limited to the interplay of impressions, including memories, in Prufrock's mind. A rather curious device complicates his reverie. By a distinction between "I" and "you," he differentiates between his thinking, sensitive character and his outward self. It may be that the poem contains traces of a medieval *débat,* as in "The Body and the Soul"; but Prufrock, in saying "you," is not speaking only to his body. He is addressing, as if looking into a mirror, his whole public personality. His motive seems to be to repudiate the inert self, which cannot act, and to assert his will. In a strict sense it is not this mirror image which is a *Doppelgänger* but the ego supervising the *monologue intérieur.* The ego alone "goes" anywhere, even in fantasy; the other, at the risk of being rebuffed with "Oh, do not ask, 'What is it?' " merely originates objections, though unfortunately this self finally decides his failure. Being no image of the heroic Prufrock he would like to be, but his own spindling, wispy frame, it necessitates his refusal of an action in which it, and not he, would be the real agent. The man of feeling can treat with no one except through his physical and psycho-

---

* The text of "The Love Song of J. Alfred Prufrock" appears on p. 575. The following footnotes are by Grover Smith.

logical mask: through it he is interpreted and by it he is condemned. Nor can the ego survive disgrace of the personality; at the end of the poem it is "we" who drown.

The epigraph to the poem expands the context of Prufrock's frustration. Guido da Montefeltro, tormented in the eighth circle of the *Inferno* (XXVII) for the sin of fraud through evil counsel, replies to Dante's question about his identity:

> If I thought my answer were to one who ever could return to the world, this flame should shake no more;

> But since none ever did return alive from this depth, if what I hear be true, without fear of infamy I answer thee.

His crime has been to pervert human reason by guile; like Ulysses he is wrapped in a flame representing his duplicity in his former life, when he knew and practiced "wiles and covert ways"—"Gli accorgimenti e le coperte vie." To Prufrock's own life this reply is also applicable. He, like Guido, is in hell, though unlike Guido, he has never participated in the active evil of the world, so that this resemblance is as ironic as the resemblance to Hamlet. But in this also there is a core of substantial truth. Prufrock is similar to Guido in having abused intellect; he has done so by channeling it into profitless fantasy. By indulging in daydreams (the soliloquy in the poem itself), he has allowed his ideal conception of woman (the sea-girls at the end) to dominate his transactions with reality. He has neither used human love nor rejected it but has cultivated an illusory notion of it which has paralyzed his will and kept him from turning desire into action. His self-detraction when he confesses that he is only a pompous fool, a Polonius instead of a Hamlet (and recognizing this fact, partly a wise Fool too), accompanies his realization that the dream itself has been only a snare, though he cannot get out of its meshes.

> I have heard the mermaids singing, each to each.

> I do not think that they will sing to me.

Failing to abandon the illusion or to be content without physical love, he despairs of life. He has advanced beyond naïve sentimentality in discovering its emptiness, but he has found nothing to replace it. His tragedy remains that of a man for whom love is beyond achievement but still within desire. His age, his shyness, and the somewhat precious and for America, at least, esoteric quality of his name, with its obtrusive initial *J* (recalling the signature T. Stearns-Eliot which Eliot used), underscore his demureness. The name Prufrock, which sounds like the man, was borrowed for him by Eliot from a St. Louis family.[1] It was a good choice.

Prufrock's thoughts start with a command to the self designated as "you" to accompany him to a distant drawing-room. His object is to declare himself to a lady—though to precisely which one of the roomful, he never specifies and perhaps has not decided. The opening image symbolizes through bathos the helpless Prufrock's subjective impression of the evening, which is like an anesthetized patient because he himself is one. By the meditated visit he might escape from the seclusion, both physical and psychological, oppressing him. That he cannot thus escape, first because of hesitancy and then because of despair, means that he will not stir from his spot at all. As the imagery shows, his world is a closed one. Various oppositions convey Prufrock's sense of impotent inferiority or isolation: the evening against the sky and the patient on the table; the streets and the room; the fog and the house; the women's transfixing eyes and the victim wriggling like a stuck

---

[1] Stephen Stepenchev, "The Origin of J. Alfred Prufrock," *Modern Language Notes,* LXVI (June, 1951), 400–401.

bug; the white, bare arms of cold day and the sensuous arms of lamplight; the proper coat and collar and the informal shirtsleeves; the clothing and the feeble limbs; the prim manners and the amorous appetite; the prophet and the ignobly severed head; the resurrection and the grave; the prince and the emotional pauper; the bright world of singing mermaids skimming the waves and the buried world of death in the sea-depths of fantasy. These all set down a record of Prufrock's longing to reach out, like grasping claws, and take life into his embrace and of his inhibition by the discrepancy between wishes and facts.

5   In his tentative urge toward action he betrays the fruitlessness of his search: the streets, stifling "retreats" with cheap hotels and with restaurants ("sawdust restaurants" in more than one sense, perhaps) littered with oyster shells like the sea floor of his emotional submersion, could lead only to a question as overwhelming to the lady as to him. And the women meanwhile are talking, no doubt tediously and ignorantly of Michelangelo, the sculptor of a strength and magnitude with which Prufrock cannot compete.[2] From the prospect of his visit he distracts himself by considering the yellow fog which sleepily laps the house and then by musing that he has plenty of time to "prepare a face," whether in order to lay a plot of momentous effect or to make small-talk over a teacup. But the recurring thought of the women leads him to speculate on their reaction to him, to the baldness he might betray if he beat too hasty a retreat, and to the ill-disguised thinness of his arms and legs. At this point he admits his first doubt, namely, whether he "dare/Disturb the universe"—a hyperbole illustrating his terrified self-consciousness. Immediately after he thus reveals his want of easy terms with life, he shows his distaste for the women as they are; both circumstances result, it appears later, from absorption in daydreams. Rejecting the voices, the eyes, and the arms (all impersonal, all monotonous, hostile, delusive), he can think of no formula of proposal but one humiliating to himself—a presumptuous obsequiousness:

> Shall I say, I have gone at dusk through narrow streets
> And watched the smoke that rises from the pipes
> Of lonely men in shirt-sleeves, leaning out of windows?

His horror of being dissected, of being "pinned," makes him recoil to the wish that he had been

>   a pair of ragged claws
> Scuttling across the floors of silent seas.[3]

With this image, just before the climax of the dramatic structure, Prufrock perceives his lack of instinct, of mindless appetite, which would have given him a realizable aim and which, of course, would have made him at home in those depths where at present he exists abnormally.

He has already spoken of the fog and smoke as if it were a cat (a Sandburg cat, no doubt) curling round the house. He now refers to the drowsy afternoon (which, correcting himself, he realizes is evening after all), saying, it "sleeps so peacefully," "stretched on the floor"—or, like his etherized self, "malingers." He is again confronting the difficulty of action rather than its unpleasantness. The difficulty lies in dread of personal inadequacy, maybe even of sexual insufficiency—"the strength to force the moment to its crisis." The climax of his reverie is shaped as he compares himself, in his feeling of being decapitated (perhaps, in effect, of being unmanned), to John the Baptist: and yet at once he disclaims

---

[2] Roberta Morgan and Albert Wohlstetter, "Observations on 'Prufrock,'" *Harvard Advocate*, CXXV, No. 3 (December, 1938), 30.

[3] Perhaps an allusion to *Hamlet*, Act II, Scene ii, lines 198–199.

the dignity of a prophet, seeing himself instead as the butt of a lackey's derision, as the butt of snickering Death. Having confessed his cowardice, he knows that it is too late for him to go, and indeed that it always was.

The remainder of the poem moves toward the image of drowning, a counterpart to the undersea image in the "ragged claws" lines. Henceforth Prufrock speaks of what *would have* happened and affirms the improbability of a favorable issue to his suit. He would have had to "bite off" and "spit out" his question in some graceless way; he would have had to "squeeze the universe into a ball" (an image in part borrowed from Marvell's "To His Coy Mistress," where it has sexual value); he would have had to rise like Lazarus from the dead (the comparison was suggested to Eliot by Dostoevsky's *Crime and Punishment*[4]) and "tell all," as Dives implored in the parable of the other Lazarus. And, at that, the answer of the lady might have been a casual rebuff. In view therefore of these impossibilities, of their clash with decorous commonplaceness and, above all, of their unacceptability because they would have brought exposure, "as if a magic lantern threw the nerves in patterns on a screen," he disclaims his pretensions. He cannot even dignify his *accidia* by associating it with that of Hamlet. Consequently he resolves, in the only positive decision he can make, to go down upon the seashore, where for a while he may masquerade in his dandyishly cuffed white-flannel trousers. He will perhaps part his hair to conceal his baldness and risk the solaces of a peach, the sole forbidden fruit he is likely to pluck. The happy mermaids, at least, will not insist that he wear a morning coat and tie. But even the mermaids, alas, will not sing to him. His vision of them has been a delusion into whose waters he has sunk deeper and deeper until, recalled to the intolerable real world by human voices in a drawing-room, he has waked and drowned in his subjective world of dreams. Like legendary sailors lulled asleep by mermaids or sirens and then dragged down to perish in the sea, Prufrock has awakened too late.

Archibald MacLeish   (1892–1982)
Who Precisely Do You Think You Are?

A year ago my friend, Mark Van Doren, was lunching with a table full of Amherst boys who astonished him by asking what they should do with their lives. "Whatever you want," said Van Doren, "just so long as you don't miss the main thing." "And what," they said, "is the main thing?" "Your lives," said Van Doren.

He was right, of course. A man can easily miss his life if he doesn't know who's living it—if he thinks a lawyer is living it or a professor of biochemistry or the head of a dry-cleaning plant or a mechanical engineer. He can wake up in his forty-fifth year and

---

[4] John C. Pope, "Prufrock and Raskolnikov," *American Literature,* XVII (November, 1945), 213–230; "Prufrock and Raskolnikov Again: A Letter from Eliot," *American Literature,* XVIII (January, 1947), 319–321.

realize that it isn't he in his bed but the treasurer of the Second National Bank. And the same thing is true, even more true, of a woman—she can come to herself, as the phrase goes, only to discover that she has no self to come to: there is no one there but the children's nurse or the chauffeur of the family station wagon, or the fourth chair in a bridge game that has been going on and on, every other Monday night, for twenty years.

So that question does present itself. To all of us. Or to all of us now, at least, in this questioning century. In simpler generations a woman could say, as Ophelia did, "We know what we are but we know not what we may become." It was only the grave that puzzled them then: the dark on the other side. With us it's the contrary: we know or think we know what we may become—it's what we are that haunts us.

Mankind? Certainly . . . but what is a man? We find it difficult to say. We know what a man was once because we have the record before us: what is literature but just that record? To Sophocles he was the wonder of the world. "Wonders are many on the earth," says the Chorus in the *Antigone,* "and of these man is the greatest." To Shakespeare he was like a god: "What a piece of work is a man! how noble in reason! how infinite in faculty! in form, in moving, how express and admirable! in action how like an angel! in apprehension how like a god! the beauty of the world! the paragon of animals!"

5   But what is man to us? Suppose you look at the folk art of the age, the graffiti of the advertising pages, the popular ballads from that world between the television programs where never is heard a discouraging word and the skies are unclouded all day. What is he there? A figure like a god? A wonder? Not precisely: a creature of rather different dimensions, a being whose dominant desire seems to be to smell sweet, to weigh less, to own the automobile everyone else will envy, and to go on smoking cigarettes even if they kill him—which they doubtless will. He has headaches, yes, sleeps badly, suffers or makes others suffer from tobacco breath, but none of this is tragic: he can always doctor himself with lozenges and pills, travel to Miami, buy a new detergent, and find at the end of it all, where Heaven used to be, a Lincoln Continental.

A satiric figure? Not in intention certainly: who would spend millions of dollars to subsidize the inanities of television merely to satirize the human race? No, the purpose is not satiric: merely the assumptions, the presuppositions. And they are not so much satiric as contemptuous. A creature presented as seeing himself solely in terms of his smell, his pills, his excitants, his soporifics and the neighbors' opinion of his possessions is a creature imagined by Jonathan Swift—a Jonathan Swift without talent, granted, but a Jonathan Swift notwithstanding.

And if you turn to literature, the literature of the time, the literature characteristic of the time and most specifically dedicated to it, the same opinion of humanity presents itself. "One of the primary features of literature (as of much activity in all the other arts) in our times," says Susan Sontag, one of the most perceptive critics of the generation, "is a chronic attachment to materials belonging to the realm of extreme situations—madness, crime, taboo sexual longings, drug addiction, emotional degradation, violent death. The motive or justification for this loyalty to extreme situations is obscure. It is felt that such situations are somehow 'more true' than others; that an art immersed in such situations is 'more serious' than other art; and finally, that only art that embraces the irrational and repellent, the violent and the outrageous, can make a valuable impact on the sluggish consciousness of the audience."

This, of course, is something more than a description of the writing of some of Miss Sontag's contemporaries: it is an account also of the beliefs about mankind on which their writing is founded. To say that the literature of "extreme situations"— of "madness, crime, taboo sexual longings, drug addiction, emotional degradation, violent death"—is felt by its authors to be "more true" means of course "more true" to man, more true to that human truth which is the measure of all literary truth. To say that an art immersed in "extreme situations" is felt to be "more serious" means more humanly serious, more worthy of serious human attention, because more *like* humanity.

Whether Miss Sontag's contemporaries would accept so blunt an interpretation of their views is questionable, but certainly the best of them would find it difficult to dissent. Man, to Samuel Beckett, is explicitly and dramatically something up to its neck in sand which would have hanged itself long ago except that the sand keeps rising. And most of the rest would agree in one form of metaphor or another. If the mirror held up by the advertising agencies is contemptuous, the mirror held up by art—by the art we call contemporary, "modern"—is derisory. The "absurdity" of human life, which the fashionable philosophers have taught us to see, has rubbed off on the human creature who lives it, and though we may call him Sisyphus and weep for him, we weep in pity—or self-pity: never as we weep for Oedipus or Lear.

And yet—and this, of course, is the heart of the matter—it is we who have produced these images: we or our surrogates, our writers, artists. And the pertinent question thus becomes the question, Why? Why have we produced them? Why has our conception of our human nature so changed in this particular time, this generation, this century? Why has the grandeur gone, the greatness, above all the wonder, so that no contemporary character on our stage could say without a snicker of self-consciousness what Hamlet said: "How infinite in faculty! in form, in moving, how express and admirable! in action how like an angel! in apprehension how like a god!"?

Is it because ours is a time without grandeur?—a time without event? On the contrary it is a great and tragic time which is also heroic as few ages have been heroic—an age which has produced, here and elsewhere, some of the most remarkable figures—remarkable both for good and for evil—the world has ever seen. It is a time of two world wars within a generation of each other with a space of hope and misery between—a time as memorable for courageous and unnoticed actions as it is for wholesale slaughters and unspeakable miseries. It is also, and at the same time, the epoch in which man has gone farther out toward the unknown, even the unknowable, than he had gone in all the centuries and millennia before. Prophecy is a fatuous and ungrateful business, but it hardly requires prophecy to foresee that men in future generations, if there are to be future generations, will look back on these few years as among the most terrible and splendid in the annals of the race.

Why then have we peopled them with pettiness and squalor? Why do we see mankind in the images we have created? Is it perhaps because we know something, in our newfound scientific knowledge, which those who lived before us did not know? Is it because we have discovered a truth about mankind which Sophocles never guessed and Shakespeare could not utter?

There are some who seem to think so. A British scientist lecturing recently at the Museum of Natural History in New York announced that "the explosive charge which, in this century, has split open the self-assurance of western man" is contained in what he called "the bland proposition" that "man is a part of nature." If it is true, he said, as it seems to be true, that "living matter is not different in kind from dead matter" then "man as a species will be shown to be no more than a machinery of atoms," and if man is no more than a machinery of atoms he cannot be a "person." It is "the nagging fear," Dr. Bronowski concluded, that we are not persons—that we are nothing but machines—which has produced the "crisis of confidence" in which we live.

But is it? That "nagging fear," if it is one, has been around for a long time. Dr. Bronowski's "bland proposition" was talked of in antiquity and stated in so many words by one of the greatest of scientific philosophers more than three hundred years ago: to

Descartes all bodies, human as well as animal, were completely mechanistic in structure and behavior. The announcement produced no "crisis of confidence" in the seventeenth century even in France—least of all in France where Jean-Jacques Rousseau was shortly to appear together with the most unquestioning confidence in man the world had ever seen or has seen since.

But is the difference, perhaps, that now we *know* what Descartes could only assert? *Do* we know? Dr. René Dubos of the Rockefeller Institute, a man who is entitled to an opinion if anybody is, apparently doubts it. "From one end of the spectrum," he says, "man appears as an ordinary physiochemical machine, complex, of course, but nevertheless re-acting with environmental forces according to the same laws that govern inanimate nature. From the other end man is seen as a creature that is rarely a passive component in the reacting system; the most characteristic aspect of his behavior is the fact that he responds actively and often creatively. . . . Man is the more human the better he is able to convert passive reactions into creative responses." What is human in man, in other words, is pre-cisely that which is not mechanical and the mechanical definition, therefore, misses its point. Dr. Dubos suggests another: "Man—the creature who can choose, eliminate, assem-ble, decide and thereby create."

It is not for us—not for me certainly— to decide the rights and wrongs of this debate founded in the discoveries of biology and psychology. But even those who have no competence in science can speak for themselves when their own emotions are called into question, and I, for one, would seriously doubt that the "nagging fear" modern humanity is alleged to feel is really fear at all, or that our "crisis of confidence," if that is the proper term for our characteristic state of mind, can be attributed to the scientific discovery that we are made of atoms like everything else.

There may be men who have thought of mankind as composed of a special human material despite the famous admonition, "Dust thou art . . . " and such men may conceiv-ably feel themselves betrayed by the demonstration that they are mere Meccano sets put together out of the common building blocks of the universe, as though a cross section of quartz had come to consciousness. If so they may think of Beckett's characters as appro-priate symbols of their state—poor potted plants to whom nothing human is possible but an occasional erotic *frisson* faintly reminiscent of a biologic role no longer feasible under the circumstances. But that most of us feel and think in terms like these I simply do not believe.

I myself have never met a man or woman, even among college students where you can meet almost anything, who was actually frightened by the thought that he might be an atomic combination rather than the cousin-german of an angel. Quite the contrary. To men of our generation a machine that can think is, if anything, more attractive than an angel and certainly more wonderful.

But if I am right, if our faith in our humanity has not been shaken by the advances of science, what has shaken it? If it is not because we know something about ourselves which our ancestors did not know, why is it that we think of our humanity as so dimin-ished? Could it conceivably be for the opposite reason?–not because we know something about ourselves earlier human beings did not know, but because we have forgotten some-thing about ourselves earlier men once knew?

Consider that famous Chorus in the *Antigone*—consider what the old men of Thebes are saying about mankind. Man, they say, is the wonder of the world. He is the master of the ageless earth, bending that mother of the gods to his will by his continuing toil. He is the master also of all living things, birds, beasts—hunting them, teaching them. He learns the use of language, of the wind-swift mind: the laws of living together in great cities built against the winter and the rain. There is nothing beyond his power—nothing but one

thing. He overcomes all chances, all the dangers, finds the remedy for every ill—every ill
but one. Death he cannot overcome.

What Sophocles' Chorus is saying, in other words, is what men throughout those
centuries were always saying, that man is the wonder of the world because, although he
dies, although he has no remedy for destiny or death, he masters nevertheless the ageless
earth, tames beasts, builds cities, races with the wind-swift mind. Heroism was never
triumph to the Greeks of the great age: heroism was Prometheus with the eagle at his
liver, Herakles among his murdered sons. And man was never anything but man, the
mortal figure dignified by its mortality, like those magnificent forms of Leonard Baskin's,
heavy with grandeur and with death.

And what has happened to that knowledge now? Nothing except that we have lost
it. Nothing except that we have turned it inside out as those philosophers do who tell our
generation that our world, *because we die,* is an absurdity: that Sisyphus is our symbol and
our sign.

There is no proof one way or the other, I suppose. Sophocles' nobly tragic world
may be a dream and ours the meaningless reality. There is no proof—but there is this to
think of: that whenever in the history of our kind men have thought of man as Sophocles
thought of him, art has flourished and the mind come clear. "What's the meaning of all
song?" asks Yeats in that curious poem in *Vacillation.* "Let all things pass away." It is a
hard saying but the truth is in it: it is when the human heart faces its destiny and notwithstanding sings—sings of itself, its life, its death—that poetry is possible.

And there is something else to think of: nothing in human life is more contemptible
than self-pity. Pride may be delusion but, even if it is, self-pity is far worse. When it comes
to that peremptory, that always haunting question, pride is the nobler fault. Who, precisely,
do you think you are? A man. A woman.

Comments and Questions

Literature is a search for answers. Its range is as wide as the total experience of the human
race. Sometimes, at its best, it plumbs depths heretofore measureless to man. Sometimes
its measure is a teaspoon, for the shallows must also be explored. It may legitimately be
read for pleasure alone, for simple recognition of the familiar or for wonder at the strange.
Its intent, however, whether overt or subtle, is to seek an answer to MacLeish's question:
"Who precisely do you think you are?" Interpreting literature can be a powerful aid to
self-analysis.

1. MacLeish's essay may be compared to Krutch's "The Tragic Fallacy," page 1112.
What is the central idea of both?

2. "Matter in motion" summarizes the theory that human beings, as well as things,
are merely material, interacting chemicals without spiritual quality. What we call courage,
for example, is simply a chemical response to stimuli. This conception bothers MacLeish,
who favors the dualism of flesh and spirit. Older literature, he shows, supports his view
and gives him confidence in his own intuitions. Nevertheless his honesty forces him to
suppose that "There is no proof one way or the other." What word denotes belief in the
unprovable? Does MacLeish use this word?

3. The author sufficiently identifies the persons to whom he alludes, but you may
wish to find out more about Susan Sontag, Dr. (Jacob) Bronowski, Dr. René Dubos, Samuel

Beckett, and Leonard Baskin. Any standard reference work will provide further information.

4. "Know thyself" is no doubt a laudable objective, but the nagging phrase "identity crisis" is a comment on how difficult it is to achieve self-knowledge. How, precisely, does literature aid the quest for self-knowledge?

Kingman Brewster, Jr. (1919–   )
In Defense of Liberal Education*

. . . My own analysis of the current assault on liberal education is that the specialization required by a complex society marches hand in hand with the economic pressure to squeeze out anything "useless." Vocationalism is the cry. To this is now added the opprobrium which attaches to anything which can be tagged as "elitist." This is especially so if it seems to reek with either self-indulgence on the one hand or an inside track to power or status on the other.

On the first point, the claim is that career usefulness in a specialized society urges more vocationalism, or at least professionalism, in college education. This is plausible if you buy a purely economic test of the value of education. In the booming fifties some economists who applied their "dismal science" to the educational "market" gave the impression that the individual and social value of education depended entirely upon the higher productive potential of the educated person compared to the less educated. The higher economic output was portrayed as the be-all and end-all of personal or public investment in higher education. The cash nexus was it.

Even back then I remember some wag telling the late Professor Seymour Harris of Harvard that the economics of higher education could be understood only if you rid your mind of concepts of market, unit cost, productivity, and marginal utility. What the teaser was trying to suggest, somewhat facetiously, was that the costs and benefits of education do not stop with the inputs and outputs which can be weighed and measured in purely economic terms.

Having popularized the cash nexus analysis of education in the fifties, it is not surprising that some commentators today, in the depressed seventies, should put the finger on liberal education as the wastrel, since it cannot easily be credited with a career or vocational pay-out.

5   Their message finds sympathetic ears among parents who would like some rationale for preferring the tuition-free trade school to the expensive liberal arts college. Certainly the critical attack finds response in the halls of the Congress and of many state legislatures. They eagerly endorse former Education Commissioner Marland's support of the vocational, while cutting back the liberal. In research they support the applied in preference to the

---

* Title provided by the editors. The following footnotes are by Kingman Brewster, Jr.

basic. They look more kindly upon the quantitative weights and measures in preference to the humanistic tradition.

To this emphasis on the career value of education in economic terms is added the political fuel of anti-intellectualism generally. This fuel is made more volatile by the charge that a liberal arts college is just four years of self-indulgence. In a somewhat contradictory posture, populist critics also complain that liberal education provides an inside track to status and power. On both counts it is subject to the charge of "elitism."

So what should our answer be?

The Aims of Liberal Learning

If I remember correctly, in the law there is something called "a plea in confession and avoidance." It says, in essence, "yes, the facts are as alleged, but what I did is not illegal." Along the same lines I think we should cheerfully admit that a liberal education *does* indulge the student. In a sense also, a liberal education *does* help to equip a person for leadership.

We should proudly confess these privileges, *provided that access to them is on the merits, as best it can be fallibly determined in the admissions process, so that opportunity for self-indulgence, opportunity for leadership is decided on the merits, not on the basis of inheritance or class or sex or race.*

If we are morally sure that no one who has the talent and the motivation for it is excluded from the opportunity for a liberal education, then we should readily admit that in a way it *is* self-indulgent; in some perspectives it *is* elitist. Instead of cringing in face of the philistines' criticism, we should glory in what a liberal education can do for the individual; we should take pride in what the liberally educated person can contribute to the quality and direction of a civilized and humane society.

Self-indulgence is pretty hard to deny, if you admit that perhaps the most fundamental value of a liberal education is that it makes life more interesting. This is true whether you are fetched up on a desert island or adrift in the impersonal loneliness of the urban hurly-burly. It allows you to see things which the under-educated do not see. It allows you to understand things which the untutored find incomprehensible. It allows you to think things which do not occur to the less learned. In short, it makes it less likely that you will be bored with life. It also makes it less likely that you will be a crashing bore to those whose company you keep. By analogy it makes the difference between the traveler who understands the local language and the traveler to whom the local language is a jumble of nonsense sounds.

A liberal education, even at its best, will not tell you how to solve all the puzzles of the universe. But it will make you wiser about the mysteries of the universe. Liberally educated people share the excitement of the effort to reduce those mysteries to rational explanation by the application of logic to fact. They can enjoy the effort to articulate human experience by rigorous and precise literary and historical expression. They can perceive revelations in expressive and symbolic form, in creative letters, in music, and the other arts. In these terms, even if you "do nothing with it," a liberal education makes life much more interesting than it otherwise would be.

It is not just an alertness to things around you, however, which makes life richer. There are at least three "senses" which are enhanced by a liberal education: a sense of place, a sense of self, and a sense of judgment.

By a *sense of place,* I do not mean latitude and longitude. I mean, rather, a sense that no person, institution, group or nation can escape the roots and evolution which give them cultural identity and distinctive meaning. Place is a matter of cultural as well as physical "turf" in all its racial, religious, sociological, and political aspects. It cannot be truly appreciated except through the lens of history. Sensitivity to comparabilities and contrasts in time and space is an important product of a liberal education.[1]

The *sense of self* also depends in no small part on an awareness of where you are, where you have been, and where you are going. Historians may supply the ship's log. Scientists, natural and social, may contribute the compass; applied scientists the charts. It takes literature and the arts to provide the suggestive insights into humanity and its condition. No one of them alone will tell you who and what you are. Even all three together will give you only a clue to where you are going but without them you are likely to remain adrift, without personal purpose or direction.

A *sense of judgment* is the last sense I mentioned: critical judgment—an informed and objective basis for deciding with some confidence what you agree with, what you like; action judgment—a basis for deciding what will work and what won't; and, part of both, but transcending all others, moral judgment—a basis for deciding what is proper, worthy, noble.

The development and refinement of all these "senses" are objectives of a liberal education.

Their development may be an indulgence, but it is not solely for the benefit of the fortunate individual. A society which does not have some members of each generation blessed with these senses will soon cease to be civilized. The vitality and continuity of any culture requires men and women who understand its values and who, because of their understanding, have a capacity to conserve and transmit the best of what has been achieved.

The more harried life becomes, the more narrowly specialized all callings become, the more important it is to have some people around who are concerned with the quality of life and mind and spirit in the society as a whole, not just some specialized corner of it.[2] If there are not some for whom leisure can be reflective and creative, the society would cease to be supportive of those who do try to add to understanding and who do try to create.

A society which disparaged its patrons, its collectors, its bibliophiles and its semi-learned journals, and amateur groups devoted to scientific and humanistic ideas, would soon cease to nurture its culture.

The charge of elitism, however, is not aimed primarily at liberally "educated" persons because they have a capacity to appreciate and enjoy the works of mind and pen and hand. It is leveled more often at the liberal arts college because, while not all educated people are leaders, advancement and prestige do seem to be enhanced by a breadth of learning.

This is not too surprising. All the senses I mentioned do, after all, contribute to a person's ability to take the measure of problems and people, to see possibilities and recognize impossibilities, to avoid the pits of dismay and the giddy heights of hubris.

When the expertise of the specialist has been exhausted; when the accumulated data do not point in an unambiguous direction, an informed intuition comes into play. When,

[1] These thoughts have drawn heavily upon a talk given by George Wilson Pierson, Larned Professor Emeritus and Historian of the University, to a regional meeting of Yale Alumni in San Francisco in March of 1965, entitled "The Humanities and Moral Man." This was reprinted in the *Yale Alumni Magazine* of October, 1965.

[2] The late Dean William Clyde DeVane was perhaps the most persistent champion of the importance of producing people who had a sense of the relatedness of things, not just an expert knowledge of their own specialized field. This was put by him with puckish eloquence in his last speech to the Annual Banquet of the *Yale Daily News* in 1960. It was reprinted in full in the *News* of April 25, 1960.

in short, wisdom requires more than knowledge, the vicarious experience of science and history, the perceptions of great literature, the sense that the struggle between good and evil defies resolution by formula or purely rational trade-off, all these stand anyone in good stead. They are essential to those who must take responsibility for decisions, especially decisions affecting others.

Of course a liberal education does not guarantee wisdom. Of course people of unusual gifts can come by understanding without formal learning. But liberal learning does increase the chance of wisdom. And wisdom does increase the ability to lead.

Comments and Questions

Kingman Brewster, Jr., was president of Yale. This essay has been taken from his 1976 *Report* to Yale alumni.

"In Defense of Liberal Education" concludes this edition of *Interpreting Literature* fittingly, for it argues that all the arts—and literature in particular—seek to expand the mind, to give pleasure, to promote awareness, to allow us "to see things which the undereducated do not see."

1. Are the goals stated above useful? If so, in what way? If not, what goals are more useful?

2. Compare the thrust of this essay with that of MacLeish's "Who Precisely Do You Think You Are?" See page 1156.

3. President Brewster identifies "three 'senses' which are enhanced by a liberal education." Discuss each of these.

4. How does the essay answer the charge that liberal education is elitist and self-indulgent? Discuss Brewster's conclusion that "the most fundamental value of a liberal education is that it makes life more interesting."

(Acknowledgments continued from p. iv).

from *The Lice* by W. S. Merwin, copyright 1967 by W. S. Merwin; and "An Annual and Perennial Problem," originally published in *A Time of Bees,* which is now included in *Merciful Disguises* by Mona Van Duyn, copyright © 1964, 1973 by Mona Van Duyn.

Mrs. W. A. Bradley for permission to reprint "Caligula" from *Caligula and Three Other Plays* by Albert Camus, translated by Stuart Gilbert, copyright © 1958 by Alfred A. Knopf, Inc.

Kingman Brewster, Jr., for permission to reprint excerpts from the 1976 Annual Report of the President, Yale University.

Broadside Press for permission to reprint "Kidnap Poem" from *Re: Creation* by Nikki Giovanni; "Booker T. and W. E. B." and "Black Poet, White Critic" by Dudley Randall; and "For Malcolm X" by Margaret A. Walker.

Cambridge University Press for permission to reprint *Hamlet* from *Shakespearian Tragedy* by H. B. Charlton.

City Lights Books for permission to reprint "Last Night in Calcutta" from *Planet News* by Allen Ginsberg, copyright © 1968 by Allen Ginsberg.

Charing Cross Music for permission to reprint lyrics of "The Sounds of Silence," copyright © 1964 by Paul Simon.

Chatto and Windus, Ltd., and Mrs. Laura Huxley for permission to reprint "Music at Night" from the book *Music at Night* by Aldous Huxley.

John Ciardi for permission to reprint "Dialogue with the Audience" from *Saturday Review,* November 22, 1958.

William E. Cole Scholarship Committee for permission to reprint "Living and Dying in Shady Valley" from *Tales from a Country Ledger,* copyright by the William E. Cole Scholarship Fund, 1981.

Columbia University Press for permission to reprint sketch of Edward Gibbon from *The Columbia Encyclopedia,* Second Edition.

Combine Music Corporation for permission to reprint lyrics of "Me and Bobby McGee" and "Sunday Mornin' Comin' Down," both copyright © 1969 by Combine Music Corporation; international copyright secured; all rights reserved.

Don Congdon Associates, Inc., for permission to reprint "There Will Come Soft Rains," copyright © 1950, renewed 1978 by Ray Bradbury.

Continental Total Media Project, Inc., for permission to reprint lyrics of "Suzanne," copyright © 1966 by Project Seven Music, Div. C.T.M.P., Inc. Corinth Books, Inc., for permission to reprint "Preface to a Twenty Volume Suicide Note," copyright © 1961 by LeRoi Jones (Imamu Amiri Baraka).

Curtis Brown, Ltd., for permission to reprint 'Miss Julie," copyright © 1955 by Elizabeth Sprigge, and "Self-Portrait as a Bear," copyright © 1969 by Donald Hall.

Frank Marshall Davis for permission to reprint "Roosevelt Smith."

J. M. Dent and Sons, Ltd., and David Higham Associates, Ltd., for permission to reprint "Do Not Go Gentle into That Good Night" and "The Force That Through the Green Fuse Drives the Flower" from *The Collected Poems of Dylan Thomas;* and "Memories of Christmas" from *Quite Early One Morning* by Dylan Thomas.

Delacorte Press/Seymour Lawrence for permission to reprint "Harrison Bergeron," excerpted from *Welcome to the Monkey House* by Kurt Vonnegut, Jr. Originally published in *Fantasy and Science Fiction.* Copyright © 1961 by Kurt Vonnegut, Jr.

Candida Donadio & Associates, Inc., for permission to reprint "August Strindberg" from *Beyond All This Fiddle* by A. Alvarez, copyright © 1968 by A. Alvarez.

Doubleday & Company, Inc., for permission to reprint "The Absurdity of the Absurd" from *The Theatre of the Absurd,* copyright © 1961, 1968, 1969 by Martin Esslin; "Brandy" from *Strictly Personal* by W. Somerset Maugham, copyright 1940, 1941; "The Colonel's Lady" from *Creatures of Circumstance,* copyright 1946 by W. Somerset Maugham; "Elegy for Jane," copyright 1950 by Theodore Roethke, and "I Knew a Woman," copyright 1954 by Theodore Roethke, both from *The Collected Poems of Theodore Roethke.*

Robert Drake for permission to reprint "Amazing Grace" from *Amazing Grace* by Robert Drake. Copyright © 1965 by Robert Drake.

Norma Millay Ellis for permission to reprint "To Jesus on His Birthday" from *Collected Poems* by Edna St. Vincent Millay, Harper & Row, copyright 1928, 1955 by Edna St. Vincent Millay and Norma Millay Ellis.

Faber and Faber Limited for permission to reprint "Lullaby," "Musée des Beaux Arts," and "The Unknown Citizen" from *Collected Shorter Poems* by W. H. Auden; "The Love Song of J. Alfred Prufrock" and "Morning at the Window" from *Collected Poems 1909–1962* by T. S. Eliot; Chapter 7 (pp. 81–95, hardbound edition) from *The Bell Jar* by Sylvia Plath; and "An Elementary School Classroom in a Slum" and "I Think Continually of Those Who Were Truly Great" from *Collected Poems* by Stephen Spender.

Fall River Music, Inc., for permission to reprint lyrics of "Where Have All the Flowers Gone?" by Pete Seeger, copyright © 1961 by Fall River Music, Inc.; all rights reserved; used by permission.

Famous Music Publishing for permission to reprint lyrics of "Gentle on My Mind" by Johnny Hartford, copyright © 1967, 1968 by Ensign Music Corporation.

Farrar, Straus & Giroux, Inc., for permission to reprint "A City of Churches" from *Sadness* by Donald Barthelme (appeared originally in *The New Yorker*); "Evening in the Sanitarium" from *The Blue Estuaries* by Louise Bogan, copyright © 1954, 1968 by Louise Bogan; "The Lottery" from *The Lottery and Other Stores* by Shirley Jackson. Copyright 1948, 1949 by Shirley Jackson. Copyright renewed © 1976, 1977 by Laurence Hyman, Barry Hyman, Mrs. Sarah Webster, and Mrs. Joanne Schnurer. "The Lottery" originally appeared in *The New Yorker*; "The Emancipators" from *The Complete Poems* by Randall Jarrell, copyright © 1969, 1971 by Mrs. Randall Jarrell; and "Skunk Hour" from *Life Studies* by Robert Lowell, copyright © 1956, 1959 by Robert Lowell; "The Magic Barrel" from *The Magic Barrel* by Bernard Malamud. Copyright © 1954, 1958, 1982 by Bernard Malamud; "Everything That Rises Must Converge" from *Everything That Rises Must Converge* by Flannery O'Connor. Copyright © 1961, 1965 by the Estate of Mary Flannery O'Connor.

Edward Francisco for permission to reprint "Lilith's Child."

Donald Hall for permission to reprint "My Son, My Executioner" from *The Alligator Bride: Poems New and Selected.*

Harcourt Brace Jovanovich for permission to reprint "The Love Song of J. Alfred Prufrock" and "Morning at the Window" from *Collected Poems 1909–1962* by T. S. Eliot, copyright 1936 by Harcourt Brace Jovanovich, Inc., copyright © 1963, 1964 by T. S. Eliot; "a/mong crum/bling people," copyright 1931, 1959 by E. E. Cummings, and "the cambridge ladies," copyright 1923, 1951 by E. E. Cummings, both from his volume, *Poems 1923–1954;* "pity this busy monster, manunkind," copyright 1944 by E. E. Cummings, renewed 1972 by Nancy T. Andrews, from *Complete Poems 1913–1962* by E. E. Cummings; "The Tragic Fallacy" from *The Modern Temper* by Joseph Wood Krutch, copyright 1929 by Harcourt Brace Jovanovich, Inc.; renewed 1957 by Joseph Wood Krutch; "The Dead in Europe" and "As a Plane Tree by the Water" from *Lord Weary's Castle,* copyright 1946, 1947 by Robert Lowell; "Flowering Judas," copyright 1930, 1958 by Katherine Anne Porter and reprinted from her volume *Flowering Judas and Other Stories:* "The Grave" from *The Leaning Tower and Other Stories,* copyright 1944, 1972 by Katherine Anne Porter; "Gib-

bon" from *Portraits in Miniature and Other Essays,* copyright 1931 by Lytton Strachey, renewed 1959 by James Strachey; "To Hell with Dying," copyright © 1967 by Alice Walker and reprinted from her volume *In Love and Trouble;* and "Museum Piece" from *Ceremony and Other Poems,* copyright 1950, 1978 by Richard Wilbur.

Harper & Row, Publishers, Inc., for permission to reprint "the ballad of chocolate Mabbie," copyright 1945 by Gwendolyn Brooks Blakely, from "The Children of the Poor," copyright 1949 by Gwendolyn Brooks Blakely, and "We Real Cool," copyright © 1959 by Gwendolyn Brooks Blakely, all from *The World of Gwendolyn Brooks;* "For John Keats, Apostle of Beauty," copyright 1925 by Harper & Row, Publishers, Inc., and "Yet Do I Marvel," copyright 1925 by Harper & Row, Publishers, Inc., both from *On These I Stand* by Countee Cullen; "Theology" from *Selected Poems* (1974) by Ted Hughes, copyright © 1961 by Ted Hughes; "Music at Night" from *Music at Night and Other Essays* by Aldous Huxley, copyright 1931, renewed 1959 by Aldous Huxley; Chapter 7 (pp. 81–95, hardbound edition) from *The Bell Jar* by Sylvia Plath, copyright © 1971 by Harper & Row, Publishers, Inc.; "What We Said" from *After Experience* by W. D. Snodgrass, copyright © 1958 by W. D. Snodgrass; "Travelling Through the Dark" from *Travelling Through the Dark* by William Stafford, copyright © 1960 by William Stafford; "The Hour of Letdown" from *The Second Tree from the Corner* by E. B. White (originally appeared in *The New Yorker*); and "I Paint What I See" from *The Fox of Peapack* by E. B. White, copyright 1933 by E. B. White.

Harvard University Press and the Trustees of Amherst College for permission to reprint selections from *The Poems of Emily Dickinson,* edited by Thomas H. Johnson, Cambridge, Mass.: The Belknap Press of Harvard University Press, copyright © 1951, 1955 by the President and Fellows of Harvard College.

James Hearst for permission to reprint "Landmark" and "Truth" from *Limited View* by James Hearst (Iowa City, Iowa: Prairie Press), copyright © 1962 by James Hearst.

The Ronald Hobbs Literary Agency for permission to reprint "A Poem for Black Hearts" from *Black Magic Poetry 1961–1967,* copyright © 1969 by LeRoi Jones (Imamu Amiri Baraka).

Holt, Rinehart and Winston, Publishers, for permission to reprint "Christmas" from *Homecoming* by Floyd Dell, copyright 1933, © 1961 by Floyd Dell; "Acquainted with the Night," "After Apple-Picking," "Departmen-

Acknowledgments

1167

tal," "The Gift Outright," "Neither Out Far nor In Deep," "Nothing Gold Can Stay," "The Secret Sits," "Stopping By Woods on a Snowy Evening," and "The Strong Are Saying Nothing" from *The Poetry of Robert Frost,* edited by Edward Connery Lathem, copyright 1923, 1928, 1930, 1939, © 1969 by Holt, Rinehart and Winston, copyright 1936, 1942, 1951, © 1956, 1958 by Robert Frost, copyright © 1964, 1967, 1970 by Lesley Frost Ballantine; "The Figure a Poem Makes" from *Selected Prose of Robert Frost,* edited by Hyde Cox and Edward Connery Lathem, copyright 1939 © 1967 by Holt, Rinehart and Winston; "To an Athlete Dying Young," "The True Lover," "When I Was One-and-Twenty," and "With Rue My Heart Is Laden" from "A Shropshire Lad"—Authorized Edition—from *The Collected Poems of A. E. Housman,* copyright 1939, 1940, © 1965 by Holt, Rinehart and Winston, copyright © 1967, 1968 by Robert E. Symons; and "How You Get Born" from *Half-Lives* by Erica Jong, copyright © 1971, 1972, 1973 by Erica Mann Jong.

Houghton Mifflin Company for permission to reprint "The Dinner-Party" from *Men, Women, and Ghosts* by Amy Lowell; "Ars Poetica," "Not Marble nor the Gilded Monuments," and "You, Andrew Marvell" from *The Collected Poems of Archibald MacLeish,* copyright 1962 by Archibald MacLeish; "Who Precisely Do You Think You Are?" from *The Continuing Journey* by Archibald MacLeish, copyright © 1967 by Archibald MacLeish; and "The Kiss" from *Love Poems* by Anne Sexton, copyright © 1967, 1968, 1969 by Anne Sexton.

Olwyn Hughes, Literary Agent, for permission to reprint "Suicide Off Egg Rock" and "Two Views of a Cadaver Room" from *The Colossus,* published by Faber and Faber, Ltd., London, copyright © 1967 by Ted Hughes.

Indiana University Press for permission to reprint "Award" by Ray Durem from *New Negro Poets: USA,* ed. Langston Hughes.

International Creative Management for Permission to reprint "The Portable Phonograph" from *The Portable Phonograph* by Walter Van Tilburg Clark, copyright © 1941, 1969 by Walter Van Tilburg Clark.

Mrs. Randall Jarrell for permission to reprint "The Emancipators" by Randall Jarrell.

Philip Larkin for permission to reprint "Aubade."

Little Brown and Company for permission to reprint "Game After Supper" from *Procedures for Underground: Poems* by Margaret Atwood, copyright © 1970 by Oxford University Press Canada; and "Very Like a Whale" from *Verses from 1929 On* by Ogden Nash, copyright 1934 by the Curtis Publishing

Company; first appeared in *The Saturday Evening Post;* and "The Oxford Method" from *Unforgotten Years* by Logan Pearsall Smith, copyright 1939.

Liveright Publishing Corporation for permission to reprint "To Brooklyn Bridge" and "North Labrador" from *The Complete Poems and Selected Letters and Prose of Hart Crane,* ed. Brom Weber, copyright 1933, © 1958, 1966 by Liveright Publishing Corporation; and "Frederick Douglass" and "Those Winter Sundays" from *Angle of Ascent: New and Selected Poems* by Robert Hayden, copyright © 1975, 1972, 1970, 1966 by Robert Hayden.

Macmillan Publishing Co., Inc., for permission to reprint "On the Road" from *The Chorus Girl and Other Stories* by Anton Chekhov, copyright 1920 by Macmillan Publishing Co., Inc., renewed 1948 by David Garnett; "Eve" from *Poems* by Ralph Hodgson, copyright 1917 by Macmillan Publishing Co., Inc., renewed 1945 by Ralph Hodgson; "The Mill" from *Collected Poems* by Edwin Arlington Robinson, copyright 1920 by Edwin Arlington Robinson, renewed 1948 by Ruth Nivison, and "Mr. Flood's Party" from *Collected Poems* by Edwin Arlington Robinson, copyright 1921 by Edwin Arlington Robinson, renewed 1949 by Ruth Nivison; "Poetry" from *Collected Poems* by Marianne Moore, copyright 1935 by Marianne Moore, renewed 1963 by Marianne Moore and T. S. Eliot; "There Will Come Soft Rains" from *Collected Poems* by Sara Teasdale, copyright 1920 by Macmillan Publishing Co., Inc., renewed 1948 by Mamie T. Wheless; "Among School Children," copyright 1928 by Macmillan Publishing Co., Inc., renewed 1956 by Georgie Yeats, "The Ballad of Father Gilligan," copyright 1906 by Macmillan Publishing Co., Inc., renewed 1934 by William Butler Yeats, "Sailing to Byzantium," copyright 1928 by Macmillan Publishing Co., Inc., renewed 1956 by Georgie Yeats, "The Second Coming," copyright 1924 by Macmillan Publishing Co., Inc., renewed 1952 by Bertha Georgie Yeats, and "The Wild Swans at Coole," copyright 1919 by Macmillan Publishing Co., Inc., renewed 1947 by Bertha Georgie Yeats, all from *Collected Poems* by William Butler Yeats, copyright 1950.

Macmillan Company of Canada for permission to reprint "Eve" from *Poems* by Ralph Hodgson, copyright 1917 by Macmillan Publishing Co., Inc., renewed 1945 by Ralph Hodgson.

The Marvell Press for permission to reprint "Church Going" from *The Less Deceived* by Philip Larkin.

William Morris Agency, Inc., for permission on behalf of the author to reprint "King of the

Bingo Game" by Ralph Ellison, copyright ©
1944 (renewed) by Ralph Ellison.

New Directions Publishing Corporation for per-
mission to reprint "In Goya's Greatest
Scenes" from *A Coney Island of the Mind* by
Lawrence Ferlinghetti, copyright © 1958 by
Lawrence Ferlinghetti; "The Pearl" (trans. by
Geoffrey M. Sargent) from *Death in Mid-
summer and Other Stories* by Yukio Mish-
ima, copyright © 1966 by New Directions
Publishing Corporation; "Ballad of the
Goodly Fere" from *Personae* by Ezra Pound,
copyright 1926 by Ezra Pound; "A Walk"
from *The Back Country* by Gary Snyder,
copyright © 1960 by Gary Snyder; "Do Not
Go Gentle into That Good Night" and "The
Force That Through the Green Fuse Drives
the Flower" from *The Poems of Dylan
Thomas,* copyright 1939 by New Directions
Publishing Corporation, copyright 1952 by
Dylan Thomas; "Memories of Christmas"
(J. M. Dent version) from *Quite Early One
Morning* by Dylan Thomas, copyright 1954
by New Directions Publishing Corporation;
"Portrait of a Lady," "This Is Just to Say," and
"Tract" from *Collected Earlier Poems* by
William Carlos Williams, copyright 1938 by
New Directions Publishing Corporation;
"October" from *O Taste and See* by Denise
Levertov, copyright © 1964 by Denise Lev-
ertov Goodman; "Dulce et Decorum Est"
from *Collected Poems of Wilfred Owen,*
copyright © 1963 by Chatto & Windus, Ltd.

John Frederick Nims for permission to reprint
"Love Poem" from *The Iron Pastoral,* copyright 1947 by John Frederick Nims.

W. W. Norton & Company for permission to reprint "Cascadilla Falls" from *Collected Poems
1951–1971* by A. R. Ammons, copyright ©
1972 by A. R. Ammons; "The Apprenticeship
of a Mass Murderer" from *Helter Skelter: The
True Story of the Manson Murders* by Vincent Bugliosi with Curt Gentry, copyright ©
1974 by Curt Gentry and Vincent Bugliosi;
"Living in Sin" and "Two Songs" from
Poems, Selected and New, 1950–1974 by
Adrienne Rich, copyright © 1975, 1973,
1971, 1969, 1966 by W. W. Norton & Company, Inc., copyright © 1967, 1963, 1962,
1961, 1960, 1959, 1958, 1957, 1956, 1955,
1954, 1953, 1952, 1951 by Adrienne Rich.

Harold Ober Associates, Inc., for permission to
reprint "I'm a Fool" by Sherwood Anderson,
copyright © 1922 by Dial Publishing Company, Inc., renewed 1949 by Eleanor Copen-
haver Anderson; and "On the Road" by
Langston Hughes, copyright © 1952 by
Langston Hughes.

The Ohio University Press, Athens, for permission to reprint "The Metaphysical Amorist"

from *Exclusions of a Rhyme* by J. V. Cunningham.

Oxford University Press Canada for permission
to reprint "Game After Supper" from *Procedures for Underground: Poems* by Margaret
Atwood, copyright © Oxford University
Press Canada.

Lora Rackstraw for permission to reprint "The
Word" by Richard Rackstraw.

Random House, Inc., Alfred A. Knopf, Inc., for
permission to reprint "August Strindberg"
from *Beyond All This Fiddle* by A. Alvarez,
copyright © 1968 by A. Alvarez; "Lullaby,"
"Musée des Beaux Arts," and "The Unknown
Citizen" from *Collected Shorter Poems
1927–1957* by W. H. Auden, copyright 1940,
renewed 1968 by W. H. Auden; "Caligula"
from *Caligula and Three Other Plays* by Albert Camus, translated by Stuart Gilbert,
copyright © 1958 by Alfred A. Knopf, Inc.;
"Nobel Prize Acceptance Speech" from *Camus at Stockholm,* translated by Justin
O'Brien, copyright © 1958 by Alfred A.
Knopf, Inc.; "The Enormous Radio," copyright © 1947 by John Cheever and reprinted
from *The Stories of John Cheever;* "The Visit"
by Friedrich Duerrenmatt, copyright © 1956
by Maurice Valency as an unpublished work
entitled "The Old Lady's Visit," adapted by
Maurice Valency from *Der Besuch der Alten
Dame* by Friedrich Duerrenmatt, copyright
© 1958 by Maurice Valency, reprinted from
Masters of Modern Drama by permission of
Random House, Inc.; "Brave Words for a
Startling Occasion" from *Shadow and Act* by
Ralph Ellison, copyright © 1963, 1964 by
Ralph Ellison; "The Bear" (7,000 word ver-
sion) by William Faulkner, copyright 1942
and renewed 1970 by Estelle Faulkner and
Jill Faulkner Summers; an expanded version
of this story appeared in *Go Down Moses* by
William Faulkner; "A Rose for Emily" from
Collected Stories of William Faulkner,
copyright 1930, renewed © 1958 by William
Faulkner; "The Bloody Sire" from *Selected
Poems* by Robinson Jeffers, copyright ©
1965 by Donnan Jeffers and Garth Jeffers;
"Shine, Perishing Republic" and "Science"
from *Selected Poetry of Robinson Jeffers,*
copyright 1925, renewed 1953 by Robinson
Jeffers; "Some Prefatory Words on Comedy"
(excerpt from pp. 3–11) from *The Thread of
Laughter: Chapters on English State Comedy
From Jonson to Maugham* by Louis Kronenberger, copyright 1952 by Louis Kronenberger; "Ile" by Eugene O'Neill, copyright 1919,
renewed 1947 by Eugene O'Neill, reprinted
from *The Long Voyage Home: Seven Plays of
the Sea* by Eugene O'Neill by permission of
Random House, Inc.; "Suicide Off Egg Rock"

and "Two Views of a Cadaver Room" from *The Colossus and Other Poems* by Sylvia Plath, copyright © 1960 by Sylvia Plath; "The Wall" by Jean-Paul Sartre, translated by Maria Jolas, copyright 1945 by Random House, Inc., reprinted from *Bedside Book of Famous French Stories* (B. Becker and R. N. Linscott, editors) by permission of New Directions Publishing Corporation and Random House, Inc.; "The Sunshine Boys" from *The Sunshine Boys* by Neil Simon, copyright © 1973 by Neil Simon; "An Elementary School Classroom in a Slum" copyright 1942, renewed 1970 by Stephen Spender, and "I Think Continually of Those Who Were Truly Great," copyright 1934, renewed 1962 by Stephen Spender, both from *Selected Poems* by Stephen Spender; "Anecdote of the Jar," "Disillusionment of Ten O'Clock," "Peter Quince at the Clavier," "The Snow Man," and "Sunday Morning" from *The Collected Poems of Wallace Stevens,* copyright 1923, renewed 1951 by Wallace Stevens; "The Playboy of the Western World," copyright 1907, renewed 1935 by the Executors of the Estate of John M. Synge, reprinted from *The Complete Works of John M. Synge;* "Harlem" from *Selected Poems of Langston Hughes,* copyright 1951 by Langston Hughes; "Autobiographia Literaria" from *The Collected Poems of Frank O'Hara,* copyright © 1967 by Maureen Granville Smith, Administratrix of the Estate of Frank O'Hara; "Bells for John Whiteside's Daughter" from *Selected Poems, Third Edition, Revised and Enlarged* by John Crowe Ransom, copyright 1924 by Alfred A. Knopf, renewed 1952 by John Crowe Ransom; and "The Astronomer," copyright © 1961 by John Updike and reprinted from *Pigeon Feathers and Other Stories* by John Updike.

Frank K. Robinson for permission to reprint "Ten Haiku."

Leo Rosten for permission to reprint "Episode near Munich: A Lost Address."

The Saturday Review for permission to reprint "Dialogue with the Audience" by John Ciardi from the November 22, 1958 issue, and "Criticism: A Many-Windowed House" by Malcolm Cowley from the August 12, 1961 issue, with permission of the authors.

Schocken Books, Inc., for permission to reprint "A Hunger Artist" from *The Penal Colony* by Franz Kafka, copyright © 1948, renewed © 1975 by Schocken Books, Inc.

Charles Scribner's Sons for permission to reprint "Quality" from *The Inn of Tranquility* by John Galsworthy, copyright 1912 by Charles Scribner's Sons, 1940 by Ada Galsworthy; "Miniver Cheevy" from *The Town Down the*

River by Edwin Arlington Robinson, copyright 1910 by Charles Scribner's Sons, renewed 1938 by Ruth Nivison.

Irwin Shaw for permission to reprint "The Eighty-Yard Run" from *Selected Stories of Irwin Shaw.*

Gary Snyder for permission to reprint "Hay for the Horses," copyright © 1966 by Gary Snyder.

The Society of Authors as the literary representative of: the Estate of John Galsworthy, for permission to reprint "Quality" from *The Inn of Tranquility* by John Galsworthy, copyright 1912 by Charles Scribner's Sons, 1940 by Ada Galsworthy; the Estate of A. E. Housman, and Jonathan Cape, Ltd., publishers of A. E. Housman's *Collected Poems,* for permission to reprint "To an Athlete Dying Young," "The True Lover," "When I Was One-and-Twenty," and "With Rue My Heart Is Laden."

Stephen Spender and Harold Taylor for permission to reprint "On Teaching Modern Poetry" from *Essays on Teaching Modern Poetry* by Stephen Spender, edited by Harold Taylor.

Stranger Music, Inc., for permission to reprint lyrics of "Stories of the Street," words and music by Leonard Cohen, copyright © 1967 by Stranger Music, Inc.; used by permission; all rights reserved.

Helen Thurber for permission to reprint "The Secret Life of Walter Mitty," copyright © 1942 James Thurber; copyright © 1970 Helen Thurber from *My World and Welcome to It,* published by Harcourt Brace Jovanovich; and "The Unicorn in the Garden," copyright © James Thurber; copyright © 1968 Helen Thurber from *Fables for Our Times,* published by Harper & Row.

Twayne Publishers, a Division of G. K. Hall & Co., Boston, for permission to reprint "Harlem Dancer" from *Selected Poems* by Claude McKay, copyright 1981 by Twayne Publishers, Inc.

Universal Publishing and Distributing Corporation for permission to reprint "At That Moment" by Raymond R. Patterson from *26 Ways of Looking at a Black Man.*

University of Chicago Press for permission to reprint excerpt from *T. S. Eliot's Poetry and Plays* by Grover Smith, 2nd. edition, copyright 1974.

Vanguard Press, Inc., for permission to reprint "In the Region of Ice" from *The Wheel of Love and Other Stories* by Joyce Carol Oates, copyright © 1970, 1969, 1968, 1967, 1966, 1965 by Joyce Carol Oates.

Viking Penguin, Inc., for permission to reprint "Araby" from *Dubliners* by James Joyce,

1170

Acknowledgments

copyright 1916 by B. W. Huebsch; definitive text copyright © 1967 by the Estate of James Joyce; "Flight" from *The Long Valley* by John Steinbeck, copyright 1938 by John Steinbeck, renewed © 1966 by John Steinbeck.

The Viking Press, Inc., for permission to reprint "The Day After Sunday" from *Times Three* by Phyllis McGinley, copyright 1952 by Phyllis McGinley; and "Résumé" from *The Portable Dorothy Parker,* copyright 1926, 1954 by Dorothy Parker.

Diane Wakoski for permission to reprint "You, Letting the Trees Stand as My Betrayer" from *The Motorcycle Betrayal Poems* by Diane Wakoski, copyright © 1971 by Diane Wakoski.

Margaret A. Walker for permission to reprint "Molly Means" from *For My People* by Margaret A. Walker, published by Yale University Press, 1942.

Bill Ward for permission to reprint lyrics from "Alabama," copyright © 1983 by Bill Ward.

Warner Brothers Music for permission to reprint lyrics from "Mister Tambourine Man" by Bob Dylan, copyright © 1964 by Warner Bros. Music; all rights reserved; used by permission.

A. Watkins, Inc., for permission to reprint "Roman Fever" from *The World Over* by Edith Wharton, copyright 1934 by Edith Wharton, renewed 1962 by William R. Tyler.

A. P. Watt & Son for permission to reprint "On the Road" by Anton Chekhov, translated by Constance Garnett from *The Chorus Girl and Other Stories,* with permission of the Executors of the Estate of Constance Garnett and Chatto & Windus, Ltd.; "Brandy" from *Strictly Personal* by W. Somerset Maugham, with permission of the Executors of the Estate of W. Somerset Maugham; "The Colonel's Lady" from *The Collected Stories of W. Somerset Maugham,* with permission of the Executors of the Estate of W. Somerset Maugham and William Heinemann Ltd.; "Three Deaths" by Leo Tolstoy from *A Trea-*

sury of Great Russian Short Stories, translated by Constance Garnett, copyright 1944, with permission of the Executors of the Estate of Constance Garnett; "Among School Children," "The Ballad of Father Gilligan," "Sailing to Byzantium," "The Second Coming," and "The Wild Swans at Coole" from *The Collected Poems of W. B. Yeats,* with permission of M. B. Yeats, Miss Anne Yeats, and the Macmillan Company of London & Basingstoke.

Wesleyan University Press for permission to reprint "Adultery" from *Poems 1957–1967* by James Dickey, copyright © 1966 by James Dickey, first appearance in *The Nation;* "Cherrylog Road" from *Helmets,* copyright © 1963 by James Dickey, first appearance in *The New Yorker;* "The Sheep Child" from *Poems 1957–1967,* copyright © 1966 by James Dickey, first appearance in *Atlantic Monthly;* "Lying in a Hammock at William Duffy's Farm in Pine Island, Minnesota" from *The Branch Will Not Break* by James Wright, copyright © 1961 by James Wright, first appearance in *Paris Review;* "A Blessing" from *The Branch Will Not Break,* copyright © 1961 by James Wright, first appearance in *Poetry;* "Counting the Mad" from *Summer Anniversaries* by Donald Justice, copyright © 1957 by Donald Justice, first appearance in *Western Review;* "The Tourist from Syracuse" from *Night Light* by Donald Justice, copyright © 1965 by Donald Justice, first appearance in *North American Review.*

John Wiley & Sons, Inc., for permission to reprint "Electric Orphic Circuit" from *Lyric Voices: Approaches to the Poetry of Contemporary Song* by Barbara Farris Graves and Donald J. McBain, copyright © 1972 by John Wiley & Sons, Inc.

Robley Wilson, Jr., for permission to reprint "The Great Teachers."

Yale University Press for permission to reprint "The Lost Pilot" from *The Lost Pilot* by James Tate, copyright © 1967.

Index of Authors
and Titles

Index of First Lines of Poems

Index of Literary and Critical Terms